fifth edition

FOR ALL PRACTICAL PURPOSES

MATHEMATICAL LITERACY IN TODAY'S WORLD

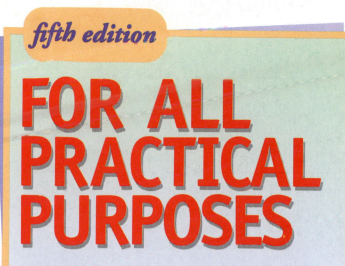

PROJECT DIRECTOR

Solomon Garfunkel, *Consortium for Mathematics and Its Applications*

CONTRIBUTING AUTHORS

PART I Management Science
Joseph Malkevitch, *York College, CUNY*
Rochelle Meyer, *Nassau Community College*
Walter Meyer, *Adelphi University*

PART II Statistics: The Science of Data
David S. Moore, *Purdue University*

PART III Coding Information
Joseph Gallian, *University of Minnesota—Duluth*

PART IV Social Choice and Decision Making
Steven J. Brams, *New York University*
Bruce P. Conrad, *Temple University*
Alan D. Taylor, *Union College*

PART V On Size and Shape
Paul J. Campbell, *Beloit College*

PART VI Modeling in Mathematics
Paul J. Campbell, *Beloit College*
Joseph Malkevitch, *York College, CUNY*
Alan D. Taylor, *Union College*

fifth edition

FOR ALL PRACTICAL PURPOSES

MATHEMATICAL LITERACY IN TODAY'S WORLD

W. H. FREEMAN AND COMPANY
NEW YORK

Publisher: Michelle Russel Julet
Marketing Manager: Kimberly Manzi
Development Editor: Randi Rossignol
Project Editor: Mary Louise Byrd
Text Designer: Circa 86, Inc.
Photo Editor: Inge King
Media and Supplements Director: Patrick Shriner
Cover/Part Opener Illustrations: Salem Krieger
Illustration Coordinator: Lou Capaldo
Illustrations: Burmar Technical Corporation
Production Coordinator: Susan Wein
Composition: Progressive Information Technologies
Manufacturing: RR Donnelley & Sons Company

Library of Congress Cataloging-in-Publication Data

For all practical purposes: introduction to contemporary mathematics
/ by COMAP—5th ed.
p.   cm.
Includes index.
ISBN 0-7167-2841-9
1. Mathematics.   I. Consortium for Mathematics and Its Applications
(U.S.)
QA7.F68 1996   96-4941
510—dc20   CIP

Printed in the United States of America

First printing 2000

CONTENTS

PART II   Statistics: The Science of Data

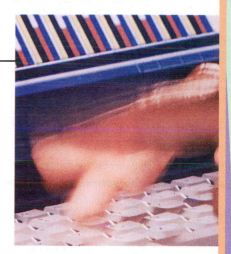

chapter 5

PRODUCING DATA   167

chapter 6

EXPLORING DATA   204

chapter 7

PROBABILITY: THE MATHEMATICS OF CHANCE   251

PART III   Coding Information

PART IV   Social Choice and Decision Making

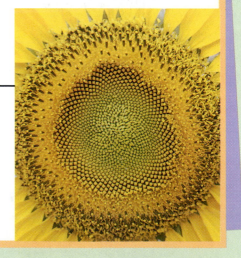

chapter 17   **SYMMETRY AND PATTERNS   629**

chapter 18

TILINGS 668

PART VI Modeling in Mathematics

chapter 19

LOGIC AND MODELING 713

chapter 20

CONSUMER FINANCE MODELS   740

The creation of a new edition of *For All Practical Purposes* is always a time for celebration at COMAP. We are immensely gratified that *For All Practical Purposes* continues to be the leading quantitative literacy text, used in over 600 college mathematics for liberal arts courses. In fact, it is fair to say that for the past 12 years, *FAPP* has led the way in defining the introductory quantitative literacy syllabus.

Our goal is to bring the excitement of contemporary mathematical thinking to every student and to help students to think logically and to read critically the mathematical information that abounds in our contemporary society. We are reminded of Thomas Jefferson's notion of an "enlightened citizenry" in which people, having acquired a broad knowledge of topics, can use sound judgment in making personal and political decisions.

New Content Features of the Fifth Edition

For All Practical Purposes continues to stress the connections between contemporary mathematics and modern society. Likewise, we continue to stress that mathematical models are our most powerful tools for solving complex problems. But mathematics is dynamic, and so our text must be flexible enough to accommodate new areas of mathematics and their new applications to our daily lives. We have also worked hard to simplify material, particularly in the chapters on decision making. Some of the important content changes are as follows:

Chapter 3 discusses how to resolve scheduling conflicts.

Nurses scheduling patient care

• Part I, **Management Science,** features an entirely new section in Chapter 3, "Planning and Scheduling," on graph coloring with applications to scheduling problems such as scheduling job interviews.

• Part II, **Statistics: The Science of Data,** has quite a bit of new material. In Chapter 5, "Producing Data," David Moore has added a new exercise set entitled, "Statistics in Practice." In Chapter 6, "Exploring Data," there are new sections on stemplots, correlation, and techniques of modern data analysis. Chapter 7, "Probability: The Mathematics of Chance," includes new material on probability histograms. And in Chapter 8, "Statistical Inference," new examples include AIDS behavioral surveys and high-stakes NAEP scores.

See Chapter 6 for new methods of data analysis.

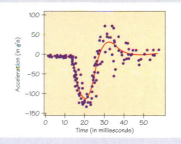

Time plot of the head of a crash test dummy as a motorcycle hits a wall, with the overall pattern calculated by a scatterplot smoother

See Chapter 13 for methods used to divide property fairly.

A checkpoint at the Berlin Wall

• **Part IV, Social Choice and Decision Making,** is a block of material that we have worked hard to keep current *and* to simplify. In Chapter 11, "Social Choice: The Impossible Dream," we have simplified the coverage of the Hare system. Chapter 12, "Weighted Voting Systems," presents a new explanation of the Banzhaf power index with an expanded treatment of counting and a simplified weighted voting notation. Chapter 13, "Fair Division," includes a new section on what happens if we "take turns." And in Chapter 14, "Apportionment," we demonstrate a new use of critical multipliers to help in our calculations.

• **Part V, On Size and Shape**
Chapter 16 features greatly expanded coverage of the mass/volume relationship, showcasing new Spotlights on the design and engineering of very tall buildings.

See Chapter 16 for a new section on how very tall buidings are designed.

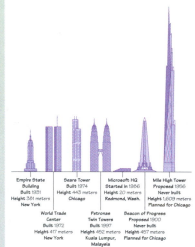

• **Part VI, Modeling in Mathematics,** is new to this edition. Although it could be argued that almost all of *For All Practical Purposes* is at heart about mathematical modeling, until now we have not made the process and art of modeling explicit. In Part VI we not only describe the modeling process and its relation to the applicability of mathematics, we illustrate that process with two new chapters. Chapter 19, "Logic and Modeling," introduces mathematical logic as a model of deductive reasoning. We have long been asked by users of *FAPP* to expand our treatment of logic and we are proud of Alan Taylor's work here. The chapter on logic is followed by Chapter 20, "Consumer Finance Models." This chapter pulls together some of the financial models from the previous edition along with coverage of models for disbursal and accumulation of funds—including new sections on valuing stock, using retirement savings, and college endowments.

For a discussion of installment loans, see Chapter 20.

Improved Pedagogy

While *For All Practical Purposes* has always been about ideas, we recognize that all mathematics texts must take advantage of the power and appeal of technology. Therefore, we have in every chapter added a new **Technology Corner** to the exercise sets. These new exercises require the students to use spreadsheet technology to solve problems. We are grateful to John Emert of Ball State University for creating the **Technology Corner**.

We have also added **Suggested Web Sites** to each chapter. These Web site references are intended to help students take more control of their experience in this course and do their own research.

Finally, we have responded to instructors' calls for more basic practice exercises with our new **Skills Check** exercises in each chapter. For the new multiple-choice questions, we thank John Emert and Kay Roebuck, both of Ball State University. Their deep familiarity with *FAPP* and insight into what will help students improve their problem-solving skills are evident in their important contribution.

Media and Supplements

The media and supplements package for the new edition has been updated to reflect the changes in the book and the growing importance of electronic media. Both students and instructors will benefit from the innovative materials available to them.

• A printed **Study Guide** has been developed to help students better understand the materials in the book and to enhance their performance in the course. Each chapter offers section-by-section summaries of the text coverage, including explanations of challenging concepts and numerous questions (with answers) designed to ensure that students fully grasp a concept before moving on. The *Study Guide* also contains chapter objectives and a practice quiz of the kinds of questions students are likely to encounter on a test.

• A new **Web Site** has been developed to serve both students and instructors using the new edition. Students will benefit from our site's chapter-by-chapter **Online Study Guide.** It includes chapter objectives to help students organize their study, flash card exercises to aid in their mastery of the text's hundreds of key terms, additional drill questions to help them build problem-solving skills, interactive exercises and chapter self-quizzes to help them prepare for tests, and Web links to show them more real-world applications of text topics. For instructors, the site features an **Online Instructor's Guide** that offers the entire contents of the printed *Instructor's Guide,* plus additional teaching tips including specific ideas on using the electronic media. There are also links to outside Web sites related to the topics and a forum where instructors teaching from *FAPP* can share ideas about using the book. The Web site address is:

www.whfreeman.com/math

• Our new **Instructor's CD-ROM** offers all the images from the textbook in two formats—as part of our **Presentation Manager Pro** software and in **JPEG files.** Presentation Manager allows instructors to prepare playlists of images for display during lectures. The JPEG files are provided for users who prefer to use commercially available presentation software.

• The printed **Instructor's Guide** has long been a useful tool for instructors using *FAPP*. It retains its popular features in this new edition including solutions to even-numbered text exercises, extensive class-tested teaching hints, detailed summaries, and suggested skill objectives.

• Our **Test Bank** comes in printed, Windows, and Macintosh formats. It offers approximately 1500 questions—50 multiple-choice and 25 short-answer questions per chapter.

• **Online Testing/Quizzing,** using questions from the Test Bank, is being offered for the first time.

• For the first time in many years, a new **Video** is being developed to illustrate topics from this textbook. Many instructors teaching from *FAPP* have long used video to demonstrate real-world applications of mathematics. We are keeping that tradition alive by undertaking new video topics. For more information about the new video, visit our Web site at www.whfreeman.com/math/.

There is also an Annenberg video series of 26 half-hour programs called **For All Practical Purposes Telecourse.** For more information on telecourse preview, purchase, or rental, please call 1-800-LEARNER, or write The Annenberg CPB Project, P.O. Box 2345, South Burlington, VT 05407-2345.

We thank the many people who have contributed to the supplements package, including the authors of supplements to previous editions. Following is a list of all of the instructors who have been involved, some of whom have worked on more than one title in this package:

John Emert, Ball State University
Chris Leary, St. Bonaventure College
Eli Passow, Temple University
Dan Reich, Temple University
Kay Meeks Roebuck, Ball State University
Sandra H. Savage, Orange Coast College

The staff of COMAP has also contributed a great deal to the supplements package.

Acknowledgments

Since the inception of *For All Practical Purposes*, we have benefited from the interest and contributions of many people, and this edition was no exception. We wish to thank our friends and colleagues who offered suggestions, comments, and corrections:

Stuart Anderson, Texas A&M University–Commerce
Terence Blows, Northern Arizona University
John Bruder, University of Alaska–Bristol Bay
Barry W. Brunson, Western Kentucky University
Judith Covington, Louisiana State University–Shreveport
Lynn D. Darragh, San Juan College
Susan T. Dean, Samford University
John Emert, Ball State University, Indiana
John C. George, Southern Illinois University at Carbondale
Jean H. Griffing, Western Kentucky University
Rodger Hammons, Morehead State University
Barbara Hargis, Middle Tennessee State University
Jean B. Harper, State University of New York–College at Fredonia
Timothy Hodges, University of Cincinnati
Francis Jones, Huntington College
Gary D. Jones, Murray State University
Darrell Kent, Washington State University
Robert Kowalczyk, University of Massachusetts, Dartmouth
Antonio M. Lopez, Jr., Loyola University, New Orleans
Ron Loser, Adams State College
Jay A. Malmstrom, Oklahoma City Community College
Denise Meeks, Pima Community College–Desert Vista Campus
James Osterburg, University of Cincinnati
Dennis Pence, Western Michigan University

Robert Pervine, Murray State University
Daniel Russow, Arizona Western College
Len Ruth, Sinclair Community College
Sandy H. Savage, Orange Coast College
Joyce H. Saxon, Morehead State University
Michael Slack, Western Michigan University
Lawrence Somer, Catholic University of America
Edward L. Thome, Murray State University
Paul J. Vesce, University of Missouri – Kansas City
Walter D. Wallis, Southern Illinois University – Carbondale
Carl Wampole, Dowling College
Monte Zerger, Adams State College
Jerad Zimmerman, Tacoma Community College

We are also grateful to the following people, who evaluated previous editions of
For All Practical Purposes:

Mark S. Anderson, Rollins College
Kathy Bavelas, Manchester Community College, Connecticut
Jerry W. Bradford, Wright State University
J. Patrick Brewer, University of Oregon
John Bruder, University of Alaska – Bristol Bay
Helen Burrier, Kirkwood Community College
Michelle Clement, Louisiana State University
Lothar A. Dohse, University of North Carolina – Asheville
John Emert, Ball State University, Indiana
Sandra Fillebrown, Saint Joseph's University
Rich France, Millersville University, Pennsylvania
Ira Gessel, Brandeis University, Massachusetts
Henry Gore, Morehouse College, Georgia
William Gratzer, Iona College
Rodger Hammons, Morehead State University
Edwin Herman, University of Oregon
Frederick Hoffman, Florida Atlantic University
Sherman Hunt, Community College of Finger Lakes
Alec Ingraham, New Hampshire College
Phillip E. Johnson, University of North Carolina – Charlotte
Karla Karstens, University of Vermont
Darrell Kent, Washington State University
Carmelita R. Keyes, Broome Community College
Antonio M. Lopez, Jr., Loyola University, New Orleans
Bennett Manvel, Colorado State University
Christopher McCord, University of Cincinnati

John G. Michaels, SUNY-Brockport
John Montgomery, University of Rhode Island
John Oprea, Cleveland State University
John L. Orr, University of Nebraska–Lincoln
James Osterburg, University of Cincinnati
Margaret A. Owens, California State University, Chico
Diane Radin, University of Texas–Austin
Sandra H. Savage, Orange Coast College
Richard Schwartz, College of Staten Island
Joanne R. Snow, Saint Mary's College
Edward R. Thome, Murray State University
Cynthia Wyels, Weber State University

We owe our appreciation to the people at W. H. Freeman and Company who participated in the preparation of this book. We wish especially to thank the editorial staff for their tireless efforts and support. Among them are Michelle Russel Julet, Publisher; Randi Rossignol, Development Editor; Mary Louise Byrd, Project Editor; Inge King, Photo Editor; Patrick Shriner, Media and Supplements Director; Trumbull Rogers, Copy Editor; Karen Osborne and Eleanor Wedge, Proofreaders; and Melanie Mays, Editorial Assistant.

We also thank the production staff at Freeman: Susan Wein, Production Coordinator; Maria Epes, Art Director; Lou Capaldo, Illustration Coordinator; and Carmen DiBartolomeo at Circa 86, Inc., Designer.

The efforts of the COMAP staff must be recognized. To the production and administrative staff—George Ward and Roland Cheyney—go all our thanks. And finally, we recognize the contribution of Laurie Aragon, the manager, who kept this project, as she does all of COMAP, running smoothly and efficiently. To everyone who helped make our purposes practical, we offer our appreciation for an exciting, exhausting, and exhilarating time.

Solomon Garfunkel, COMAP

". . . until management science was developed in the twentieth century, solutions to efficiency questions were answered by trial-and-error, 'seat-of-the-pants' approaches."

Neil Armstrong's first step on the moon's surface in July 1969 was a milestone in America's scientific and technological achievements, sure to make any short list of accomplishments in the twentieth century. Since the completion of the Apollo project's other moon landings (the last in December 1972), no one from any country has walked on the moon, nor are there specific plans by any country for any moon landings.

But mankind is now embarked on a project no less ambitious, the construction of the International Space Station. This $67-billion project aimed at placing an immense space station in orbit around the earth is a herculean task. In particular, what is remarkable about this project is that the expertise of a consortium of countries, including the United States and its former enemy Russia, is being harnessed. Will the International Space Station be the first port of call for trips to Mars, Jupiter, and beyond?

At the start of the Apollo project in the 1960s, no one really was sure if rockets would ever be able to carry humans into space. When NASA (National Aeronautics and

Space Administration) commissioned the Apollo module, it was asking several hundred companies to design, build, test, and deliver components and systems that had never been built before. The International Space Station similarly requires the construction of modularized units for assembly in space by men and robots pioneering many new materials and concepts, and with the further challenge that the people doing the designing and the work speak different languages and use different styles of engineering.

The Apollo project involved not only challenges in physical science and engineering, but also challenges in management science (operations research): how to make it all happen efficiently, economically, and on schedule. The International Space Station continues to present exactly these same challenges. Already there are concerns about the possibility of spiraling costs and delays.

However, it is not only massive projects such as Apollo, the "Chunnel" (the tunnel under the English Channel), or the International Space Station that require efficiency and timeliness. Individuals, businesses, and governments can put to use on a daily basis the same principles that were applied in the Apollo project and are being used for the International Space Station. Chapter 1 discusses how individuals or organizations, large or small, can improve efficiency in the delivery of services (such as mail and snow removal) or planning an afternoon shopping expedition. Chapters 2 and 3 present some of the planning and scheduling techniques that were pioneered in the Apollo program and are being extended to build the International Space Station. In Chapter 4, ideas that offer opportunities for production and operations problems faced by manufacturing firms and governments to trim costs using management science are explored.

The concept of efficiency is not a modern invention. For their time the Romans were masters of efficiency; otherwise, the Roman Empire would not have lasted as long as it did. However, until management science was developed in the twentieth century, solutions to efficiency questions were answered by trial-and-error, "seat-of-the-pants" approaches.

The value of putting to use a body of mathematical knowledge for operations management was first perceived during World War II. The founders of management science were mathematicians, scientists, and industrial technicians associated with the armed services who worked together to improve the war effort. In applying quantitative and qualitative techniques to project planning, these innovators founded a new branch of mathematics whose impact reaches beyond the military to every facet of our daily lives.

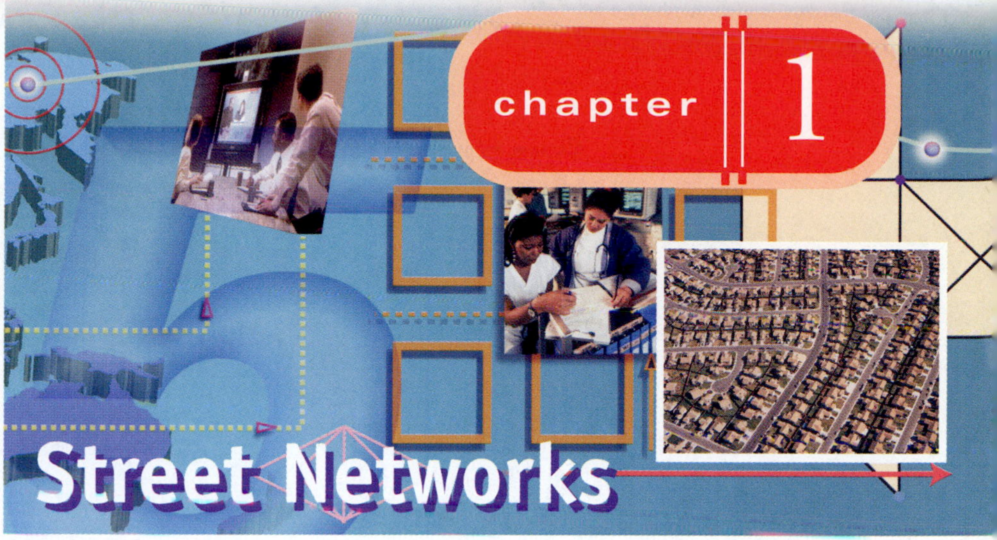

chapter 1
Street Networks

"Despite the complications of real-world problems, management science principles provide ways to understand these problems by using graphs as models."

The underlying theme of **management science,** also called **operations research,** is finding the best method for solving some problem—what mathematicians call the **optimal solution.** In some cases, it may be to finish a job as quickly as possible. In other situations, the goal might be to maximize profit or minimize cost. In this chapter our goal is to save time in traversing a street network while checking parking meters, delivering mail, or carrying out some similar task.

Let's begin by concentrating on the parking department of a city government. Most cities and many small towns have parking meters that must be regularly checked for parking violations or emptied of coins. We will use an imaginary town to show how management science techniques can help to make parking control more efficient.

Euler Circuits

The street map in Figure 1.1 is typical of many towns across the United States, with streets, residential blocks, and a village green. Our job, or that of the commissioner of parking, is to find the most efficient route for the parking-control officer, who travels on foot, to check the meters in an area. Our map shows only a small area, allowing us to start with an easy problem. But the problem occurs on a larger scale in all cities and towns and, for larger areas, there are almost unlimited possibilities for parking-control routes.

The commissioner has two goals in mind: (1) the parking-control officer must cover all the sidewalks that have parking meters without retracing any more steps

FIGURE 1.1
A street map for part of
a town.

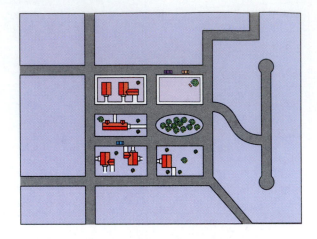

FIGURE 1.1
A street map for part of
a town.

than are necessary; and (2) the route should end at the same point from which it began, perhaps where the officer's patrol car is parked. To be specific, suppose there are only two blocks that have parking meters, the two blue-shaded blocks that are side by side toward the top of Figure 1.1. Suppose further that the parking-control officer must start and end at the upper left corner of the left-hand block. You might enjoy working out some routes by trial and error and evaluating their good and bad points. We are going to leave this problem for the moment and establish some concepts that will give us a better method to deal with this problem than trial and error.

A **graph** is a finite set of dots and connecting links. The dots are called **vertices** (a single dot is called a *vertex*), and the links are called **edges.** Each edge must connect two different vertices. A **path** is a connected sequence of edges showing a route on the graph that starts at a vertex and ends at a vertex; a path is usually described by naming in turn the vertices visited in traversing it. A path that starts and ends at the same vertex is called a **circuit.** A graph can represent our city map, a communications network, or even a system of air routes.

E X A M P L E   *Parts of a Graph*

We can see examples of these technical terms in Figure 1.2. The vertices represent cities, and the edges represent nonstop airline routes between them. We see that there is a nonstop flight between Berlin and Rome, but no such flight between New York and Berlin. There are several paths that describe how a person might travel with this airline from New York to Berlin. The path that seems most direct is New York, London, Berlin, but New York, Miami, Rome, Berlin is also such a path. An example of a circuit is Miami, Rome, London, Miami. It is a circuit because the path starts and ends at the same vertex. In this chapter we are especially

FIGURE 1.2
The edges of this graph
show nonstop routes that
an airline might offer.

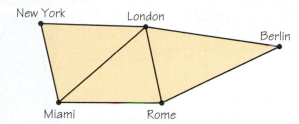

interested in circuits, just as we are in real life; most of us end our day in the same location where we start it—at home!   ◆

Returning to the case of parking control in Figure 1.1, we can use a graph to represent the whole territory to be patrolled: think of each street intersection as a vertex and each sidewalk that contains a meter as an edge, as in Figure 1.3. Notice in Figure 1.3b that the street separating the blocks is not explicitly represented; it has been shrunk to nothing. In effect, we are simplifying our problem by ignoring any distance traveled in crossing streets.

The numbered sequence of edges in Figure 1.4a shows one circuit that covers all the meters (note that it is a circuit because its path returns to its starting point). But Figure 1.4b shows another solution that is better because its circuit covers every edge (sidewalk) exactly once. In Figure 1.4b no edge is covered more than once, or *deadheaded* (a term borrowed from shipping, which means making a return trip without a load).

> Circuits that cover every edge only once are called **Euler circuits**.

FIGURE 1.3
(a) A graph superimposed upon a street map. The edges show which sidewalks have parking meters. (b) The same graph enlarged.

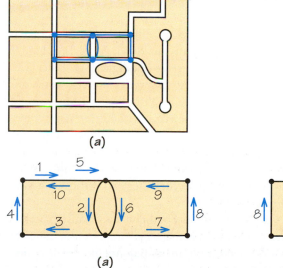
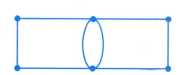

(a)   (b)

FIGURE 1.4
(a) A circuit and (b) an Euler circuit.

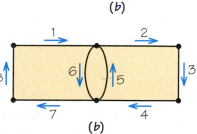

(a)   (b)

SPOTLIGHT 1.1

Leonhard Euler

Leonhard Euler

Leonhard Euler (1707–1783) was one of those rare individuals who was remarkable in many ways. He was extremely prolific, publishing over 500 works in his lifetime. But he wasn't devoted just to mathematics; he was a people person too. He was extremely fond of children and had thirteen of his own, of whom only five survived childhood. It is said that he often wrote difficult mathematical works with a child or two in his lap.

Human interest stories about Euler have been handed down through two centuries. He was a prodigy at doing complex mathematical calculations under less than ideal conditions, and continued to do them even after he became totally blind later in life. His blindness diminished neither the quantity nor the quality of his output. Throughout his life, he was able to mentally calculate in a short time what would have taken ordinary mathematicians hours of pencil-and-paper work. A contemporary claimed that Euler could calculate effortlessly, "just as men breathe, as eagles sustain themselves in the air."

Euler's mathematical mind found new mathematics in everyday life. In the old German town of Königsberg, people frequently tried to take a Sunday stroll whose route crossed each of the seven bridges in the town exactly once. Euler analyzed this local pastime using what are now known as Euler circuits.

Figure 1.4b shows an Euler circuit. These circuits get their name from the great eighteenth-century mathematician Leonhard Euler (pronounced oy′ lur), who first studied them (see Spotlight 1.1). Euler was the founder of the theory of graphs. One of his first discoveries was that some graphs have no Euler circuits at all. For example, in the graph in Figure 1.5b, it would be impossible to start at one point and cover all the edges without retracing some steps: if we try to start a circuit at the leftmost vertex, we discover that once we have left the vertex, we have "used up" the only edge meeting it. We have no way to return to our starting point except to reuse that edge. But this is not allowed in an Euler circuit. If we try to start a circuit at one of the other two vertices, we likewise can't complete it to form an Euler circuit.

As mentioned in Spotlight 1.2, realistic problems of this type will involve larger neighborhoods that might require the use of a computer. In addition, there may be other complications that might take us beyond the simple mathematics we want to stick to.

FIGURE 1.5
(a) The three shaded sidewalks cannot be covered by an Euler circuit. (b) The graph of the shaded sidewalks in part (a).

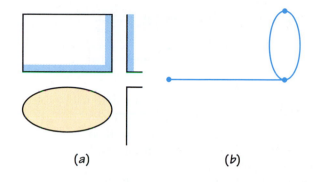

(a) *(b)*

Since we are interested in finding circuits, and Euler circuits are the most efficient ones, we will want to know how to find them. If a graph has no Euler circuit, we will want to develop the next best circuits, those having minimum deadheading. These topics make up the rest of this chapter.

SPOTLIGHT 1.2

The Human Aspect of Problem Solving

Thomas Magnanti

Thomas Magnanti, professor of operations research and management, heads the Department of Management Science at MIT's Sloan School of Management. Here are some of his observations:

Typically, a management science approach has several different ingredients. One is just structuring the problem — understanding that the problem is an Euler circuit problem or a related management science problem. After that, one has to develop the solution methods.

But one should also recognize that you don't just push a button and get the answer. In using these underlying mathematical tools, we never want to lose sight of our common sense, of understanding, intuition, and judgment. The computer provides certain kinds of insights. It deals with some of the combinatorial complexities of these problems very

nicely. But a model such as an Euler circuit can never capture the full essence of a decision-making problem.

Typically, when we solve the mathematical problem, we see that it doesn't quite correspond to the real problem we want to solve. So we make modifications in the underlying model. It is an interactive approach, using the best of what computers and mathematics have to offer and the best of what we, as human beings, with our own decision-making capabilities, have to offer.

Finding Euler Circuits

Now that we know what an Euler circuit is, we are faced with two obvious questions:

1. Is there a way to tell by calculation, not by trial and error, if a graph has an Euler circuit?
2. Is there a method, other than trial and error, for finding an Euler circuit when one exists?

Euler answered these questions in 1735 by using the concepts of valence and connectedness.

> The **valence** of a vertex in a graph is the number of edges meeting at the vertex.

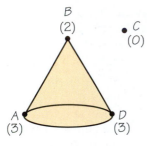

FIGURE 1.6
Valences of vertices.

Figure 1.6 illustrates the concept of valence, with vertices A and D having valence 3, vertex B having valence 2, and vertex C having valence 0. Isolated vertices such as vertex C are an annoyance in Euler circuit theory. Because they don't occur in typical applications, we henceforth assume that our graphs have no vertices of valence 0.

Figure 1.3b has four vertices of valence 2, namely, the outer corners of the graph. This graph also has two vertices of valence 4. Notice that each vertex has a valence that is an even number. We'll soon see that this is very significant.

> A graph is said to be **connected** if for every pair of its vertices there is at least one path connecting the two vertices.

Given a graph, if we can find even one pair of vertices not connected by a path, then we say that the graph is not connected. For example, the graph in Figure 1.7 is not connected because we are unable to join A to D with a path of edges. However, the graph does consist of two "pieces" or connected components, one

FIGURE 1.7
A nonconnected graph.

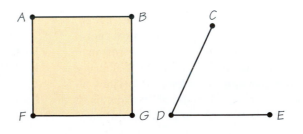

containing the vertices *A*, *B*, *F*, and *G*, the other containing *C, D*, and *E*. A connected graph will contain a single connected component. Notice that the parking-control graph of Figure 1.3b is connected.

We can now state Euler's theorem, his simple answer to the problem of detecting when a graph *G* has an Euler circuit:

1. If *G* is connected and has all valences even, then *G* has an Euler circuit.
2. Conversely, if *G* has an Euler circuit, then *G* must be connected and all its valences must be even numbers.

In the optional section "Proving Euler's Theorem," you will find an outline of a proof of this theorem.

Since the parking-control graph of Figure 1.3b conforms to the connectedness and even-valence conditions, Euler's theorem tells us that it has an Euler circuit. We already have found an Euler circuit for Figure 1.4b by trial and error. For a very large graph, however, trial and error may take a long time. It is usually quicker to check whether the graph is connected and even-valent than to find out if it has an Euler circuit.

Once we know there is an Euler circuit in a certain graph, how do we find it? Many people find that, after a little practice, they can find Euler circuits by trial and error, and they don't need detailed instructions on how to proceed. At this point you should see if you can develop this skill by trying to find Euler circuits in Figure 1.8a, Figure 1.9a, and Figure 1.10. In doing your experiments, draw your graph in ink and the circuit in pencil so you can erase. Make your graph big and clear so you won't get confused.

If you would like more guidance on how to find an Euler circuit without trial and error, here is a method that works: never use an edge that is the only link between two parts of the graph that still need to be covered. Figure 1.9b illustrates this. Here we have started the circuit at *A* and gotten to *D* via *B* and *C*, and we want to know what to do next. Going to *E* would be a bad idea because the uncovered part of the graph would then be disconnected into left and right portions. You will never be able to get from the left part back to the right part because you have just used the last remaining link between these parts. Therefore you should stay on the right side and finish that before using the edge from *D* to *E*. This kind of thinking needs to be applied every time you need to choose a new edge.

FIGURE 1.8
(a) A graph having (b) an Euler circuit.

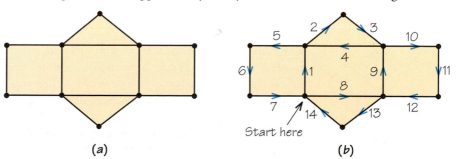

(a)   (b)

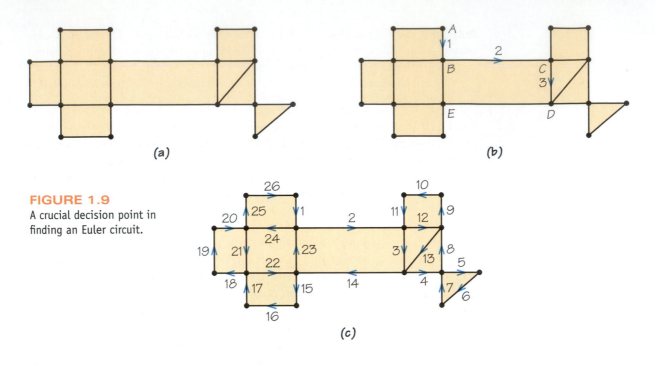

FIGURE 1.9
A crucial decision point in finding an Euler circuit.

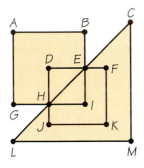

FIGURE 1.10
A graph with an Euler circuit.

Let's see how this works, starting at the beginning at *A*. From vertex *A* there are two possible edges, and neither of them disconnects the unused portion of the graph. Thus, we could have gone either to the left or down. Having gone down to *B*, we now have three choices, none of which disconnects the unused part of the graph. After choosing to go from *B* to *C*, we find that any of the three choices at *C* is acceptable. Can you complete the Euler circuit? Figure 1.9c shows one of many ways to do this.

The method just described leaves many edge choices up to you. When there are many acceptable edges for your next step, you can pick one at random. You might even flip a coin. When computers carry out algorithms of this sort, they use random number generators, which mimic the flipping of a coin.

E X A M P L E   *Finding an Euler Circuit*

Check the valences of the vertices and the connectivity of the graph in Figure 1.8a to verify that the graph does have an Euler circuit. Now try to find an Euler circuit for that graph. You can start at any vertex. When you are done, compare your solution with the Euler circuit given in Figure 1.8b. If your path covers each edge exactly once and returns to its original vertex (is a circuit), then it is an Euler circuit, even if it is not the same as the one we give. ◆

Optional   *Proving Euler's Theorem*

We'll start by proving that if a graph has an Euler circuit, then it must have only even valences and it must be connected. Let X be any vertex of the graph. We will show that the edges at X can be paired up, and this will prove that the valence is even. Every edge at X is used by the Euler circuit as an outgoing edge (leaving from X) or an incoming edge (arriving at X). If the Euler circuit starts at X, then pair up the first edge used by the circuit with the last one (when the circuit returns to X for the last time). In addition, each other edge at X that is used by the circuit as an incoming edge will be paired with the outgoing edge that is used next. Since all edges at X are used by the Euler circuit, none more than once, this pairs up the edges. But what if X is not the start of the Euler circuit? Then do the pairing like this: the first incoming edge at X is paired with the outgoing one used next, the second incoming edge at X is paired with the outgoing one used next, and so on. For example, in Figure 1.11 at vertex B we would pair up edges 2 and 3 and edges 9 and 10. At vertex C we would pair up edges 4 and 5 and edges 8 and 9. Can you see how the pairings would work at D? How about vertex A? (In studying this example, you might think it would be simpler to count the edges at a vertex to see that the valence is even. True, but our pairing method works for a graph about which we know nothing except that it has an Euler circuit.)

To see that a graph with an Euler circuit is connected, note that by following the Euler circuit around we can get from one edge to any other edge (it covers them all) using a portion of the Euler circuit. Since every vertex is on an edge (there are no vertices of 0 valence), we can get from any vertex to any other using a portion of the Euler circuit.

So far, this is not a complete proof of Euler's theorem. It is also necessary to prove that if a graph has all vertices even-valent and is connected, then an Euler circuit can be found for it. The book by Malkevitch and Meyer in the Suggested Readings section contains an elementary proof of this.   ◆

FIGURE 1.11
An Euler circuit starting and ending at *A*.

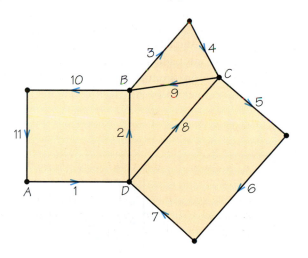

Circuits with Reused Edges

Now let's see what Euler's theorem tells us about the three-block neighborhood with parking meters, represented by dots in Figure 1.12a. Figure 1.12b shows the corresponding graph. (Since we only use edges to represent sidewalks along which the officer must walk, the sidewalk with no meters is not represented by any edge in the graph.) This graph has two odd valences, so Euler's theorem tells us that there is no Euler circuit for this graph.

Since we must reuse some edges in this graph in order to cover all edges in a circuit, for efficiency we need to keep the total length of reused edges to a minimum. This type of problem, in which we want to minimize the length of a circuit by carefully choosing which edges to retrace, is often called the **Chinese postman problem** (like parking-control routes, mail routes need to be efficient). The problem was first studied by the Chinese mathematician Meigu Guan in 1962—hence the name. Although the Euler circuit theory doesn't deal directly with reused edges or edges of different lengths, we can extend the theory to help solve the Chinese postman problem. The remainder of this chapter is dedicated to solving the Chinese postman problem and discussing applications besides parking control.

In a realistic Chinese postman problem, we need to consider the lengths of the sidewalks, streets, or whatever the edges represent, since we want to minimize the total length of the reused edges. However, to simplify things at the start, we can suppose that all edges represent the same length. (This is often called the *simplified* Chinese postman problem.) In this case, we need only count reused edges and need not add up their lengths. To solve the problem, we want to find a circuit that covers each edge and that has the minimal number of reuses of edges already covered.

To follow the procedure we are going to develop, look at the graph in Figure 1.13a, which is the same graph as in Figure 1.12b, but with labeled vertices. This graph has no Euler circuit, but there is a circuit that has only one reuse of an edge (*CG*), namely, *ABCDHGCGFBFEA*. Let's draw this circuit so that when edge *CG* is about to be reused, we install a new, extra, blue edge in the graph for the circuit to use. By duplicating edge *CG*, we can avoid reusing the edge. To duplicate an edge, we must add an edge that joins the two vertices that are already joined by the edge we want to duplicate. (It is not a good idea to join vertices that are not already connected by an edge; see Figure 1.15.) We have now created the graph of

FIGURE 1.12
(a) A street network and (b) its graphic representation.

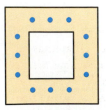
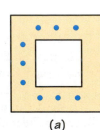
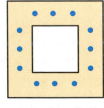

(a)

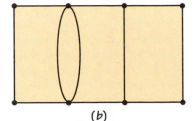

(b)

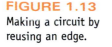

FIGURE 1.13
Making a circuit by
reusing an edge.

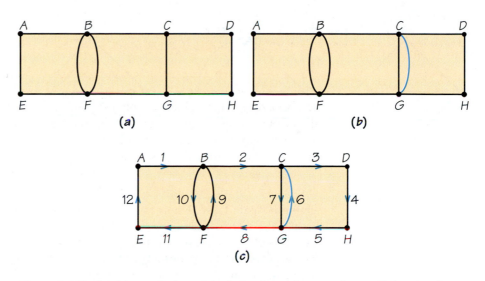

Figure 1.13b. In this graph the original circuit can be traced as an Euler circuit, using the new edge when needed. The circuit is shown in Figure 1.13c. Our theory will be based on using this idea in reverse, as follows:

1. Take the given graph and add edges by duplicating existing ones, until you arrive at a graph that is connected and even-valent.

> Adding edges to a graph to make all valences even is called **eulerizing** the graph.

We call this process eulerizing a graph, because the graph we produce will have an Euler circuit. (In our graphs, the edges we add are in color, and thus can be distinguished from the original edges, which are black. You may want to create a system to help you remember which edges are original and which are duplicates.)

2. Find an Euler circuit on the eulerized graph.
3. "Squeeze" this Euler circuit from the eulerized graph onto the original graph by reusing an edge of the original graph each time the circuit on the eulerized graph uses an added edge.

EXAMPLE *Eulerizing a Graph*

Suppose we want to eulerize the graph of Figure 1.14a. When we eulerize a graph, we first locate the vertices with odd valence. The graph in Figure 1.14a has two, *B* and *C*. Next, we add one end of an edge at each such vertex, matching the new edge up with an existing edge in the original graph. Figure 1.14b shows one way to eulerize the graph. Note that *B* and *C* have even valence in the second graph. After eulerization, each vertex has even valence. To see an Euler circuit on the eulerized

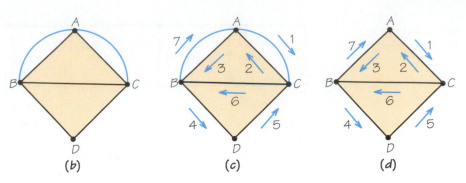

FIGURE 1.14
Eulerizing a graph.

graph in Figure 1.14c, simply follow the edges in numerical order and in the direction of the arrows, beginning and ending at vertex A. The final step, shown in Figure 1.14d, is to "squeeze" our Euler circuit into the original graph. There are two reuses of previously covered edges. Notice that each reuse of an edge corresponds to an added edge.   ◆

In the previous example we noticed that we could count how many reuses we needed by counting added edges. This is generally true in this type of problem: *if you add the new edges correctly, the number of reuses of edges equals the number of edges added during eulerization.*

Adding new edges correctly means adding only edges that are duplicates of existing edges. Doing this makes the rule, just stated in italics, always true, and so it is easy to count the needed reuses.

To see why we add only duplicate edges, examine Figure 1.15a. We need to give X and Y even valences. Adding one long edge from X to Y (Figure 1.15b) might seem like an attractive idea, but such an edge is not a duplicate of an existing edge—it runs along a series of existing edges. (Remember, to duplicate an edge means to add an edge that joins two vertices that are already joined.) Suppose we added this long edge anyhow and applied the rule in italics. We would conclude that we only needed to reuse one edge. You can see that this is wrong by imagining an Euler circuit that uses this long edge. When you squeeze the Euler circuit back into the original graph, the alternative to using the long edge will be the whole series of three edges stretching from X to Y (shown by the heavy line in Figure 1.15c).

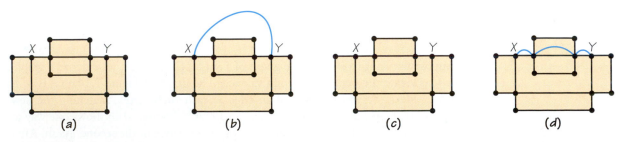

FIGURE 1.15   Eulerizing when the vertices are more than one edge apart.

If you don't add the long edge, but instead follow the rule that an added edge must duplicate an existing edge, you'll add the three edges in Figure 1.15d. Counting them will tell you the number of reuses you need (three, in this case).

Now that we have learned to eulerize, the next step is to try to get a best eulerization we can—one with the fewest added edges. It turns out that there are many ways to eulerize a graph. It is even possible that the smallest number of added edges can be achieved with two different eulerizations. This is the reason we use the phrase "a best eulerization" rather than "the best eulerization." Remember, we want a best eulerization because this enables us to find the circuit for the original graph that has the minimum number of reuses of edges.

E X A M P L E   *A Better Eulerization*

In Figure 1.16a, we begin with the same graph as in Figure 1.14, but we eulerize it in a different way—by adding only one edge (see Figure 1.16b). Figure 1.16c shows an Euler circuit on the eulerized graph, and in Figure 1.14d we see how it is squeezed onto the original graph. There is only one reuse of an edge, because we added one edge during eulerization.   ◆

The solution in Figure 1.16 is better than the solution in Figure 1.14 because one reuse is better than two. These examples suggest the following addition to our solution procedure: try to find the eulerization with the smallest number of added edges. This extra requirement makes the problem both more interesting and more difficult. For large graphs, a best eulerization may not be obvious. We can try out a few and pick the best among the ones we find, but there may be an even better one that our haphazard search does not turn up.

A systematic procedure for finding a best eulerization does exist, but the process is complicated. There is an especially easy technique for eulerizing the following special category of networks often found in our neighborhoods.

If a street network is composed of a series of rectangular blocks that form a large rectangle a certain number of blocks high by a certain number of blocks wide, the network is called *rectangular.*

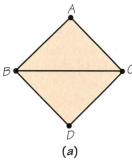

FIGURE 1.16
A better eulerization of
Figure 1.14.

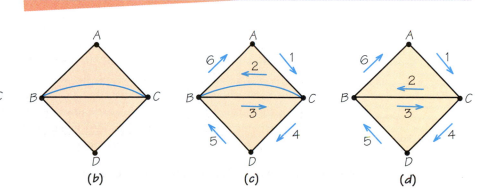

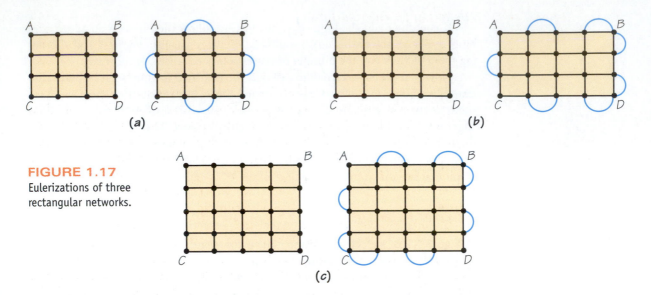

FIGURE 1.17
Eulerizations of three rectangular networks.

Examples of rectangular street networks (a 3-by-3, a 3-by-4, and a 4-by-4) are shown in Figure 1.17. The graph on the right in each pair shows a best eulerization for the rectangular street network on the left. There appear to be three different eulerization patterns, depending upon whether the rectangle height and width in the original graph are odd or even numbers. In Figure 1.17a, both lengths are 3, both odd; in Figure 1.17b, one length is odd (3) and one is even (4); in Figure 1.17c, both lengths are 4, an even number.

Although the patterns appear different, one technique can be used to create all of them. This technique can be thought of as involving an "edge walker" who walks around the outer boundary of the large rectangle in some direction, say, clockwise. He starts at any corner, say, the upper left corner. As he goes around, he adds edges by the following rules. When he comes to an odd-valent vertex, he links it to the next vertex with an added edge. This next vertex now becomes either even or odd. If it became even, he skips it and continues around, looking for an odd vertex. If it became odd (this could only happen at a corner of the big rectangle), the edge walker links it to the next vertex and then checks this vertex to see whether it is even or odd. Each of the three parts of Figure 1.17 has been eulerized by this method.

In a street network that is not rectangular, the eulerization process is started by locating all the vertices with odd valence and then pairing these vertices with each other and finding the length of the shortest path between each pair. We look for the shortest paths, since each edge on the connecting paths will be duplicated. The idea is to choose the pairings cleverly so that the sum of the lengths of those paths is the smallest it can be. With a little practice, most people can find a best or nearly best eulerization using only this idea together with trial and error and some ingenuity. Those interested in a further discussion can read the following optional section, "Finding Good Eulerizations."

Optional   *Finding Good Eulerizations*

Suppose we want a perfect procedure for eulerizing a graph. What theoretical ideas and methods could we use to build such a tool?

One building block we could use is a method for finding the shortest path between two given vertices of a graph. For example, let us focus on vertices X and Y in Figure 1.18a; both have odd valence. We can connect them with a pattern of duplicate edges, as in Figure 1.18b. The cost of this is the length of the path we duplicated from X to Y. A shorter path from X to Y, such as the one shown in Figure 1.18c, would be better. Fortunately, the *shortest-path problem* has been well studied, and we have many good procedures for solving it exactly, even in large, complex graphs. These procedures are discussed in some of the suggested readings given at the end of this chapter, but are beyond the scope of this text.

But there is more to eulerizing the graph in Figure 1.18a than dealing with X and Y. Notice that we have odd valences at Z and W. Should we connect X and Y with a path, and then connect Z and W, as in Figure 1.18d? Or should we connect X to Z and Y to W, as in Figure 1.18e? Another alternative is to use connections X to W and Y to Z, as in Figure 1.18f. It turns out that the alternatives in both Figures 1.18e and 1.18f are preferable to the one in Figure 1.18d, since they involve seven added edges, whereas Figure 1.18d uses nine.

FIGURE 1.18
Choosing among eulerizations.

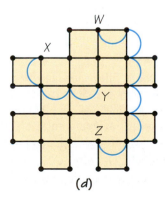

(a)

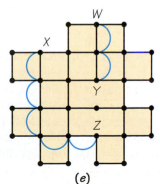

(b)

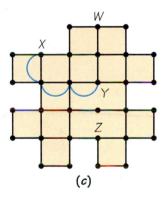

(c)

(d)

(e)

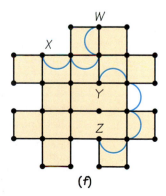

(f)

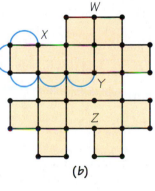

At the start, it is often not clear which alternatives are best. The problem is how to pair up vertices for connection to get a set of paths whose total length is minimal. This problem, called the *matching problem,* has also been studied and solved. As with the shortest-path problem, refer to Suggested Readings for further details. ◆

Circuits with More Complications

Euler circuits and eulerizing have many more practical applications than just checking parking meters. Almost any time services must be delivered along streets or roads, our theory can make the job more efficient. Examples include collecting garbage, salting icy roads, plowing snow, inspecting railroad tracks, and reading electric meters (see Spotlight 1.3).

Each of these problems has its own special requirements that may call for modifications in the theory. For example, in the case of garbage collection, the edges of our graph will represent streets, not sidewalks. If some of the streets are

SPOTLIGHT 1.3

Israel Electric Company Reduces Meter-Reading Task

The Beersheba branch of Israel's major electric company wanted to make the job of meter reading more efficient. When the branch managers decided to minimize the number of people required to read the electric meters in the houses of one particular neighborhood, they set a precedent by applying management science. Formerly, each person's route had been worked out by trial and error and intuition, with no help from mathematics. The whole job required 24 people, each doing a part of the neighborhood in a five-hour shift.

At first, it looks as though one would find a more efficient way of doing the work the same way as in the Chinese postman problem, but there are two important differences. First, the neighborhood was big enough to negate any possibility of having only one route assigned to one person. Instead, it was necessary to find a number of routes that, taken together, covered all the edges (sidewalks). Second, a meter reader who was done with a route was allowed to return home directly. Thus, there was no reason for the individual routes to return to their starting points; therefore, routes could be paths instead of circuits.

The Beersheba researchers found solutions to these problems by modifying the basic ideas we have described in this chapter. They managed to cover the neighborhood with 15 five-hour routes, a 40% reduction of the original 24 five-hour routes. Altogether, these routes involve a total of 4338 minutes of walking time, of which 41 minutes (less than 1%) is deadheading.

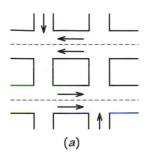

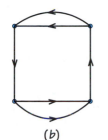

FIGURE 1.19
(a) Salt-spreading route, where each west–west street has two traffic lanes in the same direction, and (b) an appropriate digraph model.

one-way, we need to put arrows on the corresponding edges, resulting in a directed graph, or **digraph.** The circuits we seek will have to obey these arrows. In the case of salt spreaders and snowplows, each lane of a street needs to be modeled as a directed edge, as shown in Figure 1.19. Note that the arrows on the map and digraph are not in color because these arrows denote restrictions in traversal possibilities, not parts of circuits.

Like salt spreaders, street-sweeping trucks can travel in only one lane at a time and need to obey the direction of traffic. Street sweepers, however, have an additional complication: parked cars. It is very difficult to clean the street if cars are parked along the curb. Yet for overall efficiency, those who are responsible for routing street sweepers want to interfere with parking as little as possible. The common solution is to post signs specifying times when parking is prohibited, such as Thursday between 8 A.M. and 2 P.M. Because the parking-time factor is a constraint on street sweeping, it is important not only to find an Euler circuit, or a circuit with very few duplications, but a circuit that visits streets when they are free of cars. Once again, the theory can be modified to handle this constraint.

Finally, because towns and cities of any size will have more than one street sweeper, parking officer, or garbage truck, a single best route will not suffice. Instead, they will have to divide the territory into multiple routes. The general goal is to find optimal solutions while taking into account traffic direction, number of lanes, time restrictions, and divided routes (see Figure 1.20).

FIGURE 1.20   (a) Fairfield, California, USA. Today, finding optimal routes within complex street networks is often done with sophisticated computer-based color graphic systems. (b) A computer-generated street network.

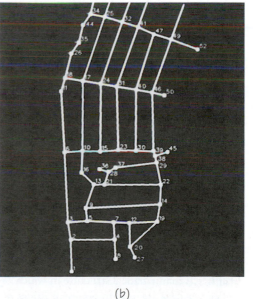

(a)   (b)

Management science makes all this possible. For example, a pilot study done in the 1970s in New York City showed that applying these techniques to street sweepers in just one district could save about $30,000 per year. With 57 sanitation districts in New York, this would amount to a savings of more than $1.5 million in a single year. In addition, the same principles could be extended to garbage collection, parking control, and other services carried out on street networks.

This plan was not adopted when first proposed. Because city services take place in a political context, several other factors come into play. For example, union leaders try to protect the jobs of city workers, bureaucrats might try to keep their departmental budgets high, and elected politicians rarely want to be accused of cutting the jobs of their constituents. Thus political obstacles can overrule management science. As mentioned in Spotlight 1.2, such human factors often arise when applying management science. Perhaps a more acceptable street-sweeping plan would have been devised for New York City if more attention had been paid to the human factors earlier.

Despite the complications of real-world problems, management science principles provide ways to understand these problems by using graphs as models. We can reason about the graphs and then return to the real-world problem with a workable solution. The results we get can have a lasting effect on the efficiency and economic well-being of any organization or community.

REVIEW VOCABULARY

Chinese postman problem   The problem of finding a circuit on a graph that covers every edge of the graph at least once and that has the shortest possible length.

Circuit   A path that starts and ends at the same vertex.

Connected graph   A graph is connected if it is possible to reach any vertex from any specified starting vertex by traversing edges.

Digraph   A graph in which each edge has an arrow indicating the direction of the edge. Such directed edges are appropriate when the relationship is "one-sided" rather than symmetric (e.g., one-way streets as opposed to regular streets).

Edge   A link joining two vertices in a graph.

Euler circuit   A circuit that traverses each edge of a graph exactly once.

Eulerizing   Adding new edges to a graph so as to make a graph that possesses an Euler circuit.

Graph   A mathematical structure in which points (called vertices) are used to represent things of interest,

and in which links (called edges) are used to connect vertices, denoting that the connected vertices have a certain relationship.

Management science   A discipline in which mathematical methods are applied to management problems in pursuit of optimal solutions that cannot readily be obtained by common sense.

Operations research   Another name for management science.

Optimal solution   When a problem has various solutions that can be ranked in preference order (perhaps according to some numerical measure of "goodness"), the optimal solution is the best-ranking solution.

Path   A connected sequence of edges in a graph.

Valence (of a vertex)   The number of edges touching that vertex.

Vertex   A point in a graph where one or more edges end.

SUGGESTED READINGS

BELTRAMI, EDWARD J. *Models for Public Systems Analysis,* Academic Press, New York, 1977. Section 5.4 deals with material similar to that in this chapter. The rest of the book gives a nice selection of applications of mathematics to plant location, manpower scheduling, providing emergency services, and other public service areas. The mathematics is somewhat more advanced than in this chapter.

COZZENS, MARGARET B., AND RICHARD P. PORTER. *Mathematics and Its Applications,* Heath, Lexington, Mass., 1987. Includes a nice discussion of Euler circuit ideas applied to DNA fragments.

MALKEVITCH, JOSEPH, AND WALTER MEYER. *Graphs,*

Models, and Finite Mathematics, Prentice Hall, Englewood Cliffs, N.J., 1974. An introductory text, which includes much the same material as in this chapter, but with a little more detail. A different algorithm for finding Euler circuits is given.

The following two references discuss the shortest-path and matching problems in depth; they are suitable for advanced students and for faculty.

ROBERTS, FRED S. *Applied Combinatorics,* Prentice Hall, Englewood Cliffs, N.J., 1984.

TUCKER, ALAN. *Applied Combinatorics,* 2nd ed., Wiley, New York, 1984.

SUGGESTED WEB SITE

www.math.harvard.edu/~hmb/isue2.2/euler/euler.html
www.informs.org   This Web site is maintained by the Institute for Operations Research and the Management Sciences, the main professional organization in these fields in the United States. It contains information of (and/or links to) news items about operations research and management science and employment opportunities and summer internships; it also has a student newsletter. Much of the material is written in a nontechnical style.

SKILLS CHECK

1. What is the valence of vertex *A* in the graph below?

   (a) 2
   (b) 1
   (c) 4

   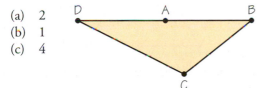

2. For the graph below, which statement is correct?

   (a)   The graph has an Euler circuit.
   (b)   One new edge is required to eulerize this graph.

   (c)   Two new edges are required to eulerize this graph.

3. For which of the situations below is it most desirable to find an Euler circuit or an efficient eulerization of the graph?

   (a)   Sweeping the sidewalks of a small town
   (b)   Planning a new highway
   (c)   Planning a parade route in Muncie, Indiana

4. Consider the path represented by the sequence of numbered edges on the graph below. Which statement is correct?

   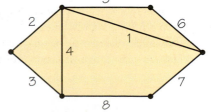

(a) The sequence of numbered edges forms an Euler circuit.

(b) The sequence of numbered edges traverses each edge exactly once, but is not an Euler circuit.

(c) The sequence of numbered edges forms a circuit, but not an Euler circuit.

5. What is the minimum number of duplicated edges needed to create a good eulerization for the graph here?

(a) 4 edges
(b) 3 edges
(c) 2 edges

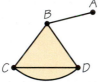

6. Suppose the edges of a graph represent streets that must be plowed after a snowstorm. In order to eulerize the graph, four edges must be added. The real-world interpretation of this is

(a) four streets will not be plowed
(b) four streets will be traversed twice
(c) four new streets would be built

7. If a graph has six vertices of odd valence, what is the absolute minimum number of edges that needs to be added (duplicated) to eulerize the graph?

(a) 6 (b) 0 (c) 3

EXERCISES ▲ *Optional.* ■ *Advanced.* ◆ *Discussion.*

Basic Concepts

1. In the graph below, the vertices represent cities and the edges represent roads connecting them. What are the valences of the vertices in this graph? (Keep in mind that *E* is part of the graph.) What might the valence of city *E* be showing about the geography?

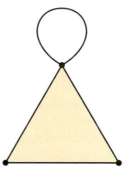

2. In the two graphs below, the vertices represent cities and the edges represent roads connecting them. In which graphs could a person located in city *A*

choose any other city and then find a sequence of roads to get from *A* to that other city?

3. Is the figure below a graph? Explain your answer

4. Jack and Jill are located in Miami and want to fly to Berlin (see Figure 1.2). Jill says she can think of three paths to get them there. Can you? Jack says that a path can repeat edges so there are more than three. Is Jack right?

5. In the graph in Figure 1.8, find the smallest possible number of edges you could remove that would disconnect the graph.

6. In the graph in Figure 1.17, find the smallest possible number of edges you could remove that would disconnect the graph.

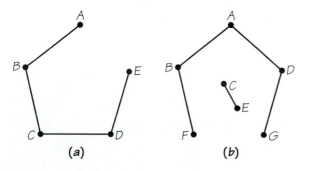

(a)   (b)

7. Is it possible that a street network gives rise to a disconnected graph? If so, draw such a network of blocks and streets and parking meters (in the style of Figure 1.12a). Then draw the disconnected graph it gives rise to.

Modeling

▲   8. For the street network in Exercise 7, draw the graph that would be useful for routing a garbage truck. Assume that all streets are two-way and that passing once down a street suffices to collect from both sides.

◆   9. A postal worker is supposed to deliver mail on all streets represented by edges in the graph below by traversing each edge exactly once. The first day the worker traverses the numbered edges in the order shown in (a), but the supervisor is not satisfied—why? The second day the worker follows the path indicated in (b), and the worker is unhappy—why? Is the original job description realistic? Why?

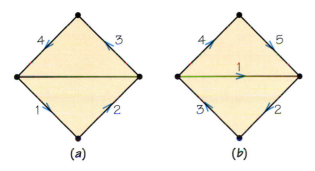

(a)   (b)

▲   10. For the street network in Exercise 9, draw the graph that would be useful for routing a snow-plow. Assume that all streets are two-way, one lane in each direction, and that you need to pass down each lane separately.

▲   11. For the street network at the top of the next column, draw the graph that would be useful for finding an efficient route for checking parking meters. (*Hint:* Notice that not every sidewalk has a meter; see Figure 1.12.)

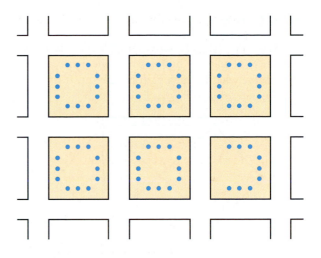

▲   12. (a) For the street network in Exercise 11, draw a graph that would be useful for routing a garbage truck. Assume that all streets are two-way and that passing once down a street suffices to collect from both sides. (b) Do the same problem on the assumption that one pass down the street only suffices to collect from one side.

13. For the street network below, draw the graph that would be useful for finding an efficient route for checking parking meters. (*Hint:* Notice that not every sidewalk has a meter; see Figure 1.12.)

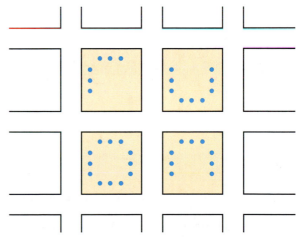

Euler Circuits

14. Examine the paths represented by the numbered sequences of edges in both parts of the figure below. Determine whether each path is a circuit. If it is a circuit, determine if it is an Euler circuit.

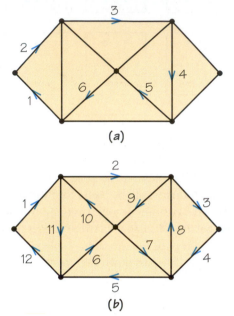

(a)

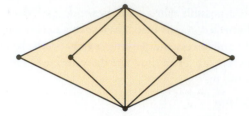

20. In the graph below, we see a territory for a parking-control officer that has no Euler circuit. How many sidewalks (edges) need to be dropped in order to enable us to find an Euler circuit?

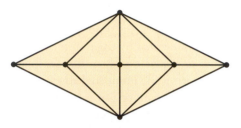

(b)

Eulerization and Squeezing

21. Find an Euler circuit on the eulerized graph (b) of the following figure. Use it to find a circuit on the original graph (a) that covers all edges and only reuses edges five times.

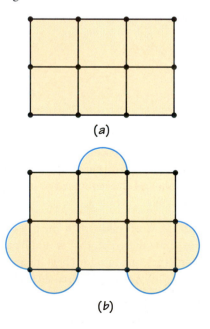

15. In Figure 1.13c, suppose we started an Euler circuit using this sequence of edges: 9, 10, 8, 7 (ignore existing arrows on the edges). What does our guideline for finding Euler circuits tell you not to do next?

16. In Figure 1.8b, suppose we started an Euler circuit using this sequence of edges: 14, 13, 8, 1, 4 (ignore existing arrows on the edges). What does our guideline for finding Euler circuits tell you not to do next?

17. Find an Euler circuit on the graph of Figure 1.15d (including the blue edges).

18. Find an Euler circuit on the right-hand graph in Figure 1.17a.

19. In the graph at the top of the next column, we see a territory for a parking-control officer that has no Euler circuit. Which sidewalk (edge) could be dropped so we could find an Euler circuit?

22. In the graph below, add one or more edges to produce a graph that has an Euler circuit.

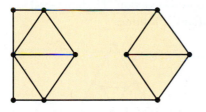

23. Can you find an eulerization with seven added edges for a 2-by-5-block rectangular street network? Can you do better than seven?

24. Squeeze the circuit shown in graph (a) below onto graph (b). Show your answers by numbered arrows on the edges.

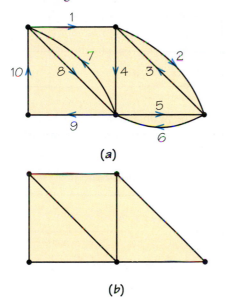

(a)

(b)

Then squeeze the circuit shown in graph (a) onto graph (b). Show your answers by numbered arrows on the edges.

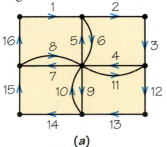

(a)

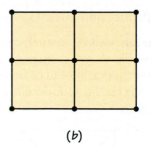

(b)

▲ 25. Eulerize these rectangular street networks using the same patterns that would be used by the "edge walker" described in the text.

(a)   A 5 × 5 rectangle
(b)   A 5 × 4 rectangle
(c)   A 6 × 6 rectangle

▲ 26. Find good eulerizations for these graphs, using as few duplicated edges as you can. See the optional section "Finding Good Eulerizations" for hints.

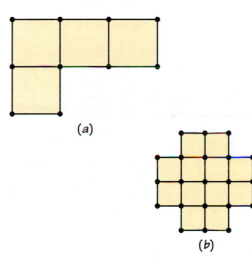

(a)

(b)

(c)

Minimum Duplication Circuits

27. A college campus has a central square with sidewalks arranged like the edges in the graph at the left. Show how all the sidewalks can be traversed efficiently in one circuit; your circuit will have to repeat some edges.

28. The figure below shows a river, some islands, and bridges connecting the islands and riverbanks. A charity fund-raiser is sponsoring a puzzle race in which entrants have to start and end at *A*, go over every bridge at least once, and end at *A*. The first one back to *A* gets a prize. Draw a graph that would be useful for finding a route that requires the least recrossing of bridges. Show what that route would be.

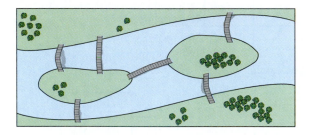

▲ 29. The year after the puzzle race described in Exercise 28, the sponsors want to do it again, but they need a new puzzle so that last year's participants won't have an unfair advantage over newcomers because of their previous experience. They can't construct new bridges or tear old ones down, so they add this rule: each of the bridges touching the right-hand island needs to be crossed at least twice. Draw a graph that would be useful for finding a route that requires the least recrossing of bridges. Show what that route would be.

▲ 30. Find a circuit in the graph below that covers every edge and has as few reuses as possible. See the optional section "Finding Good Eulerizations" for hints.

▲ 31. In the figure below, all blocks are 1000-by-1000 feet, except for the middle column of blocks, which are 1000-by-4000 feet. Find a circuit of minimum total length that covers all edges.

▲ 32. In the figure below, all blocks are 1000-by-1000 feet, except for the middle column of blocks, which are 1000-by-4000 feet. Find a circuit of minimum total length that covers all edges.

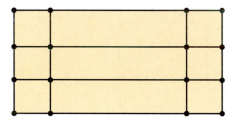

Additional Exercises

33. Which graphs (see top of left column on page 27) have Euler circuits? In the ones that do, find the Euler circuits by numbering the edges in the order the Euler circuit uses them. For the ones that don't, explain why no Euler circuit is possible.

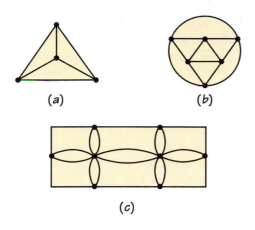

(a)   (b)

(c)

34. Find a minimum duplication circuit in a 3-by-5-block rectangular street network.

▲ **35.** Draw a graph with four vertices and all of the valences odd.

36. Find an Euler circuit on the eulerized graph (b) of the following figure. Use it to find a circuit on the original graph (a) that covers all edges and only reuses edges four times.

(a)

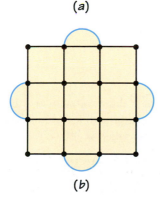

(b)

37. Which of these graphs are connected?

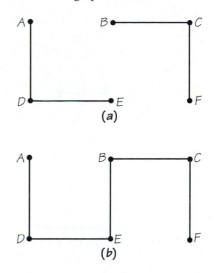

(a)

(b)

▲ **38.** In the graph below, find a circuit that covers every edge and has as few reuses as possible. See the optional section "Finding Good Eulerizations" for hints.

■ **39.** A graph G represents a street network to be traveled by a postal worker who must traverse every street twice, once for each side of the street. In graph G, the edges represent sidewalks. Does such a graph always have an Euler circuit? Explain your answer.

■ **40.** Suppose that for a certain graph it is possible to disconnect it by removing one edge. Explain why such a graph (before the edge is removed) must have at least one vertex of odd valence. (*Hint:* Show that it cannot have an Euler circuit.)

▲ 41. Find the best eulerizations you can for the two graphs below.

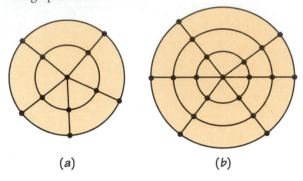

(a)   (b)

42. Each graph below represents the sidewalks to be cleaned in a fancy garden (one pass over a sidewalk will clean it). Can the cleaning be done using an Euler circuit? If so, show the circuit in each graph by numbering the edges in the order the Euler circuit uses them. If not, explain why no Euler circuit is possible.

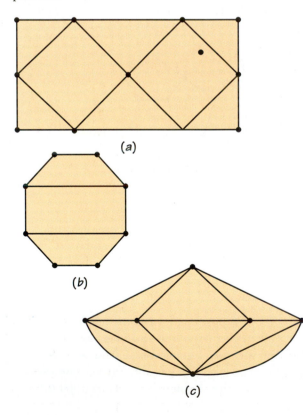

(a)

(b)

(c)

■ 43. If an edge is added to an already existing graph, connecting two vertices already in the graph, explain why the number of vertices with odd valence has the same parity before and after. (This means if it was even before, it is even after, while if it was odd before, it remains odd.)

■ 44. Any graph can be built in the following fashion: put down dots for the vertices, then add edges connecting the dots as needed. When you have put down the dots, and before any edges have been added, is the number of vertices with odd valence an even number or an odd number? What can you say about the number of vertices with odd valence when all the edges have been added (see Exercise 43)?

45. Draw the graph for the parking-control territory shown in the figure below. Label each vertex with its valence and determine if the graph is connected.

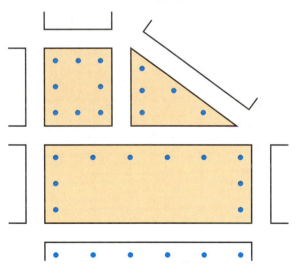

▲ 46. Eulerize these rectangular street networks using the same patterns that would be used by the "edge walker" described in the text.

(a)   A 6 × 5 rectangle
(b)   A 6 × 6 rectangle
(c)   A 5 × 3 rectangle

◆ **47.** The word *valence* is also used in chemistry. Find out what it means in chemistry and explain how this usage is similar to the use we make of it here.

■ **48.** For the street network below, draw a graph that represents the sidewalks with meters. Then find the minimum-length circuit that covers all sidewalks with meters. If you drew the graph as we recommended in this section, you would find that the shortest circuit has length 18 (it reuses every edge).

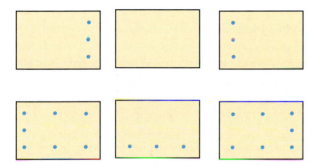

But the meter checker comes to you and says: "I don't know anything about your theories, but I have found a way to cover the sidewalks with meters using a circuit of length 10. My trick is that I don't rule out walking on sidewalks with no meters." Explain what he means and discuss whether his strategy can be used in other problems.

TECHNOLOGY CORNER

Representing a Graph

Graphs can be represented using spreadsheets. Label the vertices by letters (*A*, *B*, *C*, etc.) and the edges by numbers (1, 2, 3, etc.). Suppose each column (*A*, *B*, *C*, etc.) represents a vertex and each row (1, 2, 3, etc.) represents an edge of the graph. Then we can record each edge of the graph in the following way: in the first row, put a 1 in the two columns that represent the endpoints of edge 1. Continue, so that each row has two 1s in it. For example, the graph shown in Figure 1.21a can be represented by the spreadsheet shown in Figure 1.21b.

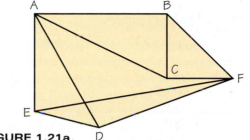

FIGURE 1.21a

	A	B	C	D	E	F
1	1	1				
2	1		1			
3	1			1		
4	1				1	
5		1				1
6		1	1			
7				1	1	
8				1		1
9					1	1
10			1			1

FIGURE 1.21b

TASK 1. Create a spreadsheet to represent the graph shown in Figure 1.22.
TASK 2. Draw a graph represented by the spreadsheet shown in Figure 1.23.

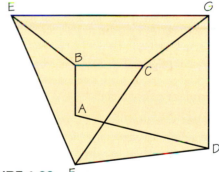

FIGURE 1.22

	A	B	C	D	E
1	1		1		
2		1	1		
3		1		1	
4		1			1
5				1	1
6	1				1

FIGURE 1.23

Calculating Vertex Degrees

When the graph is represented by a spreadsheet, calculating the degree of each vertex is easy. Use the **Sum** command to calculate the sum of each column. Since each column represents a vertex and each 1 in a column arises from an edge, the number of 1s in a column is exactly the degree of that vertex. For example, the spreadsheet shown in Figure 1.21b can be adapted to calculate vertex degrees, as shown in Figure 1.24.

	A	B	C	D	E	F
1	1	1				
2	1		1			
3	1			1		
4	1				1	
5		1				1
6		1	1			
7				1	1	
8				1		1
9					1	1
10			1			1
11						
12						
13						
14	4	3	3	3	3	4

FIGURE 1.24

Recall that a connected graph has an Euler circuit exactly when each vertex has even degree. Similarly, a connected graph has an Euler path when exactly two vertices have odd degree. The **Sum** command provides a quick method to detect when a connected graph has an Euler circuit or an Euler path.

TASK 3.　Create a spreadsheet for a graph with 10 vertices and at least 20 edges for which each column has an even number of 1s. Use the **Sum** command to compute the degree of each vertex.

TASK 4.　Draw the graph that corresponds to the spreadsheet you created in Task 3. Can you find an Euler circuit for this graph?

Exploration

If the graph is not connected, how does the spreadsheet reflect this? By looking at the spreadsheet you created for Task 3, how can you detect whether or not the corresponding graph is connected?

writing projects

1 ▶　Write a memo of three double-spaced typewritten pages to your local department of parking control (or police department) in which you suggest that management science techniques like the ones in this chapter be used to plan routes. Assume that the person to whom you are writing is not extensively trained in mathematics, but is willing to read through some technical material, provided you make it seem worth the trouble.

2 ▶　Do the same as in Writing Project 1, but to the department in charge of spreading salt on roads after snowstorms.

3 ▶　If you were making a recommendation to the mayor of New York City concerning proposed new street-sweeping routes, designed using the theory of this chapter, would you recommend that the changes be adopted or not? Write a memo (three double-spaced typewritten pages) that outlines the pros and cons as fairly as you can, and then conclude with your recommendation.

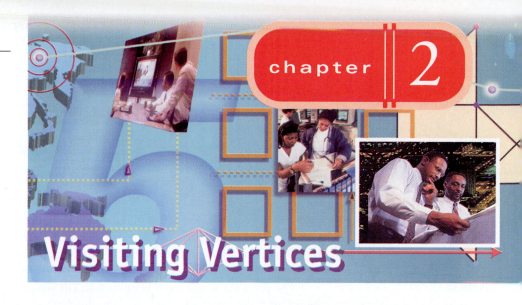

chapter 2

Visiting Vertices

"As we shall see, if Hamiltonian circuits were easy to find in any graph at all, many applied problems could be solved in a less costly way."

In the last chapter, we saw that it is relatively easy to determine if there is a circuit traversing the edges of a graph exactly once—for example, a route for street sweepers that covers the streets in a section of a city exactly once. However, the situation changes radically if we make an apparently innocuous change in the problem: When is it possible to find a route along distinct edges of a graph that visits each *vertex* once and only once in a simple circuit? For example, the wiggly line in Figure 2.1a shows a circuit we can take to tour that graph, visiting each vertex once and only once. This tour can be written *ABDGIHFECA*. Note that another way of writing the same circuit would be *EFHIGDBACE*. A different circuit visiting each vertex once and only once would be *CDBIGFEHAC* (Figure 2.1b). Do not be confused because *C* is written twice when we write down this list of vertices. We can think of the circuit as starting at any of its vertices, but we do start and end at the same vertex.

Hamiltonian Circuits

A tour, like the ones marked by wiggly edges in Figure 2.1, that starts at a vertex of a graph and visits each vertex once and only once, returning to where it started, is called a **Hamiltonian circuit.**

The concept is named for the Irish mathematician William Rowan Hamilton (1805–1865), who was one of the first to study it. (We now know that the concept was discovered somewhat earlier by Thomas Kirkman [1806–1895], a British

FIGURE 2.1
Wiggled edges illustrate
Hamiltonian circuits.

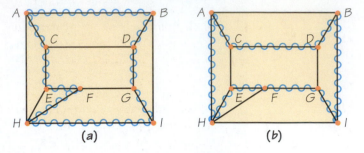

minister with a penchant for mathematics.) This problem is typical of the many new problems mathematicians create as a consequence of their professional training. In the situation here, motivated by our success in solving the problem of traversing all the *edges* of a graph, we will investigate visiting all the *vertices* of a graph.

The concepts of Euler and Hamiltonian circuits are similar in that both forbid reuse: the Euler circuit of edges, the Hamiltonian circuit of vertices. However, it is far more difficult to determine which connected graphs admit a Hamiltonian circuit than to determine which connected graphs have Euler circuits. As we saw in Chapter 1, looking at the valences of vertices tells us if a connected graph has an Euler circuit, but we have no such simple method for telling whether or not a graph has a Hamiltonian circuit.

Some special classes of graphs are known to have Hamiltonian circuits, and some special classes of graphs are known to lack them. For example, here is a method to construct an infinite family of graphs where each graph in the family cannot have a Hamiltonian circuit. Construct a vertical column of m vertices and a parallel column of n vertices, where m is bigger than n, as shown in Figure 2.2. The figure illustrates the typical case where $m = 4$ and $n = 2$. Now join each vertex on the left in the figure to every vertex on the right. As m and n vary, we get a family of different graphs.

Any graph obtained in this manner cannot have a Hamiltonian circuit. If a Hamiltonian circuit existed, it would have to include alternately vertices on the left and right of the figure. This is not possible, since the number of vertices on the left and right, m and n, respectively, are not the same. Unfortunately, it is unlikely that a method will ever be found to easily determine whether or not an arbitrarily chosen graph has a Hamiltonian circuit. As we shall see, if Hamiltonian circuits were easy to find in any graph at all, many applied problems could be solved in a less costly way.

FIGURE 2.2
An example of one graph from a family of graphs that has no Hamiltonian circuit. The number of vertices m on the left is chosen to be greater than the number of vertices n on the right. The case $m = 4$ and $n = 2$ is shown.

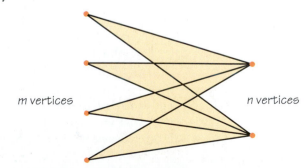

m vertices   n vertices

The Hamiltonian circuit problem and the Euler circuit problem are both examples of graph theory problems. Although we posed the Hamiltonian circuit problem merely as a variant of another graph theory problem with many applications (i.e., the Euler circuit problem), the Hamiltonian circuit problem itself has many applications. This is not unusual in mathematics. Often mathematics used to solve a particular real-world problem leads to new mathematics that suggests applications to other real-world situations.

Suppose inspections or deliveries need to be made at each vertex (rather than along each edge) of a graph. An "efficient" tour of the graph would be a route that started and ended at the same vertex and passed through all the vertices without reuse, or repetition; that is, the route would be a Hamiltonian circuit. Such routes would be useful for inspecting traffic signals or for delivering mail to drop-off boxes, which hold heavy loads of mail so urban postal carriers do not have to carry them long distances. There are many similar examples, but rather than pursue problems involving Hamiltonian circuits in general graphs, we will study instead a more important class of related problems.

E X A M P L E   *Vacation Planning*

Let's imagine that you are a college student studying in Chicago. During spring break you and a group of friends have decided to take a car trip to visit other friends in Minneapolis, Cleveland, and St. Louis. There are many choices as to the order of visiting the cities and returning to Chicago, but you want to design a

This photograph suggests some of the complexities of efficient mail delivery in a suburban environment. Sometimes services must be provided along edges (streets) and sometimes at vertices (corners).

route that minimizes the distance you have to travel. Presumably, you also want a route that cuts costs, and you know that minimizing distance will minimize the cost of gasoline for the trip. (Similar problems with different complications would arise for bus, railroad, or airplane trips.)

Imagine now that the local automobile club has provided you with the inter-city driving distances between Chicago, Minneapolis, Cleveland, and St. Louis. We can construct a graph model with this information, representing each city by a vertex and the legs of the journey between the cities by edges joining the vertices. To complete the model, we add a number called a **weight** to each graph edge, as in Figure 2.3. In this example, the weights represent the distances between the cities, each of which corresponds to one of the endpoints of the edges in the graph. (In other examples the weight might represent a cost, time, or profit.) We want to find a minimal-cost tour that starts and ends in Chicago and visits each other city once. Using our earlier terminology, what we wish to find is a **minimum-cost Hamiltonian circuit**—a Hamiltonian circuit with the lowest possible sum of the weights of its edges.

How can we determine which Hamiltonian circuit has minimum cost? There is a conceptually easy **algorithm,** or mechanical step-by-step process, for solving this problem:

1. Generate all possible Hamiltonian tours (starting from Chicago).
2. Add up the distances on the edges of each tour.
3. Choose the tour of minimum distance.

FIGURE 2.3
Road mileages between four cities.

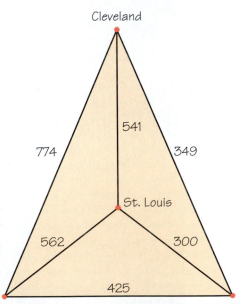

Steps 2 and 3 of the algorithm are straightforward. Thus, we need worry only about step 1, generating all the possible Hamiltonian circuits in a systematic way. To find the Hamiltonian tours, we will use the **method of trees,** as follows. Starting from Chicago, we can choose any of the three cities to visit after leaving Chicago. The first stage of the enumeration tree is shown in Figure 2.4. If Minneapolis is chosen as the first city to visit, then there are two possible cities to visit next, Cleveland and St. Louis. The possible branchings of the tree at this stage are shown in Figure 2.5. In this second stage, however, for each choice of first city we visited, there are two choices from this city to the second city visited. This would lead to the diagram in Figure 2.6.

Having chosen the order of the first two cities to visit, and knowing that no revisits (reuses) can occur in a Hamiltonian circuit, there is only one choice left for the next city. From this city we return to Chicago. The complete tree diagram showing the third and fourth stages for these routes is given in Figure 2.7. Notice, however, that because we can traverse a circular tour in either of two directions, the paths enumerated in the tree diagram of Figure 2.7 do *not* correspond to different Hamiltonian circuits. For example, the leftmost path (C–M–S–CL–C)

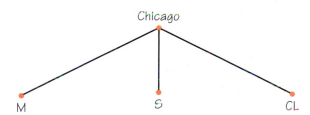

FIGURE 2.4 First stage in finding vacation-planning routes.

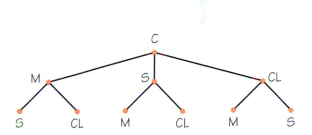

FIGURE 2.6 Complete second stage in finding vacation-planning routes.

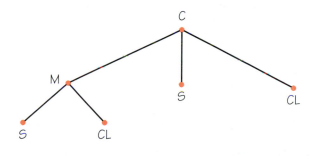

FIGURE 2.5 Part of the second stage in finding vacation-planning routes.

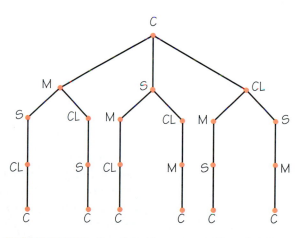

FIGURE 2.7 Completed tree enumeration of routes for vacation-planning problem.

FIGURE 2.8

The three Hamiltonian circuits for the vacation-planning problem of Figure 2.3.

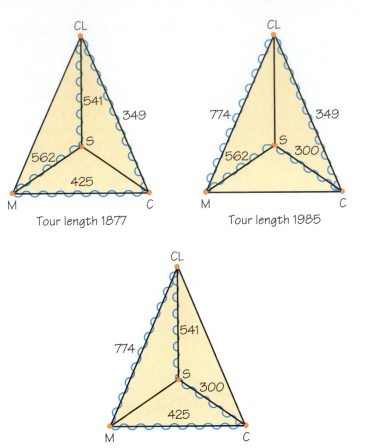

Tour length 1877

Tour length 1985

Tour length 2040

and the rightmost path (C–CL–S–M–C) represent the same Hamiltonian circuit. Thus, among what appear to be six different paths in the tree diagram, in fact, only three correspond to different Hamiltonian circuits. These three distinct Hamiltonian circuits are shown in Figure 2.8.

Note that in generating the Hamiltonian circuits we disregard the distances involved. We are concerned only with the different patterns of carrying out the visits. To find the optimal route, however, we must add up the distances on the edges to get each tour's length. Figure 2.8 shows that the optimal tour is Chicago, Minneapolis, St. Louis, Cleveland, Chicago. The length of this tour is 1877 miles.   ◆

The method of trees is not always as easy to use as our example suggests. Instead of doing our analysis for four cities, consider the general case of n cities. The graph model similar to that in Figure 2.3 would consist of a weighted graph with n vertices, with every pair of vertices joined by an edge. Such a graph is called **complete** because the edge between any pair of vertices is present in the graph. A complete graph with five vertices is illustrated in Figure 2.9.

FIGURE 2.9
A complete graph with
five vertices. Every pair of
vertices is joined by an
edge.

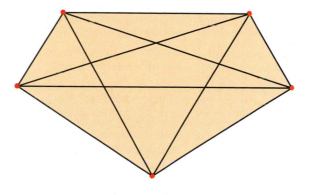

Fundamental Principle of Counting

How many Hamiltonian circuits are in a complete graph of n vertices? We can solve this problem by using the same type of analysis that emerged in the enumeration tree. The **method of trees** is a visual application of the **fundamental principle of counting,** a procedure for counting outcomes in multistage processes. Using this procedure we can count how many patterns occur in a situation by looking at the number of ways the component parts can occur. For example, if Jack has 9 shirts and 4 pair of trousers, he can wear $9 \times 4 = 36$ shirt–pants outfits. Each shirt can be worn with any of the pants. (This can be verified by drawing a tree diagram, but such a diagram is cumbersome for big numbers.)

> In general, the **fundamental principle of counting** can be stated this way: if there are a ways of choosing one thing, b ways of choosing a second after the first is chosen, . . . , and z ways of choosing the last item after the earlier choices, then the total number of choice patterns is $a \times b \times c \times \cdots \times z$.

EXAMPLE   *Counting*

Here are some other examples of how to use the fundamental principle of counting:

1. In a restaurant there are 4 kinds of soup, 12 entrees, 6 desserts, and 3 drinks. How many different four-course meals can a patron choose from? The four choices can be made in 4, 12, 6, and 3 ways, respectively. Hence, applying the fundamental principle of counting, there are $4 \times 12 \times 6 \times 3 = 864$ possible meals.

2. In a state lottery a contestant gets to pick a four-digit number that contains no zero followed by an uppercase or lowercase letter. How many such sequences of digits and a letter are there? Each of the four digits can be chosen in 9 ways (that is, 1, 2, . . . , 9), and the letter can be chosen in 52 ways (that is, $A, B, . . . , Z, a, b, . . . , z$). Hence, there are $9 \times 9 \times 9 \times 9 \times 52 = 341,172$ possible patterns.

3. A corporation is planning a musical logo consisting of four different notes from the scale C, D, E, F, G, A, and B. How many logos are there to chose from? The first note can be chosen in 7 ways, but since reuse is not allowed, the next note can be chosen in only 6 ways. The remaining two notes can be chosen in 5 and 4 ways, respectively. Using the fundamental principle of counting, $7 \times 6 \times 5 \times 4 = 840$ musical logos are possible. If reuse of notes is allowed, $7 \times 7 \times 7 \times 7 = 2401$ logos are possible.

◆

Again, in the problem of enumerating Hamiltonian circuits for the complete graph with n vertices, the city visited first after the home city can be chosen in $n - 1$ ways, the next city in $n - 2$ ways, and so on, until only one choice remains. Using the fundamental principle of counting, there are $(n - 1)! = (n - 1)(n - 2) \times \cdots \times 3 \times 2 \times 1$ routes. The exclamation mark in $(n - 1)!$ is read "factorial" and is shorthand notation for the product $(n - 1)(n - 2) \times \cdots \times 3 \times 2 \times 1$. For example, $5! = 5 \times 4 \times 3 \times 2 \times 1 = 120$.

As we saw in Figure 2.7, pairs of routes correspond to the same Hamiltonian circuit because one route can be obtained from the other by traversing the cities in reverse order. Thus, although there are $(n - 1)!$ possible routes, there are only half as many, or $(n - 1)!/2$, different Hamiltonian circuits. Now, if we have only a few cities to visit, $(n - 1)!/2$ Hamiltonian circuits can be listed and examined in a reasonable amount of time. Analysis of a 6-city problem would require generation of $(6 - 1)!/2 = 5!/2 = 120/2 = 60$ tours. But for, say, 25 cities, $24!/2$ is approximately 3×10^{23}. Even if these tours could be generated at the rate of 1 million a second, it would take 10 billion years to generate them all. Since large vacation-planning problems would take so long to solve using this method, despite its conceptual ease, it is sometimes referred to as the **brute force method** (that is, trying all the possibilities).

Traveling Salesman Problem

If the only benefit were saving money and time in vacation planning, the difficulty of finding a minimum-cost Hamiltonian circuit in a complete graph with n vertices for large values of n would not be of great concern. However, the problem we are discussing is one of the most common in operations research, the branch of mathematics concerned with getting governments and businesses to operate more efficiently. It is usually called the **traveling salesman problem (TSP)** because of its early formulation: determine the trip of minimum cost that a salesperson can make to visit the cities in a sales territory, starting and ending the trip in the same city.

Many situations require solving a TSP:

1. A lobster fisherman has set out traps at various locations and wishes to pick up his catch.
2. The telephone company wishes to pick up the coins from its pay telephone booths. (To avoid the high cost of picking up these coins, phone companies in many countries have adopted a system that uses prepurchased phone cards to operate phones. This means that there are no coins to collect!)
3. The electric (or gas) company needs to design a route for its meter readers.
4. A minibus must pick up six day campers and deliver them to camp, and later in the day return them home.
5. In drilling holes in a series of plates, the drill press operator (perhaps a robot) must drill the holes in a predetermined order.
6. Physical records, generated at automated teller machine (ATM) locations as backup in case of failure of the electronic systems, must be picked up periodically.

The meaning of cost can vary from one formulation of TSP to another. We may measure cost as distance, airplane ticket prices, time, or any other factor that is to be optimized.

In many situations, the TSP arises as a subproblem of a more complicated problem. For example, a supermarket chain may have a very large number of stores to be served from a single large warehouse. If there are fewer trucks than stores, the stores must be grouped into clusters so that one truck serves each cluster. If we then solve the TSP for every truck, we can minimize total costs for the supermarket chain. Similar vehicle-routing problems for dial-a-ride services for taking senior citizens to activity centers and for delivering children to their schools or camps often involve solving the TSP as a subproblem.

Strategies for Solving the Traveling Salesman Problem

Because the traveling salesman problem arises so often in situations where the associated complete graphs would be very large, we must find a faster method than the brute force method we have described. We need to look at our original problem in Figure 2.3, and try to find an alternative algorithm for solving it. Recall that our goal is to find the minimum-cost Hamiltonian circuit.

Nearest-Neighbor Algorithm

Let's try a new approach: starting from Chicago, first visit the nearest city, then visit the nearest city that has not already been visited. We return to the start city when no other choice is available. This approach is called the **nearest-neighbor algorithm.**

Applying this algorithm to the TSP in Figure 2.3 quickly leads to the tour of Chicago, St. Louis, Cleveland, Minneapolis, and Chicago, with a length of 2040 miles. Here is how this tour is determined. Since we are starting in Chicago, there is a choice of going to a city that is 425, 300, or 349 miles away. Since the smallest of these numbers is 300, we next visit St. Louis, which is the nearest neighbor of Chicago not already visited. At St. Louis, we have a choice of visiting next cities that are 541 or 562 miles away. Hence, Cleveland, which is nearer (541), is visited. To complete the tour, we visit Minneapolis and return to Chicago, thereby adding 774 and 425 miles to the length of the tour.

The nearest-neighbor algorithm is an example of a **greedy algorithm,** because at each stage a best (greedy) choice, based on an appropriate criterion, is made. Unfortunately, this is not the optimal tour that we saw $C-M-S-Cl-C$ was, for a total of 1877 miles. Making the best choice at each stage may not yield the best "global" solution. However, even for a large TSP, one can always find a nearest-neighbor route quickly.

Figure 2.10 again illustrates the ease of applying the nearest-neighbor algorithm, this time to a weighted complete graph with five vertices. Starting at vertex A, we get the tour $ADECBA$ (cost 2800) (Figure 2.10a). Note that the nearest-neighbor algorithm starting at vertex B yields the tour $BCADEB$ (cost 3050) (Figure 2.10b).

This example illustrates that a nearest-neighbor tour can be computed for each vertex of the complete graph being considered, and that different nearest-neighbor tours can be gotten starting at different vertices. Note that even though we may seek a tour starting at a particular vertex, say, A in Figure 2.10, since a Hamiltonian circuit can be thought of as starting at any of its vertices, we can apply

FIGURE 2.10
(a) A weighted complete graph with five vertices that illustrates the use of the nearest-neighbor algorithm (starting at A).
(b) TSP tour generated by the nearest-neighbor algorithm (starting at B).

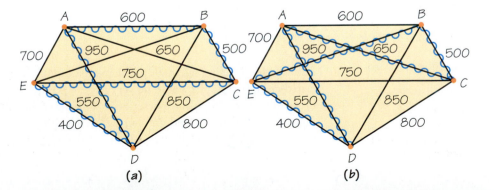

the nearest-neighbor procedure, if we wish, starting at vertex *B* (rather than at *A*). The Hamiltonian circuit we get can still be thought of as beginning at vertex *A* rather than *B*. Even for complete graphs with a large number of vertices, it would still be faster to apply nearest neighbor for each vertex and pick the cheapest of the tours generated (though such a tour might not be optimal) than to apply the brute force method.

Sorted-Edges Algorithm

Perhaps some other easy method would yield optimal solutions.

> We might start by sorting or arranging the edges of the complete graph in order of increasing cost (or, equivalently, arrange the intercity distances in order of increasing distance). Then we can select at each stage that edge of least cost that (1) never requires that three used edges meet at a vertex (since a Hamiltonian circuit uses up exactly two edges at each vertex), and that (2) never closes up a circular tour that doesn't include all the vertices. This algorithm is called the **sorted-edges algorithm.**

Applying the sorted-edges algorithm to the TSP in Figure 2.3 yields the tour Chicago, St. Louis, Minneapolis, Cleveland, and Chicago, since the edges chosen would be 300, 349, 562, 774. Here are the details of how the sorted-edges method works in this example.

First, the six weights on the edges listed in increasing order would be 300, 349, 425, 541, 562, and 774. Since the cheapest edge in this sorted list is 300, this is the first edge that we place into the tour we are building. Next we add the edge with weight 349 to the tour. The next cheapest edge would be 425, but using this edge together with those already selected would result in having three edges at a vertex (Figure 2.11a), which is not consistent with having a Hamiltonian circuit. Hence, we do not use this edge. The next cheapest edge, 541, used together with

FIGURE 2.11
(a) When three shortest edges are added in order of increasing distance, three edges at a vertex are selected, which is not allowed as part of a Hamiltonian circuit.
(b) When the edges of distances 300, 349, and 541 are selected, a circuit that does not include all vertices results.

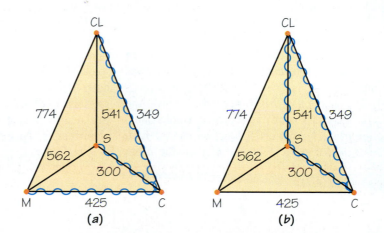

the edges already selected, would create a circuit (see Figure 2.11b) that does not include all the vertices. Thus, this edge, too, would be skipped over. However, we are able to add the edges 562 and 774 without either creating a circuit shorter than one including all the vertices or having three edges at a vertex. Hence, the tour we arrive at is Chicago, St. Louis, Minneapolis, Cleveland, and Chicago. Again, this solution is not optimal because its length is 1985. Note that this algorithm, like the nearest neighbor, is greedy.

Although the edges selected by applying the sorted-edges method to the example in Figure 2.3 are connected to each other at every stage, this does not always happen. For example, if we apply the sorted-edges algorithm to the graph in Figure 2.10a, we build up the tour first with edge *ED* (400) and then edge *BC* (500), which do not touch. The edges that are then selected are *AD*, *AB*, and *EC*, giving the circuit *EDABCE*, which is the same as the nearest-neighbor circuit starting at vertex *A*.

Although many "quick and dirty" methods for solving the TSP have been suggested and some methods give an optimal solution in some cases, none of these methods guarantees an optimal solution. Surprisingly, most experts believe that no efficient method that *guarantees* an optimal solution for the TSP will ever be found (see Spotlight 2.1).

SPOTLIGHT 2.1

NP-Complete Problems

Steven Cook, a computer scientist at the University of Toronto, showed in 1971 that certain hard, frustrating problems are equivalently difficult. This class of problems, now referred to as **NP-complete problems,** has the following characteristic: if a "fast" algorithm for solving one of these problems could be found, then a fast method would exist for all these problems.

In this context, "fast" means that as the size n of the problem grows (the number of cities gives the problem size in the traveling salesman problem), the amount of time needed to solve the problem grows no more rapidly than a polynomial function in n. (A polynomial function has the form $a_k n^k + a_{k-1} n^{k-1} + \cdots + a_1 n + a_0$.) On the other hand, if it could be shown that any problem in the class of NP-complete problems required an amount of time that grows faster than any polynomial (an exponential function, like 3^n, is an example of a function that grows faster than any polynomial) as the problem size increased, then all problems in the NP-complete class would share this characteristic. If some NP-complete problems had fast solutions, it seems likely that at least one such fast solution would have been found by now. It has been known for some time that the traveling salesman problem is an NP-complete problem; for this reason it is generally thought that no "fast" algorithm for an optimal solution for the TSP will ever be found.

Recently, mathematical researchers have adopted a somewhat different strategy for dealing with TSP problems. If finding a fast algorithm to generate optimal solutions for large problems is unlikely, perhaps one can show that the "quick and dirty" methods, usually called **heuristic algorithms,** come close enough to giving optimal solutions to be important for practical use. For example, suppose one could prove that the nearest-neighbor heuristic was never off by more than 25% in the worst case or by more than 15% in the average case. For a medium-size TSP, one would then have to choose whether to spend a lot of time (or money) to find an optimal solution or to use instead a heuristic algorithm to obtain a fairly good solution. Investigators at AT&T Research have developed many remarkably good heuristic algorithms. The best-known guarantee for a heuristic algorithm for a TSP is that it yields a cost that is no worse than one and a half times the optimal cost. Interestingly, this heuristic algorithm involves solving a Chinese postman problem (see Chapter 1), for which a "fast" algorithm is known to exist.

Throughout our discussion of the TSP we have concentrated on the goal of minimizing the cost (or time) of a tour that visited each of a variety of sites once and only once. One of the things that makes mathematical modeling exciting, however, is the subtle issues that arise in specific real-world situations (or that provide contrast between seemingly similar situations). For example, suppose the TSP situation is that of picking up day campers and taking them to and from the camp. From the point of view of the camp, it may wish to minimize the total length of time that the bus needs to pick up the campers. From the point of view of the parents of the campers, however, they may like the time their children spend on the bus to be as little as possible. For some problems, the tour that minimizes the mean (average) time that a child spends on the bus may not be the same tour that minimizes the total time of the tour. (Specifically, if the bus goes first to pick up the child the farthest from the camp, and then picks up the other children, this may yield a relatively short time on the bus for the kids, but a relatively long time for the tour itself.) It is these subtleties between problems that mathematicians go back to at a later time to examine, after the basic structure of the main problem itself is well understood. It is in this way that mathematics continues to grow, explore new ideas, and find new applications.

Minimum-Cost Spanning Trees

The traveling salesman problem is but one of many graph theory optimization problems that have grown out of real-world problems in both government and industry. Here is another.

E X A M P L E   *Pictaphone Service*

Imagine that Pictaphone service (e.g., telephone service where a video image of the callers is provided) is to be set up on an experimental basis between five cities. The

FIGURE 2.12
Costs (in millions of
dollars) of installing
Pictaphone service
between five cities.

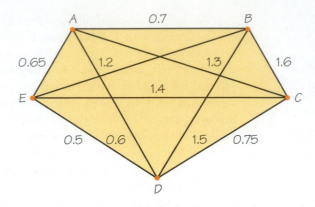

graph in Figure 2.12 shows the possible links that might be included in the Pictaphone network, with each edge showing the cost in millions of dollars to create that particular link. To send a Pictaphone message between two cities, a direct communication link is not necessary because it is possible to send a message indirectly via another city. Thus, in Figure 2.12, sending a message from *A* to *C* could be achieved by sending the message from *A* to *B*, from *B* to *E*, and from *E* to *C*, provided the links *AB, BE,* and *EC* are part of the network. We assume that the cost of relaying a message, compared with the direct communication link cost, is so small that we can neglect this amount. The problem that concerns us, therefore, is to provide service between any pair of cities in a way that minimizes the total cost of the links.

Our first guess at a solution is to put in the cheapest possible links between cities first, until all cities could send messages to any other city. Such an approach would be analogous to the sorted-edges method that was used to study the traveling salesman problem. In our example, if the cheapest links are added until all cities are joined, we obtain the connections shown in Figure 2.13a.

The links were added in the order *ED, AD, AE, AB, DC*. However, because this graph contains the circuit *ADEA* (wiggly edges in Figure 2.13b), it has redundant edges: we can still send messages between any pair of cities using relays after omitting the most expensive edge in the circuit—*AE*. After deleting an edge of a circuit, a message can still be relayed among the cities of the circuit by sending sig-

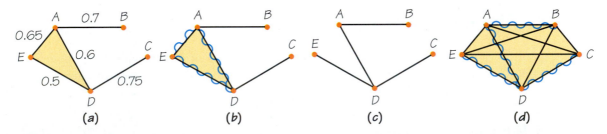

FIGURE 2.13   (a) Cities are linked in order of increasing cost until all cities are connected. (b) Circuit in part (a) highlighted. (c) Most expensive link in circuit in part (a) deleted. (d) Highlighted edges show, as a subgraph of the original graph, those links connecting the cities with minimum cost obtained using Kruskal's algorithm.

nals the long way around. After *AE* is deleted, messages from *A* to *E* can be sent via *D* (Figure 2.13c).

FIGURE 2.14
(a) A graph to help illustrate the concept of a spanning tree. (b) The wiggled edges are a tree, but not a spanning tree, since vertices *D* and *E* are not part of the tree. (c) The vertices of the graph are, however, endpoints of wiggled edges. (d) The wiggled edges are not a tree, since they contain the edges of the circuit *BDCAB*. All the vertices of the graph are, however, endpoints of wiggled edges. (e) The wiggled edges form a tree and include all of the vertices of the graph as endpoints of wiggled edges.

This procedure suggests a modified algorithm for our problem, **Kruskal's algorithm:** add the links in order of cheapest cost so that no circuits form and so that every vertex belongs to some link added (Figure 2.13d).

As in the sorted-edges method for the TSP, the edges that are added need not be connected to each other until the end.

A subgraph formed in this way will be a tree; that is, it will consist of one piece and contain no circuits. It will also include all the vertices of the original graph. A subgraph that is a tree and that contains all the vertices of the original graph is called a **spanning tree** of the original graph.

To understand these concepts better, consider the graph *G* in Figure 2.14a. The wiggled edges in Figure 2.14b would constitute a subgraph of *G* that is a tree (since it is connected and has no circuit), but this tree would not be a spanning tree of *G* since the vertices *D* and *E* would not be included. On the other hand, the wiggled edges in Figure 2.14c and 2.14d show subgraphs of *G* that include all the vertices of *G* but are not trees because the first is not connected and the second

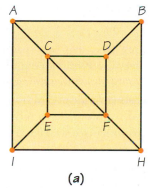

(a)

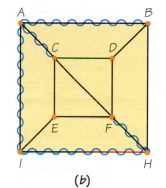

(b)

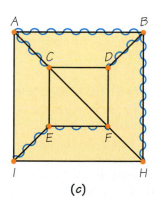

(c)

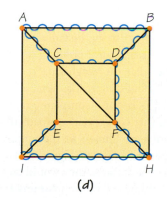

(d)

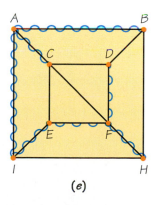

(e)

Businesspeople holding a
video conference.

contains a circuit. Figure 2.14e shows a spanning tree of *G*; the wiggled edges are connected and contain no circuit, and every vertex of the original graph is an endpoint of some wiggled edge.   ◆

Finding a **minimum-cost spanning tree,** that is, a spanning tree whose edge weights sum to a minimum value, solves the Pictaphone problem. Note that having a different goal in the Pictaphone problem led to a different mathematical question from that of finding a Chinese postman tour or TSP tour. In this application, the graph theory problem that we need to formulate to solve the applied problem was that of finding a minimum-cost spanning tree. In Figure 2.15a we have a graph model showing the costs of putting in roads to connect new houses in a suburban land-development project. Applying the algorithm we have developed, adding the edges in the order of increasing cost, but avoiding the creation of a circuit, yields as a minimum-cost spanning tree, the tree indicated by wiggled edges in Figure 2.15b. This tree is the cheapest one that makes it possible to drive between any pair of homes, though the driving distance between some of the homes will be relatively large, since only roads corresponding to wiggled edges will be built.

Remember that the weights on the edges of the graph in Figure 2.15a represent the costs of building roads, not the driving distance between the houses. Note that Figure 2.15a is not a complete graph, one in which all possible edges are included. Edges that correspond to roads that would be economically prohibitive to build have not been shown in the graph model. Also, in Figure 2.15b, the two edges of weight 5 (shown in Figure 2.15a) do not become part of the minimum-cost spanning tree, because they would create circuits with edges already chosen.

How do we know that the spanning tree found by the algorithm we developed achieves the minimum possible cost? Although this sounds very plausible, our ex-

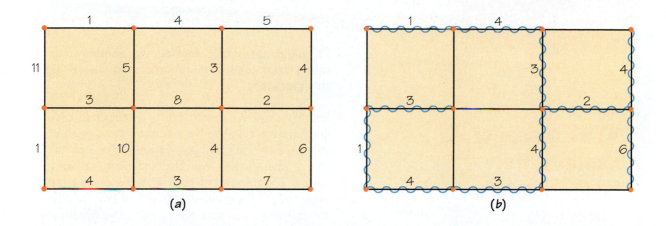

FIGURE 2.15
(a) A graph showing costs for construction of roads between houses.
(b) Wiggled edges show a minimum-cost spanning tree for the graph in part (a).

perience with the TSP should suggest caution. Remember that for the TSP, the sorted-edges algorithm, also a greedy algorithm, did not necessarily give an optimal solution! On what basis should we have more faith in our present algorithm?

Kruskal's Algorithm

The algorithm described here was first suggested by Joseph Kruskal (AT&T Research) in the mid-1950s to solve a problem in pure mathematics proposed by a Czechoslovakian mathematician. In mathematics it is surprising but not uncommon to find that ideas used to solve problems with no apparent application often turn out to have many real-world uses. Kruskal's solution to the problem of finding a minimum-cost spanning tree in a graph with weights is a good example of this phenomenon. Kruskal showed that the greedy algorithm described does yield the minimum answer, and his work led to applications of these and related ideas in designing minimum-cost computer networks, phone connections, and road and railway systems. For additional discussion of operations research in the communications industry, see Spotlight 2.2. In order to explore how one can reconstruct full information from partial information using the tree concept, see Spotlight 2.3.

Although we have mentioned many routing problems in graphs, we have not discussed one of the most obvious: finding the path between two specified, distinct vertices with the sum of the weights of the edges in the path as small as possible. (Here there is no need to cover all vertices or to cover all edges.) We have seen that the weights on the edges have many possible interpretations, including time, distance, and cost. Following are some of the many possible applications:

1. Design routes to be used by an ambulance, police car, or fire engine to get to an emergency as quickly as possible.
2. Design delivery routes that minimize gasoline use.
3. Design routes to bring soldiers to the front as quickly as possible.
4. Design a route for a truck carrying nuclear waste.

The need to find shortest paths seems natural. Next we investigate a situation where finding a longest path is the right tool.

AT&T Manager Explains How Long-Distance Calls Run Smoothly

Although long-distance calls are now routine, it takes great expertise and careful planning for a company like AT&T to handle its vast amounts of telephone traffic. Rich Wetmore was district manager of AT&T's Communications Network Operations Center in Bedminster, New Jersey. Here are his responses to questions about how AT&T handles its huge volumes of long-distance traffic and how it tracks its operations to keep things running smoothly.

How do you make sure that a customer doesn't run into a delayed signal when attempting a long-distance call?

We monitor the performance of our AT&T network by displaying data collected from all over the country on a special wallboard. The wallboard is configured to tell us if a customer's call is not going through because the network doesn't have enough capacity to handle it.

That's when we step in and take control to correct the problem. The typical control we use is to reroute the call. Instead of sending the customer's call directly to its destination, we'll route it via a third city—to someplace else in the country that has the capacity to complete the call.

It would seem that routing via another city would take longer. Is the customer aware of this process?

Routing a call via a third city is entirely transparent [imperceptible] to the customer. I'm an expert about the network, and even when I make a phone call, I have no idea how that individual call was routed. It's transparent both in terms of how far away the other person sounds and in how quickly the telephone call gets set up. With the signaling network we use, it takes milliseconds for switching systems to "talk" to each other to set up a call. So the fact that you are involved in a third switch in some distant city is something you would never know.

You want to be sure to keep costs down while supplying enough service to customers. So how do you balance company benefits with customer benefit?

In terms of making the network efficient, we want to do two things. First, we want our customers to be happy with our service and for all their calls to go through, which means we must build enough capacity in the network to allow that to happen. Second, we want to be efficient for stockholders and not spend more money than we need to for the network to be at the optimum size.

There are basically two costs in terms of building the network. There is the cost of switching systems and the cost of the circuits that connect the switching systems. Basically, you can use operations-research techniques and mathematics to determine cost trade-offs. It may make sense to build direct routing between two switching systems and use a lot of circuits, or maybe to involve three switching systems, with fewer circuits between the main two, and so on.

Common Ancestors?

New Zealand   Australia Australia and Africa   South
                              New Guinea   America

Moa   **Kiwi**   **Emu**   **Cassowary** **Ostrich**   **Rhea**
(4 species)   (3 species)   (2 species)
1 2 3 4   1   2   3   1   2

Common Australian
ancestor of kiwi, emu,
and cassowary

The branching patterns
on this tree suggest that
kiwis evolved on
Australia and then
moved to New Zealand
at a later point.

Common ancestor
of kiwi and moa

Common ancestor

In the study of ancient manuscripts different manuscripts of the same book are available, even though the original manuscript upon which they are based has been lost. Examples of this include Euclid's *Elements* and Chaucer's *Canterbury Tales*. What interests scholars is reconstructing the relationships between the manuscripts and the common ancestors of the manuscripts, even when some of the ancestors are now missing. Similarly, perceptual psychologists may be interested in which colors people perceive as being closely related and comparing these perceptions with those of people who are color blind. Finally, in studying different species biologists are interested in determining which species are more closely related to each other, including species only known in fossil form, and constructing a "tree" of life that shows which species were ancestors of others.

Reconstructions of this kind are being made possible by using graph theory, specifically using the graph theory concept of a tree. The value of the graph theory in these and many other situations is using the distance between pairs of vertices in the tree as a way of reflecting the closeness relationships that pairs of manuscripts, pairs of colors, or pairs of species have. The distance between two vertices in a tree is the sum of the weights along the one path that joins the two vertices. If there are no weights on the edges, the distance is the number of edges in the path. In some reconstruction problems a special vertex of the tree called the *root* is singled out. This root plays the role of the original common ancestor, and distances to the root are of critical interest.

In the case of species, trees of family relatedness were traditionally constructed based on similarities of bones and physical appearance. With the discovery of molecular biology, many new avenues have been opened. One can now draw trees of relatedness based on an organism's genetic material, DNA, or the proteins that the DNA codes for. The traditional trees based on physical traits often show different species as being more closely related than trees based on newer molecular biological approaches. These differences focus scholars on how to resolve the discrepancies and thereby reach a deeper understanding of the unity of life.

Critical-Path Analysis

One of the delights of mathematics is its ability to confirm the obvious in certain situations while showing that our intuition is wrong in other circumstances. Our next group of mathematical applications will illustrate this point.

One of the characteristics of recent American life seems to be its fast pace. People are interested in getting things done quickly and efficiently. This means that when you take your car in to be repaired before work, you want to know for sure that the repairs will be done when you go to pick the car up. You want the trains and the bus that take you to your doctor's appointment to run on time; and when you arrive at the doctor's office, you want a nurse to be free to take a blood sample and a throat culture. You want your outpatient appointment for an X ray at the local hospital to occur on schedule. You want the X ray to be interpreted quickly and the results reported back to your internist.

Scheduling machines and people is a big part of modern life. It is important in your own personal daily activities as well as to businesses and governments. Scheduling is involved in running a school, a hospital, an airline, or in landing a person on Mars. Perhaps surprisingly, modern mathematics is a big part of what is involved in solving scheduling problems.

Part of what makes scheduling complicated is that when one performs the tasks that make up a job, the tasks usually cannot be done in a random order. For example, to make Thanksgiving dinner one must buy and prepare the turkey before putting it in the oven, and one must set the table before serving the food.

Screens in the New York Telephone Network Control Center.

FIGURE 2.16
Typical order-requirement digraph.

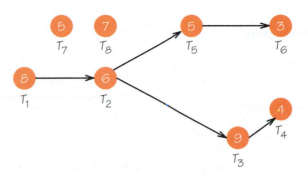

If the tasks cannot be performed in arbitrary sequence or order, we can specify the order in an **order-requirement digraph.** Digraph is short for directed graph. A digraph is a geometrical tool similar to a graph except that each edge has an arrow on it to indicate a direction for that edge. Digraphs can be used to model the fact that traffic on a street must go in one direction, or that certain tasks in a job must be completed prior to other tasks. A typical example of an order-requirement digraph is shown in Figure 2.16. There is a vertex in this digraph for each task. If one task must be done immediately before another, we draw a directed edge, or arrow, from the prerequisite task to the subsequent task. The numbers within the circles representing vertices are the times it takes to complete the tasks. In Figure 2.16 there is no arrow from T_1 to T_5 because task T_2 intervenes. Also, T_1, T_7, and T_8 have no tasks that must precede them. Hence, if there are at least three processors (i.e., people or machines) available, tasks T_1, T_7, and T_8 can be worked on simultaneously at the start of the job.

Let us investigate a typical scheduling problem faced by a business.

EXAMPLE   *Turning a Plane Around*

Consider an airplane that carries both freight and passengers. The plane must have its passengers and freight unloaded and new passengers and cargo loaded before it can take off again. Also, the cabin must be cleaned before departure can occur. Thus, the job of "turning the plane around" requires completion of five tasks:

TASK A	Unload passengers	13 minutes
TASK B	Unload cargo	25 minutes
TASK C	Clean cabin	15 minutes
TASK D	Load new cargo	22 minutes
TASK E	Load new passengers	27 minutes

The order-requirement digraph for the problem of turning an airplane around is shown in Figure 2.17. The presence or absence of an edge in the order-requirement digraph depends on the analysis made as part of the modeling process for the problem. It seems natural that one needs to have an arrow between task A and task C, since before one can clean the cabin, the passengers on the plane should have been unloaded. However, the presence of some arrows may not seem

FIGURE 2.17
Order-requirement digraph
for turning an airplane
around after landing.

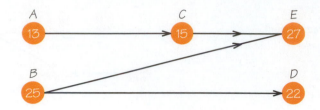

natural, say, perhaps the arrow from task *B* (unload the cargo) to task *E* (load new passengers). This arrow may be due to government rules or requirements. What matters is that the mathematics of solving the problem does not depend on the reason that the order-requirement digraph looks the way that it does. The person solving the problem constructs the order-requirement digraph and then the mathematical techniques we will develop can be applied, regardless of whether or not some business faced with a similar problem might model the problem in a different way.

Because we want to find the earliest completion time, it might seem that finding the shortest path through the digraph (i.e., path *BD* with time length 25 + 22 = 47) would solve the problem. But this approach shows the danger of ignoring the relationship between the mathematical model (the digraph) and the original problem.

The time required to complete all the tasks, *A* through *E*, must be at least as long as the time necessary to do the tasks on any particular path. Consider the path *BD*, which has length 25 + 22 = 47. Recall that here *length* of a path refers to the sum of the times of the tasks that lie along the path. Since task *B* must be done before task *D* can begin, the two tasks *B* and *D* cannot be completed before time 47. Hence, even if work on other tasks (such as *A*, *C*, and *E*) is proceeding during this period, all the tasks cannot be finished before the tasks on path *BD* are finished. The same statement is true for every other path in the order-requirement digraph. Thus, the earliest completion time actually corresponds to the length of the longest path. In the airplane example, this earliest completion time is 55 (= 13 + 15 + 27) minutes, corresponding to the path *ACE*. We call *ACE* the *critical path* because the times of the tasks on this path determine the earliest completion time.

A **critical path** in an order-requirement digraph is a longest path. The length is measured in terms of summing the task times of the tasks making up the path.

Note that if none of these tasks could go on simultaneously, the time to complete all the tasks would be 13 + 25 + 15 + 22 + 27 = 102 minutes. However, even though tasks may go on simultaneously, the length of the critical path being 55 shows that completion of the tasks in less than 55 minutes is not possible. Only by

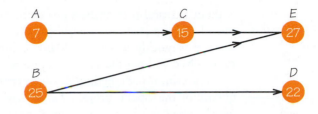

FIGURE 2.18
Order-requirement digraph for turning an airplane around with reduced times due to construction of new jetway.

speeding up the times to complete the critical-path tasks themselves can a completion time earlier than 55 time units be achieved.

Suppose it were desirable to speed the turnaround of the plane to below 55 minutes. One way to do this might be to build a second jetway to help unload passengers. For example, we could unload passengers (task *A*) in 7 minutes instead of 13. However, reducing task *A* to 7 minutes does not reduce the completion time by 6 minutes because in the new digraph (Figure 2.18) *ACE* is no longer the critical (i.e., longest) path. The longest path is now *BE*, which has a length of 52 minutes. Thus, shortening task *A* by 6 minutes results in only a 3-minute saving in completion time. This may mean that building a new jetway is uneconomical. Note also that shortening the time to complete tasks that are not on the original critical path *ACE* will not shorten the completion time at all. Speeding tasks on the critical path will shorten completion time of the job only up to the point where a new critical path is created. Also note that a digraph may have more than one longest path. ◆

Not all order-requirement digraphs are as simple as the one shown in Figure 2.17. The order-requirement digraph in Figure 2.19 has 12 paths, which can be found by exhaustive search. Examples of such paths are $T_1T_2T_3$, $T_1T_5T_9$, $T_4T_5T_9$, and $T_7T_5T_3$. (Although we have not discussed them here, fast algorithms for finding longest and shortest paths in graphs are known.) The critical path is $T_7T_8T_6$ (length 21), and the earliest completion time for all nine tasks is time 21.

These examples are typical of many scheduling problems that occur in practice (see Spotlight 2.4). Perhaps the most dramatic use of critical-path analysis is in the construction trades. No major new building project is now carried out

FIGURE 2.19
An order-requirement digraph with 12 paths, to examine how to find the length of the longest path.

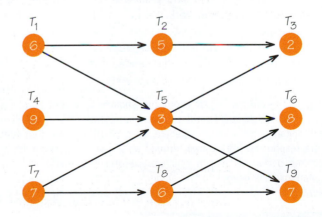

without a critical-path analysis first being performed to ensure that the proper personnel and materials are available at the right times in order to have the project finished as quickly as possible. Many such problems are too large and complicated to be solved without the aid of computers.

The critical-path method was popularized and came into wider use as a consequence of the Apollo project. As we saw in the part introduction, this project, which aimed at landing a man on the moon within 10 years of 1960, was one of the most sophisticated projects in planning and scheduling ever attempted. The dramatic success of the project can be attributed partly to the use of critical-path ideas and the related program evaluation and review technique (PERT), which helped keep the project on schedule.

In Chapter 3 we will see how mathematical ideas drawn from outside of graph theory can be used to get insight into scheduling problems.

SPOTLIGHT 2.4

Every Moment Counts in Rigorous Airline Scheduling

When people think of airline scheduling, the first thing that comes to mind is how quickly a particular plane can safely reach its destination. But using ground time efficiently is just as important to an airline's timetable as the time spent in flight. Bill Rodenhizer was the manager of control operations for an airline that provided shuttle service between Boston and New York. He is considered to be an expert on airplane turnaround time, the process by which an airplane is prepared for almost immediate takeoff once it has landed. He tells us how this well-orchestrated effort works:

Scheduling, to the airline, is just about the whole ball game. Everything is scheduled right to the minute. The whole fleet operates on a strict schedule. Each of the departments responsible for turning around an aircraft has an allotted period of time in which to perform its function. Manpower is geared to the amount of ground time scheduled for that aircraft. This would be adjusted during off-weather or bad-weather days or during heavy air-traffic delays.

Most of our aircraft in Boston are scheduled for a 42- to 65-minute ground time. Boston is the end of the line, so it is a "terminating and originating station." In plain talk, that means almost every aircraft that comes in must be fully unloaded, refueled, serviced, and dispatched within roughly an hour's time.

This is how the process works: in the larger aircraft, it takes passengers roughly 20 minutes to load and 20 minutes to unload. During this period, we will have completely cleaned the aircraft and unloaded the cargo, and the caterers will have taken care of the food. The ramp service may take 20 to 30 minutes to unload the baggage, mail, and cargo from underneath the plane, and it will take the same amount of time to load it up again. We double-crew those aircraft with heavier weights so that the work load will fit the time it takes passengers to load and unload upstairs.

While this has been going on, the fueler has fueled the aircraft. As to repairs, most major maintenance is done during the midnight shift, when all but 20 of [our] several hundred aircraft are inactive.

We all work under a very strict time frame. There are four functional departments. If any of the four cannot fit its work into its time frame, then it advises us at the control center, and we adjust the departure time or whatever, so that the other departments can coordinate their activities accordingly.

REVIEW VOCABULARY

Algorithm   A step-by-step description of how to solve a problem.

Brute force method   The method that solves the traveling salesman problem (TSP) by enumerating all the Hamiltonian circuits and then selecting the one with minimum cost.

Complete graph   A graph in which every pair of vertices is joined by an edge.

Critical path   The longest path in an order-requirement digraph. The length of this path gives the earliest completion time for all the tasks making up the job consisting of the tasks in the digraph.

Fundamental principle of counting   A method for counting outcomes of multistage processes.

Greedy algorithm   An approach for solving an optimization problem, where at each stage of the algorithm the best (or cheapest) action is taken. Unfortunately, greedy algorithms do not always lead to optimal solutions.

Hamiltonian circuit   A circuit using distinct edges of a graph that starts and ends at a particular vertex of the graph and visits each vertex once and only once. A Hamiltonian circuit can be thought of as starting at any one of its vertices.

Heuristic algorithm   A method of solving an optimization problem that is "fast," but that does not guarantee an optimal answer to the problem.

Kruskal's algorithm   An algorithm developed by Joseph Kruskal (AT&T Research) that solves the minimum-cost spanning-tree problem by selecting edges in order of increasing cost, but so that no edge forms a circuit with edges chosen earlier. It can be proved that this algorithm always produces an optimal solution.

Method of trees   A visual method of carrying out the fundamental principle of counting.

Minimum-cost Hamiltonian circuit   A Hamiltonian circuit in a graph with weights on the edges, for which the sum of the weights of the edges of the Hamiltonian circuit is as small as possible.

Minimum-cost spanning tree   A spanning tree of a weighted connected graph having minimum cost. The cost of a tree is the sum of the weights on the edges of the tree.

Nearest-neighbor algorithm   An algorithm for attempting to solve the TSP that begins at a "home" vertex and visits next that vertex not already visited that can be reached most cheaply. When all other vertices have been visited, the tour returns to home. This method may not give an optimal answer.

NP-complete problems   A collection of problems, which includes the TSP, that appear to be very hard to solve quickly for an optimal solution.

Order-requirement digraph   A directed graph that shows which tasks precede other tasks among the collection of tasks making up a job.

Sorted-edges algorithm   An algorithm for attempting to solve the TSP where the edges added to the circuit being built up are selected in order of increasing cost, but no edge is added that would prevent a Hamiltonian circuit's being formed. These edges must all be connected at the end, but not necessarily at earlier stages. The tour obtained may not have lowest possible cost.

Spanning tree   A subgraph of a connected graph that is a tree and includes all the vertices of the original graph.

Traveling salesman problem (TSP)   The problem of finding a minimum-cost Hamiltonian circuit in a complete graph where each edge has been assigned a cost (or weight).

Tree   A connected graph with no circuits.

Weight   A number assigned to an edge of a graph that can be thought of as a cost, distance, or time associated with that edge.

SUGGESTED READINGS

DOLAN, ALAN, AND JOAN ALDUS. *Networks and Algorithms: An Introductory Approach,* Wiley, Chichester, 1993. An excellent introduction to graph theory algorithms.

GUSFIELD, DAN. *Algorithms on Strings, Trees, and Sequences,* Cambridge University Press, New York, 1997. Details applications of graph theory in pattern recognition and reconstruction problems.

LAWLER, EUGENE, J. LENSTRA, RINNOY KAN, AND D. SHMOYS, EDS. *The Traveling Salesman Problem,* Prentice Hall, Englewood Cliffs, N.J., 1985. Includes survey and technical articles on all aspects of the TSP.

LUCAS, WILLIAM, FRED ROBERTS, AND ROBERT THRALL, EDS. *Discrete and Systems Models,* vol. 3: *Modules in Applied Mathematics,* Springer-Verlag, New York, 1983. Chapter 6, "A Model for Municipal Street Sweeping Operations," by A. Tucker and L. Bodin, describes street sweeping and related models in detail. Other chapters detail many recent applications of mathematics.

ROBERTS, FRED. *Applied Combinatorics,* Prentice Hall, Englewood Cliffs, N.J., 1984. The chapters on graphs and related network optimization problems are excellent.

ROBERTS, FRED. *Graph Theory and Its Applications to Problems of Society,* Society for Industrial and Applied Mathematics, Philadelphia, 1978. A very readable account of how graph theory is finding a wide variety of applications.

SUGGESTED WEB SITES

www.ics.uci.edu/~eppstein/geom.html   At this site, one can find examples of many applications of graph theory and related geometric tools.

www.ics.uci.edu/~eppstein/junkyard   A rich collection of interesting aspects of geometric mathematics.

www.informs.org   The Web page of the major professional society in operations research.

www.ing.unlp.edu.ar/cetad/mos/TSPBIB_home.html Resources about the traveling salesman problem.

mat.gsia.cmu.edu   A "hub" for resources about operations research.

SKILLS CHECK

1. Which of the following describes a Hamiltonian circuit for the graph below?

   (a)   ABCDEA
   (b)   ABEDCBDAC
   (c)   ADEBCA

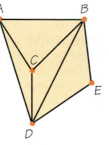

2. Using the nearest-neighbor algorithm and starting at vertex *A*, find the cost of the Hamiltonian circuit for the graph below.

   (a)   25
   (b)   26
   (c)   Another answer

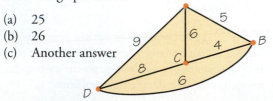

3. Using the sorted-edges algorithm, find the cost of the Hamiltonian circuit for the graph below.

   (a)   25
   (b)   26
   (c)   Another answer

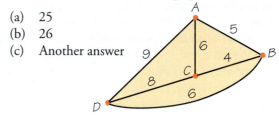

4. Using Kruskal's algorithm, find the minimum-cost spanning tree for the graph below. Which statement is true?

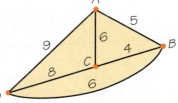

(a)   Edges *AC* and *BD* are included in the minimum-cost spanning tree.

(b)   Edges *AB* and *BD* are included in the minimum-cost spanning tree.

(c)   Edges *CD* and *BD* are included in the minimum-cost spanning tree.

5.   What is the earliest completion time (in minutes) for a job with the following order-requirement digraph?

(a)   16 minutes

(b)   17 minutes

(c)   18 minutes

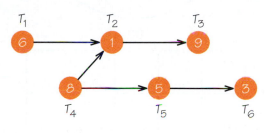

6.   Suppose that after a hurricane, a van is dispatched to pick up five nurses at their homes and bring them to work at the local hospital. Which of these techniques is most likely to be useful in solving this problem?

(a)   Finding an Euler circuit in a graph

(b)   Solving a TSP (traveling salesman problem)

(c)   Finding a minimum-cost spanning tree in a graph

7.   Paul has packed four ties, three shirts, and two pairs of pants for a trip. How many different outfits can he create?

(a)   Fewer than 10

(b)   Between 10 and 25

(c)   More than 25

EXERCISES   ▲ *Optional.*   ■ *Advanced.*   ◆ *Discussion.*

Hamiltonian Circuits

1.   For each graph below and in the first column on page 58, write a Hamiltonian circuit starting at X_1.

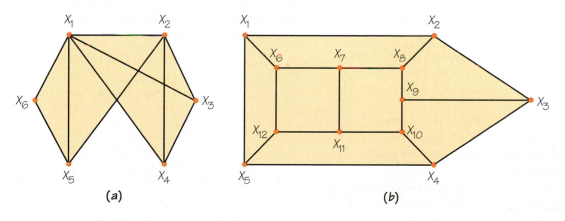

(a)   (b)

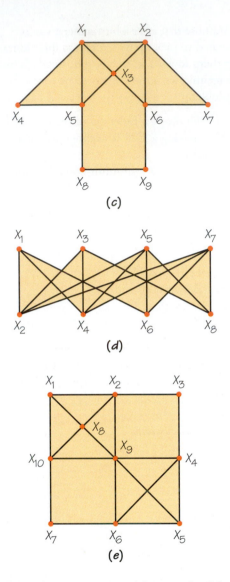

(c)

(d)

(e)

2. If the edge $X_2 X_3$ is erased from each of the graphs in Exercise 1, does the resulting graph still have a Hamiltonian circuit?

3. (a)   If the vertex X_1 and the edges attached to X_1 are removed from the graphs in Exercise 1, do the new graphs that result still have Hamiltonian circuits?
    (b)   If you think of the graphs in Exercise 1 as communications networks, what interpretation might be given to the "removal" of a vertex and the edges attached as described in (a)?

4. For each of the graphs below, add wiggly edges to indicate a Hamiltonian circuit.

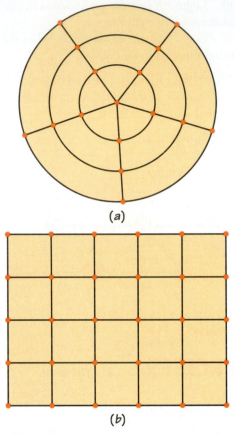

(a)

(b)

5. Suppose two Hamiltonian circuits are considered different if the collections of edges that they use are different. How many other Hamiltonian circuits can you find in the graph in Figure 2.1 different from the two discussed?

◼ 6. Explain why the tour *ACEDCBA* is not a Hamiltonian circuit for the graph at the left. Does this graph have a Hamiltonian circuit?

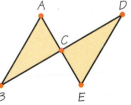

◼ 7. Do the following graphs (see page 59) have Hamiltonian circuits? If not, can you demonstrate why not?

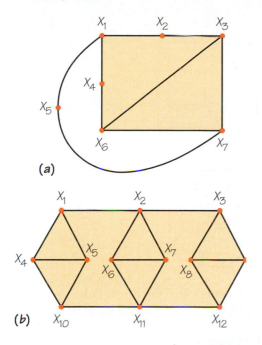

(a)

(b)

8. If an edge is added to each graph in Exercise 7 from X_2 to X_4, do the new graphs that result have a Hamiltonian circuit?

9. For each of the graphs below, determine if there is a Hamiltonian circuit.

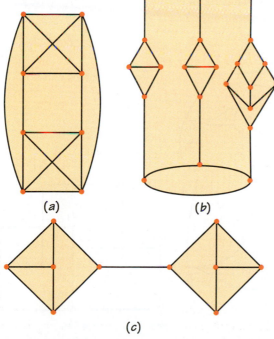

(a)   **(b)**

(c)

10. (a) The graph below is known as a four spokes and three concentric circles graph. What conditions on m and n guarantee that an m spokes and n concentric circles graph has a Hamiltonian circuit? (Assume $m \geq 2$, $n \geq 1$.)

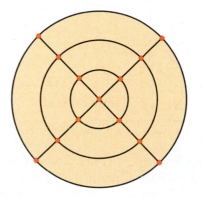

(b) The graph below is known as a 3×4 grid graph. What conditions on m and n guarantee that an $m \times n$ grid graph has a Hamiltonian circuit?

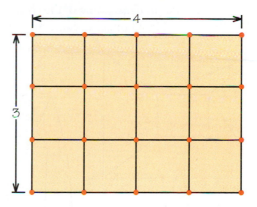

Can you think of a real-world situation in which finding a Hamiltonian circuit in an $m \times n$ grid graph would represent a solution to the problem? If an $m \times n$ grid graph has no Hamiltonian circuit, can you find a tour that repeats a minimum number of vertices and starts and ends at the same vertex?

11. The n-dimensional cube is obtained from two copies of an $(n - 1)$-dimensional cube by joining

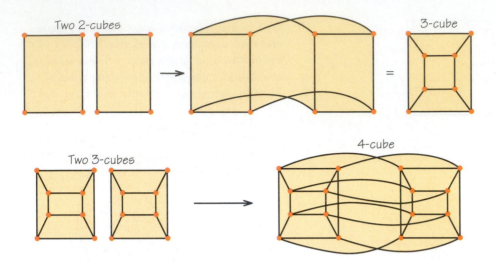

Two 2-cubes   3-cube

Two 3-cubes   4-cube

corresponding vertices. (The process is illustrated for the 3-cube and the 4-cube in the figure above.) Find formulas for the number of vertices and the number of edges of an n-cube. Can you show that every n-cube has a Hamiltonian circuit? (*Hint:* Show that if you know how to find a Hamiltonian circuit on an $(n - 1)$-cube, then you can use two copies of this to build a Hamiltonian circuit on an n-cube.)

12.   To practice your understanding of the concepts of Euler circuits and Hamiltonian circuits, determine

for each graph below if there is an Euler circuit and/or a Hamiltonian circuit. If so, write it down.

13.   If an edge is added from the vertex with subscript 2 to the vertex with subscript 4 in each graph in Exercise 12, which of the resulting graphs will have Hamiltonian circuits and which ones will have Euler circuits?

14.   Each edge of the graph on page 61 represents a two-lane highway. A grass-mowing machine is

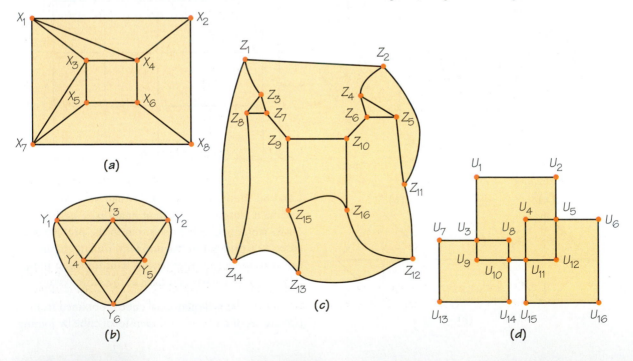

(a)

(b)

(c)

(d)

located at *A* and its operator has the job of cutting the grass along each of the edges of road shown. Can you find a tour for the mowing machine that begins and ends at *A*? Can you find such a tour that begins and ends at *A* and as the mowing is done moves along the edge of the road in the same direction as the traffic is going?

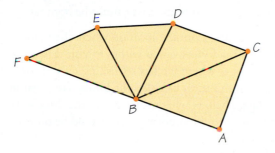

◆ 15. Give examples of real-world situations that can be modeled using a graph and for which finding a Hamiltonian circuit in the graph would be of interest.

Counting Problems

16. A lottery game ticket requires that a person select an upper- or lowercase letter followed by five different two-digit numbers (where the digits cannot both be zero). How many different ways are there to fill out a ticket?

17. (a) In designing a security system for its accounts, a bank asks each customer to choose a five-digit decimal number, all the digits to be distinct and nonzero. How many choices can the customer make?
(b) A suitcase with a liquid crystal display allows one to select a combination to lock it by choosing three capital letters that are not necessarily different. How many different choices would a thief have to go through to be sure that all the possibilities had been tried? How does this compare to a "standard" combination lock?

18. (a) For going outside on a cold winter day, Jill can choose from three winter coats, four wool scarfs, four pairs of boots, and three ski hats. How many outfits might her friends see her in? (b) If Jill insists on always wearing her green wool scarf, how many outfits might her friends see her in?

19. The notes C, D, E, F, G, A, and B are to be used to form a five-note musical logo. In how many ways can this be done if (a) no note can be repeated; (b) notes can be repeated; (c) notes can be repeated but all the notes cannot be the same?

20. Repeat Exercise 19 except that exactly one of the notes in the musical logo must be a sharp, where the note chosen to be sharped cannot appear elsewhere (e.g., BCD#AG, where D# denotes D sharp).

◆ 21. (a) In New York State one type of license plate has three letters followed by a three-digit number. Suppose the digits can be chosen from 0, 1, . . . , 9, except that all three digits cannot be zero and any letter from *A* to *Z* (repeats allowed) can be chosen. How many plates are possible?
(b) Investigate what schemes for license plates are used in your state and determine how many different plates are possible.

22. A restaurant offers 6 appetizers, 10 entrees, and 8 desserts. How many different choices for a meal can a customer make if one selection is made from each category? If three of the desserts are pies and the customer will never order pie, how many meals can the customer choose?

Traveling Salesman Problems

23. Draw complete graphs with four, five, and six vertices. How many edges do these graphs have? Can you generalize to *n* vertices? How many TSP tours would these graphs have? (Tours yielding the same Hamiltonian circuit are considered the same.)

24. Calculate the values of 5!, 6!, 7!, 8!, 9!, and 10!. Then find the number of TSP tours in the complete graph with 10 vertices.

25. The table below shows the mileage between four cities: Springfield, Ill. (S), Urbana, Ill. (U), Effingham, Ill. (E), and Indianapolis, Ind. (I).

	E	I	S	U
E	—	147	92	79
I	147	—	190	119
S	92	190	—	88
U	79	119	88	—

(a) Represent this information by drawing a weighted complete graph on four vertices.
(b) Use the weighted graph in part (a) to find the cost of the three distinct Hamiltonian circuits in the graph. (List them starting at U.)
(c) Which circuit gives the minimum cost?
(d) Would there be any difference in parts (b) and (c) if the start vertex were at I?
(e) If one applies the nearest-neighbor method starting at U, what circuit would be obtained? Does the answer change if one applies the nearest-neighbor algorithm starting at S? At E? At I?
(f) If one applies the sorted-edges method, what circuit would be obtained? Does one get the optimal answer?

26. After a party at her house, Francine (F) has agreed to drive Mary (M), Rachel (R), and Constance (C) home. If the times (in minutes) to drive between her friends' homes are shown below, what route gets Francine back home the quickest?

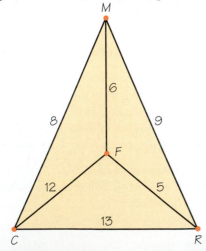

27. In Exercise 26, what route would Francine have to follow to get home as quickly as possible, assuming she promised to drive Mary home first?

28. In a situation such as that of Exercise 26, suppose that an optimal tour has been found that does not deliver a particular person home first. Does it follow that a tour that incorporates taking a particular person home first cannot be optimal?

29. Starting from the location where she moors her boat (M), a fisherwoman wishes to visit three areas A, B, and C where she has set fishing nets. If the times (in minutes) between the locales are given in the figure below, what route to visit the three sites and return to the mooring place would be optimal?

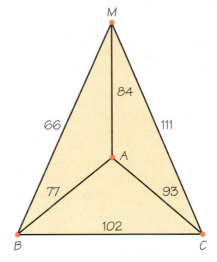

30. (a) For each of the complete graphs below and at the top of page 63, find the costs of the nearest-neighbor tour starting at A and of the tour generated by the sorted-edges algorithm.

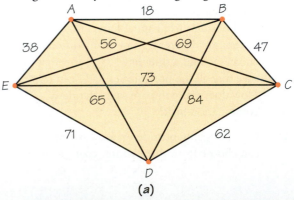

(a)

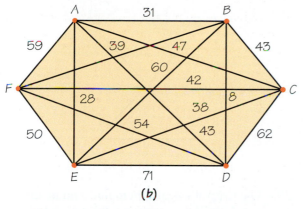

(b)

(b) How many Hamiltonian circuits would have to be examined to find a shortest route for part (a) by the brute force method?
(c) Can you invent an algorithm different from the sorted-edges and nearest-neighbor algorithms that is easy to apply for finding TSP solutions? (See Lawler et al. in Suggested Readings.)

31. An airport limo must take its six passengers to different downtown hotels from the airport. Is this a traveling salesman problem, a Chinese postman problem, or an Euler circuit problem?

32. (a) Solve the six-city TSP shown in the diagram using the nearest-neighbor algorithm starting at vertex A; starting at vertex B.
(b) Apply the sorted-edges method.

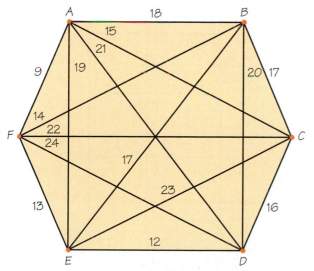

■ 33. Construct an example of a complete graph on five vertices, with distinct weights on the edges for which the nearest-neighbor algorithm starting at a particular vertex and the sorted-edges algorithm yield different solutions for the traveling salesman problem. Can you find a five-vertex complete graph with weights on the edges in which the optimal solution, the nearest-neighbor solution, and the sorted-edges algorithm solution are all different?

■ 34. If the brute force method of solving a 20-city TSP is employed, use a calculator to determine how many Hamiltonian circuits must be examined. How long would it take to determine the minimum-cost tour if the cost of tours could be computed at the rate of 1 billion per second? (Convert your answer to years by seeing how many years are equivalent to a billion seconds!)

35. Suppose one has found an optimal tour for a given 15-city TSP problem to have weight 3460. Now suppose the weights on the edges of the complete graph are increased by 30. What can you say about the optimal tour and its weight?

Trees and Spanning Trees

36. Which of the graphs below are trees?

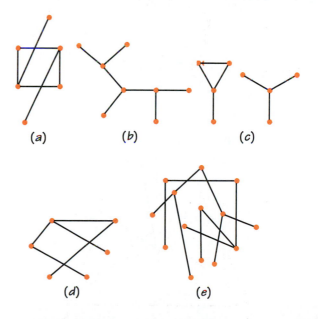

37. For each of the diagrams below explain why the wiggled edges are not
    (a) a spanning tree
    (b) a Hamiltonian circuit

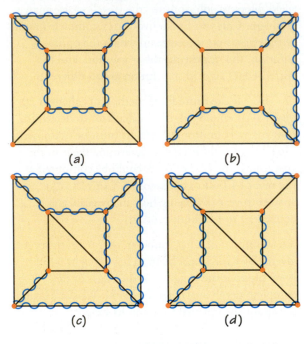

(a)   (b)

(c)   (d)

38. Find all the spanning trees in the graphs below.

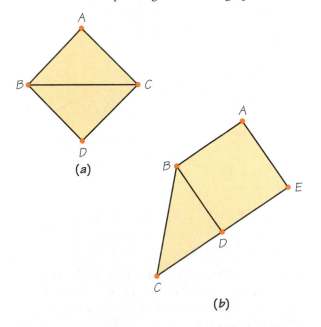

(a)

(b)

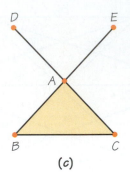

(c)

39. Use Kruskal's algorithm to find a minimum-cost spanning tree for graphs (a), (b), (c), and (d).

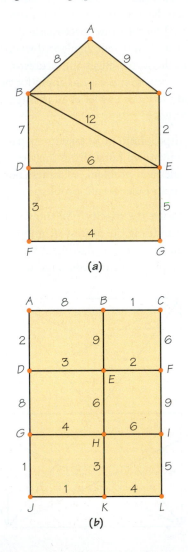

(a)

(b)

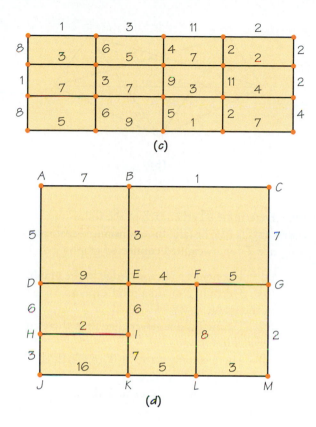

(c)

(d)

40. A large company wishes to install a pneumatic tube system that would enable small items to be sent between any of 10 locales, possibly by relay. If the nonprohibitive costs (in $100) are shown in the graph model below, between which sites should the tube be installed to minimize the total cost?

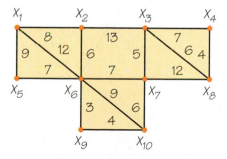

41. If the weight of each edge in Exercise 40 is increased by 1, will the tree that achieves minimum cost for the new collection of weights be the same as the one that achieves minimum cost for the original set of weights?

42. There are plans to construct a new subway system in city X. The distances between every pair of locations for the 9 stations have been computed. It is desired to build enough track so that passengers can go between any pair of the 9 stations using trains that run on the track that is built. The constructors of the subway are anxious to keep the cost to taxpayers down. It is proposed to solve this problem by finding a minimum-cost spanning tree. Does this seem reasonable? If not, under what special circumstances might it be reasonable? If, instead of a subway, freight was being sent between the 9 locations, would finding a minimal-cost spanning tree seem reasonable? Explain your reasons.

43. (a) The table shown gives the "closeness" or distance values between four objects. Can you construct a four-vertex tree with weights on its edges such that the distances between pairs of vertices of the tree (as measured by the sum of the weights on the path in the tree between these vertices) distances give rise to this table?

0	3	10	14
3	0	7	11
10	7	0	4
14	11	4	0

(b) Can you produce several real-world contexts that might give rise to the situation described here?

◆ **44.** Give examples of real-world situations that can be modeled using a weighted graph and for which finding a minimum-cost spanning tree for the graph would be of interest.

■ **45.** Can Kruskal's algorithm be modified to find a maximum-weight spanning tree? Can you think of an application for finding a maximum-weight spanning tree?

◆ 46. Find the cost of providing a relay network between the six cities with the largest populations in your home state, using the road distances between the cities as costs. Does it follow that the same solution would be obtained if air distances are used instead?

■ 47. Would there ever be a reason to find a minimum-cost spanning tree for a weighted graph in which the weights on some of the edges were negative? Would Kruskal's algorithm still apply?

48. Let G be a graph with weights assigned to each edge. Consider the following algorithm:

   (a)   Pick any vertex V of G.
   (b)   Select an edge E with a vertex at V that has a minimum weight. Let the other endpoints of E be W.
   (c)   Contract the edge VW so that edge VW disappears and vertices V and W coincide (see the following figures).

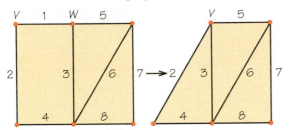

If in the new graph two or more edges join a pair of vertices, delete all but the cheapest. Continue to call the new vertex V.

   (d)   Repeat steps (b) and (c) until a single point is obtained. The edges selected in the course of this algorithm (called Prim's algorithm) form a minimum-cost spanning tree. Apply this algorithm to the following graphs.

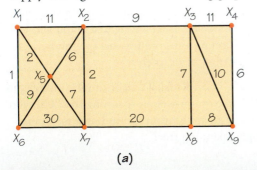

(a)

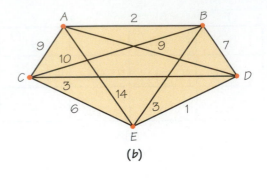

(b)

49. Determine whether each of the following statements is true or false for a minimum-cost spanning tree T for a weighted connected graph G:

   (a)   T contains a cheapest edge in the graph.
   (b)   T cannot contain a most expensive edge in the graph.
   (c)   T contains one fewer edge than there are vertices in G.
   (d)   There is some vertex in T to which all others are joined by edges.
   (e)   There is some vertex in T that has valence 3.

■ 50. In the following graphs (below and at the top of page 67), the number in the circle for each vertex is the cost of installing equipment at the vertex if relaying must be done at the vertex, while the number on an edge indicates the cost of providing service between the endpoints of the edge.

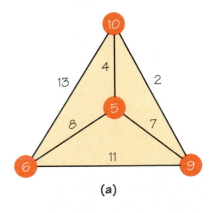

(a)

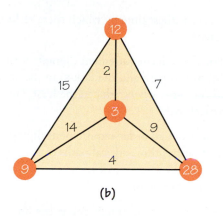

(b)

In each case, find the minimum cost (allowing relays) for sending messages between any pair of vertices, taking vertex relay costs into account. Would your answer be different if vertex relay costs are neglected? (*Warning:* Kruskal's algorithm cannot be used to answer the first question. This problem illustrates the value of having an algorithm over-relying on "brute force.")

51.   Two spanning trees of a (weighted) graph are considered different if they use different edges. Show that the graph below has different minimum-cost spanning trees, though all these different trees have the same cost.

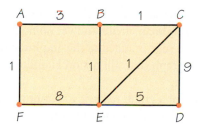

■ 52.   Suppose G is a graph such that all the weights on its edges are different numbers. Show that there is a unique minimum-cost spanning tree.

53.   Find a minimum-cost spanning tree for the complete graphs in Exercise 30.

Scheduling

54.   Find the earliest completion time and critical paths for the three order-requirement digraphs below.

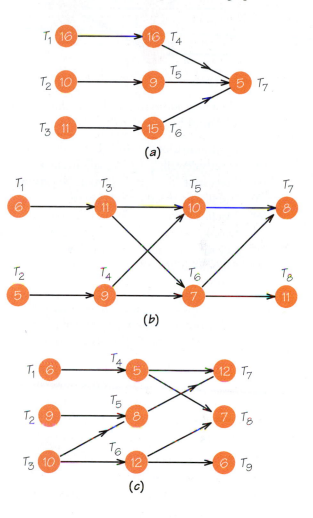

55.   Construct an example of an order-requirement digraph with three different critical paths.

■ 56.   In the order-requirement digraph on page 66, determine which tasks, if shortened, would reduce the earliest completion time and which would not. Then find the earliest completion time if task T_5 is reduced to time length 7. What is the new critical path?

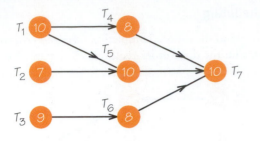

57. To build a new addition on a house, the following tasks must be completed:

(a) Lay foundation.
(b) Erect sidewalls.
(c) Erect roof.
(d) Install plumbing.
(e) Install electric wiring.
(f) Lay tile flooring.
(g) Obtain building permits.
(h) Put in door that adjoins new room to existing house.
(i) Install track lighting on ceiling.
(j) Install wall air-conditioner.

Construct reasonable time estimates for these tasks and a reasonable order-requirement digraph. What is the fastest time in which these tasks can be completed?

58. At a large toy store, scooters arrive unassembled in boxes. To assemble a scooter the following tasks must be performed:

TASK 1. Remove parts from the box.
TASK 2. Attach wheels to the footboard.
TASK 3. Attach vertical housing.
TASK 4. Attach handlebars to vertical housing.
TASK 5. Put on reflector tape.
TASK 6. Attach bell to handlebars.
TASK 7. Attach decals.
TASK 8. Attach kickstand.
TASK 9. Attach safety instructions to handlebars.

Give reasonable time estimates for these tasks and construct a reasonable order-requirement digraph.

What is the earliest time by which these tasks can be completed?

59. For the order-requirement digraph at the left, find the critical path and the task(s) in the critical path whose time, when reduced the least, creates a new critical path.

60. Construct an order-requirement digraph with six tasks that has three critical paths of length 24.

Additional Exercises

61. (a) Each of the graphs below has no Hamiltonian circuit. Is it possible to add a single new edge to these graphs and obtain a new graph that has a Hamiltonian circuit?

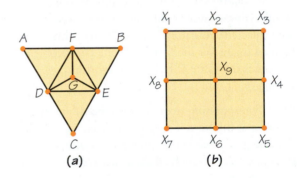

(a)　　　　　　　(b)

(b) Find an example of a graph that has no Hamiltonian circuit and yet no matter what single edge is added to the graph the result is a new graph that still has no Hamiltonian circuit.
(c) For a graph to have a Hamiltonian path, one relaxes the condition for a Hamiltonian circuit of having to start and end at the same vertex but still requires that the path include all the vertices of the graph. Do the graphs here have Hamiltonian paths?
(d) Can you think of applications situations where the concept of a Hamiltonian path would be useful?

62. The following figure represents a town where there is a sewer located at each corner (where two or more streets meet). After every thunderstorm, the department of public works wishes to have a truck start at its headquarters (at vertex H) and make an inspection of sewer drains to be sure that leaves are not clogging them. Can a route start and end at H that visits each corner exactly once? (Assume that all the streets are two-way streets.) Does this problem involve finding an Euler circuit or a Hamiltonian circuit?

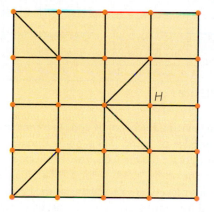

Assume that at equally spaced intervals along the blocks in this graph there are storm sewers that must be inspected after each thunderstorm to see if they are clogged. Is this a Hamiltonian circuit problem, an Euler circuit problem, or a Chinese postman problem? Can you find an optimal tour to do this inspection?

63. In the last several years regions that contain large cities that have had telephone service provided via only one area code have had to be divided into service areas with more than one area code. What is the largest number of different phone numbers that can be served using one area code? If an area code cannot begin with a zero, how many different area codes are possible?

64. For each of the graphs with weights (at the right), apply the nearest-neighbor method (starting at vertex A) and the sorted-edges method to find (it is hoped) a cheap tour.

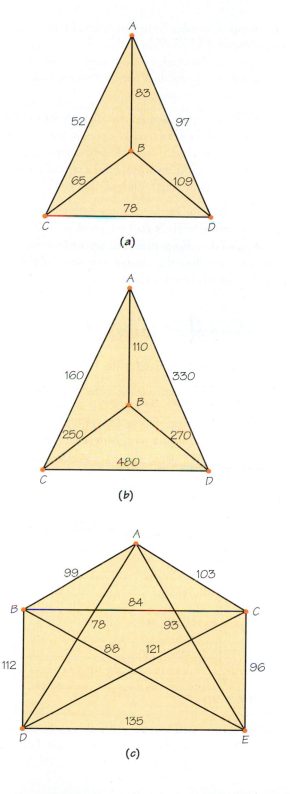

65. Suppose one has found an optimal tour for a given 10-city TSP problem to have weight 4520. Now suppose the weights on the edges of the complete graph are doubled. What can you say about the optimal tour and its weight?

66. Draw an order-requirement digraph for the following set of tasks, which make up a kitchen remodeling project, giving a reasonable estimate for the times to do the tasks involved. Find a critical path for the order-requirement digraph that you obtain.

TASKS: Clean the kitchen; scrape walls to remove old paint; prime walls; install wallpaper on walls; scrape paint on ceiling; paint ceiling; replace old floor with new floor tiles; install new stove; install new sink; install new refrigerator.

TECHNOLOGY CORNER

Finding a Low-Cost Spanning Tree

Graphs can be represented using spreadsheets so that each column (A, B, C, etc.) represents a vertex and each row (1, 2, 3, etc.) represents an edge of the graph. When there are costs associated with using the edges, we report these costs in an additional column. For example, the graph in Figure 2.12 can be represented by the spreadsheet shown in Figure 2.20.

	A	B	C	D	E	F	G
1	1	1					0.7
2		1	1				1.6
3			1	1			0.75
4				1	1		0.5
5	1					1	0.65
6					1	1	1.2
7	1				1		0.6
8			1			1	1.4
9		1			1		1.5
10	1		1				1.3

FIGURE 2.20

Representing the data in a spreadsheet eliminates any confusion about the labeling of the graph. Further-

more, spreadsheets allow you to easily sort the edges by their cost. Using the **Sort** tool, we can rearrange the rows so that less expensive edges are listed first, as shown in Figure 2.21.

	A	B	C	D	E	F	G
1				1	1		0.5
2	1				1		0.6
3	1					1	0.65
4	1	1					0.7
5			1	1			0.75
6		1				1	1.2
7	1		1				1.3
8			1			1	1.4
9		1			1		1.5
10		1	1				1.6

FIGURE 2.21

After sorting the edges by cost, mark the least expensive edge as "used." Then, going through the sorted list, locate the first edge that connects a new vertex to one of the "used" vertices. Mark it as "used." Repeat this process, always starting at the beginning of the sorted list, until every vertex is part of a "used" edge. (If there is more than one "cheapest" edge at any time, choose any one of them.) For the spreadsheet shown in Figure 2.21, edges are marked as "used" in the following order: 1, 2, 4, 5. The third edge is not used because neither of its vertices is "new."

TASK 1.   Draw the graph that corresponds to the spreadsheet shown in Figure 2.21. Mark the low-cost spanning tree found by the above procedure. Is the resulting tree the same as that found using Kruskal's algorithm?

TASK 2.   Find a low-cost spanning tree for the graph represented by the spreadsheet shown in Figure 2.22. First sort the rows by their cost, which is given in the final column. Then use the above procedure to find a low-cost spanning tree.

Finding a Low-Cost Hamiltonian Circuit

You can adapt the low-cost spanning tree procedure to find a low-cost Hamiltonian circuit (a solution to the

	A	B	C	D	E	F	G	H
1	1	1						18
2	1		1					15
3	1			1				21
4	1				1			19
5	1					1		9
6		1	1					17
7		1		1				20
8		1			1			17
9		1					1	14
10			1	1				16
11			1		1			23
12			1			1		22
13				1	1			12
14				1		1		24
15					1	1		13

FIGURE 2.22

traveling salesman problem). After sorting the rows by their cost, mark the least expensive edge as "used." Then, going through the sorted list, locate the first edge that connects a new vertex to a vertex that has only been "used" one time. Mark it as "used." Repeat this process, always starting at the beginning of the sorted list, until every vertex is part of a "used" edge. At this point, there will be two remaining vertices that have been "used" only one time. Locate the edge that connects these vertices and mark it as "used." The "used" edges will form a low-cost Hamiltonian circuit.

Using this procedure for the sorted spreadsheet shown in Figure 2.21, edges are marked as "used" in the following order: 1, 2, 4, 8, 10. The third edge is not used, since neither vertex is "new." The fifth edge is not used since "D" has been used more than once. For similar reasons, the sixth and seventh edges are not used.

TASK 3.   Find a low-cost Hamiltonian circuit for the graph whose spreadsheet is given in Task 2. Use the procedure explained above.

Reflection

In each of these procedures, will the second edge in the sorted list always be used? Do these procedures result in the same solutions as the "sorted edge" algorithms in the textbook? How are spreadsheets an effective tool in locating solutions?

writing projects

1 ▶ Write an essay about a variety of situations in which you are personally involved for which a solution of the TSP is (perhaps implicitly) required. Explain under what circumstances it might be valuable to carry out a formal mathematical solution to such TSPs rather than use an ad hoc solution.

2 ▶ Pick a situation that involves the traveling salesman model and discuss how closely the mathematics describes this situation and what features of the problem are likely to be important but have been neglected in the TSP model.

3 ▶ Construct an example, of the kind suggested on page 41, that shows that in a situation where three day campers must be picked up and brought to camp, it may make a difference if the optimization criterion is minimizing distance traveled by the camp bus versus minimizing average time that the children spend on the bus.

4 ▶ Determine the six largest cities in the state in which you live. By consulting a road atlas (or by some other means) construct the graph that represents the road distances between your hometown and these six other cities. Now apply (a) the nearest-neighbor method, (b) the sorted-edges method, and (c) the nearest neighbor from each city, and pick the minimum tour method to solve the associated TSP. Do you have reason to believe that the answers you get might include an optimum solution among them?

5 ▶ Give the pros and cons of converting between a phone system in which calls are paid for by placing coins into the phone versus a phone system that operates using prepaid cards.

6 ▶ If a housing developer must create a new system of roads to drive between any pair of houses (currently there are no roads in the area) and the paved access road, do you think the people in the new housing tract will be pleased if a minimal-cost spanning-tree approach is used by the developer in solving the problem?

"Although many
scheduling
problems are
often solved on
an ad hoc basis,
we can also use
mathematical
ideas to gain
insight. . . ."

chapter 3

Planning and Scheduling

I n a society as complex as ours, everyday problems such as providing services efficiently and on time require accurate planning of both people and machines. Take the example of a hospital in a major city. Around-the-clock scheduling of nurses and doctors must be provided to guarantee that people with particular expertise are available during each shift. The operating rooms must be scheduled in a manner flexible enough to deal with emergencies. Equipment used for X-ray, CAT, or MRI scans must be scheduled for maximal efficiency.

Although many scheduling problems are often solved on an ad hoc basis, we can also use mathematical ideas to gain insight into the complications that arise in scheduling. The ideas we develop in this chapter have practical value in a relatively narrow range of applications, but they throw light on many characteristics of more realistic and hence more complex scheduling problems.

Scheduling Tasks

Assume that a certain number of identical **processors** (machines, humans, or robots) work on a series of tasks that make up a job. Associated with each task is a specified amount of time required to complete the task. For simplicity, we assume that any of the processors can work on any of the tasks. Our problem, known as the **machine-scheduling problem,** is to decide how the tasks should be scheduled so that the completion time for the tasks collectively is as early as possible.

Even with these simplifying assumptions, complications in scheduling will arise. Some tasks may be more important than others and perhaps should be

Nurses scheduling
patient care.

scheduled first. When "ties" occur, they must be resolved by special rules. As an example, suppose we are scheduling patients to be seen in a hospital emergency room staffed by one doctor. If two patients arrive simultaneously, one with a bleeding foot, the other with a bleeding arm, which patient should be processed first? Suppose the doctor treats the arm patient first, and while treatment is going on, a person in cardiac arrest arrives. Scheduling rules must establish appropriate priorities for cases such as these.

Another common complications arises with jobs consisting of several tasks that cannot be done in an arbitrary order. For example, if the job of putting up a new house is treated as a scheduling problem, the task of laying the foundation must precede the task of putting up the walls, which in turn must be completed before work on the roof can begin.

Assumptions and Goals

To simplify our analysis, we need to make clear and explicit assumptions:

1. If a processor starts work on a task, the work on that task will continue without interruption until the task is completed.
2. No processor stays voluntarily idle. In other words, if there is a processor free and a task available to be worked on, then that processor will immediately begin work on that task.

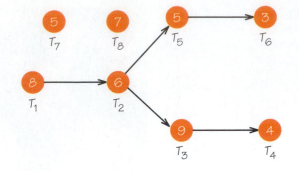

FIGURE 3.1 A typical order-requirement digraph.

3.　The requirements for ordering the tasks are given by an order-requirement digraph. (A typical example is shown in Figure 3.1, with task times highlighted within each vertex. The ordering of the tasks imposed by the order-requirement digraph represents constraints of physical reality. For example, you cannot fly a plane until it has taken fuel on board.)

4.　The tasks are arranged in a priority list that is independent of the order requirements. (The **priority list** is an ordering of the tasks according to some criterion of "importance," which may in no way reflect physical reality. For example, imagine a construction job with several tasks. Task A may have to be done before task B, but when task B is done, a monetary payment will be made. Thus, B may be given a higher priority than A. The priority list represents, from some point of view, an ordering of the tasks. Another such point of view is to order the tasks in a manner that will help the algorithm being used construct schedules with early completion times. Usually, different points of view for giving priority to tasks are not consistent. Mathematical analysis may sometimes assist in clarifying trade-offs implicit in these different points of view.)

When considering a scheduling problem, there are various goals one might wish to achieve. Among these are

1.　Minimizing the completion time of the job
2.　Minimizing the total time that processors are idle
3.　Finding the minimum number of processors necessary to finish the job by a specified time

For now we will concentrate on goal 1, finishing all the tasks at the earliest possible time. Note, however, that optimizing with respect to one criterion or goal may not optimize with respect to another. Our discussion here goes beyond what was discussed in Chapter 2 (see "Critical-Path Analysis," pages 50–54) by dealing with how to assign tasks in a job to the processors that do the work.

Air traffic controllers
manage complicated
scheduling problems.

List-Processing Algorithm

The scheduling problem we have described sounds more complicated than the traveling salesman problem (TSP). Indeed, like the TSP, it is known to be NP-complete. This means that it is unlikely that anyone will ever find a computationally fast algorithm that can find an optimal solution. Thus, we will be content to seek a solution method that is computationally fast and gives only approximately optimal answers.

The algorithm we use to schedule tasks is the **list-processing algorithm.** In describing it, we will call a task *ready* at a particular time if all its predecessors as indicated in the order-requirement digraph have been completed at that time. In Figure 3.1 at time 0 the ready tasks are T_1, T_7, and T_8, while T_2 cannot be ready until 8 time units after T_1 is started. The algorithm works as follows: at a given time, assign to the lowest-numbered free processor the first task on the priority list that is *ready* at that time and that hasn't already been assigned to a processor.

In applying this algorithm, we will need to develop skill at coordinating the use of the information in the order-requirement digraph and the priority list. It will be helpful to cross out the tasks in the priority list as they are assigned to a processor to keep track of which tasks remain to be scheduled. Let's apply this algorithm to one possible priority list, T_8, T_7, T_6, . . . , T_1, using two processors and the order-requirement digraph in Figure 3.1. The result is the schedule shown

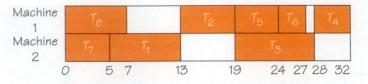

FIGURE 3.2. The schedule produced by applying the list-processing algorithm to the order-requirement digraph in Figure 3.1 using the list T_8, T_7, . . . , T_1.

in Figure 3.2, where idle processor time is indicated by white. How does the list-processing algorithm generate this schedule?

Because T_8 (task 8) is first on the priority list and ready at time 0, it is assigned to the lowest-numbered free processor, processor 1. Task 7, next on the priority list, is also ready at time 0 and thus is assigned to processor 2. The first processor to become free is processor 2 at time 5. Recall that by assumption 1, once a processor starts work on a task, its work cannot be interrupted until the task is compete. Task 6, the next unassigned task on the list, is not ready at time 5, as can be seen by consulting Figure 3.1. The reason task 6 is not ready at time 5 is that task 5 has not been completed by time 5. In fact, at time 5, the only ready task on the list is T_1, so that task is assigned to processor 2. At time 7, processor 1 becomes free, but no task becomes ready until time 13. Thus, processor 1 stays idle from time 7 to time 13. At this time, because T_2 is the first ready task on the list not already scheduled, it is assigned to processor 1. Processor 2, however, stays idle because no other ready task is available at this time. The remainder of the scheduling shown in Figure 3.2 is competed in this manner.

As the priority list is scanned from left to right to assign a processor at a particular time, we pass over tasks that are not ready to find ones that are ready. If no task can be assigned in this manner, we keep one or more processors idle until such time that, reading the priority list from the left, there is a ready task not already assigned. After a task is assigned to a processor, we resume scanning the priority list, starting over at the far left, for unassigned tasks.

When Is a Schedule Optimal?

The schedule in Figure 3.2 has a lot of idle time, so it may not be optimal. Indeed, if we apply the list-processing algorithm for two processors to another possible priority list T_1, . . . , T_8, using the digraph in Figure 3.1, the resulting schedule is that shown in Figure 3.3.

Here are the details of how this schedule was arrived at. Remember that we must coordinate the list T_1, T_2, . . . , T_8 with the information in the order-requirement digraph shown in Figure 3.3a. At time 0, task T_1 is ready, so this task is assigned to processor 1. However, at time 0, tasks T_2, T_3, . . . , T_6 are not

FIGURE 3.3
(a) A typical order-requirement digraph (repeat of Figure 3.1).
(b) The schedule produced by applying the list-processing algorithm to the order-requirement digraph in Figure 3.3a using the list $T_1, T_2, \ldots, T_8$.

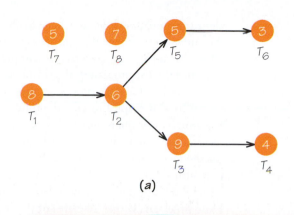

(a)

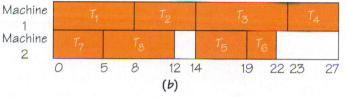

(b)

ready since their predecessors are not done. For example, T_2 is not ready at time 0 since T_1, which precedes it, is not done at time 0. The first ready task on the list, reading from left to right, that is not already assigned is T_7, so task T_7 gets assigned to processor 2. Both processors are now busy until time 5, at which point processor 2 becomes idle (Figure 3.3b).

Tasks T_1 and T_7 have been assigned; reading from left to right along the list, the first task not already assigned whose predecessors are done by time 5 is T_8, so this task is started at time 5 on processor 2; processor 2 will continue to work on this task until time 12, since the task time for this task is 7 time units. At time 8, processor 1 becomes free, and reading the list from left to right we find that T_2 is ready (since T_1 has just been completed). Thus, T_2 is assigned processor 1, which will stay busy on this task until time 14. At time 12, processor 2 becomes free, but the tasks that have not already been assigned from the list, T_3, T_4, T_5, T_6, are not ready, since they depend on T_2 being completed before these tasks can start. Thus, processor 2 stays idle involuntarily until time 14. At this time, T_3 and T_5 become ready. Since both processors 1 and 2 are idle at time 14, the lower numbered of the two, processor 1, gets to start on T_3 because it is the first ready task left to be assigned on the list scanned from left to right. Task T_5 get assigned to processor 2 at time 14. The remaining tasks are assigned in a similar manner.

The schedule shown in Figure 3.3b is optimal because the path T_1, T_2, T_3, T_4, with length 27, is the critical path in the order-requirement digraph. As we saw in Chapter 2, the earliest completion time for the job made up of all the tasks is the length of the longest path in the order-requirement digraph.

There is another way of relating optimal completion time for a scheduling problem to the completion time that is yielded by the list-processing algorithm. Suppose that we add all the task times given in the order-requirement digraph and divide by the number of processors. The completion time using the list-processing algorithm must be at least as large as this number. For example, the task times for the order-requirement digraph in Figure 3.3a sum to 47. Thus, if these tasks are scheduled on two processors, the completion time is at least $47/2 = 23.5$ (in fact, 24, since the list-processing algorithm applied to integer task times yields an integer answer), while for three processors the completion time is at least $47/3$ (in fact, 16).

Why is it helpful to take the total time to do all the tasks in a job and divide this number by the number of processors? Think of each task that must be scheduled as a rectangle that is 1 unit high and t units wide, where t is the time allotted for the task. Think of the scheduling diagram with m processors as a rectangle that is m units high and whose width W is the completion time for the tasks. The scheduling diagram is to be filled up by the rectangles that represent the tasks. How small can W be? The area of the rectangle that represents the scheduling diagram must be at least as large as the sum of all the rectangles representing tasks that are "packed" into it. The area of the scheduling diagram rectangle is mW. The combined areas of all the tasks, plus the area of rectangles corresponding to idle time, will equal mW. Width W is smallest when the idle time is zero. Thus, W must be at least as big as the sum of all the task times divided by m. Sometimes the estimate for completion time given by the list-processing algorithm from the length of the critical path gives a more useful value than the approach based on adding task times, and sometimes the opposite is true. For the order-requirement digraph in Figure 3.1, except for a schedule involving one processor, the critical-path estimate is superior. For some scheduling problems, both these estimates may be poor.

The number of priority lists that can be constructed if there are n tasks is $n!$, as can be computed using the fundamental principle of counting. For example, for eight tasks, $T_1, \ldots, T_8$, there are $8 \times 7 \times 6 \cdots \times 1 = 40{,}320$ possible priority lists. For different choices of the priority list, the list-processing algorithm we are using will schedule the tasks, subject to the constraints of the order-requirement digraph, in different ways. Different lists may yield schedules with different completion times or different schedules with the same completion time. Different priority lists may yield identical scheduling of tasks (and hence identical completion times). A little later we will see a method that can be used to select a list that, if we are lucky, will give a schedule with a relatively good completion time. In fact, no method is known, except for very specialized cases, of how to choose a list that can be guaranteed to give rise to an optimal schedule when the list algorithm is applied to it.

Strange Happenings

The list-processing algorithm involves four factors that affect the final schedule. The answer we get depends on the

1. Times of the tasks
2. Number of processors
3. Order-requirement digraph
4. Ordering of the tasks on the list

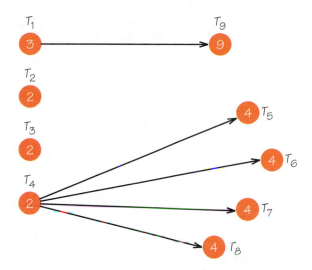

To see the interplay of these four factors, consider another scheduling problem, this one associated with the order-requirement digraph shown in Figure 3.4 (the highlighted numbers are task time lengths).

The schedule generated by the list-processing algorithm applied to the list $T_1, T_2, \ldots, T_9$, using three processors, is given in Figure 3.5.

Treating the list $T_1, \ldots, T_9$ as fixed, how might we make the completion time earlier? Our alternatives are to pursue one or more of these strategies:

1. Reduce task times.
2. Use more processors.
3. "Loosen" the constraints of the order-requirement digraph.

Let's consider each alternative in turn, changing one feature of the original problem at a time, and see what happens to the resulting schedule. If we adopt strategy 1, reducing the time of each task by one unit, it seems intuitively clear

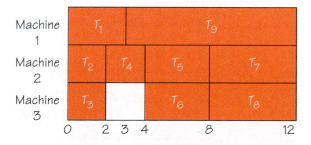

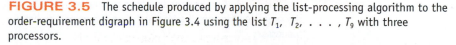

FIGURE 3.5 The schedule produced by applying the list-processing algorithm to the order-requirement digraph in Figure 3.4 using the list $T_1, T_2, \ldots, T_9$ with three processors.

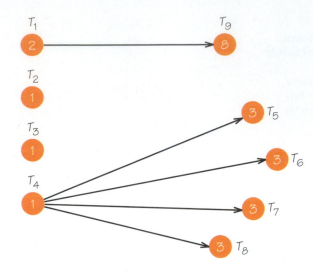

FIGURE 3.6
The order-requirement digraph obtained from the one in Figure 3.4 by reducing by one unit each of the task times shown there.

that the completion time would go down. Figure 3.6 shows the new order-requirement digraph, and Figure 3.7 shows the schedule produced for this problem, using the list-processing algorithm with three processors applied to the list $T_1, \ldots, T_9$. The completion time is now 13, longer than the completion time of 12 for the case (Figure 3.5) with longer task times. Here is something unexpected! Let's explore further and see what happens.

Next we consider strategy 2, increasing the number of machines. Surely this should speed matters up. When we apply the list-processing algorithm to the original graph in Figure 3.4, using the list $T_1, \ldots, T_9$ and four machines, we get the schedule shown in Figure 3.8. The completion time is now 15, *an even later completion time than for the previous alteration!*

Finally, we consider strategy 3, trying to shorten completion time by erasing all constraints (edges with arrows) in the order-requirement digraph shown in Fig-

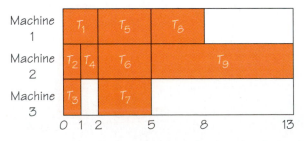
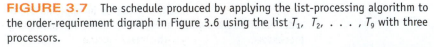

FIGURE 3.7   The schedule produced by applying the list-processing algorithm to the order-requirement digraph in Figure 3.6 using the list $T_1, T_2, \ldots, T_9$ with three processors.

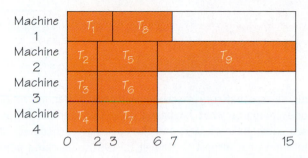
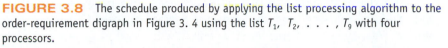

FIGURE 3.8 The schedule produced by applying the list processing algorithm to the order-requirement digraph in Figure 3. 4 using the list T_1, T_2, . . . , T_9 with four processors.

ure 3.4. By increasing flexibility of the ordering of the tasks, we might guess we could finish our tasks more quickly. Figure 3.9 shows the schedule using the list T_1, . . . T_9; now it takes 16 units! This is the worst of our three strategies to reduce completion time.

The failures we have seen here appear paradoxical at first glance, but they are typical of what can happen when a situation is too complex to analyze with naïve intuition. Sometimes our common sense leads us astray. The value of using mathematics rather than intuition or trial and error to study scheduling and other problems is that it points up flaws that can occur in unguarded intuitive reasoning.

The paradoxical behavior we see here is a consequence of the rules we set up for generating schedules. Such paradoxical behavior for the list-processing algorithm will not occur for every example you try. In fact, one has to be quite clever to design such examples. The list-processing algorithm has many nice features, including the fact that it is easy to understand and fast to implement. However, the results of the model in some cases can appear strange. Since we have been explicit about our assumptions, we could go back and make changes in these assumptions in hopes of eliminating the strange behavior. But the price we may pay is more time spent in constructing schedules and perhaps even new types of strange behavior. Unfortunately for modern society with its increasing concern with economical and efficient scheduling (see Spotlight 3.1), recent mathematical research suggests that scheduling is an intrinsically hard problem.

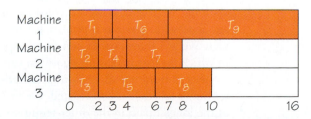
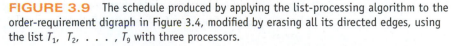

FIGURE 3.9 The schedule produced by applying the list-processing algorithm to the order-requirement digraph in Figure 3.4, modified by erasing all its directed edges, using the list T_1, T_2, ... , T_9 with three processors.

SPOTLIGHT 3.1

Scheduling in the News

An interesting comparison of scheduling occurs when one compares what happened after the San Francisco earthquake of 1993 and the opening of a new international airport in Denver in 1994.

After the earthquake, the Oakland Bay Bridge was seriously damaged, and the legendary Santa Monica Freeway, one of the most heavily used roads in the United States, had to be closed. This necessitated great inconvenience to the residents in the San Francisco Bay metropolitan area. People had to find ingenious and different ways to get to work and get business done despite the disruption. In order to get the bridge repaired and the freeway reopened, a complicated array of different contractors needed to coordinate their efforts. By offering a collection of financial incentives to finish on target or prior to scheduled dates, the bridge and freeway were repaired and made usable again earlier than originally estimated.

By comparison, the vast scheduling effort to open a new international airport to serve the Denver metropolitan area resulted in a series of announced openings and expensive delays when the scheduled dates could not be met. One of the sticking points was the development of an innovative baggage-handling system that was designed to speed travelers who started or ended their journeys in Denver or changed planes there. The idea was that passengers who required a change of planes in Denver would have a shorter layover because the baggage could be transferred between flights more quickly in the new facility than in the old one. From the beginning, the baggage-handling facility caused trouble. Inadequate time had been scheduled for the development of the system, installing it, and testing it. For this project, the scheduling went awry!

Sources: Based on David Margolick, "Quake-Damaged Freeway Reopening Ahead of Time," *New York Times,* July 27, 1994, p. A14; and Dirk Johnson, "Denver May Open Airport in Spite of Glitches," *New York Times,* July 27, 1994, p. A14.

Critical-Path Schedules

In our discussion so far, we have acted as though the priority list used in applying the list-processing algorithm was given to us in advance based on external considerations. We might, however, consider the question of whether there is a systematic method of *choosing* a priority list that yields optimal or nearly optimal schedules. We will show how to construct a specific priority list based on this principle, to which the list-processing algorithm can then be applied.

Recall from our discussion of critical-path analysis in Chapter 2 that no matter how a schedule is constructed, the finish time cannot be earlier than the length of the longest path in the order-requirement digraph. This suggests that we should try to schedule first those tasks that occur early in long paths, because they might be a bottleneck for the other tasks.

EXAMPLE   *Scheduling Two Processors*

To illustrate this method, consider the order-requirement digraph in Figure 3.10a. Suppose we wish to schedule these tasks on two processors. Initially, there are two critical paths of length 64: T_1, T_2, T_3 and T_1, T_4, T_3. Thus, we place T_1 first on the priority list. With T_1 "gone," there is a new critical path of length 60 (i.e., T_5, T_6, T_4, T_3) that starts with T_5, so T_5 is placed second on the priority list. At this stage, with T_1 and T_5 removed, we have the residual order-requirement digraph shown in Figure 3.10b. In this diagram there are paths of length 50 (T_2, T_3), 56 (T_6, T_4, T_3), 36 (T_6, T_4, T_7), and 24 (T_8, T_4, T_{10}). Since T_6 heads the path that is currently longest in length, it gets placed third in the priority list. Once T_6 is removed from Figure 3.10b, there is a tie for which is the longest path remaining, since both T_2, T_3 and T_4, T_3 are paths of length 50.

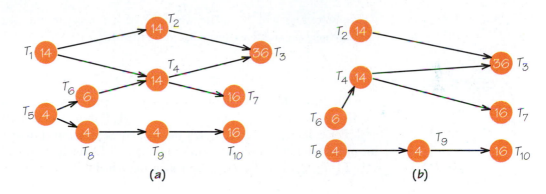

(a)   (b)

FIGURE 3.10
(a) An order-requirement digraph used to illustrate the critical-path scheduling method. (b) Residual order-requirement digraph after tasks T_1 and T_5 have been removed.

When there is a tie between two longest paths, we place next on the priority list in the lowest-numbered task heading a longest path. In the example shown here, this means that T_2 is placed next into the priority list, to be followed by T_4. Continuing in this fashion, we obtain the priority list T_1, T_5, T_6, T_2, T_4, T_3, T_8, T_9, T_7, T_{10}. Note that the order of T_7 and T_{10} was decided using the rule for breaking ties. The list-processing algorithm is now applied using this priority list and the order-requirement digraph in Figure 3.10a. We obtain the schedule in Figure 3.11. ◆

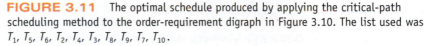

FIGURE 3.11   The optimal schedule produced by applying the critical-path scheduling method to the order-requirement digraph in Figure 3.10. The list used was T_1, T_5, T_6, T_2, T_4, T_3, T_8, T_9, T_7, T_{10}.

This example illustrates what is called **critical-path scheduling.** The algorithm for critical-path scheduling can be described for use with the order-requirement digraph defining any particular scheduling problem. The algorithm applies the list-processing algorithm using the priority list L obtained as follows:

1. Find a task that heads a critical (longest) path in the order-requirement digraph. If there is a tie, choose the task with the lower number.
2. Place the task found in step 1 next on the list L. (The first time through the process this task will head the list.)
3. Remove the task found in step 1 and the edges attached to it from the current order-requirement digraph, obtaining a new (modified) order-requirement digraph.
4. If there are no vertices left in the new order-requirement digraph, the procedure is complete; if there are vertices left, go to step 1.

This procedure will terminate when all of the tasks in the original order-requirement digraph have been placed on the list L.

The preceding example shows that critical-path scheduling can sometimes yield optimal solutions. Unfortunately, this algorithm does not always perform well. For example, the critical-path method employing four processors applied to the order-requirement digraph shown in Figure 3.12 yields the list T_1, T_8, T_9, T_{10}, T_{11}, T_5, T_6, T_7, T_{12}, T_2, T_3, T_4 and then the schedule in Figure 3.13. (Note that

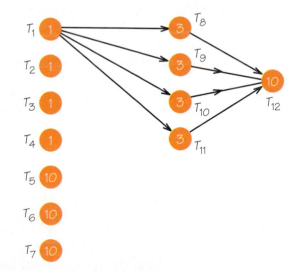

FIGURE 3.12 An order-requirement digraph used to illustrate how poorly the critical-path scheduling method can sometimes behave.

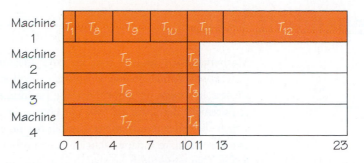

FIGURE 3.13 The schedule produced by applying the critical-path scheduling method to the order-requirement digraph in Figure 3.12 using four processors. The list used was $T_1, T_8, T_9, T_{10}, T_{11}, T_5, T_6, T_7, T_{12}, T_2 T_3, T_4$.

T_5, T_6, T_7 are thought of as heading paths of length 10.) In fact, there can be no worse schedule than this one. An optimal schedule is shown in Figure 3.14.

Many of the results we have examined so far are negative because we are dealing with a general class of problems that defy our using computationally efficient algorithms to find an optimal schedule. But we can close on a more positive note. Consider an arbitrary order-requirement digraph, but assume all the tasks take equal time. It turns out that we can always construct an optimal schedule using two processors in this situation. Ironically, we can choose among many algorithms to produce these optimal schedules. The algorithms are easy to understand (though not easy to prove optimal) and have all been discovered since 1969! Many people think that mathematics is a subject that is no longer alive, and that all its ideas and methods were discovered hundreds of years ago. As we have just seen this is not true. In fact, more new mathematics has been discovered and published in the last 30 years than during any previous 30-year period.

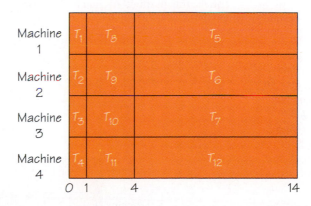

FIGURE 3.14 An optimal schedule for the order-requirement digraph in Figure 3.12 using four processors.

Independent Tasks

Mathematicians suspect that no computationally efficient algorithm for solving general scheduling problems optimally will ever be found. Owing to our limited success in designing algorithms for finding optimal schedules for general order-requirement digraphs, we will consider a special class of scheduling problems for which the order-requirement digraph has no edges with arrows. In this case we say that the tasks are independent of one another, since they can be performed in any order. (No edges with arrows in the order-requirement digraph indicates that no tasks need to precede others; that is, the tasks can be done in any order.) In this section we consider the problem of scheduling **independent tasks.**

There are two approaches we can consider. To study **average-case analysis** we might ask if the average (mean) of the completion times arrived at by using the list-processing algorithm with all the possible different lists is close to the optimal possible completion time. To study **worst-case analysis** we can ask how far from optimal a schedule obtained using the list-processing algorithm with one particular priority list can be. What is being contrasted with these two points of view is that an algorithm may work well most of the time (i.e., give an answer close to optimal) even though there may be a few cases where it performs very badly. Average-case analysis is amenable to mathematical solution but requires methods of great sophistication. For independent tasks, the worst-case analysis can be answered using a surprisingly simple argument developed by Ronald Graham of AT&T Bell Research. The idea is that if the tasks are independent, no processor can be idle at a given time and then busy on a task at a later time. We will return to Graham's worst-case analysis after exploring the problem of independent tasks in more detail.

Geometrically, we can think of the independent tasks as rectangles of height 1 whose lengths are equal to the time length of the task. Finding an optimal schedule amounts to packing the task rectangles into a longer rectangle whose height equals the number of machines. For example, Figure 3.15 shows two different

FIGURE 3.15
(a) A nonoptimal way to schedule independent tasks of time lengths 10, 4, 5, 9, 7, 7 using two processors. (b) An optimal way to schedule independent tasks of time lengths 10, 4, 5, 9, 7, 7 using two processors.

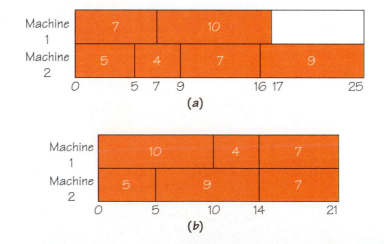

ways to schedule tasks of length 10, 4, 5, 9, 7, 7 on two machines. (For convenience, the rectangles in the case of independent tasks are labeled with their task times rather than their task numbers.) Scheduling basically means efficiently packing the task rectangles into the machine rectangle. Finding the optimal answer among all possible ways to pack these rectangles is like looking for a needle in a haystack. The list-processing algorithm produces a packing, but it may not be a good one.

What Graham's worst-case analysis showed for independent tasks is that no matter which list L one uses, if the optimal schedule requires time T, then the completion time for the schedule produced by the list-processing algorithm applied to list L with m processors is less than or equal to $(2 - 1/m)T$. For example, for two machines ($M = 2$), if an optimal schedule yields completion at time 30, then no list would ever yield a completion later than

$$(2 - \tfrac{1}{2})(30) = 45$$

Although it is of great theoretical interest, Graham's result does not provide much comfort to those who are trying to find good schedules for independent tasks.

Decreasing-Time Lists

Is there some way of choosing a priority list that consistently yields relatively good schedules? The surprising answer is yes! The idea is that when long tasks appear toward the end of the list, they often seem to "stick out" on the right end, as in Figure 3.15a.

This suggests that before one tries to schedule a collection of tasks, the tasks should be placed in a list so that longest tasks are listed first. The list-processing algorithm applied to a list arranged in this fashion is called the **decreasing-time-list algorithm.**

If we apply it to the set of tasks listed previously (10, 4, 5, 9, 7, 7), we obtain the times 10, 9, 7, 7, 5, 4 and the schedule (packing) shown in Figure 3.16. This packing is again optimal, but it is different from the optimal scheduling in Figure 3.15b. It is worth noting that the decreasing-time list and the list obtained by the

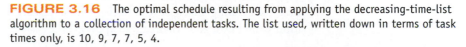

FIGURE 3.16 The optimal schedule resulting from applying the decreasing-time-list algorithm to a collection of independent tasks. The list used, written down in terms of task times only, is 10, 9, 7, 7, 5, 4.

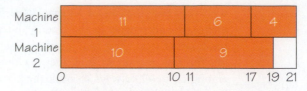

FIGURE 3.17 The nonoptimal schedule resulting from applying the decreasing-time-list algorithm to a collection of independent tasks. The list used, written down in terms of task times only, is 11, 10, 9, 6, 4.

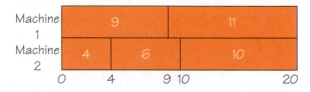

FIGURE 3.18 The optimal schedule resulting from applying the list-processing algorithm to a collection of independent tasks. The list used, written down in terms of task times only, is 9, 4, 6, 11, 10.

critical-path method discussed earlier will coincide in the case of independent tasks. The decreasing-time list can also be constructed for the case where the tasks are not independent, but for general order-requirement digraphs, the decreasing-time list does not produce particularly good schedules.

It is important to remember that the decreasing-time-list algorithm *does not guarantee* optimal solutions. This can be seen by scheduling the tasks with times 11, 10, 9, 6, 4 (Figure 3.17). The schedule has completion time 21. However, the rearranged list 9, 4, 6, 11, 10 yields the schedule in Figure 3.18, which finishes at time 20. This solution is obviously optimal, since the machines finish at the same time and there is no idle time. Note that when tasks are independent, if there are m machines available, the completion time cannot be less than the sum of the task times divided by m.

The problems we have encountered in scheduling independent tasks seem to have taken us a bit far from our goal of applying the mathematics we have developed. Sometimes mathematicians will pursue their mathematical ideas even though they have reached a point where there appear to be no applications. Fortunately, it is very common to be able to find applications for the "abstract" extensions. This is the case in the current instance.

E X A M P L E   *Photocopy Shop and Data Entry Problems*

Imagine a photocopy shop with three photocopiers. Photocopying tasks that must be completed overnight are accepted until 5 P.M. The tasks are to be done in any manner that minimizes the finish time for all the work. Because this problem involves scheduling machines for independent tasks, the decreasing-time-list algorithm would be a good heuristic to apply.

Data entry pool.

For another example, consider a data entry pool at a large corporation or college, where individual entry tasks can be assigned to any data entry specialist. In this setting, however, the assumption that the data enterers are identical in skill is less likely to be true. Hence, the tasks might have different times with different processors. This phenomenon, which occurs in real-world scheduling problems, violates one of the assumptions of our mathematical model.

Graham's result for the list-processing algorithm—that the finishing time is never more than

$$(2 - 1/m)T$$

(where T represents optimal completion time and m the number of processors)—offers us the small comfort of knowing that even the worst choice of priority list will not yield a completion time worse than twice the optimal time. Compared with the list-processing algorithm, the decreasing-time-list algorithm seems to improve completion times. Thus, it is not surprising that an improved bound or time estimate can be given for this case: the decreasing-list algorithm gives a completion time of no more than

$$[\tfrac{4}{3} - 1/(3m)]T$$

where m is the number of processors and T is the optimal time in which the tasks can be completed. In particular, when the number of processors is 2, the schedule produced by the decreasing-time-list algorithm is never off by more than 17%! Usually, the error is much less. This result is a remarkable instance of the value of mathematical research into applied problems. Note that the optimal completion time T depends on m and that Graham's theoretical analysis is necessary precisely because there is no known algorithm to compute T easily.   ◆

Bin Packing

Suppose you plan to build a wall system for your books, records, and stereo set. It requires 24 wooden shelves of various lengths: 6, 6, 5, 5, 5, 4, 4, 4, 4, 2, 2, 2, 2, 3, 3, 7, 7, 5, 5, 8, 8, 4, 4, and 5 feet. The lumberyard, however, sells wood only in boards of length 9 feet. If each board costs $8, what is the minimum cost to buy sufficient wood for this wall system?

Because all shelves required for the wall system are shorter than the boards sold at the lumberyard, the largest number of boards needed is 24, the precise number of shelves needed for the wall system. Buying 24 boards would, of course, be a waste of wood and money because several of the shelves you need could be cut from one board. For example, pieces of length 2, 2, 2, and 3 feet can be cut from one 9-foot board.

To be more efficient, we think of the boards as bins of capacity W (9 feet in this case) into which we will pack (without overlap) n weights (in this case, lengths) whose values are $w_1, \ldots, w_n$, where each $w_i \leq W$. We wish to find the minimum number of bins into which the weights can be packed. In this formulation, the problem is known as the **bin-packing problem.** Thus *bin packing* refers to finding the minimum number of bins of weight capacity W into which weights $w_1, \ldots, w_n$ (each less than or equal to W) can be packed.

At first glance, bin-packing problems may appear unrelated to the machine-scheduling problems we have been studying; however, there is a connection.

Let's suppose we want to schedule independent tasks so that each machine working on the tasks finishes its work by time W. Instead of fixing the number of machines and trying to find the earliest completion time, we must find the minimum number of machines that will guarantee completion by the fixed completion time (W). Despite this similarity between the machine-scheduling problem and the bin-packing problem, the discussion that follows will use the traditional terminology of bin packing.

By now, it should come as no surprise to learn that no one knows a fast algorithm that always picks the optimal (smallest) number of bins (boards). In fact, the bin-packing problem belongs to the class of NP-complete problems (see Spotlight 2.1, page 42), which means that most experts think it unlikely that any fast optimal algorithm will ever be found.

Bin-Packing Heuristics

We will think of the items to be packed, in any particular order, as constituting a list. In what follows we will use the list of 24 shelf lengths given for the wall system. We will consider various **heuristic** algorithms, namely, methods that can be carried out quickly but cannot be guaranteed to produce optimal results. Probably the easiest approach is simply to put the weights into the first bin until the next weight won't fit, and then start a new bin. (Once you open a new bin, don't use leftover space in an earlier, partially filled bin.) Continue in the same way until as many bins as necessary are used. The resulting solution is shown in Figure 3.19.

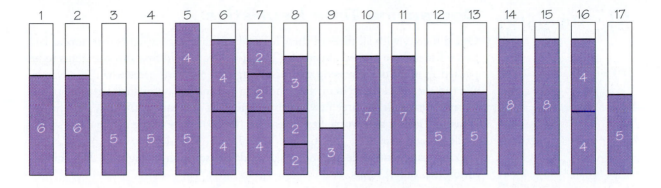

FIGURE 3.19
The list 6, 6, 5, 5, 5, 4, 4, 4, 4, 2, 2, 2, 2, 3, 3, 7, 7, 5, 5, 8, 8, 4, 4, 5 packed in bins using next fit.

This algorithm, called **next fit (NF),** has the advantage of not requiring knowledge of all the weights in advance; only the remaining space in the bin currently being packed must be remembered. The disadvantage of this heuristic is that a bin packed early on may have had room for small items that come later in the list.

Our wish to avoid permanently closing a bin too early suggests a different heuristic — **first fit (FF):** put the next weight into the first bin already opened that has room for this weight; if no such bin exists, start a new bin. Note that a computer program to carry out first fit would have to keep track of how much room was left in all the previously opened bins. For the 24 wall-system shelves the first-fit algorithm would generate a solution that uses only 14 bins (see Figure 3.20) instead of the 17 bins generated by the next-fit algorithm.

If we are keeping track of how much room remains in each unfilled bin, we can put the next item to be packed into the bin that currently has the most room available. This heuristic will be called **worst fit (WF).** The name worst fit refers to the fact that an item is packed into a bin with the most room available, that is, into which it fits "worst," rather than into a bin that will leave little room left over after it is placed in that bin (i.e., "best fit"). The solution generated by this approach looks the same as that shown in Figure 3.20. Although this heuristic also leads to 14 bins, the items are packed in a different order. For example, the first item of size 2, the tenth item in the list, is put into bin 6 in worse fit, but into bin 1 in first fit.

FIGURE 3.20
The list 6, 6, 5, 5, 5, 4, 4, 4, 4, 2, 2, 2, 2, 3, 3, 7, 7, 5, 5, 8, 8, 4, 4, 5 packed in bins using first fit. Worst fit would yield a packing that would look identical.

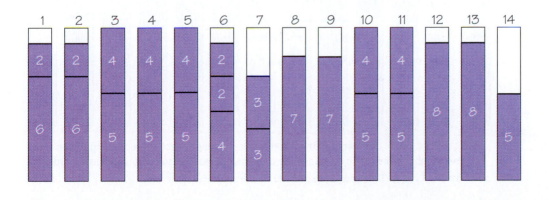

Decreasing-Time Heuristics

One difficulty with all three of these heuristics is that large weights that appear late in the list can't be packed efficiently. Therefore, we should first sort the items to be packed in order of decreasing size, assuming that all items are known in advance. We can then pack large items first and then the smaller items into leftover spaces. This approach yields three new heuristics: **next-fit decreasing (NFD), first-fit decreasing (FFD),** and **worst-fit decreasing (WFD).** Here is the original list sorted by decreasing size: 8, 8, 7, 7, 6, 6, 5, 5, 5, 5, 5, 5, 4, 4, 4, 4, 4, 4, 3, 3, 2, 2, 2, 2. Packing using first-fit-decreasing order yields the solution in Figure 3.21. This solution uses only 13 bins.

Is there any packing that uses only 12 bins? No. In Figure 3.21, there are only 2 free units (1 unit each in bins 1 and 2) of space in the first 12 bins, but 4 occupied units (two 2s) in bin 13. We could have predicted this by dividing the total length of the shelves (110) by the capacity of each bin (board): $\frac{110}{9} = 12\frac{2}{9}$. Thus, no packing could squeeze these shelves into 12 bins—there would always be at least 2 units left over for the 13th bin. (In Figure 3.21, there are 4 units in bin 13 because of the 2 wasted empty spaces in bins 1 and 2.) Even if this division has created a zero remainder, there would still be no guarantee that the items could be packed to fill each bin without wasted space. For example, if the bin capacity is 10 and there are weights of 6, 6, 6, 6, and 6, the total weight is 30; dividing by 10, we get 3 bins as the minimum requirement. Clearly, however, 5 bins are needed to pack the five 6s.

None of the six heuristic methods shown will necessarily find the optimal number of bins for an arbitrary problem. How can we decide which heuristic to use? One approach is to see how far from the optimal solution each method might stray. Various formulas have been discovered to calculate the maximum discrepancy between what a bin-packing algorithm actually produces and the best possible result. For example, in situations where a large number of bins are to be packed, FF can be off as much as 70%, but FFD is never off by more than 22%.

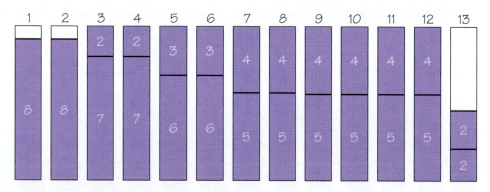

FIGURE 3.21   The bin packing resulting from applying first-fit decreasing to the wall-system numbers. The list involved, which uses the original list sorted in decreasing order, is 8, 8, 7, 7, 6, 6, 5, 5, 5, 5, 5, 5, 4, 4, 4, 4, 4, 4, 3, 3, 2, 2, 2, 2.

Of course, FFD doesn't give an answer as quickly as FF, because extra time for sorting a large collection of weights may be considerable. Also, FFD requires knowing the whole list of weights in advance, whereas FF does not. It is important to emphasize that 22% is a worst-case figure. In many cases, FFD will perform much better. Results obtained by computer simulation indicate excellent average-case performance for this algorithm.

When solving real-world problems, we always have to look at the relationship between mathematics and the real world. Thus, first-fit decreasing usually results in fewer bins than next fit, but next fit can be used even when all the weights are not known in advance. Next fit also requires much less computer storage than first fit, because once a bin is packed, it need never be looked at again. Fine-tuning of the conditions of the actual problem often results in better practical solutions and in interesting new mathematics as well. (See Spotlight 3.2 for a discussion of some of the tools mathematicians use to verify and even extend mathematical truths.)

Resolving Conflict

In attempting to understand situations that involve scheduling, one might desire to achieve a wide variety of goals. For example, in certain types of scheduling problems, as we have seen here, one is interested in optimization issues. What is the earliest completion time for getting a collection of tasks done on two identical processors? However, in other situations a different goal may arise. For example, in sports, one may have a league of baseball teams. Each team has to play some games during the day, some at night, some at home, and some away from home. In the interests of *equity*, it may be desirable for each team to play the same number of day games and night games both at home and away against each of the other teams in the league. If, for example, team *A* plays 8 games away against team *B* and 2 games at home against *B*, then if *A* wins both home games but loses 7 out of 8 away games, it may appear that *B* had an advantage due to the way its games against *A* were scheduled. Another goal of scheduling other than optimization and equity may be preventing conflicts from occurring.

We can use our knowledge of graph theory to solve some interesting scheduling problems where the goal is "conflict resolution." For example, at most colleges, every semester and summer session final examinations must be scheduled. From the point of view of students and faculty both, it would be desirable to schedule these examinations so that (1) no two examinations are scheduled at the same time when a student is enrolled in both of the courses; (2) the examinations are scheduled in as "compact" a way as possible, that is, as few time slots or days as possible. The administration of the college may share the desire for these two features and want still another property for the scheduling: (3) no more than five examinations are scheduled for any time slot. The reason for a condition such as the last might be that during the summer only five rooms with reliable enough air conditioning are available (or there might be only five rooms large enough to hold all the students taking the common final for multiple-section courses).

EXAMPLE   *Scheduling Examinations*

Small State is offering eight courses during its summer session. The table shows which pairs of courses have two or more students in the same course with an X. Only two air-conditioned lecture halls are available for use at any one time. To design an efficient way to schedule the final examinations, we can represent the information in this table by using a graph as shown in Figure 3.22a. In the graph, courses are represented by vertices and two courses are joined by an edge if there is any student enrolled in both courses.

	F	M	H	P	E	I	S	C
French (F)		X		X	X	X		X
Mathematics (M)	X				X	X		
History (H)						X	X	X
Philosophy (P)	X							X
English (E)	X	X				X		
Italian (I)	X	X	X		X		X	
Spanish (S)			X			X		
Chemistry (C)	X		X	X				

The graph theory problem we are faced with is the following: Can we assign labels to the vertices of the graph in such a way that vertices that are joined by an edge get different labels? We think of the labels as the time slots the courses are assigned for final examinations. Traditionally, in graph theory such labels are referred to as *colors.* In this language we seek to color the vertices of the graph so that vertices that are joined by an edge get different colors. Such a coloring is called a **vertex coloring.**

Figure 3.22b shows one way to color the vertices of the graph so that each vertex gets a different color. Note that numbers are being used to represent the different colors. This solution is not very valuable, however, since it means that each course be given its own time slot.

In order to minimize the number of time slots used, we assign colors so that no two vertices that are joined by an edge get the same color. Thus, vertices *F*, *M*, *I*, and *E* must get four different colors. These four colors can then be used to color the remaining vertices, ensuring that no two connected vertices have the same color.

The coloring in Figure 3.22c is a major improvement over the one in Figure 3.22b. It uses only four colors. In fact, this is the smallest number of colors that can be used. To see this, notice that the vertices *F, M, I, E* in Figure 3.22a are all joined by edges to each other. Thus, in any coloring of this graph they would

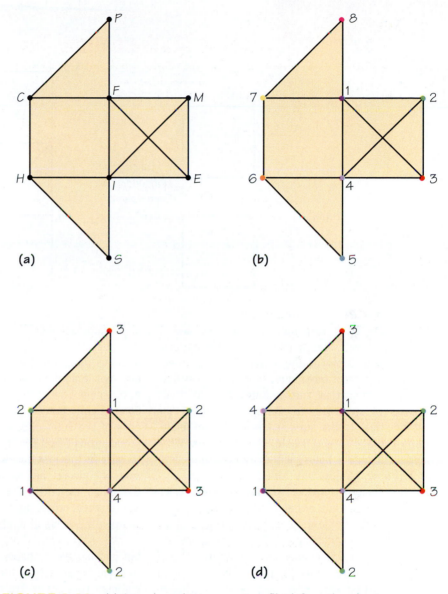

FIGURE 3.22   (a) A graph used to represent conflict information about courses. When two courses have a common student, an edge is drawn between the vertices that represent these courses. (b) A coloring of the scheduling graph with 8 colors, representing 8 time slots. Using this coloring would lead to a schedule where 8 time slots are used to schedule the examinations. This number is far from optimal.

(c) A coloring of the scheduling graph with 4 colors. This translates into a way of scheduling the examinations during 4 time slots, and it is not possible to design a schedule with fewer time slots. However, this schedule calls for the use of three different rooms, since three examinations are scheduled during time slot 2. (d) A coloring of the scheduling graph with 4 colors. This means that the examinations can be scheduled in 4 time slots. However, since each color appears only twice, all the examinations can be scheduled in two air-conditioned rooms.

Using Mathematical Tools

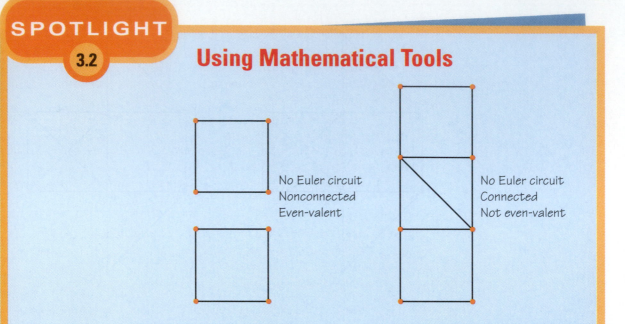

No Euler circuit
Nonconnected
Even-valent

No Euler circuit
Connected
Not even-valent

The tools of a carpenter include the saw, T square, level, and hammer. A mathematician also requires tools of the trade. Some of these tools are the proof techniques that enable verification of mathematical truths. Another set of tools consists of strategies to sharpen or extend the mathematical truths already known. For example, suppose that if A and B hold, then C is true. What happens if only A holds? Will C still be true? Similarly, if only B holds, will C still be true?

This type of thinking is of value because such questions will result either in more general cases where C holds or in examples showing that B alone and/or A alone can't imply C. For example, we saw that if a graph G is connected (hypothesis A) and even-valent (hypothesis B), then G has a tour of its edges using each edge only once (conclusion C). If either hypothesis is omitted, the conclusion fails to hold. The figures illustrate this point. On the left is an even-valent but nonconnected graph, and on the right, a connected graph with two odd-valent vertices; neither graph has an Euler circuit.

Here is another way that a mathematician might approach exending mathematical knowledge. If A and B imply C, will A and B imply both C and D, where D extends the conclusion of C? For example, not only can we prove that a connected, even-valent (hypotheses A and B) graph has an Euler circuit, but we can also show that the first edge of the Euler circuit can be chosen arbitrarily (conclusions C and D). It turns out that being able to specify the first two edges of the Euler circuit may not always be possible. Mathematicians are trained to vary the hypotheses and conclusions of results they prove, in an attempt to clarify and sharpen the range of applicability of the results.

We have seen that machine scheduling and bin packing are probably computationally difficult to solve because they are NP-complete. A mathematician could then try to find the simplest version of a bin-packing problem that would still be NP-complete: What if the items to be packed can have only eight weights? What if the weights are only one and two? Asking questions like these is part of the mathematician's craft. Such questions help to extend the domain of mathematics and hence the applications of mathematics.

require four different colors. The improved coloring in Figure 3.22c was found by trial and error.

The minimum number of colors needed to label the vertices of a graph so that no two vertices of the graph that are joined by an edge get the same color is called the (vertex) **chromatic number** of the graph.

The examination graph we have been studying has chromatic number 4, and, hence, we can schedule the eight examinations in four time slots without a conflict. Notice, however, that the coloring in Figure 3.22c schedules three different courses for the time slot corresponding to color 2. This means that not enough rooms with air conditioning will be available. Is there a way to recolor the graph with four colors so that each of the four colors is only used twice? Figure 3.22d shows that the answer is yes.

Hence, we are able to schedule the eight final examinations in four time slots, using only two air-conditioned rooms, and no student will have a conflict under this schedule!   ◆

Realistic problems to schedule government committees, high school and university final examinations, and job interviews (see Spotlight 3.3) are usually so large that graph coloring algorithms have to be incorporated into elaborate software packages to solve them.

Given any particular small graph, one can use trial and error to find the chromatic number, the minimum number of colors needed to color the vertices of that graph. Rather surprisingly, no algorithm that finds the chromatic number of a graph quickly has been found or is likely to be found. This does not mean that mathematical analysis in studying coloring problems has not been made. For example, here is a lovely theorem due to the British mathematician R. L. Brooks that applies to graphs without multiple edges:

> If G is a graph (other than a graph where each vertex is joined to every other or a circuit with odd length) with the property that its maximal valence is Δ, then the chromatic number of the graph is at most Δ.

Brooks's theorem means that if a graph has a million vertices and no vertex of valence more than 3, it can be colored with 3 or fewer colors.

Mathematicians have examined many kinds of coloring problems. One can study problems that involve the coloring of the edges of a graph rather than its vertices. Using techniques that have emerged from the study of coloring problems, problems involving such diverse contexts as scheduling government committees, using runways at airports efficiently, assigning frequencies for use by mobile pagers and cell phones, and designing timetables for public transportation have been solved—all these benefits from a problem that at first glance looks as if it belongs to recreational mathematics!

SPOTLIGHT

3.3

Scheduling Job Interviews

A group of companies is coming to campus for job interviews. The companies have been assigned the number of hours they need to cover the number of students they hope to interview during a block of consecutive hours where a representative from each company can hold interviews. Due to the fact that classes are going on at the same time, five departmental conference rooms have been made available to the companies to conduct their interviews.

The interviews will follow the school's regular hourly periods, which start at 9 A.M. and end at 4 P.M. (Companies will be scheduled for continuous interviews during lunch-hour times. Interviews cannot be scheduled beyond the end of the period that starts at 4 P.M. and ends at 5 P.M.)

Company	Time Slot Requested
A (Apricot Computers)	7
B (Big Green)	1
C (Challenge Insurance)	4, 5
D (Daisy Printers)	7, 8
E (Earnest Engine)	4, 5, 6
F (Flexible Systems)	2, 3
G (Gutter Leaders)	1, 2
H (Halley's Combs)	6, 7
I (Indelible Ink Corporation)	7, 8
J (Jay's Produce)	4, 5
K (Kelly's Detective Agency)	2, 3
L (Large Clothes)	4, 5, 6
M (Metropolitan TV)	1, 2
N (Nationwide Bank)	4, 5, 6, 7

Look at the list of time blocks that the companies requested (where $1 = 9$–10 A.M. , . . . , $8 = 4$–5 P.M.). Is it possible to accommodate all the companies that wish to do interviewing in the five rooms available while meeting their desired schedule times?

Problems of this kind seem simple enough, and you should try your hand at solving this particular one, for which a schedule does exist! However, this situation is not simple at all. The following facts are known about problems of this kind.

FACT 1. Suppose there are i interviewers, p time periods, and r rooms where interviews can be scheduled where each interviewer has specified periods during which he or she wishes to conduct interviews. Is it possible to design a schedule that meets the desired specifications? It turns out that this problem is NP-complete (see Spotlight 2.1, page 42), that is, it belongs to a large group of problems, for which among other things, the fastest known algorithms run very slowly on large-problem versions.

FACT 2. The problem just described remains NP-complete even for the case where only three rooms have to be scheduled (i.e., $p = 3$).

The moral is *surprisingly simple:* scheduling problems are very hard to solve.

However, the situation is not as hopeless as it might seem. If you look at the list of time requests for the corporations, you will note that, not surprisingly, each company has requested a contiguous block of times. It turns out that when this condition holds, it is possible to determine if there is a feasible schedule using an algorithm that works relatively quickly.

REVIEW VOCABULARY

Average-case analysis   The study of the list-processing algorithm (more generally, any algorithm) from the point of view of how well it performs on all the types of problems it may be used on and seeing on average how well it does. *See also* worst-case analysis.

Bin-packing problem   The problem of determining the minimum number of containers of capacity W into which objects of size $w_1, \ldots, w_n$ ($w_i \leq W$) can be packed.

Chromatic number   The chromatic number of a graph G is the minimum number of colors (labels) needed in any vertex coloring of G.

Critical-path scheduling   A heuristic algorithm for solving scheduling problems where the list-processing algorithm is applied to the priority list obtained by listing next in the priority list a task that heads a longest path in the order-requirement digraph. This task is then deleted from the order-requirement digraph, and the next task placed in the priority list is obtained by repeating the process.

Decreasing-time-list algorithm   The heuristic algorithm that applies the list-processing algorithm to the priority list obtained by listing the tasks in decreasing order of their time length.

First fit (FF)   A heuristic algorithm for bin packing in which the next weight to be packed is placed in the lowest-numbered bin already opened into which it will fit. If it fits in no open bin, a new bin is opened.

First-fit decreasing (FFD)   A heuristic algorithm for bin packing where the first-fit algorithm is applied to the list of weights sorted so that they appear in decreasing order.

Heuristic algorithm   An algorithm that is fast to carry out but that doesn't necessarily give an optimal solution to an optimization problem.

Independent tasks   Tasks are independent when there are no edges in the order-requirement digraph.

List-processing algorithm   A heuristic algorithm for assigning tasks to processors: assign the first ready task on the priority list that has not already been assigned to the lowest-numbered processor that is not working on a task.

Machine scheduling   The problem of assigning tasks to processors so as to complete the tasks by the earliest time possible.

Next fit (NF)   A heuristic algorithm for bin packing in which a new bin is opened if the weight to be packed next will not fit in the bin that is currently being filled; the current bin is then closed.

Next-fit decreasing (NFD)   A heuristic algorithm for bin packing where the next-fit algorithm is applied to the list of weights sorted so that they appear in decreasing order.

Priority list   An ordering of the collection of tasks to be scheduled for the purpose of attaining a particular scheduling goal. One such goal is minimizing completion time when the list algorithm is applied.

Processor   A person, machine, robot, operating room, or runway whose time must be scheduled.

Ready task   A task is called ready at a particular time if its predecessors as given by the order-requirement digraph have been completed by that time.

Vertex coloring   A vertex coloring of a graph G is an assignment of labels, which can be thought of as "colors," to the vertices of G so that vertices joined by an edge get different labels (colors).

Worst-case analysis   The study of the list-processing algorithm (more generally, any algorithm) from the point of view of how well it performs on the hardest problems it may be used on. *See also* average-case analysis.

Worst fit (WF)   A heuristic algorithm for bin packing in which the next weight to be packed is placed into the open bin with the largest amount of room remaining. If the weight fits in no open bin, a new bin is opened.

Worst-fit decreasing (WFD)   A heuristic algorithm for bin packing where the worst-fit algorithm is applied to the list of weights sorted so that they appear in decreasing order.

SUGGESTED READINGS

BRUCKER, P. *Scheduling Algorithms,* Springer-Verlag, Heidelberg, Germany, 1995. A detailed mathematical look at scheduling.

FRENCH, SIMON. *Sequencing and Scheduling,* Wiley, New York, 1982. A detailed account of a wide variety of scheduling models, most of them different from the ones treated in this chapter.

GRAHAM, RONALD. Combinatorial scheduling theory, in Lynn Steen (ed.), *Mathematics Today,* Springer-Verlag, New York, 1978, pp. 183–211. This essay on scheduling is one of many excellent accounts of recent developments in mathematics in this book.

GRAHAM, RONALD. The combinatorial mathematics of scheduling. *Scientific American,* March 1978, pp. 124–132. A very readable introduction to scheduling and bin packing.

JENSEN, T. R., AND BJARNE TOFT. *Graph Coloring Problems,* Wiley, New York, 1995. A detailed summary of what is known about coloring problems and many questions that await answering.

LAWLER, E., ET AL., Sequencing and scheduling algorithms and complexity, in S. C. Graves et al. (eds.), *Handbooks in OR and MS,* vol. 4, Elsevier, New York, 1993, pp. 445–522. A recent survey of results about scheduling.

PARKER, R. GARY. *Deterministic Scheduling Theory,* Chapman & Hall, London, 1995. A wide-ranging look at scheduling methods and their applications.

SUGGESTED WEB SITES

www.ics.uci.edu/~eppstein/geom.html   At this site, one can find examples of many applications of graph theory and related geometric tools.

www.ics.uci.edu/~eppstein/junkyard   A rich collection of interesting aspects of geometric mathematics.

www.informs.org   The Web page of the major professional society in operations research.

www.ing.unlp.edu.ar/cetad/mos/TSPBIB_home.html Resources about the traveling salesman problem.

mat.gsia.cmu.edu   A "hub" for resources about operations research.

SKILLS CHECK

1.   Given the order-requirement digraph at the right (time in minutes) and the priority list $T_1, T_2, T_3, T_4, T_5, T_6$, apply the list-processing algorithm to construct a schedule using two processors. How much time does the resulting schedule require?

   (a)   11 minutes
   (b)   13 minutes
   (c)   14 minutes

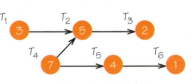

2.   A radio announcer has 10 songs of various lengths to schedule into several segments. The announcer must identify the station at least once

every 15 minutes, so the segments cannot be longer than 15 minutes. This job can be solved using the

(a)   list-processing algorithm for independent tasks.
(b)   critical-path scheduling algorithm.
(c)   worst-fit algorithm for bin packing.

3.   What is the minimum time required to complete 8 independent tasks with a total task time of 64 minutes on 4 machines?

(a)   Less than 5 minutes
(b)   Between 5 and 10 minutes
(c)   More than 10 minutes

4.   Use the decreasing-time-list algorithm to schedule these independent tasks on two machines: 6 minutes, 7 minutes, 4 minutes, 3 minutes, 6 minutes. How much time does the resulting schedule require?

(a)   13 minutes
(b)   14 minutes
(c)   More than 14 minutes

5.   Use the first-fit (FF) bin-packing algorithm to pack the following weights into bins that can hold no more than 10 lb: 6 lb, 7 lb, 4 lb, 3 lb, 6 lb. How many bins are required?

(a)   3 bins
(b)   4 bins
(c)   5 bins

6.   Use the worst-fit-decreasing (WFD) bin-packing algorithm to pack the following weights into bins that can hold no more than 10 lb: 6 lb, 7 lb, 4 lb, 3 lb, 6 lb. How many bins are holding a full 10 lb?

(a)   0 bin
(b)   1 bin
(c)   2 bins

7.   Suppose that a crew can complete in a minimum amount of time the job whose order-requirement digraph is shown below. If task T_2 is shortened from 5 minutes to 2 minutes, then what is the maximum amount by which the completion time for the entire job can be shortened?

(a)   3 minutes
(b)   2 minutes
(c)   1 minute

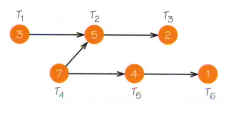

EXERCISES   ▲ *Optional.*   ■ *Advanced.*   ◆ *Discussion.*

Scheduling

1.   List as many scheduling situations as you can for these environments:

(a)   Hospital
(b)   Railroad station
(c)   Airport
(d)   Automobile repair garage
(e)   Restaurant
(f)   Your home
(g)   Your school
(h)   Police station
(i)   Firehouse

Compare and contrast the scheduling issues involved in these situtions.

2.   For the situation where a family with three children is preparing a Thanksgiving meal for 10 guests, list tasks that must be completed and the types of processors that are involved. Can any of these tasks be done simultaneously?

◆   3.   In order to get to a ski resort for a weekend vacation Jocelyn must accomplish a variety of things. She will leave work early at 1 P.M. and must get to the airport to be on a 5 o'clock shuttle to Boston. She then hopes to take a bus to get to the resort. Discuss some of the tasks that must be accomplished to get Jocelyn to the resort by 10 P.M. What are the different types of processors that are involved in getting these tasks done? Can any of these tasks be done simultaneously?

◆ 4. Discuss scheduling problems for which it is not reasonable to assume that once a processor starts a task, it would always complete that task before it works on any other task. Give examples for which this approach would be reasonable.

5. Use the list-processing algorithm to schedule the tasks in the following order-requirement digraph on

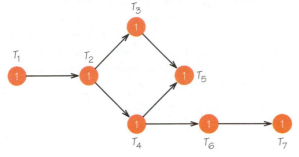

(a)   two processors using the list $T_1, \ldots, T_7$.
(b)   two processors using the list $T_1, T_2, T_3, T_4, T_6, T_5, T_7$.
(c)   Is either of the schedules that you obtain optimal?
(d)   Will adding a third processor enable the tasks to be finished by an earlier time?

6. Use the list-processing algorithm to schedule the tasks in the following order-requirement digraph on

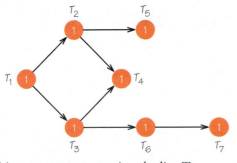

(a)   two processors using the list $T_1, \ldots, T_7$.
(b)   two processors using the list $T_1, T_2, T_3, T_4, T_6, T_5, T_7$.
(c)   Is either of the schedules that you obtain optimal?

Using the List-Processing Algorithm

7. (a)   Use the list-processing algorithm to schedule the tasks in the following order-requirement digraph on two processors, using the list $T_1, \ldots, T_{11}$. From the schedule so constructed, for each task list the start and finish time for that task.

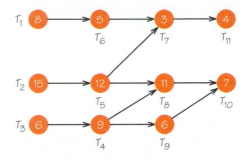

(b)   Compare your answers in part (a) with scheduling these tasks on three processors with the same list.

8. For the accompanying order-requirement digraph, apply the list-processing algorithm, using three processors for lists (a) and (b). How do the completion times obtained compare with the length of the critical path?

(a) $T_1, T_2, T_3, T_4, T_5, T_6, T_7, T_8$
(b) $T_1, T_3, T_5, T_7, T_2, T_4, T_6, T_8$
(c) $T_1, T_3, T_5, T_7, T_8, T_6, T_4, T_2$

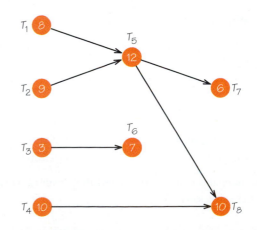

9. Consider the following order-requirement digraph:

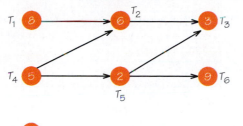

(a) Find the critical path(s).
(b) Schedule these tasks on one processor using the critical-path scheduling method.
(c) Schedule these tasks on one processor using the priority list obtained by listing the tasks in order of decreasing time.
(d) Does either of these schedules have idle time? How do their completion times compare?
(e) If two different schedules have the same completion time, what criteria can be used to say one schedule is superior to the other?
(f) Schedule these tasks on two processors using the order-requirement digraph shown and the priority list from part (b).
(g) Does the schedule produced in part (f) finish in half the time that the schedule in part (b) did, which might be expected, since the number of processors has doubled?
(h) Schedule the tasks on (i) one processor and (ii) two processors (using the decreasing-time list), assuming that each task time has been reduced by one. Do the changes in completion time agree with your expectations?

10. To prepare a meal quickly involves carrying out the tasks shown (time lengths in minutes) in the following order-requirement digraph:

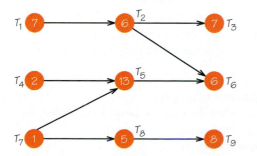

(a) If Mike prepares the meal alone, how long will it take?
(b) If Mike can talk Mary into helping him prepare the meal, how long will it take them if the tasks are scheduled using the list T_5, T_9, T_1, T_3, T_2, T_6, T_8, T_4, T_7 and the list-processing algorithm?
(c) If Mike can talk Mary and Jack into helping him prepare the meal, how long will it take if the tasks are scheduled using the same list as in part (b)?
(d) What would be a reasonable set of criteria for choosing a priority list in this situation?

11. Consider the order-requirement digraph below. Suppose one plans to schedule these tasks on two identical processors.

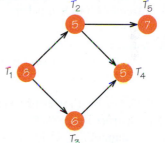

(a) How many different priority lists are there that can be used to schedule the tasks?
(b) Can all these priority lists lead to different schedules? If not, why not?
(c) Can an optimal schedule have no idle time? Can you give two different reasons why an optimal schedule must have some idle time?
(d) Is there any list that produces a schedule where the second processor has no idle time?

12. (a) In Exercise 11, how many different lists are there that do not list T_1 first?
(b) Would it make any sense not to list T_1 first in a list?
(c) Construct a list and schedule the tasks on two processors.
(d) Can you find another list that leads to a different completion time than the schedule you found for part (c)?
(e) Find a list that leads to an optimal schedule.

13. Can you find an order-requirement with five tasks for which every possible list yields exactly the same schedule?

14. Can you find an order-requirement digraph such that the schedule corresponding to every list is different?

15. At a large toy store, scooters arrive unassembled in boxes. To assemble a scooter the following tasks must be performed:

TASK 1. Remove parts from the box.
TASK 2. Attach wheels to the footboard.
TASK 3. Attach vertical housing.
TASK 4. Attach handlebars to vertical housing.
TASK 5. Put on reflector tape.
TASK 6. Attach bell to handlebars.
TASK 7. Attach decals.
TASK 8. Attach kickstand.
TASK 9. Attach safety instructions to handlebars.

(a) Give reasonable time estimates for these tasks and construct a reasonable order-requirement digraph. What is the earliest time by which these tasks can be completed?
(b) Schedule this job on two processors (humans) using the decreasing-time-list algorithm.

16. If two schedules for the same number of processors have the same completion time, can one schedule have more idle time than the other?

Independent Tasks and Other Issues

17. For the following schedules, can you produce a list so that the list-processing algorithm produces the schedule shown when the tasks are independent? What are the task times for each task?

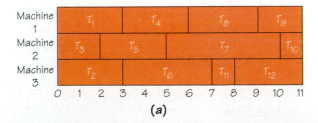

(a)

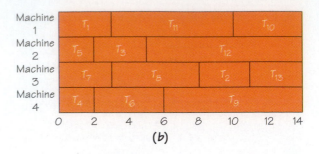

(b)

◆ 18. Once an optimal schedule has been found for independent tasks (e.g., see diagrams in Exercise 17), usually the scheduling of the tasks can be rearranged and the same optimal time achieved (i.e., one can, among other things, reorder the tasks done by a particular processor). Discuss criteria that might be used in implementing the rearrangement process.

19. The task times of 9 independent tasks T_1 to T_9 are 1, 2, 3, 4, 5, 6, 7, 8, 9.

(a) Schedule the tasks on two processors using the lists: (i) $T_1, T_2, \ldots, T_9$ and (ii) $T_9, T_8, \ldots, T_1$.
(b) Is either of the schedules you get in part (a) optimal? If not, find a list that gives an optimal schedule.

20. Repeat Exercise 19, but schedule the tasks (with the same lists) on three processors. If the schedules you get are not optimal, find a list that gives an optimal schedule.

◆ 21. Discuss different criteria that might be used to construct a priority list for a scheduling problem.

◆ 22. Some scheduling projects have due dates for tasks (i.e., times by which a given task should be completed) and release dates (i.e., times before which a task cannot have work begun on it). Give examples of circumstances where these situations might arise.

23. Can you find a schedule (use the order-requirement digraph in Figure 3.4) with a completion time earlier than 12, as shown in the following figure (page 105), using a list other than $T_1, \ldots, T_9$? If not, why not?

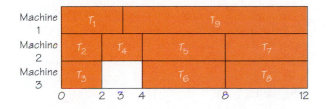

24. Given the accompanying order-requirement digraph

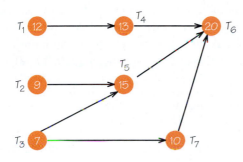

(a) Use the list-processing algorithm to schedule these seven tasks on two processors using these lists:

(i) T_1, T_3, T_7, T_2, T_4, T_5, T_6
(ii) T_1, T_3, T_2, T_4, T_5, T_6, T_7
(iii) The list obtained by listing the tasks in order of decreasing time

(b) Try to determine if any of the resulting schedules are optimal.
(c) Schedule the tasks using the critical-path scheduling method. Try to determine if this schedule is optimal.

25. A photocopy shop must schedule independent batches of documents to be copied. The times for the different sets of documents are (in minutes): 12, 23, 32, 13, 24, 45, 23, 23, 14, 21, 34, 53, 18, 63, 47, 25, 74, 23, 43, 43, 16, 16, 76.

(a) Construct a schedule using the list-processing algorithm on three machines.
(b) Construct a schedule using the list-processing algorithm on four machines.
(c) Repeat parts (a) and (b), but use the decreasing-time-list algorithm.

(d) Suppose union regulations require that an 8-minute rest period be allowed for any photocopy task over 45 minutes. Use the decreasing-time-list algorithm, with the preceding times modified to take into account the union requirement, to schedule the tasks on three human-operated machines.

26. (a) Find the completion time for independent tasks of length 8, 11, 17, 14, 16, 9, 2, 1, 18, 5, 3, 7, 6, 2, 1 on three processors, using the list-processing algorithm.
(b) Find the completion time for the tasks in part (a) on three processors, using the decreasing-time-list algorithm.
(c) Does either algorithm give rise to an optimal schedule?
(d) Repeat for tasks of lengths 19, 19, 20, 20, 1, 1, 2, 2, 3, 3, 5, 5, 11, 11, 17, 18, 18, 17, 2, 16, 16, 2.

27. Describe possible modifications for the list-processing algorithm that would allow for a

(a) machine to be "voluntarily" idle.
(b) machine to interrupt work on a task once it has begun work on the task.

28. Find a list that produces the following optimal schedule when the list-processing algorithm is applied to this list. (Assume the tasks are independent.)

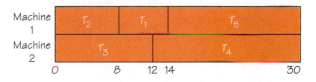

What completion time and schedule are obtained when the decreasing-time-list algorithm is applied to this list?

29. Can you think of situations other than those mentioned in the text where scheduling independent tasks on processors occurs?

30. Can you think of real-world scheduling situations in which all the tasks have the same time and

are independent? Can you find an algorithm for solving this problem optimally? (If there are n independent tasks of time length k, when will all the tasks be finished?)

31. (a) Show that when tasks to be scheduled are independent, the critical-path method and the decreasing-time-list method are identical.

(b) The (usually unknown) optimal time to complete a specific collection of independent tasks on three machines turns out to be 450 minutes.

(i) Estimate the worst possible completion time when the list-processing algorithm is used with the worst choice of priority list.

(ii) Estimate the longest possible completion time using the list-processing algorithm and the decreasing-time list.

Bin Packing

32.   Two wooden wall systems are to be made with pieces of wood with lengths shown in the accompanying diagram. If wood is sold in 10-foot planks and can be cut with no waste, what number of boards would be purchased if one uses the first-fit-decreasing, next-fit-decreasing, and worst-fit-decreasing heuristics, respectively?

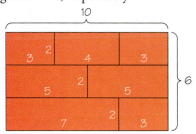

In solving this problem, does it make a difference if the 10-foot horizontal shelves and 6-foot vertical boards employ single-length pieces as compared with using pieces of boards that add up to 10- and 6-foot lengths?

33. It takes 4 seconds to photocopy one page. Manuscripts of 10, 8, 15, 24, 22, 24, 20, 14, 19, 12, 16, 30, 15, and 16 pages are to be photocopied. How many photocopy machines would be required, using the first-fit-decreasing algorithm, to guarantee that all manuscripts are photocopied in 2 minutes or less? Would the solution differ if worst-fit decreasing were used?

34. A radio station's policy allows advertising breaks of no longer than 2 minutes, 15 seconds. Using algorithms (a) and (b) below, determine the minimum number of breaks into which the following ads will fit (lengths given in seconds): 80, 90, 130, 50, 60, 20, 90, 30, 30, 40. Can you find the optimum solution? Do the same for these ads: 60, 50, 40, 40, 60, 90, 90, 50, 20, 30, 30, 50.

(a) First fit
(b) First-fit decreasing

35.   Fiberglass insulation comes in 36-inch precut sections. A plumber must install insulation in a basement on piping that is interrupted often by joints. The distances between the joints on the stretches of pipe that must be insulated are 12, 15, 16, 12, 9, 11, 15, 17, 12, 14, 17, 18, 19, 21, 31, 7, 21, 9, 23, 24, 15, 16, 12, 9, 8, 27, 22, 18 inches. How many precut sections would he have to use to provide the insulation if he bases his decision on

(a) next fit?
(b) next-fit decreasing?
(c) worst fit?
(d) worst-fit decreasing?

36.   The files that a company has for its employees dealing with utilities occupy 100, 120, 60, 90, 110, 45, 30, 70, 60, 50, 40, 25, 65, 25, 55, 35, 45, 60, 75, 30, 120, 100, 60, 90, 85 sectors. If, after operating systems are installed, a disk can store up to 480 sectors, determine the number of disks to store the utilities if each of these heuristics is used to pack the disk with files:

(a) NF   (b) NFD   (c) FF   (d) FFD

◆   37.   We have described two algorithms for bin packing called "worst fit" and "best fit" (see page

91). The words "best" and "worst" have connotations in English. However, the performance of algorithms depends on their merits as algorithms, not on the names we give them.

(a)   On the basis of experiments you perform with the best-fit and worst-fit algorithms, which one do you think is the "better" of the two?

(b)   Can you construct an example where worst fit uses fewer bins than best fit?

38.   The best-fit heuristic (see page 91) also has a "decreasing" version, where the list is first sorted in decreasing order. Using bins of capacity 10, apply the best-fit heuristic and its decreasing version to the following list: 6, 9, 5, 8, 3, 2, 1, 9, 2, 7, 2, 5, 4, 3, 7, 6, 2, 8, 3, 7, 1, 6, 4, 2, 5, 3, 7, 2, 5, 2, 3, 6, 2, 7, 1, 3, 5, 4, 2, 6.

■   39.   One pianist's recording of the complete Mozart piano sonatas takes the following times (given in minutes and seconds): 13:46, 6:15, 3:29, 5:37, 7:52, 2:55, 5:00, 4:28, 4:21, 7:39, 7:55, 6:42, 4:23, 3:52, 4:21, 4:20, 5:46, 6:29, 5:34, 6:23, 6:39, 7:19, 5:54, 6:54, 2:58, 5:22, 1:42, 5:00, 1:29, 5:47, 7:30, 8:19, 4:44, 4:57, 4:09, 14:31, 3:55, 4:04, 4:01, 6:06, 6:50, 5:27, 4:28, 5:40, 2:52, 5:16, 5:34, 3:10, 7:22, 4:40, 3:08, 6:32, 4:47, 6:59, 5:38, 7:57, 3:38. If the maximal time that can be recorded on a compact disk is 70:30, can all the music be performed on 4 compact disks? Can all the music be performed on 5 compact disks?

■   40.   In the wall-system example in the text, first fit and worst fit required equal numbers of bins (see Figure 3.20). Can you find an example where first fit and worst fit yield different numbers of bins? Can you find an example where first fit, worst fit, and next fit yield answers with different numbers of bins?

◆   41.   A common suggestion for heuristics for the bin-packing problem with bins of capacity W involves finding weights that sum to exactly W. Discuss the pros and cons of a heuristic of this type.

■   42.   A record company wishes to record all the Beethoven string quartets (16 quartets, each consisting of several consecutive parts called movements) on LPs. It wishes to complete the project on as few records as possible. Recording can be done on two sides as long as the movements are consecutive. Is this an example of a bin-packing problem? (Defend your answer.) If the project were to record the quartets on (standard) tape cassettes or compact disks, would your answer be different?

■   43.   Can you find an example of weights that, when packed into bins using first fit, use fewer bins than the number of bins used when the first-fit algorithm is applied with the first weight on the list removed?

◆   44.   Can you formulate "paradoxical" situations for bin packing that are analogous to those we found for scheduling processors?

Coloring Problems

45.   For each of the graphs below and on page 108

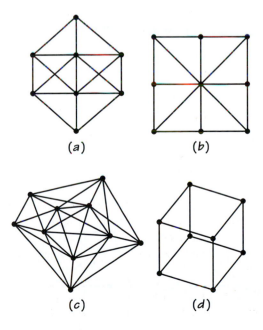

(a)   (b)

(c)   (d)

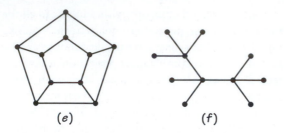

(e)　　　　　　　　　(f)

(a) color the vertices if possible with three different colors.
(b) color the vertices if possible with four different colors.
(c) find the chromatic number of the graph.

46. For each of the graphs below

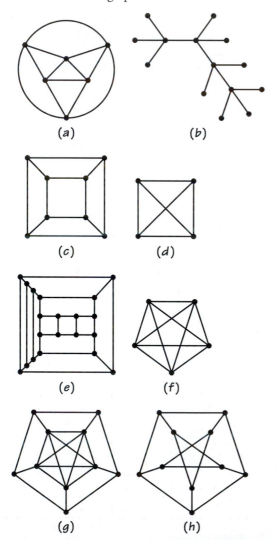

(a)　　　　　　　　　(b)

(c)　　　　　　　　　(d)

(e)　　　　　　　　　(f)

(g)　　　　　　　　　(h)

(a) color the vertices if possible with two different colors.
(b) color the vertices if possible with three different colors.
(c) find the chromatic number of the graph.

47. The owner of a pet store that is about to open wishes to display tropical fish in display tanks. The table below shows the incapatibilities between the species, in the sense that an X indicates that it is unwise to allow those species in the row and column that meet at the X to be in the same tank.

	A	B	C	D	E	F	G	H	I
A						X	X		X
B			X					X	
C		X			X			X	
D					X	X		X	
E			X	X			X		
F	X			X			X		X
G	X				X	X		X	X
H		X	X	X			X		
I	X					X	X		

(a) What is the minimum number of tanks needed to display all the fish she wishes to sell?
(b) Is it possible to display the species so that the number of species in each tank is as nearly equal as possible?

48. The managers of a zoo are planning to open a small satellite branch. The animals are to be in enclosures in which compatible animals are displayed together. The accompanying table (page 109) indicates those pairs of animals that are compatible. (Thus, an X in a particular row and column means that the animals that label this row and column can share an enclosure.)

(a) What is the minimum number of enclosures needed to avoid housing incompatible animals in the same enclosure?
(b) Is it possible to design a way to enclose the animals so that each enclosure contains the same number of animals?

(c) Why might that be desirable? Why might this approach to grouping the animals not be ideal?

	A	B	C	D	E	F	G	H	I	J
A	X	X		X	X	X	X			
B	X	X			X	X	X		X	X
C			X		X	X	X			
D	X			X	X	X	X		X	X
E	X	X	X	X	X			X	X	
F	X	X	X	X		X	X	X	X	
G	X	X	X	X		X	X	X		
H				X	X	X	X			
I		X		X	X	X			X	
J		X		X						X

49. The nine standing committees of a state legislature are designing a schedule for when the committees can meet. The matrix shown in the table below has an X in a position where the committees corresponding to the row and column have a common member, and, hence, should not be scheduled to meet at the same hour. The committees involved are Agriculture (A), Commerce (C), Consumer Affairs (CA), Education (E), Forests (F), Health (H), Justice (J), Labor (L), and Rules (R).

	A	C	CA	E	F	H	J	L	R
A		X	X			X			
C	X		X	X	X				
CA	X	X					X		X
E		X			X	X			
F		X		X		X	X		
H				X	X			X	
J			X	X				X	X
L						X	X		X
R			X				X	X	

(a) Draw a graph that will be of value in determining the minimum number of time slots the committees can meet in without any legislator having to be in two places at one time.

(b) What is the minimum number of time slots in which the committees can be scheduled without a conflict?

(c) How many different rooms are needed at any time that a committee is scheduled to meet? (Why might this issue matter?)

50. Determine the minimum number of colors, and how often each color is used, in a vertex coloring of the graphs below.

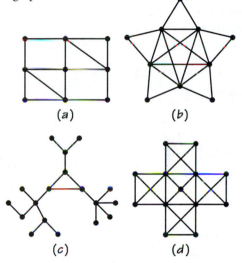

(a)   (b)

(c)   (d)

51. The faculty-student governing council at All State College has nine standing committees (e.g., Curriculum, Academic Standards, Campus Life) that are designated A, B, C, D, . . . , I for convenience. The following table shows which committees have no member in common.

	A	B	C	D	E	F	G	H	I
A		X		X		X	X		X
B	X				X	X		X	X
C				X		X	X	X	X
D	X		X			X		X	
E		X					X	X	X
F	X	X	X	X					
G	X		X		X			X	
H		X	X	X	X		X		X
I	X	X	X		X			X	

(a)   What is the minimum number of time slots in which all the committee meetings can be scheduled?

(b)   How many rooms are needed during each time slot to accommodate the committees that are scheduled to meet in that time slot?

52.   When two towns are within 145 miles of each other, the frequency used by a certain type of emergency response system for the towns would require that they be on different frequencies to avoid possible interference with each other. The table below shows the mileage distances between six towns.

	E	F	G	I	S	T
Evansville (E)		290	277	168	303	113
Ft. Wayne (F)	290		132	83	79	201
Gary (G)	277	132		153	58	164
Indianapolis (I)	168	83	153		140	71
South Bend (S)	303	79	50	140		196
Terre Haute (T)	113	201	164	71	196	

(a)   What would be the minimum number of frequencies that are needed for each town to have its emergency broadcasts not conflict with those of any other town using this system?

(b)   How many different towns would be assigned to each frequency used?

53.   Show that the vertices of any tree can be colored with two colors.

54.   Can you find a family of graphs H_n that requires n colors to color its vertices?

55.   The edge-coloring number of a graph G is the minimum number of colors needed to color the edges of G so that edges that share a common vertex get different colors. Determine the edge-coloring number for each of the graphs in Exercise 46. Can you make a conjecture about the value of the minimum number of colors needed to color the edges of any graph?

56.   Can you think of any applications that require determining the minimum number of colors to color the edges of a graph?

Additional Exercises

57.   Give examples of scheduling problems in which

(a)   processors available can be treated as if they are identical.

(b)   processors available cannot be treated as if they are identical.

58.   Consider the accompanying order-requirement digraph:

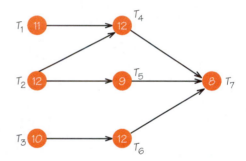

(a)   Find the length of the critical path.

(b)   Schedule these seven tasks on two processors using the list algorithm and the lists.
   (i) $T_1, T_2, T_3, T_4, T_5, T_6, T_7$
   (ii) $T_2, T_1, T_3, T_6, T_5, T_4, T_7$

(c)   Does either list lead to a completion time that equals the length of the critical path?

(d)   Show that no list can ever lead to a completion time equal to the length of the critical path (providing the schedule uses two processors).

■   59.   Could the following schedule have arisen from the list-processing algorithm? Could it have arisen from the application of the list-processing algorithm to a collection of independent tasks?

60. Can you give examples of scheduling problems for which it seems reasonable to assume that all the task times are the same?

◼ 61. Two-dimensional bin packing refers to the problem of packing rectangles of various sizes into a minimum number of $m \times n$ rectangles, with the sides of the packed rectangles parallel to those of the containing rectangle.

    (a) Suggest some possible real-world applications of this problem.
    (b) Devise a heuristic algorithm for this problem.
    (c) Give an argument to show that the problem is at least as hard to solve as the usual bin-packing problem.
    (d) If you have $1 \times m$ rectangles with total area W to be packed into a single rectangle of area $p \times q = W$, can the packing always be accomplished?

◆ 62. In what situations would packing bins of different capacities be the appropriate model for real-world situations? Suggest some possible algorithms for this type of problem.

63. A data entry group gets in 30 (independent) tasks that will take the following amounts of time (in minutes) to type: 25, 18, 13, 19, 30, 32, 12, 36, 25, 17, 18, 26, 12, 15, 31, 18, 15, 18, 16, 19, 30, 12, 16, 15, 24, 16, 27, 18, 9, 14.

    (a) Using these times as a priority list:
        (i) Use the list-processing algorithm to find the completion time for scheduling these tasks with four secretaries; with five secretaries.
        (ii) Repeat the scheduling using the decreasing-time-list algorithm.
        (iii) Can you show that any of the schedules that you get are optimal?
    (b) If one needs to finish the typing in one hour:
        (i) Use the FFD heuristic to find how many typists would be needed.
        (ii) Repeat for the NFD and WFD heuristics.
        (iii) Can you show that any of the solutions you get are optimal?

64. Find the minimum number of bins necessary to pack items of size 8, 5, 3, 4, 3, 7, 8, 8, 6, 5, 3, 2, 1, 2, 1, 2, 1, 3, 5, 2, 4, 2, 6, 5, 3, 4, 2, 6, 7, 7, 8, 6, 5, 4, 6, 1, 4, 7, 5, 1, 2, 4 in bins of capacity (a) through (d) using the first-fit and first-fit-decreasing algorithms. Can you determine if any of the packings you get are optimal?

    (a) 9
    (b) 10
    (c) 11
    (d) 12

65. Advertisements for the TV show Q are permitted to last up to a total of 8 minutes, and each group of ads can last up to 2 minutes. If the ads slated for Q last 63, 32, 11, 19, 24, 87, 64, 36, 27, 42, 63 seconds, determine if FF and FFD yield acceptable configurations for the ads.

66. Consider the following heuristic for packing bins known as *best fit*. Keep track of how much room remains in each unfilled bin and put the next item to be packed into that bin that would leave the least room left over after the item is put into the bin. (For example, suppose that bin 4 had 6 units left, bin 7 had 5 units, and bin 9 had 8 units left. If the next item in the list had size 5, then first fit would place this item in bin 4, worst fit would place the item in

bin 9, while best fit would place the item in bin 7.) If there is a tie, place the item into the bin with the lowest number. Apply this heuristic to the list 8, 7, 1, 9, 2, 5, 7, 3, 6, 4, where the bins have capacity 10.

67. Can you find a list that gives rise to the optimal schedule shown in Figure 3.14 for the order-requirement digraph in Figure 3.12?

68. Give an example to show that scheduling to minimize completion time may not minimize total idle time. (*Hint:* Assume independent tasks and use two machines for one schedule and three machines for the other schedule.)

69. When a graph has been drawn on a piece of paper so that edges only meet at vertices, the graph divides the paper up into regions called *faces*. The faces include one face, called the "infinite" face, that surrounds the whole graph. The face-coloring number of a graph G (which can be drawn in this special way) is the minimum number of colors needed to color the faces of G so that two faces that share an edge receive different colors. (Note that if two faces meet only at a vertex, they can be colored the same color.)

(a) Determine the minimum number of colors to color the faces of the graphs below and in the next column. In each case, remember to color the infinite face, which is labeled I (for "infinite").

(b) Can you think of an application of the problem of coloring the faces of a graph with a minimum number of colors?

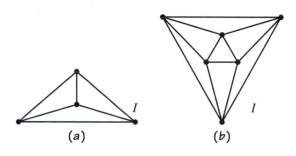

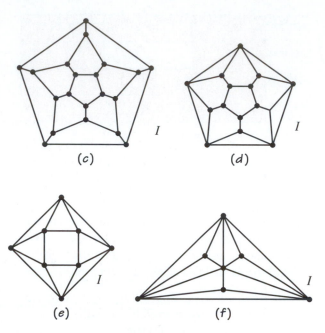

TECHNOLOGY CORNER

Using Spreadsheets to Schedule Tasks

With the use of the **Sum** function, spreadsheets provide a handy way to monitor the assignments of jobs to people or processors. Remember that "scheduling" and "bin-packing" algorithms cannot be guaranteed always to produce optimal solutions. We can use spreadsheets to experiment with different assignments of tasks as we look for efficient solutions.

For example, suppose we have 3 available employees and 30 tasks. Assume that it is known that the tasks include five each of six types: one-hour, two-hour, three-hour, four-hour, five-hour, and six-hour tasks.

First, suppose the tasks are ordered as 1, 2, 3, 4, 5, 6, 1, 2, 3, 4, 5, 6, 1, 2, 3, 4, 5, 6, 1, 2, 3, 4, 5, 6, 1, 2, 3, 4, 5, 6, and are shuffled to the three employees from this order. If each column represents an employee, this allocation of tasks is represented by the spreadsheet shown in Figure 3.23.

	A	B	C
1	1	2	3
2	4	5	6
3	1	2	3
4	4	5	6
5	1	2	3
6	4	5	6
7	1	2	3
8	4	5	6
9	1	2	3
10	4	5	6
11			
12	25	35	45

FIGURE 3.23

The sum for each column is computed at the bottom of the spreadsheet, using the **Sum** function. (As you place the tasks in the columns, you can watch the column totals grow.) Assuming all three employees should have equivalent loads, this is not an effective allocation of the tasks. However, this template can be used to explore other ways to allocate the tasks among the employees.

TASK 1.   Allocate the 30 tasks to the 3 employees by allocating longer jobs before shorter jobs. Does this result in a more equitable schedule? Can you find some way to allocate the jobs so that each employee works the same amount of time?

TASK 2.   Suppose the tasks are paired so that there are 15 jobs: 5 that require 5 hours, 5 that require 6 hours, and 5 that require 10 hours. Try at least three different allocations of these jobs to the three employees. Can you find some way to allocate the jobs so that each employee works the same amount of time?

TASK 3.   Suppose the tasks are grouped in another way so that there are 5 jobs that require 2 hours, 5

that require 8 hours, and 5 that require 11 hours. What are the most equitable ways to allocate these jobs to three employees?

Using Spreadsheets to Model Bin Packing

Suppose the 30 tasks have to be completed within 16 hours. How many employees will be needed to accomplish this job? In this situation we do not know how many employees we will need, but we do know that each column sum must be no larger than 16. As you place the jobs in the columns, you can watch the totals grow. Using the first-fit scheduling algorithm and the list 1, 2, 3, 4, 5, 6, 1, 2, 3, 4, 5, 6, . . . , the placement of the first 12 jobs results in the flowchart shown in Figure 3.24.

	A	B	C	D	E	F	G
1	1	6	5				
2	2	2	6				
3	3	3					
4	4	4					
5	5						
6	1						
7							
8							
9							
10	16	15	11	0	0	0	0

FIGURE 3.24

TASK 4.   Complete the spreadsheet shown in Figure 3.24. How do your results compare with those of one of the algorithms that uses a sorted list?

Exploration

In Task 4, what is the minimum number of employees required? Can the tasks be assigned so that each employee has the same workload?

writing projects

1 ▶ Scheduling is important for hospitals, schools, transportation systems, police services, and fire services. Pick one of these areas and write an essay about the different scheduling situations that come up, types of processors, and extent to which the assumptions of the list-processing model hold for the area you pick.

2 ▶ Write an essay that compares and contrasts the basic scheduling problem we investigated with the scheduling version of the bin-packing problem.

3 ▶ One of the oversimplifications made in our discussion of scheduling was that there were no "due dates" involved for the tasks making up a job. Develop an algorithm for solving a scheduling problem under the assumption that each task has a due date as well as a time length. You will probably want to decide on a penalty amount that will occur when a due date is exceeded.

4 ▶ Consider the problem of scheduling tasks on a single machine. Design different algorithms for achieving different goals. You will probably wish to assume that each task has a due date such that if the task is not finished by this date, some penalty payment must be made.

5 ▶ Suppose that one has found that the optimal solution to a bin-packing problem with bins of size W requires p bins. What can one say about the number of bins needed when the bin size is $2W$? (*Hint:* Be careful!)

6 ▶ Discuss the role of graph colorings for scheduling committee meetings so as to avoid conflicts. Research whether or not these ideas are used in the legislature of your home state.

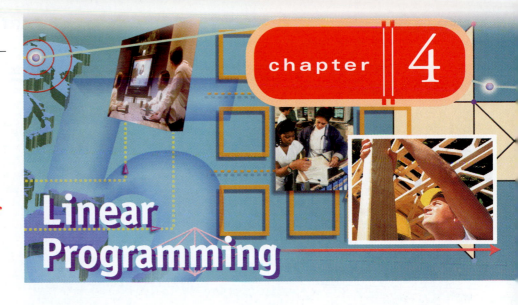

chapter 4
Linear Programming

Linear Programming

Amanager's job often calls for making very complicated decisions. One set of decisions involves planning what products the business is to make and determining what resources are needed. In the modern business world, diversification of products provides a company with stability in a climate of changing tastes and needs. So it is not surprising that companies would produce many products, some of which share resource needs. For example, any bakery uses many resources, among which are butter, sugar, eggs, and flour, to make its products: cookies, cakes, pies, and breads.

Resources can include more than just raw materials. A labor force with appropriate skills, farmland, time, and machinery are also resources. Typically, resources are limited: a farmer owns only so much land; there are only so many hours in a day; in a year of drought the wheat crop is very small. Resource availability is also limited by location and competition.

Because resources are limited, management faces important questions: How should the available resources be shared among the possible products? One goal of management is to maximize profit. How can that determine how much of each product should be produced? There are usually so many alternative product mixes that it is impossible to evaluate them all individually. Despite this complexity, millions of dollars may ride on management's decision.

In this chapter we learn about **linear programming,** a management science technique that helps a business allocate the resources it has on hand to make a particular mix of products that will maximize profit. The technique is so powerful that linear programming is said to account for over 50% and perhaps as much as 90% of all computing time used for management decisions in business.

Automated car assembly.

Linear programming is an example of "new" mathematics. It did not originate with the ancient Egyptians or Greeks, nor was it developed in Europe during the time the Western Hemisphere was being explored and settled. Linear programming came into being, along with many other management science techniques, during and shortly after World War II, in the 1940s; it is quite young as intellectual ideas go. Yet, during its short history, linear programming has changed the way businesses make decisions, from "seat-of-the-pants" methods based on guesswork and intuition to using an algorithm based on available data and guaranteed to produce an optimal decision.

Linear programming has saved businesses billions of dollars. Of all the management science techniques presented in this book, linear programming is far and away the most frequently used. It can be applied in a variety of situations, in addition to the one we study in this chapter. Some of the problems studied in Chapters 1, 2, and 3 can be viewed as linear programming problems, and examples of other uses are in Spotlight 4.1. Linear programming is an excellent example of a mathematical technique useful for solving many different kinds of problems that at first do not seem to be similar problems at all. It has been suggested that without linear programming, management science would not exist.

SPOTLIGHT

4.1

Case Studies in Linear Programming

Linear programming is not limited to mixture problems. Here are two case studies that do not involve mixture problems, yet where applying linear programming techniques produced impressive savings:

• The Exxon Corporation spends several million dollars per day running refineries in the United States. Because running a refinery takes a lot of energy, energy-saving measures can have a large effect. Managers at Exxon's Baton Rouge plant had over 600 energy-saving projects under consideration. They couldn't implement them all because some conflicted with others, and there were so many ways of making a selection from the 600 that it was impossible to evaluate all selections individually.

Exxon used linear programming to select an optimal configuration of about 200 projects. The savings are expected to be about $100 million over a period of years.

• American Edwards Laboratories uses heart valves from pigs to produce artificial heart valves for human beings. Pig heart valves come in different sizes. Shipments of pig heart valves often contain too many of some sizes and too few of others; however, each supplier tends to ship roughly the same imbalance of valve sizes on every order, so the company can expect consistently different imbalances from the different suppliers. Thus, if they order shipments from all the suppliers, the imbalances could cancel each other out in a fairly predictable way. The amount of cancellation will depend on the sizes of the individual shipments. Unfortunately, there are too many combinations of shipment sizes to consider all combinations individually.

American Edwards used linear programming to figure out which combination of shipment sizes would give the best cancellation effect. This reduced the company's annual cost by $1.5 million.

Mixture Problems

In this chapter we study how to use linear programming to solve a special kind of problem—a mixture problem.

In a **mixture problem,** limited resources are combined into products so that the profit from selling those products is a maximum.

Mixture problems are widespread because nearly every product in our economy is created by combining resources. Many different industries solve mixture problems as part of their planning. Analyzing a mixture problem requires careful reading and logic; you might think that it is not mathematics at all. But actually, analysis is extremely important because it helps us construct a mathematical model of a problem. Then we solve the problem with mathematical techniques like algebra. Without analysis we cannot solve any linear programming problem.

We will analyze small problems like those that might confront a toy or a beverage manufacturer. Both manufacturers can sell many different products on which each makes profits. There could be dozens of possible products and many resources. A manufacturer must periodically look at the quantities and prices of resources and then determine which products should be produced in which quantities in order to gain the greatest, or optimum, profit. This is an enormous task, usually requiring a computer to solve.

What does it mean to find a solution to a linear programming mixture problem? A solution to a mixture problem is a production policy that tells us how many units of each product to make.

An **optimal production policy** has two properties. First, it is possible; that is, it does not violate any of the limitations under which the manufacturer operates, such as availability of resources. Second, the optimal production policy gives the maximum profit.

Having studied the previous chapters on management science, you may sense that there must be some algorithm that will give us the optimal production policy. There are indeed such algorithms, most of which are very algebraic. Since the algebraic details of these algorithms are easily forgotten, and there are computer programs available to carry out those details, we are most interested here in the ideas behind the algorithms.

At the heart of every algorithm for linear programming are geometric ideas. This is somewhat surprising, since there seem to be no geometric ideas used to describe a mixture problem. We can see these geometric ideas clearly if we solve small linear programming problems, involving just one or two products and one or two resources, and draw some appropriate pictures, or graphs. This visualization of linear programming is readily understandable by nonmathematicians, and it has been valuable to theorists and practitioners who develop solution algorithms for linear programming. Those algorithms are used to solve problems with dozens or hundreds of products and equally large numbers of resources typical of most business applications.

We start our discussion with some very simple examples and work up to more involved ones, all of which we can solve by drawing graphs and making some relatively simple calculations. We end this chapter with a discussion of what larger problems look like and how they are typically solved.

Mixture Problems Having One Resource

One Product and One Resource: Making Skateboards

Suppose a toy manufacturer has 60 containers of plastic and wants to make and sell skateboards. The "recipe" for one skateboard requires 5 containers of plastic, plus paint and decals, which for simplicity we assume are available in essentially unlimited quantities. The profit on one skateboard is $1.00, and in order to keep things simple, we will assume that there will be customers for every skateboard produced. So the manufacturer must decide how many skateboards to make.

We see that the manufacturer can make $\frac{60}{5} = 12$ skateboards. And there seems to be no particular reason not to do exactly that, earning a profit of $1.00(12) = 12.00. We use the variable x to stand for the number of skateboards made; we see that x could be any value between 0 and 12, or algebraically, $0 \leq x \leq 12$. Those values are the *feasible set,* the particular values of our variable x that are feasible, or possible, given the available resources. Figure 4.1 shows a number line, or x-axis, with the feasible set indicated by a thick line. The problems we will discuss in this chapter will be simple enough that we will always be able to draw a picture of the feasible set. Sometimes the feasible set is called the *feasible region,* so we will use the terms *feasible set* and *feasible region* interchangeably.

x-Axis

FIGURE 4.1 Feasible region for the skateboard problem.

The **feasible set,** also called the **feasible region,** is the set of all possible solutions to a linear programming problem.

There are several features to note about our feasible region and the point within it that gives the maximum profit:

1. There are no negative values of x in the feasible region. That makes physical sense: How could one make a negative number of skateboards?
2. Any point within the feasible region represents a possible **production policy**—that is, it gives the number of skateboards (product) that it is possible to produce with the limited supply of containers of plastic (resource). The manufacturer could close shop early and spend less time making skateboards, making only 7, for a profit of $1.00(7) = 7.00.

3. The point $x = 0$ of the feasible region represents the manufacturer making no skateboards at all, having no product to sell. Eliminating the only product does not seem sensible; when we consider problems with more than one product, we will again consider whether eliminating a product is a desirable action.

4. The point where the profit is greatest, $x = 12$, happens to be an endpoint, or "corner," of the feasible region. Although this observation may not seem earthshaking in the context of this example, the realization that maximum profit always occurs at a corner point of the feasible region, in both simple and complicated problems, was a crucial insight in the development of linear programming.

The profit made can be described in terms of x: profit is the number of skateboards, x, multiplied by the profit per skateboard, 1.00, or $1.00x$. We call the formula $1.00x$ a **profit formula,** because it describes how to calculate the profit when we know the number of units, skateboards, to be made.

Common Features of Mixture Problems

Although our first mixture problem has only one product and one resource, it does contain the essential features that are common to *all* mixture problems:

Resources.   Definite resources are available in limited, known quantities for the time period in question. The resource here is containers of plastic.

Products.   Definite products can be made by combining, or mixing, the resources. In this example, the product is skateboards.

Recipes.   A recipe for each product specifies how many units of each resource are needed to make one unit of that product. Here, each skateboard uses five containers of plastic.

Profits.   Each product earns a known profit per unit. (We assume that every unit produced can be sold. More complicated mathematical models, beyond the scope of this book, are needed if we want to consider the possibility of items being produced but not sold.)

Objective.   The objective in a mixture problem is to find how much of each product to make so as to maximize the profit without exceeding any of the resource limitations.

The method we used to solve the skateboards problem is the same method we will use for more involved situations. That is, we analyze the problem, determining the resources and the products. We draw a picture, a graph, of the feasible region, and then we find a point in the feasible region that gives the maximum profit.

E X A M P L E   *Making Lemonade*

One pitcher of lemonade requires 5 lemons, and we have 40 lemons on hand. Draw the feasible region for making lemonade. What is the maximum profit we can make if we clear a profit of $1.50 per pitcher?

SOLUTION: The feasible region corresponds to $0 \leq x \leq \frac{40}{5} = 8$, shown as the thick portion of the number line in Figure 4.2. Using all the lemons and making 8 pitchers gives a maximum profit of $1.50(8) = $12.00. ◆

x-Axis

FIGURE 4.2 Feasible region for the lemonade problem.

As our manufacturing situations become more realistic, with more than one product and more than one resource, we will need a bit more algebra to draw the graph and a bit more calculation to find the point we want. But as we become engrossed in the details, it is important to remember the purpose of mixture problems: given limited resources and fixed recipes for making products from the resources, we want to find a mix of products that will result in a maximum profit. Our next problem has two products and one resource.

Two Products and One Resource: Skateboards and Dolls, Part I

Any good businessperson looks for new ways to make money. The toy manufacturer wants to expand and produce two products, skateboards and dolls. In order to keep our story simple, we will assume that most of the resources needed, such as labor, fasteners, and paint, are available in essentially unlimited quantities. The only limited resource is containers of plastic, which are needed in both products. We continue to assume that everything produced will sell. The recipe for one doll calls for 2 containers of plastic. Again, it is not difficult to see that if the original supply is again 60 containers of plastic, then the manufacturer could make $\frac{60}{2} = 30$ dolls. But then there would be no containers of plastic for skateboards. And if they make 12 skateboards, using 5 containers of plastic per board, there would be no containers of plastic for dolls. But what if they made some of each? For example, they could make 2 skateboards, using up $5(2) = 10$ containers of plastic and leaving $60 - 10 = 50$ containers of plastic. That would allow for $\frac{50}{2} = 25$ dolls.

But wait, the manufacturer is in this for profit. The company needs to know how much profit it will get from one doll. Suppose it is $0.55. Now, since we used x for the number of skateboards made, we will use y for the number of dolls. So the profit from the dolls will be $0.55y. The total profit will come from the sale of *x* skateboards plus *y* dolls, so the profit formula is $1.00*x* + $0.55*y*. We want to find a pair of numbers (*x*, *y*) that makes that profit formula as high as possible. But we don't even know what (*x*, *y*) pairs are even possible! We need to locate those **feasible points,** the points that make up the feasible set, before we even think about maximizing profit. In order to construct that region, it is helpful to summarize our problem in a *mixture chart*.

Mixture Charts

The most important skill required when solving a mixture problem is the ability to understand and model its underlying structure. This skill is as important as being able to do the subsequent algebra and arithmetic. In fact, since linear programming problems can be solved using readily available computer software, extracting the important data from the underlying structure may be the only part of the problem-solving process that must be done by a human being. Understanding the underlying structure means being able to answer these questions:

1. What are the resources?
2. What quantity of each resource is available?
3. What are the products?
4. What are the recipes for creating the products from the resources?
5. What are the unknown quantities?
6. What is the profit formula?

We will display the answers to these questions in a diagram called a **mixture chart.** Then we will translate information in our mixture chart into mathematical statements that we can use to solve the mixture problem. Figure 4.3 shows the mixture chart for Skateboards and Dolls, Part 1.

Some features are present in every mixture chart. There is a row of the chart for every product, for every type of item on which the business can make a profit. Here the products are skateboards and dolls. All the entries on a row give informa-

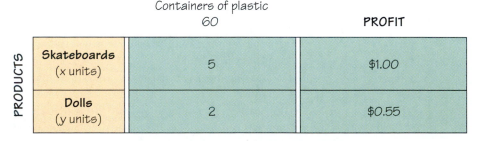

FIGURE 4.3   Mixture chart for Skateboards and Dolls, Part 1.

tion about the one product to which the row belongs. There is a column for every resource, every input to the business that comes only in limited quantities. Each resource column has information about just one of the limited resources. This problem has only one resource, containers of plastic, so it has only one resource column. (As we progress to problems with more than one resource, our mixture charts will have more columns.) There is also a column for the profit data. We will formulate a mathematical statement corresponding to the profit column and to each of the resource columns.

Each problem has specifics that are put into the mixture chart. In filling in the mixture chart, we have labeled the number of skateboards as x and the number of dolls as y, just as we did before. The recipes for the two products in terms of the number of containers of plastic they use have been entered in the column for the containers of plastic. Since each skateboard uses 5 containers of plastic, there is a 5 where the row for product skateboards meets the column for the container of plastic resource. Similarly, there is a 2 where the row for the product dolls meets the column for the container of plastic resource.

We have also entered the profit numbers in the chart. For example, in the row for dolls and the column for profits, we put $0.55 to indicate that each doll brings in a $0.55 profit. We can use the mixture chart to determine a profit formula of $1.00x + $0.55y. The $1.00 and the x are both on the row for skateboards, and the $0.55 and the y are both on the row for dolls.

E X A M P L E   *Making a Mixture Chart*

Make a mixture chart to display this situation. A clothing manufacturer has 60 yards of cloth available to make shirts and decorated vests. Each shirt requires 3 yards of material and provides a profit of $5. Each vest requires 2 yards of material and provides a profit of $2.

Solution: See the mixture chart in Figure 4.4.   ◆

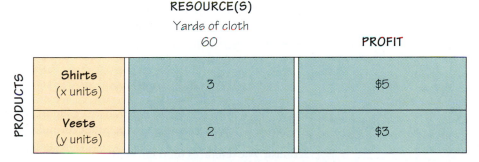

FIGURE 4.4   Mixture chart for the clothing manufacturer.

Resource Constraints

Every resource in our mixture problems gives us a *resource constraint,* an algebraic statement that says what is obvious in the physical world, "You can't use more of a resource than the amount you have available." Each resource column in the mixture chart gives us one resource constraint.

We put together the information we have about the resource, containers of plastic. There are just 60 containers of plastic, so "the number of containers of plastic used must be less than or equal to 60." That statement can be rewritten as "the number of containers of plastic used" $\leq$ 60. To translate the words in quotation marks, we reason in much the same way we did for finding our profit formula. If the manufacturer makes x skateboards, and each skateboard requires 5 containers of plastic, $5x$ containers of plastic are used. Similarly, in making y dolls, each requiring 2 containers of plastic, $2y$ containers of plastic are used up. So making x skateboards *plus* y dolls uses up $5x$ *plus* $2y$ containers of plastic, or $5x + 2y$, which cannot exceed 60. Thus we get the resource constraint $5x + 2y \leq 60$. Note that the numbers 5, 2, and 60 are all in the "container of plastic resource column" of the mixture chart.

A **resource constraint** is an inequality in a mixture problem that reflects the fact that no more of a resource can be used than what is available.

The resource constraint $5x + 2y \leq 60$ is really a combination of two mathematical statements: $5x + 2y < 60$ and $5x + 2y = 60$. The first statement, $5x + 2y < 60$, is an *inequality,* and tells us that the number of containers of plastic used to make the two products is *less than* the total number of containers of plastic available. The second statement, $5x + 2y = 60$, is an *equality,* or *equation,* and tells us that the number of containers of plastic used to make the two products is *equal to* the total number of containers of plastic available. So $5x + 2y \leq 60$ tells us that the number of containers of plastic used to make the two products must be *less than or equal to* the total number of containers of plastic available.

EXAMPLE   *Writing a Resource Constraint and a Profit Formula*

Using the numbers in the mixture chart in Figure 4.4, write a resource constraint for the cloth resource. Also write the profit formula.

SOLUTION: The resource constraint is $3x + 2y \leq 60$. The profit formula is $\$5x + \$3y$.

◆

Graphing the Constraints to Form the Feasible Region

When we have two products in a mixture problem, we use two variables, x and y. So the feasible region for a problem having two products will be a portion of the xy, or *Cartesian*, plane.

> Every point in the feasible region is a possible solution to a linear programming problem because it satisfies every constraint of that problem. For a two-product problem, the feasible region is a part of the plane. If the problem has n products, the feasible region is a portion of n-dimensional space.

How can we use a resource constraint to help us find the feasible region? In particular, how do we graph an inequality such as $5x + 2y \leq 60$? It is not difficult to draw a graph of $5x + 2y = 60$. That equation, and all the other ones we will get from resource constraints, is the equation of a straight line. Any equation having either an x term, a y term, or both, and some numerical constant, like the 60, but no other kinds of terms, always represents a line. (The equation cannot have any squared, square root, or other kind of algebraic combination of x or y.)

Constraint inequalities are always associated with equations for lines; hence the term *linear programming*. The programming does not refer to a computer but to a well-defined sequence of steps, or program of action, that solves the kinds of problems we are exploring. Here we are using program as a synonym for algorithm. With the introduction of computers into business settings, linear programming is usually carried out by running a computer program.

In order to draw a straight line, we need to know two of the points on the line. In fact, we already know two useful points, but we may not have thought of them as points. One point says that if the manufacturer makes 0 skateboards, then there are enough containers of plastic to make 30 dolls. That point, expressed in terms of the x and y coordinates of the plane, would take the general form of (x, y), and since x is the number of skateboards and y is the number of dolls, the point we want is $(0, 30)$. Another point we have already considered is the point representing 12 skateboards and 0 dolls, which we write as $(12, 0)$.

In general, when we want to draw the graph of the line portion of a resource constraint, we can substitute $x = 0$ into the equation part of the resource constraint, and find the corresponding value for y. Here's how that algebra looks:

$5x + 2y = 60$	Substitute $x = 0$ into the equation.
$5(0) + 2y = 60$	Multiply 5 by 0 and simplify.
$2y = 60$	Divide both sides of the equation by 2.
$y = 30$	

So one (x, y) point on the line is $(0, 30)$. This is the point representing our making $x = 0$ skateboards and $y = 30$ dolls.

We now follow a similar procedure for making 0 dolls; we substitute $y = 0$ into the equation $5x + 2y = 60$ and find the corresponding value of x. Starting with $5x + 2(0) = 60$ and following the same steps as in the algebra above, we get $x = 12$. So another (x, y) point on the line is $(12, 0)$. This point represents our making $x = 12$ skateboards and $y = 0$ dolls.

In Figure 4.5a we have a graph of the xy-plane showing the points $(0, 30)$ and $(12, 0)$ and a segment of the line $5x + 2y = 60$ connecting them. Every point on the line segment represents a production policy for the two products that uses up all of the containers of plastic available. Some of the points, like $(2, 25)$, give us whole products, and some of the points represent fractional products. We verify that $(2, 25)$ is on the line by substituting 2 for x and 25 for y into the equation $5x + 2y = 60$, getting $5(2) + 2(25) = 60$, which simplifies to $10 + 50 = 60$, which is a true statement. Remember, points on the xy-plane are always expressed in the form (x, y), with the x value, or coordinate, written before the y value, or coordinate.

The xy-plane has four portions, called *quadrants*. In the graph in Figure 4.5a, we only show the one in which both x and y are nonnegative because, in reality, we can never make negative quantities of our products. Reflecting that reality, we have **minimum constraints** of $x \geq 0$ and $y \geq 0$. The line segment in the graph represents all the points, or production policies, for which these properties are true: all the containers of plastic are used up, $5x + 2y = 60$, and both x and y are nonnegative. These points are part of our feasible region. We also need to identify those points corresponding to the inequality $5x + 2y < 60$; these are points corresponding to production policies that do not use up all the containers of plastic.

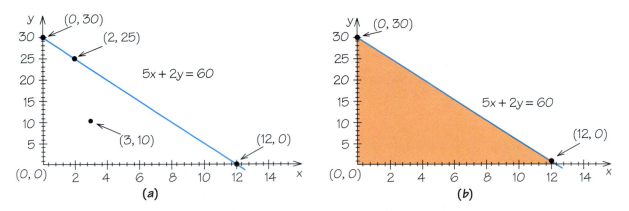

FIGURE 4.5   The feasible region for Skateboards and Dolls, Part 1. (a) Graph of $5x + 2y = 60$. (b) Shading of the half plane $5x + 2y < 60$.

Any line, such as $5x + 2y = 60$, divides the xy-plane into two parts, called *half planes*. Each of those half planes corresponds to one of two inequalities, in this case $5x + 2y < 60$ and $5x + 2y > 60$. We can determine which half plane goes with which inequality by testing one point not on the line and seeing which inequality it makes true. For example, (3, 10) is on the "down" side of the line segment. When we substitute that point into the inequality $5x + 2y < 60$, which we do by replacing the x by 3 and the y by 10, we get $5(3) + 2(10) < 60$. Simplifying gives us $15 + 20 < 60$ or $35 < 60$, which is true. Substituting the same point into the other inequality, $5x + 2y > 60$, would give $35 > 60$, which is false. So we know that the "down" side of the line segment corresponds to the inequality $5x + 2y < 60$, and the "down" side plus the line segment itself corresponds to the combination inequality $5x + 2y \leq 60$. The "up" side of the line corresponds to the inequality $5x + 2y > 60$, and thus is *not* part of the feasible region. In practice, the point (0, 0) is often used as a test point. (Can you see why?) In Figure 4.5b we show the feasible region for the skateboards and dolls problem as a shaded region in the quadrant where both x and y are nonnegative.

E X A M P L E *Drawing a Feasible Region*

In the earlier clothing manufacturer example, we developed a resource constraint of $3x + 2y \leq 60$. Draw the feasible region corresponding to that resource constraint, using the reality minimums of $x \geq 0$ and $y \geq 0$.

SOLUTION: First we find the two points where the line, $3x + 2y = 60$, crosses the axes. When $x = 0$, we get $3(0) + 2y = 60$, giving $y = \frac{60}{2} = 30$, yielding the point (0, 30). For $y = 0$, we get $3x + 2(0) = 60$, or $x = \frac{60}{3} = 20$, so we have the point (20, 0). We draw the line connecting those points. Testing the point (0, 0), we find that the "down" side of the line we have drawn corresponds to $3x + 2y < 60$. The feasible region is shown in Figure 4.6. ◆

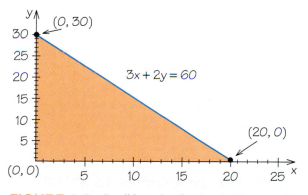

FIGURE 4.6 Feasible region for the clothing manufacturer.

Finding the Optimal Production Policy

After all this work we may think we are done, but in fact what we have just learned how to do is to draw one type of feasible region. We still must find the *optimal production policy,* a point within that region that gives a maximum profit. There are a lot of points in that region. If you only consider points with whole numbers as values for *x* or *y*, there are many points, and in fact either *x* or *y* or both of them could be some fractional number. There are so many points in this feasible region that to consider the profit at each one of them would require us to calculate profits from now until we grow very old, and still the calculations would not be done. Here is where the genius of the linear programming technique comes in, with the *corner point principle,* which we define in terms of our mixture problems.

> The **corner point principle** states that in a linear programming problem, the maximum value for the profit formula always corresponds to a **corner point** of the feasible region. (Later on in this chapter we discuss why the principle works; for now we will accept its validity.)

The corner point principle is probably the most important insight in the theory of linear programming. The geometric nature of this principle explains the value of creating a geometric model from the data in a mixture chart.

The corner point principle gives us the following method to solve a mixture problem:

1. Determine the corner points of the feasible region.
2. Evaluate the profit at each corner point of the feasible region.
3. Choose the corner point with the highest profit as the production policy.

Let's look at the feasible region we drew in Figure 4.5. It is a triangle having three corners, namely, (0, 0), (0, 30), and (12, 0). Now all we need to do is find out which of these three points gives us the highest value for the profit formula, which in this problem is $\$1.00x + \$0.55y$. We display our calculations in Table 4.1. The maximum profit for the toy manufacturer is $16.50, and that happens if the manufacturer makes 0 skateboards and 30 dolls. The point (0, 30) is called the *optimal production policy.*

> An **optimal production policy** is a corner point of the feasible region where the profit formula has a maximum value.

TABLE 4.1	Calculation of the Profit Formula for Skateboards and Dolls, Part 1

Corner Point	Value of the Profit Formula: $\$1.00x + \$0.55y$
(0, 0)	$\$1.00(0) + \$0.55(0) = \$0.00 + \$0.00 = \$0.00$
(0, 30)	$\$1.00(0) + \$0.55(30) = \$0.00 + \$16.50 = \$16.50$
(12, 0)	$\$1.00(12) + \$0.55(0) = \$12.00 + \$0.00 = \$12.00$

EXAMPLE *Finding the Optimal Production Policy*

Our analysis of the clothing manufacturer problem resulted in a feasible region with three corner points, (0, 0), (0, 30), and (20, 0). Which of these maximizes the profit formula, $\$5x + \$3y$, and what does that corner represent in terms of shirts and vests?

SOLUTION: The evaluation of the profit formula at the corner points is shown in Table 4.2. The maximum profit of $100 occurs at the corner point (20, 0), which represents making 20 shirts and no vests. ◆

TABLE 4.2	Evaluating the Profit Formula in the Clothing Example

Corner Point	Value of the Profit Formula: $\$5x + \$3y$
(0, 0)	$\$5(0) + \$3(0) = \$0 + \$0 = \$0$
(0, 30)	$\$5(0) + \$3(30) = \$0 + \$90 = \$90$
(20, 0)	$\$5(20) + \$3(0) = \$100 + \$0 = \$100$

General Shape of Feasible Regions

The shape of a feasible region for a linear programming mixture problem has some important characteristics, without which the corner point principle would not work:

1. The feasible region is a polygon in the first quadrant, where both $x \geq 0$ and $y \geq 0$. This is because the minimum constraints require that both x and y be nonnegative.

FIGURE 4.7
A feasible region may not have (a) dents or (b) holes. Graph (c) shows a typical feasible region.

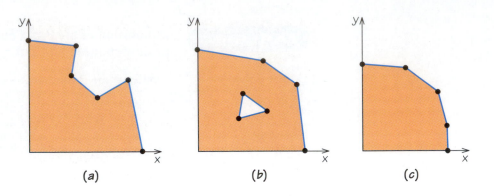

(a)   (b)   (c)

2. The region is a polygon that has neither dents (as in Figure 4.7a) nor holes (as in Figure 4.7b). Figure 4.7c is a typical example.

The Role of the Profit Formula: Skateboards and Dolls, Part 2

In practice, there are often different amounts of resources available in different time periods. The selling price for the products can also change. For example, if competition forces us to cut our selling price, the profit per unit can decrease. In order to maximize profit, it is usually necessary for a manufacturer to redo the mixture problem calculations whenever any of the numbers change.

Suppose that businesss conditions change and now the profits per skateboard and doll are, respectively, $1.05 and $0.40. Let us keep everything else about the skateboards and dolls problem the same. The change in profits would give us a new profit formula of $1.05x + $0.40y. When we evaluate the new profit formula at the corner points, we get the results shown in Table 4.3. This time the optimal production policy, the point that gives the maximum value for the profit formula, is the point (12, 0). To get the maximum profit of $12.60, the toy manufacturer should now make 12 skateboards and 0 dolls.

We see from this example that the shape of the feasible region, and thus the corner points we test, are determined by the constraint inequalities. The profit formula is used to choose an optimal point from among the corner points, so it is

TABLE 4.3	A Different Profit Formula: Skateboards and Dolls, Part 2
Corner Point	**Value of the Profit Formula: 1.05x$ + 0.40y$**
(0, 0)	$1.05(0) + $0.40(0) = $0.00 + $0.00 = $0.00
(0, 30)	$1.05(0) + $0.40(30) = $0.00 + $12.00 = $12.00
(12, 0)	$1.05(12) + $0.40(0) = $12.60 + $0.00 = $12.60

not surprising that different profit formulas give us different optimal production policies.

We started the exploration of skateboard and doll production with the idea that the toy manufacturer wanted to expand the product line from one to two products. But both linear programming solutions we have found tell the manufacturer that to maximize profit, just make one product. This is probably not an acceptable result for the manufacturer, who might want to produce both products for business reasons other than profit, such as establishing brand loyalty. And it certainly would be very difficult for the manufacturer to be ready to switch back and forth between producing either skateboards or dolls every time the profit formula changed. Linear programming is a flexible enough technique that it can accommodate the desire for there to be both products in the optimal production policy. The way this is done is by specifying that there be nonzero minimum quantities for each period.

Setting Minimum Quantities for Products: Skateboards and Dolls, Part 3

Suppose the toy manufacturer has kept track of the sales of the two products, and has discovered that no matter what, every day there has been demand for at least 4 skateboards and at least 10 dolls. It seems reasonable to set the minimum number of skateboards as 4 and the minimum number of dolls as 10. We keep the same recipes and the 60 containers of plastic. We will redo the mixture chart to include these minimums, draw a new feasible region, and find its corner points. Then we will use each of the earlier profit formulas to see which corner point is the optimal production policy in each case.

Figure 4.8 gives the mixture chart for our expanded problem. A column for minimums has been added to our mixture chart. Note that there are two sets of profits. This time when we draw the feasible region, we have the same resource constraint as we did before, namely, $5x + 2y \leq 60$, so we get the same line as we did before, and the desired inequality still is on the "down" side of that line, as in Figure 4.5b. But now we have minimum constraints that are nonzero. Let us first see what that means in terms of the skateboards. The skateboards row has a 4 in the column for minimums. That says to us "Make a minimum of 4 skateboards."

RESOURCE(S)

	Containers of plastic 60	MINIMUMS	PROFIT
Skateboards (x units)	5	4	(1) $1.00; (2) $1.05
Dolls (y units)	2	10	(1) $0.55; (2) $0.40

PRODUCTS

FIGURE 4.8 Mixture chart for Skateboards and Dolls, Part 3 (with nonzero minimums).

Another way to say this is, "The number of skateboards must be equal to or greater than 4." Since x represents the number of skateboards, we get "x must be equal to or greater than 4," which becomes the mathematical statement $x \geq 4$. Instead of the "reality minimum constraint" of $x \geq 0$, which we used earlier, now we have the nonzero minimum $x \geq 4$. Similarly, the minimum for dolls translates into $y \geq 10$.

Drawing a Feasible Region When There Are Nonzero Minimum Constraints

Figure 4.9a shows the feasible region we constructed with minimum constraints reflecting the reality that $x \geq 0$ and $y \geq 0$. We now need to incorporate the nonzero minimum constraints into that feasible region. As we did with the resource constraint, we can split a minimum constraint into two parts, an equation and an inequality. We can draw the line that corresponds to the equality and then determine which side of that line matches the inequality. First we follow these steps for the skateboards minimum. The constraint $x \geq 4$ has two parts, $x = 4$ and $x > 4$. What sort of line do we draw in the xy-plane for $x = 4$? When is a point (x, y) on the line $x = 4$? Well, clearly, x must be equal to 4, so the points look like $(4, y)$.

But what about the y value? We note that any y value will "work," because there is no y in the equation $x = 4$, so no matter what y value we choose we can never substitute it into the equation and get a false statement. So not only will any y value work, every possible y value works. If we pick two y values, we get two points, and then we can draw a line. Suppose we choose $y = 0$ and $y = 30$. We can draw the two points $(4, 0)$ and $(4, 30)$ and then draw the line they determine. We do that in Figure 4.9b. In general, any line whose equation is of the form $x =$ *some number* is a vertical line passing through the point (*that number,* 0). The y-axis is a special case, with equation $x = 0$.

When we substitute a point into the inequality $x > 4$, for example, the point $(0, 0)$, we get $0 > 4$, which is false, so we know that the point $(0, 0)$ is not on the side of the line for which $x > 4$ is true. That inequality is true for points to the right of the line $x = 4$. Thus the shaded area of Figure 4.9b shows the region of the plane for which $x \geq 4$ is true. Since $y \geq 0$ is always the case in mixture problems, the figure does not show that part of the xy-plane where y has negative values.

Now we need to draw the region where both inequalities $x \geq 4$ and $5x + 2y \leq 60$ are true. We need to find the shape that is shaded in both Figures 4.9a and 4.9b, to find the shape that is shaded twice. That shape is the intersection, or overlapping, of the two shaded regions and is shown in Figure 4.9c.

We see that the new region is a triangle, and we know the coordinates of two of its three corners. However, before we calculate the coordinates of the point labeled (?, ?) in Figure 4.9c, we should finish incorporating the minimums into the picture, so we know that our calculations are really of corner points in the final feasible region.

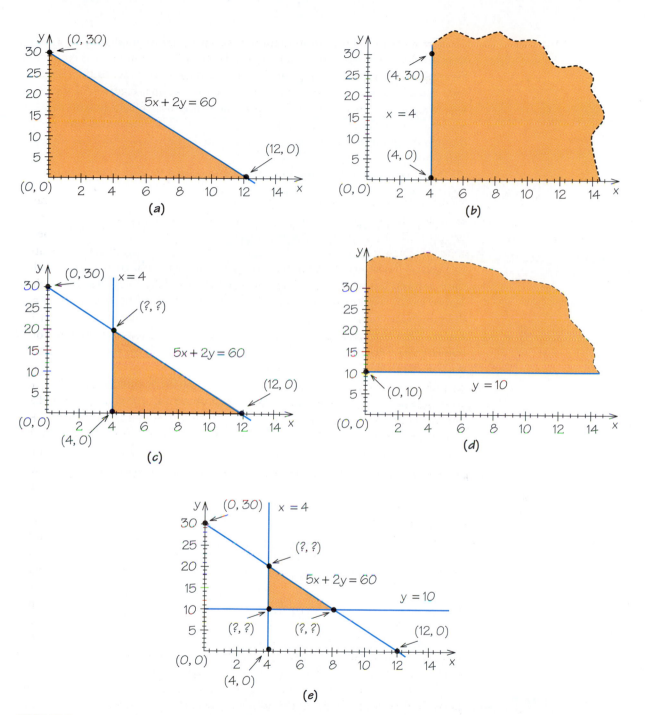

FIGURE 4.9 Feasible region for Skateboards and Dolls, Part 3 (with nonzero minimums). (a) Region where $5x + 2y \leq 60$. (b) Region where $x \geq 4$ is true (and also $y \geq 0$). (c) Region where both inequalities $x \geq 4$ and $5x + 2y \leq 60$ are true. (d) Region where $y \geq 10$ is true (and also $x \geq 0$). (e) Region where $x \geq 4$, $y \geq 10$, and $5x + 2y \leq 60$.

The other minimum constraint is $y \geq 10$. We need to graph the line $y = 10$, all of whose points are of the form $(x, 10)$. This line is horizontal; it is graphed in Figure 4.9d. The point $(0, 0)$ makes the inequality $y > 10$ false, so the region we want is the horizontal line and all the points above that line. Figure 4.9d shows the region where $y \geq 10$ is true for just those values where $x \geq 0$. In general, any line whose equation is of the form $y = some\ number$ is a horizontal line passing through the point $(0,\ that\ number)$. A special case is the x-axis, which has the equation $y = 0$.

Now we combine the shaded regions in Figures 4.9c and 4.9d, giving us, in Figure 4.9e, the feasible region for our problem.

Finding Corner Points of a Feasible Region Having Nonzero Minimums

In Figure 4.9e, we see that the feasible region for the problem is a triangle with three corners, but as yet we do not know the coordinates of any of those corners. Not to worry. We can get lots of help from the vertical and horizontal lines from the minimum constraints. First, let us work out the coordinates of the lower left corner. Since that point is on the line $x = 4$, we know its x-coordinate must be 4. Similarly, its y-coordinate must be 10, because the point is on the line $y = 10$. So the point at the lower left is $(4, 10)$.

We proceed clockwise around the boundary of the feasible region. The next corner point of the feasible region is directly above $(4, 10)$. Its x-coordinate is also 4, but we need to do some calculation to find its y-coordinate. The point is on the intersection of the lines $x = 4$ and $5x + 2y = 60$. We need to find the y-coordinate of the point that has $x = 4$ and lies on that second line. We do this by substituting 4 for x in the equation of the second line. Here is the algebra:

$5(4) + 2y = 60$	Substitute $x = 4$ into the equation.
$20 + 2y = 60$	Multiply 5 by 4.
$2y = 40$	Subtract the 20 from both sides of the equation.
$y = 20$	Divide both sides of the equation by 2.

so the coordinates of the point are $(4, 20)$.

And, finally, we find the coordinates of the third corner point of the triangle. This point has $y = 10$, so we make that substitution into the equation of the line $5x + 2y = 60$, because the point lies on that line. We get $5x + 2(10) = 60$, and then follow the same steps as we did earlier in a similar calculation. From $5x + 20 = 60$, or $5x = 40$, we get $x = 8$. So the coordinates of the point are $(8, 10)$.

E X A M P L E *Incorporating Nonzero Minimums*

Suppose the clothing manufacturer needs to make at least 4 shirts and 6 vests. Incorporate these minimums into the feasible region shown in Figure 4.6.

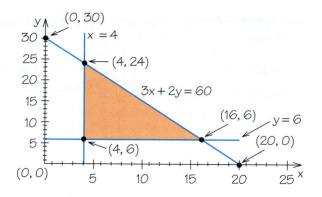

FIGURE 4.10   Feasible region for clothing manufacturer, with nonzero minimums.

SOLUTION: The minimum constraint $x \geq 4$ gives us a vertical line at $x = 4$. The part of the old feasible region to the left of that line is no longer feasible. Similarly, the minimum constraint $y \geq 6$ gives us a horizontal line. The part of the old feasible region below that line is no longer feasible. The new feasible region is shown in Figure 4.10. To find the coordinates of the new corner points, we use the equations of the two lines that meet at that corner. The point $(4, 6)$ is on the lines $x = 4$ and $y = 6$. Substituting $x = 4$ (one line) into $3x + 2y = 60$ (other line), we get $3(4) + 2y = 60$, or $2y = 60 - 12 = 48$, so $y = 24$, giving us $(4, 24)$. We get the coordinates $(16, 6)$ by substituting $y = 6$ (one line) into $3x + 2y = 60$ (other line).   ◆

Evaluating the Profit Formula at the Corners of a Feasible Region with Nonzero Minimums

Now that we have the corner points of the feasible region for making skateboards and dolls, we can find out which point gives the maximum profit. The original profit formula, $1.00x + $0.55y, gave a production policy to make no skateboards. This time all the feasible production policies have nonzero minimums, so that kind of result cannot occur. As we see from Table 4.4, the optimal production policy in this case is to make 4 skateboards and 20 dolls, for a maximum profit of $15.00. The policy calls for the absolute minimum number of skateboards, but not zero. And the "price paid for having the minimums" in this case is $16.50 (the old profit with minimums that are zeros)—$15.00 (the profit now) = $1.50.

The second profit formula, $1.05x + $0.40y, resulted in a production policy to make no dolls. With the nonzero minimums, that profit formula gives a production policy that says to make 8 skateboards and 10 dolls (check it by using the

| TABLE 4.4 | Evaluating One Profit Formula When There Are Nonzero Minimums |

Corner Point	Value of the Profit Formula: $\$1.00x + \$0.55y$
(4, 10)	$\$1.00(4) + \$0.55(10) = \$4.00 + \$5.50 = \$9.50$
(4, 20)	$\$1.00(4) + \$0.55(20) = \$4.00 + \$11.00 = \$15.00$
(8, 10)	$\$1.00(8) + \$0.55(10) = \$8.00 + \$5.50 = \$13.50$

second formula in a table like Table 4.4), the minimum number, for a profit of $12.40. And the "price paid for having the minimums" in this case is $12.60 (the old profit with the minimums that are zeros) — $12.40 (the profit now) = $0.20, a very small amount.

EXAMPLE   *Evaluating a Profit Formula*

Finish the clothing manufacturer problem by finding the corner point that maximizes the profit formula $\$5x + \$3y$.

SOLUTION: From Table 4.5 we see that the maximum profit of $98 is obtained by making 16 shirts and 6 vests. Note that the optimal production policy is still slanted toward shirts, with the manufacturer making just the minimum number of vests. ◆

| TABLE 4.5 | Evaluating the Clothing Profit Formula When There Are Nonzero Minimums |

Corner Point	Value of the Profit Formula: $\$5x + \$3y$
(4, 6)	$\$5(4) + \$3(6) = \$20 + \$18 = \$38$
(4, 24)	$\$5(4) + \$3(24) = \$20 + \$72 = \$92$
(16, 6)	$\$5(16) + \$3(6) = \$80 + \$18 = \$98$

Summary of the Pictorial Method

Before we proceed to more involved linear programming problems, let's stop and summarize the steps we are following to find the optimal production policy in a mixture problem:

1. Read the problem carefully. Identify the resources and the products.
2. Make a mixture chart showing the resources (associated with limited quantities), the products (associated with profits), the recipes for creating the products from the resources, the profit from each product, and the

amount of each resource on hand. If the problem has nonzero minimums, include a column for those as well.

3. Assign an unknown quantity, x or y, to each product. Use the mixture chart to write down the resource constraints, the minimum constraints, and the profit formula.

4. Graph the line corresponding to each resource constraint and determine which side of the line is in the feasible region. If there are nonzero minimum constraints, graph lines for them also, and determine which side of each is in the feasible region. Sketch the feasible region by putting together, that is, intersecting, the half planes from all the resource constraints plus the minimum constraints.

5. Find the coordinates of all the corner points of the feasble region. Some of these may have been calculated in order to graph the individual lines. Proceed in order around the boundary of the feasible region. Be sure that every point you consider is part of the feasible region.

6. Evaluate the profit formula for each of the corner points. The production policy that maximizes profit is the one that gives the biggest value to the profit formula.

Mixture Problems Having Two Resources

Two Products and Two Resources: Skateboards and Dolls, Part 4

We return for one last time to the toy manufacturer, now to consider two limited resources instead of one. The second limited resource will be time, the number of person-minutes available to prepare the products. Suppose that there are 360 person-minutes of labor available and that making one skateboard requires 15 person-minutes and making one doll requires 18 person-minutes. We will continue to use the original figures regarding containers of plastic, the first of our two profit formulas, and to keep the problem relatively simple, we will return to the zero minimum constraints: $x \geq 0$ and $y \geq 0$. We need a new mixture chart. In general, we will only include a column for minimums in a mixture chart if there are any nonzero minimum constraints. In Figure 4.11 we have the mixture chart for this problem.

Using the mixture chart, we can write the two resource constraints:

$$5x + 2y \leq 60 \qquad \text{for containers of plastic}$$

and

$$15x + 18y \leq 360 \qquad \text{for person-minutes}$$

We can also write the profit formula: $\$1.00x + \$0.55y$.

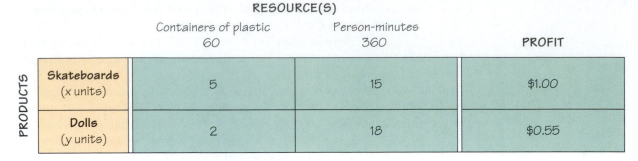

RESOURCE(S)

PRODUCTS		Containers of plastic 60	Person-minutes 360	PROFIT
	Skateboards (x units)	5	15	$1.00
	Dolls (y units)	2	18	$0.55

FIGURE 4.11 Mixture chart for Skateboards and Dolls, Part 4 (two resources).

The half plane corresponding to the plastic resource is shown in Figure 4.12a. We now need to graph the half plane corresponding to the time constraint. We find where the line $15x + 18y = 360$ intersects the two axes by substituting first $x = 0$ and then $y = 0$ into that equation. Here's how that algebra looks:

$5(0) + 18y = 360$ Substitute $x = 0$ into the equation.
$18y = 360$ Simplify.
$y = 20$ Divide both sides of the equation by 18.

So one (x, y) point on the line is $(0, 20)$. This is the point representing our making $x = 0$ skateboards and $y = 20$ dolls.

We now follow a similar procedure for making 0 dolls. We substitute $y = 0$ into the equation $15x + 18y = 360$, getting $15x + 18(0) = 360$, and carry out similar calculations to the earlier ones, getting $x = 24$. So another (x, y) point on the line is $(24, 0)$. This point represents our making $x = 24$ skateboards and $y = 0$ dolls.

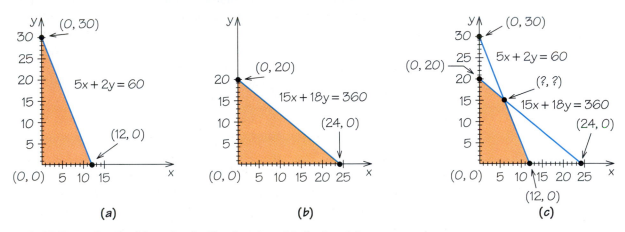

FIGURE 4.12 Feasible region for Skateboards and Dolls, Part 4 (two resources). (a) Half plane for the plastic resource constraint. (b) Half plane for the time resource constraint. (c) Intersection for the two half planes.

The line corresponding to the time constraint contains the two points (0, 20) and (24, 0). When we substitute the point (0, 0) into the inequality $15x + 18y < 360$, we get $15(0) + 18(0) < 360$, or $0 < 360$, which is true, so (0, 0) is on the side of the line that we shade. Putting all this together, we get the half plane in Figure 4.12b as the correct half plane for the time resource constraint.

We are not permitted to exceed the supply of even a single resource; therefore, the feasible region must be made up of points that are shaded twice, both in the half plane for the plastic resource constraint, shown in Figure 4.12a, and in the half plane for the time resource constraint in Figure 4.12b. As we did before with the half planes from nonzero minimum constraints, we build our feasible region by finding the intersection, or overlap, of the individual half planes in the problem. In Figure 4.12c we show the result of intersecting the half plane from the two resource constraints. Since this problem has minimums that are zeros, the shaded region in Figure 4.12c is in fact the feasible region for the problem.

We now need to find the coordinates of the corner points of the feasible region. In general, there are points in our graph that are not corner points of the feasible region. One easy way to keep track is to shade in the feasible region and then systematically move around its boundary, working from one corner point to the next. We start at the origin, (0, 0), and proceed clockwise. The next corner point is one whose coordinates we calculated in order to draw a line, so we know that it is (0, 20). For the point labeled (?, ?) we need to use a bit of algebra. And the last of the four corner points is again one whose coordinates are already known to us, namely, (12, 0).

To find the coordinates of the point that lies on the intersection of the lines $5x + 2y = 60$ and $15x + 18y = 360$, we take these two equations with two variables, or unknowns, and eliminate one of the unknowns, leaving us with an equation having just one unknown. We have solved such an equation in earlier problems. Once we know the value of one of the unknowns, we simply substitute it into the equation of the line to get the other coordinate. Here are the worked-out details:

Write the two equations with "like terms" in columns:

$$5x + 2y = 60$$
$$15x + 18y = 360$$

Pick the variable to eliminate. Here we will eliminate y. Multiply the top equation by the coefficient of that variable in the bottom equation (the top equation gets multiplied by the 18 from the $18y$). Multiply the bottom equation by the coefficient of that variable in the top equation (the bottom equation gets multiplied by the 2 from the $2y$). Change one of the two multipliers to a negative number (the 2 became a -2):

$$18(5x + 2y = 60)$$
$$-2(15x + 18y = 360)$$

Do the actual multiplication. Note that the coefficients of the variable to be eliminated are now the same except for sign; now one is + and one is −:

$$90x + \quad 36y = 1080$$
$$-30x + -36y = 720$$

Add the two equations by adding "like terms to like terms."

$(90 - 30)x + (36 - 36)y = (1080 - 720)$
$60x + 0y = 360$, so $60x = 360$ Simplify; the y variable "drops out."
$x = 6$ Divide both sides by 60, getting the coordinate for x.

Now that we know the value of one of the coordinates of the point, we are in the same place algebraically as we were when we needed to find the coordinates of a point where a resource line meets a minimum-constraint line. We just substitute the value we have, in this case $x = 6$, into either of the two *original* equations and find the corresponding value of the other coordinate. For example, if we use the equation $5x + 2y = 60$, the substitution gives us $5(6) + 2y = 60$, which yields $y = 15$. So the point at which the two lines from resource constraints cross is (6, 15). You can verify that if you picked the other original equation to find the y-coordinate, you would still get $y = 15$. In fact, substituting (6, 15) into the equation $15x + 18y = 360$ and seeing that you get a true statement is a good way to check your calculations.

Some readers may notice that other pairs of numbers will work as multipliers that will cause elimination of the y variable. That is true, and if you know ways to find pairs that work, you of course may use them. Many "tricks" involving getting the smallest values for such numbers were very useful when all calculations were done by hand. Today, since calculators are available to most of us, these "tricks" are not as important.

Now we are ready to finish the problem. In Table 4.6 we have evaluated the profit formula at the four corner points of the feasible regions. The optimal production policy for the toy manufacturer would be to make 6 skateboards and 15 dolls, for a maximum profit of $14.25.

TABLE 4.6	**The Profit at the Four Corner Points**

Corner Point	Value of the Profit Formula: $1.00x + $0.55y
(0, 0)	$1.00(0) + $0.55(0) = $0.00 + $0.00 = $0.00
(0, 20)	$1.00(0) + $0.55(20) = $0.00 + $11.00 = $11.00
(6, 15)	$1.00(6) + $0.55(15) = $6.00 + $8.25 = $14.25
(12, 0)	$1.00(12) + $0.55(0) = $12.00 + $0.0 = $12.00

EXAMPLE   *Mixtures of Two Fruit Juices: Beverages, Part 1*

A juice manufacturer produces and sells two fruit beverages: 1 gallon of cranapple is made from 3 quarts of cranberry juice and 1 quart of apple juice; and 1 gallon of appleberry is made from 2 quarts of apple juice and 2 quarts of cranberry juice. The manufacturer makes a profit of 3 cents on a gallon of cranapple and 4 cents on a gallon of appleberry. Today, there are 200 quarts of cranberry juice and 100 quarts of apple juice available. How many gallons of cranapple and how many gallons of appleberry should be produced to obtain the highest profit without exceeding available supplies? We use zeros as "reality minimums." The mixture chart for this problem is shown in Figure 4.13.

For each resource, we develop a resource constraint reflecting the fact that the manufacturer cannot use more of that resource than what is available. The number of quarts of cranberry juice needed for x gallons of cranapple is $3x$. Similarly, $2y$ quarts of cranberry are needed for making y gallons of appleberry. So if the manufacturer makes x gallons of cranapple and y gallons of appleberry, then $3x + 2y$ quarts of cranberry juice will be used. Since there are only 200 quarts of cranberry available, we get the cranberry resource constraint $3x + 2y \leq 200$. Note that the numbers 3, 2, and 200 are all in the "cranberry" column. We get another resource constraint from the column for the apple juice resource: $1x + 2y \leq 100$. We also have these minimum constraints: $x \geq 0$ and $y \geq 0$.

Finally, we have the profit formula. Since $3x$ is the profit from making x units of cranapple and $4y$ is the profit from making y units of appleberry, we get the profit formula: $3x + 4y$.

We summarize our analysis of the juice mixture problem. Maximize the profit formula, $3x + 4y$, given these constraints:

cranberry: $3x + 2y \leq 200$
apple: $1x + 2y \leq 100$
minimums: $x \geq 0$ and $y \geq 0$

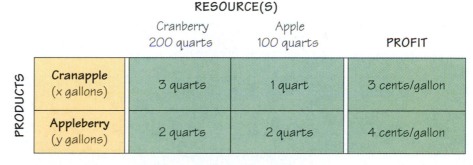

RESOURCE(S)

PRODUCTS		Cranberry 200 quarts	Apple 100 quarts	PROFIT
	Cranapple (x gallons)	3 quarts	1 quart	3 cents/gallon
	Appleberry (y gallons)	2 quarts	2 quarts	4 cents/gallon

FIGURE 4.13   A mixture chart for Beverages, Part 1.

Remember, in a mixture problem, our job is to find a production policy, (x, y), that makes all the constraints true and maximizes the profit.

Focus first on the cranberry juice constraint, $3x + 2y \leq 200$, and the associated equation $3x + 2y = 200$. We remember that when the line crosses, or intersects, the x-axis, the value of y is 0. Substituting $y = 0$ into the equation $3x + 2y = 200$ gives $3x = 200$, or $x = 200/3$, which we approximate by 66.7. So one point on the line $3x + 2y = 200$ is (66.7, 0). On the y-axis, $x = 0$. Substituting $x = 0$ into our equation $3x + 2y = 200$, we get $2y = 200$, or $y = 200/2$, giving us $y = 100$. So we have a second point on our line, namely, (0, 100). In Figure 4.14a these two points are shown and the line segment labeled $3x + 2y = 200$ was drawn by connecting them. To find out which half plane corresponds to the inequality $3x + 2y < 200$, we need only test the point (0, 0), which is not on the line. We see that $3(0) + 2(0) < 200$ is a true statement, so the inequality corresponds to the "down" side of the line, and that is the portion shaded in Figure 4.14a.

In Figure 4.14b we show the graph of the apple constraint inequality $1x + 2y \leq 100$. Note that the two points used to draw that line are (0, 50) and (100, 0), the two intercepts. (Can you find those two intercepts by substituting first $x = 0$ and then $y = 0$ into the inequality $1x + 2y \leq 100$?) You can check that the correct half plane, the one for which $1x + 2y < 100$, has been shaded by substituting the point (0, 0) into that inequality and seeing that the result you get is a true statement.

We know that a point in the feasible region must satisfy, or make true, every constraint inequality in the problem. Which points in the plane make both the cranberry and the apple constraint inequalities true? They are the points that are in

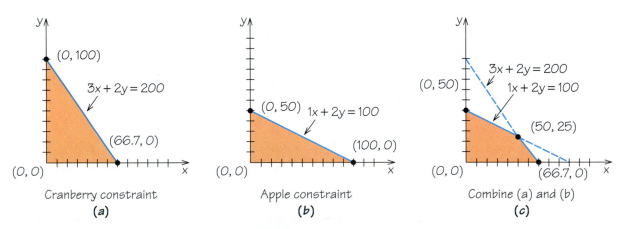

FIGURE 4.14   Feasible region for Beverages, Part 1.

the overlap of the shaded regions in Figures 4.14a and 4.14b. The feasible region satisfying both resource constraints is shown in Figure 4.14c. In this problem we also have two minimum-constraint inequalities, $x \geq 0$ and $y \geq 0$, so our graph is drawn just in the quadrant in which both x and y are nonnegative.

We now find the corner points of the feasible region in Figure 4.14c. We start at the origin, $(0, 0)$, and work our way clockwise around the boundary of the feasible region. Although we know the coordinates of the origin, it is useful to note that it is the intersection of two lines having equations $x = 0$, the y-axis, and $y = 0$, the x-axis, and corresponding to minimum constraints. These equations "solve" the problem of finding the coordinates. In general, we are trying to solve for values of x and y that satisfy both linear equations; then we will have the coordinates of the intersection.

The next corner is the intersection of the lines $x = 0$ and $1x + 2y = 100$. We found this point to be $(0, 50)$ when we sketched the line $1x + 2y = 100$.

Continuing clockwise, we come to the intersection of lines $1x + 2y = 100$ and $3x + 2y = 200$. This more general type of intersection can be solved by using multiplication and addition to eliminate one unknown, solving for the remaining unknown, and then substituting that value into an original equation to get the value of the eliminated unknown.

First, we multiply one equation by a positive value and the other by a negative value so that when the two equations are added together, one unknown gets a coefficient of zero:

$$(-3)(1x + 2y = 100) = -3x - 6y = -300$$
$$(1)(3x + 2y = 200) = 3x + 2y = 200$$

Now we add the new equations together:

$$0x - 4y = -100 \qquad \text{or} \qquad -4y = -100$$

Dividing both sides of the equation by -4, we get $y = 25$. Substituting $y = 25$ into $1x + 2y = 100$, we get $1x + 2(25) = 100$, which gives $1x + 50 = 100$, and that simplifies to $x = 50$. The point of intersection therefore seems to be $(50, 25)$. We can check our work in the other original equation: $3(50) + 2(25) = 200$ is a true statement.

The last corner point of this feasible region comes from the intersection of $3x + 2y = 200$ and $y = 0$. As with the other intersection of a resource constraint line and an axis, we already know the coordinates: $(66.7, 0)$. Note that some points we used to draw the resource constraint lines are *not* corner points of the feasible region.

When we evaluate the profit formula at these four corner points (see Table 4.7), we see that the optimal production policy is to make 50 gallons of cranapple and 25 gallons of appleberry for a profit of 250 cents.   ◆

TABLE 4.7	Finding the Optimal Production Policy for Beverages, Part I
Corner Point	**Value of the Profit Formula: $3x = 4y$ cents**
(0, 0)	$3(0)\ \ \ \ + 4(0)\ \ = 0$ cents
(0, 50)	$3(0)\ \ \ \ + 4(50) = 200$ cents
(50, 25)	$3(50)\ \ + 4(25) = 250$ cents
(66.7, 0)	$3(66.7) + 4(0)\ \ = 200$ cents (rounded)

The Corner Point Principle

In finding solutions to our mixture problems we have been using the corner point principle, which says that the highest profit value on a polygonal feasible region is always at a corner point. A feasible region has infinitely many points, making it impossible to compute the profit for each point. The corner point principle gives us a finite set of points among which we are guaranteed to find the optimal production policy. The principle turns an impossible calculation into a possible one.

This situation is reminiscent of Alexander the Great's approach to the problem of the Gordian knot, a legendary knot so large and tight and tangled that no one had been able to untie it. Alexander's solution was to slice the knot open with his sword. Mixture problems and other linear programming problems are like Gordian knots because there are infinitely many feasible points—we can't calculate the profit for all of them. The corner point principle functions like Alexander's sword and cuts through the problem. We now look at why that principle works.

You can visualize a mathematical proof of the corner point principle by imagining that each point of the plane is a tiny light bulb that is capable of lighting up. For the juice mixture example, whose feasible region is shown in Figure 4.14e, imagine what would happen if we ask this question: Will all points with profit = 360 please light up? What geometric figure do these lit-up points form?

In algebraic terms, we can restate the profit question in this way: Will all points (x, y) with $3x + 4y = 360$ please light up? As it happens, this version of the profit question is one mathematicians learned to answer hundreds of years before linear programming was born. The points that light up make a straight line because $3x + 4y = 360$ is the equation of a straight line. Furthermore, it is a routine matter to determine the exact position of the line. We call this line the **profit line** for 360; it is shown in Figure 4.15. For numbers other than 360, we would get different profit lines. Unfortunately, there are no points on the profit line for 360 that are feasible, that is, which lie in the feasible region. Therefore, the profit of

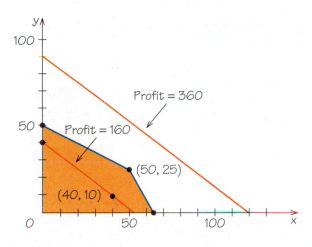

FIGURE 4.15 The profit line for 360 lies outside the feasbile region, whereas the profit line for 160 passes through the region.

360 is impossible. *If the profit line corresponding to a certain profit doesn't touch the feasible region, then that profit isn't possible.*

Because 360 is too big, perhaps we should ask the profit line for a more modest amount, say, 160, to light up. You can see that the new profit line of 160 in Figure 4.15 is parallel to the first profit line and closer to the origin. This is no accident: all profit lines for the profit formula $3x + 4y$ have the same coefficients for x and y, 3 for x and 4 for y, and since the slope of the line is determined by those coefficients, they all have the same slope. Changing the profit value from 360 to 160 has the effect of changing where the line intersects the y-axis, but it does not affect the slope.

The most important feature of the profit line for 160 is that it has points in common with the feasible region. For example, (40, 10) is on that profit line because $3(40) + 4(10) = 160$, and in addition (40, 10) is a feasible point. This means that it is possible to make 40 gallons of cranapple and 10 gallons of appleberry and that if we do so, we will have a profit of 160.

Can we do better than a 160 profit? As we slowly increase our desired profit from 160 toward 360, the location of the profit line that lights up shifts smoothly upward away from the origin. As long as the line continues to cross the feasible region, we are happy to see it move away from the origin, because the more it moves, the higher the profit represented by the line. We would like to stop the movement of the line at the last possible instant, while the line still has one or more points in common with the feasible region. It should be obvious that this will occur when the line is just touching the feasible region either at a corner point

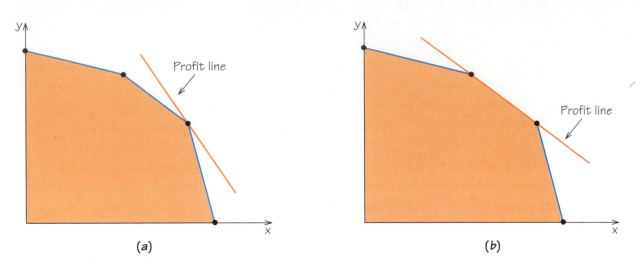

FIGURE 4.16   The highest profit will occur when the profit is just touching the feasible region, either (a) at the corner point or (b) along a line segment.

(Figure 4.16a) or along a line segment joining two corners (Figure 4.16b). That point or line segment corresponds to the production policy or policies with the maximum achievable profit. This is just what the corner point principle says: the maximum profit always occurs at a corner or along an edge of the feasible region.

Here is another way to look at the situation. Suppose that each light bulb (point of the plane) has a color determined by the profit associated with that point. All points with the same profit (i.e., points on a profit line) have the same color as shown in Figure 4.17. Furthermore, suppose the colors range continuously from violet to blue to green to yellow to red, just as they do in a rainbow. The cool colors represent low profits, the hot colors, higher ones: the higher the profit, the hotter the color. In effect, we are superimposing a straightened-out rainbow on the picture containing our feasible region. Finding the highest profit point can be thought of as finding the hottest-colored point in the feasible region.

E X A M P L E   *Adding Nonzero Minimums: Beverages, Part 2*

Suppose that in the beverage example the profit for cranapple changes from 3 cents per gallon to 2 cents and the profit for appleberry changes from 4 cents per gallon to 5 cents. You can verify that this change changes the optimal production policy to the point (0, 50)—no cranapple is produced. This result is not surprising: appleberry is giving a higher profit and the policy is to produce as much of it as possible. But suppose the manufacturer wants to incorporate nonzero minimums into the linear programming specifications so that there will always be both cranapple, x, and appleberry, y, produced. Specifically they decide that $x \geq 20$ and $y \geq 10$

FIGURE 4.17
If profit lines are colored according to the hues of the rainbow, the highest point will be the hottest-colored point in the feasible region.

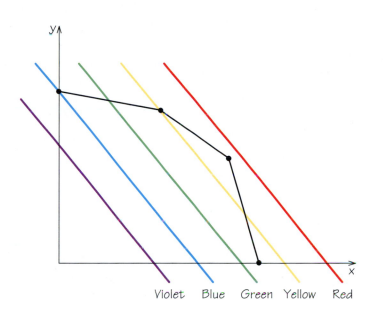

Violet   Blue   Green   Yellow   Red

are desirable minimums. Figure 4.18 is the mixture chart showing the new profit formula and the nonzero minimums along with the unchanged rest of the beverage problem.

The feasible region for Beverages, Part 1, is shown in Figure 4.19a. The feasible region for Beverages, Part 2, is shown in Figure 4.19b. You can verify that, starting at the lower left corner of the new feasible region and moving clockwise around its boundary, we have corner points (20, 10), (20, 40), (50, 25), and (60, 10). (One of those points was also a corner point of the old feasible region. Can you explain why?) Table 4.8 shows the evaluation of the profit formula at these corner points. For this modified problem the optimal production policy is to produce 20 gallons of cranapple and 40 of appleberry for a maximum profit of 240 cents.

	RESOURCE(S)			
	Cranberry juice 200 quarts	Apple juice 100 quarts	MINIMUMS	PROFIT
Cranapple (x gallons)	3	1	20	2 cents
Appleberry (y gallons)	2	2	10	5 cents

PRODUCTS

FIGURE 4.18 Mixture chart for Beverages, Part 2.

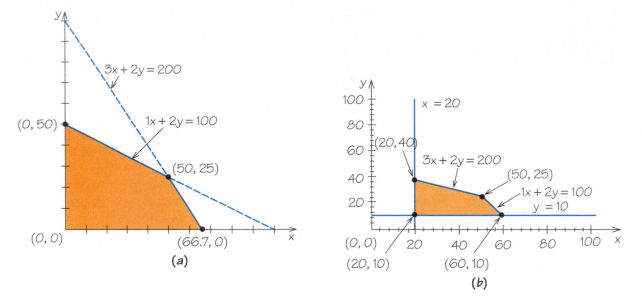

FIGURE 4.19   Feasible region for Beverages, Part 2. (a) Zero minimums. (b) Nonzero minimums.

One final note about this solution concerns the resources. The point (20, 40) is on the resource constraint line for the apple juice resource, so it represents using up all the available apple juice. We can see this by substituting into the apple juice resource constraint: $1(20) + 2(40) = 100$ is true. However, (20, 40) is *below* the line for the cranberry juice resource, indicating that there will be *slack,* or leftover, amounts of cranberry juice. Specifically, substituting (20, 40) into the cranberry juice constraint gives $3x + 2y = 3(20) + 2(40) = 60 + 80 = 140$, which is 60 quarts less than the 200 quarts available. The slack is 60 quarts of cranberry juice. Dealing with slack can be an important consideration for manufacturers. Can you see why?   ◆

TABLE 4.8	Profit Evaluation for Beverages, Part 2
Corner Point	**Value of the Profit Formula: $2x + 5y$**
(20, 10)	$2(20) + 5(10) = 40 \ + 50 \ = 90$ cents
(20, 40)	$2(20) + 5(40) = 40 \ + 200 = 240$ cents
(50, 25)	$2(50) + 5(25) = 100 + 125 = 225$ cents
(60, 10)	$2(60) + 5(10) = 120 + 50 \ = 170$ cents

Using a Computer to Calculate Profit at the Corner Points

In the Technology Corner, you will find a discussion of how to use a computer program called a spreadsheet to calculate the profit at any point in the feasible region. Of course, we know that the maximum profit will be at one of the corner points.

Computers can do all of the calculations in a linear programming problem by following an algorithm. We discuss linear programming algorithms in the next section.

Linear Programming: The Wider Picture

Characteristics of Linear Programming Algorithms

Every algorithm for solving a linear programming problem has the following three characteristics. These characteristics hold true regardless of the number of products or the number of resources in the problem.

1. The algorithm can distinguish between "good" production policies, those in the feasible set that satisfy all the constraints, and those that violate some constraint(s). There are usually many good points, each of which corresponds to some production policy; for example, "Make x units of product 1 and y units of product 2."
2. The algorithm makes use of some geometric principles—one such principle is the corner point principle—to select a special subset of the feasible set.
3. The algorithm evaluates the profit formula at points in the special subset to find which corner point actually gives the maximum profit.

The various algorithms for linear programming differ in how they find the feasible set and in how quickly the algorithm finds the production policy—corner point—that gives the optimal profit. The better algorithms are faster at finding the optimal production policy.

In practical applications, linear programming problems do not usually yield simple feasible regions in two-dimensional space. There are two ways the feasible region can be more complex:

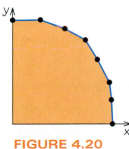

FIGURE 4.20
A feasible region with many corners.

1. Sometimes, as in Figure 4.20, we have a great many corners. The more corners there are, the more calculations we need to determine the coordinates of all of them and the profit at each one. The number of corners literally can exceed the number of grains of sand on the earth. Even with the fastest computer, computing the profit of every corner is impossible.

2. It is not possible to visualize the feasible region as a part of two-dimensional space when there are more than two products. Each product is represented by an unknown, and each unknown is represented by a dimension of space. If we have 50 products, we would need 50 dimensions and couldn't visualize the feasible region.

Another type of complication can occur even in simple two-dimensional regions: corner points can have fractional coordinates, not the integer ones we see in the specially constructed problems in this text. Making 3.75 skateboards and 5.45 dolls is not possible. Integer programming, a special type of linear programming, is used when it is not possible to use fractional answers.

The Simplex Method

Several methods are used to solve the typically large linear programming problems solved in practice. The oldest method is the **simplex method,** which is still the most commonly used. Devised by the American mathematician George Dantzig (see Spotlight 4.2), this ingenious mathematical invention makes it possible to find the best corner point by evaluating only a tiny fraction of all the corners. With the use of the simplex method, a problem that might be impossible to solve if each corner point had to be checked can be solved in a few minutes or even a few seconds on a typical business computer.

The operation of the simplex method may be likened to the behavior of an ant crawling on the edges of a polyhedron (a solid with flat sides) looking for an optimal corner point—one that gives highest profit (Figure 4.21). The ant cannot see where the optimal corner is. As a result, if it were to wander along the edges randomly, it might take a long time to reach that corner. The ant will do much better if it has a temperature clue to let it know it is getting warmer (closer to the optimal corner) or colder (farther from the optimal corner).

Think of the simplex method as a way of calculating these temperature hints. We begin at any corner. All neighboring corners are evaluated to see which ones are warmer and which are colder. A new corner is chosen from among the warmer ones, and the evaluation of neighbors is repeated—this time checking neighbors of the new corner. The process ends when we arrive at a corner all of whose neighbors are colder than it is.

Part of what the simplex method has going for it is that it works faster in practice than its worst-case behavior would lead us to believe. Although mathematicians have devised artificial cases for which the simplex method bogs down in unacceptable amounts of arithmetic, the examples arising from real applications are never like that. This may be the world's most impressive counterexample to Murphy's law, which says that if something can go wrong, it will.

Although the simplex method usually avoids visiting every corner, it may require visiting many intermediate ones as it moves from the starting corner to the optimal one. The simplex method has to search along edges on the boundary of

FIGURE 4.21
The simplex method can be compared to an ant crawling along the edges of a polyhedron, looking for the "target"—the optimal corner point.

Father of Linear Programming Recalls Its Origins

George Dantzig is professor of operations research and computer science at Stanford University. He is credited with inventing the linear programming technique called the simplex method. Since its invention in the 1940s, the simplex method has provided solutions to linear programming problems that have saved both industry and the military time and money. Dantzig talks about the background of his famous technique:

Initially, all the work we did had to do with military planning. During World War II, we were planning on a very extensive scale. The civilian population and the military were all performing scheduling and planning tasks, perhaps on a larger scale than at any time in history. And this was the case up until about 1950. From 1950 on, the whole emphasis shifted from military planning to practical planning for the civilian population, and industry picked it up.

The first areas of industry to use linear programming were the petroleum refineries. They used it for blending gasoline. Nowadays, all of the refineries in the world (except for one) use linear programming methods. They are one of the biggest users of it, and it's been picked up by every other industry you can think of—the forestry industry, the steel industry—you could fill up a book with all the different places it's used.

The question of why linear programming wasn't invented before World War II is an interesting one. In the postwar period, various technologies just evolved that had never been there before. Computers were one example. These technologies were talked about before.

You can go back in history and you'll find papers on them, but these were isolated cases that never went anywhere.

In the immediate postwar period, everything just fermented and began to happen. One of the things that began to happen was linear programming. Mathematicians as well as economists and others who do practical planning and scheduling began to ask questions: How could you formulate the process as a sort of mathematical system? How could computers be used to make this happen?

The problems we solve nowadays have thousands of equations, sometimes a million variables. One of the things that still amazes me is to see a program run on the computer—and to see the answer come out. If we think of the number of combinations of different solutions that we're trying to choose the best of, it's akin to the stars in the heavens. Yet we solve them in a matter of moments. This, to me, is staggering. Not that we can solve them—but that we can solve them so rapidly and efficiently.

The simplex method has been used now for roughly 50 years. There has been steady work going on trying to use different versions of the simplex method, nonlinear methods, and interior methods. It has been recognized that certain classes of problems can be solved much more rapidly by special algorithms than by using the simplex method. If I were to say what my field of specialty is, it is in looking at these different methods and seeing which are more promising than others. There's a lot of promise in this—there's always something new to be looked at.

the polyhedron. If it happens that there are a great many small edges lying between the starting corner and the optimal one, the simplex method must operate like a slow-moving bus that stops on every block.

In the introduction to this chapter, we noted that linear programming accounts for over 50% and possibly as much as 90% of nonroutine computer time used for management decisions. Although there are alternatives to the simplex method, much of that computer time is spent using the simplex method.

Many computer programs are available that will use the simplex method to give you an optimal production policy if you just supply the computer with the constraint inequalities and profit formula. Simplex method programs can be found in a variety of places, among which are spreadsheets, packages of mathematics programs designed for business applications or finite mathematics courses, and large "all-purpose" mathematics packages. (See Note at the end of Suggested Readings.) We hope you have access to such a program and try to use it. For this purpose, we have included some exercises (43 through 46) in this chapter that are larger and more realistic than the ones we have been solving graphically. A graphical solution is only possible for problems limited to two products; these special exercises involve more than two products.

An Alternative to the Simplex Method

In 1984, Narendra Karmarkar (see Figure 4.22), a mathematician working at Bell Laboratories, devised an alternative method for linear programming that finds the optimal corner point in fewer steps than the simplex algorithm by making use of search routes through the interior of the feasible region. The potential applica-

FIGURE 4.22
Narendra Karmarkar, a researcher at AT&T Bell Laboratories, invented a powerful new linear programming algorithm that solves many complex linear programming problems faster and more efficiently than any previous method.

tions of Karmarkar's algorithm are important to a lot of industries, including telephone communications and the airlines (see Spotlight 4.3). Routing millions of long-distance calls, for example, means deciding how to use the resources of long-distance landlines, repeater amplifiers, and satellite terminals to best advantage. The problem is similar to the juice company's need to find the best use of its stocks of juice to create the most profitable mix of products.

American Airlines worked with Karmarkar to see if his algorithm could cut fuel costs. According to Thomas Cook, director of operations research for American Airlines, "It's big dollars. We're hoping we can solve harder problems faster, and we think there's definite potential."

In the 1980s, scientists at Bell Labs applied Karmarkar's algorithm to a problem of unprecedented complexity: deciding how to economically build telephone links between cities so that calls can get from any city to any other, possibly being relayed through intermediate cities. Figure 4.23 shows one such linking. The number of possible linkings is unimaginably large, so picking the most economical one is difficult. For any given linking, there is also the problem of deciding how to economically route calls through the network to reach their destinations.

Although difficult, these problems are definitely worth solving. Nat Levine, director of the transmission facilities planning center at Bell Labs, speculated that if one found the best solution, "the savings could be in the hundreds of millions of dollars." Work on these problems at Bell Labs involved a linear programming problem with about 800,000 variables, which Karmarkar's algorithm solved in 10 hours of computer time. Scientists involved believe that the problem might have taken weeks to solve if the simplex method had been used. It appears that for some kinds of linear programming problems, Karmarkar's algorithm is a big improvement over the simplex method.

FIGURE 4.23
A map of the United States showing one conceivable network of major communication lines connecting major cities. Routing millions of calls over this immense network requires sophisticated linear programming techniques and high-speed computers.

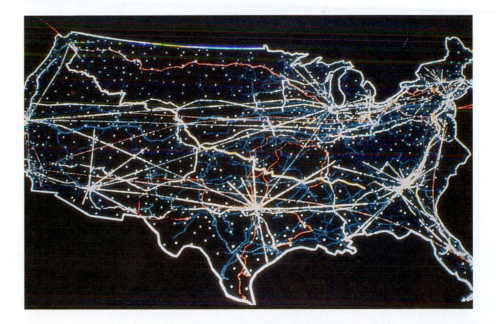

SPOTLIGHT

4.3

Finding Fast Algorithms Means Better Airline Service

Linear programming techniques have a direct impact on the efficiency and profitability of major airlines. Thomas Cook, director of operations research at American Airlines, was interviewed in 1985 concerning his ideas on why optimal solutions are essential to his business:

Finding an optimal solution means finding the best solution. Let's say you are trying to minimize a cost function of some kind. For example, we may want to minimize the excess costs related to scheduling crews, hotels, and other costs that are not associated with flight time. So we try to minimize that excess cost, subject to a lot of constraints, such as the amount of time a pilot can fly, how much rest time is needed, and so forth.

An optimal solution, then, is either a minimum-cost solution or a maximizing solution. For example, we might want to maximize the profit associated with assigning aircrafts to the schedule; so we assign large aircraft to high-need segments and small aircraft to low-load segments. Whether it's a minimum or maximum solution depends on what function we are trying to optimize.

The simplex method, which was developed some 50 years ago by George Dantzig, has been very useful at American Airlines and, indeed, at a lot of large businesses. The difference between his method and Narendra Karmarkar's is speed. Finding fast solutions to linear programming problems is also esssen-

tial. With an algorithm like Karmarkar's, which is 50 to 100 times faster than the simplex method, we could do a lot of things that we couldn't do otherwise. For example, some applications could be real-time applications, as opposed to batch applications. So instead of running a job overnight and getting an answer the next morning, we could actually key in the data or access the data base, generate the matrix, and come up with a solution that could be implemented a few minutes after keying in the data.

A good example of this kind of application is what we call a major weather disruption. If we get a major weather disruption at one of the hubs, such as Dallas or Chicago, then a lot of flights may get canceled, which means we have a lot of crews and airplanes in the wrong places. What we need is a way to put that whole operation back together again so that the crews and airplanes are in the right places. That way, we minimize the cost of the disruption as well as passenger inconvenience.

In order to solve that problem in an optimal fashion we need something as fast as Karmarkar's algorithm. In the absence of that, we'll have to come up with some heuristic ways of solving it that won't be optimal.

We can also apply fast solution methods to new problems, and even to problems that we wouldn't have tried using the simplex method. I think that's the primary reason for the excitement.

REVIEW VOCABULARY

Corner point principle   The principle that states that there is a corner point of the feasible region that yields the optimal solution.

Feasible point   A possible solution (but not necessarily the best) to a linear programming problem. With just two products, we can think of a feasible point as a point on the plane.

Feasible region   The set of all feasible points, that is, possible solutions to a linear programming problem. For problems with just two products, the feasible region is a part of the plane.

Feasible set   Another term for **feasible region.**

Linear programming   A set of organized methods of management science used to solve problems of finding optimal solutions, while at the same time respecting certain important constraints. The mathematical formulations of the constraints in linear programming problems are linear equations and inequalities. Mixture problems are usually solved by some type of linear programming.

Minimum constraint   An inequality in a mixture problem that gives a minimum quantity of a product. Negative quantities can never be produced.

Mixture chart   A table displaying the relevant data in a linear programming mixture problem. The table has a row for each product and a column for each resource, for any nonzero minimums, and for the profit.

Mixture problem   A problem in which a variety of resources available in limited quantities can be combined in different ways to make different products. It is usually desired to find the way of combining the resources that produces the most profit.

Optimal production policy   A corner point of the feasible region where the profit formula has a maximum value.

Production policy   A point in the feasible set, interpreted as specifying how many units of each product are to be made.

Profit formula   The expression, involving the unknown quantities such as x and y, that tells how much profit results from a particular production policy.

Profit line   In a two-dimensional, two-product, linear programming problem, the set of all feasible points that yield the same profit.

Resource constraint   An inequality in a mixture problem that reflects the fact that no more of a resource can be used than what is available.

Simplex method   One of a number of algorithms for solving linear programming problems.

SUGGESTED READINGS

ANDERSON, DAVID R., DENNIS J. SWEENEY, AND THOMAS A. WILLIAMS. *An Introduction to Management Science: Quantitative Approaches to Decision Making,* West, St. Paul, Minn., 1985. A business management text with seven chapters on linear programming.

BARNETT, RAYMOND A., AND MICHAEL R. ZIEGLER. *Finite Mathematics for Business, Economics, Life Sciences and Social Sciences,* 7th ed., Prentice Hall, Upper Saddle River, N.J., 1996. Chapter 5 presents both the geometric approach done here and the simplex method, with attention given to the geometric aspects of the simplex method.

GASS, SAUL I. *An Illustrated Guide to Linear Programming,* McGraw-Hill, New York, 1970. An engagingly written beginner's approach that emphasizes the formulation of problems more than algebraic technique.

GASS, SAUL I. *Decision Making, Models, and Algorithms,* Krieger, Melbourne, Fla., 1991. This unique book combines serious applied mathematics, including 12 chapters on linear programming, with a wonderful chatty style.

MEYER, WALTER. *Concepts of Mathematical Modeling,* McGraw-Hill, New York, 1984. Chapter 4 discusses several other types of linear programming problems, including minimization problems, and the "transportation problem," for which there is a special algorithm, and linear programming problems in which the corner points must have coordinates that are whole numbers, not fractions.

Note: Simplex software can be found in *Maple* (keyword is *simplex*), *Mathematica* (keyword is *LinearProgramming*), in both *Lotus 1-2-3* and *MSExcel* via *Solver,* and in other software packages, especially those intended for quantitative mathematics courses focusing on business applications.

SUGGESTED WEB SITE

www.informs.org   This Web site is maintained by the Institure for Operations Research and the Management Sciences, the main professional organization in these fields in the United States. It contains information on (and/or links to) news items about operations research and management science and employment opportunities and summer internships; it also has a student newsletter. Much of the material is written in a nontechnical style.

SKILLS CHECK

1. Where do the lines $2x + 6y = 36$ and $y = 3$ intersect?

   (a) At the point (3, 5)
   (b) At the point (9, 3)
   (c) At the point (0, 6)

2. Where do the lines $3x + y = 13$ and $2x + 3y = 18$ intersect?

   (a) At the point (3, 4)
   (b) At the point (6, 2)
   (c) At the point (3, 2)

3. Which of these points lie in the region $4x + 3y \leq 24$?

   (a) Points (5, 2) and (3, 4)
   (b) Points (2, 5) and (3, 4)
   (c) Points (5, 2) and (2, 5)

4. What is the resource constraint for this situation? Producing a bench (x) requires 2 boards, and producing a table (y) requires 5 boards. There are 25 boards available.

   (a) $x + y \leq 25$
   (b) $2x + 5y \leq 25$
   (c) $5x + 2y \leq 25$

5. What are the resource inequalities of this situation? A tart requires 3 oz. of fruit and 2 oz. of dough; a pie requires 13 oz. of fruit and 7 oz. of dough. There are 140 oz. of fruit and 90 oz. of dough available. Each tart earns 6 cents profit; each pie earns 25 cents profit.

   (a) $3x + 2y \leq 140$
   $13x + 7y \leq 90$
   $x \geq 0, y \geq 0$
   (b) $3x + 13y \leq 140$
   $2x + 7y \leq 90$
   $x \geq 0, y \geq 0$
   (c) $3x + 2y \leq 6$
   $13x + 7y \leq 25$
   $x \geq 0, y \geq 0$

6. What is the profit formula for this situation? A tart requires 3 oz. of fruit and 2 oz. of dough; a pie requires 13 oz. of fruit and 7 oz. of dough. There are 140 oz. of fruit and 90 oz. of dough available. Each tart earns 6 cents profit; each pie earns 25 cents profit.

   (a) $P = 140x + 90y$
   (b) $P = 70/3x + 18/5y$
   (c) $P = 6x + 25y$

7. Graph the feasible region identified by the inequalities

   $2x + 4y \leq 20$
   $4x + 2y \leq 16$
   $x \geq 0, y \geq 0$

8. Which of these points is *not* in the feasible region of the graph drawn in Exercise 7?

   (a) (2, 4)
   (b) (1, 1)
   (c) (10, 0)

EXERCISES   ▲ *Optional.*   ■ *Advanced.*   ◆ *Discussion.*

Note: Restrict all graphs to the first quadrant, where both x and y are positive, since that is the only part of the xy-plane needed in our mixture problems.

Graphing

1.   Using intercepts, the points where the lines cross the axes, graph each line.

    (a) $2x + 3y = 12$ (d) $7x + 4y = 42$
    (b) $3x + 5y = 30$ (e) $x = 15$
    (c) $4x + 3y = 24$ (f) $y = 4$

2.   Using intercepts, the points where the lines cross axes, graph each line.

    (a) $5x + 4y = 20$ (d) $6x + 5y = 15$
    (b) $7x + 6y = 84$ (e) $y = 9$
    (c) $4x + 5y = 60$ (f) $x = 12$

3.   Graph both lines on the same axes. Put a dot where the lines intersect. Use algebra to find the x- and y-coordinates of the point of intersection.

    (a) $3x + 4y = 18$ and $x = 2$
    (b) $3x + 5y = 45$ and $y = 6$

4.   Graph both lines on the same axes. Put a dot where the lines intersect. Use algebra to find the x- and y-coordinates of the point of intersection.

    (a) $5x + 3y = 60$ and $x = 9$
    (b) $5x + 2y = 30$ and $y = 10$

Resource-Constraint Inequalities

5.   Graph the line and half plane corresponding to the inequality, a typical constraint from a mixture problem.

    (a) $x \geq 8$ (c) $5x + 3y \leq 15$
    (b) $y \geq 5$ (d) $4x + 5y \leq 30$

6.   Graph the line and half plane corresponding to the inequality, a typical constraint from a mixture problem.

    (a) $x \geq 3$ (c) $3x + 2y \leq 18$
    (b) $y \geq 11$ (d) $7x + 2y \leq 42$

In Exercises 7–10, for each description, write an appropriate resource-constraint inequality. The unknown to use for each product is given in parentheses.

7.   One bridesmaid's bouquet (x) requires 4 roses, and one corsage (y) requires 2 roses. There are 28 roses available.

8.   Pruning a large tree (x) takes 2 hours, and pruning a small tree (y) takes 1 hour. There are 40 hours of pruning time available.

9.   Manufacturing one package of hot dogs (x) requires 6 ounces of beef, and manufacturing one package of bologna (y) requires 4 ounces of beef. There are 240 ounces of beef available.

10.   It takes 30 feet of 12-inch board to make one bookcase (x); it takes 72 feet of 12-inch board to make one table (y). There are 420 feet of 12-inch board available.

Graphing the Feasible Region

Graph the feasible region, label each line segment bounding it with the appropriate equation, and give the coordinates of every corner point.

11. $x \geq 0; y \geq 0; 2x + y \leq 8$

12. $x \geq 0; y \geq 0; 2x + 5y \leq 50$

13. $x \geq 10; y > 0; 3x + 5y \leq 120$

14. $x \geq 0; y \geq 4; x + y \leq 25$

15. $x \geq 2; y \geq 6; 3x + 2y \leq 30$

16. $x \geq 8; y \geq 5; 5x + 4y \leq 80$

Finding Points in the Feasible Region

Determine whether the points (a) (2, 4) and/or (b) (10, 6) are points of the given feasible regions:

17.   The feasible regions of Exercises 11, 13, and 15.

18.   The feasible regions of Exercises 12, 14, and 16.

19.   In the toy problem, x represents the number of skateboards and y the number of dolls. Using the version of that problem whose feasible region is presented in Figure 4.5b (page 126), and the profit formula, $2.30x + 3.70y$, write a sentence giving the maximum profit and describing the production policy that gives that profit.

20.   In the toy problem, x represents the number of skateboards and y the number of dolls. Using the version of that problem whose feasible region is presented in Figure 4.5b (page 126), and the profit formula, $5.50x + 1.80y$, write a sentence giving the maximum profit and describing the production policy that gives that profit.

Finding the Point of Intersection of Two Resource Constraints

21.   Graph both lines on the same axes. Put a dot where the lines intersect. Use algebra to find the x- and y-coordinates of the point of intersection.

(a) $5x + 4y = 22$ and $2x + 4y = 16$
(b) $2x + 2y = 14$ and $3x + 4y = 24$

22.   Graph both lines on the same axes. Put a dot where the lines intersect. Use algebra to find the x- and y-coordinates of the point of intersection.

(a) $x + 2y = 10$ and $5x + y = 14$
(b) $5x + 10y = 130$ and $7x + 4y = 112$

Graphing the Feasible Region

Graph the feasible region, label each line segment bounding it with the appropriate equation, and give the coordinates of every corner point.

23. $x \geq 0; y \geq 0; 3x + y \leq 9; x + 2y \leq 8$

24. $x \geq 0; y \geq 0; 2x + y \leq 4; 3x + 3y \leq 9$

25. $x \geq 0; y \geq 2; x + 2y \leq 10; 5x + y \leq 14$

26. $x \geq 4; y \geq 0; 5x + 4y \leq 60; x + y \leq 13$

27. $x \geq 3; y \geq 2; x + y \leq 10; 2x + 3y \leq 24$

28. $x \geq 2; y \geq 3; 3x + y \leq 18; 6x + 4y \leq 48$

Finding Points in the Feasible Region

Determine whether the points (a) (4, 2) and/or (b) (1, 3) are points of the given feasible regions:

29.   The feasible regions of Exercises 23, 25, and 27.

30.   The feasible regions of Exercises 24, 26, and 28.

Mixture Problems

Exercises 31 to 42 each has several steps leading to a complete solution to a mixture problem. Practice in a specific step of the solution algorithm can be obtained by working out just that step for several problems. The steps are

(a)   Make a mixture chart for the problem.
(b)   Using the mixture chart, write the profit formula and the resource- and minimum-constraint inequalities.
(c)   Draw the feasible region for those constraints and find the coordinates of the corner points.
(d)   Evaluate the profit information at the corner points to determine the production policy that best answers the question.
(e)   *Requires Technology.* Compare your answer with the one you get from running the same problem on a simplex algorithm computer program.

31.   A clothing manufacturer has 600 yards of cloth available to make shirts and decorated vests. Each shirt requires 3 yards of material and provides a profit of $5. Each vest requires 2 yards of material and provides a profit of $2. The manufacturer wants to guarantee that under all circumstances there are minimums of 100 shirts and 30 vests produced. How many of each garment should be made in order to maximize profit? If there are no minimum quantities, how, if at all, does the optimal production policy change?

32.   A car maintenance shop must decide how many oil changes and how many tune-ups can be scheduled in a typical week. The oil change takes 20 minutes. The tune-up requires 100 minutes. The

maintenance shop makes a profit of $15 on an oil change and $65 on a tune-up. What mix of services should the shop schedule if the typical week has available 8000 minutes for these two types of services? How, if at all, do the maximum profit and optimal production policy change if the shop is required to schedule at least 50 oil changes and 20 tune-ups?

33.   A clerk in a bookstore has 90 minutes at the end of each workday to process orders received by mail or on voice mail. The store has found that a typical mail order brings in a profit of $30 and a typical voice-mail order brings in a profit of $40. Each mail order takes 10 minutes to process and each voice-mail order takes 15 minutes. How many of each type of order should the clerk process? How, if at all, do the maximum profit and optimal processing policy change if the clerk must process at least 3 mail and 2 voice-mail orders?

34.   In a certain medical office, a routine office visit requires 5 minutes of doctors' time and a comprehensive office visit requires 25 minutes of doctors' time. In a typical week, there are 1800 minutes of doctors' time available. If the medical office clears $30 from a routine visit and $50 from a comprehensive visit, how many of each should be scheduled per week? How, if at all, do the maximum profit and optimal production policy change if the office is required to schedule at least 20 routine visits and 30 comprehensive ones?

35.   A bakery makes 600 specialty breads — multigrain or herb — each week. Standing orders from restaurants are for 100 multigrain breads and 200 herb breads. The profit on each multigrain bread is $8 and on herb bread, $10. How many breads of each type should the bakery make in order to maximize profit? How, if at all, do the maximum profit and optimal production policy change if the bakery has no standing orders?

36.   A student has decided that passing a mathematics course will, in the long run, be twice as valuable as passing any other kind of course. The student estimates that to pass a typical math course will require 12 hours a week to study and do homework. The student estimates that any other course will require only 8 hours a week. The student has available 48 hours for study per week. How many of each kind of course should the student take? (*Hint:* The profit could be viewed as 2 "value point" for passing a math course and 1 "value point" for passing any other course.) How, if at all, do the maximum value and optimal course mix change if the student decides to take at least 2 math and 2 other courses?

Problems 37 to 42 require finding the point of intersection of two lines each corresponding to a resource constraint.

37.   Webs-R-Us creates and maintains Web sites for client companies. There are two types of Web sites: "hot," sites that change their layout frequently but keep their content for long times; and "cool," sites that keep their layout for a while but frequently change their content. To maintain a "hot" site requires 1.5 hours of layout time and 1 hour for content changes. To maintain a "cool" site requires 1 hour of layout time and 2 hours for content changes. Every day Webs-R-Us has 12 hours for layout changes and 16 hours for content changes. Net profit is $50 for a set of changes on a "hot" site and $250 for a set of changes on a "cool" site. In order to maximize profit, how many of each type of site should Webs-R-Us maintain daily? How, if at all, do the maximum profit and optimal policy change if the company must maintain at least 2 "hot" and 3 "cool" sites daily?

38.   A paper recycling company uses scrap cloth and scrap paper to make two different grades of recycled paper. A single batch of grade A recycled paper is made from 25 pounds of scrap cloth and 10 pounds of scrap paper, whereas one batch of grade B recycled paper is made from 10 pounds of scrap cloth and 20 pounds of scrap paper. The company has 100 pounds of scrap cloth and 120 pounds of scrap paper on hand. A batch of grade A paper brings a profit of $500, whereas a batch of grade B paper brings a profit of $250. What amounts of each grade should be made? How, if at all, do the maximum profit and optimal production policy change if the company is required to produce at least 1 batch of each type?

39.   Jerry Murphy has a 100-acre farm that he is dividing into 1-acre plots, on each of which he builds a house. He then sells the house and land. It costs him $20,000 to build a modest house and $40,000 to build a deluxe house. He has $2,600,000 to cover these costs. The profits are $25,000 for a modest house and $60,000 for a deluxe house. How many of each type of house should he build in order to maximize profit? How, if at all, do the maximum profit and optimal production policy change if Murphy is required to build at least 20 of each type of house?

40.   The maximum production of a soft-drink bottling company is 5000 cartons per day. The company produces regular and diet drinks, and must make at least 600 cartons of regular and 1000 cartons of diet per day. Production costs are $1.00 per carton of regular and $1.20 per carton of diet. The daily operating budget is $5400. How many cartons of each type of drink should be produced if the profit is $0.10 per regular and $0.11 per diet? How, if at all, do the maximum profit and optimal bottling policy change if the company has no minimum required production?

41.   Wild Things raises pheasants and partridges to restock the woodlands and has room to raise 100 birds during the season. The cost of raising one bird is $20 per pheasant and $30 per partridge. The Wildlife Foundation pays Wild Things for the birds; the latter clears a profit of $14 per pheasant and $16 per partridge. Wild Things has $2400 available to cover costs. How many of each type of bird should they raise? How, if at all, do the maximum profit and optimal restocking policy change if Wild Things is required to raise at least 20 pheasants and 10 partridges?

42.   Lights Afire makes desk lamps and floor lamps, on which the profits are $2.65 and $4.67, respectively. The company has 1200 hours of labor and $4200 for materials each week. A desk lamp takes 0.8 hour of labor and $4 for materials; a floor lamp takes 1.0 hour of labor and $3 for materials. What production policy maximizes profit? How, if at all, do the maximum profit and optimal production policy change if Lights Afire wants to produce at least 150 desk lamps and 200 floor lamps per week?

In Exercises 43 to 46, there are more than two products in the problem. Although you cannot solve these problems using the graphical method, you can do these steps:

- ■ (a)   Make a mixture chart for each problem.
- ■ (b)   Using the mixture chart, write the resource- and minimum-constraint inequalities. Also write the profit formula.
-    (c)   *Requires Technology.* If you have a simplex method program available, run the program to obtain the optimal production policy.

43.   A toy company makes three types of toy, each of which must be processed by three machines: a shaper, a smoother, and a painter. Each Toy A requires 1 hour in the shaper, 2 hours in the smoother, and 1 hour in the painter, and brings in a $4 profit. Each Toy B requires 2 hours in the shaper, 1 hour in the smoother, and 3 hours in the painter, and brings in a $5 profit. Each Toy C requires 3 hours in the shaper, 2 hours in the smoother, and 1 hour in the painter, and brings in a $9 profit. The shaper can work at most 50 hours per week, the smoother 40 hours, and the painter 60 hours. What production policy would maximize the toy company's profit?

44.   A rustic furniture company handcrafts chairs, tables, and beds. It has three workers, Chris, Sue, and Juan. Chris can only work 80 hours per month, but Sue and Juan can each put in 200 hours. Each of these artisans has special skills. To make a chair takes 1 hour of Chris's time, 3 from Sue, and 2 from Juan. A table needs 3 hours from Chris, 5 from Sue, and 4 from Juan. A bed requires 5 hours from Chris, 4 from Sue, and 8 from Juan. Even artisans are concerned about maximizing their profit, so what product mix should they stick with if they get $100 profit per chair, $250 per table, and $350 per bed?

45.   A candy manufacturer has 1000 pounds of chocolate, 200 pounds of nuts, and 100 pounds of fruit in stock. The Special Mix requires 3 pounds of chocolate, 1 pound each of nuts and fruit, and brings in $10. The Regular Mix requires 4 pounds of chocolate, 0.5 pound of nuts, and no fruit, and brings in $6. The Purist Mix requires 5 pounds of

chocolate, no nuts or fruit, and brings in $4. How many boxes of each type should be produced to maximize profit?

46.   A gourmet coffee distributor has on hand 17,600 ounces of African coffee, 21,120 ounces of Brazilian coffee, and 12,320 ounces of Colombian coffee. It sells four blends: Excellent, Southern, World, and Special on which it makes these per-pound profits, respectively: $1.80, $1.40, $1.20, and $1.00. One pound of Excellent is 16 ounces of Colombian; it is not a blend at all. One pound of Southern consists of 12 ounces of Brazilian and 4 ounces of Colombian. One pound of World requires 6 ounces of African, 8 of Brazilian, and 2 of Colombian. One pound of Special is made up of 10 ounces of African and 6 ounces of Brazilian. What product mix should the gourmet coffee distributor prepare in order to maximize profit?

47.   Explain why finding a point of the feasible region that gives the maximum profit would be time-consuming and nearly impossible if we did not have the corner point principle.

48.   Which steps of the pictorial method are also required of a person who is solving a linear programming problem by using a simplex method computer program?

Additional Exercises

49.   Courtesy Calls makes telephone calls for businesses and charities. A profit of $0.50 is made for each business call and $0.40 for each charity call. It takes 4 minutes (on average) to make a business call and 6 minutes (on average) to make a charity call. If there are 240 minutes of calling time to be distributed each day, how should that time be spent so that Courtesy Calls makes a maximum profit? What changes, if any, occur in the maximum profit and optimal production policy if, every day, they must make at least 12 business and 10 charity calls?

50.   A refinery mixes high-octane and low-octane fuels to produce regular and premium gasolines. The profits per gallon on the two gasolines are $0.30 and $0.40, respectively. One gallon of premium gasoline is produced by mixing 0.5 gallon of each of the fuels. One gallon of regular gasoline is produced by mixing 0.25 gallon of high octane with 0.75 gallon of low octane. If there are 500 gallons of high octane and 600 gallons of low octane available, how many gallons of each gasoline should the refinery make? How, if at all, do the maximum profit and optimal production policy change if the refinery is required to produce at least 100 gallons of each gasoline?

51.   A toy manufacturer makes bikes, for a profit of $12, and wagons, for a profit of $10. To produce a bike requires 2 hours of machine time and 4 hours painting time. To produce a wagon requires 3 hours machine time and 2 hours painting time. There are 12 hours of machine time and 16 hours of painting time available per day. How many of each toy should be produced to maximize profit? How, if at all, do the maximum profit and optimal production policy change if the manufacturer must daily produce at least 2 bikes and 2 wagons?

52.   The planner for the office holiday party needs to get the maximum "happiness points" out of the choices made for the foods. There are two kinds of foods that could be purchased: fancy foods and junk foods. Each order of fancy food costs $50 per order and adds 60 "happiness points" to the party. Each order of junk food costs $30 and adds 40 "happiness points" to the party. To satisfy both the formal and the casual types at the office, it is necessary to order at least 6 fancy foods and 5 junk foods. If there is $900 to spend, how many of each kind of food should the planner order? If there are no minimum quantities, how, if at all, does the food order change?

Exercises 53 to 58 are designed to highlight areas where the interface between the linear programming model and the reality of specific situations presents us with interesting discussion possibilities. These exercises do not have "right answers." Exercise 53 gives a concrete situation that could be used in the other questions.

◆   53.   You are in charge of a business that produces sandwiches for snack bars. Make a list of your products (kinds of sandwiches), the resources you would need (sandwich ingredients), and the profit you might expect to get for each product. You need not specify the recipes numerically or the amounts of the resources available.

◆ 54. Discuss the validity of the corner point principle if the solution (x, y) to the mixture problem is required not only to lie in the feasible region but also to have integer coordinates. In the sandwich problem (Exercise 53), would there be a useful meaning to a fractional number of some kind of sandwich?

◆ 55. A linear programming analysis tells the sandwich company to stop making 7 of the 30 sandwiches in its product line. What are some business considerations that might suggest that this would be a bad business decision? How could linear programming still be used to help the sandwich company if it decided that it did not want to drop any of the 30?

◆ 56. In a mixture problem we view recipes as fixed, but in practice this is not always true. For example, bolognas having only slightly different percentages of beef and pork all taste the same to the customers. What might prompt the manufacturer to vary a recipe? What effect might the varying have on the profit function, the feasible region, and the optimal product mix?

◆ 57. Firms often give discounts for large-volume purchases. Does this necessarily contradict the assumption of a fixed (constant) profit on each unit sold? In examining this situation, you should note that discounts for large-volume purchases might apply not only to the products sold by a manufacturer but also to the prices paid by the manufacturer for resources.

◆ 58. We learn in economics that prices are determined by the interplay of supply and demand. For example, the price of a product may fall if a large quantity of it is available. In mixture problems, however, we assume a fixed (constant) profit regardless of how much is produced. Is there a contradiction here? Could the model be adjusted to incorporate this economic fact of life?

TECHNOLOGY CORNER

Solving Mixture Problems

Spreadsheets provide a dynamic environment to test scenarios. As a simple example, suppose that two jelly brands, Wholesome and Yummy, are created as a mix of juice and sugar. Each pint of Wholesome is formed as a mix of 3 cups juice and 2 cups sugar, and sells for a profit of $12. Each pint of Yummy is formed as a mix of 2 cups juice and 3 cups sugar, and sells for a profit of $10. (Much of the volume boils away during processing.) Suppose partial units are feasible, so the number of pints produced does not have to be a whole number. Assuming we have access to 12 cups of juice and 13 cups of sugar, we want to allocate these resources to maximize profits.

Let x be the amount of Wholesome produced, and y the amount of Yummy produced. Then we want to maximize $12x + 13y$ under the restrictions that the amount of juice used, $3x + 2y$, is no more than 12; and the amount of sugar used, $2x + 3y$, is no more than 13.

The spreadsheet shown in Figure 4.24 models this situation. The top row labels the columns: "x" and "y" are the number of pints of brands Wholesome and Yummy jelly produced. The next columns track the amount of juice and sugar required for the process, and the final column tracks the profit gained from the choice of x and y.

On the second row, cells **A2** and **B2** contain the number of pints of Wholesome and Yummy produced.

Cell **C2** contains the juice requirement formula:
=3*A2+2*B2
Cell **D2** contains the sugar formula:
=2*A2+3B2
Cell **E2** contains the profit formula:
=12*A2+10*B2

Spreadsheets allow one to copy formulas to relative locations. Therefore, if the cells **C2, D2,** and **E2** are selected and copied to additional rows in their columns, the spreadsheet will allow us to test several possibilities. Three scenarios are shown on the spreadsheet. The additional rows of zeros occur because no values for x and y have yet been placed on these rows.

We have the resources to produce the first scenario, one pint of each brand, as well as the second, two pints of each brand. As you would expect, the profit for the second scenario is twice that of the first. The third scenario, 2.5 pints of each brand, has a greater profit but requires more juice than is available, and is therefore not possible.

TASK 1.   Continue using the spreadsheet shown in Figure 4.24. Find more scenarios that require no more than the available juice and sugar. What production mix of Wholesome and Yummy maximizes the profit?

TASK 2.   Suppose you instead have 20 cups of juice and 15 cups of sugar. Use a spreadsheet to find a production mix that will maximize the profit.

Testing Corner Points

When a mixture problem involves only equations of straight lines, the feasible region will have corners, and the value of the profit function will be maximal at one of these corner points. In the previous exercise, there are several restrictions on the values of x and y: limited amounts of sugar and juice, and x and y must be non-negative. Therefore, four lines bound the feasible region in the previous exercise: $3x + 2y = 12$, $2x + 3y = 13$, $x = 0$, $y = 0$. By carefully plotting these four lines, you will find the four corners of this region are $(0, 0)$, $(4, 0)$, $(0, 13/3)$, and $(2, 3)$. Because of the corner point principle, these are the only four scenarios one must check in order to achieve the maximum profit possible.

TASK 3.   Determine the corner points for the situation when there are 20 cups of juice and 15 cups of sugar. Check these scenarios in order to find a production mix that maximizes the profit.

TASK 4.   Suppose you have 20 cups of juice and 15 cups of sugar, but you are required to make at least 2 pints of Wholesome and at least 2 pints of Yummy. What is the best production mix under these conditions?

Exploration

Establish a situation in which there are three products to produce and three limited resources. Suppose that you earn the same amount of profit per unit for each product. Set up a spreadsheet to model your situation,

	A	B	C	D	E
1	Whole-some	Yummy	Juice Required	Sugar Required	Profit
2	1	1	5	5	22
3	2	2	10	10	44
4	2.5	2.5	12.5	12.5	55
5				0	0
6				0	0
7				0	0
8				0	0
9				0	0
10				0	0
11				0	0

FIGURE 4.24

and attempt (by trial and error) to find a production mix which seems to maximize the profit. (Do not try to find corner points. Finding corner points is much more difficult when more than two products are involved.)

writing projects

1 ▶   Interview a local businessperson who is in charge of deciding the product mix for that business. Must this business take into consideration situations other than minimum and resource constraints? If so, what are these considerations? Find out what methods the person uses to make production policy decisions. Is linear programming used? Are other methods used? If so, what are they? Write a report of your findings, and add some of your own conclusions about the usefulness of linear programming for this business.

2 ▶   In economics, it is often useful to distinguish between a firm that has a monopoly (for example, is the only supplier of a product) and firms that supply only a small share of the market. How would the presence of a monopoly affect the relation between production and price? Would the presence of a monopoly tend to ensure the fixed-profit assumption of linear programming, or would it make it more likely that the interplay of supply and demand would have to be considered in order to have a truly realistic model?

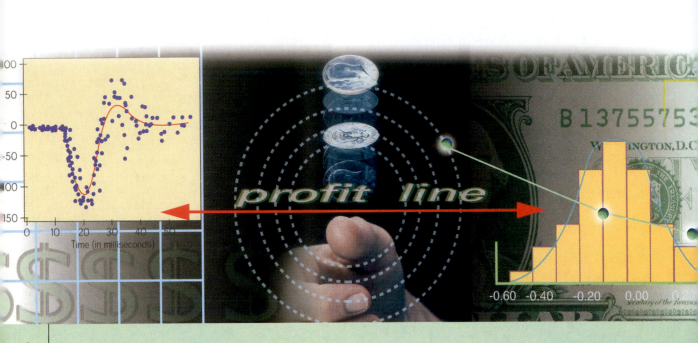

"*We can no more escape data than we can avoid the use of words.*"

Statistics is the science of collecting, organizing, and interpreting numerical facts, which we call *data*. We are bombarded by data in everyday life. Most of us associate "statistics" with the bits of data that appear in news reports: baseball batting averages, imported-car sales, the latest poll of the president's popularity, and the average high temperature for today's date. Advertisements often claim that data show the superiority of the advertiser's product. All sides in public debates about economics, education, and social policy argue from data. Yet the usefulness of statistics goes beyond these everyday examples.

Data are important in the work of many professions, so training in the science of statistics is valuable preparation for a variety of careers. Economists, financial advisers, and policy makers in government and business study the latest data on

Statistics: The Science of Data

5%

18%

32%

40%

$$-0.053 - (3)(0.14) = -0.478$$

$$\sqrt{\dfrac{p(100-p)}{n}}$$

unemployment and inflation. Physicians must understand the origin and trustworthiness of the data that appear in medical journals. Business decisions are based on market research data that reveal consumer tastes. Engineers gather data on the quality and reliability of manufactured products. Most areas of academic study make use of numbers, and therefore also make use of the methods of statistics.

We can no more escape data than we can avoid the use of words. Just as words on a page are meaningless to the illiterate or confusing to the partially educated, so data do not interpret themselves but must be read with understanding. Just as a writer can arrange words into convincing arguments or incoherent nonsense, so data can be compelling, misleading, or simply irrelevant. Statistical literacy, the ability to follow and understand arguments from data, is important for everyone.

Producing Data

"The design of trustworthy methods for producing data is our entry into the subject of statistics."

The news is full of numbers. A TV newscaster informs us that the unemployment rate has dropped to 4.7%. A Gallup poll claims that 45% of Americans are afraid to go out at night because of crime. Where do these numbers come from? Most people aren't personally interviewed to determine whether they are employed. The Gallup poll asks only a few of us if fear of being mugged keeps us indoors at night.

Another day, another headline. This one says "Study Shows Aspirin Prevents Heart Attacks." We read on and learn that the study looked at 22,000 middle-aged doctors. Half took an aspirin every other day, and the other half took a dummy pill. In the aspirin group, 139 doctors suffered a heart attack. The dummy pill group had 239 heart attacks in the same period. Is that difference large enough to show that aspirin really does prevent heart attacks?

To escape the unpleasantness of unemployment and heart attacks, we turn to our favorite advice columnist. Ann Landers has asked her female readers whether they would be content with affectionate treatment by men with no sex ever. Over 90,000 women wrote in, with 72% answering "Yes." Can it really be true that 72% of women feel that way?

How trustworthy numbers are depends first of all on where they came from. You can trust the unemployment rate, but you ought to disbelieve Ann Landers' 72%. This chapter explains why. You will learn to recognize good and bad methods of producing numerical facts, which we call *data*. Understanding how to produce trustworthy data is the first—and the most important—step toward the ability to judge whether conclusions based on data are reliable or not. The design of trustworthy methods for producing data is our entry into the subject of statistics, the science of data.

Sampling

The Bureau of Labor Statistics (see Figure 5.1) wants to know what percent of workers are unemployed. A Gallup poll wants to know what fraction of the public stays home at night because of fear of crime. A quality engineer must estimate what percent of the bearings rolling off an assembly line are defective. In all these situations we want to gather information about a large group of people or things. It is too expensive and time-consuming to contact every worker or inspect every bearing. So we gather information about only part of the group in order to draw conclusions about the whole.

> The entire group of individuals that we want information about is called the **population.** The individuals in a population may be people, animals, or things.
>
> A **sample** is a part of the population that we actually examine in order to gather information.

We often draw conclusions about a whole on the basis of a sample. Everyone has sipped a spoonful of soup and judged the entire bowl on the basis of that taste. But a bowl of soup is homogeneous, so that the taste of a single spoonful represents the whole. Choosing a representative sample from a large and varied population is not so easy. The first step is to say carefully just what population we want to describe. The second step is to say exactly what we want to measure. These preliminary steps can be complicated, as this example illustrates.

FIGURE 5.1
The Web site of the Bureau of Labor Statistics, the government office that produces data on employment, consumer prices, and workers' earnings and working conditions.

Bureau of Labor Statistics BLS

- Data
- Economy at a Glance
- Keyword Search of BLS Web Pages
- Surveys & Programs
- Publications & Research Papers
- Regional Information
- Mission, Management & Jobs
- Other Statistical Sites
- What's New
- Contact Information

E X A M P L E   *The Current Population Survey*

The government's unemployment rate comes from the Current Population Survey (CPS), a sample of about 50,000 households each month. To measure unemployment, we must first specify the population we want to describe. Which age groups will we include? Will we include illegal aliens or people in prisons? What about full-time students? The CPS defines its population as all U.S. residents (whether citizens or not) 16 years of age and over who are civilians and are not in an institution like a prison. The civilian unemployment rate announced in the news refers to this specific population.

The second question is harder: What does it mean to be "unemployed"? Someone who is not looking for work—for example, a full-time student—should not be called unemployed just because she is not working for pay. If you are chosen for the CPS sample, the interviewer first asks whether you are available to work and whether you actually looked for work in the past four weeks. If not, you are neither employed nor unemployed—you are not in the labor force.

If you are in the labor force, the interviewer goes on to ask about employment. Any work for pay or in your own business the week of the survey counts you as employed. So does at least 15 hours of unpaid work in a family business. You are also employed if you have a job but didn't work because of vacation, being on strike, or other good reason. An unemployment rate of 4.7% means that 4.7% of the sample was unemployed, using the exact CPS definitions of both "labor force" and "unemployed." ◆

Bad Sampling Methods

How can we choose a sample that is truly representative of the population? The easiest—but not the best—way to select a sample is to choose individuals close at hand. If we are interested in finding out how many people have jobs, for example, we might go to a shopping mall and ask people passing by if they are employed. A sample selected by taking the members of the population that are easiest to reach is called a **convenience sample.** Convenience samples often produce unrepresentative data.

E X A M P L E   *Convenience Samples*

A sample of mall shoppers is fast and cheap. But people at shopping malls tend to be more prosperous than typical Americans. They are also more likely to be teenagers or retired. What is more, when we decide which people to question, we will tend to choose well-dressed, respectable people and we will tend to avoid poorly dressed, unfriendly, or tough-looking individuals. In short, our shopping mall interviews will not contact a sample that is representative of the entire population, and so will not accurately reflect the nation's rate of unemployment. ◆

Exit poll surveyor with voters.

Our shopping mall sample will almost surely overrepresent middle-class and retired people and underrepresent the poor. This will happen every time we take such a sample. That is, it is a systematic error due to a bad sampling method, not just bad luck on one sample. Such a systematic difference between the results obtained by sampling and the truth about the whole population is called **bias.**

> The design of a study is **biased** if it systematically favors certain outcomes.

EXAMPLE   *Call-in Polls*

Television news programs like to conduct call-in polls of public opinion. The program announces a question and asks viewers to call one telephone number to respond "Yes" and another for "No." Telephone companies charge for these calls. The ABC network program *Nightline* once asked whether the United Nations should continue to have its headquarters in the United States. More than 186,000 callers responded, and 67% said "No."

People who spend the time and money to respond to call-in polls are not representative of the entire adult population. In fact, they tend to be the same people who call radio talk shows. People who feel strongly, especially those with strong negative opinions, are more likely to call. It is not surprising that a different, properly designed sample showed that 72% of adults say "Yes," they want the UN to stay. ◆

Call-in opinion polls are an example of *voluntary response sampling*. A voluntary response sample can easily produce 67% "No" when the truth about the population is close to 72% "Yes."

> A **voluntary response sample** consists of people who choose themselves by responding to a general appeal. Voluntary response samples are biased because people with strong opinions, especially negative opinions, are most likely to respond.

Simple Random Samples

In a voluntary response sample, people choose whether to respond. In a convenience sample, the interviewer makes the choice. In both cases, personal choice produces bias. The statistician's remedy is to allow impersonal chance to choose the sample. A sample chosen by chance allows neither favoritism by the sampler nor self-selection by respondents. Choosing a sample by chance attacks bias by giving all individuals an equal chance to be chosen. Rich and poor, young and old, black and white, all have the same chance to be in the sample.

The simplest way to use chance to select a sample is to place names in a hat (the population) and draw out a handful (the sample). This is the idea of *simple random sampling*.

> A **simple random sample (SRS)** of size n consists of n individuals from the population chosen in such a way that every set of n individuals has an equal chance to be the sample actually selected.

Picturing drawing names from a hat helps us understand what an SRS is. The same picture helps us see that an SRS is a better method of choosing samples than convenience sampling or voluntary response because it doesn't favor any part of the population. But writing names on slips of paper and drawing them from a hat is slow and inconvenient. That's especially true if, like the Current Population Survey, we must draw a sample of size 50,000. We can speed up the process by using a *table of random digits*. In practice, samplers use computers to do the work, but we can do it by hand for small samples.

A **table of random digits** is a long string of the digits 0, 1, 2, 3, 4, 5, 6, 7, 8, 9 with these two properties:

1. Each entry in the table is equally likely to be any of the 10 digits 0 through 9.
2. The entries are independent of each other. That is, knowledge of one part of the table gives no information about any other part.

Table 5.1, on page 174, is a table of random digits. The digits in the table appear in groups of five to make the table easier to read and the rows are numbered so we can refer to them, but the groups and row numbers are just for convenience. The entire table is one long string of randomly chosen digits. There are two steps in using the random digit table to choose a simple random sample:

STEP 1.   **Label**   Give each member of the population a numerical label of the *same length*. Up to 100 items can be labeled with two digits, up to 1000 items can be labeled with three digits, and so on.

STEP 2.   **Table**   To choose a simple random sample, read from Table 5.1 successive groups of digits of the length you used as labels. Your sample contains the individuals whose labels you find in the table. This gives all individuals the same chance because all labels of the same length have the same chance to be found in the table. For example, any pair of digits in the table is equally likely to be any of the 100 possible labels 00, 01, . . . , 99. Ignore any group of digits that was not used as a label or that duplicates a label already in the sample.

EXAMPLE   *Sampling Autos*

An auto manufacturer wants to select 5 of the last 50 cars produced on an assembly line for a very detailed quality inspection. Can you see why allowing the workers to choose 5 cars is likely to cause bias? To avoid bias, we will choose a simple random sample.

STEP 1.   **Label**   Give each car a numerical label. Because two digits are needed to label 50 cars, all labels will have two digits. Let's begin with 00. The labels are 00 to 49, as shown in Figure 5.2. It is also correct to use labels 01 to 50 if you prefer. Be sure to say how you labeled the members of the population.

STEP 2.   **Table**   Now go to Table 5.1. Starting at line 140 (any line will do), we find

    73063   63623   29388   89507   78553   62792   89343   27401

00	01	02	03	04	05	06	07	08	09
10	11	12	13	14	15	16	17	18	19
20	21	22	23	24	25	26	27	28	29
30	31	32	33	34	35	36	37	38	39
40	41	42	43	44	45	46	47	48	49

FIGURE 5.2   The first step in random sampling: assigning labels to 50 cars.

Because our labels are two digits long, we read successive two-digit groups from the table. Ignore groups not used as labels, like the initial 73. Also ignore any repeated labels, like the second 36 in this row, because we can't choose the same car twice. Our sample contains the cars labeled 06, 36, 23, 29, and 38.   ◆

EXAMPLE   *Sampling Housing Units*

Most national sample surveys choose their samples in stages. For example, the Current Population Survey sample design is roughly as follows:

STAGE 1.   Divide the United States into 2007 geographical areas called Primary Sampling Units, or PSUs. (See Figure 5.3.) Select a sample of 754 PSUs. This sample includes the 428 PSUs with the largest population and a random sample of the others.

STAGE 2.   Divide each PSU selected into smaller areas called "blocks." Classify the blocks into "strata" using ethnic and other information and take a random sample within each stratum of blocks.

STAGE 3.   Sort the housing units in each block selected at stage 2 into clusters of four nearby units. Interview the households in a random sample of these clusters.

FIGURE 5.3
A primary sampling unit
(PSU) for the Current
Population Survey.

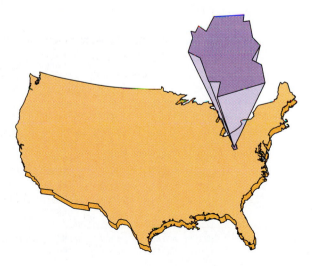

TABLE 5.1   Random Digits

101	03918	86495	47372	21870	28522	99445	38783	83307
102	10041	35095	66357	64569	08993	20429	28569	63809
103	43537	58268	80237	17407	89680	04655	24678	61932
104	64301	47201	31905	60410	80101	33382	95255	10353
105	43857	42186	77011	93839	28380	49296	63311	49713
106	91823	39794	47046	78563	89328	39478	04123	19287
107	34017	87878	35674	39212	98246	29735	09924	27893
108	49105	00755	39242	50472	39581	44036	54518	46865
109	72479	02741	75732	99808	02382	77201	44932	88978
110	84281	45650	28016	77753	39495	41847	19634	82681
111	61589	35486	59500	20060	89769	54870	75586	07853
112	25318	01995	87789	41212	74907	90734	31946	24921
113	40113	37395	51406	98099	43023	70195	07013	72306
114	58420	43526	15539	24845	15582	16780	95286	69021
115	18075	45894	09875	42869	20618	07699	80671	54287
116	52754	73124	93276	71521	59618	44966	37502	15570
117	05255	53579	08239	99174	75548	95776	42314	13093
118	76032	35569	28738	38092	74669	00749	17832	64855
119	97050	31553	32350	51491	53659	89336	36912	05292
120	29030	43074	84602	95131	22769	44680	68492	33987
121	28124	29686	63745	12313	15745	11570	20953	17149
122	97469	41277	90524	36459	22178	63785	20466	67130
123	91754	40784	38916	12949	76104	20556	34001	59133
124	84599	29798	57707	57392	91757	76994	43827	69089
125	06490	42228	94940	10668	62072	58983	10263	08832
126	30666	02218	89355	76117	75167	69005	42479	79865
127	87228	15736	08506	29759	74257	85594	75154	48664
128	45133	49229	32502	99698	68202	44704	39191	73740
129	55713	98670	57794	64795	27102	83420	26630	95009
130	20390	38266	30138	61250	07527	02014	43972	49370
131	13400	68249	32459	41627	56194	93075	50520	96784
132	08900	87788	73717	19287	69954	45917	80026	55598
133	86757	47905	16890	99047	78249	73739	97076	00525
134	19862	54700	18777	22218	25414	13151	54954	80615
135	96282	11576	59837	27429	60015	40338	39435	94021
136	17463	26715	71680	04853	55725	87792	99907	67156
137	44880	55285	95472	57551	24602	98311	63293	58110
138	61911	78152	96341	31473	58398	61602	38143	93833
139	07769	22819	58373	88466	71341	32772	93643	92855
140	73063	63623	29388	89507	78553	62792	89343	27401
141	24187	60720	74055	36902	22047	09091	79368	35408
142	06875	53335	91274	87824	04137	77579	54266	38762
143	23393	37710	46457	03553	58275	11138	18521	59667
144	00980	73632	88008	10060	48563	31874	90785	78923
145	46611	39359	98036	25351	88031	72020	13837	03121
146	56644	79453	49072	30594	73185	81691	29225	70495
147	98350	36891	04873	71321	29929	37145	95906	41005
148	17444	61728	86112	76261	92519	61569	65672	95772
149	45785	21301	89563	23018	60423	50801	70564	45398
150	54369	08513	36838	19805	67827	74938	66946	01206

As the final stage of a national sample, you must choose an SRS of 3 of the 189 clusters in a block. You need three digits to label 189 clusters. Assign the labels 001 to 189 to the clusters (000 to 188 is also OK). Then read three-digit groups from Table 5.1 Check that if you enter at line 135, the clusters chosen are those labeled 157, 001, and 117. You must skip most three-digit groups because they are not labels. ◆

Multistage random samples like the CPS offer practical advantages over a simple random sample. We don't need a list of every address in the nation, just of those in the blocks chosen at stage 2. If need be, we can make up that list by walking around these blocks. Moreover, the households to be interviewed are clustered together in relatively few locations, reducing the travel costs for the interviewers. The price paid for practicality, however, is complexity in actually choosing the sample and in interpreting the results. Because simple random sampling is the essential principle behind all random sampling and because it is also the main building block for more complex samples, we will focus our study on simple random sampling.

Statistical Estimation

We select a sample in order to get information about the population. If the sample is chosen at random, we expect it to resemble the population. So we use a result from the sample to *estimate* a characteristic of the population.

E X A M P L E   *Statistical Estimation*

A Gallup poll asked a sample of 1493 people, "Are you afraid to go outside at night within a mile of your home because of crime?" Of these people, 672 said "Yes." So the percent of the sample who said "Yes" is

$$\frac{672}{1493} = 0.45 = 45\%$$

The population for the Gallup poll is all U.S. residents age 18 and over. We don't know what percent of the population would say "Yes" if we asked them about their fear of crime. Because everyone had the same chance to be in the sample, we expect the sample to represent the population. So we estimate that about 45% of all adults are afraid to go out at night because of crime. ◆

It is unlikely that the percent of the population who are afraid to go out at night is exactly 45%. All we can claim is that the sample result is probably quite close to the truth about the population. If Gallup took another sample, it would contain different people. These people would no doubt have somewhat different views on crime. If 641 of them said "Yes" to Gallup's question, we would estimate that about

$$\frac{641}{1493} = 0.43 = 43\%$$

of all adults are afraid to go outside at night because of crime. This is *sampling variability:* when we take repeated samples from the same population, the results will vary from sample to sample. Random sampling eliminates bias in choosing a sample, but it does not eliminate variability.

One sample gives 45%, another gives 43%. Might other samples give 13% or 89%? Can we trust the results of a sample when we know that we would get a different result if we took another sample? We can. To see why, we need to look more closely at sampling variability.

There are different kinds of variability. The answers obtained by sending an interviewer to a shopping mall vary in a haphazard and unpredictable way. Repeated random samples, however, vary in a regular manner because chance was used to choose the sample. The long-run results are not haphazard. We see such long-run regularity in games of chance like tossing a coin many times. In fact, tossing a balanced coin 1493 times is just like choosing a simple random sample of 1493 from a large population, if the opinion in this particular population is evenly divided so that heads represents "Yes" and tails represents "No." Both tossing coins and choosing random samples produce results that vary, but we can say how much they will vary because they will show a regular pattern in the long run. Let's do an experiment to look at the variation in the results of many random samples.

EXAMPLE   *A Sampling Experiment*

Gallup asked a sample of 1493 adults, "Are you afraid to go outside at night within a mile of your home because of crime?" Let us suppose that, unknown to Gallup, exactly 50% of all adults would answer "Yes" to this question. Can we trust a sample of 1493 to come close to this result?

To find out, we took 1000 simple random samples from a population with exactly 50% "Yes" and recorded the percent of "Yes" responses in each sample. The first sample gave 50.2%, the second 49.2%, the third 50.4%, and so on. The sample percents do vary. Figure 5.4 shows the process of repeated sampling.

Collect all the sample percents and draw a **histogram.** The result appears in Figure 5.5. The height of each bar in the histogram shows how often the outcomes covered by the base of that bar occurred. For example, the height of the bar covering 48% to 48.5% is 80, because 80 of our 1000 samples had between 48% and 48.5% "Yes" responses. (More details about histograms appear in the next chapter.) Study of this histogram shows why we can trust estimates from samples.   ◆

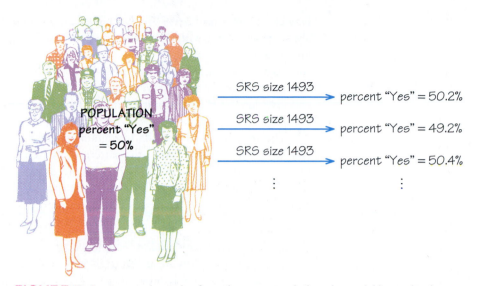

FIGURE 5.4 Repeated samples from the same population give variable results, but those results vary according to a predictable pattern.

You can see from Figure 5.5 that all 1000 samples had between 46% and 54% "Yes" responses. That is, every sample fell within four percentage points of the truth about the population. What is more, the histogram shows a regular pattern of outcomes. The center of the pattern is at 50%. The bars are tallest in the center and get shorter as we go out from the center in either direction. That is, results that are near the truth about the population are most common, and results that are further from the truth occur less often. The central 95% of the samples gave results

FIGURE 5.5

The results of 1000 samples of size 1493 drawn from a population in which 50% would say "Yes" to the questions asked.

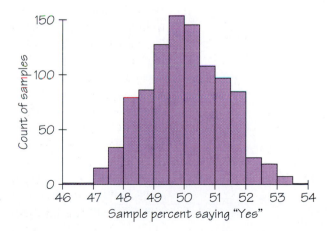

between 47.6% and 52.6% "Yes." It appears that a sample of size 1493 will almost always give a result within ± 4% of the truth and will usually (95% of the time) give a result within about ± 2.6% of the truth. So we can be pretty sure that one such sample will in fact give a result close to the result for the entire population. This is wonderful—there are almost 200 million adults in the country, and choosing just 1493 of them at random allows us to describe their opinions quite accurately.

The regular pattern of the histogram in Figure 5.5 isn't an accident. Using chance to select samples forces the pattern of the results of a large number of samples to have the regular shape that the figure displays. We don't actually have to take thousands of samples to learn what the shape is. The mathematics of chance allows us to calculate it in advance. We'll learn more about that in Chapter 8. Here are the basic facts that explain why we can trust sample estimates:

- If we take many random samples, *the pattern of results is centered about the population truth.* That center is 50% in Figure 5.5 because the truth for this population is 50%. If we take many samples from a population in which 40% would say "Yes," the results will be centered at 40%. The center of the histogram reflects the lack of bias in random sampling. Individual samples may give results above or below the truth about the population, but there is no systematic tendency to be too high or too low.
- *The spread of the pattern is controlled by the size of the sample.* Larger samples give results that cluster closer to the population truth than smaller samples do. So the larger the sample, the more confident we can be that it estimates the population truth accurately. Opinion polls usually interview between 1000 and 2000 people. The Current Population Survey uses a sample of 50,000 households because the government wants to know the unemployment rate very accurately.

Samples usually tell us how accurate their results are by giving a *margin of error.* We can't be *certain* that the sample results are as close to the population truth as the margin of error says. After all, chance chooses the sample, so it's possible to have terribly bad luck. An opinion poll about crime *might* have the bad luck to choose 1493 residents of high-crime urban neighborhoods rather than a sample that represents the entire population. That sample would give nearly 100% "Yes" answers to Gallup's question about fear of crime. Figure 5.5 shows that this will almost never happen if the truth about the whole population is 50%. The usual margin of error comes from looking at the central 95% of the outcomes in histograms like Figure 5.5.

The **margin of error** announced by most national samples says how close to the truth about the population the sample result would fall in 95% of all samples drawn by the method used to draw this one sample.

A news report says, "A new poll shows that only 34% of all Americans approve of the way the president is handling his office. The margin of error for the poll is plus or minus 3%." That means "We got this result using a method that comes within plus or minus 3% of the truth 95% of the time." This particular sample might be one of the 5% of all samples that miss by more, but knowing that we will land within the margin of error 95% of the time gives us a good idea of the poll's accuracy.

EXAMPLE *Gallup Poll Margin of Error*

In our sampling experiment, we drew many simple random samples. The Gallup poll and the Current Population Survey use more complicated sample designs. But because they use chance to choose their samples, the pattern of many sample results is still similar to Figure 5.5. The Gallup poll's statisticians tell us that their margin of error is

about ± 5% for samples of size about 600
about ± 4% for samples of size about 1000
about ± 3% for samples of size about 1500

Gallup interviewed 1514 adults and found that 53% of them oppose a longer school year. The margin of error is ± 3%. So we can be quite confident that between 50% (that's 53%—3%) and 56% (that's 53% + 3%) of all adults oppose a longer school year. ◆

Experiments

Sample surveys gather information on part of the population in order to draw conclusions about the whole. When the goal is to describe a population, statistical sampling is the right tool to use.

Suppose, however, that we want to study the response to a stimulus, to see how one variable affects another when we change existing conditions. Will a new mathematics curriculum improve the scores of sixth graders on a standard test of mathematics achievement? Will taking small amounts of aspirin daily reduce the risk of suffering a heart attack? Does a mother's smoking during pregnancy reduce the IQ of her children? Studies that simply *observe and describe* are ineffective tools for answering these questions. *Experiments* give us clearer answers.

An **observational study,** such as a sample survey, observes individuals and measures variables of interest but does not attempt to influence the responses. An **experiment,** on the other hand, deliberately imposes some *treatment* on individuals in order to observe their responses.

Experiments are the preferred method for examining the effect of one variable on another. By imposing the specific treatment of interest and controlling other influences, we can pin down cause and effect. A sample survey may show that two variables are related, but it cannot demonstrate that one causes the other. Statistics has something to say about how to arrange experiments, just as it suggests methods for sampling.

EXAMPLE   *An Uncontrolled Experiment*

The Bigfoot Mountain School District, concerned about the poor mathematics preparation of American children, adopts an ambitious new mathematics curriculum. After three years of the new curriculum, students completing sixth grade have an average achievement score 10% higher than they had before the treatment. Bigfoot Mountain pronounces the curriculum a success.

This experiment has a very simple design. A group of subjects (the students) were exposed to a treatment (the new curriculum), and the outcome (achievement test scores) was observed. Here is the design:

New curriculum $\longrightarrow$ Observe test scores

or, in general form

Treatment $\longrightarrow$ Observe response   ◆

Most laboratory experiments use a design like that in the example: apply a treatment and measure the response. In the controlled environment of the laboratory, simple designs often work well. But field experiments and experiments with human subjects are exposed to more variable conditions and deal with more variable subjects. It isn't possible to control outside factors that can influence the outcome. With greater variability comes a greater need for statistical design.

In Bigfoot Mountain, a concern for education brought about a number of simultaneous changes that could influence the students' achievement test scores. Elementary school teachers were given additional training in mathematics. A parent group began to provide classroom tutors to give children individual help with mathematics. Public concern led parents to pay more attention to their children's progress and teachers to assign more homework.

In these circumstances, mathematics achievement would have increased without a new curriculum. In fact, the new curriculum might even be *less* effective than the old. The Bigfoot Mountain experiment cannot distinguish the effects of the changes in parents and teachers from the effects of the new curriculum. Thus the new curriculum is *confounded* with the other changes that occurred at the same time.

> Variables, whether part of a study or not, are said to be **confounded** when their effects on the outcome cannot be distinguished from each other.

Randomized Comparative Experiments

The remedy for confounding is to do a *comparative experiment* in which some children are taught from the new curriculum and others from the old. The second group of children is called a **control group.** Changes in parents' attitudes and involvement, teacher retraining, and other such variables now operate equally on both groups of students, so that the effects of the new curriculum can be seen by comparison with the control group. Most well-designed experiments compare two or more treatments.

But comparison alone isn't enough to produce results we can trust. If the treatments are given to groups that differ markedly when the experiment begins, bias will result. For example, if we allow students to volunteer for the new curriculum in Bigfoot Mountain, only adventurous children who are interested in math are likely to sign up, and these students are likely to perform well. Personal choice will bias our results in the same way that volunteers bias the results of call-in opinion polls. The solution to the problem of bias is the same for experiments and for samples: use impersonal chance to select the groups.

E X A M P L E   *A Randomized Comparative Experiment*

The Bigfoot Mountain School District decides to compare the progress of 100 students taught under the new mathematics curriculum with that of 100 students taught under the old curriculum. We select the students who will be taught the new curriculum by taking a simple random sample of size 100 from the 200 available subjects. The remaining 100 students form the control group. They will continue in the old curriculum.

The result is a **randomized comparative experiment** with two groups. Figure 5.6 outlines the design in graphical form.

The selection procedure is exactly the same as it is for sampling: label and table. First, tag all 200 students with numerical labels, say, 000 to 199. Then go to the table of random digits and read successive three-digit groups. The first 100 labels encountered select the group that will be taught from the new curriculum. As usual, ignore repeated labels and groups of digits not used as labels. For example, if you begin at line 125 in Table 5.1, the first few students chosen are those labeled 064, 106, 102, 022, and 188. ◆

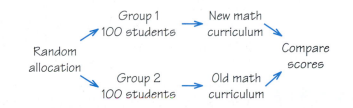

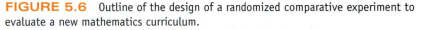

FIGURE 5.6 Outline of the design of a randomized comparative experiment to evaluate a new mathematics curriculum.

Sir Ronald A. Fisher, 1890–1962

Sir Ronald A. Fisher

The ideas and methods that we study as "statistics" were invented in the nineteenth and twentieth centuries by people working on problems that required analysis of data. Astronomy, biology, social science, and even surveying can claim a role in the birth of statistics. But if anyone can claim to be "the father of statistics," that honor belongs to Sir Ronald A. Fisher.

Fisher's writings organized statistics as a distinct field of study whose methods apply across many disciplines. He systematized the mathematical theory of statistics and invented many new techniques. The randomized comparative experiment is perhaps Fisher's greatest contribution.

Like other statistical pioneers, Fisher was driven by the demands of practical problems. Beginning in 1919, he worked on agricultural field experiments at Rothamsted in England. How should we arrange the planting of different crop varieties or the application of different fertilizers to get a fair comparison among them? Because fertility and other variables change as we move across a field, experimenters used elaborate checkerboard planting arrangements to obtain fair comparisons. Fisher had a better idea: "arrange the plots deliberately at random."

Randomized comparative experiments are a relatively new idea. They were introduced in the 1920s by Sir R. A. Fisher (see Spotlight 5.1). The Bigfoot Mountain experiment is *comparative* because it compares two treatments (the two math curricula). It is *randomized* because the subjects are assigned to the treatments by chance. Randomization creates groups that are similar to each other before we start the experiment. Comparison means that possible confounding variables act on both groups at once. The only difference between the groups is the different math curricula. So if we see a difference in performance, it must be due to the different curricula. That is the basic logic of randomized comparative experiments. We will see later that there are some fine points to worry about, but this basic logic shows why experiments can give good evidence that the different treatments really *caused* different outcomes. Randomized comparative experiments are used whenever environmental variables, such as changes in the behavior of Bigfoot Mountain parents and teachers, threaten to confound the results. Here is another example, this time comparing three treatments.

EXAMPLE   *Conserving Energy*

Many utility companies have introduced programs to encourage energy conservation among their customers. An electric company considers placing electronic indicators in households to show what the cost would be if the electricity use at that moment continued for a month. Will indicators reduce electricity use? Would cheaper methods work almost as well? The company decides to design an experiment.

One cheaper approach is to give customers a chart and information about monitoring their electricity use. The experiment compares these two approaches (indicator, chart) and also a control. The control group of customers receives information about energy conservation but no help in monitoring electricity use. The outcome is measured by total electricity used in a year. The company finds 60 single-family residences in the same city willing to participate, so it assigns 20 residences at random to each of the 3 treatments. Figure 5.7 outlines the design.

To carry out the random assignment, label the 60 households 01 to 60. Enter Table 5.1 to select an SRS of 20 to receive the indicators. Continue in Table 5.1, selecting 20 more to receive charts. The remaining 20 form the control group. ◆

FIGURE 5.7   The design of a randomized comparative experiment to compare three ways of encouraging households to conserve electricity.

Randomized comparative experiments are common tools of industrial and academic research. They are also widely used in medical research. For example, federal regulations require that the safety and effectiveness of new drugs be demonstrated by randomized comparative experiments. Let's look at an important medical experiment.

E X A M P L E   *The Physicians' Health Study*

There is some evidence that taking aspirin regularly will reduce the risk of heart attacks. Some people also suspect that regular doses of beta carotene (which the body converts into vitamin A) will help prevent some types of cancer. The Physicians' Health Study was a large experiment designed to test these claims. The subjects of this study were 22,000 male physicians at least 40 years old. Each subject took a pill every day over a period of several years. There were four treatments: aspirin alone, beta carotene alone, both, and neither. The subjects were randomly assigned to one of these treatments at the beginning of the experiment. ◆

The Physicians' Health Study example introduces several new ideas about the design of experiments. The first is the importance of the **placebo effect,** a special kind of confounding. A placebo is a fake treatment, a dummy pill that contains no active ingredient but looks and tastes like the real thing. The placebo effect is the tendency of subjects to respond favorably to any treatment, even a placebo. If subjects given aspirin, for example, are compared with subjects who receive no treatment, the first group gets the benefit of both aspirin and the placebo effect. Any beneficial effect that aspirin may have is confounded with the placebo effect. To prevent confounding, it is important that some treatment be given to all subjects in any medical experiment. In the Physicians' Health Study, all subjects took pills that looked alike. Some pills contained aspirin or beta carotene and some contained a placebo. Figure 5.8 shows the design of the experiment.

The Physicians' Health Study was a **double-blind experiment:** neither the subjects nor the experimenters who worked with them knew which treatment any subject received. Subjects might react differently if they knew they were getting "only a placebo." Knowing that a particular subject was getting "only a placebo" could also influence the researchers who interviewed and examined the subjects. So both subjects and workers were kept "blind." Only the study's statistician knew which treatment each subject received.

Finally, the Physicians' Health Study is a more elaborate experiment than our earlier examples. In the Bigfoot Mountain and electricity-use examples, we com-

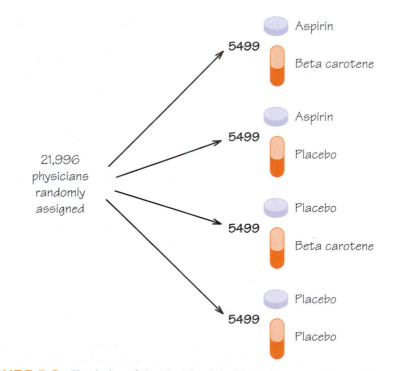

FIGURE 5.8 The design of the Physicians' Health Study, an experiment with two factors.

pare values of a single variable (Which math curriculum? Which conservation program?). The Physicians' Health Study looks at two distinct experimental variables: aspirin or not and beta carotene or not. A two-variable experiment, usually called a *two-factor experiment,* allows us to study the *interaction,* or joint effect, of the two drugs as well as the separate effects of each. For example, beta carotene may reinforce the effect of aspirin on future heart attacks. By comparing these four groups, we can study all these possible interactions. Nonetheless, the outline of the design in Figure 5.8 is similar to our earlier examples because the basic ideas of randomization and comparison of several treatments remain.

Statistical Evidence

A properly designed experiment, in the eyes of a statistician, is an experiment employing the principles of *comparison* and *randomization:* comparison of several treatments and randomization in assigning subjects to the treatments.

The future health of the subjects of the Physicians' Health Study, for example, may depend on age, past medical history, emotional status, smoking habits, and many other variables known and unknown. Randomization will, on the average, balance the groups simultaneously in all such variables. Because the groups are exposed to exactly the same environment, except for the actual content of the pills, we can say that any differences in heart attacks or cancer among the groups are caused by the medication. That is the logic of randomized comparative experiments.

Let's be a bit more careful: any difference among the groups is due *either* to the medication *or* to the accident of chance in the random assignment of subjects. It could happen, for example, that men about to have a heart attack were, just by chance, overrepresented in one of the groups. The problem is exactly the same as in random sampling, where it could happen just by chance that an SRS chooses all Republicans. Just as in sampling, we are saved by the regular pattern of chance behavior.

If we repeat the random assignment of subjects to groups many times, differences among the groups follow a regular pattern if we don't apply different treatments. This regular pattern tells us how large the differences among the four groups are likely to be if nothing but chance is operating. If we observe differences so large that they would almost never occur just by chance, we are confident that we are seeing the effects of the treatments. So it is not *any* differences that show the results of the treatments, just differences so large that chance cannot easily account for them. Differences among the treatment groups that are so large that they would rarely occur just by chance are called *statistically significant.*

An observed effect too large to attribute plausibly to chance is called **statistically significant.**

Again as in sampling, larger numbers of subjects increase our confidence in the results. The Physicians' Health Study followed 22,000 subjects in order to be quite certain that any medically important differences among the groups would be detected and that these differences could be attributed to aspirin or to beta carotene. In fact, there were significantly fewer heart attacks among the men who took aspirin than among men who took the placebo. As a result of the Physicians' Health Study, doctors often recommend that men over age 50 take small amounts of aspirin regularly. Beta carotene, on the other hand, did not significantly reduce cancer.

The logic of experimentation, the statistical design of experiments, and the laws that govern chance behavior combine to give compelling evidence of cause and effect. Only experimentation can produce fully convincing evidence of causation.

E X A M P L E   *Smoking and Health*

By way of contrast, consider the statistical evidence linking cigarette smoking to lung cancer. We can't assign groups of people to smoke or not, so a direct experiment isn't possible. The most careful studies have selected samples of smokers and nonsmokers, then followed them for many years, eventually recording the cause of death. These are called *prospective studies* because they follow the subjects forward in time. Prospective studies are comparative, but they are not experiments because the subjects themselves choose whether or not to smoke. A large prospective study of British doctors found that the death rate from lung cancer among cigarette smokers was 20 times that of nonsmokers. Another study of American men aged 40 to 79 found that the lung cancer death rate was 11 times higher among smokers than among nonsmokers. These and many other observational studies show a strong connection between smoking and lung cancer.   ◆

The connection between smoking and lung cancer is statistically significant. That is, it is far stronger than would occur by chance. We can be confident that something other than chance links smoking to cancer. But observation of samples cannot tell us *what* factors other than chance are at work. Perhaps there is something in the genetic makeup of some people that predisposes them both to nicotine addiction and to lung cancer. In that case, we would observe a strong link even if smoking itself had no effect on the lungs.

The statistical evidence that points to cigarette smoking as a cause of lung cancer is about as strong as nonexperimental evidence can be. First, the connection has been observed in many studies in many countries. This eliminates factors peculiar to one group of people, or to one specific study design. Second, there is a *dose-response relationship:* people who smoke more are more likely to get lung cancer than those who smoke less, and quitting cigarettes reduces the cancer risk. Third, specific ways in which smoking could cause cancer have been identified—cigarette smoke contains tars that have been shown by experiment to cause tumors in animals. Finally, no plausible alternative explanation is available. For example, the genetic hypothesis cannot explain the increase in lung cancer among women that occurred as more and more women became smokers. Lung cancer, which has long been the leading cause of cancer deaths in men, has now passed breast cancer as the most fatal cancer for women.

This evidence is convincing, but it is not quite as strong as the conclusive statistical evidence we get from randomized comparative experiments.

Statistics in Practice

There is more to the wise use of statistics than a knowledge of such statistical techniques as simple random samples and randomized comparative experiments. These designs for data production avoid the pitfalls of voluntary response samples or uncontrolled experiments. But there are other pitfalls that can reduce the usefulness of data even when we use a sound statistical design.

EXAMPLE *Nonresponse in Sampling*

Choosing a sample at random is only the first step in carrying out a sample survey of a large human population. You must then contact the people in the sample and persuade them to cooperate. This isn't easy. Some people are rarely at home. Others don't want to talk with an interviewer. *Nonresponse* occurs when an individual chosen for the sample can't be contacted or refuses to cooperate. Ask the rate of nonresponse before putting too much trust in a sample result. Nonresponse rates of 30% or more are common. Nonresponse is higher in cities than in rural areas, so ignoring the people who did not respond can cause bias. Opinion polls usually substitute another person from the same neighborhood to reduce the bias.

Even the 1990 census, with the resources of the government behind it, had problems with nonresponse. The census is not a sample—it tries to count everyone in the country. The census count has some bias against cities and against minorities because of nonresponse, even though census interviewers tried six times to contact nonresponders. The Census Bureau estimates that the 1990 census missed 1.8% of the overall population, but that it failed to count 4.4% of blacks and 5.0% of Hispanics.

For the 2000 census, the Bureau proposed replacing follow-up of all nonresponders with more intense pursuit of a random sample of nonresponding households plus a national sample of 750,000 households. The final counts would be based on the sample as well as on the original responses. The Supreme Court ruled that sampling cannot be used to get the counts used to apportion seats in Congress among the states, but can be used for other purposes. ◆

SPOTLIGHT 5.2

Experiments and Ethics

Charles Hennekens

Dr. Charles Hennekens, director of the Physicians' Health Study, had to concern himself with the goals, design, and implementation of his large-scale study. But other questions also arise in the course of such an experiment. Dr. Hennekens was asked about the ethics of experimenting on human health:

Much has been made of the ethical concerns about randomized trials. There are instances where it would not be ethical to do a randomized trial. When penicillin was introduced for the treatment of pneumococcal pneumonia, which was virtually 100% fatal, the mortality rate plummeted significantly. Certainly it would have been unethical to do a randomized trial, to withhold effective treatment from people who need it.

There's a delicate balance between when to do or not to do a randomized trial. On the one hand, there must be a sufficient belief in the agent's potential to justify exposing half the subjects to it. On the other hand, there must be sufficient doubt about its efficacy to justify withholding it from the other half of subjects who might be assigned to the placebos, the pills with inert ingredients. It was just these circumstances that we felt existed with regard to the aspirin and the beta carotene hypotheses.

EXAMPLE   *Is the Experiment Realistic?*

The Physicians' Health Study gave pills to middle-aged men going about their everyday lives. Many experiments, however, take place in artificial environments. A psychologist studying the effects of stress on teamwork observes teams of students carrying out tasks in a psychology laboratory under different conditions. The students know it's "just an experiment" and that the stress will only last an hour. Do the conclusions of such experiments apply to a real-life stress? An engineer uses a small pilot production process in a laboratory to find the choices of pressure and temperature that maximize yield from a complex chemical reaction. Do the results apply to a full-scale manufacturing plant?

These are not statistical questions. The psychologist and the engineer must use their understanding of psychology and engineering to judge how far their results apply. The statistical design enables us to trust the results for the students and the pilot process, but not to generalize the conclusions to other settings. ◆

When we are planning a statistical study, we must also face some *ethical questions*. Does the knowledge gained from an experiment or study justify the possible risk to the subjects? In the Physicians' Health Study, doctors gave their informed consent to take either aspirin, beta carotene, or a placebo, in any combination, as prescribed by the study designers. When it became clear that men taking aspirin had fewer heart attacks, the experiment was stopped so that all the subjects could take advantage of this new knowledge. In Spotlight 5.2 the director of the Physicians' Health Study explains why randomized comparative experiments are a mainstay of medical research and when such clinical trials are justified. Practical and ethical problems are never far from the surface when statistics is applied to real problems.

REVIEW VOCABULARY

Bias   A systematic error that tends to cause the observations to deviate in the same direction from the truth about the population whenever a sample or experiment is repeated.

Confounding   Two variables are confounded when their effects on the outcome of a study cannot be distinguished from one another.

Control group   A group of experimental subjects who are given a standard treatment or no treatment (such as a placebo).

Convenience sample   A sample that consists of the individuals who are most easily available, such as people passing by in the street. A convenience sample is usually biased.

Double-blind experiment   An experiment in which neither the experimental subjects nor the persons who interact with them know which treatment each subject received.

Experiment   A study in which treatments are applied to people, animals, or things in order to observe the effect of the treatment.

Histogram   A graph that displays how often various outcomes occur by means of bars. The height of each bar is the number of times an outcome or group of outcomes occurred in the data.

Margin of error   As announced by most national polls, the margin of error says how close to the truth about the population the sample result would fall in 95% of all samples drawn by the method used to draw this one sample.

Observational study   A study (such as a sample survey) that observes individuals and measures variables of interest but does not attempt to influence the responses.

Placebo effect   The effect of a dummy treatment (such as an inert pill in a medical experiment) on the response of subjects.

Population   The entire group of people or things that we want information about.

Randomized comparative experiment   An experiment to compare two or more treatments in which people, animals, or things are assigned to treatments by chance.

Sample   A part of the population that is actually observed and used to draw conclusions, or inferences, about the entire population.

Simple random sample   A sample chosen by chance, so that every possible sample of the same size has an equal chance to be the one selected.

Statistical significance   An observed effect is statistically significant if it is so large that it is unlikely to occur "just by chance" in the absence of a real effect in the population from which the data were drawn.

Table of random digits   A table whose entries are the digits 0, 1, 2, 3, 4, 5, 6, 7, 8, 9 in a completely random order. That is, each entry is equally likely to be any of the 10 digits and no entry gives information about any other entry.

Voluntary response sample   A sample that chooses itself by responding to a general invitation to write or call with their opinions. Such a sample is usually strongly biased.

SUGGESTED READINGS

COBB, GEORGE W. *Design and Analysis of Experiments,* Springer, New York, 1998. Chapter 1 of this more advanced text is a nice essay on designing experiments.

KALTON, GRAHAM. *Introduction to Survey Sampling,* Sage Publications, Newbury Park, Calif., 1983. A detailed but relatively nontechnical introduction to the statistics of sample surveys.

MOORE, DAVID S. *Statistics: Concepts and Controversies,* 4th ed., W. H. Freeman, New York, 1997, chapters 1 and 2. Written for liberal arts students, this book provides more extensive discussion at about the same level as *For All Practical Purposes.*

MOORE, DAVID S. *The Basic Practice of Statistics,* 2nd ed., W. H. Freeman, New York, 1999, chapter 3. Clear treatment of data production in a text on practical statistics at about the same level as *For All Practical Purposes.*

TANUR, JUDITH M. Samples and surveys. In David C. Hoaglin and David S. Moore (eds.), *Perspectives on Contemporary Statistics,* Mathematical Association of America, Washington, D.C., 1992, pp. 55–70. This essay describes the practice of sample surveys at a relatively nontechnical level.

SUGGESTED WEB SITES

Several of the most important sample surveys in the United States are conducted by the Bureau of Labor Statistics (**http://stats.bls.gov**) and the Bureau of the Census (**www.census.gov**). The Gallup Organization (**www.gallup.com**) conducts the Gallup poll; this site has excellent material on how polls are conducted. Important medical studies—many based on randomized comparative experiments—often appear in the *Journal of the American Medical Association* (**www.ama-assn.org/public/journals/jama/**) or the *New England Journal of Medicine* (**www.nejm.org**).

SKILLS CHECK

1. A marketing firm interviews 50 shoppers randomly selected from the 3500 customers at one of the mall's 23 stores yesterday. The sample in this situation is the

   (a) 50 selected shoppers.
   (b) 3500 shoppers.
   (c) 23 stores.

2. In an election for mayor there are 5 candidates and 45,000 eligible voters. A newspaper interviews 750 voters as they leave the polls. The population here is the

   (a) 5 candidates.
   (b) 45,000 eligible voters.
   (c) 750 voters interviewed.

3. A survey on the benefits of vitamins is conducted outside a health food store. This is an example of

   (a) convenience sampling.
   (b) confounding.
   (c) the placebo effect.

4. Here is a list of random numbers: 17463 26715 71680 64853. Use this list to choose 3 people from an alphabetical list of 20 people. The people chosen have labels

   (a) 17, 46, 32.
   (b) 17, 15, 16.
   (c) 17, 15, 06.

5. If Ann's sample statistic has a margin of error of ± 3% and Beth's sample statistic for the same population has a margin of error of ± 6%, then

> (a) Ann's sample gave a lower estimate of the truth about the population.
> (b) Beth's estimate is biased.
> (c) Ann's sample was larger.

6. Five students each sample 100 students to determine their favorite soda pop. Each student returns with different results. This is probably due to

> (a) bias.
> (b) sampling variability.
> (c) the use of a control group.

7. A drug test randomly selects one of three treatments for each participant. Neither the experimenter nor the participant knows which drug is chosen. This is an example of a (I) randomized comparative experiment and/or (II) double-blind experiment.

> (a) I only
> (b) II only
> (c) Both I and II

EXERCISES   ▲ *Optional.*   ■ *Advanced.*   ◆ *Discussion.*

Sampling

1. A sociologist wants to know the opinions of employed adult women about government funding for day care. She obtains a list of the 520 members of a local business and professional women's club, and mails a questionnaire to 100 of these women selected at random. Only 68 questionnaires are returned. What is the population in this study? What is the sample?

2. Home canners sometimes can vegetables in used mayonnaise jars to avoid buying special canning jars. *Organic Gardening* magazine wondered what percent of mayonnaise jars would break when used for canning. It obtained 100 mayonnaise jars and canned tomatoes in them. Only 3 of the jars broke. What is the population in this study? What is the sample?

◆   3. A member of Congress is interested in whether her constituents favor a proposed gun control bill. Her staff reports that letters on the bill have been received from 361 constituents and that 323 of these oppose the bill. What is the population of interest? What is the sample? Is this sample likely to represent the population well? Explain your answer.

Bad Sampling Methods

◆   4. A magazine for health foods and organic healing wants to establish that large doses of vitamins will improve health. The editors ask readers who have regularly taken vitamins in large doses to write in, describing their experiences. Of the 2754 readers who reply, 93% report some benefit from taking vitamins. Is the sample proportion of 93% probably higher than, lower than, or about the same as the percent of all adults who would perceive some benefit from large vitamin intake? Why? (In answering these questions, you have identified a source of bias in the sampling method.)

◆   5. In 1995, *USA Weekend* printed a box like the one below. Fine print said that a call would cost 50 cents. Do you consider the results of this opinion poll trustworthy? Explain your answer.

VOTE NOW
If you were terminally ill, would you want the right to end your life with a doctor's help?
YES: 1-900-255-2257   NO: 1-900-255-2258

◆   6.   Ann Landers once asked her female readers whether they would be content with affectionate treatment by men with no sex ever. Over 90,000 women wrote in, with 72% answering "Yes." Explain carefully why this sample is almost certainly biased. What is the *direction* of the bias? That is, is the percentage of all adult women who would be content with no sex ever lower or higher than the 72% in the sample?

◆   7.   The Miami Police Department wants to know how black residents of Miami feel about police service. A sociologist prepares several questions about the police. A sample of 300 mailing addresses in predominantly black neighborhoods is chosen, and a black police officer in uniform goes to each address to ask the questions of an adult living there. Explain why you expect the results of this sample to be biased. In what way do you think the sample results will differ from the true opinion of the population?

Simple Random Sampling

8.   A firm wants to understand the attitudes of its minority managers toward its system for assessing management performance. Below is a list of all the firm's managers who are members of minority groups. Use Table 5.1 at line 110 to choose 6 to be interviewed in detail about the performance appraisal system.

Agarwal	Dewald	Huang	Puri
Anderson	Fernandez	Kim	Richards
Baxter	Fleming	Liao	Rodriguez
Brown	Gates	Mourning	Santiago
Bowman	Goel	Naber	Shen
Castillo	Gomez	Peters	Vega
Cross	Hernandez	Pliego	Wang

9.   What kinds of programs do academic departments at a state university offer for honors students? You decide to report information from 5 randomly chosen departments in the liberal arts and sciences. Use the table of random digits starting at line 132 to select a simple random sample of 5 departments from the following list for your study. Be sure to show how you used the random digits.

Audiology	Computer	Chemistry
Communication	Sciences	Economics
Earth Sciences	English	Foreign
General Studies	Health and	Languages
Mathematics	Leisure Studies	History
Political Science	Philosophy	Physics
Statistics	Psychology	Sociology
Biological Sciences	Visual Arts	

10.   A student wishes to study the opinions of faculty at her college on the advisability of setting up a state board of higher education to oversee all colleges in the state. The college has 380 faculty members.

(a)   What is the population in this situation?
(b)   Explain carefully how you would choose a simple random sample of 50 faculty members.
(c)   Use Table 5.1 starting at line 135 to choose *only the first* 5 members of this sample.

11.   The number of students majoring in political science at Ivy University has increased substantially without a corresponding increase in the number of faculty. The campus newspaper plans to interview 25 of the 450 political science majors to learn student views on class size and other issues. You suggest a simple random sample. Explain carefully how you would choose this sample. Then use Table 5.1 starting at line 120 to select *only the first* 5 members of your sample.

■   12.   Which of the following statements are true of a table of random digits, and which are false? Explain your answers.

(a)   There are exactly four 0s in each row of 40 digits.
(b)   Each pair of digits has chance 1/100 of being 00.
(c)   The digits 0000 can never appear as a group, because this pattern is not random.

Statistical Estimation

13. You must allocate 5 tickets to a rock concert among 25 clamoring members of your club. We will use this example to illustrate sampling variability.

(a) Choose 5 at random to receive the tickets, using line 135 of Table 5.1 (ignore the asterisks).

Agassiz	Darwin	Herrnstein	Myrdal	Vogt*
Binet*	Epstein	Jimenez*	Perez*	Went
Blumenbach	Ferri	Lombrosco	Spencer*	Wilson
Chase*	Gupta*	Moll*	Thomson	Yerkes
Chen	Gutierrez	McKim*	Toulmin	Zimmer

(b) In fact, 10 of the 25 club members are female. Their names are marked with asterisks in the list. Draw 5 at random 20 times, using a different row in Table 5.1 each time [include your sample from part (a)]. Record the number of females in each of your samples. Make a histogram to display your results. What is the average number of females in your 20 samples?

(c) Do you think the club members should suspect discrimination if none of the 5 tickets go to women?

◆ **14.** An advertising agency conducts a sample survey to see how adult women react to various adjectives that might be used to describe an automobile. The firm chooses 600 women from across the country. Each woman listens to a list of adjectives, such as "elegant" and "prestigious," and says how desirable a car described this way seems to her. The possible responses are (1) highly desirable (2) somewhat desirable (3) neutral (4) not desirable. Of the women interviewed, 76% said that a car described as "elegant" was highly desirable.

(a) What is the population in this sample survey?

(b) How many of the women in the sample responded "highly desirable"?

(c) The sample used the Gallup poll's random-sampling procedure. What interval are you confident covers the true percentage of women who would say such a car was highly desirable?

15. An opinion poll asks a sample of 1324 adults whether they believe that life exists on other planets; 609 say "Yes." What percent of the sample believes in extraterrestrial life? The polling organization announces a margin of error of ±3%. What conclusion can you draw about the percent of all adults who believe that life exists on other planets?

◆ **16.** National opinion polls such as the Gallup usually take weekly samples of about 1500 people.

(a) This sample size gives a margin of error of about ±3 percentage points. Explain to someone who knows no statistics what this means.

(b) Just before a presidential election, however, the polls often increase the size of their samples to about 4000 people. Is the margin of error now more than ±3%, less than ±3%, or still equal to ±3%? Why?

◆ **17.** A news article reports that in a recent Gallup poll, 78% of the sample of 1108 adults said they believe there is a heaven. Only 60% said they believe there is a hell. The news article ends, "The poll's margin of sampling error was plus or minus four percentage points." Can we be certain that between 56% and 64% of all adults believe there is a hell? Explain your answer.

■ **18.** Random digits can be used to *simulate* the results of random sampling. Suppose that you are drawing simple random samples of size 25 from a large number of high school students and that 20% of the students are unemployed during the summer. To simulate this SRS, let 25 consecutive digits in Table 5.1 stand for the 25 students in your sample. The digits 0 and 1 stand for unemployed students, and other digits stand for employed students. This is an accurate imitation of the SRS because 0 and 1 make up 20% of the 10 equally likely digits.

Simulate the results of 50 samples by counting the number of 0s and 1s in the first 25 entries in each of the 50 rows of Table 5.1. Make a histogram like Figure 5.5 to display the results of your 50 samples. Is the truth about the population (20% unemployed, or 5 in a sample of 25) near the center of your graph? What are the smallest and largest counts of unemployed students you obtained in your 50 samples? What percent of your samples had either 4, 5, or 6 unemployed?

Experiments

The studies in Exercises 19 to 21 may produce invalid data because of confounding of outside influences with the treatment of interest. Explain in each case how confounding could influence the outcome.

◆ 19. A college student thinks that drinking herbal tea will improve the health of nursing home patients. She and some friends visit a large nursing home regularly, serving herbal tea to the residents in one wing. Residents in the other wing are not visited. After six months, the first group had fewer days ill than the second.

◆ 20. A language teacher believes that study of a foreign language improves command of English. He examines the records at his high school and finds that students who elect a foreign language do indeed score higher on English achievement tests.

◆ 21. An article in a women's magazine reported that women who nurse their babies feel warmer and more receptive toward the infants than mothers who bottle-feed. The author concluded that nursing has desirable effects on the mother's attitude toward the child.

◆ 22. It has been suggested that there is a "gender gap" in political party preference in the United States, with women more likely than men to prefer Democratic candidates. A political scientist asks each of a group of men and a group of women whether they voted for the Democratic or Republican candidate in the last congressional election. Explain carefully why this study is *not* an experiment.

◆ 23. Some people think that exercise raises the body's metabolic rate for as long as 12 to 24 hours, enabling us to continue to burn off fat after we end our workout. An exercise physiologist studying this effect asks subjects to walk briskly on a treadmill for several hours. He measures their metabolic rate before, immediately after, and 12 hours after the exercise. Is this study an experiment? Why or why not?

◆ 24. A study of the relationship between physical fitness and leadership uses as subjects middle-aged executives who have volunteered for an exercise program. The executives are divided into a low-fitness group and a high-fitness group on the basis of a physical examination. All subjects then take a psychological test designed to measure leadership, and the results for the two groups are compared. Is this an observational study or an experiment? Explain your answer.

Randomized Comparative Experiments

◆ 25. Sickle cell disease is an inherited disorder of the red blood cells that in the United States affects mostly blacks. It can cause severe pain and many complications. In 1992, the National Institutes of Health began a study of the drug hydroxyurea for treatment of sickle cell disease. The subjects were 300 adult patients who had had at least three episodes of pain from sickle cell disease in the previous year.

(a) Why would giving hydroxyurea to all 300 subjects fail to give good information about the effect of the drug?

(b) The study design was a randomized comparative experiment that compared hydroxyurea with a placebo. Outline a suitable design. Your outline should follow the model of Figure 5.6. Be sure to give the sizes of the treatment groups and to indicate the outcomes you will examine.

(c) In 1995, the experiment was stopped ahead of schedule because the hydroxyurea group had only half as many pain episodes as the control group. Explain why your design produces compelling evidence that hydroxyurea is an effective treatment for sickle cell disease.

26. Some investment advisers believe that charts of past trends in the prices of securities can help predict future prices. Most economists disagree. In an experiment to examine the effects of using charts, business students trade (hypothetically) a foreign currency at computer screens. There are 20 student subjects, named for convenience A, B, C, . . . , T. Their goal is to make as much as possible, and the best performances are rewarded with small prizes. The student traders have the price history of the foreign currency in dollars in their computers; they may or may not also have software that highlights trends. Describe a design for this experiment and use Table 5.1 to carry out the randomization required by your design.

◆ 27. A college allows students to choose either classroom or self-paced instruction in a basic mathematics course. The college wants to compare the effectiveness of self-paced and regular instruction. Someone proposes giving the same final exam to all students in both versions of the course and comparing the average score of those who took the self-paced option with the average score of students in regular sections.

(a) Explain why confounding makes the results of that study worthless.
(b) Given 30 students who are willing to use either regular or self-paced instruction, outline an experimental design to compare the two methods of instruction. Then use Table 5.1 starting at line 108 to carry out the randomization.

◆ 28. The article in the *New England Journal of Medicine* that presents the final results of the Physicians' Health Study begins with these words: "The Physicians' Health Study is a randomized, double-blind, placebo-controlled trial designed to determine whether low-dose aspirin (325 mg every other day) decreases cardiovascular mortality and whether beta carotene reduces the incidence of cancer." Doctors are expected to understand this. Explain to a doctor who knows no statistics what "randomized," "double-blind," and "placebo-controlled" mean.

◆ 29. You read in a magazine that "nonphysical treatments such as meditation and prayer have been shown to be effective in controlled scientific studies for such ailments as high blood pressure, insomnia, ulcers, and asthma." Explain in simple language what the article means by "controlled scientific studies" and why such studies can show that meditation and prayer are effective treatments for some medical problems.

30. Below are the names of 20 patients who have consented to participate in a trial of surgical treatments for angina. Outline an experiment to compare surgical treatment with a placebo (sham surgery) and use Table 5.1, beginning at line 101, to do the required randomization. (Ignore the asterisks.)

Ashley	Cravens*	Lippmann	Strong*
Bean*	Dorfman	Mark*	Tobias
Block	Garcia	Morton*	Valenzuela*
Chen	Huang*	Popkin	Washington
Chavez*	Kidder	Sosa	Williams

31. Unknown to the researchers in Exercise 30, the eight subjects whose names are marked by asterisks will have a fatal heart attack during the study period. We can observe how sampling variability operates in a randomized experiment by keeping track of how many of these eight subjects are assigned to the group that will receive the new surgical treatment. Carry out the random assignment of 10 subjects to the treatment group 20 times, keeping track of how many asterisks are on the names you choose each time. Then make a histogram of the count of heart attack victims assigned to the treatment. What is the average number in your 20 tries?

◆ 32. Explain clearly the advantage of using several thousand subjects, rather than just 20, in the experiment of Exercise 30.

■ 33.   Explain carefully how you would randomly assign the 20 subjects named in Exercise 30 to the four treatments in the Physicians' Health Study. Figure 5.8 on page 184 describes the treatments. Assign 5 of the 20 to each group. Use Table 5.1 at line 120 to carry out the randomization.

Statistical Evidence

◆ 34.   A randomized comparative experiment examined whether a calcium supplement in the diet reduces the blood pressure of healthy men. The subjects received either a calcium supplement or a placebo for 12 weeks. The researchers concluded that "the blood pressure of the calcium group was significantly lower than that of the placebo group." "Significant" in this conclusion means statistically significant. Explain what statistically significant means in the context of this experiment, as if you were speaking to a doctor who knows no statistics.

◆ 35.   The financial aid office of a university asks a sample of students about their employment and earnings. The report says that "for academic year earnings, a statistically significant difference was found between the sexes, with men earning more on the average. No significant difference was found between the earnings of black and white students." Explain both of these conclusions, for the effects of sex and of race on average earnings, in language understandable to someone who knows no statistics.

Statistics in Practice

◆ 36.   A common form of nonresponse in telephone surveys is "ring-no-answer." That is, a call is made to an active number but no one answers. The Italian National Statistical Institute looked at nonresponse to a government survey of households in Italy during the periods January 1 to Easter and July 1 to August 31. All calls were made between 7 and 10 P.M., but 21.4% gave "ring-no-answer" in one period versus 41.5% "ring-no-answer" in the other period. Which period do you think had the higher rate of no

answers? Why? Explain why a high rate of nonresponse makes sample results less reliable.

◆ 37.   The *wording of questions* can strongly influence the results of a sample survey. Here are two wordings for the same question.

> (a)   Should laws be passed to eliminate all possibilities of special interests giving huge sums of money to candidates?
> (b)   Should laws be passed to prohibit interest groups from contributing to campaigns, or do groups have a right to contribute to the candidates they support?

One of these questions drew 40% favoring banning contributions; the other drew 80% with this opinion. Which question produced the 40% and which got 80%? Explain why the results were so different.

◆ 38.   Do those high center brake lights, required on all cars sold in the United States since 1986, really reduce rear-end collisions? Randomized comparative experiments with fleets of rental and business cars, done before the lights were required, showed that the third brake light reduced rear-end collisions by as much as 50%. Alas, requiring the third light in all cars led to only a 5% drop. Explain why the experiment did not realistically imitate conditions after the lights were required.

Additional Exercises

◆ 39.   Ms. Caucus is her party's candidate in the Second Congressional District of Indiana. The party wants to know what percent of registered voters would vote for Ms. Caucus if the election were held tomorrow. A polling firm contacts 800 voters, of whom 456 say they would vote for Ms. Caucus. What is the population that the poll seeks information about? What is the sample? Explain to someone who knows no statistics the advantage of a sample of 800 voters over a sample of 200 voters.

◆ 40.   Sampling from a list that contains only part of the population is a common cause of bias in sampling. In each of the following examples, explain why this source of bias may be present.

(a)   To assess public opinion on a proposal to reduce welfare and unemployment payments, a polling firm selects a sample by random digit dialing. That is, they use a computer to dial residential telephone numbers at random.

(b)   To assess the reaction of her constituents to the same proposal, a member of Congress uses her free-mailing privilege to send a questionnaire to every registered voter in her district.

◆   **41.**   The advice columnist Ann Landers regularly invites her readers to respond to questions asked in her newspaper column. On one occasion, she asked, "If you had it to do over again, would you have children?" Almost 10,000 parents wrote in, of whom 70% said "No." Shortly afterward, a national poll asked a random sample of 1400 parents the same question; 90% of this sample said "Yes." Which of these polls is more trustworthy, and why?

42.   Joan's small accounting firm serves 30 business clients. Joan wants to interview a sample of 5 clients in detail to find ways to improve client satisfaction. To avoid bias, she chooses an SRS of size 5. Use Table 5.1 at line 123 to choose the SRS from Joan's client list.

A-1 Plumbing	Accent Printing	Balloons Inc.
Anderson	Bailey Trucking	Blue Print
Construction	Best's Camera	Specialties
Bennett	Shop	Computer
Hardware	Classic Flowers	Answers
Central Tree	Fleisch Realty	Hernandez
Service	JL Records	Electronics
Darlene's Dolls	MagicTan	Keiser
Johnson	River City	Construction
Commodities	Books	Peerless Machine
Liu's Chinese	Satellite Services	Riverside Tavern
Restaurant	Tire Specialties	Scotch Wash
Photo Arts	Action Sport	Von's Video
Rustic Boutique	Shop	Store
Sewer's Center		

■   **43.**   The Internal Revenue Service plans to examine an SRS of individual federal income tax returns from each state. One variable of interest is the proportion of returns claiming itemized deductions. The total number of tax returns in a state varies from more than 13 million in California to fewer than 220,000 in Wyoming.

(a)   Will the margin of error for estimating the proportion change from state to state if an SRS of 2000 tax returns is selected in each state? Explain your answer.

(b)   Will the margin of error change from state to state if an SRS of 1% of all tax returns is selected in each state? Explain your answer.

■   **44.**   The last stage of the Current Population Survey chooses addresses within small areas called blocks. The method used is *systematic random sampling*. An example will illustrate the idea of a systematic sample. Suppose that we must choose 4 addresses out of 100. Because $100/4 = 25$, we can think of the list as four lists of 25 addresses. Choose 1 of the first 25 at random, using Table 5.1. The sample contains this address and the addresses 25, 50, and 75 places down the list from it. If 13 is chosen, for example, then the systematic random sample consists of the addresses numbered 13, 38, 63, and 88.

(a)   Use Table 5.1 to choose a systematic random sample of 5 addresses from a list of 200. Enter the table at line 120.

(b)   Like an SRS, a systematic sample gives all individuals the same chance to be chosen. Explain why this is true, then explain carefully why a systematic sample is nonetheless *not* an SRS.

◆   **45.**   An experiment that claimed to show that meditation lowers anxiety proceeded as follows. The experimenter interviewed the subjects and rated their level of anxiety. Then the subjects were randomly assigned to two groups. The experimenter taught one group how to meditate and they meditated daily for a month. The other group was simply told to relax more. At the end of the month, the experimenter interviewed all the subjects again and rated their anxiety level. The meditation group now had less anxiety. Psychologists said that the results were suspect because the ratings were not blind. Explain what this means and how lack of blindness could bias the reported results.

46.   Ignoring all practical difficulties and moral issues, outline the design of an experiment that would settle the question of whether cigarette smoking causes lung cancer.

◆   47.   In a test of the effects of persistent pesticides, researchers will feed a diet contaminated with DDT to rats for 60 days after weaning. Then they will measure the rats' nerve responses to assess the effects of the DDT.

(a)   Explain why the experimenters should also study a control group of rats that are fed the same diet uncontaminated with DDT.
(b)   If 20 newly weaned male rats are available, outline the design of the experiment and use Table 5.1 starting at line 123 to carry out the randomization.

48.   Will providing child care for employees make a company more attractive to women, even those who are unmarried? You are designing an experiment to answer this question. You prepare recruiting material for two fictitious companies, both in similar businesses in the same location. Company A's brochure does not mention child care. There are two versions of Company B's material, identical except that one describes the company's on-site child-care facility. Your subjects are 40 unmarried women who are college seniors seeking employment. Each subject will read recruiting material for both companies and choose the one she would prefer to work for. You will give each version of Company B's brochure to

half the women. You expect that a higher percentage of those who read the description that includes child care will choose Company B.

(a)   Outline an appropriate design for the experiment.
(b)   The names of the subjects appear below. Use Table 5.1, beginning at line 131, to do the randomization required by your design. List the subjects who will read the version that mentions child care.

Abrams	Danielson	Gutierrez	Lippman	Rosen
Adamson	Durr	Howard	Martinez	Sugiwara
Afifi	Edwards	Hwang	McNeill	Thompson
Brown	Fluharty	Iselin	Morse	Travers
Cansico	Garcia	Janle	Ng	Turing
Chen	Gerson	Kaplan	Quinones	Ullmann
Cortez	Green	Kim	Rivera	Williams
Curzakis	Gupta	Lattimore	Roberts	Wong

◆   49.   Fizz Laboratories, a pharmaceutical company, has developed a new pain-relief medication. Sixty patients suffering from arthritis and needing pain relief are available. Each patient will be treated and asked an hour later, "About what percentage of pain relief did you experience?"

(a)   Why should Fizz not simply administer the new drug and record the patients' responses?
(b)   Outline the design of an experiment to compare the drug's effectiveness with that of aspirin and of a placebo.
(c)   Should patients be told which drug they are receiving? How would this knowledge probably affect their reactions?
(d)   If patients are not told which treatment they are receiving, the experiment is single-blind. Should this experiment be double-blind also? Explain.

■   50.   Is the number of days a letter takes to reach another city affected by the day of the week it is mailed and whether or not the ZIP code is used? Describe briefly the design of a two-factor experiment to investigate this question. Be sure to specify the treatments exactly and to tell how you will handle outside variables such as the time of day the letter is mailed.

◆ **51.** Exercise 50 illustrates the use of a statistically designed experiment to answer questions that arise in everyday life. Select a question of interest to you that an experiment might answer and carefully discuss the design of an appropriate experiment.

■ **52.** Corn is an important part of the feed of many farm animals. Normal corn is low in the amino acid lysine. Animals may grow faster if they eat new varieties of corn with increased amounts of lysine. Researchers conduct an experiment to compare a new variety, called floury-2, with normal corn. They mix corn–soybean meal diets using each type of corn at each of three protein levels, 12% protein, 16% protein, and 20% protein. There are thus six diets in all. Ten one-day-old male chicks are assigned to each diet, and their weight gains after 21 days are recorded.

(a) This experiment has two factors. What are they?

(b) Outline the design of the experiment. Be sure to use randomization. (You need not actually carry out the randomization required by your design.)

◆ **53.** The many connections on the bottom of electronic circuit boards are soldered by passing the board through a standing wave of molten solder. An engineer wants to study the effect the speed of the conveyor belt that carries the circuit boards has on the quality of the soldering. The speeds to be compared are 20, 25, and 30 feet per minute. The outcome variable is the number of improperly soldered connections among the 2000 connections on a circuit board.

(a) The engineer plans to process 10 boards at each conveyor speed. Why should she assign the speeds at random to the 30 boards, rather than simply process the first 10 at 20 feet per minute, the second 10 at 25 feet per minute, and so on?

(b) Outline the design of a randomized comparative experiment, beginning with boards numbered 1 through 30 in the order in which they will be soldered.

(c) Enter Table 5.1 at line 130 to carry out the randomization required. List the sequence of 30 conveyor speeds that the engineer will use when she carries out the experiment.

◆ **54.** A psychologist reports that "in our sample, ethnocentrism was significantly higher among church attenders than among nonattenders." Explain what this means in language understandable to someone who knows no statistics. Do not use the word "significance" in your answer.

◆ **55.** The cigarette industry has adopted a voluntary code requiring that models appearing in its advertising must appear to be at least 25 years old. Studies have shown, however, that consumers think many of the models are younger. Here is a quote from a study that asked whether different brands of cigarettes use models that appear to be of different ages:

[Statistical analysis] revealed that the brand variable is highly significant, indicating that the average perceived age of the models is not equal across the 12 brands. As discussed previously, certain brands such as Lucky Strike Lights, Kool Milds, and Virginia Slims tended to have younger models. [From Michael B. Maziz et al., Perceived age and attractiveness of models in cigarette advertisements, *Journal of Marketing*, 56 (January 1992): 22–37.]

Explain to someone who knows no statistics what "highly significant" means and why this is good evidence of differences among all advertisements of these brands even though the subjects saw only a sample of ads.

TECHNOLOGY CORNER

Generating Random Numbers

There are several ways to generate numbers randomly. You can use a table of random numbers, such as Table 5.1. You can draw cards from a deck, ignoring face cards. You can ask someone to make up numbers. You can also produce random numbers using a spreadsheet. The spreadsheet shown in Figure 5.9 includes random numbers between 0 and 99 from each of these four sources.

The first column uses line 142 of the random number table in Table 5.1. The second column was produced by asking someone for random numbers between 0 and 99. The third column uses playing cards to generate random numbers: Face cards (Jack, Queen, King) are ignored, the "10" card is read as a "0" card, and all other denominations are read as their normal numbers. The spreadsheet shows the results of repeatedly shuffling, drawing, and replacing these cards: Ace, 7, 10, 3, Jack, 9, 4.

The fourth column uses the spreadsheet's random number generator, **=RandBetween (0, 99).** Each time the spreadsheet evaluates this command, a random number between 0 and 99 will be produced. While each entry in the fourth column has this same command, different values are produced. (In fact, because spreadsheets tend to continually update formulae, it may recompute a value for these entries each time another entry is added anywhere on the spreadsheet. It is possible to turn off this feature.)

TASK 1.　Create and complete a spreadsheet like the example in Figure 5.9.

Using Histograms to Display Data

Histograms provide a way to display and compare data. To create a histogram using the spreadsheet, first determine the categories into which the data are separated. In the spreadsheet shown in Figure 5.10, categories for 0 to 19, 20 to 39, 40 to 59, 60 to 79, and 80 to 99 are listed in the "Categories" column. Then select **Histogram** from the **Data Analysis Tools.** Select the

	A	B	C	D	E
1	Table	Human	Cards	Spreadsheet	
2					
3	6	34	17	0	
4	87	54	3	36	
5	55	87	94	21	
6	33	31		2	
7	35	9		69	
8	91			78	
9	27			87	
10	48			74	
11	78			1	
12	24			55	
13	4			47	
14	13			14	
15	77			6	
16	75			3	
17	79			46	
18	54			67	
19	26			45	
20	63			17	
21	87			30	
22	62			97	

FIGURE 5.9

column of data to be organized, and then the column of categories to be used. A frequency table is created. The second column indicates how many data are in each of the categories. To create a graph, first rename the first column entries to describe the categories, as shown below. Then select both columns, click the **Graph** icon and follow the steps to produce a graph. (The bars of a histogram should be adjacent to one another. If the bars have gaps between them, select the bars, click **Format** from the taskbar menu, select the **Options** for the **Selected Data Series,** and set the **Gap Width** to be 0.)

Even though random number tables and spreadsheet random number generators are unbiased, natural variability is evident. Notice that the two histograms look different and (perhaps) a bit unbalanced.

TASK 2.　Create histograms for your spreadsheet data created in Task 1. How do your resulting histograms compare to one another? Do you think this variation is due *entirely* to variability?

	A	B	C	D	E	F	G	H
1	Table	Human	Cards	Spreadsheet		Categories		
2								
3	6	34	17	56		19		
4	87	54	3	12		39		
5	55	87	94	6		59		
6	33	31		59		79		
7	35	9		29		99		
8	91			86				
9	27			71				
10	48			56				
11	78			35				
12	24			34				
13	4			45				
14	13			60				
15	77			34				
16	75			91				
17	79			72				
18	54			48				
19	26			40				
20	63			31				
21	87			21				
22	62			61				
23								
24	Bin	Frequency						
25	0 to 19	3						
26	20 to 39	5						
27	40 to 59	3						
28	60 to 79	6						
29	80 to 89	3						
30	More	0						
31								
32								
33								
34								
35								
36	Bin	Frequency						
37	0 to 19	7						
38	20 to 39	3						
39	40 to 59	4						
40	60 to 79	4						
41	80 to 89	2						
42	More	0						
43								
44								
45								
46								
47								

Random Number Table Data

Spreadsheet Random Numbers

FIGURE 5.10

TASK 3. Create a spreadsheet where the first column lists the students in your class. Using the spreadsheet random number generator, assign each person to one of three exercise regimens: daily jogs, daily weight training, or no exercise.

TASK 4. Suppose your class is infected with a deadly, alien virus. There are three experimental drugs that may work separately or in combination to kill the virus. Create a spreadsheet in which the first column lists the students and the next three columns represent the three experimental drugs. Randomly determine which drug or drugs each person will take.

Exploration

When the number of data increases, natural variability tends to become less significant. Using the spreadsheet random number generator, create sets of 50, 100, and 500 random numbers between 0 and 99. Construct histograms for each set. How do these graphs compare?

writing projects

1 ▶ Go to the Web site of the Gallup Organization (**www.gallup.com**). There you will find archives of recent press releases put out by the Gallup poll. Choose a poll topic of interest to you and summarize the poll results. Now examine the press release in detail: Does Gallup give the exact questions asked? The margin of error? Warnings about nonresponse and other sources of additional errors? Finally, return to the Gallup home page to read the account of how the polls are conducted. Write a brief summary of the statistical sampling design used.

2 ▶ Articles in the press often describe medical findings based on an experiment. The conclusion of the Physicians' Health Study that taking aspirin regularly helps prevent heart attacks is an example. Many of the medical studies reported appear in the *Journal of the American Medical Association* or the *New England Journal of Medicine*. A news article is released the same day that the journal appears.

Find an article in a newspaper or magazine that deals with a recent medical study. Describe the purpose and design of the study. Was it an experiment? What were the conclusions of the study, and how well grounded do you think they are?

Add a brief critique of the news article's presentation. Does the article mention a control group? Does it mention random assignment of the subjects? If the article concerns an observational study, does it warn against causal conclusions?

Optional: Locate the medical journal report in your library or on-line. Use the actual report for your critique of the news article.

3 ▶ Choose an issue of current interest to students at your school. Prepare a short (no more than five questions) questionnaire to determine opinions on this issue. Choose a sample of about 25 students, administer your questionnaire, and write a brief description of your findings. Also write a short discussion of your experiences in designing and carrying out the survey.

(Although 25 students are too few for you to be statistically confident of your results, this project centers on the practical work of a survey. You must first identify a population; if it is not possible to reach a wider student population, use students enrolled in this course. Did the subjects find your questions clear? Did you write the questions so that it was easy to tabulate the responses? At the end, did you wish you had asked different questions?)

4 ▶ Polls play a large role in American politics. Let's concentrate on polls that attempt to predict the outcome of elections. There are two types. Polls taken ahead of the election ask "If the election were held today, for whom would you vote?" *Exit polls* interview voters as they leave their polling place. Television networks use exit polls for election-night predictions before the official vote count is complete.

Some countries have laws restricting election forecasts. In France, no poll results can be published in the week before a presidential election. Belgium, Italy, and Portugal have similar laws. Do you think this is wise policy? Why? (You can find detailed comments on election polls in *Statistics: Concepts and Controversies,* listed in Suggested Readings.)

5 ▶ Although experiments with human subjects raise special ethical questions, there are also ethical issues associated with any study that collects data from human subjects. Here are two of these issues. Address one of them in a brief essay.

■ Any institution that receives federal funds must have an *Institutional Review Board (IRB)* that reviews in advance all studies that use human subjects. The IRB is charged with protecting the welfare of the subjects. What is the name of your college's IRB? Who are the members? Are there representatives from outside the college, and if so, how are they chosen? What guidelines does your IRB follow? Do you have any suggestions for strengthening the protection of subjects offered by the IRB's review process?

■ Suppose that you are conducting a sample survey that gathers opinions from subjects. Ethical standards require that you give potential subjects some information about the survey and get their *informed consent* to participate. What kinds of information should respondents be given in order to decide whether to participate? (Perhaps they expect to spend 10 minutes, but the survey takes an hour. Perhaps questions about sex and drugs appear without warning.) Should respondents always be told who is sponsoring the poll? (If so, will knowing that the Republican National Committee is the sponsor affect their answers?) Should a poll always offer to send respondents a copy of the final report so they can see how their information is being used? (That's expensive.)

Exploring Data

"... data are useful only if we can organize them and present them so that their meaning is clear."

chapter **6**

Exploring Data

A flood of data is a prominent feature of modern society. Data, or numerical facts, are essential for making decisions in almost every area of life and work. Like other great floods, the flood of numbers threatens to overwhelm us. We must control the flood by careful organization and interpretation. A corporate data base, for example, contains an immense volume of data—on employees, sales, inventories, customer accounts, equipment, taxes, and other topics. These data are useful only if we can organize them and present them so that their meaning is clear. The penalties for ignoring data can be severe— several banks have suffered billion-dollar losses from unauthorized trades in financial markets by their employees, trades that were hidden in a mass of data that the banks' management did not examine carefully.

Any set of data contains information about some group of *individuals*. The information is organized in *variables*.

Individuals are the objects described by a set of data. Individuals may be people, but they may also be animals or things. A **variable** is any characteristic of an individual. A variable can take different values for different individuals.

E X A M P L E   *A Corporate Data Set*

Figure 6.1 displays a small part of the data set in which CyberStat Corporation records information about its employees. The *individuals* described are the em-

FIGURE 6.1

Part of a data set
displayed by the Excel
spreadsheet program.

	A	B	C	D	E	F
1	Name	Age	Gender	Race	Salary	Job Type
2	Fleetwood, Delores	39	Female	White	62,100	Management
3	Perez, Juan	27	Male	White	47,360	Technical
4	Wang, Lin	22	Female	Asian	18,250	Clerical
5	Johnson, LaVerne	48	Male	Black	77,600	Management
6						

Enter   NUM

FIGURE 6.1

Part of a data set displayed by the Excel spreadsheet program.

ployees. Each row records data on one individual. Each column contains the values of one *variable* for all the individuals. In addition to the person's name, there are 5 variables. Gender, race, and job type are variables that classify the employees and do not take numerical values. Age and salary do take numerical values. You can see that age is measured in years and salary in dollars.

Most data tables follow this format—each row is an individual, and each column is a variable. This data set appears in a *spreadsheet* program that has rows and columns ready for your use. Spreadsheets are commonly used to enter and transmit data, and spreadsheet programs also have functions for basic statistics. ◆

Statistical tools and ideas help us examine data in order to describe their main features. This examination is called **exploratory data analysis.** Like an explorer crossing unknown lands, we want first to simply describe what we see. In this chapter we use both numbers and pictures to explore data. Here are two principles that provide the tactics for exploratory analysis of data.

1. First examine each variable individually. Then move on to study the relationships among several variables.
2. Begin with a graph or graphs. Then add numerical summaries of specific aspects of the data.

These principles also organize the material in this chapter. We start with data on a single variable, then move to relations among several variables. In each setting, we first display the data in graphs, then add numerical summaries.

Displaying Distributions: Histograms

The **distribution** of a variable tells us what values the variable takes and how often it takes each value. Data analysis begins with graphical displays of the distribution of a single variable.

Numerical variables often take many values. A graph of the distribution is clearer if nearby values are grouped together. The most common graph of the distribution of one numerical variable is a **histogram.**

E X A M P L E   *Making a Histogram*

Table 6.1 presents the percent of residents aged 65 years and over in each of the 50 states. To make a histogram of this distribution, proceed as follows:

1. Divide the range of the data into classes of equal width. The data in Table 6.1 range from 5.2 to 18.5, so we choose as our classes

$$5.0 < \text{percent over } 65 \leq 6.0$$
$$6.0 < \text{percent over } 65 \leq 7.0$$
$$\vdots$$
$$18.0 < \text{percent over } 65 \leq 19.0$$

Be sure to specify the classes precisely so that each individual falls into exactly one class. A state with 6.0% of its residents aged 65 or older would fall into the first class, but 6.1% falls into the second.

TABLE 6.1	Percent of Population 65 Years Old and Over, by State, 1996				
State	**Percent**	**State**	**Percent**	**State**	**Percent**
Alabama	13.0	Louisiana	11.4	Ohio	13.4
Alaska	5.2	Maine	13.9	Oklahoma	13.5
Arizona	13.2	Maryland	11.4	Oregon	13.4
Arkansas	14.4	Massachusetts	14.1	Pennsylvania	15.9
California	10.5	Michigan	12.4	Rhode Island	15.8
Colorado	11.0	Minnesota	12.4	South Carolina	12.1
Connecticut	14.3	Mississippi	12.3	South Dakota	14.4
Delaware	12.8	Missouri	13.8	Tennessee	12.5
Florida	18.5	Montana	13.2	Texas	10.2
Georgia	9.9	Nebraska	13.8	Utah	8.8
Hawaii	12.9	Nevada	11.4	Vermont	12.1
Idaho	11.4	New Hampshire	12.0	Virginia	11.2
Illinois	12.5	New Jersey	13.8	Washington	11.6
Indiana	12.6	New Mexico	11.0	West Virginia	15.2
Iowa	15.2	New York	13.4	Wisconsin	13.3
Kansas	13.7	North Carolina	12.5	Wyoming	11.2
Kentucky	12.6	North Dakota	14.5		

SOURCE: *Statistical Abstract of the United States,* 1997.

2. Count the number of individuals in each class. Here are the counts.

Class	Count	Class	Count	Class	Count
5.1 to 6.0	1	10.1 to 11.0	4	15.1 to 16.0	4
6.1 to 7.0	0	11.1 to 12.0	8	16.1 to 17.0	0
7.1 to 8.0	0	12.1 to 13.0	13	17.1 to 18.0	0
8.1 to 9.0	1	13.1 to 14.0	12	18.1 to 19.0	1
9.1 to 10.0	1	14.1 to 15.0	5		

3. Draw the histogram. First mark the scale for the variable whose distribution you are displaying on the horizontal axis. Here it's "percent of state residents age 65 and over." The scale runs from 5 to 19 because that is the span of the classes we chose. The vertical axis contains the scale of counts. Each bar represents a class. The base of the bar covers the class, and the bar height is the class count. There is no horizontal space between the bars unless a class is empty, so that its bar has height zero. Figure 6.2 is our histogram. ◆

The bars of a histogram should cover the entire range of values of a variable. When the possible values of a variable have gaps between them, extend the bases of the bars to meet halfway between two adjacent possible values. For example, in a histogram of the ages in years of university faculty, the bars representing 25 to 29 years and 30 to 34 years would meet at 29.5.

Our eyes respond to the *area* of the bars in a histogram. Because the classes are all the same width, area is determined by height. You must use your judgment in choosing classes to display the shape. Too few classes will give a "skyscraper" graph, with all values in a few classes with tall bars. Too many will produce a "pancake" graph, with most classes having one or no observations. Neither choice will give a good picture of

FIGURE 6.2

Histogram of the percent of state residents age 65 and over.

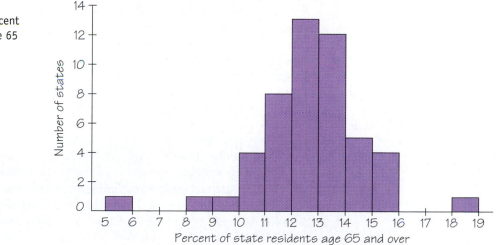

the shape of the distribution. Statistics software will choose the classes for you; the computer's choice is usually a good one, but you can change it if you want.

Interpreting Histograms

Making a statistical graph is not an end in itself. The purpose of the graph is to help us understand the data. After you make a graph, always ask, "What do I see?" Once you have displayed a distribution, you can see its important features as follows.

> In any graph of data, look for the **overall pattern** and for striking **deviations** from that pattern. You can describe the overall pattern of a histogram by its **shape, center,** and **spread.** We will soon learn how to describe center and spread numerically. An important kind of deviation is an **outlier,** an individual value that falls outside the overall pattern.

EXAMPLE   *Describing a Distribution*

Look again at the histogram in Figure 6.2. *Shape:* The distribution has a *single peak.* It is roughly *symmetric*—that is, the pattern is similar on both sides of the peak. *Center:* The midpoint of the distribution is close to the single peak at about 13%. That is, roughly half the observations lie on either side of 13%. *Spread:* The spread is about 10% to 16% if we ignore the four most extreme observations.

   Outliers: Two states stand out in the histogram of Figure 6.2. You can find them in the table once the histogram has called attention to them. Florida has 18.5% of its residents over age 65, and Alaska has only 5.2%. Once you have spotted outliers, look for an explanation. Some outliers are due to mistakes, such as typing 5.0 as 50. Other outliers point to the special nature of some observations. Florida, with its many retired people, has many residents over 65 and Alaska, the northern frontier, has few. ◆

   When you describe a distribution, concentrate on the main features. Look for major peaks, not for minor ups and downs in the bars of the histogram. Look for clear outliers, not just for the smallest and largest observations. Look for rough *symmetry* or clear *skewness.*

> A distribution is **symmetric** if the right and left sides of the histogram are approximately mirror images of each other. A distribution is **skewed to the right** if the right side of the histogram (containing the observations with larger values) extends much farther out than the left side. It is **skewed to the left** if the left side of the histogram extends much farther out than the right side.

Data displayed on a laptop computer.

Distributions of real data are usually only roughly symmetric. We consider Figure 6.2 (without the outliers) to be approximately symmetric. Here is an example of a skewed distribution.

EXAMPLE **Shakespeare's Words**

Figure 6.3 shows the distribution of lengths of words used in Shakespeare's plays. This distribution also has a single peak but is skewed to the right. That is, there are many short words (3 and 4 letters) and few very long words (10, 11, or 12 letters), so that the right tail of the histogram extends out much farther than the left tail. ◆

FIGURE 6.3
Histogram of the lengths of words used in Shakespeare's plays.

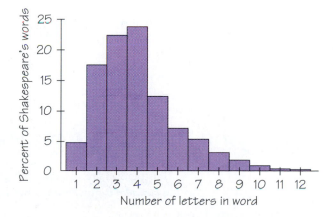

Outliers are one kind of deviation that you should notice when inspecting a histogram. The next example illustrates another type of deviation from the overall pattern.

E X A M P L E   *Quality Control*

Figure 6.4 presents data from a study by the quality expert W. Edwards Deming (see Spotlight 6.1). The data concern the size of steel rods used in a manufacturing process. The histogram displays the diameters of 500 steel rods, as reported by the manufacturer's inspectors. The rod diameters are measured to the nearest thousandth of a centimeter, so each bar in the histogram shows how often one measurement occurred.

We see an overall pattern in the size of the rods: the distribution is approximately symmetric, centered at 1.002 centimeters and falling off rapidly both above and below. There is also a deviation from this pattern: the *gap* at 0.999 centimeter.

Rods smaller than 1.000 cm will be loose in their bearings. The inspectors are supposed to reject them. The empty 0.999 class in the histogram, with the taller than expected bar for 1.000 centimeter, shows that the inspectors are passing rods that measure 0.999 centimeter by recording them as 1.000 centimeter. The inspectors don't realize that just one-thousandth of a centimeter can be crucial. With better training of the inspectors, the missing 0.999 class filled in and the distribution became quite regular.   ◆

FIGURE 6.4
Deming's illustration of the effects of improper inspection: A histogram with a gap.

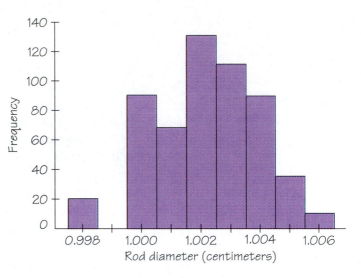

Displaying Distributions: Stemplots

Histograms are not the only graphical display of distributions. For small data sets, a *stemplot* is quicker to make and presents more detailed information.

To make a **stemplot:**

1. Separate each observation into a **stem** consisting of all but the final (rightmost) digit and a **leaf,** the final digit. Stems may have as many digits as needed, but each leaf contains only a single digit.
2. Write the stems in a vertical column with the smallest at the top, and draw a vertical line at the right of this column.
3. Write each leaf in the row to the right of its stem, in increasing order out from the stem.

SPOTLIGHT

6.1

W. Edwards Deming

From one point of view, statistics is about understanding variation. Elimination of variation in products and processes is the central theme of statistical quality control. So it is not surprising that a statistician should become the leading guru of quality management. In the final decades of his long life, W. Edwards Deming (1900–1993) was one of the world's most influential consultants to management.

Deming grew up in Wyoming and earned a doctorate in physics at Yale. Working for the U.S. Department of Agriculture in the 1930s, he became acquainted with the young field of statistics and in particular with statistical process control, newly invented by Walter Shewhart of AT&T. In 1939 he moved to the U.S. Census Bureau as an expert on sampling.

The work that made Deming famous began after he left the government in 1946. He visited Japan to advise on a census, and returned to lec-

W. Edwards Deming

ture on quality control. He earned a large following in Japan, which named its premier prize for industrial quality after him. As Japan's reputation for excellence in manufacturing grew, Deming's fame grew with it. Blunt-spoken and even abrasive, he told corporate leaders that most quality problems are system problems for which management is responsible. He urged breaking down barriers to worker involvement and constant search for causes of variation.

EXAMPLE   *Making a Stemplot*

For the "over 65" percents in Table 6.1, the whole number part of the observation is the stem and the final digit (tenths) is the leaf. The Alabama entry, 13.0, has stem 13 and leaf 0. Stems can have as many digits as needed, but each leaf must consist of only a single digit. Figure 6.5 is the stemplot for the data in Table 6.1.

◆

```
 5 │ 2
 6 │
 7 │
 8 │ 8
 9 │ 9
10 │ 2 5
11 │ 0 0 2 2 4 4 4 4 6
12 │ 0 1 1 3 4 4 5 5 5 6 6 8 9
13 │ 0 2 2 3 4 4 4 5 7 8 8 8 9
14 │ 1 3 4 4 5
15 │ 2 2 8 9
16 │
17 │
18 │ 5
```

FIGURE 6.5   A stemplot of the percent of state residents age 65 and over.

A stemplot looks like a histogram turned on end. The stemplot in Figure 6.5 resembles the histogram in Figure 6.2. The stemplot, unlike the histogram, preserves the actual value of each observation. We interpret stemplots like histograms, looking for the overall pattern and for any outliers.

You can choose the classes in a histogram. The classes (the stems) of a stemplot are given to you. You can get more flexibility by rounding the data so that the final digit after rounding is suitable as a leaf. Do this when the data have too many digits. For example, data like

  3.468   2.567   2.981   1.095 ···

would have too many stems if we took the first three digits as the stem and the final digit as the leaf. You can round these data to

  3.5   2.6   3.0   1.1···

before making a stemplot.

Describing Center: Mean and Median

A description of a distribution almost always includes a measure of its center or average. The most common measure of center is the ordinary arithmetic average, or *mean*.

> To find the **mean** of a set of observations, add their values and divide by the number of observations. If the n observations are $x_1, x_2, \ldots, x_n$, their mean is
>
> $$\overline{x} = \frac{x_1 + x_2 + \cdots + x_n}{n}$$

The bar over the x indicates the mean of all the x-values. Pronounce the mean $\overline{x}$ as "x-bar." This notation is very common. When writers who are discussing data use $\overline{x}$ or $\overline{y}$, they are talking about a mean.

E X A M P L E   *Calculating the Mean*

A study in Switzerland examined the number of hysterectomies (removal of the uterus) performed in a year by doctors. Here are the data for a sample of 15 male doctors.

27   50   33   25   86   25   85   31   37   44   20   36   59   34   28

A stemplot shows that the distribution is skewed to the right and that there are two outliers on the high side:

```
2 | 05578
3 | 13467
4 | 4
5 | 09
6 |
7 |
8 | 56
```

The mean number of hysterectomies performed by these doctors is

$$\overline{x} = \frac{x_1 + x_2 + \cdots + x_n}{n}$$

$$= \frac{27 + 50 + 33 + \cdots + 28}{15}$$

$$= \frac{620}{15} = 41.3$$

In practice, you can key the data into your calculator and hit the $\bar{x}$ key. You don't have to actually add and divide. But you should know that this is what the calculator is doing. ◆

The mean is the average value. Another way to measure center is to give the midpoint, the value with half the observations below it and half above. This is the idea of the *median*. Here is the full rule for finding the median.

> To find the **median M** of a distribution:
>
> 1. Arrange all observations in order of size, from smallest to largest.
> 2. If the number *n* of observations is odd, the median *M* is the center observation in the ordered list. The location of the median is found by counting $(n + 1)/2$ observations up from the bottom of the list.
> 3. If the number *n* of observations is even, the median *M* is the average of the two center observations in the ordered list. The location of the median is again $(n + 1)/2$ from the bottom of the list.

Be sure to write down each individual observation in the data set, even if several observations repeat the same value. And be sure to arrange the observations in order of size before locating the median. The middle observation in the haphazard order in which the observations first come has no importance. Note that the recipe $(n + 1)/2$ gives the position of the median in the ordered list of observations, *not* the median itself.

EXAMPLE *Calculating the Median*

To find the median for our sample of 15 male doctors, first arrange the observations in order:

20   25   25   27   28   31   33   34   36   37   44   50   59   85   86

There are $n = 15$ observations, so the location of the median is

$$\frac{n + 1}{2} = \frac{16}{2} = 8$$

The median is the 8th observation in the ordered list. Therefore $M = 34$.

The study also looked at a sample of 10 female Swiss doctors. The numbers of hysterectomies performed by these doctors (arranged in order) were

5   7   10   14   18   19   25   29   31   33

The location of the median is

$$\frac{n+1}{2} = \frac{11}{2} = 5.5$$

The location 5.5 means "halfway between the fifth and sixth observations in the ordered list." So the median is the average of these two observations:

$$M = \frac{18+19}{2} = 18.5$$

The typical female doctor performed many fewer hysterectomies than the typical male doctor. This was one of the important conclusions of the study. Notice that whenever the number of observations n is odd, the median is one of the observations in the list. When n is even, the median lies midway between two observations.   ◆

This example illustrates an important difference between the mean and the median. *The mean is strongly influenced by a few extreme observations.* In particular, the mean of a right-skewed distribution is larger than the median. The median number of hysterectomies performed by the male doctors was 34, but the few large values (85 and 86) in the right tail of the distribution pull the mean up to 41.3. In practice, you must ask yourself whether the "midpoint" (the median) or the "average" (the mean) is a better description of the center of the data.

Describing Spread: The Quartiles

The mean and median provide two different measures of the center of a distribution. But a measure of center alone can be misleading. The Census Bureau reports that in 1997 the median income of American households was $37,005. Half of all households had incomes below $37,005, and half had higher incomes. But these figures do not tell the whole story. Two nations with the same median household income are very different if one has extremes of wealth and poverty and the other has little variation among households. A drug with the correct mean concentration of active ingredient is dangerous if some batches are much too high and others much too low. We are interested in the *spread* or *variability* of incomes and drug potencies as well as their centers. The simplest useful numerical description of a distribution consists of both a measure of center and a measure of spread.

One way to measure spread is to give the smallest and largest observations. For example, the percent of residents over age 65 in the states ranges from 5.2% in Alaska to 18.5% in Florida. These single observations show the full spread of the data, but they may be outliers. We can improve our description of spread by also looking at the spread of the middle half of the data. The *quartiles* mark out the middle half. Count up the ordered list of observations, starting from the smallest.

The *first quartile* lies one-quarter of the way up the list. The *third quartile* lies three-quarters of the way up the list. In other words, the first quartile is larger than 25% of the observations, and the third quartile is larger than 75% of the observations. The second quartile is the median, which is larger than 50% of the observations. That is the idea of quartiles. We need a rule to make the idea exact. The rule for calculating the quartiles uses the rule for the median.

To calculate the **quartiles:**

1. Arrange the observations in increasing order and locate the median M in the ordered list of observations.
2. The **first quartile Q_1** is the median of the observations whose position in the ordered list is to the left of the location of the overall median.
3. The **third quartile Q_3** is the median of the observations whose position in the ordered list is to the right of the location of the overall median.

EXAMPLE   *Calculating Quartiles*

The numbers of hysterectomies performed by our sample of 15 male doctors were (arranged in order):

20   25   25   27   28   31   33   **34**   36   37   44   50   59   85   86

There is an odd number of observations, so the median is the middle one, the bold 34 in the list. The first quartile is the median of the 7 observations to the left of the median. This is the 4th of these 7 observations, so $Q_1 = 27$. If you want, you can use the recipe for the location of the median with $n = 7$:

$$\frac{n + 1}{2} = \frac{7 + 1}{2} = 4$$

The third quartile is the median of the 7 observations to the right of the median, $Q_3 = 50$. The overall median is left out of the calculation of the quartiles when there is an odd number of observations.

For the 10 female doctors, the data are (again arranged in increasing order):

5   7   10   14   18 | 19   25   29   31   33

There is an even number of observations, so the median lies midway between the middle pair. Its location is between the 5th and 6th values, marked by | in the list. The first quartile is the median of the first 5 observations, because these are the observations to the left of the location of the median. Check that $Q_1 = 10$ and $Q_3 = 29$. When the number of observations is even, all the observations enter into the calculation of the quartiles. ◆

Some software packages use a slightly different rule to find the quartiles, so computer results may be a bit different from your own work. Don't worry about this. The differences will always be too small to be important.

The Five-Number Summary and Boxplots

The smallest and largest observations tell us little about the distribution as a whole, but they give information about the tails of the distribution that is missing if we know only Q_1, M, and Q_3. To get a quick summary of both center and spread, combine all five numbers.

> The **five-number summary** of a distribution consists of the smallest observation, the first quartile, the median, the third quartile, and the largest observation, written in order from smallest to largest. In symbols, the five-number summary is
>
> $$\text{Minimum} \quad Q_1 \quad M \quad Q_3 \quad \text{Maximum}$$

These five numbers offer a reasonably complete description of center and spread. The five-number summaries for the hysterectomy example are

    20   27   34   50   86

for the male doctors and

    5   10   18.5   29   33

for the female doctors. The five-number summary of a distribution leads to a new graph, the *boxplot*. Figure 6.6 shows boxplots for the Swiss doctors.

> .A **boxplot** is a graph of the five-number summary. A central box spans the quartiles, with a line marking the median. Lines extend out from the box to the smallest and largest observations.

FIGURE 6.6
Side-by-side boxplots comparing the number of hysterectomies performed by male and female Swiss doctors.

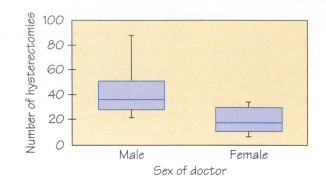

You can draw boxplots either horizontally or vertically. Be sure to include a numerical scale in the graph. When you look at a boxplot, first locate the median, which marks the center of the distribution. Then look at the spread. The quartiles show the spread of the middle half of the data, and the extremes (the smallest and largest observations) show the spread of the entire data set.

Because boxplots show less detail than histograms or stemplots, they are best used for side-by-side comparison of more than one distribution, as in Figure 6.6. We can see at once that female doctors in general perform far fewer hysterectomies than men. In fact, the upper extreme for females falls below the male median. You can also see that the female distribution has less spread. In particular, it lacks the few very large observations that stretch out the distribution for the men.

Describing Spread: The Standard Deviation

Although the five-number summary is the most generally useful numerical description of a distribution, it is not the most common. That distinction belongs to the combination of the mean with the *standard deviation.* The mean, like the median, is a measure of center. The standard deviation, like the quartiles and extremes in the five-number summary, measures spread. The standard deviation and its close relative, the *variance,* measure spread by looking at how far the observations are from their mean.

E X A M P L E   *Understanding the Standard Deviation*

A person's metabolic rate is the rate at which the body consumes energy. Metabolic rate is important in studies of weight gain, dieting, and exercise. Here are the metabolic rates of 7 men who took part in a study of dieting. (The units are calories per 24 hours. These are the same calories used to describe the energy content of foods.)

 1792   1666   1362   1614   1460   1867   1439

Figure 6.7 displays the data as points above the number line, with their mean marked by an asterisk (*). The arrows mark two of the deviations from the mean.

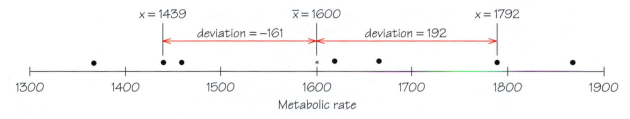

FIGURE 6.7   The variance and standard deviation measure spread by looking at the deviations of observations from their mean.

These deviations show how spread out the data are about their mean. Some of the deviations are positive and some are negative. Squaring the deviations makes them all positive. Observations far from the mean in either direction will have large positive squared deviations. So a reasonable measure of spread is the average of the squared deviations. This average is called the *variance*. The variance is large if the observations are widely spread about their mean; it is small if the observations are all close to the mean.

But the variance has the wrong units: if we measure metabolic rate in calories, the variance of the metabolic rates is in squared calories. Taking the square root of the variance gets us back to calories. The square root of the variance is the *standard deviation*. ◆

The **variance s^2** of a set of observations is an average of the squares of the deviations of the observations from their mean. In symbols, the variance of n observations $x_1, x_2, \ldots, x_n$ is

$$s^2 = \frac{(x_1 - \bar{x})^2 + (x_2 - \bar{x})^2 + \cdots + (x_n - \bar{x})^2}{n - 1}$$

The **standard deviation s** is the square root of the variance s^2.

In practice, use software or your calculator to obtain the standard deviation from keyed-in data. Doing an example step-by-step will help you understand how the variance and standard deviation work, however.

E X A M P L E   *Calculating the Standard Deviation*

To find the standard deviation of the 7 metabolic rates, first find the mean:

$$\bar{x} = \frac{1792 + 1666 + 1362 + 1614 + 1460 + 1867 + 1439}{7}$$

$$= \frac{11{,}200}{7} = 1600 \text{ calories}$$

The deviations shown in Figure 6.7 are the starting point for calculating the variance and the standard deviation.

Observations x_i	Deviations $x_i - \bar{x}$	Squared deviations $(x_i - \bar{x})^2$
1792	$1792 - 1600 = \quad 192$	$192^2 = \quad 36{,}864$
1666	$1666 - 1600 = \quad 66$	$66^2 = \quad 4{,}356$
1362	$1362 - 1600 = -238$	$(-238)^2 = 56{,}644$
1614	$1614 - 1600 = \quad 14$	$14^2 = \quad 196$
1460	$1460 - 1600 = -140$	$(-140)^2 = 19{,}600$
1867	$1867 - 1600 = \quad 267$	$267^2 = 71{,}289$
1439	$1439 - 1600 = -161$	$(-161)^2 = 25{,}921$
	sum $= \quad 0$	sum $= 214{,}870$

The variance is the sum of the squared deviations divided by one less than the number of observations:

$$s^2 = \frac{214{,}870}{6} = 35{,}811.67$$

The standard deviation is the square root of the variance:

$$s = \sqrt{35{,}811.67} = 189.24 \text{ calories} \quad \blacklozenge$$

More important than the details of hand calculation are the properties that determine the usefulness of the standard deviation:

- s measures spread about the mean and should be used only when the mean is chosen as the measure of center.
- $s = 0$ only when there is *no spread*. This happens only when all observations have the same value. Otherwise $s > 0$. As the observations become more spread out about their mean, s gets larger.
- s has the same units of measurement as the original observations. For example, if you measure metabolic rates in calories, s is also in calories. This is one reason to prefer s to the variance s^2, which is in squared calories.
- Like the mean $\bar{x}$, s is strongly influenced by a few extreme observations. For example, the standard deviation of the hysterectomy data for male doctors is 20.61. (Use your calculator to verify this.) If we omit the two extreme obervations 85 and 86, the standard deviation drops to 10.97.

We now have a choice between two descriptions of the center and spread of a distribution: the five-number summary, or $\bar{x}$ and s. Because $\bar{x}$ and s are sensitive to extreme observations, they can be misleading when a distribution is strongly skewed or has outliers. In fact, because the two sides of a skewed distribution have different spreads, no single number such as *s* describes the spread well. The five-number summary, with its two quartiles and two extremes, does a better job.

> The five-number summary is usually better than the mean and standard deviation for describing a skewed distribution or a distribution with outliers. Use $\bar{x}$ and *s* only for reasonably symmetric distributions that are free of outliers.

Although the standard deviation is widely used, it is not a natural or convenient measure of the spread of a distribution. The real reason for the popularity of the standard deviation is that it is the natural measure of spread for *normal distributions,* an important class of distributions that we will meet in the next chapter.

Displaying Relations Between Two Variables

The examples we have looked at so far considered only a single variable, such as the number of hysterectomies performed by a doctor. Now we will examine data for two variables, emphasizing the nature and strength of the relationship between the variables. To study a relationship, we measure both variables on the same individuals. Often, we think that one of the variables explains or influences the other.

> A **response variable** measures an outcome of a study. An **explanatory variable** explains or influences changes in a response variable.

EXAMPLE *Natural Gas Consumption*

Sue is about to install solar panels to reduce the cost of heating her house in the midwest. In order to know how much the solar panels help, she records her consumption of natural gas before the panels are installed. Gas consumption is higher in cold weather, so the relationship between outside temperature and gas consumption is important.

Table 6.2 gives data for 9 months. The response variable is the average amount of natural gas consumed each day during the month, in hundreds of cubic feet. The explanatory variable is the average number of heating degree-days each day during the month. (Heating degree-days are the usual measure of demand for heating. One degree-day is accumulated for each degree a day's average temperature falls below 65°F. An average temperature of 20°F, for example, corresponds to 45 degree-days.)

TABLE 6.2	Natural Gas Consumption of a Household								
	Oct	Nov	Dec	Jan	Feb	Mar	Apr	May	June
Degree-days per day	15.6	26.8	37.8	36.4	35.5	18.6	15.3	7.9	0.0
Gas consumed per day (100 cubic feet)	5.2	6.1	8.7	8.5	8.8	4.9	4.5	2.5	1.1

Looking at the numbers in the table, we can see that more degree-days (colder temperatures) go with higher gas consumption. But the shape and strength of the relationship are not fully clear. To display and interpret these data, we need a graph. Figure 6.8a is a *scatterplot* of Sue's data. ◆

A **scatterplot** shows the relationship between two numerical variables measured on the same individuals. The values of one variable appear on the horizontal axis, and the values of the other variable appear on the vertical axis. Each individual in the data appears as the point in the plot fixed by the values of both variables for that individual.

Always plot the explanatory variable, if there is one, on the horizontal axis (the *x*-axis) of a scatterplot. As a reminder, we usually call the explanatory variable *x* and the response variable *y*. If there is no explanatory–response distinction, either variable can go on the horizontal axis. Degree-days appear on the horizontal scale and gas consumption on the vertical scale in Figure 6.8a because degree-days is the explanatory variable. The weather affects gas consumption; gas consumption does not explain the weather.

FIGURE 6.8

Natural gas consumption versus degree days.
(a) A scatterplot. (b) A regression line and its use for prediction.

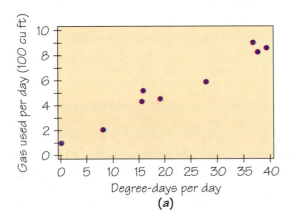

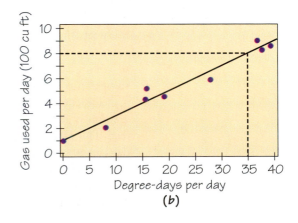

Just as when we examined distributions of a single variable, we look for an overall pattern in a scatterplot and then for any striking deviations from that pattern.

> You can describe the overall pattern of a scatterplot by the **form, direction,** and **strength** of the relationship.

The *form* of the relationship between degree-days and gas consumption is clear: the points have a straight-line pattern. We can represent the overall pattern of the relationship by drawing a straight line through the points of the scatterplot. Figure 6.8b shows such a line. As degree-days increase, gas consumption also increases; that is the *direction* of the relationship. The points in the plot lie very close to the line, so the relationship is quite *strong*. The number of degree-days explains most of the variation in gas consumption. A weaker straight-line relationship would show more scatter of the points about a generally straight-line pattern. The scatter reflects the effects of other factors, such as use of gas for cooking or turning down the thermostat when the family is away from home. These effects are relatively small. There are no *outliers* (points far outside the overall straight-line pattern) or other important deviations.

Regression Lines

Sue wants to use her data to predict how much gas she will use for any outside temperature (in degree-days). She can do this by drawing a line through the straight-line pattern on the scatterplot in Figure 6.8a.

> A **regression line** is a straight line that describes how a response variable y changes as an explanatory variable x changes. We often use a regression line to predict the value of y for a given value of x.

The points in Figure 6.8a lie so close to a line that it is easy to draw a regression line on the graph by using a transparent straightedge. This gives us a line on the graph, but not an equation for the line. There is also no guarantee that the line we fit by eye is the best line for predicting gas consumption. There are statistical techniques for finding from the data the equation of the best line (with various meanings of "best"). We will soon discuss the most common of these techniques called *least squares regression*. The line in Figure 6.8b is the least squares regression line for Sue's data. All statistical software packages and many calculators will calculate the least squares line for you, so that a line is often available with little work.

You should therefore know how to use a line fitted to the data even if you do not learn the details of how to get the equation from the data.

In writing the equation of a line, we use x for the explanatory variable because this is plotted on the horizontal or x-axis, and y for the response variable. Any line has an equation of the form

$$y = a + bx$$

The number b is the *slope* of the line, the amount by which y changes when x increases by one unit. The slope is usually important in a statistical setting, because it is the rate of change of the response y as x increases. The number a is the *intercept,* the value of y when $x = 0$.

E X A M P L E   *Interpreting Slope and Intercept*

A computer program tells us that the least squares regression line computed from Sue's data is

$$y = 1.23 + 0.202x$$

The slope of this line is $b = 0.202$. This means that gas consumption increases by 0.202 hundred cubic feet per day when there is one more degree-day per day. The intercept is $a = 1.23$. When there are no degree-days (that is, when the average temperature is 65°F or above), gas consumption will be 1.23 hundred cubic feet per day. The slope and intercept are estimates based on fitting a line to the data in Table 6.2. We do not expect every month with no degree-days to average exactly 1.23 hundred cubic feet of gas per day. The line represents only the overall pattern of the data.   ◆

The purpose of a regression line is to predict the value of the response variable for a given value of the explanatory variable. A line drawn on a scatterplot can be used for making predictions with a straightedge and pencil. If the equation of the line is available, we can simply substitute the given value of the explanatory variable into the equation.

After installing solar panels, Sue wants to know how much she has saved in heating costs. She cannot simply compare before-and-after gas usage, because the winters before and after will not be equally severe. Instead, she can use the regression line to predict how much gas she would have used without the solar panels. Comparing this prediction with the actual amount used will show her savings.

E X A M P L E   *Predicting Gas Consumption*

The next February averages 35 degree-days per day. How much gas would Sue have used without the solar panels? Figure 6.8b illustrates using the regression line for prediction. First locate 35 on the horizontal axis. Go up to the regression line and then over to the gas consumption scale. We predict that slightly more than 800 cubic feet per day will be consumed.

We can give a more exact prediction using the equation of the regression line. This equation is

$$y = 1.23 + 0.202x$$

In this equation, x is the number of degree-days per day during a month and y is the predicted gas consumption per day, in hundreds of cubic feet. Our predicted gas consumption for a month with $x = 35$ degree-days per day is

$$y = 1.23 + (0.202)(35)$$
$$= 8.3 \text{ hundred cubic feet per day}$$

This prediction will almost certainly not be exactly correct for the next month that has 35 degree-days per day. But the past data points lie so close to the line that we can be confident that gas consumption in such a month will be quite close to 830 cubic feet per day. ◆

Correlation

A scatterplot displays the form, direction, and strength of the relationship between two quantitative variables. *Linear* (straight-line) relationships are important because a line is a simple pattern that is quite common. We say a linear relation is strong if the points lie close to a line, and weak if they are widely scattered about a line. Our eyes are not good judges of how strong a relationship is. We need to follow our strategy for data analysis by using a numerical measure to supplement the graph. *Correlation* is the measure we use.

The **correlation** measures the direction and strength of the linear relationship between two quantitative variables. Correlation is usually written as r.

Suppose that we have data on variables x and y for n individuals. The values for the first individual are x_1 and y_1, the values for the second individual are x_2 and y_2, and so on. The means and standard deviations of the two variables are $\bar{x}$ and s_x for the x values, and $\bar{y}$ and s_y for the y values. The correlation r between x and y is

$$r = \frac{1}{n-1} \sum \left(\frac{x_i - \bar{x}}{s_x} \right) \left(\frac{y_i - \bar{y}}{s_y} \right)$$

SPOTLIGHT 6.2

Florence Nightingale

Florence Nightingale (1820–1910) won fame as a founder of the nursing profession and as a reformer of health care. As chief nurse for the British army during the Crimean War, from 1854 to 1856, she found that lack of sanitation and disease killed large numbers of soldiers hospitalized by wounds. Her reforms reduced the death rate at her military hospital from 42.7% to 2.2%, and she returned from the war famous. She at once began a fight to reform the entire military health care system, with considerable success.

One of the chief weapons Florence Nightingale used in her efforts was data. She had the facts, because she reformed record keeping as well as medical care. She was a pioneer in using graphs to present data in a vivid form that even generals and members of Parliament could understand. Her inventive graphs are a landmark in the growth of the new science of statistics. She considered statistics essential to understanding any social issue and tried to introduce the study of statistics into higher education.

Remember that the summation sign Σ means "add these terms for all the individuals." The formula for the correlation r helps us see what correlation is, but in practice you should use software or a calculator that finds r from keyed-in values of two variables x and y. Exercise 28 asks you to calculate a correlation step-by-step from the definition to solidify its meaning. A table layout like that we used for the variance on page 220 is helpful.

The correlation uses the deviations of the x and y observations from their means. So the sign of r shows the direction of the relationship between x and y. Height and weight, for example, tend to move together. People who are above average in height tend to also be above average in weight. People who are below average in height tend to also have below-average weight. So the deviations from the mean that are multiplied to form the sum for r are mostly both positive or both negative. Their products are therefore mostly positive, so that r is positive.

More detailed study of the formula gives more detailed properties of r. Here is what you need to know in order to interpret correlation.

1. Correlation makes no use of the distinction between explanatory and response variables. It makes no difference which variable you call x and which you call y in calculating the correlation.
2. Correlation measures the strength of linear relationships only. Correlation does not describe curved relationships between variables, no matter how strong they are.
3. The sign of r describes the direction of the relationship. Positive r indicates a positive association: the variables tend to move together. Negative

r indicates negative association: the variables tend to move in opposite directions.

4. The correlation *r* is always a number between −1 and 1. Values of *r* near 0 indicate a very weak linear relationship. The strength of the linear relationship increases as *r* moves away from 0 and toward either −1 or 1. Values of *r* close to −1 or 1 indicate that the points lie close to a straight line. The extreme values *r* = −1 and *r* = 1 occur only in the case of a perfect linear relationship, when the points in a scatterplot lie exactly along a straight line. The scatterplots in Figure 6.9 illustrate how values of *r* closer to 1 or −1 correspond to stronger linear relationships.

5. The correlation *r* does not change when we change the units of measurement of *x*, *y*, or both. Measuring height in inches rather than centimeters and weight in pounds rather than kilograms does not change the correlation between height and weight. The correlation *r* itself has no unit of measurement; it is just a number.

6. Like the mean and standard deviation, the correlation is strongly affected by a few outlying observations.

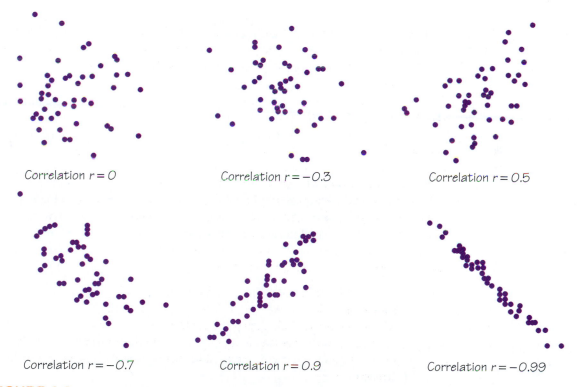

Correlation *r* = 0

Correlation *r* = −0.3

Correlation *r* = 0.5

Correlation *r* = −0.7

Correlation *r* = 0.9

Correlation *r* = −0.99

FIGURE 6.9 How correlation measures the strength of a straight-line relationship. Patterns closer to a straight line have correlations closer to 1 or −1.

Figure 6.8 shows a very strong positive linear relationship between degree-days and natural gas consumption. The correlation is $r = 0.989$, close to the $r = 1$ of a perfect straight line. Check this on your calculator using the data in Table 6.2.

Least Squares Regression

When a scatterplot shows a linear relation between an explanatory variable x and a response variable y, we want to draw a line to describe the relationship. The points will rarely lie exactly on a line, so our problem is to find the line that best fits the points. To do this, we must first say what we mean by the "best-fitting" line.

Suppose that we want to use our line to predict y for given values of x, as Sue used degree-days to predict gas consumption. The error in our prediction is measured in the y, or vertical, direction. So we want to make the vertical distances of the points from the line as small as possible. A line that fits the data well does not pass entirely above or below the plotted points, so some of the errors will be positive and some negative. Their squares, however, will all be positive. The *least squares regression line* makes the sum of the squares of the errors as small as possible.

> The **least squares regression line** of y on x is the line that makes the sum of the squares of the vertical distances of the data points from the line as small as possible.

The least squares idea says what we mean by the best-fitting line. We must still learn how to find this line from the data. Given n observations on variables x and y, what is the equation of the least squares line? Here is the solution to this mathematical problem.

> We have data on an explanatory variable x and a response variable y for n individuals. From the data, calculate the means $\bar{x}$ and $\bar{y}$ and the standard deviations s_x and s_y of the two variables, and their correlation r. The least squares regression line is the line
>
> $$y = a + bx$$
>
> with **slope**
>
> $$b = r\frac{s_y}{s_x}$$
>
> and **intercept**
>
> $$a = \bar{y} - b\bar{x}$$

This equation gives insight into the behavior of least squares regression by showing that it is related to the means and standard deviations of the x and y observations and to the correlation between x and y. In practice, you don't need to calculate the means, standard deviations, and correlation first. Statistical software or your calculator will give the slope b and intercept a of the least squares line from keyed-in values of the variables x and y. Use your calculator to verify that the equation for the least squares line from Sue's gas consumption data is indeed $y = 1.23 + 0.202x$, as we claimed earlier. Your calculator will report more decimal places for the intercept and slope.

EXAMPLE   *Do Heavy People Burn More Energy?*

Metabolic rate, the rate at which the body consumes energy, is important in studies of weight gain, dieting, and exercise. Table 6.3 gives data on the lean body mass and resting metabolic rate for 12 women and 7 men who are subjects in a study of dieting. Lean body mass, given in kilograms, is a person's weight leaving out all fat. Metabolic rate is measured in calories burned per 24 hours, the same calories used to describe the energy content of foods. The researchers believe that lean body mass is an important influence on metabolic rate.

Figure 6.10 is a scatterplot of the data. Because we think that body mass helps explain metabolic rate, we plot body mass on the horizontal x-axis. We have also added a feature to the scatterplot: two different plotting symbols distinguish the female and male subjects. This allows us to see that, while the women as a group have lower body mass than the men, the nature of the relationship is similar for both genders. We will therefore do calculations for all 19 subjects together.

The scatterplot shows a moderately strong positive linear relationship. The correlation $r = 0.865$ describes the strength of the relationship more exactly. The line on the plot is the least squares regression line for predicting metabolic rate

TABLE 6.3	Lean Body Mass and Metabolic Rate						
Subject	Sex	Mass (kg)	Rate (cal)	Subject	Sex	Mass (kg)	Rate (cal)
1	M	62.0	1792	11	F	40.3	1189
2	M	62.9	1666	12	F	33.1	913
3	F	36.1	995	13	M	51.9	1460
4	F	54.6	1425	14	F	42.4	1124
5	F	48.5	1396	15	F	34.5	1052
6	F	42.0	1418	16	F	51.1	1347
7	M	47.4	1362	17	F	41.2	1204
8	F	50.6	1502	18	M	51.9	1867
9	F	42.0	1256	19	M	46.9	1439
10	M	48.7	1614				

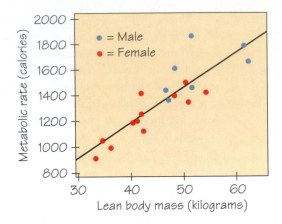

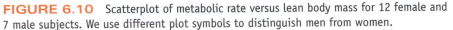

FIGURE 6.10 Scatterplot of metabolic rate versus lean body mass for 12 female and 7 male subjects. We use different plot symbols to distinguish men from women.

from lean body mass. The equation of this line is

$$y = 113.165 + 26.879x$$

The slope of the line tells us that on the average the subjects burn about 27 more calories per day for every additional kilogram of body mass. The intercept $a = 113.165$ is needed to draw the line but has no statistical interpretation. Body mass $x = 0$ is impossible, so we can't speak of the value of metabolic weight when $x = 0$. ◆

Modern Data Analysis

Scatterplots, correlation, and regression are basic tools for describing the relationship between two variables. What if the form of the relationship is more complex than a straight line? What if we have many variables rather than just two? Software and computer graphics allow us to display and describe complicated relationships. Here are two examples.

E X A M P L E   *A Motorcycle Crash Test*

Crash a motorcycle into a wall. The rider, fortunately, is a dummy with an instrument to measure acceleration (change of velocity) mounted in its head. Figure 6.11 is a scatterplot of the acceleration of the dummy's head against time in milliseconds. Acceleration is measured in g's, or multiples of the acceleration due to gravity at the earth's surface. The motorcycle approaches the wall at a constant speed (acceleration near 0). As it hits, the dummy's head snaps forward and decelerates violently (negative acceleration reaching more than 100 g's), then snaps back again (up to 75 g's) and wobbles a bit before coming to rest.

The scatterplot has a clear overall pattern, but it does not obey a simple form such as linear. Moreover, the strength of the pattern varies, from quite strong at the left of the plot to weaker (much more scatter) at the right. Statistical software includes a *scatterplot smoother* that deals with this complexity and draws a line on the plot to represent the overall pattern. ◆

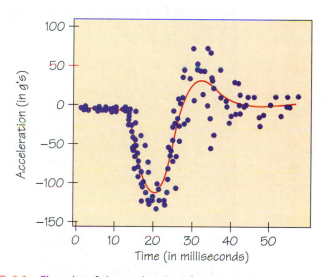

FIGURE 6.11 Time plot of the acceleration of the head of a crash test dummy as a motorcycle hits a wall, with the overall pattern calculated by a scatterplot smoother.

So far we have looked only at plots for two variables. What if we want to display a third variable in the same plot? Because we have already used the horizontal and vertical directions of the graph, there is only one direction left, moving out of and into the page. Three-dimensional plots are hard to see clearly unless we use color or motion (or both) to help us gain perspective. Computer graphics can supply color and motion, allowing us to see data on several variables at once.

EXAMPLE   *Images of the Earth*

The large plates that make up the earth's crust are pushed apart at ridges in mid-ocean where hot magma (melted rock) wells up from below. Scientists study this seafloor spreading by combining data from several sources, including instruments planted two miles down at the bottom of the ocean. Figure 6.12 is a computer graphic image of the data from a study in the South Pacific.

The top panel shows the topography of the ocean floor. Latitude and longitude coordinates locate the area. The ridge separating two plates runs down the center, and small underwater volcanos can be seen on either side. The second panel displays small variations in gravity that help distinguish different kinds of rock. The third panel adds data from tracking the velocity of earthquake waves, and shows the structure of the magma underneath the earth's crust. The panels are lined up so that scientists can visually compare several variables at many locations to understand a geological process that shapes our planet. ◆

FIGURE 6.12

The seafloor in the South Pacific near a midocean ridge. This computer graphic shows the topography and measurements on gravity and earthquake wave velocity as well as location on the earth's surface. (This image was provided by D. S. Scheirer of Brown University. The study is reported in several papers in the May 22, 1998, issue of *Science.*)

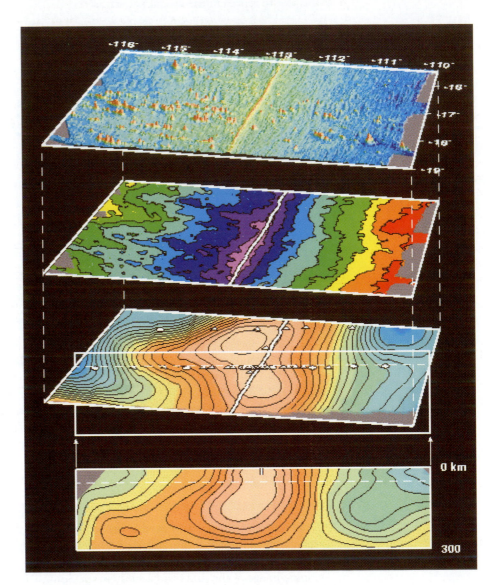

REVIEW VOCABULARY

Boxplot   A graph of the five-number summary. A box spans the quartiles, with an interior line marking the median. Lines extend out from this box to the extreme high and low observations.

Correlation   A measure of the direction and strength of the linear relationship between two variables. Correlations take values between 0 (no linear relationship) and ± 1 (perfect straight-line relationship).

Distribution   The pattern of outcomes of a variable. The distribution describes what values the variable takes and how often each value occurs.

Exploratory data analysis   The practice of examining data for unanticipated patterns or effects, as opposed to seeking answers to specific questions.

Five-number summary   A summary of a distribution of values consisting of the median, the first and third quartiles, and the largest and smallest observations.

Histogram   A graph of the distribution of outcomes (often divided into classes) for a single variable. The height of each bar is the number of observations in the class of outcomes covered by the base of the bar. All classes should have the same width.

Individuals   The people, animals, or things described by a data set.

Least squares regression line   A line drawn on a scatterplot that makes the sum of the squares of the vertical distances of the data points from the line as small as possible. The regression line can be used to predict the response variable y for a given value of the explanatory variable x.

Mean   The ordinary arithmetic average of a set of observations. To find the mean, add all the observations and divide the sum by the number of observations summed.

Median   The midpoint of a set of observations. Half the observations fall below the median and half fall above.

Outlier   A data point that falls clearly outside the overall pattern of a set of data.

Quartiles   The first quartile of a distribution is the point with 25% of the observations falling below it; the third quartile is the point with 75% below it.

Regression line   Any line that describes how a response variable y changes as we change an explanatory variable x. The most common such line is the least squares regression line.

Response variable, explanatory variable   A response variable measures an outcome of a study. An explanatory variable attempts to explain the observed outcomes.

Scatterplot   A graph of the values of two variables as points in the plane. Each value of the explanatory variable is plotted on the horizontal axis and the value of the response variable for the same individual is plotted on the vertical axis.

Skewed distribution   A distribution in which observations on one side of the median extend notably farther from the median than do observations on the other side. In a right-skewed distribution, the larger observations extend farther to the right of the median than the smaller observations extend to the left.

Standard deviation   A measure of the spread of a distribution about its mean as center. It is the square root of the average squared deviation of the observations from their mean.

Stemplot   A display of the distribution of a variable that attaches the final digits of the observations as leaves on stems made up of all but the final digit.

Symmetric distribution   A distribution with a histogram or stemplot in which the part to the left of the median is roughly a mirror image of the part to the right of the median.

Variable   Any measured characteristic of an individual.

Variance   A measure of the spread of a distribution about its mean. It is the average squared deviation of the observations from their mean. The square root of the variance is the standard deviation.

SUGGESTED READINGS

CLEVELAND, WILLIAM S. *The Elements of Graphing Data,* Wadsworth, Monterey, Calif., 1985. A careful study of the most effective elementary ways to present data graphically, with much sound advice on improving simple graphs.

MOORE, DAVID S. *The Basic Practice of Statistics,* 2nd ed., W. H. Freeman, New York, 1999. The first two chapters of this text provide a more extensive treatment of displaying and describing data for one and two variables. They cover the material of this chapter in more detail and present much new material on both technique and interpretation.

ROSSMAN, ALLAN J. *Workshop Statistics: Discovery with Data,* Springer-Verlag, New York, 1996. An excellent source of hands-on activities that concentrates on describing data.

TUFTE, EDWARD R. *The Visual Display of Quantitative Information,* Graphics Press, Cheshire, Conn., 1983. A beautifully printed book with both historic and contemporary graphs and suggestions for both statisticians and graphic artists.

VELLEMAN, PAUL F., AND DAVID C. HOAGLIN. Data analysis. In David C. Hoaglin and David S. Moore (eds.), *Perspectives on Contemporary Statistics,* Mathematical Association of America, Washington, D.C., 1992, pp. 19–39. A conceptual essay that presupposes knowledge of the basic techniques described in this chapter and in the text by Moore.

SUGGESTED WEB SITES

Web sites don't feature how to make histograms or scatterplots. They do provide lots of interesting sets of real data. The *Data and Story Library* **lib.stat.cmu.edu/DASL/** has both data and the background needed to use them. The Chance Web site **www.dartmouth.edu/~chance/** features current news items that involve statistics and also an archive of data. The electronic *Journal of Statistics Education* has both articles about teaching statistics and a data archive. You can find JSE on the American Statistical Association's Web site, **www.amstat.org**.

SKILLS CHECK

1. The heights of your cousins are (in inches) 40, 36, 18, 38, 30, 34. Which are outliers?

   (a)   40 only
   (b)   18 only
   (c)   both 18 and 40

2. To the right is a histogram of the ages of adults in your restaurant. Which statement is true?

   (a)   The histogram is roughly symmetric.
   (b)   The histogram is skewed to the right.
   (c)   The class from 58 to 68 represents 8 outliers.

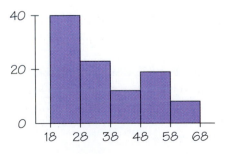

3. Here are 7 measured weights (in pounds): 4, 7, 5, 6, 5, 11, 4. Find their median.

(a)   5
(b)   6
(c)   5.5

4. Here are 7 measured weights (in pounds): 4, 7, 5, 6, 5, 11, 4. Find their mean.

(a)   5
(b)   6
(c)   6.6

5. The five-number summary includes

(a)   the mean and standard deviation.
(b)   the median and mean.
(c)   the quartiles.

6. The mean of the data 4, 5, 5, 7, 6, 6, 9 is 6. What is the standard deviation?

(a)   2.67
(b)   1.63
(c)   1.51

7. The daily ice consumption y at a park (in pounds) is related to the high temperature x (in degrees F). Suppose the least squares regression line is $y = 50 + 20x$. Suppose the high temperature today is 70°F. Predict the ice consumption.

(a)   1 pound
(b)   190 pounds
(c)   1450 pounds

EXERCISES ▲ *Optional.* ■ *Advanced.* ◆ *Discussion.*

Many exercises require use of a calculator (or software) that will find mean, standard deviation, correlation, and the slope and intercept of the least squares regression line from keyed-in data.

Displaying Distributions

1.   To the right is a small part of a data set that describes the fuel economy of 1998 model motor vehicles.

Make and Model	Vehicle Type	Transmission Type	Number of Cylinders	City MPG	Highway MPG
⋮					
BMW 318I	Subcompact	Automatic	4	22	31
BMW 318I	Subcompact	Manual	4	23	32
Buick Century	Midsize	Automatic	6	20	29
Chevrolet Blazer	4WD	Automatic	6	16	20
⋮					

What are the individuals and the variables in these data?

2.   Environmental Protection Agency regulations require automakers to give the city and highway gas mileages for each model of car. Table 6.4 (see page 236) gives the highway mileages (miles per gallon) for 26 midsize 1998 car models.

(a)   Make a histogram of the highway mileages of these cars.
(b)   Describe the main features (shape, center, spread, outliers) of the distribution of highway mileage.
(c)   The government imposes a "gas guzzler" tax on cars with low gas mileage. Which of these cars do you think are subject to the tax?

TABLE 6.4	Highway Gas Mileage for 1998 Model Midsize Cars		
Model	**MPG**	**Model**	**MPG**
Acura 3.5RL	25	Lexus GS300	23
Audi A6 Quattro	26	Lexus LS400	25
Buick Century	29	Lincoln Mark VIII	26
Cadillac Catera	24	Mazda 626	33
Cadillac Eldorado	26	Mercedes-Benz E320	29
Chevrolet Lumina	29	Mercedes-Benz E420	26
Chrysler Cirrus	30	Mitsubishi Diamante	24
Dodge Stratus	28	Nissan Maxima	28
Ford Taurus	28	Oldsmobile Aurora	26
Honda Accord	29	Rolls-Royce Silver Spur	16
Hyundai Sonata	27	Saab 900S	25
Infiniti I30	28	Toyota Camry	30
Infiniti Q45	23	Volvo S70	25

3.   The histogram in Figure 6.13 displays data on the hour at which the first flash of lightning was observed each day during a study in Colorado. Describe this distribution: Is it roughly symmetric or distinctly skewed? Where is the center? Are there any outliers or gaps?

4.   The total return on a stock is the change in its market price plus any dividend payments made. Total return is usually expressed as a percent of the beginning price. Figure 6.14 is a histogram of the distribution of total returns for all 1528 stocks listed on the New York Stock Exchange in one year. Like Figure 6.3, it is a histogram of the percents in each class rather than a histogram of counts. [From John K. Ford, Diversification: How many stocks will suffice? *American Association of Individual Investors Journal* (January 1990): 14–16.]

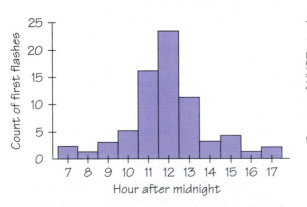

FIGURE 6.13   The distribution of the time of the first lightning flash each day at a site in Colorado.

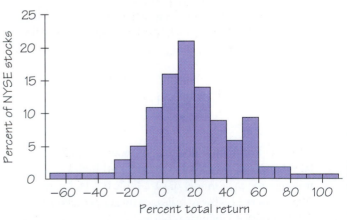

FIGURE 6.14   The distribution of percent total return for all New York Stock Exchange common stocks in one year.

(a) Describe the overall shape of the distribution of total returns.

(b) What is the approximate median of this distribution? (That is, what is the value with roughly half the stocks having lower returns and half having higher returns?)

(c) Approximately what were the smallest and largest total returns? (This describes the spread of the distribution.)

(d) A return less than zero means that an owner of the stock lost money. About what percent of all stocks lost money?

5.   In 1798 the English scientist Henry Cavendish measured the density of the earth in a careful experiment with a torsion balance. Here are his 29 repeated measurements of the same quantity (the density of the earth relative to that of water) made with the same instrument. [From S. M. Stigler, Do robust estimators work with real data? *Annals of Statistics*, 5(1977): 1055–1078.]

5.50	5.47	5.29	5.55	5.75	5.27
5.57	4.88	5.34	5.34	5.29	5.85
5.42	5.62	5.26	5.30	5.10	5.65
5.61	5.63	5.44	5.36	5.68	5.39
5.53	5.07	5.46	5.79	5.58	

(a) Make a stemplot of the data.

(b) Describe the distribution: Is it approximately symmetric, or distinctly skewed? Are there gaps or outliers?

6.   A fisheries researcher compiled the following data on lengths (in millimeters) of 6-year-old white female crappies:

217	230	220	221	225	223
219	217	225	228	234	222
231	222	220	222	222	223
225	214	221	233	227	234
223	225	253	220	213	224
235	283	210	218	235	231

(a) Make a stemplot of the data.

(b) Now make a histogram as well. The data range from 210 to 283 mm. Group them into 5 classes of width 15 mm starting with

$$210 \le \text{length} < 225$$

as the leftmost class.

(c) Describe the distribution: Is it roughly symmetric or clearly skewed? Are there gaps or outliers?

Describing Distributions

7.   Table 6.3 gives the lean body masses and metabolic rates for 7 men and 12 women. Compare the distributions of body mass for men and women, using the five-number summary and side-by-side boxplots. What do the data show?

8.   Return to the gas mileages in Table 6.4.

(a) Find the five-number summary.

(b) Use your calculator to find the mean and the standard deviation.

(c) Remove the Rolls-Royce and repeat your calculations. Which of your measures change, and by how much? What general fact does this example illustrate?

9.   Here are the percents of the popular vote won by the successful candidate in each of the presidential elections from 1948 to 1996:

Year	1948	1952	1956	1960	1964
Percent	49.6	55.1	57.4	49.7	61.1

Year	1968	1972	1976	1980	1984
Percent	43.4	60.7	50.1	50.7	58.8

Year	1988	1992	1996		
Percent	53.9	43.2	49.2		

(a) Make a histogram of the winners' percents.

(b) What is the median percent of the vote won by the successful candidate in presidential elections?

(c)   Call an election a landslide if the winner's percent falls at or above the third quartile. Find the third quartile. Which elections were landslides?

■ 10.   The level of various substances in the blood influences our health. Here are measurements of the level of phosphate in the blood of a patient, in milligrams of phosphate per deciliter of blood, made on 6 consecutive visits to a clinic:

    5.6   5.2   4.6   4.9   5.7   6.4

A graph of only 6 observations gives little information, so we proceed to compute the mean and standard deviation.

(a)   Find the mean from its definition. That is, find the sum of the 6 observations and divide by 6.
(b)   Find the standard deviation from its definition. That is, find the deviations of each observation from the mean, square the deviations, then obtain the variance and the standard deviation.
(c)   Now enter the data into your calculator and use the mean and standard deviation buttons to obtain $\bar{x}$ and s. Do the results agree with your hand calculations?

■ 11.   Some people worry about how many calories they consume. *Consumer Reports* magazine (June 1986, pp. 366–367) measured the calories in 20 brands of beef hot dogs, 17 brands of meat hot dogs, and 17 brands of poultry hot dogs. Here is computer output describing the beef hot dogs:

```
Mean = 156.8  Standard deviation = 22.64
Min = 111  Max = 190  N = 20
Median = 152.5  Quartiles = 140, 178.5
```

the meat hot dogs:

```
Mean = 158.7  Standard deviation = 25.24
Min = 107  Max = 195  N = 17
Median = 153  Quartiles = 139, 179
```

and the poultry hot dogs:

```
Mean = 122.5  Standard deviation = 25.48
Min = 87  Max = 170  N = 17
Median = 129  Quartiles = 102, 143
```

Use this information to make side-by-side boxplots of the calorie counts for the three types of hot dogs. Write a brief comparison of the distributions. Will eating poultry hot dogs usually lower your calorie consumption compared with eating beef or meat hot dogs?

12.   Return to the data on lengths of fish given in Exercise 6.

(a)   Find the five-number summary of this distribution. What range of lengths contains the middle 50% of the distribution?
(b)   From the shape of the distribution, do you expect the mean to be larger than the median, smaller than the median, or about the same as the median? Find the mean and verify your expectation.
(c)   Find the standard deviation. Based on the shape of the distribution, are $\bar{x}$ and s acceptable summary measures of center and spread?

13.   Find the five-number summary of Cavendish's measurements of the density of the earth in Exercise 5. How is the symmetry of the distribution reflected in the five-number summary?

14.   The mean of the 23 measurements in Exercise 5 was Cavendish's best estimate of the density of the earth. Find this mean. Then find the standard deviation. (Because of the symmetry of the distribution, it can be summarized by $\bar{x}$ and s.)

◆ 15.   The distribution of individual incomes in the United States is strongly skewed to the right. In 1997, the mean and median incomes of the top 1% of Americans were $330,000 and $675,000. Which of these numbers is the mean and which is the median? Explain your reasoning.

◆ 16.   A news article reports that of the 411 players on National Basketball Association rosters in February 1998, only 139 "made more than the league average salary" of $2.36 million. Is $2.36 million the mean or median salary for NBA players? How do you know?

17.   Scores of adults on the Stanford-Binet IQ test have mean 100 and standard deviation 15. What is the variance of scores on this test?

■ 18.   Here are the numbers of home runs that Babe Ruth hit in his 15 years with the New York Yankees, 1920 to 1934:

54   59   35   41   46   25   47   60
54   46   49   46   41   34   22

The current major league single-season home-run record is held by Mark McGwire. Here are McGwire's home run counts for 1987 to 1988:

49   32   33   39   22   42   9   9
39   52   58   70

A *back-to-back stemplot* helps us compare two distributions. Write the stems as usual, but with a vertical line both to their left and to their right. On the right, put leaves for Ruth. On the left, put leaves for McGwire. Arrange the leaves on each stem in increasing order out from the stem. Now write a brief comparison of Ruth and McGwire as home-run hitters. (McGwire was injured in 1993 and there

was a baseball strike in 1994. How do these events appear in the data?)

Displaying Relations

◆   19.   Manatees are large, gentle sea creatures that live along the Florida coast. Many manatees are killed or injured by powerboats. Table 6.5 gives data on powerboat registrations (in thousands) and the number of manatees killed by boats in Florida in the years 1977 to 1990.

(a)   We want to examine the relationship between number of powerboats and number of manatees killed by boats. Which is the explanatory variable?
(b)   Make a scatterplot. Describe the direction, form, and strength of the relationship. Are there any outliers or other important deviations?

◆   20.   How does the fuel consumption of a car change as its speed increases? The table on page 240 gives data for a British Ford Escort. Speed is measured in kilometers per hour, and fuel consumption is measured in liters of gasoline used per 100 kilometers traveled. [Based on T. N. Lam, Estimating fuel consumption from engine size, *Journal of Transportation Engineering*, 111 (1985): 339–357.]

TABLE 6.5	Florida Powerboats and Manatee Deaths, 1977–1990				
Year	Boats (thousands)	Manatees Killed	Year	Boats (thousands)	Manatees Killed
1977	447	13	1984	559	34
1978	460	21	1985	585	33
1979	481	24	1986	614	33
1980	498	16	1987	645	39
1981	513	24	1988	675	43
1982	512	20	1989	711	50
1983	526	15	1990	719	47

Speed (km/hr)	Fuel used (liters/100 km)	Speed (km/hr)	Fuel used (liter/100 km)
10	21.00	90	7.57
20	13.00	100	8.27
30	10.00	110	9.03
40	8.00	120	9.87
50	7.00	130	10.79
60	5.90	140	11.77
70	6.30	150	12.83
80	6.95		

(a)   Make a scatterplot. (Which is the explanatory variable?)

(b)   Describe the form of the relationship. Explain why the form of the relationship makes sense.

(c)   How would you describe the direction of this relationship?

(d)   Is the relationship reasonably strong or quite weak? Explain your answer.

Regression Lines

21.   Researchers studying acid rain measured the acidity of precipitation in a Colorado wilderness area for 150 consecutive weeks. Acidity is measured by pH. Lower pH values show higher acidity. The acid rain researchers observed a linear pattern over time. They reported that the least squares regression line

$$\text{pH} = 5.43 - (0.0053 \times \text{weeks})$$

fit the data well. [W. M. Lewis and M. C. Grant, Acid precipitation in the western United States, *Science,* 207 (1980): 176–177.]

(a)   Draw a graph of this line. Explain in plain language what the line says about how pH was changing over time.

(b)   According to the regression line, what was the pH at the beginning of the study (weeks = 1)? At the end (weeks = 150)?

(c)   What is the slope of the regression line? Explain clearly what this slope says about the rate of change in pH.

22.   Continue your study of the manatee data in Table 6.5. Here are four more years of manatee data:

| 1991 | 716 | 53 | 1993 | 716 | 35 |
| 1992 | 716 | 38 | 1994 | 735 | 49 |

(a)   Start with your scatterplot from Exercise 19. If Florida decided to freeze powerboat registrations at 716,000, about how many manatees would be killed by boats each year? Draw a line by eye on your graph to make the prediction.

(b)   Add the new data to your graph. In fact, powerboat registrations remained at 716,000 for the next three years. How accurate was your prediction?

■ 23.   Suppose that in some far future year 2 million powerboats are registered in Florida. Extend the fitted line you found in the previous exercise and use it to predict manatees killed. Explain why this prediction is very unreliable. (Using a fitted line to predict the response to an x value outside the range of the data used to fit the line is called *extrapolation.* Extrapolation often produces unreliable predictions.)

24.   Concrete road pavement gains strength over time as it cures. Highway engineers use regression lines to predict the strength after 28 days (when curing is complete) from measurements made after 7 days. Let x be strength (in pounds per square inch) after 7 days and y the strength after 28 days. One set of data gave the least squares regression line to be

$$y = 1389 + 0.96x$$

(a)   Explain in words what the slope 0.96 tells us about the curing of concrete.
(b)   A test of some new pavement after 7 days shows that its strength is 3300 pounds per square inch. Predict the strength of this pavement after 28 days.

Femur	38	56	59	64	74
Humerus	41	63	70	72	84

Correlation and Least Squares Regression

25.   Exercise 20 gives data on gas used versus speed for a small car. Make a scatterplot if you did not do so in Exercise 20. Calculate the correlation (use your calculator or software). Explain why r is small despite a strong relationship between speed and gas used.

26.   Find the equation of the least squares regression line for the manatee data in Table 6.5. Use the equation to predict manatee deaths in a future year when 716,000 powerboats are registered in Florida. Compare this prediction with your eyeball prediction in Exercise 22.

27.   If women always married men who were 2 years older than themselves, what would be the correlation between the ages of husband and wife? (*Hint:* Draw a scatterplot for several ages.)

28.   *Archaeopteryx* is an extinct beast having feathers like a bird but teeth and a long bony tail like a reptile. Only six fossil specimens are known. Because these specimens differ greatly in size, some scientists think they are different species rather than individuals from the same species. If the specimens belong to the same species and differ in size because some are younger than others, there should be a straight-line relationship between the lengths of a pair of bones from all individuals. An outlier from this relationship would suggest a different species. At the top of the next column are data on the lengths (in centimeters) of the femur (a leg bone) and the humerus (a bone in the upper arm) for the five specimens that preserve both bones. [From M. A. Houck et al., Allometric scaling in the earliest fossil bird, *Archaeopteryx lithographica*, *Science*, 247 (1990): 195–198.]

(a)   Make a scatterplot. Do you think that all five specimens come from the same species?

(b)   Find the correlation r step-by-step. That is, find the mean and standard deviation of the femur lengths and of the humerus lengths. (Use your calculator for means and standard deviations.) Then find the deviations from the mean and use the formula for r.
(c)   Now enter these data into your calculator and use the calculator's correlation function to find r. Check that you get the same result as in part (b).

29.   A food industry group asked 3368 people to guess the number of calories in each of several common foods. Table 6.6 (see page 242) displays the average of their guesses and the correct number of calories.

(a)   We think that how many calories a food actually has helps explain people's guesses of how many calories it has. With this in mind, make a scatterplot of these data.
(b)   Find the correlation r (use your calculator). Explain why your r is reasonable based on the scatterplot.
(c)   The guesses are all higher than the true calorie counts. Does this fact influence the correlation in any way? How would r change if every guess were 100 calories higher?
(d)   The guesses are much too high for spaghetti and snack cake. Circle these points on your scatterplot. Calculate r for the other eight foods, leaving out these two points. Explain why r changed in the direction that it did.

30.   Continue your exploration of the true versus guessed calories data from Table 6.6.

(a)   Use your calculator to find the least squares regression line of guessed calories on true calories. Do this twice, first for all 10 data points and then leaving out spaghetti and snack cake.

TABLE 6.6	Guessed and True Calories in 10 Foods	
Food	Guessed Calories	Correct Calories
8 oz whole milk	196	159
5 oz spaghetti with tomato sauce	394	163
5 oz macaroni with cheese	350	269
One slice wheat bread	117	61
One slice white bread	136	76
2-oz candy bar	364	260
Saltine cracker	74	12
Medium-size apple	107	80
Medium-size potato	160	88
Cream-filled snack cake	419	160

SOURCE: Wheat Industry Council, reported in *USA Today*, October 20, 1983.

(b)   Plot both lines on your scatterplot from the previous exercise. (Make one line dashed so you can tell them apart.) Does including the two outliers move the regression line substantially?

31.   Find the equation of the least squares regression line for the gas versus speed data in Exercise 20. Make a scatterplot and draw your line on the plot. This is the line that best fits these data (in the sense of least squares), but you would not use it for prediction.

32.   We gave the equation of the regression line of gas consumption y on degree-days x for the data in Table 6.2 as $y = 1.23 + 0.202x$. Enter the data from Table 6.2 into your calculator.

(a)   Use your calculator's regression function to find the equation of the least squares regression line.
(b)   Use your calculator to find the mean and standard deviation of both x and y and their correlation r. Find the slope b and intercept a of the regression line from these, using the equation of the least squares regression line. Verify that in both part (a) and part (b) you get

the equation in the example. (Results may differ slightly because of rounding off.)

◆   33.   A strong relationship between two variables does *not* always mean that one of the variables causes changes in the other. Someone says, "There is a strong positive correlation between the number of firefighters at a fire and the amount of damage the fire does. So sending lots of firefighters just causes more damage." Explain why this reasoning is wrong.

◆   34.   A strong relationship between two variables does *not* always mean that one of the variables causes changes in the other. A study shows that there is a positive correlation between the size of a hospital (measured by its number of beds x) and the median number of days y that patients remain in the hospital. Does this mean that you can shorten a hospital stay by choosing a small hospital? Explain.

■   35.   Changing the units of measurement can greatly alter the appearance of a scatterplot. Consider the following data:

x	−4	−4	−3	3	4	4
y	0.5	−0.6	−0.5	0.5	0.5	−0.6

(a)   Draw x and y axes each extending from -6 to 6. Plot the data on these axes.

(b)   Calculate the values of new variables $x^* = x/10$ and $y^* = 10y$, starting from the values of x and y. Plot y^* against x^* on the same axes using a different plotting symbol. The two plots are very different in appearance.

(c)   Use your calculator to find the correlation between x and y. Then find the correlation between x^* and y^*. How are the two correlations related? Explain why this isn't surprising.

■   36.   Use the equation for the least squares regression line to show that this line always passes through the point $(\bar{x}, \bar{y})$. That is, set $x = \bar{x}$ and show that the line predicts that $y = \bar{y}$.

Additional Exercises

37.   Table 6.7 gives the populations of the states (in thousands of people). Make a stemplot or histogram of the populations. Briefly describe the shape, center, and spread of the distribution of population. Be sure to give appropriate numerical measures of center and spread. Explain why the shape of the distribution is not surprising. Are there any states that you consider outliers?

38.   New York Yankee outfielder Roger Maris broke Babe Ruth's major league single-season home run record in 1961 and held the record until Mark McGwire hit 70 home runs in 1998. Here are Maris's home run counts in his 10 years in the American League:

14   28   16   39   61   33   23   26   8   13

Maris's record 61 home runs is an outlier in these data.

(a)   Use your calculator to find the mean $\bar{x}$ and the standard deviation s.

(b)   Use your calculator to find $\bar{x}$ and s for the nine observations that remain when you leave out the outlier. How does the outlier affect the values of $\bar{x}$ and s?

TABLE 6.7	**Population of the States (Thousands of People)**						
State	**Pop**	**State**	**Pop**	**State**	**Pop**	**State**	**Pop**
AL	4,273	IL	11,847	MT	879	RI	990
AK	607	IN	5,841	NE	1,652	SC	3,699
AZ	4,428	IA	2,852	NV	1,603	SD	732
AR	2,510	KS	2,572	NH	1,162	TN	5,320
CA	31,878	KY	3,884	NJ	7,988	TX	19,128
CO	3,823	LA	4,351	NM	1,713	UT	2,000
CT	3,274	ME	1,243	NY	18,185	VT	589
DE	725	MD	5,072	NC	7,323	VA	6,675
DC	543	MA	6,092	ND	644	WA	5,533
FL	14,400	MI	9,594	OH	11,173	WV	1,826
GA	7,353	MN	4,658	OK	3,301	WI	5,160
HI	1,184	MS	2,716	OR	3,204	WY	481
ID	1,189	MO	5,359	PA	12,056		

■   39.   A common criterion for detecting suspected outliers in a set of data is as follows:

I.   Find the quartiles Q_1 and Q_3 and the *interquartile range, IQR* = $Q_3 - Q_1$. The interquartile range is the spread of the central half of the data.

II.   Call an observation an outlier if it falls more than $1.5 \times IQR$ above the third quartile or below the first quartile.

Applying this criterion, is the Rolls-Royce a suspected outlier in the gas mileage data of Table 6.4? Are Alaska or Florida outliers in the over-65 data of Table 6.1?

40.   Table 6.8 gives the survival times (in days) of 72 guinea pigs after they were infected by tubercle bacilli in a medical study. Make a histogram of these data. Is the survival-time distribution approximately symmetric or strongly skewed? Based on the shape of the distribution, would you prefer the five-number summary or $\bar{x}$ and s as a numerical description? Compute the numerical description you chose.

◆   41.   Find the mean and the median survival time for the guinea pigs in Table 6.8. Explain from the overall shape of the distribution the relationship between the two measures of center.

■   42.   This is a standard deviation contest. You must choose four numbers from the whole numbers 0 to 10, with repeats allowed.

(a)   Choose four numbers that have the smallest possible standard deviation.
(b)   Choose four numbers that have the largest possible standard deviation.
(c)   Is more than one choice possible in either part (a) or part (b)? Explain.

◆   43.   Choose a set of interesting data from the *Statistical Abstract of the United States* or an almanac (for example, school dropout rates for the states or per capita incomes of nations). Make a histogram of the data and describe the pattern and any outliers. Then give a numerical description of the data.

■   44.   Colleges announce an "average" SAT score for their entering freshmen. Usually a college would like this "average" to be as high as possible. A *New York Times* article noted that "private colleges that buy lots of top students with merit scholarships prefer the mean, while open-enrollment public institutions like medians." Use what you know about the behavior of means and medians to explain these preferences.

45.   Give an example of a small set of data for which the mean is larger than the third quartile.

◆   46.   A mutual fund company's newsletter says, "A well-diversified portfolio includes assets with low

TABLE 6.8	Guinea Pig Survival Times (Days)								
43	45	53	56	56	57	58	66	67	73
74	79	80	80	81	81	81	82	83	83
84	88	89	91	91	92	92	97	99	99
100	100	101	102	102	102	103	104	107	108
109	113	114	118	121	123	126	128	137	138
139	144	145	147	156	162	174	178	179	184
191	198	211	214	243	249	329	380	403	511
522	598								

SOURCE: T. Bjerkedal, Acquisition of resistance in guinea pigs infected with different doses of virulent tubercle bacilli, *American Journal of Hygiene,* 72 (1960): 130–148.

correlations." The newsletter includes a table of correlations between the returns on various classes of investments. For example, the correlation between municipal bonds and large-cap stocks is 0.50 and the correlation between municipal bonds and small-cap stocks is 0.21.

(a)   Rachel invests heavily in municipal bonds. She wants to diversify by adding an investment whose returns do not closely follow the returns on her bonds. Should she choose large-cap or small-cap stocks for this purpose? Explain.
(b)   If Rachel wants an investment that tends to increase when the return on her bonds drops, what kind of correlation should she look for?

47.   Some people think that the behavior of the stock market in January predicts its behavior for the rest of the year. Take the explanatory variable x to be the percent change in a stock market index in January and the response variable y to be the change in the index for the entire year. We expect a positive correlation between x and y because the change during January contributes to the full year's change. Calculation from data for the years 1960 to 1997 gives:

$$\bar{x} = 1.75\% \qquad s_x = 5.36\% \qquad r = 0.596$$
$$\bar{y} = 9.07\% \qquad s_y = 15.35\%$$

(a)   What is the equation of the least squares line for predicting full-year change from January change?
(b)   The mean change in January is $\bar{x} = 1.75\%$. Use your regression line to predict the change in the index in a year in which the index rises 1.75% in January. What do you notice about your result? (See Exercise 36.)

◆   48.   There is some evidence that drinking moderate amounts of red wine reduces the risk of heart attacks. Table 6.9 gives data on wine consumption and deaths from heart disease in 19 developed countries as of 1989. Wine consumption is measured as liters of alcohol from drinking wine, per person. The heart-disease death rate is deaths per 100,000 people.

(a)   Make a scatterplot of these data arranged to show the possible influence of wine consumption on heart-disease deaths.
(b)   The equation of the least squares regression line of heart-disease death rate on wine consumption is

$$y = 260.56 - 22.969x$$

Draw this line on your scatterplot.
(c)   Use the regression line to predict the heart-disease death rate in a country where

TABLE 6.9	Wine Consumption and Heart-Disease Deaths for Selected Countries				
Country	**Alcohol from Wine**	**Heart-Disease Death Rate**	**Country**	**Alcohol from Wine**	**Heart-Disease Death Rate**
Australia	2.5	211	Netherlands	1.8	167
Austria	3.9	167	New Zealand	1.9	266
Belgium/Lux.	2.9	131	Norway	0.8	227
Canada	2.4	191	Spain	6.5	86
Denmark	2.9	220	Sweden	1.6	207
Finland	0.8	297	Switzerland	5.8	115
France	9.1	71	United Kingdom	1.3	285
Iceland	0.8	211	United States	1.2	199
Ireland	0.7	300	Germany (West)	2.7	172
Italy	7.9	107			

SOURCE: *New York Times,* December 28, 1994, from M. H. Criqui, University of California, San Diego.

TECHNOLOGY CORNER

Computing the Mean and Standard Deviation

Spreadsheets provide an easy means to copy formulas. This feature is useful when computing the mean and standard deviation for a set of data. In Figure 6.15, 15 random rolls of a die are listed in the "x" column. To compute the mean of these data, first add the data, using the function =**Sum(B2:B16)**. With the sum at **B18**, you can then compute the mean by dividing the sum by the number of data, n, using the function =**B18/15**.

To use the formula for variance in this chapter, we need to compute the difference between each data entry and the mean. Enter the mean in location **C2** and the difference in location **D2** using the formula =**B2−C2**. Square this difference in location **E2** using the formula =**D2^2**. After the first row of

these three columns is created, the remaining rows can be created by cutting and pasting these formulas.

Sum the terms in the last column and divide this sum by $(n − 1)$ to compute the variance. If the variance is at **E20**, the standard deviation can be found by computing the square root: =**Sqrt(E20)**.

TASK 1.   Generate the results of 50 rolls of a die, using a die or the spreadsheet's random number generator. Following the example above, compute the mean and standard deviation of your data.

TASK 2.   Use the **Sort** command to arrange your data from smallest to largest. Use this ordering to find the median and quartiles for your data.

Computing the Least Squares Line

The least squares line can be identified by computing its slope and y-intercept. Using formulas slightly different from those in this chapter, the slope and intercept can be computed from the following items: x, y, x^2, xy. The spreadsheet shown in Figure 6.15 includes columns for x, y, x^2, and xy. The formulas for entries **C2** and **D2** are given by =**A2*A2** and =**A2*B2**. Copy these formulas to complete the third and fourth columns.

Then use the **Sum** function to compute the sum of each column. The entries on row 13 correspond to the values x, y, x^2, xy. The slope is computed from these values by the formula =**(E13*D13−B13*A13)/(E13*C13−A13*A13)**. Since **E13** reports the number of data, the y-intercept is computed by the formula =**B13/E13−C15*A13/E13**.

Select the x and y data and graph these points, using a Scatterplot Graph. Notice that the data tend to generally follow a line. Using the computed slope and y-intercept, note that the least squares line passes through the points (0, 2.3) and (6, 12). This line is drawn atop the scatterplot on the spreadsheet shown in Figure 6.16.

	A	B	C	D	E	F
1		x	mean	(x-mean)	(x-mean)^2	
2		2	3.6	−1.6	2.56	
3		6		2.4	5.76	
4		6		2.4	5.76	
5		1		−2.6	6.76	
6		1		−2.6	6.76	
7		1		−2.6	6.76	
8		5		1.4	1.96	
9		4		0.4	0.16	
10		6		2.4	5.76	
11		3		−0.6	0.36	
12		3		−0.6	0.36	
13		1		−2.6	6.76	
14		6		2.4	5.76	
15		5		1.4	1.96	
16		4		0.4	0.16	
17						
18	sum	54			57.6	
19	mean	3.6				
20				variance	4.114286	
21			standard deviation		2.02837	

FIGURE 6.15

	A	B	C	D	E
1	x	y	x^2	xy	
2	1	5	1	5	
3	6	8	36	48	
4	4	8	16	32	
5	4	7	16	28	
6	2	8	4	16	
7	4	10	16	40	
8	4	9	16	36	
9	1	3	1	3	
10	2	7	4	14	
11	1	5	1	5	
12					
13	29	70	99	227	10
14					
15	least squares slope		1.610738		
16	y intercept		2.328859		
17					

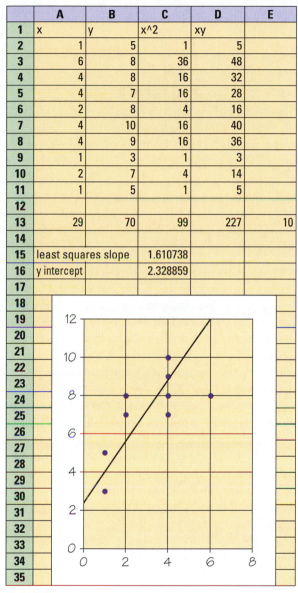

FIGURE 6.16

TASK 3. Perform the following experiment: roll a white die and a black die. Let x be the value of the white die and y be the sum of the dice. Repeat this experiment 20 times. Then create a scatterplot of the data and compute the least squares line for the data.

TASK 4. Locate a newspaper's financial report for two different days. Choose 20 stocks of regional interest, and enter their prices on the first day in the x column and their prices the second day in the y column. Create a scatterplot of the data and compute the least squares line for the data.

Then test your model by choosing 10 additional stocks, locating their prices on the first day and using the least squares line to estimate their prices on the second day. How accurate are these estimates?

Exploration

As the number of observations increases, what changes occur to the mean, median, quartiles, variance, and standard deviation? Simulate 20, 100, and 500 rolls of a die, and compute these values in each case. Which of these values remain reasonably constant? Which of these values change significantly? Why?

writing projects

1 ▶ Part of analyzing data is to watch for implausible numbers. Here is part of a report on the problem of vacation cruise ships polluting the sea by dumping garbage overboard that appeared in *Condé Nast Traveler* magazine in June 1992:

> On a seven-day cruise, a medium-size ship (about 1,000 passengers) might accumulate 222,000 coffee cups, 72,000 soda cans, 40,000 beer cans and bottles, and 11,000 wine bottles.

Are these numbers plausible? Write a short essay arguing your position, with some arithmetic to back up your conclusion.

2 ▶ Thinking about numbers requires more than just the ability to do the calculations. Has the income of Americans gone down in recent decades? Here are some data that feature in the debate over this question. After adjusting for the effects of inflation, the median money income of U.S. households rose from $33,181 in 1970 to $35,492 in 1996. That's a gain of just 7% in 26 years. Per capita money income (total income divided by total number of people), on the other hand, increased from $12,070 in 1970 to $18,136 in 1996. That's a gain of 50%. All of these numbers come from the Bureau of Labor Statistics, so they are trustworthy.

Write a brief essay explaining this apparently contradictory trend. The effect of extreme observations on the median and the mean plays a role. So do changes in American households over the past decades. (A household consists of all people living together at the same address.)

3 ▶ Graphs good and bad fill the news media. Some publications, such as *USA Today*, make particularly heavy use of graphs to present data. Collect several graphs (at leave five) from newspapers and magazines (not from advertisements). Use them as examples in a brief essay about the clarity, accuracy, and attractiveness of graphs in the news. You can find information on what makes good graphs in the books by Tufte and by Cleveland listed in Suggested Readings.

4 ▶ Armed with software, you can begin to explore larger sets of data. Go to the Web site **www.stat.purdue.edu/~dsmoore/data** and download the file **gpa.dat**. This file contains data on all 78 seventh-grade students in a rural midwestern school. There are five variables recorded in order for each student: GPA, the student's grade point index; IQ, score on an IQ test; AGE, age in years; GENDER, with 1 = female and 2 = male; SC, overall score on a psychological test that measures "self-concept."

First examine the distribution of GPA for these students. Write a brief description, including numerical measures, of the overall pattern of the distribution. Are there any outliers or other unusual features? Then examine the relationship between IQ score and GPA. Do students with higher IQ tend to get higher grades? Is the relationship strong? Are there unusual points?

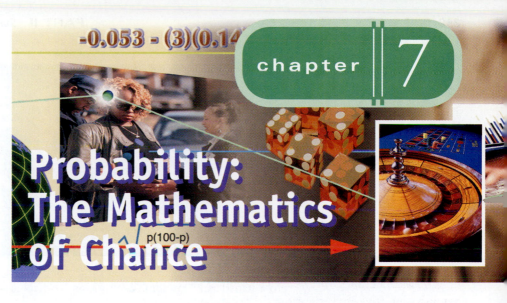

chapter 7

Probability: The Mathematics of Chance

$-0.053 - (3)(0.14$

$p(100-p)$

> *"It is a remarkable fact that the aggregate result of many thousands of chance outcomes can be known with near certainty."*

Have you ever wondered how gambling, which is a recreation or an addiction for individuals, can be a business for the casino? A business requires predictable revenue from the service it offers, even when the service is a game of chance. Individual gamblers may win or lose. They can never say whether a day at the casino will turn a profit or a loss. But the casino isn't gambling. Casinos are consistently profitable, and state governments make money both from running lotteries and from taxing other forms of gambling.

It is a remarkable fact that the aggregate result of many thousands of chance outcomes can be known with near certainty. The casino need not load the dice, mark the cards, or alter the roulette wheel. It knows that in the long run each dollar bet will yield its five cents or so of revenue. It is therefore good business to concentrate on free floor shows or inexpensive bus fares to increase the flow of dollars bet. The flow of profit will follow.

Gambling houses are not alone in profiting from the fact that a chance outcome many times repeated is firmly predictable. For example, although a life insurance company does not know *which* of its policyholders will die next year, it can predict quite accurately *how many* will die. It sets its premiums by this knowledge, just as the casino sets its jackpots.

A phenomenon is called **random** if individual outcomes are uncertain but the long-term pattern of many individual outcomes is predictable.

Casino dice.

To a statistician, "random" does not mean "haphazard." Randomness is a kind of order, an order that emerges only in the long run, over many repetitions. Many phenomena, both natural and of human design, are random. The life spans of insurance buyers and the hair color of children are examples of natural randomness. Indeed, quantum mechanics asserts that at the subatomic level the natural world is inherently random. Probability theory, the mathematical description of randomness, is essential to much of modern science.

Games of chance are examples of randomness deliberately produced by human effort. Casino dice are carefully machined, and their drilled holes, called pips, are filled with material equal in density to the plastic body. This guarantees that the side with six pips has the same weight as the opposite side, which has only one pip. Thus, each side is equally likely to land upward. All the odds and payoffs of dice games rest on this carefully planned randomness.

Statisticians and casino managers both rely on planned randomness, although statisticians use tables of random digits rather than dice and cards. The reasoning of statistical inference rests on planned randomness and on the mathematics of probability, the same mathematics that guarantees the profits of casinos and insurance companies. The mathematics of chance is the topic of this chapter.

What Is Probability?

The mathematics of chance, the mathematical description of randomness, is called *probability theory*. Probability describes the predictable long-run patterns of random outcomes.

E X A M P L E *Coin Tossing*

When you toss a coin, there are only two possible outcomes, heads or tails. Figure 7.1 shows the results of tossing a coin 1000 times. For each number of tosses from 1 to 1000, we have plotted the proportion of those tosses that gave a head. The first toss was a head, so the proportion of heads starts at 1. The second toss was a

FIGURE 7.1
Proportion of heads versus number of tosses in tossing a coin. The proportion of heads eventually settles down to the probability of a head.

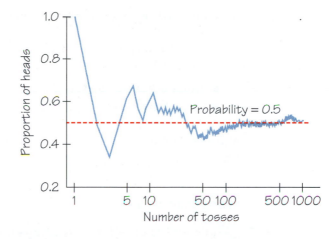

tail, reducing the proportion of heads to 0.5 after two tosses. The next three tosses gave a tail followed by two heads, so the proportion of heads after five tosses is 3/5, or 0.6.

The proportion of tosses that produce heads is quite variable at first, but it settles down as we make more and more tosses. Eventually this proportion gets close to 0.5 and stays there. We say that 0.5 is the *probability* of a head. The probability 0.5 appears as a horizontal line on the graph. ◆

> The **probability** of any outcome of a random phenomenon is the proportion of times the outcome would occur in a very long series of repetitions.

We might suspect that a coin has probability 0.5 of coming up heads just because the coin has two sides. As Exercises 7.1 and 7.2 illustrate, such suspicions are not always correct. The idea of probability is empirical. That is, it is based on observation rather than theorizing. Probability describes what happens in very many trials, and we must actually observe many trials to pin down a probability.

Will it land heads or tails?

Probability Models

Gamblers have known for a long time that the fall of coins, cards, or dice stabilizes into definite patterns in the long run. France gave birth to the mathematics of probability in the seventeenth century when gamblers turned to mathematicians for advice (see Spotlight 7.1). The idea of probability rests on the observed fact that the average result of many thousands of chance outcomes can be known with near certainty. But a definition of probability as "long-run proportion" is vague. Who can say what "the long run" is? Instead, we give a mathematical description of *how probabilities behave,* based on our understanding of long-run proportions. To see how to proceed, think first about a very simple random phenomenon, tossing a coin once. When we toss a coin, we cannot know the outcome in advance. What do we know? We are willing to say that the outcome will be either heads or tails. We believe that each of these outcomes has probability 1/2. This description of coin tossing has two parts:

- A list of possible outcomes
- A probability for each outcome

Such a description is the basis for all probability models. Here is the vocabulary we use:

> The **sample space *S*** of a random phenomenon is the set of all possible outcomes.
>
> An **event** is any outcome or any set of outcomes of a random phenomenon. That is, an event is a subset of the sample space.
>
> A **probability model** is a mathematical description of a random phenomenon consisting of two parts: a sample space *S* and a way of assigning probabilities to events.

The sample space *S* can be very simple or very complex. When we toss a coin once, there are only two possible outcomes, heads or tails. So the sample space is *S* = {H, T}. If we draw a random sample of 1500 U.S. residents age 18 and over, as Gallup polls do, the sample space contains all possible choices of 1500 of the more than 200 million adults in the country. This *S* is extremely large. Each member of *S* is a possible Gallup poll sample, which explains the term *sample space*.

E XAMPLE   *Rolling Dice*

Rolling two dice is a common way to lose money in casinos. There are 36 possible outcomes when we roll two dice and record the up faces in order (first die, second die). Figure 7.2 displays these outcomes. They make up the sample space *S*. "Roll a 5" is an event, call it *A*, that contains four of these 36 outcomes:

If the dice are carefully made, experience shows that each of the 36 outcomes in Figure 7.2 comes up equally often. So a reasonable probability model assigns probability 1/36 to each outcome.

In craps and other games, all that matters is the *sum* of the pips on the up faces. Let's change the random outcomes we are interested in: roll two dice and

FIGURE 7.2
The possible outcomes for rolling two dice.

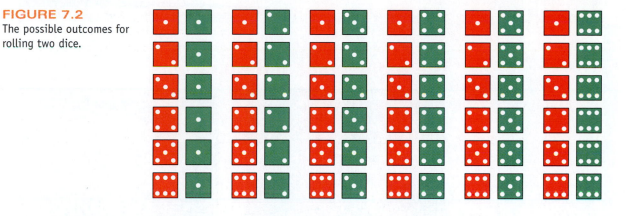

count the pips on the up faces. Now there are only 11 possible outcomes, from a sum of 2 for rolling a double one through 3, 4, 5, and on up to 12 for rolling a double six. The sample space is now

$$S = \{2, 3, 4, 5, 6, 7, 8, 9, 10, 11, 12\}$$

Comparing this S with Figure 7.2 reminds us that we can change S by changing the detailed description of the random phenomenon we are describing. The outcomes in this new sample space are *not* equally likely, because there are six ways to roll a 7 and only one way to roll a 2 or a 12.   ◆

Probability Rules

There are many ways to assign probabilities, so it is convenient to start with some general rules that any assignment of probabilities to outcomes must obey. These facts follow from the idea of probability as "the long-run proportion of repetitions on which an event occurs."

1. **Any probability is a number between 0 and 1.** Any proportion is a number between 0 and 1, so any probability is also a number between 0 and 1. An event with probability 0 never occurs, and an event with probability 1 occurs on every trial. An event with probability 0.5 occurs in half the trials in the long run.
2. **All possible outcomes together must have probability 1.** Because some outcome must occur on every trial, the sum of the probabilities for all possible outcomes must be exactly 1.
3. **If two events have no outcomes in common, the probability that one or the other occurs is the sum of their individual probabilities.** If one event occurs in 40% of all trials, a different event occurs in 25% of all trials, and the two can never occur together, then one or the other occurs on 65% of all trials because 40% + 25% = 65%.

SPOTLIGHT

7.1

The Mathematical Bernoullis

Jakob Bernoulli

Johann Bernoulli

Few families have made more contributions to mathematics than the Bernoullis of Basel, Switzerland. No fewer than seven Bernoullis, over three generations spanning the years between 1680 and 1800, were distingushed mathematicians. Five of them helped build the new mathematics of probability.

Jakob (1654–1705) and Johann (1667–1748) were sons of a prosperous Swiss merchant, but they studied mathematics against the will of their practical father. Both were among the finest mathematicians of their times, but it was Jakob who concentrated on probability. He was the first to see clearly the idea of a long-run proportion as a way of measuring chance.

Johann's son Daniel (1700–1782) and Jakob and Johann's nephew Nicholas (1687–1759) also studied probability. Nicholas saw that the pattern of births of male and female children could be described by probability. Despite his own rebellion against his father's strictures, Johann tried to make his son Daniel a merchant or a doctor. Daniel, undeterred, became yet another Bernoulli mathematician. In the field of probability, he worked to fairly price games of chance and gave evidence for the effectiveness of inoculation against smallpox.

The Bernoulli family in mathematics, like their contemporaries the Bachs in music, is an unusual example of talent in one field appearing in successive generations. The Bernoullis' work helped probability to grow from its birthplace in the gambling hall to a respectable tool with worldwide applications.

We can use mathematical notation to state Rules 1 to 3 more concisely. Capital letters near the beginning of the alphabet denote events. If A is any event, we write its probability as $P(A)$. Here are our probability rules in formal language. As you apply these rules, remember that they are just another form of intuitively true facts about long-run proportions.

> **Rule 1.** The probability $P(A)$ of any event A satisfies $0 \leq P(A) \leq 1$.
>
> **Rule 2.** If S is the sample space in a probability model, then $P(S) = 1$.
>
> **Rule 3.** Two events A and B are **disjoint** if they have no outcomes in common and so can never occur simultaneously. If A and B are disjoint,
>
> $$P(A \text{ or } B) = P(A) + P(B)$$
>
> This is the **addition rule for disjoint events.**

E X A M P L E   *Probabilities for Rolling Dice*

Figure 7.2 displays the 36 possible outcomes of rolling two dice. For casino dice it is reasonable to assign the same probability to each of the 36 outcomes in Figure 7.2. Because all 36 outcomes together must have probability 1 (Rule 2), each outcome must have probability 1/36.

What is the probability of rolling a 5? Because the event "roll a 5" contains the four outcomes displayed in the previous example, the addition rule (Rule 3) says that its probability is

$$P(\text{roll a } 5) = P(\;\blacksquare\;\blacksquare\;) + P(\;\blacksquare\;\blacksquare\;) + P(\;\blacksquare\;\blacksquare\;) + P(\;\blacksquare\;\blacksquare\;)$$

$$= \frac{1}{36} + \frac{1}{36} + \frac{1}{36} + \frac{1}{36}$$

$$= \frac{4}{36} = 0.111$$

What about the probability of rolling a 7? In Figure 7.2 you will find six outcomes for which the sum of the pips is 7. The probability is 6/36, or about 0.167. Continue in this way to get the full probability model (sample space and assignment of probabilities) for rolling two dice and summing the pips on the up faces. Here it is:

Outcome	2	3	4	5	6	7	8	9	10	11	12
Probability	1/36	2/36	3/36	4/36	5/36	6/36	5/36	4/36	3/36	2/36	1/36

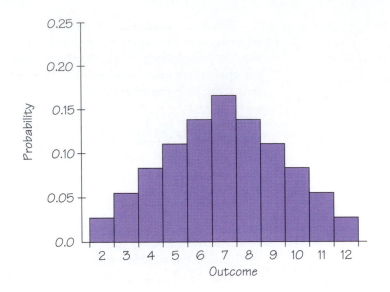

Figure 7.3 is a **probability histogram** of this probability model. The height of each bar shows the probability of the outcome at its base. Because the heights are probabilities, they add to 1. Think of Figure 7.3 as an idealized picture of the results of very many rolls of a die. As an idealized picture, it is perfectly symmetric.

This model assigns probabilities to individual outcomes. To find the probability of an event, just add the probabilities of the outcomes that make up the event. For example,

$$P(\text{outcome is odd}) = P(3) + P(5) + P(7) + P(9) + P(11)$$

$$= \frac{2}{36} + \frac{4}{36} + \frac{6}{36} + \frac{4}{36} + \frac{2}{36}$$

$$= \frac{18}{36} = \frac{1}{2} \quad \blacklozenge$$

This example illustrates one way to assign probabilities to events: assign a probability to every individual outcome, then add these probabilities to find the probability of any event. If such an assignment is to satisfy the rules of probability, the probabilities of all the individual outcomes must sum to exactly 1.

> To give a **probability model for a finite sample space,** assign a probability to each individual outcome. These probabilities must be numbers between 0 and 1 and must have sum 1. The probability of any event is the sum of the probabilities of the outcomes making up the event.

E X A M P L E   *High School Academic Rank*

Select a first-year college student at random and ask what his or her academic rank was in high school. Here are the probabilities, based on proportions from a large sample survey of college students:

Rank	Top 20%	Second 20%	Third 20%	Fourth 20%	Lowest 20%
Probability	0.41	0.23	0.29	0.06	0.01

Check that these probabilities sum to 1. Here are the probabilities of some events.

$$P(\text{student is in top 40\%}) = P(\text{top 20\%}) + P(\text{second 20\%})$$
$$= 0.41 + 0.23 = 0.64$$
$$P(\text{student is } not \text{ in top 20\%}) = 0.23 + 0.29 + 0.06 + 0.01$$
$$= 0.59$$

Can you see why the probability that a student is *not* in the top 20% is one minus the probability that the student chosen *is* in the top 20%? ◆

Equally Likely Outcomes

A simple random sample gives all possible samples an equal chance to be chosen. Rolling two casino dice gives all 36 outcomes the same probability. When randomness is the product of human design, it is often the case that the outcomes in the sample space are all equally likely. Rules 1 and 2 force the assignment of probabilities in this case.

> If a random phenomenon has k possible outcomes, all equally likely, then each individual outcome has probability $1/k$. The probability of any event A is
>
> $$P(A) = \frac{\text{count of outcomes in } A}{\text{count of outcomes in } S}$$
> $$= \frac{\text{count of outcomes in } A}{k}$$

EXAMPLE   *Random Digits*

The successive digits in Table 5.1 (page 174) were produced by a careful randomization that makes each entry equally likely to be any of the 10 candidates. Because the total probability must be 1, the probability of each of the 10 outcomes must be 1/10. That is, the probability model is

Outcome	0	1	2	3	4	5	6	7	8	9
Probability	0.1	0.1	0.1	0.1	0.1	0.1	0.1	0.1	0.1	0.1

Figure 7.4 displays this model in a probability histogram.

We can find the probability of any event by counting its outcomes. Here are two events, with the outcomes that they contain:

A = {odd outcome} = {1, 3, 5, 7, 9}
B = {outcome less than or equal to 3} = {0, 1, 2, 3}

We see that $P(A) = 0.5$ and $P(B) = 0.4$. The event {A or B} contains 7 outcomes,

{A or B} = {0, 1, 2, 3, 5, 7, 9}

so it has probability 0.7. This is *not* the sum of $P(A)$ and $P(B)$, because A and B are *not* disjoint events. Outcomes 1 and 3 belong to both A and B.   ◆

FIGURE 7.4
Probability histogram showing the probabilities for generating a random digit between 0 and 9.

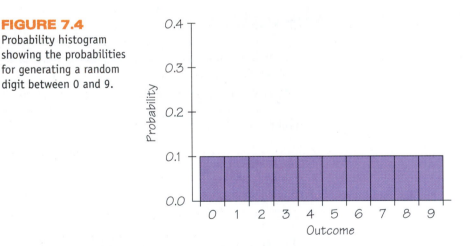

When outcomes are equally likely, finding probabilities leads to the study of counting methods, called **combinatorics.** Combinatorics is an important area of mathematics in its own right. We will start with the multiplication method that we called the *fundamental principle of counting* in Chapter 2.

E X A M P L E   *Code Words*

A computer system assigns log-in identification codes to users by choosing three letters at random. All three-letter codes are therefore equally likely. What is the probability that the code assigned to you has no *x* in it?

First count the total number of code words. There are 26 letters that can occur in each position in the word. Any of the 26 letters in the first position can be combined with any of the 26 letters in the second position to give 26×26 choices. (This is true because the order of the letters matters, so that *ab* and *ba* are different choices.) Any of the 26 letters can then follow in the third position. The number of different codes is

$$26 \times 26 \times 26 = 17{,}576$$

Now count the number of code words that have no *x*. These codes are made up the other 25 letters. So there are

$$25 \times 25 \times 25 = 15{,}625$$

such codes. The probability that your code has no *x* is therefore

$$P(\text{no } x) = \frac{\text{number of codes with no } x}{\text{number of codes}}$$

$$= \frac{15{,}625}{17{,}576} = 0.889$$

Suppose that the computer is programmed to avoid repeated letters in the identification codes. Any of the 26 letters can still appear in the first position. But only the 25 remaining letters are allowed in the second position, so that there are 26×25 choices for the first two letters in the code. Any of these choices leaves 24 letters for the third position. The number of different codes without repeated letters is

$$26 \times 25 \times 24 = 15{,}600$$

Codes with no *x* are allowed one fewer choice in each position. There are

$$25 \times 24 \times 23 = 13{,}800$$

such codes. The probability that your code has no *x* is then

$$P(\text{no } x) = \frac{\text{number of codes with no } x}{\text{number of codes}}$$

$$= \frac{13{,}800}{15{,}600} = 0.885$$

Eliminating repeats slightly lowers your chance of avoiding an *x*.   ◆

The preceding example makes use of two rules about counting that we often apply in finding probabilities:

> *Counting Rule A.* Suppose we have a collection of n distinct items. We want to arrange k of these items in order, and the same item can appear several times in the arrangement. The number of possible arrangements is
>
> $$n \times n \times \cdots \times n = n^k$$
>
> *Counting Rule B.* Suppose we have a collection of n distinct items. We want to arrange k of these items in order, and any item can appear no more than once in the arrangement. The number of possible arrangements is
>
> $$n \times (n - 1) \times \cdots \times (n - k + 1)$$

In the example, n (the number of letters available) is first 26, then 25, and k (the number of letters to be arranged to make a code) is 3. It is easier to think your way through the counting than to memorize the recipes.

E X A M P L E   *How Many Orderings?*

A jury of 7 students is seated in a row of 7 chairs to judge a speaking competition. In how many orders can the students sit?

Because each chair holds only one student, no repeats are allowed. This is the case described by rule B with n and k both equal to 7. To think through the problem, proceed like this: any of the 7 students can sit in the first chair; then any of the 6 who remain can sit in the second chair; and so on. The number of arrangements is therefore

$$7 \times 6 \times 5 \times 4 \times 3 \times 2 \times 1 = 5040$$

(This number is often called 7!, read "seven factorial.")   ◆

The Mean of a Probability Model

Suppose you are offered this choice of bets, each costing the same: bet A pays \$10 if you win and you have probability 1/2 of winning, while bet B pays \$10,000 and offers probability 1/10 of winning. You would very likely choose B even though A offers a better chance to win, because B pays much more if you win. It would be foolish to decide which bet to make just on the basis of the probability of winning. How much you can win is also important. When a random phenomenon has numerical outcomes, we are concerned with their amounts as well as with their probabilities.

What will be the average payoff of our two bets in many plays? Recall that the probabilities are the long-run proportions of plays on which each outcome occurs. Bet A produces $10 half the time in the long run and nothing half the time. So the average payoff should be

$$\left(\$10 \times \frac{1}{2}\right) + \left(\$0 \times \frac{1}{2}\right) = \$5$$

Bet B, on the other hand, pays out $10,000 on 1/10 of all bets in the long run. Bet B's average payoff is

$$\left(\$10,000 \times \frac{1}{10}\right) + \left(\$0 \times \frac{9}{10}\right) = \$1000$$

If you can place many bets, you should certainly choose B. Here is a general definition of the kind of "average outcome" we used to compare the two bets.

Suppose that the possible outcomes $s_1, s_2, \ldots, s_k$ in a sample space S are numbers, and that p_j is the probability of outcome s_j. The **mean** μ of this probability model is

$$\mu = s_1 p_1 + s_2 p_2 + \cdots + s_k p_k$$

Earlier, we met the mean $\bar{x}$, the average of n observations that we actually have in hand. The mean μ, on the other hand, describes the probability model rather than any one collection of observations. You can think of μ as a theoretical mean that says what average outcome we expect in the long run.

E X A M P L E   *Mean Household Size*

What is the mean size of an American household? Here is the distribution of the size of households according to Census Bureau studies:

Inhabitants	1	2	3	4	5	6	7
Proportion of households	0.25	0.32	0.17	0.15	0.07	0.03	0.01

If we imagine selecting a single household at random, the size of the household chosen has probability model given by the table. The mean μ is the mean household size in the population. This mean is

$$\mu = (1)(0.25) + (2)(0.32) + (3)(0.17) + (4)(0.15) + (5)(0.07)$$
$$+ (6)(0.03) + (7)(0.01)$$
$$= 2.6$$

Figure 7.5 is a probability histogram of the distribution of household size, with the mean $\mu = 2.6$ marked.

In this case, the mean μ is the average size of all American households. If we took a random sample of, say, 100 households and recorded their sizes, we would call the average size for this sample $\bar{x}$. A second random sample would no doubt give a somewhat different value of $\bar{x}$. So $\bar{x}$ varies from sample to sample, but μ, which describes the distribution of probabilites, is a fixed number.   ◆

The mean μ is an average outcome in two senses. The definition says that it is the average of the possible outcomes, not weighted equally but weighted by their probabilites. More likely outcomes get more weight in the average. An important fact of probability, the *law of large numbers,* says that μ is the average outcome in another sense as well.

Observe any random phenomenon having numerical outcomes with finite mean μ. According to the **law of large numbers,** as the random phenomenon is repeated a large number of times

■ The proportion of trials on which each outcome occurs gets closer and closer to the probability of that outcome, and
■ The mean $\bar{x}$ of the observed values gets closer and closer to μ.

These facts can be stated more precisely and then proved mathematically. The law of large numbers brings the idea of probability to a natural completion. We first observed that some phenomena are random in the sense of showing long-run regularity. Then we used the idea of long-run proportions to motivate the basic laws of probability. Those laws are mathematical idealizations that can be used without interpreting probability as proportion in many trials. Now the law of large numbers tells us that in many trials the proportion of trials on which an outcome occurs will always approach its probability.

The law of large numbers also explains why gambling can be a business. The winnings (or losses) of a gambler on a few plays are uncertain—that's why gambling is exciting. It is only *in the long run* that the mean outcome is predictable.

FIGURE 7.5
Probability histogram
showing the probabilities
for the number of people
in a randomly chosen
household. The mean
household size is
$\mu = 2.6$ people.

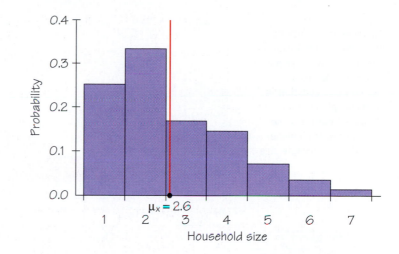

The house plays tens of thousands of times. So the house, unlike individual gamblers, can count on the long-run regularity described by the law of large numbers. The average winnings of the house on tens of thousands of plays will be very close to the mean of the distribution of winnings. Needless to say, this mean guarantees the house a profit.

Sampling Distributions

Sampling, in a way, is a lot like gambling. Both rely on the deliberate use of chance. We want to apply probability to describe the results of sampling. At first glance, this is a formidable task. Suppose that we choose a simple random sample of size 100 from the more than 200 million adults in the United States. All possible samples are equally likely — that is the definition of simple random sampling. There are an immense number of possible samples, so that finding probabilities by counting is not appealing. There are mathematical shortcuts, but there is also another way: rather than counting, we can actually choose a large number of samples and observe the outcomes. In practice, we program a computer to imitate (the formal word is *simulate*) drawing many samples. Let's try it.

E X A M P L E   *A Sampling Experiment*

In Chapter 5, we looked at a Gallup poll that asked a sample of 1493 people "Are you afraid to go outside at night within a mile of your home because of crime?" Ask that question of a simple random sample of 100 adults; 48 say "Yes." That's 48% of the sample. Take another simple random sample of 100 adults; this time, 50% say "Yes." This is **sampling variability:** when we take repeated samples from the same population, the results will vary from sample to sample.

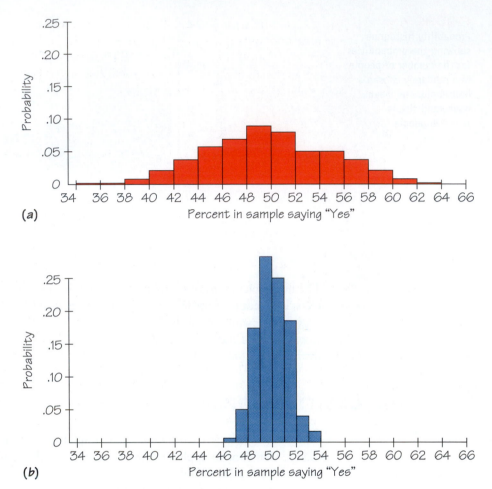

Sampling distributions that show the behavior of the percent of a sample who say "Yes" to an opinion poll question in many simple random samples from the same population. (a) Sample size 100. (b) Sample size 1493.

Figure 7.6a is a histogram of the percents who said "Yes" to the question in 1000 simple random samples from the same population. It shows the regular pattern of outcomes that is characteristic of random sampling. Now we can use the language of probability to describe this pattern.

One of the classes in the histogram covers the range

46% < percent saying "Yes" ≤ 48%

Exactly 70 of the 1000 samples had outcomes in this class. Because 1000 samples is a large number of repetitions of the random sampling, the proportion of outcomes that fall in this class is close to the probability of the class. So we estimate that the probability of getting an outcome greater than 46% but no larger than 48% is 70/1000, or 0.07. The height of the bar above that class in Figure 7.6a is 0.07. ◆

Statisticians call a number that is computed from a sample a **statistic.** The percent of our sample of 100 people who said "Yes" to the poll question is a statistic. The histogram in Figure 7.6a displays the sampling variability of this statistic by assigning probabilities to its possible values. These probabilities make up the *sampling distribution* of the statistic.

> The **sampling distribution** of a statistic is the distribution of values taken by the statistic in all possible samples of the same size from the same population.

Strictly speaking, the sampling distribution is the ideal pattern that would emerge if we looked at all possible samples of size 100 from our population. We could display this ideal distribution with a probability histogram. A distribution obtained from a fixed number of trials, like the 1000 trials in Figure 7.6a, is only an approximation to the sampling distribution. One of the uses of probability theory in statistics is to obtain exact sampling distributions without actually drawing many samples. The interpretation of a sampling distribution is the same, however, whether we obtain it by actual sampling or by the mathematics of probability.

Let's try a second sampling experiment. The Gallup poll asked 1493 people, not 100 people, about their fear of crime. We will take 1000 simple random samples of 1493 people. For each of these samples, calculate the percent who say that they are afraid to go out because of crime. Figure 7.6b displays the distribution of the 1000 sample percents, using the same scale as Figure 7.6a. This is the sampling distribution for this statistic.

EXAMPLE   *Examining Sampling Distributions*

Let's apply our tools for describing distributions to the two sampling distributions in Figure 7.6. We will examine the *shape, center,* and *spread* of these distributions.

Both distributions share a distinctive shape. They are quite symmetric, with a single peak in the center. There are no outliers to disturb the pattern. Both are centered very close to 50%. In fact, the mean outcomes are 50.11 for samples of size 100 and 50.03 for samples of size 1493. The distribution of results for samples of size 1493 is much less spread out than the distribution for samples of 100 people—that is, the histogram in Figure 7.6b is taller and narrower than that in Figure 7.6a. The standard deviations of the 1000 sample results are 4.986 for the smaller samples and 1.289 for the larger samples.

In fact, the population from which we drew all of our samples contained exactly 50% who would say "Yes" to Gallup's question about fear of crime. The centers of the sampling distributions are very close to 50%. This reflects the lack of bias in simple random sampling. The spread of the sample results goes down as we take larger samples. So large samples usually give results close to the truth about the population.   ◆

Our sampling experiment has both produced an approximate assignment of probabilities (without counting) and taught us a bit about how the sampling distribution behaves when we increase the size of the sample. Our goal is to learn enough about the mathematics of probability to get more exact results than sampling experiments provide. In the next chapter we'll learn specific recipes for the mean and standard deviation of the sampling distributions that Figure 7.6 approximates. The first step is to study the distinctive shape of these distributions. They are *normal distributions.* That is the topic to which we now turn.

Normal Distributions

Although they differ in variability, the histograms in Figures 7.6a and 7.6b have similar shapes in other respects. Both are symmetric, with centers close to 50%. The tails fall off smoothly on either side, with no outliers. Suppose that we represent the shape of each histogram by drawing a smooth curve through the tops of the bars. If we do this carefully—using the actual probabilities of the outcomes rather than estimates from only 1000 samples—the two curves we obtain will be quite close to two members of the family of *normal curves.* The two normal curves appear in Figure 7.7.

Normal curves introduce a new way of describing probabilites. We can describe an assignment of probabilities to the values of a statistic by a probability histogram. The height of any bar is the probability of the outcomes spanned by the

FIGURE 7.7
The normal curves that approximate the sampling distributions in Figure 7.6. The taller curve is for sample size 1493, the flatter curve for smaller samples of size 100. Each curve has area exactly 1 beneath it.

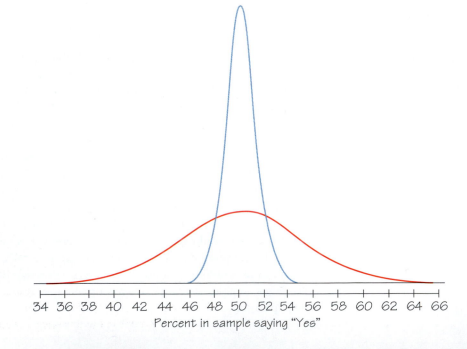

34 36 38 40 42 44 46 48 50 52 54 56 58 60 62 64 66
Percent in sample saying "Yes"

base of that bar. Because all bars have the same width, their area (height times width) is proportional to the probability. Normal curves can be thought of as approximations to a histogram of probabilities in which area is exactly equal to probability. Normal curves are easier to work with than histograms because many bars are replaced by a single smooth curve. Normal curves have the property that the total area under the curve is exactly 1, corresponding to the fact that all outcomes together have probability 1.

> A normal curve assigns probabilities to outcomes as follows: the probability of any interval of outcomes is the area under the normal curve above that interval. The total area under any normal curve is exactly 1.

EXAMPLE *Probability as Area Under a Curve*

Figure 7.8 is another drawing of the normal curve for the sampling distribution of Figure 7.6b. This curve assigns probabilities for the percent of a simple random sample of size 1493 who say "Yes" to Gallup's question about fear of crime.

The shaded area is the area under the normal curve between 50% and 52%. This area is 0.44. So the probability that between 50% and 52% of the people in a randomly chosen sample will say "Yes" is 0.44. ◆

FIGURE 7.8
Probability as area under a normal curve. The area 0.44 is the probability of an outcome between 50 and 52.

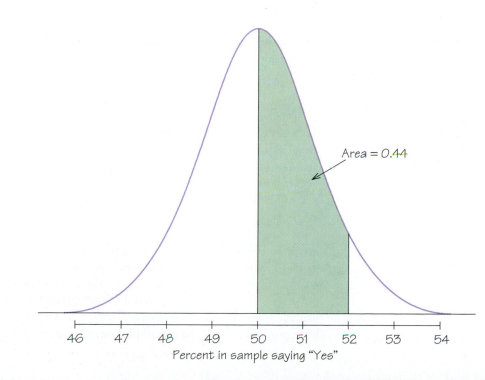

Area = 0.44

Percent in sample saying "Yes"

Our first method of assigning probabilities was to give a probability to each individual outcome, then add these probabilities to get the probability of any event. Probability as area under a curve is the second important method of assigning probability. It is easier when there are many individual outcomes falling close together. Curves of different shapes describe different assignments of probability. We will emphasize the normal curves, because they describe probability in several important situations. An assignment of probabilities to outcomes by a normal curve is a **normal probability distribution.**

Figures 7.6 and 7.7 demonstrate that the sampling distribution of a sample proportion from a simple random sample is close to a normal distribution. This is not just a matter of artistic judgment. It is a mathematical fact, first proved by Abraham DeMoivre in 1718. Some other common statistics, such as the mean $\bar{x}$ of a large sample, also have sampling distributions that are approximately normal. A normal curve will not exactly describe a specific set of outcomes, such as our 1000 sample percentages. It is an idealized distribution that is convenient to use and gives a good approximation to the actual distribution of outcomes.

There is a close connection between describing an assignment of probability to numerical outcomes and describing a set of data. Histograms can be used for both tasks. Similarly, smooth curves such as the normal curves can replace histograms for describing large sets of data as well as for assigning probabilites. Many sets of data are approximately described by normal distributions. The normal distributions therefore deserve more detailed study.

The Shape of Normal Curves

Normal curves can be specified exactly by an equation, but we will be content with pictures like Figures 7.7 and 7.8. All normal curves are symmetric and bell-shaped, with tails that fall off rapidly. The center of the symmetric normal curve is the center of the distribution in several senses. It is the mean μ for the assignment of probabilities. It is also the median in the sense that half the probability (half the area under the curve) lies on each side of the center. When probabilities are assigned as areas under a symmetric curve, the mean μ is also the median of the distribution.

The mean and median of a skewed distribution are not equal. Figure 7.9, for example, shows a *right-skewed distribution.* The right tail of the curve is much longer than the left. The prices of new houses are an example of a skewed distribution—there are many moderately priced houses and a few extravagantly priced mansions out in the right tail. Those mansions pull the mean, or average price, up, so that it is greater than the median. The mean price of new houses sold in 1997 was $176,000, but the median price for these same houses was only $146,000.

As we saw in Chapter 6, even the most cursory description of data on a single variable should include a measure of spread in addition to a measure of center or location. What about the spread of a normal curve? *Normal curves have the special*

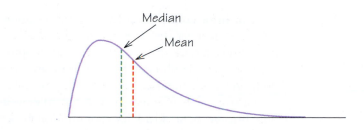

property that their spread is completely measured by a single number, the standard deviation. We learned in the last chapter how to calculate the standard deviation from a set of observations. For normal distributions, the standard deviation (like the mean) can be found directly from the curve.

> The **mean** of a normal distribution lies at the center of symmetry of the normal curve.
>
> To find the **standard deviation** of a normal distribution, run a pencil along the normal curve from the center (the mean) outward. At first, the curve falls ever more steeply as you go out; farther from the mean it falls ever less steeply. The two points where the curvature changes are located one standard deviation on either side of the mean.

With a little practice, you can locate the change-of-curvature points quite accurately. For example, Figure 7.10 shows the distribution of heights of American women ages 18 to 24. The shape of the curve is normal, with mean (and median) height $\mu = 64.5$ inches. The two change-of-curvature points are at 62 inches and 67 inches. The standard deviation of the distribution is the distance of either of these points from the mean, or 2.5 inches.

FIGURE 7.10
Locating the mean and standard deviation on a normal curve. For this normal curve, $\mu = 64.5$ and $\sigma = 2.5$.

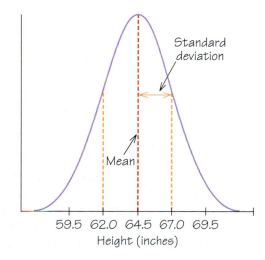

The usual notation for the standard deviation of a probability distribution is σ, the Greek letter sigma. Just as for the mean μ, it is possible to find σ for any distribution directly from the assignment of probabilities. Again just as for the mean, we distinguish between s, the standard deviation of a given set of observations, and σ, the standard deviation of a probability distribution.

In Chapter 6, we often used the quartiles to indicate the spread of a distribution. Because the standard deviation completely describes the spread of any normal distribution, it tells us where the quartiles are. Here are the facts:

> The first quartile of any normal distribution is located 0.67σ below the mean; the third quartile is 0.67σ above the mean.

E X A M P L E   *Heights of Young Women*

The distribution of heights of young women, shown in Figure 7.10, is approximately normal, with mean $\mu = 64.5$ inches and standard deviation $\sigma = 2.5$ inches. The quartiles lie 0.67σ, or

$$(0.67)(2.5) = 1.7 \text{ inches}$$

on either side of the mean. The first quartile is $64.5 - 1.7$, or 62.8 inches. The third quartile is $64.5 + 1.7$, or 66.2 inches. Figure 7.11 marks the quartiles on the normal curve. They contain between them the middle 50% of women's heights.

◆

FIGURE 7.11
The quartiles of a normal distribution are located 0.67 standard deviation on either side of the mean. For this normal curve, $\mu = 64.5$ and $\sigma = 2.5$.

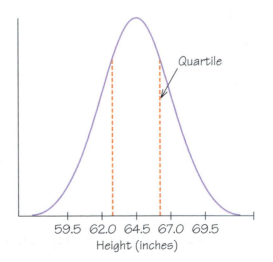

The mean and standard deviation of normal curves have a special property: *the shape of a normal distribution is completely specified by giving μ and σ.* A measure of center and a measure of spread are not sufficient to determine the exact shape of most distributions of data, but the mean and standard deviation are enough when the distribution is normal. Changing the mean of a normal curve does not change its shape; it only moves the curve to a new location. Changing the standard deviation does change the shape. A normal curve with a smaller standard deviation is taller and narrower (has less spread) than one with a larger standard deviation. You can see this by comparing the two normal curves for our random sampling experiments in Figure 7.7. Both normal curves have the same mean, but the curve for samples of size 1493 has the smaller standard deviation.

The 68–95–99.7 Rule

One consequence of the fact that the mean and standard deviation completely specify a normal distribution is that all normal distributions are the same when we record observations in terms of how many standard deviations they lie from the mean. In particular, the probability that an observation falls within one, two, or three standard deviations of the mean is the same for all normal distributions. The probability of an outcome falling within one standard deviation on either side of the mean is 0.68. If we go out two standard deviations from the mean, the probability is 0.95. Finally, the probability of falling within three standard deviations of the mean is almost 1, or 0.997 to be exact. These facts can be derived mathematically from the equation of a normal curve. They are not true for distributions with other shapes.

Figure 7.12 illustrates these facts expressed in terms of percents. Together, we call them the *68–95–99.7 rule* for normal distributions.

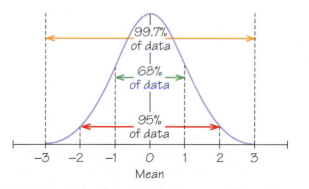

FIGURE 7.12 The 68–95–99.7 rule for normal distributions.

According to the **68–95–99.7 rule,** in any normal distribution:

- 68% of the observations fall within one standard deviation of the mean.
- 95% of the observations fall within two standard deviations of the mean.
- 99.7% of the observations fall within three standard deviations of the mean.

Using the three numbers in the 68–95–99.7 rule, we can quickly derive helpful information about any normal distribution. More detailed information can be gleaned from tables of areas under the normal curves, but the 68–95–99.7 rule is adequate for our purposes.

EXAMPLE *Heights of Young Women*

The heights of women between the ages of 18 and 24 are roughly normally distributed, with mean $\mu = 64.5$ inches and standard deviation $\sigma = 2.5$ inches. One standard deviation below the mean is $64.5 - 2.5$, or 62 inches. Similarly, one standard deviation above the mean is $64.5 + 2.5$, or 67 inches. The "68" part of the 68–95–99.7 rule says that about 68% of women are between 62 and 67 inches tall. Because two standard deviations are 5 inches, we know that 95% of young women are between $64.5 - 5$ and $64.5 + 5$, that is, between 59.5 and 69.5 inches tall. Almost all women have heights within three standard deviations of the mean, or between 57 and 72 inches. Few women are 6 feet (72 inches) tall or over. ◆

EXAMPLE *SAT Scores*

The distribution of scores on tests such as the SAT college entrance examinations is close to normal. SAT scores are adjusted so that the mean score is about $\mu = 500$ and the standard deviation is about $\sigma = 100$. This information allows us to answer many questions about SAT scores.

- *How high must a student score to fall in the top 25%?*
  The third quartile is $(0.67)(100) = 67$ points above the mean. So scores above 567 are in the top 25%.
- *What percent of scores fall between 200 and 800?*
  Scores of 200 and 800 are three standard deviations on either side of the mean. The 99.7 part of the 68–95–99.7 rule says that 99.7% of all scores lie in this range. (In fact, 200 and 800 are the lowest and highest scores that are reported on the SAT. The few scores higher than 800 are reported as 800.)

FIGURE 7.13
Using the 68–95–99.7 rule to find the percent of SAT scores that are above 700. For this normal curve, $\mu = 500$ and $\sigma = 100$.

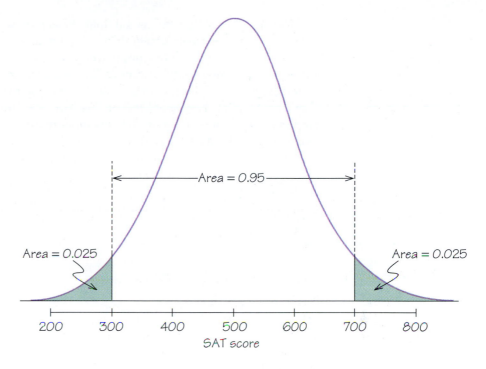

■ *What percent of scores are above 700?*
A score of 700 is two standard deviations above the mean. By the 95 part of the 68–95–99.7 rule, 95% of all scores fall between 300 and 700 and 5% fall below 300 or above 700. Because normal curves are symmetric, half of this 5% are above 700. So a score above 700 places a student in the top 2.5% of test-takers.

Sketching a normal curve with the points one, two, and three standard deviations from the mean marked can help you use the 68–95–99.7 rule. Figure 7.13 shows the distribution of SAT scores with the areas needed to find the percent of scores above 700. ◆

The Central Limit Theorem

The significance of normal distributions is explained in part by a key fact in probability theory known as the *central limit theorem*. This theorem says that the distribution of any random phenomenon tends to be normal if we average it over a large number of independent repetitions. The central limit theorem allows us to analyze and predict the results of chance phenomena if we average over many observations.

We have already seen the central limit theorem at work in our random sampling experiment. A single person drawn at random says either "Yes" or "No" to the opinion poll question. Only two outcomes are possible, and there is no normal curve in sight. However, the percent of "Yes" answers when 100 people are drawn at random roughly follows a normal distribution. You can think of the percent of "Yes" answers as an average of "Yes" or "No" over the 100 people. When we sample 1493 people, the percent of "Yes" responses represents an average over a larger number of people and is even closer to a normal curve.

Our sampling experiment showed that samples of size 1493 have much less spread than samples of size 100. We describe spread by the standard deviation of the normal distribution of outcomes. The central limit theorem makes the relationship of standard deviation to sample size explicit. Here is a more exact statement:

> The **central limit theorem** states that
>
> - A sample mean or sample proportion from n trials on the same random phenomenon has a distribution that is approximately normal when n is large.
> - The mean of this normal distribution is the same as the mean for a single trial.
> - The standard deviation of this normal distribution is the standard deviation for a single trial divided by $\sqrt{n}$.

Pay attention to the fact that the standard deviation of a mean or proportion decreases with the square root of the number of observations, $\sqrt{n}$. This is true for all values of n, not just when n is large enough that the central limit theorem says that the distribution is close to normal.

EXAMPLE   *Averages Are Less Variable Than Individuals*

Choose a single young woman at random. The resulting height varies in repeated random selections, with standard deviation $\sigma = 2.5$ inches.

Now choose 5 young women at random and take the mean $\bar{x}$ of their heights. The mean $\bar{x}$ varies in repeated samples, with standard deviation

$$\sigma_{\bar{x}} = \frac{\sigma}{\sqrt{n}}$$

$$= \frac{2.5}{\sqrt{5}} = \frac{2.5}{2.236} = 1.118 \text{ inches}$$

The notation $\sigma_{\bar{x}}$ reminds us that this is the standard deviation of the distribution of $\bar{x}$, not the standard deviation σ of a single observation.   ◆

That averages $\bar{x}$ of several observations are less variable than individual observations is an important statistical fact. For example, the average of 25 observations ($\sqrt{25} = 5$) from the same population has standard deviation 1/5 as large as the standard deviation for an individual. The average of 100 observations ($\sqrt{100} = 10$) has a standard deviation 1/10 as large as the standard deviation of a single observation. Because of the square root, to cut the standard deviation of a sample mean or proportion in half, we must multiply the sample size by 4, not just by 2.

Applying the Central Limit Theorem

We can use the central limit theorem to see just how good a business gambling can be for a casino. Let's look at just one of the many bets that a casino offers.

E X A M P L E   *Red or Black in Roulette*

An American roulette wheel has 38 slots, of which 18 are black, 18 are red, and 2 are green (see Figure 7.14). When the wheel is spun, the ball is equally likely to

FIGURE 7.14
A gambler may win or lose at roulette, but in the long run the casino always wins.

come to rest in any of the slots. Gamblers can place a number of different bets in roulette. One of the simplest wagers chooses red or black. A bet of one dollar on red will pay off an additional dollar if the ball lands in a red slot. Otherwise, the player loses his dollar. When gamblers bet on red or black, the two green slots belong to the house.

State Lotteries

Gambling on chance outcomes goes back to ancient times. Both public and private lotteries were common in the early years of the United States. After disappearing for a century or so, government-run gambling reappeared in 1964, when New Hampshire caused a furor by introducing a lottery to raise public revenue without raising taxes. The furor subsided quickly as larger states adopted the idea, until almost all states outside the South now sponsor lotteries. State lotteries made gambling acceptable as entertainment. By 1998, only three states had no form of legal gambling.

State governments like the idea of raising revenue without raising taxes. Casinos, however, carry heavy social costs in increased crime and in the troubles of gambling addicts who waste their own and their families' resources. One University of Illinois study estimated that costs to social and police agencies raise state expenses by about three times the amount that gambling brings into the state treasury.

The most popular game in state lotteries is Lotto, in which players choose (for example) 6 numbers out of 49 in the hope of matching the randomly drawn winning numbers. The odds against winning Lotto are enormous (6,991,908 to 1 for choosing 6 numbers out of 49). Of course, the payoff is also enormous. Lotteries are a bad

bet, because the state pays out only about half of the money wagered. Many casino games do better, as the roulette example in the text illustrates.

Regular Lotto players can't even rely on the central limit theorem. The mean payoff for a $1 bet is about 50 cents—but this mean is spread over a very few winners and very many losers. The variation on a single play is so large that no humanly possible number of plays, even with the help of that $\sqrt{n}$, can reduce the variation enough to allow a useful prediction. The only compensation almost all Lotto players receive is the pleasure of imagining themselves rich. Casino owners do better. One of them, Donald Trump, says, "I've never gambled in my life. To me, a gambler is someone who plays slot machines. I prefer to own slot machines."

If we decide to bet on red, there are only two possible outcomes: win or lose. We win if the ball stops in one of the 18 red slots. We lose if it lands in one of the 20 slots that are black or green. Because casino roulette wheels are carefully balanced so that all slots are equally likely, the probabilities are

$$P(\text{win } \$1) = 18/38$$
$$P(\text{lose } \$1) = 20/38$$

The mean outcome of a single bet on red is found in the usual way:

$$\mu = (1)\left(\frac{18}{38}\right) + (-1)\left(\frac{20}{38}\right)$$

$$= -\frac{2}{38} = -0.053$$

The law of large numbers says that the mean μ is the average outcome of a very large number of individual bets. In the long run, gamblers will lose (and the casino will win) an average of 5.3 cents per bet. ◆

Just as when we ask only one person's opinion, there is no normal curve in sight when a gambler makes only one bet on red in roulette. But the central limit theorem ensures that the average outcome of many bets follows a distribution that is close to normal. Suppose that we place 50 bets in an evening's play. The mean outcome $\bar{x}$ is the overall gain (or loss) divided by 50. If we win 30 and lose 20 times, the overall gain is $10, an average winnings of $\bar{x} = \$0.20$ per bet. If we continue to gamble night after night, placing 50 bets each night, our average winnings per bet will vary from night to night. A histogram of these values will follow a normal distribution. Figure 7.15 shows the results of many trials of 50 bets each. The normal curve superimposed on the histogram is the distribution given by the central limit theorem in this case.

We know that the mean of the normal distribution in Figure 7.15 is the same as the mean of a single bet, -0.053. What is the standard deviation? We know

FIGURE 7.15
The distribution of winnings in repeated bets on red or black in roulette.

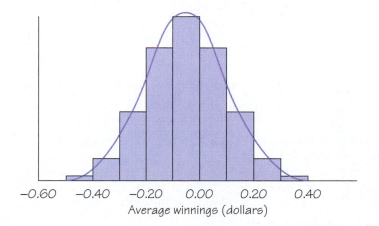

Average winnings (dollars)

that it is $\sigma/\sqrt{50}$, where σ is the standard deviation of the distribution of individual bets. Individual bets do not have a normal distribution, but their distribution is so simple that we can find the standard deviation starting from the idea of the variance as the average squared deviation from the mean. Just as in the case of the mean, "average" here is found by using the probabilities of the outcomes.

> Suppose that the possible outcomes $s_1, s_2, \ldots, s_k$ in a sample space S are numbers, and that p_j is the probability of outcome s_j. The **variance** σ^2 of this probability model is
>
> $$\sigma^2 = (s_1 - \mu)^2 p_1 + (s_2 - \mu)^2 p_2 + \cdots + (s_k - \mu)^2 p_k$$
>
> The **standard deviation** σ is the square root of the variance.

EXAMPLE   *Red or Black in Roulette*

We saw that the mean for betting red or black is $\mu = -0.053$. The variance and standard deviation of the outcome of a single bet are

$$\sigma^2 = (1 - (-0.053))^2 \frac{18}{38} + (-1 - (-0.053))^2 \frac{20}{38}$$

$$= (1.053)^2 \frac{18}{38} + (-0.947)^2 \frac{20}{38}$$

$$= 0.9972$$

$$\sigma = \sqrt{0.9972} = 0.9986$$

The standard deviation of the mean outcome $\bar{x}$ for 50 bets is therefore

$$\frac{\sigma}{\sqrt{n}} = \frac{0.9986}{\sqrt{50}} = 0.14$$

Check this by locating the change-of-curvature points of the normal curve in Figure 7.15. ◆

What will be the experience of a habitual gambler who places 50 bets per night? Almost all average nightly winnings will fall within three standard deviations of the mean, that is, between

$$-0.053 + (3)(0.14) = 0.367$$

and

$$-0.053 - (3)(0.14) = -0.473$$

The total winnings after 50 bets will therefore fall between

$$(0.367)(50) = 18.35$$

and

$$(-0.473)(50) = -23.65$$

The gambler may win as much as $18.35 or lose as much as $23.65. Gambling is exciting because the outcome, even after an evening of bets, is uncertain. It is possible to walk away a winner. It's all a matter of luck.

The casino, however, is in a different position. It doesn't want excitement, just a steady income. The house bets with all its customers—perhaps 100,000 individual bets on black or red in a week. The distribution of average customer winnings on 100,000 bets is very close to normal, and the mean is still the mean outcome for one bet, -0.053, a loss of 5.3 cents per dollar bet. The standard deviation is much smaller when we average over 100,000 bets. It is

$$\frac{\sigma}{\sqrt{n}} = \frac{0.9986}{\sqrt{100,000}} = 0.003$$

Here is what the spread in the casino's average result looks like after 100,000 bets:

$$
\begin{aligned}
\text{Spread} &= \text{mean} \pm 3 \text{ standard deviations} \\
&= -0.053 \pm (3)(0.003) \\
&= -0.053 \pm 0.009 \\
&= -0.044 \text{ to } -0.062
\end{aligned}
$$

Because the casino covers so many bets, the standard deviation of the average winnings per bet becomes very small. And because the mean is negative, almost all outcomes will be negative. The gamblers' losses and the casino's winnings are almost certain to average between 4.4 and 6.2 cents for every dollar bet.

The gamblers who collectively place those 100,000 bets will lose money. The probable range of their losses is:

$$(-0.044)(100,000) = -4400$$
$$(-0.062)(100,000) = -6200$$

The gamblers are almost certain to lose—and the casino is almost certain to take in—between $4400 and $6200 on those 100,000 bets. What's more, we have seen from the central limit theorem that the more bets that are made, the narrower is the range of possible outcomes. That is how a casino can make a business out of gambling. The more money that is bet, the more accurately the casino can predict its profits.

REVIEW VOCABULARY

Addition rule for disjoint events   If two events are disjoint, the probability that one or the other occurs is the sum of their individual probabilities.

Central limit theorem   The average of many independent random outcomes is approximately normally distributed. When we average n independent repetitions of the same random phenomenon, the resulting distribution of outcomes has mean equal to the mean outcome of a single trial and standard deviation proportional to $1/\sqrt{n}$.

Combinatorics   The branch of mathematics that counts arrangements of objects.

Disjoint events   have no outcomes in common.

Equally likely outcomes   occur when every possible outcome of a random phenomenon has the same probability. If there are k outcomes, each has probability $1/k$.

Event   Any collection of possible outcomes of a random phenomenon. An event is a subset of the sample space.

Law of large numbers   As a random phenomenon is repeated many times, the mean $\bar{x}$ of the observed outcomes approaches the mean μ of the probability model.

Mean of a probability model   The average outcome of a random phenomenon with numerical values. When possible values $s_1, s_2, \ldots, s_k$ have probabilities $p_1, p_2, \ldots, p_k$, the mean is the average of the outcomes weighted by their probabilities, $\mu = s_1 p_1 + s_2 p_2 + \cdots + s_k p_k$.

Normal distributions   A family of probability models that assign probabilities to events as areas under a curve. The normal curves are symmetric and bell-shaped. A specific normal curve is completely described by giving its mean μ and its standard deviation σ.

Probability   A number between 0 and 1 that gives the long-run proportion of repetitions of a random phenomenon on which an event will occur.

Probability histogram   A histogram that displays a probability model when the outcomes are numerical. The height of each bar is the probability of the outcome or group of outcomes at the base of the bar.

Probability model   A sample space S together with an assignment of probabilities to events. If probabilities $P(s)$ are assigned to individual outcomes s in S, they must be numbers between 0 and 1 that add to exactly 1. A probability model can also assign probabilities to events as areas under a curve. In this case, the total area under the curve must be exactly 1.

Random phenomenon   A phenomenon is random if it is uncertain what the next outcome will be but each outcome nonetheless tends to occur in a fixed proportion of a very long sequence of repetitions. These long-run proportions are the probabilities of the outcomes.

Sample space   A list of all possible outcomes of a random phenomenon.

Sampling distribution   The distribution of values taken by a statistic when many random samples are drawn under the same circumstances. A sampling distribution consists of an assignment of probabilities to the possible values of a statistic.

Sampling variability   The random variability in the value of a statistic (such as a sample mean or sample proportion) when random samples are drawn repeatedly from the same population.

68–95–99.7 rule   In any normal distribution, 68% of the observations lie within one standard deviation on either side of the mean; 95% lie within two standard deviations of the mean; and 99.7% lie within three standard deviations of the mean.

Standard deviation of a normal curve   The standard deviation σ of a normal curve is the distance from the mean to the change-of-curvature points on either side.

Standard deviation of a probability model   A measure of the variability of a probability model. When the possible values $s_1, s_2, \ldots, s_k$ have probabilities $p_1, p_2, \ldots, p_k$, the variance is the average (weighted by probabilities) of the squared deviations from the mean, $\sigma^2 = (s_1 - \mu)^2 p_1 + (s_2 - \mu)^2 p_2 + \cdots + (s_k - \mu)^2 p_k$. The standard deviation σ is the square root of the variance.

Statistic   A number computed from a sample, such as a sample mean or sample proportion. In random sampling, the value of a statistic will vary in repeated sampling.

SUGGESTED READINGS

MOSTELLER, FREDERICK, ROBERT E. K. ROURKE, AND GEORGE B. THOMAS. *Probability with Statistical Applications,* Addison-Wesley, Reading, Mass., 1970. A rich treatment of basic probability that requires only high school algebra but is somewhat sophisticated.

OLKIN, INGRAM, LEON J. GLESER, AND CYRUS DERMAN. *Probability Models and Applications,* 2nd ed., Macmillan, New York, 1994. This book is distinguished by an emphasis on the use of probability to describe real phenomena and by outstanding examples of modeling. In level it falls between Mosteller et al. and Snell.

SNELL, J. LAURIE. *Introduction to Probability,* Random House, New York, 1988. A calculus-based text aimed at undergraduate mathematics majors. Recommended here because of its excellent examples and historical remarks, and in particular because Snell makes good use of BASIC programs that are included in the text.

SUGGESTED WEB SITES

You can find animated simulations on the Web that demonstrate important facts about probability and sampling distributions. Most such sites are at college or university mathematics or statistics departments. Unfortunately, they change frequently. A Web search on a phrase such as "probability applet" will turn up more than you have time to play with.

As of early 1999, David Lane of Rice University (http://www.ruf.rice.edu/~lane/hyperstat/index.html) offers both a number of applets and a good list of "Related Projects" to browse.

SKILLS CHECK

1. We will flip a coin and roll a die. Then we will report the number on the die and whether the coin is heads or tails. How many outcomes are in the sample space?

   (a) 6
   (b) 8
   (c) 12

2. A sample space contains 3 outcomes: A, B, C. Which of the following is a legitimate assignment of probabilities to the outcomes?

   (a) $P(A) = .3$ $P(B) = .6$ $P(C) = .1$
   (b) $P(A) = .5$ $P(B) = .4$ $P(C) = .4$
   (c) $P(A) = .7$ $P(B) = -.2$ $P(C) = .5$

3. There are 3 black and 7 blue socks in a drawer. We reach in and pull one out. What is the probability that it is black?

   (a) 3/10
   (b) 3/7
   (c) 1/2

4. An attaché case has a 3-digit code lock. How many possible codes are there?

   (a) 30
   (b) 729
   (c) 1000

5. Each raffle ticket costs $2. Of 200 tickets sold, one will win $100 and another will win $50. What is your mean value of one play?

   (a) $0.75
   (b) $1.25
   (c) −$1.25

6. The working life of a watch battery is normally distributed with mean 2 years and standard deviation 0.75 year. What is the probability that it will last less than 6 months?

(a) 5%
(b) 2.5%
(c) less than 1%

7. The working life of a watch battery is normally distributed with mean 2 years and standard deviation

0.75 year. Suppose a sample of 16 is drawn from a production run and tested. What is the standard deviation $\sigma_{\bar{x}}$ of the mean result?

(a) 0.75 year
(b) 0.1875 year
(c) 0.0469 year

EXERCISES   ▲ *Optional.*   ■ *Advanced.*   ◆ *Discussion.*

What Is Probability?

1. Hold a penny upright on its edge under your forefinger on a hard surface, then snap it with your other forefinger so that it spins for some time before falling. Based on 50 spins, estimate the probability of heads.

2. You may feel that it is obvious that the probability of a head in tossing a coin is about 1/2 because the coin has two faces. Such opinions are not always correct. The previous exercise asked you to spin a penny rather than toss it—that changes the probability of a head. Now try another variation. Stand a penny on edge on a hard, flat surface. Pound the surface with your hand so that the penny falls over. What is the probability that it falls with heads upward? Make at least 50 trials to estimate the probability of a head.

3. Open your local telephone directory to any page and note whether the last digit of each of the first 100 telephone numbers on the page is odd or even. How many of the digits were odd? What is the approximate probability that the last digit of a telephone number is odd?

4. The table of random digits (Table 5.1 on page 174) was produced by a random mechanism that gives each digit probability 0.1 of being a 0.

What proportion of the first 200 digits in the table are 0s? This proportion is an estimate of the true probability, which in this case is known to be 0.1.

5. You read in a book on poker that the probability of being dealt three of a kind in a five-card poker hand is 1/50. Explain in simple language what this means.

6. Probability is a measure of how likely an event is to occur. Match one of the probabilities that follow with each statement about an event. (The probability is usually a much more exact measure of likelihood than is the verbal statement.)

0, 0.01, 0.3, 0.6, 0.99, 1

(a) This event is impossible. It can never occur.
(b) This event is certain. It will occur on every trial of the random phenomenon.
(c) This event is very unlikely, but it will occur once in a while in a long sequence of trials.
(d) This event will occur more often than not.

Probability Models and Rules

In each of Exercises 7 to 9, describe a reasonable sample space for the random phenomena mentioned. In some cases, more than one choice is possible.

7.   Toss a coin 10 times.

   (a)   Count the number of heads observed.
   (b)   Calculate the percent of heads among the outcomes.
   (c)   Record whether or not at least five heads occurred.

8.   A female lab rat is about to give birth. You count the number of offspring in the litter. (We don't know how large rat litters can be, but you can set a reasonable upper limit if you want.)

9.   Subjects in a clinical trial are assigned at random to either the new treatment group or the control group. For the next subject, you record treatment or control, male or female, and smoker or nonsmoker.

10.   All human blood can be typed as one of O, A, B, or AB, but the distribution of the types varies a bit with race. Here is the distribution of the blood type of a randomly chosen black American:

Blood type	O	A	B	AB
Probability	0.49	0.27	0.20	?

   (a)   What is the probability of type AB blood? Why?
   (b)   Maria has type B blood. She can safely receive blood transfusions from people with blood types O and B. What is the probability that a randomly chosen black American can donate blood to Maria?

11.   If you draw an M&M candy at random from a bag of the candies, the candy you draw will have one of six colors. The probability of drawing each color depends on the proportion of each color among all candies made.

   (a)   Here are the probabilities of each color for a randomly chosen plain M&M:

Color	Brown	Red	Yellow	Green	Orange	Blue
Probability	0.3	0.2	0.2	0.1	0.1	?

What must be the probability of drawing a blue candy?
   (b)   The probabilities for peanut M&M's are a bit different. Here they are:

Color	Brown	Red	Yellow	Green	Orange	Blue
Probability	0.2	0.1	0.2	0.1	0.1	?

What is the probability that a peanut M&M chosen at random is blue?
   (c)   What is the probability that a plain M&M is any of red, yellow, or orange? What is the probability that a peanut M&M has one of these colors?

12.   Las Vegas Zeke, when asked to predict the Atlantic Coast Conference basketball champion, follows the modern practice of giving probabilistic predictions. He says, "North Carolina's probability of winning is twice Duke's. North Carolina State and Virginia each have probability 0.1 of winning, but Duke's probability is three times that. Nobody else has a chance." Has Zeke given a legitimate assignment of probabilities to the eight teams in the conference? Explain your answer.

13.   Government data assign a single cause for each death that occurs in the United States. The data show that the probability is 0.45 that a randomly chosen death was due to cardiovascular (mainly heart) disease, and 0.22 that it was due to cancer. What is the probability that a death was due either to cardiovascular disease or to cancer? What is the probability that the death was due to some other cause?

Equally Likely Outcomes

14.   Abby, Deborah, Julie, Sam, and Roberto work in a firm's public relations office. Their employer must choose two of them to attend a conference in Paris. To avoid unfairness, the choice will be made by drawing two names from a hat. (This is an SRS of size 2.)

   (a)   Write down all possible choices of two of the five names. This is the sample space.
   (b)   The random drawing makes all choices equally likely. What is the probability of each choice?
   (c)   What is the probability that Julie is chosen?
   (d)   What is the probability that neither of the two men (Sam and Roberto) is chosen?

15.   A couple plans to have three children. There are 8 possible arrangements of girls and boys. For example, GGB means the first two children are girls and the third child is a boy. All 8 arrangements are (approximately) equally likely.

   (a)   Write down all 8 arrangements of the sexes of three children. What is the probability of any one of these arrangements?
   (b)   Starting from this probability model, find the probability model for the number of girls the couple has. Make a probability histogram of this model.
   (c)   Use your model from part (b) to find the probability of at least two girls.
   (d)   Return to your model in (a). Use this model to find the probability of at least two girls. You should get the same result as in (c).

■   16.   A computer assigns three-letter log-in identification codes at random as in the example on page 261. If we take the vowels to be a, e, i, o, u, and y, what is the probability that your code contains no vowels if repeated letters are allowed? If no repeats are allowed?

■   17.   The computer in Exercise 16 is

reprogrammed to assign log-in codes of the form consonant-vowel-consonant. The consonants and vowels are both chosen at random and the consonants can repeat. What is the probability that your code does not contain an x?

■   18.   Suppose that a computer assigns three-character log-in codes that may contain the digits 0 to 9 as well as letters, with repeats allowed. What is now the probability that your code contains no x? What is the probability that your code contains no digits?

■   19.   The personal identification numbers (PINs) for automatic teller machines and telephone calling cards usually consist of four digits. You notice that most of your PINs have at least one 0, and you wonder if the issuers use lots of 0s to make the numbers easy to remember. What is the probability that a PIN chosen at random has at least one 0?

The Mean of a Probability Model

20.   What is the mean number of pips observed in rolling a single fair die?

21.   In Exercise 15 you found a probability model for the genders of three children. Compute the mean number of girls such couples will have.

22.   The distribution of grades (A = 4, B = 3, and so on) in Professor Lopez's economics course is

Grade	0	1	2	3	4
Probability	0.10	0.15	0.30	0.30	0.15

Find the average (that is, the mean) grade in this course. Make a probability histogram for the distribution of grades and mark the mean on your histogram.

■   23.   A state lottery Pick 3 game offers a choice of several bets. You choose a three-digit number and bet $1. The lottery commission announces the winning three-digit number, chosen at random, at the end of each day. The "box" pays $83.33 if the number you choose has the same digits as the winning number, in any order. Otherwise, you lose your dollar. Find the mean winnings for a bet on the box. (Assume that you chose a number having three distinct digits.)

24.   The numbers racket is a well-entrenched illegal gambling operation in most large cities. One version works as follows: you choose one of the 1000 three-digit numbers 000 to 999 and pay your local numbers runner a dollar to enter your bet. Each day, one three-digit number is chosen at random and pays off $600. If you bet on any other number, you lose your dollar. What is the mean payoff? Joe makes one bet every day for many years. Explain what the law of large numbers says about Joe's results as he keeps on betting.

25.   An American roulette wheel has 38 slots numbered 0, 00, and 1 to 36. The ball is equally likely to come to rest in any of these slots when the wheel is spun. The slot numbers are laid out on a board on which gamblers place their bets. One column of numbers on the board contains a multiple of 3, that is, 3, 6, 9, . . . , 36. A gambler places a $1 column bet that pays out $3 if any of these numbers comes up.

(a)   What is the probability of winning?
(b)   What are the mean winnings for one play, taking into account the $1 cost of each play?

Sampling Distributions

26.   Let us illustrate the idea of a sampling distribution in the case of a very small sample from a very small population. The population is the scores of 10 students on an exam:

Student	0	1	2	3	4	5	6	7	8	9
Score	82	62	80	58	72	73	65	66	74	62

The parameter of interest is the mean score μ in this population. The sample is an SRS of size $n = 4$ drawn from the population. Because the students are labeled 0 to 9, a single random digit from Table 5.1 chooses one student for the sample.

(a)   Find the mean of the 10 scores in the population. This is the population mean μ.
(b)   Use Table 5.1 to draw an SRS of size 4 from this population. Write the four scores in your sample and calculate the mean $\bar{x}$ of the sample scores. This statistic is an estimate of μ.
(c)   Repeat this process 10 times using different parts of Table 5.1. Make a histogram of the 10 values of $\bar{x}$. You are constructing the sampling distribution of $\bar{x}$. Is the center of your histogram close to μ?

27.   Table 6.8 (page 244) gives the survival times of 72 guinea pigs in a medical experiment. Consider these 72 animals to be the population of interest.

(a)   Make a histogram of the 72 survival times. This population is strongly skewed to the right.
(b)   Find the mean of the 72 survival times. This is the population mean μ. Mark μ on the x-axis of your histogram.
(c)   Label the members of the population 01 to 72 and use Table 5.1 to choose an SRS of size $n = 12$. What is the mean survival time $\bar{x}$ for your sample? Mark the value of $\bar{x}$ with a point on the axis of your histogram from (a).
(d)   Choose four more SRSs of size 12, using different parts of Table 5.1. Find $\bar{x}$ for each sample and mark the values on the axis of your histogram from (a). Would you be surprised if all five $\bar{x}$'s fell on the same side of μ? Why?
(e)   If you chose a large number of SRSs of size 12 from this population and made a histogram of the $\bar{x}$ values, where would you expect the center of this sampling distribution to lie?

Normal Distributions

28. The distribution of heights of adult American men is approximately normal, with mean 69 inches and standard deviation 2.5 inches. Draw a normal curve on which this mean and standard deviation are correctly located. (*Hint:* Draw the curve first, then mark the horizontal axis.)

29. Using the normal distribution described in Exercise 28 and the 68–95–99.7 rule, answer the following questions about the heights of adult American men:

    (a) What percent of men are taller than 74 inches?

    (b) Between what heights do the middle 95% of American men fall?

    (c) What percent of men are shorter than 66.5 inches?

30. What are the quartiles of the distribution of heights of American men in Exercise 28?

31. The number of flaws per square yard in a type of carpet material varies with mean 1.6 flaws per square yard and standard deviation 1.2 flaws per square yard. The population distribution cannot be normal, because a count takes only whole-number values. An inspector samples 200 square yards of the material, records the number of flaws found in each square yard, and calculates $\bar{x}$, the mean number of flaws per square yard inspected. If this inspection were repeated many times, what range of values would contain the middle 95% of the many $\bar{x}$'s?

32. Figure 7.16 shows a probability distribution that is not symmetric. The mean and median do not coincide. Which of the points marked is the mean of the distribution, and which is the median? Explain your answer.

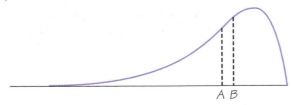

                                 A B

FIGURE 7.16   A skewed distribution.

33. Scores on the Wechsler Adult Intelligence Scale (a standard "IQ test") for the 20 to 34 age group are approximately normally distributed with $\mu = 110$ and $\sigma = 25$.

    (a) About what percent of people in this age group have scores above 110?

    (b) About what percent have scores above 160?

    (c) What are the quartiles of the distribution of scores? Explain in simple language what these two numbers tell us.

34. The army reports that the distribution of head circumference among soldiers is approximately normal with mean 22.8 inches and standard deviation 1.1 inches.

    (a) What percent of soldiers have head circumference greater than 23.9 inches?

    (b) The army plans to make helmets in advance to fit the middle 95% of head circumferences. Soldiers who fall outside this range will get custom-fitted helmets. What head circumferences are small enough or big enough to require custom fitting?

The Central Limit Theorem

35. The SAT scores of high school seniors have a distribution that is approximately normal with mean $\mu = 500$ and standard deviation $\sigma = 100$.

    (a) Choose one senior at random. What is the probability that his or her score is higher than 500? Higher than 600?

    (b) Now choose an SRS of 4 seniors. What is the probability that their mean score is higher than 500? Higher than 600?

36. Juan makes a measurement in a chemistry laboratory and records the result in his lab report. The standard deviation of students' lab measurements is $\sigma = 10$ milligrams. Juan repeats the measurement 3 times and records the mean $\bar{x}$ of his 3 measurements.

(a)   What is the standard deviation of Juan's mean result? (That is, if Juan kept on making 3 measurements and averaging them, what would be the standard deviation of all his $\bar{x}$'s?)
(b)   How many times must Juan repeat the measurement to reduce the standard deviation of $\bar{x}$ to 5? Explain to someone who knows no statistics the advantage of reporting the average of several measurements rather than the result of a single measurement.

37.   A student organization is planning to ask a sample of 50 students if they have noticed AIDS education brochures on campus. The sample percentage who say "Yes" will be reported. Their statistical advisor says that the standard deviation of this percentage will be about 7%. What would the standard deviation be if the sample contained 100 students rather than 50?

◆ 38.   How large a sample is required in the setting of Exercise 37 to reduce the standard deviation of the percentage who say "Yes" from 7% to 3.5%? Explain to someone who knows no statistics the advantage of taking a larger sample in a survey of opinion.

■ 39.   In Exercise 25 you found the mean winnings for a $1 column bet in roulette. They are of course negative—in the long run, players lose and the house wins. Now find the standard deviation for this type of bet. Compare your results with those in the examples for a bet on red or black. Is there any reason to prefer one bet over the other?

■ 40.   In Exercise 24 you found the mean winnings for a numbers game. They are of course negative—in the long run, players lose and the house wins. Now find the standard deviation for single plays of this game. Use the central limit theorem to give the spread (mean ± 3 standard deviations) for a daily player's winnings after a year (365 plays) and after 10 years (3650 plays).

Additional Exercises

41.   Choose a student at random and record the number of dollars in bills (ignore change) that he or she is carrying. Give a reasonable sample space S for this random phenomenon. (We don't know the largest amount that a student could reasonably carry, so you will have to make a choice in stating the sample space.)

◆ 42.   Here is the distribution of marital status for American women aged 25 to 29 years:

Outcome	Never married	Married	Widowed	Divorced
Probability	0.376	?	.003	.062

(a)   If this is to be a legitimate probability model, what must be the probability that a woman in this age group is married?
(b)   It does not make sense to speak of the mean for this model. Why not?

◆ 43.   A bridge deck contains 52 cards, four of each of the 13 face values ace, king, queen, jack, ten, nine, . . . , two. You deal a single card from such a deck and record the face value of the card dealt. Give an assignment of probabilities to these outcomes that should be correct if the deck is thoroughly shuffled. Give a second assignment of probabilities that is legitimate (that is, obeys the rules of probability) but differs from your first choice. Then give a third assignment of probabilities that is *not* legitimate, and explain what is wrong with this choice.

■ 44.   Automobile license plate numbers in Indiana consist of seven characters. The first two describe the county in which the car is licensed, the third is a letter, and the last four are digits. You are hoping for a plate on which these four digits are identical (like 7777). If letters and digits are assigned at random, what is your probability of receiving such a plate?

■ 45. Automobile license plates in Hawaii consist of three letters followed by three digits.

(a) How many different license plates are possible in Hawaii?
(b) A visitor to Honolulu observes that all license plates seem to begin with one of E, F, G, or H. How many license plates are possible if all plates begin with one of these letters?
(c) Suppose that a state allowed license plates consisting of any six letters or digits in any order. How many different license plates would then be possible?

■ 46. A monkey at a keyboard presses three keys and hits the letters *a*, *g*, and *s* in random order. How many possible three-letter "words" can the monkey type using only these letters? Which of these are meaningful English words? What is the probability that the word the monkey typed is meaningful?

47. You are about to visit a new neighbor. You know that the family has four children, but you do not know their age or sex. Write down all possible arrangements of girls and boys in order from youngest to oldest, such as BBGG (the two youngest are boys, the two oldest girls). The laws of genetics say that all of these arrangements are equally likely.

(a) What is the probability that the oldest child is a girl?
(b) What is the probability that the family has at least three boys?
(c) What is the probability that the family has at least three children of the same sex?

48. A study selected a sample of fifth-grade pupils and recorded how many years of school they eventually completed. Based on this study we can give the following probability model for the years of school that will be completed by a randomly chosen fifth grader:

Years	4	5	6	7	8
Probability	0.010	0.007	0.007	0.013	0.032

Years	9	10	11	12
Probability	0.068	0.070	0.041	0.752

(a) Verify that this is a legitimate probability model.
(b) What outcomes make up the event "The student completed at least one year of high school?" (High school begins with the ninth grade.) What is the probability of this event?
(c) What is the mean number of years of school completed?

■ 49. Keno is a favorite game in casinos, and similar games are popular with the states that operate lotteries. Balls numbered 1 to 80 are tumbled in a machine as the bets are placed, then 20 of the balls are chosen at random. Players select numbers by marking a card. Here are two of the simpler Keno bets. For each, give the probability model for the outcomes and find the mean and the standard deviation of the winnings. Is there any reason to prefer one bet over the other?

(a) A $1 bet on "Mark 1 number" pays $3 if the single number you mark is one of the 20 chosen; otherwise you lose your dollar.
(b) A $1 bet on "Mark 2 numbers" pays $12 if both your numbers are among the 20 chosen. The probability of this is about 0.06. Is Mark 2 a more or a less favorable bet than Mark 1?

■ 50. Here is a simple way to create a probability model that has specified mean μ and standard deviation σ: there are only two outcomes, $\mu - \sigma$ and $\mu + \sigma$, each with probability 0.5. Use the definition of the mean and variance for probability models to show that this model does have mean μ and standard deviation σ.

◆ 51. The psychologist Amos Tversky did many studies of our perception of chance behavior. In its obituary of Tversky (June 6, 1996), the *New York Times* cited the following example:

(a) Tversky asked subjects to choose between two public health programs that affect 600 people. One has probability 1/2 of saving all 600 and probability 1/2 that all 600 will die. The other is guaranteed to save exactly 400 of the 600 people. Find the mean number of people saved by the first program.

(b)   Tversky then offered a different choice. One program has probability 1/2 of saving all 600 and probability 1/2 of losing all 600, while the other will definitely lose exactly 200 lives. What is the difference between this choice and that in (a)?

(c)   Given option (a), most subjects choose the second program. Given option (b), most subjects choose the first program. Do the subjects appear to use means in making their decisions? Why do you think their choices differed in the two cases?

◆   52.   The table below contains the results of 100 repetitions of the drawing of a simple random sample of size 200 from a large lot of bearings, 10% of which do not conform to the specifications. The numbers in the table are the percents of nonconforming bearings in each sample of 200.

8.5	11.5	9	13.5	7.5	8.5	9	6.5	8	9
10	7.5	9	8	10.5	8.5	9	9.5	8	11.5
10	9	9	8.5	9.5	6.5	13.5	11	11.5	13
8.5	6.5	8	7	12	11	8	10.5	12	10.5
15	12	8.5	7	8	8	8.5	12	10.5	8
8.5	11.5	9	11.5	11	12	11.5	11.5	10	9.5
10	9	10	12.5	8	12	12	12	7.5	11
11	8	14	7.5	11	4.5	9.5	8	9.5	9.5
12.5	12	10	7.5	10.5	12.5	12	9.5	9.5	10
14	9	8.5	8.5	12.5	8.5	8.5	9	9.5	9

Give an estimated sampling distribution for the sample proportion in this situation by recording each outcome and the proportion of trials on which it occurred. Make a histogram of the distribution and describe its shape. Is the center close to 10%? Is the distribution roughly symmetric? Does it appear approximately normal? Find the mean outcome from your distribution. Is it close to 10%?

53.   The concentration of the active ingredient in capsules of a prescription painkiller varies according to a normal distribution with $\mu = 10\%$ and $\sigma = 0.2\%$.

(a)   What is the median concentration? Explain your answer.

(b)   What range of concentrations covers the middle 95% of all the capsules?

(c)   What range covers the middle half of all capsules?

54.   Answer the following questions for the painkiller in Exercise 53:

(a)   What percent of all capsules have a concentration of active ingredient higher than 10.4%?

(b)   What percent have a concentration higher than 10.6%?

55.   The length of human pregnancies from conception to birth varies according to a distribution that is a approximately normal with mean 266 days and standard deviation 16 days.

(a)   Between what values do the lengths of the middle 95% of all pregnancies fall?

(b)   How short are the shortest 2.5% of all pregnancies?

56.   The *deciles* of a distribution are the points having 10% (lower decile) and 90% (upper decile) of the observations falling below them. The lower and upper deciles contain between them the central 80% of the data. The lower and upper deciles of any normal distribution are located 1.28 standard deviations on either side of the mean. What score is needed to place you in the top 10% of the distribution of SAT scores (normal with mean 500 and standard deviation 100)?

57.   Based on the information in Exercises 55 and 56, how short are the shortest 10% of human pregnancies?

TECHNOLOGY CORNER

Designing a Game of Chance

Casino games and other games of chance are designed to offer the temptation of a large jackpot, occasionally pay out smaller prizes, and ensure a small average outcome in favor of the proposer of the game. Consider the following game: You pay $1 and then pull a card out of each of three shuffled 52-card decks. If all three cards are the same, you win the jackpot. If two of the three cards match, you win a smaller prize. Of the $52^3 = 140,608$ possible ways that three cards could be pulled, 52 will earn the jackpot and another 7956 will earn the smaller prize.

The spreadsheet shown in Figure 7.17 models a situation where the jackpot is $1000 and the smaller prize is $10. The probabilities that the prizes will be earned are $52/(52^3)$ for the jackpot and $7956/(52^3)$ for the smaller prize. On average, about 90 cents is paid out every time the game is played, and the player pays one dollar for each game. Therefore, the casino earns about 10 cents on each play of the game.

	A	B	C	D
1	prize	probability	prize*probability	
2	$1,000.00	0.000369822	0.36982	
3	$ 10.00	0.053440088	0.53440	
4				
5		total	0.90422	
6		cost	$ 1.00	
7		average income	−0.09578	

FIGURE 7.17

TASK 1.   Most casinos set their games to earn about 5 cents for each dollar game. Find values for the prizes so that the above game meets this target.

TASK 2.   In order to make the game more enticing, you declare that pulling three identical aces will earn a Super Jackpot. Pulling three identical non-aces will earn a smaller jackpot, and pulling two matching cards will still earn a small prize. Set values for the prizes so that the jackpots are large and the game still earns the casino about 5 cents for each dollar game.

Simulating the Game with a Spreadsheet

Suppose the 52 cards are numbered 1 to 52, starting with the four aces. The spreadsheet shown in Figure 7-18 uses the **=RandBetween(1,52)** function to randomly choose a number between 1 and 52 in each of the first three columns. In the fourth column, the spreadsheet checks to see if all three numbers match. For example, to detect if A1, B1, and C1 all match, use the function **=And(A1=B1, B1=C1)**. This function has the value False when the three numbers are different. To check if at least two numbers match, the fifth column uses the function **=Or (A1=B1, A1=C1, B1=C1).** The spreadsheet allows you to build the example by constructing the first row and copying the first row onto the next nine rows. Therefore, this spreadsheet simulates 10 games, a cost of $10.

Each time the spreadsheet is recalculated, new random numbers are chosen and a new round of games is created. The final column tabulates the number of times a *pair* of matching cards were drawn in each of 10 rounds. (A triple was not hit during this simulation.) In this simulation, the final column totals 11. If each small prize is $10, the player receives $110 for an investment of $100.

TASK 3.   Simulate ten $100 investments like the example above. Of the ten, how many returned more money than was invested?

	A	B	C	D	E	F	G
1	35	30	17	FALSE	FALSE	outcomes:	2
2	14	46	48	FALSE	FALSE		1
3	10	28	20	FALSE	FALSE		2
4	11	29	36	FALSE	FALSE		1
5	29	26	16	FALSE	FALSE		1
6	25	9	6	FALSE	FALSE		0
7	21	50	33	FALSE	FALSE		2
8	8	41	41	FALSE	TRUE		1
9	22	29	48	FALSE	FALSE		0
10	17	30	43	FALSE	FALSE		1
11							
12				match 3	match at least 2		

FIGURE 7.18

TASK 4.   Is it possible to reset the values of the prizes so that the jackpots are still high, the average return to the casino is about 5 cents for each game, and the player in your previous simulations generally wins back most of the investment? Find a compromise prize structure that addresses these aspects.

Exploration

If you play this game many times, statistically speaking you should lose very little per game. However, since the jackpots will be earned very rarely, you may have to play a long time before you recoup your investments by earning a large jackpot. On average, about how long do you think you would need to play the game before winning a jackpot?

writing projects

1 ▶   "France gave birth to the mathematics of probability in the seventeenth century when gamblers turned to mathematicians for advice." Some of the mathematicians in question were Pierre de Fermat and Blaise Pascal. Do some reading to learn more about the origins of probability theory and write a brief essay describing the role of Fermat and Pascal. (One good source is Carl B. Boyer, *A History of Mathematics,* Wiley, New York, 1991.)

2 ▶   State-run lotteries are common in the United States and in other countries, as Spotlight 7.2 suggests. Write a brief essay describing current state lotteries in the United States. How much money do they take in? How is the money that is kept used? What are the trends in the games offered? What other forms of gambling do revenue-hungry states license? (You can often find recent information about lotteries in the press. Consult, for example, the indexes to the *New York Times* in your library.)

3 ▶   Most people "overreact" to risks that have very low probability of occurring. The probability of dying from an airplane crash, a terrorist attack, or a tornado, for example, is extremely small. Yet public opinion and personal decisions often act as if these risks were as probable as death from an automobile accident or a heart attack. Write a brief essay describing how people assess risks, and what factors besides probability influence their actions. One reference is Richard J. Zeckhauser and W. Kip Vicusi, Risk within reason, *Science,* May 4, 1990, pp. 559–564.

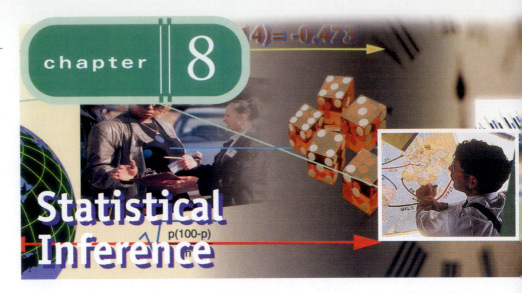

chapter 8

Statistical Inference

Inference is the process of reaching conclusions from evidence. Evidence can come in many forms. In a murder trial, evidence might be presented by the testimony of a witness, by a record of telephone conversations, or by DNA analysis of blood samples. In statistical inference, the evidence is provided by data. Informal statistical inference is often based on graphical presentation of data. Formal inference, the topic of this chapter, uses the language of probability to say how confident we are that our conclusion is correct.

EXAMPLE   Was the Draft Lottery Unfair?

During the Vietnam era, young men were selected for the military draft by a lottery. The first draft lottery was held in 1970. News reports soon suggested that the lottery was biased against men born late in the year. Figure 8.1 is a scatterplot of draft number (low numbers were drafted first) against birth date counting from January 1. The line on the plot was produced by a scatterplot smoother. It shows a trend toward lower numbers late in the year. The trend is not very strong, so we might well ask whether the outcome was simply due to chance rather than to systematic bias in the lottery. After all, any lottery will show some deviation from perfect uniformity due to the play of chance.

A calculation of the probabilities shows, however, that a trend as strong as that in Figure 8.1 has probability less than 1 in 1000 in a truly random drawing. This calculation convinced everyone that the draft lottery was not a random drawing. Investigation showed that the process of mixing capsules containing the birth dates had been poorly done. ◆

FIGURE 8.1
Scatterplot of draft lottery numbers (1 to 366) versus date of birth (1 to 366 starting with January 1). The overall pattern is described by a scatterplot smoother. It appears that the lottery favored men born earlier in the year.

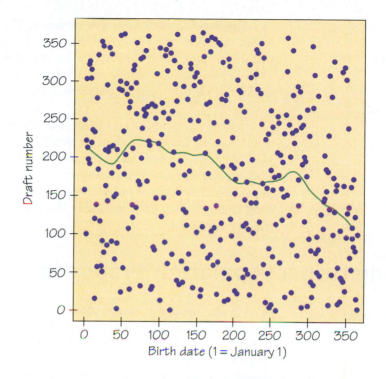

Drawing conclusions in mathematics is a matter of starting from a hypothesis and using logical argument to prove without doubt that the conclusion follows. This is a *deductive argument* from hypothesis to consequences. Statistics argues in almost the reverse order. If the lottery process was biased, we expect birth dates late in the year to have systematically lower draft numbers. There is such a trend in the data, so this is evidence in favor of the claim that the lottery was biased. This is an *inductive argument* from consequences back to a hypothesis. Inductive arguments do not produce proof. The lower draft numbers late in the year *might* be just bad luck. *Statistical inference uses probability to say how strong an inductive argument is.* The trend observed in 1970 would almost never occur (probability less than 0.001) in a random drawing. That is strong evidence for the claim that the lottery was not truly random.

E X A M P L E   *Can We Trust an Opinion Poll?*

How can we trust the results of a random sample, knowing that a second sample would usually yield a different result? A Gallup poll of 1493 people finds that 45% are afraid to go out at night within a mile of their homes because of fear of crime. A second random sample would select a different 1493 people and give a result different from 45%. Knowing this, what can we say about the population of more than 200 million American adults on the basis of Gallup's sample?

A probability calculation tells us that 95% of Gallup's samples give a result within three percentage points of the truth about the population. We now realize that we are quite safe to believe that the truth for all adults lies between 42% and 48%. Because Gallup's sample will often miss by more than 1%, however, we can't confidently say that the truth lies between 44% and 46%.   ◆

In both examples, a probability calculation answered the question, "What would happen if we did this many times?" In many random lotteries, only 1 in 1000 would give a trend as strong as that observed in the draft lottery. In many Gallup poll samples, 95% would give a result within ± 3% of the truth for the population. This kind of probability statement is characteristic of statistical inference. Understanding how probability is employed is the key to understanding statistical inference.

Estimating a Population Proportion

We will use a simplified version of the Gallup crime survey to introduce an important type of statistical inference. Like most national sample surveys, the Gallup poll uses a complex multistage sampling design. Suppose that we instead drew a *simple random sample* of 1500 adults and discovered that 675 of the people in this sample were afraid to go out at night because of crime. The **sample proportion** who stay home from fear of crime is

$$\hat{p} = \frac{675}{1500} = 0.45 = 45\%$$

We will call a sample proportion $\hat{p}$ (read as "p hat"). We will always express sample proportions as percents.

The sample proportion $\hat{p} = 45\%$ refers to the 1500 people in this particular sample. We really want to know the *population proportion,* the percent (call it p) of all adult Americans who stay home at night for fear of crime. To discuss statistical inference intelligently, we must keep straight which numbers describe the sample and which describe the population.

> A number such as p that describes a population is called a **parameter.** A number such as $\hat{p}$ that is calculated from a sample is called a **statistic.**

It is easy to remember that **p**arameters belong to **p**opulations and **s**tatistics belong to **s**amples because the first letters agree. In an inference problem, parameters are usually unknown. We do not know, for example, the true proportion p of all adults who stay home at night for fear of crime. We use the statistic $\hat{p}$, which we know because we actually interviewed the sample, to estimate the unknown p. *Our goal is not simply to estimate p, but to say how accurate our estimate is.* To do this, we ask "What would happen if we took many samples? How close to the unknown p would the estimate $\hat{p}$ usually fall?"

To answer this question, we turn to the *sampling distribution* of $\hat{p}$. This is the distribution of values taken by the sample proportion as it varies from sample to sample in a large number of samples from the same population. We have simulated sampling distributions in earlier chapters. Now we want the mathematical facts. Here they are.

Choose a simple random sample of size n from a large population of which the percent p have some characteristic of interest. Let $\hat{p}$ be the percent of the sample having that characteristic. Then

- The sampling distribution of $\hat{p}$ is *approximately normal* and is closer to a normal distribution when the sample size n is large.
- The *mean* of the sampling distribution is exactly p.
- The *standard deviation* of the sampling distribution is

$$\sigma_{\hat{p}} = \sqrt{\frac{p(100 - p)}{n}}$$

To remind ourselves that this standard deviation belongs to the distribution of $\hat{p}$, we write it as $\sigma_{\hat{p}}$.

Figure 8.2 presents this sampling distribution as a normal curve. Both the center (mean) and spread (standard deviation) of this curve carry important statistical messages.

First, the mean of the curve is the true proportion p of people afraid to go out at night. This fact says that $\hat{p}$ has no bias or systematic error as an estimator of the unknown p. In repeated sampling our result will sometimes be high and sometimes low, but the long-run average result, the mean of the sampling distribution, will be correct. Of course, in practice we don't know the numerical value of the parameter p. But we now know that, whatever value p has, the observed values of the statistic $\hat{p}$ cluster around it as shown in Figure 8.2.

Being correct on the average is not good enough. A good estimator must also be highly repeatable in the sense of giving nearly the same answer in repeated samples. Repeatability is described by the spread of the sampling distribution, as measured by its standard deviation. If we repeated the sampling many times, making waves of telephone calls to randomly selected numbers, each time we would get a value of the sample proportion $\hat{p}$ somewhere along the curve in Figure 8.2. How far from the true p these sample results lie depends on the standard deviation $\sigma_{\hat{p}}$ of this normal curve. The standard deviation gets smaller as the sample size n gets

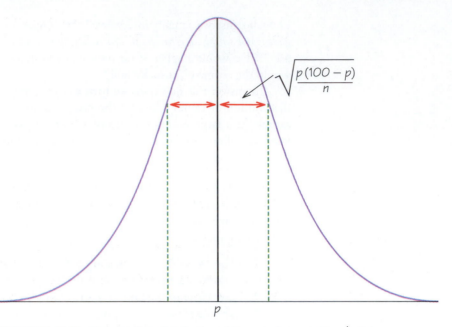

FIGURE 8.2 The sampling distribution of the sample proportion $\hat{p}$. It is approximately normal, with mean p and standard deviation $\sqrt{p(100 - p)/n}$.

larger. Our simulations in Chapter 7 (Figure 7.6, page 266) showed this effect. Now we know the exact relationship between n and the standard deviation. *The standard deviation depends on the square root* $\sqrt{n}$. To cut the spread of the sampling distribution in half, we must take four times as many observations.

E X A M P L E   *Sampling Distribution for the Crime Survey*

Suppose that in fact 40% of all adults fear to go out at night because of crime. That is, suppose that $p = 40\%$. Take a simple random sample of size $n = 1500$ people. In repeated samples, the sample percent $\hat{p}$ will vary according to a normal distribution with

$$\text{mean} = p = 40\%$$

$$\text{standard deviation } \sigma_{\hat{p}} = \sqrt{\frac{p(100 - p)}{n}}$$

$$= \sqrt{\frac{(40)(60)}{1500}} = \sqrt{1.6} = 1.265\%$$

In practice the value of the parameter p is unknown. Our calculations show that the standard deviation of $\hat{p}$ is small. So the sample percent $\hat{p}$ will usually lie quite close to p.

Suppose now that the truth about the population is $p = 50\%$ rather than 40%. The mean of the sampling distribution moves to 50%. The standard deviation changes to

$$\sigma_{\hat{p}} = \sqrt{\frac{p(100 - p)}{n}}$$

$$= \sqrt{\frac{(50)(50)}{1500}} = \sqrt{1.67} = 1.29\%$$

The standard deviation $\sigma_{\hat{p}}$ does not change very much when p changes. That is, when we take a sample of the same size from different populations, the center of the sampling distribution of $\hat{p}$ moves to the true p for each population, but the spread stays about the same.

The size of the sample is the major influence on the spread. Suppose that we took a sample of only $n = 375$ instead of 1500 people from a population for which $p = 40\%$. The mean of the distribution of $\hat{p}$ is still 40% — the sample size doesn't change the center of the sampling distribution. But the standard deviation increases to

$$\sigma_{\hat{p}} = \sqrt{\frac{p(100 - p)}{n}}$$

$$= \sqrt{\frac{(40)(60)}{375}} = \sqrt{6.4} = 2.53\%$$

Because the new sample size 375 is one-fourth of 1500, the new standard deviation 2.53% is twice as large as the previous result 1.265%. That's the $\sqrt{n}$ effect in action. ◆

Confidence Intervals

Our poll of 1500 people found that $\hat{p} = 45\%$. This is our best guess for the population percent p. How close to the true p is our guess likely to be? Well, $\hat{p}$ varies normally. The 95 part of the 68–95–99.7 rule says that $\hat{p}$ falls within two standard deviations of the true p (the mean of the sampling distribution) in 95% of all samples. So our guess based on this one sample is likely to be within two standard deviations, that is, within

$$2\sigma_{\hat{p}} = 2\sqrt{\frac{p(100 - p)}{1500}}$$

of the true p.

The catch is that this standard deviation depends on the unknown p. Fortunately, as the example demonstrated, $\sigma_{\hat{p}}$ changes only slowly as p changes, as long as p is not very close to either 0% or 100%. Because $\hat{p}$ is close to p, we simply substitute $\hat{p} = 45\%$ for the unknown p in the formula for the standard deviation. To indicate that the standard deviation is estimated rather than known exactly, we call it $s_{\hat{p}}$.

EXAMPLE   *Estimated Standard Deviation for the Crime Survey*

We want to estimate the standard deviation of our observed sample proportion. The sample size was $n = 1500$, and for p we use the estimate $\hat{p} = 45\%$, based on our survey. The estimated standard deviation is

$$s_{\hat{p}} = \sqrt{\frac{(45)(55)}{1500}}$$
$$= \sqrt{1.65} = 1.285\% \quad \blacklozenge$$

Here, then, is our conclusion: in 95% of all samples, the sample proportion $\hat{p}$ will fall within 2×1.285, or about 2.6%, of the unknown population proportion p. We took one sample and got $\hat{p} = 45\%$. So we conclude that the p lies in the interval

45% ± 2.6%

or between 42.4% and 47.6%. We say that we are *95% confident* in this conclusion because we got the interval by calculating how close to p the sample proportion will lie in 95% of all samples. Our interval is a 95% *confidence interval* for estimating the unknown population proportion.

In mathematical terms, the probability is 0.95 that the sample proportion $\hat{p}$ will fall within ±2.6% of the unknown true fraction p of all adults who are afraid to go out at night because of crime. Figure 8.3 makes the idea clearer. The normal curve at the top of the figure is the sampling distribution of $\hat{p}$. As we take many samples, the actual values of $\hat{p}$ vary according to this distribution. The values of $\hat{p}$ observed in 25 samples appear as dots below the curve, together with the confidence intervals that extend out 2.6% on either side of the observed $\hat{p}$. The true population proportion p is marked by the vertical line. Although the intervals vary from sample to sample, all but one of these samples gave a confidence interval that covers the true p. To say that these are 95% confidence intervals is just to say that the interval covers the true p in 95% of all samples and misses in only 5%. Be sure you understand that this 95% and 5% refer to what would happen if we continued to take samples forever. In a small number of samples, the number of confidence intervals that fail to cover the true p may be a bit more or less than 5% of the samples. In Figure 8.3, for example, 1 out of 25, or 4%, of the confidence intervals fails to contain *p*.

> A 95% **confidence interval** is an interval obtained from the sample data by a method that in 95% of all samples will produce an interval containing the true population parameter.

You can see in Figure 8.3 that a confidence interval from one particular sample can either hit or miss the unknown true parameter. We don't know whether our sample is one of the 95% that hit or one of the 5% that miss. To say that our interval 45% $\pm$ 2.6% is a 95% confidence interval means "We got this interval by a method that catches the true parameter 95% of the time."

FIGURE 8.3
The behavior of 95% confidence intervals in repeated sampling. The interval changes from sample to sample, but in the long run, 95% of all samples produce intervals that contain the true value of *p*.

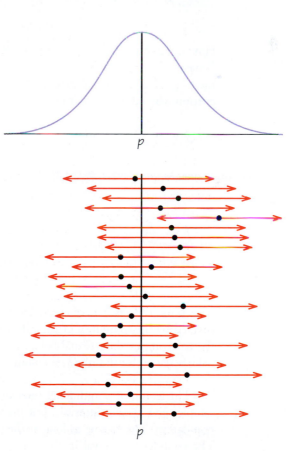

We have now accomplished two things: we have seen what "95% confidence" means, and we have actually found a 95% confidence interval for estimating a population proportion. Here is the recipe for this interval.

A **95% confidence interval for a population proportion p,** based on a simple random sample of size n, is

$$\hat{p} \pm 2s_{\hat{p}} = \hat{p} \pm 2\sqrt{\frac{\hat{p}(100 - \hat{p})}{n}}$$

Remember that both p and $\hat{p}$ are measured in percent. This recipe is only approximately correct, but it is quite accurate when the sample size n is large.

EXAMPLE   *Risky Behavior in the Age of AIDS*

How common is behavior that puts people at risk of AIDS? The National AIDS Behavioral Surveys interviewed a random sample of 2673 adult heterosexuals. Of these, 170 had had more than one sexual partner in the past year. The sample proportion who admit to multiple partners is

$$\hat{p} = \frac{170}{2673} = 6.36\%$$

A 95% confidence interval for the proportion p of all adult heterosexuals with multiple partners is therefore

$$\hat{p} \pm 2\sqrt{\frac{\hat{p}(100 - \hat{p})}{n}} = 6.36 \pm 2\sqrt{\frac{(6.36)(93.64)}{2673}}$$
$$= 6.36 \pm 0.94$$
$$= 5.42\% \text{ to } 7.30\%$$

As is often the case, there are practical difficulties that cause additional errors *not* covered by the margin of error. It is likely that some people were reluctant to tell the truth about their sexual behavior. The survey result probably underestimates risky behavior by an unknown amount. ◆

The length of a confidence interval depends on the size n of the sample: larger samples give shorter intervals. But the interval does *not* depend on the size of the population. This is true as long as the population is much larger than the sample. The confidence interval in the example works for a sample of 2673 from a city with 100,000 adults as well as for a sample of 2673 from a nation of 200 million.

What matters is how many people we interview, not what percent of the population we contact.

Any confidence interval has two essential pieces: the interval itself and the confidence level. The interval usually has the form

estimate $\pm$ margin of error

The estimate is a sample statistic such as $\hat{p}$ that estimates the unknown parameter. The margin of error indicates how accurate this estimate is. In the AIDS survey example, the estimate is 6.36% and the margin of error is $\pm 0.94\%$.

The *confidence level* states how confident we are that our interval contains the true parameter. Although 95% confidence is common, you can hold out for higher confidence, such as 99%, or be satisfied with lower confidence, such as 90%. Our 95% confidence interval was based on the middle 95% of a normal distribution. A 99% confidence interval requires the middle 99% of the distribution and so is wider (has a larger margin of error). Similarly, a 90% confidence interval is shorter than a 95% interval obtained from the same data. There is a trade-off between how closely we can pin down the parameter (the margin of error) and how confident we can be in the result.

E X A M P L E   *Understanding the News*

The results of opinion polls and other sample surveys are common in the news. News reports often give a margin of error but rarely state a confidence level. (See Spotlight 8.1 for an exception.) A news report of our crime survey would say "The survey found that 45% of all Americans are afraid to go out at night because of crime. The margin of error in the survey is plus or minus 2.6 percentage points."

We need to know both the margin of error and the confidence level, because higher confidence requires a larger margin of error. There is an unspoken understanding in news releases: almost all public opinion polls announce the margin of error for 95% confidence. So if a story about an opinion poll gives a margin of error without a confidence level, you can usually assume 95%.   ◆

The Bureau of Labor Statistics, on the other hand, chooses to announce the monthly unemployment rate at the 90% level of confidence. Basing its conclusions on the Current Population Survey of 50,000 households, the bureau says that the published unemployment rate is within $\pm 0.2\%$ (two-tenths of 1 percent) of the figure it would get if it interviewed all workers. When the headlines announce a 5.9% unemployment rate, the bureau is saying—with 90% confidence—that between 5.7% and 6.1% of the labor force is out of work.

Opinion polls often have margins of error of about $\pm 3\%$. The much smaller margin of error for the announced unemployment rate is due to the much larger sample interviewed by the Current Population Survey. Larger samples give smaller margins of error at the same confidence level. However, the square root of n that

SPOTLIGHT 8.1

How the Poll Was Taken

On June 15, 1998, the *New York Times* published an article by Steve Lohr and Marjories Connelly titled "Most Regard Microsoft Favorably, a Poll Shows." At a time when the government was attacking the giant software company under antitrust laws, a public opinion poll showed that 55% of adults had a favorable opinion of Microsoft. The *Times* printed some details of the poll in a box titled "How the Poll Was Conducted." Here are some excerpts.

The latest *New York Times*/CBS News Poll is based on telephone interviews conducted June 7 to June 9 with 1,126 adults throughout the United States.

The sample of telephone exchanges called was randomly selected by a computer from a complete list of more than 42,000 active residential exchanges across the country. Within each exchange, random digits were added to form a complete telephone number, thus permitting access to both listed and unlisted numbers. Within each household, one adult was designated by a random procedure to be the respondent for the survey.

. . . In theory, in 19 cases out of 20 the results based on such samples will differ by no more than three percentage points in either direction from what would have been obtained by seeking out all American adults.

. . . In addition to sampling error, the practical difficulties of conducting any survey of public opinion may introduce other sources of error into the poll. Variations in question wording or the order of questions, for instance, can lead to somewhat different results.

appears in the calculations shows that in order to reduce our margin of error by half, we need a sample size four times bigger. To obtain a very small margin of error, the Current Population Survey takes the trouble to interview a sample of 50,000 people, compared with the Gallup poll's usual 1500. The Gallup poll can afford to be 3% off. The unemployment rate must be more exact because so many economic and political decisions depend on it.

Estimating a Population Mean

The statistician's tool kit contains many different confidence intervals, matching the many different population parameters we may wish to estimate. We have met the confidence interval for estimating a population proportion p. Now we want to estimate a population mean. We have used the **sample mean** $\bar{x}$ of a sample of observations to describe the center of a set of data. Now we will use the sample mean $\bar{x}$ to estimate the unknown mean μ of the entire population from which the sample is drawn. We use μ, the symbol for the mean of a probability distribution, for the population mean because it is the mean of the distribution of the results of drawing one individual at random from the population. The sample mean $\bar{x}$ is a statistic that will vary in repeated samples, while the population mean μ is a parameter, a fixed number. Fortunately, the new confidence interval for estimating μ is quite similar to the familiar confidence interval for estimating p, because both intervals are based on a normal sampling distribution.

EXAMPLE   *NAEP Quantitative Scores*

The National Assessment of Educational Progress (NAEP) includes a short test of quantitative skills, covering mainly basic arithmetic and the ability to apply it to realistic problems. Scores on the test range from 0 to 500. For example, a person who scores 233 can add the amounts of two checks appearing on a bank deposit slip; someone scoring 325 can determine the price of a meal from a menu; a person scoring 375 can transform a price in cents per ounce into dollars per pound.

In a recent year, 840 men 21 to 25 years of age were in the NAEP sample. Their mean quantitative score was $\bar{x} = 272$. These 840 men are a simple random sample from the population of all young men. On the basis of this sample, what can we say about the mean score μ in the population of all 9.5 million young men of these ages?   ◆

The law of large numbers tells us that the sample mean $\bar{x}$ from a large random sample will be close to the unknown population mean μ. Because $\bar{x} = 272$, we guess that μ is "somewhere around 272." To make "somewhere around 272" more precise, we ask: "How would the sample mean $\bar{x}$ vary if we took many samples of 840 young men from this same population?" The answer is given by the *central limit theorem* (page 276).

> Draw a simple random sample of size n from a large population that has mean μ and standard deviation σ. When the sample size n is large, the **sampling distribution of the sample mean $\bar{x}$** is approximately normal with mean μ and standard deviation $\sigma/\sqrt{n}$.

We can add a new fact to this familiar statement. *If the distribution of individuals in the population is normal, then the sampling distribution of $\bar{x}$ is exactly normal.* This is true for samples of any size. Figure 8.4 shows the relation between the distribution of a single observation drawn from a normally distributed population and the distribution of the mean of several (in this case 10) observations. The mean of several observations is less variable than individual observations.

To make use of the sampling distribution of $\bar{x}$, we must know the standard deviation σ for the population. From past experience, we know that the standard deviation of NAEP scores in the population of all young men is close to $\sigma = 60$. Now we have the information we need to give a confidence interval for the mean score.

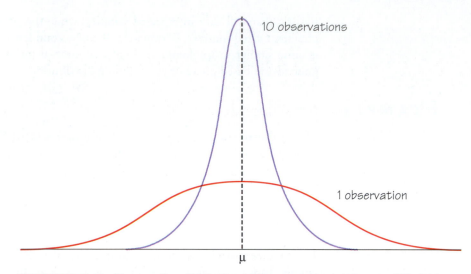

FIGURE 8.4 The sampling distribution of the sample mean $\bar{x}$ from an SRS of 10 observations compared with the distribution of a single observation.

E X A M P L E　　*Estimating the Mean NAEP Score*

The normal sampling distribution of $\bar{x}$ has mean equal to the unknown population mean μ. The standard deviation of the sampling distribution is

$$\sigma_{\bar{x}} = \frac{\sigma}{\sqrt{n}}$$

$$= \frac{60}{\sqrt{840}} = 2.1$$

By the 95 part of the 68–95–99.7 rule, $\bar{x}$ will fall within two standard deviations of μ in 95% of all samples. Two standard deviations is 2×2.1, or 4.2 points. We observed $\bar{x} = 272$ in our sample. So we are 95% confident that the population mean μ lies in the interval

$$272 \pm 4.2$$

or between 267.8 and 276.2.　◆

Here is the recipe that summarizes our development. The confidence interval again has the form

estimate $\pm$ margin of error

The estimate is now the sample mean $\bar{x}$.

Suppose that a population has unknown mean μ and known standard deviation σ. Draw a simple random sample of size n from this population and calculate the sample mean $\bar{x}$. A **95% confidence interval for the population mean μ** is

$$\bar{x} \pm 2\sigma_{\bar{x}} = \bar{x} \pm 2\frac{\sigma}{\sqrt{n}}$$

This interval is correct if the population has a normal distribution and approximately correct for large samples in other cases.

Often in practice the standard deviation σ of the population is not known in advance. Then we must estimate σ by the standard deviation s of the sample. If we have a large sample, s will be close to σ and the substitution will have little effect on the confidence interval.

Here is another example of estimating a population mean.

EXAMPLE *Estimating Dust in Coal Mines*

Because the mean of several observations is less variable than a single observation, it is good practice to take the average of several observations when accuracy is important. The amount of dust in the atmosphere of coal mines is measured by exposing a filter in the mine and then weighing the dust collected by the filter. The weighing is not perfectly precise. Repeated weighings of the same filter will vary according to a normal distribution. The values that would be obtained in many weighings form the population we are interested in. The mean μ of this population is the true weight (that is, there is no bias in the weighing). The population standard deviation describes the precision of the weighing; it is known to be $\sigma = 0.08$ milligram (mg). Each filter is weighed three times and the mean weight is reported.

For one filter the three weights are

123.1 mg   122.5 mg   123.7 mg

What is the 95% confidence interval for the true weight μ?

First compute the sample mean:

$$\bar{x} = \frac{123.1 + 122.5 + 123.7}{3}$$

$$= \frac{369.3}{3} = 123.1 \text{ mg}$$

Then the 95% confidence interval is

$$\bar{x} \pm 2 \frac{\sigma}{\sqrt{n}} = 123.1 \pm 2 \frac{0.08}{\sqrt{3}}$$

$$= 123.1 \pm (2)(0.046) = 123.1 \pm 0.09$$

We are 95% confident that the true weight is between 123.01 mg and 123.19 mg.

◆

Statistical Process Control

Statistical methods are widely used to gather social and economic information and in research on a wide variety of subjects. Most of our examples to this point, from the Current Population Survey and the National Assessment of Educational Progress to the Physicians' Health Study and the National AIDS Behavioral Surveys, have illustrated these two types of applications of statistics. Statistics also contributes to the drive to improve the quality of manufactured products. Along with new technology and new management emphases such as cooperating with workers and suppliers, statistical ideas are an important part of any manufacturer's efforts to compete in the global marketplace. In this section we look at one simple but important statistical tool for monitoring and improving quality, the control chart.

E X A M P L E   *Monitoring Computer Screens*

A manufacturer of computer video screens must control the tension on the mesh of fine wires that lies behind the surface of the screen. Too much tension will tear the mesh, and too little will allow wrinkles. Tension is measured by an electrical

TABLE 8.1	The Means $\bar{x}$ from 20 Samples of Size 4		
Sample	**$\bar{x}$**	**Sample**	**$\bar{x}$**
1	269.5	11	264.7
2	297.0	12	307.7
3	269.6	13	310.0
4	283.3	14	343.3
5	304.8	15	328.1
6	280.4	16	342.6
7	233.5	17	338.8
8	257.4	18	340.1
9	317.5	19	374.6
10	327.4	20	336.1

device with output readings in millivolts (mV). The proper tension is 275 mV. Some variation is always present in the production process. When the process is operating properly, the standard deviation of the tension readings is $\sigma = 43$ mV.

The operator measures the tension on a sample of 4 screens each hour. The mean $\bar{x}$ of each sample estimates the mean tension μ for the process at the time of the sample. Table 8.1 shows the observed $\bar{x}$'s for 20 consecutive hours of production. How can we use these data to keep the process stable?   ◆

A plot against time helps us see whether or not the process has been disturbed. Figure 8.5 is a plot of the successive sample means against the order in which the samples were taken. Because the target value for the process mean is $\mu = 275$ mV, we draw a *center line* at that level across the plot. The means from the later samples fall above this line and are consistently higher than those from earlier samples. This suggests that the process mean μ may have shifted upward, away from its target value of 275 mV. But perhaps the drift in $\bar{x}$ simply reflects the natural variation in the process. We need to back up our graph by calculation.

FIGURE 8.5
Plot of sample mean tension measurements for computer screens versus time. The line is the target value 275.

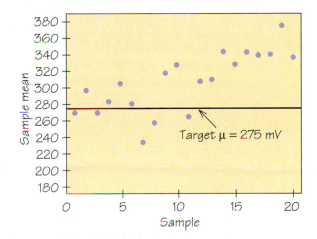

We expect $\bar{x}$ to have a distribution that is close to normal. Not only are the tension measurements roughly normal, but also the central limit theorem effect implies that sample means will be closer to normal than individual measurements. If the standard deviation of the individual screens remains at $\sigma = 43$ mV, the standard deviation of $\bar{x}$ from 4 screens is

$$\sigma_{\bar{x}} = \frac{\sigma}{\sqrt{n}} = \frac{43}{\sqrt{4}} = 21.5$$

As long as the mean remains at its target value $\mu = 275$ mV, the 99.7 part of the 68–95–99.7 rule says that almost all values of $\bar{x}$ will lie between

$$\mu - 3\sigma_{\bar{x}} = 275 - (3)(21.5) = 210.5 \text{ mV}$$
$$\mu + 3\sigma_{\bar{x}} = 275 + (3)(21.5) = 339.5 \text{ mV}$$

We therefore draw dashed *control limits* at these two levels on the plot.

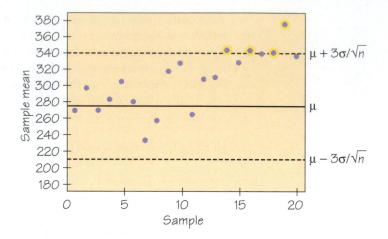

FIGURE 8.6 An $\bar{x}$ control chart for computer screen mesh tension. The dashed control limits set boundaries for the variation expected when the process is undisturbed.

Figure 8.6 is the control chart for the observations from Figure 8.5. Four points, which are circled on the plot, lie above the upper control limit of the control chart. It is unlikely (probability less than 0.003) that a particular point would fall outside the control limits if μ and σ remain at their target values. These points are therefore good evidence that the distribution of the production process has changed. It appears that the process mean moved up at about sample number 14. In practice, the operators search for a disturbance in the process as soon as the first out-of-control point is noticed, that is, after sample number 14. Lack of control might be caused by a new operator, a new batch of mesh, or a breakdown in the tensioning apparatus. The out-of-control signal alerts us to the change before a large number of defective screens is produced. Here is a summary of the steps in constructing a control chart such as Figure 8.6.

To monitor the stability of a process with given standards μ and σ, make an $\bar{x}$ **control chart** as follows:

- Plot the means $\bar{x}$ of regular samples of size n against time.
- Draw a horizontal *center line* at μ.
- Draw horizontal *control limits* at $\mu \pm 3\sigma/\sqrt{n}$.

Any $\bar{x}$ that does not fall between the control limits is evidence that the process is *out of control*.

Statistical ideas form the basis for control charts. First, we recognize that all processes have variation. Our goal is not to eliminate variation but to distinguish the natural variation in the process from the extra variation that warns us of a disturbance. Second, we use the normal sampling distribution of $\bar{x}$ and the 68–95–99.7 rule to specify the range of natural variation. Third, we combine this formal inference with a graph of the data that can be used in the factory by people with little statistical training.

Why sample only four screens each hour? The purpose of statistical process control is not to check the function of the screens; they will be rigorously tested when completed. Rather, the goal is to monitor the process of positioning the mesh and correct any malfunctions quickly. It is not practical to check every screen at every stage of manufacture. Instead, statistical sampling techniques give a quick and economical way to keep the process running smoothly. Control charts based on samples keep down costs by catching malfunctions quickly, allowing a faulty process to be corrected immediately. This eliminates the need to repair or scrap products at the end of the assembly line.

In practice, we look not only for individual points beyond the control limits but for other suspicious patterns as well.

E X A M P L E **The "Run of 9" Signal**

One common out-of-control signal is a *run* of 9 consecutive points above or below the center line. Such a run is unlikely if the process mean remains at the target used to draw the center line — it is just like getting 9 heads in a row when tossing a coin. So a run suggests that the mean has moved away from the center line.

In the $\bar{x}$ chart shown in Figure 8.6, the "run of 9" signal does not give an out-of-control signal until sample number 20. The "one point out" signal alerts us at sample 14. In this case the run signal was slow to detect lack of control. When the process mean slowly drifts away from its target value, however, the run signal will often give an out-of-control signal before any individual point falls outside the control limits. That is why it is common practice to use the one-point-out signal and the run signal simultaneously. ◆

The Perils of Data Analysis

Statistical designs for collecting data may, like the Physicians' Health Study, involve experimentation. Or they may use sampling procedures such as those used in the Current Population Survey and also for process control. In both cases, we rely on randomization and the mathematics of probability to compute sampling distributions. From a sampling distribution we can obtain results that have known levels of confidence.

However, formal statistical inference, as reflected in levels of confidence, is secondary to well-designed data collection and to insight into the behavior of data. Inference is useless for voluntary response samples and can't correct flaws such as nonresponse in a sample survey. Moreover, the effects of *hidden variables* can make even an apparently clear inference misleading. We saw in Chapter 5 that a well-designed experiment can control for confounding of hidden variables with explanatory variables. When an experiment is not possible, we may need to do some statistical detective work. Let's look at an example. Although the example is imaginary, it is based on a real situation.

EXAMPLE   *Which Hospital Is Safer?*

To help consumers make informed decisions about health care, the government releases data about patient outcomes in hospitals. You want to compare Hospital A and Hospital B, which serve your community. Table 8.2 presents data on the survival of patients after surgery in these two hospitals. All patients undergoing surgery in a recent time period are included. "Survived" means that the patient lived at least 6 weeks following surgery.

Hospital A loses 3% (63/2100) of its surgery patients, and Hospital B loses only 2% (16/800). It seems that you should choose Hospital B if you need surgery.   ◆

TABLE 8.2	Survival of Surgery Patients at Two Hospitals	
	Hospital A	**Hospital B**
Died	63	16
Survived	2037	784
Total	2100	800

Table 8.2 is a **two-way table.** When variables simply place subjects into categories, such as died–survived, we cannot draw a scatterplot to display the relationship between them. Instead we display the counts in a two-way table and see the relationship by comparing percents. Comparison of the percents of patients who died shows that Hospital B has a lower death rate. Let's look more closely.

EXAMPLE   *The Hidden Variable Strikes*

Not all surgery cases are equally serious. Later in the government report you find data on the outcome of surgery broken down by the condition of the patient before the operation. Patients are classified as being in either "poor" or "good" condi-

TABLE 8.3	Survival of Surgery Patients at Two Hospitals, by Condition				
	Good Condition			**Poor Condition**	
	Hospital A	Hospital B		Hospital A	Hospital B
Died	6	8	**Died**	57	8
Survived	594	592	**Survived**	1443	192
Total	600	600	Total	1500	200

tion. The more detailed data appear in Table 8.3. Check that the entries in the original two-way table are just the sums of the "poor" and "good" entries in this pair of tables.

Hospital A beats Hospital B for patients in good condition: only 1% (6/600) died in Hospital A, compared with 1.3% (8/600) in Hospital B. Hospital A wins again for patients in poor condition, losing 3.8% (57/1500) to Hospital B's 4% (8/200). So Hospital A is safer for both patients in good condition and patients in poor condition. You should choose Hospital A if you are facing surgery. ◆

This example provides a warning about statistical evidence, especially when the data do not come from an experiment. When we ignore the condition of the patients, Hospital B seems safer, even though Hospital A does better for both classes of patients. How can A do better in both groups, yet do worse overall? Look at the data. Hospital A is a medical center that attracts seriously ill patients from a wide region. It had 1500 patients in poor condition. Hospital B had only 200 such cases. Because patients in poor condition are more likely to die, Hospital A has a higher death rate despite its superior performance for each class of patients. Table 8.2 is misleading because it does not take account of the condition of the patients. Statistical inference based simply on the data in Table 8.2 would be equally misleading.

Even if we produce data carefully and analyze them properly, we can't absolutely guarantee correct conclusions. There is always some chance, however small, that random selection will lead to a false conclusion. The strength of statistical inference is that the chance of a false conclusion is known and can be controlled by setting the confidence level as high as we think necessary.

Statistics does not produce proof. But in a world where proof is always wanting and most evidence is uncertain, statistical evidence is often the best evidence available.

REVIEW VOCABULARY

Confidence interval   An interval computed from a sample by a method that has a known probability of producing an interval containing the unknown parameter. This probability is called the *confidence level.* Confidence intervals usually have the form

estimate $\pm$ margin of error

Control chart   A graph showing the value of a statistic for successive samples (for example, one sample each hour or one sample each shift). The graph also contains a *center line* at the target value for the process parameter and *control limits* that the statistic will rarely fall outside of unless the process drifts away from the target. The purpose of a control chart is to monitor a process over time and signal when some unusual source of variation interferes with the process.

Parameter   A number that describes the population. In statistical inference, the goal is often to estimate an unknown parameter or make a decision about its value.

Sample mean   The mean (arithmetic average) $\bar{x}$ of the observations in a sample. The sample mean from a simple random sample is used to estimate the unknown mean μ of the population from which the sample was drawn.

Sample proportion   The proportion $\hat{p}$ of the members of a sample having some characteristic (such as agreeing with an opinion poll question). The sample proportion from a simple random sample is used to estimate the corresponding proportion p in the population from which the sample was drawn.

Statistic   A number that describes a sample. A statistic can be calculated from the sample data alone and does not involve any unknown parameters of the population.

Two-way table   A table showing the counts or percentages of outcomes classified according to two variables (such as surgery patients classified by both their condition and whether or not they survive).

SUGGESTED READINGS

MOORE, DAVID S. *The Basic Practice of Statistics,* 2nd ed., Freeman, New York, 1999. Chapter 6 of this text presents the reasoning of inference in detail. Chapters 7 and 8 discuss the practical use of inference about means and proportions.

MOSES, LINCOLN E. The reasoning of statistical inference. In David C. Hoaglin and David S. Moore (eds.), *Perspectives on Contemporary Statistics,* Mathematical Association of America, Washington, D.C., 1992, pp. 107–122. This broad essay on the nature of inference requires some knowledge of probability and should be read after the introductory text just cited.

SUGGESTED WEB SITES

It is both interesting and instructive to see how major polling organizations describe the accuracy of their sample surveys. You can find the full news releases that the Gallup poll sends to the news media at **www.gallup.com.** For the Harris poll, visit **www.louisharris.com** and look under "Harris Poll This Week." The monthly news releases for the unemploy-ment rate are stored by the Bureau of Labor Statistics at **stats.bls.gov.** Look under "News Releases" and then under "Employment & Unemployment" for releases with the title "Employment Situation." The National Council on Public Polls (**www.ncpp.org**) has statements on "Principles of Disclosure" and "20 Questions for Journalists" that make interesting reading.

SKILLS CHECK

1. A random sample of 10 bags of sugar has a mean weight of 4.9 pounds, less than the mean weight 5.05 pounds of all bags of sugar produced. In this example 4.9 is

   (a)   a statistic.
   (b)   a parameter.
   (c)   a sample.

2. To determine the interest in a new park, 300 residents are polled; 135 are in favor of the park. What is the sample proportion $\hat{p}$?

   (a)   0.45%
   (b)   40.5%
   (c)   45%

3. A simple random sample of 400 residents of a town is asked about a new fire station; 144 are in favor. What is the approximate standard deviation of the sample proportion $\hat{p}$ in this setting?

   (a)   6%
   (b)   2.4%
   (c)   about 1%

4. Bags of sugar produced by a company have a mean weight of 5.05 pounds and a standard deviation of 0.05 pound. Four bags are chosen at random and a mean weight is found. What is the standard deviation of the sampling distribution for the mean weight?

   (a)   0.0125 pound
   (b)   0.025 pound
   (c)   0.1 pound

5. A random sample of 2000 residents in Centerville found that 45 had never had chicken pox. Find a 95% confidence interval for the true proportion of Centerville residents who have never had chicken pox.

   (a)   2.25% ± 0.3316%
   (b)   2.25% ± 0.6632%
   (c)   2.25% ± 0.2199%

6. Bags of sugar produced by a company have a mean weight of 5.05 pounds and a standard deviation of 0.05 pound. The company uses 95% control limits for a process control chart for this procedure. A random sample of 9 bags is selected and weighed, with a sample mean weight of 5.09 pounds. Which of the following statements is true?

   (a)   The sample mean weight is out of control.
   (b)   The sample mean weight is not out of control.
   (c)   There is not enough information given.

7. Here is a two-way table for admission into a private club. Find the percentage of males admitted.

	Male Applicants	Female Applicants
Admitted	20	20
Denied	30	10

   (a)   20%
   (b)   25%
   (c)   40%

EXERCISES   ▲ *Optional.*   ■ *Advanced.*   ◆ *Discussion.*

Estimating a Population Proportion

Identify each of the boldface numbers in Exercises 1 to 3 as either a *parameter* or a *statistic*.

1. A random sample of female college students has a mean height of **65** inches, which is greater than the **63**-inch mean height of all adult American women.

2. A researcher carries out a randomized comparative experiment with young rats to investigate the effects of a toxic compound in food. She feeds the control group a normal diet. The experimental group receives a diet with 2500 parts per million of the toxic material. After 8 weeks, the mean weight gain is **335** grams for the control group and **289** grams for the experimental group.

3. A telemarketing firm in Los Angeles uses a device that dials residential telephone numbers in that city at random. Of the first 100 numbers dialed, **48%** are unlisted. This is not surprising because **52%** of all Los Angeles residential phones are unlisted.

4. Tonya wants to estimate what proportion of the students in her dormitory like the dorm food. She interviews a simple random sample of 50 of the 680 students living in the dormitory. She finds that 14 think the dorm food is good.

   (a) Describe the population and explain in words what the parameter p is.
   (b) Give the value (in percents) of the statistic $\hat{p}$ that estimates p.
   (c) If, in fact, 25% of all students like the food, what are the mean and standard deviation of the sampling distribution of $\hat{p}$?

5. PTC is a substance that has a strong bitter taste for some people and is tasteless for others. The ability to taste PTC is inherited. About 75% of Italians can taste PTC, for example. You want to estimate the proportion of Americans with at least one Italian grandparent who can taste PTC. Suppose that the 75% estimate for Italians holds true in this population and you test 500 people. Sketch the normal curve that shows how the proportion $\hat{p}$ in your sample that can taste PTC will vary if you take many samples.

6. In a midwestern state, 84% of the households have Christmas trees at holiday time. A sample survey asks a random sample of 400 households "Did you have a Christmas tree this year?" What is the sampling distribution of the percent who say "Yes"?

7. The standard deviation $\sigma_{\hat{p}}$ of a sample proportion $\hat{p}$ varies with the true value of the population proportion p. Fortunately, it does not vary greatly unless p is near 0% or 100%. Suppose that the size of the sample is $n = 1500$. Evaluate $\sigma_{\hat{p}}$ for $p = $ 30%, 40%, 50%, 60%, and 70%. Then evaluate $\sigma_{\hat{p}}$ for $p = $ 0%, 10%, and 20%. In which range does $\sigma_{\hat{p}}$ change most rapidly as p changes? Make a graph of $\sigma_{\hat{p}}$ against p.

Confidence Intervals

◆ 8. The report of a sample survey of 1500 adults says, "With 95% confidence, between 27% and 33% of all American adults believe that drugs are the most serious problem facing our nation's public schools." Explain to someone who knows no statistics what the phrase "95% confidence" means in this report.

◆ 9. The Gallup poll asked a random sample of 1005 adults whether they favored bilingual education or immersion training in English for non-English-speaking students in public schools. Sixty-three percent of the sample favored immersion. The press release stated that this poll has a 3% margin of error. Explain carefully to someone who knows no statistics what is meant by a "3% margin of error."

10. Suppose that the poll in Exercise 9 had used a simple random sample of size 1005, of whom 60% favored immersion. Give a 95% confidence interval for the percent of all adults who would favor immersion if asked.

11. In a recent year, 73% of first-year college students responding to a national survey identified "being very well off financially" as an important personal goal. A state university finds that 132 of a simple random sample of 200 of its first-year students say that this goal is important. Give a 95% confidence interval for the percentage of all first-year students at the university who would identify being well-off as an important personal goal.

12. The U.S. Forest Service is considering additional restrictions on the number of vehicles allowed to enter Yellowstone National Park. To assess public reaction, the service asks a simple random sample of 150 visitors if they favor the proposal. Of these, 89 say "Yes." Give a 95% confidence interval for the proportion of all visitors to Yellowstone who favor the restrictions. Are you 95% confident that more than half are in favor? Explain your answer.

♦ 13. The *New York Times* and CBS News conducted a nationwide poll of 1048 randomly selected 13- to 17-year-olds. Of these teenagers, 692 had a television in their room and 189 named Fox as their favorite television network. We will act as if the sample were a simple random sample.

   (a) Give 95% confidence intervals for the proportion of all people in this age group who have a TV in their room and the proportion who would choose Fox as their favorite network.
   (b) The news article says that "In theory, in 19 cases out of 20, the poll results will differ by no more than three percentage points in either direction from what would have been obtained by seeking out all American teenagers." Explain how your results agree with this statement.

♦ 14. Have efforts to promote equality for women gone far enough in the United States? A poll

on this issue by the cable network MSNBC contacted 1019 adults. A newspaper article about the poll said that "Results have a margin of sampling error of plus or minus 3 percentage points."

   (a) Overall, 54% of the sample (550 of 1019 people) answered "Yes." Find a 95% confidence interval for the proportion in the adult population who would say "Yes" if asked. Is the report's claim about the margin of error roughly right? (Assume that the sample is a simple random sample.)
   (b) The news article said that 65% of men, but only 43% of women, think that efforts to promote equality have gone far enough. Explain why we do not have enough information to give confidence intervals for men and women separately.
   (c) Would a 95% confidence interval for women alone have a margin of error less than 0.03, about equal to 0.03, or greater than 0.03? Why? You see that the news article's statement about the margin of error for poll results is a bit misleading.

Exercises 15 to 18 are based on the following situation. A news report says that a national opinion poll of 1500 randomly selected adults found that 43% thought they would be worse off during the next year. The news report went on to say that the margin of error in the poll result is ±3 percentage points with 95% confidence.

♦ 15. Which of the following sources of error are included in the poll's margin of error?

   (a) The poll dialed telephone numbers at random and so missed all people without phones.
   (b) Nonresponse: some people whose numbers were chosen never answered the phone in several calls or answered but refused to participate in the poll.
   (c) There is chance variation in the random selection of telephone numbers.

◆　16.　Would a 90% confidence interval based on the poll results have a margin of error less than ±3 percentage points, equal to ±3 percentage points, or greater than ±3 percentage points? Explain your answer.

◆　17.　If the poll had interviewed 1000 persons rather than 1500 (and still found 43% believing they would be worse off), would the margin of error for 95% confidence be less than ±3 percentage points, equal to ±3 percentage points, or greater than ±3 percentage points? Explain your answer.

◆　18.　Suppose that the poll had obtained the outcome 43% by a similar random sampling method from all adults in New York State (population 18 million) instead of from all adults in the United States (population 270 million). Would the margin of error for 95% confidence be less than ±3 percentage points, equal to ±3 percentage points, or greater than ±3 percentage points? Explain your answer.

Estimating a Population Mean

19.　A shipment of machined parts has a critical dimension that is normally distributed with mean 12 centimeters and standard deviation 0.01 centimeter. The acceptance sampling team measures a random sample of 25 of these parts. What is the sampling distribution of the sample mean $\bar{x}$ of the critical dimension for these parts?

20.　The scores of students on the ACT college entrance examination in a recent year had the normal distribution with mean $\mu = 18.6$ and standard deviation $\sigma = 5.9$.

(a)　What range of scores contains the middle 95% of all scores?
(b)　If the ACT scores of 25 randomly selected students are averaged, what range contains the middle 95% of the averages $\bar{x}$?

21.　Errors in careful measurements often have a distribution that is close to normal. Experience shows that the error in a surveying method varies when a measurement is repeated according to a normal distribution with mean 0 (that is, the procedure does not systematically overestimate or underestimate the true distance) and standard deviation 0.03 meter. A surveyor repeats each measurement three times and uses the mean of the three measurements as the final value. The error in this value is the mean $\bar{x}$ of the errors in the three individual measurements.

(a)　What is the distribution of the mean error $\bar{x}$ when the surveyor measures many distances?
(b)　Between what values do 95% of the errors fall?

22.　A study of the career paths of hotel general managers sent questionnaires to a simple random sample of 160 hotels belonging to major U.S. hotel chains. There were 114 responses. The average time these 114 general managers had spent with their current company was $\bar{x} = 11.78$ years. We do not know the population standard deviation σ, but the sample standard deviation was $s = 3.2$ years. Because the sample is large, s will be close to σ. Give a 95% confidence interval for the mean number of years general managers of major-chain hotels have spent with their current company.

23.　A laboratory scale is known to have a standard deviation of $\sigma = 0.001$ gram in repeated weighings. Suppose that scale readings in repeated weighings are normally distributed, with mean equal to the true weight of the specimen. Three weighings of a specimen give (in grams)

　　　3.412　　　3.414　　　3.415

Give a 95% confidence interval for the true weight of the specimen. What are the estimate and the margin of error in this interval?

◆　24.　Here are the IQ test scores of 31 seventh-grade girls in a midwest school district:

114	100	104	89	102	91
114	114	103	105	108	130
120	132	111	128	118	119
86	72	111	103	74	112
107	103	98	96	112	112
93					

(a)   We expect the distribution of IQ scores to be close to normal. Make a stemplot of the distribution of these 31 scores. Does your plot show outliers, clear skewness, or other nonnormal features?

(b)   Treat the 31 girls as a simple random sample of all seventh-grade girls in the school district. Suppose that the standard deviation of IQ scores in this population is known to be $\sigma = 15$. Give a 95% onfidence interval for the mean score in the population.

(c)   In fact, the scores are those of all seventh-grade girls in one of the several schools in the district. Explain carefully why your confidence interval from (b) cannot be trusted.

◆   **25.**   Find the margin of error for 95% confidence in Exercise 23 if we weigh each specimen twelve times rather than three times. Check that your result is half as large as the margin of error you found in Exercise 23. Explain why you knew without calculating that the new margin of error would be half as large.

◆   **26.**   The National Assessment of Educational Progress (NAEP) test was also given to a sample of 1077 women of ages 21 to 25 years. Their mean quantitative score was 275. Take it as known that the standard deviation of all individual scores is $\sigma = 60$.

(a)   Give a 95% confidence interval for the mean score μ in the population of all young women.

(b)   Suppose that the same result, $\bar{x} = 275$, had come from a sample of 250 women. Give the 95% confidence interval for the population mean μ in this case.

(c)   Then suppose that a sample of 4000 women had produced the sample mean $\bar{x} = 275$, and again give the 95% confidence interval for μ.

(d)   What are the margins of error for samples of size 250, 1077, and 4000? How does increasing the sample size affect the margin of error of a confidence interval?

27.   A milk processor monitors the number of bacteria per milliliter in raw milk received for processing. A random sample of 10 one-milliliter specimens from milk supplied by one producer gives the following data:

5370	4890	5100	4500	5260
5150	4900	4760	4700	4870

Suppose it is known that the bacteria count varies normally and that the standard deviation is $\sigma = 265$ per milliliter. Give a 95% confidence interval for the mean bacteria count per milliliter in this producer's milk.

◆   **28.**   A radio talk show invites listeners to enter a dispute about a proposed pay increase for city council members. "What yearly pay do you think council members should get? Call us with your number." In all, 958 people call. The mean pay they suggest is $\bar{x} = \$8740$ per year, and the standard deviation of the responses is $s = \$1125$. For a large sample such as this, s is very close to the unknown population σ. The station calculates the 95% confidence interval for the mean pay μ that all citizens would propose for council members to be $\$8667$ to $\$8813$.

(a)   Show that the station's calculation is correct.

(b)   Nonetheless, their conclusion does not describe the population of all the city's citizens. Explain why.

Statistical Process Control

In assessing control charts, use both the "one-point-out" and the "run of 9" signals for lack of control.

29.   A maker of auto air conditioners checks a sample of 4 thermostatic controls from each hour's production. The thermostats are set at 75°F and then placed in a chamber where the temperature is raised gradually. The temperature at which the thermostat turns on the air conditioner is recorded. The standard for the process mean is $\mu = 75°$. Past experience indicates that the response temperature of properly adjusted thermostats varies with $\sigma = 0.5°$. The mean response temperature $\bar{x}$ for each hour's sample is plotted on an $\bar{x}$ control chart. Calculate the center line and control limits for this chart.

30. The width of a slot cut by a milling machine is important to the proper functioning of a hydraulic system for large tractors. The manufacturer checks the control of the milling process by measuring a sample of 5 consecutive items during each hour's production. The mean slot width for each sample is plotted on an $\bar{x}$ control chart. The target width for the slot is $\mu = 0.8750$ inch. When properly adjusted, the milling machine should produce slots with mean width equal to the target value and standard deviation $\sigma = 0.0012$ inch. What center line and control limits should be drawn on the $\bar{x}$ chart?

31. It is common for laboratories to keep a control chart for a measurement process based on regular measurements of a standard specimen. Suppose that you are maintaining a control chart for the scale in Exercise 23 by weighing a 5-gram standard weight three times at regular intervals. What should be the center line of your chart? What are the control limits?

32. The diameter of a bearing deflector in an electric motor is supposed to be 2.205 centimeters (cm). Experience shows that when the manufacturing process is properly adjusted, it produces items with mean 2.2050 cm and standard deviation 0.0010 cm. A sample of 5 consecutive items is measured once each hour. Here are the sample means $\bar{x}$ for the past 12 hours:

Hour	1	2	3	4
$\bar{x}$	2.2047	2.2047	2.2050	2.2049

Hour	5	6	7	8
$\bar{x}$	2.2053	2.2043	2.2036	2.2042

Hour	9	10	11	12
$\bar{x}$	2.2038	2.2045	2.2026	2.2040

Make an $\bar{x}$ control chart for the deflector diameter. Use both the "one-point-out" and the "run of nine" signals to assess the control of the process. At what point should action have been taken to correct the process as the hourly point was added to the chart?

Exercises 33 to 35 are based on the following data: A pharmaceutical manufacturer forms tablets by compressing a granular material that contains the active ingredient and various fillers. The hardness of a sample from each lot of tablets is measured in order to control the compression process. The target values for the hardness are $\mu = 11.5$ and $\sigma = 0.2$. Table 8.4 gives three sets of data, each representing $\bar{x}$ for 20 successive samples of $n = 4$ tablets.

33. Make an $\bar{x}$ control chart for data set A in Table 8.4. The process mean μ shifted suddenly to a new value while these data were being collected. Does the chart show lack of control? How? At about which sample do you think that the mean changed?

34. The process mean μ remained stable at its target value $\mu = 11.5$ while the data in data set B of Table 8.4 were collected. The sample means vary, but this is just expected random variation. Make an $\bar{x}$ control chart and comment on what it shows.

35. Data set C in Table 8.4 (on the facing page) illustrates the effect of a steady drift in the mean of the population. The process remains stable for the first 10 samples. Then the process mean μ drifts steadily upward. Make an $\bar{x}$ control chart for these data. Are there any indications of lack of control? Is the upward drift in μ visible on the chart?

TABLE 8.4	Three Sets of $\bar{x}$ from 20 Samples of Size 4		
Sample	Data Set A	Data Set B	Data Set C
1	11.602	11.627	11.495
2	11.547	11.613	11.475
3	11.312	11.493	11.465
4	11.449	11.602	11.497
5	11.401	11.360	11.573
6	11.608	11.374	11.563
7	11.471	11.592	11.321
8	11.453	11.458	11.533
9	11.446	11.552	11.486
10	11.522	11.463	11.502
11	11.664	11.383	11.534
12	11.823	11.715	11.624
13	11.629	11.485	11.629
14	11.602	11.509	11.575
15	11.756	11.429	11.730
16	11.707	11.477	11.680
17	11.612	11.570	11.729
18	11.628	11.623	11.704
19	11.603	11.472	12.052
20	11.816	11.531	11.905

The Perils of Data Analysis

36. How is the hatching of water python eggs influenced by the temperature of the snake's nest? Researchers assigned newly laid eggs to one of three temperatures: hot, neutral, or cold. Hot duplicates the extra warmth provided by the mother python, and cold duplicates the absence of the mother. Here are the data on the number of eggs and the number that hatched. [From R. Shine, T. R. L. Madsen, M. J. Elphick, and P. S. Harlow, The influence of nest temperatures and maternal brooding on hatchling phenotypes in water pythons, *Ecology*, 78 (1997): 1713–1721.]

	Eggs	Hatched
Cold	27	16
Neutral	56	38
Hot	104	75

(a) Make a two-way table of temperature by outcome (hatched or not).

(b) Calculate the percent of eggs in each group that hatched. The researchers anticipated that cold water would reduce hatching. Do the data support that anticipation?

◆ 37. In a study of the effect of parents' smoking habits on the smoking habits of high school students, researchers interviewed students in eight high schools in Arizona. The results appear in the following two-way table. (From S. V. Zagona, ed., *Studies and Issues in Smoking Behavior,* University of Arizona Press, Tucson, 1967, pp. 157–180.)

	Student Smokes	Student Does Not Smoke
Both parents smoke	400	1380
One parent smokes	416	1823
Neither parent smokes	188	1168

Describe the association between the smoking habits of parents and their high school children by computing and comparing several percents. Then summarize the results in plain language.

38. Firearms are second to motor vehicles as a cause of nondisease deaths in the United States. Here are counts from a study of all firearm-related deaths in Milwaukee, Wisconsin, between 1990 and 1994. We want to compare the types of firearms used in homicides and in suicides. We suspect that long guns (shotguns and rifles) will more often be used in suicides because many people keep them at home for hunting. Make a careful comparison of homicides and suicides. What do you find about long guns versus handguns? [From S. W. Hargarten et al., Characteristics of firearms involved in fatalities, *Journal of the American Medical Association,* 275 (1996): 42–45.]

	Homicides	Suicides
Handgun	468	124
Shotgun	28	22
Rifle	15	24
Not specified	13	5
Total	524	175

◆ 39. Here are the numbers of flights on time and delayed for two airlines at five airports in one month. Overall on-time percentages for each airline are often reported in the news. Lurking variables can make such reports misleading. (Data from reports submitted by airlines to the Department of Transportation, from A. Barnett, How numbers can trick you, *Technology Review,* October 1994, pp. 38–45.)

	Alaska Airlines		America West	
	On Time	Delayed	On Time	Delayed
Los Angeles	497	62	694	117
Phoenix	221	12	4840	415
San Diego	212	20	383	65
San Francisco	503	102	320	129
Seattle	1841	305	201	61

(a) What percent of all Alaska Airlines flights were delayed? What percent of all America West flights were delayed? These are the numbers usually reported.

(b) Now find the percent of delayed flights for Alaska Airlines at each of the five airports. Do the same for America West.

(c) America West does worse at *every one* of the five airports, yet does better overall. That sounds impossible. Explain carefully, referring to the data, how this can happen. (The weather in Phoenix and Seattle lies behind what you see.)

◆ 40. Whether a convicted murderer gets the death penalty seems to be influenced by the race of the victim. Here are data on 326 cases in which the defendant was convicted of murder. [From M. Radelet, Racial characteristics and imposition of the death penalty, *American Sociological Review,* 46 (1981): 918–927.]

White Defendant			Black Defendant		
	Death Penalty			Death Penalty	
	Yes	No		Yes	No
White victim	19	132	White victim	11	52
Black victim	0	9	Black victim	6	97

(a)   Use these data to make a two-way table of defendant's race (white or black) versus death penalty (yes or no).
(b)   Show that Simpson's paradox holds: a higher percentage of white defendants are sentenced to death overall, but for both black and white victims a higher percent of black defendants are sentenced to death.
(c)   Use the data to explain why the paradox holds in language that a judge could understand.

Additional Exercises

◆   41.   A student reads that a 95% confidence interval for the mean NAEP quantitative score for men of ages 21 to 25 is 267.8 to 276.2. Asked to explain the meaning of this interval, the student says, "95% of all young men have scores between 267.8 and 276.2." Is the student right? Justify your answer.

◆   42.   The "Technology" column in the *New York Times* of May 29, 1995, reported that a survey of users of the Internet found that males outnumbered females by nearly 2 to 1. This was a surprise, because earlier surveys had put the ratio of men to women closer to 9 to 1. Later in the article we find this information:

Detailed surveys were sent to more than 13,000 organizations on the Internet; 1,468 usable responses were received. According to Mr. Quarterman, the margin of error is 2.8 percent, with a confidence level of 95 percent.

(a)   What was the response rate for this survey? (The response rate is the percent of the planned sample that responded.)
(b)   Do you think that the small margin of error is a good measure of the accuracy of the survey's results? Explain your answer.

◆   43.   A *New York Times* poll on women's issues interviewed 1025 women randomly selected from the United States, excluding Alaska and Hawaii. The poll found that 47% of the women said they do not get enough time for themselves.

(a)   The poll announced a margin of error of ±3 percentage points for 95% confidence in its conclusions. What is the 95% confidence interval for the percent of all adult women who think they do not get enough time for themselves?
(b)   Explain to someone who knows no statistics why we can't just say that 47% of all adult women do not get enough time for themselves.
(c)   Then explain clearly what "95% confidence" means.

■   44.   When the statistic that estimates an unknown parameter has a normal distribution, a 95% confidence interval for the parameter has the form

$$\text{estimate} \pm 2\sigma_{\text{estimate}}$$

In a complex sample survey design, estimates and their standard deviations require elaborate computations. But when we are given the estimate and its standard deviation, we can calculate a confidence interval for μ without knowing the formulas that led to the numbers given.

A report based on the Current Population Survey estimates the unemployment rate in the United States in June 1998 as 4.7%. (That is, 4.7% of civilians at least 16 years old who wanted work were not employed.) The report also says that the standard deviation of this estimate is 0.11%. The Current Population Survey uses an elaborate multistage sampling design to select a sample of about 50,000 households. The sampling distribution of the estimated unemployment rate is approximately normal. Give a 95% confidence interval for the unemployment rate in the population.

45.   A simple random sample of students at Upper Wabash Tech is asked whether they favor limiting enrollment in crowded majors as a way of keeping the quality of instruction high. The student government suspects that the plan will be unpopular among freshmen, who have not yet been admitted to a major. Here are the responses for freshmen and seniors.

	Favor	Oppose
Freshmen	40	160
Seniors	80	20

(a)   Give a 95% confidence interval for the percent of all freshmen who support the plan.
(b)   Give a 95% confidence interval for the percent of all seniors who support the plan.

◆ 46.   Sulfur compounds cause "off-odors" in wine, so winemakers want to know the odor threshold, the lowest concentration of a compound that the human nose can detect. The odor threshold for dimethyl sulfide (DMS) in trained wine tasters is about 25 micrograms per liter of wine (μg/l). The untrained noses of consumers may be less sensitive, however. Here are the DMS odor thresholds for 10 untrained students:

```
31    31    43    36    23
34    32    30    20    24
```

Assume that the standard deviation of the odor threshold for untrained noses is known to be $\sigma = 7$ μg/l.

(a)   Make a stemplot to verify that the distribution is roughly symmetric with no outliers. (More data confirm that there are no systematic departures from normality.)
(b)   Give a 95% confidence interval for the mean DMS odor threshold among all students.
(c)   Are you confident that the mean odor threshold for students is higher than the published threshold, 25 μg/l? Why?

◆ 47.   U.S. Treasury bills are safe investments, but how much do they pay investors? Here are data on the total return (in percent) on Treasury bills for the years 1970 to 1996.

Year	1970	1971	1972	1973
Return	6.45	4.37	4.17	7.20
Year	1974	1975	1976	1977
Return	8.00	5.89	5.06	5.43
Year	1978	1979	1980	1981
Return	7.46	10.56	12.18	14.71
Year	1982	1983	1984	1985
Return	10.84	8.98	9.89	7.65
Year	1986	1987	1988	1989
Return	6.10	5.89	6.95	8.43
Year	1990	1991	1992	1993
Return	7.72	5.46	3.50	3.04
Year	1994	1995	1996	
Return	4.37	5.60	5.13	

(a)   Make a histogram of these data, using bars 2 percentage points wide. What kind of deviation from normality do you see? Thanks to the central limit theorem, we can nonetheless treat $\bar{x}$ as approximately normal.
(b)   Suppose that we can regard these 27 years' results as a random sample of returns on Treasury bills. Give a 95% confidence interval for the long-term mean return. (Assume you know that the standard deviation of all returns is $\sigma = 2.75$%.)
(c)   The rate of inflation during these years averaged about 5.5%. Are you convinced that Treasury bills have a mean return higher than 5.5%? Why?

■ 48. We used the sampling distribution of $\hat{p}$ and the 68–95–99.7 rule to give a 95% confidence interval for a population proportion p.

(a) Explain carefully why

$$\hat{p} \pm \sqrt{\frac{\hat{p}(100 - \hat{p})}{n}}$$

is a 68% confidence interval for p.
(b) Give the recipe for a 99.7% confidence interval for p.

■ 49. Use the result of the Exercise 48(a) and the data in Exercise 12 to give a 68% confidence interval for the percent of visitors to Yellowstone who support restricting the number of vehicles allowed into the park. Compare the width of the 68% interval with that of the 95% interval from Exercise 12 and explain the difference in plain language.

■ 50. Use the result of Exercise 48(b) and the data in Exercise 9 to give a 99.7% confidence interval for the percent of all adults who favor immersion for non-English-speaking schoolchildren. Compare the width of the 99.7% interval with that of the 95% confidence interval from Exercise 10. What is the reason for the difference in widths?

■ 51. The upper and lower deciles of any normal distribution are located 1.28 standard deviations above and below the mean. (The lower decile is the point with probability 10% below it; the upper decile has probability 90% below it.)

(a) Use this information to give a recipe for an 80% confidence interval for a population proportion p based on the sample proportion $\hat{p}$ that is accurate for large sample sizes n.
(b) Give an 80% confidence interval for the proportion of visitors to Yellowstone favoring vehicle restrictions, using the data in Exercise 12.

■ 52. The upper and lower deciles of any normal distribution are located 1.28 standard deviations above and below the mean.

(a) Use this information to give a recipe for an 80% confidence interval for the mean μ of a normal population based on the sample mean $\bar{x}$ of a simple random sample of size n.
(b) Give an 80% confidence interval for the mean IQ score in Exercise 24.

■ 53. The rate of return on a stock varies from month to month. We can use a control chart to see if the pattern of variation is stable over time or whether there are periods during which the stock was unusually volatile by comparison with its own long-run pattern. Here are the mean monthly rates of return (in percent) for Wal-Mart stock for 38 six-month periods, in time order from left to right along the rows. The data begin in January 1973 and end in December 1990.

− 11.78	1.68	7.88	− 11.01	19.72
1.66	1.13	2.70	− 0.60	5.91
2.95	0.05	1.88	6.46	2.25
8.05	4.10	2.08	4.02	11.36
8.13	0.12	1.30	− 1.27	6.59
3.01	8.68	− 1.52	6.64	− 3.20
2.92	0.63	3.49	2.94	5.86
− 0.25	6.02	5.87		

We can treat these as the means $\bar{x}$ from 38 samples of 6 consecutive observations each. We will plot them on an $\bar{x}$ control chart.

(a) For the center line, use the mean of the $\bar{x}$'s, called $\bar{\bar{x}}$ in quality control. This is the same as the mean of the 228 individual monthly returns.
(b) The standard deviation of the 228 monthly returns includes both long-term and short-term variation and will generally be too

large for effective control. Instead, it is common to average the standard deviations of the 38 samples. The result is $\bar{\bar{s}} = 9.450$. If $\bar{\bar{x}}$ estimates the mean μ and $\bar{s}$ estimates σ, what are the control limits for an $\bar{x}$ control chart?

(c)   Make the chart. Look for points out of control and for runs of 9. Were there periods during these 19 years when the returns on Wal-Mart stock were out of control?

■   54.   Here are the row and column totals for a two-way table with two rows and two columns:

a	b	50
c	d	50
60	40	100

Find *two different* sets of counts a, b, c, and d for the body of the table that give these same totals. This shows that the relationship between two variables cannot be obtained from the two individual distributions of the variables.

■   55.   Recent studies have shown that earlier reports underestimated the health risks associated with being overweight. The error was due to overlooking lurking variables. In particular, smoking tends both to reduce weight and to lead to early death. Illustrate the perils of ignoring hidden variables by a simplified version of this situation. That is, make up a table of overweight (yes or no) by early death (yes or no) by smoker (yes or no) such that:

- Overweight smokers and overweight nonsmokers both tend to die earlier than those not overweight.
- But when smokers and nonsmokers are combined into a two-way table of overweight by early death, persons who are not overweight tend to die earlier.

TECHNOLOGY CORNER

Testing the Spreadsheet's Random Number Generator

In this unit we have relied on the spreadsheet's random number generator as a substitute for a fair coin, a fair die, or a well-shuffled deck. Have these simulations really been fair and unbiased? We can use samples and confidence intervals to answer this question.

In order to simulate flipping a coin, we can choose a random number between 0 and 1, using the command **=RandBetween(0,1).** If we assume the software is fair, then the probability that "1" is chosen is $p = 0.5$. If 10 samples are taken, 95% of the time the observed sample $\hat{p}$ is within the 95% confidence interval: 0.5 ± 0.316, or between 0.184 and 0.816. That is, between 2 and 8 of 10 samples should be "1"s (at least 95% of the time) if the coin is fair.

TASK 1.   Conduct the experiment just described above. Compute the sum of 10 random numbers generated by the command **=RandBetween(0,1).** Repeat this experiment for a total of 20 times. How often did the number of "1"s fall outside the acceptable range?

TASK 2.   If larger samples are taken, the size of the 95% confidence interval is reduced. Increase the sample size to 100 and calculate the resulting confidence interval. Then compute the sum of 100 random numbers generated by the command **=RandBetween(0,1).** Repeat this experiment 20 times. How often did the number of "1"s fall outside the acceptable range?

Estimating μ Using a Sample $\bar{x}$

Often, one uses the sample mean $\bar{x}$ to estimate the true value of the population mean μ. The spreadsheet shown in Figure 8.7 lists 5 sample weighings (in grams) for a certain product. Each individual weight is accurate with a standard deviation of $\sigma = 0.05$ gram. Based on these values, the sample mean and sample standard deviation $\sigma_{\bar{x}} = \sigma/\sqrt{n}$ are computed. The endpoints of a 95% confidence interval for the sample mean are computed by adding and subtracting $\sigma_{\bar{x}}$ from the sample mean.

	A	B	C	D
1	38.85		sigma	0.05
2	38.76		sample mean	38.804
3	38.80		n	5
4	38.83		sigma/sqrt(n)	0.022361
5	38.78			
6			interval min	38.75928
7	194.02	sum	interval max	38.84872

FIGURE 8.7

TASK 3.   Replicate the spreadsheet shown in Figure 8.7 for the following five weighings: 38.82, 38.76, 38.75, 38.75, 38.81.

TASK 4.   Use the function $=25.5 +$ **RandBetween(5,25)/50** to generate "weighings." The standard deviation is approximately $\sigma = 0.1$. Produce 5 samples and calculate a 95% confidence interval for the "true" weight.

Exploration

Suppose you are required by contract to ensure that your sample variance $\sigma_{\bar{x}}$ is no more than 0.01. Each weighing costs time and money, but more accurate scales tend to be more expensive. How do you find a compromise between the expense of multiple weighings and the expense of a more accurate scale? Create a scenario that addresses these issues.

writing projects

1 ▶   How do polling organizations describe the accuracy of their results? Spotlight 8.1 shows the *New York Times*'s practice. Go to the Gallup Organization Web site (**www.gallup.com**) and look at the press release for a recent Gallup poll. Then go to the Bureau of Labor Statistics (BLS) archive of news releases (**stats.bls.gov/newsrels.htm**) and look at the latest "Employment Situation" news release in the "Employment & Unemployment" section.

In both news releases, look for the part of the news release that describes the sampling methods

used, the margin of error for the result, and sources of error that are not included in the margin of error. In the case of the BLS, pay attention only to information about the Current Population Survey. Write a brief comparison of the two discussions. Why do you think that Gallup says much less than the BLS?

2 ▶   The margin of error announced for a sample survey takes into account the chance variation due to random sampling. In practice, survey results can be in error for other reasons. Some subjects can't be contacted, others lie or don't remember information, and the wording of the questions will influence the responses. These are the "practical difficulties" mentioned in Spotlight 8.1.

Write a brief discussion of the most important practical difficulties encountered in opinion polls and other surveys of human populations. You will want to read more on the subject. Some sources are Section 1.5 of *Statistics: Concepts and Controversies* (see Suggested Readings in Chapter 5) and the article by P. E. Converse and M. W. Traugott, Assessing the accuracy of polls and surveys, *Science*, 234 (1986): 1094–1098.

3 ▶   There are many confidence intervals for use in settings other than the two described in this chapter. One common setting is to estimate the difference between *two* population proportions, p_1 and p_2. For example, p_1 could be the proportion of women and p_2 the proportion of men who stay home at night due to fear of crime. Read an account of the confidence interval for $p_1 - p_2$ in a statistical methods text (for example, in Section 8.2 of Moore's *The Basic Practice of Statistics*). Then explain carefully how this new confidence interval arises from the same reasoning we have used: find an estimate, discover that the sampling distribution of the estimate is at least approximately normal, learn the standard deviation of this normal distribution, and go out two standard deviations from the estimate to get 95% confidence.

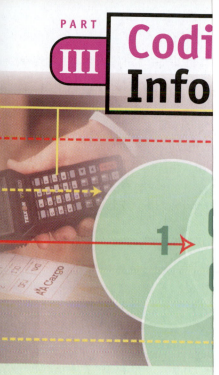

PART

III

Codi
Info

alphabet, a
application:
the makeup
invented a
and even VC
recent decad
data. For exa
fax machines
errors in the
services such
that only tho

Financial
reception thr
examine som

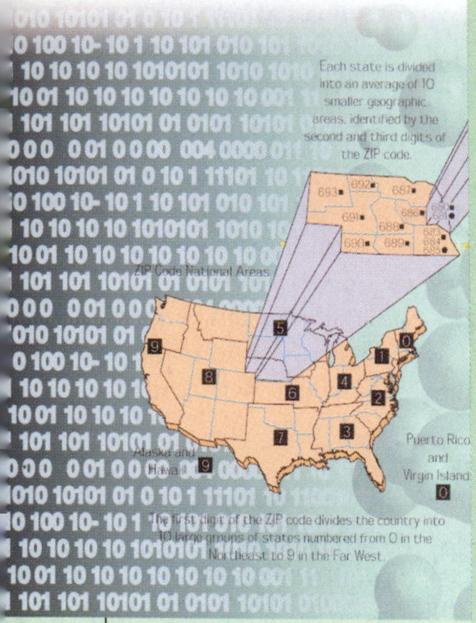

"Codes existed tho
years ago: hierogly
Greek alphabet, a
Roman numerals.

inexpensive,
today are m
numbers hav
correctly ent
Identificatio
as sex, date

Identific
represent inf

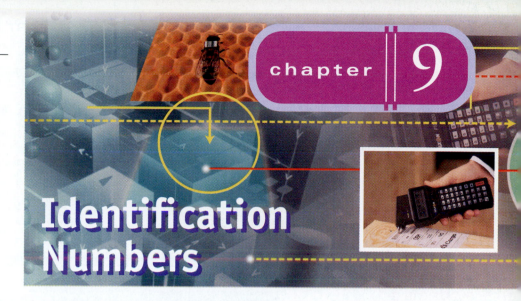

chapter 9

Identification Numbers

" . . . many items you encounter daily have identification numbers that code data."

Modern identification numbers have at least two functions. Obviously, an identification number should unambiguously identify the person or thing to which it is associated. Not obvious is a "self-checking" aspect of the number.

Look at the ISBN printed on the back of this book. The number 0-7167-3514-8 distinguishes this book from all others. The last digit "8" is there solely to detect errors that may occur when the ISBN is entered into a computer. Look at the bottom of the airline ticket shown in Figure 9.1. Notice the letters "ck" (for "check") above the last digit of the stock control number and above the last digit of the document number. They also are there for the purpose of error detection. Grocery items, credit cards, overnight mail, magazines, personal checks, traveler's checks, soft-drink cans, automobiles, and many other items you encounter daily have identification numbers that code data and include check digits for error detection. In this chapter we examine some of the methods that are used to assign identification numbers and check digits.

Let us begin by considering the U.S. Postal Service money order shown in Figure 9.2. The first 10 digits of the 11-digit number 63024383845 simply identify the money order. The last digit, 5, serves as **error-detecting code** or mechanism. Let us see how this mechanism works. The eleventh (last) digit of a Postal Service money order number is the remainder obtained when the sum of the first 10 digits of the number is divided by 9. In our example the last digit is 5 because $6 + 3 + 0 + 2 + 4 + 3 + 8 + 3 + 8 + 4 = 41$ and the remainder when 41 is divided by 9 is 5.

Now suppose instead of the correct number, the number 63054383845 (an error in the fourth position) were entered into a computer programmed for error detection of money orders. The machine would divide the sum of the first 10 digits

FIGURE 9.1

Airline ticket with identification number 127881879532 and check digit 1; stock control number 3026164775 and check digit 4.

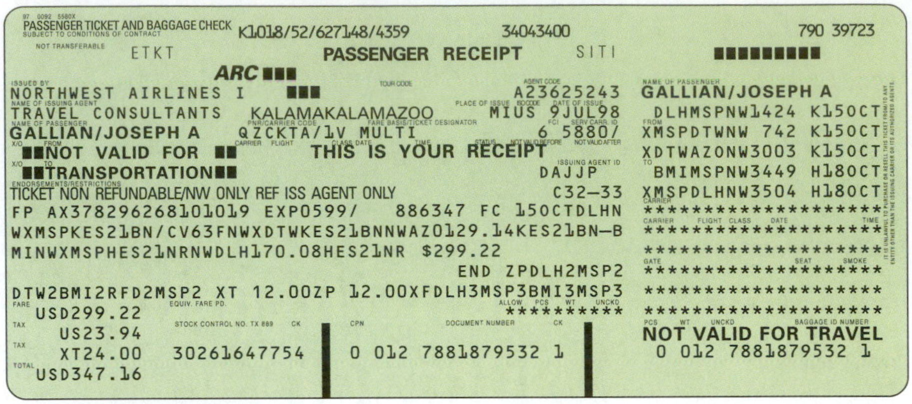

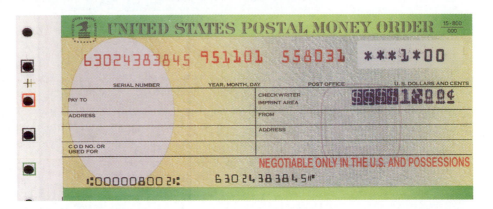

FIGURE 9.2

Money order with identification number 6302438384 and appended check digit 5. The check digit is the remainder upon dividing the sum of the digits by 9.

FIGURE 9.3

Traveler's check with identification number 387505055 and check digit 7. The check digit is chosen so that the sum of all the digits including the check digit is evenly divisible by 9. Notice that the check digit is included as part of the identification number along the bottom but not included in the upper right corner. The number along the bottom is read by a computer.

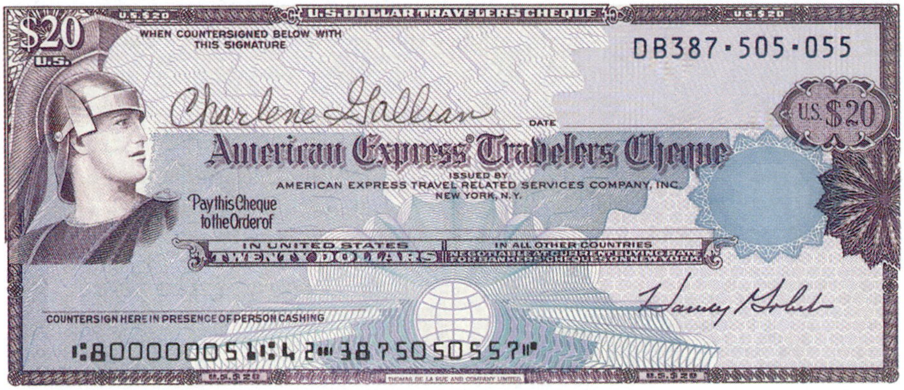

of the entered number, 44, by 9 and obtain a remainder of 8. Since the last digit of the entered number is 5 rather than 8, the entered number cannot be correct. This crude method of error detection will not detect the mistake of replacing a 0 with a 9, or vice versa. Nor will it detect the transposition of digits, such as 63204383845 instead of 63024383845 (the digits in positions three and four have been transposed).

American Express (see Figure 9.3) and VISA traveler's checks also utilize a check digit determined by division by 9. In these cases, the check digit is chosen so that the sum of the digits, including the check digit, is evenly divisible by 9.

E X A M P L E   *The American Express Travelers Cheque*

The American Express Travelers Cheque with the identification number 387505055 has check digit 7 because $3 + 8 + 7 + 5 + 0 + 5 + 0 + 5 + 5 = 38$ and $38 + 7$ is evenly divisible by 9. ◆

The scheme used on airline tickets, Federal Express mail, UPS packages, and Avis and National rental cars assigns the remainder upon division by 7 of the number itself as the check digit (see Figure 9.1) rather than dividing the sum of the digits by 7. For example, the check digit for the number 540047 is 4 since $540047 = 7 \times 77149 + 4$. This method will not detect the substitution of 0 for a 7, 1 for an 8, 2 for a 9, or vice versa. However, unlike the Postal Service method, it will detect transpositions of adjacent digits with the exceptions of the pairs 0, 7; 1, 8; or 2, 9. For example, if 5400474 were entered into a computer as 4500474 (the first two digits are transposed), the machine would determine that the check digit should be 3 since $450047 = 7 \times 64292 + 3$. Because the last digit of the entered number is not 3, the error has been detected.

The scheme used on grocery products, the so-called *Universal Product Code (UPC)*, is more sophisticated. Consider the number 0 38000 00127 7 found on the bottom of a box of corn flakes. The first digit identifies a broad category of goods, the next five digits identify the manufacturer, the next five the product, and the last is a check. Suppose this number were entered into a computer as 0 58000 00127 7 (a mistake in the second position). How would the computer recognize the mistake?

The computer is programmed to carry out the following computation: add the digits in positions 1, 3, 5, 7, 9, 11 and triple the result; then add this tally to the sum of the remaining digits. If the result doesn't end with a 0, the computer knows the entered number is incorrect.

For the incorrect corn flakes number, we have $((0 + 8 + 0 + 0 + 1 + 7) \times 3) + (5 + 0 + 0 + 0 + 2 + 7) = (16 \times 3) + 14 = 62$. Since 62 doesn't end with 0, the error is detected. Notice that had we used the correct digit 3 in the second position instead of 5, the sum would have ended in a 0 as it should. This simple scheme detects *all* single-position errors and about 89% of all other kinds of errors.

The U.S. banking system uses a variation of the UPC scheme that appends check digits to the numbers assigned to banks. Each bank has an eight-digit identification number $a_1 a_2 \cdots a_8$ together with a check digit a_9 so that a_9 is the last digit of $7a_1 + 3a_2 + 9a_3 + 7a_4 + 3a_5 + 9a_6 + 7a_7 + 3a_8$. The numbers 7, 3, and 9 used in this formula are called **weights.** The weights were carefully chosen so that all single-digit errors and most transposition errors are detected. (The use of different weights in adjacent positions permits the detection of most transposition errors.) See Spotlight 9.1.

SPOTLIGHT
9.1

Bank Checks

What do the string of numbers at the bottom of a check represent? Here is the answer.

0710	the bank's Federal Reserve District, office, and state or special collection arrangement
0001	the bank's identification number
3	the check digit
22 633 78	the checking account number
0134	the check number

E X A M P L E   *Bank Identification Number*

The First Chicago Bank has the number 071000013 on the bottom of all its checks. The check digit 3 is the last digit of $7 \cdot 0 + 3 \cdot 7 + 9 \cdot 1 + 7 \cdot 0 + 3 \cdot 0 + 9 \cdot 0 + 7 \cdot 0 + 3 \cdot 1 = 33$. ◆

One of the most efficient error-detection methods is one used by all major credit card companies, as well as by many libraries, blood banks, photofinishing companies, German banks, and the Wisconsin and South Dakota driver's license departments. It is called **Codabar.** Say a bank intends to issue a credit card with the identification number 312560019643001. It must then add an extra digit for error detection. This is done as follows. Add the digits in positions 1, 3, 5, 7, 9, 11, 13, and 15 and double the result: $(3 + 2 + 6 + 0 + 9 + 4 + 0 + 1) \times 2 = 50$. Next, count the number of digits in positions 1, 3, 5, 7, 9, 11, 13, and 15 that exceed 4 and add this to the total. For our example, only 6 and 9 exceed 4, so the count is 2 and our running total is 52. Now add in the remaining digits: $52 + (1 + 5 + 0 + 1 + 6 + 3 + 0) = 68$.

The check digit is whatever is needed to bring the final tally to a number that ends with 0. Since $68 + 2 = 70$, the check digit for our example is 2. This digit is appended to the end of the number the bank issues for identification purposes. Errors in input data are detected by applying the same algorithm to the input, including the check digit. If the correct number is entered into a computer, the result will end in a zero. If the result doesn't end with a zero, a mistake has been made. The credit card shown in Figure 9.4 is reproduced from an ad promoting the Citibank VISA card. Notice that the check digit on the card is not valid since the Codabar algorithm yields

$$(4 + 2 + 0 + 1 + 3 + 5 + 7 + 9) \times 2 + 3$$
$$+ (1 + 8 + 0 + 2 + 4 + 6 + 8) + 0 = 94$$

FIGURE 9.4
VISA card with an invalid Codabar number.

which does not end in 0. This method allows computers to detect 100% of single-position errors and about 98% of other common errors.

Besides detecting errors, the check digit offers partial protection against fraud. A person who wanted to create a phony credit card number, bank account number, or driver's license number would have to know the appropriate check digit scheme for the number to go unchallenged by the computer. (See Spotlight 9.2.)

SPOTLIGHT

9.2

Credit Card Fraud

In 1994 a computer program designed to create credit card numbers began to appear on on-line computer services such as America Online and many electronic bulletin boards. Known as the Credit Master, the program uses legitimate bank codes and produces the correct check digit. Only 3 to 5% of the numbers the program produces actually correspond to active accounts. The program cannot produce the expiration date or the holder's name, which are often checked before spending is authorized. Credit card companies say that they know of no significant losses as the result of

Credit Master. "We consider it as a threat, but the formula was never meant to be high-tech security screening," said Dennis Fiene, director of fraud control for Visa.

Source: Adapted from Ashley Dunn, "A pirate computer program builds credit card numbers," *New York Times,* March 19, 1995, p. 18.

SPOTLIGHT 9.3

VIN System

Automobiles and trucks are given a vehicle identification number (VIN) by the manufacturer. A typical VIN has 17 alphanumeric characters that code information, such as country where the vehicle was built, manufacturer, make, body style, engine type, plant where the vehicle was built, model year, model, type of restraint, a check digit, and a production sequence number. The check digit is calculated by converting the 26 consecutive letters of the alphabet respectively, to the numbers 1,2,3,4,5,6,7,8,9,1,2,3,4,5,6,7,8, 9,2,3,4,5,6,7,8,9 (note the anomaly after the second 9) so as to obtain a 16-digit number $a_1 a_2 \cdots a_{15} a_{16}$ that is weighted with 8,7,6,5,4,3,2, 10,9,8,7,6,5,4,3,2. The check digit is the remainder when the weighted sum $8 \cdot a_1 + 7 \cdot a_2 + \cdots + 3 \cdot a_{15} + 2 \cdot a_{16}$ is divided by 11 unless the remainder is 10, in which case an X is used instead. The check digit is inserted in position 9.

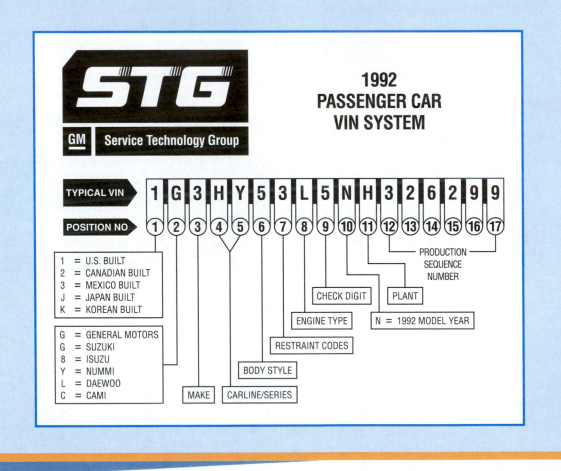

Thus far we have not discussed any schemes that detect 100% of single errors and 100% of transposition errors. The **International Standard Book Number (ISBN)** method used throughout the world is one that detects all such errors. (See the copyright page and the back of this book.)

A correctly coded 10-digit ISBN $a_1 a_2 \cdots a_{10}$ has the property that $10a_1 + 9a_2 + 8a_3 + 7a_4 + 6a_5 + 5a_6 + 4a_7 + 3a_8 + 2a_9 + a_{10}$ is evenly divisible by 11. Consider the ISBN of the book you are now reading: 0-7167-3514-8. The initial digit 0 indicates that the book is published in an English-speaking country (*not* that the book is written in English). The next block of digits—7167—identifies the publisher, W. H. Freeman and Company. The third block—3514—is assigned by the publisher and identifies this particular book. The last digit, 8, is the check digit.

Let us verify that this number is a legitimate possibility. We must compute
$$10 \cdot 0 + 9 \cdot 7 + 8 \cdot 1 + 7 \cdot 6 + 6 \cdot 7 + 5 \cdot 3 + 4 \cdot 5 + 3 \cdot 1 + 2 \cdot 4 + 8 = 209.$$
Since $209 = 11 \cdot 19$, it is evenly divisible by 11, and no error has been detected.

How can we be sure that this method detects 100% of the single-position errors? Well, let us say that a correct number is $a_1 a_2 a_3 a_4 a_5 a_6 a_7 a_8 a_9 a_{10}$ and that a mistake is made in the second position. (The same argument applies equally well in every position.) We can write this incorrect number as $a_1 a'_2 a_3 a_4 a_5 a_6 a_7 a_8 a_9 a_{10}$, where $a'_2 \neq a_2$. Now in order for this error to go undetected, it must be the case that $10a_1 + 9a'_2 + 8a_3 + 7a_4 + 6a_5 + 5a_6 + 4a_7 + 3a_8 + 2a_9 + a_{10}$ is evenly divisible by 11. Then, since both $10a_1 + 9a_2 + 8a_3 + 7a_4 + 6a_5 + 5a_6 + 4a_7 + 3a_8 + 2a_9 + a_{10}$ and $10a_1 + 9a'_2 + 8a_3 + 7a_4 + 6a_5 + 5a_6 + 4a_7 + 3a_8 + 2a_9 + a_{10}$ are divisible by 11, so is their difference:

$$(10 \cdot a_1 + 9 \cdot a_2 + 8 \cdot a_3 + \cdots + 1 \cdot a_{10})$$
$$- (10 \cdot a_1 + 9 \cdot a'_2 + 8 \cdot a_3 + \cdots + 1 \cdot a_{10}) = 9 \cdot (a_2 - a'_2)$$

Because a_2 and a'_2 are distinct digits between 0 and 9, their difference must be one of $\pm 1, \ldots, \pm 9$. Thus the only possibilities for the number $9 \cdot (a_2 - a'_2)$ are $\pm 9, \pm 18, \pm 27, \pm 36, \pm 45, \pm 54, \pm 63, \pm 72, \pm 81, \pm 90$, and none of these is divisible by 11. So, a single-position error cannot go undetected.

Since this method, in contrast to the others we have described, detects all single-position errors and all transposition errors, why is it not used more? Well, it does have a drawback. Say the next title published by Freeman is to have 1910 for the third block. (All Freeman books begin with 0-7167-.) What check digit should be assigned? Call it a. Then $10 \cdot 0 + 9 \cdot 7 + 8 \cdot 1 + 7 \cdot 6 + 6 \cdot 7 + 5 \cdot 1 + 4 \cdot 9 + 3 \cdot 1 + 2 \cdot 0 + a = 199 + a$. Since the next integer after 199 that is divisible by 11 is 209, we see that $a = 10$. But appending 10 to the existing 9-digit number would result in an 11-digit number instead of a 10-digit one. This is the only flaw in the ISBN scheme. To avoid this flaw, publishers use an X to represent the check digit 10. As a result not all ISBNs consist solely of digits (some end with X). Publishers could avoid this inconsistency by simply refraining from using numbers that require an X.

At this point the reader might naturally ask, "Why are there so many different methods for achieving the same purpose?" Like many practices in the "real world," historical accident and lack of knowledge about existing methods seem to be the explanation.

Many identification numbers utilize both alphabetic and numerical characters. One of the most prevalent of these was developed in 1975 and is called **Code 39.** Code 39 permits the 26 uppercase letters A through Z and the digits 0 through 9. Because Code 39 has been chosen by the Department of Defense, the automotive companies, and the health industry for use by their suppliers it has become the workhorse of nonretail business.

A typical example of a Code 39 number is 210SA0162322ZAY. The last character is the "check." The check character is determined by assigning the letters A through Z the numerical values 10 through 35, respectively. The original number, composed of the digits 0 through 9 and letters A through Z, is now converted to a string $a_1, a_2, \ldots, a_{14}, a_{15}$, where the a_i are integers between 0 and 35. The check character a_{15} is chosen so that $15a_1 + 14a_2 + 13a_3 + \cdots + 2a_{14} + a_{15}$ is divisible by 36. Finally a_{15} is converted to its alphabetic counterpart if it is greater than 9 (for example, 13 is converted to D).

SPOTLIGHT 9.4

German Banknotes

Germany is one of few countries in the world that includes a check digit on its currency. Each German banknote has a 10-character serial number comprising letters and numbers. To compute the check digit, the letters are converted to numbers and complicated schemes for weighing the numbers in each position and for calculating the check digit are employed. Interestingly, the method used to calculate the check digit is not commutative (that is, a times b need not be the same as b times a). For example, in this unusual mathematical system, 4 times 5 is 9 but 5 times 4 is 6. Using a noncommutative system of calculation results in greater error-detection capability than is possible with a commutative system. The banknote shown here features the mathematician Carl Gauss. The last digit is the check digit.

German banknote with serial number DZ6768309Y and check digit 9.

E X A M P L E   *Code 39 Number 210SA0162322ZA*

Let us examine the Code 39 method for the number 210SA0162322ZA. Here is how we determine the check character. First we convert the alphabetic characters to their numerical counterparts: $210SA0162322ZA \rightarrow$ 2, 1, 0, 28, 10, 0, 1, 6, 2, 3, 2, 2, 35, 10. Then we compute

$$15 \cdot 2 + 14 \cdot 1 + 13 \cdot 0 + 12 \cdot 28 + 11 \cdot 10 + 10 \cdot 0 + 9 \cdot 1 + 8 \cdot 6$$
$$+ 7 \cdot 2 + 6 \cdot 3 + 5 \cdot 2 + 4 \cdot 2 + 3 \cdot 35 + 2 \cdot 10 = 30 + 14 + 0 + 336$$
$$+ 110 + 0 + 9 + 48 + 14 + 18 + 10 + 8 + 105 + 20 = 722$$

Now we select a_{15} so that $722 + a_{15}$ is divisible by 36. Since 722 divided by 36 has a remainder of 2 ($722 = 36 \cdot 20 + 2$), we choose a_{15} as 34. Finally, we convert 34 to Y. Thus the number becomes 210SA0162322ZAY.   ◆

In many applications of Code 39 the seven special characters -, ., space, \$, /, +, and % are permitted. These characters are assigned the numerical values 36 through 42, respectively. In these applications the check character is determined by the remainder upon division by 43 instead of 36.

The ZIP Code

Identification numbers occasionally **encode** geographical data. **ZIP codes,** social security numbers, and telephone numbers are prime examples. In 1963 the U.S. Postal Service numbered every American post office with a five-digit ZIP code. The numbers begin with zeros at the point farthest east—00601 for Adjuntas, Puerto Rico—and work up to nines at the point farthest west—99950 for Ketchikan, Alaska (see Figure 9.5). Here's what the five digits mean.

Let's use one of the ZIP codes for Lincoln, Nebraska, as an example:

68588

6   The first digit represents one of 10 geographical areas, usually a group of states. The numbers begin at points farthest east (0) and end at the points farthest west (9).

85   The second two digits, in combination with the first, identify a central mail-distribution point known as a sectional center. The location of a sectional center is based on geography, transportation facilities, and population density; although just four centers serve the entire state of Utah, there are six of them for New York City alone.

88   The last two digits indicate the town, or local post office. The order is often alphabetic for towns within a delivery area—for example, towns with names beginning with A usually have low numbers. (There are many exceptions to this, such as towns that came into existence after the

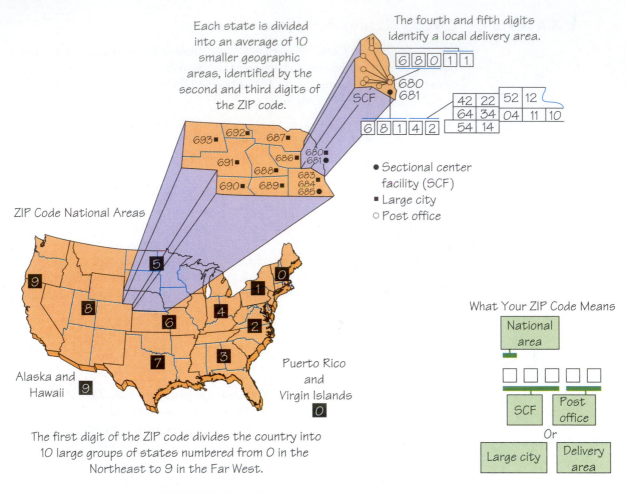

Each state is divided into an average of 10 smaller geographic areas, identified by the second and third digits of the ZIP code.

The fourth and fifth digits identify a local delivery area.

SCF

● Sectional center facility (SCF)
■ Large city
○ Post office

ZIP Code National Areas

Alaska and Hawaii

Puerto Rico and Virgin Islands

What Your ZIP Code Means

National area

SCF · Post office

Or

Large city · Delivery area

The first digit of the ZIP code divides the country into 10 large groups of states numbered from 0 in the Northeast to 9 in the Far West.

FIGURE 9.5 ZIP code scheme.

ZIP code scheme was created.) In many cases the largest city in a region will be given the digits 01 and surrounding towns assigned succeeding digits alphabetically, as shown below for the Farmville, Virginia, area.

Andersonville	23911	Hampden-Sydney	23943
Boydton	23917	Kenbridge	23944
Buckingham	23921	Keysville	23947
Burkeville	23922	Lunenburg	23952
Charlotte Court House	23923	Meherrin	23954
Chase City	23924	Nottoway	23955
Clarksville	23927	Pamplin	23958

Crewe	23930	Phenix	23959
Cullen	23934	Prospect	23960
Darlington Heights	23935	Red Oak	23964
Dillwyn	23936	Rice	23966
Drakes Branch	23937	Skipwith	23968
Dundas	23938	Victoria	23974
Farmville	23901	Wylliesburg	23976
Green Bay	23942		

In 1983 the U.S. Postal Service added four digits to the ZIP code. When four digits are added after a dash—for example, 68588-1234—the number is called the **ZIP + 4 code.** Mail with the ZIP + 4 coding benefits from cheaper bulk rates, being easier to sort with automated equipment. It's also helpful for businesses that wish to sort the recipients of their mailings by geographical location. The first two numbers of the four-digit suffix represent a delivery sector, which may be several blocks, a group of streets, several office buildings, or a small geographical area. The last two numbers narrow the area further: they might denote one floor of a large office building, a department in a large firm, or a group of post office boxes.

For businesses that receive an enormous volume of mail the ZIP + 4 code permits automation of in-house mailroom sorting. For example, the first seven digits of all mail sent the University of Minnesota, Duluth, are 55812-24. The school has designated nine pairs of digits for the last two positions to direct the mail to the appropriate dormitory or apartment complex.

Bar Codes

In modern applications bar codes and identification numbers go hand in hand. Bar coding is a method for automated data collection. It is a way to transmit information rapidly, accurately, and efficiently to a computer.

A **bar code** is a series of dark bars and light spaces that represent characters.

To **decode** the information in a bar code, a beam of light is passed over the bars and spaces via a scanning device, such as a hand-held wand or a fixed-beam device. The dark bars reflect very little light back to the scanner, whereas the light spaces reflect much light. The differences in reflection intensities are detected by the scanner and converted to strings of 0s and 1s that represent specific numbers and letters. Such strings are called a *binary coding* of the numbers and letters.

> Any system for representing data with only two symbols is a **binary code.**

Hand-held scanner
reading the shipping bar
code on a crate.

ZIP Code Bar Code

The simplest bar code is the **Postnet code** used by the U.S. Postal Service and commonly found on business reply forms (see Figure 9.6). For a ZIP + 4 code there are 52 vertical bars of two possible lengths (long and short). The long bars at the beginning and end are called *guard bars* and together provide a frame for the remaining 50 bars. In blocks of five, the 50 bars within the guard bars represent the ZIP + 4 code and a tenth digit for error correction. Each block of five is composed of exactly two long bars and three short bars, according to the pattern shown below:

Decimal Digit	Bar Code
1	ııı‖
2	ıı‖ı
3	ıı‖ıı
4	ı‖ıı
5	ı‖ıı
6	ı‖ıı
7	‖ıı
8	‖ı‖ı
9	‖ı‖ı
0	‖ıı

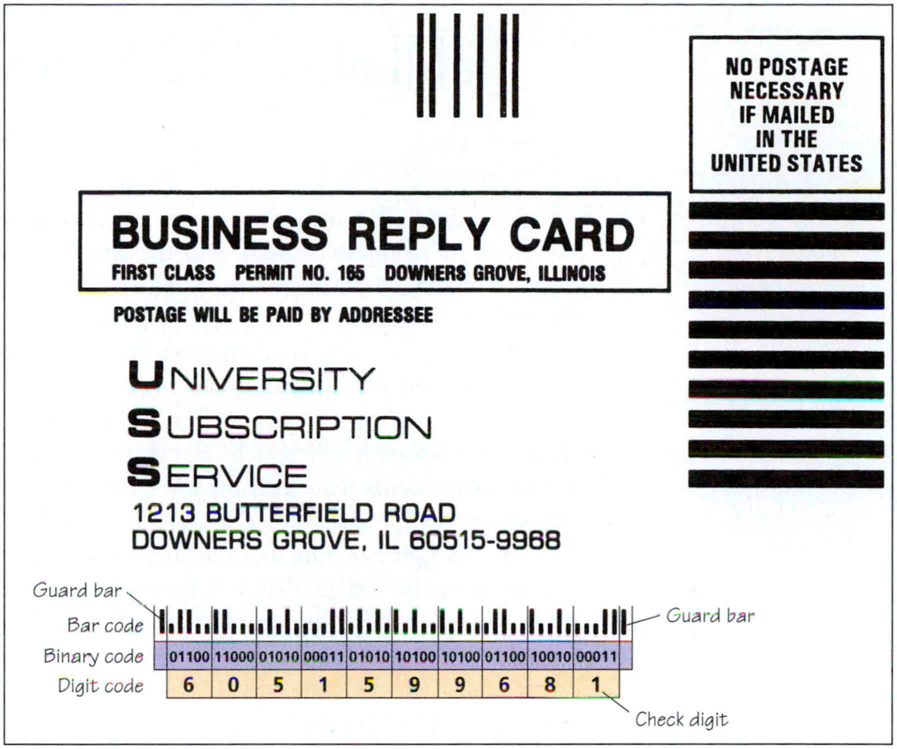

FIGURE 9.6 ZIP + 4 bar code.

The tenth digit of a Postnet code number is a check digit chosen so that the sum of the nine digits of the ZIP + 4 code and the tenth one is evenly divisible by 10. That is, the check digit C for the ZIP + 4 code $a_1a_2 \cdots a_9$ is the digit with the property that the sum $a_1 + a_2 + \cdots + a_9 + C$ ends with 0. For example, the ZIP + 4 code 80321-0421 has the check digit 9 since $8 + 0 + 3 + 2 + 1 + 0 + 4 + 2 + 1 = 21$ and $21 + 9 = 30$ ends with 0.

Because each digit is represented by exactly two long bars and three short ones, any error in reading or printing a single bar would result in a block of five with only one long bar or three long bars. In either case, the error is detected. (This is the reason behind the choice of five bars to code each digit rather than four bars. With five bars per digit, there are exactly 10 arrangements composed of two long bars and three short bars. Any misreading of a single bar in such a block is therefore recognizable, since it does not match any other of the blocks for the 10 digits.) And since the block location of the error is known, the check digit permits the correction of the error. Let's look at an example of an incorrectly printed bar code and see how the error is correctable.

The scanner ignores the guard bars at the beginning and the end and reads the remaining bars in blocks of five as shown in the illustration on the following page. (We have inserted dividing lines for readability.)

3   0   7   2   2   ?   9   0   1   7

Since the sixth block has only one long bar, it is an incorrect one. To correct the error, the computer linked with the bar code scanner sums the remaining 9 digits to obtain 31. Since the sum of all 10 digits ends with 0, the correct value for the sixth digit must be 9.

Beginning in 1993, large organizations and businesses that wanted to receive reduced rates for ZIP + 4 bar-coded mail were required to use a 12-digit bar code called the *delivery-point bar code*. This code permits machines to sort a letter into the order in which it will be delivered by the carrier. (Mail for the first location on a mail route occurs first, mail for the second location on a route occurs second, and so on.)

The 12-digit bar code uses the Postnet bar scheme to code the 12-digit string composed of the 9-digit ZIP + 4 number followed by the last two digits of the street address or box number and a check digit chosen so that the sum of all 12 digits is evenly divisible by 10. For example, a letter addressed to 1738 Maple Street with ZIP + 4 code 55811-2742 would have the Postnet bar code for the digits 558112742384 (38 is from the street address and 4 is the check digit).

The UPC Bar Code

The bar code that we encounter most often is the **Universal Product Code (UPC).** The UPC was first used on grocery items in 1973 and has since spread to most retail products. The UPC bar code translates a 12-digit number into bars that can be quickly and accurately read by a laser scanner. The number has four components—two five-digit numbers sandwiched between two single digits—as shown in Figure 9.7.

Here is what the four components represent:

5   The first digit identifies the kind of product. For example, a 2 signals random-weight items, such as cheese or meat; a 3 means drug and certain health-related products; a 4 means products marked for price reduction by the retailer; a 5 signals cents-off coupons (see Figure 9.7).

43000   The next five digits identify the manufacturer. This number is assigned by the Uniform Code Council in Dayton, Ohio.

21031   The next five digits are assigned by the manufacturer to identify the product, and can include size, color, or other important information (but not price).

9   The final digit is the check digit. This digit is often not printed, but it is always included in the bar code.

FIGURE 9.7

UPC identification number 5 43000 21031 9. The initial 5 indicates the number is a manufacturer's coupon. The block 43000 identifies the manufacturer as Kraft General Foods. The block 21031 identifies the product. The last digit, 9, is a check digit.

Each digit of the UPC code is represented by a space divided into seven modules of equal width, as illustrated in Figure 9.8. How these seven modules are filled depends on the digit being represented and whether the digit being represented is part of the manufacturer's number or the product number. In every case there are two light "spaces" and two dark bars of various thicknesses that alternate. A UPC code has on each end two long bars of one module thickness separated by a light space of one module thickness. These three modules are called the *guard bar*

FIGURE 9.8

UPC bar coding for a left-side 6 and a left-side 0.

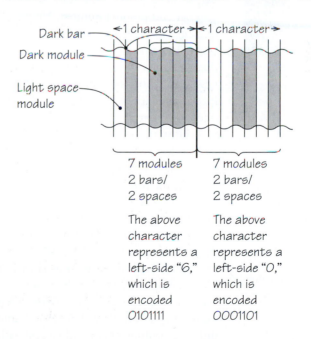

FIGURE 9.9
UPC bar code format.

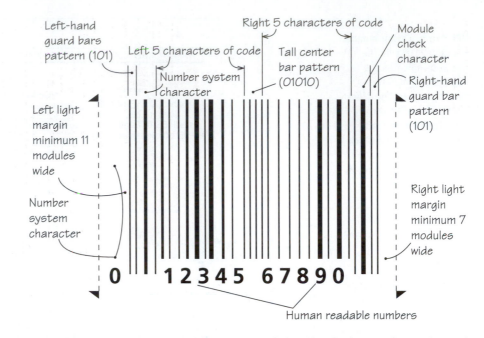

patterns (Figure 9.9). The guard bar patterns define the thickness of a single module of each type. They are not part of the identification number. The manufacturer's number and the product number are separated by a center bar pattern consisting of the following five modules: a light space, a (long) dark bar, a light space, a (long) dark bar, and a light space (see Figure 9.9). The center bar pattern is not part of the identification number but merely serves to separate the manufacturer's number and product number. Figure 9.8 shows how the digits 6 and 0 in a manufacturer's number are coded.

Observe the following pattern in Figure 9.8: a light space of one module thickness, a dark bar of one module thickness, a light space of one module thickness, a dark bar of four module thickness. Symbolically such a pattern of light spaces and dark bars is represented as 0101111. Here each 0 means a one-module-thickness light space and each 1 means a one-module-thickness dark bar. Figure 9.10 illustrates how the thicknesses of the spaces and bars are translated into a binary code.

Table 9.1 shows the binary code for all digits. Notice that the code for the digits in the product number (the block of five digits on the right side) can be obtained from the code for the digits in the manufacturer's number (the block of digits on the left side), and vice versa, by replacing each 0 by a 1 and each 1 by a 0. Thus the code 0111011 for 7 in a manufacturer's number becomes 1000100 in the product number. Also notice that each manufacturer's number has an odd number of 1s, whereas each product number has an even number of 1s. This permits a computer linked with an optical scanner to determine whether the bar code was scanned left to right or right to left. (If the first block of digits has an even number of 1s for each digit, the scanning is being done right to left.) Thus scanning can be done in either direction without ambiguity.

Entomologist Stephen Buchmann developed a reliable, inexpensive way to track bees using the same technology that supermarkets use to speed up the checkout lines and keep track of inventory. He glued bar code labels onto the backs of 100 bees and placed a laser scanner above the hive. In the past, the researchers marked bees with paint or tags, but the monitoring of activity required the presence of a human observer.

FIGURE 9.10
Translation of bars and space modules into binary code (see top of bars). The guard pattern defines a single module thickness for a bar and a space.

TABLE 9.1	Binary UPC Coding	
Digit	Manufacturer's Number	Product Number
0	0001101	1110010
1	0011001	1100110
2	0010011	1101100
3	0111101	1000010
4	0100011	1011100
5	0110001	1001110
6	0101111	1010000
7	0111011	1000100
8	0110111	1001000
9	0001011	1110100

Optional   *Encoding Personal Data*

Consider this social security number: 189-31-9431. What information about the holder can be deduced from the number? Only that the holder obtained it in Pennsylvania (see Spotlight 9.5). Figure 9.11 shows an Illinois driver's license number: I225-1637-2133. What information about the holder can be deduced from this number? This time we can determine the date of birth, sex, and much about the person's name.

These two examples illustrate the extremes in coding personal data. The social security number has no personal data encoded in the number. It is entirely determined by the place and time it is issued, not the individual to whom it is assigned. In contrast, in some states the driver's license numbers are entirely determined by personal information about the holders. It is no coincidence that the unsophisticated social security numbering scheme predates computers. Agencies that have large data bases that include personal information such as names, sex, and dates of birth find it convenient to encode these data into identification numbers. Examples

FIGURE 9.11
Illinois driver's license.

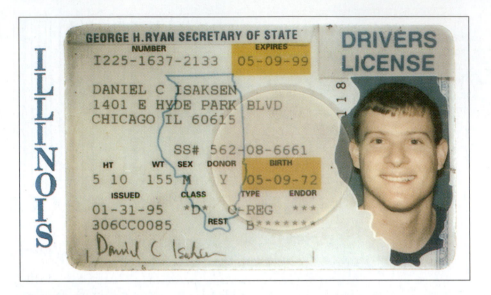

of such agencies are the National Archives (where census records are kept), genealogical research centers, the Library of Congress, and state motor vehicle departments.

There are many methods in use to encode personal data such as name, sex, and date of birth. Perhaps the most widely used application of these methods is to assign driver's license numbers in some states. Coding license numbers solely from personal data enables automobile insurers, government entities, and law enforcement agencies to determine the number from the personal data.

Many states encode the surname, first name, middle initial, date of birth, and sex by quite sophisticated schemes (see Figure 9.11).

In one scheme the first four characters of the license number are obtained by applying the **Soundex Coding System** to the surname as follows:

1. Delete all occurrences of h and w. (For example, Schworer becomes Scorer and Hughgill becomes uggill.)
2. Assign numbers to the remaining letters as follows:

   a, e, i, o, u, y → 0
   b, f, p, v → 1   1 → 4
   c, g, j, k, q, s, x, z → 2   m, n → 5
   d, t → 3   r → 6

3. If two or more letters with the same numerical value are adjacent, omit all but the first. (For example, Scorer becomes Sorer and uggill becomes ugil.)
4. Delete the first character of the original name if still present. (Sorer becomes orer.)
5. Delete all occurrences of a, e, i, o, u, and y.
6. Retain only the first three digits corresponding to the remaining letters;

SPOTLIGHT 9.5

Social Security Numbers

The first three digits of social security numbers show where the number was applied for. Changes in population have forced some numbers to be moved or assigned out of sequence over the years.

001–003	New Hampshire	387–399	Wisconsin	526–527	Arizona
004–007	Maine	400–407	Kentucky	& 600–602	
008–009	Vermont	408–415	Tennessee	528–529	Utah
010–034	Massachusetts	416–424	Alabama	530	Nevada
035–039	Rhode Island	425–428	Mississippi	531–539	Washington
040–049	Connecticut	& 587–588		540–544	Oregon
050–134	New York	429–432	Arkansas	545–573	California
135–158	New Jersey	433–439	Louisiana	& 602–626	
159–211	Pennsylvania	440–448	Oklahoma	574	Alaska
212–220	Maryland	449–467	Texas	575–576	Hawaii
221–222	Delaware	468–477	Minnesota	577–579	District of Columbia
223–231	Virginia	478–485	Iowa	580	Virgin Islands
232–236	West Virginia	486–500	Missouri	580–584	Puerto Rico
232, 237–246	North Carolina	501–502	North Dakota	& 596–599	
247–251	South Carolina	503–504	South Dakota	586	Guam
252–260	Georgia	505–508	Nebraska	586	American Samoa
261–267	Florida	509–515	Kansas	586	Philippines
& 589–595		516–517	Montana	700–728	*through July 1, 1963,*
268–302	Ohio	518–519	Idaho		*reserved for railroad*
303–317	Indiana	520	Wyoming		*employees*
318–361	Illinois	521–524	Colorado		
362–386	Michigan	525 & 585	New Mexico		

Source: Social Security Administration.

append trailing zeros if fewer than three letters remain; precede the three digits by the first letter of the surname.

Figure 9.12 shows three examples.

What is the advantage of this method? It is an error-correcting scheme. Indeed, it is designed so that likely misspellings of a name nevertheless result in the correct coding of the name. For example, frequent misspellings of the name Erickson are Ericksen, Eriksen, Ericson, and Ericsen. Observe that all of these yield the same coding as Erickson. If a law enforcement official, a genealogical researcher, a librarian, or an airline reservation agent wanted to pull up the file from a data bank for someone whose name was pronounced "Erickson," the correct spelling

Step 1   Step 2
Schworer → Scorer → Scorer
220606

Step 3   Step 4   Step 5   Step 6
→   Sorer → orer → rr → S-660
20606   0606   66

Step 1   Step 2
Hughgill → uggill → uggill
022044

Step 3   Step 4   Step 5   Step 6
→   ugil → ugil → gl → H-240
0204   0204   24

Step 1   Step 2
Schmidlapper → Scmidlapper → Scmidlapper
22503401106

Step 3   Step 4   Step 5   Step 6
→   Smidlaper → midlaper → mdlpr → S-534
250340106   50340106   534116

FIGURE 9.12   The Soundex Coding System.

isn't essential because the computer searches for records that are coded as E-625 for all spelling variations. (The Soundex system was designed for the U.S. Census Bureau when much census data were obtained orally. Airlines use a somewhat different system called the *Davidson Consonant Code*.)

There are many schemes for encoding the date of birth and the sex in driver's license numbers. For example, the last five digits of Illinois and Florida driver's license numbers capture the year and date of birth as well as the sex. In Illinois, each day of the year is assigned a three-digit number in sequence beginning with 001 for January 1. However, each month is assumed to have 31 days. Thus, March 1 is given the number 063 since both January and February are assumed to have 31 days. These numbers are then used to identify the month and day of birth of male drivers. For females, the scheme is identical except 600 is added to the number. The last two digits of the year of birth, separated by a dash (probably to obscure that fact that they represent the year of birth), are listed in the fifth and fourth positions from the end of the driver's license number. Thus, a male born on October 13, 1940, would have the last five digits 4-0292 ($292 = 9 \cdot 31 + 13$), whereas a female born on the same day would have 4-0892. The scheme to identify birth date and sex in Florida is the same as in Illinois except each month is assumed to have 40 days and 500 is added for women. For example, the five digits 4-9585 belong to a woman born on March 5, 1949. ◆

REVIEW VOCABULARY

Bar code   A code that employs bars and spaces to represent information.

Binary code   A coding scheme that uses two symbols, usually 0 and 1.

Codabar   An error-detection method used by all major credit card companies, many libraries, blood banks, and others.

Code   A group of symbols that represent information together with a set of rules for interpreting the symbols.

Code 39   An alphanumeric code that is widely used on nonretail items.

Decoding   Translating code into data.

Encoding   Translating data into code.

Error-detecting code   A code that detects certain types of errors.

International Standard Book Number (ISBN)   A 10-digit identification number used on books through-

out the world that contains a check digit for error detection.

Postnet code   The bar code used by the U.S. Postal Service for ZIP codes.

Soundex Coding System   An encoding scheme for surnames based on sound.

Universal Product Code (UPC)   A bar code and identification number that are used on most retail items. The UPC code detects 100% of all single-digit errors and most other types of errors.

Weights   Numbers used in the calculation of check digits.

ZIP code   A five-digit code used by the U.S. Postal Service to divide the country into geographical units to speed sorting of the mail.

ZIP + 4 code   The nine-digit code used by the U.S. Postal Service to refine ZIP codes into smaller units.

SUGGESTED READINGS

COLLINS, D. J., AND N. WHIPPLE. *Using Bar Code,* Data Capture Institute, Duxbury, Mass., 1990. Contains extensive information on bar codes.

DAVIDSON, L. Retrieval of misspelled names in an airline passenger record system, *Communications of the Association for Computing Machinery,* 5 (1962): 169–171. Describes the method used by airlines (the Davidson Consonant Code) to store and retrieve passenger names.

GALLIAN, J. Assigning driver's license numbers, *Mathematics Magazine,* 64 (1992): 13–22. Discusses various methods used by the states to assign driver's license numbers. Several of these methods include check digits for error detection.

GALLIAN, J. The mathematics of identification numbers, *College Mathematics Journal,* 22 (1991): 194–202. A comprehensive survey of check digit schemes that are associated with identification numbers.

GALLIAN, J. Error detection methods, *ACM Computing Surveys,* 28 (1996): 504–517. A detailed description of numerous error-detection methods.

GALLIAN, J., AND S. WINTERS. Modular arithmetic in the marketplace, *American Mathematical Monthly,* 95 (1988): 548–551. A detailed analysis of the check digit schemes presented in this chapter. In particular, the error-detection rates for the various schemes are given.

HARMAN, C. K., AND R. ADAMS. *Reading Between the Lines,* Helmers, Peterborough, N.H., 1989. Contains extensive information on bar codes.

PHILIPS, LAWRENCE. Hanging on the Metaphone, *Computer Language,* 7 (December 1990): 39–43. Describes a sound-based retrieval algorithm that in some respects is superior to Soundex.

ROUGHTON, KAREN, AND DAVID A. TYCKOSEN. Browsing with sound: Sound-based codes and automated authority control, *Information Technology and Libraries,* 4 (June 1985): 130–136. Explains the Soundex system and the Davidson Consonant Code and their uses. The Davidson Consonant Code is a sound-based retrieval algorithm used by airline passengers retrieval systems.

WAGNER, N., AND P. PUTTER. Error detecting decimal digits, *Communications of the Association for Computing*

Machinery, 32 (1989): 106–110. Describes the experience of two mathematicians hired by a large mail-order company to make recommendations for an error-correction scheme for the company's account numbers. They recommended a four-digit method.

SUGGESTED WEB SITES

http://www.d.umn.edu/~jgallian/fapp5   This Web site enables users to calculate check digits using the various methods discussed in this chapter. Also included are the methods used by several states to assign driver's license numbers.

http://www.upl.cs.wisc.edu/cgi-bin/wilic   This site enables users to determine a Wisconsin driver's

license number from the person's name and date of birth. Moreover, after the user enters a valid Wisconsin driver's license number, the site will list many possible names that will produce the number, as well as the date of birth corresponding to the entered number.

SKILLS CHECK

1. Suppose a U.S. Postal Service money order is numbered 1012065994X, and the last digit is obliterated. What is the missing digit?

   (a)   1
   (b)   8
   (c)   The missing digit cannot be determined.

2. Suppose an American Express Travelers Cheque is numbered X425036790, and the first digit is obliterated. What is the missing digit?

   (a)   0
   (b)   9
   (c)   The missing digit cannot be uniquely determined.

3. Is the number 105408970012 a legitimate airline ticket number?

   (a)   Yes.
   (b)   No, but if the final digit is changed to a 5, the resulting number 105408970015 is legitimate.

   (c)   No, but if the final digit is changed to a 6, the resulting number 105408970016 is legitimate.

4. Determine the check digit that should be appended to the UPC code 0-14300-25433.

   (a)   1
   (b)   9
   (c)   Another number

5. Determine the check digit that should be appended to the bank identification number 01500085.

   (a)   1
   (b)   9
   (c)   Another number

6. Suppose the ISBN 0-1750-3549-0 is incorrectly reported as 0-1750-3540-0. Which of the following statements is true?

   (a)   This error will not be detected by the check digit.

(b) While this particular error will be detected, the check digit does not detect all single-digit errors in ISBNs.

(c) Any single-digit error in an ISBN is detectable by the check digit.

7. Suppose that the Postnet code is incorrectly reported as 20001-5800-7. You know that only the sixth digit is incorrectly reported. Which of these statements is true?

(a) It is impossible to determine the correct digit for the sixth position.

(b) It is possible to determine the correct digit in this case. However, it was necessary to know which digit was incorrectly reported.

(c) It is possible to determine the correct digit in this case. Moreover, it was not necessary to know which digit was incorrectly reported.

EXERCISES ▲ *Optional.* ■ *Advanced.* ◆ *Discussion.*

Postnet Codes

1. Determine the ZIP + 4 code and check digit for each of the following Postnet bar codes.:

(a)
(b)
(c)

2. Determine the ZIP + 4 code and check digit for each of the following Postnet bar codes:

(a)
(b)
(c)

3. In each Postnet bar code below, exactly one mistake occurs (that is, a long bar appears instead of a short one, or vice versa). Determine the correct ZIP code.

(a)
(b)
(c)

4. Below is a 12-digit delivery-point bar code. Determine the ZIP + 4 number, the last two digits of the street address, and the check digit.

5. Explain why any two errors in a particular block of five bars in a Postnet are always detectable. Explain why not all such errors can be corrected.

Identification Numbers

6. Determine the check digit for a money order with identification number 7234541780.

7. Determine the check digit for a money order with identification number 395398164.

8. Suppose a money order with the identification number and check digit 21720421168 is erroneously copied as 27750421168. Will the check digit detect the error? Explain your reasoning.

9. Determine the check digit for the United Parcel Service (UPS) identification number 873345672.

10. Determine the check digit for the Avis rental car with identification number 540047.

11. Determine the check digit for the airline ticket number 30860422052.

12. Determine the check digit for the UPC number 05074311502.

13. Determine the check digit for the UPC number 38137009213.

14. Determine the check digit for the ISBN 0-669-33907.

15. Determine the check digit for the ISBN 0-669-19493.

16. Determine the check digit for the bank number 09100001.

17. Determine the check digit for the bank number 09190204.

18. Determine if the Master Card number 3541 0232 0033 2270 is valid.

19. Use the Codabar scheme to determine the check digit for the number 300125600196431.

20. Determine the check character for the Code 39 number 210SA0162305ZA. (Assume the code uses only 36 characters.)

21. Determine the check character for the number 3050-0000 HEAD using the 43-character Code 39 scheme. (Be sure to include the hyphen and space as characters.)

22. Change 173 into Postnet code.

23. Is there any mathematical reason for a check digit to be at the end of an identification number? Explain your reasoning.

24. Suppose the first block of a UPC bar code following the guard bar pattern a scanner reads is 1000100. Is the scanner reading left to right or right to left?

25. For some products, such as soft-drink cans and magazines, an 8-digit UPC number called Version E is used instead of the 12-digit number. The method of calculating the eighth digit, which is the check digit, depends on the value of the seventh digit. Use the fact that the check digit a_8 for a UPC Version E identification number $a_1a_2a_3a_4a_5a_6a_7$, where a_7 is 0, 1, or 2, is chosen so that $a_1 + a_2 + 3a_3 + 3a_4 + a_5 + 3a_6 + a_7 + a_8$ is divisible by 10 to determine the check digit for the following Version E numbers:

    (a) 0121690
    (b) 0274551
    (c) 0760022
    (d) 0496580

26. Use the fact that the check digit a_8 for a UPC Version E identification number $a_1a_2a_3a_4a_5a_6a_7$, where a_7 is 4, is chosen so that $a_1 + a_2 + 3a_3 +$

$a_4 + 3a_5 + 3a_6 + a_8$ is divisible by 10 to determine the check digit for the following Version E numbers:

    (a) 0754704
    (b) 0774714
    (c) 0724444

■ 27. The ISBN 0-669-03925-4 is the result of a transposition of two adjacent digits not involving the first or last digit. Determine the correct ISBN.

28. Explain why the bank scheme will detect the error $751 \cdots \rightarrow 157 \cdots$, but the UPC scheme will not.

29. Suppose the check digit a_9 for bank checks were chosen to be the last digit of $3a_1 + 7a_2 + a_3 + 3a_4 + 7a_5 + a_6 + 3a_7 + 7a_8$ instead of the way described in the chapter. How would this compare with the actual check digit?

Encoding Personal Data (Optional)

30. Determine the Soundex code for Smith, Schmid, Smyth, and Schmidt.

31. Determine the Soundex code for Skow, Sachs, Lennon, Lloyd, Ehrheart, and Ollenburger.

32. Determine the last five digits of an Illinois driver's license number for a male born on July 18, 1942.

33. In Florida the last three digits of the driver's license number of a female with birth month m and birth date b are $40(m - 1) + b + 500$. For both males and females, the fourth and fifth digits from the end give the year of birth. Determine the last five digits of a Florida driver's license number for a female born on July 18, 1942.

Additional Exercises

34. In Florida the last three digits of the driver's license number of a male with birth month m and birth date b are $40(m - 1) + b$. For both males and females, the fourth and fifth digits from the end give the year of birth. Determine the dates of birth of

people with the numbers whose last five digits are 42218 and 53953.

35.   For driver's license numbers issued in New York prior to September 1992, the last two digits were the year of birth. The three digits preceding the year encoded the sex and the month and day of birth. For a woman with birth month m and birth date b the three digits were $63m + 2b + 1$. For a man with birth month m and birth date b the three digits were $63m + 2b$. Determine the birth months, birth dates, and sexes of drivers with the three digits 248 and 601 preceding the year.

■ 36.   The state of Utah appends a ninth digit a_9 to an eight-digit driver's license number $a_1a_2 \cdots a_8$ so that $9a_1 + 8a_2 + 7a_3 + 6a_4 + 5a_5 + 4a_6 + 3a_7 + 2a_8 + a_9$ is divisible by 10.

(a)   If the first eight digits of a Utah license number are 14910573, what is the ninth digit?

(b)   Suppose a legitimate Utah license number 149105767 is miscopied as 149105267. How would you know a mistake was made? Is there any way you could determine the correct number? Suppose you know the error was in the seventh position, could you correct the mistake?

(c)   If a legitimate Utah number 149105767 were miscopied as 199105767, would you be able to tell a mistake was made? Explain.

(d)   Explain why any transposition error involving adjacent digits of a Utah number would be detected.

37.   Form all possible strings consisting of exactly three a's and two b's and arrange the strings in alphabetical order (for example, the first two possibilities are *aaabb* and *aabab*). Do you see any relationship between your list and the Postnet code?

■ 38.   Suppose the check digit a_{10} of ISBN numbers were chosen so that $a_1 + 2a_2 + 3a_3 + 4a_4 + 5a_5 + 6a_6 + 7a_7 + 8a_8 + 9a_9 + 10a_{10}$ is divisible by 11 instead of the way described in the chapter.

How would this compare with the actual check digit?

■ 39.   The Canadian province of Quebec assigns a check digit a_{12} to an 11-digit driver's license number $a_1a_2 \cdots a_{11}$ so that $12a_1 + 11a_2 + 10a_3 + 9a_4 + 8a_5 + 7a_6 + 6a_7 + 5a_8 + 4a_9 + 3a_{10} + 2a_{11} + a_{12}$ is divisible by 10. Criticize this method. Describe all single-digit errors that are undetected by this scheme. How does the transposition of two adjacent digits of a number affect the check digit of a number?

40.   Most recently published books include a bar code on the back cover that has the ISBN above the bars and a 13-digit identification number below the bars. Examine several books with a bar code on the back cover. How does the number below the bar code differ from the UPC code? How is the number below the bar code related to the ISBN number? Given the fact that the last digit in the number below the bar code is a check digit, determine how it is calculated.

41.   Determine the check digit for the VIN JM1GD222J1581570. (See Spotlight 9.3 for a description of the method to be used.)

42.   Below is an actual identification number and bar code from a roll of wallpaper. What appears to be wrong with them? Speculate on the reason for the apparent violation of the UPC format.

5 011419 194056

Building Regulations: 1985 Class 0
FINE ART WALLCOVERINGS LTD.
HOLMES CHAPEL, CHESHIRE
MADE IN ENGLAND
FABRIQUE EN ANGLETERRE

43.   The state of Washington encodes the last two digits of the year of birth into driver's license numbers (in positions 8 and 9) by subtracting the two-digit number from 100. For example, a person born in 1942 has 58 in positions 8 and 9, whereas a person born in 1971 has 29 in positions 8 and 9. Speculate on the reason for subtracting the birth year from 100.

44. Driver's license number assignment schemes that utilize personal data occasionally produce the same number for different people. Speculate about circumstances under which this is more likely to occur.

■ 45. Consider a UPC number in which the digits 7 and 2 appear consecutively (that is, the number has the form $\cdots 72 \cdots$). Will the error caused by transposing these digits (that is, the number is taken as $\cdots 27 \cdots$) be detected? What if the digits 6 and 2 are transposed instead? State the general criterion for the detection of an error of the form

$$\cdots ab \cdots \longrightarrow \cdots ba \cdots$$

using the UPC scheme.

▲ 46. Apply the Soundex code to common ways to misspell your name. Do they give the same code as your name does?

◆ 47. The Canadian postal system has assigned each geographical region a six-character code composed of alternating letters and digits, such as P7B5E1 and K7L3N6. Discuss the advantages this scheme has over the five-digit ZIP code used in the United States.

48. Speculate on the reason why telephone numbers, social security numbers, and serial numbers on most currency do not have check digits.

TECHNOLOGY CORNER

U.S. Postal Service Money Orders

The final digit of a USPS money order is computed by adding the first 10 digits, dividing this sum by 9, and reporting the remainder. For example, in the spreadsheet shown in Figure 9-13, the 10 digits are listed in a column and the sum is calculated, which is then divided by 9. The repeating decimal digit of the quotient is the check digit.

	A	B
1	Money Order digits	
2	8	
3	9	
4	3	
5	9	
6	4	
7	6	
8	0	
9	9	
10	2	
11	8	
12		
13	58	sum
14	6.444444	sum/9
15	4	check digit

FIGURE 9.13

TASK 1. Find all single-digit errors that can go undetected in the spreadsheet shown in Figure 9-13.

TASK 2. Create a spreadsheet that computes the check digit for American Express Travelers Cheques. Determine if the following is a legitimate identification number for an AmEx Travelers Cheque: 3291023916.

UPC Codes

Some identification numbers, including UPC codes, use a weighted scheme. A UPC code with digits $a_1 \, a_2 \cdots a_{12}$ is assumed to be error-free when the sum $3a_1 + a_2 + 3a_3 + a_4 + \cdots + 3a_{11} + a_{12}$ is a multiple of 10. The spreadsheet shown in Figure 9-14 illustrates these calculations.

TASK 3. Sometimes transposed digits in a UPC code can go undetected. Is it possible to exchange two adjacent digits in the above example without the error being detected?

TASK 4. Create a spreadsheet that models the ISBN coding scheme. If the ISBN number of this textbook

	A	B	C	D
1	UPC digits	weights	digit*weight	
2	0	3	0	
3	7	1	7	
4	7	3	21	
5	2	1	2	
6	7	3	21	
7	2	1	2	
8	5	3	15	
9	7	1	7	
10	9	3	27	
11	5	1	5	
12	2	3	6	
13	7	1	7	
14				
15			120	sum

FIGURE 9.14

is incorrectly entered so that three consecutive digits are scrambled, does the scheme detect the error? Try a few examples.

Exploration

Create a set of weights that, when multiplied by the digits of your social security number, sums to a multiple of 10. Can you choose weights so that any single digit error is detected?

writing projects

1 ▶   Prepare a report on coded information in your location. Possibilities for investigation include driver's license numbers in your state; student ID numbers and bar codes at your school; bar codes used by your school library and city library. Identify the coding schemes and, when possible, determine whether a check digit is employed. Include samples. The Suggested Readings for this chapter contain information that will assist you.

2 ▶   Prepare a report on the driver's license coding schemes used by Minnesota, Michigan, Maryland, and Washington (the first three states use the same method). J. Gallian's "Assigning Driver's License Numbers" (see Suggested Readings) has the information you will need.

3 ▶   Imagine that you are employed by a small company that doesn't use identification numbers and bar codes for its employees or products. As requested by your boss, prepare a report discussing the various methods and make a recommendation.

4 ▶   The Davidson Consonant Code and Metaphone are two text-retrieval algorithms based on sound that are alternatives to Soundex. Prepare a report on either of these encoding schemes. The article by Roughton and Tyckosen and the one by Philips (see Suggested Readings) contain the information you will need.

5 ▶   Prepare a report on the check digit method used on German currency. J. Gallian's article "Error Detection Methods" (see Suggested Readings) has the information you will need.

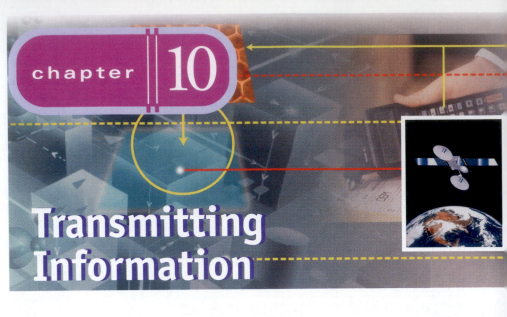

chapter 10

Transmitting Information

> "... mathematicians and engineers have devised highly sophisticated schemes to build extra information in messages composed of 0s and 1s."

Data stored in computers may be modified by naturally occurring radiation; information transmitted from communication satellites and space probes is subject to a variety of elecromagnetic interference; compact discs are corrupted by dust, dirt, scratches, and fingerprints; magnetic tapes deteriorate; and entry of data into computers by humans is subject to frequent error. In this chapter we illustrate a mathematical method for correcting errors. We also illustrate a way data can be coded to reduce transmission time and storage space, and ways to securely transmit secret messages.

Binary Codes

Because of the way computers are built, in high-tech applications such as compact disc players, fax machines, high-definition television, modems, and signals sent back from space probes, data are represented as strings of 0s and 1s rather than the usual digits 0 through 9 and letters A through Z. Recall from Chapter 9 that a system for coding data with 0s and 1s is called a *binary code*. There are many binary codes in use. In this section we will illustrate one way binary codes can be devised so that errors can be corrected.

The idea behind error-correction schemes is simple and one you often use. To illustrate, suppose you are reading the employment section of a newspaper and you see the phrase "must have a minimum of bive years experience." Instantly you detect an error since "bive" is not a word in the English language. Moreover, you are fairly confident that the intended word is "five." Why so?

Because "five" is a word and it makes the phrase sensible. In other phrases, words such as "bike" or "give" might be sensible alternatives to "bive." Using the extra information provided by the context, we are often able to infer the intended meaning when errors occur.

Over the past 40 years mathematicians and engineers have devised highly sophisticated schemes to build extra information into messages composed of 0s and 1s that often permits one to infer the correct message even though the message may have been received incorrectly (see Spotlight 10.1). As a simple example, let's say that our message is 1001. We will build extra information into this message with the aid of the diagram in Figure 10.1. Begin by placing the four message digits in the four overlapping regions I, II, III, IV, with the digit in position 1 (starting at the left of the sequence) in region I, the digit in position 2 in region II, and so on. For regions V, VI, and VII, assign 0 or 1 so that the total number of 1s in each circle is even. See Figure 10.2.

We have now encoded our message 1001 using the diagram as 1001101. Now suppose that this encoded message is received as 0001101 (an error in the first position). How would we know an error was made? We place each digit from the received message in its appropriate region as in Figure 10.3.

Noting that in both circles A and B there is an odd number of 1s, we instantly realize that something is wrong, since the intended message had an even number of 1s in each circle. How do we correct the error? Since circles A and B have the wrong parity (parity refers to the oddness or evenness of a number: even integers have **even parity**; odd integers have **odd parity**) and C does not, the error is located in the portion of the diagram in circles A and B, but not in circle C; that is, region I (see Figure 10.4). Here we also see the advantage of using only 0s and 1s to encode data. If you have only two possibilities and one of them is incorrect, then the other one must be correct. Since the 0 in region I is incorrect, we know 1 is correct. This technique can be used to encode all 16 possible binary messages of

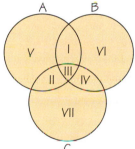

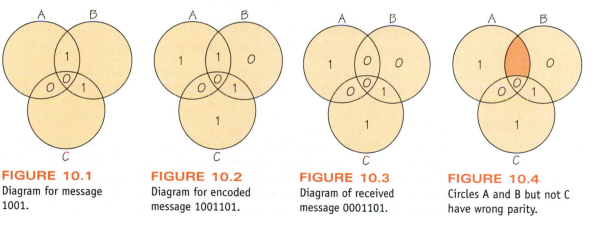

FIGURE 10.1
Diagram for message 1001.

FIGURE 10.2
Diagram for encoded message 1001101.

FIGURE 10.3
Diagram of received message 0001101.

FIGURE 10.4
Circles A and B but not C have wrong parity.

SPOTLIGHT 10.1

The Ubiquitous Reed–Solomon Codes

Irving Reed and Gustave Solomon at the Jet Propulsion Laboratory in 1989 monitor the encounter of *Voyager 2* with Neptune.

One of the mathematical ideas underlying current error-correcting techniques for everything from computer hard disk drives to CD players was first introduced in 1960 by Irving Reed and Gustave Solomon. Reed–Solomon codes made possible the stunning pictures of the outer planets sent back by the space probes *Voyager 1* and *2*. They make it possible to scratch a compact disc and still enjoy the music.

"When you talk about CD players and digital audio tape and now digital television, and various other digital imaging systems that are coming—all of those Reed–Solomon [codes] as an integral part of the system," says Robert McEliece, a coding theorist at Caltech.

Why? Because digital information consists of 0s and 1s, and a physical device may occasionally confuse the two. *Voyager 2*, for example, was transmitting data at incredibly low power—barely a whisper—over billions of miles. Error-correcting codes are a kind of safety net, mathematical insurance against the vagaries of an imperfect material world.

In 1960, the theory of error-correcting codes was only about a decade old. Through the 1950s, a

number of researchers began experimenting with a variety of error-correcting codes. But the Reed–Solomon paper, McEliece says, "hit the jackpot." "In hindsight it seems obvious," Reed recently said. However, he added, "coding theory was not a subject when we published the paper." The two authors knew they had a nice result; they didn't know what impact the paper would have.

Four decades later, the impact is clear. The vast array of applications, both current and pending, has settled the questions of the practicality and significance of Reed–Solomon codes. Billions of dollars in modern technology depend on ideas that stem from Reed and Solomon's original work.

Source: Adapted from an article by Barry Cipra, with permission from *SIAM News*, January 1993, p. 1. © by SIAM. All rights reserved.

length 4, as shown in the right column of Table 10.1. The encoded messages are called *code words.* The extra three digits appended to each string of length 4 provides the "extra information" that is sufficient to infer the intended four-digit message as long as the received seven-digit message has at most one error. If a received message has two or more errors, this method will not always yield the correct message.

TABLE 10.1

Message		Code Word
0000	→	0000000
0001	→	0001011
0010	→	0010111
0100	→	0100101
1000	→	1000110
1100	→	1100011
1010	→	1010001
1001	→	1001101
0110	→	0110010
0101	→	0101110
0011	→	0011100
1110	→	1110100
1101	→	1101000
1011	→	1011010
0111	→	0111001
1111	→	1111111

Encoding with Parity-Check Sums

In practice, binary messages consist of strings longer than four digits, and diagrams are too cumbersome for encoding them and decoding them. Rather, the messages are encoded by appending extra digits determined by the parity of various sums of certain portions of the messages. We illustrate this method for the 16 messages shown in the left column of Table 10.1. (See also Spotlight 10.2.)

Our goal is to take any binary string $a_1a_2a_3a_4$ and append three check digits $c_1c_2c_3$ so that any single error in any of the seven positions can be corrected. This is done as follows: choose

$c_1 = 0$ if $a_1 + a_2 + a_3$ is even
$c_1 = 1$ if $a_1 + a_2 + a_3$ is odd
$c_2 = 0$ if $a_1 + a_3 + a_4$ is even
$c_2 = 1$ if $a_1 + a_3 + a_4$ is odd
$c_3 = 0$ if $a_2 + a_3 + a_4$ is even
$c_3 = 1$ if $a_2 + a_3 + a_4$ is odd

The sums $a_1 + a_2 + a_3$, $a_1 + a_3 + a_4$, and $a_2 + a_3 + a_4$ are called **parity-check sums.** They are so named because their function is to guarantee that the sum of various components of the encoded message is even. Indeed, c_1 is defined so that

SPOTLIGHT
10.2

Neil Sloane

In the middle of Neil Sloane's office, which is in the center of AT&T Bell Laboratories, which in turn is at the heart of the Information Age, there sits a tidy little pyramid of shiny steel balls stacked up like oranges at a neighborhood grocery. Sloane has been pondering different ways to pile up balls of one kind or another for most of his professional life. Along the way he has become one of the world's leading researchers in the field of sphere packing, a field that has become indispensable to modern communications. Without it we might not have modems or compact discs or satellite photos of Neptune. "Computers would still exist," says Sloane. "But they wouldn't be able to talk to one another."

To exchange information rapidly and correctly, machines must code it. As it turns out, designing a code is a lot like packing spheres: both involve cramming things together into the tightest possible arrangement. Sloane, fittingly, is also one of the world's leading coding theorists, not least because he has studied the shiny steel balls on his desk so intently.

Here's how a code might work. Imagine, for example, that you want to transmit a child's drawing that used every one of the 64 colors found in a jumbo box of Crayola crayons. For transmission, you could code each of those colors as a number—say, the integers from 1 to 64. Then you could divide the image into many small units, or pixels, and assign a code to each one based on the color it contains. The transmission would then be a steady stream of those numbers, one for each pixel.

In digital systems, however, all those numbers would have to be represented as strings of 0s and

Neil Sloane
at work, wearing his famous "Codemart" T-shirt (952 points in a sphere).

1s. Because there are 64 possible combinations of 0s and 1s in a six-digit string, you could handle the entire Crayola palette with 64 different six-digit "code words." For example, 000000 could represent the first color, 000001 the next color, 000010 the next, and so on.

But in a noisy signal two different code words might look practically the same. A bit of noise, for example, might shift a spike of current to the wrong place, so that 001000 looks like 000100. The receiver might then wrongly color someone's eyes. An efficient way to keep the colors straight in spite of noise is to add four extra digits to the six-digit code words. The receiver, programmed to know the 64 permissible combinations, could now spot any other combination as an error introduced by noise and it would automatically correct the error to the "nearest" permissible color.

In fact, says Sloane, "If any of those ten digits were wrong, you could still figure out what the right crayon was."

Source: Adapted from an article by David Berreby, *Discover*, October 1990.

$a_1 + a_2 + a_3 + c_1$ is even. (Recall that this is precisely how the value in region V was defined.) Similarly, c_2 is defined so that $a_1 + a_2 + a_4 + c_2$ is even, and c_3 is defined so that $a_2 + a_3 + a_4 + c_3$ is even.

Let us revisit the message 1001 we considered in Figure 10.1. Then $a_1a_2a_3a_4 = 1001$ and

$c_1 = 1$ since $1 + 0 + 0$ is odd
$c_2 = 0$ since $1 + 0 + 1$ is even

and

$c_3 = 1$ since $0 + 0 + 1$ is odd

So, because $c_1c_2c_3 = 101$, we have $1001 \rightarrow 1001101$.

Now how is the intended message determined from a received encoded message? This process is called **decoding.** Say, for instance, that the message 1000, which has been encoded using parity check sums as $u = 1000110$, is received as $v = 1010110$ (an error in the third position). We simply compare v with each of the 16 code words (that is, the possible correct messages) in Table 10.1 and decode it as the one that differs from v in the fewest positions. (Put another way, we decode v as the code word that agrees with v in the most positions.) In the situation that there is more than one code word that differs from v in the fewest positions, we do not decode. To carry out this comparison it is convenient to define the distance between two strings of equal length.

> The **distance between two strings** of equal length is the number of positions in which the strings differ.

For example, the distance between $v = 1010110$ and $u = 1000110$ is 1, since they differ in only one position (the third). In contrast, the distance between 1000110 and 0111001 is 7, since they differ in all seven positions. Thus our decoding procedure is simply to decode any received message v as the code word v' that is "nearest" to v in the sense that among all distances between v and code words, the distance between v and v' is a minimum. (If there is more than one possibility for v', we do not decode.) Table 10.2 shows the distance between $v = 1010110$ and all 16 code words. From this table we see that v will be decoded as u, since it differs from u in only one position while it differs from all others in the table in at least two positions. This method is called *nearest-neighbor decoding.*

> The **nearest-neighbor decoding** method decodes a received message as the code word that agrees with the message in the most positions.

TABLE 10.2

v	1010110	1010110	1010110	1010110	1010110	1010110	1010110	1010110
code word	0000000	0001011	0010111	0100101	1000110	1100011	1010001	1001101
distance	4	5	2	5	1	4	3	4
v	1010110	1010110	1010110	1010110	1010110	1010110	1010110	1010110
code word	0110010	0101110	0011100	1110100	1101000	1011010	0111001	1111111
distance	3	4	3	2	5	2	6	3

Assuming that errors occur independently, the nearest-neighbor method decodes each received message as the one it most likely represents.

The scheme we have just described was first proposed in 1948 by Richard Hamming, a mathematician at Bell Laboratories. (See Spotlight 10.3.) It is one of an infinite number of codes that are called the *Hamming codes.*

Strings of 0s and 1s obtained from all possible k-tuples of 0s and 1s by appending extra 0s and 1s using parity-check sums, as illustrated earlier, are called *binary linear codes.* The strings with the appended digits are called *code words.*

A **binary linear code** consists of words composed of 0s and 1s obtained from all possible k-tuple messages by using parity-check sums to append check digits to the messages. The resulting strings are called **code words.**

You should think of a binary linear code as a set of n-tuples where each n-tuple is composed of two parts: the message part, consisting of the original k-digit messages, and the remaining check digit part.

The longer the messages are, the more check digits are required to correct errors. For example, binary messages consisting of six digits require four check digits to ensure that all messages with one error can be decoded correctly. Where there is no possibility of confusion, it is customary to denote an n-tuple $(a_1, a_2, \ldots, a_n)$ more concisely as $a_1 a_2 \cdots a_n$, as we did in Table 10.1.

Given a binary linear code, how can we tell if it will correct errors and how many errors it will detect? It is remarkably easy. We examine all the code words to find one that has the fewest number of 1s excluding the code word consisting entirely of 0s. Call this minimum number of 1s in any nonzero code word the weight of the code and denote it by t.

The **weight of a code** is the minimum number of 1s that occur among all nonzero code words of that code.

SPOTLIGHT
10.3

Richard Hamming

Richard Hamming (right) and Fred Gruenberger discuss complicated computer technology.

Richard W. Hamming was born in Chicago, Illinois, on February 11, 1915. He graduated from the University of Chicago with a B.S. degree in mathematics. In 1939, he received an M.A. degree in mathematics from the University of Nebraska, and in 1942, a Ph.D. in mathematics from the University of Illinois.

During the latter part of World War II, Hamming was at Los Alamos, where he was involved in computing atomic bomb designs. In 1946, he joined Bell Telephone Laboratories, where he worked in mathematics, computing, engineering, and science.

When Hamming arrived at Bell Laboratories, the Model V computer there had over 9000 relays and over 50 pieces of Teletype apparatus. It occupied about 1000 square feet of floor space and weighed some 10 tons. (In computing power it equaled some of today's hand-held calculators.) The input was entered into the machine via a punched paper tape, which had two holes per row. Each row was read as a unit. The sensing relays would prevent further computation if more or less

than two holes appeared in a given row. Similar checks were used in nearly every step of a computation. If such a check failed when the operating personnel were not present, the problem had to be rerun. This inefficiency led Hamming to investigate the possibility of automatic error correction. Many years later he said to an interviewer:

> Two weekends in a row I came in and found that all my stuff had been dumped and nothing was done. I was really aroused and annoyed because I wanted those answers and two weekends had been lost. And so I said, "Damn it, if the machine can detect an error, why can't it locate the position of the error and correct it?"

In 1950, Hamming published his famous paper on error-correcting codes, resulting in the use of Hamming codes in modern computers and a new branch of information theory. Hamming died at the age of 82 in 1998.

Source: Adapted from T. Thompson, *From Error-Correcting Codes Through Sphere Packing to Simple Groups* (Washington, D. C.: Mathematical Association of America, 1983).

If t is odd, the code will correct any $(t - 1)/2$ or fewer errors; if t is even, the code will correct any $(t - 2)/2$ or fewer errors. If we prefer simply to detect errors rather than to correct them (as is often the case in applications), the code will detect any $t - 1$ or fewer errors.

Applying this test to the code in Table 10.1, we see that the weight is 3, so it will correct any $(3 - 1)/2 = 1$ error or it will detect any $3 - 1 = 2$ errors. Be careful here. We must decide *in advance* whether we want our code to correct single errors or detect double errors. It can do whichever we choose, but not both. If we decide to detect errors, then we will not decode any message that was not among our original list of encoded messages (just as "bive" is not a word in the English language). Instead, we simply note that an error was made and, in most applications, request a retransmission. An example of this occurs when a bar code reader at the supermarket detects an error and it does not emit a sound (in effect, requesting a rescanning). On the other hand, if we decide to correct errors, we will decode any received message as its nearest neighbor.

Here is an example of another binary linear code. Let the set of messages be {000, 001, 010, 100, 110, 101, 011, 111} and append three check digits c_1, c_2, and c_3 using

$c_1 = 0$ if $a_1 + a_2 + a_3$ is even
$c_1 = 1$ if $a_1 + a_2 + a_3$ is odd
$c_2 = 0$ if $a_1 + a_3$ is even
$c_2 = 1$ if $a_1 + a_3$ is odd
$c_3 = 0$ if $a_2 + a_3$ is even
$c_3 = 1$ if $a_2 + a_3$ is odd

For example, if we take $a_1a_2a_3$ as 101, we have

$c_1 = 0$ since $1 + 0 + 1$ is even
$c_2 = 0$ since $1 + 1$ is even
$c_3 = 1$ since $0 + 1$ is odd

So we encode 101 by appending 001, that is, $101 \rightarrow 101001$. The entire code is shown in Table 10.3.

Since the minimum number of 1s of any nonzero code word is 3, this code will either correct any single error or detect any double error, whichever we choose.

It is natural to ask how the method of appending extra digits with parity-check sums enables us to detect or even correct errors. Error detection is obvious. Think of how a computer spell checker works. If you type "bive" instead of "five," the spell checker detects the error because the string "bive" is not on its list of valid words. On the other hand, if you type "give" instead of "five," the spell checker will not detect the error since "give" is a valid word.

Our error-detection scheme works the same way, except that if we add extra digits to ensure that our code words differ in many positions, say t positions, then

TABLE 10.3

Message		Code Word
000	$\rightarrow$	000000
001	$\rightarrow$	001111
010	$\rightarrow$	010101
100	$\rightarrow$	100110
110	$\rightarrow$	110011
101	$\rightarrow$	101001
011	$\rightarrow$	011010
111	$\rightarrow$	111100

even $t - 1$ mistakes will not convert one code word into another code word. And if every pair of code words differs from each other in at least three positions, we can correct any single error since the incorrect received word will differ from the correct code word in one position, but it will differ from all others in two or more positions. Thus, in this case, the correct word is the "nearest neighbor." So the role of the parity-check sums is to ensure that code words differ in many positions. For example, consider the code in Table 10.1. The messages 1000 and 1100 differ in only the second position. But the two parity-check sums $a_1 + a_2 + a_3$ and $a_2 + a_3 + a_4$ will guarantee that encoded words for these messages will have different values in positions 5 and 7 as well as position 2. It is the job of mathematicians to discover the appropriate parity-check sums to correct several errors in long, complicated codes.

SPOTLIGHT
10.4

Jessie MacWilliams

An important contributor to coding theory was Jessie MacWilliams. Born in 1917 in England, she received a B.A. in 1938 and an M.A. degree in 1939 from Cambridge University and then came to the United States to study at Johns Hopkins University. After a year at Johns Hopkins, she went to Harvard, where she studied a second year. In 1955, with three children aged 13, 11, and 9, MacWilliams became a programmer at Bell Labs, where she learned about coding theory. Although she made a major discovery about codes while a programmer, she could not obtain a promotion to a math research position without a Ph.D. degree. She completed some of the requirements for the Ph.D. while working full time at Bell Labs and looking after her family. She then returned to Harvard for a year (1961–1962) and finished her degree. Interestingly, both MacWilliams and her daughter Ann were studying mathematics at Harvard at the same time.

Jessie MacWilliams

MacWilliams returned to Bell Labs, where she remained until her retirement in 1983. While at Bell Labs she made many contributions to the subject of error-correcting codes, including *The Theory of Error-Correcting Codes,* written jointly with Neil Sloane—a book that is still a leader in the field. One of her results of great theoretical importance is known as the "MacWilliams identity." She died on May 27, 1990, at the age of 73.

Data Compression

Binary linear codes are fixed-length codes. In a fixed-length code each code word is represented by the same number of digits (or symbols). In contrast, the Morse code (see Figure 10.5), designed for the telegraph, is a **variable-length code.** That is, a code in which the number of symbols for each code word may vary.

Notice that in the Morse code the letters that occur most frequently have the shortest coding, whereas the letters that occur the least frequently have the longest coding. By assigning the code in this manner, telegrams could convey more information per line than would be the case for fixed-length codes or a randomly assigned variable-length coding of the letters. The Morse code is an example of data compression. Figure 10.6 shows a typical frequency distribution for letters in English-language text material.

Data compression is the process of encoding data so that the most frequently occurring data are represented by the fewest symbols.

Let us illustrate the principles of data compression with a simple example. Biologists are able to describe genes by specifying sequences composed of the four letters A, T, G, and C, which represent the four nucleotides adenine, thymine, guanine, and cytosine, respectively. One way to encode a sequence such as AAACAGTAAC in fixed-length binary form would be to encode the letters as

$$A \longrightarrow 00 \qquad C \longrightarrow 01 \qquad T \longrightarrow 10 \qquad G \longrightarrow 11$$

The corresponding binary code for the sequence AAACAGTAAC is then

00000001001110000001

FIGURE 10.5
Morse code.

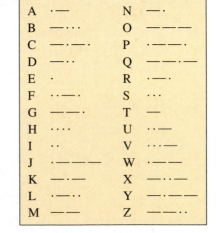

A	·—	N	—·
B	—···	O	———
C	—·—·	P	·——·
D	—··	Q	——·—
E	·	R	·—·
F	··—·	S	···
G	——·	T	—
H	····	U	··—
I	··	V	···—
J	·———	W	·——
K	—·—	X	—··—
L	·—··	Y	—·——
M	——	Z	——··

FIGURE 10.6

A widely used frequency table for letters in normal English usage.

	A	B	C	D	E	F	G	H	I	J	K	L	M
Percentage:	8	1.5	3	4	13	2	1.5	6	6.5	0.5	0.5	3.5	3

	N	O	P	Q	R	S	T	U	V	W	X	Y	Z
Percentage:	7	8	2	0.25	6.5	6	9	3	1	1.5	0.5	2	0.25

On the other hand, if we knew from experience that the hierarchy of occurrence of the letters is A, C, T and G (that is, A occurs most frequently, C second most frequently, and so on), and that A occurs much more frequently than T and G together, the most efficient binary encoding would be

$$A \longrightarrow 0 \qquad C \longrightarrow 10 \qquad T \longrightarrow 110 \qquad G \longrightarrow 111$$

For this encoding scheme the sequence AAACAGTAAC is encoded as

0001001111100010

Notice that this binary sequence has 20% fewer digits than our previous sequence, in which each letter was assigned a fixed length of 2 (16 digits versus 20 digits). However, to realize this savings, we have made decoding more difficult. For the binary sequence using the fixed length of two symbols per character, we decode the sequence by taking the digits two at a time in succession and converting them to the corresponding letters. For the compressed coding, we can decode by examining the digits in groups of three.

E X A M P L E *Decode 0001001111100010*

Consider the compressed binary sequence 0001001111100010. Look at the first three digits: 000. Since our code words have one, two, or three digits and neither 00 nor 000 is a code word, the sequence 000 can only represent the *three* code words 0, 0, and 0. Now look at the next three digits: 100. Again, since neither 1 nor 100 is a code word, the sequence 100 represents the *two* code words 10 and 0. The next three digits, 111, can only represent the code word 111 since the other three code words all contain at least one 0. Next consider the sequence 110. Since neither 1 nor 11 is a code word, the sequence 110 can only represent 110 itself. Continuing in this fashion, we can decode the entire sequence to obtain AAACAGTAAC.

The following observation can simplify the decoding process for compressed sequences. Note that 0 only occurs at the end of a code word. Thus each time you see a 0, it is the end of the code word. Also, because the code words 0, 10 and 110 end in a 0, the only circumstances under which there are three consecutive 1s is when the code word is 111. So, to quickly decode a compressed binary sequence using our coding scheme, insert a comma after every 0 and after every three consecutive 1s. The digits between the commas are code words. ◆

E X A M P L E   *Code AGAACTAATTGACA and Decode the Result*

Recall: A → 0, C → 10, T → 110, and G → 111, So

AGAACTAATTGACA ⟶ 0111001011000110110110100

To decode the encoded sequence we insert commas after every 0 and after every occurrence of 111 and convert to letters:

0,111,0, 0,10,110,0, 0,110,110,111,0,10,0
A, G, A,A,C, T, A,A, T,   T,   G, A, C,A   ◆

Modern data compression schemes were first invented in the 1950s (see Spotlight 10.5). They are now routinely used by modems and fax machines for data transmissions and by computers for data storage. In many cases data compression results in a savings of up to 50% on telephone charges or storage space.

Cryptography

Thus far we have discussed ways in which data can be encoded to detect errors or correct errors in transmission. In many situations there is also a desire for security against unauthorized interpretation of coded data (that is, a desire for secrecy). The process of disguising data is called **encryption. Cryptology** is the study of methods to make and break secret codes.

Historically, encryption was used primarily for military and diplomatic transmissions. Today encryption is pivotal for securing electronic transfers of funds and for authenticating such transactions. In September of 1998 history was made when President Clinton and Ireland's Prime Minister Bertie Ahern used digital signatures to sign an intergovernmental document. Each leader had a unique signing code and a digital certificate that served as a "digital ID," thereby ensuring that the document was approved by them. Although modern encryption schemes are extremely complex, we will illustrate the fundamental concepts involved with two simple examples.

A method used by premium television services such as HBO, Showtime, and the Disney Channel utilizes a monthly **password,** a subscriber sequence called a key, and the addition of binary sequences. We add two binary sequences $a_1a_2 \cdots a_n$ and $b_1b_2 \cdots b_n$ as follows:

$$
\begin{array}{c}
a_1a_2 \cdots a_n \\
+ \underline{b_1b_2 \cdots b_n} \\
c_1c_2 \cdots c_n
\end{array}
$$

where $c_i = 0$ if $a_i = b_i$ and $c_i = 1$ if $a_i \neq b_i$. Equivalently, $c_i = 0$ if $a_i + b_i$ is 0 or 2 and $c_i = 1$ if $a_i + b_i$ is 1. (Add a_i and b_i in the ordinary way but replace 2 by 0.)

SPOTLIGHT 10.5

David Huffman

Large networks of IBM computers use it. So do high-definition televisions, modems, and a popular electronic device that takes the brainwork out of programming a videocassette recorder. All these digital wonders rely on the results of a 40-year-old term paper by an MIT graduate student—a data compression scheme known as Huffman encoding.

In 1951 David Huffman and his classmates in an electrical engineering graduate course on information theory were given the choice of a term paper or a final exam. For the term paper, Huffman's professor had assigned what at first appeared to be a simple problem. Students were asked to find the most efficient method of representing numbers, letters, or other symbols using binary code. Huffman worked on the problem for months, developing a number of approaches, but none that he could prove to be the most efficient. Finally, he despaired of ever reaching a solution and decided to start studying for the final. Just as he was throwing his notes in the garbage, the solution came to him. "It was the most singular moment of my life," Huffman says. "There was the absolute lightning of sudden realization. It was my luck to be there at the right time and also not have my professor discourage me by telling me that other good people had struggled with the problem," he says. When presented with his student's discovery, Huffman recalls, his professor exclaimed: "Is that all there is to it!"

David Huffman

"The Huffman code is one of the fundamental ideas that people in computer science and data communications are using all the time," says Donald Knuth of Stanford University. Although others have used Huffman's code to help make millions of dollars, Huffman's main compensation was dispensation from the final exam. He never tried to patent an invention from his work and experiences only a twinge of regret at not having used his creation to make himself rich. "If I had the best of both worlds, I would have had recognition as a scientist, and I would have gotten monetary rewards," he says. "I guess I got one and not the other."

But Huffman has received other compensation. A few years ago an acquaintance told him that he had noticed that a reference to the code was spelled with a lowercase "H." Remarked his friend to Huffman, "David, I guess your name has finally entered the language."

Source: Adapted from an article by Gary Stix, *Scientific American*, September 1991, pp. 54, 58.

Encrypting a message.

E X A M P L E   *Sum of Binary Sequences*

11000111	00111011	10011100
+ 01110110	+ 01100101	+ 10011100
10110001	01011110	00000000

The data security method we describe hinges on the fact that the sum of two binary sequences $a_1 a_2 \cdots a_n + b_1 b_2 \cdots b_n = 00 \cdots 0$ if and only if the sequences are identical.

Beginning in 1984, HBO scrambled its signal. To unscramble the signal, a cable system operator or dish owner who pays a monthly fee has to have a password that is changed monthly. The password is transmitted along with the scrambled signal. Although HBO uses binary sequences of length 56, we will illustrate the method with sequences of length 8.

Let us say that the password for this month is p. Each subscriber of the service is assigned a sequence uniquely associated with him or her called a **key.** Let us say that the list of keys issued by HBO to its customers is $k_1, k_2, \ldots .$ HBO transmits the password p, and the encrypted sequences $k_1 + p, k_2 + p, \ldots$ (that is, one sequence for each authorized user). A microprocessor in each subscriber's decoding box adds its key, say k_i, to each of the encrypted sequences. That is, it calculates $k_i + (k_1 + p), k_i + (k_2 + p), \ldots .$ As it does so, the microprocessor compares each of these calculated sequences with the correct password p. When one of the sequences matches p, the microprocessor will unscramble the signal. Notice that the correct password p will be produced precisely when k_i is added to $k_i + p$, since $k_i + (k_i + p) = (k_i + k_i) + p = 00 \cdots 0 + p = p$ and $k_i + (k_j + p) \neq p$ when $k_j \neq k_i$. (That is, key k_i "unlocks" the encrypted sequence $k_i + p$ and no other.) If a subscriber with key k_i fails to pay the monthly bill, HBO can terminate the service by not transmitting the sequence $k_i + p$ the next month. ◆

E X A M P L E   *Encryption and Decoding*

Suppose the password for this month is $p = 10101100$ and your key is $k = 00111101$. One of the sequences transmitted by HBO is $k + p$:

$$
\begin{array}{r}
00111101 \\
+\ 10101100 \\
\hline
10010001
\end{array}
$$

Your decoder box adds your key $k = 00111101$ to each of the sequences received. Eventually, it finds the sequence obtained by adding the password to your key (namely, $p + k = 10010001$) and calculates

$$
\begin{array}{r}
00111101 \\
+\ 10010001 \\
\hline
10101100
\end{array}
$$

to obtain the password p. Once the password has been found, the decoder descrambles the signal.

One might suspect that a computer hacker could find the password by simply trying a large number of possible keys until one "unlocks" the password. But with sequences of length 56 there are 2^{56} possible keys, of which fewer than a million are used by HBO to scramble its monthly password. The number 2^{56} is so large (it exceeds 72 quadrillion), however, that even if one tries a billion possible keys, the chance of finding one that works is essentially 0. ◆

Optional   *Public Key Cryptography*

In the mid-1970s Ron Rivest, Adi Shamir, and Len Adleman devised an ingenious method that permits each person who is to receive a secret message to publicly tell how to scramble messages sent to him or her. And even though the method used to scramble the message is known publicly, only the person for whom it is intended will be able to unscramble the message.

Before presenting this idea, we first introduce a method of counting that you often use. For example, if it is now September, what month will it be 25 months henceforth? Of course, you answer October, but the interesting fact is that you didn't arrive at the answer by starting with September and counting off 25 months. Instead, without even thinking about it, you simply observed that $25 = 12 \cdot 2 + 1$ and you added one month to September. Similarly, if it is now Wednesday, you know that in 23 days it will be Friday. This time, you arrived at your answer by noting that $23 = 7 \cdot 3 + 2$, so you added 2 days to Wednesday instead of counting off 23 days. Likewise, if your electricity is off for 26 hours, you know you must advance your clock 2 hours, since $26 = 2 \cdot 12 + 2$. Surprisingly, this simple idea has numerous important applications in mathematics and computer science.

Before describing the method for transmitting messages secretly, it is convenient to introduce a notation for the kind of arithmetic described in the previous paragraph. For any positive integers a and n we write a mod n (read: "a modulo n" or just "a mod n") to be the remainder when a is divided by n. Thus,

$$3 \bmod 2 = 1 \text{ since } 3 = 1 \cdot 2 + 1$$
$$6 \bmod 2 = 0 \text{ since } 6 = 2 \cdot 3 + 0$$
$$4 \bmod 3 = 1 \text{ since } 4 = 1 \cdot 3 + 1$$
$$15 \bmod 3 = 0 \text{ since } 15 = 5 \cdot 3 + 0$$
$$12 \bmod 10 = 2 \text{ since } 12 = 1 \cdot 10 + 2$$
$$37 \bmod 10 = 7 \text{ since } 37 = 3 \cdot 10 + 7$$
$$98 \bmod 85 = 13 \text{ since } 98 = 1 \cdot 85 + 13$$
$$342 \bmod 85 = 2 \text{ since } 342 = 4 \cdot 85 + 2$$
$$62 \bmod 85 = 62 \text{ since } 62 = 0 \cdot 85 + 62$$

Arithmetic involving mod n is called **modular arithmetic.** One rule of modular arithmetic we will need is

$$(ab) \bmod n = ((a \bmod n)(b \bmod n)) \bmod n$$

This rule allows you to replace integers greater than or equal to n with integers less than n to simplify calculations. You should think of the rule as saying, "Mod before you multiply." ◆

EXAMPLE   *Modular Arithmetic*

$$(17 \cdot 23) \bmod 10 = ((17 \bmod 10)(23 \bmod 10)) \bmod 10$$
$$= (7 \cdot 3) \bmod 10 = 21 \bmod 10 = 1$$

$$(22 \cdot 19) \bmod 8 = ((22 \bmod 8)(19 \bmod 8)) \bmod 8$$
$$= (6 \cdot 3) \bmod 8 = 18 \bmod 8 = 2$$

$$(100 \cdot 8) \bmod 85 = ((100 \bmod 85) \cdot (8 \bmod 85)) \bmod 85$$
$$= (15 \cdot 8) \bmod 85 = 120 \bmod 85 = 35 \quad ◆$$

We now describe the Rivest, Shamir, and Adleman method by way of a simple example that nevertheless illustrates the essential features of the method. Say we wish to send the message "IBM." We convert the message to digits by replacing A by 1, B by 2, . . . , and Z by 26. So the message IBM becomes 9213. The person to whom the message is to be sent has picked two primes p and q, say, $p = 5$ and $q = 17$ (recall that a *prime* is an integer greater than 1 whose only divisors are 1 and itself), and a number r that has no divisors in common with the least common multiple m of $(p - 1) = 4$ and $(q - 1) = 16$ other than 1, say, $r = 3$, and published $n = pq = 85$ and r in a public directory. The receiver also must find a number s so that $r \cdot s = 1 \bmod m$ (this is where knowledge of p and q is necessary). That is, $3 \cdot s = 1 \bmod 16$. The number is 11. (The number s can be found by calculating successive powers of $r \bmod m$; when 1 is reached, the previous power of r is s. In our example we have

$$3 \bmod 16 = 3, \qquad 3^2 \bmod 16 = 9, \qquad 3^3 \bmod 16 - 11, \qquad 3^4 \bmod 16 = 1$$

so $s = 3^3 \bmod 16 = 11$.)

We consult this directory to find n and r, then send the "scrambled" numbers $9^3 \bmod 85$, $2^3 \bmod 85$, and $13^3 \bmod 85$ rather than 9, 2, and 13 and the receiver will unscramble them. Thus we send

$$9^3 \bmod 85 = 49$$
$$2^3 \bmod 85 = 8$$

and

$$13^3 \bmod 85 = 72$$

Now the receiver must take the numbers he or she receives, 49, 8, and 72, and convert them back to 9, 2, and 13 by calculating $49^{11} \bmod 85$, $8^{11} \bmod 85$, and $72^{11} \bmod 85$.

The calculation of $49^{11} \bmod 85$ can be simplified as follows:[1]

$$49 \bmod 85 = 49$$
$$49^2 \bmod 85 = 2401 \bmod 85 = 21$$
$$49^4 \bmod 85 = 49^2 \cdot 49^2 \bmod 85 = 21 \cdot 21 \bmod 85 + 441 \bmod 85$$
$$= 16 \bmod 85$$
$$49^8 \bmod 85 = 49^4 \cdot 49^4 \bmod 85 = 16 \cdot 16 \bmod 85 = 1$$

So $49^{11} \bmod 85 = (49^8 \bmod 85)(49^2 \bmod 85)(49 \bmod 85)$

$$= (1 \cdot 21 \cdot 49) \bmod 85$$
$$= 1029 \bmod 85$$
$$= 9 \bmod 85$$

Thus, the receiver has correctly determined the code for "I." The calculations for $8^{11} \bmod 85$ and $72^{11} \bmod 85$ are left as exercises for the reader. Notice that without knowing how pq factors, one cannot find the least common multiple of $p - 1$ and $q - 1$ (in our case, 16), and therefore the s that is needed to determine the intended message.

The procedure just described is called the **RSA public key encryption scheme** after Rivest, Shamir, and Adleman, who developed the method. The scheme is practical and secure because there exist efficient methods for finding very large prime numbers (say about 100 digits long) and for multiplying large numbers, but no efficient algorithm for factoring large integers (say about 200 digits long).

The algorithm is summarized below (page 376). (In practice, the messages are not sent one letter at a time. Rather, the entire message is converted to decimal form, with

---

[1] To determine $49^2 \bmod 85$ with a calculator, enter 49×49 to obtain 2401, then divide 2401 by 85 to obtain 28.247058. Finally, enter $2401 - (28 \times 85)$ to obtain 21.

A represented by 01, B by 02, . . . , and a space by 00. The message is then broken up into blocks of uniform size and the blocks are sent. See step 2 under Sender.)

Receiver

1. Pick very large primes p and q and compute $n = pq$.
2. Compute the least common multiple of $p - 1$ and $q - 1$; let us call it m.
3. Pick r so that it has no divisors in common with m other than 1 (any such r will do).
4. Find s so that $rs = 1$ modulo m (there is always exactly one such s between 1 and m).
5. Publicly announce n and r, but keep p, q, and s secret.

Sender

1. Convert the message to a string of digits.
2. Break up the message into uniformly sized blocks of digits, appending 0s in the last block if necessary; call them $M_1, M_2, \ldots, M_k$. For example, for a string such as 2105092315, we would use $M_1 = 2105$, $M_2 = 0923$, $M_3 = 1500$.
3. Check to see that the greatest common divisor of each M_i and n is 1. If not, n can be factored and the code is broken. (In practice, the primes p and q are so large that they exceed all M_i, so this step may be omitted.)
4. Calculate and send $R_i = M_i^r \bmod n$.

Receiver

1. For each received message R_i, calculate $R_i^s \bmod n$.
2. Convert the string of digits back to a string of characters.

Why does this method work? It works because of a basic property of modular arithmetic and the choice of r. It so happens that the number m has the property that for each x having no common divisors with n except 1, we have $x^m = 1 \bmod n$. So, because each message M_i has no common divisors with n except 1, and r was chosen so that $rs = 1 + mt$ for some t, we have modulo n:

$$R_i^s = (M_i^r)^s = M_i^{rs} = M_i^{1+mt} = M_i(M_i^m)^t = M_i 1^t = M_i \quad \blacklozenge$$

REVIEW VOCABULARY

Binary linear code   A code consisting of words composed of 0s and 1s obtained by using parity-check sums to append check digits to messages.

Code words   Words from a binary linear code.

Cryptography   The study of how to make and break secret codes.

Data compression   The process of encoding data so that the most frequently occurring data are represented by the fewest symbols.

Decoding   The process of translating received words into code words.

Distance between two messages   The distance between two messages is the number of positions in which they differ.

Encryption   The process of encoding data to protect against unauthorized interpretation.

Even parity   Even integers are said to have even parity.

Key   A string used to decode data.

Modular arithmetic   Addition and multiplication involving modulo n.

Nearest-neighbor decoding   A method that decodes a received message as the code word that agrees with the message in the most positions.

Odd parity   Odd integers are said to have odd parity.

Parity-check sums   Sums of digits whose parities determine the check digits.

Password   A word used to encode data.

RSA public key encryption   A method of encoding that permits each person to announce publicly the means by which secret messages are to be sent to him or her.

Variable-length code   A code in which the number of symbols for each code word may vary.

Weight of a code   The minimum number of 1s that occur among all nonzero code words of a code.

SUGGESTED READINGS

DENEEN, L. Secret encryption with public keys, *UMAP Journal,* 8 (1987): 9–29. Describes several ways in which modular arithmetic can be used to code secret messages, from a simple scheme used by Julius Caesar to the RSA public key encryption method.

KAHN, DAVID. *Codebreakers: The Story of Secret Writing,* Macmillan, New York, 1967. A monumental, illustrated history.

KORHEIM, ALAN G. *Cryptography: A Primer,* Wiley, New York, 1981. An introduction to cryptography.

MCELIECE, R. The reliability of computer memories, *Scientific American,* 252 (1985): 88–95. Discusses why and how error-correcting codes are employed in computer memories.

RICHARDS, I. The invisible prime factor, *American Scientist,* 70 (1982): 176–179. Explains how elementary number theory and modular arithmetic can be used to test whether an integer is prime and how prime numbers can be used to create secret codes that are extremely difficult to break.

THOMPSON, T. *From Error-Correcting Codes Through Sphere Packing to Simple Groups,* Mathematical Association of America, Washington, D.C., 1983. Chapter 1 of this award-winning book gives a fascinating historical account of the origins of error-correcting codes.

SUGGESTED WEB SITES

http://hotwired.com   This site features the latest news about encryption schemes and applications.

http://www.estamp.com   This site describes a new Web-based on-line postage service.

http://www.rsa.com   This site provides information about a variety of cryptosystems and their many applications to computing and business.

http://d.umn.edu/~jgallian/fapp5   This Web site implements the nearest-neighbor decoding method for 7-digit binary strings using the code given in Table 10.1.

SKILLS CHECK

1.   If you use the circular diagram method to encode the message 1011, what is the encoded message?

   (a)   1011001
   (b)   1011010
   (c)   1010001

2.   Suppose the message 1010010 is received and decoded using the nearest-neighbor method. What message is recovered?

   (a)   1010
   (b)   1011
   (c)   1110

3. What is the distance between received words 1011001 and 1000101?

   (a) 0

   (b) 1

   (c) 3

4. Use the encoding scheme $A \rightarrow 0$, $B \rightarrow 10$, $C \rightarrow 11$ to decode the sequence 010110.

   (a) ABCB

   (b) ABCA

   (c) ABACA

5. What is the sum of the binary sequences 1011001 and 1001101?

   (a) 0100110

   (b) 0010100

   (c) 1011101

6. Using modular arithmetic, 3^5 mod 20 is equal to

   (a) 3

   (b) 12

   (c) 15

7. Use the RSA scheme with $n = 91$ and $s = 5$ to decode the message "4."

   (a) "11"

   (b) "20"

   (c) "23"

EXERCISES   ▲ *Optional.*   ■ *Advanced.*   ◆ *Discussion.*

Binary Codes

1. Use the diagram method shown in Figures 10.1 and 10.2 to verify the code words in Table 10.1 for the messages 0101, 1011, and 1111.

2. Use the diagram method to decode the received messages 0111011 and 0100110.

3. Find the distance between each of the following pairs of words:

   (a) 11011011 and 10100110

   (b) 01110100 and 11101100

4. Referring to Table 10.1, use the nearest-neighbor method to decode the received words 0000110 and 1110100.

5. If the code word 0110010 is received as 1001101, how is it decoded using the diagram method?

6. Suppose a received word has the diagram arrangement shown at the right:

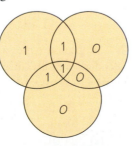

What can we conclude about the received word?

Parity-Check Sums

7. Determine the binary linear code that consists of all possible three-digit messages with three check digits appended using the parity-check sums $a_2 + a_3$, $a_1 + a_3$, and $a_1 + a_2$. (That is, $c_1 = 0$ if $a_2 + a_3$ is even; $c_1 = 1$ if $a_2 + a_3$ is odd; and similarly for c_2 and c_3.)

8. Let C be the code

   {0000000, 1110100, 0111010, 0011101, 1001110, 0100111, 1010011, 1101001}

What is the error-correcting capability of C? What is the error-detecting capability of C?

9. Find all code words for binary messages of length 4 by adding three check digits using the parity-check sums $a_2 + a_3 + a_4$, $a_2 + a_4$, and $a_1 + a_2 + a_3$. Will this code correct any single error?

10. Consider the binary linear code

   $C =$ {00000, 10011, 01010, 11001, 00101, 10110, 01111, 11100}

Use nearest-neighbor decoding to decode 11101 and 01100. If the received word 11101 has exactly one error, can you determine the intended code word? Explain your reasoning.

11. Construct a binary linear code using all eight possible binary messages of length 3 and appending three check digits using the parity-check sums $a_1 + a_2$, $a_2 + a_3$, and $a_1 + a_2 + a_3$. Decode each of the received words

001001, 011000, 000110, 100001

by the nearest-neighbor method.

12. Add the following pairs of binary sequences:

(a) 10111011 and 01111011
(b) 11101000 and 01110001

13. All binary linear codes have the property that the sum of two code words is another code word. Use this fact to determine which of the following sets cannot be a binary linear code:

(a) {0000, 0011, 0111, 0110, 1001, 1010, 1100, 1111}
(b) {0000, 0010, 0111, 0001, 1000, 1010, 1101, 1111}
(c) {0000, 0110, 1011, 1101}

Cryptography

14. The *Caesar cipher* encrypts messages by replacing each letter of the alphabet with the letter shown beneath it

ABCDEFGHIJKLMNOPQRSTUVWXYZ
DEFGHIJKLMNOPQRSTUVWXYZABC

Use the Caesar cipher to encrypt the message RETREAT. Determine the intended message corresponding to the encrypted message DWWDFN.

▲ 15. Use the RSA scheme with $p = 5$, $q = 17$, and $r = 3$ to determine the numbers sent for the message VIP.

▲ 16. Use the RSA scheme with $p = 5$, $q = 17$, and $r = 3$ to decode the received numbers 52 and 72.

▲ 17. In the RSA scheme with $p = 5$, $q = 17$, and $r = 5$, determine the value of s.

▲ 18. Why can't we use the RSA scheme with $p = 7$, $q = 11$, and $r = 3$?

▲ 19. Assume that the letters of the alphabet have been converted to integers according to the correspondence $A \rightarrow 0$, $B \rightarrow 1$, $C \rightarrow 2$, . . . , $Z \rightarrow 25$. Write a formula that describes the result of applying the Casesar cipher (see Exercise 14) to the integer x. (*Hint:* Use modular arithmetic.)

Data Compression

■ 20. Suppose we code a five-symbol set $\{A, B, C, D, E\}$ into binary form as follows:

$$A \longrightarrow 0, B \longrightarrow 10, C \longrightarrow 110,$$
$$D \longrightarrow 1110, \text{ and } E \longrightarrow 1111$$

Convert the sequence to *AEAADBAABCB* into binary code. Determine the sequence of symbols represented by the binary code 01000110100011111110.

■ 21. Use the code in Exercise 20 to convert the sequence *EABAADABB* into binary code. Determine the sequence of letters represented by the binary code 001000110011110111010.

■ 22. Devise a variable-length binary coding scheme for a six-symbol set $\{A, B, C, D, E, F\}$. Assume that A is the most frequently occurring symbol, B is the second most frequently occurring symbol, and so on.

23. Judging from the Morse code, what are the three most frequently occurring consonants in English text material? What is the most frequently occurring vowel?

24. In English, the letter H occurs more often than D, G, K, and W, but in Morse code, H has a longer code than D, G, K, and W. Speculate on the reason for this apparent violation of data compression principles.

25. Explain why the Morse code must include a space after each letter but fixed-length codes do not.

Additional Exercises

26. Let $v = a_1 a_2 \cdots a_n$ and $u = b_1 b_2 \cdots b_n$ be binary sequences. Explain why the number of 1s in $v + u$ is the same as the distance between u and v.

27. Extend the code words listed in Table 10.1 to eight digits by appending a 0 to words of even weight and a 1 to words of odd weight. What is the error-detecting and error-correcting capability of the new code?

28. Suppose the weight of a binary linear code is 6. How many errors can the code correct? How many errors can the code detect?

29. How many code words are there in a binary linear code that has all possible messages of length 5 with three check digits appended?

■ **30.** Explain why no binary linear code with three message digits and three check digits can correct all possible double errors.

■ **31.** A *ternary* code is formed by starting with all possible strings of a fixed length composed of 0s, 1s, and 2s and appending extra digits that are also 0s, 1s, or 2s. Form a ternary code by appending to each message $a_1 a_2$ the checks digits $c_1 c_2$ using:

$c_1 = 0$ if $a_1 + a_2$ is 0 or 3
$c_1 = 1$ if $a_1 + a_2$ is 1 or 4
$c_1 = 2$ if $a_1 + a_2$ is 2
$c_2 = 0$ if $2a_1 + a_2$ is 0, 3, or 6
$c_2 = 1$ if $2a_1 + a_2$ is 1 or 4
$c_2 = 2$ if $2a_1 + a_2$ is 2 or 5

■ **32.** Use the ternary code in Exericse 31 and the nearest-neighbor method to decode the received word 1211.

■ **33.** Suppose a ternary code is formed by starting with all possible strings of length 4 composed of 0s, 1s, and 2s and appending two extra digits that are also 0s, 1s, and 2s. How many code words are there in this code? How many possible received words are there in this code?

▲ **34.** For each part below explain how modular arithmetic can be used to answer the question.

(a) If today is Wednesday, what day of the week will it be in 16 days?
(b) If a clock (with hands) indicates that it is now 4 o'clock, what will it indicate in 37 hours?
(c) If a military person says it is now 0400, what time would it be in 37 hours? (Instead of A.M. and P.M., military people use 1300 for 1 P.M., 1400 for 2 P.M., and so on.)
(d) If it is now July 20, what day will it be in 65 days?
(e) If the five-digit odometer of an automobile reads 97,000 miles now, what will it read in 12,000 miles?

TECHNOLOGY CORNER

Hamming Codes

The spreadsheet shown in Figure 10.7 models the parity-check routine for 7-digit code words. A code word is valid when each of the three digit sums in the right column has even parity. Each of these sums is defined as a function of the entries in the first column. For example, the entry at **D1** is **=A1+A2+A3+A5**. By these calculations, each of the sums has even parity, and therefore the code word 0001011 is valid.

	A	B	C	D
1	0		sum of 1,2,3,5:	0
2	0		sum of 1,3,4,6:	2
3	0		sum of 2,3,4,7:	2
4	1			
5	0			
6	1			
7	1			

FIGURE 10.7

TASK 1.   Use the spreadsheet in Figure 10.7 to find examples of valid code words with one, two, three, four, five, and six 1s, if possible.

TASK 2.   Create a parity-check routine for a 10-digit binary code word. Include four check digits, each of which is obtained by adding together five of the ten digits. Assuming each of these check-digit sums should be even, find a valid code word. Can your routine detect any single error in the code word you found?

RSA Encryption

The RSA encryption routine utilizes several variables that must satisfy certain conditions. For example, the numbers p and q in Figure 10.8 must be primes. The number m is computed using the formula **=Lcm(C1-1,C2-1)**. The number r is chosen to have no common divisors, other than 1, with m. The number s must be chosen so that the number $rs \bmod m$ is 1. The value of $rs \bmod m$ can be computed using the formula **=Mod(C5*C6, C4)**. In the spreadsheet shown in Figure 10.8, $s = 35$ makes $rs \bmod m = 1$.

TASK 3.   Using the values $n = 221$ and $r = 11$, encode the message $M = 42$ by calculating $R = M^r \bmod n$. Then use the secret value $s = 35$ to decode the message R by calculating $R^s \bmod n$. After encoding and decoding, was the original message returned?

TASK 4.   Select three-digit primes for p and q. Compute n and m. Choose an appropriate r, then search for a valid s.

	A	B	C
1		p	13
2		q	17
3		n=pq	221
4		m=lcm(p-1,q-1)	48
5		r	11
6		s	35
7		rs mod m	1

FIGURE 10.8

Exploration

Using your individual p and q, prepare a public list of each person's personal n and r. Use these numbers to encode messages. (Be sure that in each case the message M and the number n share no common divisors other than 1.) When you have received an encoded message, use your secret s to decode the message.

When p and q are small, it is possible to break a code, knowing only n and r. Knowing only the values n and r, use the spreadsheet to try to guess the values of p, q, and r.

writing projects

1 ▶   Prepare a report on cryptography. Discuss at least three methods of encryption. Discuss the interface between computers and cryptography.

2 ▶   Prepare a report on applications of modular arithmetic. Explain the calculation of the check digits described in Exercises 7, 9, 11, and 31 with modular arithmetic. Use modular arithmetic to describe the error-detection schemes used in Chapter 9.

3 ▶   Prepare a report on the early history of error-correcting codes. The reference by Thompson (see Suggested Readings) has the information you will need.

4 ▶   Prepare a report on the electronic postage service that is available over the Internet (see Suggested Web Sites for a Web address).

5 ▶   A Smart Card is a card the size of a credit card that has a built-in microprocessor and memory. Soon, consumers will be able to use a Smart Card in combination with a network like the Internet to make secure monetary transactions and to authenticate remote users accessing private intranets. Use the Internet to find information about Smart Card technology and prepare a report on your findings.

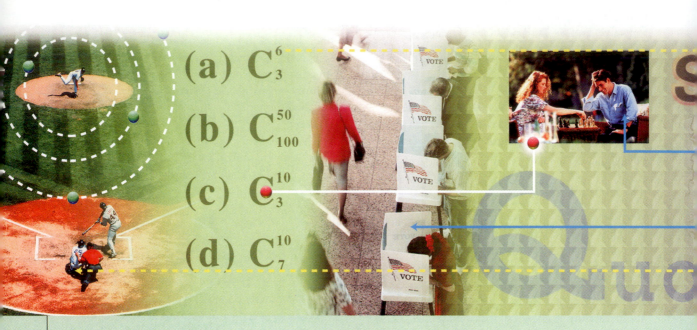

$$\text{(a) } C_3^6$$

$$\text{(b) } C_{100}^{50}$$

$$\text{(c) } C_3^{10}$$

$$\text{(d) } C_7^{10}$$

> "... *a new profession is emerging devoted to thinking mathematically about human affairs.*"

A revolution currently taking place in the field of mathematics is its application to the study of human beings—their behavior, values, interactions, conflicts, and decision making, as well as their interface with modern technology and various institutions. This revolution could eventually prove as far-reaching as the turning of mathematics to the study of physical objects and their motion some three centuries ago. As mathematics and computers play an increasingly important role in our understanding of social institutions, a new profession is emerging devoted to thinking mathematically about human affairs.

In particular, decision making is being influenced profoundly by modern mathematics, and several particularly mathematical areas have been created primarily to assist in arriving at sound decisions. While many aspects involved in arriving at a decision are cultural rather than quantitative, there are many ingredients of contemporary decision making that are mathematical in nature; some of these are addressed by mathematical models that are developed in Part IV.

In Chapter 11 we discuss the important problem of social choice. How does a group of individuals, each with his or her own set of values, select one outcome from a

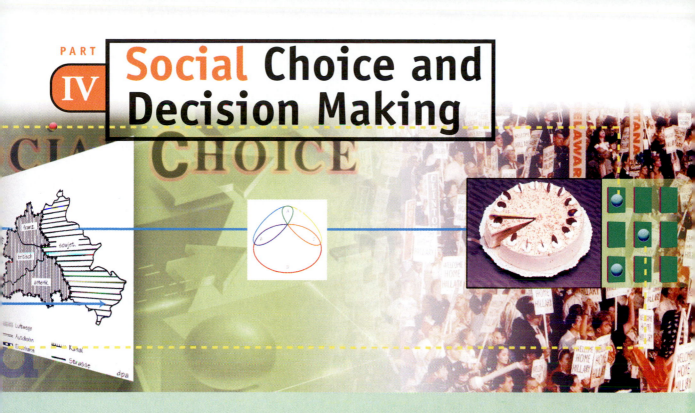

list of possibilities? This problem arises frequently in a democratic society and even in authoritarian institutions where decisions are made by more than one person. While "majority rule" is a good system for deciding an election involving just two candidates, there is no perfect way of deciding an election when three or more candidates are running. Group decision making is often a strategic encounter, and citizens need to be aware of the difficulties that can arise when some participants have an incentive to manipulate the outcome.

In Chapter 12 we consider decision-making bodies in which the individual voters or parties do not have equal power. In particular, we will look at weighted voting systems such as the electoral college, stockholders in a corporation, or political parties in a national assembly, in which the voters cast different numbers of votes. While the notion of power is central in political science, it is typically difficult to quantify. We will find that a voter's power in such a system may not be proportional to the number of votes that he or she is entitled to cast. We describe two well-known indices for measuring power in weighted voting systems that will enable us to assess the fairness of weighted voting systems.

A general theme of Part IV concerns the idea of fairness in decision making. In Chapter 13 this becomes most explicit. Here we describe some fair-decision schemes in which a group of individuals with different values can be assured of each receiving what he or she views as a fair share when dividing up objects like cakes or the goods in an estate. An important theme of this chapter is finding procedures that produce "envy-free" allocations, in which each person gets a largest portion (as he or she values the cake or other goods) and hence does not envy anybody else.

In Chapter 14 we discuss the apportionment problem, which is to round a set of fractions to whole numbers while preserving their sum; of course, the sum of the original fractions must be a whole number to start. Apportionment problems occur when resources must be allocated in integer quantities — for instance, when college administrators allocate faculty positions to each department.

The most important apportionment problem is the allocation of seats in the U.S. House of Representatives to the 50 states. It is this problem that initiated the study of apportionment, when President George Washington vetoed the first congressional apportionment bill.

Chapter 15 introduces the mathematical field called game theory, which describes situations involving two or more decision makers having different goals. Game theory provides a collection of models to assist in the analysis of conflict and cooperation. It prescribes optimal strategies for games of total conflict in which one player's gain is equal to the other player's loss. It also provides insights into more cooperative situations in which players are trying to coordinate their choices, as well as encounters of partial conflict that involve aspects of both competition and cooperation. Particular games, including those known as Prisoners' Dilemma and Chicken, provide us with insights into certain social paradoxes that we routinely meet in our daily lives.

We briefly introduce an extension of game theory, called the theory of moves, which is designed to model strategic situations in which players think beyond the immediate consequences of departing from an outcome. Such farsighted thinking has favorable consequences in games like Prisoners' Dilemma.

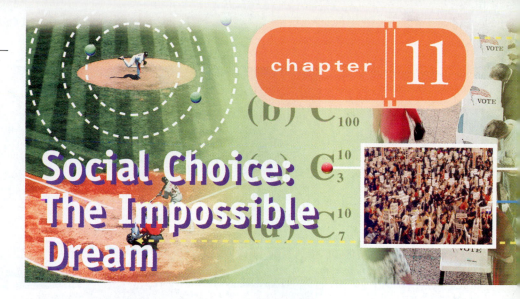

chapter 11

Social Choice: The Impossible Dream

"The goal is to find such procedures that will result in an outcome that 'reflects the will of the people'."

The basic question of *social choice,* of how groups can best arrive at decisions, has occupied social philosophers and political scientists for centuries. Indeed, voting is a subject that lies at the very heart of representative government and participatory democracy.

Social choice theory attempts to address the problem of finding good procedures that will turn individual preferences for different candidates—or *alternatives,* as they are often called—into a single choice by the whole group. The goal is to find such procedures that will result in an outcome that "reflects the will of the people."

This search for good voting systems, as we shall see, is plagued by a variety of counterintuitive results and disturbing outcomes. In fact, it turns out that one can prove (mathematically) that no one will ever find a completely satisfactory voting system for three or more alternatives.

The elections with which we are most familiar—those at the national political level—typically involve only two candidates. Ignoring the electoral college, such elections pose little difficulty in theory or practice: each voter casts a vote for one of the two candidates, and the majority wins. We will begin our discussion of voting systems with this two-alternative case.

On the other hand, there are real-world situations where elections must be held to choose a single winner among three or more candidates, as in the presidential election of 1992 in which George Bush, Bill Clinton, and Ross Perot were the candidates. The procedure used in that election—ignoring the electoral college—was *plurality voting,* wherein a ballot is a choice for one of the three, and the candidate with the most votes wins.

Bill Clinton–Bob Dole in a presidential debate, 1996.

Plurality voting, however, is not the only method that can be used to elect a single candidate from a choice of three or more, and we will investigate several other methods in this chapter. Most of these methods (the one called *approval voting* is the exception) use a ballot in which a voter provides a rank ordering of the candidates (without ties) indicating the order in which he or she prefers the candidates.

A ballot consisting of such a rank ordering of candidates (which we often picture as a vertical list with the most preferred candidate on top and the least preferred on the bottom) is called a *preference list,* or, more completely, an **individual preference list,** since it is a statement of the preferences of one of the individuals who is voting.

Ballots that are preference lists allow each voter to make a much clearer statement of his or her preferences than do ballots that correspond to a single vote for a single candidate. Such ballots (preference lists) are already used in a wide range of applications, such as rating football teams and scoring track meets.

We present four particular methods of choosing a winner when there are three or more alternatives. For each method, we illustrate the failure of some natural property that one would like to have satisfied by any voting system that is being used. Finally, we face the fact that the unfortunate shortcomings of the particular procedures we have presented are largely unavoidable. There are difficulties with elections involving three or more candidates that are simply insurmountable.

Elections with Only Two Alternatives

When choosing between two alternatives, the first type of voting to suggest itself is **majority rule:** each voter indicates a preference for one of the two candidates, and the candidate with the most votes wins. Majority rule has at least three desirable properties:

1. All voters are treated equally. That is, if any two voters were to exchange (marked) ballots prior to submitting them, the outcome of the election would be the same.
2. Both candidates are treated equally. That is, if a new election were held and every voter were to reverse his or her vote, then the outcome of the previous election would be reversed as well.
3. If a new election were held and a single voter were to change his or her ballot from being a vote for the loser of the previous election to being a vote for the winner of the previous election, and everyone else voted exactly as before, then the outcome of the new election would be the same as the outcome of the previous election.

It is easy to devise voting systems for two alternatives in which these fail, but each such voting system quickly reveals its undesirability. For example, condition 1 is not satisfied by a *dictatorship* (whereby all ballots except that of the dictator are ignored); condition 2 is not satisfied by *imposed rule* (whereby candidate X wins regardless of who votes for whom); and condition 3 is not satisfied by *minority rule* (whereby the candidate with the fewest votes wins).

But maybe there are voting systems in the two-alternatives case that are superior to majority rule in the sense of satisfying the three properties just listed *and* some other properties that we might also wish to have satisfied. This, however, turns out not to be the case. In 1952, Kenneth May proved the following:

> If the number of voters is odd, and we are interested only in voting systems that never result in a tie, then majority rule is the *only* voting system for two alternatives that satisfies the three conditions just listed.

This is an important and elegant result. **May's theorem** says that, for two alternatives, our work in finding a good voting system is done.

Elections with Three or More Alternatives: Procedures and Problems

In sharp contrast with the case of two alternatives is the situation in which there are three or more candidates. Here, we find no shortage of procedures that suggest themselves and that seem to represent perfectly reasonable ways to choose a winner from among three or more alternatives. Closer inspection, however, reveals shortcomings with all of these. We illustrate this with a consideration of four well-known procedures. Additional procedures (and additional shortcomings) can be found in the exercises.

In what follows, we assume that a ballot is an individual preference list. We allow ties in the election result and assume that, in the real world, either the number of voters is so large that ties in the election result will virtually never occur or that they can be broken by some kind of random device.

Plurality Voting and the Condorcet Winner Criterion

In **plurality voting,** only first-place votes are considered. Thus, while we will consider plurality voting in the context of preference lists, a ballot might just as well be a single vote for a single candidate. The candidate with the most votes wins, even though this may be considerably fewer than one-half the total votes cast. This is perhaps the most common system in use today. It is how we chose Bill Clinton over George Bush and Ross Perot in 1992.

Political rally in Washington, D.C.

E X A M P L E   *Plurality Voting and Senator Alfonse D'Amato*

On November 3, 1998, Alfonse D'Amato was defeated by Chuck Schumer in the U.S. Senate race in New York State. This brought an end to an 18-year reign by this moderate Republican. Of the many elections in which D'Amato took part, none is more interesting than the one that first brought him to power.

In 1980, D'Amato was opposed by two liberals: Elizabeth Holtzman and the late Jacob Javits. Reasonable estimates (based largely on exit polls) suggest that voters ranked the three candidates according to the following table.

22%	23%	15%	29%	7%	4%
D	D	H	H	J	J
H	J	D	J	H	D
J	H	J	D	D	H

Plurality voting led to D'Amato winning with 22% + 23% = 45% of the vote to 15% + 29% = 44% for Holtzman, and 7% + 4% = 11% for Javits. In this example, however, Holtzman was what is called a **Condorcet winner:** she would have defeated each of the other candidates in a head-to-head (i.e., a "one-on-one") election. That is, Holtzman would have defeated D'Amato in a two-candidate contest

15% + 29% + 7% = 51% (for Holtzman)

to

22% + 23% + 4% = 49% (for D'Amato)

and she would have defeated Javits in a two-candidate contest

22% + 15% + 29% = 66% (for Holtzman)

to

23% + 7% + 4% = 34% (for Javits)   ◆

A voting procedure is said to satisfy the **Condorcet winner criterion (CWC)** provided that, for every possible sequence of preference lists, either (1) there is no Condorcet winner (as is often the case), or (2) there is a Condorcet winner (which, if it exists, is always unique) and it is the unique winner of the election.

The Condorcet winner criterion is certainly a property that one would like to see satisfied. However, the D'Amato–Holtzman–Javits election shows that plurality voting fails to satisfy the Condorcet winner criterion.

Perhaps a more fundamental drawback of plurality voting is the extent to which the ballots provide no opportunity for a voter to express any preferences except for naming his or her top choice. No use is made, for example, of the fact that a candidate may be no one's first choice but everyone's close second choice.

Finally, there is yet another shortcoming of plurality voting. It is subject to what is called *manipulability:* there are elections in which it is to a voter's advantage to submit a ballot that misrepresents his or her true preferences. For example, in the presidential election of 1992, many voters who ranked Ross Perot over George Bush and Bill Clinton chose to vote for Bush or Clinton rather than "throw away" their vote on a candidate who they felt had no chance. As we move on to consider voting systems that make more significant use of a voter's rank ordering of the candidates, we will see that manipulability becomes even more of an issue.

The Borda Count and Independence of Irrelevant Alternatives

In many elections that use preference lists as ballots, the goal is to arrive at a final group rank ordering of all the contestants that best expresses the desires of the electorate. The purpose is not only to determine the winner, say, the class valedictorian, but also to arrive at who finished second, third, and so on, as in the case of one's rank in his or her senior class. In other applications, such as an election to a hall of fame, the first few finishers each receive the award, while the remaining nominees are also-rans.

One common mechanism for achieving this objective is to assign points to each voter's rankings and then to sum these for all voters to obtain the total points for each candidate. If there are 10 candidates, for example, then we could assign 10 points to each first-place vote for a given candidate, 9 points for each second-place vote, 8 for each third, and so forth. The candidate with the highest total number of points is the winner. Subsequent positions are assigned to those with the next-highest tallies.

A voting method that assigns points in a nonincreasing manner to each voter's subsequent ranking and then sums these points to arrive at a group's final ranking is called a *rank method.* The special case in which there are n alternatives with each first-place vote worth $n - 1$ points, each second-place vote worth $n - 2$ points, and so on down to each last-place vote worth zero points is known as the **Borda count.**

Rank methods other than the Borda count are not uncommon. For example, a track meet can be thought of as an "election" in which each event is a "voter" and each of the schools competing is a "candidate." If the order of finish in the 100-meter dash is School A, School B, School C, School D, then points are often awarded to each school as follows: 5 points for first place, 3 for second place, 2 for third place, and 1 for fourth place.

Sports polls often use point assignments that qualify as rank methods according to our definition. The following example provides an illustration of this.

EXAMPLE *Rank Methods and a Football Poll*

The 1998 preseason college football poll, conducted by the Associated Press, was reported as follows:

AP TOP 25

The Top Twenty Five teams in The Associated Press preseason college football poll, with first-place votes in parentheses, 1997 records, total points based on 25 points for a first place vote through one point for a 25th place vote and ranking in 1997 final poll:

	Record	Pts	Pv
1. Ohio St. (30)	10-3	1,668	12
2. Florida St. (22)	11-1	1,663	3
3. Florida (5)	10-2	1,547	4
4. Nebraska (4)	13-0	1,534	2
5. Michigan (4)	12-0	1,475	1
6. Kansas St. (2)	11-1	1,335	8
7. UCLA (1)	10-2	1,331	5
8. Arizona St. (2)	9-3	1,256	14
9. LSU	9-3	1,237	13
10. Tennessee	11-2	1,094	7
11. West Virginia	7-5	985	—
12. North Carolina	11-1	864	6
13. Penn St.	9-3	804	16
14. Texas A&M	9-4	760	20
15. Colorado St.	11-2	631	17
16. Virginia	7-4	620	—
17. Syracuse	9-4	608	21
18. Washington	8-4	494	18
19. Georgia	10-2	480	10
20. Wisconsin	8-5	444	—
21. Southern Miss.	9-3	341	19
22. Notre Dame	7-6	291	—
23. Michigan St.	7-5	211	—
24. Arizona	7-5	208	—
25. Auburn	10-3	201	11

Others receiving votes: Texas 145, Southern Cal 121, Georgia Tech 86, Missouri 72, Colorado 60, Oklahoma St. 31, Purdue 30, Mississippi 24, Mississippi St. 21, Utah 17, Brigham Young 10, Miami 10, Wake Forest 9, Oregon 8, Arkansas 7, Kentucky 4, Washington St. 4, Tulane 3, Marshall 2, South Carolina 2, Louisiana Tech 1, Toledo 1.

An interesting question is whether or not this is a ranking system. For example, if it is, what are the alternatives, and how many of them are there? In fact, this *can* be regarded as a ranking system, but the number of alternatives is not 25. That is, although 25 football teams appeared on each ballot, at least one ballot included Toledo, for example, while other ballots definitely did not.

To regard this as a ranking system, we must consider the set of alternatives to be the entire set of eligible college football teams; and we must interpret each ballot as listing all teams other than that voter's top 25 in, say, alphabetical order and coming below that voter's top 25. The point assignments are then as in the newspaper clipping, except that we also assign zero points for a 26th-place vote, zero points for a 27th-place vote, and so on. This is why, in the definition of ranking system, we said "assigns points in a *nonincreasing* manner" instead of "assigns points in a *descending* manner."

We can use this poll to illustrate how total points are arrived at with a ranking method. Let's see how Ohio State might have earned the 1668 points it is reported to have in the AP poll. We know that it had 30 first-place votes, and each first-place vote was worth 25. We also know the total number of ballots was 70 (because they give the number of first-place votes that each team received and $30 + 22 + 5 + 4 + 4 + 2 + 1 + 2 = 70$).

Thus, one possibility is that Ohio State received

30 first-place votes (at 25 points each)
13 second-place votes (at 24 points each)
13 third-place votes (at 23 points each)
13 fourth-place votes (at 22 points each)
1 fifth-place vote (at 21 points)

The total would then be:

$$(30)(25) + (13)(24) + (13)(23) + (13)(22) + (1)(21) = 1668. \quad \blacklozenge$$

The Borda count certainly seems to be a reasonable way to choose a winner from among several alternatives (or to arrive at a group ranking of the alternatives). It also has its shortcomings, however, one of which is the failure of a property known as *independence of irrelevant alternatives.*

To describe this property, suppose that an election yields one alternative (call it *A*) as a winner and another alternative (call it *B*) as a nonwinner. Suppose that a new election is now held and that, although some of the voters may have changed their preference lists, no one who had previously ranked *A* over *B* changed his or her list so as now to have *B* over *A*.

If this new election were to yield *B* as a winner, then *B*—in terms of the outcome of the election—would have moved up to at least a tie with *A* on the basis of ballot changes involving alternatives *other than A* or *B*. One could argue that these other alternatives ought to be irrelevant to the question of whether *A* is more desirable than *B* or *B* is more desirable than *A*.

A voting system is said to satisfy **independence of irrelevant alternatives (IIA)** if it is impossible for an alternative B to move from nonwinner status to winner status unless at least one voter reverses the order in which he or she had B and the winning alternative ranked.

The following illustration shows that the Borda count fails to satisfy independence of irrelevant alternatives. Suppose the initial five ballots are as here:

	Number of Voters		
Rank	**3**	**2**	**Points**
First	A	C	2
Second	B	B	1
Third	C	A	0

We calculate the total number of points for each alternative as follows:

A: $(2)(3) + (0)(2) = 6$
B: $(1)(3) + (1)(2) = 5$
C: $(0)(3) + (2)(2) = 4$

The winner is A (with 6 points), and B is a nonwinner (with 5 points). But now suppose that the two voters (on the right) change their ballots by moving C down between A and B. The lists then become

	Number of Voters		
Rank	**3**	**2**	**Points**
First	A	B	2
Second	B	C	1
Third	C	A	0

For this new election, we calculate the total number for each alternative:

A: $(2)(3) + (0)(2) = 6$
B: $(1)(3) + (2)(2) = 7$
C: $(0)(3) + (1)(2) = 2$

prevail. Assume that two of the three voters do prefer the proposed bill *N* over the existing law *O*, as indicated in this table of preferences:

	Voter		
	A	*B*	*C*
First choice	*N*	*N*	*O*
Second choice	*O*	*O*	*N*

In a direct comparison between the outcomes *N* and *O*, *N* will win by a vote of 2 to 1. Nevertheless, voter *C* may attempt to defeat *N* by the following maneuver. He proposes to modify the new bill *N* with an amended version called *M*, chosen so that *A* prefers *M* most of all and *B* prefers *M* least of all. This may be done, perhaps, by merely shifting some of the proposed reward in bill *N* from *B* to *A*.

For *C*'s strategy to work, he must behave (i.e., vote) as if *O* were still his first choice but as if he liked *M* better than *N*. This may require deception on the part of *C*.

What effect will this have? Standard practice requires amendments to be considered, one at a time, before the main motion is brought to the floor. Thus, the voting method we find in use here is sequential pairwise voting with the agenda

M   N   O

Moreover, the sequence of preference lists is the following (which the reader will want to compare with those in the voting paradox of Condorcet):

	Voter		
	A	*B*	*C*
First choice	*M*	*N*	*O*
Second choice	*N*	*O*	*M*
Third choice	*O*	*M*	*N*

When voting between *M* and *N*, *M* wins over *N* by 2 to 1. At the second step, *O* beats *M* by 2 to 1. Thus, voter *C* has tricked the others into defeating *N* and maintaining the status quo, *O*. Voter *A* should have noticed this tactic and resisted the temptation to initially vote for the fleeting amendment *M*. In reality, however, *C* could have publicized amendment *M* in *A*'s district, making it difficult for her to vote no, even if she saw *C*'s trick (which is familiar to virtually all legislators). ◆

In the course of a long, complex agenda and heated debate, we must be continuously on guard to avoid being manipulated into voting against our own long-range interests. Those designing the agenda can often rig it in their own favor. For example, one contingent might stack up a larger number of popular outcomes and pit them against a *single* highly desired one in an attempt to eliminate this single outcome at an early stage of the agenda. As a general rule of thumb, it's best to enter the more preferred outcomes at a later stage of the agenda. The chances of survival may increase when there are fewer competing alternatives and fewer remaining votes to be taken.

It would be nice, of course, to have a voting system that is not vulnerable to this kind of deceptive strategy. This turns out to be too much to ask. In the early 1970s, Allan Gibbard and Mark Satterthwaite independently proved that in a context similar to the ones we have considered, there is no social choice procedure, except a dictatorship, that completely avoids situations wherein it is better for at least one of the voters to mark his or her ballot in an insincere way. Thus, in terms of strategy, honesty may not be the best policy.

Impossibility

Nothing in the remarkable body of work produced by Nobel laureate Kenneth J. Arrow of Stanford University is as well known or widely acclaimed as the result known as **Arrow's impossibility theorem** (see Spotlight 11.1). How, though, can one mathematically prove that it is *impossible* to find a voting system that satisfies certain properties?

Our goal here is to consider a version of Arrow's theorem and at least to sketch the argument behind it. This version is taken from the 1995 text cited in Suggested Readings and uses stronger hypotheses than Arrow's original theorem. (Essentially, the CWC is replacing Arrow's assumption of Pareto and nondictatorship.)

The framework for our present considerations will be the same one with which we have been working. Ballots will be preference lists (without ties), and the outcome of an election will be either a single alternative (the winner) or a group of alternatives (tied for the win). We *do* demand of any social choice procedure that it definitely produce at least one winner when confronted by any sequence of preference lists.

Recall that the first two examples of social choice procedures that we considered were plurality voting and the Borda count. Moreover, we showed that plurality voting failed to satisfy the Condorcet winner criterion (CWC) and that the Borda count failed to satisfy independence of irrelevant alternatives (IIA). The theorem we want to prove here is the following:

> There does not exist, and never will exist, *any* social choice procedure that satisfies both the CWC and IIA.

SPOTLIGHT
11.1

Kenneth J. Arrow

Kenneth Arrow

For centuries, mathematicians have been in search of a perfect voting system. Finally, in 1951, economist Kenneth Arrow proved that finding an absolutely fair and decisive voting system is impossible. Arrow is the Joan Kenney Professor of Economics, as well as a professor of operations research, at Stanford University. In 1972, he received the Nobel Memorial Prize in Economic Science for his outstanding work in the theory of general economic equilibrium. His numerous other honors include the 1986 von Neumann Theory Prize for his fundamental contributions to the decision sciences. He has served as president of the American Economic Association, the Institute of Management Sciences, and other organizations. Dr. Arrow talks about the process by which he developed his famous impossibility theorem and his ideas on the laws that govern voting systems:

My first interest was in the theory of corporations. In a firm with many owners, how do the owners agree when they have different opinions, for example, about the prospects of the company? I was thinking of stockholders. In the course of this, I realized that there was a paradox involved—that majority voting can lead to cycles. I then dropped that discussion because I was frustrated by it.

I happened to be working with The RAND Corporation one summer about a year or two later. They were very interested in applying concepts of rationality, particularly of game theory, to military and diplomatic affairs. That summer, I felt not like an economist but instead like a general social scientist or a mathematically oriented social scientist. There was tremendous interest in game theory, which was then new.

Some there asked me, "What does it mean in terms of national interest?" I said, "Oh, that's a very simple matter," and he said, "Well, why don't you write us a little memorandum on the subject." Trying to write that memorandum led to a sharper formulation of the social-choice question, and I realized that I had been thinking of it earlier in that other context.

I think that society must choose among a number of alternative policies. These policies may be thought of as quite comprehensive, covering a number of aspects: foreign policy, budgetary policy, or whatever. Now, each individual member of the society has a preference, or a set of preferences, over these alternatives. I guess that you can say one alternative is better than another. And these individual preferences have a property I call rationality or consistency, or more specifically, what is technically known as transitivity: if I prefer a to b, and b to c, then I prefer a to c.

Imagine that society has to make these choices among a set. Each individual has a preference ordering, a ranking of these alternatives. But we really want society, in some sense, to give a ranking of these alternatives. Well, you can always produce a ranking, but you would like it to have some properties. One is that, of course, it be responsive in some sense to the individual rankings. Another is that when you finish, you end up with a real ranking, that is, something that satisfies these consistency, or transitivity, properties. And a third condition is that when choosing between a number of alternatives, all I should take into account are the preferences of the individuals among those alternatives. If certain things are possible and some are impossible, I shouldn't ask individuals whether they care about the impossible alternatives, only the possible ones.

It turns out that if you impose the conditions I just stated, there is no method of putting together the individual preferences that satisfies all of them.

The whole idea of the axiomatic method was very much in the air among anybody who studied mathematics, particularly among those who studied the foundations of mathematics. The idea is that if you want to find out something, to find the properties, you say, "What would I like it to be?" [You do this] instead of trying to investigate special cases. And I was really accustomed to this approach. Of course, the actual process did involve trial and error.

But I went in with the idea that there was some method of handling this problem. I started out with some examples. I had already discovered that these led to some problems. The next thing that was reasonable was to write down a condition that I could outlaw. Then I constructed another example, another method that seemed to meet that problem, and something else didn't seem very right about it. Then I had to postulate that we have some other property. I found I was having difficulty satisfying all of these properties that I thought were desirable, and it occurred to me that they couldn't be satisfied.

After having formulated three or four conditions of this kind, I kept on experimenting. And lo and behold, no matter what I did, there was nothing that would satisfy these axioms. So after a few days of this, I began to get the idea that maybe there was another kind of theorem here, namely, that there was no voting method that would satisfy all the conditions that I regarded as rational and reasonable. It was at this point that I set out to prove it. And it actually turned out to be a matter of only a few days' work.

It should be made clear that my impossibility theorem is really a theorem [showing that] the contradictions are possible, not that they are necessary. What I claim is that given any voting procedure, there will be some possible set of preference orders for individuals that will lead to a contradiction of one of these axioms.

But you say, "Well, okay, since we can't get perfection, let's at least try to find a method that works well most of the time." Then when you do have a problem, you don't notice it as much. So my theorem is not a completely destructive or negative feature any more than the second law of thermodynamics means that people don't work on improving the efficiency of engines. We're told you'll never get 100% efficient engines. That's a fact—and a law. It doesn't mean you wouldn't like to go from 40% to 50%.

More specifically, we claim that if a "voting rule" of some kind were to be found that satisfied both the CWC and IIA, then, when confronted by the three preference lists occurring in the voting paradox of Condorcet, this voting rule would *fail* to produce a winner (and thus not be a social choice procedure in the sense that we are using the phrase). Let's see why this is true.

The argument really comes in three separate, but extremely similar, pieces—one for each of the three alternatives. Piece 1 argues that alternative A can't be among the winners; piece 2 that B can't be among the winners; and piece 3 that C can't be among the winners. We'll do piece 1 and leave the others for the interested reader. The sequence of preference lists that we are considering is the following:

	Number of Voters		
Rank	1	1	1
First	A	B	C
Second	B	C	A
Third	C	A	B

Our starting point, however, will be to ask what our hypothetical voting rule must do when confronted by a slightly different sequence of preference lists:

	Number of Voters		
Rank	1	1	1
First	A	C	C
Second	B	B	A
Third	C	A	B

Here, alternative C is clearly a Condorcet winner, and thus it must be the unique winner of the election contested under our hypothetical voting rule. Therefore, C is a winner and A is a nonwinner (for *this* sequence of preference lists).

However, because our hypothetical voting rule satisfies independence of irrelevant alternatives, we know that alternative A will remain a nonwinner as long as no one reverses his or her ordering of A and C. But to arrive at the preference lists from the voting paradox, we can move B (the alternative that is irrelevant to A and C) up one slot in the second voter's list.

Thus, because of IIA, we know that alternative A is a nonwinner when our voting rule is confronted by the preference lists from the voting paradox of Condorcet. This is one-third of the argument. As we mentioned before, similar arguments (see Exercise 23) show that B and C are also nonwinners when our voting rule is confronted by the preference lists from the voting paradox of Condorcet. Therefore, we have shown that no voting system that is guaranteed to produce at least one winner can satisfy both CWC and IIA.

A Better Approach? Approval Voting

Elections in which there are only two candidates present no problem. Majority rule is, as we have seen, an eminently successful voting system in both theory and practice. If there are three or more candidates, however, the situation changes quite dramatically. While several voting systems suggest themselves (plurality, the Borda count, sequential pairwise voting, and the Hare system), each fails to satisfy one or more desired properties (the Condorcet winner criterion, independence of irrelevant alternatives, the Pareto condition, and monotonicity). Manipulability is an ever-present problem. Moreover, when all is said and done, Arrow's impossibility theorem says that any search for an ideal voting system of the kind we have discussed is doomed to failure.

Where does this leave us? More than intellectual issues are at stake here: over 550,000 elected officials serve in approximately 80,000 governments in the United States. Whether it is a small academic department voting on the best senior thesis or a democratic country electing a new leader, multicandidate elections will be contested in one way or another. If there is no perfect voting system—and perhaps not even a best voting system (whatever that may mean; that is, best in what way?)—what can we do?

Perhaps the answer is that different situations lend themselves to different voting systems, and what is required is a judicious blend of common sense with an awareness of what the mathematical theory has to say. For example, while both the Hare system and the Borda count are subject to manipulability, it is clearly easier to manipulate the latter (recall the quote of Jean-Charles de Borda on page 394). Thus, people may tend to vote more sincerely, rather than strategically, if the Hare system is used instead of the Borda count. This may be a consideration when choosing a voting system for a faculty governance system, for example.

For national political elections, there are also practical considerations. The kind of ballot we are considering (an individual preference list) is certainly more complicated than the ballots we now employ, and preference lists cannot be used with existing voting machines. There is, however, a voting system that avoids the practical difficulties caused by the type of ballot being used that has much else to commend it. It is called *approval voting*.

Under **approval voting,** each voter is allowed to give one vote to as many of the candidates as he or she finds acceptable. No limit is set on the number of candidates for whom an individual can vote. Voters show disapproval of other candidates simply by not voting for them.

The winner under approval voting is the candidate who receives the largest number of approval votes. This approach is also appropriate in situations where more than one candidate can win, for example, in electing new members to an exclusive society such as the National Academy of Sciences or the Baseball Hall of Fame.

Approval voting was proposed independently by several analysts in the 1970s. Probably the best-known official elected by approval voting today is the secretary-general of the United Nations. In the 1980s, several academic and professional societies initiated the use of approval voting. Examples include the Institute of Electrical and Electronics Engineers (IEEE), with about 400,000 members, and the National Academy of Sciences. In Eastern Europe and some former Soviet republics, approval voting has been used in the form wherein one disapproves of (instead of approving of) as many candidates as one wishes.

Is approval voting the perfect voting system? Certainly not. For example, the type of ballot used limits the extent to which voter preferences can be expressed. However, it is certainly a voting system with much potential, and the reader wishing to explore it in more detail can start with Brams and Fishburn's 1983 monograph, listed in Suggested Readings.

REVIEW VOCABULARY

Agenda   An ordering of the alternatives for consideration. Often used in sequential pairwise voting.

Approval voting   A method of electing one or more candidates from a field of several in which each voter submits a ballot that indicates which candidates he or she approves of. Winning is determined by the total number of approvals a candidate obtains.

Arrow's impossibility theorem   Kenneth J. Arrow's discovery that any voting system can give undesirable outcomes.

Borda count   A voting system for elections with several candidates in which points are assigned to voters' preferences and these points are summed for each candidate to determine a winner.

Condorcet's voting paradox   The observation that two-thirds of society can prefer A to B, two-thirds prefer B to C, and two-thirds prefer C to A.

Condorcet winner   A Condorcet winner in an election is a candidate who, based on the ballots, would have defeated every other candidate in a one-on-one contest.

Condorcet winner criterion (CWC)   A voting system satisfies the Condorcet winner criterion if, for every election in which there is a Condorcet winner, it wins the election when that voting system is used.

Hare system   A voting system for elections with several candidates in which candidates are successively eliminated in an order based on the number of first-place votes.

Independence of irrelevant alternatives (IIA)   A voting system satisfies independence of irrelevant alternatives if the only way a candidate (call him A) can go from losing one election to being among the winners of a new election (with the same set of candidates and voters) is for at least one voter to reverse his or her ranking of *A* and the previous winner.

Individual preference list   A ballot that provides a rank ordering of candidates, from best to worst, in the eyes of that individual voter.

Majority rule   A voting system for elections with two candidates (and an odd number of voters) in which the candidate preferred by more than half the voters is the winner.

May's theorem   Kenneth May's discovery that, for two alternatives and an odd number of voters, majority rule is the only voting system satisfying three natural properties.

Monotonicity   A voting system satisfies monotonicity provided that ballot changes favorable to one alternative (and not favorable to any other alternative) can never hurt that alternative.

Pareto condition   A voting system satisfies the Pareto condition provided that every voter's ranking of one alternative higher than another precludes the possibility of this latter alternative winning.

Plurality voting   A voting system for elections with several candidates in which the candidate with the most first-place votes wins.

Sequential pairwise voting   A voting system for elections with several candidates in which one starts with an agenda and pits the candidates against each other in one-on-one contests (based on ballots that are preference lists), with losers being eliminated as one moves along the agenda.

Sincere voting   Submitting a ballot that represents a voter's true preferences.

Strategic voting   Submitting a ballot that does not represent a voter's true preferences.

SUGGESTED READINGS

AUMANN, ROBERT, AND SERGIU HART, EDS. *Handbook of Game Theory with Economic Applications,* Vol. II, Elsevier, Amsterdam, 1994. Chapter 30 (by Steven Brams) and chapter 31 (by Hervé Moulin) provide intermediate to advanced treatments of voting procedures and social choice.

BLACK, DUNCAN. *The Theory of Committees and Elections,* Kluwer, Dordrecht, The Netherlands, 1986. The historical highlights and developments of voting methods in the nineteenth and twentieth centuries are traced in this economist's volume.

BRAMS, STEVEN J., AND PETER C. FISHBURN. *Approval Voting,* Birkhäuser, Boston, 1983. This volume is a research-level work on developments in the recently popular (but rediscovered) method now called approval voting. The first chapter, however, is an elementary exposition of this voting method and its uses.

FARQUHARSON, ROBIN. *Theory of Voting,* Yale University Press, New Haven, Conn., 1969. This is an elementary but historically important monograph.

KELLY, JERRY S. *Social Choice Theory,* Springer-Verlag, New York, 1988. This text for undergraduates provides an extensive treatment of voting theory.

MALKEVITCH, JOSEPH, AND WALTER MEYER. *Graphs, Models and Finite Mathematics,* Prentice Hall, Englewood Cliffs, N.J., 1974. In chapter 10 there is an introduction to the problem of voting, including a discussion of the properties desired of any voting method (Arrow's axioms).

MERRILL, SAMUEL III. *Making Multicandidate Elections More Democratic,* Princeton University Press, Princeton, N.J., 1988. This is a well-written treatment of voting from quite a practical point of view.

NURMI, HANNU. *Comparing Voting Systems,* Reidel, Dordrecht, The Netherlands, 1987. This monograph provides an excellent treatment, at a somewhat more technical level, of the topics dealt with in this chapter.

SARRI, DONALD G. *The Geometry of Voting,* Springer-Verlag, New York, 1994. This monograph provides an advanced treatment of voting that focuses on ranking methods like the Borda count.

TAYLOR, ALAN D. *Mathematics and Politics: Strategy, Voting, Power, and Proof,* Springer-Verlag, New York, 1995. Chapters 5 and 10 give an expanded treatment of the topics considered here, with proofs included. It is also intended for nonmajors.

SUGGESTED WEB SITES

http://fsmat.htu.tuwien.ac.at/~zahi/wahl.html
"The Voting Page," this site contains additional topics from the theory of voting, including yes–no voting and power indices (as discussed in Chapter 14).

http://bcn.boulder.co.us/government/
approvalvote/goodsoc.html   An article entitled "Approval Voting and the Good Society," by Steven J. Brams.

SKILLS CHECK

1.   Thirty students who need to choose a day for their final exam have the following set of preference lists.

	12 Students	8 Students	10 Students
First choice	Friday	Thursday	Wednesday
Second choice	Wednesday	Wednesday	Thursday
Third choice	Thursday	Friday	Friday

Which day will be selected if they use majority rule?

(a)   Wednesday
(b)   Thursday
(c)   Friday
(d)   No winner can be chosen.

2.   Thirty students who need to choose a day for their final exam have the following set of preference lists.

	12 Students	8 Students	10 Students
First choice	Friday	Thursday	Wednesday
Second choice	Wednesday	Wednesday	Thursday
Third choice	Thursday	Friday	Friday

Which day will be selected if they use plurality voting?

(a)   Wednesday
(b)   Thursday
(c)   Friday
(d)   No winner can be chosen.

3.   Thirty students who need to choose a day for their final exam have the preference schedule shown below.

	12 Students	8 Students	10 Students
First choice	Friday	Thursday	Wednesday
Second choice	Wednesday	Wednesday	Thursday
Third choice	Thursday	Friday	Friday

Which day will be selected if they use the Borda count?

(a)   Wednesday
(b)   Thursday
(c)   Friday
(d)   No winner can be chosen.

4.   Thirty students who need to choose a day for their final exam have the preference schedule shown below.

	12 Students	8 Students	10 Students
First choice	Friday	Thursday	Wednesday
Second choice	Wednesday	Wednesday	Thursday
Third choice	Thursday	Friday	Friday

Which day will be selected if they use the Hare system?

(a) Wednesday   (c) Friday
(b) Thursday   (d) No winner can be chosen.

5. Thirty students who need to choose a day for their final exam have the preference schedule shown below.

	12 Students	8 Students	10 Students
First choice	Friday	Thursday	Wednesday
Second choice	Wednesday	Wednesday	Thursday
Third choice	Thursday	Friday	Friday

Which day is the Condorcet winner?

(a) Wednesday
(b) Thursday
(c) Friday
(d) There is no Condorcet winner.

6. Thirty students mark those days that would be acceptable for the exam.

	Number of Students					
Students	8	6	4	4	4	4
Wednesday		X	X	X		X
Thursday	X			X	X	X
Friday			X	X	X	

Which day will be selected using approval voting?

(a) Wednesday   (c) Friday
(b) Thursday   (d) No winner can be chosen.

7. Each of four candidates is evaluated to be acceptable or unacceptable. The candidate that the most voters evaluate to be acceptable wins. This voting method is an example of

(a) sequential pairwise voting.
(b) approval voting.
(c) majority rule.

EXERCISES   ▲ *Optional.*   ■ *Advanced.*   ◆ *Discussion.*

Elections with Only Two Alternatives

1. In a few sentences, explain why a dictatorship (the voting procedure for two alternatives that is described on page 387) satisfies conditions (2) and (3) on page 387, but not (1).

2. In a few sentences, explain why imposed rule (the voting procedure for two alternatives that is described on page 387) satisfies conditions (1) and (3) on page 387, but not (2).

3. In a few sentences, explain why minority rule (the voting procedure for two alternatives that is described on page 387) satisfies conditions (1) and (2) on page 387, but not (3).

■ 4. Find (or invent) a voting rule for two alternatives that satisfies

(a) condition (1) on page 387, but neither (2) nor (3).
(b) condition (2) on page 387, but neither (1) nor (3).
(c) condition (3) on page 387, but neither (1) nor (2).

Elections with Three or More Alternatives: Procedures and Problems

5. (Everyone wins.) Consider the following set of preference lists:

	Number of Voters						
Rank	3	1	1	1	1	1	1
First	A	A	B	B	C	C	D
Second	D	B	C	C	B	D	C
Third	B	C	D	A	D	B	B
Fourth	C	D	A	D	A	A	A

Note that the first list is held by three voters, not just one. Calculate the winner using

(a) plurality voting.
(b) the Borda count.
(c) the Hare system.
(d) sequential pairwise voting with the agenda A, B, C, D.

6. Consider the following set of preference lists:

	Number of Voters				
Rank	2	2	1	1	1
First	C	D	C	B	A
Second	A	A	D	D	D
Third	B	C	A	A	B
Fourth	D	B	B	C	C

Calculate the winner using

(a) plurality voting.
(b) the Borda count.
(c) the Hare system.
(d) sequential pairwise voting with the agenda B, D, C, A.

7. Consider the following set of preference lists:

	Number of Voters					
Rank	2	2	1	1	1	1
First	A	E	A	B	C	D
Second	B	B	D	E	E	E
Third	C	D	C	C	D	A
Fourth	D	C	B	D	A	B
Fifth	E	A	E	A	B	C

Calculate the winner using

(a) plurality voting.
(b) the Borda count.
(c) the Hare system.
(d) sequential pairwise voting with the agenda B, D, C, A, E.

8. Consider the following set of preference lists:

	Number of Voters				
Rank	1	1	1	1	1
First	A	B	C	D	E
Second	B	C	B	C	D
Third	E	A	E	A	C
Fourth	D	D	D	E	A
Fifth	C	E	A	B	B

Calculate the winner using

(a) plurality voting.
(b) the Borda count.
(c) the Hare system.
(d) sequential pairwise voting with the agenda A, B, C, D, E.

9. Consider the following set of preference lists:

	Number of Voters				
Rank	2	2	1	1	1
First	A	B	A	C	D
Second	D	D	B	B	B
Third	C	A	D	D	A
Fourth	B	C	C	A	C

Calculate the winner using

(a) plurality voting.
(b) the Borda count.
(c) the Hare system.
(d) sequential pairwise voting with the agenda B, D, C, A.

10. Consider the following set of preference lists:

	Number of Voters				
Rank	2	2	1	1	1
First	C	E	C	D	A
Second	E	B	A	E	E
Third	D	D	D	A	C
Fourth	A	C	E	C	D
Fifth	B	A	B	B	B

Calculate the winner using

(a) plurality voting.
(b) the Borda count.
(c) the Hare system.
(d) sequential pairwise voting with the agenda A, B, C, D, E.

11. In a few sentences, explain why plurality voting satisfies

(a) the Pareto condition.
(b) monotonicity.

12. In a few sentences, explain why the Borda count satisfies

(a) the Pareto condition.
(b) monotonicity.

13. In a few sentences, explain why sequential pairwise voting satisfies

(a) the Condorcet winner criterion.
(b) monotonicity.

14. In a few sentences, explain why the Hare system satisfies the Pareto condition.

15. Consider the following two elections among candidates $A, B,$ and C:

	Number of Voters			
Rank	1	1	1	1
First	A	A	B	C
Second	B	B	C	B
Third	C	C	A	A

	Number of Voters			
Rank	1	1	1	1
First	A	A	B	B
Second	B	B	C	C
Third	C	C	A	A

(a) Use these two elections to show that plurality voting does not satisfy independence of irrelevant alternatives.
(b) Use these two elections to show that the Hare system does not satisfy independence of irrelevant alternatives.

16. Construct ballots for the alternatives $A, B,$ and C to show that the Borda count does not satisfy the Condorcet winner criterion.

■ 17. Suppose we have 3 voters and 4 alternatives and suppose the sequence of preference lists is as follows:

	Number of Voters		
Rank	1	1	1
First	A	C	B
Second	B	A	D
Third	D	B	C
Fourth	C	D	A

Show that if the voting system being used is sequential pairwise voting with a fixed agenda, and if you have agenda-setting power (i.e., you get to choose the order), then you can arrange for whichever alternative you want to win the election. (Your answer will consist of the 4 agendas you find—perhaps by trial and error—and the calculation of which alternative is the winner for each in sequential pairwise voting.)

■ 18. Suppose the following preference lists represent the true preferences of the 17 voters involved:

Rank	Number of Voters			
	7	5	4	1
First	A	C	B	A
Second	B	A	C	B
Third	C	B	A	C

(a)   Find the winner of the election if the Hare system is used and everyone votes sincerely.

(b)   Find the winner if the voter on the far right votes strategically.

19.   Show that the nonmonotonicity of the Hare system can also be demonstrated by the following 17-voter, 4-alternative election. (In a number of recent books, this example is used to show the nonmonotonicity of the Hare system. The easier 13-voter, 3-alternative example given in the text was pointed out to us by Matt Gendron, an undergraduate at Union College.)

Rank	Number of Voters			
	7	5	4	1
First	A	C	B	D
Second	D	A	C	B
Third	B	B	D	A
Fourth	C	D	A	C

20.   The following example illustrates how badly the Hare system can fail to satisfy monotonicity. Consider the following sequence of preference lists:

Rank	Number of Voters			
	7	6	5	3
First	A	B	C	D
Second	B	A	B	C
Third	C	C	A	B
Fourth	D	D	D	A

(a)   Show that A is the unique winner if the Hare system is used.

(b)   Find the winner using the Hare system in the new election wherein the 3 voters on the right all move A from last place on their preference lists to first place on their preference lists.

Insurmountable Difficulties: From Paradox to Impossibility

21.   Suppose we have 10 candidates (A, B, C, D, E, F, G, H, I, and J). Exhibit 10 ballots so that if each ballot were to be held by 10% of the electorate, then 90% of the voters would prefer A to B, 90% would prefer B to C, and so on down to 90% preferring I to J and then 90% preferring J to A. (*Hint:* Mimic the pattern for the three-candidate case that gave us Condorcet's voting paradox.)

22.   Construct a real-world example (perhaps involving yourself and two friends) where the individual preference lists for three alternatives are as in the voting paradox of Condorcet.

■   23.   Complete the proof of the version of Arrow's theorem from the text by showing that neither B nor C can be a winner in the situation described. (Your argument will be almost word-for-word the same as the proofs of what is in the text.)

Additional Exercises

24.   How many different ways can a voter

(a)   rank 3 choices (when ties are not allowed)?

(b)   rank 4 alternatives (without ties)?

(c)   rank n potential outcomes (without ties)?

25.   How many different ways can a voter

(a)   rank 3 choices when ties are not allowed, but *incomplete* rankings can be submitted (e.g., a first choice without giving a second or third choice)?

(b)   rank 3 choices when ties are allowed and *complete* rankings are required?

26. Ten board members vote by approval voting on eight candidates for new positions on their board as indicated in the following table. An X indicates an approval vote. For example, voter 1, in the first column, approves of candidates A, D, E, F, and G, and disapproves of B, C, and H.

	Voters									
Candidates	1	2	3	4	5	6	7	8	9	10
A	X	X	X			X	X	X		X
B		X	X	X	X	X	X	X	X	
C			X					X		
D	X	X	X	X	X		X	X	X	X
E	X		X		X		X		X	
F	X		X	X	X	X	X	X		X
G	X	X	X	X	X			X		
H		X			X		X		X	X

(a) Which candidate is chosen for the board if just one of them is to be elected?
(b) Which candidates are chosen if the top four are selected?
(c) Which candidates are elected if 80% approval is necessary and at most four are elected?
(d) Which candidates are elected if 60% approval is necessary and at most four are elected?

27. To be elected to the Baseball Hall of Fame a player must be retired for five years and receive a vote from 75% of some 420 actual voters. (A few eligible voters often do not cast a ballot.) In the election for January 1993 there were 423 voters, and the top five finishers (and their number of votes) were

Reggie Jackson (396)
Phil Niekro (278)
Orlando Cepeda (252)
Tony Perez (233)
Steve Garvey (176)

(a) Who was elected in 1993?
(b) How many more votes would Perez have needed to have been elected?
(c) What percent of the voters who did not vote for Garvey would have had to change and vote for him in order for Garvey to have been elected?
▲ (d) Is there any way in which a voter can vote in an insincere manner to help or hurt the chances of some player?

28. A player remains on the ballot for the Baseball Hall of Fame for 15 years provided he receives 5% of the votes cast each year. Some other players (and their votes) in the 1993 election were

Mickey Lolich (43)
Thurman Munson (40)
Rusty Staub (32)
Bill Maddock (19)
Ron Cey (8)

Which of these five players meets the 5% cutoff criterion (for the 423 votes cast) for remaining on the ballot for the 1994 election?

29. Consider the following set of preference lists:

	Number of Voters						
Rank	1	1	1	1	1	1	1
First	C	D	C	B	E	D	C
Second	A	A	E	D	D	E	A
Third	E	E	D	A	A	A	E
Fourth	B	C	A	E	C	B	B
Fifth	D	B	B	C	B	C	D

Calculate the winner using

(a) plurality voting.
(b) the Borda count.
(c) sequential pairwise voting with the agenda A, B, C, D, E.
(d) the Hare system.

30. An interesting variant of the Hare system was proposed by the psychologist Clyde Coombs. It operates exactly as does the Hare system, but instead of deleting alternatives with the fewest first-place votes, it deletes those with the most last-place votes.

(a)   Use the Coombs procedure to find the winner if the ballots are as in Exercise 29.

(b)   Show that for two voters and three alternatives, it is possible to have ballots that result in one alternative winning if the Coombs' procedure is used and a tie between the other two if the Hare system is used.

31.   The 45 members of a school's football team vote on three nominees, *A*, *B*, and *C*, by approval voting for the award of "most improved player" as indicated in the following table. An X indicates an approval vote.

	Number of Voters							
Nominee	7	8	9	9	6	3	1	2
A	X			X	X		X	
B		X		X		X	X	
C			X		X	X	X	

(a)   Which nominee is selected for the award?

(b)   Which nominee gets announced as runner-up for the award?

(c)   Note that two of the players "abstained," that is, approved of none of the nominees. Note also that one person approved of all three of the nominees. What would be the difference in the outcome if one were to "abstain" or "approve of everyone"?

TECHNOLOGY CORNER

Borda Counts

The spreadsheet shown in Figure 11.1 lists seven potential spring break destinations and the number of points assigned to each destination by Chris, Kim, Jan, and Tony, using a Borda count method. The first choice receives 7 points, the second receives 6 points, and so on. For example, Chris's first choice is Cincinnati and last choice is Boston. Assume that the rankings in this spreadsheet represent the sincere preferences of each person.

	A	B	C	D	E	F	G
1		Chris	Kim	Jan	Tony		Totals
2	Atlanta	6	2	5	3		16
3	Boston	1	7	6	2		16
4	Cincinnati	7	5	2	4		18
5	Denver	5	1	3	7		16
6	Evansville	3	6	1	5		15
7	Fresno	4	4	7	1		16
8	Gainesville	2	3	4	6		15

FIGURE 11.1

In order to compute the total number of points for each potential destination, use the **Sum** command to add together the four individual scores for each city. Since Cincinnati received the most points, it appears that the group is going to Cincinnati.

TASK 1.   Jan is rather unhappy with the present situation, since Cincinnati is Jan's last choice. Knowing the preferences of the other people, how can Jan change her own preference list in order that Atlanta is chosen instead? Use the spreadsheet shown in Figure 11.1 to explore how Jan's changes can impact the destination sums.

TASK 2.   Seeing Jan's changes, Kim is now unhappy, since Atlanta is Kim's next-to-last choice. Knowing the preferences of Chris and Tony, as well as Jan's new preferences, what impact can Kim make by revising his preference list?

Approval Voting

Since the previous method proved too tempting for insincerity, the group decides to instead declare which cities to which each person would prefer to go. The results of this approval voting are shown in the spreadsheet shown in Figure 11.2. Chris and Tony choose their top three selections, Kim chooses his top two selections, and Jan chooses her top five selections. Each approval is marked by a "1," and the number of votes is tallied as before. Since Denver receives the most votes, Denver appears to be the chosen destination.

TASK 3.   But Kim is unhappy, since Denver was his last choice. Assuming the other three people's votes are known, how can Kim change his approval votes so that another destination beats or ties with Denver?

	A	B	C	D	E	F	G
1		Chris	Kim	Jan	Tony		Totals
2	Atlanta	1		1			2
3	Boston		1	1			2
4	Cincinnati	1					1
5	Denver	1		1	1		3
6	Evansville		1		1		2
7	Fresno			1			1
8	Gainesville			1	1		2

FIGURE 11.2

TASK 4.   Suppose instead that Kim and Jan secretly agree to work together and the votes of Chris and Tony remain unchanged. How can Kim and Jan change their votes so that a city other than Denver is chosen?

Exploration

Create a spreadsheet that lists 10 possible local lunch destinations, showing the ranked preferences of 12 people, including yourself. If you change your own responses, how much impact can you have on the overall results?

writing projects

1 ▶   In the 1992 presidential election, the final results were as follows:

Candidates	Number of Votes	Percentage of Votes
Clinton	43,727,625	43
Bush	38,165,180	38
Perot	19,236,411	19

Making reasonable assumptions about voters' preference schedules, discuss how the election might have turned out under the different voting methods discussed in this chapter.

2 ▶   Frequently in presidential campaigns, the winner of the first few primaries is given front-runner status that can lead to the nomination of his or her party. Moreover, there are often several candidates running in early primaries such as New Hampshire. Consider a recent election (for example, the 1996 Republican primaries), and discuss how the nominating process might have proceeded through the campaign if approval voting had been used to decide primary winners.

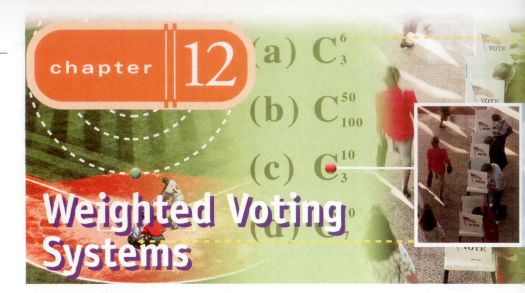

$$\text{(a) } C^6_3 \qquad \text{(b) } C^{50}_{100} \qquad \text{(c) } C^{10}_3$$

Weighted Voting Systems

"The power of a participant in a weighted voting system is the ability of the participant to influence a decision."

A **weighted voting system** is a decision-making procedure in which the participants have varying numbers of votes. Weighted voting is most commonly encountered in shareholder elections. When the shareholders of a public corporation elect a board of directors, each shareholder is entitled to one vote per share owned. Shareholders who own relatively large numbers of shares usually have greater influence in such an election than the small shareholders do.

Another important example is the electoral college, which uses a weighted voting system to elect the president of the United States (see Spotlight 12.1). In addition, some legislative bodies have such strong party discipline that each legislator always votes as dictated by his or her party. These legislatures are weighted voting systems in which the participants are the political party organizations, each of which is entitled to a number of votes equal to the size of its delegation in the legislature.

The *power* of a participant in a weighted voting system is the ability of the participant to influence a decision. We shall study two ways of measuring power, the *Banzhaf power index* and the *Shapley–Shubik power index.* We shall see that either of these indices provides a more accurate measure of a participant's power than the number of votes that the participant is entitled to cast.

How Weighted Voting Works

SMILE, Ltd., is a group dental practice with five dentists, organized as a professional corporation. Dr. Ruth Smith, who founded the practice, holds 9 shares of

Democratic National Convention, Chicago, 1996.

stock in the corporation. Her husband, Ralph, who is not a dentist, also owns 9 shares. The other dentists in the practice also own shares in the corporation; the details are listed in Table 12.1.

When a decision regarding the corporation is to be made, each of the six shareholders casts one vote for every share owned. There are 30 shares in all, and a simple majority (16 votes) is necessary to pass a motion.

A **coalition** is a set of voters that has formed to support or oppose a measure that is up for a vote. A coalition may consist of all the voters or any subset of the voters. It may consist of just one voter, or it may even be *empty*. For example, if the voting body is unanimously in favor of a motion, then the coalition opposing the motion is empty. If a coalition has enough votes to pass the measure, it is called a

TABLE 12.1	Weighted Voting, SMILE, Ltd.
Shareholder	**Number of Shares**
Ruth Smith, D.D.S.	9
Ralph Smith, C.P.A.	9
Albert Mansfield, D.D.S.	7
Katherine Ide, D.D.S.	3
Gary Lambert, D.D.S.	1
Marjorie Edwards, D.D.S.	1
Total	30

SPOTLIGHT
12.1

The Electoral College

In a presidential election, we don't actually vote for a candidate. The voters in each state vote for electors to represent their state in the electoral college. The number of electors allotted to a state is equal to the size of its congressional delegation; thus a state with one congressional district gets three electors, since it has one representative in the U.S. House of Representatives and two senators. A state with 25 representatives and 2 senators would be entitled to 27 electors.

States typically require their electors to vote as blocs. For example, the candidate who gets a plurality in California's election gets all 54 of California's electoral votes, while the candidate who carries Delaware gets all 3 of Delaware's electoral votes. In effect, the electoral college is a weighted voting system with 51 participants (the states and the District of Columbia). The weights range from 3 to 54, and the quota is a simple majority of the 538 electors, or 270.

winning coalition; otherwise it is a **losing coalition.** In SMILE, Ltd., the Smiths have enough votes to be a winning coalition. A winning coalition can also consist of one of the Smiths and Dr. Mansfield. There are also larger winning coalitions, because any of the shareholders may join one of these coalitions to form a coalition with even more votes.

The winning coalitions that include any or all of Drs. Ide, Lambert, or Edwards would still be winning coalitions without their support. Between them, these dentists have only five votes, so even if they combined all of their votes with one of the Smiths' nine votes, the total would be only 14—not enough to form a winning coalition. A coalition consisting of these three dentists and Dr. Mansfield would have only 12 votes and would also be a losing coalition. To form a winning coalition, at least two of the three more powerful shareholders, and no one else, is needed.

In this situation, Drs. Ide, Lambert, and Edwards have no voting power. We have a technical term for a voter who, although he or she may join a winning coalition, is never essential to form one: such a voter is a **dummy.**

Notation for Weighted Voting

To describe a weighted voting system, it is necessary to specify the number of votes that each voter has. This number is called the voter's **weight.** The number of votes necessary to pass a measure is called the **quota** for the voting system, and it too must be specified in the description of a weighted voting system. The shorthand notation

$$[q:w_1, w_2, \ldots, w_n]$$

is used to describe a weighted voting system with a quota q and n voters whose weights are $w_1, w_2, \ldots, w_n$. In this notation, the voting system used by SMILE, Ltd., was [16:9, 9, 7, 3, 1, 1].

If a voting system is to reach an unambiguous decision, it is important not to permit two winning coalitions to oppose each other. For this reason, we will require the quota to be more than half the sum of the weights of all the voters. Since each winning coalition must have more than half of the votes, the opposing voters will have less than half of the votes and will not form a winning coalition. To guarantee that a motion will pass when the voters favor it unanimously, we will also require that the quota be not more than the sum of the voting weights. To summarize, assuming that there are n voters, we are requiring that

$$q > \frac{1}{2}(w_1 + w_2 + \cdots + w_n)$$

and

$$q \leq w_1 + w_2 + \cdots + w_n$$

For example, the quota for SMILE, Ltd., has to be more than 15, since there are 30 votes in all. It is 16, but it could be 17, 18, or any larger number up to 30. Changing the quota can affect the way power is distributed. For example, with a quota of 17, a coalition consisting of one of the Smiths and Dr. Mansfield, with only 16 votes, is losing. If these two convinced Dr. Lambert, Dr. Ide, or Dr. Edwards to join them, they would form a winning coalition. Thus, if the quota were 17, there would be no dummies.

A **blocking coalition** is a subset of voters opposing a motion, with enough votes to defeat it. In a voting system with total weight w and quota q, any coalition with weight more than $w - q$ is a blocking coalition. For example, in SMILE, Ltd., $w = 30$, $q = 16$, and $w - q = 14$; so any coalition with 15 or more votes is a blocking coalition.

Winning coalitions always have enough votes to block a measure (remember that they have more than half the votes), but there can be blocking coalitions whose votes total less than the quota for winning. For a simple example, consider a voting system with four voters, each with one vote, and a quota of three votes to pass a measure. Any coalition of two voters opposing a measure is a blocking coalition, although these voters could not pass any measure they favored without being joined by a third voter.

In a criminal trial, the jury's decision to convict or to acquit must be unanimous, so a winning coalition requires all of the jurors. If the jury cannot agree on a verdict, a mistrial is declared and the prosecution has the right to demand a new trial. There is only one winning coalition, but every coalition with at least one member is a blocking coalition.

If the voting weight of one voter meets or exceeds the quota for passing a measure, then that voter is called a **dictator.** The other voters in the system are dummies.

The Banzh

Stock certificates.

EXAMP

SPOTLIGHT 12.2

Power Indices

Lloyd S. Shapley   *John F. Banzhaf III*   *Martin Shubik*

The first widely accepted numerical index for assessing power in voting systems was the Shapley–Shubik index, developed in 1954 by a mathematician, Lloyd S. Shapley, and an economist, Martin Shubik. A particular voter's power as measured by this index is proportional to the number of different *permutations* (or orderings) of the voters in which he or she has the potential to cast the pivotal vote—the vote that first turns from losing to winning.

The Banzhaf power index was introduced in 1965 by John F. Banzhaf III, a law professor who is also well known as the founder of the antismoking organization, ASH (Action on Smoking and Health). The Banzhaf index is the one most often cited in court rulings, perhaps because Banzhaf brought several cases to court and continues to file *amicus curiae* briefs when courts evaluate weighted voting systems. A voter's Banzhaf index is the number of different possible voting *combinations* in which he or she casts a critical vote—a vote in favor of a motion that is necessary for the motion to pass, or a vote against a motion that is essential for its defeat.

EXAMPLE *Critical Voters*

Consider a committee of three members, whom we will call *A*, *B*, and *C*. The chair of the committee, *A*, has two votes, while *B* and *C* each have one. The quota is three, and thus our shorthand notation for this voting system is

$$[3:2, 1, 1]$$

The coalition {*A*, *B*, *C*} is a winning coalition, since it has all four votes. Suppose that *A* decides to leave the coalition. We can indicate this situation schematically as follows:

A	B	C	Votes	Outcome
Yes	Yes	Yes	4	Pass
↓				
No	Yes	Yes	2	Fail

By changing her vote, *A* has changed the outcome. In this coalition, *A* is a critical voter.

Now let's go back to the original coalition and see what happens if *B* changes his vote.

A	B	C	Votes	Outcome
Yes	Yes	Yes	4	Pass
	↓			
Yes	No	Yes	3	Pass

This time, the outcome doesn't change, so *B* is not a critical voter in this coalition. Since *C* has the same power as *B*, he is also not a critical voter in the coalition. ◆

EXAMPLE *Winning and Blocking*

In the committee with members *A*, *B*, and *C*, and voting system [3:2, 1, 1], *A* and *B* have formed a coalition to vote in favor of measure *X* and to oppose another measure, *Y*. Member *C* is voting against *X* and for *Y*. Since the coalition {*A*, *B*} has 3 votes (2 for *A*, and 1 for *B*), it is a winning coalition for *X* and a blocking coalition for *Y*. When voting for *X*, both *A* and *B* are critical voters, because their votes add up to the quota. It only takes 2 votes to block a measure. If *A* leaves the coalition and joins with *C*, the measure *Y* will pass, so *A* is a critical voter in the blocking coalition. The voter *B* is not critical since *A* can block *Y* without *B*. ◆

In calculating the Banzhaf power index, the following principle is useful:

Extra Votes Principle

A winning coalition with total weight *w* has *w − q* **extra votes.** The critical voters in the coalition are those whose weight exceeds the coalition's extra votes.

The proof of the extra votes principle rests on the fact that if a voter in a winning coalition has weight exceeding the coalition's extra votes, then without that voter's support, the coalition's total weight would fall below the quota, and the coalition would be losing. Thus the voter is critical.

To calculate the Banzhaf index of a given voting system, make a list of the winning and blocking coalitions, and use the extra votes principle to identify the critical votes in each coalition. A voter's Banzhaf index is then the number of coalitions in which he or she appears as a critical voter.

EXAMPLE   *Calculating the Banzhaf Index*

We will calculate the Banzhaf index for the committee with voting system [3:2, 1, 1].

The winning coalitions are all those whose weights sum to 3 or 4, and we will start by making a list of them:

Weight	Winning Coalitions	Extra Votes
3	$\{A, B\}, \{A, C\}$	0
4	$\{A, B, C\}$	1

All members of the coalitions with 0 extra votes are critical voters. Since A is the only voter with more than 1 vote, she is the only critical voter in the coalition that has 1 extra vote. We have thus found that A is a critical voter in three winning coalitions, while B and C are each critical voters in one coalition.

Blocking coalitions have total weights of 2, 3, or 4. Here is a list of the blocking coalitions:

Weight	Blocking Coalitions	Extra Votes
2	$\{A\}, \{B, C\}$	0
3	$\{A, B\}, \{A, C\}$	1
4	$\{A, B, C\}$	2

Again, all voters in the coalitions with 0 extra votes are critical. In the blocking coalitions with 1 extra vote, only A is critical. The 4-vote blocking coalition $\{A, B, C\}$ has 2 extra votes. Since no voter has more than 2 votes, no one is a critical voter in this coalition. Voter A is critical in three blocking coalitions, while B and C are each critical in one. Adding up winning and blocking critical votes, we find that the Banzhaf index of A is 6, while B and C each have a Banzhaf index of 2. We will say that the Banzhaf index of this system is (6, 2, 2).   ◆

The Banzhaf index provides a comparison of the voting power of the participants in a voting system. In the three-member committee, we saw that A, with a Banzhaf index of 6, is three times as powerful as B or C. To determine the way voting power is distributed, we can add the numbers of critical voters for all three voters together to get $6 + 2 + 2 = 10$ critical votes in all. Thus A has $\frac{6}{10} = 60\%$ of the voting power, while B and C each have 20%.

Consider the following three voting systems:

System I: [2:1, 1, 1]
System II: [3:2, 1, 1]
System III: [3:1, 1, 1]

We have studied System II and found that its Banzhaf index is (6, 2, 2). The voters are equally powerful in systems I and III, but there is a distinction. System III requires a unanimous vote to pass a measure. There is only one winning coalition, in which all three voters are critical, and each voter is critical in the blocking coalition where he or she stands alone against the other two voters. The Banzhaf index for System III is therefore (2, 2, 2). In System I, coalitions of total weight 2 or 3 can either block or win. There are no critical voters in the coalition of weight 3, since it has 1 extra vote. In the coalitions of weight 2, all voters are critical. A voter A is therefore critical in two winning coalitions, $\{A, B\}$ and $\{A, C\}$, and in the same coalitions (with "No" voters rather than "Yes" voters) as blocking coalitions. Thus A, and each of the other voters, has a Banzhaf index of 4.

We cannot detect the difference between Systems I and III by comparing the power shares of the voters, since in both systems, power is equally divided. Since the Banzhaf index of the voters in System III is less than in System I, we can see that the individual voters in System III have less influence than they do in System I.

In the examples that we have discussed so far, each participant was a critical voter in equal numbers of winning coalitions and blocking coalitions, and you might wonder if this was by coincidence. It was not, because when a critical voter defects from a winning coalition, the opposing coalition becomes a blocking coalition, and the same voter is now a critical voter in that blocking coalition. If a critical voter defects from a blocking coalition, its opposing coalition would win, and the same voter would cast a critical vote in the new winning coalition. For example, in System II the winning coalitions and blocking coalitions for voter A correspond to each other as follows:

Winning Coalition		Blocking Coalition
$\{A, B, C\}$	$\longleftrightarrow$	$\{A\}$
$\{A, B\}$	$\longleftrightarrow$	$\{A, C\}$
$\{A, C\}$	$\longleftrightarrow$	$\{A, B\}$

In calculating the Banzhaf power index of a voting system it is useful to know that each participant is a critical voter in exactly the same number of blocking coalitions as in winning coalitions. Thus, a voter's Banzhaf index can be determined by counting the winning coalitions in which he or she is a critical voter, and doubling the result to account for the blocking coalitions.

E X A M P L E   *A Corporation with Four Shareholders*

A corporation has shareholders A, B, C, and D with 40, 30, 20, and 10 shares, respectively. They use the weighted voting system

[51:40, 30, 20, 10]

Table 12.2 shows a list of all the winning coalitions and the extra votes that each has. The four columns at the right are marked to indicate the critical voters in each coalition.

TABLE 12.2	Winning Coalitions in the Four-Stockholder Corporation					
Coalition	Weight	Extra Votes	A	B	C	D
$\{A, B, C, D\}$	100	49				
$\{A, B, C\}$	90	39	×			
$\{A, B, D\}$	80	29	×	×		
$\{A, C, D\}$	70	19	×		×	
$\{A, B\}$	70	19	×	×		
$\{B, C, D\}$	60	9		×	×	×
$\{A, C\}$	60	9	×		×	
Critical votes			5	3	3	1

By doubling the numbers of critical votes shown in the table, we arrive at the Banzhaf index for the corporation: (10, 6, 6, 2). In this model, A has

$$\frac{10}{10 + 6 + 6 + 2}$$

or approximately 42% of the voting power, while B and C each have 25% (even though B has more shares than C). Shareholder D has the remaining 8% of the power. ◆

How to Count Combinations

A **combination** is a list of voters in a voting system indicating how each voted on an issue.

In a voting system with just one voter, there are two possible outcomes of a vote: yes (Y) or no (N). With two voters, there are four possible outcomes: YY, NY, YN, NN. Each time a new voter joins a voting system, the number of possible outcomes doubles. Thus, with three voters, the first two can vote in the four ways just listed, while the third voter votes Y: YYY, NYY, YNY, NNY. The first two voters could vote in the same four ways while the third votes N: YYN, NYN, YNN, NNN. To determine the number of voting combinations in a system with n voters, we can double repeatedly to obtain 2^n possible outcomes.

Now let us consider a system with n voters and ask, in how many of the 2^n voting combinations would there be exactly k (Y) votes and $n - k$ (N) votes. For example, if $n = 4$ we could group the $2^4 = 16$ outcomes in five groups as follows:

Number of Y Votes	Voting Combinations
0	NNNN
1	YNNN, NYNN, NNYN, NNNY
2	YYNN, YNYN, YNNY, NYYN, NYNY, NNYY
3	NYYY, YNYY, YYNY, YYYN
4	YYYY

Thus, if $k = 2$, we see that there are 6 voting combinations with 2 Y and 2 N votes.

The number of voting combinations of n voters having k Y votes and $n - k$ N votes is denoted C_k^n. When speaking, people often refer to C_k^n as "n choose k." According to the list of combinations for $n = 4$, $C_0^4 = 1$, $C_1^4 = 4$, $C_2^4 = 6$, $C_3^4 = 4$, and $C_4^4 = 1$.

Let us determine C_2^5. Instead of listing the voting combinations, we will list the two-voter coalitions, taken from a set of voters $\{A, B, C, D, E\}$.

Coalitions involving A: $\{A, B\}, \{A, C\}, \{A, D\}, \{A, E\}$
Coalitions involving B: $\{B, A\}, \{B, C\}, \{B, D\}, \{B, E\}$
Coalitions involving C: $\{C, A\}, \{C, B\}, \{C, D\}, \{C, E\}$
Coalitions involving D: $\{D, A\}, \{D, B\}, \{D, C\}, \{D, E\}$
Coalitions involving E: $\{E, A\}, \{E, B\}, \{E, C\}, \{E, D\}$

There are 5×4 combinations listed, but each coalition appears twice on the list. For example, $\{B, D\}$ is listed as a coalition involving B and as a coalition involving

D. To correct for the double counting, we must divide the number of combinations on the list by 2 to obtain

$$C_2^5 = \frac{5 \times 4}{2} = 10$$

A similar formula could be used to find C_2^4:

$$C_2^4 = \frac{4 \times 3}{2} = 6$$

This is a special case of a general formula for C_k^n.

$$C_k^n = \frac{n \times (n - 1) \times (n - 2) \times \cdots \times (n - k + 1)}{k \times (k - 1) \times (k - 2) \times \cdots \times 1}$$

An easy way to remember the formula for C_k^n is that both the numerator and the denominator each have k (the number of yes votes) factors; the factors of the numerator start with n (the total number of voters) and count down, while the factors of the denominator start with k and count down. Many scientific calculators have keys for calculating C_k^n.

EXAMPLE   *Using the Combination Formula*

To determine the number of voting combinations with three Y votes and three N votes that can occur in a set of six voters, we calculate

$$C_3^7 = \frac{7 \times 6 \times 5}{3 \times 2 \times 1} = 35 \quad \blacklozenge$$

Calculating C_k^n can be simplified by making a simple observation. If there are n voters, C_k^n is the number of ways that k of the voters could vote Y while $n - k$ vote N. If each voter should change his or her vote, a voting combination with $n - k$ Y votes and k N votes would be obtained. Therefore, the number of combinations with k Y voters from a set of n is equal to the number of combinations with $n - k$ Y voters from a set of n. In symbols,

Duality Formula

$$C_{n-k}^n = C_k^n$$

E X A M P L E   *Using the Duality Formula*

Let us calculate C_{23}^{25}. If we do not use the duality formula, it will be necessary to work with a fraction in which both the numerator and the denominator are determined by multiplying 23 numbers together. In the duality formula, put $n = 25$ and $k = 23$. Then $n - k = 2$, so

$$C_{23}^{25} = C_2^{25} = \frac{25 \times 24}{2} = 300 \quad \blacklozenge$$

Efficient counting methods make it possible to compute the Banzhaf power index of large weighted voting systems. The method of counting combinations applies to systems in which most of the voters have equal weights, as in the following example.

E X A M P L E   *A Seven-Person Committee*

The chairperson of a committee has three votes. There are six ordinary members, each of whom casts one vote. The quota for passing a measure is five, so we are considering a voting system

$$[5:3, 1, 1, 1, 1, 1, 1]$$

We will calculate the Banzhaf power index for each person in the committee.

Let M be an ordinary number, with weight 1. By the extra votes principle, M will be a critical voter in all winning coalitions with no extra votes. These coalitions have exactly five votes, including that of M. We can build such coalitions by including the chairperson and one other member along with M, or by not including the chairperson and including four other members with M.

There are C_4^5 ways to assemble a five-vote coalition consisting of M and four of the five *other* ordinary members, and C_1^5 ways to choose one of the *other* ordinary members to join M and the chairperson to form a winning coalition. By the duality formula, $C_4^5 = C_1^5$, and we know that $C_1^5 = 5$. Therefore there are $5 + 5 = 10$ winning coalitions in which M is critical. The Banzhaf power index of M (and each of the other ordinary members) is 20, counting the 10 winning coalitions and an equal number of blocking coalitions.

The chairperson C is a critical voter in any winning coalition with not more than two extra votes. Thus, C must be joined by at least two, and not more than four, ordinary members. There are C_2^6 ways to choose 2 ordinary members to join the chairperson, C_3^6 ways to choose 3, and C_4^6 ways to choose 4. The number of winning coalitions in which C is a critical voter is thus $C_2^6 + C_3^6 + C_4^6$. Since $C_2^6 = \frac{6 \times 5}{2 \times 1} = 15$, $C_3^6 = \frac{6 \times 5 \times 4}{3 \times 2 \times 1} = 20$, and $C_4^6 = C_2^6$ by duality, this is a total of 50 winning coalitions, and counting 50 blocking coalitions as well, the Banzhaf power index of C is 100. We say that the Banzhaf index of the committee as a whole is

$$(100, 20, 20, 20, 20, 20, 20)$$

The total number of critical votes is $100 + 6 \times 20 = 220$. Thus, according to the Banzhaf model, the chairperson has $\frac{100}{220}$, or about 45%, of the power in the committee, and each of the other members has about 9% of the power.   ◆

In voting systems where there are voters with many different weights, other counting methods must be used. For example, in the presidential election years 1992, 1996, and 2000, the electoral college of the United States has 21 different weights, ranging from 3 to 54 votes. The brute force method is completely impractical: the participants are the 50 states and the District of Columbia, so there are $2^{51} = 2,251,799,813,685,248$ coalitions to examine. This would take over 70 years at one million per second. Advanced counting methods make it possible to compute the Banzhaf index of the electoral college in a few minutes with a home

TABLE 12.3 **The Electoral College**			
States	Electoral Votes	Nominal Power (%)	Banzhaf Power (%)
CA	54	10.04	11.14
NY	33	6.13	6.20
TX	32	5.95	6.00
FL	25	4.65	4.63
PA	23	4.28	4.25
IL	22	4.09	4.06
OH	21	3.90	3.87
MI	18	3.35	3.30
NJ	15	2.79	2.75
NC	14	2.60	2.56
GA, VA	13	2.42	2.38
IN, MA	12	2.23	2.19
MO, TN, WA, WI	11	2.04	2.01
MD, MN	10	1.86	1.82
AL, LA	9	1.67	1.64
AZ, CO, CT, KY, OK, SC	8	1.49	1.46
IA, MS, OR	7	1.30	1.28
AR, KS	6	1.12	1.09
NE, NM, UT, WV	5	0.93	0.91
HI, ID, ME, NV, NH, RI	4	0.74	0.73
AK, DE, DC, MT, ND, SD, VT, WY	3	0.56	0.55

Note: A state's nominal power is the number of electoral votes that it has, expressed as a percentage of the total number of electoral votes for the nation (538). A state's Banzhaf power is the Banzhaf power index, expressed as a percentage of the total number of critical votes for all states in all winning and blocking coalitions (9,426,404,631,750,950 critical votes in all).

computer. Table 12.3 displays the result of one such calculation, done by using a method described in the article by Paul J. Affuso and Steven J. Brams cited in the Suggested Readings for this chapter. The same method is implemented at the Web address cited in this chapter.

Equivalent Voting Systems

The purpose of a weighted voting system is to determine which coalitions are winning and which are losing. But if there are just two voters, A and B, how many really different voting systems are there? We can agree that the empty coalition ({}) is surely a losing coalition and that the unanimous coalition ({A, B}) must be a winning coalition. Therefore there are only three distinct voting systems involving A and B: in the first, unanimous consent is required for each measure, so the only winning coalition is {A, B}. In the second, A is the dictator, and the winning coalitions are {A} and {A, B}. In the third voting system B is the dictator, and the winning coalitions are {B} and {A, B}. Of course, there is an infinite number of ways that we can assign weights to the voters and a quota for passing measures in this two-voter system. However, there are only three ways to distribute the voting power: A as dictator, B as dictator, or consensus rule.

> Two voting systems are **equivalent** if there is a way for all of the voters of the first system to exchange places with the voters of the second system and preserve all winning coalitions.

For example, the weighted voting systems [50:49, 1] and [4:3, 3], involving pairs of voters A, B and C, D, respectively, are equivalent because in each system, unanimous support is required to pass a measure. We could have A exchange places with C, and B exchange places with D.

Now consider two voting systems involving the same pair of voters, A, B. In the first, [2:2, 1], A is a dictator, while in the second, [5:3, 6], B dictates. To show that the two systems are equivalent, have A and B exchange places *with each other*. Here, the pairing is $A \leftrightarrow B$, $B \leftrightarrow A$. The winning coalitions for the first system, {A} and {A, B}, correspond to the winning coalitions {B}, {A, B} of the second, so the systems are equivalent. "Equivalent" does not mean "the same." The system where A dictates to B is not the same as the system where B dictates to A. The systems are equivalent because each has a dictator and thus they have the same underlying structure.

Every two-voter system is equivalent either to a system with a dictator or to one that requires consensus. As the number of voters increases, the number of

TABLE 12.4	Voting Systems with Three Participants		
System	Minimal Winning Coalitions	Quota: Weights	Banzhaf Index
Dictator	{A}	[3:3, 1, 1]	(8, 0, 0)
Clique	{A, B}	[4:2, 2, 1]	(4, 4, 0)
Majority	{A, B}, {A, C}, {B, C}	[2:1, 1, 1]	(4, 4, 4)
Chair veto	{A, B}, {A, C}	[3:2, 1, 1]	(6, 2, 2)
Unanimous	{A, B, C}	[3:1, 1, 1]	(2, 2, 2)

different types of voting systems increases. Table 12.4 lists all five types of three-voter systems. Each of these systems can be presented as a weighted voting system, and suitable weights are given in the table. If we want to make a similar list of all types of four-voter systems, we can start by making each three-voter system into a four-voter system. This is done by putting a fourth voter into the system, without including him or her in any of the minimal winning coalitions. This makes the fourth voter a dummy. There are nine more four-voter systems that don't have any dummies. It is interesting to try to list as many of these systems as you can.

A winning coalition in which every member is a critical voter is called a **minimal winning coalition.**

A voting system can be completely described by listing the minimal winning coalitions. All other winning coalitions are formed by adding voters to minimal winning coalitions.

EXAMPLE *Minimal Winning Coalitions in the Four-Shareholder Corporation*

Table 12.2 lists the five winning coalitions in the corporation with voting system [51:40, 30, 20, 10]. The minimal ones are those in which each voter is marked as critical: {A, B}, {A, C}, and {B, C, D}. ◆

The essential properties of a voting system are apparent when we find the minimal winning coalitions. For example, if some voter belongs to all of the minimal winning coalitions, that voter has veto power. Any voter who doesn't belong to any minimal winning coalition is a dummy. In the four-shareholder corporation, we see that there are no dummies, and no one has veto power either.

FIGURE 12.1
Minimal winning coalitions for the four-shareholder corporation.

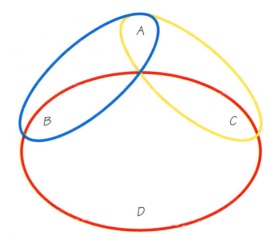

When listing the minimal winning coalitions of a voting system, you should be alert for two pitfalls:

a. If two minimal winning coalitions are distinct, each must have a voter who does not belong to the other.
b. Every pair of minimal winning coalitions has to overlap, with at least one voter in common.

Figure 12.1 displays the minimal winning coalitions of the four-shareholder corporation. You can see that property (a) is satisfied, because no minimal winning coalition lies within the boundary of another; and that (b) is also satisfied, because every pair of minimal winning coalitions have at least one voter in common.

An easy way to construct a new voting system is to specify a set of minimal winning coalitions satisfying requirements (a) and (b).

E X A M P L E   *A Five-Voter System*

Five voters, *A*, *B*, *C*, *D*, and *E*, are split into two committees, {*A*, *B*, *C*} and {*C*, *D*, *E*}. (Notice that *C* belongs to both committees.) The voting rule is that to pass a measure, at least one of the committees has to approve unanimously. The minimal winning coalitions of this voting system are the two committees (see Figure 12.2).

This five-voter system is not equivalent to any weighted voting system. We can see why by supposing for a moment that we have assigned weights to the voters and a quota so that these are the minimal winning coalitions. Since {*A*, *B*, *C*, *D*}

FIGURE 12.2
The five-voter system: minimal winning coalitions.

REVIEW VOCABULARY

Banzhaf power index   A numerical measure of power for participants in a voting system. A participant's Banzhaf index is the number of winning or blocking coalitions in which he or she is a critical voter.

Blocking coalition   A set of participants in a voting system that can prevent a measure from passing by voting against it.

C_k^n The number of combinations of n voters with k "yes" votes and $n - k$ "no" votes. This number, referred to as "n choose k," is given by the formula

$$C_k^n = \frac{n \times (n-1) \times \cdots \times (n-k+1)}{k \times (k-1) \times \cdots \times 1}.$$

Remember that the numerator is the product of k numbers starting with n and counting down; the denominator is the product of k numbers starting with k and counting down.

Coalition   A set consisting of some, all, or none of the participants in a voting system.

Combination   A list of voters indicating the vote of each on an issue. There is a total of 2^n combinations in an n-element set, and C_k^n combinations with k "yes" votes and $n - k$ "no" votes.

Critical voter   A member of a winning coalition whose vote is essential for the coalition to win, or a member of a blocking coalition whose vote is essential for the coalition to block.

Dictator   A participant in a voting system who can pass any issue even if all other voters oppose it, and block any issue even if all other voters approve it.

Duality formula $C_k^n = C_{n-k}^n$.

Dummy   A participant who has no power in a voting system. A dummy is never a critical voter in any winning or blocking coalition, and is never the pivotal voter in any permutation.

Equivalent voting systems   Two voting systems are equivalent if there is a way for all of the voters of the first system to exchange places with the voters of the second system and preserve all winning coalitions.

Extra votes   The number of votes in excess of the quota that a winning coalition has.

Extra votes principle   The critical voters in the coalition are those whose weights are more than the extra votes of the coalition. For example, if a coalition has 12 votes and the quota is 9, there are 3 extra votes. The critical voters in the coalition are those with more than 3 votes.

Factorial   If n is a positive integer, the factorial of n (denoted $n!$) is the product of all the positive integers less than or equal to n. It is usually a big number: 10! is a seven-digit number, 9000! is a seven-page number.

Losing coalition   A coalition that does not have the voting power to get its way.

Minimal winning coalition   A winning coalition that will become losing if any member defects. Each member is a critical voter.

Permutation   A specific ordering from first to last of the elements of a set; for example, an ordering of the participants in a voting system.

Pivotal voter   The first voter in a permutation who, with his or her predecessors in the permutation, will form a winning coalition. Each permutation has one and only one pivotal voter.

Quota   The minimum number of votes necessary to pass a measure in a weighted voting system.

Shapley–Shubik power index   A numerical measure of power for participants in a voting system. A participant's Shapley–Shubik index is the number of permutations of the voters in which he or she is the pivotal voter, divided by the number of permutations ($n!$ if there are n participants).

Veto power   A voter has veto power if no issue can pass without his or her vote. A voter with veto power is a one-person blocking coalition.

Weight   The number of votes assigned to a voter in a weighted voting system, or the total number of votes of all voters in a coalition.

Weighted voting system   A voting system in which the participants can have different numbers of votes. It can be represented as $[q : w(A_1), w(A_2), \ldots, w(A_n)]$, where $A_1, \ldots, A_n$ are the voters, $w(A_1), \ldots, w(A_n)$ represent the numbers of votes held by these voters, and q is the quota necessary to win.

Winning coalition   A set of participants in a voting system who can pass a measure by voting for it.

SUGGESTED READINGS

AFFUSO, PAUL J., AND STEVEN J. BRAMS. Power and size: A new paradox, *Theory and Decision,* 7(1976): 29–56. This paper explains a technique involving algebra for calculating the Banzhaf and Shapley–Shubik power indices.

BANZHAF, JOHN F. III. Weighted voting doesn't work, *Rutgers Law Review,* 19 (1965): 317–343. The author defines the Banzhaf index and uses it to show that the weighted voting system in use by the Nassau County Board of Supervisors was unfair.

BANZHAF, JOHN F. III. One man, 3.312 . . . votes: A mathematical analysis of the electoral college, *Villanova Law Review,* 13 (1968): 304–332. The author shows that voters residing in the more populous states have more power to influence the outcome of a presidential election. The same issue has commentaries on Banzhaf's analysis (pp. 333–346). Another commentary appears in the same *Review,* 14 (1968): 86–96.

BRAMS, STEVEN J. *Game Theory and Politics,* Free Press, New York, 1975. Chapter 5 treats the Shapley–Shubik and Banzhaf indices.

BRAMS, STEVEN J. *The Presidential Election Game,* Yale University Press, New Haven, Conn., 1978.

BRAMS, STEVEN J., W. F. LUCAS, AND P. D. STRAFFIN, JR., EDS. *Political and Related Models. Modules in Applied Mathematics,* vol. 2, Springer-Verlag, New York, 1983. Chapters 9–11 are devoted to measuring power in weighted and other types of voting systems. The Banzhaf and Shapley–Shubik indices are the focus of chapters 9 and 11; chapter 10 is about an index based on counting minimal winning coalitions.

FELSENTHAL, DAN S., AND MOSHE MACHOVER. *The Measurement of Voting Power: Theory and Practice, Problems and Paradoxes,* Edward Elgar, Cheltenham, UK, 1998. This monograph covers the Shapley–Shubik and Banzhaf indices thoroughly. It includes a thorough analysis of an extremely important weighted voting system: the Council of Ministers of the European Community.

Iannucci v. *Board of Supervisors of Washington County.* 20 N.Y. 2d 244, 251, 229 N.E. 2d 195, 198, 282 N.Y.S. 2d 502, 507 (1967). This code will help a law librarian find this case for you. It opened a "mathematical quagmire."

LAMBERT, JOHN P. Voting games, power indices, and presidential elections, *UMAP Journal,* 9(3) (1988): 213–267.

LUCAS, WILLIAM F. *Fair Voting: Weighted Votes for Unequal Constituencies,* COMAP: HistoMAP Module 19, Lexington, Mass., 1992. An introduction to the power indices with emphasis on the historical aspects.

TAYLOR, ALAN D. *Mathematics and Politics: Strategy, Voting Power, and Proof,* Springer-Verlag, New York, 1995. Chapter 4 covers weighted voting systems and their analysis using the Shapley–Shubik and Banzhaf indices. It has no mathematical prerequisites, but it does include carefully written logical arguments that must be carefully read.

SUGGESTED WEB SITE

www.math.temple.edu/~cow/bpi.html This site has an interactive program that will calculate the Banzhaf index of weighted voting systems.

SKILLS CHECK

1. What would be the quota for a voting system that has a total of 20 voters and uses a simple majority quota?

   (a)   10
   (b)   11
   (c)   20

2. For the weighted voting system $[q:w(A), w(B), w(C)] = [65:60, 30, 10]$, which statement is true?

   (a) A is a dictator.
   (b) B has veto power.
   (c)   Every person has power.

3. Two daughters each hold six votes and a son has the remaining two votes for a trust fund. Which statement is true?

   (a)   The son is a dummy voter.
   (b)   The son is not a dummy voter but has less power than a daughter.
   (c)   The three children have equal power.

4. Which voters A, B, C, D in the weighted voting system $[10:4, 4, 3, 2]$ have veto power?

   (a)   No one
   (b) A and B only
   (c)   Everyone

5. What is the value of C_2^6?

   (a)   12
   (b)   15
   (c)   32

6. For the weighted voting system $[6:4, 3, 2, 1]$, find the Banzhaf power index for the voter with three votes.

   (a)   3
   (b)   6
   (c)   14

7. Calculate the Shapley–Shubik power index for the three-vote voter in the weighted voting system $[6:4, 3, 2, 1]$.

   (a)   1/4
   (b)   5/24
   (c)   1/12

EXERCISES   ▲ *Optional.*   ■ *Advanced.*   ◆ *Discussion.*

How Weighted Voting Works

◆   1.   A committee has 9 members. What constitutes a winning coalition, and what constitutes a blocking coalition, if

   (a)   majority rules?
   (b)   a two-thirds majority is required to pass a motion?
   (c)   a unanimous vote is required to pass a motion?

What if the committee has only 8 members?

◆   2.   Is it possible to have a weighted voting system in which more votes are required to block a measure than to pass a measure?

◆   3.   For each of the following weighted voting systems, list

   1.   all winning coalitions containing the first voter.

2. all blocking coalitions containing the first voter.

3. all voters that have veto power.

4. all dummy voters.

(a) [51:52, 48]
(b) [2:1, 1, 1]
(c) [3:2, 2, 1]
(d) [8:5, 4, 3]
(e) [51:45, 43, 8, 4]
(f) [51:28, 27, 26, 19]
(g) [16:10, 10, 10, 1]
(h) [21:10, 10, 10, 10, 1]

4. List all of the winning coalitions of a committee of four members, *A*, *B*, *C*, and *D*, with voting system [51:30, 25, 24, 21].

5. How would the list in Exercise 4 change if the quota were increased to

(a) 52?
(b) 55?
(c) 58?

6. Voter *A* in Exercise 4 would like to have veto power. How much should the quota be increased to give her, and no one else, veto power?

The Banzhaf Power Index

7. (a) List the 16 possible combinations of how four voters, *A*, *B*, *C*, and *D*, can vote either yes (Y) or no (N) on an issue.
(b) List the 16 subsets of the set {*A*, *B*, *C*, *D*}.
◆ (c) How do the lists in parts (a) and (b) correspond to each other?
(d) In how many of the combinations in part (a) is the vote

(i) 4 Y to 0 N?
(ii) 3 Y to 1 N?
(iii) 2 Y to 2 N?

8. Calculate the number of extra votes for each of the winning coalitions found in Exercise 4. Identify the winning coalitions in which

(a) *A* is a critical voter.
(b) *B* is a critical voter.

9. Calculate the Banzhaf index for the voting system in Exercise 4.

10. The system in Exercise 4 is modified by increasing the quota to

(a) 52
(b) 55
(c) 58
(d) 73
(e) 76
(f) 79
(g) 82

Calculate the Banzhaf index in each case. (*Hint:* Increasing the quota will reduce the number of extra votes in each of the original coalitions. When the number of extra votes becomes negative, the coalition is losing and you can cross it off the list. As the number of extra votes decreases, a member of a coalition who was originally not a critical voter will become a critical voter.)

11. Calculate the Banzhaf index for each of the weighted voting systems in Exercise 3.

12. Calculate the following:

(a) C_3^6
(b) C_{100}^{50}
(c) C_3^{10}
(d) C_7^{10}

13. Calculate the following:

(a) C_4^6
(b) C_2^{100}
(c) C_{98}^{100}
(d) C_5^{10}

14. The Board of Supervisors of Nassau County, New York, is a historically important example of a weighted voting system (see Spotlight 12.3). Before it was declared unconstitutional by a federal district court in 1993, the weighted voting system of the

Board of Supervisors was changed several times. The weights in use since 1958 were as follows:

Year	Quota	Weights					
		H_1	H_2	N	B	G	L
1958	16	9	9	7	3	1	1
1964	58	31	31	21	28	2	2
1970	63	31	31	21	28	2	2
1976	71	35	35	23	32	2	3
1982	65	30	28	15	22	6	7

Here H_1 is the presiding supervisor, always from the community of Hempstead, H_2 is the second supervisor from Hempstead, and N, B, G, and L are the supervisors from North Hempstead, Oyster Bay, Glen Cove, and Long Beach.

◆ (a) From 1970 on, more than a simple majority was required to pass any measure. Give an argument in favor of this policy from the viewpoint of a supervisor who would benefit from it, and an argument against the policy from the viewpoint of a supervisor who would lose some power.
(b) In which years were some supervisors dummy voters?
(c) Suppose the two Hempstead supervisors always vote together. In which years are some of the supervisors dummy voters?
(d) Assume that the two Hempstead supervisors always agree, so that the board is in effect a five-voter system. Determine the Banzhaf index of this system in each year.
(e) In 1982, a special supermajority of 72 votes was needed to pass measures that required a two-thirds majority. If the two Hempstead supervisors vote together, what is the Banzhaf index of the resulting five-voter system?
◆ (f) Table 12.7 gives the 1980 census for each municipality, the number of votes assigned to each supervisor, and the Banzhaf index for each supervisor in 1982. Do you think the voting scheme was fair?

Equivalent Voting Systems

15. Consider a four-person voting system with voters A, B, C, and D. The winning coalitions are $\{A, B, C, D\}$, $\{A, B, C\}$, $\{A, B, D\}$, $\{A, C, D\}$, and $\{A, B\}$.

(a) List the minimal winning coalitions.
(b) List the minimal blocking coalitions.
(c) Determine the Banzhaf power index for this voting system.
(d) Find an equivalent weighted voting system.

TABLE 12.7   Nassau County Board of Supervisors, 1982

Supervisor from	Population	Number of Votes	Banzhaf Power Index	
Quota			65	72
Hempstead (Presiding)	738,517	30	30	26
Hempstead		28	26	22
North Hempstead	218,624	15	18	18
Oyster Bay	305,750	22	22	18
Glen Cove	24,618	6	2	2
Long Beach	43,073	7	6	6
Totals	1,321,582	108	104	92

16. A committee has a chairperson and six ordinary members. It uses majority rule, except that the chairperson is only allowed to vote when it is necessary to break a tie. Give an equivalent weighted voting system for the committee. What would happen if one of the members is absent?

◆ 17. A five-member committee has the following voting system. The chairperson can pass or block any motion that she supports or opposes, provided that at least one other member is on her side. Show that this voting system is equivalent to the weighted voting system $[4:3, 1, 1, 1, 1]$.

18. Calculate the Banzhaf index for the weighted voting system in Exercise 17.

19. Which of the following voting systems are equivalent to weighted voting systems? Find the weights and quota for those that are.

   (a) A committee of three faculty and the dean. To pass a measure, at least two faculty members and the dean must vote yes.
   (b) A committee of three faculty, the dean, and the provost. To pass a measure, two faculty, the dean, and the provost must vote yes.
   (c) A four-member faculty committee and a three-member administration committee vote separately on each issue. The measure passes if it receives the support of a majority of each of the committees.

20. Calculate the Banzhaf index of each of the voting systems in Exercise 19.

◆ 21. How many *distinct* (nonequivalent) voting systems with four voters can you find? Systems that have dummies don't count. The challenge is to find all nine.

The Shapley–Shubik Power Index

22. For the voting system in Exercise 4, list all permutations of the voters in which

   (a) *A* is the pivotal voter.
   (b) *B* is the pivotal voter.

23. Calculate the Shapley–Shubik index for the system in Exercise 4.

24. Calculate the Shapley–Shubik index for the weighted voting system in Exercise 17.

25. Calculate the Shapley–Shubik index of each of the voting systems in Exercise 19.

Systems with Large Numbers of Voters

26. A corporation has 120 shares of stock outstanding. There are 100 shareholders who own one share each, and one shareholder who owns 20 shares. To pass an issue, owners representing 61 shares must vote yes. Determine the Shapley–Shubik index of each shareholder.

■ 27. Estimate the power of the shareholders of the corporation in Exercise 26, as measured by the Banzhaf index.

Miscellaneous Problems

◆ 28. The vice president of the United States is allowed to break ties in the U.S. Senate. How does his or her Banzhaf power index compare with that of an individual senator?

29. Determine the Shapley–Shubik power index for the four-person voting system described in Exercise 15.

30. A corporation has four shareholders and a total of 100 shares. The quota for passing a measure is the votes of shareholders owning 51 or more shares. The number of shares owned are as follows:

   A 48 shares
   B 23 shares
   C 22 shares
   D 7 shares

All transactions must be in whole numbers of shares; sales of fractional shares are not permitted.

   (a) List the winning coalitions and compute the number of extra votes for each. Make a separate list of the losing coalitions and compute the number of votes that would be needed to make the coalition winning.

(b)   How many shares can A sell to B without causing any of the winning coalitions listed in part (a) to lose, or any of the losing coalitions in part (a) to win?

(c)   How many shares can A sell to D without changing the sets of winning or losing coalitions?

(d) E, who now owns none of the stock, would like to buy some. How many shares can A sell to E without changing the winning coalitions? Note that since E is now a dummy, he must remain a dummy after the trade.

(e)   How many shares can D sell, without changing the set of winning coalitions, to A, B, C, or E? Again, it is conceivable that D would be able to sell more to one stockholder than to another.

(f)   How many shares can D sell to A, B, C, or E without becoming a dummy?

(g)   How many shares can B sell to C without changing the set of winning coalitions?

31.   Which of the following voting systems is equivalent to the voting system in use by the corporation in Exercise 30?

(a) $[3:1, 1, 1, 1]$
(b) $[3:2, 1, 1, 1]$
(c) $[5:3, 1, 1, 1]$
(d) $[5:3, 2, 1, 1]$
(e) $[5:3, 2, 2, 2]$

32.   Determine the Banzhaf and Shapley–Shubik power indices for the corporation in Exercise 30.

33.   (a)   Show that $C_3^5 + C_4^5 = C_4^6$.
(b)   Show that $C_5^9 + C_6^9 = C_6^{10}$.
◆   (c)   Explain why the following combinatorial identity is true.

$$C_{k-1}^n + C_k^n = C_k^{n+1}$$

(*Hint:* Consider k-member coalitions in an $n + 1-$ member committee. Count those that have the chairperson as a member, and those that do not include the chairperson.)

34.   A nine-member committee has a chairperson and eight ordinary members. A motion can pass if and only if it has the support of the chairperson and at least two other members, or if it has the support of all eight ordinary members.

(a)   Find an equivalent weighted voting system.
(b)   Determine the Banzhaf power index.
(c)   Determine the Shapley–Shubik power index.

35.   Consider the $2m$-person voting system in which each participant has one vote and a simple majority wins. In the notation for weighted voting systems, this system can be expressed as

$$[m + 1:1, \ . \ . \ . \ , 1]$$

Assume that all voting combinations are equally likely. What is the probability that a voter will be a critical voter, when $m = 1, 2, 3, 4, 5, 6,$ or 7?

36.   The New York City Board of Estimate consists of the mayor, the comptroller, the city council president, and the presidents of each of the five boroughs. It employed a voting system in which the city officials each had two votes and borough presidents each had one; the quota to pass a measure was six. This voting system was declared unconstitutional by the U.S. Supreme Court in 1989 (*Morris* v. *Board of Estimate*).

(a)   Describe the minimal winning coalitions.
■   (b)   Determine the Banzhaf power index.

37.   Here is a proposed weighted voting system for the New York City Board of Estimate that is based on the populations of the boroughs (see Exercise 36):

$$[71:35, 35, 35, 11.3, 7.3, 9.6, 6.0, 1.8]$$

Find a simpler system of weights that yields an equivalent voting system.

38.   The United Nations Security Council has five permanent members: China, France, Russia, the United Kingdom, and the United States, and 10 other members that serve 2-year terms. To resolve a

dispute not involving a member of the council, nine votes, including the votes of each of the permanent members, are required. (Thus each permanent member has veto power.)

◆ (a) Show that this voting system is equivalent to the weighted voting system in which each permanent member has 7 votes, each ordinary member has 1 vote, and the quota is 39.

■ (b) Compute the Banzhaf index for the Security Council.

■ (c) Compute the Shapley–Shubik index for the Security Council. (This is harder than computing the Banzhaf index.)

◆ (d) Which index is most appropriate for measuring power in the Security Council?

▲ 39. The ABC College Student Senate is a five-member body with simple majority rule; each member has one vote. Two members of the senate, A and B, have a pact to vote together.

(a) In how many voting combinations do A and B cast the same vote?

(b) Say that $\{A, B\}$ is a critical voter in a voting combination if the result of the vote would be reversed if both A and B defected. In how

many of the voting combinations in part (a) is $\{A, B\}$ a critical voter?

(c) In how many voting combinations in part (a) would Senator C, who is not involved in a pact, be a critical voter?

(d) How does A's pact with B affect the probability that A will be a critical voter? How does it affect C's chance of being a critical voter?

▲ 40. Senators A and B have quarreled in the ABC College Student Senate (see Exercise 39). In the future, they will never be on the same side of *any* issue.

(a) In how many voting combinations will A and B be on opposite sides?

(b) In how many of the voting combinations in part (a) is A a critical voter?

(c) In how many of the voting combinations in part (a) is C a critical voter?

(d) How does the quarrel affect the distribution of power, as compared to independent voting?

41. The political spectrum of the Israeli Parliament following the May 17, 1999, election is shown below. Which party has the pivot position?

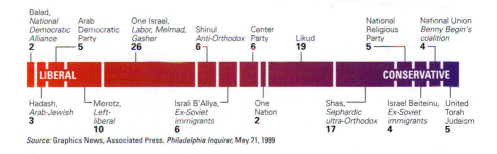

Source: Graphics News, Associated Press. *Philadelphia Inquirer*, May 21, 1999

TECHNOLOGY CORNER

A Three-Person Weighted Voting System

The 3rd through the 10th rows of the spreadsheet shown in Figure 12.3 demonstrate the ways that three people can cast their ballots. Here, "1" indicates "yes" and "0" indicates "no." Assume that Peter has 4 votes, Paul has 3 votes, Mary has 2 votes, and a (simple majority) quota of 5 votes is needed to pass a motion. This is the weighted voting system [5:4, 3, 2].

To compute the number of votes represented by position A3, B3, and C3, the following formula is placed at position D3: $=4*A3 + 3*B3 + 2*C3$. The formula can then be copied and pasted at positions D4 through D10. (Because spreadsheets define positions in a relative fashion, the position numbers in the formula will change when the formula is copied.)

Noting that the quota is 5, one can then manually mark each row as a "pass" or "fail," as shown in the final column.

TASK 1.   Even though Peter, Paul, and Mary have different numbers of votes, they have the same power in this system. Use the spreadsheet shown in Figure 12.3 to justify this fact.

TASK 2.   Change the spreadsheet shown in Figure 12.3 to model the weighted voting system

[6:5, 4, 3]. How do the incidents of passing or failing under this model compare to those of the original system [5:4, 3, 2]? How do they compare to the incidents under the system [8:7, 6, 5]?

TASK 3.   What is the smallest quota for [q:4, 3, 2] in which the three people do not have equal power?

A Four-Person Weighted Voting System

By copying and pasting, one can create a spreadsheet model for four people. From the first example, copy the rectangle with corners A3, C3, A10, C10, and paste it in the spreadsheet shown in Figure 12.4 as the rectangle with corners at B3, D3, B10, D10, and also as the rectangle with corners B11, D11, B18, D18. Put a "1" at A3 and copy it onto A4 through A10. Put a "0" at A11 and copy it onto A12 through A18. The resulting grid demonstrates the 16 ways that four people can vote on an issue. Suppose the weighted voting system is [q:5, 4, 2, 2] and place formulas in the "votes" column, as before, to compute the number of votes for each row.

	A	B	C	D	E	F
1	Chris (5)	Jay (4)	Erin (2)	Olaf (2)		quota: ?
2					votes	
3	1	1	1	1	13	
4	1	1	1	0	11	
5	1	1	0	1	11	
6	1	1	0	0	9	
7	1	0	1	1	9	
8	1	0	1	0	7	
9	1	0	0	1	7	
10	1	0	0	0	5	
11	0	1	1	1	8	
12	0	1	1	0	6	
13	0	1	0	1	6	
14	0	1	0	0	4	
15	0	0	1	1	4	
16	0	0	1	0	2	
17	0	0	0	1	2	
18	0	0	0	0	0	

FIGURE 12.4

	A	B	C	D	E
1	Peter (4)	Paul (3)	Mary (2)		quota: 5
2				votes	
3	1	1	1	9	pass
4	1	1	0	7	pass
5	1	0	1	6	pass
6	1	0	0	4	fail
7	0	1	1	5	pass
8	0	1	0	3	fail
9	0	0	1	2	fail
10	0	0	0	0	fail

FIGURE 12.3

TASK 4. What is the Banzhaf power index for the "simple majority" weighted voting system [7 : 5, 4, 2, 2]? How does it compare to the Banzhaf power index for the "two-thirds" weighted voting system [9 : 5, 4, 2, 2]?

Exploration

Copy and paste to create a spreadsheet for six people to model the weighted voting system [q : 4, 4, 3, 3, 3, 3]. Find a quota for which all players have equal power. Can you also find a quota for which the power is not equal?

writing projects

1 ▶ The most important weighted voting system in the United States is the electoral college (see Spotlights 12.1 and 12.4). Three alternate methods to elect the president of the United States have been proposed:

- *Direct election.* The electoral college would be abolished, and the candidate receiving a plurality of the votes would be elected. Most versions of this system include a runoff election or a vote in the House of Representatives in cases where no candidate receives more than 40% of the vote.
- *District system.* In each congressional district, and in the District of Columbia, the candidate receiving the plurality would select one elector. Furthermore, in each state, including the District of Columbia, the candidate receiving the plurality would receive two electors. In effect, the unit rule would be retained for the District of Columbia and for states with a single congressional district. Larger states would typically have electors representing both parties.
- *Proportional system.* Each state and the District of Columbia would have fractional electoral votes assigned to each candidate in proportion to the number of popular votes

received. Under this system, President Clinton, who received 158,220 popular votes out of 182,115 cast in the District of Columbia in 1996, would have received

$$\frac{158,220}{182,115} \times 3 = 2.6064$$

of the District's 3 electoral votes. Obviously, there would be no actual electors involved in the process.

Should the present electoral college, operating under the unit rule, be replaced by one of these systems? A starting point to answer this question is the article by John Banzhaf III, "One Man, 3.312 . . . Votes" (1968). Another reference is "The A Priori Voting Strength of the Electoral College," by I. Mann and L. S. Shapley, in the anthology edited by Martin Shubik (1964). Another reference is *The Presidential Election Game,* by Steven Brams (1978), which contains useful references to Senate hearings on electoral college reform.

2 ▶ Write an essay on weighted voting in the Council of Ministers of the European Community. Compute the Banzhaf and Shapley–Shubik indices for the system as it was in 1958. In later years, the number of member nations increased significantly, and you may have to refer to published computations to determine the indices. If they differ significantly in their allocation of power, which index represents the true balance of power best? *The Measurement of Voting Power,* by Felsenthal and Machover, is a useful reference.

3 ▶ Obtain up-to-date populations of the 50 states and District of Columbia. Using the methods of apportionment described in Chapter 14, determine the voting weight of each state in the electoral college. Finally, determine the Banzhaf index for each state, thus updating Table 12.3. Sources for this project include the Web site of the U.S. Census Bureau (**www.census.gov**) and the Banzhaf calculator (**www.math.temple.edu/~cow/bpi.html**).

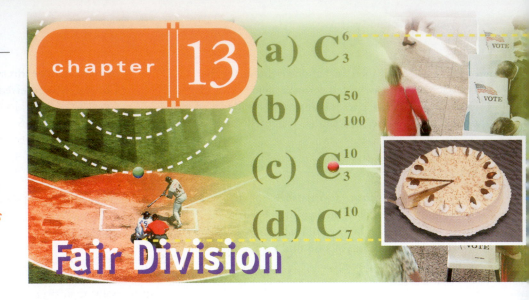

chapter 13

Fair Division

$$\text{(a) } C^6_3$$

$$\text{(b) } C^{50}_{100}$$

$$\text{(c) } C^{10}_3$$

$$\text{(d) } C^{10}_7$$

" . . . an early lesson in fair division occurs in elementary school, with the choosing of sides for a spelling bee or when picking up teams on the playground."

"Gimme the Plaza, the jet, and $150 million, too."

—Headline, *New York Post,* February 13, 1990, reporting Ivana Trump's divorce settlement demands of husband, Donald

Though hardly typical, the 1991 divorce ending the 13-year marriage of Donald and Ivana Trump was one of an estimated 1,187,000 divorces in the United States that year. Few of them involved distributing marital property that included a 118-room mansion, a 282-foot yacht, and a small airline, as was the case in the Trumps' divorce. Many, however, gave rise to the same difficulties—and opportunities—in deciding exactly who gets what in a breakup.

How are divisions of assets in a divorce handled today? The answer often seems to be, "Not very well," even in states like New York where there are domestic relation laws regarding equitable distribution of assets when a marriage dissolves. The point is that an asset that is of considerable value to one party (for reasons ranging from personal circumstances to sentimentality) may be of little interest to the other.

Thus, a property settlement is perhaps the only aspect of a divorce that provides an opportunity for some kind of win-win situation. If the two parties place different values on the items to be distributed (or the issues to be resolved), then there should be settlements (allocations) that leave each party feeling that he or she has been met more than halfway.

454

Divorces are one example of what is called a **fair-division problem.** In general, a fair-division problem consists of a group of individuals, called **players,** and either a single object (like a cake) or some set of objects (like property in a divorce). A **fair-division procedure** or **fair-division scheme** is a method for solving a fair-division problem in which each player has a way to realize a share that he or she considers fair in his or her own value system.

These considerations bring us to the two questions we address in this chapter:

1. Have real-world problems such as divorce settlements led to the development of new mathematics that has potential applications in such contexts?
2. If so, is the mathematics of interest in its own right, in the sense of involving nontrivial questions and answers that shed light on the fundamental issue of fairness?

We begin this chapter with a procedure developed within the last few years called the *adjusted winner procedure.* To describe this procedure we revisit the Trump divorce and analyze it using this new procedure, as was initially done by Catherine Duran (see Suggested Readings in this chapter).

Then, turning to inheritances, we describe an old allocation scheme that was discovered by the Polish mathematician Bronislaw Knaster during World War II. This is followed by a discussion of an extremely basic fair-division scheme—taking turns—and the question of strategy in this context.

Bridging the gap between schemes with obvious real-world potential, such as divorce and inheritance procedures, and schemes that address fundamental mathematical questions of fair division (as do the procedures treated later in this chapter) is the ancient two-person scheme known as divide-and-choose. An application of this scheme to the Law of the Sea Treaty is described.

Divide-and-choose sets the stage for the mathematical investigations of fair division that have gone on for the past half-century. These investigations have often been phrased within the metaphor of "cake cutting." We present four cake-cutting schemes. The first two of these—found by Steinhaus and Banach–Knaster in the 1940s—yield allocations that are "proportional," meaning that each player receives what he or she perceives to be at least his or her fair share of the cake. The last two of these—found by Selfridge–Conway in 1960 and Brams–Taylor in 1992—yield allocations that are "envy-free" in the sense that each player receives what he or she perceives to be a piece at least tied for largest.

The Adjusted Winner Divorce Procedure

In this section we present a recently developed scheme, called the *adjusted winner procedure,* for handling property settlements in a divorce or in an inheritance involving only two heirs. Generalizations of the adjusted winner scheme to three or more parties are somewhat less satisfactory, and so we will introduce a different, and much older, scheme in the next section to handle such cases. This older scheme, however, has the drawback that it requires each party to have an adequate bankroll with which to work.

EXAMPLE   *The Trump Divorce*

Although Ivana had initially estimated Donald's assets to be in the $5 billion range, public disclosures by Donald later revealed his financial instability, and by early 1991, both Donald and Ivana were willing to attempt an out-of-court settlement.

Of course, we have no way of knowing the exact values and states of mind of Donald and Ivana Trump at the time of these negotiations, and we can only offer a rough approximation of the actual items involved, as some assets were taken back by the bank in default proceedings. Child custody, we should note, had already been settled to the satisfaction of both.

For the sake of a fairly realistic illustration, let us take as the marital assets the following: a 45-room mansion in Greenwich, Connecticut; the 118-room Mar-a-Lago mansion in Palm Beach, Florida; an apartment in the Trump Plaza; a 50-room Trump Tower triplex; and just over a million dollars in cash and jewelry.

The starting point of the adjusted winner scheme is to have each party (independently and simultaneously) distribute 100 points over the items in a way that reflects their relative worth to that party. In practice, this is at best a daunting task, and one that may require a considerable amount of assistance from a trained facilitator. For our example—given what we know—let's assume that Donald and Ivana used the following point assignments:

Marital Asset	Point Allocations	
	Donald	Ivana
Connecticut estate	10	38
Palm Beach mansion	40	20
Trump Plaza apartment	10	30
Trump Tower triplex	38	10
Cash and jewelry	2	2

Some of the reasons behind the point totals are as follows. In the four marital agreements signed by the Trumps over the years, Ivana had always received the Connecticut estate, indicating that it was probably worth more to her than to him. The Palm Beach mansion was purely a vacation home to Ivana, but represented an important business opportunity for Donald. The Trump Plaza apartment was home to Ivana and the children (thus explaining its relative importance

Trump Tower, Midtown Manhattan.

to her), while Donald was living at the triplex (thus explaining its relative importance to him). The cash and jewelry were not much of an issue (but one we need in order to illustrate fully the adjusted winner procedure).

The adjusted winner procedure now allocates the property as follows:

1. Each party is initially given each asset for which he or she placed more points than the other party. Thus, Donald initially receives the Palm Beach mansion (40 of his points) and the Trump Tower triplex (38 of his points), while Ivana initially receives the Connecticut estate (38 of her points) and the Trump Plaza apartment (30 of her points). Notice that Donald now has $40 + 38 = 78$ of his points and Ivana only has $38 + 30 = 68$ of her points. The issue upon which they placed the same number of points (the cash and jewelry, on which each placed 2 points) now goes to Ivana, because she has fewer points so far. This increases her point total to $68 + 2 = 70$.

2. We now start transferring assets from Donald to Ivana until their point totals are equalized. The order in which this is done—that is, which assets get transferred before which others—is extremely important and determined as follows.

The assets which Donald currently has are arranged, from left to right, so that the fractions

$$\frac{\text{Donald's point value of the asset}}{\text{Ivana's point value of the asset}}$$

increase (or stay the same) as we scan from left to right. For our example, the fractions for the two items Donald has are

40/20 (Palm Beach)   38/10 (triplex)

We now transfer, in the preceding order, assets (or fractions thereof) from Donald to Ivana until equality of points is achieved.

If we were to transfer the Palm Beach mansion (worth 40 points to Donald and 20 points to Ivana) completely to Ivana, then she would have far more points than Donald: $70 + 20 = 90$ of her points to $78 - 40 = 38$ of his points.

Hence, we want to find what fraction—call it x—of the mansion Donald should retain, while giving the rest—namely, $1 - x$—to Ivana. For example, if Donald retains $\frac{4}{5}$ of the mansion, then Ivana will get $1 - \left(\frac{4}{5}\right) = \frac{1}{5}$ of the mansion. The points Donald receives from his fraction of the mansion will be x times 40, while the points Ivana receives from her fraction of the mansion will be $1 - x$ times 20. Thus, to equalize points we want x to satisfy the following:

$$38 + 40x = 70 + 20(1 - x)$$

That is, Donald receives 38 of his points from the Trump Tower triplex, and 40 times x of his points from his fraction x of the Palm Beach mansion. Ivana receives 70 of her points from the Connecticut estate, the Trump Plaza apartment, and the cash and jewelry, while she receives 20 times $1 - x$ of her points from her fraction $1 - x$ of the Palm Beach mansion.

Solving for x yields the following:

$$38 + 40x = 70 + 20 - 20x$$
$$38 + 40x = 90 - 20x$$
$$60x = 52$$
$$x = 52/60$$

With $x = \frac{52}{60}$, the number of his points that Donald receives is

$$38 + 40 \times (52/60) = 38 + 2080/60 \approx 38 + 34.7 = 72.7$$

Similarly, the number of her points that Ivana receives is

$$70 + 20 \times (8/60) = 70 + 160/60 \approx 70 + 2.7 = 72.7$$

Thus, equality of points is achieved when Donald retains $\frac{52}{60}$ (about 87%) ownership of the Palm Beach mansion, and Ivana gets the remaining $\frac{8}{60}$ (about 13%) ownership. ◆

In point of fact, the actual settlement reached by Ivana and Donald Trump was extremely close to that produced by the adjusted winner procedure: Donald received the Trump Tower triplex, and Ivana received the Connecticut estate, the Trump Plaza apartment, and the cash and jewelry. And what about the Palm Beach mansion that gets split 87–13 by the adjusted winner procedure? In reality, Ivana was awarded use of it for one month a year as a vacation home—not too far off the kind of split we came up with here.

Having seen how the adjusted winner procedure works, one must now ask the following question: Exactly what is it about the allocation produced by this scheme that would make one want to use it? The answer is given by the following theorem (whose proof can be found in the 1996 monograph by Brams and Taylor cited in Suggested Readings):

Theorem: For two parties, the **adjusted winner procedure** produces an allocation, based on each player's assignment of 100 points over the items to be divided, that has the following properties:

1. The allocation is **equitable:** this means that both players receive the same number of points.
2. The allocation is **envy-free:** this means that neither player would be happier with what the other received.
3. The allocation is **Pareto-optimal:** this means that no other allocation, arrived at by any means, can make one party better off without making the other party worse off.

Economists consider Pareto optimality (named after the nineteenth-century Italian scholar Vilfredo Pareto) to be an extremely important property. The fact that the adjusted winner procedure produces an allocation that is efficient in this sense leads one to hope that it can and will play a future role in real-world dispute resolution.

The Knaster Inheritance Procedure

The adjusted winner procedure can be applied in the case of an inheritance if there are only two heirs. For *more than two heirs,* there is quite a different scheme, the **Knaster inheritance procedure,** first proposed by Bronislaw Knaster in 1945. It has a drawback, though, in that it requires the heirs to have a large amount of cash at their disposal.

E X A M P L E   *A Four-Person Inheritance*

Suppose (for the moment) that there is just one object—a house—and four heirs—Bob, Carol, Ted, and Alice. Knaster's scheme begins with each heir bidding (simultaneously and independently) on the house. Assume, for example, that the bids are

Bob	Carol	Ted	Alice
$120,000	$200,000	$140,000	$180,000

Carol, being the high bidder, is awarded the house. Her fair share, however, is only one-fourth of the $200,000 she thinks the house is worth, and so she places $150,000 (which is three-fourths of the $200,000 she bid) into a temporary "kitty."

Each of the other heirs now withdraws from the kitty his or her fair share, that is, one-fourth of his or her bid. Thus

Bob withdraws $120,000/4 = $30,000
Ted withdraws $140,000/4 = $35,000
Alice withdraws $180,000/4 = $45,000

Thus, from the $150,000 kitty, a total of $30,000 + $35,000 + $45,000 = $110,000 is withdrawn, and each of the four heirs now feels that he or she has the equivalent of one-fourth of the estate. Moreover, there is a $40,000 surplus ($150,000 kitty − $110,000 withdrawn), which is now divided equally among the four heirs (so each receives an additional $10,000). The final settlement is:

Bob	Carol	Ted	Alice
$40,000	house − $140,000	$45,000	$55,000

This illustrates Knaster's procedure for the simple case in which there is only one object. But what do we do if our same four heirs have to divide an estate consisting of, say, a house (as before), a cabin, and a boat? The easiest answer is to handle the estate one object at a time (proceeding for each object as we just did for the house). To illustrate, assume that our four heirs submit the following bids:

	Bob	Carol	Ted	Alice
House	$120,000	$200,000	$140,000	$180,000
Cabin	60,000	40,000	90,000	50,000
Boat	30,000	24,000	20,000	20,000

We have already settled the house. Let's handle the cabin the same way. Thus, Ted is awarded the cabin based on his high bid of $90,000. His fair share is one-fourth of this, so he places three-fourths of $90,000 (which is $67,500) into the kitty.

Bob withdraws from the kitty $60,000/4 = $15,000. Carol withdraws $40,000/4 = $10,000, and Alice withdraws $50,000/4 = $12,500. Thus, from the $67,500 kitty, a total of $15,000 + $10,000 + $12,500 = $37,500 is withdrawn.

The surplus left in the kitty is thus $30,000, and this is again split equally ($7500 each) among the four heirs. The final settlement on the cabin is:

Bob	Carol	Ted	Alice
$22,500	$17,500	cabin − $60,000	$20,000

If we were now to do the same for the boat (we leave the details to the reader), the corresponding final settlement would be

Bob	Carol	Ted	Alice
boat − $20,875	$7625	$6625	$6625

Putting the three separate analyses (house, cabin, and boat) together, we get a final settlement of

Bob: boat + ($40,000 + $22,500 − $20,875 = $41,625)
Carol: house + (−$140,000 + $17,500 + $7625 = −$114,875)
Ted: cabin + ($45,000 − $60,000 + $6625 = −$8375)
Alice: $55,000 + $20,000 + $6625 = $81,625. ◆

Notice that in the final settlement, Carol gets the house, but she must put up $114,875 in cash (and Ted gets the cabin, but he must put up $8375 in cash). This cash is then disbursed to Bob and Alice. In practice, Carol's having this amount of cash available may be a real problem. This is the key drawback to Knaster's procedure. Nevertheless, Knaster's procedure shows again that whenever some participants have different evaluations of some objects, there is an allocation in which everyone obtains more than a fair share.

Taking Turns

For many of us, an early lesson in fair division occurs in elementary school with the choosing of sides for a spelling bee or when picking up teams on the playground. In terms of importance, these pale in comparison with the issue of property settlement in a divorce. Remarkably, however, the same fair-division scheme — *taking turns* — is often used in both.

Taking turns is fairly self-explanatory. With two parties (and that's all we'll consider here), one party selects an object, then the other party selects one, then the first party again, and so on. But in this context, there are several interesting questions that suggest themselves:

1. How do we decide who chooses first?
2. Because choosing first is often quite an advantage, shouldn't we compensate the other party in some way, perhaps by giving him or her extra choices at the next turn?
3. Should a player always choose the object he or she most favors from those that remain, or are there strategic considerations that players should take into account?

The answer to question 1 is often "toss a coin," but there are other possibilities—for example, the two parties could "bid" for the right to go first, as in an auction. The answer to question 2 is less clear, but we outline a discussion of the issue it raises in one of the Writing Assignments. Question 3, on the other hand, is remarkably interesting, and it is this one that we want to pursue.

Let's look at an easy example. Suppose that Bob and Carol are getting a divorce, and their four main possessions, ranked from best to worst by each, are as follows:

	Bob's Ranking	Carol's Ranking
Best	Pension	House
Second best	House	Investments
Third best	Investments	Pension
Worst	Vehicles	Vehicles

If Carol knows nothing of Bob's preferences, then we can assume that she will choose sincerely—selecting at her turn whichever item she most prefers from those not yet chosen. Now, if Bob is also sincere, and if he chooses first, the items will be allocated as follows:

First turn:	Bob takes the pension
Second turn:	Carol takes the house
Third turn:	Bob takes the investments
Fourth turn:	Carol is left with the vehicles

Hence, Bob gets his first and third favorites (the pension and the investments). However, if Bob opens by choosing the house—and bypassing the pension for the moment—then the allocation will be as follows:

First turn:	Bob takes the house
Second turn:	Carol takes the investments
Third turn:	Bob takes the pension
Fourth turn:	Carol is left with the vehicles

Thus, by being insincere, Bob does better—getting his first and second favorites (the pension and the house).

In general, then, what is the optimal strategy for rational players to use, assuming that both know the preferences of the other? The answer is something called the **bottom-up strategy** discovered by the mathematicians D. A. Kohler and R. Chandrasekarean in 1969. We will illustrate it with an example.

Suppose we have five objects—a, b, c, d, e—and Bob is choosing first. Suppose that Bob and Carol have the following rankings of the objects (called **preference lists** in what follows):

Bob	Carol
a	c
b	e
c	d
d	a
e	b

It will turn out that Bob should open with c (his third choice) followed by Carol's choice of d (skipping over e, for the moment). Bob will then take a, Carol will follow with e, and finally Bob will get b. Bob gets his first, second, and third choices without selecting his first choice first! Where does this come from?

The intuition here is quite easy. Let's make two assumptions about rational players: a rational player will never choose his or her least preferred alternative, and a rational player will avoid wasting a choice on an object that he or she knows will remain available, and thus can be chosen later.

With these assumptions as motivation, let's return to the preceding example and think about the mental calculation Bob will go through in deciding what his first choice will be. Bob knows the eventual sequence of choices will fill in all of the following blanks:

Bob: _____   _____   _____
Carol: _____   _____

Now, working mentally from right to left, Bob knows that Carol will not choose b, because it is the bottom thing on her list. Thus, he will get stuck with b, and so he will avoid wasting anything but his last choice on alternative b. Thus, Bob can pencil in alternative b as his last choice:

Bob: _____   _____   _b_
Carol: _____   _____

Bob, placing himself momentarily in Carol's shoes, knows she will reason the same way, and thus he pencils Carol in for the bottom alternative, e, on his list:

Bob: _____   _____   _b_
Carol: _____   _e_

Mentally now, Bob reasons as if alternatives *b* and *e* never existed (and the choice sequence had been Bob–Carol–Bob), and continues to pencil in alternatives from right to left, with Bob working from bottom to top on Carol's preference list and Carol working from bottom to top on Bob's preference list. This yields the following sequence of choices mentally penciled in by Bob:

Bob:　　　__*c*__　　　　　　　__*a*__　　　　　　__*b*__
Carol:　　　　　　__*d*__　　　　　　__*e*__

Remember, this is just a mental calculation that Bob went through to decide upon the actual choice—in this case, *c*—with which he will open. Bob has no guarantee that Carol will, in fact, respond with *d*.

Of course, in describing a strategy, this only explains the procedure Bob goes through in deciding what his first choice will be. Nevertheless, such a **first-choice strategy** can be repeatedly applied with a player recognizing that "what's done is done." Thus, a player with a first-choice strategy can proceed each time it is his or her turn to choose by acting as if he or she were making a first choice among the alternatives not yet chosen.

This bottom-up strategy can also be viewed as a procedure that a mediator (or arbitrator) could use to specify a division of several objects between two parties. Given the preference lists of both parties, the mediator could construct a list—exactly as we did for Bob and Carol above—and then offer this to the parties as the suggested allocation. In effect, the mediator is simultaneously playing the role of two rational parties who choose to employ optimal strategies.

Divide-and-Choose

There are vast mineral resources under the seabed, all of which, one might argue, should be available to both the developed and the developing countries. In the absence of some kind of agreement, however, what is to prevent the developed countries from mining all of the most promising tracts before the developing countries have reached a technological level where they can begin their own mining operations? Such an agreement went into effect on November 16, 1994, with 159 signatories (including the United States). It was called the **Convention of the Law of the Sea,** and it protects the interests of the developing countries by means of the following fair-division procedure.

Whenever a developed country wants to mine a portion of the seabed, that country must propose a division of the portion into two tracts. An international mining company called the Enterprise, funded by the developed countries but representing the interests of the developing countries through the International Seabed Authority, then chooses one of the two tracts to be reserved for later use by the developing countries.

The preceding rules constitute a fair-division procedure known as **divide-and-choose:** one party divides the object into two parts in any way that he desires, and the other party chooses whichever part she wants.

As a fair-division procedure, the origins of divide-and-choose go back at least 5000 years. The Hebrew Bible tells the story of Abram (later to be called Abraham) and Lot, who settled a dispute over land via a proposed division by Abram—"If you go north, I will go south; and if you go south, I will go north" (Gen. 13:8–9)—and a choice (of the plain of Jordan) by Lot. Divide-and-choose resurfaced about 2000 years later in Hesiod's book *Theogony.* The Greek gods Prometheus and Zeus had to divide a portion of meat. Prometheus began by placing the meat into two piles, and Zeus selected one.

Actually, a fair-division procedure consists of both rules and strategies, and all we have described so far are the rules of divide-and-choose. But the strategies here are quite obvious: the divider makes the two parts equal in his estimation, and the chooser selects whichever piece she feels is more valuable.

Rules and strategies differ from each other in the following sense: a referee could determine if a rule were being followed, even without knowing the preferences of the players. Strategies represent choices of how players follow the rules, given their individual preferences (and any other knowledge and/or goals they may have).

The strategies on which we will focus in our discussion of fair-division procedures are those that require no knowledge of the preferences of the other players and yet provide some kind of minimal degree of satisfaction even in the face of collusion by the other players. For example, the strategies just given for divide-and-choose guarantee each player a piece that he or she would not wish to trade for that received by the other.

There are, to be sure, other strategic considerations that might be relevant. For example, in divide-and-choose, would you rather be the divider or the chooser? The answer, given our assumptions that nothing is known of the preferences of the others, is to be the chooser. However, if you knew the preferences of your opponent (and her value of spite), then you might want to be the divider.

As a final comment on strategic considerations, we need only look to the origins of the well-known expression "the lion's share." It comes from one of Aesop's fables, as reported by Todd Lowry in *Archaeology of Economic Ideas* (1987, p. 130):

It seems that a lion, a fox, and an ass participated in a joint hunt. On request, the ass divides the kill into three equal shares and invites the others to choose. Enraged, the lion eats the ass, then asks the fox to make the division. The fox piles all the kill into one great heap except for one tiny morsel. Delighted at this division, the lion asks, "Who has taught you, my very excellent fellow, the art of division?" to which the fox replies, "I learnt it from the ass, by witnessing his fate."

Cake-Division Schemes: Proportionality

The modern era of fair division in mathematics began in Poland during World War II (see Spotlight 13.1). At this time, Hugo Steinhaus asked what is, in retrospect, the obvious question: What is the "natural" generalization of divide-and-

SPOTLIGHT

13.1

Fifty Years of Cake Cutting

Will this cake be divided fairly?

The modern era of cake cutting began with the investigations of the Polish mathematician Hugo Steinhaus during World War II. His research, and that of dozens of others over the past half-century, involved dealing with two fundamental difficulties. First, allocation schemes that work in the context of two or three players often do not generalize easily to the context of four or more players. Second, procedures that yield envy-free allocations are considerably harder to obtain than procedures that yield proportional allocations.

The mathematics inspired by these two difficulties over the past 50 years constitutes a rather elegant corner of the large and important area of fair division. Steinhaus's investigations in the 1940s led to his observation that there is a rather natural extension of divide-and-choose to the case of three players. This is the "lone-divider scheme" choose to three or more people? The metaphor that has been used in this context, going back at least to the English political theorist James Harrington (1611–1677), is a cake. We picture different players valuing different parts of the cake differently because of concentrations of certain flavors or depth of frosting. (Don't, however, think of a layer cake, because that is a context in which the difficult

described on page 468. Steinhaus's method was generalized to an arbitrary number of players by Harold W. Kuhn of Princeton University in 1967.

Unable to extend his scheme from three to four players, Steinhaus proposed the problem to some Polish colleagues. Two of them, Stefan Banach and Bronislaw Knaster, solved this problem in the mid-1940s by producing the "last-diminisher scheme" described on page 469.

In addition to the schemes devised by Banach, Knaster, and Kuhn, there are other well-known constructive procedures for obtaining a proportional allocation among four or more players. One of these is due to A. M. Fink of Iowa State University and appears in Exercise 26.

Another constructive procedure of note, although different in flavor from the others, is the 1961 recasting by Lester E. Dubins and Edwin H. Spanier of the University of California at Berkeley of the last-diminisher method as a "moving-knife scheme" (illustrated in Exercise 28). The trade-off here involves giving up the "discrete" nature of the last-diminisher method in exchange for the conceptual simplicity of the moving knife.

Although the existence of an envy-free allocation (even for four or more players) was known to Steinhaus in the 1940s, the first constructive procedure for producing an envy-free allocation among three players was not found until around 1960. At that time, John L. Selfridge of Northern Illinois University and, later but independently, John H. Conway of Princeton University found the elegant scheme presented on pages 473–474. Although never published by either, the scheme was quickly and widely disseminated by Richard K. Guy of the University of Calgary and others; eventually it appeared in several treatments of the problem by different authors.

In 1980, a moving-knife procedure for producing an envy-free allocation among three players was found by Walter R. Stromquist of Daniel Wagner Associates. Then, another scheme, capable of being recast as a moving-knife solution of the three-player case, was found by a law professor at the University of Virginia, Saul X. Levmore, and a former student of his, Elizabeth Early Cook.

In 1992, Steven J. Brams, a political scientist at New York University, and Alan D. Taylor, a mathematician at Union College, succeeded in finding a constructive procedure for producing an envy-free allocation among four or more players. In 1994, Brams, Taylor, and William S. Zwicker (also from Union College) found a moving-knife solution to the four-person envy-free problem. No moving-knife scheme is known that will produce an envy-free allocation among five or more players.

"envy-free" questions we ask can be answered by simply dividing each layer equally among the players.) Thus, we ask the following:

> Can one devise a **cake-division scheme** for n players—that is, a procedure that the players can use to allocate a cake among themselves (no outside arbitrators)—so that each player has a strategy that will guarantee her a piece with which she is "satisfied," even in the face of collusion by the others?

As we have seen, divide-and-choose is a cake-division scheme for two players, if by "satisfied" we mean either "thinks his piece is of size or value at least one-half" or "does not want to trade what she received for what anyone else received." These two notions of satisfaction are so important that we define them precisely.

> A cake-division scheme (for n players) will be called **proportional** if each player's strategy guarantees him a piece of size or value at least $1/n$ of the whole in his own estimation. It will be called **envy-free** if each player's strategy guarantees him a piece he considers to be at least tied for largest.

It turns out that for $n = 2$, a scheme is envy-free if and only if it is proportional; that is, for $n = 2$, the two notions of fair division are exactly the same. For $n > 2$, however, all we can say is that an envy-free scheme is automatically proportional. For example, if a three-person allocation is not proportional, then one player (call him Bob) thinks that he received less than one-third. Bob then feels that the other two are sharing more than two-thirds between them, and thus that at least one of the two (call her Carol) must have more than one-third. But then Bob will envy Carol, and so the allocation is not envy-free. Since all nonproportional allocations fail to be envy-free, it follows that if an allocation is envy-free, then it must be proportional.

Many schemes that are proportional, however, fail to be envy-free, as we shall soon show. Thus, proportional schemes are fairly easy to come by, but envy-free schemes are fairly hard to come by.

EXAMPLE   *The Steinhaus Proportional Procedure for Three Players (Lone Divider)*

Given three players—Bob, Carol, and Ted—we have Bob divide the cake into three pieces, call them X, Y, and Z, each of which he thinks is of size or value exactly one-third. Let's speak of Carol as "approving of a piece" if she thinks it is of size or value at least one-third. Similarly, we will speak of Ted as "approving of a piece" if the same criterion applies. Notice that both Carol and Ted must approve of at least one piece.

If there are distinct pieces, say, X and Y, with Carol approving of X and Ted approving of Y, then we give the third piece, Z, to Bob (and, of course, X to Carol and Y to Ted), and we are done. The problem case is where both Carol and Ted approve of only one piece and it is the *same* piece.

Thus, let's assume that Carol and Ted approve of only one piece, X, and hence (of more importance to us) both *disapprove* of piece Z. Let XY denote the result of putting piece X and piece Y back together to form a single piece. Notice that both Carol and Ted think that XY is at least two-thirds of the cake, since both disapprove of Z. Thus, we can give Z to Bob and let Carol and Ted use divide-and-choose on XY. Since half of two-thirds is one-third, both Carol and Ted are guaranteed a proportional share (as is Bob, who approved of all three pieces).   ◆

The method just described, which guarantees proportional shares but is not necessarily envy-free and is sometimes called the **lone-divider method,** was discovered by Hugo Steinhaus around 1944. Unfortunately, it does not extend easily to more than three players. It was left to Steinhaus's students, Stefan Banach and Bronislaw Knaster, to devise a method for more than three players. Picking up where Steinhaus left off (and traveling in quite a different direction), they devised the proportional scheme that today is referred to as the **last-diminisher method.** Like the lone-divider method, it is proportional but not envy-free. We illustrate it for the case of four players (Bob, Carol, Ted, and Alice), and we include both the rules and the strategies that guarantee each player his or her fair share.

E X A M P L E   *The Banach–Knaster Proportional Procedure for Four or More Players (Last Diminisher)*

Bob cuts from the cake a piece that he thinks is of size one-fourth and hands it to Carol. If Carol thinks the piece handed her is larger than one-fourth, she trims it to size one-fourth in her estimation, places the trimmings back on the cake, and passes the diminished piece to Ted. If Carol thinks the piece handed her is of size at most one-fourth, she passes it unaltered to Ted.

Ted now proceeds exactly as did Carol, trimming the piece to size one-fourth if he thinks it is larger than this and passing it (diminished or unaltered) on to Alice. Alice does the same, but, being the last player, simply holds onto the piece momentarily instead of passing it to anyone.

Notice that everyone now thinks the piece is of size at most one-fourth, and the last person to trim it (or Bob, if no one trimmed it) thinks the piece is of size exactly one-fourth. Thus, the procedure now allocates this piece to the last person who trimmed it (and to Bob if no one trimmed it).

Assume for the moment that it was Ted who trimmed the piece last, and so he takes this piece and exits the game. Bob, Carol, and Alice all think that at least three-fourths of the cake is left, and so they can start the process over with (say) Bob beginning by cutting a piece from what remains that he thinks is one-fourth of the original cake. Carol and Alice are both given a chance to trim it to size one-fourth in their estimation, and again, the last one to trim it takes that piece and exits the game. The two remaining players both think that at least half the cake is left, and so they can use divide-and-choose to divide it between themselves and thus be assured of a piece that is of size at least one-fourth in their estimation.   ◆

For a concrete illustration of the last-diminisher method for the simple case where there are only three players (Bob, Carol, and Ted), suppose that all three players view the cake as having 18 units of "value," with each unit of value represented by a small square. Suppose, however, that the players value various parts of the cake differently (or that Bob views the cake as being perfectly rectangular, whereas Carol and Ted see it as skewed in opposite ways). We represent this pictorially as follows:

Bob

Carol

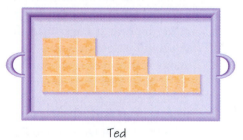

Ted

In step 1, Bob cuts from the cake a piece—call it *A*—that he considers to be of size or value one-third (because there are only three players this time). We'll assume he does this by making a vertical cut as follows:

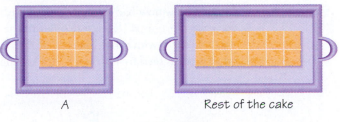

Bob's view

From Carol's point of view (or value system), the piece *A* appears to contain only 3 of the 18 units of value:

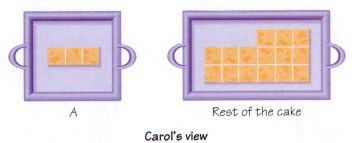

Carol's view

Because Carol thinks that *A* represents less than one-third of the cake, she passes *A* unaltered to Ted. Now Ted sees *A* as follows:

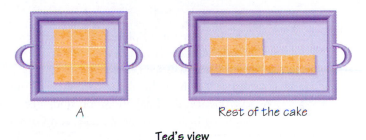

Ted's view

Thus, Ted thinks that *A* represents one-half of the cake (9 out of 18 units of value), and so he will trim it to what he thinks is one-third (6 out of 18 units of value). Let's assume that he does this with another vertical cut, with the trimmed version of *A* now called *A′*.

Ted's view

Everyone has now had a chance to diminish the piece A that Bob initially cut from the cake. Portion A', therefore, goes to the last person to trim it, namely, Ted. So Ted takes A' (which he thinks is of size $\frac{6}{18} = \frac{1}{3}$) and exits the game. Notice that what is left is seen by Bob and Carol as follows:

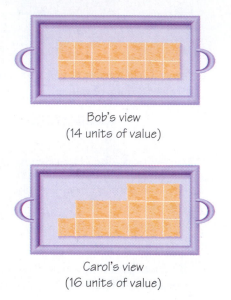

Bob's view
(14 units of value)

Carol's view
(16 units of value)

The final step has Bob and Carol use divide-and-choose. Note that if Bob is the divider and elects to make a vertical cut (halving the middle column of squares), then Carol will see the division as leaving 6 squares to the left of the cut and 10 squares to the right of the cut. She will thus choose the piece to the right of the cut. Hence, the final allocation finds Ted thinking he has 6/18 of the cake, Bob thinking he has 7/18 of the cake, and Carol thinking she has 10/18 of the cake.

Cake-Division Schemes: The Problem of Envy

Divide-and-choose has a property that neither of the last two procedures possesses: it can assure each player of a piece of cake he or she considers the largest or tied for the largest. In the case of only two players, this means that each player can get what he or she perceives to be at least half the cake, no matter what the other player does. Thus, divide-and-choose is an envy-free procedure.

Steinhaus's $n = 3$ proportional procedure (the lone-divider method) is not envy-free. For example, consider the case where Carol and Ted both find one piece unacceptable (and this piece is given to Bob). Carol and Ted will not envy each other when one divides and the other chooses, but Bob may think that this is not a 50–50 split. Indeed, if Bob divided the cake initially into what he thought was three equal pieces, an unequal split of the remaining two-thirds of the cake by Carol and Ted means that Bob will prefer the larger of these two pieces to the one-third he got. Consequently, Bob will envy the person who got this larger piece.

Neither is the last-diminisher method envy-free. For example, if Bob initially cuts a piece of cake of size one-fourth, and no one else trims it, then Bob receives this piece and exits the game. If Carol is the one to make the next initial cut, she may well cut a piece from the cake that she thinks is of size one-fourth, but that Bob thinks is of size considerably more than one-fourth. But Bob is out of the game. Thus, if Ted and Alice think this piece is of size less than one-fourth, then Carol receives it, and so Bob will envy Carol.

Nevertheless, there do exist cake-division schemes that are envy-free. We present two of these in what follows.

E X A M P L E   *The Selfridge–Conway Envy-Free Procedure for Three Players*

We start with a cake and three people. The point we wish to arrive at is an envy-free allocation of the entire cake among the three people in a finite number of steps. This task may seem formidable; however, quite often in mathematics, an important part of solving a problem involves breaking the problem into identifiable parts. In this case, let us call our starting point A and the final point we wish to reach C. Now let us identify an appropriate in-between point B that makes going from A to C—via B—more manageable. Our in-between point B is the following:

> *Point B:* Getting a constructive procedure that gives an envy-free allocation of *part* of the cake.

Can we constructively obtain three pieces of cake, whose union may not be the whole cake, which can be given to the three people so that each thinks he or she received a piece at least tied for largest? This turns out to be quite easy, with the solution due to John Selfridge and John Conway, who arrived at it independently around 1960. The following process and strategies do the trick:

1. Player 1 cuts the cake into three pieces he considers to be the same size. He hands the three pieces to player 2.
2. Player 2 trims at most one of the three pieces so as to create at least a two-way tie for largest. Setting the trimmings aside, player 2 hands the three pieces (one of which may have been trimmed) to player 3.
3. Player 3 now chooses, from among the three pieces, one that he considers to be at least tied for largest.
4. Player 2 next chooses, from the two remaining pieces, one that she considers to be at least tied for largest, with the proviso that if she trimmed a piece in step 2, and player 3 did not choose this piece, then she must now choose it.
5. Player 1 receives the remaining piece.

Let us reconsider the five steps of this trimming procedure to assure ourselves that each player experiences no envy. Recall that player 1 cuts the cake into three pieces, and player 2 trims one of these three pieces. Now player 3 chooses, and, as the first to choose, he certainly envies no one. Player 2 created a two-way tie for largest, and at least one of these two pieces is still available after player 3 selects his piece. Hence, player 2 can choose one of the tied pieces she created and will envy no one. Finally, player 1 created a three-way tie for largest and, because of the proviso in step 4, the trimmed piece is not the one left over. Thus, player 1 can choose an untrimmed piece and therefore will envy no one.

So far we have gone from point A to point B: starting with a cake and three players, we have constructively obtained (in finitely many steps) an envy-free allocation of all of the cake, except the part T that player 2 trimmed from one of the pieces. We will now describe how T can be allocated among the three players in such a way that the resulting allocation of the whole cake is envy-free. (This is the rest of the **Selfridge–Conway envy-free procedure.**)

The key observation for the $n = 3$ case is that player 1 will not envy the player who received the trimmed piece, even if that player were to be given all of T. Recall that player 1 created a three-way tie and received an untrimmed piece. The union of the trimmed piece and the trimmings yields a piece that player 1 considers to be exactly the same size as the one he received. Thus, assume that it is player 3 who received the trimmed piece (it could as well be player 2). Then player 1 will not envy player 3, however T is allocated.

The next step ensures that neither player 2 nor player 3 will envy another player when it comes time to allocate T. Let player 2 cut T into three pieces she considers to be the same size. Let the players choose which of the three pieces they want in the following order: player 3, player 1, player 2.

To see that this yields an envy-free allocation, notice that player 3 envies no one, because he is choosing first. Player 1 does not envy player 2, because he is choosing ahead of her; and player 1 does not envy player 3 because, as pointed out earlier, player 1 will not envy the player who received the trimmed piece. Finally, player 2 envies no one, because she made all three pieces of T the same size.

Hence, for $n = 3$, the Selfridge–Conway procedure will give an envy-free allocation of all the cake except T, followed by an allocation of T that gives an envy-free allocation of all the cake.   ◆

A naive attempt to generalize to $n = 4$ what we have done for $n = 3$ would proceed as follows: we would begin by having player 1 cut the cake into four pieces he considers to be the same size. Then we would have players 2 and 3 trim some pieces (but how many?) to create ties for the largest. Finally, we would have the players choose from among the pieces—some of which would have been trimmed—in the following order: player 4, player 3, player 2, player 1.

This approach fails because player 1 could be left in a position of envy. In order to understand how the approach could fail, consider how many pieces player 3 might have to trim in order to create a sufficient supply of pieces tied for largest so that he is guaranteed to have one available when it is his turn to choose. Player 3 might have to trim one piece to create a two-way tie for largest. Player 2 might need to trim two pieces to create a three-way tie for largest (since, if there were only a two-way tie for largest, player 3 might further trim one of these pieces and player 4 might choose the other). This leaves player 1 in a possible position of envy, because we could have a situation where player 2 trims two pieces and player 3 trims a third piece, and player 4 then chooses the only untrimmed piece. If this happens, player 1, by being forced to choose a trimmed piece, will definitely envy player 4.

All is not lost, however, since there are slight modifications of the Selfridge–Conway procedure that will work for arbitrary n. We describe one such modification for the case $n = 4$.

E X A M P L E   **The 1992 Envy-Free Procedure for Four or More Players (the Trimming Procedure)**

With four or more players, the new idea we introduce is to have the first player cut the cake into more pieces than there are players. For simplicity, we illustrate this with four players.

1. Player 1 cuts the cake into *five* pieces she considers to be the same size. She hands the five pieces to player 2.
2. Player 2 trims at most two of the five pieces so as to create at least a three-way tie for largest. Setting the trimmings aside, player 2 hands the five pieces—one or two of which may have been trimmed—to player 3.
3. Player 3 trims at most one of the five pieces she has been handed so as to create at least a two-way tie for largest. This, of course, may involve further trimming of a piece that player 2 already trimmed in step 2. She sets her trimmings aside with those of player 2, handing the further altered collection of five pieces to player 4.
4. Player 4 now chooses from among the five pieces, some of which may have been trimmed by player 2 and/or player 3, a piece that he considers to be at least tied for largest. (The remaining steps now reverse the order of initial play.)
5. Player 3 chooses next, from among the four remaining pieces, a piece that she considers to be at least tied for largest, with the proviso that if she trimmed a piece in step 3, and player 4 did not choose this piece, then player 3 must choose it now.
6. Player 2 chooses next, from among the three remaining pieces, a piece that he considers to be at least tied for largest, with the proviso that if he trimmed a piece or pieces in step 2, and one of these is still available, then he must now choose such a piece.
7. Player 1 now chooses, from the remaining two pieces, one that was not trimmed.

This time, check the procedure on your own to be certain that it achieves an envy-free allocation of part of the cake. Notice, however, that for $n = 4$ we not only have the trimmings from steps 2 and 3 left over but also one of the five pieces, perhaps now trimmed, with which we started.

Thus, we have again gone from point A to point B: starting with a cake and n players, we have constructively obtained (in finitely many steps) an envy-free allocation of part of the cake. Our next step (before arriving at C) is a fairly small one:

> *Point B′:* Getting a constructive procedure that gives an envy-free allocation of all the cake, but using *infinitely* many steps.

The intuition behind the infinite scheme is simple: one applies the **trimming procedure,** a scheme that yields an envy-free allocation of part of the cake, over and over again, with each application yielding an envy-free allocation of part of what was left over from the previous application. Eventually the whole cake is allocated.

The next question for the $n = 4$ case is how to get from point $B′$ to point C, where the whole cake is allocated in a finite number of steps. That is, how do we make the infinite scheme finite? Our approach mirrors what we did in the $n = 3$ case: if two players have different preferences, then we arrange the partial-allocation scheme so that each player thinks he received a piece of cake strictly larger than the other player.

Eventually, when the size of the crumb is sufficiently small (in the eyes of these two players), then neither will care if the other player should get the whole crumb (because both will think his piece is already larger than the other's piece, even with the crumb added to it). This is just a glimpse of what is needed; full details of the trimming procedure can be found in the article by Brams and Taylor in Suggested Readings.   ◆

Thus, there is a solution to the problem of envy-freeness that obviates the need for an endless process of finer and finer divisions. Practically speaking, however, it is only necessary to know that the trimmings become progressively smaller; then one can stop this procedure when what remains no longer matters much to the players.

Although we have used the metaphor of cake cutting throughout our discussion of the problem of envy, the idea of successive trimming is nonetheless applicable to problems of fair division other than parceling out the last crumbs of a cake. The main practical problem in applying the trimming procedure is that many fair-division problems involve goods that cannot be divided up at all, much less trimmed in fine amounts. Such goods are said to be indivisible.

It is interesting to recall that when the Allies agreed in 1944 to partition Germany into sectors after World War II (first stage), they at first did not reach agreement about what to do with Berlin. Subsequently, they decided to partition Berlin itself into sectors (second stage), even though this city fell 110 miles within the Soviet sector. Berlin was simply too valuable a "piece" for the Western Allies (Great

Britain, France, and the United States) to cede to the Soviets, which suggests how, after a leftover piece is trimmed off, it can be subsequently divided under the trimming procedure.

Yet, what if a large piece like Berlin is not divisible? In the settlement of an estate, this might be the house, which may be worth half the estate to the claimants. In this situation, there may be no alternative but to sell this big item and use the proceeds to make the remaining estate more liquid or, in our terms, "trimmable."

The division of Berlin after World War II.

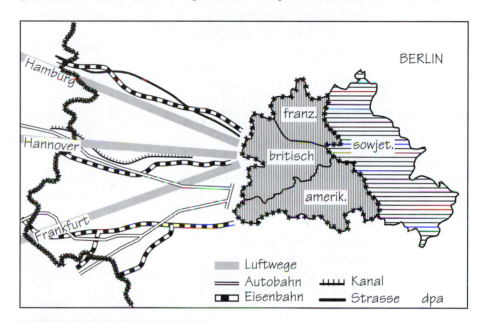

A checkpoint at the Berlin Wall.

REVIEW VOCABULARY

Adjusted winner procedure   A fair-division procedure introduced by Steven Brams and Alan Taylor in 1993. It works only for two players, and begins by having each player independently spread 100 points over the items to be divided so as to reflect the relative worth of each object to that player. The allocation resulting from this procedure is equitable, envy-free, and Pareto-optimal. It requires no cash from either player, but one of the objects may have to be divided or shared by the two players.

Bottom-up strategy   A bottom-up strategy is a strategy under an alternating procedure in which sophisticated choices are determined by working backwards.

Cake-division scheme   A fair-division procedure that uses a cake as a metaphor. Such procedures involve finding allocations of a single object that is finely divisible, as opposed to the situation encountered with either the adjusted winner procedure or Knaster's procedure. In a cake-division scheme, each player has a strategy that will guarantee her a piece with which she is "satisfied," even in the face of collusion by the others.

Convention of the Law of the Sea   An agreement based on divide-and-choose that protects the interests of developing countries in mining operations under the sea.

Divide-and-choose   A fair-division procedure (or cake-division scheme) for dividing an object or several objects between two players. This method produces an allocation that is both proportional and envy-free (the two being equivalent when there are only two players).

Envy-free   A fair-division procedure is said to be envy-free if each player has a strategy that can guarantee him or her a share of whatever is being divided that is at least as large (or at least as desirable) as that received by any other player, no matter what the other players do.

Equitable   An allocation (resulting from a fair-division procedure like adjusted winner) is said to be equitable if each player believes he or she received the same fractional part of the total value.

Fair-division problem   A problem that involves the dividing up of an object or set of objects among several individuals (players) so that each individual considers the part he or she receives to be a fair portion.

Fair-division procedure   A method for solving a fair-division problem. Each participant in the procedure must have a way of realizing a share that he or she views as fair in his or her own value system.

First-choice strategy   A strategy for an alternating procedure that indicates only what a player's first choice should be.

Knaster inheritance procedure   A fair-division procedure for any number of parties that begins by having each player (independently) assign a dollar value (a "bid") to the item or items to be divided so as to reflect the absolute worth of each object to that player. The allocation resulting from this procedure leaves each party feeling that he or she received a dollar value at least equal to his or her fair share (and often more so). It never requires the dividing or sharing of an object, but it may require that the players have a large amount of cash on hand.

Last-diminisher method   A cake-division scheme introduced by Stefan Banach and Bronislaw Knaster in the 1940s. It works for any number of players and produces an allocation that is proportional but not, in general, envy-free.

Lone-divider method   A cake-division scheme introduced by Hugo Steinhaus in the 1940s. It works only for three players and produces an allocation that is proportional but not, in general, envy-free.

Pareto-optimal   When no other allocation, achieved by any means whatsoever, can make any one player better off without making some other player worse off.

Player   A participant in a fair-division scheme.

Preference lists   Rankings of the items to be allocated, from best to worst, by each of the participants.

Proportional   A fair-division procedure is said to be proportional if each of n players has a strategy that can guarantee him or her a share of whatever is being divided that he or she considers to be at least $1/n$ of the whole in size or value.

Selfridge–Conway procedure   A cake-division scheme introduced independently by John Selfridge and John Conway around 1960. It works only for three players but produces an allocation that is envy-free (as well as proportional).

Taking turns   A fair-division procedure in which two or more parties alternate selecting objects.
Trimming procedure   A cake-division scheme introduced by Steven Brams and Alan Taylor in 1992. It works for any number of players, requires only finitely many steps, and produces an allocation that is envy-free (as well as proportional).

SUGGESTED READINGS

BRAMS, S. J., AND A. D. TAYLOR. An envy-free cake division protocol, *American Mathematical Monthly,* 102 (1995): 9–18. Brams and Taylor describe in detail the finite version of their envy-free procedure for $n = 4$; in addition, they review earlier work on "protocols" (step-by-step procedures) that led up to their constructive solution of the envy-freeness problem for $n > 3$.

BRAMS, S. J., AND A. D. TAYLOR. *Fair Division: From Cake-Cutting to Dispute Resolution,* Cambridge University Press, Cambridge, 1996. Brams and Taylor provide a book-length treatment of the kinds of topics introduced in this chapter, as well as divide-and-choose in the political arena, moving-knife schemes for cake cutting, and fairness as it applies to different auction and election procedures.

BRAMS, S. J., AND A. D. TAYLOR. *The Win-Win Solution: Guaranteeing Fair Shares to Everybody,* Norton, New York, 1999. Brams and Taylor do more with adjusted winner, as well as divide-and-choose and taking turns.

DUBINS, L. E., AND E. H. SPANIER. How to cut a cake fairly, *American Mathematical Monthly,* 68 (1961): 1–17. This article gives some extensions of the simple fair-division concepts introduced in this chapter.

DURAN, C. Trump v. Trump: A fair division analysis, unpublished, 1995. This paper, written while Catherine Duran was an undergraduate in a Diplomacy and Negotiation class taught by Steven Brams at New York University, contains the analysis of the Trump divorce using the adjusted winner procedure.

KUHN, H. W. On games of fair division, in Martin Shubik (ed.), *Essays in Mathematical Economics,* Princeton University Press, Princeton, N.J., 1968, pp. 29–37. This article provides extensions of, and additional references to, the fair-division concepts presented in this chapter.

ROBERTSON, J., AND W. WEBB. *Cake Cutting Algorithms: Be Fair if You Can,* A. K. Peters, Wellesley, Mass., 1998. Robertson and Webb cover a great deal of cake-cutting ground in a text that includes exercises.

STEINHAUS, H. *Mathematical Snapshots.* Oxford University Press, Oxford, 1960. A brief but significant introduction to both fair division and apportionment is provided in this popular book on interesting mathematical topics.

SUGGESTED WEB SITES

http://www.math.hmc.edu/~su/fairdivision/
This is called "The Fair Division Page." It was put together by Francis Su of Harvey Mudd College, and has a number of interesting links related to work done by Su and his students.

http://www.maa.org/mathland/mathland_5_13. html   At this site, Ivars Peterson discusses some recent work by Bryan Dawson of Emporia State University in Kansas on taking turns and the sports draft.

http://www.mcn.org/c/rsurratt/conflict.html
This page is called "The Mediator." It contains fair and envy-free conflict resolution methods inspired by the adjusted winner technique in Chapter 13.

SKILLS CHECK

1. In a fair-division procedure, the goal for each participant is to (I) receive an identical portion or (II) receive what is perceived as a fair portion.

    (a) I
    (b) II only
    (c) Both I and II

2. Chris and Terry must make a fair division of three objects. They assign points to the objects, and use the adjusted winner procedure. What does Chris end up with?

Object	Chris	Terry
Boat	30	20
Land	50	60
Car	20	20

    (a) Boat and car
    (b) Boat and land
    (c) Boat, car, and part of the land

3. If you use the Knaster inheritance procedure to divide a single object and if each person bids a different price, then

    (a) each person will receive more than his or her perceived fair share.
    (b) some persons, but not every person, will receive more than their perceived fair share.
    (c) the successful bidder is the only person who will receive more than his or her perceived fair share.

4. Chris and Terry use the Knaster inheritance procedure to divide a coin collection. Chris bids $1000 and Terry bids $800. What is the outcome?

    (a) Chris gets the coins and pays Terry $200.
    (b) Chris gets the coins and pays Terry $450.
    (c) Chris gets the coins and pays Terry $500.

5. Four children bid on two objects. Using the Knaster inheritance procedure, what does Adam end up with after the division?

Object	Adam	Beth	Carl	Dietra
House	$80,000	$75,000	$90,000	$60,000
Car	$10,000	$12,000	$13,000	$15,000

    (a) House and cash
    (b) Car and cash
    (c) Cash only

6. Two people use the divide-and-choose procedure to divide a field. Suppose Jeff divides and Karen chooses. Which statement is true?

    (a) Karen always believes she gets more than her fair share.
    (b) Karen can guarantee that she always gets at least her fair share.
    (c) Karen can possibly believe she gets less than her fair share.

7. Suppose seven people will share a cake using the last-diminisher method. To begin, Scott cuts a piece and passes it to each of the other six people, but no one trims the piece. Then

    (a) Scott gets this piece.
    (b) the last person who is handed the piece keeps it.
    (c) the piece is returned to the cake and someone else cuts a piece.

EXERCISES   ▲ *Optional.*   ■ *Advanced.*   ◆ *Discussion.*

The Adjusted Winner Procedure

1. Suppose that Calvin and Hobbes discover a sunken pirate ship and must divide their loot. They assign points to the items as follows:

Object	Calvin's Points	Hobbes's Points
Cannon	10	5
Anchor	10	20
Unopened chest	15	20
Doubloon	11	14
Figurehead	20	30
Sword	15	6
Cannon ball	5	1
Wooden leg	2	1
Flag	10	2
Crow's nest	2	1

Use the adjusted winner procedure to determine a fair allocation of the loot. (Exercise 1 courtesy of Erica DeCarlo.)

2. This exercise illustrates how the adjusted winner procedure can be used to resolve disputes as well as to achieve fair allocations. Suppose Mike and Phil are roommates in college, and they encounter serious conflicts during their first week at school. Their resident adviser decides to use the adjusted winner procedure to resolve the dispute. The issues agreed upon, and the (independently assigned) points, turn out to be the following:

Issue	Mike's Points	Phil's Points
Stereo level	4	22
Smoking rights	10	20
Room party policy	50	25
Cleanliness	6	3
Alcohol use	15	15
Phone time	1	8
Lights-out time	10	2
Visitor policy	4	5

Use the adjusted winner procedure to resolve this dispute. (Exercise 2 courtesy of Erica DeCarlo.)

3. Make up an example involving two people and several *objects* for which the adjusted winner procedure can be used, and then use the adjusted winner procedure to determine a fair division.

4. Make up an example involving two people and several *issues* for which the adjusted winner procedure can be used, and then use the adjusted winner procedure to determine a fair resolution of the dispute.

The Knaster Inheritance Procedure

5. If John bids $28,225 and Mary bids $32,100 on their aging parents' old classic car, which they no longer drive, how would you reach a fair division?

6. John and Mary inherit their parents' old house and classic car. John bids $28,225 on the car and $55,900 on the house. Mary bids $32,100 on the car and $59,100 on the house. How should they arrive at a fair division?

7. Can you modify your fair-division scheme in Exercise 6 so that both John and Mary receive one of the two objects while still considering the allocation as fair?

8. Describe a fair division for three heirs, *A*, *B*, and *C*, who inherit a house in the city, a small farm, and a valuable sculpture, and who submit sealed bids (in dollars) on these objects as follows:

	A	*B*	*C*
House	145,000	149,999	165,000
Farm	135,000	130,001	128,000
Sculpture	110,000	80,000	127,000

9. Describe a fair division for three children, *E*, *F*, and *G*, who inherit equal shares of their parents'

classic car collection and who submit sealed bids (in dollars) on these five cars as follows:

	E	F	G
Duesenberg	18,000	15,000	15,000
Bentley	18,000	24,000	20,000
Ferrari	16,000	12,000	16,500
Pierce-Arrow	14,000	15,000	13,500
Cord	24,000	18,000	22,000

Taking Turns

10.   Suppose that Bob and Carol rank a series of objects, from most preferred to least preferred, as follows:

Bob	Carol
Car	Boat
Investments	Investments
CD player	Car
Boat	Washer–dryer
Television	Television
Washer–dryer	CD player

Assume that Bob and Carol use the bottom-up strategy and that Bob gets to choose first. Determine Bob's first choice, and the final allocation.

11.   Repeat Exercise 10 under the assumption that Carol gets to choose first.

12.   Mark and Fred have inherited a number of items from their parents' estate, with no indication of who gets what. They rank the items from most preferred to least preferred as follows:

Mark	Fred
Truck	Boat
Tractor	Tractor
Boat	Car
Car	Truck
Tools	Motorcycle
Motorcycle	Tools

Assume that Mark and Fred use the bottom-up strategy and that Mark gets to choose first. Determine Mark's first choice and the final allocation.

13.   Repeat Exercise 12 under the assumption that Fred gets to choose first.

Divide-and-Choose

14.   Suppose that Bob, Carol, and Ted view a cake as pictured in the example illustrating the Banach–Knaster scheme (see page 470). Assume that all cuts that will be made are vertical.

(a)   If Bob and Carol use divide-and-choose to divide the cake between them, how large a piece will each receive (assuming they follow the suggested strategies that go with divide-and-choose)?

(b)   If Carol and Ted use divide-and-choose to divide the cake between them, how large a piece will each receive (assuming they follow the suggested strategies that go with divide-and-choose)?

15.   If you and another person are using divide-and-choose to divide something between you, would you rather be the divider or the chooser? (Assume that neither of you knows anything about the preferences of the other.)

16.   Suppose that Bob and Carol view a cake as pictured in the example illustrating the Banach–Knaster scheme (see page 470). Assume that all cuts that will be made are vertical. Assume that Bob and Carol know how each other values the cake, and that neither is spiteful. Suppose they are to divide the cake using the *rules*, but not necessarily the *strategies*, of divide-and-choose.

(a)   Is Bob better off being the divider or the chooser? Why?

(b)   Discuss this in relation to Exercise 15.

Cake-Division Schemes: Proportionality

17.   Suppose that players 1, 2, and 3 view a cake as follows:

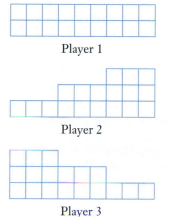

Notice that each player views the cake as having 18 square units of area (or value). Assume that each player regards a piece as acceptable if and only if it is at least $\frac{18}{3} = 6$ square units of area (his or her "fair share"). Assume also that all cuts made correspond to vertical lines.

(a)   Provide a total of three drawings to show how each player views a division of the cake by player 1 into three pieces he or she considers to be the same size or value. Label the pieces A, B, and C.

(b)   Identify two of these pieces that player 2 finds acceptable, and two that player 3 finds acceptable.

(c)   Show that a feasible assignment of fair pieces can be achieved by letting the players choose in the following order: player 3, player 2, player 1. Indicate how many square units of value each player thinks he or she received. Is there any other order in which players can choose pieces (in this example) that also results in a feasible assignment?

18.   Suppose that players 1, 2, and 3 view a cake as follows:

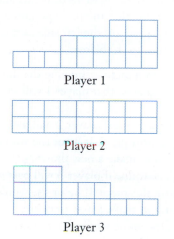

(a)   Provide a total of three drawings to show how each player views a division of the cake by player 1 into three pieces he or she considers to be the same size or value. Label the pieces A, B, and C. (We are still assuming that all cuts correspond to vertical lines, so this will require a cut along a vertical center line of some of the squares.)

(b)   Show that neither player 2 nor player 3 finds more than one of the three pieces acceptable (with "acceptable" defined as in Exercise 17).

(c)   Identify a single piece that player 2 and player 3 agree is *not* acceptable. (There are actually two such pieces; for definiteness, find the one on the right.)

(d)   Assume that players 2 and 3 give the piece from part (c) to player 1. Suppose they reassemble the rest and players 2 and 3 divide it between themselves using divide-and-choose (with a single vertical cut). Determine what size piece each of the three players will think he or she received (1) if player 2 divides and player 3 chooses, and (2) if player 3 divides and player 2 chooses.

19. Suppose players 1, 2, and 3 view a cake as in Exercise 18. Illustrate the last-diminisher method (still restricting attention to vertical cuts and, in addition, assuming that the piece potentially being diminished is a piece off the left side of the cake) by following steps (a)–(h) below:

(a) Draw a picture showing the third of the cake (6 squares) that player 1 will slice off the cake.

(b) Determine if player 2 will pass or further diminish this piece. If he or she would further diminish it, make a new drawing.

(c) Determine if player 3 will pass or further diminish this piece. If he or she would further diminish it, make a new drawing.

(d) Determine who receives the piece cut off the cake and what size or value he or she thinks it is. (Actually, we knew what size the person receiving this first piece would think it was, assuming he or she followed the prescribed strategy. How did we know this?)

(e) Finish the last-diminisher method using divide-and-choose on what remains, with the lowest-numbered player who remains doing the dividing.

(f) Redo step (e) with the other player doing the dividing.

(g) Redo step (e), but with the last two players using the last-diminisher method directly, instead of divide-and-choose (with the order as in step (e)).

(h) Redo step (g) with the order reversed.

20. Suppose players 1, 2, and 3 view the cake as in Exercise 18. Illustrate the envy-free procedure for $n = 3$ (yielding an allocation of part of the cake) by following steps (a)–(c) below. Again, restrict attention to vertical cuts.

(a) Provide a total of three drawings to show how each player views a division of the cake by player 1 into three pieces he or she considers to be the same size or value. Label the pieces A, B, and C. (This is the same as Exercise 18a.)

(b) Redraw the picture from player 2's view, and illustrate the trimming of piece A that he or she would do. Label the trimmed piece A' and the actual trimmings T.

(c) Indicate which piece each player would choose (and what he or she thinks its size is) if the players choose in the following order: player 3, player 2, player 1, according to the envy-free procedure on pages 473–474. Does the proviso in step 4 come into play here?

21. Apply the remainder of the Selfridge–Conway procedure from pages 473–474 to what was obtained in Exercise 20 by completing (a)–(c) below:

(a) Draw a picture of T from each player's view.

(b) The procedure calls for the player (other than player 1) who did not receive the trimmed piece to divide T into three pieces he or she considers to be the same size. Here, that would be player 2. Illustrate this division, and label the pieces X, Y, Z.

(c) Indicate which parts of T (and the sizes or values) the players will choose when they go in the following order: player 3, player 1, player 2.

■ 22. Consider the trimming procedure for four people described on pages 475–476. Explain why each player experiences no envy.

23. In generalizing the $n = 4$ envy-free procedure to arbitrary n, player 1 cuts the cake into $2^{n-2} + 1$ pieces. For $n = 4$, we had $2^{n-2} + 1 = 5$. Suppose that $n = 5$. Then $2^{n-2} + 1 = 9$. Determine how many pieces each player must trim to make the procedure work for $n = 5$.

▲ 24. Suppose that $n = 5$, and we begin by having player 1 cut the cake into 16 pieces of the same size. Suppose player 2 creates an eight-way tie, then player 3 creates a four-way tie, and, finally, player 4 creates a two-way tie. Let the players now choose in the following order: player 5, player 4, player 3, player 2, player 1. Show that no provisos about choosing trimmed pieces are needed to ensure envy-freeness.

▲ 25. Consider the envy-free procedure for $n = 4$, wherein player 1 cuts the cake into five pieces he considers to be the same size. Since he (player 1) gets an untrimmed piece, he thinks the size of the left-over L_1 from the first stage is at most 4/5 of the original cake. (He may think it as little as 1/5 if the other players did no trimming, leaving only one of the five pieces he cut for the second stage.) If we now do the same thing with L_1, then he will think the size of the leftover L_2 from the second stage is at most $(4/5)(4/5) = 16/25 = .64$ of the cake. How large a portion of the cake will he think the maximum size of the eleventh leftover is? Is the size of this leftover less than 1/10 of the cake?

Additional Exercises

26. The Banach–Knaster last-diminisher method is not the only well-known cake-division scheme that yields a proportional allocation for any number of players. There is also one due to A. M. Fink (sometimes called the *lone-chooser method*). For three players (Bob, Carol, and Ted) it works as follows:

(i) Bob and Carol divide the cake into two pieces using divide-and-choose.
(ii) Bob now divides the piece he has into three parts that he considers to be the same size. Carol does the same with the piece she has.
(iii) Ted now chooses whichever of Bob's three pieces that he (Ted) thinks is largest, and Ted chooses whichever of Carol's three pieces that he thinks is largest.
(iv) Bob keeps his remaining two pieces, as does Carol.

(a) Explain why Ted thinks he is getting at least one-third of the cake.

(b) Explain why Bob and Carol each think they are receiving at least one-third of the cake.
(c) Explain why, in general, this scheme is not envy-free.

27. In A. M. Fink's scheme (described in Exercise 26), suppose that a fourth person (Alice) comes along after Bob, Carol, and Ted have already divided the cake among themselves so that each of the three thinks he or she has a piece of size at least one-third. Mimic what was done in the three-person case to obtain an allocation among the four that is proportional. (*Hint:* Begin by having Bob, Carol, and Ted divide the pieces they have into a certain number—how many?—of equal parts.)

28. There is a moving-knife version of the Banach–Knaster scheme that appears in the Dubins–Spanier paper in Suggested Readings. To describe it, we picture the cake as being rectangular, and the procedure beginning with a referee holding a knife along the left edge, as illustrated below.

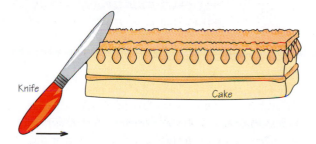

Assume, for the sake of illustration, that there are four players (Bob, Carol, Ted, and Alice). The referee starts moving the knife from left to right over the cake (keeping it parallel to the position in which it started) until one of the players (assume it is Bob) calls "cut." At this time, a cut is made, and the piece to the left of the knife is given to Bob, and he exits the game. The knife starts moving again, and the process continues. The strategies are for each player to call "cut" whenever it would yield him or her a piece of size at least one-fourth.

(a)   Explain why this procedure produces an allocation that is proportional.

(b)   Explain why the resulting allocation is not, in general, envy-free.

(c)   Explain why, if you are not the first player to call "cut," there is a strategy different from the one suggested that is never worse for you, and sometimes better.

29.   There is a two-person moving-knife cake-division scheme due to A. K. Austin that leads to each player receiving a piece of cake that he or she considers to be of size exactly one-half. It begins by having one of the two players (Bob) place two knives over the cake, one of which is at the left edge, and the other of which is parallel to the first and placed so that the piece between the knives (A in the picture below) is of size exactly one-half in Bob's estimation.

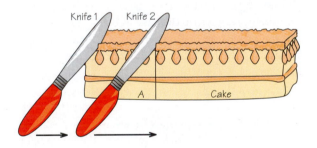

If Carol agrees that this is a 50–50 division, we are done. Otherwise, Bob starts moving both knives to the right—perhaps at different rates—so that the piece between the knives remains of size one-half in his eyes. Carol calls "stop" at the point when she also thinks the piece between the two knives is of size exactly one-half.

(a)   If the knife on the right were to reach the right-hand edge, where would the knife on the left be?

(b)   Explain why there definitely is a point where Carol thinks the piece between the two knives is of size exactly one-half. (*Hint:* If Carol thinks the piece is too small at the beginning, what will she think of it at the end?)

30.   Suppose we have three items (X, Y, and Z) and three people (Bob, Carol, and Ted). Assume that each of the people spreads 100 points over the items (as in adjusted winner) to indicate the relative worth of each item to that person:

Item	Bob	Carol	Ted
X	40	30	30
Y	50	40	30
Z	10	30	40

For each of the following allocations, indicate

(a)   whether or not it is proportional.

(b)   whether or not it is envy-free.

(c)   whether or not it is equitable.

(d)   for the ones that are *not* Pareto-optimal, another allocation that makes one person better off without making anyone else worse off.

Allocation 1:   Bob gets Z, Carol gets Y, and Ted gets X. (This is not Pareto-optimal.)

Allocation 2:   Bob gets Y, Carol gets Z, and Ted gets X. (This is not Pareto-otpimal.)

Allocation 3:   Bob gets X, Y, and Z. (This *is* Pareto-optimal; explain why.)

Allocation 4:   Bob gets Y, Carol gets X, and Ted gets Z. (This is Pareto-optimal.)

Allocation 5:   Bob gets X, Carol gets Y, and Ted gets Z. (This is Pareto-optimal.)

TECHNOLOGY CORNER

The Knaster Inheritance Procedure

The spreadsheet shown in Figure 13.1 models the situation where four heirs use the Knaster procedure to divide an inheritance of a house, car, and boat. Each heir establishes bids for the items, in rows 2, 3, and 4 of columns B, C, D, E. The maximum bid for each item is given in the last column, using the **Max** command. For example, the entry in position G2 is computed as =**Max(B2:E2)**.

Each person's bid for the estate is given in row 6, using the **Sum** command. For example, Adam's valuation of the estate is in position **B6,** computed as =**Sum(B2:B4)**. Assuming each heir is to receive an equal share, each person's perceived share is computed by dividing the value in the 6th row by 4. For example, the entry in position **B7** is computed as =**B6/4.**

Each item is acquired by the person who values it most highly. Therefore, Beth buys the house for $90,000, Chris buys the boat for $2400, and Danielle buys the car for $5600. These costs are manually entered in the 8th row, and the balance due is calculated on the 9th row. Here, a negative number indicates a balance due to the estate. But by adding these amounts, a surplus to the estate arises, as shown in entry **G9**, computed as =**Sum(B9:E9)**. This surplus is divided evenly among the heirs, and added back to their balances in the final line.

TASK 1.   Suppose that the estate also includes a collection of jewelry. Danielle values this collection at $3000, but each of the other three heirs values it at $2000. As the high bidder, Danielle will receive the jewelry and the other heirs will receive compensation for their portion. Adjust the spreadsheet above to reflect these changes.

TASK 2.   Two children are equal heirs to a collection of four sculptures. Kim places a higher bid for two of the items, and Chris places a higher bid for the other two items. Set bids for each item and create a spreadsheet that models the Knaster procedure for distribution of the estate.

	A	B	C	D	E	F	G
1		Adam	Beth	Chris	Danielle		Max Price
2	Car	5000	5500	5200	5600		5600
3	House	85000	90000	86000	88000		90000
4	Boat	2000	1600	2400	2200		2400
5							
6	Estate Sum	92000		97100	93600	95800	
7	Estate Portion	23000		24275	23400	23950	
8	Items Received			−90000	−2400	−5600	
9	Balance	23000		−65725	21000	18350	surplus:	−3375
10	Surplus Funds	843.75		843.75	843.75	843.75	
11	Total Received	23843.75		−64881.25	21843.75	19193.75	
12				and House	and Boat	and Car	

FIGURE 13.1

The Adjusted Winner Procedure

The spreadsheet shown in Figure 13.2 models the adjusted winner procedure for an estate with three items. Point allocations are entered in rows 2, 3, and 4 of columns B and C. The last column shows the ratio of Jack's allocations to Jill's allocations.

Jack placed more points on the car and boat, so he is initially given these items. Likewise, Jill placed more points on the house, so she is initially given it. However, part of the house must be given to Jack in order that both Jack and Jill eventually have equal point totals. Entry E9 represents the part of the house that goes to Jack. The point total for Jack's portion of the house, shown in entry **B9**, is then computed as =**70*E9.** The point total for Jill's portion of the house, shown in entry **C9**, is computed as =**80*E9.** Different

	A	B	C	D	E
1		Jack	Jill	ratio:Jack/Jill	
2	House	70	80	0.875	
3	Car	20	15	1.33333333	
4	Boat	10	5	2	
5					
6	Total	100	100		
7					
8	Assets	Jack	Jill		
9	House	21	56	part to Jack: 0.3	
10	Car	20			
11	Boat	15			
12	Total	56	56		

FIGURE 13.2

values in entry **E9** will result in different point totals. For this example, an entry of .3 (meaning Jack gets 30% of the house) results in a distribution where each person believes they received 56% of the estate.

TASK 3.   Suppose Jill actually does not want the car or the boat, but wants to keep as much of the house as possible. Assuming she knows how Jack will assign his points, how should Jill change her point assignment in order to get a larger percentage of the house?

TASK 4.   Assume that Jill assigns all of her points to the house, and Jack knows this before he assigns his points. If Jack wants to get the car, the boat, and as much of the house as possible, how should he assign his points?

Exploration

The Knaster procedure shown in Figure 13.1 can be adjusted for situations where the heirs do not share equally in the inheritance. Adjust rows 7 and 10 in the spreadsheet in order to model the situation where Beth receives 50% of the estate, Chris receives 30% of the estate, and Adam and Danielle each receive 10% of the estate.

writing projects

1 ▶   It turns out that there is no way to extend the adjusted winner procedure to three or more players. That is, there are point assignments by three players to three objects so that no allocation satisfies the three desired properties of equability (equal points), envy-freeness, and Pareto optimality. On the other hand, there are separate procedures that will realize any two of the three properties. Thus, trade-offs must be made, and these may depend on the circumstances. Discuss your feelings regarding the relative importance of the three properties and circumstances that may affect the choice of which two of the three properties one might wish to have satisfied.

2 ▶   If we use taking turns to divvy up a collection of objects between two people (Bob and Carol), then there is an obvious advantage to going first. Assume that we have decided that Bob will, in fact, choose first (say, by the toss of a coin). Let's think about how Carol might be compensated. First of all, if there are only three objects, then the "choice sequence" Bob–Carol–Carol seems to be the only reasonable one. Do you agree? For four objects, however, there are two choice sequences that suggest themselves: Bob–Carol–Carol–Carol and Bob–Carol–Carol–Bob. Do you think that one of these is obviously more fair than the other? What if there are four essentially identical objects? What if both Bob and Carol value object *A* twice as much as *B*, and *B* twice as much as *C*, and *C* twice as much as *D*? What sequences suggest themselves for 5 objects? For 8 objects? (For more on this, see the book *The Win-Win Solution* in Suggested Readings.)

3 ▶   One of the most important differences between the three-person and the *n*-person envy-free procedures is that the latter procedure may take more than two stages. And, of course, the more stages there are, the more cuts and trimmings that may be necessary. Do you consider this a serious practical problem, or is it mainly a theoretical problem? Why?

chapter 14

Apportionment

". . . who but a politician would care so much about rounding fractions?"

The Apportionment Problem

The U.S. Constitution requires that seats in the House of Representatives "shall be apportioned among the several states within this union according to their respective Numbers. . . ." The total number of representatives—not specified in the Constitution—started at 105 in 1790 and steadily increased until 1910, when Congress permanently fixed the House size at 435 seats.

The apportionment problem arises because it is unlikely that any state's fair share of the House will be a whole number. For example, in the census of 1790, the population of the United States was found to be 3,615,920. The state populations ranged from 55,540 for Delaware to 630,560 for the most populous state, Virginia. Virginia's fair share of the 105 seat House was

$$\frac{\text{population of Virginia}}{\text{population of the United States}} \times 105$$

or

$$\frac{630,560}{3,615,920} \times 105 = 18.310 \text{ seats}$$

Delaware's share was

$$\frac{55,540}{3,615,920} \times 105 = 1.613 \text{ seats}$$

The 106th Congress of the
United States in session.

Should these numbers be rounded to give Delaware 2 representatives and Virginia 18? Then each Virginia representative would be responsible for $\frac{630,560}{18} = 35,031$ constituents, while each of the 2 Delaware representatives would represent half of Delaware's population, or 27,770 people.

> The **apportionment problem** is to round a set of fractions so that their sum is maintained at its original value. The rounding procedure must not be an arbitrary one, but one that can be applied consistently. Any such rounding procedure is called an **apportionment method.**

The House of Representatives is the best-known and most frequently studied case of political apportionment. Some half-dozen different apportionment methods have been seriously considered for use by the Congress. In addition to the *Hill–Huntington method* that is currently used, three other methods have been implemented in the past: the methods of *Thomas Jefferson, Alexander Hamilton,* and *Daniel Webster.*

Apportionment problems often involve political institutions—who but a politician would care so much about rounding fractions?—but they do arise in other contexts. Here is an example. A high school has one mathematics teacher who teaches all geometry, precalculus, and calculus classes. She has time to teach a total of five sections. One hundred students are enrolled as follows: 52 for geometry, 33 for precalculus, and 15 for calculus. How many sections of each course should be scheduled? Since 52% of the students are taking geometry, 52% of the 5 sections available, or 2.6 sections should be for geometry. The precalculus share is

33% of 5, or 1.65 sections, and the calculus share, 15% of 5, equals 0.75 section. The apportionment will be the actual numbers of sections taught, which have to be whole numbers. It is tempting to round each of these quantities to the nearest whole number, assigning 3 sections to geometry, 2 sections to precalculus, and 1 to calculus. This makes 6 sections in all—too many! The purpose of an apportionment method is to find an equitable way to round a set of numbers like this without increasing or decreasing the sum.

Although many apportionment problems do not involve the House of Representatives, our terminology refers to *states, populations,* and a *house size.* In a course-scheduling problem, the states are the subjects, the populations are the numbers of students enrolled in each subject, and the house size is the total number of sections to be taught.

Let n be the number of states. The populations of these states will be denoted

$$p_1, p_2, \ldots, p_i, \ldots, p_n$$

and the total population will be

$$p = p_1 + p_2 + \cdots + p_n$$

A state's fair share of the congressional districts is called its *quota.* To calculate a state's quota, multiply its fraction of the total population by the house size.

> In an apportionment problem, the **quota** is the exact share that would be allocated *if a whole number were not required.* State i, with population p_i, has quota
>
> $$q_i = \frac{p_i}{p} \times h$$

An apportionment is given by n whole numbers

$$a_1, a_2, \ldots, a_i, \ldots, a_n$$

with a_i representing the number of representatives given to state i. Ideally, each state's apportionment should be close to its quota. It is unrealistic to expect that for any state $a_i = q_i$, because a_i has to be a whole number and q_i is unlikely to be a whole number. In choosing an apportionment method, we must decide what we mean by the phrase "a_i should be close to q_i." Apportionment involves rounding, and there are many ways to round. *Rounding down* means discarding the fractional part of a number q to obtain a whole number that we will denote by $\lfloor q \rfloor$. Thus, $\lfloor 7.00001 \rfloor = 7$, $\lfloor 7 \rfloor = 7$, and $\lfloor 6.99999 \rfloor = 6$. *Rounding up* gives the next whole number, $\lceil q \rceil$. Thus, $\lceil 7.00001 \rceil = 8$, but $\lceil 7 \rceil = 7$.

The first apportionment method that we will consider uses *both* of these rounding methods.

The Hamilton Method

The first apportionment method considered by Congress was the *method of largest fractions*, or the *method of Alexander Hamilton.*

> With the **Hamilton method,** state i receives either its **lower quota,** which is the integer part of its quota (in the notation just introduced, $\lfloor q_i \rfloor$), or its **upper quota,** $\lceil q_i \rceil$, obtained by rounding the quota up to the next integer value. The states that receive their upper quotas are those whose quotas have the largest fractional parts.

Implementing the Hamilton method is a three-step procedure. First, calculate each state's quota. Second, tentatively assign to each state its lower quota of representatives. Each state whose quota is not a whole number loses a fraction of a seat at this stage, so the total number of seats assigned at this point is less than the House size h. This leaves additional seats to be apportioned, so the final step is to allot the remaining seats, one each, to the states whose quotas have the largest fractional parts.

It is possible that a tie will be encountered, in which the quotas of two states have identical fractional parts, but in practice, ties rarely occur when large populations are involved.

The apportionment method of largest fractions, also known as the Hamilton method, was named for Alexander Hamilton.

The Hamilton method provoked the first presidential veto in U.S. history when George Washington rejected an apportionment bill that was based on it. Washington's objection was that the fractions of seats gained by some states in the third step of the Hamilton apportionment were not related to the states' total populations.

E X A M P L E   *Hamilton's Apportionment of the House of Representatives*

In 1790, there were 15 states, and the House had 105 seats. Table 14.1 displays the calculations leading to Alexander Hamilton's proposed apportionment.

The quotas shown in the table were calculated by using the formula

$$q_i = \frac{p_i}{p} \times h$$

where $p = 3,615,920$ is the total population and $h = 105$. We can rearrange the formula as

$$q_i = \frac{h}{p} \times p_i = \frac{105}{3,615,920} \times p_i$$

TABLE 14.1 **Apportioning the House of Representatives by the Hamilton Method**

State	Population	Quota	Lower Quota	Apportionment
Virginia	630,560	18.310	18	18
Massachusetts	475,327	13.803	13 ↑	14
Pennsylvania	432,879	12.570	12 ↑	13
North Carolina	353,523	10.266	10	10
New York	331,589	9.629	9 ↑	10
Maryland	278,514	8.088	8	8
Connecticut	236,841	6.877	6 ↑	7
South Carolina	206,236	5.989	5 ↑	6
New Jersey	179,570	5.214	5	5
New Hampshire	141,822	4.118	4	4
Vermont	85,533	2.484	2	2
Georgia	70,835	2.057	2	2
Kentucky	68,705	1.995	1 ↑	2
Rhode Island	68,446	1.988	1 ↑	2
Delaware	55,540	1.613	1 ↑	2
Totals	3,615,920	105	97	105

If you are using a calculator to follow the entries in the table, divide 105 by 3,615,920 first, and store the result in memory. Then each quota can be figured by recalling the result in memory and multiplying the individual state population.

The table shows that if each state were given its lower quota, only 97 seats would have been apportioned. The remaining 8 seats go to the 8 states whose quotas had the largest fractional parts, and these are marked in the table.   ◆

President Washington's veto prevented the Hamilton method from being used in 1792, but it was adopted by Congress in 1850 and remained in use until 1900. The half-century of experience with the Hamilton method revealed a paradox.

Paradoxes of the Hamilton Method

A *paradox* is a fact that seems obviously false. The first Hamilton apportionment paradox, called the *Alabama paradox,* was discovered in 1881. As part of the reapportionment procedure mandated by the Constitution, the Census Bureau had supplied Congress with a table of congressional apportionments for a range of different house sizes from 275 to 350, based on the 1880 census. The table revealed a strange phenomenon. With a 299-seat House, Alabama's quota was 7.646. The fractional part ranked twentieth of the 38 states, and that was just enough to give Alabama its upper quota of $\lceil 7.646 \rceil = 8$ seats. Illinois and Texas, with quotas of 18.640 and 9.640, respectively, ranked below Alabama and received their lower quotas: 18 for Illinois and 9 for Texas. The next column of the table, corresponding to a house size of 300 seats, showed changes in the apportionments for each of these three states: Alabama now had 7 seats instead of 8, while Illinois and Texas received increased apportionments of 19 seats and 10 seats, respectively. Alabama had *lost* a seat as a result of an increase in the house size. This happened because the Illinois and Texas quotas increased more than Alabama's quota did. With a 300-seat House, Alabama's quota increased to 7.671, Illinois's to 18.702, and Texas's to 9.672. Since the fractional parts of the quotas for Illinois and Texas were larger, those states were given their upper quotas, and Alabama was left with its lower quota.

> The **Alabama paradox** occurs when a state loses a seat as the result of an increase in the house size.

E X A M P L E   *A Mathematics Department Meets the Alabama Paradox*

A mathematics department has 30 teaching assistants to cover recitations for college algebra, calculus I, calculus II, calculus III, and contemporary mathematics. The enrollments of these courses are given in Table 14.2. The department will use the Hamilton method to apportion the teaching assistants to the five subjects. In this problem, the house size is $h = 30$ (the number of teaching assistants) and the

TABLE 14.2	Apportioning 30 Teaching Assistants			
Course	Enrollment	Quota	Lower Quota	Apportionment
College algebra	188	7.52	7	7
Calculus I	142	5.68	5 ↑	6
Calculus II	138	5.52	5	5
Calculus III	64	2.56	2 ↑	3
Contemporary mathematics	218	8.72	8 ↑	9
Totals	750	30.00	27	30

population is $p = 750$. Using the formula for calculating the quota given on page 493, we see that each subject's quota is given by dividing its enrollment by 750 and multiplying by 30. Equivalently, the quota of subject i, with enrollment p_i, is

$$q_i = \frac{30}{750} \times p_i = 0.04 \times p_i$$

The lower quotas add up to 27, so the three courses whose quotas have the largest fractional parts, calculus I and III and contemporary mathematics, are entitled to their upper quotas.

After these calculations were finished, the graduate school authorized the department to hire an additional teaching assistant. With 31 teaching assistants, the quotas will be obtained by multiplying the subject enrollments by $31 \div 750 = 0.0413333$. Table 14.3 displays the rest of the calculations. The calculus III instructor will be dismayed, since the increased number of teaching assistants has caused her course to *lose* one section. ◆

TABLE 14.3	Apportioning 31 Teaching Assistants			
Course	Enrollment	Quota	Lower Quota	Apportionment
College algebra	188	7.771	7 ↑	8
Calculus I	142	5.869	5 ↑	6
Calculus II	138	5.704	5 ↑	6
Calculus III	64	2.645	2	2
Contemporary mathematics	218	9.011	9	9
Totals	750	31.000	28	31

The size of the House of Representatives is now fixed at 435 members, so the Alabama paradox cannot occur. A second paradox, called the *population paradox,* is associated with a fixed house size. In Exercise 3 we consider a situation involving an imaginary country with four states and a 100-seat legislature, apportioned by the Hamilton method. The new census shows substantial increases in population for the three largest states and a slight loss of population for the smallest state. In the new apportionments, the largest and smallest states both gain seats, while the middle two states lose seats. Thus the smallest state lost population and gained a seat, while the middle two states gained population and lost seats.

> The **population paradox** occurs when one state's population increases and its apportionment decreases, while simultaneously another state's population increases proportionally less, or decreases, and its apportionment increases.

Divisor Methods

The Jefferson Method

The Constitution requires that congressional districts be drawn so that the population of each is at least 30,000. President Washington could have vetoed the Hamilton apportionment bill because Delaware's population of only 55,540 was too small for the two congressional districts assigned to it. Thomas Jefferson proposed an apportionment method, now called the **Jefferson method,** to replace the Hamilton method.

Jefferson selected a minimum district population d. Each state's population is divided by d, and the result is rounded *down* to obtain the state's apportionment. The actual number that Jefferson used was $d = 33,000$. Thus Virginia's apportionment was

$$\left\lfloor \frac{\text{population of Virginia}}{33,000} \right\rfloor = \left\lfloor \frac{630,560}{33,000} \right\rfloor = \lfloor 19.108 \rfloor = 19$$

The Jefferson method is one of a class of apportionment methods called *divisor methods.*

> A **divisor method** of apportionment determines each state's apportionment by dividing its population by a common divisor d and rounding the resulting quotient. Divisor methods differ in the rule used to round the quotient.

Thomas Jefferson favored a method of apportionment biased in favor of states with large populations.

With the Jefferson method, a state's apportionment is determined by calculating how many complete d-person districts will fit in that state. As long as $d \geq 30{,}000$, the requirement that congressional districts have a population of at least 30,000 will be satisfied.

The divisor must be carefully chosen to achieve the correct house size. In 1790, $d = 30{,}000$ would have resulted in larger apportionments for several states and a House size of 112, while $d = 36{,}000$ would have decreased several apportionments, and the House size would have been 91.

Critical Multipliers

We shall use a modification of the Jefferson method that uses multipliers instead of divisors. The first step is to calculate the quota for each state and to round the quotas down to obtain the lower quotas. A state's lower quota will be its **tentative apportionment.** The sum of these tentative apportionments will be less than the house size, so some of them will have to increase. To determine which states are to receive increased apportionments, we calculate a critical multiplier for each.

Let n_i be the tentative apportionment of a state, and let q_i be its quota. The **critical multiplier** m_i for that state is

$$m_i = \frac{n_i + 1}{q_i}$$

The reason for this is that when each quota is multiplied by a number M that is greater than 1, the larger quotas are increased more than the small ones. For example, to increase a small quota such as 1.5 to the next whole number, 2, you need $M = 1.3333$. To increase a larger quota such as 52.5 to *one more than the next whole number*, 54, only takes $M = 54 \div 52.5 = 1.0286$.

With the Hamilton method, each state starts with its lower quota, and some states are given their upper quotas to fill the House. There is no way for a state to receive less than its lower quota or more than its upper quota, so the Hamilton method does satisfy the quota condition. This was obvious to the Congress in 1850, so it based its apportionment on the Hamilton method.[1]

The Jefferson method, however, is not troubled by the Alabama and population paradoxes. Consider the Alabama paradox, in which a state loses a seat as a result of an increase in the House size. With any apportionment method, the apportionments of some states must increase when the size of the House increases. The Jefferson method awards seats in order of critical multipliers. When the House size increases, the next seat will go to the state with the smallest critical multiplier. There is no opportunity for a state to lose a seat.

Congress has never used an apportionment method that satisfies the quota condition and avoids the paradoxes. It would be desirable to use such a method, and in the 1970s, the mathematicians Michel L. Balinski and H. Peyton Young set out to find one. They succeeded in finding a method, which they called the *quota method*, that satisfies the quota condition (as the Hamilton method does) and avoids the Alabama paradox (as the Jefferson method does). However, the population paradox remained. They subsequently proved that the only apportionment methods that are free of the population paradox are the divisor methods. Since it is also known that every divisor method is capable of violating the quota condition, Balinski and Young have proved an impossibility theorem like Kenneth Arrow's theorem that there is no completely satisfactory way to decide multicandidate elections based on voter preference schedules (see Chapter 11). No apportionment method is free of paradoxes and satisfies the quota condition.

The Webster Method

> The **Webster method** is the divisor method that rounds the quota to the nearest whole number, rounding up when the fractional part is greater than or equal to $\frac{1}{2}$, and rounding down when the fractional part is less than $\frac{1}{2}$.

There is no standard notation like $\lfloor q \rfloor$ and $\lceil q \rceil$ to denote the rounding of q to the nearest whole number. We will use $\langle q \rangle$ to denote this rounding. The Webster and Jefferson methods are immune to the Alabama and population paradoxes, and

---

[1] The origins of the Hamilton method had been forgotten in 1850, and the method was named for Congressman Samuel Vinton, who had rediscovered the method.

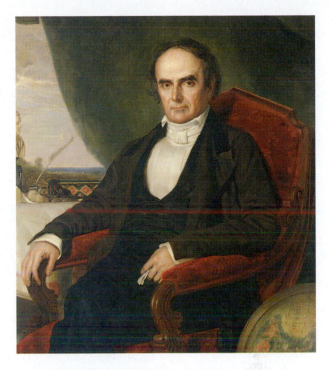

Statesman and orator Daniel Webster (1782–1852), who developed a divisor method for apportioning the U.S. House of Representatives.

neither satisfies the quota condition. However, in many respects, Webster's is a better method than Jefferson's. While the Jefferson method obviously favors the large states, the Webster method is neutral, favoring neither the large nor the small states. Furthermore, while the Jefferson method almost always gives the most populous state more than its upper quota, the Webster method would never have violated the quota condition in any of the 21 congressional apportionments that have occurred since 1790.

EXAMPLE   *Apportioning Classes*

The mathematics department of a high school has staff to teach a total of 17 seconds. The enrollments for the five courses that are offered are shown in Table 14.4. We will use the Webster method to decide how many sections to allot to each course. The first step is to calculate the quotas. The total enrollment is $p = 577$, and the house size is $h = 17$, so, using the formula on page 493, the quota for subject i is

$$q_i = \frac{17}{577} \times p_i = 0.202946 \times p_i$$

where p_i is the number of students enrolled in subject i. The quotas are shown in Table 14.4. If the sum of the tentative apportionments had been equal to 17, our job would be finished: they would be the actual apportionments. In this example, the sum turns out to be 19, so we must reduce the number of sections apportioned by 2.

TABLE 14.4   Apportioning Classes by the Webster Method

Subject	Enrollment	Quota	Tentative Apportionment	Critical Multiplier	Adjusted Quota	New Tentative Apportionment
Algebra I	155	4.56675	5	0.98538	4.5588	5
Geometry	124	3.65340	4	0.95801	3.6470	4
Algebra II	158	4.65514	5	0.96667	4.6470	5
Precalculus	85	2.50435	3	0.99826	2.49999	2
Calculus	55	1.62046	2	0.92566	1.6176	2
Totals	577	17	19	—	16.9704	18

To decide which courses should be given fewer sections, we calculate a critical multiplier for each, just as we did with the Jefferson method. Our critical multipliers will now be less than one, since we need the adjusted quotas to be less than the original quotas.

If the tentative apportionment of a course is n_i, then the critical multiplier for that subject is

$$m_i = \frac{n_i - 0.5}{q_i}$$

If we multiply the quota q_i by any number *less than* m_i, the product $\bar{q}_i$ will be less than $n_i - 0.5$, because

$$\bar{q}_i < m_i \times q_i = \frac{n_i - 0.5}{q_i} \times q_i = n_i - 0.5$$

Therefore $\bar{q}_i$ will be rounded to either $n_i - 1$ or some lesser value, because all numbers less than $n_i - 0.5$ are rounded to something less than n_i. Table 14.4 displays the critical multipliers.

The critical multiplier for precalculus, $M_1 = 0.99826$, is closest to 1.00000. The **adjusted quotas** are obtained by multiplying the original quotas by M_1, and the new tentative apportionments result from rounding these numbers.

The only course whose tentative apportionment has changed is precalculus. The new critical multiplier is based on the new tentative apportionment of 2, and is equal to $(2 - 0.5) \div 2.50435 = 0.59896$. The other critical multipliers are not changed, and we can see in Table 14.4 that the multiplier closest to 1.00000 is now that of algebra I, $M_2 = 0.98538$. When we multiply the quotas by M_2, we get the following new adjusted quotas:

Subject	Adjusted Quota	Apportionment
Algebra I	4.49998	4
Geometry	3.59999	4
Algebra II	4.58708	5
Precalculus	2.46774	2
Calculus	1.59677	2
Total	16.75146	17

The final apportionment is given by rounding these new adjusted quotas. ◆

With the Webster method, the sum of the initial tentative apportionments may be equal to the house size—in which case they are the final apportionments—or it may be larger or smaller. If too many seats were apportioned initially (as in the example), adjust the quotas by multiplying all of them by the critical multiplier that is closest to 1.00000.

If the sum of the rounded quotas is less than the house size, it is necessary to increase the apportionments of some of the states. To decide which states are to receive additional seats, we calculate, as before, a critical multiplier for each. Since we are increasing some apportionments, the critical multipliers will be greater than 1.

When the tentative apportionments given by the Webster method add up less than the house size, the formula for the critical multiplier for state i is

$$m_i = \frac{n_i + 0.5}{q_i}$$

where n_i is the tentative apportionment and q_i is the quota for state i.

Multiplying all of the quotas by a multiplier $M > 1$ *inflates* them, whereas if $M < 1$, the quotas are *deflated*. When the quotas are inflated, the larger states benefit, since their inflated quotas are likely to be the first ones to reach the rounding point. This is analogous to what happens when every employee of a company receives a 3% pay increase. If a worker has an annual salary of $25,000, she will receive a $750 raise. The company president, who makes $800,000 per year, gets a $24,000 raise.

When the quotas are deflated, the less populous states will benefit, since they will lose less than the larger states. Let us return to our analogy with salaries. An across-the-board 3% pay cut will cost the worker $750 per year and will cost the company president $24,000.

Since the Webster method is just as likely to inflate the quotas as it is to deflate them, it is a neutral method; that is, it is just as likely to favor small states as large states.

The Hill–Huntington Method

The **Hill–Huntington method** is a divisor method that has been used to apportion the U.S. House of Representatives since 1940. Like the Jefferson and Webster methods, the apportionment is calculated by rounding the quotas, after adjusting them if necessary. The only difference between the three divisor methods is in the rounding procedure.

The Hill–Huntington rounding procedure is related to the **geometric mean.** Consider the rectangle $\mathcal{R}$ displayed in Figure 14.1. The area of $\mathcal{R}$ is the product of the lengths A and B, or AB. The geometric mean of A and B is defined to be the length E of the edge of a square $\mathcal{S}$ with the same area as $\mathcal{R}$. The area of $\mathcal{S}$ is E^2, so $E^2 = AB$, and therefore $E = \sqrt{AB}$.

Given a positive number q, let q^* be the geometric mean of $\lfloor q \rfloor$ and $\lceil q \rceil$. The Hill–Huntington rounding of a number q is equal to

$$\lfloor q \rfloor \quad \text{if } q < q^*$$

and

$$\lceil q \rceil \quad \text{if } q \geq q^*$$

For example, suppose that $q = 7.485$. Jefferson and Webster would round 7.485 down to 7. Since $\lfloor 7.485 \rfloor = 7$ and $\lceil 7.485 \rceil = 8$, the geometric mean is $q^* = \sqrt{7 \times 8} = 7.48331\cdots$, which is less than 7.485. Therefore, the Hill and Huntington rounding of 7.485 is $\lceil 7.485 \rceil = 8$. We will use $\langle\!\langle q \rangle\!\rangle$ for the Hill–Huntington rounding of a number q.

FIGURE 14.1
The edge, E, of the square is the geometric mean of the edges of the rectangle (A and B), since the two figures have the same area.

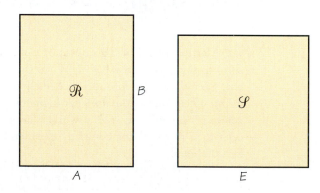

Hill–Huntington apportionment calculations follow the general plan of the Jefferson and Webster methods. Round each state's quota the Hill–Huntington way to obtain a first tentative apportionment. If the sum of the tentative apportionments is equal to the House size, the job is finished. If not, a list of critical multipliers must be constructed, each chosen to be just sufficient to change the corresponding state's apportionment by one seat in the desired direction. If n_i is the number of seats apportioned tentatively to a state, and the total apportionment is too small, the multiplier for that state is

$$m_i = \frac{\sqrt{n_i (n_i + 1)}}{q_i}$$

If m_i is used as the multiplier, the adjusted quota for state i will be $\sqrt{n_i (n_i + 1)}$, just enough to warrant rounding the quota to $n_i + 1$. Of course, states with critical multipliers less than m_i will also receive increased apportionments.

If the total apportionment is too large, the critical multiplier for state i is

$$m_i = \frac{\sqrt{n_i (n_i - 1)}}{q_i}$$

With m_i as multiplier, the adjusted quota of state i would be equal to $\sqrt{n_i (n_i - 1)}$, the cutoff number for rounding down to $n_i - 1$. If further adjustments are necessary, the critical multiplier of the state whose apportionment was changed is recalculated, and the process is repeated.

A zero apportionment is impossible with the Hill–Huntington method, because the rounding point for quotas between 0 and 1 is $\sqrt{0 \times 1} = 0$. Any such quota will be rounded to 1.

E X A M P L E   *Apportionment of the 1790 Congress, Revisited*

The calculations leading to the Hill–Huntington apportionment of the Congress are given in Table 14.5. The rounded quotas add up to 106, more than the House size of 105, so we have to adjust the quotas. The table shows the critical multipliers. The critical multiplier that is closest to 1.00000 is Pennsylvania's, 0.9936. This multiplier is used to adjust the quotas, and we see that Pennsylvania will lose a seat, while the other apportionments will remain the same.   ◆

Which Divisor Method Is the Best?

The three divisor methods that we have considered often given different results. When this happens, a state that is favored by the method not in use will often argue that the apportionment was unfair. Spotlight 14.1 summarizes a Supreme

TABLE 14.5	Apportioning the House of Representatives by the Hill–Huntington Method					
State	**Population**	**Quota**	q^*	**Tentative Appor- tionment**	**Critical Multiplier**	**Adjusted Quota**	**Final Appor- tionment**
Virginia	630,560	18.310	18.493	18	0.9554	18.193	18
Massachusetts	475,327	13.803	13.491	14	0.9773	18.186	14
Pennsylvania	432,879	12.570	12.490	13	0.9936	12.490	12
North Carolina	353,523	10.266	10.488	10	0.9241	10.200	10
New York	331,589	9.629	9.487	10	0.9852	9.567	10
Maryland	278,514	8.088	8.485	8	0.9252	8.036	8
Connecticut	236,841	6.877	6.481	7	0.9243	6.833	7
South Carolina	206,236	5.989	5.477	6	0.9145	5.951	6
New Jersey	179,570	5.214	5.477	5	0.8577	5.181	5
New Hampshire	141,822	4.118	4.472	4	0.8412	4.092	4
Vermont	85,533	2.484	2.449	3	0.9861	2.468	3
Georgia	70,835	2.057	2.449	2	0.6875	2.044	2
Kentucky	68,705	1.995	1.414	2	0.7088	1.982	2
Rhode Island	68,446	1.988	1.414	2	0.7114	1.975	2
Delaware	55,540	1.613	1.414	2	0.8768	1.603	2
Totals	3,615,920	105	—	106	—	104.328	105

Court case about this issue. We can try to decide which divisor method is fairest by comparing the apportionments actually produced by the methods.

Let a_i be the apportionment given to a state whose population is p_i. The quotient $\dfrac{a_i}{p_i}$ is called the **representative share.** It represents the share of a congressional seat given to each citizen of the state.

In an ideal apportionment, every state would have the same representative share. Since this is impossible, we can measure how close a given apportionment is to being ideal. One way (but, as we will see, not the only way) to do this is as follows. We are given an apportionment done by some method. This method could be Webster, Hamilton, or an old-fashioned smoke-filled room. We would compute the representative share for each state, and identify the state that has the largest share and the state that has the smallest. The discrepancy between these two values is a measure of how far the apportionment is from being perfectly equitable. It can be shown that among all conceivable apportionments, the one for which this discrepancy is the least is provided by the Webster method. Thus, while no appor-

SPOTLIGHT

14.1

A Legal Challenge to Apportionment

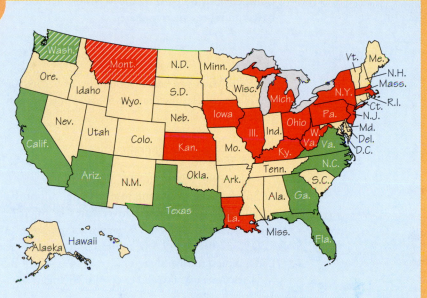

In 1991, the Census Bureau reported the new apportionment that would be in effect for the congressional elections in the years 1992–2000. Several states lost representatives: New York lost 3, and Ohio and Pennsylvania lost 2 apiece. Montana, whose apportionment decreased from 2 to 1, sustained the greatest percentage loss, and Montana sued to restore the lost seat. As precedents, Montana referred to the two famous cases, *Baker* v. *Carr* and *Wesberry* v. *Sanders,* in which the Supreme Court requires legislative and congressional district boundaries to be drawn so as to make district populations equal.

Montana argued that the correct apportionment would be the one that met the *Baker* and *Wesberry* criterion of having districts as nearly equal in population as possible, and asked the Court to require the Census Bureau to recompute the apportionments using the Dean method, a divisor method that minimizes differences in district populations. This would have resulted in the transfer of a congressional seat from Washington to Montana.

The *Montana* case coincided with another federal lawsuit, *Massachusetts* v. *Mosbacher,* which asked the Court to order the apportionment to be calculated by the Webster method. If Massachusetts had won this suit, it would have gained an additional seat, but Montana would not have benefited.

In *U.S. Department of Commerce* v. *Montana,* the Supreme Court unanimously rejected Montana's claim. The opinion of the Court, written by Justice Stevens, pointed out that *intra*state districts, which were the subject of the *Baker* and *Wesberry* cases, could be equalized in population by drawing district boundaries correctly. Since congressional districts can't cross state lines, some inequity is inevitable in congressional apportionment. The opinion conceded that there were alternatives to the Hill–Huntington method, but concluded that the choice of apportionment method was best left to Congress.

Note: In the map, states colored red lost seats and those colored green gained seats.

tionment can be perfect, the Webster method is the fairest when comparisons are based on representative share.

E X A M P L E   *Inequity in the 77th Congress*

In 1940, Michigan had a population of 5,256,106 and was apportioned 17 seats in the House of Representatives. This apportionment gave each citizen of Michigan a representative share of

$$\frac{17}{5,256,106} = 0.000003234 \text{ seat}$$

or 3.234 microseats (a microseat is one-millionth of a seat).

To calculate representative shares in microseats, divide the state's apportionment by its population, *expressed in millions*. Arkansas—with a population of 1,949,387, or 1.949,387 million—received 7 seats, so each citizen of that state had a representative share of $7 \div 1.949,387 = 3.591$ microseats.

Arkansas was favored over and Michigan by

$$3.591 - 3.234 = 0.357 \text{ microseats}$$

If a seat had been transferred from Arkansas to Michigan, then the representative share for a Michigander would have been $18 \div 5.256,106 = 3.425$ microseats, while each Arkansan would have been left with a representative share of $6 \div 1.949,387 = 3.078$ microseats.

Now Michigan, with the larger representative share, has the advantage, but the discrepancy,

$$3.425 - 3.078 = 0.347 \text{ microseats}$$

is less than it was before the transfer was made. In terms of representative share, it would have been more equitable to have given Arkansas 6 seats and Michigan 18 seats. In the Webster apportionment, the seats would have been distributed in this way since that method minimizes discrepancies in representative share. This shows that the Webster method is better than the Hill–Huntington method, which was used in the 1940 apportionment, *if we view minimizing discrepancies in representative share as of prime importance.* ◆

Another way to compare apportionments is by computing the *district population* of each state.

The **district population** of state i is $p_i \div a_i$. It represents the average population of a congressional district in the state.

EXAMPLE   *Comparing District Populations*

If we consider differences in district population rather than representative share, it was correct to give Michigan 17 seats and Arkansas 7 in the 1940 apportionment. The district population for Michigan was

$$\frac{\text{population of Michigan}}{\text{Michigan's apportionment}} = \frac{5{,}256{,}106 \text{ people}}{17 \text{ districts}}$$

$$= 309{,}183 \text{ people per district}$$

The district population for Arkansas was $1{,}949{,}387 \div 7 = 278{,}484$. The Arkansas average district population was 30,689 smaller than Michigan's. If Michigan had 18 seats and Arkansas had 6, Michigan would have a smaller district population, 292,006, while Arkansas's would have increased to 324,898. This adjustment in apportionment would have increased the inequity between the two states, since now Arkansas would be worse off than Michigan by 32,892 in district population. ◆

For state i, the representative share is $\dfrac{a_i}{p_i}$, and the district population is $\dfrac{p_i}{a_i}$;

thus,

$$\text{representative share} = \frac{1}{\text{district population}}$$

Thus it is surprising that the two ways of evaluating the fairness of an apportionment would disagree, but we have just seen that it is possible for them to do so. Those who think it is most important for states to have representative shares as nearly equal as possible would say that Michigan should have 18 seats and Arkansas should have 6, but those who prefer to focus on district population instead of representative share would say that the two states should have 17 and 7 seats, respectively.

A mathematician, Edward V. Huntington, suggested a compromise between the two measures of inequity that we have considered: differences in representative share and differences in district populations. He pointed out that if *relative differences* are compared instead of absolute differences, then either district population or representative share would give identical comparisons of apportionments.

Given two positive numbers A and B, with $A > B$, the **absolute difference** is $A - B$, and the **relative difference** is the quotient $\dfrac{A - B}{B} \times 100\%$.

For any two states, it turns out that the *relative difference* in district popula- tions is equal to the relative difference in representative share (see Exercise 23). Therefore, an apportionment method that minimizes *relative* difference in repre- sentative shares will also minimize the relative difference in district populations. The Hill–Huntington method gives the apportionment in which the relative dif- ferences in representative shares (or district populations) is as small as possible.

EXAMPLE   *Relative Inequity in the 77th Congress*

Recall that Michigan was given 17 seats in the 77th Congress and had a represen- tative share of 3.234 microseats. Arkansas had 7 seats and a representative share of 3.591 microseats. The relative difference was

$$\frac{3.591 - 3.234}{3.234} \times 100\% = 11.02\%$$

Thus, Arkansas was 11.02% better represented in the 77th Congress than Michi- gan was.

If Michigan had 18 seats and Arkansas had 6, the relative difference in repre- sentative shares would be found by subtracting the smaller representative share (Arkansas's) from the larger (Michigan's), and expressing the result as a percentage of the smaller representative share. Thus, the relative difference would have been

$$\frac{3.425 - 3.078}{3.078} \times 100\% = 11.27\%$$

in Michigan's favor. Since the relative inequity was less when Michigan had 17 seats and Arkansas had 7, the Hill–Huntington method gave this apportionment. Spotlight 14.2 tells how the Arkansas–Michigan apportionment in 1940 influ- enced the decision of Congress to adopt the Hill–Huntington method. ◆

Since each divisor method can lead to a slightly different apportionment, one way to decide which apportionment method to use is to decide, in a political de- bate, which type of inequity should be minimized. Challenges to apportionments have followed this approach (see Spotlight 14.1).

An apportionment method could also be chosen by minimizing *bias* in favor of large or small states. We have seen that the Jefferson method favors large states and that the Webster method is neutral. What about the Hill–Huntington method?

Bias in a divisor method is in favor of large states when the quotas are adjusted by using a multiplier $M > 1$. If the quotas must be adjusted downward—that is, $M < 1$—small states are favored. Because the rounding point for the Webster method is half-way between whole numbers, $M > 1$ is just as likely to occur as $M < 1$. The geometric mean q^* used by the Hill–Huntington method is closer to

Mathematics and Politics: A Strange Mixture

Walter F. Willcox   *Edward V. Huntington*

The first American to consider apportionment from a theoretical point of view was Walter Willcox (1861–1964), who strongly advocated the Webster method and had computed the apportionment of 1900. His arguments convinced the Congress to use the Webster method again in 1910. In 1911, Joseph Hill, a statistician at the Census Bureau, proposed the Hill–Huntington method — with the strong endorsement of Edward V. Huntington, a mathematics professor at Harvard.

In 1920, the two methods were in competition. There were significant differences in the apportionments determined by the two methods, and the result was Washington gridlock: no apportionment bill passed during the decade, and the 1910 apportionments were retained throughout the 1920s. In preparation for the 1930 census results, the National Academy of Sciences formed a committee to study the issue of apportionment. In 1929, the academy's committee endorsed the Hill–Huntington method.

The 1930 census was remarkable in that the apportionments calculated by the Webster method were the same as the Hill–Huntington apportionments. The House was therefore reapportioned, but the method used could be claimed to be either one of the competing methods. The coincidence was almost repeated in the 1940 census, but there was one difference. The Hill–Huntington method gave the last seat to Arkansas, while Webster's method gave it to Michigan (see page 508). At the time, Michigan was a predominantly Republican state, and Arkansas was in the Democratic column. The vote on the apportionment bill split strictly along party lines, with Democrats supporting the Hill–Huntington method and Republicans voting for the Webster method. Since the Democrats had the majority, the Hill–Huntington method became the law.

$\lfloor q \rfloor$ than to $\lceil q \rceil$ (see Exercise 15). This means that a random number q is more likely to be greater than q^* and thus rounded up to $\lceil q \rceil$ than it is to be less than q^* and rounded down to $\lfloor q \rfloor$. The difference between the Webster and Hill–Huntington ways of rounding is not significant for relatively large numbers. For example, if q is a number between 50 and 51, then $q^* = 50.498$. Therefore, q will be rounded up to 51 by Hill–Huntington if it is larger than 50.498. The Webster method would round q to 51 if $q \geq 50.500$. The differences are more significant when rounding smaller numbers. Thus, Hill–Huntington rounds all numbers between 0 and 1 up to 1; Webster rounds numbers in the range of 0.500–1 up to 1. When the Hill–Huntington method is used for apportionment, the sum of the tentative apportionments is more likely to exceed the House size than it is to be less. Therefore, it is more likely that $M < 1$ than $M > 1$. This favors the less populous states.

REVIEW VOCABULARY

$\lfloor q \rfloor$ The result of rounding a number q down; for example, $\lfloor \pi \rfloor = 3$.

$\lceil q \rceil$ The resulting of rounding a number q up to the next integer; for example, $\lceil \pi \rceil = 4$.

$\langle q \rangle$ The result of rounding a number q in the usual way: round down if the fractional part of q is less than 0.5, and round up otherwise. For example, $\langle \frac{86}{57} \rangle = 2$. This notation is not standard and is used only in this text.

$\langle\langle q \rangle\rangle$ The result of rounding a number q the Hill–Huntington way: round down if q is less than the geometric mean of $\lfloor q \rfloor$ and $\lceil q \rceil$, and round up otherwise. For example, to compute $\langle\langle 2.45 \rangle\rangle$, calculate the geometric mean of $\lfloor 2.45 \rfloor = 2$ and $\lceil 2.45 \rceil = 3$, which is $\sqrt{2 \times 3} \approx 2.449$. Since $2.45 > 2.449$, we round up: $\langle\langle 2.45 \rangle\rangle = 3$.

Absolute difference of two numbers   The result of subtracting the smaller number from the larger.

Adjusted quota   The product of the state's quota and a multiplier. The purpose of adjusting the quotas is to correct a failure of the rounded quotas to sum to the house size.

Alabama paradox   A state loses a representative solely because the size of the House is increased. This paradox is possible with the Hamilton method but not with divisor methods.

Apportionment method   A systematic way of computing solutions of apportionment problems.

Apportionment problem   To round a list of fractions to whole numbers in a way that preserves the sum of the original fractions.

Critical multiplier   An adjustment factor that, applied to a state's quota, is just enough to change that state's tentative apportionment. The following table lists formulas for critical multipliers for some divisor methods. In the table, q stands for the state's quota and n is its tentative apportionment.

Method	Critical Multiplier Causing Tentative Apportionment	
	To Increase	**To Decrease**
Jefferson	$\dfrac{n + 1}{q}$	Not necessary
Webster	$\dfrac{n + 0.5}{q}$	$\dfrac{n - 0.5}{q}$
Hill–Huntington	$\dfrac{\sqrt{n(n + 1)}}{q}$	$\dfrac{\sqrt{n(n - 1)}}{q}$

District population   A state's population divided by its apportionment.

Divisor method   One of many apportionment methods in which the apportionments are determined by multiplying the quotas for the states by a common factor to obtain adjusted quotas. The apportionments are calculated by rounding the adjusted quotas. Divisor methods differ in their rounding rules. The methods of Jefferson, Webster, and Hill–Huntington are divisor methods.

Geometric mean For positive numbers A and B, the geometric mean is defined to be $\sqrt{A \times B}$.

Hamilton method An apportionment method advocated by Alexander Hamilton. This method assigns to each state either its lower quota or its upper quota. The states that receive their upper quotas are those whose quotas have the largest fractional parts.

Hill–Huntington method A divisor method, named for the statistician Joseph Hill and the mathematician Edward V. Huntington, that minimizes relative differences in both representative shares and district populations. It is based on the Hill–Huntington way of rounding, so a state's apportionment is $\langle\langle \bar{q}_i \rangle\rangle$, where $\bar{q}_i$ is the state's adjusted quota.

Jefferson method A divisor method invented by Thomas Jefferson, based on rounding all fractions down. Thus, if $\bar{q}_i$ is the adjusted quota of state i, the state's apportionment is $\lfloor \bar{q}_i \rfloor$.

Lower quota The result of rounding a state's quota down to a whole number. A state whose quota is q has a lower quota equal to $\lfloor q \rfloor$.

Population paradox If changes in population cause one state's apportionment to decrease and another's to decrease, although the first state's population increased and the second state's population had increased proportionally less or had actually decreased, the population paradox has occurred. This paradox is possible with all apportionment methods *except* divisor methods.

Quota A state's quota is the number of seats it would receive if fractional seats could be awarded. The quota for state i is $q_i = \dfrac{p_i}{p} \times h$, where p_i is the population of the state, p is the total population, and h is the house size.

Quota condition A requirement that in every situation each state's apportionment is equal to either its lower quota or its upper quota. The Hamilton method satisfies this requirement but divisor methods do not.

Relative difference The relative difference between two positive numbers is obtained by subtracting the smaller number from the larger, and expressing the result as a percentage of the smaller number. Thus, the relative difference of 120 and 100 is 20%.

Representative share A state's representative share is the state's apportionment divided by its population. It is intended to represent the amount of influence a citizen of that state would have on his or her representative.

Tentative apportionment When apportioning by use of a divisor method, a state's tentative apportionment is initially obtained by rounding its quota, using the rounding rule associated with the method. In the process of calculating the apportionment, a state's tentative apportionment changes as it acquires or loses seats.

Upper quota The result of rounding a state's quota up to a whole number. A state whose quota is q has an upper quota equal to $\lceil q \rceil$.

Webster method A divisor method of apportionment invented by Representative Daniel Webster. It is based on rounding fractions the usual way, so that the apportionment for state i is $\langle \bar{q}_i \rangle$, where $\bar{q}_i$ is the adjusted quota for state i. The Webster method minimizes differences of representative share between states.

SUGGESTED READINGS

BALINSKI, M. L., AND H. P. YOUNG. *Fair Representation: Meeting the Ideal of One Man, One Vote,* Yale University Press, New Haven, Conn., 1982. In the 1970s, Balinski and Young analyzed apportionment methods in depth. Their point of view was to postulate the desirable properties of an apportionment method as axioms and to deduce which method is best from the axioms. This book combines an account of the history of apportionment of the U.S. House of Representatives with the results of their research.

COMMONWEALTH OF MASSACHUSETTS V. *MOSBACHER,* 785 Federal Supplement 230 (District of Massachusetts 1992). This opinion concerns a suit by Massachusetts to increase its representation. The Commonwealth argued that the Bureau of the Census did not fairly assign federal employees that are stationed abroad to their home states, but this part of the opinion is not of interest to us. However, Massachusetts also claimed that the Hill–Huntington method was an unfair method of apportionment, and asked the Court to replace that method with the Webster method. The discussion of this portion of the claim is Section D of the opinion, and starts on page 253. The Federal Supplement is available in law libraries.

ERNST, LAWRENCE R. Apportionment methods for the House of Representatives and the court challenges, *Management Science,* 40 (1994): 1207–1227. Ernst, who wrote briefs for the government in both the *Montana* and the *Massachusetts* cases, reviews the apportionment problem and the arguments in favor of and against each of the divisor methods. The article includes a summary of the arguments used by both sides in the two court cases.

LUCAS, W. F. The apportionment problem, in S. J. Brams, W. F. Lucas, and P. D. Straffin, Jr., eds., *Political and Related Models,* Springer-Verlag, New York, 1983, pp. 358–396. An introduction to apportionment, written at a somewhat more advanced level than the presentation in this text.

U.S. DEPARTMENT OF COMMERCE V. *MONTANA,* 112 Supreme Court 1415 (1992). This opinion, available in any law library, gives the grounds for rejecting the *Montana* suit to replace the Hill–Huntington method with the Dean method.

YOUNG, H. PEYTON. *Equity,* Princeton University Press, Princeton, N.J., 1994. Chapter 3 covers apportionment and focuses on which apportionment method is the most equitable.

SUGGESTED WEB SITE

www.census.gov This site contains a two-page history of apportionment of the Congress.

SKILLS CHECK

1. A county is divided into three districts with populations: Southern, 3600; Western, 3100; Northeastern, 1600. There are six seats on the county council to be apportioned. What is the quota for the Southern district?

(a) 0.43
(b) 3
(c) 2.6

2. The Hill–Huntington method of apportionment

(a) is currently used to apportion the House of Representatives.

(b) is not a divisor method.
(c) always rounds up the fractional parts.

3. A county is divided into three districts with the following populations: Southern, 3600; Western, 3100; Northeastern, 1600. There are ten seats on the school board to be apportioned. What is the apportionment for the Northeastern district using the Jefferson method?

(a) 1
(b) 2
(c) 3

4. A county is divided into three districts with the following populations: Southern, 3600; Western, 3100; Northeastern, 1600. There are ten seats on the school board to be apportioned. What is the apportionment for the Southern district using the Webster method?

(a) 4
(b) 5
(c) 6

5. A county is divided into three districts with the following populations: Southern, 3600; Western, 3100; Northeastern, 1600. There are ten seats on the school board to be apportioned. If the Hill–Huntington method is used instead of the Webster method, how do the results differ?

(a) The apportionments are the same.
(b) Southern gains an extra seat and Western

loses a seat if the Hill–Huntington method is used instead of the Webster method.
(c) Southern gains an extra seat and Northeastern loses a seat if the Hill–Huntington method is used instead of the Webster method.

6. The geometric mean of 6 and 7 is

(a) 6.5.
(b) less than 6.5.
(c) more than 6.5.

7. The relative difference of 6 and 7 is

(a) 1.
(b) approximately 14.29%.
(c) approximately 16.67%.

EXERCISES   ▲ *Optional.*   ■ *Advanced.*   ◆ *Discussion.*

The Hamilton Method

1. A country has a parliament with 577 seats. In an election, the Democratic Socialists receive 323,829 votes; the Social Democrats, 880,702 votes; the Christian Democrats, 5,572,614 votes; the Greens, 1,222,498 votes; and the Communists, 111,224 votes. The number of seats won by each party is to be proportional to the number of votes cast in its favor. Calculate the quota for each party and apportion the seats by the Hamilton method.

2. A very small country has three states, with populations of 59,000, 76,000, and 14,000. Use the Hamilton method to apportion the seats of the 35-seat National Legislature. Repeat the calculation for 36, 37, 38, 39, and 40 seats. Does the Alabama paradox occur?

3. A country has four states, *A*, *B*, *C*, and *D*. Its house of representatives has 100 members, and by law, the Hamilton method is used to apportion it. A new census is taken, and the house is reapportioned. Here are the data:

State	Old Census	New Census
A	5,525,381	5,657,564
B	3,470,152	3,507,464
C	3,864,226	3,885,693
D	201,203	201,049
Totals	13,060,962	13,251,770

(a) Apportion the house using the old census.
(b) Reapportion, using the new census.
(c) Explain how this is an example of the population paradox.

4. Suppose that a country has three states, with populations 254,000, 153,000, and 103,000, respectively. The legislature has 102 seats. Show that

if the Hamilton method is used to apportion seats, a tie will result. How would you suggest breaking the tie?

Divisor Methods

◆ 5. Show that for any number q,
$$\langle q \rangle = \lfloor q + 0.5 \rfloor.$$

6. A small high school has one mathematics teacher who can teach a total of five sections. The subjects that she teaches, and their enrollments, are as follows: geometry, 43; algebra, 42; calculus, 12. Apportion sections to the subjects using the Hamilton, Jefferson, and Webster methods.

7. Repeat Exercise 6 using the following enrollments: geometry, 76; algebra, 19; calculus, 20.

8. A three-state country has a legislature with 36 seats. The states have populations of 155,000, 105,000, and 100,000. Show that a tie will result if the seats are apportioned by the Webster method.

9. A country has a 100-seat parliament with one major party, the National party, and 10 splinter parties. In a recent election, the National party received 87.85% of the vote. The splinter parties received the following percentages: 1.26, 1.25, 1.24, 1.23, 1.22, 1.21, 1.20, 1.19, 1.18, and 1.17.

◆ (a) What is the best apportionment for the parliament?

(b) Compute the apportionments according to the methods of Hamilton, Jefferson, and Webster.
(c) Do any of the methods in part (b) violate the quota condition? That is, does some party receive either more than its upper quota or less than its lower quota?

10. A country with a 100-seat parliament has an election in which one party captures 92.15% of the vote. Five splinter parties receive the following percentages of the vote: 1.59, 1.58, 1.57, 1.56, and 1.55. Answer all the questions in Exercise 9.

■ 11. Suppose that the Jefferson method is used to apportion the House according to the 1990 census. Decide the contest between Massachusetts and Oklahoma for the last seat available to them. The population figures are given in Exercise 24. (*Hint:* Start with the assumption that Massachusetts already has 10 seats and Oklahoma has 5 and compare their critical multipliers.)

The Hill–Huntington Method

12. Find the geometric mean of each pair of numbers.

(a) 0, 1
(b) 1, 2
(c) 2, 3
(d) 3, 4

13. A high school has one math teacher, who can teach five sections. Fifty-six students have enrolled in the algebra class, 28 have signed up for geometry, and 7 students will take calculus. Use the Hill–Huntington method to decide how many sections of each course to schedule.

14. One year later, the high school described in Exercise 13 still has just one math teacher, who teaches five sections. The enrollments are algebra, 36; geometry, 61; and calculus, 3. Apportion the classes by the Webster and Hill–Huntington methods. Which apportionment do you think the school principal would prefer?

◆ 15. (a) Show that for any positive numbers A and B, the geometric mean is less than the arithmetic mean (the arithmetic mean of A and B is equal to $(A + B)/2$), except when $A = B$; then the two means are equal. (*Hint:* Show that the triangle below is a right triangle.)

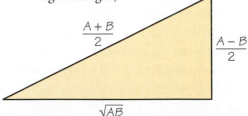

(b)   Show that for any number $q \geq 0$, the following inequality holds:

$$\langle q \rangle > \langle\langle q \rangle\rangle$$

(c)   Explain why the inequality established in (b) implies that the Hill–Huntington method favors smaller states more than the Webster method.

■   16.   Suppose that the governor of Kansas believes that the population of his state was undercounted. What increase in population would be large enough to entitle Kansas to take a seat from Ohio, if the apportionment is by the Hill–Huntington method? The data needed for this problem are given in Exercise 21.

■   17.   Ties can occur when the Hill–Huntington method is used to apportion, if two states have identical populations, or if the number of states is larger than the House size. Is there any other way that ties can occur with this method?

Which Divisor Method Is Best?

18.   Determine the relative difference between the numbers 5 and 7.

19.   Jim is 72 inches tall and Alice is 65 inches tall. What is the relative difference of their heights?

20.   In the 1991 apportionment of Congress, the average congressional district in Pennsylvania had a population of 567,843. The corresponding figure for New Jersey was 596,049.

(a)   Which state is the more favored in this apportionment?
(b)   What is the relative difference in the district sizes?

21.   According to the 1990 census, the population of Ohio was 10,887,325; Ohio was apportioned 19 House seats. The population of Kansas was 2,485,600, and Kansas received 4 House seats.

(a)   Determine the average congressional district sizes for these states.

(b)   Determine the relative difference in these district sizes.
(c)   Suppose a seat were transferred from Ohio to Kansas, giving Ohio 18 seats and Kansas 5. What would the relative difference in district sizes now be?

22.   Table 14.6 shows the Hill–Huntington apportionments for several states, based on the 1970 census.

(a)   Which state has the largest district size, and which has the smallest?
(b)   If a seat were transferred from the state with the smallest district size to the one with the largest, would the inequity be less (as measured by absolute difference in district size)?
(c)   If a seat were transferred from the state with the smallest district size to the one with the largest, would the inequity be less (as measured by relative difference in district size)?

(d)   Citizens of which state have the largest representative share? The smallest?

(e)   If a seat were transferred from the state with the smallest representative share to the one with the largest, would the inequity be less (as measured by absolute difference in representative share)?

(f)   Which state would benefit from a change of apportionment method, and which method would that state prefer?

TABLE 14.6   **Some 1970 Apportionments**

State	Population	Apportionment
California	20,098,863	43
Connecticut	3,050,693	6
Montana	701,573	2
Oregon	2,110,810	4
South Dakota	673,247	2

◆   23.   Let the populations of states A and B be p_A and p_B, respectively. The apportionments will be a_A and a_B. Assuming that district populations for state A are larger than district populations in state B, show that the relative difference in district populations is

$$\frac{p_A a_B - p_B a_A}{p_B a_A} \times 100\%$$

Also show that this expression is equal to the relative difference in representative share. Hence the relative difference in district populations is equal to the relative difference in representative shares.

24.   In *Massachusetts* v. *Mosbacher,* Massachusetts contested its 1991 apportionment, claiming a systematic census undercount of Massachusetts residents living abroad. Another issue in the suit was the claim by Massachusetts that the Hill–Huntington method of apportionment is unconstitutional, because it does not reflect the "one person, one vote" principle as well as the Webster method does. Massachusetts sought an additional House seat that had been awarded to Oklahoma. Would Massachusetts have gained a seat from Oklahoma if the Webster method had been used to apportion the House of Representatives in 1991? Use the following populations and Hill–Huntington apportionments:

State	Population	Apportionment
Massachusetts	6,029,051	10
Oklahoma	3,145,585	6

Additional Exercises

◆   25.   Here is an apportionment method that should please everyone! Just give each state its upper quota. Of course, the House size would vary.

(a)   Show that the House size will be more than the planned house size h.
(b)   Do you think California would be enthusiastic about this method, or would that state prefer to give each state its *lower* quota?

26.   A country has five states, with populations 5,576,330, 1,387,342, 3,334,241, 7,512,860, and 310,968. Its House of Representatives is apportioned by the Hamilton method.

(a)   Calculate the apportionments for house sizes of 82, 83, and 84. Does the Alabama paradox occur?
(b)   Repeat the calculations for house sizes of 89, 90, and 91.

27.   A country that is governed by a parliamentary democracy has two political parties, the Liberals and the Tories. The number of seats awarded to a party is supposed to be proportional to the number of votes it receives in the election. Suppose the Liberals receive 49% of the vote. If the total number of seats in parliament is 99, how many seats do the Liberals get with the Hamilton method? With the Webster method? With the Jefferson method?

◆   28.   A country with a parliamentary government has two parties that capture 100% of the vote between them. Each party is awarded seats in proportion to the number of votes received.

(a)   Show that the Webster and Hamilton methods will always give the same apportionment in this two-party situation.
(b)   Show that the Alabama and population paradoxes cannot occur when the Hamilton method is used to apportion seats between two parties or states.
(c)   Show that the Webster method satisfies the quota condition when the seats are apportioned between two parties or states.
(d)   Will the Jefferson and the Hill–Huntington methods also yield the same apportionments as the Hamilton method?

29.   If the 1790 Congress were apportioned by the Webster method, would the result differ from the Hill–Huntington method (see Table 14.5)?

30.   The following apportionment method was invented by Congressman William Lowndes of South Carolina in 1822. Lowndes starts, as Hamilton does, by giving each state its lower quota.

But where Hamilton apportions the remaining seats to the states whose quotas have the largest fractional parts—in other words, the states for which the *absolute difference* between q_i and $\lfloor q_i \rfloor$ is greatest—Lowndes gives the extra seats to the states where the *relative* difference between q_i and $\lfloor q_i \rfloor$ is greatest, raising as many as necessary to their upper quotas to fill the House.

◆ (a) Would this method be more beneficial to states with large populations or small populations, as compared with the Hamilton method?

◆ (b) Does the Lowndes method satisfy the quota condition?

◆ (c) Would there be any trouble with paradoxes with the Lowndes method?

◆ (d) Use the method to apportion the 1790 House of Representatives.

■ 31. The Hill–Huntington method, based on the 1990 census, apportioned 9 seats to Washington, based on a population of 4,887,941. The figures for Massachusetts are given in Exercise 24. How much would have to be added to the population of Massachusetts to entitle that state to take a seat from Washington, if apportionment is done by

(a) the Hill–Huntington method?

(b) the Webster method?

32. John Quincy Adams, the sixth president of the United States, proposed that the House of Representatives should be apportioned by a divisor method in which a state's apportionment is $\lceil \bar{q} \rceil$, where $\bar{q}$ is the state's adjusted quota.

(a) Will the factor used to adjust the quotas be less than 1, greater than 1, or sometimes greater, sometimes less than 1?

(b) Does the method favor small states or large states?

(c) Find a formula for a state's critical multiplier in terms of the state's tentative apportionment n_i and its quota is q_i.

33. The Marquis de Condorcet, who proposed a criterion for deciding elections (see Chapter 11), also designed a divisor method for apportionment. His rounding rule was to round numbers whose fractional parts are less than 0.4 down and to round up otherwise.

(a) Show that the Condorcet rounding of a number q is $\lfloor q + 0.6 \rfloor$.

(b) Does the method favor large states, small states, or is it neutral?

(c) Find a formula for a state's critical multiplier in terms of the state's tentative apportionment n_i and its quota is q_i.

◆ 34. The U.S. Constitution requires that each state shall be apportioned at least one seat in the House of Representatives.

(a) Show that the Hill–Huntington method is consistent with this requirement. What about the methods of Hamilton, Jefferson, and Webster?

(b) Does the Adams method (see Exercise 32) meet the requirement?

■ (c) The Dean method is the divisor method that minimizes absolute differences in district population. Using this information, explain why a Dean apportionment will never give any state zero seats, unless the house size is less than the number of states.

■ 35. Let $q_1, q_2, \ldots, q_n$ be the quotas for n states in an apportionment problem, and let the apportionments assigned by some apportionment method be denoted $a_1, a_2, \ldots, a_n$. The *absolute deviation* for state i is defined to be $|q_i - a_i|$; it is a measure of the amount by which the state's apportionment differs from its quota. The *maximum absolute deviation* is the largest of these numbers. Show that the Hamilton method always gives the least possible maximum absolute deviation.

◆ 36. The choice of a divisor method for apportioning sections to classes according to class enrollments, as in the senior high school example, depends on what the school principal considers most important.

(a)   The principal wants to set a minimum class size. For example, if the minimum class size is 20, and 39 students are signed up for English III, there would be one section, since there are not enough students for two sections with enrollment of at least 20. If there were 40 students, there would be two sections. The minimum class size is adjusted so that as many sections as possible are running. What apportionment method should she use, and what will the minimum class size be?

■   (b)   The principal prefers to set a maximum class size. For example, if the maximum class size is 33, and 67 students are taking history I, there will be three sections, because there are too many students to fit in two 33-student sections. If there were only 66 taking history I, there would be two sections. The maximum class size is adjusted so that as many sections as possible are running. What apportionment method should she use, and what will the maximum class size be? (*Hint:* This divisor method is not described in the text but is mentioned in one of the previous exercises.)

(c)   The principal wants to treat students as equitably as possible, so that the differences between students' share of teachers varies as little as possible from one course to another. What apportionment method should she use now?

(d)   The principal wants to minimize relative difference in class size. What divisor method would work best for her?

(e)   The principal wants to cancel any class that has an enrollment of just one student. Which apportionment methods should she avoid using?

TECHNOLOGY CORNER

The Hamilton Apportionment Method

The Hamilton method apportions to each state either its upper or lower quota. The states that receive their upper quotas are those whose quotas have the largest fractional parts. We will use a spreadsheet to compute the quota for each state and to compare the fractional parts so that it is easy to determine which states will be awarded extra seats.

Let's use a spreadsheet to duplicate Table 14.1 on page 493, which displays the apportionment of the 1790 House of Representatives, calculated by the Hamilton method. You should have your computer on, with a blank spreadsheet before you. Column **A** of the table consists of labels. Start by entering the heading **State** in cell **A1**. Move down to cell **A2** and type **Virginia,** and continue, typing the remaining 14 state names. Finally, type the word **Totals** in cell **A17**. Move to cell **B1** and enter the word **Population.** The rest of column **B** contains the state population data, which must be copied from Table 14.1. The computer can find the total population if you select cells, starting at **B17** and going up to **B2,** and then select the summation icon Σ on the toolbar.

Enter the column heading **Quota** in cell **C1**. Now let's compute the quotas. Starting with Virginia's, type the following formula in **C2**:

$$=105*B2/B\$17$$

This formula asks the computer to multiply the entry in cell **B2** by 105 and divide the result by the entry in cell **B17**. The dollar sign in the formula will be explained later, but don't forget to include it.

You could retype the formula 14 times to fill in the rest of column **C**, but that is not necessary. Make sure that cell **C2** is still active, select Edit on the menu bar, and then select Copy from the pull-down menu. Now select cells **C3--C16,** and select Paste from the Edit menu. The formula in cell **C2** will be copied to the 14 cells below it. The copying is *relative,* in the sense that you will find the formula

$$=105*B3/B\$17$$

in cell **C3.** The computer changes the reference cell **B2** to **B3** automatically. We want that to happen, because otherwise we would just get another copy of Virginia's quota, not that of Massachusetts. We do not want the reference to cell **B17** to change to **B18** and so on as we move down, and the dollar sign tells the spreadsheet not to change this reference when copying it to another location in column **B.** Finally, we can get the sum of the quotas by copying the formula in cell **B17** and pasting it in cell **C17.** This sum should equal 105. (Why?)

Column **D** will contain the lower quotas. After typing the column heading **Lower quota** in cell **D1,** enter $=INT(C2)$ in cell **D2.** The **INT** function rounds numbers down by truncating their fractional parts. By copying this formula and pasting it to cells **D3--D16,** the lower quota for each state is determined. Copy the sum formula in **C17** to **D17** to obtain the sum of the lower quotas. Since this sum is 97, we have to increase the apportionments of the 8 states whose quotas have the largest fractional parts. Enter the labels **Fraction** in cell **E1** and **Apportionment** in **F1.** We will fill in the rest of column **F** by entering $=C2-D2$ in **F2** and copying it to **D3--D16.** Now select cells **A2--F16** and go to Data on the menu bar. Select Sort and a dialogue box will appear. Indicate column **F** as the sort key and select **OK.** You will find your table is now in increasing order by fractional part of quota. You can enter the apportionments in column **E,** giving the first 7 states (which have the lesser fractions) their lower quotas, and the remaining 8 states their upper quotas. Figure 14.2 shows the spreadsheet as it appears at this point. If you want to make the table look like Table 14.1, re-sort the block **A2--F16,** this time selecting column **B** as the key, with descending order.

TASK 1. The Mathematics Department expects enrollments of 199 in Precalculus, 453 in Calculus I, 177 in Calculus II, 323 in Calculus III, 36 in Advanced Calculus, 133 in Differential Equations,

	A	B	C	D	E	F
				Lower		Appor-
1	State	Population	Quota	Quota	Fraction	tionment
2	Georgia	70835	2.0569247	2	0.0569247	2
3	Maryland	278514	8.08756	8	0.08756	8
4	New Hampshire	141822	4.1182631	4	0.1182631	4
5	New Jersey	179570	5.2143991	5	0.2143991	5
6	North Carolina	353523	10.26569	10	0.2556903	10
7	Virginia	630560	18.310361	18	0.3103608	18
8	Vermont	85533	2.4837289	2	0.4837289	2
9	Pennsylvania	432879	12.57005	12	0.5700499	13
10	Delaware	55540	1.6127846	1	0.6127846	2
11	New York	331589	9.6287653	9	0.6287653	10
12	Massachusetts	475327	13.802666	13	0.8026657	14
13	Connecticut	236841	6.8774489	6	0.8774489	7
14	Rhode Island	68446	1.9875523	1	0.9875523	2
15	South Carolina	206236	5.9887332	5	0.9887332	6
16	Kentucky	68705	1.9950732	1	0.9950732	2
17	Total	3615920	105	97		105

FIGURE 14.2

44 in Geometry, 227 in Linear Algebra, 78 in Numerical Analysis, and 20 in Modern Algebra. There are 13 professors, each of whom teaches 3 sections. Use the Hamilton method to determine how many sections of each course that the department should offer. After the assignments are made, one of the professors gets a grant, and now she teaches only one course. Which courses will have reduced numbers of sections?

Divisor Methods

Divisor methods work by rounding each state's quota in a particular way to obtain the apportionment. The sum of the rounded quotas can be either more or less than the house size, and it is usually necessary to adjust the quotas by multiplying them all by a common factor, so that when they are rounded the sum is equal to the house size. The adjustment factor necessary to change the number of seats apportioned to a given state is called that state's *critical multiplier.* We perform the adjustments in stages, starting with the state with critical multiplier closest to 1.

With the Jefferson method the quotas are all rounded down. To compute the Jefferson apportionment of the 1790 House of Representatives, you can re-use columns **A--D** of the spreadsheet that we constructed for the Hamilton apportionment. The only alteration necessary is that the label in cell **D1** should be changed from **Lower quota** to **Tentative Apportionment.** Column **E** should be labeled **Critical Multiplier.** Enter **=(D2+1)/C2** in cell **E2** and copy and paste it to the range **E3--E16.** The smallest critical multiplier is used to adjust the quotas. Put the label **Adjusted quota** in **F1,** and the formula **=MIN(E$2:E$16)*C2** in **F2.** Copy this formula to the range **F3--F16.** (Can you explain the dollar signs in the formula?) Finally, place the label **New Tentative Apportionment** in **G1.** Select the cell range **C2--C17,** copy it, and paste it to **G2.** You will find the rounded adjusted quota for each state in column **G** and the sum of these in **G17.** Now the fun begins.

Column **G** is identical to column **D,** except that the new tentative apportionment for South Carolina is 6, while the old one was 5. Move the cursor to cell **D9**—the location of South Carolina's old tentative apportionment—and type the number 6. When you press the **Enter** key, you will see the adjusted quotas have changed to reflect this change. Now Kentucky's tentative apportionment, shown in column **G,** has increased from 1 to 2. Make the corresponding change in cell **C14** by overwriting its contents with a 2, and watch the spreadsheet change to reflect this new entry. At each of these steps, you will see the total number of seats apportioned increase: now we have 99. The next apportionment to change is that of Rhode Island, and so the process continues until a total apportionment of 105 is reached. Figure 14.3 displays the spreadsheet.

The Jefferson spreadsheet can be streamlined, because columns **F** and **G** are unnecessary. We know that at each step, the apportionment that changes is the one that has the critical multiplier closest to 1. To assist in locating that multiplier, place the formula **=MIN(E3:E16)** in **E17.** When we change the apportionment of the state with this multiplier, its critical multiplier changes, and it is likely that another state will have the critical multiplier closest to 1.

	A	B	C	D	E	F	G
1	State	Population	Quota	Tentative Appor-tionment	Critical Multiplier	Adjusted Quota	New Tentative Appor-tionment
2	Virginia	630560	18.310361	18	1.0376639	18.425036	18
3	Vermont	85533	2.4837289	2	1.2078613	2.4992841	2
4	South Carolina	206236	5.9887332	6	1.1688616	6.0262397	6
5	Rhode Island	68446	1.9875523	1	1.0062628	2	2
6	Pennsylvania	432879	12.57005	12	1.0342043	12.648774	12
7	North Carolina	353523	10.26569	10	1.0715305	10.329983	10
8	New York	331589	9.6287653	9	1.0385548	9.6890688	9
9	New Jersey	179570	5.2143991	5	1.1506599	5.2470561	5
10	New Hampshire	141822	4.1182631	4	1.2141041	4.1440552	4
11	Massachusetts	475327	13.802666	13	1.0142968	13.88911	13
12	Maryland	278514	8.08756	8	1.1128202	8.1382111	8
13	Kentucky	68705	1.9950732	2	1.5037042	2.007568	2
14	Georgia	70835	2.0569247	2	1.458488	2.0698069	2
15	Delaware	55540	1.6127846	1	1.2400912	1.6228852	1
16	Connecticut	236841	6.8774489	6	1.0178193	6.9205213	6
17	Total	3615920	105	99			100

FIGURE 14.3

TASK 2. Use the Jefferson method to apportion sections of the mathematics courses, using the populations given in Task 1, and assuming that 39 sections will be taught. Which subject gains a section, and which loses one, when the method is changed from Hamilton's to Jefferson's?

To implement the Webster method, where rounding is done in the usual way, we will use the format of the streamlined Jefferson spreadsheet, with only columns **A--E.** The tentative apportionments are initially done by rounding the quotas. Type **=ROUND(C2,0)** in **D2.** This tells the computer to round the entry in **C2** to 0 decimal places. This formula is copied to cells **D3--D16** to give the tentative apportionments. If we are lucky, the sum of these tentative apportionments will be equal to the house size, and the job is finished. If we have to adjust the quotas, we need to put the critical multipliers in column **E.**

If the tentative apportionments add up to *more* than the house size, all multipliers must be less than 1. In this case the formula for the critical multiplier **=(D2-.5)/C2** should be typed in **E2** and copied to the cells below **E2.** The largest of these (closest to 1) belongs to the state whose apportionment must decrease, and to locate the state that will be affected, we enter **=MAX(E3:E16)** in **E17.** When the change in the tentative apportionment of the state with that critical multiplier is made in column **D,** its critical multiplier will decrease, and another state will probably lose the next seat—if the tentative apportionments do not yet sum to the house size.

If the sum of the tentative apportionments is *less* than the house size, the critical multipliers, given by =**(D2+.5)/C2** in **E2,** will be greater than 1. This time we increase the apportionment of the state that has the critical multiplier closest to 1.

TASK 3. Use the Webster method to apportion sections of the Mathematics courses, using the populations in Task 1. Assume that 39 sections will be taught and then recompute the apportionment assuming that two professors have received grants, so that only 35 sections can be taught.

The Hill–Huntington Method

Your spreadsheet does not have a built-in function for Hill–Huntington rounding, which rounds a number down if it is less than the geometric mean of the integers immediately above and below it. To improvise, we will use column **D** for geometric mean of these numbers. Thus, enter the formula

$$=SQRT(INT(C2)*INT(C2+1))$$

in **D2.** As usual, this formula must be copied to the cells below **D2.** Now enter the following in **E2:**

$$=INT(C2) + INT((C2+1)/(D2+1))$$

Since **INT((C2+1)/(D2+1))** is equal to 0 if the quota in **C2** is less than the geometric mean in **D2** and 1 otherwise, the number in **E2** is the Hill–Huntington rounding of the quota. Copy the formula in **E2** to the cells below it to determine the tentative apportionment for each state. Form the sum of the tentative apportionments; if it is equal to the house size, the job is finished. If the tentative apportionments add up to more than the house size, we have to compare critical multipliers, computed as

follows:

Enter in **F2** the formula

$$=SQRT(E2*(E2-1))/C2$$

and copy this formula to the cells below in column **F.** Decrease the apportionment of the state whose critical multiplier is closest to 1. If the sum of the tentative apportionments is less than the house size the formula in **F2** is

$$=SQRT(E2*(E2+1))/C2,$$

which is greater than 1. The state with the critical multiplier closest to 1 now gains a seat. The spreadsheet for the 1790 apportionment by the Hill–Huntington method is shown in Figure 14-4. You will see that the sum of the rounded quotas was 106, so it was necessary to reduce the apportionment of one state. The critical multiplier that is closest to 1 is Pennsylvania's so the apportionment, shown in column **G,** gives Pennsylvania 12 seats.

TASK 4. Repeat Task 3, using the Hill–Huntington method. There are 35 sections available. Now imagine that 41 sections are available, and reapportion.

Exploration

You would think that if you double the house size, each state's apportionment would double, but does that really happen? Experiment with the 1790 House of Representatives, assuming a house size of 210. Do any of the methods that we have studied give twice as many seats to each state as they did for the 105-seat house? As a second experiment, reapportion the 1790 House of Representatives, assuming 35 seats. You will find that although 35 seats is exactly one-third of the actual house size, no method gives each state one-third of the apportionment that it would get in a house with 105 seats. Which methods leave the smaller states without any seats?

writing projects

1 ▷ Does the Hill–Huntington method best reflect the intentions of the founding fathers, as these intentions were set down in the Constitution and in the debate during the 1787 Constitutional Convention? Good sources of information here include the following publications listed in Suggested Readings: *Fair Representation,* by Balinski and Young; *Equity,* by Young; "Apportionment Methods," by Ernst; and the two court opinions, *Massachusetts* v. *Mosbacher* and *U.S. Department of Commerce* v. *Montana.* This writing project requires that you state your answer to the question and make a case for it.

2 ▷ Suppose that in 1990, Congress reverted to its nineteenth-century habit of increasing the House size with every reapportionment so that no state would have a decrease in the size of its delegation. How many seats would have been added to the House, and which states would have gotten them? (*Warning:* The apportionments of some states might *increase* as a result of this practice.) As the first step of this project, look up the populations and apportionments for the 50 states in an almanac, or on the Census Bureau's Web site, **www.census.gov.**

3 ▷ A computer is required for this project. Use a spreadsheet to calculate the Hill–Huntington apportionment of the U.S. House of Representatives that would result from the latest census data. You can find the data on the Census Bureau's Web site (**www.census.gov**); go to the index and look for state populations. Reapportion using the Webster method. Finally, compute the apportionment by the Dean method. This method is like the Hill–Huntington method, with only one difference: the *harmonic mean* is used instead of the geometric mean. The harmonic mean of two numbers A and *B* is

$$\frac{2AB}{A + B}$$

Thus, adjusted quotas are rounded down when they are less than the harmonic mean of the lower and upper quotas, and rounded up otherwise. The Dean method minimizes differences in district populations.

With this information, predict the squabbles between states that will occur as a result of the next apportionment.

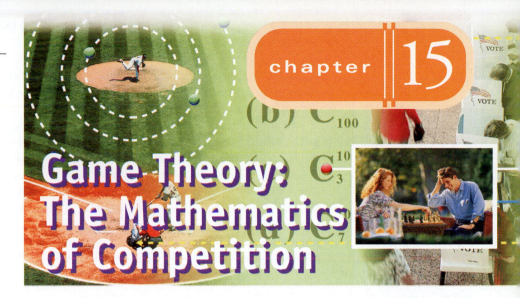

chapter 15

Game Theory: The Mathematics of Competition

onflict has been a central theme throughout human history and in literature. It arises whenever two or more individuals, with different values or goals, compete to try to control the course of events. *Game theory* uses mathematical tools to study situations involving both conflict and cooperation. Its study was greatly stimulated by the publication in 1944 of the monumental *Theory of Games and Economic Behavior* by John von Neumann and Oskar Morgenstern (see Spotlight 15.1).

The *players* in a game, who may be people, organizations, or even countries, choose from a list of options available to them—that is, courses of action they may take—that are called **strategies.** The strategies chosen by the players lead to *outcomes,* which describe the consequences of their choices. We assume that the players have *preferences* for the outcomes: they like some more than others.

Game theory analyzes the **rational choice** of strategies—that is, how players select strategies to obtain preferred outcomes. Among areas to which game theory has been applied are bargaining tactics in labor–management disputes, resource-allocation decisions in political campaigns, military options in international crises, and the use of threats by animals in habitat acquisition and protection.

Unlike the subject of *individual* decision making, which researchers in psychology, statistics, and other disciplines study, game theory analyzes situations in which there are at least two players, who may find themselves in conflict because of different goals or objectives. The outcome depends on the choices of *all* the players. In this sense decision making is *collective,* but this is not to say that the players necessarily cooperate when they choose strategies. Indeed, many strategy choices are noncooperative, such as those between combatants in warfare or competitors in sports. In these encounters, the adversaries' objectives may be at cross-purposes: a gain for one means a loss for the other. But in many activities, especially in economics and politics, there may be joint gains that can be realized from cooperation.

Most interactions probably involve a delicate mix of cooperative and noncooperative behavior. In business, for example, firms in an industry cooperate to gain tax breaks even as they compete for shares in the marketplace.

In the next two sections we present several simple examples of two-person games of **total conflict,** in which what one player wins the other player loses, so cooperation never benefits the players. We distinguish two different kinds of solutions to such games. Next we analyze two well-known games of **partial conflict,** in which the players can benefit from cooperation but may have strong incentives not to cooperate. We then turn to the analysis of a larger three-person voting game, in which we show how to eliminate undesirable strategies in stages. Finally, we offer some general comments on solving matrix games and discuss different applications of game theory.

Two-Person Total-Conflict Games: Pure Strategies

For some games with two players, determining the best strategies for the players is straightforward. We begin with such a case.

E X A M P L E   *A Location Game*

Two young entrepreneurs, Henry and Lisa, plan to locate a new restaurant at a busy intersection in the nearby mountains. They agree on all aspects of the restaurant except one. Lisa likes low elevations, whereas Henry wants greater heights—the higher, the better. In this one regard, their preferences are diametrically opposed. What is better for Henry is worse for Lisa, and likewise what is good for Lisa is bad for Henry.

The layout for their location problem is shown in Figure 15.1. Observe that three routes, Avenue A, Boulevard B, and County Road C (blue lines), run in an

FIGURE 15.1
The road map for the location example.

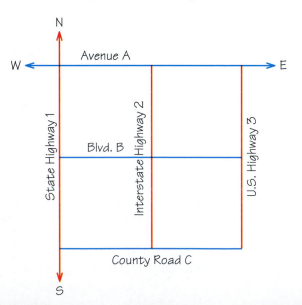

TABLE 15.1	Heights (in thousands of feet) of the Nine Intersections		
		Highways	
Routes	1	2	3
A	10	4	6
B	6	5	9
C	2	3	7

east–west direction, and that three highways, numbered 1, 2, and 3 (red lines), run in a north–south direction. Table 15.1 shows the altitudes at the nine corresponding intersections; the same information (which is in thousands of feet) is shown in three dimensions in Figure 15.2.

To maximize the number of customers, Henry and Lisa agree that the restaurant should be at a location where one of the east–west routes intersects one of the three highways. But they cannot agree on which intersection, so they decide to turn their decision into the following competitive game: Henry will select one of the three routes, A, B, or C, and Lisa will simultaneously choose one of the three highways, 1, 2, or 3.

Henry is pessimistic and considers the lowest—for him, the worst—elevations of each route. These are the numbers 4, 5, and 2, which are the respective

FIGURE 15.2
Three-dimensional road map showing Henry's and Lisa's possible choices.

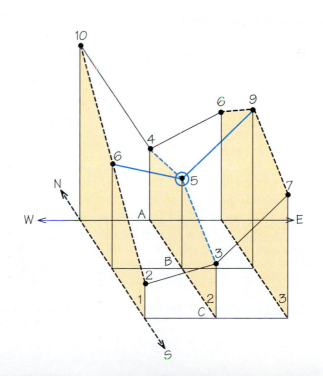

SPOTLIGHT
15.1

Historical Highlights

John von Neumann

Oskar Morgenstern

As early as the seventeenth century, such outstanding scientists as Christiaan Huygens (1629–1695) and Gottfried W. Leibniz (1646–1716) proposed the creation of a discipline that would make use of the scientific method to study human conflict and interactions. Throughout the nineteenth century, several leading economists created simple mathematical models to analyze particular examples of competitive encounters. The first general mathematical theorem on this subject was proved by the distinguished logician Ernst Zermelo (1871–1956) in 1912. It stated that any finite game with perfect information, such as checkers or chess, has an optimal solution in *pure* strategies; that is, no randomization or secrecy is necessary. A game is said to have *perfect information* if at each stage of the play, every player is aware of all past moves by itself and others as well as all future choices that are possible. This theorem is an example of an *existence theorem:* it demonstrates that there must exist a best way to play such a game, but it does not provide a detailed plan for playing a complex game, like chess, to achieve victory.

The famous mathematician F. E. Émile Borel (1871–1956) introduced the notion of a *mixed,* or randomized, strategy when he investigated some elementary duels around 1920. The fact that every two-person, *zero-sum* game must have optimal mixed strategies and an *expected value* for the game was proved by John von Neumann

(1903–1957) in 1928. Von Neumann's result was extended to the existence of equilibrium outcomes in mixed strategies for multiperson games that are either *constant-sum* or *variable-sum* by John F. Nash, Jr. (1931–   ), in 1951.

Modern game theory dates from the publication in 1944 of *Theory of Games and Economic Behavior* by the Hungarian-American mathematician John von Neumann and the Austrian-American economist Oskar Morgenstern (1902–1977). They introduced the first general model and solution concept for multiperson *cooperative games,* which are primarily concerned with coalition formation (by economic cartels, voting blocs, and military alliances) and the resulting distribution of gains or losses. Several other suggestions for a solution to such games have since been proposed. These include the value concept of Lloyd S. Shapley (1923–   ), which relates to fair allocation and economic prices and serves as well as an index of voting power (see Chapter 12).

The French artist George Mathieu designed a medal for the Paris Musée de la Monnaie in 1971 to honor game theory. It was the seventeenth medal to "commemorate 18 stages in the development of Western consciousness." The first medal was for the Edict of Milan in A.D. 313. Game theory also has a mascot, the tiger, arising from the Princeton University tiger and the Russian abbreviation of the term "game theory" (ТЕОРИЯ ИГР).

row minima, indicated in the right-hand column of Table 15.2. He notes that the highest of these values is 5. By choosing the corresponding route, B, Henry can guarantee himself an altitude of at least 5000 feet.

> The number 5 in the right-hand column is referred to as the **maximin,** which is circled in Table 15.2. It is the maximum value of the minimum numbers in the three rows in the table. The strategy that corresponds to the maximin (for Henry, Route B) is called his **maximin strategy.**

Lisa likewise does a worst-case analysis and lists the highest—for her, the worst—elevations for each highway. These numbers, 10, 5, and 9, are the column maxima and are listed in the bottom row of Table 15.2. From Lisa's point of view, the best of these outcomes is 5. If she picks Interstate Highway 2, then she is assured of an elevation of no more than 5000 feet.

> The number 5 in the bottom row of Table 15.2 is referred to as the **minimax,** which is circled in the table. It is the minimum value of the maximum numbers in the three columns. The strategy that corresponds to the minimax (for Lisa, Highway 2) is called her **minimax strategy.**

To summarize, Henry has a strategy that will ensure the height is 5000 or higher, and Lisa has a strategy that will ensure the height is 5000 or lower. The height of 5000 at the intersection of Route B and Highway 2 is, simultaneously, the lowest value along Boulevard B and the highest along Interstate Highway 2. In other words, the maximin and the minimax are both equal to 5000 for the location game.

TABLE 15.2 **Heights (in thousands of feet) in Table 15.1, with the Row Minima and Column Maxima**

| | Routes | Lisa Highways | | | Row minima |
		1	2	3	
Henry	A	10	4	6	4
	B	6	5	9	⑤
	C	2	3	7	2
	Column maxima	10	⑤	9	

When the maximin and the minimax are the same, the resulting outcome is called a **saddlepoint.**

The reason for the term *saddlepoint* should be clear from the saddle-shaped payoff surface shown in Figure 15.2. The middle point on a horse saddle is simultaneously the lowest point along the spine of the horse and the highest point between the rider's legs. (In Figure 15.2, the rider would be facing leftward or rightward.) In our example, one might also think of the saddlepoint as a mountain pass: as one drives through the pass, the car is at a high point on a highway (in the north–south direction) and at a low point on a route (in the east–west direction).

The resolution of this contest is for Henry to pick B and Lisa to pick 2. This puts them at an elevation of 5000, which is simultaneously the maximin and the minimax.

If a game has a saddlepoint (5 in our example), it gives the **value** of the game. Players can guarantee at least this value by choosing their maximin and minimax strategies (B for Henry and 2 for Lisa).

There is no need for secrecy in a game with a saddlepoint. Even if Henry were to reveal his choice of B in advance, Lisa would be unable to use this knowledge to exploit him. In fact, both players can use the height information in our example to compute the optimal strategy for their opponent as well as for themselves. In games with saddlepoints, players' worst-case analyses lead to the best *guaranteed* outcome—in the sense that each player can ensure that he or she does not do worse than a certain amount (5 in our example)—and may do better (if the opponent deviates from a maximin or minimax strategy). ◆

Another well-known game with a saddlepoint is tic-tac-toe. Two players alternately place an **X** or an **O**, respectively, in one of the nine unoccupied spaces in a 3 × 3 grid. The winner is the first player to have three **X**'s, or three **O**'s, in either the same row, the same column, or along a diagonal.

An explicit list of all strategies for either the first- or second-moving player in tic-tac-toe is long and complicated, because it specifies a complete plan for all possible contingencies that can arise. For the first-moving player, for example, a strategy might say "put an **X** in the middle square, then an **X** in the corner if your opponent puts an **O** in a noncorner position, etc." While, initially, young children find this game interesting to play, before long they discover that each player can always prevent the other player from winning by forcing a tie, making the game quite boring. All strategies that force a tie, it turns out, are a saddlepoint in tic-tac-toe.

EXAMPLE *The Restricted-Location Game*

Assume in our location game that Henry and Lisa are informed by the county officials that it is against the law to locate a restaurant on either Boulevard B or Interstate Highway 2. These two choices, which provided our earlier solution, are now forbidden. The resulting location game without these two strategies is given in Table 15.3 (with payoffs again expressed in thousands of feet).

As before, Henry and Lisa can each do a worst-case analysis. Henry is worried about the minimum number in each row, and Lisa is concerned with the maximum number in each column. These are listed in the right column and bottom row, respectively, in Table 15.4.

Henry sees that his maximin is 6, so he can guarantee a height of 6000 feet or more by choosing Route A. Likewise, Lisa observes that her minimax is 7, so she can keep the elevation of the restaurant down to 7000 feet or less by selecting Highway 3. There is a gap of 1 (=7 − 6) between the minimax and maximin. When the maximin is less than the minimax, as in this case, then a game does *not* have a saddlepoint, but it does have a value (described in the next section).

If Henry does play his maximin strategy, Route A, and Lisa plays her minimax strategy, Highway 3, then the resulting payoff is 6. However, Henry may be motivated to gamble in this case by playing his other strategy, Route C; if Lisa sticks to her conservative strategy, Highway 3, then the payoff is 7. Henry will have gained one unit (1000 feet), going from 6 to 7.

TABLE 15.3 Heights (in thousands of feet) Without Boulevard B and Interstate Highway 2

		Highways	
Routes		1	3
A		10	6
C		2	7

TABLE 15.4 Heights (in thousands of feet) in Table 15.3, with Row Minima and Column Maxima

		Lisa Highways		
	Routes	1	3	Row minima
Henry	A	10	6	⑥
	C	2	7	2
	Column maxima	10	⑦	

This is, however, a risky move. If Lisa suspected it, she might counter by selecting Highway 1. The payoff would then be 2, the best for Lisa and the worst for Henry. So Henry's gamble to gain one unit (6 to 7) by moving has the risk that he might lose 4 units (6 to 2) if Lisa also moves.

But then there is no incentive for Lisa to play her nonminimax strategy (that is, to play Highway 1) if she believes Henry, in turn, will move back to his maximin strategy (Route A), leading to a payoff of 10. This is worse than 6 from her viewpoint. ◆

In two-player games that have saddlepoints, like our original 3 × 3 location game and tic-tac-toe, each player can calculate the maximin and minimax strategies for both players before the game is even played. Once the solution has been determined by either mathematical analysis or practical experience (as was probably true of tic-tac-toe), there may be little interest in actually playing the game.

But this is decidedly not the case for much more complex games, like chess, whose solution has not yet been determined—and is unlikely to be in the foreseeable future. Even though computers are able to beat world champions on occasion, the computer's winning moves will not necessarily be optimal against those of *all* other opponents. Nevertheless, we know that chess, like tic-tac-toe, has a saddlepoint; what we do not know is whether it yields a win for white, a win for black, or a draw.

Unlike chess, many games, like the 2 × 2 restricted-location game, do not have an outcome that can always be guaranteed. These games, which include poker, involve uncertainty and risk. One desires in such games not to have one's strategy detected in advance, because this information can be exploited by an opponent. It is no surprise, then, that poker players are told to keep a "poker face," revealing nothing about their likely moves. But this advice is not very helpful in telling the players what actually to do in the game, such as how many cards to ask for in draw poker.

Chess players apply the reasoning of TOM (see pages 562–563) when they think ahead to consequences of moves, countermoves, and so on.

We will show that there are optimal ways to play two-person total-conflict games without a saddlepoint so as not to reveal one's choices. But their solution is by no means as straightforward as that of games with a saddlepoint.

Two-Person Total-Conflict Games: Mixed Strategies

Probably most competitive games do not have a saddlepoint, like that we found in our first location-game example. Rather, as is illustrated in our restricted-location game—in which the maximin and minimax were not the same—players must try to keep secret their strategy choices, lest their opponent use this information to his or her advantage.

In particular, players must take care to conceal the strategy they will select until the encounter actually takes place, when it is too late for the opponent to alter his or her choice. If the game is repeated, a player will want to *vary* his or her strategy in order to surprise the opponent.

In parlor games like poker, players often use the tactic of *bluffing*. This tactic involves a player's sometimes raising the stakes when he has a low hand so that opponents cannot guess whether or not his hand is high or low—and may, therefore, miscalculate whether to stay in or drop out of the game (a player would prefer opponents to stay in when he has a high hand and drop out when he has a low hand). In military engagements, too, secrecy and even deception are often crucial to success.

In many sporting events, a team tries to surprise or mislead the opposition. A pitcher in baseball will not signal the type of pitch he or she intends to throw in advance, varying the type throughout the game to try to keep the batter off balance. In fact, we next consider a confrontation between a pitcher and batter in more detail.

The pitcher and the batter use mixed strategies.

TABLE 15.5	Batting Averages in a Baseball Duel			
		Pitcher		Row
		F	C	minima
Batter	F	.300	.200	(.200)
	C	.100	.500	.100
	Column maxima	(.300)	.500	

EXAMPLE   A Duel Game

Assume that a particular baseball pitcher can throw either a blazing fastball or a slow curve into the strike zone and so has two strategies: *fast* (denoted by F) and *curve* (C). The pitcher faces a batter who attempts to guess, before each pitch is thrown, whether it will be a fastball or a curve, giving the batter also two strategies: guess F and guess C. Assume that the batter has the following batting averages, which are known by both players.

- .300 if the batter guesses fast (F) and the pitcher throws fast (F)
- .200 if the batter guesses fast (F) and the pitcher throws curve (C)
- .100 if the batter guesses curve (C) and the pitcher throws fast (F)
- .500 if the batter guesses curve (C) and the pitcher throws curve (C)

A player's batting average is the number of times he hits safely divided by his number of times at bat. If a batter hit safely 3 times out of 10, for example, his average would be .300.

This game is summarized in Table 15.5. We see from the right-hand column in the table that the batter's maximin is .200, which is realized when he selects his first strategy, F. Thus, the batter can "play it safe" by always guessing a fastball, which will result in his batting .200, hardly enough for him to remain on the team.

We see from the bottom row of the table that the pitcher's minimax is .300, which is obtained when he throws fast (F). Note that the batter's maximin of .200 is less than the pitcher's minimax of .300, so this game does not have a saddle-point. There is a gap of .100 ($=.300 - .200$) between these two numbers.

Each player would like to play so as to win as much for himself of the .100 payoff in the gap as possible. That is, the batter would like to average more than .200, whereas the pitcher wants to hold the batter down to less than .300. ◆

A Flawed Approach

If the batter and pitcher in our example consider how they might outguess each other, they might reason along the following lines:

1. *Pitcher* (to himself): If I choose strategy *F*, I hold the batter down to .300 (the minimax) or less. However, the batter is likely to guess *F* because it guarantees him at least .200 (his maximin), and it actually provides him with .300 against my *F* pitch. In this case, the batter wins all the .100 payoff in the gap.
2. *Batter* (to himself): Knowing that the pitcher is reasoning as in step 1, he will try to surprise me with *C*. So I should fool him and guess *C*. I would thus average .500, which will show him up for trying to gamble and out-guess me!
3. *Pitcher* (to himself): But if the batter is thinking as in step 2—that is, guessing *C*—I, on second thought, should really throw *F*. This will lead to an average of only .200 for the batter and teach him to not try to out-guess me!

This type of cyclical reasoning can go on forever: I think that he thinks that I think that he thinks. . . . It provides no resolution of the players' decision problem.

Clearly, there is no pitch, or guess, that is best in all circumstances. Nevertheless, both the pitcher and the batter *can* do better, but not by trying to anticipate the choices of each other. The answer to their problem lies in the notion of a *mixed strategy*.

A Better Idea

The play of many total-conflict games requires an element of surprise, which can be realized in practice by making use of a mixed strategy.

A **mixed strategy** is a particular randomization over a player's strategies (which henceforth we call **pure strategies**—the definite options a player can choose—to distinguish them from mixed strategies). Each one of the player's pure strategies is assigned some probability, indicating the relative frequency with which the pure strategy will be played. The specific pure strategy that will be used in any given play of the game is selected by some appropriate probabilistic mechanism or random device.

Note that a pure strategy is a special case of a mixed strategy, with the probability of 1 assigned to just one pure strategy and 0 to all the rest. When a player resorts to a mixed strategy, the resulting outcome of the game is no longer predictable in advance. Rather, it must be described in terms of the probabilistic notion of an *expected value*.

If each of the n payoffs $s_1, s_2, \ldots, s_n$ will occur with the probabilities p_1, $p_2, \ldots, p_n$, respectively, then the average, or **expected value E,** is given by

$$E = p_1 s_1 + p_2 s_2 + \cdots + p_n s_n$$

We assume that the probabilities sum to 1 and that each probability p_i is never negative. That is, we assume that $p_1 + p_2 + \cdots + p_n = 1$, and $p_i \geq 0$ $(i = 1, 2, \ldots, n)$.

To see how mixed strategies and expected values are used in the analysis of games, we turn to what is perhaps the simplest of all competitive games without a saddlepoint.

E X A M P L E   *Matching Pennies*

In matching pennies, each of two players simultaneously shows either a head H or a tail T. If the two coins match, with either two heads or two tails, then the first player (Player I) receives both coins (a win of 1 for Player I). If the coins do not match, that is, if one is an H and the other is a T, then the second player (Player II) receives the two coins (a loss of 1 for Player I). These wins and losses for Player I are shown in Table 15.6.

The game in Table 15.6 is described by a **payoff matrix.** The rows and columns correspond to the strategies of the two players, and the numerical entries give the payoffs to Player I when these strategies are chosen.

Although the entries in our earlier tables for the location game also gave payoffs, they were not monetary, as here. A game represented by a payoff matrix is called *a game in strategic form.*

TABLE 15.6	**Wins and Losses for Player I in Matching Pennies**		
		Player II	
		H	*T*
Player I	*H*	1	−1
	T	−1	1

The two rows in Table 15.6 correspond to Player I's two pure strategies, H and T, and the two columns to Player II's two pure strategies, also H and T. The numbers in the table are the corresponding winnings for Player I and losses for Player II. If two H's or two T's are played, Player I wins 1 from Player II. When both an H and a T are played, Player I pays out 1 to Player II.

It is fruitless for one player to attempt to outguess the other in this game. They should instead resort to mixed strategies and use expected values to estimate their likely gains or losses.

The best thing for Player I to do is randomly to select H half the time and T half the time. This mixed strategy can be expressed as

$$(p_H, p_T) = (p_1, p_2) = (p, 1 - p) = (\tfrac{1}{2}, \tfrac{1}{2})$$

Note that the probabilities of choosing H (p) and T ($1 - p$) do indeed sum to 1, as required; in particular, when $p = \frac{1}{2}$, $1 - p = 1 - \frac{1}{2} = \frac{1}{2}$.

This mixture can be realized in practice by the flip of a coin. Player I's resulting expected value is

$$E_H = \tfrac{1}{2}(1) + \tfrac{1}{2}(-1) = 0$$

whenever Player II plays H (first column of Table 15.6), and

$$E_T = \tfrac{1}{2}(-1) + \tfrac{1}{2}(1) = 0$$

whenever Player II plays T (second column).

> Player I's average outcome of 0 is the **(mixed-strategy) value** of the game; unlike the use of this notion in games with a saddlepoint, the value here can only be realized by the use of mixed strategies.

The value of 0 is really an expected value and so must be understood in a statistical sense. That is, in a given play of the game, Player I will either win 1 or lose 1. However, his or her expectation over many plays of this game is 0. The optimal mixed strategy for Player II is likewise a 50–50 mix of H and T, which also leads to an expectation of 0, making the game fair.

> A game is **fair** if its value is 0 and, consequently, it favors neither player when at least one player uses an *optimal* (mixed) strategy—one that guarantees that the resulting payoff is the best that this player can obtain against all possible strategy choices (pure or mixed) by an opponent.

Player II gains nothing by knowing that Player I is using the optimal mixed strategy $(\frac{1}{2}, \frac{1}{2})$. However, Player I must not reveal to Player II whether H or T will be displayed *in any given play* of the game before Player II makes his or her own choice of H or T. Even without this information, if Player II knew that Player I was using a particular *nonoptimal* mixed strategy $(p_1, p_2) = (p, 1 - p)$, where $p \neq \frac{1}{2}$—that is, not choosing a 50–50 mixture between H and T—then Player II could take advantage of this knowledge and increase his or her average winnings over time to something greater than the value of 0. (See Exercise 14.) ◆

EXAMPLE   *Nonsymmetrical Matching*

In this game, Players I and II can again show either heads H or tails T. When two H's appear, Player II pays $5 to Player I. When two T's appear, Player II pays $1 to Player I. When one H and one T are displayed, then Player II collects $3 from Player I. Note that although the sum of Player I's gains ($5 + $1 = $6) when there are two H's or two T's, and the sum of Player II's gains ($3 + $3 = $6) otherwise, are the same, the game is nonsymmetrical.

A **nonsymmetrical** two-person total-conflict game is one in which the row player's gains ($5 and $1 in our example) are different from the column player's gains (always $3), except when there is a tie (not possible in our example, but possible in tic-tac-toe). In matching pennies, the payoff for winning is the same for each player, so the game is *symmetrical*.

The game just described in given by the payoff matrix in Table 15.7, which shows the payoffs that Player I receives from Player II. A worst-case analysis, like that which solved our initial location game, is of little help here. Player I may lose $3 whether he plays H or T, making his maximin −3. Player II can keep her losses down to $1 by always playing T (and thus avoiding the loss of $5 when two H's appear), so Player II's minimax is 1. However, if Player II chooses T and Player I knows this, then Player I will also play T and collect $1 from Player II. Can Player II do better than lose $1 in each play of the game?

TABLE 15.7 Payoffs for Player I in a Nonsymmetrical Matching Game

		Player II	
		H	*T*
Player I	*H*	5	−3
	T	−3	1

Consider the situation where Player I uses a mixed strategy $(p_H, p_T) = (p, 1 - p)$, which involves playing H with probability $1 - p$ and playing T with probability p, where $0 \leq p \leq 1$. Against Player II's pure strategy H, Player I's expected value is

$$E_H = (5)(p) + (-3)(1 - p) = 8p - 3$$

Against Player II's pure strategy T, Player I's expected value is

$$E_T = (-3)(p) + 1(1 - p) = -4p + 1$$

These two linear equations in the variable p are depicted in Figure 15.3. Note that the four points where these two lines intersect the two vertical lines, $p = 0$ and $p = 1$, are the four payoffs appearing in the payoff matrix.

The point at which the lines given by E_H and E_T intersect can be found by setting $E_H = E_T$, yielding

$$8p - 3 = -4p + 1$$
$$12p = 4$$

so $p = \frac{1}{3}$. To the left of $p = \frac{1}{3}$, $E_T > E_H$, and to the right $E_H > E_T$; at $p = \frac{1}{3}$, $E_H = E_T$. If Player I chooses $(p_H, p_T) = (p, 1 - p) = (\frac{1}{3}, \frac{2}{3})$, he can ensure

$$E_H = 8(1/3) - 3 = E_T = -4(1/3) + 1 = -1/3$$

regardless of what Player II does.

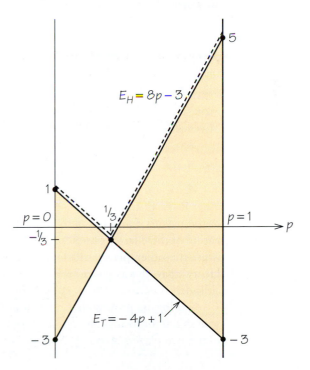

In other words, Player I's optimal mixed strategy is to pick H and T with probabilities $\frac{1}{3}$ and $\frac{2}{3}$, respectively, which gives Player I an expected value of $-\frac{1}{3}$. As can be seen from Figure 15.3, $-\frac{1}{3}$ is the highest expected value that Player I can guarantee against *both* strategies H and T of Player II. Although T yields Player I a higher expected value for $p < \frac{1}{3}$, and H yields him a higher expected value for $p > \frac{1}{3}$, Player I's choice of $(p_H, p_T) = (\frac{1}{3}, \frac{2}{3})$ protects him against an expected loss greater than $-\frac{1}{3}$, which neither of his pure strategies does (each may produce a maximum loss of -3). Put another way, the intersection of E_H and E_T at $p = \frac{1}{3}$ is the minimum of the function given by E_T to the left and E_H to the right (shown by the dashed line in Figure 15.3). If Player II had more than two strategies, this approach to finding a minimum that puts a floor on Player I's expected loss can be extended.

A similar calculation for Player II results in the same optimal mixed strategy $(\frac{1}{3}, \frac{2}{3})$ and expected value $-\frac{1}{3}$. But because the payoffs for Player II are losses, $-\frac{1}{3}$ means that she gains $\frac{1}{3}$ on the average.

This game is therefore unfair, even though the sum of the amounts ($6) that Player I might have to pay Player II when he loses is the same as the sum that Player II might have to pay Player I when she loses. Interestingly, it is Player II, who will win an average of $33\frac{1}{3}$ cents each time the game is played, who is favored, even though she may have to pay more to Player I when she loses (a maximum of $5) than Player I will ever have to pay her (a maximum of $3). ◆

The symmetrical and nonsymmetrical matching games are examples of what are called *zero-sum games.*

> A **zero-sum game** is one in which the payoff to one player is the negative of the corresponding payoff to the other, so the sum of the payoffs to the two players is always zero. These games can be completely described by a payoff matrix, in which the numbers represent the payoffs to Player I, while their negatives are the payoffs to Player II.

Zero-sum games are total-conflict games in which what one player wins the other loses. But not all total-conflict games are zero-sum—in particular, the sum of the payoffs could be some other constant than zero. Nevertheless, the strategic nature of these latter games is the same as that of zero-sum games: what one player wins, the other player still loses. This was true in our location game, in which Henry's payoff was greater the higher the altitude, and Lisa's greater the lower the altitude.

Scoring in professional chess tournaments usually assigns a payoff of 1 for winning, 0 for losing, and $\frac{1}{2}$ to each player for a tie, making the sum of the payoffs to the two players always 1. Such games are called **constant-sum,** which can readily be converted to zero-sum games. Thus, chess could as well be scored -1 for a loss, $+1$ for a win, and 0 for a tie, making the constant 0 in this case. Although constant-sum and zero-sum games have the same strategic nature, constant-sum games are a more general class because the constant need not be zero.

The solution in the symmetrical version of matching pennies illustrated how the mixed strategy of $(\frac{1}{2}, \frac{1}{2})$ guarantees each player the value of 0, but we did not give a *solution technique* for finding optimal mixed strategies. In the nonsymmetrical version of matching pennies, by contrast, we illustrated a procedure that can be applied to *every* payoff matrix in which each player has only two strategies.

We must use more complex methods, which we will not describe here, to find mixed-strategy solutions when one or both players have more than two strategies. However, one should always check first to see whether a game has a saddlepoint before employing any technique for finding optimal mixed strategies.

In our next example, which is the earlier duel between the pitcher and the batter given by the 2×2 payoff matrix in Table 15.4, we already showed that there is no saddlepoint. Thus, the solution will necessarily be in mixed strategies, and we now proceed to find it.

EXAMPLE   *The Duel Game Revisited*

In Table 15.8, we add probabilities, which we explain next, to Table 15.5, where F indicates fastball and C indicates curve ball. The pitcher should use a mixed strategy $(p_1, p_2) = (p_F, p_C) = (p, 1 - p)$. The probabilities p and $1 - p$ (where $0 \le p \le 1$) are indicated below the game matrix and under the corresponding strategies, F and C, for the pitcher. If the pitcher plays a mixed strategy $(p, 1 - p)$ against the two pure strategies, F and C, for the batter, he realizes the respective expected values:

$$E_F = (.3)p + .2(1 - p) = .1p + .2$$
$$E_C = (.1)p + .5(1 - p) = -.4p + .5$$

As in the nonsymmetrical matching-pennies game, the solution to this game occurs at the intersection of the two lines given by E_F and E_C. Setting the equations of these lines equal to each other yields $p = .6$, giving $E_F = E_C = E = .260$.

TABLE 15.8	A Baseball Duel with Probabilities			
		Pitcher		
		F	**C**	
Batter	F	.300	.200	q
	C	.100	.500	$1 - q$
		p	$1 - p$	

Thus, the pitcher should use his optimal mixed strategy that selects F with probability $p = 3/5$ and C with probability $1 - p = 2/5$. This choice will hold the batter down to a batting average of .260, which is the value of the game. We stress that .260 is an average and must be interpreted in a statistical manner. It says that about one time in four the batter will get a hit, but not what will happen on any particular time at bat.

Assume that the batter uses a mixed strategy $(q_1, q_2) = (q_F, q_C) = (q, 1 - q)$, as indicated to the right of the game matrix in Table 15.8. This mixed strategy, when played against the pitcher's pure strategies, F and C, results in the respective expected values:

$$E_F = (.3)q + .1(1 - q) = .2q + .1$$
$$E_C = (.2)q + .5(1 - q) = -.3q + .5$$

The intersection of these two lines occurs at the point $q = .8$, giving $E_F = E_C = E = .260$. The batter's optimal mixed strategy is, therefore, $(q_F, q_C) = (\frac{4}{5}, \frac{1}{5})$, which gives him the same batting average of .260.   ◆

We have seen that the outcome of .260, which is the value of the game, occurs when either the pitcher selects his optimal mixed pitching strategy $(\frac{3}{5}, \frac{2}{5})$ or the batter selects his optimal mixed guessing strategy $(\frac{4}{5}, \frac{1}{5})$. This particular result holds true for every two-person zero-sum game; it is the fundamental theorem for such games and is known as the *minimax theorem*.

The **minimax theorem** guarantees that there is a unique game value (.260 in our example), and an optimal strategy for each player, so that either player alone can realize at least this value by playing this strategy, which may be pure or mixed.

While our previous examples illustrated this theorem, they are not a proof of it, which can be found in advanced game theory texts.

Partial-Conflict Games

The 2×2 matrix games presented so far have been total-conflict games: one player's gain was equal to the other player's loss. Although most parlor games, like chess or poker, are games of total conflict, and therefore constant-sum, most real-life games are surely not. (Elections, in which there are usually a clear-cut winner and one or more losers, probably come as close to being games of total conflict as we find in the real world.) We will consider two games of partial conflict, in which the players' preferences are not diametrically opposed, that have often been used to model many real-world conflicts.

> Games of partial conflict are **variable-sum games,** in which the sum of pay-offs to the players at the different outcomes varies.

There is some mutual gain to be realized by both players if they can cooperate in partial-conflict games, but this may be difficult to do in the absence of either good communication or trust. When these elements are lacking, players are less likely to comply with any agreement that is made. *Noncooperative games* are games in which a binding agreement cannot be enforced. Even if communication is allowed in such games, there is no assurance that a player can trust an opponent to choose a particular strategy that he or she promised to select.

In fact, the players' self-interests may lead them to make strategy choices that yield both lower payoffs than they could have achieved by cooperating. Two partial-conflict games illustrate this problem later in the chapter.

EXAMPLE   *Prisoners' Dilemma*

Prisoners' Dilemma is a two-person variable-sum game. It provides a simple explanation of the forces at work behind arms races, price wars, and the population problem. In these and other similar situations, the players can do better by cooperating. But there may be no compelling reasons for them to do so, unless the players have credible threats of retaliation for not cooperating. The term *Prisoners' Dilemma* was first given to this game by Princeton mathematician Albert W. Tucker (1905–1994) in 1950.

Before defining the formal game, we introduce it through a story, which involves two persons, accused of a crime, who are held incommunicado. Each has two choices: to maintain his or her innocence, or to sign a confession accusing the partner of committing the crime.

Now it is in each suspect's interest to confess and implicate the partner, thereby trying to receive a reduced sentence. Yet if both suspects confess, they ensure a bad outcome—namely, they are both found guilty. What is good for the prisoners as a pair—to deny having committed the crime, leaving the state with insufficient evidence to convict them—is frustrated by their pursuit of their own individual rewards.

Prisoners' Dilemma, as we already noted, has many applications, but we will use it here to model a recurrent problem in international relations: arms races between antagonistic countries, which earlier included the superpowers but now include such countries as India and Pakistan and Israel and some of its Arab neighbors.

For simplicity, assume there are two nations, Red and Blue. Each can independently select one of two policies:

A: Arm in preparation for a possible war (noncooperation).
D: Disarm, or at least negotiate an arms-control agreement (cooperation).

There are four possible outcomes:

(D, D):   Red and Blue disarm, which is *next best* for both because, while advantageous to each, it also entails certain risks.

(A, A):   Red and Blue arm, which is *next worst* for both, because they spend needlessly on arms and are comparatively no better off than at (D, D).

(A, D):   Red arms and Blue disarms, which is *best for Red* and *worst for Blue*, because Red gains a big edge over Blue.

(D, A):   Red disarms and Blue arms, which is *worst for Red* and *best for Blue*, because Blue gains a big edge over Red.

This situation can be modeled by means of the matrix in Table 15.9, which gives the possible outcomes that can occur. Here, Red's choice involves picking one of the two rows, whereas Blue's choice involves picking one of the two columns.

We assume that the players can rank the four outcomes from best to worst, where 4 = best, 3 = next best, 2 = next worst, and 1 = worst. Thus, the higher the number, the greater the payoff, but these payoffs are only **ordinal:** they indicate an ordering of outcomes from best to worst, but they say nothing about the *degree* to which a player prefers one outcome over another. To illustrate, if a player despises the outcome that he or she ranks 1 but sees little difference among the outcomes ranked 4, 3, and 2, the "payoff distance" between 4 and 2 will be less than that between 2 and 1, even though the numerical difference between 4 and 2 is greater.

The ordinal payoffs to the players for choosing their strategies of A and D are shown in Table 15.10, where the first number in the pair indicates the payoff to the row player (Red), and the second number the payoff to the column player (Blue). Thus, for example, the pair (1, 4) in the second row and first column signifies a payoff of 1 (worst outcome) to Red and a payoff of 4 (best outcome) to Blue. This outcome occurs when Red unilaterally disarms while Blue continues to arm, making Blue, in a sense, the winner and Red the loser.

Let us examine this strategic situation more closely. Should Red select strategy A or D? There are two cases to consider, which depend on what Blue does:

TABLE 15.9	The Outcomes in an Arms Race, as Modeled by Prisoners' Dilemma	
		Blue
		A	*D*
Red	*A*	Arms race	Favors red
	D	Favors blue	Disarmament

TABLE 15.10	Ordinal Payoffs in an Arms Race, as Modeled by Prisoners' Dilemma	
	Blue	
	A	**D**
Red A	(2, 2)	(4, 1)
D	(1, 4)	(3, 3)

- If Blue selects *A*: Red will receive a payoff of 2 for *A* and 1 for *D*, so it will choose *A*.
- If Blue selects *D*: Red will receive a payoff of 4 for *A* and 3 for *D*, so it will choose *A*.

In both cases, Red's first strategy (*A*) gives it a more desirable outcome than its second strategy (*D*). Consequently, we say that *A* is Red's **dominant strategy,** because it is always advantageous for Red to choose *A* over *D*.

In Prisoners' Dilemma, *A* dominates *D* for Red, so we presume that a rational Red would choose *A*. A similar argument leads Blue to choose *A* as well, that is, to pursue a policy of arming. Thus, when each nation strives to maximize its own payoffs independently, the pair is driven to the outcome (*A*, *A*), with payoffs of (2, 2). The better outcome for both, (*D*, *D*), with payoffs of (3, 3), appears unobtainable when this game is played noncooperatively.

The outcome (*A*, *A*), which is the product of dominant strategy choices by both players in Prisoners' Dilemma, is a *Nash equilibrium*.

When no player can benefit by departing unilaterally (i.e., by itself) from its strategy associated with an outcome, the strategies of the players constitute a **Nash equilibrium.** (Technically, while it is the set of strategies that define the equilibrium, the choice of these strategies leads to an outcome that we shall also refer to as the equilibrium.)

Note that in Prisoners' Dilemma, if either player departs from (*A*, *A*), the payoff for the departing player who switches to *D* drops from 2 to 1 at (*D*, *A*) and (*A*, *D*). Not only is there no benefit from departing, but there actually is a loss, with the *D* player punished with its worst payoff of 1. These losses would presumably deter each nation from moving away from the Nash equilibrium of (*A*, *A*), assuming the other nation sticks to *A*.

Even if both nations agreed in advance jointly to pursue the socially beneficial outcome, (D, D), (3, 3) is unstable. This is because if either nation alone reneges on the agreement and secretly arms, it will benefit, obtaining its best payoff of 4. Consequently, each nation would be tempted to go back on its word and select A. Especially if nations have no great confidence in the trustworthiness of their opponents, they would have good reason to try to protect themselves against defection from an agreement by arming.

> **Prisoners' Dilemma** is a two-person variable-sum game in which each player has two strategies, cooperate or defect. Defect dominates cooperate for both players, even though the mutual-defection outcome, which is the unique Nash equilibrium in the game, is worse for both players than the mutual-cooperation outcome.

Note that if 4, 3, 2, and 1 in Prisoners' Dilemma were not just ranks but numerical payoffs, their sum would be $2 + 2 = 4$ at the mutual-defection outcome and $3 + 3 = 6$ at the mutual-cooperation outcome. At the other two outcomes, the sum, $1 + 4 = 5$, is still different, illustrating why Prisoners' Dilemma is a variable-sum game.

In real life, of course, people often manage to escape the noncooperative Nash equilibrium in Prisoners' Dilemma. Either the game is played within a larger context, wherein other incentives are at work, such as cultural norms that prescribe cooperation (though this is just another way of saying that defection from (D, D) is not rational, rendering the game not Prisoners' Dilemma), or the game is played on a repeated basis—it is not a one-shot affair—so players can induce cooperation by setting a pattern of rewards for cooperation and penalties for noncooperation.

In a repeated game, factors like reputation and trust may play a role. Realizing the mutual advantages of cooperation in costly arms races, players may inch toward the cooperative outcome by slowly phasing down their acquisition of weapons over time, or even destroying them (the United States and Russia have begun doing exactly this). They may also initiate other productive measures, such as improving their communication channels, making inspection procedures more reliable, writing agreements that are truly enforceable, or imposing penalties for violators when their violations are detected (as may be possible by reconnaissance or spy satellites).

Prisoners' Dilemma illustrates the intractable nature of certain competitive situations that blend conflict and cooperation. The standoff that results at the Nash equilibrium of (2, 2) is obviously not as good for the players as that which they could achieve by cooperating—but they risk a good deal if the other player defects.

The fact that the players must forsake their dominant strategies to achieve the (3, 3) cooperative outcome (see Table 15.10) makes this outcome a difficult one to sustain in one-shot play. On the other hand, assume that the players can threaten each other with a policy of tit-for-tat in repeated play: "I'll cooperate on each round unless you defect, in which case I will defect until you start cooperating again." If these threats are credible, the players may well shun their defect strategies and try to establish a pattern of cooperation in early rounds, thereby fostering the choice of (3, 3) in the future. Alternatively, they may look ahead, in a manner that will be described at the end of this chapter, to try to stabilize (3, 3). ◆

E X A M P L E *Chicken*

Let us look at one other two-person game of partial conflict, known as *Chicken,* which also can lead to troublesome outcomes. Two drivers approach each other at high speed. Each must decide at the last minute whether to swerve to the right or not swerve. Here are the possible consequences of their actions:

1. Neither driver swerves, and the cars collide head-on, which is the worst outcome for both because they are killed (payoff of 1).
2. Both drivers swerve—and each is mildly disgraced for "chickening out"—but they do survive, which is the next-best outcome for both (payoff of 3).
3. One of the drivers swerves and badly loses face, which is his next-worst outcome (payoff of 2), whereas the other does not swerve and is perceived as the winner, which is her best outcome (payoff of 4).

These outcomes and their associated strategies are summarized in Table 15.11.

If both drivers persist in their attempts to "win" with a payoff of 4 by not swerving, the resulting outcome will be mutual disaster, giving each driver his or her worst payoff of 1. Clearly, it is better for both drivers to back down and each obtain 3 by swerving, but neither wants to be in the position of being intimidated into swerving (payoff of 2) when the other does not (payoff of 4).

TABLE 15.11	Payoffs in a Driver Confrontation, as Modeled by Chicken		
		Driver 2	
		Swerve	Not swerve
Driver 1	Swerve	(3, 3)	(2, 4)
	Not swerve	(4, 2)	(1, 1)

Notice that neither player in Chicken has a dominant strategy. His or her better strategy depends on what the other player does: swerve if the other does not, don't swerve if the other player swerves, making this game's choices highly interdependent, which is characteristic of many games. The Nash equilibria in Chicken, moreover, are (4, 2) and (2, 4), suggesting that the compromise of (3, 3) will not be easy to achieve because both players will have an incentive to deviate from it in order to try to be the winner.

> **Chicken** is a two-person variable-sum game in which each player has two strategies: to swerve to avoid a collision or not to swerve and possibly cause a collision. Neither player has a dominant strategy. The compromise outcome, in which both players swerve, and the disaster outcome, in which both players do not, are not Nash equilibria; the other two outcomes, in which one player swerves and the other does not, are Nash equilibria.

In fact, there is a third Nash equilibrium in Chicken, but it is in mixed strategies, which can only be computed if the payoffs are not ranks, as we have assumed here, but numerical values. Even if the payoffs were numerical, however, it can be shown that this equilibrium is always worse for both players than the cooperative (3, 3) payoffs. Moreover, it is implausible that players would sometimes swerve and sometimes not—randomizing according to particular probabilities—in the actual play of this game, compared with either trying to win outright or reaching a compromise.

The two pure-strategy Nash equilibria in Chicken suggest that, insofar as there is a "solution" to this game, it is that one player will succeed when the other caves in to avoid the mutual-disaster outcome. But there certainly are real-life cases in which a major confrontation was defused and a compromise of sorts was achieved in Chicken-type games. This fact suggests that the one-sided solution given by the two pure-strategy Nash equilibria may not be the only pure-strategy solution, especially if the players are farsighted and think about the possible untoward consequences of their actions.

International crises, labor–management disputes, and other conflicts in which escalating demands may end in wars, strikes, and other catastrophic outcomes have been modeled by the game of Chicken. But Chicken, like Prisoners' Dilemma, is only one of the 78 essentially different 2×2 ordinal games, in which each player can rank the four possible outcomes from best to worst.

Chicken and Prisoners' Dilemma, however, are especially disturbing, because the cooperative (3, 3) outcome in each is not a Nash equilibrium. Unlike a constant-sum game, in which the losses of one player are offset by the gains of the other, *both* players can end up doing badly—at (2, 2) in Prisoners' Dilemma and (1, 1) in Chicken—in these variable-sum games. ◆

Larger Games

We have shown how to compute optimal pure and mixed strategies, and the values ensured by using them, in 2×2 constant-sum games. In 2×2 variable-sum games, we focused on Nash equilibria as a solution concept in Prisoners' Dilemma and Chicken, but we found that this notion of a stable outcome did not justify the choice of cooperative strategies in either of these games.

We turn next to a somewhat larger game, in which there are three players, each of whom can choose among three strategies, which is technically a $3 \times 3 \times 3$ game. In this game, we eliminate certain undesirable strategies, but in stages, to arrive at a Nash equilibrium that seems quite plausible.

If one of the three players has a dominant strategy in the $3 \times 3 \times 3$ game, we suppose this player will choose it, thereby reducing the game to a 3×3 game between the other two players. (Of course, if no player has a dominant strategy in a three-person game, it cannot be reduced in this manner to a two-person game.)

If this game is not one of total conflict, the minimax theorem, which guarantees players the value in a two-person zero-sum game, is not applicable. Even if the game were zero-sum, the fact that we assume the players in the $3 \times 3 \times 3$ game can only rank outcomes, not assign numerical values to them, means that they cannot calculate optimal mixed strategies in it.

The problem in finding a solution to the reduced 3×3 game is not a lack of Nash equilibria. Rather, there are too many! So the question becomes which, if any, are likely to be selected by the players. Specifically, is one more appealing than the others? The answer is "yes," but it requires extending the idea of dominance, discussed in the previous section, so its successive application in different stages of play.

E X A M P L E   *The Paradox of the Chair's Position — And an Escape*

The $3 \times 3 \times 3$ game we analyze involves voting, illustrating the applicability of game theory to politics. There is also a tie-in to the analysis of weighted voting in Chapter 12, because one of the players (the chair in the voting body), while not having more votes than the others, can break ties. This would seem to make the chair more powerful, in some sense, than the other players.

As we shall see, however, rather than making the chair more powerful—as we earlier measured voting power—the possession of a tie-breaking vote backfires, preventing the chair from obtaining a preferred outcome. However, we do indicate a possible escape for the chair from this unenviable position.

The power indices described in Chapter 12 do not take into account the preferences of the differently weighted players—all combinations (Banzhaf index) or permutations (Shapley–Shubik index) were assumed to be equally likely. But as we shall show next, the greater resources that a player like the chair has do not always translate into greater **power,** by which we mean the ability of a player to obtain a preferred outcome.

The 1994 Nobel Memorial Prize in Economics

John C. Harsanyi

John F. Nash

The Nobel Memorial Prize in Economics was awarded to three game theorists in 1994, marking the fiftieth anniversary of the publication of von Neumann and Morgenstern's *Theory of Games and Economic Behavior* (see Spotlight 15.1, page 528). The recipients were as follows:

• *John C. Harsanyi* (1920–) of the University of California, Berkeley, a Hungarian-American who emigrated from Hungary to Australia in 1950 and then to the United States in 1956. He is well known for extending game theory to the study of ethics and how societal institutions, each of whose members' satisfaction can be measured against that of others, choose among alternatives. His other major contribution was to give a precise definition to "incomplete information" in games in which players may be thought of as different types, and probabilities assigned to each type. His analysis of such games is applicable to the modeling of many real-life conflicts in which there are severe constraints on the information that players have about each other. Harsanyi was trained in both mathematics and economics; he also has strong interests in philosophy.

• *John F. Nash* (1928–) of Princeton University, an American mathematician who did path-breaking work in both noncooperative game theory (the "Nash equilibrium" is named after him) and cooperative game theory, especially on bargaining, in which axioms or assumptions are specified and a unique solution that satisfies these axioms is derived. Nash

Reinhard Selten

obtained his results in the early 1950s, when he was only in his 20s, after which he became mentally ill and was unable to work. Fortunately, he has made a remarkable recovery and has now resumed research.

• *Reinhard Selten* (1930–) of the University of Bonn, a German mathematician who proposed significant refinements in the concept of a Nash equilibrium that help to distinguish those that are most plausible in games (often there are many such equilibria, which creates a selection problem). Some of his work on equilibrium selection was done in collaboration with Harsanyi. Selten is also noted for pioneering work on developing game-theoretic models in evolutionary biology. He is an advocate of experimental testing of game-theoretic

solutions to determine those that are most likely to be chosen by human subjects, and using these empirical results to refine the theory.

Other contemporary game theorists have also made important advances in the theory, including Lloyd S. Shapley (1923–), an American mathematician who proposed the cooperative game-theoretic solution concept known as the "Shapley value." He extended this work with Robert J. Aumann (1930–), a mathematician who was born in Germany, emigrated as a child to the United States before World War II, and then moved to Israel. Aumann also gave a precise formulation to "common knowledge," developing some of its consequences in games, and proposed the notion of a "correlated equilibrium," which has been helpful in understanding how players coordinate their choices in games.

Game theory has provided important theoretical foundations in economics, starting with microeconomics but now extending to macroeconomics and international economics. It also has been increasingly applied in political science, especially in the study of voting, elections, and international relations. In addition, game theory has contributed major insights in biology, particularly in understanding the evolution of species and conditions under which animals—humans included—fight each other for territory or act altruistically. It has also illuminated certain fields in philosophy, including ethics, philosophy of religion, and political philosophy, and inspired many experiments in social psychology.

One would suppose that the chair of a voting body, if he or she has a tie-breaking vote in addition to a regular vote, *would* have more power than other members. Yet, under circumstances to be spelled out shortly, the chair may actually be at a disadvantage relative to the other members.

THE PARADOX: To illustrate this problem, suppose there is a set of three voters, $V = \{X, Y, Z\}$, and a set of three alternatives, $A = \{x, y, z\}$, from which the voters choose. Assume that voter X prefers x to y to z, indicated by xyz; voter Y's preference is yzx; and voter Z's is zxy. These preferences give rise to a *Condorcet voting paradox* (discussed in Chapter 11), because the social ordering, according to majority rule, is *intransitive:* although a majority (voters X and Z) prefer x to y, and a majority (voters X and Y) prefer y to z, a majority (voters Y and Z) prefer z to x. So there is no *Condorcet winner*—an alternative that would beat all others in separate pairwise contests. Instead, every alternative can be beaten by one other.

Assume that the voting procedure used by the three voters, who choose from among the three alternatives, is the **plurality procedure,** under which the alternative with the most votes wins. If there is a three-way tie (there can never be a two-way tie if there are three voters), we assume the chair X can break the tie, giving the chair what would appear to be an edge over the other two voters, Y and Z.

To begin, assume that voting is sincere.

Under **sincere voting,** every voter votes for his or her most-preferred alternative, based on his or her true preferences, without taking into account what the other players might do (see Chapter 11, page 394).

In this case, X will prevail by being able to break the tie in favor of x. However, X's apparent advantage disappears if voting is "sophisticated," as demonstrated below.

To see why, first note that X has a dominant strategy of "vote for x": it is never worse and sometimes better than her other two strategies, whatever the other two voters do. Thus, if the other two voters vote for the same alternative, it wins, and X cannot do better than vote sincerely for x, so voting sincerely is never worse. On the other hand, if the other two voters disagree, X's tie-breaking vote (along with her regular vote) for x will be decisive in x's selection, which is X's best outcome.

Given the dominant choice of x on the part of X, Y and Z face the strategy choices shown in Figure 15.4. Y has one, and Z has two, **dominated strategies,** which are never better and sometimes worse than some other strategy, whatever the other two voters do. For example, observe that "vote for x" by Y always leads to his worst alternative, x. The dominated strategies are crossed out in the top matrix in Figure 15.4.

This leaves Y with two *undominated* strategies that are neither dominant nor dominated; "vote for y" and "vote for z." "Vote for y" is better than "vote for z" if Z chooses y (leading to y rather than x), whereas the reverse is the case if Z chooses

FIRST REDUCTION

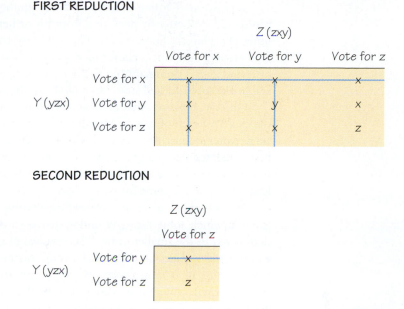

SECOND REDUCTION

FIGURE 15.4 Sophisticated voting, given *X* chooses "vote for *x*." The dominated strategies of each voter are crossed out in the first reduction, leaving two (undominated) strategies for *Y* and one (dominant) strategy for *Z*. Given these eliminations, *Y* would then eliminate "vote for *y*" in the second reduction, making *z* the sophisticated outcome.

z (leading to *z* rather than *x*). By contrast, *Z* has a dominant strategy of "vote for *z*," which leads to outcomes at least as good and sometimes better than his other two strategies.

If voters have complete information about each other's preferences, then they can perceive the situation in terms of the top matrix in Figure 15.4 and eliminate the dominated strategies that are crossed out (first reduction). The elimination of these strategies gives the bottom matrix in Figure 15.4. Then *Y*, choosing between "vote for *y*" and "vote for *z*" in this matrix, would cross out "vote for *y*" (second reduction), now dominated because that choice would result in *x*'s winning due to the chair's tie-breaking vote. Instead, *Y* would choose "vote for *z*" (hence, not *Y*'s sincere strategy), ensuring *z*'s election, which is *Z*'s best outcome but only the next-best outcome for *Y*. In this manner, *z*, which is not the first choice of a majority and could in fact be beaten by *y* in a pairwise contest, becomes the sophisticated outcome.

The successive elimination of dominated strategies by voters—insofar as this is possible—beginning in our example with *X*'s of choice of *x* in favor of *y* and *z*, is called **sophisticated voting.**

Sophisticated voting results in a Nash equilibrium, because none of the three players can do better by departing from his or her sophisticated strategy when the other two players choose theirs. This is clearly true for X, because x is her dominant strategy; given X's choice of x, z is dominant for Z; and given these choices by X and Z, z is dominant for Y. These "contingent" dominance relations, in general, make sophisticated strategies a Nash equilibrium.

Observe, however, that there are four other Nash equilibria in this game. First, the choice of each of x, y, or z by all three voters are all Nash equilibria, because no single voter's departure can change the outcome to a different one, much less a better one, for that player. In addition, the choice of x by X, y by Y, and x by Z—resulting in x—is also a Nash equilibrium, because no voter's departure would lead to a better outcome for him or her.

In game-theoretic terms, sophisticated voting produces a different and smaller game in which some formerly undominated strategies in the larger game become dominated in the smaller game. The removal of such strategies, sometimes in several successive stages, in effect enables sophisticated voters to determine what outcomes eventually *will* be chosen by eliminating those outcomes that definitely *will not* be chosen. Voters can thereby ensure that their worst outcomes will not be chosen by successively removing dominated strategies, given the presumption that other voters do likewise.

How does sophisticated voting affect the chair's presumed extra voting power? The chair's tie-breaking vote is not only not helpful, but it is positively harmful: it guarantees that X's worst outcome (z) will be chosen if voting is sophisticated! This situation, in which the chair's tie-breaking vote hurts rather than helps the chair, is called the **paradox of the chair's position.**

Given this unfortunate state of affairs for the chair, we might ask whether a chair, or the largest voting faction in a voting body comprising three factions—none of which commands a majority—has any recourse. It would appear not: the sophisticated outcome, z, is supported by both Y and Z, which no voting strategy of X can upset.

AN ESCAPE: A chair is often in the unique position, after the other voters have already committed themselves, of being the last voter to have to make a strategy choice. However, this position does not furnish a ready solution to the chair's problem if voting is truly sophisticated, for sophisticated voting implies that voters act upon both their own preferences and a knowledge of the preferences of the other voters. Therefore, the order of voting is immaterial: all voters can predict sophisticated choices beforehand and act accordingly. Thus, even a chair's (unexpected) deviation from a sophisticated strategy cannot effect a better outcome for it.

But now assume that the chair, by virtue of her position, can obtain information about the preferences of the other two voters, but they cannot obtain information about her preference. Further, assume that each of the two regular members is informed of the other's preference. If voting is to be sophisticated, the chair's preference must be made known to the regular member; however, the chair is not compelled to tell the truth. The question is: Can a chair, by announcing a preference different from her true preference, induce a more preferred sophisticated outcome?

Recall that the chair, having a tie-breaking vote, will always have a dominant strategy, which happens to be her sincere choice in our example, if voting is sophisticated. Indeed, the other voters need only know (and believe) her announced first choice, and not her complete preference scale, to determine what her sophisticated strategy will be.

A **deception strategy** on the part of the chair is any *announced* most-preferred alternative that differs from her sincere choice. Her deception is **tacit** if she chooses the strategy she announces, thereby not revealing her deception, which may be considered a specific form of strategic voting (Chapter 11, page 394).

Tacit deception will be profitable for the chair if it induces an outcome that the chair prefers to the sophisticated outcome, based on her sincere preferences.

In our example, the chair (X), by announcing her first choice to be y instead of x, can induce the sophisticated outcome y, which she would prefer to z. This can be seen from the reductions shown in Figure 15.5. Note that the first-reduction matrix gives the outcomes as Y and Z *perceive* them, after X's deceptive announcement of y as her first choice (it does not matter in what order she ranks x and z below y).

Y's elimination of dominated strategies "vote for x" and "vote for z," and Z's elimination of dominated strategy "vote for y," give the second-reduction matrix shown in Figure 15.5, which cannot be reduced further since Z's two remaining strategies both yield y. Thus, tacit deception, by changing the outcome from z to y, is profitable for X (as well as Y).

Suppose now that X, as the chair, actually chooses "vote for x" after announcing her (insincere) preference for y. Then the sophisticated outcome she induces will be x, her first preference. In other words, the chair can induce her most-preferred outcome by announcing a false preference for y and, contrary to her announcement, voting sincerely for x in the end. Because y, the tacit-deception outcome, is not a Nash equilibrium, X can benefit by voting for x, contrary to her announced preference for y.

Such **revealed deception** involves announcing a deception strategy but then voting contrary to the announcement.

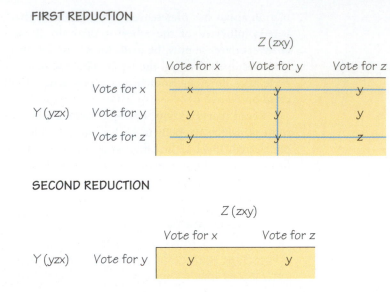

FIGURE 15.5 Tacit-deception outcome, given *X* chooses "vote for *y*." The dominated strategies of each voter are crossed out in the first reduction, leaving two (undominated) strategies for *Z* and one (dominant) strategy for *Y*. Given these eliminations, *Z*'s two undominated strategies, both yielding *y*, remain undominated in the second reduction—so no strategies are in fact crossed out. The (manipulated) outcome is *y*, whichever of *Z*'s two remaining strategies he chooses, making the *y* the tacit-deception outcome. If *X* actually voted for *x* after falsely announcing a first choice of *y*, the (manipulated) outcome would be *x*; however, *X*'s deception would be revealed.

Recall that an insincere announcement by the chair improves her position somewhat, inducing her next-best outcome (*y*) when deception remains tacit. However, when this announcement is followed instead by the chair's vote for her most preferred alternative (*x*)—flouting this announcement—then the chair can achieve her best outcome (*x*).

Of course, revealed deception becomes apparent after the vote, unless it is secret, and probably cannot be used very frequently. If it were, the chair's announcements would quickly lose credibility and thus their inducement value.

The deception-strategy game we have described for the chair can also be played by a regular member if he or she is privy to information that the chair and the other regular members are not. (The results of such special knowledge will not duplicate those for the chair, however, because the chair has an extra resource—her tie-breaking vote.) We shall not carry this analysis further, though, because our main purpose has been to demonstrate that there is a resolution of sorts to the paradox of the chair's position. It requires, however, that the information available to some players in the game be restricted, which has the effect of endowing one player (the chair) with still greater resources.

This, it must be admitted, is a rather deceptive way out of a problem that seems genuine. If voting is sophisticated, the chair, despite the added weight of her position, will not necessarily enjoy greater control over outcomes than the other members. In fact, the reverse might be the case, as the paradox demonstrates.

Clearly, power defined as control over outcomes is not synonymous with power defined as control over resources (e.g., a tie-breaking vote or simply more votes). The strategic situation facing voters intervenes and may cause them to reassess their sincere strategies in light of the additional resources that a chair possesses. In so doing, they may be led to "gang up" against the chair—that is, to vote in such a way as to undermine the impact of her extra resources—handing the chair a worse outcome than she would have achieved without them. These resources in effect become a burden to bear, not power to wield.

We stress that Y and Z do not form a coalition against X in the sense of coordinating their strategies and agreeing to act together in a cooperative game, wherein binding agreements are possible. Rather, they behave as isolated individuals; at most they could be said to form an "implicit coalition." Such a coalition does not imply even communication between its members but simply choices based on their common perceived strategic interests. ◆

So far we have used payoff matrices to describe games in strategic forms. In these games, the row and column players' choices of strategies led to an outcome from which each player received a payoff. These strategy choices were assumed to be simultaneous.

In the next example of a larger game, we start by assuming simultaneous choices and show what outcome would occur. Then we assume that the choices of the players need not be simultaneous, and one player considers moving first. We will use a "game tree" to analyze the *sequential choices* players can then make, as occurs when first you move, then I move, and so on, which are called *games in extensive form*. As we will see, the outcome in such a game may be wholly different from what it is in a game with simultaneous choices, which raises the question of which game is the most realistic model of a situation.

EXAMPLE *A Truel*

A *truel* is like a duel, except that there are three players. Each player can either fire, or not fire, his or her gun at either of the other two players. We assume the goal of each player is, first, to survive and, second, to survive with as few other players as possible. Each player has one bullet and is a perfect shot, and no communication (e.g., to pick out a common target) that results in a binding agreement with other players is allowed, making the game noncooperative. We will discuss the answers that simultaneous choices, on the one hand, and sequential choices, on the other, give to what it is optimal for the players to do in the truel.

If choices are simultaneous, *at the start of play, each player fires at one of the other two players, killing that player.*

Why will the players all fire at each other? Because their own survival does not depend an iota on what they do. Since they cannot affect what happens to themselves, but can only affect how many others survive (the fewer the better, according to the postulated secondary goal), they should all fire away at each other. (Even if the rules of the play permitted shooting oneself, the primary goal of survival would preclude committing suicide.) In fact, the players all have dominant strategies to shoot at each other, because whether or not a player survives—we will discuss shortly the probabilities of doing so—he or she does at least as well shooting an opponent.

The game, and optimal strategies in it, would change if (1) the players were allowed more options, such as to fire in the air and thereby disarm themselves, or (2) they did not have to choose simultaneously, and a particular order of play were specified. Thus, if the order of play were A, followed by B and C choosing simultaneously, followed by any player with a bullet remaining choosing, then A would fire in the air and B and C would subsequently shoot each other. (A is no threat to B or C, so neither of the latter will fire at A; on the other hand, if B or C did not fire immediately at the other, each would not survive to get in the last shot, so they both fire.) Thus, A will be the sole survivor. In 1992, a modified version of this scenario was played out in late-night television programming among the three major television networks, with ABC's effectively going first with "Nightline," its well-established news program, and CBS and NBC dueling on which host, David Letterman or Jay Leno, to choose for their entertainment shows. Regardless of their ultimate choices, ABC "won" when CBS and NBC were forced to divide the entertainment audience.

To return to the original game (all choose simultaneously), the players' strategies of all firing have two possible consequences: either one player survives (even if two players fire at the same person, the third must fire at one of them, leaving only one survivor), or no player survives (if each player fires at a different person). In either event, there is no guarantee of survival. In fact, if each player has an equal probability of firing at one of the two other players, the probability that any particular player will survive is only .25.

The reason is that if the three players are A, B, and C, A will be killed when either B fires at him or her, C does, or both do. The only circumstance in which A will survive is if B and C fire at each other, which gives A one chance in four.

If choices are sequential, no player will fire at any other, so all will survive.

At the start of the truel, all the players are alive, which satisfies their primary goal of survival, though not their secondary goal of surviving with as few others as possible. Now assume that A contemplates shooting B, thereby reducing the number of survivors, and cannot fire into the air. But looking ahead, A knows that by firing first and killing B, he or she will be defenseless and be immediately shot by C, who will then be the sole survivor.

It is in A's interest, therefore, not to shoot anybody at the start, and the same logic applies to each of the other players. Hence, everybody will survive, which is a happier outcome than when choices are simultaneous, in which case everyone's primary goal is not satisfied — or, quantitatively speaking, satisfied only 25% of the time. ◆

While sequential choices produce a "happier" outcome, do they provide a plausible model of a strategic situation that mimics what people might actually think and do in such a situation? We believe that the players in the truel, artificial as this kind of shoot-out may seem, would be motivated to think ahead, given the dire consequences of their actions. Therefore, they would hold their fire, knowing that if one fired first, he or she would be the next target.

In Figure 15.6, we show this logic somewhat more formally with a **game tree,** in which A has three strategies, as indicated by the three branches that sprout from A: not shoot, shoot B ($S \rightarrow B$), or shoot C ($S \rightarrow C$). The latter two branches, in turn, give survivors C and B, respectively, two strategies: not shoot ($\overline{S}$) or shoot A ($S \rightarrow A$).

We assume that the players rank the outcomes as follows, which is consistent with their primary and secondary goals: $4 =$ best (lone survivor), $3 =$ next best (survivor with one other), $2 =$ next worst (survivor with two others), and $1 =$ worst (nonsurvivor). These payoffs are given for ordered triples (A, B, C); thus ($3, 3, 1$) indicates the next-best payoffs for A and B and the worst payoff for C.

FIGURE 15.6
A game tree of a truel.

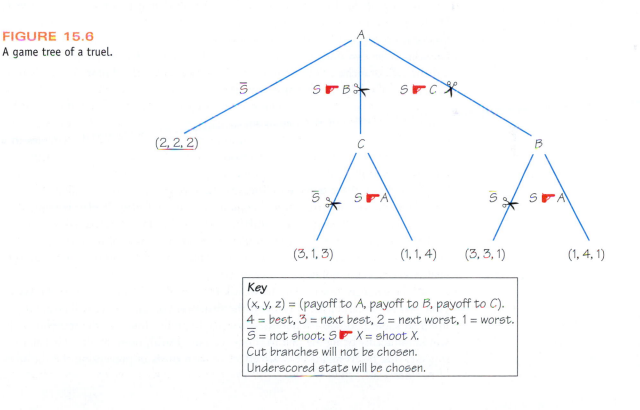

Key
(x, y, z) = (payoff to A, payoff to B, payoff to C).
4 = best, 3 = next best, 2 = next worst, 1 = worst.
$\overline{S}$ = not shoot; $S \rightarrow X$ = shoot X.
Cut branches will not be chosen.
Underscored state will be chosen.

Note that play necessarily terminates when there is only one survivor, as is the case at (1, 1, 4) and (1, 4, 1). To keep the tree simple, we assume that play also terminates when either A initially or B or C subsequently chooses $\overline{S}$, giving outcomes of (2, 2, 2), (3, 3, 1), and (3, 1, 3), respectively. Of course, we could allow the two or three surviving players in the latter cases to make subsequent choices in an extended game tree, but this example is meant only to illustrate the analysis of a game tree, not be the definitive statement on truel possibilities (more will be explored in the exercises).

In a game in extensive form represented by a game tree, players work backwards, starting the analysis at the bottom of the tree. (By "bottom" we mean where play terminates; because this is where the tree branches out, the tree looks upside down in Figure 15.6.) The players then work up the tree, using backward induction. **Backward induction** is a reasoning process in which players, working backward from the last possible moves in a game, anticipate each other's rational choices.

To illustrate, because C prefers (1, 1, 4) to (3, 1, 3), we indicate that C would not choose by "cutting" this branch with a scissors; similarly, B would not choose $\overline{S}$. Thus, if play got to the bottom of the tree, C would shoot A (choose $S \rightarrow A$) if C were the survivor, and B would shoot A (choose $S \rightarrow A$) if B were the survivor, following A's shooting C or B, respectively.

Moving up to the next level, A would know that if he or she chose $S \rightarrow B$, (1, 1, 4) would be the outcome; if he or she chose $S \rightarrow C$, (1, 4, 1) would be the outcome, making one or the other the outcome from the bottom level. Choosing between these two outcomes and (2, 2, 2), A would prefer the latter, so A would cut the two branches, $S \rightarrow B$ and $S \rightarrow C$. Hence, A would choose $\overline{S}$, terminating play with nobody's shooting anybody else.

This, of course, is the conclusion we reached earlier, based on the reasoning that if A shot either B or C, he or she would end up dead, too. Because we could allow each player, like A, to choose among his or her three initial strategies in a $3 \times 3 \times 3$ game, and subsequently make moves and countermoves from the initial state (if feasible), the foregoing analysis applies to all players.

Underlying the completely different answers given by the simultaneous and sequential choices in a truel is a change in the rules of play. If play is sequential, the players do not have to fire simultaneously at the start, as assumed in a $3 \times 3 \times 3$ strategic-form game. Rather, a player who moves first (A in our example)—and then the later players—would not fire, given that play continues until all bullets are expended or nobody chooses to fire.

In the extensive-form analysis, we ask of each player (it need not be A): Given your present situation (all alive), and the situation you anticipate will ensue if you fire first, should you do so? Because each player prefers living to the state he or she would induce by being the first to shoot (certain death), none shoots. This analysis suggests that truels might be more effective than duels in preventing the outbreak of conflict.

We will not try to develop this argument into a more general model. The main point is that a game tree allows for a look-ahead approach whereby players compare the present state with possible future states—perhaps several steps ahead—to determine which moves to make. These choices, as we have seen, may lead to radically different outcomes compared with those based on simultaneous choices.

Using Game Theory

Solving Games

Given any payoff matrix, the first thing we ask is whether it is zero-sum (or constant-sum). If so, we check to see whether it has a saddlepoint by determining the minimum number of each row and the maximum number of each column, as we did in several earlier examples. If the maximum of the row minima (maximin) is equal to the minimum of the column maxima (minimax), then the game has a saddlepoint. The resulting value, and the corresponding pure strategies, provide a solution to the game.

This value will appear in the payoff matrix as the smallest number in its row and the largest in its column. In the 3×3 location game, this number was 5 (5000 feet).

Like our voting game, dominated strategies can successively be eliminated in the 3×3 location game. Thus, Route B dominates Route C, and Highway 2 dominates Highway 3; having made these eliminations, Highway 2 dominates Highway 1; having made this elimination, Route B dominates Route A. Thus, Highway 2 and Route B survive the successive eliminations, yielding the saddlepoint of 5. The successive-elimination procedure therefore provides an alternative method for finding the saddlepoint in this 3×3 location game. Unfortunately, it does not work to find the saddlepoint in *all* two-person zero-sum games bigger than 2×2.

Recall that instead of eliminating dominated strategies in the 3×3 location game, we eliminated Route B and Highway 2, which dominated other strategies, to obtain the 2×2 restricted-location game in Table 15.3. In this game, there were no dominated strategies and, hence, no saddlepoint.

If a two-person zero-sum game does not have a saddlepoint, which was the case not only in the restricted-location game but also for matching pennies, the nonsymmetrical matching game, and the baseball duel, the solution will be in mixed strategies. To find the optimal mix in a 2×2 game, we calculate the expected value to a player from choosing its first strategy with probability p and its second with probability $1 - p$, assuming that the other player chooses its first pure strategy (yielding one expected value) and its second pure strategy (yielding another expected value).

Setting these two expected values equal to each other yields a unique value for p that gives the optimal mix, $(p, 1 - p)$, with which the player should choose its first and second strategies. Substituting the numerical solution of p back into either expected-value equation gives the value of the game, which each player can guarantee for itself, whatever strategy its opponent chooses.

Several general algorithms have been developed since 1945 to find mixed-strategy solutions to large constant-sum games. This work has mostly been done in the field of linear programming, using such algorithms as the simplex method of G. B. Dantzig and the more recent method of N. K. Karmarkar (see Chapter 4).

In variable-sum games, we also begin by successively eliminating dominated strategies, if there are any. The outcomes that remain do not depend on the numerical values we attach to them but only on their ranking from best to worst by the players, as illustrated in the three-person voting example.

Care must be taken in interpreting this solution, however. It began with the choice of a dominant strategy by the chair (X) — and her elimination of her two dominated strategies. Presuming these eliminations, Y and Z were then able to eliminate their own dominated strategies in the first reduction, and Y in turn eliminated a dominated strategy in the second reduction, leading finally to the outcome z, supported by Y and Z.

This solution is a fairly demanding one, because it assumes considerable calculational abilities on the part of the players. Less demanding, of course, is that players simply choose their dominant strategies, as is possible in Prisoners' Dilemma, but of course games may not have such strategies.

In the game of Chicken, for example, neither player has a dominant (or dominated) strategy, so the game cannot be reduced. In such situations, we ascertain what outcomes are Nash equilibria. There are two (in pure strategies) in Chicken, suggesting that the only stable outcomes in this game occur when one player gives in and the other does not. In Prisoners' Dilemma, by comparison, the choice by the players of their dominant strategies singles out the mutual-defection outcome as the unique Nash equilibrium, which is worse for both players than the cooperative outcome.

In both Chicken and Prisoners' Dilemma, there seems no good reason for the choice of the (3, 3) cooperative outcome, at least if each game is played only once, because this outcome is not a Nash equilibrium. However, there is an alternative theory, called the "theory of moves," that assumes different rules of play and renders the cooperative outcomes in both Prisoners' Dilemma and Chicken stable (i.e., if the players think ahead).

Theory of moves (TOM) is a dynamic theory that describes optimal strategic choices in strategic-form games in which the players, thinking ahead, can make moves and countermoves.

TOM is *dynamic* in the sense that it allows players, after choosing strategies that lead to an outcome in a payoff matrix, to make subsequent moves and countermoves, with row's being able to move vertically by changing his row strategy, and column's being able to move horizontally by changing her column strategy. The reasoning that the players use in deciding whether to move or not move is backward induction, as illustrated earlier in the truel.

We informally illustrate this reasoning in Prisoners' Dilemma, starting from each of the four possible outcomes:

- If the play starts at the noncooperative (2, 2) outcome, players are stuck, no matter how far ahead they look, because as soon as one player departs, the other player, enjoying its best outcome at (4, 1) or (1, 4), will not move on. *Result:* The players stay at the noncooperative outcome.
- If play starts at the cooperative (3, 3) outcome, then neither player will defect, because if he or she does, the other player will also defect, and they both will end up worse off at (2, 2). Thinking ahead, therefore, neither player will defect. *Result:* The players stay at the cooperative outcome.
- If play starts at one of the (4, 1) or (1, 4) win–lose outcomes, the player doing best (4) will know that if he or she does not move to the cooperative (3, 3) outcome, his or her opponent will move to the noncooperative (2, 2) outcome, inflicting on the best-off player a next-worst (2) outcome. Therefore, it is in this player's interest—as well as his or her opponent's—that the best-off player act cooperatively and move to (3, 3), anticipating that if he or she does not, the (2, 2) rather than the (3, 3) outcome will be chosen. *Result:* The best-off player will move to the cooperative outcome, where play will stop.

Thus TOM does not predict unconditional cooperation in Prisoners' Dilemma but, instead, makes it a function of the starting point of play. As in the truel, a change in rules from simultaneous choices to sequential choices can induce cooperation.

The calculations we have described for Prisoners' Dilemma, which are grounded in backward induction and could be formalized by a game tree, are not, we believe, beyond the ability of most players. Farsighted players *can* escape the dilemma in Prisoners' Dilemma, provided play begins at a state other than the noncooperative one. (But we must be careful in interpreting this result: with the change in the rules, the original game changes, so this "solution" to Prisoners' Dilemma is not for the original dilemma.) Similar reasoning in Chicken indicates that if play starts at the cooperative (3, 3) outcome, players will stay at this outcome, but the reasoning in this game is somewhat more complicated than in Prisoners' Dilemma.

Practical Applications

The element of surprise, as captured by mixed strategies, is essential in many encounters. For example, mixed strategies are used in various inspection procedures and auditing schemes to deter potential cheaters; by making inspection or auditing choices random, they are rendered unpredictable.

Investigators or regulatory agencies monitor certain accounts as well as take various actions to check for faults, errors, or illegal activities. The investigators include bank auditors, customs agents, insurance investigators, and quality control experts. The National Bureau of Standards is responsible for monitoring the accuracy of measuring instruments and for maintaining reliable standards. The Nuclear Regulatory Agency demands an accounting of dangerous nuclear material as part of its safeguards program. The Internal Revenue Service attempts to identify those cheating on taxes.

Military or intelligence services may wish to intercept a weapon hidden among many decoys or plant a secret agent disguised to look like a respectable individual. Because it is prohibitively expensive to check the authenticity of each and every possible item or person, efficient methods need to be used to check for violations. Both optimal detection and optimal concealment strategies can be modeled as a game between an inspector trying to increase the probability of detection and a violator trying to evade detection.

Some of these games are constant-sum: the violator "wins" when the evasion is successful and "loses" when it is not. On the other hand, cheating on arms-control agreements may well be variable-sum if both the inspector and the cheater would

Soviet General Secretary Mikhail Gorbachev and U.S. President Ronald Reagan sign the Intermediate Range Nuclear Forces Treaty in Washington, D.C., on December 8, 1987.

prefer that no cheating occur to there being cheating and public disclosure of it. The latter could be an embarrassment to both sides, especially if it undermines an arms-control agreement both sides wanted and the cheating is not too serious.

We alluded earlier to the strategy of bluffing in poker, which is used to try to keep the other player or players guessing about the true nature of one's hand. The optimal probability with which one should bluff can be calculated in a particular situation (see Exercise 17). Besides poker, bluffing is common in many bargaining situations, whereby a player raises the stakes (e.g., labor threatens a strike in labor–management negotiations), even if it may ultimately have to back down if its "hand is called."

Perhaps the greatest value of game theory is the framework it provides for understanding the rational underpinnings of conflict in the world today. As a case in point, a confrontation over the budget between the Democratic President Bill Clinton and the Republican Congress resulted in the shutdown of part of the federal government on two occasions between November 1995 and January 1996. Many government workers were frustrated in not being able to do their jobs, even though they knew they would be paid for not working, not to mention the many citizens either greatly hurt or substantially inconvenienced by the shutdown.

Viewed as a game of Chicken, in which each side wanted to get its way not only for the moment but also to establish a precedent for the future, this conflict was not so foolish as it might seem at first glance. The Northern Ireland conflict, which was settled by a peace agreement in April 1998 after 30 years of fighting and more than 3200 deaths, can be viewed in similar terms. As another example, the constant price wars among the airlines suggest competitors caught up in a Prisoners' Dilemma, in which they all suffer from lower fares but cannot avoid their dominant strategies of not cooperating, perhaps to try to seize a quick advantage or hurt the competition even more (and possibly even eliminate a competitor). To be sure, if the airlines cooperate by colluding on fares, which is definitely not advantageous to consumers, the consumers may be thought of as a collective player whose interests are represented by the government. The government can prosecute the airlines for price fixing, or the consumers themselves can file a class-action suit in a "larger" game.

All in all, game theory offers fundamental insights into conflicts at all levels, especially its *seemingly* irrational features which, on second look, are often well conceived and effective.

REVIEW VOCABULARY

Backward induction   A reasoning process in which players, working backward from the last possible moves in a game, anticipate each other's rational choices.

Chicken   A two-person variable-sum symmetric game in which each player has two strategies: to swerve to avoid a collision, or not to swerve and cause a collision if the opponent has not swerved. Neither player has a dominant strategy; the compromise outcome, in which both players swerve, is not a Nash equilibrium, but the two outcomes in which one player swerves and the other does not are Nash equilibria.

Constant-sum game   A game in which the sum of payoffs to the players at each outcome is a constant, which can be converted to a zero-sum game by an appropriate change in the payoffs to the players that does not alter the strategic nature of the game.

Deception strategy   A player's announcement of a false preference to induce other players to choose strategies favorable to the deceiver.

Dominant strategy   A strategy that is sometimes better and never worse for a player than every other strategy, whatever strategies the other players choose.

Dominated strategy   A strategy that is sometimes worse and never better for a player than some other strategy, whatever strategies the other players choose.

Expected value E   If each of the n payoffs, s_1, s_2, . . . , s_n occurs with respective probabilities p_1, p_2, . . . , p_n, then the expected value E is

$$E = p_1 s_1 + p_2 s_2 + \cdots + p_n s_n$$

where $p_1 + p_2 + \cdots + p_n = 1$ and $p_i \geq 0$ ($i = 1, 2, . . . , n$).

Fair game   A zero-sum game is fair when the (expected) value of the game, obtained by using optimal strategies (pure or mixed), is zero.

Game tree   A symbolic tree, based on the rules of play in a game, in which the vertices, or nodes, of the tree represent choice points, and the branches represent alternative courses of action that the players can select.

Maximin   In a two-person zero-sum game, the largest of the minimum payoffs in each row of a payoff matrix.

Maximin strategy   In a two-person zero-sum game, the pure strategy of the row player corresponding to the maximin in a payoff matrix.

Minimax   In a two-person zero-sum game, the smallest of the maximum payoffs in each column of a payoff matrix.

Minimax strategy   In a two-person zero-sum game, the pure strategy of the column player corresponding to the minimax in a payoff matrix.

Minimax theorem   The fundamental theorem for two-person constant-sum games, stating that there always exist optimal pure or mixed strategies that enable the two players to guarantee the value of the game.

Mixed strategy   A strategy that involves the random choice of pure strategies, according to particular probabilities. A mixed strategy of a player is optimal if it guarantees the value of the game.

Nash equilibrium   Strategies associated with an outcome such that no player can benefit by choosing a different strategy, given that the other players do not depart from their strategies.

Nonsymmetrical game   A two-person constant-sum game in which the row player's gains are different from the column player's gains, except when there is a tie.

Ordinal game   A game in which the players rank the outcomes from best to worst.

Paradox of the chair's position   This paradox occurs when being chair (with a tie-breaking vote) hurts rather than helps the chair if voting is sophisticated.

Partial-conflict game   A variable-sum game in which both players can benefit by cooperation, but they may have strong incentives not to cooperate.

Payoff matrix   A rectangular array of numbers. In a two-person game, the rows and columns correspond to the strategies of the two players, and the numerical entries give the payoffs to the players when these strategies are selected.

Plurality procedure   A voting procedure in which the alternative with the most votes wins.

Power   The ability of a player to induce a preferred outcome.

Prisoners' Dilemma   A two-person variable-sum symmetric game in which each player has two strategies, cooperate or defect. Cooperate dominates defect for both players, even though the mutual-defection outcome, which is the unique Nash equilibrium in the game, is worse for both players than the mutual-cooperation outcome.

Pure strategy   A course of action a player can choose in a game that does not involve randomized choices.

Rational choice   A choice that leads to a preferred outcome.

Revealed deception   Involves falsely announcing a strategy to be dominant but subsequently choosing another strategy—inconsistent with one's announcement—that reveals one's deception.

Saddlepoint   In a two-person constant-sum game, the payoff that results when the maximin and the minimax are the same, which is the value of the game. The saddlepoint has the shape of a saddle-shaped surface and is also a Nash equilibrium.

Sincere voting   Voting for one's most-preferred alternative in a situation.

Sophisticated voting   Involves the successive elimination of dominated strategies by voters.

Strategy   One of the courses of action a player can choose in a game; strategies are mixed or pure, depending on whether they are selected in a randomized fashion (mixed) or not (pure).

Tacit deception   Involves falsely announcing a strategy to be dominant, and subsequently choosing this strategy—consistent with one's announcement—thereby not revealing one's deception.

Theory of moves (TOM)   A dynamic theory that describes optimal choices in strategic-form games in which players, thinking ahead, can make moves and countermoves.

Total-conflict game   A zero-sum or constant-sum game, in which what one player wins the other player loses.

Value   In a two-person zero-sum game, if there is a saddlepoint, this is the value; otherwise, it is the expected payoff resulting when the players choose their optimal mixed strategies.

Variable-sum game   A game in which the sum of the payoffs to the players at the different outcomes varies.

Zero-sum game   A constant-sum game in which the payoff to one player is the negative of the payoff to the other player, so the sum of the payoffs to the players at each outcome is zero.

SUGGESTED READINGS

AUMANN, ROBERT J., AND SERGIU HART, EDS. *Handbook of Game Theory with Economic Applications,* Elsevier, Amsterdam, 1992 (vol. 1), 1994 (vol. 2). A comprehensive treatment of game theory and its applications, developed in long chapters written by leading experts. A third (and final) volume is forthcoming.

BAIRD, DOUGLAS G., ROBERT H. GERTNER, AND RANDAL C. PICKER. *Game Theory and the Law,* Harvard University Press, Cambridge, Mass., 1994. A good treatment of how game theory informs various branches of the law.

BINMORE, KEN. *Fun and Games: A Text on Game Theory,* Heath, Lexington, Mass., 1992. This best-selling text is a provocative introduction to game theory at an elementary–intermediate level.

BRAMS, STEVEN J. *Biblical Games: A Strategic Analysis of Stories in the Old Testament,* MIT Press, Cambridge, Mass., 1980. About 20 stories of conflict and intrigue in the Hebrew Bible are modeled as simple games, in many of which God is a player. By and large, Brams argues, the players made rational choices.

BRAMS, STEVEN J. *Negotiation Games: Applying Game Theory to Bargaining and Arbitration,* Routledge, New York, 1990. Game-theoretic models of negotiation have been developed in several disciplines; this book provides a survey of different models and applications.

BRAMS, STEVEN J. *Superpower Games: Applying Game Theory to Superpower Conflict,* Yale University Press, New Haven, Conn., 1985. The superpower conflict, as it existed during the cold war (roughly from 1945 to

1990), has evaporated since the demise of the Soviet Union, but the models developed in this book to study deterrence, arms races, and the verification of arms-control agreements are relevant to conflicts between other countries today.

BRAMS, STEVEN J. *Theory of Moves,* Cambridge University Press, New York, 1994. Describes in detail the theory of moves and applies it to a wide range of conflicts.

BRAMS, STEVEN J., AND JEFFREY M. TOGMAN, "Cooperation Through Threats: The Northern Ireland Case." *PS: Political Science and Politics,* 31(1):34–43 (March 1998).

DIXIT, AVINASH, AND BARRY NALEBUFF. *Thinking Strategically: The Competitive Edge in Business, Politics, and Everyday Life,* Norton, New York, 1991. A best-selling popular treatment of applications of game theory, with many stimulating examples.

GARDNER, ROY. *Game Theory for Business and Economics,* Wiley, New York, 1995. A good introduction to game theory and its business and economic applications, with many examples.

GIBBONS, ROBERT. *Game Theory for Applied Economists,* Princeton University Press, Princeton, N.J., 1993. There are a number of texts on game-theoretic models in economics, many at an advanced level; this is an intermediate-level text that emphasizes applications.

LUCE, R. DUNCAN, AND HOWARD RAIFFA. *Games and Decisions: Introduction and Critical Survey,* Wiley, New York, 1957; Dover, New York, 1989. This venerable survey of classic game theory presents two-person constant-sum and variable-sum games in chapters 4 and 5. Several different algorithms for solving the zero-sum case are given in appendix 6; the minimax theorem, and its equivalence to the "duality theorem" in linear programming, are given in appendixes 2 and 5.

MCDONALD, JOHN. *The Game of Business,* Doubleday, New York, 1975; Anchor, New York, 1977. A superb collection of cases in which elementary tools of game theory are used to explicate some classic battles in the business world.

MORROW, JAMES D. *Game Theory for Political Scientists,* Princeton University Press, Princeton, N.J., 1994. Develops tools of game theory and discusses game-theoretic models used in political science.

NASAR, SYLVIA. *A Beautiful Mind,* Simon & Shuster, New York, 1998. A biography of John Nash that is also a fascinating account of the early history of game theory.

POUNDSTONE, WILLIAM. *Prisoner's Dilemma: John von Neumann, Game Theory, and the Puzzle of the Bomb,* Doubleday, New York, 1992. A history of game theory as well as a biography of its mathematician founder, including his views on the use of nuclear weapons.

SIGMUND, KARL. *Games of Life: Explorations in Ecology, Evolution, and Behavior,* Oxford University Press, Oxford, 1993. Game theory is placed in the broader context of evolutionary models in biology and related fields in a very readable account.

STRAFFIN, PHILIP D. *Game Theory and Strategy,* Mathematical Association of America, Washington, D.C., 1993. An elementary but sophisticated introduction to game theory and several interesting applications.

TAYLOR, ALAN D. *Mathematics and Politics: Strategy, Voting, Power and Proof,* Springer-Verlag, New York, 1995. A mathematics textbook in which game theory and theory of moves are used to model power, voting, and conflict and escalation processes.

WEIBULL, JÖRGEN. *Evolutionary Game Theory,* MIT Press, Cambridge, Mass., 1995. Applications of game theory in biology, especially the study of evolution, have grown rapidly, and this is an advanced, up-to-date treatment.

WILLIAMS, JOHN D. *The Compleat Strategyst: Being a Primer on the Theory of Games of Strategy,* McGraw-Hill, New York, 1954, rev. 1966; Dover, New York, 1986. This gem, which contains many simple illustrations, is a humorous primer on two-person zero-sum games.

SUGGESTED WEB SITES

Martin Osborne's home page (game theory and applications): **http://www.socsci.mcmaster. ca/~econ/faculty/osborne**

Alvin Roth's Game Theory and Experimental Eco-

nomics Page: **http://www.economics. harvard.edu/~aroth/alroth.html**

David Levine's Economics and Game Theory Page: **http://levine.sscnet.ucla.edu/**

SKILLS CHECK

1. In the following two-person zero-sum game, the payoffs represent gains to the row Player I and losses to column Player II.

$$\begin{bmatrix} 3 & 7 & 2 \\ 8 & 5 & 1 \\ 6 & 9 & 4 \end{bmatrix}$$

What is the maximin strategy for Player I?

   (a)   Play the first row.
   (b)   Play the second row.
   (c)   Play the third row.

2. In the following two-person zero-sum game, the payoffs represent gains to row Player I and losses to column Player II.

$$\begin{bmatrix} 3 & 7 & 2 \\ 8 & 5 & 1 \\ 6 & 9 & 4 \end{bmatrix}$$

What is the maximax strategy for Player II?

   (a)   Play the first column.
   (b)   Play the second column.
   (c)   Play the third column.

3. In a two-person zero-sum game, suppose the first player chooses the third row as the maximin strategy and the second player chooses the first column as the minimax strategy. Based on this information, which of the following statements is true?

   (a)   This game definitely has no saddlepoint.
   (b)   This game may or may not have a saddlepoint.
   (c)   This game definitely has a saddlepoint.

4. In the game of matching pennies, Player I wins a penny if the coins match; Player II wins a penny if the coins do not match. Given this information, it can be concluded that the 2×2 matrix which represents this game

   (a)   has two "−1"s and two "1"s.
   (b)   has four "1"s.
   (c)   has four "−1"s.

5. In the following game of batter-versus-pitcher in baseball, the batter's batting averages are given in the game matrix.

		Pitcher	
		Fastball	**Curve**
Batter	**Fastball**	.400	.200
	Curve	.100	.500

What is the pitcher's optimal strategy?

   (a)   Throw more curves than fastballs.
   (b)   Throw more fastballs than curves.
   (c)   Throw about the same number of curves and fastballs.

6. In the following game of batter-versus-pitcher in baseball, the batter's batting averages are given in the game matrix.

		Pitcher	
		Fastball	Curve
Batter	Fastball	.400	.200
	Curve	.100	.500

What is the batter's optimal strategy?

(a)   Expect more curves than fastballs.
(b)   Expect more fastballs than curves.
(c)   Expect about the same number of curves and fastballs.

7. Consider the following partial-conflict game, played in a noncooperative manner.

		Player II	
		Choice A	Choice B
Player 1	Choice A	(4, 4)	(1, 3)
	Choice B	(3, 1)	(2, 2)

What outcomes constitute a Nash equilibrium?

(a)   Only when both players select A.
(b)   Only when both players select A or both select B.
(c)   Only when one player selects A and the other selects B.

EXERCISES   ▲ *Optional.*   ■ *Advanced.*   ◆ *Discussion.*

Total-Conflict Games

Consider the following five two-person zero-sum games, wherein the payoffs represent gains to the row Player I and losses to the column Player II:

1. $\begin{bmatrix} 6 & 5 \\ 4 & 2 \end{bmatrix}$

2. $\begin{bmatrix} 0 & 3 \\ -5 & 1 \\ 1 & 6 \end{bmatrix}$

3. $\begin{bmatrix} -2 & 3 \\ 1 & -2 \end{bmatrix}$

4. $\begin{bmatrix} 13 & 11 \\ 12 & 14 \\ 10 & 11 \end{bmatrix}$

5. $\begin{bmatrix} -10 & -17 & -30 \\ -15 & -15 & -25 \\ -20 & -20 & -20 \end{bmatrix}$

(a)   Which of these games have saddlepoints?
(b)   Find the maximin strategy of Player I, the minimax strategy of Player II, and the value for those games given in part (a).

(c)   List dominated strategies in these games that the players should avoid because the resulting payoffs are worse than those for some alternative strategy.

Solve the following three games of batter-versus-pitcher in baseball, wherein the pitcher can throw one of two pitches and the batter can guess either of these two pitches. The batter's batting averages are given in the game matrix.

6.

		Pitcher	
		Fastball	Curve
Batter	Fastball	.300	.200
	Curve	.100	.400

7.

		Pitcher	
		Fastball	Knuckleball
Batter	Fastball	.500	.200
	Knuckleball	.200	.300

8.

		Pitcher	
		Blooperball	Knuckleball
Batter	Blooperball	.400	.200
	Knuckleball	.250	.250

9.   A businessman has the choice of either not cheating on his income tax or cheating and making $1000 if not audited. If caught cheating, he will pay a fine of $2000 in addition to the $1000 he owes. He feels good if he does not cheat and is not audited (worth $100). If he does not cheat and is audited, he evaluates this outcome as −$100 (for the lost day). Viewing the game as a two-person zero-sum game between the businessman and the tax agency, what are the optimal mixed strategies for each player and the value of the game?

10.   When it is third down and short yardage to go for a first down in American football, the quarterback can decide to run the ball or pass it. Similarly, the other team can commit itself to defend more heavily against a run or a pass. This can be modeled as a 2×2 matrix game, wherein the payoffs are the probabilities of obtaining a first down. Find the solution of this game.

		Defense	
		Run	Pass
Offense	Run	.5	.8
	Pass	.7	.2

11.   You have the choice of either parking illegally on the street or else parking in the lot and paying $16. Parking illegally is free if the police officer is not patrolling, but you receive a $40 parking ticket if she is. However, you are peeved when you pay to park in the lot on days when the officer does not patrol, and you are willing to assess this outcome as costing $32 ($16 for parking plus $16 for your time, inconvenience, and grief). It seems reasonable to assume that the police officer ranks her preferences in the order (1) giving you a ticket, (2) not patrolling with you parked in the lot, (3) patrolling with you in the lot, and (4) not patrolling with you parked illegally.

(a)   Describe this as a matrix game, assuming that you are playing a zero-sum game with the officer.
(b)   Solve this matrix game for its optimal mixed strategies and its value.

◆   (c)   Discuss whether it is reasonable or not to assume that this game is zero-sum.
◆   (d)   Assuming that you play this parking game each working day of the year, how do you implement an optimal mixed strategy?

12.   Describe how a pure strategy for a player in a matrix game can be considered as merely a special case of a mixed strategy.

■   13.   (a)   Describe in detail *one* pure strategy for the player who moves first in the game of tic-tac-toe. (This strategy must tell how to respond to all possible moves of the other player.) (*Hint:* You may wish to make use of the symmetry in the 3×3 grid in this game; that is, there are one "center" box, four "corner" boxes, and four "side" boxes.)
         (b)   Is your strategy optimal in the sense that it will guarantee the first player a tie (and possibly a win) in the game?

14.   In the matching-pennies example, consider the case where Player I favors heads H over tails T. For example, assume that Player I plays H three-fourths of the time and T only one-fourth of the time—a nonoptimal mixed strategy. What should Player II do if he knows this?

15.   Assume in the nonsymmetrical matching example that Player II is using the nonoptimal mixed strategy $(p, 1 - p) = (\frac{1}{2}, \frac{1}{2})$; that is, he is playing H and T with the same frequency. What should Player I do in this case if she knows this?

16.   You plan to manufacture a new product for sale next year, and you can decide to make either a small quantity, in anticipation of a poor economy and few sales, or a large quantity, hoping for brisk sales. Your expected profits are indicated in the following table.

		Economy	
		Poor	Good
Quantity	Small	$500,000	$300,000
	Large	$100,000	$900,000

If you want to avoid risk and believe that the economy is playing an optimal mixed strategy against you in a two-person zero-sum game, then what is your optimal mixed strategy and the resulting expected value? Discuss some alternative ways that you may go about making your decision.

■　17.　Consider the following miniature poker game with two players, I and II. Each antes $1. Each player is dealt either a high card H or a low card L, with probability ½. Player I then folds or bets $1. If Player I bets, then Player II either folds, calls, or raises $1. Finally, if II raises, I either folds or calls.

Most choices by the players are rather obvious, at least to anyone who has played poker: if either player holds H, that player always bets or raises if he or she gets the choice. The question remains of how often one should bluff—that is, continue to play (by calling or raising) while holding a low card in the hope that one's opponent also holds a low card.

This poker game can be represented by the following matrix game, wherein the payoffs are the expected winnings for Player I (depending upon the random deal) and the dominated strategies have been eliminated:

		Player II (when holding L)		
		Folds	Calls	Raises
Player I (when holding L)	Folds initially	−.25	0	.25
	Bets first and folds later	0	0	−.25
	Bets first and calls later	−.25	−.25	0

(a)　Are there any strategies in this matrix game that a player should avoid playing?
(b)　Solve this game.
(c)　Which player is in the more favored position?
(d)　Should one ever bluff?

Partial-Conflict Games

Consider the following three two-person variable-sum games. Discuss the players' possible behavior

when these games are played in a noncooperative manner (i.e., with no prior communication or agreements). The first payoff is to the row player; the second, to the column player. Are the Nash equilibria in these games sensible? Why or why not?

18.

	Player II	
Player I	(4, 4)	(1, 3)
	(3, 1)	(2, 2)

19.　Battle of the sexes:

		She buys a ticket for:	
		Boxing	Ballet
He buys a ticket for:	Boxing	(4, 3)	(2, 2)
	Ballet	(1, 1)	(3, 4)

20.

	Player II	
Player I	(2, 1)	(4, 2)
	(1, 4)	(3, 3)

Larger Games

21.　For the preferences of the players given in the text—*xyz* for *X* (chair), *yzx* for *Y*, and *zxy* for *Z*—verify that the strategy choices of *x* by *X*, *y* by *Y*, and *x* by *Z* are a Nash equilibrium. Does this equilibrium seem to you defensible as the social choice by the voters? Under what circumstances might the voters choose these strategies rather than their sophisticated strategies?

22.　What is the sophisticated outcome, and the sophisticated strategies of voters, if the preferences of *X* (chair), *Y*, and *Z* are *xyz*, *yxz*, and *zyx*, respectively? What are the other Nash equilibria in this game? Can tacit or revealed deception help the chair?

23.　Assume that the preferences of the three voters are the same as those in Exercise 22, but *X* does not have a tie-breaking vote. What is the sophisticated outcome? Can tacit or revealed deception help *X*?

24. Assume that the preference of Y in Exercise 22 changes from yxz to yzx, but the preferences of the other two voters remain the same. When there is no chair, show that all three possible outcomes can occur under sophisticated voting. Can tacit or revealed deception ensure X, Y, or Z's best outcome if that voter has a tie-breaking vote?

25. Extend the game tree of the truel in Figure 15.6 to allow the additional possibility that if A does not shoot initially, then B has the choice of shooting or not shooting C. Will A, in fact, not shoot initially, and will B then shoot C?

26. Extend the game tree in Exercise 25 to still another level to allow for the possibility that if A does not shoot initially, and B shoots C, then A has the choice of shooting or not shooting B. What will happen in this case?

27. Change Exercise 26 to allow for the possibility that if A does not shoot initially, and B shoots *or does not shoot* C, then A has the choice of shooting or not shooting B. What will happen in this case?

◆ **28.** What general conclusions would you draw in light of your answers to Exercises 25, 26, and 27?

Additional Exercises

Consider the following three two-person zero-sum games, wherein the payoffs represent gains to the row Player I and losses to the column Player II:

29. $\begin{bmatrix} 3 & 6 \\ 5 & 4 \end{bmatrix}$

30. $\begin{bmatrix} -1 & 3 \\ 2 & 0 \end{bmatrix}$

31. $\begin{bmatrix} 6 & 5 & 6 & 5 \\ 1 & 4 & 2 & -1 \\ 8 & 5 & 7 & 5 \\ 0 & 2 & 6 & 2 \end{bmatrix}$

(a) Which of these games have saddlepoints?
(b) Find the optimal strategy for Player I and for Player II, and the value for those games given in part (a).
(c) List dominated strategies in these games that the players should avoid because the resulting payoffs are worse than those for some alternative strategy.

32. Consider the game played between the opposing goalie and a soccer player who, after a penalty, is allowed a free kick. The kicker can elect to kick toward one of the two corners of the net, or else aim for the center of the goal. The goalie can decide to commit in advance (before the kicker's kick) to either one of the sides, or else remain in the center until he sees the direction of the kick. This two-person zero-sum game can be represented as follows, wherein the payoffs are the probability of scoring a goal:

		Goalie		
		Breaks left	Remains center	Breaks right
Kicker	Kicks left	.5	.9	.9
	Kicks center	.1	0	.1
	Kicks right	.9	.9	.5

If we assume that decisions between the left or right side are made symmetrically (i.e., with equal probabilities), then this game can be represented by a 2×2 matrix, where $.7 = (\frac{1}{2})(.5) + (\frac{1}{2})(.9)$:

		Goalie	
		Remains center	Breaks side
Kicker	Kicks center	0	1
	Kicks side	.9	.7

Find the optimal mixed strategies for the kicker and goalie and the value of this game.

■ 33. (a) Describe in detail *one* pure strategy for the player who moves second in the game of tic-tac-toe.
(b) Is your strategy in part (a) optimal in the sense that it will guarantee the second player a tie (and possibly a win) in the game?

▲ 34. Find a two-person zero-sum game with a saddlepoint in which the successive elimination of dominated strategies does *not* lead to the saddlepoint (unlike the 3×3 location game; you may restrict yourself to 3×3 games).

35. On an overcast morning, deciding whether to carry your umbrella can be viewed as a game between yourself and nature as follows:

		Weather	
		Rain	No rain
You	Carry umbrella	Stay dry	Lug umbrella
	Leave it home	Get wet	Hands free

Let's assume that you are willing to assign the following numerical payoffs to these outcomes, and that you are also willing to make decisions on the basis of expected values (that is, average payoffs):

(Carry umbrella, rain) $= -2$
(Carry umbrella, no rain) $= -1$
(Leave it home, rain) $= -5$
(Leave it home, no rain) $= 3$

(a) If the weather forecast says there is a 50% chance of rain, should you carry your umbrella or not? What if you believe there is a 75% chance of rain?

(b) If you are conservative and wish to protect against the worst case, what pure strategy should you pick?
(c) If you are rather paranoid and believe that nature will pick an optimal strategy in this two-person zero-sum game, then what strategy should you choose?
(d) Another approach to this decision problem is to assign payoffs to represent what your *regret* will be after you know nature's decision. In this case, each such payoff is the best payoff you could have received under that state of nature, minus the corresponding payoff in the previous table:

		Weather	
		Rain	No Rain
You	Carry umbrella	$0 = (-2) - (-2)$	$4 = 3 - (-1)$
	Leave it home	$3 = (-2) - (-5)$	$0 = 3 - 3$

What strategy should you select if you wish to minimize your maximum possible regret?

Consider the two following two-person variable-sum games. Discuss the players' possible behavior when these games are played in a noncooperative manner (i.e., with no prior communication or agreements). The first payoff is to the row player, the second to the column player.

36.

	Player II	
Player I	(2, 4)	(4, 3)
	(1, 2)	(3, 1)

37.

	Player II	
Player I	(3, 4)	(2, 3)
	(1, 2)	(4, 1)

■ 38.   Under a voting system called approval voting, a voter can vote for as many alternatives as he or she wishes. (If there are three alternatives, the only undominated strategies of a voter under approval voting are to vote for his or her best, or two best, choices.) If voters X, Y, and Z have paradox-of-voting preferences of *xyz*, *yzx*, and *zxy*, and X is the chair, show that x is the sophisticated outcome, obtained by all voters voting for their two best choices.

▲ 39.   Show by example that approval voting is not immune to the paradox of the chair's position.

40.   If a fourth player is added to the original truel, show that every player will have an incentive to shoot another (as in a duel).

	A	B	C	D	E
1		Pitched Fastball	Pitched Curveball	Batter's Mix (1-q,q)	Batter's Expectations (E_F,E_C)
2	Expected Fastball	0.250	0.150	0.75	0.213
3	Expected Curveball	0.100	0.400	0.25	0.211
4	Pitcher's Mix (1-p,p))	0.63	0.37		
5	Pitcher's Expectations (E_F,E_C)	0.2125	0.2125		

FIGURE 15.7

TECHNOLOGY CORNER

Modeling Mixed Strategies with Two Alternatives

Spreadsheets allow the analysis of mixed strategies. For example, a mixing of fastballs and curveballs for pitcher and batter can be modeled by the spreadsheet shown in Figure 15.7.

The four decimals in the upper left corner indicate the probabilities that the batter will make a hit when the batter expects a fastball or curveball and the pitcher throws a fastball or curveball. Entries **D2** and **D3** contain the probabilities that the pitcher will throw a fastball and a curveball. In the situation modeled in the spreadsheet, the pitcher throws about times as many fastballs as curveballs. Similarly, entries **B4** and **C4** model the situation where the batter anticipates about twice as many fastballs as curveballs. Each pair of entries must sum to 1. For this reason, entry **D3** can be defined as =1-D2 and entry **C4** can be defined as =1-B4. The pitcher wants to mix the throws to minimize the overall batting average; the batter wants to mix her anticipations to maximize the average. In this chapter we found these optimal mixes by solving for the intersection of lines. Using spreadsheets, we can immediately see the effects of various mixes by pitcher and batter.

The batter's expected values for anticipating a fastball and a curveball are computed using the formula =B2*B4+C2*C4 in entry **E2** and the formula =B3*B4+C3*C4 in entry **E3**. Formulas for the batter's expected value of pitching a fastball and a curveball are computed in entries **B5** and **C5** using the formulas =B2*D2+B3*D3 and =B2*D2+B3*D3. An optimal mixed solution produces the same expected value in each of these four locations (ignoring slight rounding variations). In this scenario, the pitcher's 3-to-1 mix and the batter's 63% to 37% mix is expected to yield an overall hit average of about .212.

TASK 1.   Suppose the batter works hard on hitting fastballs, and improves her hit record for fastballs, when anticipated, from .250 to .350. Recompute the pitcher's mix and batter's mix which solve the resulting mixed strategy. How does the batter's overall hit average change?

TASK 2.   Suppose the batter has a goal of raising her overall hitting average to at least .270. Assuming her fastball hit record (when anticipated) is .350, how high must she raise her curveball hit record (when anticipated) from its present .400 in order to achieve this goal? (Remember that the pitcher's and batter's ratios should change when the .400 is raised.)

Modeling Mixed Strategies with More Than Two Alternatives

Spreadsheets can easily be adapted to model situations with more than two alternatives. The spreadsheet in Figure 15.8 models a situation in which the batter and the pitcher choose among three different types of pitches. As before, each expected value for the batter is a sum of products. For example, entry **F2**, computed as **=B2*B5+C2*C5+D2*D5,** is the expected value of anticipating a fastball. Likewise, the pitcher's expected value for throwing a fastball, entry **B6**, is computed as **=B2*E2+B3*E3+B4*E4.** For the model shown in Figure 15.8, the mixed strategy leads to an overall hitting average of .180.

TASK 3.   In the model shown in Figure 15.8, what mix of pitches solves the mixed strategy? What mix of throws does the batter anticipate?

TASK 4.   Suppose the batter improves her ability to hit curveballs (when anticipated) so that her average rises from .200 to .400. Find the optimal mixes for pitcher and batter in this situation.

Exploration

For the model of Figure 15.8, suppose the batter notices that the pitcher never throws knuckleballs, and switches to a 50–50 mix of fastballs and curveballs. How will the pitcher change his mix of throws? Assuming the batter notices the pitcher's new mix, how might the batter change her mix?

writing projects

1 ▸ In tennis, one player often prefers to play from the baseline while her opponent prefers a serve-and-volley game (i.e., likes to come to the net). The baseline player attempts to hit passing shots. This player has a choice of hitting "down the line" or "crosscourt." The net player must often guess correctly which direction the ball will go in order to cover the shot. Formulate this situation as a duel game and discuss appropriate strategies for the players.

2 ▸ Consider a conflict that you, personally, had—with a parent, a boss, a girlfried or boyfriend, or some other acquaintance—in which each of you had to make a choice without being sure of what the other person would do. What strategies did you seriously consider adopting, and what options do you think the other person considered? What plausible outcomes do you think each set of strategy choices would have led to? How would you rank

	A	B	C	D	E	F
1		Pitched Fastball	Pitched Knuckleball	Pitched Curveball	Batter's Mix (p_F,p_K,p_C)	Batter's Expectations (E_F,E_K,E_C)
2	Expected Fastball	0.300	0.150	0.150	0.4	0.18
3	Expected Knuckleball	0.100	0.300	0.200	0.2	0.18
4	Expected Curveball	0.100	0.150	0.200	0.4	0.18
5	Pitcher's Mix (p_F,p_K,p_C)	0.2	0	0.8		
6	Pitcher's Expectations (E_F,E_K,E_C)	0.18	0.18	0.18		

FIGURE 15.8

these outcomes from best to worst, and how do you think the other player would have ranked them? Analyze the resulting game, and state whether you think you and the other person made optimal choices. If not, what upset your or the other person's rationality?

3 ▶ It is sometimes argued that game theory does not take account of the (irrational?) emotions of people, such as anger, jealousy, or love. What is your opinion about this question? Give an example, real or hypothetical, that supports your position, paying particular attention to whether the players acted consistently with, or contrarily to, their preferences.

4 ▶ Quentin Tarantino's films *Reservoir Dogs* (1992) and *Pulp Fiction* (1994) both have truels, but the choices that the characters make in each are completely different. Does the truel analysis offer any insight into why?

log$_{10}$ y = b + a log$_{10}$ x

LOGA

> *"Mathematicians search for and classify numerical, geometrical, and even abstract patterns."*

Mathematics is the study of patterns and relationships. It can be used to characterize the spiral growth of a sunflower's seeds, measure increase in populations, and calculate the effects of travel near the speed of light.

Mathematicians search for and classify numerical, geometrical, and even abstract patterns. In these chapters we follow some of those searches, concentrating on geometrical patterns, but also looking at what geometry

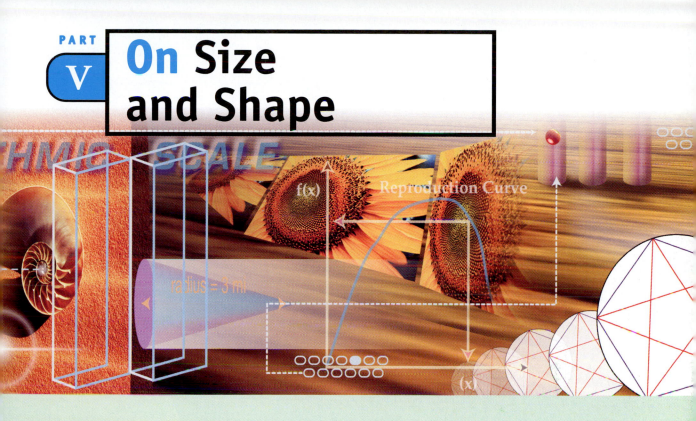

can express about some numerical patterns. Examining the underlying patterns helps explain why some of the objects in the world around us have the shapes that they do and trains us to recognize the same patterns as they arise in contemporary problems.

We investigate patterns in some BIG things: King Kong, tall trees, high mountains, large populations, the universe, and even symmetries that extend infinitely in all directions. We look at how an animal's size can greatly influence its form.

Intertwined with size, shape is also a theme for these chapters. We examine why the shape of an animal must change as the animal grows. We ask: What is the shape of the universe? We analyze what shapes crystals can have. We enjoy the patterned beauty of African crafts and the prints of M. C. Escher.

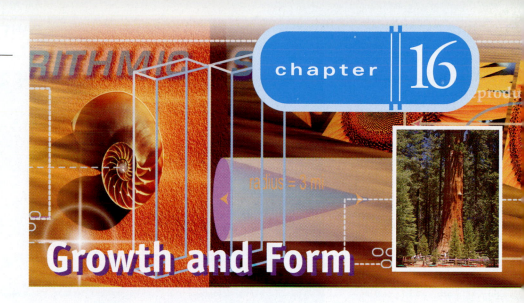

chapter 16

Growth and Form

Fantasy films have made us familiar with assorted giant creatures, including King Kong, Godzilla, and the 50-foot-high grasshoppers in *The Beginning of the End.* We also find supergiants in literature, such as the giant of "Jack and the Beanstalk," Giant Pope and Giant Pagan of *The Pilgrim's Progress,* and the Brobdingnagians of *Gulliver's Travels.*

Much as we appreciate those stories, even from an early age we don't really believe in monsters and giants. But could such beings ever exist? What problems would their enormous size cause them? How would they have to adapt in order to cope? (See Figure 16.1.)

Every species survives by adapting to its environment. In particular, it faces the **problem of scale:** how to adapt and survive at the different sizes from the beginning of life to the final size of a mature adult. For example, consider the giant panda, which ranges from barely 1 lb at birth to 275 lb in adulthood. A baby panda is at risk of being crushed by its mother; an adult panda needs to eat a great deal of food.

As a contrasting example, consider the horse. If a newborn foal weighed as little as a newborn panda, the foal would be too small to keep up with the moving herd and could not survive. An adult horse weighs much more than a panda and has to consume much more food; but the horse can move much more quickly and cover great distances, to take advantage of wide-ranging sources of sustenance.

There have been large land mammals (mammoths) and huge sea mammals (the blue whale) — not to mention the dinosaurs. But the tallest humans have been only 9 to 10 feet tall; the largest mammoth was 16 feet at the shoulder (about twice as tall as an elephant); and even the tallest dinosaur, *Supersaurus,* stood only 40 feet high.

FIGURE 16.1
Could King Kong
actually exist?

But what about supergiants and utterly huge monsters? That they have never existed suggests that there are physical limits to size. In fact, with a few simple principles of geometry, we can show not only that lizards and apes of such size are impossible, but also that none of the living beings and objects in our world could exist, unchanged in shape, on a vastly different scale, larger or smaller.

Geometric Similarity

The powerful mathematical idea that we use is *geometric similarity.*

> Two objects are **geometrically similar** if they have the same shape, regardless of the materials of which they are made.

Similar objects need not be of the same size, but measurements of corresponding distances on the two objects must be proportional. For example, when a photo is enlarged, it is enlarged by the same factor in both the horizontal and vertical directions—in fact, in any direction whatever (such as a diagonal). We call this enlargement factor the *linear scaling factor.*

> The **linear scaling factor** of two geometrically similar objects is the ratio of a length of any part of the second to the corresponding part of the first.

FIGURE 16.2
Two geometrically similar
photographs.

In the photos in Figure 16.2, the linear scaling factor is 3; the enlargement is three times as wide and three times as high as the original. In fact, every pair of points goes to a new pair of points three times as far apart as the original ones.

We notice that the enlargement can be divided into $3 \times 3 = 9$ rectangles, each the size of the original. Hence, the enlargement has $3 \times 3 = 3^2 = 9$ times the area of the original. More generally, if the linear scaling factor is some general number L (not necessarily 3), the resulting enlargement has an area $L \times L = L^2$ ("L squared") times the area of the original.

> *The area of a scaled-up object goes up with the square of the linear scaling factor.*

We symbolize the relationship between the area A and the linear scaling factor L by

$$A \propto L^2$$

where the symbol $\propto$ is read as "is proportional to" or "scales as."

What about enlarging three-dimensional objects? If we take a cube and enlarge it by a linear scaling factor of 3, it becomes three times as long, three times as high, and three times as deep as the original (see Figure 16.3).

What about volume? The enlarged cube has three layers, each with $3 \times 3 = 9$ little cubes, each the same size as the original. Thus, the total volume is $3 \times 3 \times 3 = 3^3 = 27$ times as much as the original cube.

> *The* volume *of a scaled-up object goes up with the* cube *of the linear scaling factor.*

Denoting the volume by V, we can write

$$V \propto L^3$$

Thus, for an object enlarged by a linear scaling factor of L, the enlargement has L^3 ("L cubed") $= L \times L \times L$ times the volume of the original. Like the relationship between surface area and L^2, this relationship holds even for irregularly shaped objects, such as science fiction monsters.

We observe, however, that the area of each face (side) of the enlarged cube is $3^2 = 9$ times as large as that of a face of the original cube, just as the area of the photo enlarged by a factor of 3 has nine times the area of the original. Since this fact is true for all six faces, the total surface area of the enlarged cube is nine times as much as the total surface area of the original cube.

More generally, for objects of any shape, the total *surface area* of a scaled-up object goes up with the *square* of the linear scaling factor. Thus, the surface area of an object scaled up by a factor of L is L^2 times the surface area of the original; this feature holds true even for irregular shapes.

Before we discuss scaling real three-dimensional objects, you should understand the pitfalls of the language for describing increases and decreases.

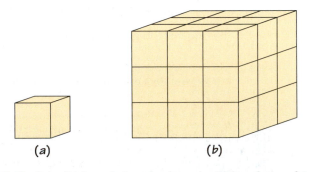

(a)   (b)

FIGURE 16.3   Cube (b) is made by enlarging cube (a) by a factor of 3.

The Language of Growth, Enlargement, and Decrease

In 1976, the average price of a home in Madison [Wisconsin] was $38,323—about 108 percent less than in 1988.

—*Madison Business*, March 1991, p. 38.

House prices in Madison rose substantially, but we explore why this is an incorrect and confusing way to say so. In 1988 the average price was $80,000, which you can verify was 2.08 times the 1976 average price. What the author meant to say, in correct language, is that the 1988 price was 208% *of* the 1976 price, or that the 1988 price was 108% *more than* the 1976 price.

> "x% of A" or "x% as large as" means $\frac{x}{100} \times A$.
>
> "x% more than A" means A plus x% of A, in other words, $(1 + \frac{x}{100}) \times A$. Saying that A has "increased by x%" means the same thing.
>
> "x% less than A" means A minus x% of A, in other words, $(1 - \frac{x}{100}) \times A$. Saying that A has "decreased by x%" means the same thing.

So, to say "108% less than" $80,000 would mean $80,000(1 - \frac{108}{100}) = \$80,000 (1 - 1.08) = \$80,000(-0.08) = -\$6400$. Clearly this is not what the author intended to say.

The terms "of," "times," and "as much as" refer to *multiplication* of the original amount, while the terms "more," "larger," and "greater" refer to *adding* to the original amount. For instance, "five times as much" means the same as "four times more than" (the original plus four times as much in addition). Similarly, the relationship of the original amount to the larger amount can be expressed in multiplicative terms ("one-fifth as much," "20% as much") or in subtractive terms ("four-fifths less than," "80% less than").

These two ways of expressing change are similar in their phrasing, and people (even people in the media) often say "five times more than" when they mean "five times as much" (or even "five times less than" when they mean "one-fifth as much"). All you can do is be aware of the potential confusion, try to figure out what was meant, and be careful in your own expression. In particular, *don't use both* times *and* more *together*.

Finally, in discussions of percent we need to distinguish *percent* from percentage *points:* if support for the president has decreased from 60% to 30%, it has dropped 30 *percentage points* but decreased 50% (because the drop of 30 percentage points is 50% of the original 60 percentage points).

E X A M P L E   *What About Those Homes?*

Returning to the Madison home prices, how can we state correctly what the author was trying to say? The 1976 figure, $38,323, is about 0.48 times the 1988 figure of $80,000 (38,323/80,000 = 0.48), or 48% of $80,000; so the writer could say "about 48% of what it is in 1988" or "about 52% less than in 1990."

What if the writer wanted to use the 1976 figure as a base (i.e., as the 100% for the calculation)? The 1988 price is about 2.08 times the 1976 price, so the 1988 price is "208% of," or "108% more than," the 1976 price.

Caution: The dollar comparisons here can be misleading, since they do not take into account that a dollar was worth less in purchasing power in 1988 than in 1976, because of inflation. Shortly we will explore the "numerical similarity" of dollars in different years and show how to take inflation into account.

Another caution: What does the author mean by "average": the mean or the median (see pages 213–215)? Prices of houses are skewed, with a small number of very expensive houses (as noted on page 270), and the mean may be much larger than the median. Government statisticians and economists usually use the median. The Madison housing article notes that the median price in 1976 was $34,000, so the $38,323 "average" must be the mean.   ◆

Numerical Similarity

House prices in different years are not directly comparable, in part because of inflation—a dollar today is not worth the same as a dollar in 1976. However, based on measures of inflation, we can determine the equivalent today of a 1976 price, or how much a 1976 dollar would be worth today.

The official measure of inflation is the Consumer Price Index (CPI), prepared by the Bureau of Labor Statistics. We describe and use here the CPI-U, the index for all urban consumers, which covers about 80% of the U.S. population and is the index of inflation that is usually referred to in newspaper and magazine articles.

Each month, the Bureau of Labor Statistics determines the average cost of a "market basket" of goods, including food, housing, transportation, clothing, and other items. It compares this cost to the cost of the same (or comparable) goods in a base period. The base period used to construct the CPI-U is 1982–1984. The index for 1982–1984 is set to 100, and the CPI-U for other years is calculated by using the proportion

$$\frac{\text{CPI for other year}}{100} = \frac{\text{cost of market basket in other year}}{\text{cost of market basket in base period}}$$

For example, the cost of the market basket in 1976 (in 1976 dollars) was 0.569 times the cost in 1982–1984 (in 1982–1984 dollars), so the CPI for 1976 is 100×0.569, or 56.9.

TABLE 16.1		U.S. Consumer Price Index (1982–1984 = 100)							
—	—	1931	15.2	1951	26.0	1971	40.5	1991	136.2
—	—	1932	13.7	1952	26.6	1972	41.8	1992	140.3
1913	9.9	1933	13.0	1953	26.7	1973	44.4	1993	144.5
1914	10.0	1934	13.4	1954	26.9	1974	49.3	1994	148.2
1915	10.1	1935	13.7	1955	26.8	1975	53.8	1995	152.4
1916	10.9	1936	13.9	1956	27.2	1976	56.9	1996	156.9
1917	12.8	1937	14.4	1957	28.1	1977	60.6	1997	160.5
1918	15.1	1938	14.1	1958	28.9	1978	65.2	1998	163.0
1919	17.3	1939	13.9	1959	29.1	1979	72.6	1999 (est.)	166.0
1920	20.0	1940	14.0	1960	29.6	1980	82.4	2000 (est.)	168.9
1921	17.9	1941	14.7	1961	29.9	1981	90.9		
1922	16.8	1942	16.3	1962	30.2	1982	96.5		
1923	17.1	1943	17.3	1963	30.6	1983	99.6		
1924	17.1	1944	17.6	1964	31.0	1984	103.9		
1925	17.5	1945	18.0	1965	31.5	1985	107.6		
1926	17.7	1946	19.5	1966	32.4	1986	109.6		
1927	17.4	1947	22.3	1967	33.4	1987	113.6		
1928	17.1	1948	24.1	1968	34.8	1988	118.3		
1929	17.1	1949	23.8	1969	36.7	1989	124.0		
1930	16.7	1950	24.1	1970	38.8	1990	130.7		

Note: This is the CPI-U index, which covers all urban consumers, about 80% of the U.S. population. Each index is an average for all cities for the year. The basis for the index is the period 1982–1984, for which the index was set equal to 100. SOURCE: http://stats.bls.gov/

Table 16.1 shows the average CPI for each year from 1913 through 1998, with estimates for 1999 and 2000. This table can be used to convert the cost of an item in dollars for one year to what it would cost in dollars in a different year, using the proportion

$$\frac{\text{cost in year A}}{\text{cost in year B}} = \frac{\text{CPI for year A}}{\text{CPI for year B}}$$

EXAMPLE   *The Price of a House and the Value of a Dollar*

We convert the average cost of a Madison house in year 1976 dollars into a price in year 2000 dollars.

We see from Table 16.1 that the CPI for 1976 is 56.9 and the CPI for 2000 is estimated to be 168.9. The average cost of a Madison house in 1976 was $38,323.

Using the proportion, we have

$$\frac{\text{cost in 2000}}{\text{cost in 1976}} = \frac{\text{CPI for 2000}}{\text{CPI for 1976}}$$

or

$$\frac{\text{cost in 2000}}{\$38{,}323} = \frac{168.9}{56.9}$$

so that

$$\text{cost in 2000} = \$38{,}323 \times \frac{168.9}{56.9} = \$38{,}323 \times 2.968 = \$113{,}757$$

The 2.968 is the *scaling factor* for converting 1976 dollars to 2000 dollars. What we are observing is a proportion, or *numerical similarity,* between 1976 dollars and 2000 dollars, analogous to the geometrical similarity that we studied earlier. To convert from 2000 dollars to 1976 dollars, we would multiply by 1/2.968, or 0.337.   ◆

We now move from scaling up one-dimensional dollars and two-dimensional photographs toward examining similarities between three-dimensional objects, including animals, buildings, and trees. Scaling three-dimensional objects involves considering the scaling of physical quantities such as distance, weight, area, and volume. Before we consider the possibility of a King Kong or a building ten times as tall as the Sears Tower in Chicago, we need to discuss the units in which quantities are measured.

Measuring Length, Area, Volume, and Weight

We start with a brief introduction to the common units in which various physical quantities are measured, together with a handy table of scaling factors (often called *conversion factors*) and examples of how to convert successfully from one system of units to another.

U.S. Customary System

You are probably familiar with the common units of the *U.S. Customary System* of measurement and their abbreviations. But please examine Table 16.2 and pay close attention to the systematic way of converting from one unit to another and to the expression of approximate numbers in scientific notation. The symbol ≈ means "is approximately equal to."

TABLE 16.2	Units of the U.S. Customary System

Distance:
1 mile (mi) = 1760 yards (yd) = 5280 feet (ft) = 63,360 in.
1 yard (yd) = 3 feet (ft) = 36 in.
 1 foot (ft) = 12 inches (in.)

Area:
1 square mile = 1 mi × 1 mi = 5280 ft × 5280 ft
$$= 27,878,400 \text{ ft}^2 \approx 28 \times 10^6 \text{ ft}^2$$
$$= 63,360 \text{ in.} \times 63,360 \text{ in.}$$
$$= 4,014,489,600 \text{ in.}^2 \approx 4 \times 10^9 \text{ in.}^2$$
$$= 640 \text{ acres}$$
1 acre = 43,560 ft^2

Volume:
1 cubic mile = 1 mi × 1 mi × 1 mi
$$= 5280 \text{ ft} \times 5280 \text{ ft} \times 5280 \text{ ft}$$
$$= 147,197,952,000 \times \text{ft}^3$$
$$\approx 147 \times 10^9 \times \text{ft}^3$$
$$= 63,360 \text{ in.} \times 63,360 \text{ in.} \times 63,360 \text{ in.}$$
$$\approx 2.5 \times 10^{14} \text{ in.}^3$$
1 U.S. gallon (gal) = 4 U.S. quarts (qt) = 231 in.^{3}, exactly

Weight:
1 ton (t) = 2000 pounds (lb)

Metric System

With the notable exception of the United States, almost every country of the world uses the same measurement system in science, industry, and commerce — the metric system. It was first proposed in France by Gabriel Mouton, Vicar of Lyons, in 1670, and was adopted in France in 1795. The fundamental unit of length, the *meter,* was originally defined to be one ten-millionth of the distance from the North Pole to the equator, as measured on the meridian through Paris. Later, the meter was redefined as the distance between two lines marked on a platinum-iridium bar kept at the International Bureau of Weights and Measures, near Paris, where the bar is kept at a temperature of 0°C. Finally, in 1960 the meter was redefined in terms of a standard reproducible in any laboratory, namely, 1,650,763.73 times the wavelength of the orange-red light emitted by atoms of the gas krypton-86 when an electrical charge is passed through them.

All other units of length, area, and volume are *defined* in terms of the meter; for example, a centimeter is a hundredth of a meter. The metric unit of weight, the *kilogram,* is defined as the weight of a platinum-iridium standard.

Table 16.3 lists the units of the metric system.

TABLE 16.3   **Units of the Metric System**

Distance:

 1 meter (m) = 100 centimeters (cm)

1 kilometer (km) = 1000 meters (m)

    = 100,000 centimeters (cm) = 1×10^5 cm

Area:

1 square meter (m²) = 1 m × 1 m

     = 100 cm × 100 cm = 10,000 (cm²) = 1×10^4 cm²

 1 hectare (ha) = 10,000 m²

Volume:

  1 liter (l) = 1000 cm³ = 0.001 m³

1 cubic meter (m³) = 1 m × 1 m × 1 m

    = 100 cm × 100 cm × 100 cm

    = 1,000,000 cm³ = 1×10^6 cm³ (or cc)

Weight:

1 kilogram (kg) = 1000 grams (g)

Converting Between Systems

What are the scaling factors between the U.S. Customary System and the metric system? Since 1960, the fundamental units of the U.S. Customary System, the yard (for length) and the pound (for weight), have been *defined* in terms of metric units, so that we have

 1 yd = 0.9144 m, exactly

 1 lb = 0.45359237 kg, exactly

The scaling factors for other units are shown in Table 16.4.

  We illustrate how to convert a measurement in one unit to the corresponding measurement in a different unit.

E X A M P L E *What's That in Feet?*

A foreign student tells her American student friends that she is 160 cm tall. They naturally ask how much that is in feet and inches.

  We approach the conversion by using the scaling factor that 1 cm = 0.393701 in.:

 160 cm = 160 × 1 cm ≈ 160 × 0.393701 in.

$$\approx 62.9 \text{ in.} = 62.9 \text{ in.} \times \frac{1 \text{ ft}}{12 \text{ in.}} \approx \frac{62.9}{12} \text{ ft} \approx 5.25 \text{ ft}$$

TABLE 16.4	Conversions Between the U.S. Customary System and the Metric System

Distance:
1 in. = 2.54 cm, exactly
 1 ft = 12 in. = 12 × 2.54 cm = 30.48 cm = 0.3048 m, exactly
1 yd = 0.9144 m, exactly
1 mi = 5280 ft = 5280 × 30.48 cm
      = 160,934.4 cm, exactly ≈ 1.61 km
1 cm ≈ 0.3937 in. ≈ 0.4 in.
 1 m ≈ 39.37 in. ≈ 3.281 ft
1 km ≈ 0.621 mi

Area:
1 hectare (ha) = 2.47 acres

Volume:
1 cubic meter (m^3) = 1000 liters = 264.2 U.S. gallons = 35.31 ft^3
      1 liter (l) = 1000 cm^3 = 1.057 U.S. quarts (qt)

Weight:
1 lb = 0.45359237 kg, exactly
1 kg ≈ 2.205 lb

However, since we normally give height in feet and a whole number of inches, the height is

$$62.9 \text{ in.} = 5 \times (12 \text{ in.}) + 2.9 \text{ in.} = 5 \text{ ft} + 2.9 \text{ in.} \approx 5 \text{ ft } 3 \text{ in.}$$

Another way to approach the problem is by means of a proportion, similar to the one used with the CPI:

$$\frac{\text{height in inches}}{\text{height in cm}} = \frac{\text{length of 1 inch in inches}}{\text{length of 1 inch in cm}} = \frac{1 \text{ in.}}{2.54 \text{ cm}}$$

Comparison of a meter stick with a yardstick, a liter with a quart, and a kilogram with a pound.

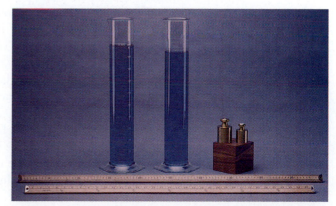

so that

$$\text{height in inches} = \text{height in cm} \times \frac{1 \text{ in.}}{2.54 \text{ cm}}$$

$$= 160 \text{ cm} \times \frac{1 \text{ in.}}{2.54 \text{ cm}} \approx 62.9 \text{ in.} \quad \blacklozenge$$

Scaling Real Objects

Real three-dimensional objects are made of matter, which has volume and mass. **Mass** is the aspect of matter that is affected by forces, according to physical laws. For example, your mass reacts to the gravitational force of the earth by staying close to it (and your mass exerts an equal force on the earth that tends to keep the earth close to you). We perceive the mass of an object when we try to move it (as in throwing a ball). When we try to lift an object, we perceive its mass as weight, due to the gravitational force that the earth exerts on it. As we will see, gravity exerts an enormous effect on the size and shape that objects and beings can assume.

Suppose that the two cubes in Figure 16.3 are made of steel, and that the first is 1 ft on a side and the second is 3 ft on a side. For each, its bottom face supports the weight of the entire cube. **Pressure** is the force per unit area, so the pressure exerted on the bottom face by the weight of the cube is equal to the weight of the cube divided by the area of the bottom face, or

$$P = \frac{W}{A}$$

A cubic foot of steel weighs about 500 lb (we say it has a **density** of 500 lb per cubic foot). The first cube weighs 500 lb and has a bottom face with area 1 ft^2, so the pressure exerted on this face is 500 lb/ft^2.

The second cube is 3 feet on a side. The area of the bottom face has increased with the square of the linear scaling factor, so it is $3^2 \times 1$ ft^2 = 9 ft^2. As we learned earlier in this chapter, volume goes up with the cube of the linear scaling factor. So this larger cube has a volume of $3^3 \times 1$ = 27 ft^3. Because both cubes are made of the same steel, the larger cube has 27 times as much steel as the smaller; hence it weighs 27 times as much as the smaller cube, or 27×500 lb = 13,500 lb.

When we divide this weight by the area of the bottom face (9 ft^2), we find that the pressure exerted on the bottom face is 1500 lb/ft^2, or three times the pressure on the bottom face of the original cube. This makes sense because over each 1 ft^2 area stands 3 ft^3 of steel. In general, if the linear scaling factor for the cube is

L, the pressure on the bottom face is L times as much. Using the notation of proportionality, we have $A \propto L^2$ and $W \propto V \propto L^3$, so

$$P = \frac{W}{A} \propto \frac{L^3}{L^2} \propto L$$

EXAMPLE *What About a 10-Foot Cube?*

If we scale the original cube of steel up to a cube 10 ft on a side, then the dimensions are

10 ft $\times$ 10 ft $\times$ 10 ft

The total volume is

$$V = \text{length} \times \text{width} \times \text{height}$$
$$= 10 \text{ ft} \times 10 \text{ ft} \times 10 \text{ ft} = 1000 \text{ ft}^3$$

The weight of the cube is

$$W = V \times \text{density}$$
$$= 1000 \text{ ft}^3 \times 500 \text{ lb/ft}^3 = 500,000 \text{ lb}$$

The area of the bottom face is

$$A = \text{length} \times \text{width}$$
$$= 10 \text{ ft} \times 10 \text{ ft} = 100 \text{ ft}^2$$

The pressure on the bottom face is

$$P = \frac{W}{A} = \frac{500,000 \text{ lb}}{100 \text{ ft}^2} = 5000 \text{ lb/ft}^2$$

This is 10 *times*—not "10 times *more* than"—the pressure on the bottom face of the original 1-foot cube. ◆

At some scale factor, the pressure on the bottom face will exceed the steel's ability to withstand that pressure—and the steel will deform under its own weight. That point for steel is reached for a cube about 3 miles on a side—the pressure exerted by the cube's weight exceeds the resistance to crushing (ability to withstand pressure, or **crushing strength**) of steel, which is about 7.5 million lb/ft². Since a mile is 5280 ft, a 3-mile-long cube of steel would be more than 15,000 times as long as the original 1-foot cube; that is, the linear scaling factor is more than 15,000. The pressure on the bottom face of the cube would therefore be more than 15,000 times as much as for the 1-foot cube, or 15,000 × 500 lb/ft² = 7.5 million lb/ft².

SPOTLIGHT
16.1

A Mile-High Building?

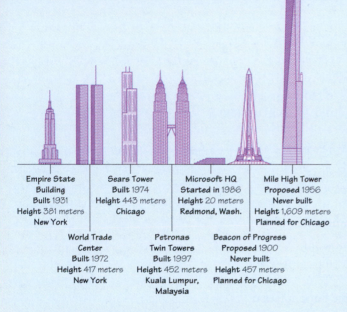

Empire State Building
Built 1931
Height 381 meters
New York

Sears Tower
Built 1974
Height 443 meters
Chicago

Microsoft HQ
Started in 1986
Height 20 meters
Redmond, Wash.

Mile High Tower
Proposed 1956
Never built
Height 1,609 meters
Planned for Chicago

World Trade Center
Built 1972
Height 417 meters
New York

Petronas Twin Towers
Built 1997
Height 452 meters
Kuala Lumpur, Malaysia

Beacon of Progress
Proposed 1900
Never built
Height 457 meters
Planned for Chicago

In 1956, the famous American architect Frank Lloyd Wright (1867–1959) proposed a mile-high tower for the Chicago waterfront. In the text, we focus on the problem of holding up the weight of such a structure, which would have to involve stronger materials and thicker walls and supporting columns.

But there are other limits to the height of a building. Some of these can also be addressed by similar strategies. For example, the bending of the building in the wind, which can go up dramatically with height, can be controlled by making the building stiffer.

Note: Drawings not to scale.

A mile-high building, however, might not be at all practical. For example, the enormous number of people (perhaps 100,000) living, working, or visiting in such a building would create enormous traffic problems (pedestrian, parking, deliveries) for blocks around.

Cost per square foot of usable area is an important economic consideration. Even if the building had the same width all the way up (as opposed to tapering near the top, like the Empire State Building), the space in the upper floors might not justify their additional expense. With increasing height, an increasingly larger proportion of the cross-sectional area of all floors of the building must be devoted to services, such as elevators, plumbing, and conduits for heat and air conditioning. It's not that there are more people on the top floors (or that they use more water than people on other floors!). But everyone entering the building and going to any floor needs to start in an elevator on the ground floor, so there must be more elevators and more elevator shafts. In an emergency evacuation, the people must walk down!

The architects of the Petronas Twin Towers, however, maintain that the main limit on height of a building is human physiology. Differences in air pressure between the top and bottom of a building impose a limit on how fast elevators can rise or drop without discomfort to passengers, thereby enforcing long travel times for "vertical commuters." Human psychology might also present some limits.

EXAMPLE   **What About the Petronas Towers?**

At 1482.6 ft (451.9 m), the twin Petronas Towers in Kuala Lumpur, Malaysia, are the tallest buildings in the world, if we don't count radio and television antennas. What is the pressure on the bottom of their walls?

The towers are made of reinforced concrete, which weighs about 160 lb/ft³. Over each square foot of bottom surface of one of their walls stands 1462 ft³ of reinforced concrete, which weighs $1482.6 \times 160 = 237,000$ lb. The pressure at the bottom of the wall, from the wall's weight alone, is 237,000 lb/ft². That's not counting the contents of the tower, which also must be supported!

Could we have a Super Petronas Tower 10 times as high? The bottom of its walls would have to support 2.4 million lb/ft². The crushing strength of reinforced concrete is about 8.5 million lb/ft³, which would leave some safety margin. (See Spotlight 16.1 for more on tall buildings.)   ◆

Sorry, No King Kongs

Unfortunately, the resistance of bone to crushing is not nearly as great as that of steel. This fact helps to explain why there couldn't be any King Kongs (unless they were made of steel!). A King Kong scaled up by a factor of 20 would weigh $20^3 = 8000$ times as much. Though the weight increases with the cube of the linear scaling factor, the ability to support the weight—as measured by the cross-sectional area of the bones, like the area of the bottom face of the cube in Figure 16.3—increases only with the square of the linear scaling factor.

These simple consequences of the geometry of scaling apply not only to super-monsters but also to other objects, such as trees and mountains.

How Tall Can a Tree Be?

Galileo suggested that no tree could grow taller than 300 feet (see Spotlight 16.2). The world's tallest trees are giant sequoias, which grow only on the west coast of the United States, and hence were unknown to Galileo. They can grow to almost 370 feet (Figure 16.4).

What can limit the height of a tree? If the roots do not adequately anchor it, a tall tree can blow over. (This, in fact, happened in 1990 to the world's then tallest tree, the Dyerville Giant, a giant sequoia in Humboldt Redwoods State Park in California.) The tree could buckle or snap under its own weight and the force of a strong wind. The wood at the bottom will begin to crush if there is too much weight above. Finally, there is a limit to how far the tree can lift water and minerals from the roots to the leaves.

Could a tree be a mile high? To make an easy but rough estimate of the pressure at the base of the tree due to gravity, let's model the tree as a perfectly vertical cylinder. Over each square foot at the bottom, there is 5280 ft³ of cells of wood,

FIGURE 16.4
Even these giant sequoias can grow no taller than their form and materials allow.

SPOTLIGHT

16.2

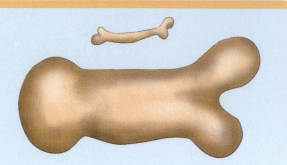

Galileo and the Problem of Scale

The Italian physicist Galileo Galilei (1564–1642) was the first to describe the problem of scale, in 1638, in his *Dialogues Concerning Two New Sciences* (in which he also discussed the idea of the earth revolving around the sun):

One bone, with another three times as long and thick enough to perform the same function in a scaled-up animal.

You can plainly see the impossibility of increasing the size of structures to vast dimensions either in art or in nature; likewise, the impossibility of building ships, palaces, or temples of enormous size in such a way that their oars, yards, beams, iron-bolts, and, in short, all their other parts will hold together; nor can nature produce trees of extraordinary size because the branches would break down under their own weight, so also would it be impossible to build up the bony structures of men, horses, or other animals so as to hold together and perform their normal functions if these animals were to be increased enormously in height; for this increase in height can be accomplished only by employing material which is harder and stronger than usual, or by enlarging the size of the bones, thus changing their shape until the form and appearance of the animals suggests a monstrosity.

To illustrate briefly, I have sketched a bone whose natural length has been increased three times and whose thickness has been multiplied until, for a corre-spondingly large animal, it would perform the same function which the small bone performs for its small animal. From the figures shown here you can see how out of proportion the enlarged bone appears. Clearly then if one wishes to maintain in a great giant the same proportion of limb as that found in an ordinary man he must either find a harder and stronger material for making the bones, or he must admit a diminution of strength in comparison with men of medium stature; for if his height be increased inordinately he will fall and be crushed under his own weight. Whereas, if the size of a body be diminished, the strength of that body is not diminished in proportion; indeed the smaller the body the greater its relative strength. Thus a small dog could probably carry on his back two or three dogs of his own size; but I believe that a horse could not carry even one of his own size.

Translated by Henry Crew and Alfonso De Salvo, and published by Macmillan, 1914, and Northwestern University, 1946.

which we can think of as a column of water. To calculate how much that weighs, we first translate 1 ft^3 into metric measurement:

$$1 \text{ ft}^3 = (12 \text{ in.})^3 = (12 \times 2.54 \text{ cm})^3 = 28{,}316 \text{ cm}^3$$

A reason to convert to cubic centimeters is the convenient fact that water weighs just about exactly 1 gram per cubic centimeter. Now, 1 ft^3 of water weighs about $28{,}300 \text{ g} = 28.3 \text{ kg} = 28.3 \times 2.20 \text{ lb} \approx 62 \text{ lb}$. Consequently, 5280 ft^3 of water weighs $5280 \times 62 \text{ lb} \approx 327{,}000 \text{ lb}$, so the pressure on the bottom layer would be about 327,000 lb/ft^2.

Actually, freshly cut wood weighs only about *half* as much as water, so the pressure on the bottom layer would be half this figure, or 164,000 lb/ft^2. This is still an overestimate, however, since we assumed that the tree does not taper. A tree that tapers steadily looks like an elongated cone; using a more realistic cone model (as we will do in the next section for a mountain), the pressure at the bottom of the tree is one-third of 164,000 lb/ft^2, or 55,000 lb/ft^2.

A biological organism needs a safety factor of at least two to four times the absolute minimum physical limits, so a tree a mile high would need from 110,000 to 220,000 lb/ft^2 of upward pressure for water and minerals. Tension in the string of water molecules from root to leaf ranges from 80,000 to 3.2 million lb/ft^2, for different kinds and heights of trees, so this consideration does not rule out mile-high trees.

However, at more than about 500 lb/in.^{2} = 70,000 lb/ft^2, the bottom of the tree would begin to crush under the weight above. On this point, the mile-high tree is barely feasible, with little margin of safety.

These considerations suggest that trees a mile high might be *physically* possible, but others suggest a lower maximum height. In addition, there are also biological considerations. The taller the tree, the greater the area from which it must draw water and minerals, for which nearby trees also compete. Moreover, for a tree to grow very tall, it would have to live for a very long time. Evolution and time may select against extremely tall trees; or maybe, for no reason at all, they have just never evolved. ◆

E X A M P L E   *How High Can a Mountain Be?*

Gravity and the physical characteristics of wood limit the height of trees. Gravity also limits the height of mountains. Mountains differ in composition and shape, and some assumptions about those features are necessary to do any calculating. We want to make realistic assumptions that make it easy to estimate how high a mountain can be. In effect, we build a simple mathematical model of a mountain.

Let's suppose that the mountain is made entirely of granite, a common material in many mountains, and let's assume that the granite has uniform density. Granite weighs 165 lb/ft^3 and has a crushing strength of about 4 million lb/ft^2.

In the interests of both realism and simplicity, we assume that the mountain is in the shape of a cone whose width at the base is the same as its height. Let's model Mount Everest: the tallest earth mountain, it is about 6 miles high. The base, then, is a circle with a distance across (or diameter) of 6 miles. The radius of the circle is half the diameter, so the model Everest has a radius of 3 miles measured at the base (Figure 16.5). Since we are taking such a round number for the height of Everest, we record as significant only the first two digits of the results of the calculations.

What does the model Everest weigh? The relevant formula is

weight = density × volume

FIGURE 16.5
Model of Mt. Everest as a
cone of granite.

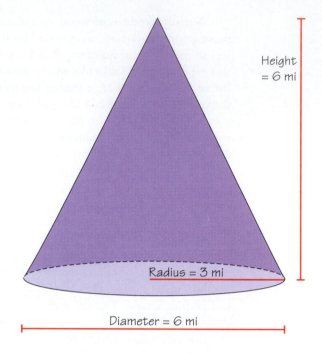

We already know the density of granite (165 lb/ft³), so to find the weight we need the formula for the volume of a cone of radius r and height h:

$$\text{volume} = \frac{1}{3}\,\pi r^2 h$$

For Everest, the radius is 3 miles and the height is 6 miles; π (pi) is about 3.14. Using those values in the formula, we find that the model Everest has a volume of about 57 cubic miles.

To find the weight of 57 cubic miles of granite, we need to convert units, since the density is given in pounds per cubic foot. Let's convert to units of feet:

$$
\begin{aligned}
1\text{ mi}^3 &= 1\text{ mi} \times 1\text{ mi} \times 1\text{ mi} \\
&= 5280\text{ ft} \times 5280\text{ ft} \times 5280\text{ ft} \\
&\approx 1.5 \times 10^{11}\text{ ft}^3
\end{aligned}
$$

Thus

$$57\text{ mi}^3 \approx 57 \times 1.5 \times 10^{11}\text{ ft}^3 \approx 8.6 \times 10^{12}\text{ ft}^3$$

So we have

$$
\begin{aligned}
\text{weight of mountain} &= 165\text{ lb/ft}^3 \times 8.6 \times 10^{12}\text{ ft}^3 \\
&\approx 1.4 \times 10^{15}\text{ lb} \\
&\approx 1.4 \text{ quadrillion lb}
\end{aligned}
$$

Now that we know the weight of the mountain, we want to find out what the pressure is on the base of the cone and compare that with the crushing strength of granite. (Everest is standing, so if our model is any good, that pressure will be below the crushing strength.) Physics tells us that the weight of the mountain is spread evenly over the base of the cone (though we are oversimplifying the geology underlying mountains). Since

$$\text{pressure} = \frac{\text{weight}}{\text{area}}$$

we need to calculate the area of the base of the cone. The shape is a circle, and the familiar formula

$$\text{area} = \pi r^2$$

gives an area of 28 square miles for a radius of 3 miles.

Once again, we need to convert units in order to express the pressure in pounds per square foot, the units in which the crushing strength is expressed. We get

$$\text{area} = 28 \text{ mi}^2 = 28 \times 5280 \text{ ft} \times 5280 \text{ ft} \approx 8 \times 10^8 \text{ ft}^2$$

Then

$$\begin{aligned} \text{pressure} &= \frac{\text{weight}}{\text{area}} \\ &= \frac{1.4 \times 10^{15} \text{ lb}}{8 \times 10^8 \text{ ft}^2} \\ &= 1.8 \times 10^6 \text{ lb/ft}^2 \end{aligned}$$

This number is below the crushing strength of granite, 4×10^6 lb/ft^2, with a safety factor of about 2.

For a mountain to come close to the limitation of the crushing strength of granite, it would have to be only about twice as high as Everest, or about 10 miles high. Other physical considerations suggest a maximum height of at most 15 miles. That no current mountains are that high may be a consequence of the earth's high amount of volcanic activity and the structural deformation of the earth's crust. ◆

What about mountains made of other materials—glass, ice, wood, old cars? They couldn't be nearly as high; the pressure would cause glass to flow, ice to melt, and old cars to compact. What about mountains on another planet? Their potential height depends on the gravity of the planet.

Solving the Problem of Scale

A large change in scale forces a change in either materials or form. A major manifestation of the scaling problem is the tension between weight and the need to support it. For example, a real building or machine must differ from a scale model: the balsa wood or plastic of the model would never be strong enough to use for the real thing, which must use aluminum, steel, or reinforced concrete. So one way to compensate for the problem of scale is to use stronger materials in the scaled-up object.

Another way to compensate is to redesign the object so that its weight is better distributed. Let's go back to the original cube. It supports all its weight on its bottom face. In the version scaled up by a factor of 3, each small cube of the bottom layer has a bottom face that is supporting that cube's weight plus the weight of the other two cubes piled on top of it.

Let's redesign the scaled-up cube, concentrating for simplicity only on the front face, with its nine small cubes. We take the three cubes on top and move them to the bottom, alongside the three already there. We take the three cubes on the second level, cut each in half, and put a half cube over each of the six ground-level cubes (see Figure 16.6). We have the same volume and weight that we started with, but now there is less pressure on the bottom face of each small cube. Of course, the new design is not geometrically similar to the object that we started with—it's no longer a cube. We have solved the scaling problem by changing the proportions and redistributing the weight.

We observe in nature both strategies for adaptation to scaling: change of materials and change of form. Smaller animals generally do not have bony internal skeletons; larger animals generally do. Animals made of similar materials but differing greatly in size, such as a mouse and an elephant, most certainly differ in shape. If a mouse were scaled up to the size of an elephant, its legs could no longer support it; it would need the disproportionately thicker legs of the elephant. It would also need the elephant's thick hide to contain its tissue.

Some dinosaurs, like *Supersaurus* (which weighed 30 tons), had special adaptations to lighten their weight, such as hollow bones, just as some birds have. (Hol-

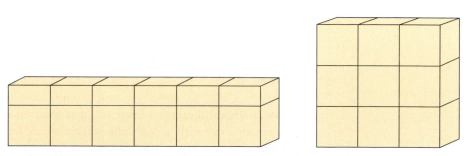

FIGURE 16.6   Nine small cubes rearranged to support greater weight.

low bonds also turn out to be stronger, a paradox that Galileo analyzed. Of two bones of the same weight and length, the hollow one is wider across at its midpoint, because of the air it contains; and the greater the width, the greater the resistance to fracture.)

Falls, Jumps, and Flight

The need to support weight can be thought of as a tension between volume and area. As an object is scaled up, its volume and weight go up together, as long as the density remains constant (for example, no air bubbles introduced into the steel to make it into a Swiss cheese!). At the same time, the ability to support the weight goes up with the cross-sectional area, like the bottom face of the steel cube.

> **Area-volume tension** is a result of the fact that as an object is scaled up, the volume increases faster than the surface area and faster than areas of cross sections.

Since volume V is proportional to the cube of the linear scaling factor L, we have $V \propto L^3$, or, taking each side to the one-third power, $L \propto V^{1/3}$. The fact that surface area A is proportional to the square of the linear scaling factor becomes

$$A \propto L^2 \propto (V^{1/3})^2 = V^{2/3}$$

so that surface area scales as the two-thirds power of volume.

Area-volume tension has many practical consequences, some of them related to our childhood fantasies. We can forget about humans "leaping tall buildings in a single bound," "soaring like an eagle," diving miles below the sea, and jumping from airplanes without parachutes. Consider the following examples.

E X A M P L E   *Falls*

Area-volume tension affects how animals respond to falling, another of gravity's effects. A mouse may be unharmed by a 10-story fall and a cat by a 2-story fall, but a human may well be injured by falling down while running, walking, or even just standing.

What is the explanation? The energy acquired in falling is proportional to the weight of the falling object, hence to its volume. This energy must be absorbed either by the object or by what it hits, or must be otherwise dissipated at impact—for example, as sound. The fall is absorbed over part of the surface area of the object, just as the weight of the cube was distributed over its base. With scaling up, volume—hence weight, hence falling energy—goes up much faster than area. As volume increases, the hazards of falling from the same height increase. ◆

EXAMPLE   *Jumps*

A flea can jump about 2 feet vertically, many times its own height. Many people believe that if a flea were as large as a person, it could jump a thousand feet into the air. Imagining—against our earlier arguments—that there could be so large a flea, we know its limits: a scaled-up flea could jump about the same height as a small flea. The strength of a muscle is proportional to its cross-sectional *area* (see Spotlight 16.3). A jump involves suddenly contracting the muscle through its length, so it turns out that the ability to jump is proportional to the *volume* of muscle. But the volume of the flea and the volume of its leg muscles go up in proportion.

Let's say that a real flea's leg muscles account for 1% of its body. If we scale the flea up to the size of a person (without any change in its form), the enlarged flea's leg muscles would still make up 1% of its body. For either flea, each bit of muscle has the same power: in a jump, it propels 100 times its own weight, and it can do so to the same height. Both the weight of the flea and the power of its legs go up proportionately. In fact, the maximum heights that people, fleas, grasshoppers, and kangaroos can jump are all within a factor of 3.   ◆

EXAMPLE   *Flight*

Wouldn't it be nice to be able to fly? Well, you have to be able to stay up. The power necessary for sustained flight is proportional to the **wing loading,** which is the weight supported divided by the area of the wings. We know that in scaling up, weight grows with the cube of the length of the bird or plane, and wing area with the square of the length. So the wing loading is proportional to the length of the flying object.

For example, if a bird or plane is scaled up proportionally by a factor of 4, it weighs $4^3 = 64$ times as much but has only $4^2 = 16$ times as much wing area. So each square foot of wing must support 4 times as much weight.

Once you're up, you have to keep moving. Hovering helicopters, hummingbirds, and insects maintain lift by moving their wings directly rather than through forward motion. To stay level, an airborne object must fly fast enough to maintain the lift on the wings. The minimum necessary speed is proportional to the square root of the wing loading. Combining this fact with the first consideration, we conclude that the minimum speed goes up with the square root of the length. A bird scaled up by a factor of 4 must fly $\sqrt{4} = 2$ times as fast.

Take, for instance, a sparrow, whose minimum speed is about 20 miles per hour (mph). An ostrich is 25 times as long as a sparrow, so the minimum speed for an ostrich would be $\sqrt{25} \times 20 = 100$ mph. Have you seen any flying ostriches lately? Heavy birds have to fly fast or not at all!

Of course, ostriches are not just scaled-up sparrows, nor are eagles. The larger flying birds have disproportionately larger wings than a sparrow, to keep the wing loading down. The largest animal ever to have taken to the air was *Quetzalcoatlus northropi,* a flying reptile of 65 million years ago, with a wingspan of 36 feet and a weight of about 100 pounds.

SPOTLIGHT 16.3

"Take That, King Richard!"

Did wearing armor give an advantage to the shorter warrior?

Shakespeare painted Richard III as a humpbacked Machiavellian monster. Did Richard have an advantage in armored combat because he was short? That suggestion was made some years ago by one of the leading modern historians of the Tudor era, Garrett Mattingly.

Between a short man and a tall man, height increases by the linear dimension — from 5 feet 2 inches, say, to 6 feet — while the surface of the body increases as the square. Since it's the surface of the body that the armorer must plate with steel, the armor of a short warrior, like Richard, would be lighter than a tall warrior's by a lot more than the few inches' difference in height would indicate. So Richard's notorious deadliness in battle would have been possible at least in part because his armor, while protecting him as well as the big man's, left him less encumbered.

After the lecture, someone said to Mattingly that he had grasped the right idea — but by the wrong end. Muscle power, the listener claimed, is a matter of bulk — and physical volume goes up by the cube, whereas the surface to be protected goes up by the square. So the large warrior should have more strength left over than the little guy after putting on his armor. And the large warrior, swinging a bigger club, can deliver a far more punishing blow — because the momentum of the club depends on its weight, which goes up with its volume, which means by the cube. Richard was at a terrible disadvantage.

But wait a minute, a second listener said. That's true about the club — but not about the muscles. The strength of a muscle is proportional not to its bulk but to the area of its cross section. And since the cross section of muscles increases by the square, just as the surface of the body does, the big guy, plated out, has no more, or less, advantage over the little guy than if both were naked.

But hang on, a third person interjected — an engineer. That's right about the muscles, but it's not right about the armor. The weight of the armor increases not simply with the increase in the surface area that it must cover but slightly faster. There must be reinforcing ribs. Or else the metal must be significantly thicker overall. So maybe Richard had an advantage.

Armor was made as thin as possible. Thickness, reinforcement, and structural stiffening were concentrated where opponents' weapons were likely to hit. From these strong, shaped places, the metal tapered away, until the sheet steel was as thin as the lid of a coffee can at the sides of the rib cage beneath the arms, or across the fingers, or at the cheek of a helmet.

Source: Horace F. Judson, *The Search for Solutions* (Baltimore: Johns Hopkins University Press, 1987), pp. 54–56.

You have to stay up, you have to keep moving—and you have to get up there. Here basic aerodynamics imposes further limits. Paleontologists originally thought that *Quetzalcoatlus northropi* weighed 200 pounds and had a 50-foot wingspan. Even though that works out to just about the same wing loading as for 100 pounds and a wingspan of 36 feet, other considerations from aerodynamics show that at 200 pounds, the reptile wouldn't have been able to get off the ground.   ◆

Keeping Cool (and Warm)

Area-volume tension is also crucial to an animal's maintenance of thermal equilibrium. Both warm-blooded and cold-blooded animals gain or lose heat from the environment in proportion to body surface area.

Warm-Blooded Animals

A warm-blooded animal usually is losing heat; its basal metabolism, or rate of food intake needed to maintain body heat, depends primarily on the amount of its surface area, the temperature of its environment, and the insulation provided by its coat or skin. Other factors being equal, a scaled-up mammal scales up its food consumption by *surface area* (proportional to the square of the linear scaling factor), *not by volume* (proportional to its cube). For example, a mouse eats about half of its weight in food every day, while a human consumes only about one-fiftieth of its own weight.

Thus, the metabolic rate must be proportional to the surface area. Using the symbolism of proportionality, we can find how the metabolic rate changes with the mass of the animal. We know that mass is proportional to volume, which in turn is proportional to the square of length, or

$$M \propto V \propto L^3$$

Taking each side to the one-third power, we have

$$M^{1/3} \propto V^{1/3} \propto L \qquad \text{or} \qquad L \propto M^{1/3}$$

Meanwhile, the metabolic rate (call it P) is proportional to surface area, so

$$P \propto A \propto L^2 \propto (M^{1/3})^2 = M^{2/3}$$

So, based on area-volume tension, we would expect metabolic rate to scale as the two-thirds power of body mass.

But it doesn't—instead, it scales as the *three-quarters* power of body mass. The least-squares line (see Chapter 6) through the points in the "mouse-to-elephant" curve of Figure 16.7 has a slope of 0.74, very close to the three-quarters predicted by theory.

FIGURE 16.7
Metabolic rates for mammals and birds, when plotted against body mass on logarithmic coordinates, tend to fall along a single straight line. Adapted from Benedict (1938).

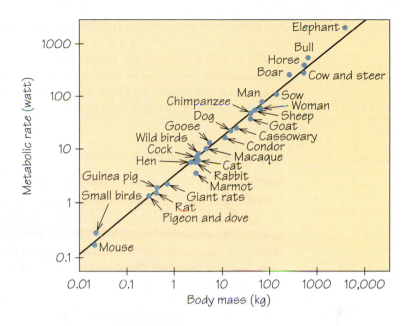

Why the difference from the two-thirds that area-volume tension would predict? And does the small difference between two-thirds and three-quarters matter? The answers lie in further considerations from geometry, physiology, and physics. A plant or animal needs a network of vessels (like the blood system) to transport resources to, and wastes away from, every part of the animal's tissues. The terminal branches (in the blood system, capillaries) tend to be just about the same size in all species, for reasons of the physics involved. To minimize the energy involved in transport, the network of vessels needs to be organized like a fractal-like tree, with smaller vessels branching off larger ones. With same-size terminal branches, minimization of energy demands that the metabolic rate scale as the three-quarters power of body mass. The branching makes it possible for the circulatory system of a whale, which has 10^7 times the mass of a mouse, to have only 70% more branches than that of the mouse.

E X A M P L E   *Dives*

Sperm whales (and some other species) regularly hold their breath and stay under water for an hour. Why can't we? In part, because we aren't as large as whales. A mammal's breath-holding ability depends on how much air it can hold in its lungs, which is proportional to its mass, and on how fast it uses up the air—in other words, on its metabolic rate, which is proportional to the three-quarters power of its mass. Hence, the limit of duration of a dive should be proportional to

$$\frac{M}{M^{3/4}} = M^{1/4}$$

For a 90,000-lb sperm whale, that limit is proportional to $90,000^{1/4} = 17.3$, while the corresponding figure for a 150-lb human is $50^{1/4} = 3.5$. So the sperm whale should be able to hold its breath for about $17.3/3.5 \approx 5$ times as long. However, humans cannot hold their breath for one-fifth of an hour (12 minutes)! That fact tells us that the whale must have some special adaptation—such as larger than proportional lungs, or a lower than predicted metabolism—to make its long dives possible. ◆

Cold-Blooded Animals

Mammals and birds regulate their metabolism and maintain a constant internal body temperature. Cold-blooded animals, such as alligators or lizards, have a somewhat different problem. They absorb heat from the environment for energy, but they must also dissipate any excess heat to keep their temperature below unsafe levels. The amount of heat that must be gained or lost is proportional to total volume, because the entire animal must be warmed or cooled. But the heat is exchanged through the skin, so the rate is proportional to surface area.

Dimetrodon was a large mammal-like reptile that roamed present-day Texas and Oklahoma 280 million years ago (see Figure 16.8). *Dimetrodon* had a great "sail" or fan on its back. As an individual grew, and as the species evolved, the sail grew. But it did not grow according to *geometric similarity*, the kind of growth we refer to as *proportional growth*.

> **Proportional growth** is a growth according to geometric similarity: the length of every part of the organism enlarges by the same linear scaling factor.

FIGURE 16.8
Dimetrodon may have evolved a sail to absorb and dissipate heat efficiently.

Instead, the area of *Dimetrodon*'s sail grew precisely in proportion to the volume of the animal, a fact that strongly suggests to paleontologists that the sail was a temperature-regulating organ that was able to absorb or radiate heat. So, an individual *Dimetrodon* twice as long would have eight ($= 2^3$) times as much weight and volume and also a sail with eight times as much area. If it had grown according to geometric similarity, the sail would have been twice as high and twice as wide, and hence would have had only four times as much sail area. Larger specimens of *Dimetrodon* didn't look quite like scaled-up smaller ones; we would say that the sail grew disproportionately large compared to the rest of the animal.

Dimetrodon was a large animal, but the need for heat regulation is even more acute for smaller animals. Like human babies, small animals can lose heat quickly, because of their high ratio of surface area to volume. Leading paleontologists now believe that birds (most of whom are quite small) evolved from dinosaurs and that feathers are modified reptilian scales. Though not a prevailing view, it has been hypothesized that the wings of birds and insects evolved originally not for flight but as temperature control devices.

Some scientists have speculated that African Pygmies are small in part because a small body is better able to lose heat in the hot, humid climate of the Ituri Forest where Pygmies live. Other scientists have suggested that ancestors of human beings began walking on two legs in part to keep cool in a hot climate. Walking upright exposes much less area of the body to the rays of the sun than walking on all fours and also reduces the amount of water needed by about one-half.

Similarity and Growth

Although a large change of scale forces adaptive changes in materials or form, within narrow limits—perhaps up to a factor of 2—creatures can grow according to a law of similarity, that is, they can grow proportionally, so that their shape is preserved. A striking example of such growth is that of the chambered nautilus (*Nautilus pompilius*). Each new chamber that is added onto the nautilus shell is larger than but geometrically similar to the previous chamber, and the shape of the shell as a whole—an *equiangular*, or *logarithmic*, spiral—remains the same (see Figure 16.9).

Most living things grow over the course of their lives by a factor greater than 2. We've seen with *Dimetrodon* that a big specimen was not just a scaled-up small one. Nor is a human adult simply a scaled-up baby. Relative to the length of the body, a baby's head is much larger than an adult's. The arms of the baby are disproportionately shorter than an adult's. In the growth from baby to adult, the body does not scale up as a whole. But different parts of the body scale up, each with a different scale factor. That is, a baby's eyes grow at one rate to perhaps twice their original size, while the arms grow at another rate, to about four times their original size.

SPOTLIGHT 16.4

Helping to Find Missing Children

  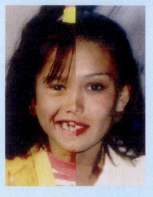

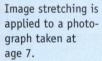 Image stretching is applied to a photograph taken at age 7.

Age progression to age 17.

It can be valuable to be able to predict what a developing organism will look like in the future. For example, what does a child look like now who was kidnapped six years ago, at age 3?

At the National Center for Missing & Exploited Children (NCMEC) in Arlington, Virginia, a computer and a more sophisticated version of the graph-paper technique are used to answer such questions. Computer age-progression specialists scan photographs of both the missing child at age 3 and an older sibling or a biological parent at age 9 into a computer. Then the face of the 3-year-old is stretched, depending on age, to reflect craniofacial growth and merged with the image of the sibling or parent at 9 years old. The result is a rough idea of what the missing child may look like. As mathematicians and biologists refine their models of how faces change over time, this technique will improve. It may even become possible to gain an idea of how a child may look at age 40 or 65.

FIGURE 16.9
A chambered nautilus
shell.

Although the laws for growth can be much more complicated than proportional growth (or even the allometric growth that we discuss in the next section), more sophisticated mathematics—for example, differential geometry, the geometry of curves and surfaces—permits analysis of complex and interlocking scalings. For a model of the process in which a baby's head changes shape to grow into an adult head, we can use graph paper: first, we put a picture of the baby's skull on graph paper, then we determine how to deform the grid until the pattern matches an adult skull (see Figure 16.10 and Spotlight 16.4). The same idea lies at the heart of computerized "morphing," the process in which the face of one film character can be made to change smoothly into the face of another, with different scalings for different parts of the face.

FIGURE 16.10
Modeling the changes in
the shape of a human
head from infancy to
adulthood.

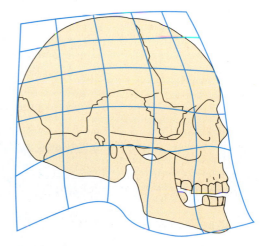

Allometry

If we measure the arm length or head size for humans of different ages and compare these measurements with body height, we observe that humans do not grow proportionally, that is, in a way that maintains geometric similarity. The head of a newborn baby may be one-third of the baby's length, but an adult's head is usually close to one-seventh of the individual's height. The arm, which at birth is one-third as long as the body, is by adulthood closer to two-fifths as long (see Figure 16.11a).

Ordinary graphing provides a way to test for differential growth. We can plot body height on the horizontal axis and arm length on the vertical axis (see Figure 16.11b). A straight line would indicate proportional growth, that is, according to geometric similarity; and we do get a straight line from age 9 months (0.75 years) or so on up. Up to age 9 months or so, we get a curve, which indicates that the ratio of arm length to height does not remain constant over the first year.

Is there an orderly law by which we can relate arm length to height? Let's plot again, this time using a different scale. For this **logarithmic scale,** we mark off equal units, as usual. But instead of labeling the marked points with 0, 1, 2, 3, etc., we label them with the corresponding powers of 10: $10^0 = 1$, $10^1 = 10$, $10^2 = 100$, $10^3 = 1000$, etc., which are also called **orders of magnitude.** Plotting a point on such a scale is not easy, since the point midway between 1 and 10 is not 5.5, but instead is closer to 3. Special graph paper (available in most college bookstores) marks smaller divisions and makes it easier to plot; paper marked with log scales on both axes is called **log-log paper,** while **semilog paper** has a logarithmic scale on just one axis. Also, many computer plotting packages can produce logarithmic scales.

We could use a logarithmic scale for either height or arm length, or for both. Using logarithmic scales for both, as in Figure 16.11c, the data plot closely to a straight line. Looking carefully, we can discern two different straight lines: a steeper one that fits early development (we will see shortly that it has slope 1.2), and a less steep one (with slope 1.0) that fits development after 9 months of age.

The change from one line to another after 9 months indicates a change in pattern of growth. The pattern after 9 months, characterized by the straight line with slope 1, is indeed proportional growth (sometimes called **isometric growth**). For the pattern before 9 months, we know from the slope (1.2) being greater than 1 that arm length is increasing relatively faster than height. That earlier growth also follows a definite pattern, called *allometric growth.*

> **Allometric growth** is the growth of the length of one feature at a rate proportional to a power of the length of another.

We have seen that in geometric scaling, area grows according to the square (second power) and volume according to the cube (third power) of length, so we can say that they grow allometrically with length.

FIGURE 16.11
(a) The proportions of the human body change with age. (b) A graph of human body growth on ordinary graph paper. The numbers shown beside the points indicate the age in years; they correspond to the stage of human development shown in part a. (c) A graph of human body growth on log-log paper.

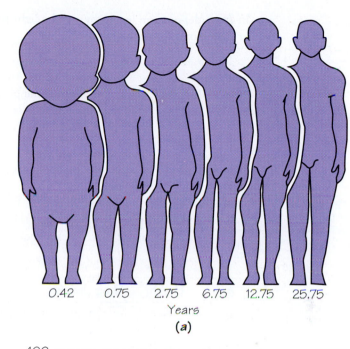

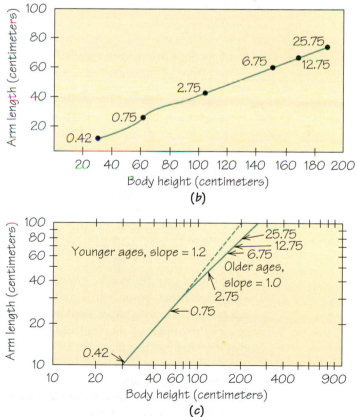

If we denote arm length by y and height by x, a straight-line fit on log-log paper corresponds to the algebraic relation

$$\log_{10} y = B + a \log_{10} x$$

where a is the slope of the line and B is the point where the graph crosses the vertical axis. If we raise 10 to the power of each side, we get

$$y = bx^a$$

where $b = 10^B$. This equation describes a **power curve:** y is a constant multiple of x raised to a certain power.

We can find approximate values for a for each of the two lines in the log-log plot from the coordinates of the points at the ends of the line. Those are the points for ages 0.42, 0.75, and 25.75. The observations and the corresponding logarithms are:

Age	Height	Log (height)	Arm Length	Log (arm length)
0.42	30.0	1.48	10.7	1.03
0.75	60.4	1.78	25.1	1.40
25.75	180.8	2.26	76.9	1.89

The slope for the line from age 0.42 to age 0.75 is the vertical change over the horizontal change, both converted to log units:

$$\frac{\log 25.1 - \log 10.7}{\log 60.4 - \log 30.0} = \frac{1.40 - 1.03}{1.78 - 1.48} = \frac{0.37}{0.30} \approx 1.2$$

The slope for the line from age 0.75 to age 25.75 is

$$\frac{\log 76.9 - \log 25.1}{\log 180.8 - \log 60.4} = \frac{1.89 - 1.40}{2.26 - 1.78} = \frac{0.49}{0.48} \approx 1.0$$

So $a = 1.2$ up to 9 months, and $a = 1.0$ after 9 months. Up to 9 months, arm length grows according to $(\text{height})^{1.2}$; after 9 months, arm length grows according to $(\text{height})^{1.0}$. We get $y = bx^{1.0}$, which is a linear relationship describing proportional growth, that is, growth according to geometric similarity. On ordinary graph paper, proportional growth appears as a straight line, allometric growth as a curve. On log-log paper, both patterns appear as straight lines.

The technique of allometry has been used in the last few years by paleontologists to determine that all of the six known specimens identified as the earliest fossil bird *Archaeopteryx* are indeed from the same species, and that the minute fossil and puzzling fish known as *Palaeospondylus* (found only in Scotland) is probably just the larval stage of some better-known fish. ◆

Conclusion

We have examined the problem of scale and noted that a large change in scale forces a change in either materials or form. A particular instance of the problem of scale is area-volume tension, and we have seen how an animal's size and geometric shape affect its abilities to move and to keep itself warm or cool.

In this chapter we have explored the limitations on life imposed by dwelling in three dimensions. In Chapter 20 we will see that dimensionality also imposes surprising limits on artistic creativity in devising patterns.

REVIEW VOCABULARY

Allometric growth   A pattern of growth in which the length of one feature grows at a rate proportional to a power of the length of another feature.

Area-volume tension   A result of the fact that as an object is scaled up, the volume increases faster than the surface area and faster than areas of cross sections.

Crushing strength   The maximum ability of a substance to withstand pressure without crushing or deforming.

Density   Weight per unit volume.

Geometrically similar   Two objects are geometrically similar if they have the same shape, regardless of the materials of which they are made. They need not be of the same size. Corresponding linear dimensions must have the same factor of proportionality.

Isometric growth   Proportional growth.

Linear scaling factor   The number by which each linear dimension of an object is multiplied when it is scaled up or down; that is, the ratio of the length of any part of one of two geometrically similar objects to the length of the corresponding part of the second.

Logarithmic scale   A scale on which equal divisions correspond to powers of 10.

Log-log paper   Graph paper on which both the vertical and the horizontal scales are logarithmic scales, that is, the scales are marked in orders of magnitude 1, 10, 100, 1000, . . . , instead of 1, 2, 3, 4, ...

Mass   The aspect of matter that is affected by forces, according to physical laws.

Orders of magnitude   Powers of 10.

Power curve   A curve described by an equation $y = bx^a$, so that y is proportional to a power of x.

Pressure   Weight divided by area.

Problem of scale   As an object or being is scaled up, its surface and cross-sectional areas increase at a different rate from its volume, forcing adaptations of materials or shape.

Proportional growth   Growth according to geometric similarity: the length of every part of the organism enlarges by the same linear scaling factor.

Semilog paper   Graph paper on which only one of the scales is a logarithmic scale.

Wing loading   Weight supported divided by wing area.

SUGGESTED READINGS

DEWDNEY, A. K. *200% of Nothing: An Eye-Opening Tour Through the Twists and Turns of Math Abuse and Innumeracy,* Wiley, New York, 1993.

DIAMOND, JARED M. Why are Pygmies small? *Nature,* 354 (1991): 111–112.

DUDLEY, BRIAN A. C. *Mathematical and Biological Interrelations,* Wiley, New York, 1977. Excellent and gentle extended introduction to graphing, scale factors, and logarithmic plots.

FLASPOHLER, DAVID C., FRANK MASTRIANNA, AND RICHARD PULSKAMP. *The Consumer Price Index: What Does It Mean?* 2nd ed. UMAP Modules in Undergraduate Mathematics and Its Applications: Module 639. COMAP, Inc., Lexington, Mass., 1994. Reprinted in *UMAP Modules: Tools for Teaching, 1993,* COMAP, Inc., Lexington, Mass., 1994.

GOULD, STEPHEN JAY. Size and shape. In *Ever Since Darwin,* Norton, New York, 1977, chapter 21.

HALDANE, J. B. S. On being the right size. In *Possible Worlds and Other Papers,* Harper, New York, 1928. Reprinted in James R. Newman (ed.), *The World of Mathematics,* vol. 2, Simon & Schuster, New York, 1956, pp. 952–957. Also reprinted in John Maynard Smith (ed.), *On Being the Right Size and Other Essays by J. B. S. Haldane,* Oxford University Press, Oxford, 1985, pp. 1–8. Succinctly surveys area-volume tension, flying, the size of eyes, and even the best size for human institutions.

HILDEBRANDT, STEFAN, AND ANTHONY J. TROMBA. *Mathematics and Optimal Form,* Scientific American Library, New York, 1985.

MCMAHON, T. A., AND J. T. BONNER. *On Size and Life,* Scientific American Library, New York, 1983. Astonishingly beautiful and informative book on the effects of size and shape on living things.

MINEYEV, ANATOLY. Trees worthy of Paul Bunyan: Why do trees grow so tall—but no taller? *Quantum,* 4 (January/February 1994): 4–10.

NIKLAS, KARL J. *Plant Allometry: The Scaling of Form and Process,* University of Chicago Press, Chicago, 1994.

SCHMIDT-NIELSEN, KNUT. *Scaling: Why Is Animal Size So Important?* Cambridge University Press, New York, 1984.

STEVENS, PETER S. *Patterns in Nature,* Atlantic Monthly Press, Boston, 1974. Splendid treatment of the problem of scale and other physical phenomena in nature: flows, meanders, branching, trees, soap films, cracking, and packing.

THOMPSON, D'ARCY. *On Growth and Form,* Cambridge University Press, Cambridge, 1917, 1961. "A discourse on science as though it were a humanity" (J. T. Bonner); this was the first book to describe in quantitative terms the processes of growth and shaping of biological forms.

TREFIL, JAMES S. What would a giant look like? In *The Unexpected Vista: A Physicist's View of Nature,* chapter 10, pp. 156–171, Scribner, New York, 1983. Explanation of the effects of scaling up. In Trefil's illustration on p. 162, however, the eyes of the giants are unrealistically large.

WENT, F. W. The size of man. *American Scientist,* 56 (1968): 400–413. Demonstrates a schism between the macroworld and the molecular world, by comparing human life with that of an ant.

WEST, GEOFFREY B., JAMES H. BROWN, AND BRIAN J. ENQUIST. A general model for the origin of allometric scaling laws in biology. *Science,* 276 (April 4, 1997): 122–126; nontechnical summary on p. 34. Derives the three-quarters-power scaling law.

WGBH EDUCATIONAL FOUNDATION AND PEACE RIVER FILMS. *Nova: The Shape of Things,* 1985. Distributed by Vestron Video, Box 4000, Stamford, CT 06907.

ZHERDEV, A. Horseflies and flying horses: Questions of scale in the animal kingdom. *Quantum,* 4 (May/June 1994): 32–37, 59–60.

SUGGESTED WEB SITES

http://physics.nist.gov/News/TechBeat/9501beat.html   Proposed redefinition of the kilogram.

http://hyperarchive.lcs.mit.edu/HyperArchive.html   Program to convert units.

http://www.missingkids.com/   National Center for Missing and Exploited Children.

http://www.usmint.gov   U.S. Mint.

http://www.kcnet.com/~marc/bmi.html   Body mass index calculator and further links.

SKILLS CHECK

1. You want to enlarge a small 3-inch by 5-inch photograph to a 12-inch by 20-inch copy. Assuming that the cost of photographic paper is proportional to its area, and that 3-inch by 5-inch reprints cost 40 cents each, how much would you expect to pay for the large copy?

   (a) $1.60
   (b) $3.20
   (c) $6.40

2. If a model car is built to a scale of 1 to 40, and the actual car has a turning circle of 37 feet, what should be the turning circle of the model?

   (a) 11.1 inches
   (b) 0.925 inches
   (c) 1480 feet

3. If a medium 10-inch pizza costs $8 and a similar 14-inch pizza costs $14, which is the better buy?

   (a) The 10-inch pizza
   (b) The 14-inch pizza
   (c) They are about the same price.

4. An artist plans to melt 100 pennies and reform a larger penny proportional to an ordinary coin. What is the linear scaling factor of the large penny, compared to the ordinary penny?

   (a) 100 to 1
   (b) 10 to 1
   (c) 4.64 to 1

5. You bought your English textbook for $40 in 1997. The earlier edition sold for $37 in 1992. Comparing the converted cost, which book is more expensive? (Assume the 1997 CPI is 160.5 and the 1992 CPI is 140.3.)

   (a) The 1997 book
   (b) The 1992 book
   (c) The books are about the same price.

6. Coffee costs about $5 per pound in the United States. If a Canadian dollar exchanges for 75 U.S. cents and a kilogram is about 2.2 pounds, what is the equivalent cost in Canadian dollars?

   (a) $3.03 Canadian per kilogram
   (b) $8.25 Canadian per kilogram
   (c) $14.67 Canadian per kilogram

7. A sculpture weighs 140 pounds and is supported by three legs each of which is 0.5 inch by 0.5 inch by 2 inches high. How much pressure do the legs exert on the table?

   (a) 47 lb/in.^{2}
   (b) 105 lb/in.^{2}
   (c) 187 lb/in.^{2}

EXERCISES   ▲ *Optional.*   ■ *Advanced.*   ◆ *Discussion.*

Most of the exercises require a calculator; one that offers square roots will suffice.

Geometric Similarity

1. Suppose you are printing photographs from negatives of so-called 35-millimeter film, whose frames are just about 1 inch by $1\frac{1}{2}$ inches (the actual size is 24 mm (millimeters) by 36 mm).

   (a) First you make some contact prints, which are exactly the same size as the negatives. What is the scaling factor of a contact print?
   (b) One enlargement that you want to make is to be three times as high and three times as wide as the negative. What is the linear scaling factor for this print? How does its area compare with the area of the negative?

(c)   What is the scaling factor for a 4-by-6 print? What is the area of the print?

(d)   The size of so-called 3-by-5 prints can vary, depending on whether the print has a border or not; a common size is about $3\frac{1}{16}$ by $4\frac{19}{32}$ inches. Is this print geometrically similar to the negative?

(e)   The cost of photographic paper is very nearly proportional to the area of the paper. Suppose you are comparing the cost of getting 3-by-5 enlargements versus 4-by-6 enlargements, and let's assume for the sake of simplicity that the prints are exactly 3 in. by 5 in. and 4 in. by 6 in. The smaller prints cost 17 cents each, and the larger cost 50 cents each. From what you know about scaling, what can you say about the relative cost of the two kinds of prints?

(f)   Based on the amount of paper used, what would you expect a 7-by-10 print to cost, considering the cost of the 3-by-5 prints in part (e)? Considering the cost of the 4-by-6 prints in part (e)?

2.   The area of a circle of radius r is πr^2; expressed in terms of the diameter, $d = 2r$, the area is $\frac{1}{4}\pi d^2$. If we apply a linear scaling factor L to the diameter of a circle, then—as in the case of the square that we considered in the text—the area of the scaled circle changes with L^2, the square of the linear scaling factor. A natural application of this idea, of course, is to your local pizza parlor and the prices on its menu. The actual prices at the pizza restaurant closest to Beloit College are $6, $7, $7.95, and $8.95, respectively, for small (10-inch), medium (12-inch), large (14-inch), and extra large (16-inch) cheese pizzas.

(a)   What is the linear scaling factor for an extra large pizza compared to a small one?

(b)   How many times as large in area is the extra large pizza compared to the small one?

(c)   How much pizza does each size give per dollar? What "hidden" assumptions are you making about how the pizzas are scaled up?

(d)   The corresponding prices for a pizza with "the works" are $8.25, $9.75, $11.95, and $13.95. Is there any size of these for which you get more pizza per dollar than some size of the cheese pizzas?

3.   The human figures in Lego sets are 4 cm tall (without hats or helmets).

(a)   What is the linear scaling factor of a Lego figure if it represents a human who is 180 cm tall?

(b)   How does the volume of a real human compare with the volume of a Lego figure?

(c)   The jeep in one Lego set is 10 cm long. Using the linear scaling factor of part (a), how long would a real jeep be?

4.   Dollhouses and their furnishings are usually built to a scale of exactly 1 in. to 1 ft, meaning that an item 1 ft long in a real house is 1 in. long in a dollhouse.

(a)   What is the linear scaling factor for a dollhouse?

(b)   If a dollhouse were made of the same materials as a real house, how would their weights compare?

5.   Two geometric figures are *similar* if they have the same shape but not necessarily the same size. Indicate whether the geometric figures described below are always, sometimes, or never similar.

(a)   Two squares
(b)   Two isosceles triangles
(c)   Two equilateral triangles
(d)   Two pentagons
(e)   Two regular pentagons
(f)   Two rectangles
(g)   A square and a rectangle
(h)   Two circles
(i)   A regular pentagon and a regular hexagon
(j)   Two angles

6.   Identify each of the following statements as either true or false.

(a)   Every polygon is similar to itself.
(b)   If polygon A is similar to polygon B and polygon B is similar to polygon C, then polygon A is similar to polygon C.

(c)   Corresponding interior angles of similar polygons are congruent.

7.   One of the famous geometry problems of Greek antiquity was the *duplication of the cube*. Our knowledge of the history of the problem comes from the third century B.C. from Eratosthenes of Cyrene, who is famous for his estimate of the circumference of the earth. According to him, the citizens of Delos were suffering from a plague. They consulted the oracle, who told them that to rid themselves of the plague, they must construct an altar to a particular god that would be geometrically similar to the existing one but double the volume.

(a)   How would the volume of the new altar compare with the old if each of its linear dimensions were doubled?

(b)   What should the linear scaling factor be for the new altar? (The problem intended by the oracle was to construct with straightedge and compasses a line segment equal in length to this particular linear scaling factor. Not until the nineteenth century was the task shown to be impossible. Eratosthenes relates that the Delians interpreted the problem in this sense, were perplexed, and asked Plato about it. Plato told them that the god didn't really want an altar of double the volume but wished to shame them for their "neglect of mathematics and their contempt for geometry.")

8.   The declining purchasing power of the dollar and the short life of a dollar bill in circulation suggest that the dollar bill be abolished in favor of a dollar coin. The Susan B. Anthony dollar coin of 1979–1981 was a failure with the U.S. public, who found it too small and light. Starting in the year 2000, there will be a new gold-colored dollar depicting Sacagawea, a Shoshone Indian who guided explorers Meriwether Lewis and William Clark in their 1804–1805 expedition to the Pacific Ocean. But even this coin may be too little (in size and weight) too late (a dollar today is worth less than half what it was in 1978). Suppose that you are put in charge of planning a new *$5* coin (whom should it depict?). The sole requirement is that the coin be

made of the same material as the current U.S. 25-cent piece but, unlike the Anthony and Sacagawea coins, weigh four times as much. A quarter can be described geometrically as a circular cylinder approximately $\frac{15}{16}$ in. in diameter and $\frac{1}{16}$ in. thick. Since your new dollar should weigh four times as much, it needs to have four times the volume of a quarter. (You may find it helpful that the formula for the volume of a cylinder is $\pi \times (\text{diameter}/2)^2 \times \text{height}$.)

(a)   A member of your public advisory panel suggests that the requirement will be fulfilled if you just double the diameter and double the thickness. What do you tell this individual, in the most diplomatic terms?

(b)   If you go along with the member's suggestion to double the diameter, how thick does the coin need to be?

(c)   Another member of the board feels that doubling the diameter would produce a coin too large to be convenient and proposes instead that you scale up the quarter proportionally (she took a course from an earlier edition of this book). What would the dimensions be for this new $5 piece?

The Susan B. Anthony dollar, to be replaced by the dollar coin in the year 2000.

The young Native American Sacagawea portrayed in relief.

The Language of Growth, Enlargement, and Decrease

9.   Criticize the following statement, which appears on sacks of the product, and write a correct version.

> "Erin's Own Irish sphagnum moss peat. It enriches your soil and makes your growing easier. Compressed to $2\frac{1}{2}$ times normal volume."

10.   Criticize the following claims, which were cited in the *New York Times* of 9/25/87 and 10/21/87:

(a)   A new dental rinse "reduces plaque on teeth by over 300%."
(b)   An airline working to decrease lost baggage has "already improved 100% in the last six months."
(c)   "If interest rates drop from 10% to 5%, that is a 100% reduction."

Numerical Similarity

11.   Here are some problems on using the Consumer Price Index (CPI) (see Table 16.1):

(a)   I bought my first LP record in 1965, at list price, for $4.98. How much would that be in 2000 dollars? How does that compare with the list price of a CD today?
(b)   My father bought a Royal portable typewriter in 1940 for $40. What would be the equivalent price in 2000 dollars?
(c)   My first-semester college mathematics book cost $10.75 in 1962. What would be the equivalent price in 2000 dollars? How does that compare to what you paid for this book? (My book had black and white text and figures, with no photographs, color or otherwise.)
(d)   In 1970, before the OPEC oil embargo, gasoline cost about 25 cents per gallon. In 1974, after the embargo, it cost about 70 cents per gallon. What would be the equivalent prices in 2000 dollars? How do they compare to the price of gasoline today?

12.   From the CPI table (see Table 16.1), you can determine the rate of inflation from one year to the next. For example, you find the rate of inflation from 1996 to 1997 by subtracting the two index numbers and dividing by the earlier one: (160.5 − 156.9)/156.9 = 0.023 = 2.3%. Similarly, knowing the rate of inflation, you can compute one index number from another. (Thus, from learning the rate of inflation from newspapers, you can add entries to the CPI table for years past 1998.)

(a)   What was the rate of inflation from 1980 to 1981?
(b)   For a 3% rate of inflation per year from 2000 on, what would the CPI be in 2003?
(c)   Gasoline costs about $1.10 per gallon in mid-1992, when Ross Perot proposed increasing the federal tax on gasoline by 10 cents each year for five years in order to pay for investments in U.S. infrastructure and to reduce dependence on oil imports. Assume that from 1992 to 1997, the price of gasoline (exclusive of Perot's proposed tax) went up according to the CPI and that in 1997 there was in addition the proposed additional $0.50 tax per gallon. What would the price of gasoline have been in 1997?
(d)   Compare your answer to part (c) with your answers to Exercise 11, part (d). Discuss possible conclusions.

13.   In Germany the fuel efficiency of cars is measured in terms of liters of gasoline used per 100 kilometers traveled. On a recent trip there, driving a subcompact car, we averaged 6.5 liters per 100 km. What is the equivalent in miles per gallon?

Measuring Length, Area, Volume, and Weight

14.   A *light-year* is not a measure of time but of distance; it is how far light travels in a year. Light travels at 2.9979×10^8 m/sec in a vacuum.

(a)   How long is a light-year in kilometers?
(b)   In miles?
(c)   In angstroms (1 Å = 10^{-10} m)?

The Macintosh program Convert, available from http://hyperarchive.lcs.mit.edu/HyperArchive.html, can convert many kinds of units. You can explore such units as tuns (volume), blinks (time), and barns (length).

15. Consider a real locomotive that weighs 88 tons and an HO-gauge scale model of it, for which the linear scaling factor is 1/87.

(a) How much would an exact scale model weigh, in tons?
(b) What assumptions are involved in your answer to part (a)?
(c) How much would an exact scale model weigh, in pounds?
(d) In kilograms?
(e) In metric tonnes (1 metric tonne = 1000 kg)?

16. An ad for a software package for data analysis included a data set on tropical rain forests and deforestation. The data were given in hectares and were accompanied by the statement "A hectare equals 10,000 mi^2 or 2471 acres." What conversion factors should have appeared instead?

17. Gasoline is sold in the United States by the U.S. gallon and in Canada by the liter (1 U.S. gallon = 231 cu in.; 1 liter = 1000 cm^3). What is the equivalent cost, in U.S. dollars per U.S. gallon, for gasoline in Canada priced at 45 Canadian cents per liter, when one Canadian dollar exchanges for 66 cents U.S.?

18. In 1991, Edward N. Lorenz, a meteorologist who was an early researcher into chaos and dynamical systems, received the Kyoto Prize in Basic Sciences, consisting of a gold medal and 45 million Japanese yen. If US$1 = ¥125 at the time, what was the value of the cash award in 1991 U.S. dollars?

19. In 200 B.C., Eratosthenes measured the circumference of the earth and expressed the result as 250,000 *stadia* (plural of *stadium*). In *The American Heritage Dictionary,* Second College Edition (Houghton Mifflin, Boston, 1982), we read for the second meaning of "stadium": "An ancient Greek measure of distance . . . equal to about 185 kilometers, or 607 feet." The name of the unit came from the length of a racecourse that was a bit less than an eighth of a mile long. If the numbers in the definition are correct, what are the correct units that should have appeared?

Sorry, No King Kongs

20. The weight of a 1-ft cube of steel is 500 lb. What is the pressure on the bottom face in

(a) pounds per square inch?
(b) atmospheres (1 atm = 14.7 lb/sq in.)?

21. In an article on adding organic matter to soil, the magazine *Organic Gardening* (March 1983) said, "Since a 6-inch layer of mineral soil in a 100-square-foot plot weighs about 45,000 pounds, adding 230 pounds of compost will give you an instant 5% organic matter."

(a) What is the density of the mineral soil, according to the quotation?
(b) How does this density compare with that of steel?
(c) How do you think the quotation should be revised to be accurate?

22. A mature gorilla weighs 400 lb and stands 5 ft tall.

(a) Give an estimate of its weight when it was half as tall.
(b) What assumptions are involved in your estimate?
(c) A mature gorilla's two feet together have a combined area of about 1 ft^2. When the gorilla is standing on its feet, what is the pressure on its feet, in pounds per square inch?

23. Suppose King Kong is a gorilla scaled up with a linear scaling factor of 10.

(a) How much does King weigh?
(b) What is the pressure on King's feet, in pounds per square inch?

24.   You may have wanted to have a waterbed but found that waterbeds were not allowed in your building. Apart from the danger of flood if the bed should puncture or leak, there is the consideration of the weight.

    (a)   If a queen-size mattress is 80 in. long by 60 in. wide by 12 in. high, and water weighs 1 kg/liter, how much does the water in the mattress weigh in pounds?

    (b)   If the weight of the mattress and frame is carried by four legs, each 2 in. by 2 in., what is the pressure, in pounds per square inch, on each leg?

    (c)   How does the pressure on the legs of the waterbed compare with the pressure that a person exerts on his or her feet—for example, a 130-lb person with a total foot area of about one-quarter of a square foot in contact with the ground?

    (d)   If you aren't allowed to have a waterbed, how about a spa (hot tub)? Find the weight of the water in a spa that is in the shape of a cylinder 6 ft in diameter and 3.5 ft deep. (*Hint:* The volume of a cylinder is $\pi r^2 h$, where r is the radius and h is the height.)

25.   What does the largest giant sequoia tree weigh? Model the tree as a (very elongated) cone, supposing that the tree is 360 ft high and has a circumference of 40 ft at the base, and that the density of the wood is 31 lb/cu ft. (The volume of a cone of height h and radius r is $\frac{1}{3}\pi r^2 h$.)

Falls, Jumps, and Flights

26.   (Adapted from George Knill and George Fawcett, Animal form or keeping your cool, *Mathematics Teacher,* May 1982, 395–397.) The movie *Them* features enormous ants (about 8 m long and about 3 m wide). We can investigate how feasible such a scaled-up insect is by considering its oxygen consumption. A common ant, which is about 1 cm long, needs about 24 milliliters of oxygen per second for each cubic centimeter of its volume. Since an ant does not have lungs, it must absorb the oxygen through its "skin," which it can do at a rate of about 6.2 milliliters per second per square centimeter. Suppose that the tissues of a scaled-up ant would have the same need for oxygen for each cubic centimeter, and that its skin could absorb oxygen at the same rate, as a normal ant. Compared to a common ant, how many times as large is an enormous ant's

    (a)   length?

    (b)   surface area?

    (c)   volume?

    (d)   What proportion of such an ant's oxygen need could its skin supply?

What can you conclude about the existence of such insects?

27.   In the children's story *Peter Pan,* Peter and Wendy can fly. We may suppose that they are 4 ft tall, so they are about 12 times as tall as a sparrow is long. What should their minimum flying speed be?

28.   Icarus of Greek legend escaped from Crete with his father, Daedalus, on wings made by Daedalus and attached with wax. Against his father's advice, Icarus flew too close to the sun; the wax melted, the wings fell off, and he fell into the sea and drowned. What must have been his minimum cruising speed? What assumptions does your answer involve?

Keeping Cool (and Warm)

◆   29.   Smaller birds and mammals generally maintain higher body temperatures than larger ones. Explain why you would expect this to be so. (Adapted from A. Zherdev, Horseflies and flying horses, *Quantum,* May/June 1994, 32–37, 59–60.)

◆   30.   Some humans, such as the Bushmen of the Kalahari Desert in Africa, live in desert environments, where it is important to be able to do without water for periods of time. Would you expect such an environment to favor short or tall individuals? (Adapted from A. Zherdev, Horseflies and flying horses, *Quantum,* May/June 1994, 32–37, 59–60.)

31. The branching of trees is similar to the branching of systems in the bodies of animals. For similar reasons, the area of the cross section of the tree at its base scales as the three-fourths power of the tree's mass, that is, $A \propto M^{3/4}$. Assume that most of the mass is in the trunk and model the tree either as a tall cylinder ($V = \pi r^2 h$) or as a cone ($V = \pi r^2 h/3$). Show that the diameter d of a tree is approximately proportional to the three-halves power of the height, that is, $d \propto h^{3/2}$.

Allometry

▲ **32.** Listed below are the winning times in the 1983 World Rowing Championships for rowing shells with one, two, four, and eight oars. The men's times are for 2000 m, the women's for 1000 m. Convert the times to speed, in meters per minute. For men and women separately, plot speed versus number of oars on ordinary graph paper, and then on log-log paper. If you don't have log-log paper available, use a calculator to take the logarithms (LOG_{10}) of all the numbers and graph these values on ordinary graph paper.

Event	Number of Oars	Men (2000 m)	Women (1000 m)
Single sculls	1	6:49.75	3:36.51
Pairs without coxswain	2	6:35.85	—
Fours without coxswain	4	6:14.83	3:26.68
Eights (with coxswain)	8	5:34.39	2:56.22

Is the relationship proportional? Allometric?

Additional Exercises

For Exercises 33 and 34, refer to the following: An ancient measure of length, the *cubit* was the distance from the elbow to the tip of the middle finger of a person's outstretched arm. So the length of a cubit depended on the person, though there was some attempt at standardization. Most estimates place the length of a cubit between 17 and 22 in.

33. Goliath (of David and Goliath, as related in the Bible [I Samuel 17:4]) was "six cubits and a span." A span was originally the distance from the tip of the thumb to the tip of the little finger when the hand is fully extended, about 9 in. What range of heights would this indicate for Goliath, in feet and inches? In centimeters?

34. According to classical Greek sources, Pythagoras (sixth century B.C.) used geometric scaling to model the height of Hercules, the heroic figure of classical mythology in the epic poems of Homer. Pythagoras compared the lengths of two racecourses, one (according to tradition) paced off by Hercules and the other by a man of average height. Both were 600 "paces" long, but the one established by Hercules was longer because of Hercules's longer stride (600 "Herculean" paces versus 600 paces by a normal man). A normal man in the time of Pythagoras would have been about 5 ft tall.

(a) If the distance paced off by Hercules was 30% longer than the other racecourse, how tall was Hercules? What does your calculation assume?

(b) In fact, the ancient sources do not give the original data but only the two conflicting answers that Hercules was 4 cubits tall and 4 cubits 1 foot tall. What range does this give for the height of Hercules, in feet and inches? In centimeters?

◆ **35.** Recent years have seen the beginnings of human-powered controlled flight, in the *Gossamer Condor* and other superlightweight planes. The *Gossamer Condor* is far longer than an ostrich, but it flies at only 12 mph. How can it?

◆ **36.** Jonathan Swift's Gulliver also traveled to Lilliput, where the Lilliputians were human-shaped but only about 6 in. tall. In other words, they were geometrically similar in shape to ordinary human beings but only one-twelfth as tall. What would a Lilliputian weigh?

Are Lilliputians ruled out by the size-shape and area-volume considerations in this chapter? If you think they are, what considerations do you find convincing? If not, why not?

37.   [Contributed by Charlotte Chell of Carthage College, Kenosha, Wisconsin.] A 6-ft indoor holiday tree needs four strings of lights to decorate it. How many strings of lights are needed for an outdoor tree that is 30 ft high?

38.   What would you expect an individual *Quetzalcoatlus northropi* to weigh if it had half the wingspan of an adult? If an individual weighed half as much as an adult, what would you expect its wingspan to be?

◆   39.   The TV series *All in the Family* featured Archie Bunker, his wife, Edith, his daughter, Gloria, and her friend (and later husband), Michael (called "Meathead" by Archie). This family provides a way to visualize the changes over the past 20 years in the economic situation of a U.S. blue-collar family. The series began in 1973. Archie is a factory worker, about 50 years old, with at most a high school degree, earning about $13,000 then. Gloria, living at home and employed half-time, earns about $2000. Michael earns about $10,000 at his factory job.

We consider a similar family in 1979, the Trapps, with people of the same ages, education, and social background as before. The 50-year-old factory worker Art earns about $12,600. To help support them, his wife, Enid, is employed, earning about $9000. Their daughter, Gina, is married to Martin ("Cheddarhead"), who earns about $15,000 at the cheese factory, while Gina is at home with their children.

We move now to 2000 and yet another family with the same age structure, the Sands. Patriarch Arnie earns about $34,000 at his job, while his wife, Eve, makes $12,000. Their daughter, Gwen, is married to Matt ("Muttonhead"), who earns $25,000 (when he isn't laid off from the meat-packing plant). Gwen works, too, earning $12,000;

but day-care expenses for their son cost $5000 per year.

Use the Consumer Price Index (see Table 16.1) to convert all of these figures to 2000 dollars, and then compare the relative situations of these similar families in 1973, 1979, and 1998.

(Thanks to Paul Solman of PBS's *MacNeil-Lehrer Newshour* for the idea and some of the data.)

40.   The *body-mass index* (BMI) is the basis for the National Heart, Lung and Blood Institute's new weight guidelines. BMI is body weight (in kilograms) divided by the square of height (in meters). A BMI of 25 through 29 is considered "overweight"; a BMI of 30 or over is considered "obese." Some 55% of American adults have a BMI of 25 or above. (*Note:* BMI is not a useful measure for young children, pregnant or breastfeeding women, frail elderly, or very muscular people.)

(a)   Calculate the BMI for a woman 160 cm tall who weighs 65 kg. Is she overweight according to the institute's guidelines?
(b)   How much in kilos must a man weigh who is 190 cm tall if he is not to be considered overweight according to the institute's guidelines?
(c)   Calculate your own BMI.
(d)   Suppose that weight and height are measured instead in U.S. Customary units of pounds and inches. We can still calculate body weight divided by the square of height, using these units. What conversion factor is necessary to convert this number to the BMI?
(e)   Since body weight is average density times body volume, BMI is average density times a quantity that has units of length. Discuss whether BMI makes sense as a measure of being overweight. Would dividing by a different power of height make for a better measure?

41.   Maybe some trees could grow to a mile high, but they just don't live long enough to have the

chance. In this problem we try to determine how fast the height of a tree increases. How much mass the tree adds each year is determined by how much water is pumped to the treetop, and that in turn is determined by the area of the tree rings involved. Here are two relevant facts about trees:

- You may have noticed from tree stumps that as a tree grows older, its annual rings get thinner. Although the width of the ring varies somewhat from year to year with the amount of rainfall and other factors, the total *area* of each annual ring is roughly the same over the years, meaning that *the tree adds roughly the same amount of mass each year.* Call that amount a; then the mass M of the tree is $M = at$, where t is its age in years.
- Over a large range of tree sizes and tree species, the diameter d of a tree of a species is approximately proportional to the three-halves power of the height h of the tree (different species have different constants of proportionality). Thus, $d \propto h^{3/2}$ (see Exercise 31).

Now, if we assume that the bulk of the mass of the tree is in the trunk, and if we model the trunk either as a long cylinder or as a thin cone, the mass is proportional to the volume, so $M \propto d^2 h$. Then

$$at = M \propto d^2 h \propto (h^{3/2})^2 h = h^4$$

so $h \propto t^{1/4}$. In other words, the tree grows as the fourth root of its age.

(a) Suppose a tree grows to 20 m in 30 years. How tall will it be (if it lives long enough) when it is 60 years old?
(b) How long would it take the tree in part (a) to grow to be 40 m tall?
(c) Giant sequoias can reach 100 m after about 1000 years. If it kept on growing at the same rate of addition of mass, how long would it take a giant sequoia to grow to 200 m?

TECHNOLOGY CORNER

Comparing Prices Using the Consumer Price Index

A spreadsheet can allow instant computation of changing prices, using the Consumer Price Index (CPI). The CPI for certain years is transferred from Table 16.1 to columns **D** and **E** in the spreadsheet shown in Figure 16.12. A current price and the current CPI are placed in entries **A2** and **B2**. Entry **F2** computes the equivalent cost in 1920 dollars, using the formula $=$**A2/B2*E2**. If entries **A3** and **B3** are defined as $=$**A2** and $=$**B2**, these formulas can be copied to the remaining entries of Columns **A, B,** and **F.** For example, a car which cost about $3200 in 1970 costs about $14,000 today.

TASK 1. In 1950, a new Ford tractor cost about $900. In restored condition, this tractor now sells for about $7500. In year 1950 dollars, how does its present value compare? In year 2000 dollars, how does its current value compare to its original cost?

TASK 2. Assume that the minimum wage is (somewhat) tied to the CPI so that its real value is constant. Based on today's minimum wage (in year 2000 dollars), approximately when did the minimum wage surpass $1 per hour? Approximately when did it surpass $2, $3, and $4 per hour?

	A	B	C	D	E	F
1	Today's Cost	Today's CPI		Year	CPI	Cost
2	$14,000.00	170		1920	20.0	$1,647.06
3	$14,000.00	170		1930	16.7	$1,375.29
4	$14,000.00	170		1940	14.0	$1,152.94
5	$14,000.00	170		1950	24.1	$1,984.71
6	$14,000.00	170		1960	29.6	$2,437.65
7	$14,000.00	170		1970	38.8	$3,195.29
8	$14,000.00	170		1980	82.4	$6,785.88
9	$14,000.00	170		1990	130.7	$10,763.53
10	$14,000.00	170		1995	152.4	$12,550.59

FIGURE 16.12

Estimating Area and Volume of a House

Based on the length, width, and height of a house, one can estimate its footing (length times width), outer sides (length plus width times height), and volume (length times width times height). Assuming each story requires approximately 10 feet of height, the floor space of the house can be estimated as the volume divided by 10. The spreadsheet in Figure 16.13 allows us to compare several different configurations, based on the values in the first three columns. The entries in the remaining columns have computed values based on the entries of the first three. For example, entry **E2** has the formula **=2*(A2+B2)*C2**.

	A	B	C	D	E	F	G
1	Length	Width	Height	Footing	Sides	Volume	Floor Space
2	60	24	20	1440	3360	28800	2880
3	50	15	10	750	1300	7500	750
4	48	20	30	960	4080	28800	2880
5				0	0	0	0
6				0	0	0	0
7				0	0	0	0

FIGURE 16.13

Task 3. According to the spreadsheet in Figure 16.13, a 2-story 60 ft × 24 ft house and a 3-story 48 ft × 20 ft house have about the same amount of floor space. However, the 2-story house would require less external woodwork or brick. Can you find dimensions of another home with about the same amount of floor space which would require even less external woodwork?

Task 4. For a single-story house with 2000 square feet of floor space, what dimensions will minimize the needed footing?

Exploration

Many slanted roofs are modeled on a "5–12–13" right triangle. The roof rises 5 feet for every 12 feet that it covers, using 13 feet of roofing, so that 13 feet of roofing cover every 12 feet of house width. Assume these houses have a two-piece roof with two vertical triangular ends. Create a formula that computes the amount of roofing needed. Recompute the area of the external sides to include the two triangular ends.

writing projects

1 ▶ A human infant at birth usually weighs between 5 and 10 pounds and has a height (length) between 1 and 2 feet, with the shorter babies having the lesser weight. Considering the weight and height of an adult human, give an argument that human growth must not be just proportional growth.

2 ▶ The principle that area scales with the square of length, and volume with the cube, has important consequences for the depiction and interpretation of data in graphic form. Suppose we wish to indicate in an artistic way that the weekly income of a U.S. carpenter is twice that of a carpenter in (mythical) Rotundia. We draw one moneybag for the Rotundian and another one "twice as large" for the

American. [Illustration from Darrell Huff, *How to Lie with Statistics,* Norton, 1954, p. 69.]

What's the problem? Well, first, people tend to respond to graphics by comparing areas. Since the larger moneybag is twice as high and twice as wide as the smaller one, the image of it on the page has four times the area. Second, we are used to interpreting depth and perspective in drawings in terms of three-dimensional objects. Since the larger bag is also twice as thick as the smaller, it has eight times the volume. The graphic leaves the subconscious impression that the U.S. carpenter earns eight times as much, instead of twice as much. With these ideas in mind, evaluate the depictions of data below.

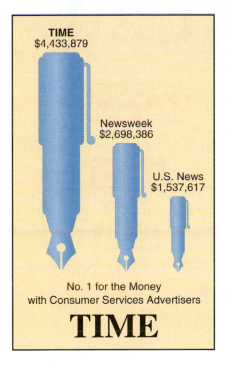

(a) Advertising spending in three prominent newsmagazines. [From *Time* magazine, as reproduced in David S. Moore, *Statistics: Concepts and Controversies,* 4th ed., W. H. Freeman, 1997, p. 207.]

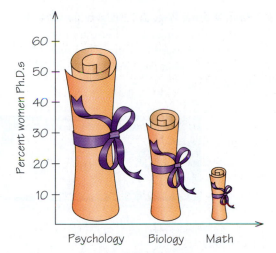

(b) Percentages of Ph.D.s earned by women in three fields. [From *Science,* 260 (April 16, 1993), 409, as reproduced in Jessia Utts, *Seeing Through Statistics,* Duxbury, 1996, p. 142.]

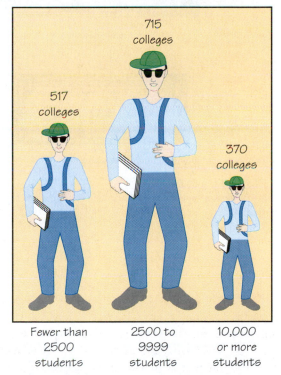

(c) U.S. colleges as classified by enrollment. [From David S. Moore, *Statistics: Concepts and Controversies,* 4th ed., W. H. Freeman, 1997, p. 217.]

3 ▶ As in Writing Project 2, evaluate the depictions below and on the facing page. [Illustrations reproduced or adapted from Edward R. Tufte, *The Visual Display of Quantitative Information,* Graphics Press, 1983, pp. 70, 69, and 57.]

1958—Eisenhower

1963—Kennedy

1968—Johnson

1973—Nixon

1978—Carter

1984—Reagan

1990—Bush

1993—Clinton

(a) Value of the dollar.

(b)   The shrinking family doctor.

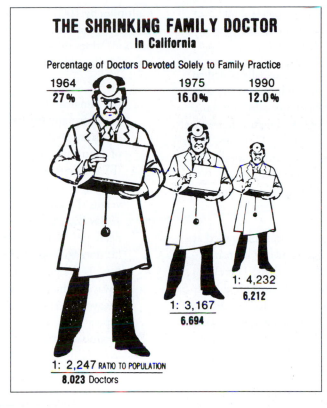

THE SHRINKING FAMILY DOCTOR
In California

Percentage of Doctors Devoted Solely to Family Practice

1964	1975	1990
27%	16.0%	12.0%

1: 4,232
6,212

1: 3,167
6,694

1: 2,247 RATIO TO POPULATION
8,023 Doctors

This line, representing 18 miles per gallon in 1978, is 0.6 inch long.

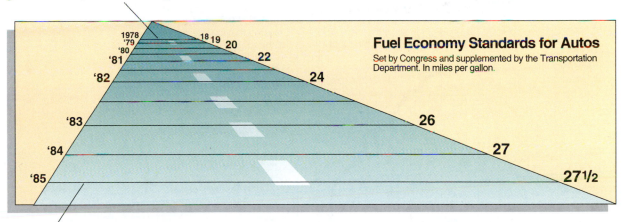

Fuel Economy Standards for Autos
Set by Congress and supplemented by the Transportation Department. In miles per gallon.

1978 '79 '80 '81 '82 '83 '84 '85

18 19 20 22 24 26 27 27½

This line, representing 27.5 miles per gallon in 1985, is 5.3 inches long.

New York Times, August 9, 1978, p. D2.

(c)   Fuel economy standards for autos.

4 ▶ With the ideas of Writing Projects 2 and 3 in mind, collect and evaluate similar depictions of data from magazines and newspapers.

5 ▶ Dolls and human figures are usually scaled to be geometrically similar to actual humans. But are dolls designed to represent babies or adult humans? Go to a toy store and measure the height, the vertical height of the head, and the arm length of some dolls and other figures. Scale your measurements to compare them with Figure 16.11; from that comparison, try to estimate the ages of the humans that the figures resemble.

6 ▶ On July 11, 1994, the Russian ruble traded at 3736 rubles to the U.S. dollar. One day later, it traded at 3926 rubles to the U.S. dollar. There are two competing practices for stating how much one currency has depreciated (lost value) against another. Option A, used by the International Monetary Fund and the British periodical *The Economist,* takes the difference in the first country (here, 3926 − 3736) and divides it by the new trading value (3926) and

multiplies by 100 to get a result in percent (here, 4.84%). Option B, sometimes called the "popular method," does the same, but divides by the old trading value instead of the new value (getting 5.09%).

(a)   Calculate the results for both methods for the Jamaican dollar, which traded at J$1.78 to US$1 in January 1983 and at J$5.50 to US$1 for most of 1985. Does it make sense to speak of a currency depreciating more than 100%?

(b)   Calculate the value (in current U.S. dollars) of one Jamaican dollar in January 1983 versus the value of one Jamaican dollar in 1985. By what percentage has this value declined? With which of your answers to part (a) does this number agree?

(c)   Is the percentage obtained from Option A always higher than that from Option B? or always lower? or neither? Which would you expect a person to use who wanted to make a decline seem large?

(d)   Critique the data display below and offer alternatives.

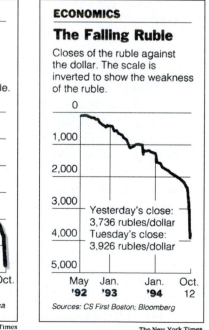

ECONOMICS

The Falling Ruble

Weekly closes of the ruble against the dollar. The scale is inverted to show the growing weakness of the ruble.

Source: CS First Boston; Bank of America

The New York Times

ECONOMICS

The Falling Ruble

Closes of the ruble against the dollar. The scale is inverted to show the weakness of the ruble.

Yesterday's close: 3,736 rubles/dollar
Tuesday's close: 3,926 rubles/dollar

Sources: CS First Boston; Bloomberg

The New York Times

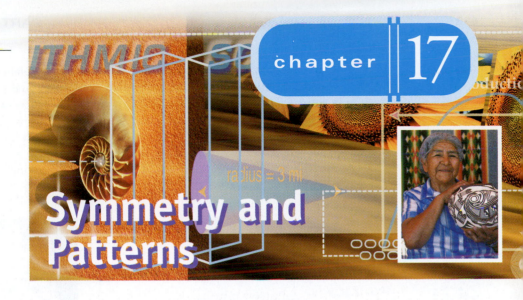

chapter | 17

Symmetry and Patterns

"The senses delight in things duly proportional." So said the famous philosopher-theologian Thomas Aquinas more than 700 years ago, in noting human aesthetic appreciation. In this chapter we examine some of the elements of that aesthetic appreciation, particularly what we call *symmetry.*

What is symmetry and what does mathematics have to do with it? Symmetry, like beauty, is very difficult to define. Dictionary definitions talk about "correspondence of form on opposite sides of a dividing line or plane or about a center or an axis," "correspondence, equivalence, or identity among constituents of an entity," and "beauty as a result of balance or harmonious arrangement" (*American Heritage Dictionary,* 3rd ed.).

In the narrowest sense, symmetry refers to "mirror-image" correspondence between parts of an object. Crystals, in both their appearance and their atomic structure, provide examples of symmetry in this sense. Taken in a wider sense, though, symmetry includes notions of *balance, similarity,* and *repetition.*

It is our sense of symmetry that leads us to appreciate patterns. As we noted in the introduction to this part of the book, *mathematics is the study of patterns,* and we will see here that mathematics gives important insights into symmetry.

Spirals

Patterns abound in nature. The successive sections of the beautiful chambered nautilus grow according to a very strict and specific spiral pattern, a broader kind of symmetry. This spiral has the property that it has the same shape at any size: a photographic enlargement superimposed on it would fit exactly.

629

Botanists have long appreciated other spirals. In plant growth from a central stem, the shoots, leaves, and seeds often occur in a spiral pattern known as **phyllotaxis.** For instance, the scales of a pineapple or a pinecone are arranged in spirals (Figure 17.1), as are the seeds of a sunflower (Figure 17.2a) and the petals on a daisy. Like the chambers of the nautilus in Figure 17.2b, the spirals on these plants are geometrically similar to one another, and they are arranged in a regular way, with balance and "proportion." These plants have a kind of symmetry we would naturally call **rotational.**

FIGURE 17.1
Spirals of scales on a pinecone: 8 right, 13 left.

Fibonacci Numbers

Associated with the geometric symmetry of phyllotaxis, there is also a kind of *numeric symmetry,* with a "proportion" in the sense of a ratio of numbers. Strangely, the number of spirals in plants with phyllotaxis is not just any whole number but always comes from a particular sequence of numbers, called the *Fibonacci numbers* (see Spotlight 17.1).

Fibonacci numbers occur in the sequence

   1, 1, 2, 3, 5, 8, 13, 21, 34, 55, 89, 144, 233, 377, . . .

This sequence begins with the numbers 1 and 1 again, and each next number is obtained by adding the two preceding numbers together.

Sometimes a sequence of numbers is specified by stating the value of the first term or first several terms and then giving an equation to calculate succeeding terms from preceding ones. This is called a *recursive rule,* and the sequence is said

FIGURE 17.2
(a) This sunflower has 55 spirals in one direction and 89 spirals in the other direction. (b) A chambered nautilus shell.

to be defined by **recursion.** Let's denote the nth Fibonacci number by F_n; then the Fibonacci sequence can be defined by

$$F_1 = 1, F_2 = 1, \qquad \text{and} \qquad F_{n+1} = F_n + F_{n-1} \qquad \text{for } n \geq 2$$

The recursive rule just expresses in algebraic form that the next Fibonacci number is the sum of the previous two.

Look at the sunflower in Figure 17.2a. You see a set of spirals running in the counterclockwise direction and another set in the clockwise direction. It is (just barely) possible to count the number of spirals in both directions; in the sunflower there are 55 in one and 89 in the other direction—two consecutive Fibonacci numbers. In the case of the pineapple, there are three sets of spirals, one each along the three directions through each hexagonally shaped scale. For the common grocery pineapple *(Ananas comosus),* there are always 8 spirals to the right, 13 to the left, and 21 vertically—again, consecutive Fibonacci numbers.

Why are the numbers of spirals in plants the same numbers that appear next to each other in a purely mathematical sequence? The question has been the subject of extensive research, and there is no easy answer; there are several intricate theories about the dynamics involved in the plant's growth.

The Golden Ratio

During the last several centuries, an attractive myth arose that the ancient Greeks considered a specific numerical proportion essential to beauty and symmetry. Known variously in modern times as the *golden ratio,* **golden mean,** or even

SPOTLIGHT 17.1

Leonardo Pisano Bigollo ("Fibonacci")

Born in Pisa in 1170, Leonardo Pisano Bigollo has been known as "Fibonacci" for the past century and a half. This nickname, which refers to his descent from an ancestor named Bonaccio, is modern, and there is no evidence that he was known by it in his own time.

Leonardo was the greatest mathematician of the Middle Ages. His stated purpose in his book *Liber abbaci* (1202) was to introduce calculation with Hindu-Arabic numerals into Italy, to replace the Roman numerals then in use. Other books of his treated topics in geometry, algebra, and number theory.

We know little of Leonardo's life apart from a short autobiographical sketch in the *Liber abbaci:*

I joined my father after his assignment by his homeland Pisa as an officer in the customhouse located at Bugia [Algeria] for the Pisan merchants who were often there. He had me marvelously instructed in the Arabic-Hindu numerals and calculation. I enjoyed so

Leonardo Pisano ("Fibonacci")
A portrait of unlikely authenticity.

much the instruction that I later continued to study mathematics while on business trips to Egypt, Syria, Greece, Sicily, and Provence and there enjoyed discussions and disputations with the scholars of those places. [L. E. Sigler, *Leonardo Pisano Fibonacci, The Book of Squares: An Annotated Translation into Modern English,* Academic Press, New York, 1987.]

The *Liber abbaci* contains a famous problem about rabbits, whose solution is now called the Fibonacci sequence. Leonardo did not write further about it.

divine proportion, this proportion was investigated by Euclid in Book II of his *Elements.* Recent research reveals little evidence connecting this proportion to Greek aesthetics, but we pursue the golden ratio briefly because of its intimate connection to the Fibonacci sequence and because it does have appeal as a standard for beautiful proportion.

The value of the **golden ratio,** which is usually denoted by the Greek letter phi (ϕ), is

$$\phi = \frac{1 + \sqrt{5}}{2} = 1.618034\ldots$$

The basic aesthetic claim is that a **golden rectangle**—one whose height and width are in the ratio of 1 to ϕ—is the most pleasing of all rectangles. The Greeks treated lengths geometrically, so for them it was important to construct lengths using straightedge and compass; in Spotlight 17.2 we show how to construct a golden rectangle that is 1 unit by ϕ units.

What would make anyone think that this is such an attractive ratio? And where did it come from? The answer lies not in Fibonacci numbers but in the Greeks' pursuit of balance in their study of geometry.

Given two line segments of different lengths, one way to find another length that "strikes a balance" between the two is to average them. For lengths l (the larger) and w (the smaller), their *arithmetic mean* (average) is $m = (l + w)/2$, and it satisfies

$$l - m = m - w$$

The length m strikes a balance between l and w, in terms of a common difference from the two original lengths. More generally, the arithmetic mean of n numbers or lengths is their sum divided by n.

The Greeks, however, preferred a balance in terms of ratios rather than differences. They sought a length s, the *geometric mean,* that gives a common ratio

$$l \div s = s \div w \qquad \text{or} \qquad \frac{l}{s} = \frac{s}{w}$$

Hence $lw = s^2$, which expresses the geometric fact that s is the side of a square, the area of which is the same as the area of a rectangle that is l by w (the Greeks thought in terms of geometrical objects). In geometry, the geometric mean s is called the *mean proportional* between l and w (see Figure 17.3).

The quantity $s = \sqrt{lw}$ is the **geometric mean** of l and w. More generally, the geometric mean of n numbers is the nth root of the product of all n factors: the geometric mean of $x_1, \ldots, x_n$ is $\sqrt[n]{x_1 \cdots x_1}$. For example, the geometric mean of 1, 2, 3, and 4 is $\sqrt[4]{1 \times 2 \times 3 \times 4} = \sqrt[4]{24} = 24^{1/4} \approx 2.213$.

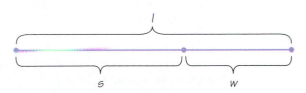

FIGURE 17.3 The line segment of length l is divided so that the length of s is the geometric mean between l and $w = l - s$; the dividing point divides the length l in the golden ratio.

SPOTLIGHT

17.2

How the Greeks Constructed a Golden Rectangle

In constructing a golden rectangle, the Greeks started from a one-by-one square (shown in black in the figure), which they made by constructing perpendiculars at the two ends of a horizontal segment of unit length. To extend the square to a golden rectangle, they bisected the original segment to get a new point that divides it into two pieces of length one-half each. Using this new point and a compass opening equal to the distance from it to a far corner of the square, they could cut off an interval of length ϕ.

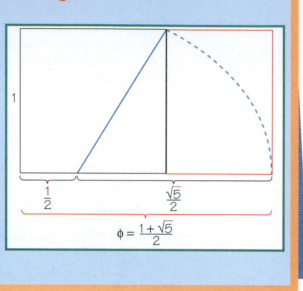

$$1$$

$$\frac{1}{2} \qquad \frac{\sqrt{5}}{2}$$

$$\phi = \frac{1+\sqrt{5}}{2}$$

The ancient Greeks found symmetry and proportion in the geometric mean, but the geometric mean also has important practical applications (see Spotlight 17.3).

The Greeks were interested in the problem of cutting a single line segment of length l into lengths s and w, where $l = w + s$, so that s would be the mean proportional between w and l. Surprisingly, the ratio ϕ arises, as we show. Denote the common ratio

$$\frac{l}{s} = \frac{s}{w}$$

by x. Substituting $l = s + w$, we get

$$x = \frac{l}{s} = \frac{s + w}{s} = \frac{s}{s} + \frac{w}{s} = 1 + \frac{w}{s}$$

But w/s is just $1/x$, so we have

$$x = 1 + \frac{1}{x}$$

Multiplying through by x gives

$$x^2 = x + 1 \qquad \text{or} \qquad x^2 - x - 1 = 0$$

This is a quadratic equation of the form

$$ax^2 + bx + c = 0$$

with $a = 1$, $b = -1$ and $c = -1$. We apply the famous quadratic formula

$$x = \frac{-b \pm \sqrt{b^2 - 4ac}}{2a}$$

to get the two solutions

$$x = \frac{1 + \sqrt{5}}{2} = 1.618034 \ldots \qquad \text{and} \qquad \frac{1 - \sqrt{5}}{2} = -0.618034 \ldots$$

We discard the negative solution since it does not correspond to a length. The first solution is the golden ratio ϕ. It occurs often in other contexts in geometry, for example, ϕ is the ratio of a diagonal to a side of a regular pentagon (see Figure 17.4).

Thanks to recent work of Roger Herz-Fischler (Wilfrid Laurier University) and George Markowsky (University of Maine), we know that the term "golden ratio" was not used in antiquity and that there is no evidence that the Great Pyramid was designed to conform to ϕ, that the Greeks used ϕ in the proportions of the

FIGURE 17.4
In a pentagon with equal sides, ϕ is the ratio of a diagonal to a side. The five-pointed star formed by the diagonals was the symbol of the followers of the ancient Greek mathematician Pythagoras.

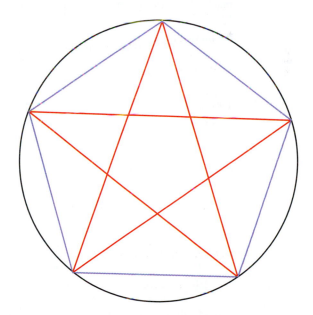

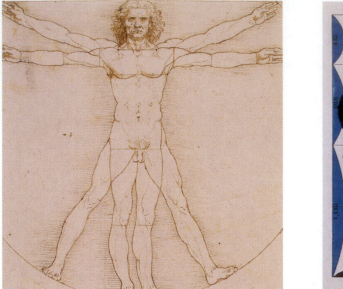 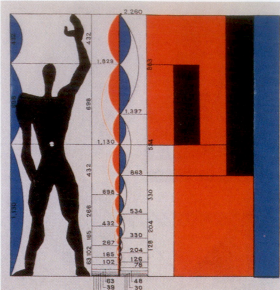

FIGURE 17.5   (a) There is no evidence that Leonardo used ϕ in his drawings of the human figure. (b) Le Corbusier, however, did use ϕ in his "Modular" scale of proportions.

Parthenon, or that Leonardo da Vinci used ϕ in proportions for the human figure (Figure 17.5a). Moreover, experiments show that people's preferences for dimensions of rectangles cover a wide range, with golden rectangles not holding any special place. The impressionists Gustave Caillebotte (1848–1894) and Georges Seurat (1859–1891) may have used the golden ratio to design some of their paintings, but we do not have any historical evidence that they claimed or intended to do so.

It is true that human bodies exhibit ratios close to the golden ratio, as you can see by comparing your overall height to the height of your navel. The twentieth-century Swiss-born architect Le Corbusier (Charles-Edouard Jeanneret [1887–1965]) used the golden ratio (including a navel-height feature) as the basis for his "Modulor" scale of proportions. (Figure 17.5b).

There are intriguing connections between the spiral of the nautilus and the spirals of the sunflower and between the golden ratio and the Fibonacci sequence. The nautilus shape follows what is known as an *equiangular* or *logarithmic* spiral, which in its turning determines a sequence of golden rectangles (Figure 17.6). The spirals of the sunflower are in fact approximations to a logarithmic spiral. The mathematical reason for this connection is that the ratios of consecutive Fibonacci numbers

$$\frac{1}{1} \quad \frac{2}{1} \quad \frac{3}{2} \quad \frac{5}{3} \quad \frac{8}{5} \quad \frac{13}{8} \quad \frac{21}{13} \cdots$$
$$1.0 \quad 2.0 \quad 1.5 \quad 1.666\ldots \quad 1.6 \quad 1.625 \quad 1.615\ldots$$

provide alternately under- and overapproximations to $\phi = 1.618034 \ldots$

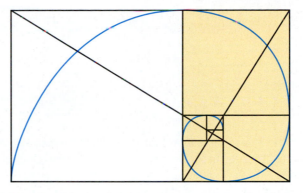

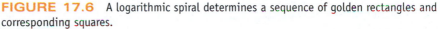

FIGURE 17.6 A logarithmic spiral determines a sequence of golden rectangles and corresponding squares.

Balance in Symmetry

The spiral distribution of the seeds in a sunflower head and the spiraling of leaves around a plant stem are instances of *similarity* and *repetition,* two key aspects of symmetry; they also illustrate *balance,* which refers to regularity in *how* the repetitions are arranged. In considering patterns with repetition, we distinguish the individual element or figure of the design (sometimes called the *motif*) from the *pattern* of the design—*how the copies of the motif are arranged.*

The problem that we will work on for the rest of this chapter is to classify the fundamentally different ways that a flat design can be symmetric. The ideas that we discuss were used by chemists and crystallographers to discover how many different crystalline forms are possible. Although there is a limitless number of different chemicals, and of motifs that people can make, what is quite surprising is that there is only a limited number of ways that atoms of a chemical or motifs of a design can be arranged in a symmetrical way.

How can we possibly enumerate the ways that designs can be put together without counting all the actual designs themselves? The key mathematical idea is to look not at the motifs that make up the patterns, but what you can *do* to the pattern without changing its appearance. This is what we pursue in the next section.

Rigid Motions

Mathematicians describe a variety of kinds of symmetry by using the geometric notion of a *rigid motion,* also known as an **isometry** (which means "same size"). A rigid motion is a specific kind of variation on the original pattern: we pick it up and move it, perhaps rotate it, possibly flip it over—but we *don't change its size or shape.* (To connect this concept with the language of Chapter 16, the original figure and its image are not just geometrically similar but congruent—the same size.)

SPOTLIGHT 17.3

A New Consumer Price Index: An Application of the Geometric Mean

In 1999, the Bureau of Labor Statistics (BLS) began using the geometric mean—instead of the arithmetic mean (average)—in calculating the Consumer Price Index (CPI), which tracks changes in the cost of the goods and services that people buy.

Using the geometric mean is intended to take into account substitutions that consumers make when prices change. For example, if the price of beef goes up but the price of chicken doesn't, consumers may buy less beef and substitute chicken (because it is cheaper) for some beef.

Suppose that, overall, U.S. families consume equal dollar values of beef and chicken. A typical family might consume weekly 5 lb of beef at $4/lb and 10 lb of chicken at $2/lb, for $20 each and a total cost of $40. We say that beef and chicken each have a relative *market share* of 0.5 (50% beef, 50% chicken, by dollar value).

What if beef goes up to $6/lb but chicken stays at $2/lb? The *relative price change* in beef is $6/$4 = 1.5 and the relative price change in chicken is $2/$2 = 1.00 (i.e., no change). If the average family continues to eat just as much beef and chicken as before, the cost is now $50, an increase of 25%. Since $30 goes for beef and $20 for chicken, the relative market shares (0.6 and 0.4) have changed. The *relative price change* for the family's meat is $50/$40 = 1.25, which is just the arithmetic mean (average) of the two relative price changes (1.50 and 1.00). A more general formulation is

Relative price change

$$= (\text{old market share of beef}) \frac{\text{new cost of beef}}{\text{old cost of beef}}$$

$$+ (\text{old market share of chicken}) \times$$

$$\frac{\text{new cost of chicken}}{\text{old cost of chicken}}$$

$$= 0.5 \times \frac{6.00}{4.00} + 0.5 \times \frac{2.00}{2.00}$$

$$= \frac{1.50 + 1.00}{2} = 1.25$$

A family that eats no beef sees no increase; a family that eats only beef sees an increase of 50%. The CPI is an average over *all* families, weighted by the dollar value that each consumes.

If instead we use the geometric mean, we get a relative price change of $\sqrt{1.50 \times 1.00} = 1.225$. The more general formulation is

Relative price change

$$= \left(\frac{\text{new cost of beef}}{\text{old cost of beef}} \right)^{(\text{old market share of beef})}$$

$$\times \left(\frac{\text{new cost of chicken}}{\text{old cost of chicken}} \right)^{(\text{old market share of chicken})}$$

$$= \left(\frac{6.00}{4.00} \right)^{0.5} \times \left(\frac{2.00}{2.00} \right)^{0.5}$$

$$= \sqrt{1.50 \times 1.00} = 1.225$$

This relative price change, which is interpreted as a 22.5% increase in the cost of living, is slightly less than the 25% using the arithmetic mean.

The intention of the CPI is to measure the cost of living, that is, the change in the cost of goods and services that still yield the same level of satisfaction to consumers. The use of the arithmetic mean presumes that a family will go on buying the same weight of beef and chicken (5 lb beef; 10 lb chicken) as before; the use of the geometric mean presumes that a family will respond to changes in prices by buying the same *relative dollar value* of each meat as before. Using the geometric mean, the presumption is that, on average, families will purchase 1.225 times as much dollar value of meat as before, or $40 \times 1.225 = \$49$. Of this, $24.50 (12.25 lb) would be chicken and the same dollar value $24.50 (4.08 lb) would be beef, so the relative market shares do not change. This substitution, which involves buying 0.92 lb less beef and substituting for it 2.25 lb of chicken, is supposed to yield the "same satisfaction" as the $20 (5 lb) of beef and $20 (10 lb) of chicken earlier, at a 22.5% increase in cost.

Since the geometric mean is always less than or equal to the arithmetic mean (see Exercise 11), the effect of using the geometric mean is a smaller CPI and a lower figure for inflation, perhaps 0.25% less per year than using the arithmetic mean would produce. Since social security payments, some wage increases, and income tax rates are automatically geared to the CPI, the result will be lower increases in social security payments and in wages, plus higher taxes for many taxpayers. The net effect on the federal budget will be a large increase in revenues and a large decrease in expenditures.

Figure 17.7 shows the results of various motions applied to the rectangle in Figure 17.7a. In Figure 17.7b, each side is shrunk by 50%: not a rigid motion, because the size of the rectangle changes. For Figure 17.7c, we imagine that the rectangle has rigid sides but hinges at the corner; like an unbraced bookshelf, it sags: again, this is not a rigid motion because the shape of the rectangle changes. In Figure 17.7d we rotate the rectangle 90° (a quarter turn) clockwise around the center of the rectangle: this is a rigid motion. Similarly, in Figure 17.7e, rotating by 180° (a half turn) is a rigid motion.

In Figure 17.7f we reflected the rectangle along a vertical mirror down the middle: could you tell? The right and left halves have exchanged places.

Figure 17.7g shows the result of reflecting across a diagonal of the rectangle. All reflections and all rotations are rigid motions. So are all **translations,** which move every point in the plane a certain distance in the same direction.

FIGURE 17.7

Results of various motions applied to a rectangle:
(a) the original rectangle;
(b) 50% reduction (not a rigid motion); (c) sagging (not a rigid motion);
(d) quarter turn;
(e) half turn; (f) reflection along the vertical line down the middle;
(g) reflection along a diagonal line.

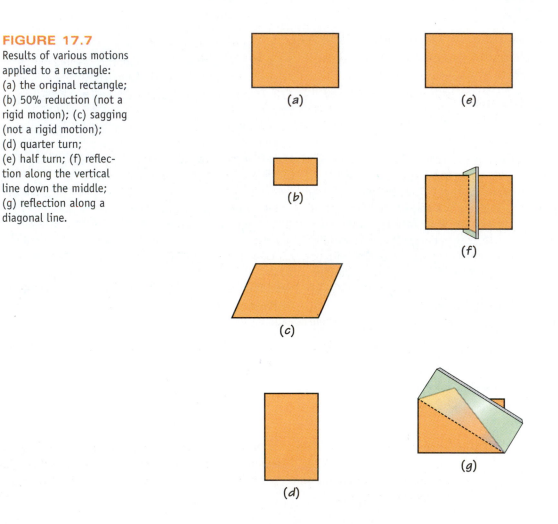

FIGURE 17.8
Glide reflection of
(a) footprints; (b) design
elements on a pot from
San Ildefonso Pueblo.

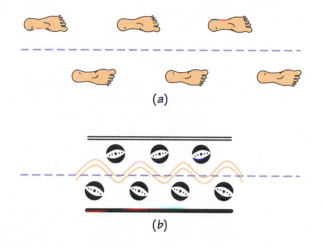

(a)

(b)

The only remaining kind of rigid motion in the plane is a hybrid of reflection and translation. Known as a **glide reflection,** it is the kind of pattern that your footprints make as you walk along: each successive element of the design (footprint) is a reflection of the previous one (Figure 17.8). The motion combines, in an integral way, translation ("glide") with a reflection across a line that is parallel to the direction of the translation.

A **rigid motion** is one that preserves the size and shape of figures; in particular, any pair of points is the same distance apart after the motion as before. Any rigid motion of the plane must be one of:

- Reflection (across a line)
- Rotation (around a point)
- Translation (in a particular direction)
- Glide reflection (across a line)

Performing one rigid motion after another results in a rigid motion that (surprisingly) must be one of the four types that we have just explored.

Preserving the Pattern

In terms of symmetry, we are especially interested in rigid motions like those of Figures 17.7e and 17.7f that **preserve the pattern**—that is, ones for which the pattern looks exactly the same, *with all the parts appearing in the same places,* after the motion is applied.

SPOTLIGHT 17.4

"Strive Then to Be Perfect"

Stand in front of a mirror and look at yourself. Are your left and right sides exactly symmetrical? Not on the inside, of course, but externally? What about the part in your hair, freckles on your face, evenness of your shoulders, outward bending of your ears?

It turns out that animals—including people—have a preference for bilateral symmetry, according to recent studies. That preference is for as perfect a symmetry as possible, so that even slight deviations from exact symmetry can make an individual less desirable to others.

In some cases, symmetry may signal fitness. For example, the more symmetrical that a flower is, the more nectar it produces, making it a better food source for pollinating insects. And the insects do prefer symmetrical flowers, thereby giving them a better chance of being pollinated than less perfect ones.

Symmetry, as a proxy for fitness, may affect mate selection by animals. Fruit flies and female barn swallows prefer males with symmetrical tails; a particular parasite can lead to an uneven tail.

Symmetrical racehorses may run faster; male lions with lopsided facial whisker-spot patterns die younger. Female zebra finches prefer males with symmetrical leg bands.

What about people? Computer-generated symmetrical female faces, generated from composites of individual photos, appear more attractive to men than photos of actual women. Studies also indicate that "symmetrical" men tend to have an earlier first sexual experience, more sexual partners, and more extramarital affairs. Women desiring fertile partners may want to consider a study that indicates that low sperm counts and poor sperm motility are associated with lack of symmetry of the hands. However, to what extent such symmetry in people signals individual or genetic fitness is yet to be determined.

You might enjoy thinking of applying these motions as a game, "The Pattern Game": you turn your back, I apply a transformation, then you turn back and see if you can tell if anything is changed.

The 90° rotation of Figure 17.7a into Figure 17.7d does not preserve the pattern. The moved rectangle doesn't fit exactly over the original rectangle. On the other hand, the 180° rotation in Figure 17.7e does preserve the pattern. It's true that the top of the original rectangle is now on the bottom of the transformed version, but you can't tell that has happened, because you can't distinguish the two. If you had turned your back while the motion was applied, you wouldn't be able to tell that anything had been done. A rotation by any multiple of 180° would also preserve the pattern.

Similarly, the reflection across the vertical line in Figure 17.7f preserves the pattern, while the one in Figure 17.7g, where the reflection line is along a diagonal, does not. Spotlight 17.4 discusses possible biological consequences of reflection symmetry or imperfections in it.

The pattern of footsteps in Figure 17.8a is not preserved under reflection along the direction of walking—there is not a left footprint directly across from a right footprint. The pattern is preserved under a glide reflection along the direction of walking, as well as by a translation of two steps, or one of four steps, and so on—but not by a translation of one step.

Analyzing Patterns

Given a pattern, we analyze it by determining which rigid motions preserve the pattern. These are often referred to as the **symmetries of the pattern.** We then can classify the pattern by which rigid motions preserve it.

We may think of a pattern as a recipe for repeating a figure (motif) indefinitely. Of course, any pattern we see in nature or art has only finitely many copies of the figure; but if the recipe for repetition is clear, we may imagine that we are looking at just a part of a pattern that extends indefinitely.

Patterns in the plane can be divided into those that have indefinitely many repetitions in

- no direction—the **rosette patterns**
- exactly one direction (and its reverse)—the **strip patterns**
- more than one direction—the **wallpaper patterns**

A rosette pattern describes the possible symmetries for a flower. There is just one flower in the pattern; the repetition aspect of symmetry consists of the repetition of the petals around the stem. Translations and glide reflections do not come into play. The pattern is preserved under a rotation by certain angles, corresponding to the number of petals. There may or may not be reflections that preserve it, depending on whether the petal itself has reflection symmetry. Most flowers do (Figure 17.9, left), but some do not. An everyday example of the rosette pattern—

FIGURE 17.9 (*left*) Flower with petals with reflection symmetry. (*right*) Pinwheel.

a human-made one — that does not have reflection symmetry is a pinwheel (Figure 17.9, right). If there is no reflection symmetry, the motif of the pattern (the element that is repeated) is an entire petal; if there is reflection symmetry, the motif is just half a petal, because the entire pattern can be generated by rotation and reflection of a half petal. The fact that these are the only possibilities is sometimes called *Leonardo's theorem,* after Leonardo da Vinci, who, in the course of planning the design of churches, needed to decide if chapels and niches could be added without destroying the symmetry of the central design.

Leonardo realized that there were two different classes of rosettes, the ones without reflection symmetry *(cyclic rosettes)* and the ones with reflection symmetry *(dihedral rosettes)* (see Figure 17.9). The respective notations for the patterns are *cn* and *dn*, where *n* is the number of times that the rosette coincides with its original position in one complete turn around the center. It coincides with itself for every rotation of $360°/n$. A cyclic pattern has no lines of reflection symmetry, while the dihedral pattern *dn* has *n* different lines of reflection symmetry. The flower in Figure 17.9 has a dihedral pattern, because each petal has reflection symmetry. The pinwheel in Figure 17.9 has pattern *c8*.

Strip Patterns

We illustrate the different kinds of strip patterns, and their "ingredient" symmetries, with patterns in the art of the Bakuba people of the Democratic Republic of the Congo, who are noted for their fascination with pattern and symmetry (see Spotlight 17.5).

All of the strip patterns offer repetition and **translation symmetry** along the direction of the strip. For simplicity, we will always position the pattern so that its repetition runs horizontally.

It may be that the pattern has no other rigid motions that preserve it apart from translation, as in Figure 17.10a.

The simplest other rigid motion to check for preservation of the pattern is reflection across a line. For a strip pattern, the center line of the strip may be a reflection line; if so, as in Figure 17.10b, we say that the pattern has symmetry across a horizontal line. There may instead be reflection across a *vertical* axis, such as the vertical lines through or between the V's in Figure 17.10c.

What kind of rotational symmetry can a strip pattern have? The only possibility for a strip pattern is a rotation by 180° (a half-turn), since any other angle won't even bring the strip back into itself. (We don't count rotations of 360° or integer multiples [full turns], since any pattern is preserved under these.) Figure 17.10d shows a strip pattern that is unchanged by a 180° rotation about any point at the center of the small crosshatched regions.

FIGURE 17.10
Bakuba patterns.
(a) Carved stool; (b) pile
cloth; (c) pile cloth;
(d) embroidered cloth;
(e) embroidered cloth;
(f) carved back of wooden
mask; (g) carved box.

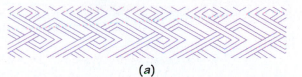

(a)

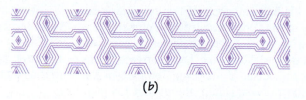

(b)

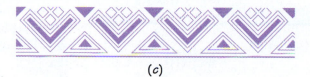

(c)

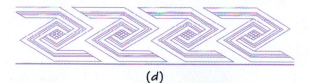

(d)

(e)

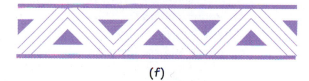

(f)

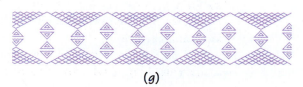

(g)

SPOTLIGHT

17.5

Patterns Created by the Bakuba People

Among the Bakuba people of the Democratic Republic of the Congo (shaded area of map), it is considered an achievement to invent a new pattern, and every Bakuba king had to create a new pattern at the outset of his reign. The pattern was displayed on the king's drum throughout his reign and, for some kings, on his dynastic statue.

When missionaries first showed a motorcycle to a Bakuba king in the 1920s, he showed little interest in it. But the king was so enthralled by the novel pattern the tire tracks made in the sand that he had it copied and gave it his name.

Source: Adapted from Jan Vansina, *The Children of Woot*, University of Wisconsin Press, Madison, 1978, p. 221.

Two women with raffia cloths from the Bakuba village of Mbelo, July 1985; Mpidi Muya with embroidered raffia cloth (left) and Muema Kenye with plush and embroidered raffia cloth (right).

The pattern made by tire tracks fascinated the Bakuba people.

What about glide reflections? A row of alternating p's and b's has glide reflection:

Glide	P	P	P	P	P	P	P	P	P
Reflection	P	P	P	P	P	P	P	P	P
	b	b	b	b	b	b	b	b	b
Glide reflection	p	b	p	b	p	b	p	b	p

For glide reflection, a p is translated as far as the next b and is then reflected upside down. Figure 17.10e shows a Bakuba pattern whose only symmetry (except for translation) is glide reflection.

Having examined symmetries on strip patterns, we can ask: What *combinations* of the four are possible? It turns out that apart from the five kinds of patterns we have already seen, there are only two other possibilities: we can have vertical line reflection, half-turns, and glide reflection, either with (Figure 17.10f) or without horizontal line reflection (Figure 17.10g).

Mathematical analysis reveals:

There are only seven ways to repeat a pattern along a strip.

That this number is so small is quite surprising, since there are myriad different design elements (motifs). The key idea is that two designs may look entirely different yet share the same pattern of reproducing their design elements.

Symmetry Groups

We mentioned earlier that the key mathematical idea about detecting and analyzing symmetry is to look not at the motifs of a pattern but at its symmetries, the transformations that preserve the pattern.

The symmetries of a pattern have some notable properties:

- If we combine two symmetries by applying first one and then the other, we get another symmetry.
- There is an identity, or "null," symmetry that doesn't move anything, but leaves every point of the pattern exactly where it is.
- Each symmetry has an inverse or "opposite" that undoes it and also preserves the pattern. A rotation is undone by an equal rotation in the opposite direction, a reflection is its own inverse, and a translation or glide reflection is undone by another of the same distance in the opposite direction.

■ In applying a number of symmetries one after the other, we may combine consecutive ones without affecting the result.

These properties are common to many kinds of mathematical objects; they characterize what mathematicians call a *group*. Various collections of numbers and numerical operations that are already familiar to you are groups.

EXAMPLE   *A Group of Numbers*

The positive real numbers form a group under multiplication:

■ Multiplying two positive real numbers yields another positive real number.
■ The positive real number 1 is an identity element.
■ Any positive real number x has an inverse $1/x$ in the collection.
■ In multiplying several numbers together, it doesn't matter if we first multiply together some adjacent pairs of numbers, that is, it doesn't matter how we group or parenthesize the multiplication. For instance, $2 \times 3 \times 4 \times 5$ is equal to $2 \times (3 \times 4) \times 5 = 2 \times 12 \times 5$ and also to $(2 \times 3) \times 4 \times 5 = 6 \times 4 \times 5$. ◆

A **group** is a collection of elements $\{A, B, \ldots\}$ and an operation $\circ$ between pairs of them such that the following properties hold:

closure: The result of one element operating on another is itself an element of the collection ($A \circ B$ is in the collection).
identity element: There is a special element I, called the identity element, such that the result of an operation involving the identity and any element is that same element ($I \circ A = A$ and $A \circ I = A$).
inverses: For any element, A, there is another element, called its inverse and denoted A^{-1}, such that the result of an operation involving an element and its inverse is the identity element ($A \circ A^{-1} = I$ and $A^{-1} \circ A = I$).
associativity: The result of several consecutive operations is the same regardless of grouping or parenthesizing, provided the consecutive order of operations is maintained: $A \circ B \circ C = A \circ (B \circ C) = (A \circ B) \circ C$.

The group of symmetries that preserve a pattern is called the **symmetry group of the pattern.**

E X A M P L E   *The Symmetry Group of a Rectangle*

Consider the rectangle of Figure 17.11. Its symmetries, the rigid motions that bring it back to coincide with itself (even as they interchange the labeled corners), are

- the identity symmetry I, which leaves every point where it is
- a 180° (half-turn) rotation R around its center
- a reflection V in the vertical line through its center
- a reflection H in the horizontal line through its center

You should convince yourself that these four elements form a group. Combining any pair by applying first one and then the other is equivalent to one of the others; for example, applying first V and then H is the same as applying R, that is, $H \circ V = R$ (check this by following where the corner A goes to under the operations). The element I is an identity element. Each element is its own inverse. Try some examples to verify that associativity holds. For instance, $R \circ H \circ V = (R \circ H) \circ V = R \circ (H \circ V)$; in other words, applying V followed by H followed by R, we get the same result if we combine the first two and then apply the third, or if we combine the second two and apply the first followed by that combination. ◆

FIGURE 17.11

A rectangle, with reflection symmetries and 180° rotation symmetry marked.

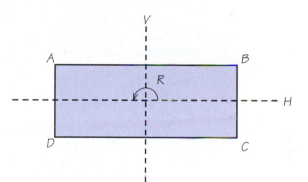

E X A M P L E   *Symmetry Groups of Strip Patterns*

Each of the strip patterns of Figure 17.10 is distinguished by a different group of symmetries. The pattern of Figure 17.10a is preserved only by translations. If we let T denote the smallest translation to the right that preserves the pattern, then the pattern is also preserved by $T \circ T$ (which we write as T^2), by $T \circ T \circ T = T^3$, and so forth. Although the pattern looks the same after each of these translations by different distances, we can tell these translations apart if we number each copy of the motif and observe which other motif it is carried into under the symmetry. For instance, T^2 takes each motif into the motif two to the right. The symmetry

T has an inverse T^{-1} among the symmetries of the pattern: the smallest translation to the *left* that preserves the pattern; and $T^{-1} \circ T^{-1}$ (which we write as T^{-2}), $T^{-1} \circ T^{-1} \circ T^{-1} = T^{-3}$, and so forth also are symmetries. The entire collection of symmetries of the pattern is

$$\{. \ . \ . \ , T^{-3}, T^{-2}, T^{-1}, I, T, T^2, T^3, \ . \ . \ .\}$$

From this listing, you see that it is natural to think of the identity I as being T^0. All of the strip patterns are preserved by translations, so the symmetry group of each includes the *subgroup* of all translations in this list. We say that the group is generated by T, and we write the group as $<T>$, where between the angle brackets we list symmetries (generators) that, in combination, produce all of the group elements.

The symmetry group of Figure 17.10e includes in addition a glide reflection G and all combinations of the glide reflection with the translations. Doing two glide reflections is equivalent to doing a translation, which we express as $G^2 = T$; the glide is only "half as far" as the shortest translation that preserves the pattern. Check that $G \circ T = T \circ G$. The symmetry group of the pattern is

$$\{. \ . \ . \ , G^{-3}, G^{-2} = T^{-1}, G^{-1}, I, G, G^2 = T, G^3, \ . \ . \ .\} = <G>$$

The pattern of Figure 17.10c is preserved by vertical reflections at regular intervals. If we let V denote reflections at a particular location, the other reflections can be obtained as combinations of V and T. The symmetry group of the pattern is

$$\{. \ . \ . \ , T^{-3}, T^{-2}, T^{-1}, I, T, T^2, T^3, \ . \ . \ . \ ;$$
$$. \ . \ . \ , T^{-3}V, T^{-2}V, T^{-1}V, V, TV, T^2V, T^3V, \ . \ . \ .\}$$

This group is notable because not all of its elements satisfy the *commutative property* that $A \circ B = B \circ A$, which you are used to for numerical operations ($a + b = b + a$, $a \times b = b \times a$). In fact, we do not have $VT = TV$, but instead $VT = T^{-1}V$, a fact that you should verify by labeling one of the V shapes in the pattern and observing where it is carried by each of these three combinations of symmetries. We can express the group as $<T, V \mid VT = T^{-1}V>$, where we list the generators and indicate relations among them.   ◆

We have made a transition from thinking about patterns in geometrical terms to reasoning about them in algebraic notation—in effect, applying one branch of mathematics to another. This kind of cross-fertilization is characteristic of contemporary mathematics.

The concept of a group is a fundamental one in the mathematical field of abstract algebra. The generality ("abstractness") is exactly why groups and other algebraic structures arise in so many applications, in areas ranging from crystallography, quantum physics, and cryptography, to error-correcting codes (see Chapters 9 and 10), anthropology (describing kinship systems; see Ascher [1991])—and analyzing symmetries of patterns.

Notation for Patterns

It's useful to have a standard notation for patterns, for purposes of communications. Crystallographers' notation is the one more commonly used. For the strip patterns, it consists of four symbols (an example is *pma2*):

1. The first symbol is always a *p*, which indicates that the pattern repeats (is "periodic") in the horizontal direction.
2. The second symbol is *m* if there is a vertical line of reflection, or a *1* otherwise.
3. The third symbol is

   ■ *m* (for "mirror") if there is a horizontal line of reflection (in which case there is also glide reflection),
   ■ *a* (for "alternating") if there is a glide reflection but no horizontal reflection, or
   ■ *1* if there is no horizontal reflection or glide reflection.

4. The fourth symbol is *2* if there is half-turn rotational symmetry, or *1* otherwise.

A *1* always means that the pattern does not have the symmetry corresponding to that position.

In the notation

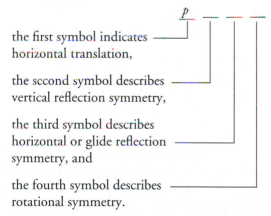

the first symbol indicates horizontal translation,

the second symbol describes vertical reflection symmetry,

the third symbol describes horizontal or glide reflection symmetry, and

the fourth symbol describes rotational symmetry.

Figure 17.12 gives a flowchart for identifying the seven ways patterns repeat, together with the notations for them.

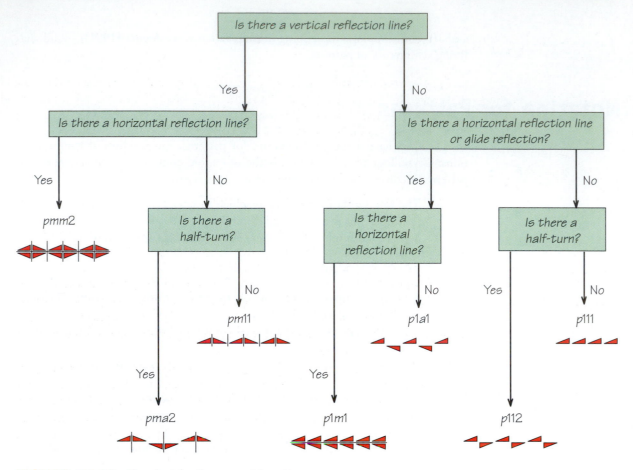

FIGURE 17.12   Flowchart for the seven strip patterns.

E X A M P L E   *Bakuba Patterns*

We use the flowchart of Figure 17.12 to analyze some of the Bakuba patterns of Figure 17.10.

Figure 17.10a does not have a vertical reflection, so we branch right, and the pattern notation begins to take shape as *p1_ _*. The figure does not have a horizontal reflection, nor a glide reflection, so we branch right again, filling in the third position in the notation, to get *p11_*. A half-turn preserves part but not all of the pattern, so we conclude that we have a *p111* pattern.

Figure 17.10b does not have vertical reflection, so we branch right, to *p1_ _*. The figure does have horizontal reflection, so we branch left and left, concluding that the pattern is *p1m1*.

Figure 17.10f has vertical reflection, so we branch left, to *pm_ _*. The figure does not have horizontal reflection, so we branch right but cannot yet fill in the third symbol. The figure does have a half-turn symmetry (and glide symmetry, too), with center on the middle of the three lines between any pair of closest triangles. So the pattern is *pma2*.   ◆

Imperfect Patterns

In applying these classification schemes to patterns on real objects, we need to take into account that the pattern itself may not be perfectly rendered. Also, patterns that are not on flat surfaces—for example, the pattern around the rim of a bowl or around the body of a jar—require some latitude in interpretation.

E X A M P L E   *Patterns on Pueblo Pottery*

The pitchers in Figure 17.13 are from a thousand-year-old Pueblo site at Starkweather Ruin near Reserve, New Mexico. We consider the patterns on the main bodies of the pitchers, which continue on the back sides. We suppose that they could be unwrapped and continued as strip patterns, and we consider them as such. We disregard the patterns on the spouts and handles.

We immediately come up against the question of the perfectness of the patterns. In Figure 17.13a the "teeth" on the left design element on the main body are "sharper" than those on the right. (The "teeth" represent the zigzagging of lightning bolts.) Is this lack of pattern, or just lack of perfection in executing one? For our analysis, we opt for the latter.

Similarly, what are we to make of the diagonal lines on the pitcher in Figure 17.13b? In the narrowest interpretation, these lines are part of the pattern and any rigid motion that is to qualify as a symmetry of the pattern must preserve them. More liberally, we may consider the lines as a kind of shading, a way to make the region appear gray; indeed, to an observer at a distance, that is the effect of the lines.

FIGURE 17.13   Reserve black-on-white pitchers from the Pueblo II horizon (A.D. 900–1100), excavated 1935–1936 from Starkweather Ruin by Professor Paul H. Nesbitt and students from Beloit College.

For the pattern on the body of the pitcher in Figure 17.13c, we notice that the jagged white line in the design element on the left has three "steps," while that in the one on the right has four. If we were really strict, we would decide that the two are different design elements. But we do detect a similarity of the two that we do not want to deny totally; we attribute the variations in the jagged lines to artistic license and for our purposes consider the two jagged lines to be the same. ◆

We follow the flowchart in Figure 17.12 and get the following:

- Figure 17.13a: Is there a vertical reflection? *No.* Is there a horizontal reflection or glide reflection? *No.* Is there a half-turn? *No.* Hence the pattern is *p111.*
- Figure 17.13b (narrow interpretation of the diagonal lines): Is there a vertical reflection? *No.* Is there a horizontal reflection or glide reflection? *No.* Is there a half-turn? *Yes* (e.g., around the center of each cross). The pattern is *p112.*
- Figure 17.13b (liberal interpretation—diagonal lines as shading, their direction doesn't have to be preserved): Is there a vertical reflection? *Yes* (e.g., on a vertical line through the center of a cross). Is there a horizontal reflection? *Yes* (e.g., through the center of a cross). The pattern is *pmm2.*
- Figure 17.13c: Is there a vertical reflection? *No.* Is there a horizontal reflection or glide reflection? *No.* Is there a half-turn? *Yes* (e.g., around the center of each jagged white line). The pattern is *p112.* (This pitcher has the interesting feature that the patterns on the neck and the body are mirror images of each other.)

Women made the pots at Starkweather; they strongly preferred the symmetry of half-turns; very few of the pots have any reflection symmetry, either reflection or glide. The avoidance of reflection symmetry was a consistent feature of pottery of the indigenous peoples of the Western Hemisphere.

REVIEW VOCABULARY

Divine proportion Another term for the golden ratio.

Fibonacci numbers The numbers in the sequence 1, 1, 2, 3, 5, 8, 13, 21, 34, . . . (each number after the second is obtained by adding the two preceding numbers).

Geometric mean The geometric mean of two numbers a and b is $\sqrt{ab}$.

Glide reflection A combination of translation (= glide) and reflection in a line parallel to the translation direction. Example: pbpbpb.

Golden ratio, golden mean The number $\phi = \frac{1+\sqrt{5}}{2} = 1.618. . . .$

Golden rectangle A rectangle the lengths of whose sides are in the golden ratio.

Group A group is a collection of elements with an operation on pairs of them such that the collection is closed under the operation, there is an identity for the operation, each element has an inverse, and the operation is associative.

Isometry Another word for rigid motion. Angles and distances, and consequently shape and size, remain unchanged by a rigid motion. (For plane figures there are only four possible isometries: reflection, rotation, translation, and glide reflection.)

Phyllotaxis   The spiral pattern of shoots, leaves, or seeds around the stem of a plant.

Preserves the pattern   A transformation preserves a pattern if all parts of the pattern look exactly the same after the transformation has been performed.

Recursion   A method of defining a sequence of numbers, in which the next number is given in terms of previous ones.

Rigid motion   A motion that preserves the size and shape of figures; in particular, any pair of points is the same distance apart after the motion as before.

Rosette pattern   A pattern whose only symmetries are rotations about a single point and reflections through that point.

Rotational symmetry   A figure has rotational

symmetry if a rotation about its "center" leaves it looking the same, like the letter S.

Strip pattern   A pattern that has indefinitely many repetitions in one direction.

Symmetry of the pattern   A transformation of a pattern is a symmetry of the pattern if it preserves the pattern.

Symmetry group of a pattern   The group of symmetries that preserve the pattern.

Translation   A rigid motion that moves everything a certain distance in one direction.

Translation symmetry   An infinite figure has translation symmetry if it can be translated (slid, without turning) along itself without appearing to have changed. Example: AAA

Wallpaper pattern   A pattern in the plane that has indefinitely many repetitions in more than one direction.

SUGGESTED READINGS

ASCHER, MARCIA. *Ethnomathematics: A Multicultural View of Mathematical Ideas,* Brooks/Cole, 1991, chapter 3. The logic of kin relations (pp. 66–83) shows that kinship systems have the structure of dihedral groups.

BOLES, MARTHA, AND ROCHELLE NEWMAN. *The Golden Relationship: Art, Math & Nature, Book 1: Universal Patterns; Book 2: The Surface Plane,* Pythagorean Press, Bradford, Mass., 1992.

BROWNE, MALCOLM W. Can't decide if that centerfold is a perfect 10? Just do the math, *New York Times* (October 20, 1998) (national edition), D5. http://www.nytimes.com/library/national/science/102098sci-essay. html.

CRISLER, NANCY. *Symmetry & Patterns,* COMAP, Inc., Lexington, Mass., 1995.

CROWE, DONALD W. *Symmetry, Rigid Motions and Patterns,* HiMAP Module 4, COMAP, Inc., Lexington, Mass., 1987. Reprinted in smaller format in *The UMAP Journal,* 8: 207–236 (1987). Instructional module on rigid motions of the plane, strip patterns, and wallpaper patterns, with worksheets.

GALLIAN, JOSEPH A. Symmetry in logos and hubcaps, *American Mathematical Monthly,* 97(3): 235–238 (March 1990).

GALLIAN JOSEPH A. Finite plane symmetry groups, *Journal of Chemical Education,* 67(7): 549–550 (July 1990). Hubcap examples.

HARGITTAI, ISTVÁN, AND MAGDOLNA HARGITTAI. *Symmetry: A Unifying Concept,* Shelter Publications, Bolinas, Calif., 1994.

HERZ-FISCHLER, ROGER. *A Mathematical History of Division in Extreme and Mean Ratio,* Wilfrid Laurier University Press, Waterloo, Ont., Canada, 1987. Reprint with a new preface, under the title *Mathematical History of the Golden Number,* Dover, New York, 1998.

HOGGATT, VERNER E., JR. *Fibonacci and Lucas Numbers,* Houghton Mifflin, New York, 1969.

HUNTLEY, H. E. *The Divine Proportion,* Dover, New York, 1970.

MARKOWSKY, GEORGE. Misconceptions about the golden ratio, *College Mathematics Journal,* 23(1): 2–19 (January 1992).

MARTIN, GEORGE E. *Transformation Geometry: An Introduction to Symmetry,* Springer-Verlag, New York, 1982.

O'DAFFER, PHARES G., AND STANLEY R. CLEMENS. *Geometry: An Investigative Approach,* Addison-Wesley, Reading, Mass., 1976, chapters 1–5. A gentle introduction to the geometry of symmetry, with lots of examples and illustrations. Chapter 4 gives an elementary proof that there are only four kinds of rigid motions in the plane.

RUNION, GARTH E. *The Golden Section and Related Curiosa,* Scott, Foresman, Glenview, Ill., 1972.

SIBLEY, THOMAS Q. *Geometric Patterns: A Study in Symmetry,* Saint John's University, Collegeville, Minn., 1989.

STEWART, IAN. Mathematical recreations: Daisy, Daisy, give me your answer, do, *Scientific American,* 272(1): 96–99 (January 1995). Explains the occurrence of Fibonacci numbers in plants based on the dynamics of plant growth and the efficient packing of seeds into spiral faces.

WASHBURN, DOROTHY K., AND DONALD W. CROWE. *Symmetries of Culture: Theory and Practice of Plane Pattern Analysis,* University of Washington Press, Seattle, 1988. An introduction to the mathematics of symmetry, splendidly illustrated with photographs of patterns from cultures all over the world. Includes a complete analysis of patterns with two colors. Appendixes contain proofs of the facts that there are only four rigid motions in the plane and that there are exactly seven strip patterns.

SUGGESTED WEB SITES

Computer Software for Tiling. **http://www.geom.umn.edu/software/tilings** Lists programs for various platforms that allow the user to create designs featuring the rosette, strip, and wallpaper patterns.

Escher Web Sketch. **http://www-sphhys.unil.ch/escher/** Interactive Web program that allows a user to design repeating patterns. Choose a wallpaper pattern using crystallographic notation and draw on the screen a colored design for the motif, and the program then reproduces the motif using the pattern. The software (for Windows, Macintosh, and Unix) can also be downloaded.

Kali. **http://www.geom.umn.edu/java/Kali/** Interactive Web program that lets the user draw pictures under the action of rosette, strip, or wallpaper groups. Versions for various platforms can be downloaded.

RepTiles. **ftp://ftp.uni-bielefeld.de/pub/math/tiling/reptiles/RepTiles2.0.1.hqx** Interactive Macintosh application for designing wallpaper patterns, plus systematically generating all possible periodic tilings of the plane by applying "topological transformations" and "symmetry."

SKILLS CHECK

1. What is the geometric mean of 4 and 36?

   (a) 12
   (b) 16
   (c) 20

2. Which of the following rectangles is an approximate golden rectangle?

   (a) 10 by 16
   (b) 6 by 13
   (c) 8 by 11

3. Which of the following letters has a rotation isometry?

    (a)   S   (b)   K   (c)   Y

4. Assume the following two patterns continue in both directions. Which of these patterns has a reflection isometry?   ZZZZZZZZ
UUUUUUUU

    (a)   ZZZZZZZZ only
    (b)   UUUUUUUU only
    (c)   neither

5. What isometries does this strip pattern have?

    JΓ   JΓ   JΓ   JΓ

    (a)   Translation and glide reflection only
    (b)   Translation and rotation only
    (c)   Translation, rotation, and glide reflection only

6. What isometries does this wallpaper pattern have?

    (a)   Translation and reflection only
    (b)   Translation and rotation only
    (c)   Translation, rotation, and reflection

7. What isometries does this wallpaper pattern have?

    (a)   Translation only
    (b)   Translation and reflection only
    (c)   Translation, rotation, and reflection

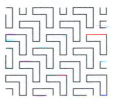

EXERCISES   ▲ *Optional.*   ■ *Advanced.*   ◆ *Discussion.*

Fibonacci Numbers

1. Examine the "scales" on the surface of a pineapple, which are arranged in spirals (parastichies) around the fruit. Note that there are spirals in three distinct directions. For each direction, how many spirals are there?

2. Repeat Exercise 1, but for a pinecone from your area.

3. Repeat Exercise 1, but for a sunflower.

4. Here are two primitive models of natural increase of biological populations, similar to those Fibonacci hypothesized around the year 1200. A pair of newborn male and female rabbits is placed in an enclosure to breed.

    (a) Suppose that the rabbits start to bear young one month after their own birth. This may be unrealistic for rabbits, but we could substitute another species for which it is realistic; Fibonacci used rabbits. At the end of each month, they have another male–female pair, which in turn matures and starts to bear young one month later. Assuming that none of the rabbits dies, how many pairs of rabbits will there be at the end of six months from the start (just before any births for that month)? (*Hint:* Draw a month-by-month chart of the situation at the end of the month, just before any births.)

    (b) Repeat part (a), but assume instead that the rabbits start to bear young exactly two months after their own birth.

The Golden Ratio

5. Put the golden ratio $\phi = (1 + \sqrt{5})/2$ into the memory of your calculator.

    (a) Look at the value of ϕ. Now square it (either use the x^2 button or multiply it by itself). What do you observe?

(b)   Back to ϕ. Now take its reciprocal (either use the $1/x$ button or divide it into 1). What do you observe?
(c)   What formula explains what you saw in part (a)?
(d)   What formula explains what you saw in part (b)?

6.   The golden ratio satisfies the equation $x^2 = x + 1$.

(a)   Show that $(1 - \phi)$ also satisfies the equation.
(b)   Use part (a) to show that $(1 - \phi) = (1 - \sqrt{5})/2$ is the other solution to $x^2 - x - 1 = 0$.

7.   The geometric mean has interpretations in both arithmetic and geometry.

(a)   Find the geometric mean of 3 and 27.
(b)   Find the length of a side of a square that has the same area as a rectangle that is 4 by 64.

8.   Here's further practice on arithmetic and geometric interpretations of the geometric mean:

(a)   Find the geometric mean of 4 and 9.
(b)   You are to make a golden rectangle with 6 inches of string. How wide should it be, and how high?

9.   Another sequence closely related to the Fibonacci sequence is the Lucas sequence, which is formed using the same recursive rule but different starting numbers. The nth Lucas number L_n is given by

$L_1 = 1, L_2 = 3$, and $L_{n+1} = L_n + L_{n-1}$ for $n \geq 2$

(a)   Calculate L_3 through L_{10}.
(b)   Calculate the ratio of successive terms of the Lucas sequence:

$$\frac{L_2}{L_1}, \frac{L_3}{L_2}, \ldots, \frac{L_{10}}{L_9}$$

What do you notice?

10.   For a sequence specified by a recursive rule, finding an explicit expression for the nth term is not easy, nor is the form necessarily simple. An exact expression for the nth term of the Fibonacci sequence is given by the Binet formula:

$$F_n = \frac{1}{\sqrt{5}}\left(\frac{1 + \sqrt{5}}{2}\right)^n - \frac{1}{\sqrt{5}}\left(\frac{1 - \sqrt{5}}{2}\right)^n$$

(a)   Verify the formula for $n = 1$ and $n = 2$ (by multiplying out, not by using a calculator).
(b)   Use the Binet formula and your calculator to find F_5.
(c)   In fact, the second term on the right of the equation gets closer and closer to 0 as n gets large. Since we know that the Fibonacci numbers are integers, we can just round off the result of calculating the first term. Find F_{13} by calculating the first term with your calculator and rounding.

11.   For two positive numbers x and y, show that the arithmetic mean $(x + y)/2$ is always greater than or equal to the geometric mean $x^{1/2}y^{1/2} = \sqrt{xy}$. (*Hint:* Suppose that the claim is false, so that $(x + y)/2 < \sqrt{xy}$.) Square both sides of the inequality, bring all terms to one side, factor, and observe a contradiction.

12.   You may remember having to work problems like, "If Joe can dig a ditch in 3 days, and Sam can dig it in 4, how long will it take the two of them working together?" The answer is related to the *harmonic mean* of 3 and 4. The formula for the harmonic mean of two numbers x and y is

$$\frac{2}{1/x + 1/y}$$

(a)   Calculate the answer for Joe and Sam, which is *one-half* of the harmonic mean of 3 and 4. Explain why this is the correct answer.
(b)   Show that the harmonic mean of two positive numbers is always less than or equal to the geometric mean. (Thus, in light of Exercise 11, we have the general conclusion that

$H \leq G \leq A$, where H stands for the harmonic mean, G for the geometric mean, and A for the arithmetic mean.) (*Hint:* Suppose that the claim is false. Simplify the fraction that is the harmonic mean, square both sides of the inequality, and proceed as in Exercise 11.)

(c)   Show once more that the harmonic mean of two positive numbers is always less than the geometric mean, but this time do it with less work: let $A = 1/x$ and $B = 1/y$, and discover one connection (equation) between the harmonic mean of x and y and the arithmetic mean of A and B, and a second connection between the geometric mean of x and y and the geometric mean of A and B. Then use Exercise 11 on A and B.

(d)   What should be the formula for the geometric mean of three numbers? of n numbers?

(e)   As in part (d), but for the harmonic mean.

13.   (Adapted from Martin Gardner, *Mathematical Circus,* Knopf, New York, 1979.) Here is a trick to "prove" that you can calculate faster than a person with a calculator. Turn your back and ask a friend to write down any two positive integers, then add them to get a third, then add the second and third to get a fourth, etc., adding each time the last two until there are 10 numbers. Have your friend show you the list, whereupon you write down right away the total of all 10, while your friend begins to add them up on the calculator (to prove that you're right). The secret: the total is always 11 times the 7th number, and multiplying by 11 is pretty easy to do in your head (just add each pair of neighboring digits, carrying if necessary). Suppose that your friend writes down m and n as the first two numbers; show that indeed the total of all 10 numbers is 11 times the 7th number.

14.   (Adapted from Martin Gardner, *Mathematical Circus,* Knopf, New York, 1979.) The game of Fibonacci Nim begins with n counters. Two players take turns removing at least one counter, but no more than twice as many as the opponent just did. The winner is the player who takes the last counter. One other rule: the first player may not win immediately by taking all the counters on the first turn!

(a)   Play this game taking turns with an opponent and starting with different numbers n of counters and try to come up with a strategy for one player or the other to win. (*Hint:* The key is that any positive integer can be represented uniquely as a sum of Fibonacci numbers.)

(b)   As in part (a), but with the rule changes that the player who takes the last counter loses and the first player may not take all but one counter.

Preserving the Pattern

15.   Determine whether each of the following statements is always true or sometimes false. (Drawing some sketches may be helpful.)

(a)   A line reflection preserves collinearity of points. That is, if the points A, B, and C are in a straight line (collinear), then their images reflected in some other line also lie in a straight line.

(b)   A line reflection preserves betweenness. That is, if the collinear points A, B, and C (with B between A and C) are reflected about a line, then the image of B is between the images of A and C.

(c)   The image of a line segment under a line reflection is a line segment of the same length.

(d)   The image of an angle under a line reflection is an angle of the same measure.

(e)   The image of a pair of parallel lines under a line reflection is a pair of parallel lines.

16.   Determine whether each of the following statements is always true or sometimes false. (Drawing some sketches may be helpful.)

(a)   The image of a pair of perpendicular lines under a line reflection is a pair of perpendicular lines.

(b)   The image of a square under a line reflection is a square.

(c)   Label the vertices of a square A, B, C, and D in a clockwise direction. Then their images A', B', C', and D' under a line reflection also follow a clockwise direction.

(d)   The perimeter of a geometric figure is equal to the perimeter of its image under a line reflection.

(e)   The image of a vertical line under a line reflection is always a vertical line.

17.   Which of the capital letters of the alphabet have

(a)   a horizontal line of reflection symmetry?

(b)   a vertical line of reflection symmetry?

(c)   rotational symmetry? (Assume that each letter is drawn in the most symmetric way. For example, the upper and lower loops of "B" should be the same size.)

18.   Repeat Exercise 17 for the lowercase letters.

19.   In *The Complete Walker III* (3rd ed., Knopf, New York, 1984, p. 505), Colin Fletcher's answer to "What games should I take on a backpacking trip?" is the game he calls "Colinvert": "You strive to find

words with meaningful mirror (or half-turn) images." Some of the words he found are

MOM   WOW   pod   MUd   bUM

(a)   Which of his words reflect into themselves?

(b)   Which of his words rotate into themselves?

(c)   Find some more words or phrases of these various types—the longer, the better.

20.   Repeat Exercise 19, but for words written vertically instead of horizontally.

Analyzing Patterns

21.   Give the notation (e.g., *d4* or *c5*) for the symmetry patterns of the rosettes in hubcaps (a) through (c), disregarding the logos in the centers.

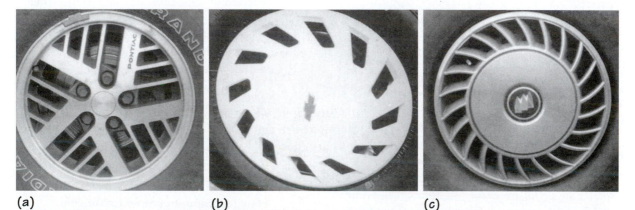

(a)   (b)   (c)

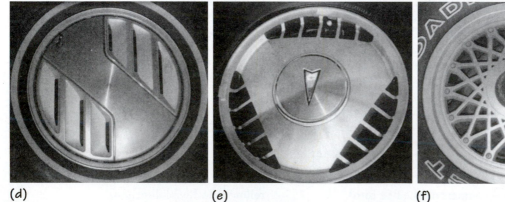

(d)   (e)   (f)

(Can you identify the make of car and year for each hubcap?)

22.   Repeat Exercise 21, for hubcaps (d) through (f).

23.   Repeat Exercise 21, for corporate logos (a) through (c). (Can you identify the corporations?)

(a)   (b)   (c)

24.   Repeat Exercise 21, for corporate logos (d) through (f).

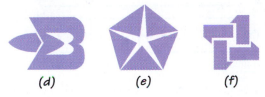

(d)   (e)   (f)

25.   For each of the shapes in parts (a) through (e) of the accompanying figure, determine all lines of symmetry.

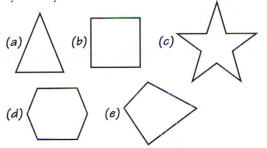

26.   Repeat Exercise 25, but for the shapes in parts (f) through (j).

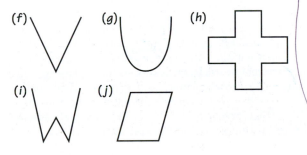

Strip Patterns

27.   For each of the following strip patterns, identify the rigid motions that preserve the pattern:

   (a)   AAAAAAAAAA   (c)   0000000000
   (b)   BBBBBBBBBB   (d)   FFFFFFFFFF

28.   Repeat Exercise 27, but for

   (a)   NNNNNNNNNN   (c)   dbpqdbpqdbpq
   (b)   bdbdbdbdbd

Symmetry Groups

29.   What is the group of symmetries of

   (a)   an equilateral triangle (all three sides equal)?
   (b)   an isosceles triangle (two equal sides) that is not equilateral?
   (c)   a scalene triangle (no pair of sides equal)?

30.   What is the group of symmetries of a square?

31.   Explain, by referring to the properties of a group, whether the collection of all real numbers is a group under the operation of (a) addition; (b) multiplication.

32.   (a)   Give a numerical example to show that the operation of subtraction on the integers is not associative.
   (b)   Repeat part (a), but for division on the positive real numbers.

33.   What are the elements of the group of symmetries of (a) Figure 17.10b? (b) Figure 17.10f?

34.   What are the elements of the group of symmetries of (a) Figure 17.10d? (b) Figure 17.10g?

35.   What are the elements of the group of symmetries of the dihedral pattern $d8$ (see the flower in Figure 17.9)?

36.   What is the group of symmetries of the cyclic pattern $c8$?

Notation for Patterns

37. Use the flowchart in Figure 17.12 to identify (by International Crystallographic Union notation) the types of the strip patterns from Hungarian needlework, shown in the illustration below.

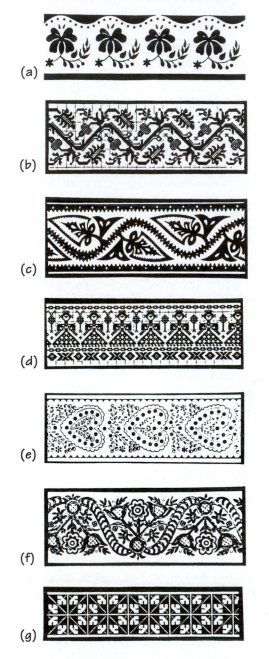

38. [Contributed by Margaret A. Owens, California State University, Chico.] In each of the four accompanying examples, two adjacent triangles of an infinite strip are shown.

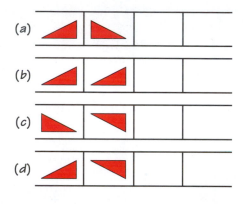

For each example

(a)   Determine a motion (translation, reflection, rotation, or glide reflection) that takes the first (= left) triangle to the second (= right) one.

(b)   Draw the next four triangles of the infinite strip that would result if the second triangle is moved to the next space by another motion of the same kind, and so on.

(c)   Identify (by notation) the resulting strip as one of the seven possible strip patterns.

Hungarian needlework designs. (a) Edge decoration of table cover from Kalocsa, southern Hungary. (b) Pillow end decoration from Tolna County, southwest Hungary. (c) Decoration patched onto a long embroidered felt coat of Hungarian shepherds in Bihar County, eastern Hungary. (d) Embroidered edge decoration of bed sheet from the eighteenth century. (Note the deviations from symmetry in the lower stripes of the pattern.) (e) Shirt from Karád, southwest Hungary. (f) Pillow decoration pattern from Torockó (Rimetea), Transylvania, Romania. (G) Grape leaf pattern from the territory east of the river Tisza.

Imperfect Patterns

39. Repeat Exercise 37, for the accompanying eight strip patterns, all of which appear on the brass straps for a single lamp from nineteenth-century Benin in West Africa. [From H. Ling Roth, *In Great Benin*.] Note that the patterns are roughly carved, so you will need to discern the intent of the artist.

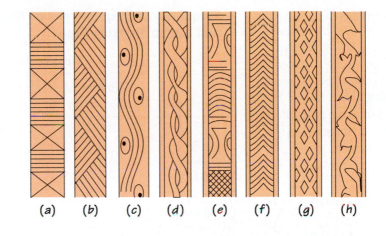

(a)   (b)   (c)   (d)   (e)   (f)   (g)   (h)

40. Repeat Exercise 37, for the accompanying patterns from San Ildefonso Pueblo, New Mexico.

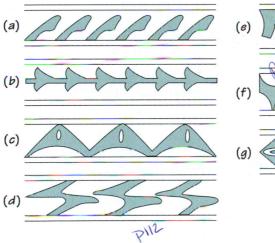

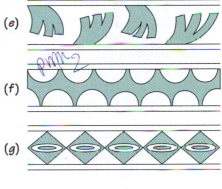

Additional Exercises

41. For positive integers *a* and *n*, the expression *a* and *n* means remainder when *a* is divided by *n*. Thus, 23 mod 4 = 3, since 15 = 5·4 + 3, and we say that "23 is equivalent to 3 modulo 4" (see Chapter 10 for further details about this *modular arith-* metic). Every positive integer is equivalent to either 0, 1, 2, or 3 modulo 4. Consider the collection of elements {0 1, 2, 3} and the operation $\oplus$ on them defined by $a \oplus b = (a + b) \bmod 4$. Show that under this operation, the collection forms a group.

42. The table at the right shows comparative data about the frequency of occurrence of strip designs of various types on pottery (Mesa Verde, United States) and smoking pipes (Begho, Ghana, Africa) from two continents.

Frequency of Strip Designs on Mesa Verde Pottery and Begho Smoking Pipes

Strip Type	Mesa Verde		Begho	
	Number of Examples	Percentage of Total	Number of Examples	Percentage of Total
p111	7	4	4	2
p1m1	5	3	9	4
pm11	12	7	22	10
p112	93	53	19	8
p1a1	11	6	2	1
pma2	27	16	9	4
pmm2	19	11	165	72
Totals	174		230	

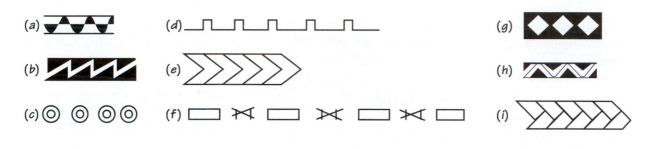

(a) Which types of motions appear to be preferred for designs from each of the two localities?

(b) What other conclusions do you draw from the data of this table?

(c) On the evidence of the table alone, in which locality is each of the strip patterns in the illustration above most likely to have been found?

TECHNOLOGY CORNER

Generating Fibonacci Numbers with a Spreadsheet

The recursive definition of Fibonacci numbers can easily be incorporated into a spreadsheet. The first column of Figure 17.14 lists the first 10 Fibonacci numbers. The first two numbers of the sequence are placed in entries **A2** and **A3.** Entry **A4** is defined as the sum of entries **A2** and **A3,** using the formula **=A2+A3.** This formula can then be copied to compute additional Fibonacci numbers.

The ratios of consecutive Fibonacci numbers are computed in the second column. Entry **B3** is defined by the function **=A3/A2.** This formula can then be

	A	B	C
1	Fib number F_n	Ratio F_n/F_(n-1)	
2	1		
3	1	1	
4	2	2	
5	3	1.5	
6	5	1.666666667	
7	8	1.6	
8	13	1.625	
9	21	1.615384615	
10	34	1.619047619	
11	55	1.617647059	

FIGURE 17.14

	A	B
1	Term	Ratio
2	1	
3	1	1
4	1	1
5	3	3
6	5	1.666667
7	9	1.8
8	17	1.888889
9	31	1.823529
10	57	1.83871
11	105	1.842105

FIGURE 17.15

copied to compute ratios of subsequent Fibonacci numbers.

TASK 1. We know that the ratios in the second column are drifting toward the golden ratio. How far into the sequence must we go until the first four decimal places of the ratio are fixed as 1.6180 . . . ?

TASK 2. To convert this sequence to the Lucas sequence, change the entry **A3** from 1 to 3. How far into the sequence must we now go until the first four decimal places of the ratio become fixed?

Another Recursive Sequence

Consider the sequence whose first three terms are 1, 1, 1. Each subsequent term is defined as the sum of the previous *three* terms. The spreadsheet in Figure 17.15 shows the first 10 terms and the ratios of consecutive terms.

TASK 3. The ratios of this sequence are also drifting toward a number. Extend the spreadsheet until the first four decimal places of this number become fixed.

TASK 4. If any or all of the first three terms of this sequence are changed, do the resulting ratios still drift toward the same number?

Exploration

Extend the original spreadsheet in Figure 17.15 until the first six decimal places of the ratio are fixed. Then extend until the first eight decimal places are fixed. Extend again until the first 10 decimal places are fixed. As you continue to extend the spreadsheet until 12, 14, 16, or more decimal places are fixed, are about the same number of *additional* terms required each time? Does the number of additional terms tend to increase or decrease?

writing projects

1 ▶ The Fibonacci Association is devoted to fostering interest in Fibonacci and related numbers. In November 1988, the society's journal, *The Fibonacci Quarterly,* published "Suppose More Rabbits Are Born" (pp. 306–311), by Shari Lynn Levine (a high school student when she wrote it). The article begins: "How would Fibonacci's age-old sequence be redefined if, instead of bearing one pair of baby rabbits per month, the mature rabbits bear two pairs of baby rabbits per month?" The article goes on to discuss properties of the resulting "Beta-nacci" sequence and the sequences that result from even greater rabbit fertility. Here we ask you to

rediscover some of Shari's results about the Beta-nacci sequence:

(a)   How many rabbits will there be each month for the first 12 months?

(b)   What is the recursive rule for the nth Beta-nacci number B_n?

(c)   For the terms of the sequence in part (a), calculate the ratios B_{n+1}/B_n of successive terms. (*Motivating hint:* It's not the golden ratio this time.)

(d)   Suppose that the ratio of successive terms approaches a number x. We show how to find x exactly. For very large n, we have $B_{n+1} \approx xB_n$ $\approx x^2 B_{n-1}$. Substituting these values into the recursive rule for the sequence and dividing by B_{n-1} gives us the equation $x^2 = x + 2$. Solve this equation for x (you can use the quadratic formula). Make a table of values of $3B_n$ versus 2_n. From the evidence, can you suggest a formula for B_n?

2 ▶ Generalize Writing Project 1, parts (a) through (d)

(a)   to the case of each pair of rabbits having three pairs of rabbits (the "Gamma-nacci" sequence).

(b)   to the case of each pair of rabbits having q pairs of rabbits.

3 ▶ Our emphasis in this chapter is on the patterns and practicality of symmetry. Fibonacci numbers and the golden ratio also have applications in efficient searching. Suppose, for example, that you need to determine the location and depth of the deepest point in the ocean along a particular transit line 1000 m long to within $t = 10$ m on either side. (Another setting would be trying to determine the thickest point of a seam of gold.) Suppose also that it doesn't make sense to try to take observations any closer than $\epsilon = 5$ m apart (it's hard to keep the boat closely enough positioned during a sounding). You could just take soundings every 10 m, starting from one end and continuing until you reach the low point. But provided the ocean slopes steadily down

on both sides toward the low point, a more efficient approach would be to use either *Fibonacci search* or *golden ratio search*.

Both follow the same general procedure: initially pick a pair of test points, which divide the search area into three regions (left, middle, right).

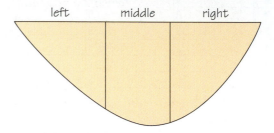

Determine the depth at the test points; if the right test point is deeper, eliminate the left region, and vice versa (see the figure below, where we eliminate the left region). In the remaining interval, determine a new test point that is located symmetrically with regard to the already-tested point, and proceed as before to eliminate the new right or the new left region (see figure below).

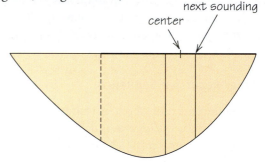

The two search methods differ only in how the first pair of test points is picked. If the major concern is to determine the location of the deepest point, the most efficient approach is Fibonacci search: determine the number n of steps needed (based on how accurately you need to know the position) and take the first pair of test points at a distance from each endpoint of

$$\frac{F_{n-1}}{F_n} L + \frac{(-1)^n}{F_n} \epsilon$$

where L is the length of the original interval, F_n is the nth Fibonacci number, and ϵ is the closest together that you could take two soundings.

If you are more concerned with determining the depth at the deepest point, you can't specify in advance how many steps you will need. The most efficient approach is therefore golden ratio search: take the first pair of test points at a distance from each endpoint of ϕL, where L is the length of the original interval and ϕ is the golden ratio. You keep taking soundings until the depths of two consecutive soundings are close enough together for your purposes, or until you reach the limit of how close together you can take soundings.

For example, suppose that (unknown to you) the depth d in km at a distance x km along the transit line is given by $d(x) = x^3 - x$ for $0 \leq x \leq 1$. The actual deepest point is $d = 0.3849$ (385 m) at $x = 0.5774$ (577 m along the transit line).

(a) How many soundings would it take to determine, within 10 m, where the deepest point is if you start at the left ($x = 0$) and take soundings every 10 m?

(b) The number of soundings required by Fibonacci search is the smallest n for which $F_n \geq L/t$, where t is the tolerance for error — that is, how accurately you need to know

where the deepest point is. For $L = 1000$ m and $t = 10$ m, what is n?

(c) Determine for the Fibonacci search of part (b) the locations of the first two test points, and then the location of the next test point.

(d) Determine for golden ratio search the locations of the first two test points, and then the location of the next test point.

(e) Each step of golden ratio search reduces the length of the search interval by a factor of ϕ; after N steps, the interval has length $L\phi^N$. For the preceding numerical values, what is the largest N can be before the next step would require you to take a sounding closer than ϵ to the last one?

(f) Fibonacci and golden ratio searches are the most efficient search techniques when there is a simple minimum or maximum without intervening ups and downs. Suggest other possible applications.

4 ▶ Visit the World Wide Web site **http://www.sphhys.unil.ch/escher/,** which features an interactive Java program called Escher Web Sketch. Experiment with choosing wallpaper patterns using crystallographic notation. For each, draw on the screen a colored design for the motif; the program will reproduce the motif using the pattern.

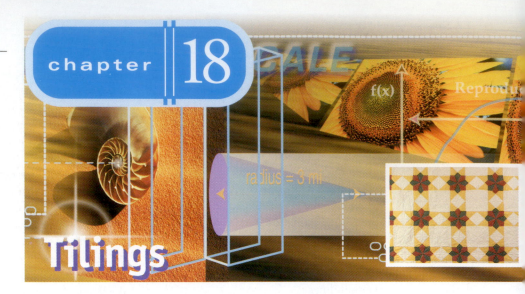

chapter || 18

Tilings

When our ancestors used stones to cover the floors and walls of their houses, they selected shapes and colors to form pleasing designs. We can see the artistic impulse at work in mosaics, from Roman dwellings to Muslim religious buildings (see Figure 18.1). The same intricacy and complexity arise in other decorative arts—on carpets, fabrics, baskets, and even linoleum.

Such patterns have one feature in common: they use repeated shapes to cover a flat surface, without gaps or overlaps. If we think of the shapes as tiles, we can call the pattern a *tiling,* or *tessellation.* Even when efficiency is more important than aesthetics, designers value clever tiling patterns. In manufacturing, for example, stamping the components from a sheet of metal is most economical if the shapes of the components fit together without gaps—in other words, if the shapes form a tiling.

A **tiling** is a covering of the entire plane with nonoverlapping figures.

The major mathematical question about tilings is: Given one or more shapes (in specific sizes) of tiles, can they tile the plane? And, if so, how?

The surprising answer to the first question is that it is undecidable. That is, given any arbitrary set of tile shapes, there is no way to determine for certain if they can tile the plane or not. For some particular sets of tiles, we can exhibit tilings, and for others, we can prove that there can't be any tiling. In this chapter we will see examples of both situations. But mathematicians have proved that there is no algorithm (mechanical step-by-step process) that can tell for any set of tile

FIGURE 18.1
Mosaic tile dome built by
Abbas I, Safavid dynasty
(1611–1638), Iran.

shapes which of the two situations happens. (See Spotlight 11.1, pages 402–403, for other examples of "unattainable ideals.")

Given this sobering (and puzzling) limitation, we begin our investigation of tilings by considering the simplest kinds of tiles and tilings.

Regular Polygons

The simplest tilings use only one size and shape of tile, and they are known as *monohedral tilings.*

> A **monohedral tiling** is a tiling that uses only one size and shape of tile.

In particular, we are interested especially in tiles that are **regular polygons,** figures all of whose sides are the same length and all of whose angles are equal. A square is a regular polygon with four equal sides and four equal interior angles; a triangle with all sides equal (an **equilateral triangle**) is also a regular polygon. A polygon with five sides is a pentagon, one with six sides is a hexagon, and one with n sides is an ***n*-gon.** Regular polygons are especially interesting because of their high degree of symmetry; each has the reflection and rotation symmetries of a dihedral rosette pattern (see Chapter 17). In three dimensions, the corresponding highly symmetrical figures are called *regular polyhedra* (see Spotlight 18.1).

SPOTLIGHT 18.1

Regular Polyhedra and Buckyballs

The three-dimensional analogue of a regular polygon is a regular polyhedron, a convex solid whose faces are regular polygons all alike (same number of sides, same size), with each vertex surrounded by the same number of polygons. Although there are infinitely many regular polygons, there are only five regular polyhedra, a fact proved by Theaetetus (414–368 B.C.); they were called the *Platonic solids* by the ancient Greeks.

If the restriction that the same number of polygons meet at each vertex is relaxed, five additional convex polyhedra are obtained, all of whose faces are equilateral triangles. If we allow more than one kind of regular polygon, thirteen further convex polyhedra are obtained, known as the *semiregular polyhedra* or *Archimedean solids* (although there is no documented evidence that Archimedes studied them—but Kepler did catalogue them all). The truncated icosahedron, whose faces are pentagons and hexagons, is known throughout the world (once inflated) as a regulation soccer ball. Drawings of it appear in the work of Leonardo da Vinci.

The truncated icosahedron is also the structure of C_{60}, a form of carbon known as buckminsterfullerene and, more familiarly, the "buckyball." Sixty carbon atoms lie at the 60 vertices of this molecule, which was discovered in 1985. It is named after R. Buckminster Fuller (1895–1983), inventor and promoter of the geodesic dome. The molecule resembles a dome.

The buckyball is part of a family of carbon molecules, the *fullerenes,* in which each carbon atom is joined to three others. Thirty years before the discovery of fullerenes, mathematicians had shown that a convex polyhedron in which every vertex has three edges must have 12 pentagon faces and may have any number of hexagon faces, from 0 on up, except for 1.

That there must be 12 pentagons follows from a famous equation due to Leonhard Euler (1707–1783). For any convex polyhedron, it must be true that $v - e + f = 2$, where v is the number of vertices, e is the number of edges, and f is the number of faces of the polyhedron.

The five regular polyhedra.

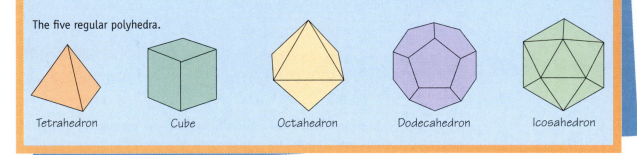

Tetrahedron   Cube   Octahedron   Dodecahedron   Icosahedron

By a convention dating back to the ancient Babylonians, angles are measured in degrees. An **exterior angle** of a polygon is one formed by one side and the extension of an adjacent side (Figure 18.2). Proceeding around the polygon in the same direction, we see that each **interior angle** (the angle inside a polygon formed by two adjacent sides) is paired with an exterior angle. If we bring all the exterior angles together at a single point, they will add up to 360° (see Figure 18.2). If the

FIGURE 18.2
The exterior angles of a regular hexagon, like those of any regular polygon, add up to 360°. Each interior angle measures 60°.

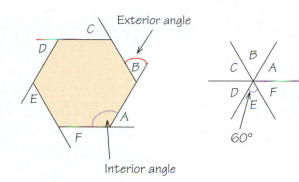

Exterior angle

Interior angle

60°

polygon has n sides, then each exterior angle must measure $360/n$ degrees. For example, a square with $n = 4$ sides has 4 exterior angles, each measuring 90°; a pentagon with $n = 5$ sides has 5 exterior angles, each measuring 72°; whereas a regular hexagon with $n = 6$ sides has 6 exterior angles, each measuring 60°. Notice that each exterior angle plus its corresponding interior angle make up a straight line, or 180°. For a regular polygon with more than six sides, the interior angle is between 120° and 180°. This last consideration will prove crucial shortly.

Regular Tilings

A monohedral tiling whose tile is a regular polygon is called a **regular tiling.**

A square tile is the simplest case. Apart from varying the size of the square, which would change the scale but not the pattern of the tiling, we can get different tilings by offsetting one row of squares some distance from the next.

However, there is only one tiling that is edge-to-edge:

In an **edge-to-edge tiling,** the edge of a tile coincides entirely with the edge of a bordering tile (see Figure 18.3 for a tiling that is not edge-to-edge and another that is).

For simplicity, from now on we consider only edge-to-edge tilings. In them (even in ones with tiles of different shapes and sizes), edges of different tiles meet at points that are surrounded by tiles and their edges.

Any tiling by squares can be refined to one by triangles by drawing a diagonal of each square; but these triangles are not regular (equilateral). Equilateral triangles can be arranged in rows by alternately inverting triangles; as with squares, there is only one pattern of equilateral triangles that forms an edge-to-edge tiling.

FIGURE 18.3
(a) A tiling that is not edge-to-edge; the horizontal edges of two adjoining squares do not exactly coincide. (b) A tiling by right triangles that is edge-to-edge.

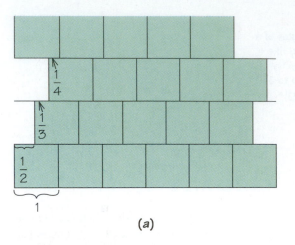

(*a*)

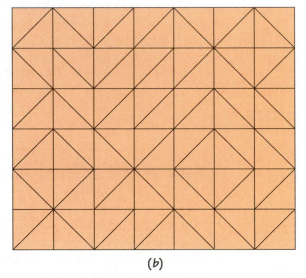

(*b*)

What about tiles with more than four sides? An edge-to-edge tiling with regular hexagons is easy to construct (see the upper right pattern in Figure 18.5, on page 674).

However, if we look for a tiling with regular pentagons, we won't find one. How do we know whether we're just not being clever enough or there really isn't one to be found? This is the kind of question that mathematics is uniquely equipped to answer. In the other sciences, phenomena may exist even though we have not observed them; such was the case for bacteria before the invention of the microscope. In the case of an edge-to-edge tiling with regular pentagons, we can conclude with certainty that there is no edge-to-edge tiling with regular pentagons.

The proof is very easy. As we calculated earlier, the interior angles of a pentagon are each 108°. At a point where several pentagons meet, how many can meet there? The total of all of the angles around a point must be 360°. As you can see in

FIGURE 18.4
Polygons that come together at a vertex in a tiling must have interior angles that add up to 360° — no less, no more.

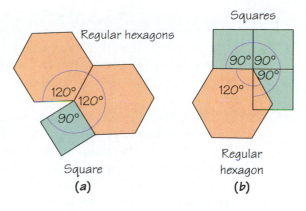

Figure 18.4, four pentagons at a point would be too many (their angles would add to 4 × 105° = 420°, so they'd have to overlap), and three would be too few (their angles would add to 3 × 108° = 324°, so some of the area wouldn't be covered). Since 108 does not evenly divide 360, *regular pentagons can't tile the plane.*

With this argument, we can do something that is a favorite with mathematicians: we can generalize it. Its main idea is a criterion for when a regular polygon can tile the plane: when the size of its interior angles divides 360 evenly. We can apply this criterion to determine exactly which other regular polygons can tile the plane.

E X A M P L E   *Identifying the Edge-to-Edge Regular Tilings*

A regular hexagon has interior angles of 120°; 120 divides 360 evenly, and 3 regular hexagons fit together exactly around a point. A regular 7-gon—or any regular polygon with more than six sides—has interior angles that are larger than 120° but smaller than 180°. Now 360 divided by 120 gives 3, and 360 divided by 180 gives 2—and there aren't any other possibilities in between. Angles between 180° and 120° divided into 360° will give a result between 2 and 3, and consequently not an integer. So there are no edge-to-edge regular tilings of the plane with polygons of more than 6 sides. ◆

The only edge-to-edge regular tilings are the ones with equilateral triangles, with squares, and with regular hexagons.

The follow-up question, of course, is which *combinations* of regular polygons of different numbers of sides can tile the plane edge-to-edge? The arrangement of polygons around a vertex in an edge-to-edge tiling is the **vertex figure** for that vertex.

A systematic tiling that uses a mix of regular polygons with different numbers of sides but in which all vertex figures are alike—the same polygons in the same order—is called a **semiregular tiling** (see Figure 18.5).

As before, the technique of adding up angles at a vertex (to be 360°) can eliminate some impossible combinations, such as "square, hexagon, hexagon" (Figure 18.4). Once we have found an arrangement that is numerically possible, we must confirm the actual existence of each tiling by constructing it (i.e., show that it is geometrically possible). For example, even though a possible arrangement of regular polygons around a point is "triangle, square, square, hexagon," it is not possible to construct a tiling with that vertex figure at every vertex.

The result of such an investigation is that in a semiregular tiling no polygon can have more than 12 sides. In fact, polygons with 5, 7, 9, 10, or 11 sides do not occur either. Figure 18.5 exhibits all of the semiregular tilings.

If we abandon the restriction about the vertex figures being the same at every vertex, then there are *infinitely many* systematic edge-to-edge tilings with regular polygons, even if we continue to insist that all polygons with the same number of sides have the same size.

FIGURE 18.5
The three regular tilings and the eight semiregular tilings, plus one tiling that does not belong to either group. Can you identify it?

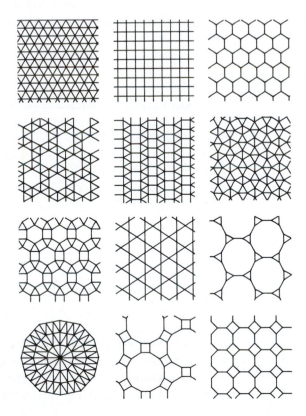

Tilings with Irregular Polygons

What about edge-to-edge tilings with irregular polygons, which may have some sides longer than others, or some interior angles larger than others? We will look just at monohedral tilings (in which all tiles have the same size and shape) and investigate in turn what triangles, **quadrilaterals** (four-sided polygons), hexagons, and so forth, can tile the plane.

The most general shape of triangle has all sides of different lengths and all interior angles of different sizes. Such a triangle is called a **scalene triangle,** from the Greek word for "uneven." We can always take two copies of a scalene triangle and fit them together to form a **parallelogram,** a quadrilateral whose opposite sides are parallel (Figure 18.6a). It's easy to see that we can then use such parallelograms to tile the plane, by making strips and then fitting layers of strips together edge-to-edge (Figure 18.6b). So:

Any triangle can tile the plane.

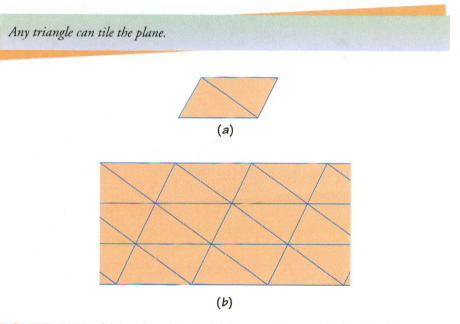

(a)

(b)

FIGURE 18.6   (a) A scalene triangle. (b) Every scalene triangle tiles the plane.

What about quadrilaterals? We have seen that squares tile the plane, and rectangles certainly will, too; and we have just noted that any parallelogram will tile. What about a quadrilateral (four-sided polygon) with its opposite sides not parallel, as in Figure 18.7a? The same technique as for triangles will work. We fit together two copies of the quadrilateral, forming a hexagon whose opposite sides are parallel. Such hexagons fit next to each other to form a tiling, as in Figure 18.7b.

The quadrilaterals shown in Figure 18.7 are all **convex.** If you take any two points on the tile (including the boundary), the line segment joining them lies

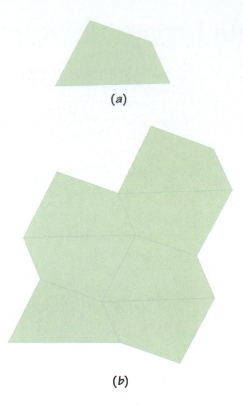

entirely within the tile (again, including the boundary). The quadrilateral of Figure 18.8a is not convex, but the same approach works for using it to form a tiling (Figure 18.8b). So:

Any quadrilateral, even one that is not convex, can tile the plane.

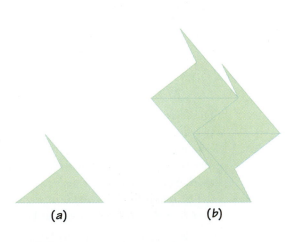

We could hope that such success would extend to irregular polygons with any numbers of sides, but it doesn't. The situation for convex hexagons was determined by K. Reinhardt in his 1918 doctoral thesis. He showed that for a convex hexagon to tile, it must belong to one of three classes, and that every hexagon in those classes will tile. Examples of the three classes are shown in Figure 18.9, together with their characterizations. Notice that tilings with a hexagon of type 2 (Figure 18.9b) use both ordinary and mirror-image versions of the hexagon.

Exactly three classes of convex hexagons can tile the plane.

FIGURE 18.9
The three types of convex hexagon tile.

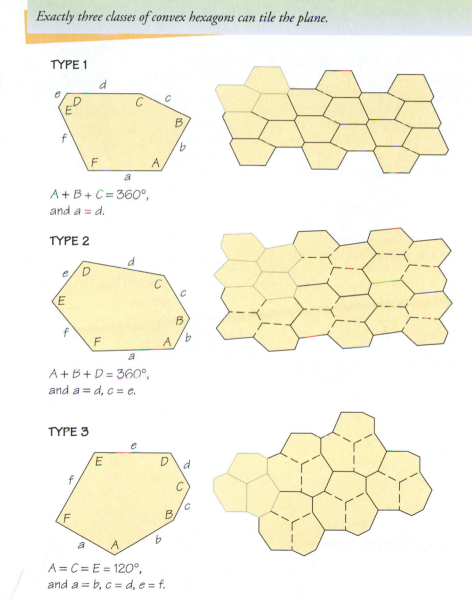

TYPE 1

$A + B + C = 360°$,
and $a = d$.

TYPE 2

$A + B + D = 360°$,
and $a = d, c = e$.

TYPE 3

$A = C = E = 120°$,
and $a = b, c = d, e = f$.

SPOTLIGHT
18.2

In Praise of Amateurs

R.B. Kershner's claim to have found all convex pentagons that tile was reported by Martin Gardner in his column in *Scientific American,* which was read by many amateur puzzle enthusiasts, including Richard James III and Marjorie Rice. James found a tiling that Kershner had missed, a discovery that Gardner reported in a later column.

Rice, a San Diego housewife and mother of five, read about James's new tile. "I thought I would like to understand these fascinating patterns better and see if I could find still another type. It was like a delightful new puzzle to me." Her search became a full-scale assault on the problem, lasting two years.

Rice had no formal education in mathematics beyond a high school general mathematics course. She not only worked out her own method of attack but also invented her own notation as well, both of which were far from the conventional ways that mathematicians use.

"I began drawing little diagrams on my kitchen counter when no one was there, covering them up quickly if someone came by, for I didn't wish to have to explain what I was doing to anyone. Soon I realized that many interesting patterns were possible but did not pursue them further, for I was searching for a new type and a few weeks later, I found it." Over the next two years, she found three additional new tilings.

What makes a person pursue a problem so steadfastly as Marjorie Rice? She was not trained

Marjorie Rice

to do this, nor paid to do it, but obviously gained personal satisfaction in her patient and persistent search.

She was born in 1923 in St. Petersburg, Florida, a first child. At age 5, she began school in a one-room country school with eight grades and two dozen pupils.

"When I was in the 6th or 7th grade, our teacher pointed out to us one day the Golden Section in the proportions of a picture frame. This immediately caught my imagination and though it was just a passing incident, I never forgot it. I've . . . been especially interested in architecture and the ideas of architects and planners such as

Underlying grid for Marjorie Rice's *Fish,* based on one of her unusual tilings by pentagons.

Buckminster Fuller. I've come across the Golden Section again in my reading and considered its use in painting and design."

After high school, Marjorie Rice worked until her marriage in 1945. She was drawn back into mathematics by her children, finding solutions to their homework problems "by unorthodox means, since I did not know the correct procedures." She became especially interested in textile design and the works of M. C. Escher. As she pursued the pentagonal tilings, she produced some beautiful geometric designs and imaginative Escher-like patterns (see Figure 18.19 and the figure here).

"I enjoy puzzles of all kinds, crosswords, jigsaw puzzles, mathematical puzzles and games, and have purchased books of mathematical puzzles over the years. Those of a geometric nature are a special delight."

The intense spirit of inquiry and the keen perception of all they encounter are the forte of all such amateurs. No formal education provides these gifts. Lack of a mathematical degree separates these "amateurs" from the "professionals," yet their curiosity and ingenious methods make them true mathematicians.

Source: Adapted from Doris Schattschneider, "In Praise of Amateurs," in *The Mathematical Gardner,* edited by David A. Klarner, pp. 140–166, plus Plates I–III, Wadsworth, Belmont, Calif., 1981.

Reinhardt also explored convex pentagons and found five classes that tile. For example, any pentagon with two parallel sides will tile. Reinhardt did not complete the solution, as he did for hexagons, by proving conclusively that no other pentagons could tile; he claimed that it would be very tedious to finish the analysis. Still, he felt that he had found them all. In 1968, after 35 years of working on the problem on and off, R. B. Kershner, a physicist at Johns Hopkins University, discovered three more classes of pentagons that will tile. Kershner was sure that he had found all pentagons that tile, but again did not offer a complete proof, which "would require a rather large book."

When an account of the "complete" classification into eight types appeared in *Scientific American* (July 1975), the article provoked an amateur mathematician to discover a ninth type! A second amateur, Marjorie Rice, a housewife with no formal education in mathematics beyond high school "general mathematics" 36 years earlier, devised her own mathematical notation and found four more types over the next two years (see Spotlight 18.2). A fourteenth type was found by a mathematics graduate student in 1985. Since then, no new types have been discovered, yet no one knows if the classification is complete.

With the situation so intricate for convex pentagons, you might think that it must be still worse for polygons with seven or even more sides. In fact, however, the situation is remarkably simple, as Reinhardt proved in 1927:

A convex polygon with seven or more sides cannot tile.

M. C. Escher and Tilings

The Dutch artist M. C. Escher (1898–1972) was inspired by the great variety of decoration in tilings in the Alhambra, a fourteenth-century palace built during the last years of Islamic dominance in Spain. He devoted much of his career of making prints to creating tilings with tiles in the shapes of living beings (a practice forbidden to Muslims). Those prints of interlocking animals and people have inspired awe and wonder among people all over the world. Figures 18.10–18.13 illustrate a few of his drawings and finished works. Like Marjorie Rice, he too developed his own mathematical notation for the different kinds of patterns for the tilings.

Tiling by Translations

You may wonder just how much liberty can be taken in shaping a tile, and how you might be able to design an Escher-like tiling yourself.

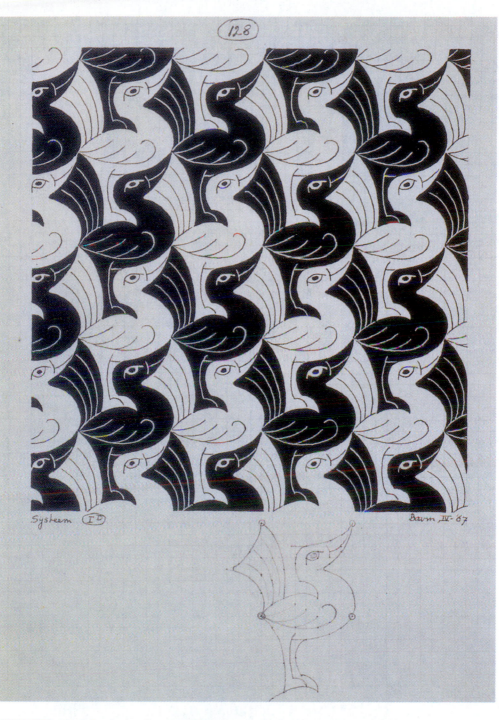

FIGURE 18.10 Escher No. 128 [*Bird*], from Escher's 1941–1942 notebook.

FIGURE 18.11
(a) Escher No. 67 [*Horseman*], from Escher's 1941–1942 notebook, and (b) sketch showing the tile design for the *Horseman* print.

(a)

(b)

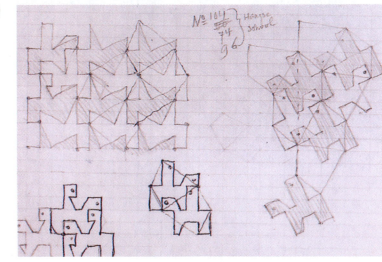

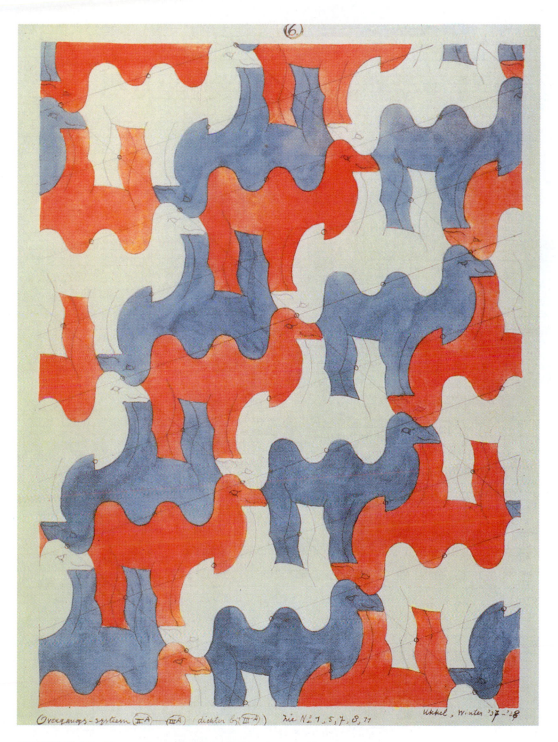

FIGURE 18.12 Escher No. 6 [*Camel*], from Escher's 1941–1942 notebook.

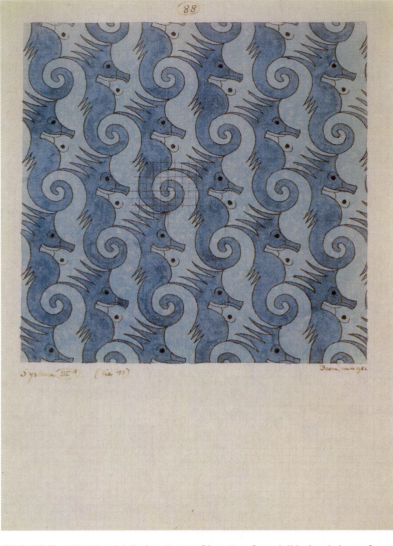

(b)

FIGURE 18.13   (a) Escher No. 88 [*Sea Horse*], and (b) the skeleton for No. 88 from Escher's 1941–1942 notebook.

The simplest case is when the tile is just *translated* in two directions, that is, copies are laid edge-to-edge in rows, as in Figure 18.10. Each tile must fit exactly into the ones next to it, including its neighbors above and below. We say that each tile is a **translation** of each other one, since we can move one to coincide with another without doing any rotation or reflection.

When is it possible for a tile to cover the plane in this manner? The boundary of the tile must be divisible into matching pairs of opposing parts that will fit together. Figures 18.10 and 18.11 illustrate two basic ways that this can happen. In the first, two opposite pairs of sides match; in the second, three opposite pairs of sides match.

> A tile can tile the plane by translations if either
>
> ■ there are four consecutive points A, B, C, and D on the boundary such that
>
> the boundary part from A to B is congruent by translation to the boundary part from D to C, and
> the boundary part from B to C is congruent by translation to the boundary part from A to D (see Figure 18.14a)
>
> ■ or there are six consecutive points A, B, C, D, E, and F on the boundary such that the boundary parts AB, BC, and CD are congruent by translation, respectively, to the boundary parts ED, FE, and AF (see Figure 18.15b).

The tiles for each of Figures 18.10 and 18.11 are shown in outline form in Figure 18.14, together with points marked to show how the tiles fulfill the criteria.

FIGURE 18.14
Individual tiles traced from the Escher prints of Figures 18.10 – 18.13, with points marked to show how they fulfill the criteria for tiling by translations or by translations and half-turns.

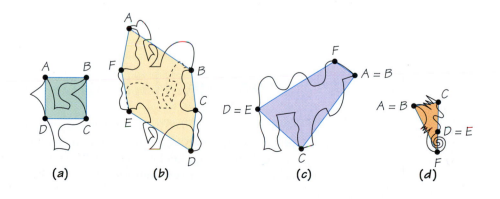

(a)   (b)   (c)   (d)

To create tilings, you can proceed exactly as Escher did. His notebooks show that he designed his patterns in just the way that we now describe.

E X A M P L E   *Tiling the Plane Using a Parallelogram*

For the first case of the theorem, start from a parallelogram, make a change to the boundary on one side, then copy that change to the opposite side. Similarly, change one of the other two sides and copy that change on the side opposite it (Figure 18.15). Revise as necessary, always making the same change to opposite sides. You might find it useful (as Escher did) to make your designs on graph paper, or you can work by cutting and taping together pieces of heavy paper. ◆

FIGURE 18.15
How to make an Escher-like tiling by translations, from a parallelogram base.

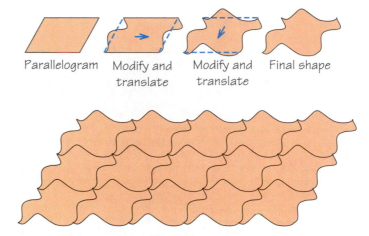

Parallelogram   Modify and translate   Modify and translate   Final shape

E X A M P L E   *Tiling the Plane Using a Hexagon*

For the second case, start from a **par-hexagon,** one whose opposite sides are equal and parallel; this is one of the kinds of hexagons that tile the plane. Again, make a change on one boundary and copy the change to the opposite side, and do this for all three pairs of opposite sides (Figure 18.16). ◆

Of course, there is a real art to being able to make the resulting tile resemble an animal or human figure!

Tiling by Translations and Half-Turns

If the tiling is to allow half-turns, so that some of the figures are "upside down," the part of the boundary of a right-side-up figure has to match the corresponding part of itself in an upside-down position. For that to happen, that part of the boundary must be **centrosymmetric,** that is, symmetric about (unaltered by) a

FIGURE 18.16
How to make an Escher-like tiling by translations, from a par-hexagon base.

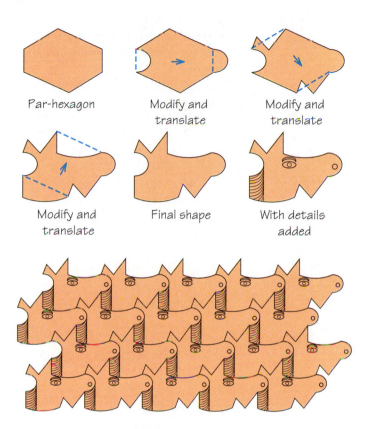

Par-hexagon   Modify and   Modify and
                     translate   translate

Modify and   Final shape   With details
translate   added

180-degree rotation around its midpoint. The key to some of Escher's more sophisticated monohedral designs, and the fundamental principle behind some further easy recipes for making Escher-like tilings, is the **Conway criterion,** formulated by John H. Conway of Princeton University:

A tile can tile the plane by translations and half-turns if there are six consecutive points on the boundary (some of which may coincide, but at least three of which are distinct)—call them *A, B, C, D, E,* and *F*— such that

■ the boundary part from *A* to *B* is congruent by translation to the boundary part from *E* to *D*, and
■ each of the boundary parts *BC, CD, EF,* and *FA* is centrosymmetric.

The first condition means that we can match up the two boundary parts exactly, curve for curve, angle for angle. The second condition means that each of the remaining boundary parts is brought back into itself by a half-turn around its center. Either condition is automatically fulfilled if the boundary part in question is a straight-line segment.

The tiles for each of Figures 18.12 and 18.13 are shown in outline form in Figure 18.14, together with points marked to show how the tiles fulfill the Conway criterion.

Once again, you can make Escher-like tilings by starting from simple geometric shapes that tile. This time, the starting geometric tile can be any triangle or any quadrilateral.

E X A M P L E　*Tiling the Plane Using a Triangle*

For a triangle, modify half of one side, then rotate that side around its center point to extend the modification to the rest of the side, thereby making the new side centrosymmetric. Then you may do the same to the second and third sides (Figure 18.17). ◆

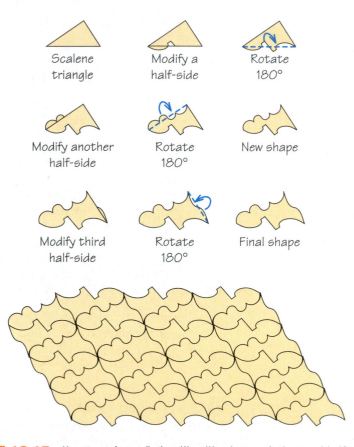

FIGURE 18.17　How to make an Escher-like tiling by translations and half-turns, from a scalene triangle base.

E X A M P L E   *Tiling the Plane Using a Quadrilateral*

For the quadrilateral, do the same, modifying each of the four sides, or as many as you wish (Figure 18.18). ◆

FIGURE 18.18
How to make an Escher-like tiling by translations and half-turns, from a quadrilateral base.

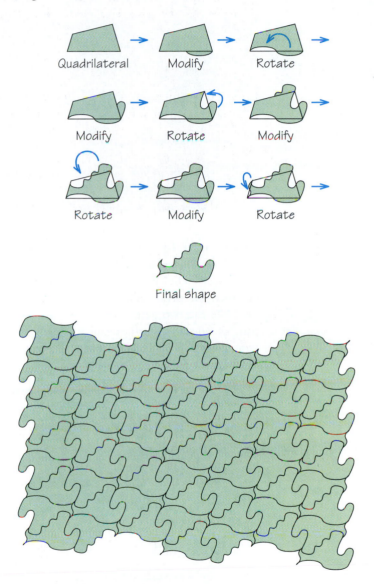

The same approach will work with some of the sides of some pentagons and hexagons that tile. Because not all sides can be modified, there is less freedom for designing tiles, so it is more difficult to make the resulting tiles resemble intended

FIGURE 18.19
Fish, by Marjorie Rice,
based on one of her
unusual tilings by
pentagons.

figures. Figure 18.19 shows the beautiful results achieved by Marjorie Rice, using one of the unusual tilings by pentagons that she discovered.

The sketches in Escher's notebook in Figures 18.10–18.13 indicate how he designed the prints whose tiles you see in Figure 18.14. For Figure 18.14a, he modified the two pairs of sides of a square. For Figure 18.14b, he modified the pairs of sides of a par-hexagon that became a tile made up of a pair of dark and light knights. This figure also has a reflection symmetry, taking a leftward-facing light knight to a rightward-facing dark knight. However, we have not discussed criteria for when you can start with a tile (e.g., a single knight) and produce a tiling with this symmetry. In Figure 18.14c, the blue overlay shows how the tile could be made by modifying half of every side of a general quadrilateral, though Figure 18.12 shows that Escher actually designed the tiling from a parallelogram base. Regarding Figure 18.14d, Figure 18.13 shows that Escher used a triangle base. He did not use the procedure that we noted earlier, in which half of every side is modified. Instead, he treated the triangle as a quadrilateral, in which two adjacent sides (*CD* and *DF*) happen to continue on in a straight line.

Further Considerations

All the patterns that we have exhibited and discussed so far have been **periodic tilings.** If we transfer a periodic tiling to a transparency, it is possible to slide the transparency a certain distance horizontally, without rotating it, until the transparency exactly matches the tiling everywhere. We can also achieve the same result by moving the transparency some second direction (possibly vertically) a certain (possibly different) distance.

In a periodic tiling you can identify a **fundamental region**—a tile, or a block of tiles—with which you can cover the plane by translations at regular intervals. For example, in Figure 18.10, a single bird forms a fundamental region. In Figure 18.12, two adjacent camels, one right-side up and one upside down, form a fundamental region. In the terminology of Chapter 17, the periodic tilings are ones that are preserved under translations in more than two directions. (In this chapter we are concerned with the design elements more than with the patterns, which were the main topic of Chapter 17.)

Nonperiodic Tilings

A **nonperiodic tiling** is a tiling in which there is no regular repetition of the pattern by translation.

The lower left pattern in Figure 18.5 (page 674), with its expanding rings of triangles, does not have any regular repetition by translation.

In Figure 18.3a (page 672), the second row from the bottom is offset one-half of a unit to the right from the bottom row, the third row from the bottom is offset one-third of a unit further, and so forth. Since the sum $\frac{1}{2} + \frac{1}{3} + \frac{1}{4} + \cdots + \frac{1}{n}$ never adds up to exactly a whole number, there is no direction (horizontal, vertical, or diagonal) in which we can move the entire tiling and have it coincide exactly with itself.

EXAMPLE *A Random Tiling*

Consider the usual edge-to-edge square tiling. For each square, flip a coin; depending on the result, divide the square into two right triangles by adding either a rising or a falling diagonal (see Figure 18.3b, page 672). Because what happens in each individual square is unconnected to what happens in the rest of the tiling, the tiling by right triangles that is produced by this procedure has no chance of being periodic. ◆

The Penrose Tiles

For all known cases, if a single tile can be used to make a nonperiodic tiling of the plane, then it can also be used to make a periodic tiling. It is still an open question whether this property is true for every possible shape. In 1993, Conway discovered an example in three dimensions of a single convex polyhedron that tiles space nonperiodically but cannot be used to make a periodic tilogy.

For a long time mathematicians also tended to believe the more general assertion that if you can construct a nonperiodic tiling with a set of one *or more* tiles, you can construct a periodic tiling from the same tiles. But in 1964 a set of tiles was found that permits only nonperiodic tiling. It contains 20,000 different shapes! Over the next several years, smaller sets were discovered with the same property, with as few as 100 shapes. But it was still amazing when in 1975 Roger Penrose, a mathematical physicist at Oxford, announced a set that would tile only nonperiodically—consisting of just two tiles! (See Figure 18.20 and Spotlight 18.3.)

Penrose called his tiles "darts" and "kites" and both of these *Penrose tiles* can be obtained from a single rhombus. (A **rhombus** is a quadrilateral with four equal sides and equal opposite interior angles.) The particular rhombus from which the Penrose tiles are constructed has interior angles of 72° and 108°. If we cut the longer diagonal in two pieces so that the longer piece is the golden ratio $((1 + \sqrt{5})/2 \approx 1.618)$ times as long as the shorter (see Chapter 17), and connect the dividing point to the remaining corners, we split the rhombus into a dart and a kite (Figure 18.20).

Since the two Penrose pieces come from a rhombus, and a rhombus can be replicated to tile the plane periodically, the rules for fitting the Penrose pieces together do not allow the periodic rhombus arrangement. We may label the front and back vertices of the dart with H (for head) and its two wing tips with T (for tail), and do the reverse for the kite. Then the rule is that only vertices with the same letter may meet: heads must go to heads, and tails to tails.

A prettier method of enforcing the rules, proposed by Conway, is to draw circular arcs of different colors on the pieces and require that adjacent edges must

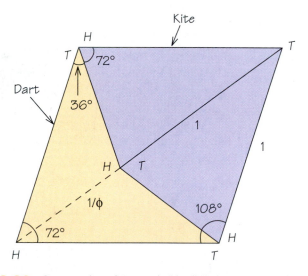

FIGURE 18.20 Construction of Penrose's "dart" (beige area) and "kite" (blue area). The length $1/\phi \approx 0.618$ is the golden ratio.

SPOTLIGHT 18.3

Roger Penrose

Roger Penrose, a professor at the University of Oxford, received a doctorate in mathematics but has been seriously interested in physics for many years; he was one of the first to conjecture the existence of black holes. He discovered what are now called the Penrose pieces in 1973. His latest endeavors have been devoted to trying to establish that the mind is not a machine, that is, that the ideas and concepts of artificial intelligence cannot explain human consciousness.

Roger Penrose

join arcs of the same color. The result is the pretty patterns of Figure 18.21. In fact, Conway thinks of the darts as children, each with two hands. The rule for fitting the pieces together is that children are required to hold hands. Penrose patterns become dancing circles of children.

FIGURE 18.21
A Penrose tiling with specially marked tiles, forming what is known as the cartwheel tiling.

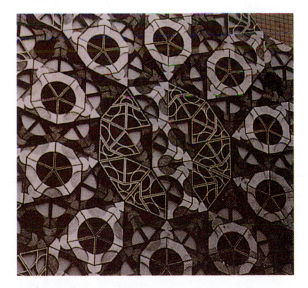

FIGURE 18.22   A Penrose nonperiodic tiling made with two rhombus shapes.

FIGURE 18.23   A modification of a Penrose tiling by refashioning the kites and darts into bird shapes.

FIGURE 18.24

A Penrose tiling by kites and darts, colored with five colors. A Penrose tiling can always be colored using four colors, in such a way that two tiles that share an edge have different colors. Whether a Penrose tiling can be colored in such a way using only three colors is an unsolved problem; we know, though, that if one Penrose tiling can be colored using three colors, all Penrose tilings can.

Figure 18.22 shows a tiling by a different pair of pieces, both rhombuses, that tile the plane only nonperiodically. Figure 18.23 shows a modification of the Penrose pieces into two bird shapes. Figure 18.24 shows a coloring of one particular tiling with the Penrose pieces so that no two adjacent pieces have the same color.

Although tilings with Penrose's pieces cannot be periodic, the tilings possess unexpected symmetry. As you recall, we have explored our intuitions of symmetry in terms of *balance, similarity,* and *repetition.* Patterns made with the Penrose pieces certainly involve repetition, but it is the balance in the arrangement that we seek.

What balance can there be in a nonperiodic pattern? It turns out that some Penrose patterns have a single line of reflection. But most surprising of all is that every Penrose pattern has a kind of fivefold rotational symmetry.

EXAMPLE   *Fivefold Symmetry*

Look again at Figure 18.20, which shows how to split a rhombus into the Penrose dart and kite pieces. Except in the recess of the dart and the matching part of the kite, all of the internal angles of the kite and of the dart are either 72° or 36°. Now, 72° goes into 360° five times, and 36° goes into 360° ten times. If we recall that it is the interior angles that matter in arranging polygons around a point, we see why it might be possible for a Penrose pattern to have fivefold or tenfold rotational symmetry.

A Penrose pattern with tenfold rotational symmetry is impossible, but there are exactly two Penrose patterns that tile the entire plane with fivefold rotational symmetry about one particular point. We show finite parts of these patterns in Figure 18.25. For each pattern, the center of rotational symmetry is at the center of the figure, surrounded either by five darts or by five kites.

For any other Penrose pattern, the pattern as a whole does not have fivefold rotational symmetry. However, what is surprising is that the pattern must have arbitrarily large finite regions with fivefold rotational symmetry. You can see this feature in the regions of Figure 18.22 that are enclosed by yellow lines. In Conway's metaphor, whenever a chain of children (darts) closes, the region inside has fivefold symmetry.   ◆

Conway invented a process called *inflation* that takes any Penrose pattern into a different Penrose pattern with larger darts and kites. The inflation operation (we don't give the details here) systematically cuts up the darts and kites into triangles and regroups the triangles into larger darts and kites.

Proceeding by contradiction, we can use inflation to show that a Penrose pattern must be nonperiodic. Suppose (contrary to what we want to establish) that some Penrose pattern is periodic, that is, it has translation symmetry. Let d be the distance along the translation direction to the first repetition. Performing inflation does the same thing to each repetition, so the inflated pattern must still have translation symmetry and a distance d along the translation direction to the first repetition. Keep on performing inflation, time after time, until the darts and kites are so large that they are more than d across. The pattern, as we have just argued, must still have translation symmetry at a distance d, but it can't, because there's no repetition inside a single tile! We reach a contradiction. So what's wrong? Our initial

FIGURE 18.25
Successive deflation (that is, the systematic cutting up of large tiles into smaller ones) of patches of tiles of a Penrose nonperiodic tiling.

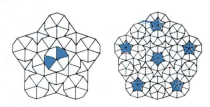

supposition, that the pattern was periodic in the first place, must have been erroneous. We conclude that all Penrose tilings are nonperiodic.

Despite their being nonperiodic, all Penrose patterns are somewhat alike, in the following remarkable sense:

> *Any finite region in one Penrose pattern is contained somewhere inside every other Penrose pattern; in fact, it occurs infinitely many times in every Penrose pattern.*

The nonperiodicity of Penrose tilings found a surprising application in 1997 — to bathroom tissue. Quilted bathroom tissue needs to be embossed with a pattern to keep the layers together (Figure 18.26). If the pattern is regular, then the multiple layers on the roll can produce lumpy ridges and grooves; using a non-repeating Penrose pattern averts the lumpiness. (However, the company used Penrose's pattern without his permission, and Penrose sued.)

FIGURE 18.26   Sir Roger Penrose, an eminent British mathematician, discovered how to tile a surface with a pattern of flat geometric shapes in a way that is never quite repeated. In doing so he illustrated fivefold symmetry, something that wasn't supposed to exist. Not an idea that would be particularly marketable to people redoing their bathrooms, one might think, but apparently useful for making quilted bathroom tissue, which must be embossed with a design that never repeats itself. Otherwise, layers upon layers of the same pattern build up ridges and grooves and the roll becomes lumpy. Penrose's design smooths out the bumps.

Penrose tilings have another feature that allows us to characterize them as *quasiperiodic,* or somewhere between periodic and random. (Noting the precise definition of this term would take us too far afield.) Robert Ammann introduced onto the two rhombic Penrose pieces used in Figure 18.22 lines that are now known as *Ammann bars.* In any Penrose tiling, these bars line up into five sets of parallel lines, each set rotated 72° from the next, forming a pentagonal grid (Figure 18.27). The distance between two adjacent parallel bars is one of only two values, either *A* or *B*. Do you want to guess what the ratio of the longer *A* is to the shorter *B*? You don't think it could possibly be anything but the golden ratio of chapter 17, do you? And so it is.

E X A M P L E   *Musical Sequences*

What about the order in which the *A*'s and *B*'s occur, as we move from left to right in Figure 18.27? Is there any pattern to that? From the limited part of the pattern we can observe, we see the sequence as

   ABAABABABAABABA

You might think from the figure that the pattern continues repeating the group

   ABAAB

indefinitely; after all, there are five symbols in this group. But such is not the case. Known as a musical sequence, the sequence of intervals between Ammann bars is nonperiodic—it cannot be produced by repeating any finite group of symbols. We can think of it as a one-dimensional analogue of a Penrose tiling.

FIGURE 18.27
Penrose tilings with Ammann bars. Specially placed lines on the tiles produce five sets of parallel bars in different directions.

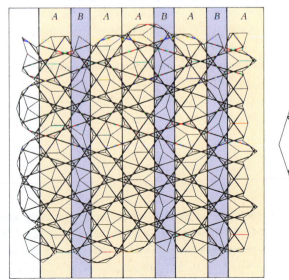

There is some regularity in musical sequences. Two B's can never be next to each other, nor can we have three A's in a row. Just as any finite part of any Penrose tiling occurs infinitely often in any other Penrose tiling, any finite part of any musical sequence appears infinitely often in any other one. The order of the symbols is neither periodic nor random, but between the two—quasiperiodic.

These sequences are called *musical* sequences because musicians represent the large-scale structure of songs in terms of the letters A and B. For example, a common pattern for popular songs is *AABA*, indicating that the first, second, and fourth verses have the same melody, but the third verse has a different melody.   ◆

The ratio of darts to kites in an infinite Penrose tiling, or of A's to B's in a musical sequence, is exactly the golden ratio, approximately 1.618. So if you are going to play with sets of Penrose pieces and see what kinds of patterns you can create, you will need about 1.6 times as many darts as kites.

As pointed out by geometers Marjorie Senechal (Smith College) and Jean Taylor (Rutgers University), Penrose tilings have three important properties:

- They are constructed according to rules that force nonperiodicity.
- They can be obtained from a substitution process (inflation and deflation) that features self-similarity.
- They are quasiperiodic.

Research of the late 1980s indicates that these properties are somewhat independent, meaning that one or two may be true of a tiling without all three being true.

Quasicrystals and Barlow's Law

Although Penrose's discovery was a big hit among geometers and in recreational mathematics circles in the mid-1970s, few people thought that his work might have practical significance. In the early 1980s some mathematicians even generalized Penrose tilings to three dimensions, using solid polyhedra to fill space nonperiodically. Like the two-dimensional Penrose patterns, these have orderly fivefold symmetry but are nonperiodic.

Yet in 1982 scientists at the U.S. National Bureau of Standards discovered unexpected fivefold symmetry while looking for new ultrastrong alloys of aluminum (mixtures of aluminum with other metals).

Manganese doesn't ordinarily alloy with aluminum, but the experimenters were able to produce small crystals of alloy by cooling mixtures of the two metals at a rate of millions of degrees per second. Following routine procedures, chemist Daniel Shechtman began a series of tests to determine the atomic structure of the special crystals. But there was nothing routine about what he found: the atomic structures of the manganese-aluminum crystals were so startling that it took Shechtman three years to convince his colleagues they were real.

Why did he encounter such resistance? His patterns—and the crystals that produced them—defied one of the fundamental laws of crystallography. Like our discovery that the plane cannot be tiled by regular pentagons, **Barlow's law,** also called the **crystallographic restriction,** says that a crystal can have only rotational symmetries that are twofold, threefold, fourfold, or sixfold. Since crystals are periodic, if there were a center of fivefold symmetry, there would have to be many such centers. Barlow proved this impossible.

Peter Barlow was a nineteenth-century British mathematician whose name survives today in the name of a book of mathematical tables. His argument was a very simple proof by contradiction, similar to Conway's proof in which we saw earlier that Penrose patterns are not periodic. Suppose (contrary to what we intend to show) that there is more than one fivefold rotation center. Let A and B be two of these that are closest together (see Figure 18.28). Rotate the pattern of Figure 18.28 by one-fifth of a turn clockwise around B, which carries A to some point A'. Since the pattern has fivefold symmetry around B, the point A', which is the image of the fivefold center A, must itself be a fivefold center. Now use A as a center and rotate the pattern by one-fifth of a turn counterclockwise, which carries B to some point B'; as we just argued in the case of A', B' must also be a fivefold center. But A' and B' are closer together than A and B, which is a contradiction. Hence our original supposition must be false, and a pattern can have at most one fivefold rotation center (as the patterns in Figure 18.25 in fact do) and so cannot be periodic.

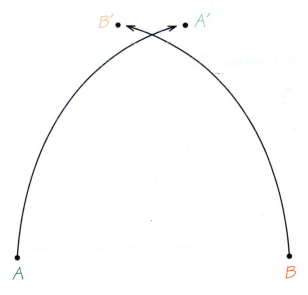

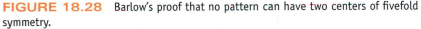

FIGURE 18.28   Barlow's proof that no pattern can have two centers of fivefold symmetry.

Quasicrystals

In 1984, working at the University of Pennsylvania, Paul Steinhardt and Don Levine did a computer simulation of what a three-dimensional Penrose pattern would be like; they decided to call such structures quasicrystals. Later that fall, their chemist colleague Daniel Shechtman showed that quasicrystals really exist; he produced images of an alloy of aluminum and manganese that were amazingly similar to images from the computer simulations. In short order, sevenfold, ninefold, and other symmetries were also shown to occur in real materials.

In 1991 Sergei Burkov showed that quasiperiodic tilings can be made using only a single kind of 10-sided tile, *provided the tiles are allowed to overlap*. With overlaps, the resulting patterns are no longer tilings; they are called *coverages*. In late 1998, scientists presented electron microscope photos that demonstrated that atoms really do form such coverages.

The current theory is that quasicrystals are packings of copies of a single type of atom cluster, with each cluster sharing atoms with its neighbors, that is, overlapping nearby clusters. The clusters form a quasiperiodic pattern that maximizes their density, thereby minimizing the energy of the atoms involved.

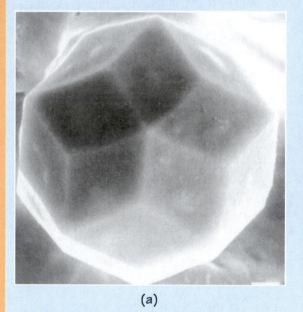

(a)

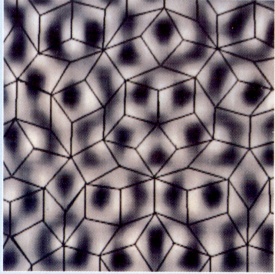

(b)

(a) A scanning electron microscope image of the quasicrystal alloy $Al_{5???}Li_3Cu$. The fivefold symmetry can be seen in the five rhombic faces that meet at a single point in the center of the photograph, forming a starlike shape.

(b) This image of the quasicrystal material $AL_{65}Co_{20}Cu_{15}$ was obtained with a scanning tunneling microscope; the resulting image has been overlaid with a nonperiodic tiling to display the local fivefold symmetry.

Barlow's law, as a mathematical theorem, shows that fivefold symmetry is impossible in a periodic tiling of the plane or of space. Chemists, for good theoretical and experimental reasons, believe that crystals are modeled well by three-dimensional tilings. An array of atoms with no symmetry whatever would not be considered a crystal. Yet until Penrose's discovery, no one realized that nonperiodic tilings—or arrays of atoms—can have the regularity of fivefold symmetry.

Chemists could simply say that Shechtman's alloys aren't crystals. In the classic sense they aren't, but in other respects they do resemble crystals. It is scientifically more fruitful to extend the concept of crystal to include them rather than rule them out; they are now known as *quasicrystals* (see Spotlight 18.4).

Once again, as so often happens in history, pure mathematical research anticipated scientific applications. Penrose's discovery, once just a delightful piece of recreational mathematics, has prompted a major reexamination of the theory of crystals.

REVIEW VOCABULARY

Barlow's law, or the **crystallographic restriction**
A law of crystallography that states that a crystal may have only rotational symmetries that are twofold, threefold, fourfold, or sixfold.

Centrosymmetric Symmetric by 180 degrees rotation around its center.

Convex A geometric figure is convex if for any two points on the figure (including its boundary), all the points on the line segment joining them also belong to the figure (including its boundary).

Conway criterion A criterion for determining whether a shape can tile by means of translations and half-turns.

Edge-to-edge tiling A tiling in which adjacent tiles meet only along full edges of each tile.

Equilateral triangle A triangle with all three sides equal.

Exterior angle The angle outside a polygon formed by one side and the extension of an adjacent side.

Fundamental region A tile or group of adjacent tiles that can tile by translation.

Interior angle The angle inside a polygon formed by two adjacent sides.

Monohedral tiling A tiling with only one size and shape of tile (the tile is allowed to occur also in "turned-over," or mirror-image, form).

n-gon A polygon with n sides.

Nonperiodic tiling A tiling in which there is no repetition of the pattern by translation.

Parallelogram A convex quadrilateral whose opposite sides are equal and parallel.

Par-hexagon A hexagon whose opposite sides are equal and parallel.

Periodic tiling A tiling that repeats at fixed intervals in two different directions, possibly horizontal and vertical.

Quadrilateral A polygon with four sides.

Regular polygon A polygon all of whose sides and angles are equal.

Regular tiling A tiling by regular polygons, all of which have the same number of sides and are the same size; also, at each vertex, the same kinds of polygons must meet in the same order.

Rhombus A parallelogram all of whose sides are equal.

Scalene triangle A triangle no two sides of which are equal.

Semiregular tiling A tiling by regular polygons; all polygons with the same number of sides must be the same size.

Tiling A covering of the plane without gaps or overlaps.

Translation A rigid motion that moves everything a certain distance in one direction.

Vertex figure The pattern of polygons surrounding a vertex in a tiling.

SUGGESTED READINGS

CHOW, WILLIAM W. Automatic generation of interlocking shapes, *Computer Graphics and Image Processing*, 9 (1979): 333–353. Shows how to design a computer program to draw interlocking patterns.

CHOW, WILLIAM W. Interlocking shapes in art and engineering, *Computer Aided Design*, 12 (1980): 29–34. Discusses applications to sheet material manufacturing (e.g., fabrication of gloves, can openers, forks, key blanks, and bunk bed brackets).

CHUNG, FAN, AND SHLOMO STERNBERG. Mathematics and the buckyball, *American Scientist*, 81 (1993): 56–71.

FOSTER, LORRAINE. *The Alhambra Past and Present: A Geometer's Odyssey.* Illustrates strip and wallpaper patterns from the Alhambra in Spain.

GARDNER, MARTIN. Mathematical games: Extraordinary nonperiodic tiling that enriches the theory of tiles, *Scientific American* (January 1977): 110–121, 132, and front cover. Reprinted with additional material in Martin Gardner, *Penrose Tiles to Trapdoor Ciphers,* Freeman, New York, 1989, pp. 1–29.

GARDNER, MARTIN. Mathematical games: On tessellating the plane with convex polygon tiles, *Scientific American* (July 1975): 112–117, 132. Reprinted with additional material in Martin Gardner, *Time Travel and Other Mathematical Bewilderments,* Freeman, New York, 1988, pp. 163–176.

GRÜNBAUM, BRANKO, AND G. C. SHEPHARD. *Tilings and Patterns,* Freeman, New York, 1987. Abbreviated edition: *Tilings and Patterns: An Introduction.*

HALES, THOMAS. The Kepler Conjecture. http://www.math.lsa.umich.edu/~hales/countdown/.

KORYEPIN, V. Penrose patterns and quasi-crystals: What does tiling have to do with a high-tech alloy? *Quantum,* 4 (4): 13–19 (January/February 1994); 4 (5): 59–62 (March/April 1994).

LEE, KEVIN. *Tesselmania!* Computer program for producing Escher-like tilings for Macintosh or Windows. The Learning Company; school pricing at http://www.learningco.com/school/products/subject/mp/tmd/price.htm.

PETERSON, IVARS. A quasicrystal construction kit. *Science News* 155 (23 January 1999): 60–61.

RANUCCI, ERNEST, AND JOSEPH TEETERS. *Creating Escher-Type Patterns,* Creative Publications, Oak Lawn, Ill., 1977.

SCHATTSCHNEIDER, DORIS. Will it tile? Try the Conway criterion! *Mathematics Magazine,* 53 (1980): 224–233.

SCHATTSCHNEIDER, DORIS. In praise of amateurs, in David A. Klarner, ed., *The Mathematical Gardner,* Wadsworth, Belmont, Calif., 1981, pp. 140–166, plus Plates I–III.

SCHATTSCHNEIDER, DORIS. *Visions of Symmetry: Notebooks, Periodic Drawings, and Related Work of M. C. Escher,* Freeman, New York, 1990.

SCHATTSCHNEIDER, DORIS. Penrose puzzles, *SIAM News,* 28 (6): 8, 14 (July 1995). Review of various commercial puzzles based on variations on the Penrose pieces, distributed by Kadon Enterprises (1227 Lorene Drive, Suite 16, Pasadena, MD 21122; 410-437-2163) and World of Escher (14542 Brook Hollow Boulevard, no. 250, San Antonio, TX 78232-3810; 800-237-2232).

SEYMOUR, DALE, AND JILL BRITTON. *Introduction to Tessellations,* Dale Seymour Publications, Palo Alto, Calif., 1989. An excellent introduction to tessellations, including how to make Escher-like tessellations.

TEETERS, JOSEPH L. How to draw tessellations of the Escher type, *Mathematics Teacher,* 67: 307–310 (1974).

Tessellation Winners: Original Student Art, 2 vols. *Book One: The First Contest, 1989–90,* and *Book Two: The Second Contest, 1991–92,* Dale Seymour Publications, Palo Alto, Calif., 1991, 1993.

URBAN, KNUT W. From tilings to coverings, *Nature* 396: 14–15 (5 November 1998).

WAGON, STAN. *Mathematica in Action,* W. H. Freeman, New York, 1991, chapter 4. How to generate Penrose tilings using the Mathematica software.

SUGGESTED WEB SITES

Computer Software for Tiling.
http://www.geom.umn.edu/software/tilings   Lists programs for various platforms that allow the user to design tilings.

Java Penrose Tiler.
http://www.aie.nl/~geert/java/public/Penrose.html
Interactive Web program that allows the user to build Penrose tilings.

Quasitiler.
http://www.geom.umn.edu/apps/quasitiler
Interactive Web program that draws Penrose tilings and their generalizations in higher dimensions.

KaleidoTile.
ftp://geom.umn.edu/pub/software/Kaleidotile
Interactive Macintosh program that lets the user design tilings on the plane, the sphere, and the hyperbolic plane. Spherical tilings can be realized as polyhedra.

SKILLS CHECK

1. What is the exterior angle of a regular octagon?

    (a) 30°
    (b) 45°
    (c) 135°

2. Which of the following polygons *cannot* tile the plane?

    (a) Regular hexagon
    (b) Regular pentagon
    (c) Non-rectangle parallelogram

3. Regular octagons and squares can form a semiregular tiling of the plane with

    (a) 2 octagons and 1 square at each vertex.
    (b) 2 octagons and 2 squares at each vertex.
    (c) a varying configuration at the vertices.

4. A semiregular tiling has a square, a regular dodecagon (12-gon), and another regular polygon at each vertex. What is this other polygon?

    (a) Another square
    (b) Another dodecagon
    (c) A hexagon

5. Can the tile below be used to create a tiling of the plane?

    (a) No.
    (b) Yes, using only translations.
    (c) Yes, using translations and half-turns.

6. Can the tile below be used to create a tiling of the plane?

    (a) No.
    (b) Yes, using only translations.
    (c) Yes, using translations and half-turns.

7. Penrose tilings are

    (a) Periodic.
    (b) Random.
    (c) Quasiperiodic.

EXERCISES   ▲ *Optional.*   ■ *Advanced.*   ◆ *Discussion.*

Hint: For the exercises about determining whether a shape will tile the plane, you should make a number of copies of the shape and experiment with placing them. One easy way to make copies is to trace the shape onto a piece of paper, staple half a dozen other blank sheets behind that sheet, and use scissors to cut through all the sheets along the edges of the traced shape on the top sheet.

Regular Polygons

1.   Determine the measure of an exterior angle and of an interior angle of a regular octagon (eight sides).

2.   Determine the measure of an exterior angle and of an interior angle of a regular decagon (ten sides).

3.   Discover a formula for the measure of an interior angle of a regular *n*-gon.

4.   Using the formula from Exercise 3 and either your calculator or a short computer program, make a chart of the interior angle measures of regular polygons with 3, 4, . . . , 12 sides.

Regular Tilings

5.   Give a numerical reason why a semiregular tiling could not include both polygons with 12 sides and polygons with 8 sides (with or without any polygons with other numbers of sides).

6.   The lower left corner of Figure 18.5 (page 674) shows a tiling by isosceles triangles.

(a)   Use the center vertex to determine the measures of the angles of the isosceles triangle tile.

(b)   Every vertex except the center vertex has the same vertex figure, in terms of the measures of the angles surrounding the vertex. What is that vertex figure?

Tilings with Irregular Polygons

7.   For each of the tiles below, show how it can be used to tile the plane. (Adapted from *Tilings and Patterns,* by Branko Grünbaum and G. C. Shephard, Freeman, New York, 1987, p. 25.)

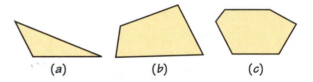

(a)   (b)   (c)

8.   You know that a regular pentagon cannot tile the plane. Suppose you cut one in half. Can this new shape tile the plane? (See page 635 for a regular pentagon that you can trace.)

Tiling by Translations

Refer to tiles (a) through (g), below and on the facing page, in doing Exercises 9 and 10.

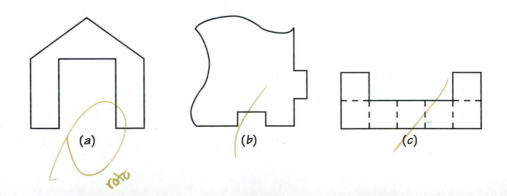

(a)   (b)   (c)

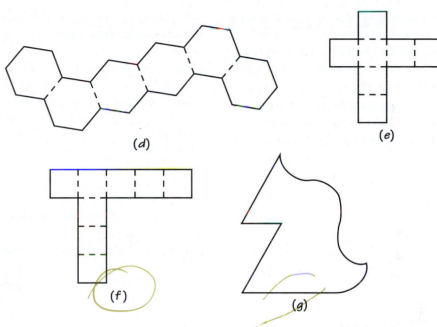

(d)

(e)

(f)

(g)

9. For each of the tiles (a) through (c), determine if it can be used to tile the plane by translations. (From *Tiling the Plane,* by Frederick Barber et al., COMAP, Lexington, Mass., 1989, pp. 1, 8, 9.)

10. Repeat Exercise 9, but for the tiles (d) through (g).

11. Start from a parallelogram of your choice and modify it to tile the plane by translations. (You will probably find it useful to do your work on graph paper.) Can you draw a design on the tile so as to make an Escher-like pattern?

12. Start from a par-hexagon of your choice and modify it to tile the plane by translations. (You will probably find it useful to do your work on graph paper. If you choose a regular hexagon, there is special graph paper, ruled into regular hexagons, that would be particularly useful.) Can you draw a design on the tile so as to make an Escher-like pattern?

Tiling by Translations and Half-Turns

Refer to tiles (a) through (g) in doing Exercises 13 and 14.

13. For each of the tiles (a) through (c), determine if it can be used to tile the plane by translations and half-turns.

14. Repeat Exercise 13, but for tiles (d) through (g).

15. Show how an arbitrary pentagon with two parallel sides can tile the plane.

16. Shown below is a pentagonal tile of type 13, discovered by Marjorie Rice. Show how it can tile the plane. (*Hint:* Carefully trace and cut out a dozen or so copies and try fitting them together.) The parts of this pentagon satisfy the following relations: $A = C = D = 120°$, $B = E = 90°$, $2A + D = 360°$, $2C + D = 360°$, $a = e$, and $a + e = d$.

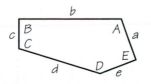

(Adapted from "In Praise of Amateurs," by Doris Schattschneider, in *The Mathematical Gardner,* edited by David A. Klarner, Wadsworth, Belmont, Calif., 1981, p. 162.)

17.   Start from a triangle of your choice and modify it to tile the plane by translations and half-turns. (You will probably find it useful to do your work on graph paper.) Can you draw a design on the tile so as to make an Escher-like pattern?

18.   Start from a quadrilateral of your choice and modify it to tile the plane by translations and half-turns. (You will probably find it useful to do your work on graph paper.) Can you draw a design on the tile so as to make an Escher-like pattern?

Additional Exercises

■   19.   Use the chart of interior-angle measures from Exercise 4 to determine all of the possible vertex figures of regular polygons (with at most 12 sides) surrounding a point.

■   20.   Which of the vertex figures of Exercise 19 do not occur in a semiregular tiling?

■   21.   In addition to the vertex figures of Exercise 19, exactly five others are possible, each involving one polygon with more than 12 sides. None of these vertex figures leads to a semiregular tiling. The five many-sided polygons involved in these five vertex figures have 15, 18, 20, 24, and 42 sides. Determine the other polygons in these vertex figures.

▲   22.   In the text we discuss criteria and methods for generating Escher-like patterns that involve just translations or translations and half-turns. A slight variation on one of those methods allows construction of tilings that feature a tile and its mirror image.

Begin with a parallelogram made from two congruent isosceles triangles, as shown in the figure. Each of these triangles has two sides equal; be sure that the two triangles are arranged so that they have one of the equal sides in common, forming a diagonal of the parallelogram.

Make any modification to half of the third side of one of the triangles. Mirror-reflect that modification across the side, then translate the

reflection to become the modification of the other half of the side. Take the complete modification of this side and translate it to become the modification of the opposite side of the parallelogram.

Modify in any way one of the two remaining sides of the parallelogram, and make the same modification to the opposite side (that is, translate the modification, without rotation or reflection). Then make the mirror-reflection of this modification the modificiation of the diagonal of the parallelogram.

The result is a modified parallelogram that tiles by translation and splits into two pieces that are mirror images of each other. Escher used a similar technique, but starting from a par-hexagon made from two quadrilaterals, in his *Horseman* print, as shown in his sketch in Figure 18.11a.

Use this technique to produce a tiling of your own design. Can you draw a design on the tile so as to make an Escher-like pattern?

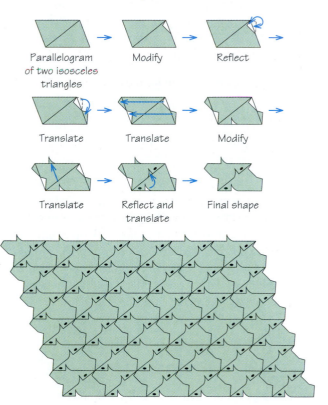

▲ 23. Show that the modified parallelogram in Exercise 22 fulfills the Conway criterion, by identifying the six points of the criterion.

▲ 24. The rabbit problem in Chapter 17 (Exercise 4, page 657) can lead us directly into nonperiodic patterns and musical sequences. Let A denote an adult pair of rabbits and B denote a baby pair. We will record the population at the end of each month, just before any births, in a particular systematic way—as a string of A's and B's. At the end of their second month of life, a rabbit pair will be considered to be adult. At the end of the first month, the sequence is just A, and the same is true at the end of the second month. When an adult pair A has a baby pair B, we write the new B immediately to the right of the A. So at the end of the third month, the sequence is AB; at the end of the fourth, it is ABA, since the first baby pair is now adult; at the end of the fifth month we have ABAAB.

Mathematicians and computer scientists call this manner of generating a sequence a *replacement system*. At each stage we replace each A by AB and each B by A.

(a) What is the sequence at the end of the sixth month?
(b) Why can't we ever have two B's next to each other?
(c) Why can't we ever have three A's in a row?
(d) Show that from the fourth month on, the sequence for the current month consists of the sequence for last month followed by the sequence for two months ago.

TECHNOLOGY CORNER

Computing Exterior and Interior Angles with a Spreadsheet

The spreadsheet in Figure 18.29 computes the exterior and interior angles for regular polygons. After entering the value at **A2**, entry **A3** can be entered as **=A2+1** and copied to the remainder of the column. The exterior angle of a regular polygon with n sides is computed as $360°/n$. Therefore, entry **B2** can be computed as **=360/A2**. Since an interior angle and an exterior angle sum to 180°, entry **C2** can be computed as **=180−B2**. Each of these formulas can be copied down the column to subsequent entries.

	A	B	C
1	Number of sides	Exterior angle	Interior angle
2	3	120	60
3	4	90	90
4	5	72	108
5	6	60	120

FIGURE 18.29

TASK 1. Extend the spreadsheet to include polygons with up to 20 sides. Which of these polygons have interior angles whose measure (in degrees) is a whole number? Are there any polygons with more than 20 sides that also have this type of interior angle?

TASK 2. When polygons form a tiling, the interior angles at each vertex add up to exactly 360°. Using the data in your spreadsheet, explain why it is not possible to create a regular tiling using a polygon with more than six sides.

Designing Semiregular Tilings

The two additional columns shown in Figure 18.30 allow us to find combinations of regular polygons that can form semiregular tilings. A semiregular tiling includes several different regular polygons, but each vertex of the resulting tiling has the same structure. The number of each type of polygon we propose to place at a vertex is indicated in column **D**. Based on these numbers, the final column computes the sum of the interior angles at a vertex. The tiling is valid only when the sum of angles is 360°. To compute this sum, entry **E2** has the formula **=D2*C2**. This formula is copied to the subsequent entries of the column, and the column is then summed in entry **E7**.

	A	B	C	D	E	F
1	Number of sides	Exterior angle	Interior angle	Number selected	Interior angles	
2	3	120	60	1	60	
3	4	90	90	2	180	
4	5	72	108		0	
5	6	60	120	1	120	
6						
7				4	360	sums

FIGURE 18.30

TASK 3. Figure 18.30 shows the combination for a valid semiregular tiling with one triangle, two squares, and one hexagon at each vertex. Find a valid combination of polygons that includes two hexagons at each vertex.

TASK 4. Extend the spreadsheet to include polygons with up to 12 edges. Find another valid combination that uses three distinct polygons.

Exploration

If a combination creates a semiregular tiling, the angle sum at each vertex is 360°. However, not every arrangement of polygons about a vertex can be extended to form a tiling. For example, the combination indicated in Figure 18.30 forms a tiling only if the squares are not adjacent. The combination found in Task 3 includes two hexagons. Is a similar restriction for the case found in Task 3 also necessary?

writing projects

1 ▶ We can define inflation and deflation of a sequence of A's and B's, and musical sequences themselves, without reference to Penrose patterns, and thereby arrive at an example of a nonperiodic pattern in one dimension. Inflation consists of replacing each A by AB and each B by A, and deflation consists of replacing each AB by A and each A by B; inflation and deflation undo each other on musical sequences. Call a sequence *musical* if it results from applying inflation to the sequence consisting of a single B. Then inflation and deflation preserve musicality: if we inflate or deflate a musical sequence, we get another musical sequence. Another way to think of this relationship is that a musical sequence is self-similar under inflation and deflation.

(a)   Let the lone B be considered the first stage of inflation. Show that at the nth stage of inflation, for $n \geq 3$, there are F_n (the nth Fibonacci number) symbols in the sequence, of which F_{n-1} are A's and F_{n-2} are B's.

(b)   Show that no musical sequence contains AAA or BB.

(c)   Show that no musical sequence ends in AA or in $ABAB$.

(d)   Show that apart from the lone sequence B, every musical sequence is an initial subsequence of all the succeeding musical sequences.

(e)   Slightly modified, deflation can be used to check whether a finite block of A's and B's can belong to a musical sequence or not. First, if the block has length greater than one, we may suppose that it begins with an A (why?); so at any stage of the deflation with a block beginning with B, we may add an initial A. Second, we add the additional deflation rule to replace an ending AA with BA. If at any stage of this modified deflation we arrive at two or more B's in a row, or three or more A's in a row, then the original block could not be part of a musical sequence; otherwise, the original block will eventually deflate to a single symbol, at which point we conclude that the original block is a part of a musical sequence. Check the two blocks $ABAABABAAB$ and $ABAABABABA$.

(f)   Since from part (d) we know that each application of inflation to a musical sequence simply extends it, then by successive inflation we build an infinite sequence. Show that as we approach this limiting sequence, the ratio of B's to A's tends toward the golden ratio ϕ.

(g) Conclude from part (f) that the sequence cannot be periodic, nor settle into a period after a finite "burn-in" period. Thus, the sequence is nonperiodic. (*Hint:* ϕ is not a rational number, that is, it cannot be represented as a ratio m/n of whole numbers m and n.)

(h) Show that any finite block of A's and B's that occurs in the infinite sequence must occur over and over again (just as any patch of tiles in a Penrose pattern occurs infinitely often in the pattern). Thus, the infinite sequence is self-similar.

2 ▶ Get computer software for tiling and make some tilings of your own. Check for software for your computing platform at http://www.geom.umn.edu/software/tilings/TilingSoftware.html.

Arithmetic

> *"The essence of mathematical modeling is controlled simplification."*

Problems, problems, problems! Life is full of problems. Do mathematicians approach problems in a special way—a way different from the way other "specialists" attack problems? As befits the subject sometimes described as the science of studying patterns, mathematics has paid attention to the pattern by which one can be helped to understand and solve problems. The branch of mathematics that deals with applying and using mathematics to solve problems outside mathematics, often referred to as "real-world" problems, is called mathematical modeling.

Mathematical modeling involves constructions called models. Models are tools that mathematicians create in order to help them understand and solve real-world problems. These tools, like the tools that are used by other professionals (physicians, lawyers, and others), have evolved over long periods of time. Much of what is being done has significantly extended the domain of areas in which mathematics has been useful, resulting in a broad array of new technologies (e.g., medical imaging, wireless telephony) and improvements in old ones (e.g., fuel-efficient planes, better weather forecasts). Whereas at the end of the nineteenth century, applications of mathematics

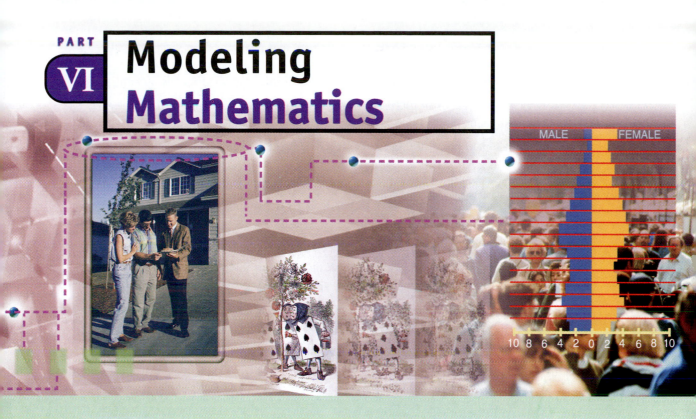

were mostly confined to physics and engineering, at the start of the twenty-first century, mathematics is being applied to every conceivable discipline. Hence, the title of this book!

The essence of mathematical modeling is controlled simplification. Faced with a complex situation, it can be hard to see the forest for the trees. In simplification, what is being disregarded and what is being zoomed in on are carefully noted.

Here are two situations that benefit by the modeling approach:

1. Design a good route for driving from New York to Los Angeles.
2. Design a good route for getting Charles Lindbergh from New York's Roosevelt Field (on Long Island, near New York City) to Paris.

In the first situation we must be able to see at a glance the possible roads from New York to Los Angeles and the terrain they cover, where they cross major rivers such as the Hudson and Mississippi, what the choices are for going over the Rocky Mountains or avoiding high altitudes. The solution is obvious: we need a map including the interstate highway system for the country. A map is a model that can be folded and placed in a glove compartment. It show rivers, mountains, and deserts, all drawn to scale to display the pros and cons of different road routes by contrasting driving distances with physical terrain to be covered. Although the earth is a sphere, flat road maps typically do not attempt to take this fact into account. For the problem at hand, the major existing roads and not the shortest distance from New York to Los Angeles is what matters. Joining New York and Los Angeles by a straight line and asserting that this line would be a good route would be silly: no road would follow this route exactly. Controlled simplification solves the problem.

In the second situation, Lindbergh was faced with flying an aircraft to Paris in a way that minimized the amount of fuel needed. He needed a short route since planes of that time had trouble carrying their payload and fuel. A flat map of the world on which he could have joined New York and Paris with a straight line, the shortest distance between two points in a plane, would not have met his needs. For Lindbergh's situation a flat map is the wrong model. Shortest routes on the earth can best be understood by looking at a spherical globe to represent the earth. Although the earth is, in fact, not a perfect sphere, for many purposes treating it as if it were a sphere is good enough. Using mathematical methods for the geometry of a sphere, one can find the shortest route between two points on the surface of a sphere. (The route would be a part of a circle that goes through the center of the sphere and includes the start and destination points, New York and Paris.) For Lindbergh to have taken the globe, however, would have been unnecessary: after having planned the best route, he did not need to consult the globe again. Also, globes are hard to store in a glove compartment! He was better off taking a few more ounces of fuel.

These examples, finding a convenient automobile route from New York to Los Angeles and finding a shortest air route from New York to Paris, though superficially similar, require very different models — a map versus a globe. In the chapters that follow, the process of controlled simplification will be illustrated, and the power and flexibility of mathematics will unfold before your eyes.

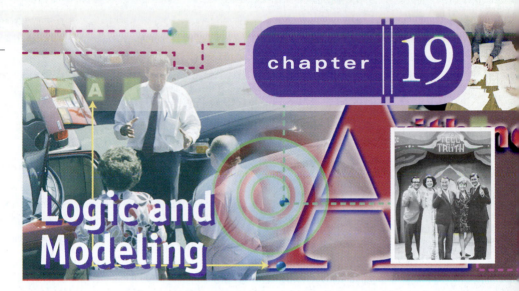

chapter 19

Logic and Modeling

"The English language is remarkably expressive. Unfortunately, it is also extremely complicated."

In the preface to the first edition of *For All Practical Purposes,* we find the following sentence:

> [This book] represents our efforts to bring the excitement of contemporary mathematical thinking to the nonspecialist, as well as help him or her develop the capacity to engage in logical thinking and to read critically the technical information with which our contemporary society abounds.

In part, *For All Practical Purposes* has met this challenge of developing the capacity to think logically by illustrating how mathematical models can be used to analyze real-world problems. But isn't this challenge itself a real-world problem? If we want to understand what "critical thinking" is, perhaps we can do so by constructing a mathematical model that we can analyze.

Historically, this modeling approach is exactly what was done by mathematicians like George Boole in the nineteenth century. The model created was something now called "symbolic logic." In a well-known text on mathematical logic, author H. B. Enderton begins with the following paragraph:

> Symbolic logic is a mathematical model of deductive thought. Or at least that was true originally; as with other branches of mathematics it has grown beyond the circumstances of its birth. Symbolic logic is a model in much the same way that modern probability theory is a model for situations involving chance and uncertainty.

Symbolic logic really involves the study of two different models of deductive thought. The first model is called **propositional logic.** In spite of being, as Enderton says, "woefully inadequate for interesting [mathematical] deductions," it certainly plays a role in analyzing our everyday use of the English language. The second model is called **first-order logic.** It is, again to quote Enderton, "admirably suited to deductions encountered in mathematics."

In this chapter, we study symbolic logic, with our main emphasis on propositional logic. We will see that what arises is not only a model of important real-world objects ("logically correct deductions"), but an area of mathematics that is rich in deep questions and profound theorems.

The English Language

The English language is remarkably expressive. Unfortunately, it is also extremely complicated. In their book *Sweet Reason,* logicians Tymoczko and Henle point out that the following are all grammatically correct and meaningful English sentences:

Buffalo!
Buffalo buffalo.
Buffalo buffalo buffalo.

The last sentence, for example, asserts that a certain kind of animal confuses others of the same species. We're not saying that this is a *true* assertion—actually, we have no idea of how effectively these animals communicate. But it is a grammatically correct and meaningful sentence, and this allows for the possibility that it is true and the possibility that it is false.

And if language itself is complicated, then logical arguments are even more so. In his 1896 text on symbolic logic, writer and mathematician Charles Dodgson (perhaps better known to the reader as Lewis Carroll, author of *Alice's Adventures in Wonderland*) logically concludes—and correctly so—that "Amos Judd loves cold mutton," based on the following seven assumptions:

1. All the policemen on this beat sup with our cook.
2. No man with long hair can fail to be a poet.
3. Amos Judd has never been in prison.
4. Our cook's "cousins" all love cold mutton.
5. None but policemen on this beat are poets.
6. None but her "cousins" ever sup with our cook.
7. Men with short hair have all been in prison.

Variants of this kind of argument are standard fare on graduate program tests such as the Law School Admissions Test (LSAT) and the Medical College Admissions Test (MCAT). It turns out that propositional logic can be a great help in dealing with this kind of question.

We'll return to arguments like Dodgson's in a moment. Our immediate goal, however, is to set up a formal language that captures some (but not all) of the key aspects of the English language, and to analyze the idea of "logical deduction" within the context of this formal language. This analysis will open the door to investigations that not only explain Dodgson's conclusion about Amos Judd loving cold mutton but also probe some of the deepest questions of the past century regarding the limitations of computers and mathematics.

The gardeners paint the Queen's rose trees red.

The Basic Symbols of Propositional Logic

The objects that we are trying to model are declarative sentences—also called "propositions." This rules out certain kinds of legitimate English sentences like questions and exclamations. We will model declarative sentences by using uppercase letters: A, B, C, P, Q, R, etc. These will be called **sentence symbols.**

For example, if we were trying to analyze Charles Dodgson's earlier argument, we might introduce the following sentence symbols:

B   suggested by the sentence "Amos Judd is a policeman on this beat."
S   suggested by the sentence "Amos Judd sups with our cook."

Associated with each declarative sentence is another declarative sentence called its **negation.** For example, the negation of the sentence "Amos Judd is a policeman on this beat" is the sentence "Amos Judd is not a policeman on this beat." As a symbol for negation we will use ¬. Thus, if B denotes "Amos Judd is a policeman on this beat" then ¬B denotes "Amos Judd is not a policeman on this beat."

The English language also contains connectives that combine two declarative sentences to form a third (much as addition combines two numbers to yield a third). Perhaps the first two such connectives that spring to mind are "and" and "or," but we will momentarily postpone consideration of those two and focus on another. The connective on which we will focus is "implies."

Let's return to Dodgson's first statement: "All the policemen on this beat sup with our cook." What this tells us about Amos Judd (the character of interest) is the following:

> If Amos Judd is a policeman on this beat, then Amos Judd sups with our cook.

With our propositional symbols B and S as before, this sentence has the form "if B then S." Sentences of this form are extremely important in mathematics. In fact, it has been suggested that mathematics could be defined as the study of all "if–then" statements.

What kind of symbol should we use in our formal language to denote "if–then"? We certainly don't want to mix symbols (B and S) with words ("if" and "then") in our formal lanaguage. We also don't want to work with two separate symbols—one for "if" and one for "then." The answer lies in accepting a bit of less familiar phraseology from the English language, and agreeing to rewrite if–then sentences as "implies" sentences. For example, the sentence

> If Amos Judd is a policeman on this beat, then Amos Judd sups with our cook.

becomes

> Amos Judd is a policeman on this beat implies [that] Amos Judd sups with our cook.

This one-word connective "implies" can now be replaced in our formal language by a symbol $\Rightarrow$. Thus, $B \Rightarrow S$ denotes the assertion that can be read as "Amos Judd is a policeman on this beat implies [that] Amos Judd sups with our cook." Equivalently, $B \Rightarrow S$ denotes the assertion "If Amos Judd is a policeman on this beat, then Amos Judd sups with our cook."

In an if–then statement, the "if part" is called the **antecedent** and the "then part" is called the **consequent.** However, in the English language, an if–then statement is not always written with the antecedent following the "if" and the consequent following the "then." For example, the following sentences all mean the same thing:

> If Amos Judd is a policeman, then Amos Judd sups with our cook.
> Amos Judd sups with our cook if Amos Judd is a policeman.
> Amos Judd is a policeman only if Amos Judd sups with our cook.
> Only if Amos Judd sups with our cook is Amos Judd a policeman.

When analyzing the English language, it is important that we recognize all of these as if–then statements. Then, when confronted with one of the less familiar versions—for example, "Only if Amos Judd sups with our cook is Amos Judd a policeman"—we can mentally rearrange it into the simple form of the first one, "If Amos Judd is a policeman, then Amos Judd sups with our cook."

This completes our discussion of what we will take as the basic (also called "primitive") symbols of our formal language. In summary:

The basic symbols of propositional logic are:

- Sentence symbols P, Q, R, . . .
- The negation symbol ¬
- The implication symbol ⟹

We expand this list shortly (adding symbols for "and," for "or," and for "if and only if"). But let's pause in the formal development for a moment and look at one of the immediate benefits of what we have done so far.

Using Symbolism in Analytical Reasoning

How can Dodgson conclude that Amos Judd loves mutton? There are really only three facts of logic (or common sense, if you prefer) that we need:

(i)   Knowing that ¬¬P is true is the same as knowing that P itself is true. Essentially this says that something is true if and only if (that is, precisely when) it is not the case that it is false.

(ii)   If we know that P ⟹ Q is true and we know that P is true, then we also know that Q is true.

(iii)   If we know that P ⟹ Q is true and we know that Q is false, then we also know that P is false.

EXAMPLE

Let's illustrate (i), (ii), and (iii). For (i), let P be the statement, "Amos Judd is a policeman." Then ¬¬P is the assertion "It is not the case that Amos Judd is not a policeman." Thus, ¬¬P is certainly awkward, but it is clearly true if and only if Amos Judd is, in fact, a policeman.

Now, suppose again that P is the statement "Amos Judd is a policeman" and let Q be the statement "Amos Judd sups with our cook." In both (ii) and (iii), we are assuming that we know the truth of the assertion P ⟹ Q, which, in this example, is the following:

"If Amos Judd is a policeman, then Amos Judd sups with our cook."

To be sure, (ii) is the most straightforward; it says that if we also know that Amos Judd is, in fact, a policeman, then we can conclude that he sups with our cook. For (iii), however, we are assuming that we know that Amos Judd does *not* sup with our cook (i.e., Q is false). How do we know that Amos Judd is *not* a policeman? Well, if he were a policeman, then—by our assumption that $P \Rightarrow Q$ is true—we could conclude that Amos Judd sups with our cook (contrary to what we just said we are assuming). Thus, we must be able to conclude that Amos Judd is not a policeman (i.e., that P is false.)   ◆

Assertion (iii) is extremely important. It gives rise to a definition and an observation that is worth recording:

The **contrapositive** of $P \Rightarrow Q$ is the assertion $\neg Q \Rightarrow \neg P$. For example, the contrapositive of "If Amos Judd is a policeman, then Amos Judd sups with our cook" is the statement "If Amos Judd does *not* sup with our cook, then Amos Judd is *not* a policeman." An if–then statement is true if and only if its contrapositive is true—they are simply two ways of asserting exactly the same thing.

With these facts of logic (or common sense) at our disposal, let's translate Dodgson's assumptions into symbolic form (so that we can get on with the analysis of the argument that eventually concludes that Amos Judd loves cold mutton). We begin by rephrasing each assumption as a statement about Amos Judd.

(1) All the policemen on this beat sup with our cook.   becomes   If Amos Judd is a policeman on this beat, then Amos Judd sups with our cook.

(2) No man with long hair can fail to be a poet.   becomes   If Amos Judd has long hair, then Amos Judd is a poet.

(3) Amos Judd has never been in prison.   becomes   unchanged (it is already a statement about Amos Judd)

(4) Our cook's "cousins" all love cold mutton.   becomes   If Amos Judd is a cousin of our cook, then Amos Judd loves cold mutton.

(5) None but policemen on this beat are poets.   becomes   If Amos Judd is not a policeman on this beat, then Amos Judd is not a poet.

(6) None but her "cousins" ever sup with our cook.   becomes   If Amos Judd is not a cousin of our cook, then Amos Judd does not sup with her.

(7) Men with short hair have all been in prison.   becomes   If Amos Judd has short hair, then Amos Judd has been in prison.

Notice that care must be taken in getting the correct assertions in lines (5) and (6). Saying, for example, that "None but Republicans are honest" is not literally saying that Republicans are honest (although everyday usage would carry with it the implication that at least *some* Republicans are honest). What it is asserting is that if someone is *not* a Republican, then he or she is definitely *not* honest.

Our next step is to introduce sentence symbols to denote the various basic declarative sentences involved:

B	for	"Amos Judd is a policeman on this beat."
S	for	"Amos Judd sups with our cook."
H	for	"Amos Judd has long hair."
P	for	"Amos Judd is a poet."
J	for	"Amos Judd has been in prison." (using "J" for "jail")
M	for	"Amos Judd loves cold mutton."
C	for	"Amos Judd is a cousin of our cook."

We have some options in choosing what we take as "basic declarative sentences." For example, we could have chosen "Amos Judd has *never* been in prison" instead of "Amos Judd has been in prison." We chose the latter only to make our basic declarative sentences uniform in the sense that none of them uses the word "not." Such a choice, however, is a matter of taste and has no effect on the subsequent analysis.

We can now restate our assumptions in the formal language we have set up.

(1) $B \Rightarrow S$ (If Amos Judd is a policeman on this beat, then Amos Judd sups with our cook.)

(2) $H \Rightarrow P$ (If Amos Judd has long hair, then Amos Judd is a poet.)

(3) $\neg J$ (Amos Judd has never been in prison.)

(4) $C \Rightarrow M$ (If Amos Judd is a cousin of our cook, then Amos Judd loves cold mutton.)

(5) $\neg B \Rightarrow \neg P$ (If Amos Judd is not a policeman on this beat, then Amos Judd is not a poet.)

(6) $\neg C \Rightarrow \neg S$ (If Amos Judd is not a cousin of our cook, then Amos Judd does not sup with her.)

(7) $\neg H \Rightarrow J$ (If Amos Judd has short hair, then Amos Judd has been in prison.)

This is the point at which we take advantage of modeling. Although we have the sentences in English at our disposal, these are the very things that made the analysis difficult in the first place. If it were easy to sort out the relevance of long hair and prison to the loving of cold mutton, then we wouldn't need a model.

Thus, we will ignore the original sentences (these are part of the real world) and work simply with the letters B, S, H, etc., and the symbols $\Rightarrow$ and $\neg$ (these are part of the model). We know how to manipulate things in the model using our previous three facts of logic:

(i)   We know P is true if and only if we know $\neg\neg$P is true;

(ii)   If we know P $\Rightarrow$ Q is true and we know P is true, then we know Q is true; and

(iii)   If we know P $\Rightarrow$ Q is true and we know Q is false, then we know P is false.

So let's get on with the analysis (in the model). We begin with the single assumption that is not an implication: $\neg$J in (3). This, together with $\neg$H $\Rightarrow$ J from (7), gives us H (actually, it gives us $\neg\neg$H, but this is the same as H). Thus we know H is true. Now (2) tells us that H $\Rightarrow$ P, and so we can conclude P. Using $\neg$B $\Rightarrow$ $\neg$P (5), together with P, gives us B, and B $\Rightarrow$ S by (1). Thus, we can conclude S. Now S, taken together with $\neg$C $\Rightarrow$ $\neg$S from (6), allows us to conclude C. Finally, we have C $\Rightarrow$ M in (4), and we can conclude that M is true.

Now, returning to the real world, we can conclude that Amos Judd loves mutton (which is what M stood for), as desired. This completes our analysis.

When first confronting an analysis such as this, there is a temptation to translate the result of each step back into English before taking the next step. This temptation is the result of a natural insecurity that is present when one begins modeling in a new context; one is seeking reassurance by periodically checking the model against the real world as one proceeds. Although this seeking of reassurance is not a bad instinct, the reader should realize that such checking is—assuming one has confidence in the model—not at all necessary. The validity of our argument is no more dependent on the meanings of H or P than is the truth of the assertion $x + y = y + x$ dependent on what numbers are represented by x and y.

There is another way to get at this derivation of M from these seven assumptions that some might find preferable to what we just did. This alternate analysis involves making use of the contrapositives in an organized fashion. To illustrate this, we will begin by repeating the list of seven assumptions, but this time, we will also include, beside each implication, its contrapositive (denoted with a "c" for "contrapositive"):

(1)	B $\Rightarrow$ S	(1c)	$\neg$S $\Rightarrow$ $\neg$B
(2)	H $\Rightarrow$ P	(2c)	$\neg$P $\Rightarrow$ $\neg$H
	(3) $\neg$J		
(4)	C $\Rightarrow$ M	(4c)	$\neg$M $\Rightarrow$ $\neg$C
(5)	$\neg$B $\Rightarrow$ $\neg$P	(5c)	P $\Rightarrow$ B
(6)	$\neg$C $\Rightarrow$ $\neg$S	(6c)	S $\Rightarrow$ C
(7)	$\neg$H $\Rightarrow$ J	(7c)	$\neg$J $\Rightarrow$ H

Now, starting with $\neg$J again, we get a sequence of implications—depicted with labels over the arrows to show which assumption is being used—as follows:

$$(7c) \quad (2) \quad (5c) \quad (1) \quad (6c) \quad (4)$$
$$\neg J \Rightarrow H \Rightarrow P \Rightarrow B \Rightarrow S \Rightarrow C \Rightarrow M$$

The reader should recognize that this is quite a quick and mechanical way to arrive at the conclusion that Amos Judd loves mutton.

Truth and Falsity for ¬ and ⇒

The English sentences in which we are interested are not only declarative sentences (as opposed to exclamations or questions) but ones that have a definite **truth value** T (for true) or F (for false). This rules out certain assertions (of considerable interest in other contexts), such as "This sentence is false." (Think about it—if the assertion is true, it must be false; if it's false, it must be true.)

The question we address here is the following. Suppose we know the truth or falsity of two basic declarative sentences such as "2 + 2 = 4" (true) and "Bertrand Russell is the Pope" (false, but relevant to a historical anecdote that we will relate momentarily). If P denotes the first assertion and Q denotes the second, what truth value should we assign to the sentences $P \Rightarrow Q$ and $Q \Rightarrow P$? Actually, it should be pretty clear that $P \Rightarrow Q$ is false (think about it). But the truth or falsity of $Q \Rightarrow P$ should strike the reader as less obvious. We'll return to this as well.

First of all, however, let's deal with the easy case of negation. Suppose we know that a sentence P is true. What can we say about the sentence ¬P? This is trivial: if a sentence is true, then its negation is false. Conversely, if a sentence is false, then its negation is true. These observations about the truth and falsity of ¬P can be summarized with two statements:

1. If P is true, then ¬P is false.
2. If P is false, then ¬P is true.

As a shorthand for expressing these two assertions, we might write the following:

P	¬P
T	F
F	T

This is a very simple example of what is known as a **truth table.** It is an organized presentation—in the form of a table—of all possible assignments of T for true and F for false to the sentence symbols (which will generally be several upper-case letters, but for this example is just P), and the resulting assignments of Ts and Fs to some propositional sentence built up from these symbols using ¬ and/or ⇒. With the example at hand, the sentence is just ¬P. Some additional examples will help to clarify the idea of a truth table.

What should the truth table for $P \Rightarrow Q$ look like? As a starting point, we note that there are now four basic statements concerning the truth and falsity of $P \Rightarrow Q$ that need to be completed:

1. If P is true and Q is true, then $P \Rightarrow Q$ is __?__.
2. If P is true and Q is false, then $P \Rightarrow Q$ is __?__.
3. If P is false and Q is true, then $P \Rightarrow Q$ is __?__.
4. If P is false and Q is false, then $P \Rightarrow Q$ is __?__.

These four statements correspond to the four possibilities for the truth and falsity of P and Q. The corresponding truth table (with the last column not yet filled in) is as follows:

P	Q	$P \Rightarrow Q$
T	T	?
T	F	?
F	T	?
F	F	?

Our first claim is that there are two situations in which we can all agree on the truth or falsity of $P \Rightarrow Q$. Let's fill these in and see if we all do, in fact, agree.

P	Q	$P \Rightarrow Q$
T	T	T
T	F	F
F	T	?
F	F	?

The point is that $P \Rightarrow Q$ means "if P, then Q" and this, if we expand the English, means "if P is true, then Q is true." Hence, in the first two lines—where P is true—there seems no doubt that $P \Rightarrow Q$ is true when Q is true (line 1) and false when Q is false (line 2). For example, if P is the statement "You mow my lawn" and Q is the statement "I will give you $20," then line (1) corresponds to a promise kept (you mowed my lawn and I gave you $20) and line (2) corresponds to a promise broken (you mowed my lawn and I failed to give you $20). It is natural to assign truth to a kept promise and falsity to a broken promise. But in this example, lines (3) and (4) correspond to a promise neither broken nor kept (you didn't mow my lawn).

Of course, not every if–then statement corresponds to what we would normally think of as a promise. For example, the statement "If $2 + 2 = 5$, then

Bertrand Russell is the Pope" hardly seems like a promise, but we nevertheless want to assign it a truth value. But even if we stick with promises, we have a choice of identifying truth with "promise kept" or falsity with "promise broken."

In fact, we opt for the latter. Thus, P $\Rightarrow$ Q is regarded as false only if it corresponds to a broken promise—a situation where P is true and Q is false. In all other situations—in particular, in all situations where the antecedent P is false—the implication P $\Rightarrow$ Q is regarded as true. Thus, for example, the statement "If 2 + 2 = 5, then Bertrand Russell is the Pope" is true.

Moreover, we claim that this decision is the one most faithful to our everyday use of the English language. Many authors justify this by asserting that identifying falsity with promises broken is the only natural thing to do. But is this really more compelling than identifying truth with promises kept? The fact is that while a discussion of promises provides a nice way to remember when implications are false, the real decision of when implications are regarded as true can be better justified in other ways (see the Writing Assignments at the end of the chapter).

In summary, P $\Rightarrow$ Q is false only if P is true and Q is false. If P is false, then P $\Rightarrow$ Q is true, regardless of whether Q is true or false.

We can now complete the truth table for P $\Rightarrow$ Q.

P	Q	P $\Rightarrow$ Q
T	T	T
T	F	F
F	T	T
F	F	T

The truth or falsity of P $\Rightarrow$ Q is also related to the validity of arguments, and we will say more about this later in the chapter. For the moment, however, let us foreshadow this connection by an old anecdote that recounts a time when the great British mathematician and philosopher Bertrand Russell was trying to explain to a group of nonacademics why it is that if one has a false axiom to work with, then one can prove anything as a theorem. (This is true, and related to the fact that P $\Rightarrow$ Q is true whenever P is false—regardless of what Q is.)

Russell was at this point challenged with the task of proving that he was the Pope, given the assumption that 2 + 2 = 5. (Recall that we agreed that the statement "If 2 + 2 = 5, then Bertrand Russell is the Pope" is true.) Russell responded roughly as follows: Well, we are assuming that 2 + 2 = 5, but I can prove that 2 + 2 = 4. Thus, we know that 4 = 5. Subtracting 3 from each side of this equation gives 1 = 2. Now, surely you will agree that the Pope and I are two. Hence, the Pope and I are one.

Needless to say, one should take this with a grain of salt.

The Other Connectives

In our formal language, we certainly want something that models the word "and" as it is used in the English language. The symbol commonly used for this is $\wedge$, so we read "P $\wedge$ Q" as "P and Q." There is no ambiguity as to when P $\wedge$ Q is true: this happens precisely when P is true and Q is true.

For example, if P is the statement "Amos Judd is a policeman" and Q is the statement "Amos Judd is a poet" then P $\wedge$ Q is the statement "Amos Judd is a policeman *and* Amos Judd is a poet." This is clearly false if Amos Judd fails to be a policeman or fails to be a poet (or fails to be either).

In summary then, the truth table for P $\wedge$ Q is as follows:

P	Q	P $\wedge$ Q
T	T	T
T	F	F
F	T	F
F	F	F

Why are we just getting to "and" now, and why didn't we introduce it as one of the primitive symbols of our formal language? The answer is that we really don't need a symbol for "and." If we have $\neg$ and $\Rightarrow$, then we could use "$\neg(P \Rightarrow \neg Q)$" in place of "P $\wedge$ Q" because—in terms of truth and falsity—they mean exactly the same thing (although, at first sight, this is far from obvious). Let's see why this is true.

We'll start with an example in English (but the reader should not get his or her hopes for enlightenment too high yet). As before, let P be the statement "Amos Judd is a policeman" and Q be the statement "Amos Judd is a poet." Our claim is that the following two sentences are equivalent:

(*)   "Amos Judd is a policeman and Amos Judd is a poet."
(**)   "Amos Judd's being a policeman does not imply that he fails to be a poet."

Few of us will find the equivalence of (*) and (**) obvious. It's a little clearer if we rephrase (**) as "It is not true that Amos Judd's being a policeman implies that he fails to be a poet," but the use of the phrase "it is not true that" seems a little artificial.

We can, however, settle the matter of the equivalence of "$\neg(P \Rightarrow \neg Q)$" and "P $\wedge$ Q" completely by the use of a truth table. That is, we can show that regardless of what the truth values of P and Q are, the sentence "$\neg(P \Rightarrow \neg Q)$" is true precisely when the sentence "P $\wedge$ Q" is true.

In constructing the truth table for "$\neg(P \Rightarrow \neg Q)$" we will begin with a column for P and a column for Q, since these are the sentence symbols that occur in

"¬(P ⟹ ¬Q)." These two columns will be filled in as before, giving the four possibilities TT, TF, FT, and FF. The last column of the truth table will have the sentence "¬(P ⟹ ¬Q)" at the top. In between, we will have columns labeled ¬Q and P ⟹ ¬Q to serve as "scratchwork" that we use in arriving at the Ts and Fs in the last column. Thus, we will fill out the table in five steps (first step: fill in column one; second step: fill in column two; etc.).

To illustrate the construction of the truth table, we'll pick up the procedure at the end of step three, where we have filled in the column for P, the column for Q, and the column for ¬Q (which is just the opposite of what we have in the column for Q):

P	Q	¬Q
T	T	F
T	F	T
F	T	F
F	F	T

In step four, we will fill in the column for P ⟹ ¬Q, remembering that this is true unless the antecedent (P) is true and the consequent (¬Q) is false (so the column labeled Q can be ignored in this step):

P	Q	¬Q	P ⟹ ¬Q
T	T	F	F
T	F	T	T
F	T	F	T
F	F	T	T

In step five, we will fill in the column for ¬(P ⟹ ¬Q), which is easy—it is just the opposite of the column we just filled in for P ⟹ ¬Q:

P	Q	¬Q	P ⟹ ¬Q	¬(P ⟹ ¬Q)
T	T	F	F	T
T	F	T	T	F
F	T	F	T	F
F	F	T	T	F

The point of constructing this truth table is to illustrate the fact that if we were to omit the scratchwork columns for ¬Q and P ⟹ ¬Q in this table, then we'd have:

P	Q	¬(P ⟹ ¬Q)
T	T	T
T	F	F
F	T	F
F	F	F

which is identical (except for the heading in the last column) to the truth table for P ∧ Q. Thus, we have used truth tables to show that regardless of whether P is true or false, and regardless of whether Q is true or false, the sentence ¬(P ⟹ ¬Q) is true precisely when the sentence P ∧ Q is true (and false precisely when the sentence P ∧ Q is false).

The connective "or" is a little more tricky. Sometimes, in English, we use "or" in the exclusive sense: "Eat your supper or you'll be sent to bed." Those of us who grew up hearing this understood it to mean that if we ate our supper then we wouldn't be sent to bed (at least not for anything to do with the evening meal). It turns out to be most useful to use "or" in the inclusive sense—corresponding to "and/or" in the English language. For example, a requirement for graduating with honors in mathematics might be to write an honors thesis or to take two additional upper-level mathematics classes. A student who, in fact, did both (the thesis and the extra courses) would certainly expect to receive honors.

The symbol for "or" is ∨. Thus, P ∨ Q will be regarded as false only if both P and Q are false, and so the truth table for P ∨ Q is as follows:

P	Q	P ∨ Q
T	T	T
T	F	T
F	T	T
F	F	F

It turns out that the sentence P ∨ Q is true precisely in the same situations where the sentence ¬P ⟹ Q is true, as an examination of its truth table will show.

P	Q	¬P	Q	¬P ⟹ Q
T	T	F	T	T
T	F	F	F	T
F	T	T	T	T
F	F	T	F	F

(We have chosen to add a scratchwork column in which we repeated Q simply to make it easier to fill in the last column while looking at the two columns immediately to its left.)

Actually, the equivalence of P ∨ Q and ¬P ⟹ Q is easier to see with English sentences than it was for P ∧ Q and ¬(P ⟹ ¬Q). For example, if P is the statement "Amos Judd is a policeman" and Q is "Amos Judd is a poet," then we are claiming that the following two sentences are simply different ways of saying the same thing:

(*)   "Amos Judd is a policeman or Amos Judd is a poet."
(**)   "If Amos Judd is not a policeman, then Amos Judd is a poet."

With the inclusive use of "or" it is easy to see that the negation of "P and Q" is the sentence "not P or not Q" and the negation of "P or Q" is the sentence "not P and not Q." In particular (and this is also important for the kind of analytical reasoning done on standardized tests), the negation of an "and sentence" is an "or sentence" and vice versa. The reader should check this with the example wherein P is the statement "Amos Judd is a policeman" and Q is the statement "Amos Judd is a poet."

There is one other connective in the English language that we make considerable use of in mathematics. It corresponds to the phrase "if and only if," and it is so common in mathematics that it is almost universally abbreviated as "iff." We are continually asserting that something is true "precisely when" something else is true. For example, we just said that ¬P ⟹ Q is true precisely when P ∨ Q is true. This is equivalent to saying that ¬P ⟹ Q is true iff P ∨ Q is true.

The symbol in our formal language that will correspond to "if and only if" is ⟺. Its truth table is as follows:

P	Q	P ⟺ Q
T	T	T
T	F	F
F	T	F
F	F	T

For example, suppose we were to assert (as we did) that P ⟹ Q is true iff ¬P ∨ Q is true. We'd mean by this that, for all four possibilities of assigning true and false to P and Q (i.e., TT, TF, FT, and FF), the resulting assignment of T or F to P ⟹ Q is the same as the assignment to ¬P ∨ Q. This is easily seen to be true:

P	Q	P ⟹ Q
T	T	T
T	F	F
F	T	T
F	F	T

P	Q	¬P ∨ Q
T	T	T
T	F	F
F	T	T
F	F	T

Asserting that these two truth tables have the same last column is equivalent to asserting that the truth table for $(P \Rightarrow Q) \Leftrightarrow (\neg P \vee Q)$ has all Ts in its right-hand column. This is easily checked:

P	Q	P⇒Q	¬P	Q	¬P∨Q	(P⇒Q)⇔(¬P∨Q)
T	T	T	F	T	T	T
T	F	F	F	F	F	T
F	T	T	T	T	T	T
F	F	T	T	F	T	T

Propositional sentences with all Ts in the right-hand column of their truth table correspond to assertions that are true regardless of the truth of the simple declarative sentences (represented by the Ps, Qs, etc.) out of which they are made. These are called tautologies.

> A **tautology** is a propositional sentence that is true for every possible assignment of Ts and Fs to the sentence symbols in the sentence.

Thus, $(P \Rightarrow Q) \Leftrightarrow (\neg P \vee Q)$ is an example of a tautology. There are several reasons why it is important (at least theoretically) to be able to determine when a propositional sentence is a tautology. For example, we have already seen that the question of whether or not two sentences like $P \Rightarrow Q$ and $\neg P \vee Q$ are equivalent is the same as the question of whether the single sentence $(P \Rightarrow Q) \Leftrightarrow (\neg P \vee Q)$ is a tautology.

As another example of the usefulness of the idea of a tautology, consider our original question of whether or not one could logically conclude M (from our Amos Judd loves mutton example) from the seven assumptions: $B \Rightarrow S$; $H \Rightarrow P$; $\neg J$; $C \Rightarrow M$; $\neg B \Rightarrow \neg P$; $\neg C \Rightarrow \neg S$; $\neg H \Rightarrow J$. This is the same as asking if the following sentence is a tautology:

$$[(B \Rightarrow S) \wedge (H \Rightarrow P) \wedge (\neg J) \wedge (C \Rightarrow M) \wedge (\neg B \Rightarrow \neg P) \wedge (\neg C \Rightarrow \neg S)$$
$$\wedge (\neg H \Rightarrow J)] \Rightarrow M$$

Truth tables provide a mechanical procedure for determining whether or not a propositional sentence is a tautology. We'll demonstrate with an example.

EXAMPLE

Is the sentence $(P \Rightarrow \neg P) \Rightarrow \neg P$ a tautology? To answer this question, we simply construct the truth table:

P	¬P	P⇒¬P	¬P	(P⇒¬P)⇒¬P
T	F	F	F	T
F	T	T	T	T

Since there are only Ts in the last column, we conclude that the sentence $(P \Rightarrow \neg P) \Rightarrow \neg P$ is, in fact, a tautology.   ◆

Notice, however, that as far as using truth tables to check valid arguments, there are some real practical limitations. For example, checking whether or not

$$[(B \Rightarrow S) \wedge (H \Rightarrow P) \wedge (\neg J) \wedge (C \Rightarrow M) \wedge (\neg B \Rightarrow \neg P) \wedge (\neg C \Rightarrow \neg S) \wedge (\neg H \Rightarrow J)] \Rightarrow M$$

is a tautology by truth tables requires $2^7 = 128$ lines in the table (because there are seven sentence symbols: B, S, H, P, J, C, and M).

Tautologies have all Ts in their last column. Also of interest are those propositional sentences that have *at least one T* in their last column. Such a sentence is said to be **satisfiable.** Studying satisfiable sentences is, in a sense, the same as studying tautologies because of the following fact (which should be clear after a moment's reflection): a sentence is satisfiable if and only if its negation is *not* a tautology. Thus, truth tables also provide a completely mechanical method to test for satisfiability. Is there a "better" way to test a propositional sentence for satisfiability? We consider this question next.

An Important Open Question

Computers rely on mechanical procedures, or algorithms, to solve problems. Unfortunately, there are certain problems that we now know can never be solved by a computer. For example, it would be nice if a computer could check other computer programs to see if there are any so-called infinite loops (i.e., instructions that would send it along an infinite path in a vain attempt to accomplish that for which it was intended). It has been mathematically proven that no such algorithm will ever exist—this is known as the "unsolvability of the **halting problem.**"

On the other hand, there are a number of tasks that can be done by a computer, but for which the only known algorithms (that are guaranteed to work) involve so many steps, in general, that it is impractical for some real-world problems. One example is the so-called traveling salesman problem discussed in Chapter 2. Another example is that of determining if a given propositional sentence is, or is not, satisfiable (the **satisfiability problem**).

There are naive algorithms to solve the traveling salesman problem and the satisfiability problem. In both cases, the algorithms consist of checking all the different possibilities that are available. With the traveling salesman problem, this means looking at all possible routes (and doing an easy calculation to determine the cost associated with each such path). In the case of the satisfiability problem, this means constructing the truth table (and doing an easy check to see if there is at least one T in the last column).

But if there are n propositional constants, there are 2^n rows in the truth table. And 2^n is a very large number compared to n (for example, if $n = 20$, then 2^n is over a million). Hence, this is an "exponential algorithm" as opposed to a "polynomial algorithm" (i.e., one that would require only n^k steps for some fixed k).

This brings us to Spotlight 2.1 on page 42 in Chapter 2. A problem is said to be "NP-complete" if the existence of a "fast algorithm" for it would immediately yield a fast algorithm for all problems in a well-defined class that includes many important problems like the traveling salesman problem. It turns out that not only is the satisfiability problem NP-complete, but it is the very problem used by Stephen Cooke in his 1971 breakthrough result in the field.

Thus, we now have, as one of the most important open questions in the field of theoretical computer science, the following:

Is there an algorithm for solving the satisfiability problem that is "substantially better" than the use of truth tables?

This is called the "**P = NP problem**," although we won't digress here to discuss what P and NP stand for (we mention it only so that if the reader hears reference to the "P = NP problem," he or she will know what is being talked about).

A Model of Deduction

Gottfried Wilhelm Leibniz (1646–1716), one of the co-inventors of calculus (along with Isaac Newton), envisioned all of mathematics as being eventually reduced to algorithmic computations. Today, we know that will never be the case. For example, although additive number theory can be done by a computer, as can multiplicative number theory, there will never be an algorithm that can correctly determine the truth or falsity of every number-theoretic sentence involving both addition and multiplication.

So how do we determine what is mathematically true? The answer is that we prove theorems. That is, we assume that certain statements are true (these are called *axioms*), and then we derive from them (via so-called laws of inference) the truth of some other statements (these are called *theorems*). The demonstration of this logical deduction is called a *proof*.

Can we model this activity within propositional logic? In a sense, we already have. Let's give one illustration.

Suppose we take as axioms the following seven statements:

(1) $B \Rightarrow S$

(2) $H \Rightarrow P$

(3) $\neg J$

(4) $C \Rightarrow M$

(5) $\neg B \Rightarrow \neg P$

(6) $\neg C \Rightarrow \neg S$

(7) $\neg H \Rightarrow J$

Now, as rules of inference, let's agree to take the following:

(i)   If we have $P \Rightarrow Q$ and we have P, then we can write down Q. This is called **modus ponens,** and is often depicted as follows:

$$\frac{\begin{array}{c} P \Rightarrow Q \\ P \end{array}}{\therefore Q}$$

(ii)   If we have $P \Rightarrow Q$ and we have $\neg Q$, then we can write down $\neg P$. This is called **modus tollens,** and is often depicted as follows:

$$\frac{\begin{array}{c} P \Rightarrow Q \\ \neg Q \end{array}}{\therefore \neg P}$$

(iii) We can replace P by $\neg\neg P$ and vice versa. This is called **double negation.**

With these axioms and rules of inference, we can now justify our previous conclusion (that Amos Judd loves cold mutton) via a formal demonstration — that is, a "proof" — that these seven "axioms" yield M as a "theorem."

Statement	Justification
$\neg J$	axiom 3
$\neg H \Rightarrow J$	axiom 7
$\neg\neg H$	modus tollens
H	double negation
$H \Rightarrow P$	axiom 2
P	modus ponens
$\neg\neg P$	double negation
$\neg B \Rightarrow \neg P$	axiom 5
$\neg\neg B$	modus tolens
B	double negation
$B \Rightarrow S$	axiom 1
S	modus ponens
$\neg\neg S$	double negation
$\neg C \Rightarrow \neg S$	axiom 6
$\neg\neg C$	modus tollens
C	double negation
$C \Rightarrow M$	axiom 4
M	modus ponens

Derivations such as this notwithstanding, propositional logic is still not adequate to model the kind of deductions done in mathematics. First-order logic, to which we next turn (if only briefly), certainly is.

First-Order Logic

To see the kind of language we really need to serve as a model for everyday mathematics, let's take a look at one of the most famous unsolved problems in all of mathematics: the twin-prime conjecture.

Simply stated, the twin-prime conjecture asserts that there are infinitely many numbers y with the property that y and $y + 2$ are both prime, in which case we would say that y and $y + 2$ are "twin primes." For example, 17 and 19 are twin primes. What kind of a language would we need in order to write the twin-prime conjecture in some kind of symbolic form?

We certainly need variables (such as y), and we probably need symbols for addition and multiplication (we could use $+$ and $\cdot$ as usual), as well as for the ordering of the natural numbers (let's use $>$). We may also need names for certain numbers (like 1).

But the real key turns out to be the need for symbols—so-called "quantifiers"—that correspond to the phrases "for every x, . . ." and "there exists an x

SPOTLIGHT 19.1

The Continuum Hypothesis

Working mathematicians do not sit with a list of axioms on their desk as they work. Yet they try to construct proofs in an effort to discover truth (and to gain understanding). For the working mathematician, however, a "proof" is an argument—written in an informal language like English—that the mathematical community will find convincing.

Remarkably though, there is a set of axioms—the so-called Zermello–Frankel axioms with the axiom of choice (denoted ZFC)—from which all known mathematics can be formally derived (using only a couple of rules of inference, one of which is modus ponens). The overwhelming feeling of the mathematical community today is that any informal argument that would generally be found to be convincing by mathematicians can be translated into a formal proof from the axioms of ZFC.

But with any axiom system, there are two important questions. First of all, is the axiom system free of contradictions? This is called *consistency*. An axiom system that is inconsistent allows one to prove both the truth and the falsity of some mathematical assertion, and so it is quite worthless. In fact, an inconsistent system actually allows one to prove the truth and falsity of *every* mathematical assertion—recall Bertrand Russell's "proof" that he and the Pope are one.

The second question is whether or not the axiom system is powerful enough to settle (at least in theory) every mathematical question. This is called *completeness*.

Early in the twentieth century, when the axioms of ZFC were first introduced, the hope was that mathematicians would be able to prove that this axiom system (or perhaps some variant of it) is both consistent and complete. Both hopes were shattered in the 1930s by the remarkable work of such that . . ." The symbols used for these phrases are the **universal quantifier** $\forall$ (read as "for all") and the **existential quantifier** $\exists$ (read as "there exists").

Now, asserting that there are infinitely many natural numbers with a certain property is equivalent to asserting that for every natural number x there exists a natural number y that is larger than x and that has the property. Thus, the assertion,

"There are infinitely many natural numbers such that . . . "

can be phrased in our language as

"$\forall x \exists y$ such that $y > x$ and . . . "

Let's agree to omit the phrase "such that" and just put in brackets or parentheses. Now, the twin-prime conjecture can be stated in our formal language as

"$\forall x \, \exists y \, [y > x \wedge \forall u \, \forall v \, [(u > 1 \wedge v > 1) \Rightarrow \neg(y = u \cdot v \vee y + 1 + 1 = u \cdot v)]]$"

This asserts that there are infinitely many y's with the property that neither y nor $y + 2$ can be written as a product of two integers u and v, both of which are greater than 1.

a young Austrian logician named Kurt Gödel. He showed that systems like ZFC were, of mathematical necessity, either inconsistent or incomplete.

Mathematicians believe that ZFC is consistent. But this belief also forces us to accept (by Gödel's work) that there are mathematical statements that we can neither prove nor disprove on the basis of the axioms of ZFC. In fact, logicians in the twentieth century have identified a great many such statements. One of the first—and perhaps the most important—is the so-called *Continuum Hypothesis*.

The Continuum Hypothesis is the assertion that every infinite set of real numbers (like the set of rational numbers or the set of irrational numbers) can be put either in one-to-one correspondence with the set of natural numbers $\{1, 2, 3, . . .\}$ or in one-to-one correspondence with the set of reals itself. It turns out (although this is far from obvious) that the rationals have the former property and the irrationals have the latter property.

In 1940, Kurt Gödel showed that it is impossible to *disprove* the Continuum Hypothesis from the axioms of ZFC (unless the axioms are inconsistent), and he conjectured that a *proof* of the Continuum Hypothesis from ZFC was similarly impossible. This conjecture was established in 1964 by Paul Cohen. Thus, the Continuum Hypothesis is a mathematical statement that can be neither proved nor disproved on the basis of the axioms of ZFC (unless these axioms are inconsistent).

Mathematical logicians have spent the last third of the twentieth century identifying a wide variety of other mathematical statements that can be neither proved nor disproved from the axioms of ZFC. In the process of such identifications, logicians are also hoping to find additional axioms that can be added to ZFC, with the hope that these additional axioms will allow questions like the Continuum Hypothesis to be settled. Although no such additional axiom has surfaced that the mathematical community finds sufficiently compelling to add to ZFC, one can expect the hunt to go on, as mathematical logic continues into the twenty-first century as one of the most exciting and active areas of mathematical research.

First-order logic, in general, has all the basic symbols of propositional logic ($\Rightarrow$, $\neg$, etc.), as well as an infinite supply of variables (the x's and y's), an infinite supply of operation and relation symbols (like $+$, $\cdot$, $<$, etc.), and an infinite supply of constants (like 1). It also has the quantifiers $\forall$ and $\exists$ (but they can only be applied to variables like x, y, z, as opposed to *sets* of variables).

The analogue of a tautology in first-order logic is a sentence that is true no matter how the operations and relations are interpreted. There is, however, no analogue for truth tables in the context of first-order logic. And there never will be. It is known that no algorithm will ever exist for testing whether or not a first-order sentence is a tautology in this sense.

But we can now ask if there are axioms and rules of inference that would allow us to deduce exactly the tautologies. In the absence of an algorithm (like that provided by truth tables), this is an extremely important question. The answer is yes—there are elegant axiom systems accomplishing exactly this. But the study of these is quite another question, and we will leave it for quite another course (although Spotlight 19.1 provides a glimpse of some twentieth-century axiomatics in the context of a remarkable assertion known as the Continuum Hypothesis).

REVIEW VOCABULARY

Antecedent   The "if part" of an "if–then" sentence.

Consequent   The "then part" of an "if–then" sentence.

Contrapositive   The contrapositive of the statement "if P, then Q" is the statement "if not Q, then not P."

Double negation   The fact that P is true if and only if $\neg\neg$P is true.

Existential quantifier   The symbol $\exists$, which is read as "there exists."

First-order logic   A model of deduction that includes the existential and universal quantifiers as applied to variables ranging over individuals (as opposed to sets of individuals).

Halting problem   The fact that there will never exist an algorithm for determining of an arbitrary computer program whether or not it has an infinite loop.

Modus ponens   The rule of inference that allows one to conclude Q based on having P and P $\Rightarrow$ Q.

Modus tollens   The rule of inference that allows one to conclude $\neg$P based on having $\neg$Q and P $\Rightarrow$ Q.

P = NP problem   The problem of finding an algorithm for satisfiability of propositional sentences that operates in polynomial time instead of exponential time (as truth tables do).

Propositional logic   A model of deduction that includes sentence symbols as well as symbols for the connectives (e.g., $\neg$ and $\Rightarrow$).

Satisfiability   A propositional sentence is said to be satisfiable if there is at least one T in the final column of its truth table. The satisfiability problem is the problem of determining if a given propositional sentence is satisfiable.

Symbols of propositional logic   The basic symbols taken were sentence symbols (P, Q, etc.) as well as those for negation ($\neg$) and implies ($\Rightarrow$). The defined connectives were "and" ($\wedge$), "or" ($\vee$), and "if and only if" ($\Leftrightarrow$).

Tautology   A propositional sentence is said to be a tautology if there are all Ts in the final column of its truth table.

Truth table   A truth table for a propositional sentence is an organized tabular presentation of all possible ways of assigning Ts and Fs to the sentence symbols involved, and the resulting Ts and Fs assigned to the sentence.

Universal quantifier   The symbol $\forall$, which is read as "for all."

SUGGESTED READINGS

ENDERTON, H. B. *A Mathematical Introduction to Logic,* Academic Press, New York, 1972. This is a well-written undergraduate text on mathematical logic designed for mathematics majors. The nontechnical parts can be effectively used as reference material for those who want to go further than the present chapter.

JEFFREY, R. *Formal Logic: Its Scope and Limits,* 3rd ed., McGraw-Hill, New York, 1991. Jeffrey, a philosopher at Princeton University, provides a very enjoyable (and not too technical) introduction to the field.

MACHOVER, M. *Set Theory, Logic, and Their Limitations,* Cambridge University Press, Cambridge, 1996. Another outstanding text in the field.

TYMOCZKO, T., AND J. HENLE. *Sweet Reason: A Field Guide to Modern Logic,* W. H. Freeman, New York, 1995. A wonderful introduction to logic, written by a mathematician (Henle) and a philosopher (Tymoczko) working together. A real delight.

SUGGESTED WEB SITES

http://www.rbjones.com/rbjpub/logic/index.htm
This page is entitled "What Is Logic." It contains links to a number of topics in logic (although often at a slightly advanced level).

http://csli-www.stanford.edu/hp/   This page is called "Logic Software from CSLI." It contains links to various kinds of logic software developed by experts in the field.

SKILLS CHECK

1. The statement "A if not B" can be written as

   (a) $A \Rightarrow \neg B$.
   (b) $\neg B \Rightarrow A$.
   (c) $A \vee B$.

2. The logical statement "$\neg A \wedge B$" can be read as

   (a) B and not A.
   (b) neither A nor B.
   (c) if A then B.

3. If C is the statement "The water is clear" and S is the statement "The water is safe," then which of the following is equivalent to the statement "The water is safe if it is clear"?

   (a) $C \Rightarrow S$
   (b) $S \Rightarrow C$
   (c) $C \Leftrightarrow S$

4. If D is the statement "Donald is a duck" and S is the statement "All ducks swim," then which of the following is equivalent to the statement "Donald swims"?

   (a) $D \vee S$
   (b) $D \Rightarrow S$
   (c) $D \wedge S$

5. If P is true and Q is false, then which one of the following is true?

   (a) $P \vee Q$
   (b) $P \wedge Q$
   (c) $P \Rightarrow Q$

6. If $P \vee Q$ is true and $P \wedge Q$ is true, then

   (a) P must be true.
   (b) either P or Q must be false.
   (c) Q must be false.

7. If $P \Rightarrow Q$ is false, then

   (a) P and Q must both be false.
   (b) P must be false.
   (c) P must be true.

EXERCISES ▲ *Optional.* ■ *Advanced.* ◆ *Discussion.*

The English Language, The Basic Symbols of Propositional Logic, and Using Symbolism in Analytical Reasoning

Note: Exercises 1–4 refer to the following question (taken from the Analytical Reasoning section of a review manual for the LSAT prepared by the Research and Education Association, Piscataway, N.J.).

> Betty, Eva, and Maria were planning on going to a party together. However, the day before the party, two of the women had an argument, such that the following resulted: If Betty went, then Maria did not go. Eva went only if Betty went. If Maria went, then either Betty or Eva did not go. Maria went to the party. The question is: How many of these young women went to the party?

1.　Let B, E, and M denote the sentences "Betty went to the party," "Eva went to the party," and "Maria went to the party," respectively. Translate the three if–then statements into symbolic terms using ¬, ⟹, ∨, ∧, and ⟺. (Be especially careful with "Eva went only if Betty did.")

2.　One of the implications involves ¬B ∨ ¬E. Write down (in symbolic form) the negation of this.

3.　Using as "axioms" the three given if–then statements and the assumption that Maria went (i.e., M is true), provide an informal derivation (as on page 720) that allows the question to be answered.

4.　Beside each of the three implications from Exercise 1, write its contrapositive. Now, starting with M, write a short chain of implications (as on page 721) that allows the question to be answered.

Note: Exercises 5–8 refer to the following question (taken from the Analytical Reasoning section of a review manual for the LSAT prepared by the Research and Education Association, Piscataway, N.J.).

> Curly is a ringmaster of a one-ring circus, and he must decide what acts will perform during this Saturday's matinee. The matinee runs for only one hour, and acts must be scheduled according to how long they take to set up, perform, and take down. He is considering six acts for the matinee: the knife-thrower, the trapeze artists, the clowns, Dynamo the Human Cannonball, the elephants, and finally, Pogo, the Dancing Dog.
>
> Either Dynamo the Human Cannonball or the clowns must perform, as both acts draw big crowds and hence big profits. If the knife-thrower performs, then there won't be time for the trapeze artists to perform. If the elephants perform, then the trapeze artists will not be able to perform because of setup problems. Either the elephants or Pogo the Dancing Dog must perform, since there must be at least one animal act for the children in the audience. If the trapeze artists do not perform, then the clowns will not be able to perform, since the clown act is tied into the trapeze act. As it turns out, Dynamo the Human Cannonball will not perform, as he broke both arms in an automobile accident.

5.　Choose sentence symbols to denote the statements relevant to the problem (e.g., K may denote the sentence "The knife-thrower will perform.") Now, using these six sentence symbols, together with ¬, ∨, and ⟹, write down the sentences in our formal language corresponding to the six statements in the second paragraph.

6.　The first and fourth sentences in the second paragraph are or-statements. Rewrite them as implies statements. (If P ∨ Q is true, what must follow from the falsity of P?)

7.　Using as "axioms" the five if–then statements from Exercises 5 and 6, and the assumption that Dynamo the Human Cannonball will not perform, provide an informal derivation (as on page 720) that allows the question of exactly who will perform to be answered.

8.　Beside each of the five implications from Exercises 5 and 6, write its contrapositive. Now, starting with the assumption that Dynamo the Human Cannonball will not perform, write a short chain of implications (as on page 721) that allows the question of exactly who will perform to be answered. (The chain of implications will split at one point, because two conclusions follow from the assumption that the trapeze artists will perform. In your chain of implications, have one arrow here go up at a 45-degree angle, and one go down at a 45-degree angle.)

Note: Exercises 9–11 refer to the following question (taken from the Analytical Reasoning section of a review manual for the LSAT prepared by the Research and Education Association, Piscataway, N.J.).

> Alvin, Frank, George, Henry, Sam, and Irving are planning a week-long fishing trip to Lake Carlisle. However, two days before they were to depart, they argued over what type of bait was best for catching trout. The argument became quite heated, and some of the men were so angry with the others that they decided they would not go if the others went.
>
> If both Sam and Alvin went, then Irving went. If Irving went, then George went. If Frank went, then Sam also went. Either Sam or Henry will go. Alvin went, but George did not.

9. Choose sentence symbols to denote the statements relevant to the problem. Now, using these six sentence symbols, together with ¬, ∨, ∧, and ⟹, write down the sentences in our formal language corresponding to the six statements in the second paragraph.

10. Using as "axioms" the statements from Exercise 9, provide an informal derivation (as on page 720) that allows the question of exactly who went fishing to be answered.

11. Beside each of the implications from Exercise 9, write its contrapositive. Write a short chain of implications (as on page 721 of the text) that allows the question of exactly who will perform to be answered. The chain will branch as in Exercise 8. Start the line with ¬G, and use "A" over the arrow from ¬(S ∧ A) to ¬S.

Truth and Falsity for ¬ and ⟹ and the Other Connectives

12. Use a truth table to verify that the following is a tautology:

$$\neg(P \Rightarrow Q) \Leftrightarrow (P \wedge \neg Q)$$

13. Use a truth table to verify that the following is a tautology:

$$\neg(P \Leftrightarrow Q) \Leftrightarrow ((P \wedge \neg Q) \vee (\neg P \wedge Q))$$

14. Use a truth table to verify that the following is a tautology:

$$P \wedge (Q \vee R) \Leftrightarrow (P \wedge Q) \vee (P \wedge R)$$

15. Use a truth table to verify that the following is a tautology:

$$P \vee (Q \wedge R) \Leftrightarrow (P \vee Q) \wedge (P \vee R)$$

16. The logical connective "I" is called the "Sheffer stroke." Its truth table is the same as that for ¬(P ∧ Q). Show that both ¬ and ⟹ can be defined in terms of just the Sheffer stroke (and thus we could have taken it alone in place of ¬ and ⟹ in our list of basic propositional symbols).

17. Construct a truth table for the "exclusive disjunction" $\veebar$ where $P \veebar Q$ means that exactly one of P and Q is true.

18. Verify that the following is a tautology (where $P \veebar Q$ is defined in Exercise 17):

$$P \veebar Q \Leftrightarrow (P \vee Q) \wedge \neg(P \wedge Q)$$

19. Use truth tables to determine if the following sentences are tautologies:

(a) $\neg[(P \Leftrightarrow Q) \Rightarrow (P \wedge \neg Q)]$
(b) $(\neg P \wedge \neg Q) \Leftrightarrow \neg(P \vee Q)$
(c) $\neg P \Leftrightarrow (P \Rightarrow \neg Q)$

20. Use truth tables to determine if the following sentences are tautologies:

(a) $(P \vee Q) \vee \neg P$
(b) $(P \Rightarrow (Q \Rightarrow R)) \Rightarrow ((P \Rightarrow Q) \Rightarrow (P \Rightarrow R))$
(c) $(P \Rightarrow Q) \vee (Q \Rightarrow P)$

A Model of Deduction

21. Redo Exercise 3, but with the derivation as formal as the one on page 731.

22. Redo Exercise 7, but with the derivation as formal as the one on page 731. (*Hint:* Replace "D ∨ C" by "¬D ⇒ C" and replace "E ∨ P" by "¬E ⇒ P.")

23. Redo Exercise 10, but with the derivation as formal as the one on page 731. (*Hint:* Replace "S ∧ A ⇒ I" by "¬I ⇒ (S ⇒ ¬A)" and replace "S ∨ H" by "¬S ⇒ H.")

First-Order Logic

24. In the same first-order language in which the twin-prime conjecture was stated, write down the assertion that every even number greater than 2 is composite. (*Hint:* This says that for all $x > 2$, and for all y, if x equals 2 times y, then x is not prime.)

25. In the same first-order language as in Exercise 24, write down a sentence that asserts there are infinitely many primes.

26. Another famous open problem in number theory is Goldbach's conjecture. It asserts that every even number greater than 4 is the sum of two odd primes. Show that this can be written in the same first-order language that was used for the twin-prime conjecture.

TECHNOLOGY CORNER

Building Truth Tables

The spreadsheet in Figure 19.1 constructs a four-row truth table for statements P and Q. Spreadsheets use the words **True** and **False** as logical values. The first two columns list all the possible ways that statements P and Q could be true or false. To compute the value of "P and Q", entry **C2** has the formula **=And (A2, B2)**. In a similar way, entry **D2** has the formula **=Or (A2, B2)** and entry **E2** has the formula **=Not (D2)**. These formulas can then be copied to the remaining entries of the columns.

	A	B	C	D
1	P	Q	P and Q	P or Q
2	TRUE	TRUE	TRUE	TRUE
3	TRUE	FALSE	FALSE	TRUE
4	FALSE	TRUE	FALSE	TRUE
5	FALSE	FALSE	FALSE	FALSE

FIGURE 19.1

TASK 1. Add columns to the spreadsheet for "Not(P)" and "Not(Q)." Then compute the values of "Not(P) and Not(Q)" and "Not(P) or Not (Q)."

TASK 2. In your extended spreadsheet, which columns have exactly the same entries? What does this mean?

The spreadsheet in Figure 19.2 has an additional statement R. The first three columns list the eight ways that statements P, Q, and R can be true or false. The additional columns are added in the same way as before.

TASK 3. Construct four additional columns for "Q and R," "P or Q," "P or R," and "Q or R."

TASK 4. Construct columns for the statement "(P and Q) or (P and R)" and the statement "P and (Q or R)." How are these two statements related?

	A	B	C	D	E
1	P	Q	R	P and Q	P and R
2	TRUE	TRUE	TRUE	TRUE	TRUE
3	TRUE	FALSE	TRUE	FALSE	TRUE
4	FALSE	TRUE	TRUE	FALSE	FALSE
5	FALSE	FALSE	TRUE	FALSE	FALSE
6	TRUE	TRUE	FALSE	TRUE	FALSE
7	TRUE	FALSE	FALSE	FALSE	FALSE
8	FALSE	TRUE	FALSE	FALSE	FALSE
9	FALSE	FALSE	FALSE	FALSE	FALSE

FIGURE 19.2

Exploration

Constuct a column for the statement "(P or Q) and (P or R)". Then find another statement (with one "and" and one "or") that yields exactly the same column.

writing projects

1 ▶ (Adapted from T. Tymoczko and J. Henle, *Sweet Reason: A Field Guide to Modern Logic,* W. H. Freeman, New York, 1995.) Let's say that a word is *n-strong* if *n* successive occurrences of the word—using only a colon, period, and quotation marks as punctuation—constitute a meaningful sentence in the English language. If we were asked, for example, to name a word that can be used in a sentence as both a noun and a verb, we might answer, "Buffalo: 'buffalo buffalo buffalo'" (thus stating our answer—the first buffalo in the sentence—and then an example—"buffalo buffalo buffalo"—of a sentence in which the word occurs as both a noun and a verb). This shows that "buffalo" is 4-strong. Suppose we were now asked if we could name a word that is 4-strong. How might we respond? Where does this lead us?

2 ▶ Dodgson's problem as to whether Amos Judd loves mutton or not could also be solved by a truth table. Discuss how this could (in theory) be done, and why it is extremely impractical.

3 ▶ If we think of $P \Rightarrow Q$ as a promise, then, clearly, broken promises correspond to instances where $P \Rightarrow Q$ is false, and kept promises correspond to instances where $P \Rightarrow Q$ is true. Discuss whether you find it more compelling to declare $P \Rightarrow Q$ to be false only if it corresponds to a broken promise (and true in all other situations), or to declare $P \Rightarrow Q$ to be true only if it corresponds to a kept promise (and false in all other situations).

4 ▶ Suppose there are two men in the town: Tom, who is a policeman and a poet, and Harry, who is neither a policeman nor a poet. Consider the following statements:

(i) Every man in this town who is a policeman is a poet.
(ii) For all *x*, if *x* is a policeman in this town, then *x* is a poet.
(iii) If Tom is a policeman, then Tom is a poet, and if Harry is a policeman, then Harry is a poet.

Discuss whether or not you would believe that these three statements are equivalent *even if* you knew nothing about the occupations of Tom and Harry. Can you conclude anything about how truth must be assigned to statements like "If Harry is a policeman, then Harry is a poet" in situations where Harry is not a policeman?

5 ▶ We showed that it suffices to take only ¬ and $\Rightarrow$ as basic symbols in our formal language, since we could then define ∧, ∨, and ⇔ in terms of these. But how do we know that we haven't missed a binary connective? For example, what if someone were to say to us, "Here's the truth table for the connective *":

P	Q	P * Q
T	T	F
T	F	T
F	T	T
F	F	T

How do you know it can be defined in terms of ¬ and $\Rightarrow$? There is a completely mechanical way to do this. In this example, the sentence would be $(P \wedge \neg Q) \vee (\neg P \wedge Q) \vee (\neg P \wedge \neg Q)$. Explain how this would work in general.

Consumer Finance Models

How much interest will your savings account earn in the next year? How much will the payment be on your credit card loan, your car loan, or your home mortgage? How much would you need to save each month to pay for a child's college education? How much should you save for retirement? These are problems of daily life for which mathematics provides custom-tailored models. In this chapter we examine the mathematics of finance and models for accumulation and disbursal of funds.

Good mathematical models are often versatile and flexible, and the financial models of this chapter indeed apply broadly to important problems in other areas of life. Growth of money at interest is like growth of some biological populations. Inflation of a currency or depreciation of an asset is like the decay of a radioactive substance. Finding out how long a retirement "nest egg" will last is similar to determining how long before a nonrenewable resource, such as oil or coal, may be exhausted. Managing a trust fund, such as the endowment of a college, presents problems similar to management of a renewable biological resource, such as a forest or a fishery.

Models for Savings

When you open a savings account, your primary concerns are the safety and the growth of the "population" of your savings. Suppose that you deposit $1000 in an account that, you are told, "pays interest at a rate of 10%, compounded and paid annually." Assuming that you make no other deposits or withdrawals, how much is in the account after 1, 2, or 5 years?

The $1000 is the **principal,** the **initial balance** of the account. At the end of one year, **interest** is added. The amount of interest is 10% of the principal, or

$$10\% \times \$1000 = 10 \times 0.01 \times \$1000 = 0.10 \times \$1000 = \$100$$

in this case. (You can think of the symbol "%" as standing for "$\times 0.01$.") So the balance at the beginning of the second year is $1100. During the second year the interest is also 10%—not of the *initial* balance of $1000 but of the *new* balance of $1100—so at the end of the second year, 10% of $1100, or $110, is added to the account.

Thus, during the second year you earn interest on both the principal of $1000 and on the $100 interest earned during the first year. Interest that is paid on both the principal and on the accumulated interest is known as **compound interest.** You receive more interest during the second year than during the first, that is, the account grows by a greater amount during the second year. At the beginning of the third year the account contains $1210, so at the end of the third year you receive $121 in interest. Again this is larger than the amount you received at the end of the preceding year. Moreover, the increase during the third year,

$$\text{third-year interest} - \text{second-year interest} = \$121 - \$110 = \$11$$

is larger than the increase during the second year,

$$\text{second-year interest} - \text{first-year interest} = \$110 - \$100 = \$10$$

Thus, not only is the account balance increasing each year, but the amount added also increases each year.

Banks and savings institutions often compound interest more often than once a year, for example, quarterly (four times per year). With an interest rate of 10% per year and quarterly compounding, you get one-fourth of the rate, or 2.5%, paid in interest each quarter. The quarter (3 months) is the **compounding period,** or the time elapsing before interest is paid.

Consider again a principal of $1000. At the end of the first quarter, you have the original balance plus $25 interest, so the balance at the beginning of the second quarter is $1025. During the second quarter you receive interest equal to 2.5% of $1025, or $25.63, so the balance at the end of the second quarter is $1050.63. Continuing in this manner, you find that the balance at the end of the first year is $1103.81. (You should "read" all calculations in this chapter by confirming them on your calculator.)

Even though the account was advertised as paying 10% interest (the *nominal rate*), the interest for the year is 10.381% of the principal. The 10.381% is the *effective rate* or *equivalent yield.*

The **nominal rate** is the stated rate of interest on which any compounding is based.

The **effective rate** is the actual percentage increase in the account. It is also called the **equivalent yield,** since an account with this nominal rate would earn the same increase without compounding.

The nominal rate for a year is called the **annual (percentage) rate (APR),** and the effective rate is called the **annual (equivalent) yield** or **annual percentage yield (APY).**

If interest is compounded monthly (12 times per year) or daily (365 times per year), the resulting balance is even larger. A comparison of yearly, quarterly, monthly, and daily compounding for an interest rate of 10% is shown in Table 20.1. We will shortly summarize results in a general formula.

From now on, we will express all interest rates as decimals. For example, 10% is 0.10; to convert a percentage to a fraction, divide the percentage by 100, by moving the decimal point two places to the left. An interest rate of 0.10 is the same as 10%, or 10/100; an interest rate r is the same as $100r\%$.

TABLE 20.1	**Comparing Compound Interest: The Value of $1000, at 10% Annual Interest, for Different Compounding Periods**				
Years	Compounded Yearly	Compounded Quarterly	Compounded Monthly	Compounded Daily	Compounded Continuously
1	1100.00	1103.81	1104.71	1105.16	1105.17
5	1610.51	1638.62	1645.31	1648.61	1648.72
10	2593.74	2685.06	2707.04	2717.91	2718.28

The Mathematics of Geometric Growth

We look for the underlying mathematical pattern of compounding. For quarterly compounding, you have at the end of the first quarter

initial balance + interest = $1000 + $1000(0.025) = $1000(1 + .025)

and at the end of the second quarter

$$\begin{aligned}\text{initial balance + interest} &= \$1000(1 + 0.025) \\ &\quad + [\$1000(1 + 0.025)](0.025) \\ &= [\$1000(1 + 0.025)] \times (1 + 0.025) \\ &= \$1000(1 + 0.025)^2\end{aligned}$$

The pattern continues in this way, so that you have $1000(1 + 0.025)^4$ at the end of the fourth quarter.

You use the calculator button marked $\boxed{y^x}$ to evaluate expressions like $(1.0125)^2$: enter 1.012, push $\boxed{y^x}$, enter 2, and push $\boxed{=}$; you get 1.02515625.

More generally, with an initial balance of P and an interest rate $r\ (= 100r\%)$ per compounding period, you have at the end of the first compounding period

$$P + Pr = P(1 + r)$$

This amount can be viewed as a new starting balance. Hence, in the next compounding period, the amount $P(1 + r)$ grows to

$$P(1 + r) + P(1 + r)r = P(1 + r)(1 + r) = P(1 + r)^2$$

The pattern continues, and we reach the following conclusion:

Compound interest formula: If a principal P is deposited in an account that pays interest at an effective rate r per compounding period, then after n compounding periods the account contains the amount

$$A = P(1 + r)^n$$

The amount added each compounding period is proportional to the amount present. This type of growth is called *geometric growth.*

Geometric growth (also called **exponential growth**) is growth proportional to the amount present.

EXAMPLE   *Compound Interest*

Suppose that you have a principal of $P = \$1000$ invested at 10% nominal interest per year. Using the compound interest formula $A = P(1 + r)^n$, you can determine the amount in the account after 10 years, which varies according to the compounding period:

■ *Annual compounding.* The annual rate of 10% gives $r = 0.10$, and after 10 years the account has

$$\$1000(1 + 0.10)^{10} = \$1000(1.10)^{10} = \$1000(2.59374)$$
$$= \$2593.74$$

■ *Quarterly compounding.* Then $r = 0.10/4 = 0.025$, and after 10 years (40 quarters) the account contains

$$\$1000(1 + \tfrac{0.10}{4})^{40} = \$1000(1.025)^{40} = \$1000(2.68506)$$
$$= \$2685.06$$

■ *Monthly compounding.* Then $r = 0.10/12 = 0.008333$. The amount in the account after 10 years (120 months) is

$$\$1000(1 + \tfrac{0.10}{12})^{120} = \$1000(1.00833333)^{120} = \$1000(2.70704)$$
$$= \$2707.04$$

These entries are found in the last row of Table 20.1.   ◆

Suppose that you want to make a one-time deposit now, of amount P, that will grow to a specific amount A in n years from now by earning interest at an effective rate of $100r\%$ per year. The quantities A, P, r, and n are related through the compound interest formula, $A = P(1 + r)^n$. The quantity P is called the **present value** of the amount A to be paid n years in the future.

E X A M P L E   *Certificate of Deposit*

Suppose that you will need \$15,000 to pay for a year of college for your child 18 years in the future, and you can buy a certificate of deposit whose interest rate of 10% compounded quarterly is guaranteed for that period. How much do you need to deposit?

     We have $A = \$15,000$, $r = 0.10/4 = 0.025$, and $n = 72$. The compound interest formula gives

$$\$15,000 = A = P(1 + r)^n = P(1.025)^{72} = 5.91723P$$

so $P = \$15,000/5.91723 = \$2534.94$.   ◆

E X A M P L E   *Money Market Account*

In some cases you know the principal, the current balance, and the interval of time, and you want to learn the interest rate. For example, money market funds typically report earnings to investors each month, based on interest rates that vary from day to day. The investor may want to know an average rate of interest for the month, but often the monthly statement does not report one. We find the equivalent average *daily* effective rate, from which we calculate the annual yield. The compound interest formula gives the end-of-month balance as $A = P(1 + r)^n$, where P is the balance at the beginning of the month, r is the average daily interest rate, and n is the number of days that the statement covers. So we have

$$\frac{A}{P} = (1 + r)^n$$

Changing each quantity to the other side and taking the nth root of each side gives

$$1 + r = \left(\frac{A}{P}\right)^{1/n}, \qquad r = \left(\frac{A}{P}\right)^{1/n} - 1$$

Suppose that the monthly statement from the fund reports a beginning balance (P) of \$7373.93 and a closing balance (A) of \$7416.59 for 28 days (n). We thus have

$$r = \left(\frac{7416.59}{7373.93}\right)^{1/28} - 1 = (1.005785246)^{0.035714286} - 1$$

$$= 0.000206042$$

Thus the average daily effective rate is 0.0206042%. Compounding daily, for a year we would have $(1 + 0.000206042)^{365} = 1.0780972$, for an annual yield of 7.81%. ◆

Arithmetic Growth

Under another method of paying interest, called **simple interest,** interest is paid only on the original balance, no matter how much interest has accumulated. With simple interest, for a principal of \$1000 and a 10% interest rate, you receive \$100 interest at the end of the first year; so at the beginning of the second year, the account contains \$1100, as before. But at the end of the second year, you again receive only \$100; so at the beginning of the third year, the account contains \$1200. In fact, at the end of each year you receive just \$100 in interest. This method yields less than if interest is compounded.

The amounts in accounts paying interest at 10% per year with compound and simple interest are shown in Table 20.2 and in the graph in Figure 20.1, which

TABLE 20.2	The Growth of $1000: Compound Interest vs. Simple Interest	
Years	Amount in Account from Compounded Interest	Amount from Simple Interest
1	1100.00	1100.00
2	1210.00	1200.00
3	1331.00	1300.00
4	1464.10	1400.00
5	1610.51	1500.00
10	2593.74	2000.00
20	6727.50	3000.00
50	117,390.85	6000.00
100	13,780,612.34	11,000.00

FIGURE 20.1
The growth of $1000:
compound interest and
simple interest.

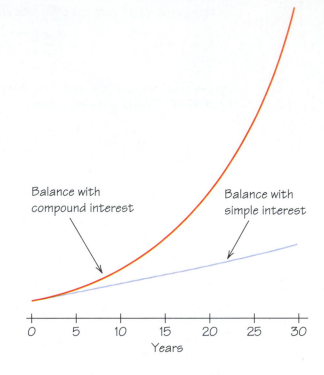

Balance with
compound interest

Balance with
simple interest

Years

dramatically illustrate the growth of money at compound interest compared to simple interest.

Simple interest is seldom used in today's financial institutions. However, we frequently observe the corresponding kind of growth, called *arithmetic growth,* in other contexts.

Arithmetic growth (also called **simple growth**) is growth by a constant amount in each time period.

The population of medical doctors in the United States grows arithmetically, since the fixed number of medical schools each graduate the same total number of doctors each year (and the number of doctors dying is also fairly constant). On the other hand, general human populations tend to grow geometrically because the number of children born—the "interest"—increases as the population—the "balance"—increases.

The distinction between arithmetic growth and geometric growth is fundamental to the major theory of demographer and economist Thomas Malthus (1766–1834). He claimed that human populations grow geometrically but food supplies grow arithmetically, so that populations tend to outstrip their ability to feed themselves (see Spotlight 20.1).

Thomas Malthus

Thomas Malthus (1766–1834), a nineteenth-century English demographer and economist, based a well-known prediction on his perception of the different patterns of growth of the human population and the "population" of food supplies.

He believed that human populations increase geometrically but food supplies increase arithmetically—so that the increase in food supplies will eventually be unable to match increases in population. He concluded, however, that over the long run there would be restrictions on the natural growth of human populations too, including war, disease, and starvation—hardly an optimistic forecast and, doubtless, responsible for the dreary image associated with his views.

Thomas Malthus

The situation of nuclear waste generated by a nuclear power plant is more complicated. The absolute volume of waste added each year depends on the fixed size and output of the power plant, not on the growing amount of waste in storage. Hence the volume of waste grows arithmetically. What about the total amount of radioactive material in the storage dump? The waste is a mixture of radioactive and nonradioactive substances; over time, the radioactive ingredients decay slowly into nonradioactive ones. While the radioactivity of waste already in storage is decreasing, new amounts of radioactive material are being added each year. The situation requires a hybrid model that incorporates positive arithmetic growth (adding to the dump) accompanied by negative geometric growth (radioactive decay). The situation is like turning on the faucet to the bathtub while leaving the drain hole open; what happens to the height of water in the tub depends on how fast water runs in versus how fast it runs out.

A Limit to Compounding

The rows in Table 20.1 show a trend: more frequent compounding yields more interest. But, as the frequency of compounding increases, the interest tends to a limiting amount, shown in the far right column.

Why is this so? Basically, because the extra interest from more frequent compounding is *interest on interest*. For example, in the first row of Table 20.1, the $3.81 extra interest from compounding quarterly is interest on the $100 yearly interest. The $3.81 is less than 10% of the $100 because the $100 interest is not on deposit for the whole year, since just part of it is credited to the account (and begins earning interest) at the end of each quarter. As compounding is done more and more often, smaller and smaller amounts of interest on interest are added.

How can we determine the limiting amount? Let's suppose that the initial balance is $1, and that we keep track at all stages of even the smallest fractions of a dollar.

We first suppose an interest rate of 100% per year compounded n times per year; later we examine interest rates closer to the ones in stable economies. For an initial balance of $1, the amount at the end of one year is—from the compound interest formula, with $P = \$1$ and $r = 100\%$—

$$A = \$1 \times \left(1 + \frac{100\%}{n}\right) = \$\left(1 + \frac{1.00}{n}\right)^n$$

As n increases, this amount, which is just $(1 + 1/n)^n$, gets closer and closer to a special number called $e \approx 2.71828$ (see Spotlight 20.2). This is illustrated in Table 20.3, where the dots (ellipses) indicate that more decimal places follow.

For a nominal interest rate r, the amount that $1 grows to when compounded n times during the year is

$$\left(1 + \frac{r}{n}\right)^n$$

SPOTLIGHT 20.2

The Number *e*

The number e is similar to the number π in several respects. Both arise naturally, π in finding the area and circumference of circles, and e in compounding interest continuously (e is also the base for the system of "natural" logarithms). In addition, neither is rational (expressible as the ratio of two integers, such as 7/2) nor even algebraic (the solution of a polynomial equation with integer coefficients, such as $x^2 = 2$); we say that they are *transcendental* numbers. Finally, no pattern has ever been found in the digits of the decimal expansion of either number.

TABLE 20.3	Yield of \$1 at 100% Interest, Compounded *n* Times per Year

n	$\left(1 + \frac{1}{n}\right)^n$
1	2.0000000 . . .
5	2.4883200 . . .
10	2.5937424 . . .
50	2.6915880 . . .
100	2.7048138 . . .
1,000	2.7169239 . . .
10,000	2.7181459 . . .
100,000	2.7182682 . . .
1,000,000	2.7182818 . . .
10,000,000	2.7182818 . . .

As n is made larger and larger, the limiting amount is e^r, and the interest method is called **continuous compounding**. The effective rate is $(e^r - 1)$. (You can calculate powers of e using the $\boxed{e^x}$ button on your calculator; on some calculators, this button is the $\boxed{\text{2nd}}$ function of the button marked $\boxed{\text{LN}}$ or $\boxed{\ln x}$. For example, to calculate $e^{0.10}$, enter 0.10, push $\boxed{\text{2nd}}$, then push $\boxed{\ln x}$; you get 1.105170918.)

E X A M P L E   *Continuous Compounding*

For \$1000 at an annual rate of 10%, compounded n times in the course of a single year, the balance at the end of the year is

$$\$1000\left(1 + \frac{0.10}{n}\right)^n$$

This quantity gets closer and closer to $\$1000e^{0.1} = \$1105.17$ . . . as the number of compoundings n is increased. No matter how frequently interest is compounded—daily, hourly, every second, infinitely often ("continuously")—the original \$1000 at the end of one year cannot grow beyond \$1105.17. The values after 5 and 10 years are shown in the lower rows of Table 20.1. ◆

According to the **continuous interest formula**, for a principal P, deposited in an account at the nominal annual rate of $r = 100r\%$ compounded continuously,

- ■ After 1 year, the account contains $A = Pe^r$
- ■ After m years, it contains $A = Pe^{rm}$

It makes virtually no difference whether compounding is done daily or continuously over the course of a year. Most banks apply a daily periodic rate (based on compounding continuously) to the balance in the account each day and post interest daily (rounded to the nearest cent). The daily nominal rate is $r/365$, so each day the balance of the account is multiplied by $e^{r/365}$, the daily effective rate. Except for the rounding in posting interest, the effect is the same as continuous compounding throughout the year, since the compound interest formula gives $A = P(e^{r/365})^{365}$, which is the same as Pe^r from the continuous interest formula.

Also, it makes virtually no difference whether the bank treats a year as

- 365 days with daily nominal interest rate $r/365$ (the *365 over 365 method*) — this is the usual method for daily compounding; or
- 360 days with daily interest rate $r/360$ (the *360 over 360 method*) — this is the usual method for loans with equal monthly installments, since 360 is evenly divisible into 12 equal "months" of 30 days. The daily interest is greater than for the 365 over 365 method, but there are fewer days in the year.

Table 20.4 gives a comparison of different interest methods. ◆

TABLE 20.4	**Comparing Methods of Compounding Interest**				
Method	**Compounding Periods per Year**	**Rate per Period**	**Formula per One Year**	**Effective Rate**	**Effective Rate for $r = 5\%$**
360 over 360, daily	360	$r/360$	$P\left(1 + \frac{r}{360}\right)^{360}$	$\left(1 + \frac{r}{360}\right)^{360} - 1$	5.12674%
365 over 365, daily	365	$r/365$	$P\left(1 + \frac{r}{365}\right)^{365}$	$\left(1 + \frac{r}{365}\right)^{365} - 1$	5.12675%
Continuous			Pe^r	$e^r - 1$	5.12711%

A Model for Accumulation

The compound interest formula tells the fate over time of a single deposited amount, but another common question that arises in finance is: What size deposit do you need to make *on a regular basis,* in an account with a fixed rate of interest, to have a specified amount at a particular time in the future?

This question is important in planning for a major purchase in the future, accumulating a retirement nest egg, paying off a mortgage, or making installment payments on a car. Later we apply the results to calculate the amount of a nonrenewable resource used up over a number of years.

EXAMPLE   *A Savings Plan*

An individual saves $100 per month, deposited directly into her credit union account on payday, the last day of the month. The account earns 5% per year, compounded daily (just simple compounding, without continuous compounding during the day). How much will she have at the end of 5 years, assuming that the credit union continues to pay the same interest rate?

Note that she makes the first deposit at the end of the first month and the last deposit at the end of the sixtieth month. Although the months differ in length and the credit union compounds daily using the 365 over 365 method, we get virtually the same result by assuming instead that each month has 30 days and the 360 over 360 method is used.

The daily interest rate is 5%/360 = 0.000138889, so the amount earned for a 30-day month is

$$(1.000138889)^{30} - 1 = 1.0041751 - 1 = 0.004175073$$
$$= 0.4175073\%$$

Call this monthly rate r.

It's easier to look at the deposits in reverse time order. The last deposit is deposited on the last day of the 5 years, so it earns no interest and contributes just $100 to the total.

The second last deposit earns interest for 1 month, contributing $100(1 + r)$.

Similarly, the third last deposit is on deposit for 2 months, contributing $100(1 + r)^2$.

Continuing in the same way, we find that the first deposit earns interest for 59 months and contributes $100(1 + r)^{59}$. The total of all of the contributions is

$$\$100 + \$100(1 + r)^1 + \$100(1 + r)^2 + \cdots + \$100(1 + r)^{59}$$
$$= \$100[1 + (1 + r)^1 + (1 + r)^2 + \cdots + (1 + r)^{59}]$$

This expression is known as a **geometric series,** because the successive terms grow geometrically: each succeeding term is a constant common growth rate—here, $(1 + r)$—times the preceding term. There is a formula for the sum of such a series, which we give for a geometric series with ratio x:

$$1 + x + x^2 + x^3 + \cdots + x^{n-1} = \frac{x^n - 1}{x - 1}$$

That this formula works for all x (except $x = 1$) can be confirmed by multiplying both sides by $(x - 1)$ and watching terms on the left cancel (you should do this confirmation for $n = 4$).

In our example, we have $x = 1 + r$, and the formula becomes

$$1 + (1 + r)^1 + (1 + r)^2 + \cdots + (1 + r)^{n-1} = \frac{(1 + r)^n - 1}{r}$$

We have $n - 1 = 59$, or $n = 60$ months, and $r = 0.0041751$, the interest rate per month. The total accumulation is

$$A = \$100 \left[\frac{(1 + 0.004175073)^{60} - 1}{0.004175073} \right] = \$6802.36 \quad \blacklozenge$$

In general terms, we have

For a uniform deposit of d per period (deposited at the end of the period) and an interest rate r per period, the amount A accumulated is given by the **savings formula:**

$$A = d \left[\frac{(1 + r)^n - 1}{r} \right]$$

The savings formula involves four quantities: A, d, r, and n. If any three are known, the fourth can be found. A common situation is for A, r, and n to be known, with d (the regular payment) to be found, since the practical concern for most people is how much their monthly payment will be.

Sometimes the purpose of a savings plan is to accumulate a fixed sum by a certain date. Such savings plans are called **sinking funds.**

EXAMPLE   *A Sinking Fund*

Suppose that a couple wishes to save for the college education of their child. They begin saving a regular amount d per month after the child is born and want to have $100,000 available when the child turns 18. How much do they have to save each month, if their account earns 6.5% interest per year, compounded daily?

Again, for simplicity, we can calculate as if each month has 30 days and the savings institution uses the 360 over 360 method. The daily nominal rate is $6.5\%/360 = 0.000180556\%$, so the effective monthly rate (for a 30-day month) is

$$r = (1.000180556)^{30} - 1 = 1.005430885 - 1 = 0.005430885$$
$$= 0.5430885\%$$

We have $A = \$100,000$, $r = 0.005430885$, and $n = 12 \times 18 = 216$. Applying the savings formula, we have

$$\$100,000 = d \left[\frac{(1.005430885)^{216} - 1}{0.005430885} \right] = d((593.21)$$

so $d = \$100,000/593.21 = \$168.57$. $\quad \blacklozenge$

A common situation that you are likely to encounter is a loan—for a house, a car, or college expenses—to be paid back in equal periodic installments. Your payments are said to **amortize** the loan. Each payment pays the current interest and also repays part of the principal. *As the principal is reduced, less of each payment goes to interest and more toward paying of the principal.*

Let's suppose that Sally buys a house for $100,000 with a loan that she will pay off over 30 years in equal monthly installments. Suppose that the interest rate for her loan is 6.00%. Let's figure out how much her monthly payment needs to be.

Imagine changing the setup slightly so that now Sally is borrowing the entire sum ($100,000) for 30 years, and we think of her monthly payments as the savings fund that she's building up to pay off the loan at the end of the term. The interest rate of 6.00% on the loan is compounded monthly, so the monthly rate is 0.5%. At the end of 30 years, the principal and interest on the loan will (by the compound interest formula) amount to

$$\$100{,}000 \times (1 + 0.005)^{30 \times 12} = \$602{,}257.52$$

On the other hand, saving d each month for 30 years at 6.00% interest compounded monthly, we know from the savings formula that Sally will accumulate

$$d\left[\frac{(1 + 0.005)^{360} - 1}{0.005}\right]$$

To make d just the right amount to pay off the loan exactly, we need to solve the equation

$$d\left[\frac{(1 + 0.005)^{360} - 1}{0.005}\right] = \$100{,}000 \times (1 + 0.005)^{30 \times 12} = \$602{,}257.52$$

for the value of d, getting $d = \$599.55$ as Sally's monthly payment.

We put this in a more general setting:

Let the principal be P, the effective interest rate per period r, the payment at the end of each period d, and let there be n periods. Then the **amortization formula** is

$$P(1 + r)^n = d\left[\frac{(1 + r)^n - 1}{r}\right]$$

Examining this equation, you see the compound interest formula on the left and the savings formula on the right. You can think of paying off the loan as making payments to a savings account, earning interest at the same rate as the loan, which will exactly balance principal and interest on the loan at the end of the loan term.

EXAMPLE   *Installment Loans*

You decide to buy a new Wheelmobile car. After a down payment, you need to finance (borrow) $12,000. After comparing interest rates offered by the car dealership, local banks, and your credit union, the best rate that you can find is 7.9% (compounded monthly) over 48 months. What will your monthly payment be?

We have $P = \$12,000$, monthly interest rate $r = .079/12 = .006583333$, and $n = 48$. Using the amortization formula, we have

$$\$12,000(1.006583333)^{48} = d\left[\frac{1.006583333^{48} - 1}{.006583333}\right]$$

$$\$16,442.53 = d\,(56.2345), \qquad d = \$292.39$$

How much interest do you pay? Altogether, you make payments totaling $48 \times \$292.39 = \$14,034.72$, so your interest is $\$14,034.72 - \$12,000 = \$2,034.72$.

Note that if you had gone for a Plushmobile instead, with $24,000 to be financed, you would have borrowed twice as much, and your monthly payment also would have been twice as much.   ◆

A Model for Financial Derivatives

Financial markets trade everything from agricultural commodities (corn, orange juice, coffee) to precious metals (gold, silver), from national currencies (dollars, euros) to corporate stocks and bonds. In recent years, an increasing share of such trading has turned from the objects themselves to less tangible entities based on them, known as *financial derivatives*. Traditional derivatives include mutual funds, in which a purchaser owns shares in a company that itself owns and manages a portfolio of corporate stocks and bonds; commodities futures, in which an agricultural producer contracts to sell a commodity at a definite point in the future for a price agreed to in advance; and options.

An option allows (but does not require) an investor to acquire an asset (which may itself be a commodity or corporate stocks or bonds) during a particular interval at a price fixed in advance. Part of an employee's pay package may be options to acquire stock in the company. Options may be bought and sold, but a vexing problem for many years was how to assess accurately the worth of an option. How can you determine the value of an option to buy 100 million German marks at $0.55 per mark at any time between now and next Tuesday, or an option to buy 100 shares of Apple Computer at $25 per share before January 1?

One widely used pricing formula for valuing financial derivatives is the *Black-Scholes formula* (see Spotlight 20.3). In the next example, we examine a simpler model for valuing an option that still incorporates the main ideas.

Nobel Prize for a Model in Economics

The 1997 Nobel Memorial Prize in Economics was awarded to Robert C. Merton of Harvard University and Myron S. Scholes of Stanford University for their method of valuing financial derivatives. Together with the late Fischer Black in the 1970s, they formulated a mathematical model with appropriate assumptions and solved the resulting equation. At the time, Black was a mathematician with Arthur D. Little consultants in Boston, Scholes was a professor of finance at M.I.T., and Merton was an assistant to the economist Paul Samuelson at M.I.T.; all then were under age 30.

The major achievement of Merton, Black, and Scholes was to incorporate variability of market prices into the formula for the value of an option. They realized that the risk involved in the market is already implicitly taken into account in the stock's current price and its volatility, and they were able to find the right formulation for incorporating the risk into the value of the option. Black and Scholes actually modeled the rate of change of the option value and then used methods from calculus to work backwards to calculate the value and the formula itself.

This fairly complicated formula is based on simplifying assumptions (no stock dividends, no transaction costs, fixed price volatility, fixed interest rate, efficient market) plus a major modeling assumption. That modeling assumption is that the change in the price of the stock, as a percentage of the price, has a fixed component proportional to elapsed time (price trends upward over time) plus a random component deriving from volatility (so the price also can jump around). The random component is modeled using the normal distribution of Chapter 7.

EXAMPLE *Valuing an Option*

Suppose that you are interested in an Internet company named Interjunk, but you're not sure whether or not to buy into it just now. You could buy a share of stock now for $100 or else buy an option to purchase a share of stock a year from now for $100, called the *exercise price* (or strike price) of the option. The value of the option depends on the current price of the stock: the higher the price of the stock now, the more likely that it will be more than $100 a year from now, and hence the more valuable the option. As time goes by, if the price of the stock goes up, the value of the option does too—but not quite as much, because there is still uncertainty about what will happen between then and expiry. What would be a fair price for such an option?

The answer depends on what you expect to happen to the price of the stock. Suppose (for simplicity, but unrealistically) that the consensus in the market is that there are only two possibilities: there is a 50% chance that the stock price a year from now will be $200, and a 50% chance that it will be $80.

If you buy a share of stock, the expected value of that share a year from now is $(0.50) \times \$200 + (0.50) \times \$80 = \$140$, for an expected profit of $140 − $100 = $40.

If you buy an option for some cost $C, you have a 50% chance of exercising it. Half the time you wind up with a share of stock that costs you only $100 but is worth $200, netting you $100; the other half of the time, the stock price is at $80 and the option is worth nothing. Either way, you paid $C for the option. Your expected profit is $(0.50) \times \$100 + (0.50) \times \$0 - \$C = \$50 - \$C$.

What should you be willing to pay for the option? If you pay less than $10, you expect on average to make a greater profit than the $40 you could make by buying the stock now; if you pay more than $10 for the option, you would be better off instead buying the stock now. So the value of the option is $10.

We could refine our model slightly to take into account alternative investments. Suppose that you can earn a risk-free 10% on U.S. Treasury obligations. Suppose further that you have $110 on hand and are going to invest it all in some combination of stock, Treasuries, and options.

STRATEGY 1.   Buy the stock ($100), put the rest into Treasuries ($10). You expect to realize $40 from the stock and $1 from the Treasuries, for $41.

STRATEGY 2.   Buy an option ($10), put the rest into Treasuries ($100). You expect to realize $40 from the option and $10 from the Treasuries, for a total of $50.

Of course, the rest of the investors in the market can do the same calculations, and it is readily apparent that an option is worth more—hence should be priced higher—than the $10 used in these calculations. An option is worth closer to $20.

◆

Exponential Decay

In times of economic inflation, prices increase. When the rate of inflation is constant, the compound interest formula can be used to project prices.

EXAMPLE   *Inflation*

Suppose that there is constant 3% annual inflation from mid-2000 through mid-2004. What will be the projected price in mid-2004 of an item that costs $100 in mid-2000.

The compound interest formula applies with $P = \$100$, $r = 3\%$, and $n = 4$. The projected price is $A = P(1 + r)^n = \$100(1 + 0.03)^4 = \$112.55$.   ◆

During constant-rate inflation, prices grow geometrically (exponentially) and the value of the dollar goes down geometrically.

Exponential decay is geometric growth with a negative rate of growth.

Let i represent the rate of inflation; what costs $1 now will cost $\$(1 + i)$ this time next year. For example, if the inflation rate were $i = 25\%$, then what costs $1 now would cost $1.25 this time next year. A dollar next year would buy only 0.8 ($= 1/1.25$) times as much as a dollar buys today. In other words, a dollar next year would be worth only $0.80 in today's dollars—by next year, a dollar would have lost 20% of its purchasing power. We say that the **present value** of a dollar next year would be $0.80. Notice that although the inflation rate is 25%, the loss in purchasing power is 20%. For a general inflation rate i, a dollar a year from now will buy only a fraction of what a dollar today can buy; that fraction, the present value of a dollar a year from now, is

$$\frac{1}{1 + i} - \frac{1 + i - i}{1 + i} = \frac{1 + i}{1 + i} = \frac{i}{1 + i} = 1 - \frac{i}{1 + i}$$

In other words, a dollar a year from now is worth $\$[1 - i/(i + 1)]$ today, and the loss in purchasing power is the fraction $i/(i + 1)$. (You should calculate what these expressions become for $i = 25\%$.) The quantity $-i(1 + i)$ behaves like a negative interest rate. We can use the compound interest formula to find the value of P dollars n years from now as $A = P(1 + r)^n = P(1 - [i/(i + 1)])^n$.

The actual posted price of an item, at any time, is said to be in **current dollars.** That price can be compared with prices at other times by converting all prices to **constant dollars,** dollars of a particular year.

EXAMPLE   *Deflated Dollars*

Suppose that there is 25% annual inflation from mid-2000 through mid-2004. What will be the value of a dollar in mid-2004 in constant 2000 dollars?

We have $i = 0.25$, so $r = -i/(i + 1) = -0.25/1.25 = -0.20$. This, not the 25%, is the negative interest rate, the rate at which the dollar is losing purchasing power. We have $n = 4$ years, so the value of \$1 four years from mid-2000 is, in 2000 dollars,

$$\$1(1 + r)^4 = \$(1 - 0.20)^4 = (0.80)^4 = \$0.41. \quad \blacklozenge$$

In the example, we may think of the value of the dollar as "depreciating" 20% per year. Depreciation of the value of equipment is similar.

EXAMPLE   *Depreciation*

If you bought a car at the beginning of 1996 for \$10,000 and its value in current dollars depreciates steadily at a rate of 15% per year, what will be its value at the beginning of 2001 in current dollars?

We have $P = \$10,000$, $r = -0.15$, and $n = 5$. The compound interest formula gives $A = P(1 + r)^n = \$10,000(1 - 0.15)^5 = \$4437$ $\blacklozenge$

Exponential decay is characteristic of radioactive materials. A radioactive substance emits particles and decreases in quantity at a predictable continuous rate. The amount of radioactive substance remaining is given by the continuous interest formula. The rate r is usually written instead as $-\lambda$; the positive quantity λ is called the *decay constant*.

Alternatively, the rate of decay of the substance can be described in terms of the *half-life*. A substance that is decaying geometrically never completely vanishes, even after millions of years. Since there is no time until it is all gone, we settle for measuring how long it takes until half of it is gone.

Growth Models for Biological Populations

The economic models for savings are flexible and can be applied to other arenas. We now use a geometric growth model to make rough estimates about sizes of human populations, using for the growth rate r the difference between the annual birth rate and the annual death rate, for which the technical term is the **rate of natural increase.** In the terminology of financial models, this is the effective rate.

Birth and death rates rarely remain constant for very long, so projections must be made with extreme care. In addition, we exclude the effect of net migration. In the short run, predictions based on the model may provide useful information. Let's apply this model to two questions about the population of the United States.

EXAMPLE   *Predicting U.S. Population*

U.S. Census estimates agree on a population of 272 million at the beginning of 2000. It is increasing at an average growth rate of 0.7% per year. What is the anticipated population at the beginning of the year 2003? What is it if the rate of natural increase is instead 0.4% per year, or 1.0% per year?

We apply the compound interest formula with initial population size ("principal") 272 million. Using a year as the compounding period and the formula $A = P(1 + r)^n$, where $n = 3$, the projected population size in 2003 for a rate $r = 0.007$ is

$$
\begin{aligned}
\text{population in 2003} &= (\text{population in 2000}) \times (1 + \text{growth rate})^3 \\
&= 272,000,000(1 + 0.007)^3 \\
&= 272,000,000(1.02115) \approx 278,000,000
\end{aligned}
$$

Because the original estimates of population and growth rate are approximations, we don't copy down all the digits from the calculator, but instead round off; the result of a calculation can't be more precise than the ingredients.

In the same way, with a growth rate of 0.4% per year, we predict a population of 275 million, while a growth rate of 1.0% per year yields a prediction of 280 million. So an uncertainty of three-tenths of one percentage point, or 0.003, in the growth rate has major implications, even over fairly short time horizons. The presence or absence of 5 million people would have a significant impact on our social and economic systems! Indeed, much of the concern over long-range funding of the social security programs results from uncertainties over birth and immigration rates. Figure 20.2 gives a graph of the U.S. population in 2000, structured by age and sex. ◆

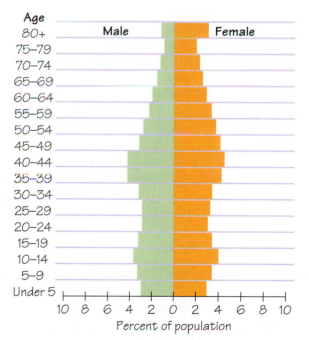

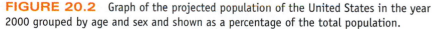

FIGURE 20.2 Graph of the projected population of the United States in the year 2000 grouped by age and sex and shown as a percentage of the total population.

Rates of natural increase in most Third World countries are much higher than in industrialized nations, sometimes 3% per year or more. With its growth rate of 3.1%, Africa's most populous country, Nigeria, whose population was 122 million in mid-1998, will have 200 million by the middle of 2015, an increase of 65%. Projections of this sort are at the root of worldwide concern over the ability to provide sufficient food and other resources for all people.

Nonrenewable Resources

People use resources, some of which are renewable but others are not. In this section, we model depletion of nonrenewable resources; in the next, we treat renewable resources.

A **nonrenewable resource** is one that does not tend to replenish itself; gasoline, coal, and natural gas are important examples, while lottery winnings or an inheritance could be examples from personal affairs. There is no practical way to recover or reconstitute these resources after use. Some substances, such as aluminum or the sand used to make glass, are potentially recyclable; but to the extent that we do not recycle them, they too are nonrenewable.

For a renewable resource, there is only a fixed supply S (in some convenient units) that is available. Even without human population increases, we face dwindling nonrenewable natural resources. We are interested in the question: How long will the supply of a resource last?

As long as the rate of use of the resource remains constant, the answer is easy. If we are using U units per year and continue using U units per year, then the supply will last S/U years. This kind of calculation is the basis for statements such as "at the current rate of consumption, U.S. coal reserves will last 500 years," or that the U.S. strategic reserve of gasoline (stored in salt domes in the South) would last 60 days.

However, the rate of use of resources tends to increase with increasing population and with higher "standard of living." For example, projections for use of electric power are often based on assumptions that the use will increase by some fixed percentage each year. This is the simplest situation (apart from constant usage), and one that we can easily model to give an important perspective.

Suppose that $U_1 = U$ is the rate of use of the resource in the first year (this year), and that usage increases $r = 0.05 = 5\%$ each year. Then the usage in the second year is

$$U_2 = U_1 + 0.05U_1 = 1.05U$$

and usage in the third year is

$$U_3 = U_2 + 0.05U_2 = 1.05U_2 = 1.05(1.05U) = (1.05)^2 U$$

Generalizing, we see that usage in year i will be $(1.05)^{i-1}U$. Total usage over the next 5 years, for example, will be

$$U + (1.05)^1 U + (1.05)^2 U + (1.05)^3 U + (1.05)^4 U$$

This situation should remind you of our earlier study of accumulation of regular deposits plus interest. Here the usage U corresponds to a deposit and the increasing rate of use r corresponds to the interest rate. We may think of the situation as making regular withdrawals (with interest) from a fixed supply of the nonrenewable resource. The savings formula gives

$$A = d\,\frac{(1 + r)^n - 1}{r}$$

In translating to the resource situation, A is the accumulated amount of the resource that has been used up at the end of n years, and U is the initial rate of use. We have

$$A = U\left[\frac{(1 + r)^n - 1}{r}\right]$$

To find out how long the supply S will last, we set the supply S equal to the cumulative use A over n years and then determine what n will be. We have

$$S = U\left[\frac{(1 + r)^n - 1}{r}\right]$$

We perform some algebra to isolate the term involving n, getting

$$(1 + r)^n = 1 + \frac{S}{U}\,r$$

At this point, to isolate n, we need to take the natural logarithm of both sides. We get

$$\ln\left[(1 + r)^n\right] = n \ln\,(1 + r) = \ln\left(1 + \frac{S}{U}\,r\right)$$

which gives the final expression

$$n = \frac{\ln\,[1 + (S/U)r]}{\ln\,(1 + r)}$$

This expression may look complicated, but it is quite easy to evaluate on a calculator for particular values of S/U and r.

The expression S/U is called the *static reserve,* and n is called the *exponential reserve.*

> The **static reserve** is how long the supply S will last at a particular constant rate of use U, namely, S/U units of time.
>
> The **exponential reserve** is how long the supply S will last at an initial rate of use U that is increasing by a proportion r each year, namely
>
> $$\frac{\ln\,[1\,+\,(S/U)r]}{\ln(1\,+\,r)}$$
>
> units of time.

EXAMPLE   *U.S. Coal Reserves*

We noted earlier that measured reserves of U.S. coal would last about 500 years at the current rate of use, so the static reserve for this resource is 500 years. How long would the supply last if the rate of use increases 5% per year? The corresponding exponential reserve is

$$n = \frac{\ln\,[1\,+\,(500)(0.05)]}{\ln 1.05} = \frac{\ln 26}{\ln 1.05} = 65 \text{ years}$$

That's quite a difference!   ◆

We must not take such projections as exact predictions. Estimates of supplies of a resource may underestimate how much is available, and previously unknown sources may be discovered or the technology improved to extract previously unavailable supplies. In addition, as supplies dwindle, the economic considerations of supply, demand, and price come into play. We will never completely run out of oil; it will always be available "at a price."

However, we must not take such projections lightly, either, since we are discussing resources that, once used, are gone forever. In any projection, it is very important to examine the assumptions, since small differences in the rate of increase of use can make big differences in the exponential reserve.

EXAMPLE   *Using Up Retirement Savings*

Suppose you begin retirement with $1 million in savings, and you don't trust banks or the stock market, so you keep it all under your mattress. (In the next section, we'll see what happens if you are more conventional.) Suppose it costs you

$50,000 per year to live at your accustomed standard of living and there is no inflation. How long will your retirement nest egg last? The static reserve is $1,000,000/$50,000/\text{year} = 20$ years. If, however, there is constant 5% per year inflation, then it will cost you increasingly more per year to live, so you should realize that your savings will last only for the length of the exponential reserve, which is

$$n = \frac{\ln(1 + 20(0.05))}{\ln 1.05} = 14.2 \text{ years}$$

You have a fine strategy if you expect to live just 14 more years and want to die broke! ◆

Renewable Resources

A **renewable natural resource** is a resource that tends to replenish itself, such as fish, wildlife, and forests. We would like to know how much of a resource we can harvest and still allow for the resource to replenish itself.

E X A M P L E   College Endowment

Donors sometimes give money to colleges and universities to fund specific prizes, scholarships, or professorships, which they would like to see continue in perpetuity. The college invests the donor's money, so that this resource renews itself, and "harvests" the earnings to fund the project. Suppose that the college can earn 8% on its endowed funds. Then an individual who wants to make a one-time donation to fund an annual full scholarship (tuition, books, room and board) of $20,000 needs to donate enough so that the fund earns that much; the donation needs to be $20,000/0.08 = $250,000.

However, the current cost of $20,000 will increase with inflation. If the donor wants each year's future interest to cover that year's full cost, the donation needs to be larger. If the college endowment earns 8% but there is 3% inflation in the annual cost, the net interest is only 5%, and the amount of the donation needs to be $20,000/0.05 = $400,000. ◆

Other renewable resources are biological populations. We concentrate on the subpopulation with commercial value. For a forest, this might be trees of a commercially useful species and appropriate size. We measure the population size as its **biomass**, the mass of the population expressed in units of equal value. For example, we measure the size of a fish population in terms of pounds rather than numbers of fish, and a forest not by counting the trees but by estimating the number of board feet of usable timber.

Salmon swimming up-
stream to reproduce.

Reproduction Curves

In this chapter we have used several models to analyze and predict population growth. As models, they include many simplifications. Real populations may behave like one of the models we have discussed, or like other known models. But the complicated factors that can affect populations, such as climatic or economic change, may mean that the only way to understand the population is to plot a graph of its size over time. Whether the growth of a population can be described by one of the formulas that we have developed or by a table of measurements collected by counting, there are useful techniques to analyze the growth of the population and help us make decisions about managing it. The situation that we will be thinking about most is managing a population of renewable resources, such as trees or fish, to make the most of them.

We use a figure called a **reproduction curve,** which predicts next year's population size (biomass) based on this year's size. Although the precise shape of the curve varies from one population to another, the shape shown in Figure 20.3 is

FIGURE 20.3
A typical reproduction curve.

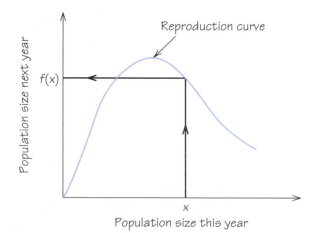

typical. It shows next year's size (on the vertical axis) as a function of this year's size (on the horizontal axis). For all possible sizes, the reproduction curve shows the change in size from one year to the next, taking into account growth of continuing members and addition of new members, minus losses due to death and other factors.

Let x on the horizontal axis be a typical size of the population in the current year. The size *next* year is given by the height of the curve above the point marked x. This value is denoted by $f(x)$. (You can think of f as standing for "function of," or even as "forthcoming.")

Figure 20.4 shows the same reproduction curve, plus the broken line $y = x$ (which makes a 45° angle with the horizontal axis). You could trace what happens for various choices for x. For an x for which the curve is above the broken line, next year's size ($f(x)$) is larger than this year's (x). In Figure 20.4, the **natural increase,** or gain in population size, is shown as the length of the green vertical line from the broken line to the curve, which in algebraic terms is $f(x) - x$. For an x for which the curve is below the broken line, next year's size is smaller than this year's and $f(x) - x$ is negative. For the size labeled x_e, for which the curve crosses the broken line, the size is the same next year as this year; this is the *equilibrium population size.*

An **equilibrium population size** is one that does not change from year to year.

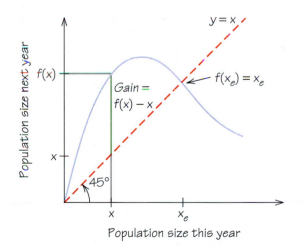

FIGURE 20.4 Depiction of the natural increase (gain) in population from one year to the next. The population size x_e is the equilibrium population size, for which the population one year later is the same, or $f(x_e) = x_e$.

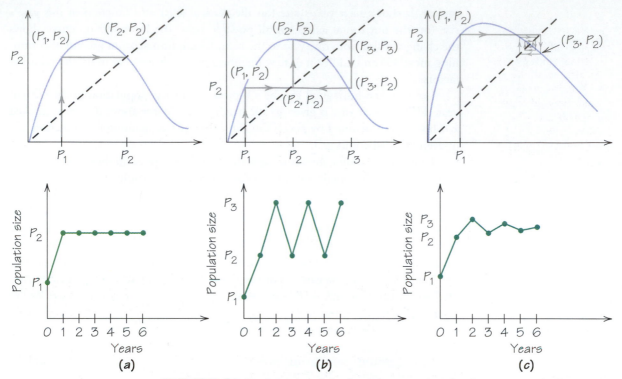

FIGURE 20.5 Examples of the dynamics, over time, for the same reproduction curve but different starting populations. (a) The population goes in one year to the equilibrium population and stays there year after year. (b) After initial adjustment, the population cycles between values over and under the equilibrium population. (c) The population spirals in toward the equilibrium population.

The line $y = x$ provides a convenient way to trace the evolution of the population over several years (see Figure 20.5), by alternating steps vertically to the curve and horizontally to the line $y = x$. Begin with the first year's population on the horizontal axis, go up vertically to the curve; the height is the population in the second year. Proceed horizontally from the curve over to the line $y = x$. Proceeding vertically from there to the curve yields a height that is the population in the third year.

Figure 20.5 shows several traces for the same reproduction curve, each starting from a different initial population on the horizontal axis. The resulting variation is quite surprising—it can even be "chaotic" in a very specific mathematical sense, showing how apparently random behavior can result from strict deterministic rules.

Sustained-Yield Harvesting

Many biological populations are harvested by predators (including humans). **Yield** is the amount harvested at each harvest. We focus on sustained-yield harvesting, which is important to timber companies and other enterprises that extract a natural resource over a long period.

FIGURE 20.6
The reproduction curve, with the population size x_M corresponding to the maximum sustainable yield. The maximum sustainable yield is the greatest vertical distance from the 45° line to the reproduction curve.

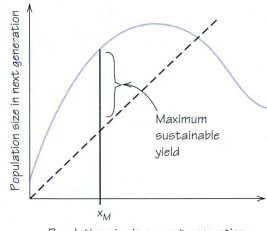

A **sustained-yield harvesting policy** is a policy that if continued indefinitely will maintain the same yield.

For a sustainable yield, the same amount is harvested every year and the population remaining after each year's harvest is the same. To achieve this stability, the harvest must exactly equal the natural increase each year, the length of the green vertical line in Figure 20.4.

Each value of x between 0 and x_e determines a different vertical line and corresponding sustained-yield harvest. This harvest can vary from 0 (for $x = 0$ or $x = x_e$) up to some maximum value (for some x between 0 and x_e). A goal for a timber company or a fishery is to harvest the **maximum sustainable yield:** to select an x whose vertical line is as long as possible, marked as x_M in Figure 20.6.

Considerations from Economics

The costs of harvesting should be taken into account in our analysis. We consider two models: one for a cattle ranch and one for either a fishing boat or a tree farm.

We assume that the price p received is the same for each harvested unit and does not depend on the size of our harvest. In effect, we assume that our operation is a small part of the total market, not substantially affecting overall supply and hence price.

We want to stay in business, so we do not extinguish the resource for quick profits. For any given population size, we harvest just the natural increase.

E X A M P L E   *Cattle Ranching*

We assume that the cost of raising and bringing a steer to market is the same for every steer and does not depend on how many steers we bring to market. Since the

FIGURE 20.7
The unit cost, unit revenue, and unit profit of harvesting one unit, as a function of population size, for the cattle ranch.

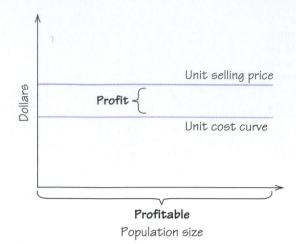

cost does not depend on the population size, the cost curve is a horizontal line (Figure 20.7).

As long as the selling price per unit is higher than the harvest cost per unit, we make a profit. The points of view of economics and biology agree, since the maximum profit occurs for the maximum sustainable yield. ◆

E X A M P L E   *Fishing and Logging*

In this model we assume that the cost of harvesting a unit of the population decreases as the size of the population increases; this is the familiar principle of **economy of scale.** For example, the same fishing effort yields more fish when fish are more abundant. Similarly, a logger's harvest costs per tree are less when the trees are clumped together; this is the logger's motivation to clear-cut large stands.

The cost curve slopes downward and to the right, as in Figure 20.8. The size of the population from which one unit is harvested is shown on the horizontal axis; the cost of harvesting a single unit is measured on the vertical axis.

FIGURE 20.8
The unit cost, as a function of population size, for fishing or logging.

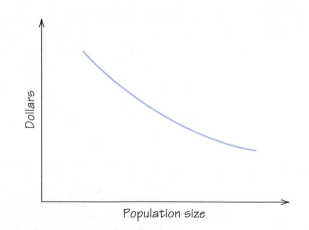

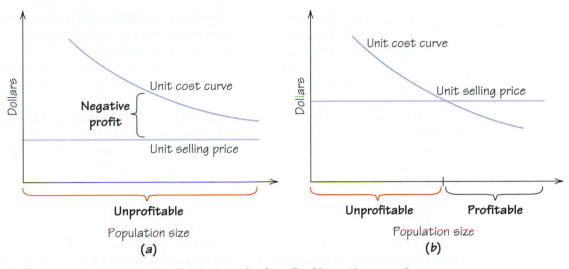

FIGURE 20.9 The unit cost, unit revenue, and unit profit of harvesting one unit, as a function of population size, for fishing or logging. (a) The market price is below harvesting cost for all population sizes. (b) The operation is profitable for populations above a certain minimum size.

An optimal harvesting policy depends on the relation between price and costs. There are two cases, as shown in Figure 20.9:

■ *The unit cost curve lies entirely above the unit price line:* The price for a harvested unit is less than the cost of harvesting it, no matter how large the population. It is impossible to make a profit.

■ *The unit cost curve intersects the unit price line:* Above a certain population size, the price for a harvested unit is more than the cost of harvesting it, so profit is

FIGURE 20.10
Regions of profitability for sustained-yield policy, with the economically optimal population size x_0 marked.

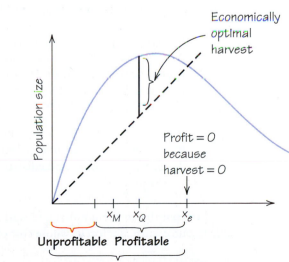

possible (Figure 20.10). Some population size, call it x_Q, gives a maximum net profit. Using calculus, it can be shown that x_Q is actually larger than x_M, the population that gives the maximum sustainable yield. Compared to harvesting the maximum sustainable yield, economic considerations result in harvesting less, but also in maintaining a larger stock of the population.   ◆

Our simple models fail to take into account a very critical feature of a modern economy that we already explored earlier in this chapter: the time value of money, as measured by the interest capital can earn. In the next section we see one important explanation of why biological populations are susceptible to overexploitation and even extinction.

Why Eliminate a Renewable Resource?

In some instances, such as the passenger pigeon, populations have been harvested to extinction. In other cases the whole ecosystem has been destroyed (see Spotlight 20.4). Why would anyone eliminate a renewable resource? Our approach helps explain why.

Sustained-yield policies involve revenues that will be received, year after year, in the future. The value of these revenues should be discounted to reflect the lost investment income that we could earn if instead we had the revenues today. For funds invested at a return of $100r\%$ per year, compounded annually, the present value P of an amount A to be received in n years in the future is related to A by the compound interest formula $A = P(1 + r)^n$.

The economic goal is to maximize the sum of the present values of all future receipts from harvesting. The optimal harvesting policy thus must depend on the expected rate of return r. We don't delve into the details of the calculations here, but instead just give the results of the analysis.

Again there are several cases to consider:

1. The unit cost of harvesting exceeds the unit price received, for all population sizes. Then it is impossible to make a profit.
2. For some population size x, the unit cost of harvesting equals the unit price received. Then there is a size between x and x_e (the equilibrium population size) for which the present value of the total return is maximized and the population and its yield are sustained.
3. The unit price exceeds the unit cost for *all* population sizes.

    ■ For r small, the situation is the same as in the second case just cited.
    ■ For larger r, the economically optimal policy may be to harvest the entire population immediately—extinguish the resource—and invest the proceeds.

Let's put this in the simplest and starkest terms. Suppose that you own a valuable resource, such as a forest, whose cost of harvesting is small relative to the value

The Tragedy of Easter Island

Easter Island

Easter Island is famous for its isolation — 1400 miles to the nearest island — and for its hundreds of huge stone statues. For 30,000 years before the arrival of people in about A.D. 400, Easter Island maintained a lush forest, with several species of land birds. By the time of the first visit by Europeans in 1722, the island was barren, denuded of all trees and bushes over 10 feet high, and with no native animals larger than an insect. The 2000 or so islanders had only three or four leaky canoes made of small pieces of wood.

What happened? Careful analysis of pollen in soil samples tells the sad story. The settlers and their descendants cut wood to plant gardens, build canoes, make sledges and rollers to move the huge statues, and burn for cooking and warmth in the winter. In addition to crops they raised and chickens that they had brought to the island and cultivated, they ate palm fruit, fish, shellfish, the meat and eggs of birds, and the meat of porpoises that they hunted from seagoing canoes. The population of the island grew to 7000 (or perhaps even 20,000).

By 1500, the forest was gone. Most tree species, all land birds, half of the seabirds, and all large and medium-sized shellfish had been extinguished. There was no firewood, no wood for sledges and rollers to transport hundreds of statues at various stages of completion, and no wood for seaworthy canoes. Without canoes, fishing declined and porpoises could not be taken. Stripping the trees exposed the soil, which eroded, so crop yields fell off. The people continued raising chickens, but warfare and cannibalism ensued. By 1700, the population had crashed to 10–25% of its former size.

Why didn't the people notice earlier what was happening, imagine the consequences of keeping on as they had been, and act to avert catastrophe? After all, the trees did not disappear overnight.

From one year to the next, changes may not have been very noticeable. The forests may have been regarded as communal property, with no one charged with limiting exploitation or ensuring new growth. There was no quantitative assessment of the resources available and need for conservation versus the long-term needs of the "public works" program of erecting statues. Moreover, the religion of the people, the prestige of the chiefs, and the livelihood of hundreds depended on the statue industry. There was no perceived need to limit the population and no technology for birth control. Once the large trees were gone, there was no means for excess population to emigrate.

Adapted from Jared Diamond, "Easter's end," *Discover,* 16 (8) (August 1995): 63–69.

of the resource. If the rate at which the forest population grows is greater than what you can earn on other investments, it pays to let the forest keep on growing.

On the other hand, if the forest is growing more slowly than the rate of return on other investments, the economically optimal harvesting policy is to cut down all the trees now and invest the money. You could then start raising cattle on the land—and right there you have the scenario that is resulting in deforestation all over the world.

The sobering fact is that *very few economically significant renewable resources can sustain annual growth rates over 10%*. Many, like whales and most forests, have growth rates in the 4% to 5% range. These values—even a growth rate of 10%—are far below the return investors expect on their investment. For example, until recent deregulation, Wisconsin electric utilities were guaranteed 14.25% profit; and venture capital firms expect to exceed 25% profit.

The concept of maximum sustainable yield is an attractive ideal if expectations of investors are low enough. However, there are still difficult problems:

- One problem is "the tragedy of the commons," discussed by ecologist Garrett Hardin. Several hundred years ago, English shepherds would graze their flocks together on common land. The grass of the commons could support only a fixed number of sheep. Each shepherd could reasonably think that adding just one or two more sheep to his flock would not over-tax the commons; yet if each did so, there could be disaster, with all the sheep starving. Many natural-products industries, such as fisheries, are a form of commons; small overexploitation by each harvester can produce disastrous results for all.

- How, in the presence of human needs or greed, can we anticipate and prevent overexploitation and possible extinction of a resource? By and large, it has been politically impossible to force a harvesting industry to reduce current harvests to assure stability in the future.

- In some industries, such as a fishery, growth of the population may be abundant one year but meager another, so that a steady yield cannot be sustained without damaging the resource. A few good years in a row may provoke increased investment in fishing capacity; then attempting to harvest at the same levels in succeeding normal or below-normal years results in overfishing. This exact scenario destroyed the California sardine fishery in the 1930s, the Peruvian anchovy fishery in 1972, and much of the North Atlantic fishery in the 1980s.

REVIEW VOCABULARY

Amortization formula   Formula for installment loans that relates the principal P, effective interest rate r per period, the payment d at the end of each period, and the number of periods to pay off the loan:

$$P(1 + r)^n = d\left[\frac{(1 + r)^n - 1}{r}\right]$$

Amortize   To repay in regular installments.

Annual (equivalent) yield, annual percentage yield   Effective rate on an annual basis.

Annual percentage rate   Nominal rate on an annual basis.

Arithmetic growth   Growth by a constant amount in each time period.

Biomass   A measure of a population in common units of equal value.

Compound interest   The method of paying interest on both the principal amount and the accumulated interest in an account.

Compound interest formula   Formula for the amount in an account that pays compound interest periodically. For an initial principal P and effective rate r per compounding period, the amount after n compounding periods is $A = P(1 + r)^n$.

Compounding period   The interval that elapses before interest is calculated on an account.

Constant dollars   Costs are expressed in constant dollars if inflation or deflation has been taken into account by converting all costs to their equivalent in dollars of a particular year.

Continuous compounding   Payment of interest in the amount toward which compound interest tends with more and more frequent compounding.

Continuous interest formula   Formula for the amount in an account that pays interest compounded continuously. For an initial principal P and nominal annual rate r, the amount after m years is $A = Pe^{rm}$.

Current dollars   The actual cost of an item is said to be in current dollars; inflation or deflation has not been taken into account.

e   The base for continuous compounding, geometric (exponential) growth, and natural logarithms; $e = 2.71828.\ \ldots$

Economy of scale   Costs per unit decrease with increasing volume.

Effective rate   The percentage increase in an account after one year.

Equilibrium population size   A population size that does not change from year to year.

Equivalent yield   Effective rate.

Exponential decay   Geometric growth with a negative rate of growth.

Exponential growth   Geometric growth.

Exponential reserve   How long a fixed amount of a resource will last at a constantly increasing rate of use.

Geometric growth   Growth proportional to the (increasing) amount present.

Geometric series   A sum of terms, each of which is the same constant times the previous term, that is, the terms grow geometrically.

Initial balance   Initial deposit in a bank account.

Interest   Money earned on financial investments, such as bank accounts.

Maximum sustainable yield   The largest harvest that can be repeated indefinitely.

Natural increase   The growth of a population that is not harvested.

Nominal rate   The stated rate of interest per year, on which any compounding is based.

Nonrenewable resource   A resource that does not tend to replenish itself.

Present value   The value today of money to be received in the future.

Principal   Initial balance.

Rate of natural increase   Birth rate minus death rate, the annual rate of population growth without taking into account net migration.

Renewable natural resource   A resource that tends to replenish itself; examples are fish, forests, wildlife.

Reproduction curve   A curve that shows population size in the next year plotted against population size in the current year.

Savings formula   Formula for the amount in an account to which a regular deposit is made (equal for each period) and interest is credited, both at the end of each period. For a regular deposit of d and an interest rate r per period, the amount A accumulated is

$$A = d \left[\frac{(1 + r)^n - 1}{r} \right]$$

Simple growth Arithmetic growth.
Simple interest The method of paying interest on only the initial balance in an account and not on any accrued interest.

Sinking fund A savings plan to accumulate a fixed sum by a certain date.
Static reserve How long a fixed amount of a resource will last at a constant rate of use.
Sustained-yield harvesting policy A harvesting policy that can be continued indefinitely while maintaining the same yield.
Yield The amount harvested at each harvest.

SUGGESTED READINGS

ARROW, KENNETH A., ET AL. Economic growth, carrying capacity, and the environment, *Science,* 268: 520–521 (April 28, 1995). Letters: Economic growth and environmental policy: 1549–1551 (June 16, 1995).

BARTLETT, ALBERT A. Forgotten fundamentals of the energy crisis, *American Journal of Physics,* 46 (9): 876–888 (September 1978).

CLARK, COLIN. Some socially relevant applications of calculus, *The Two-Year College Mathematics Journal,* 4 (2): 1–15 (Spring 1973). Gives a mathematical approach to animal resource economics.

CLARK, COLIN. The mathematics of overexploitation, *Science,* 181: 630–634 (August 17, 1973).

COHEN, JOEL. *How Many People Can the Earth Support?* Norton, New York, 1995.

COHEN, JOEL. Ten myths of population, *Discover,* 17 (4) (April 1996): 42–47.

DIAMOND, JARED. Easter's end, *Discover,* 16 (8)(August 1995): 63–69.

HARDIN, GARRETT. The tragedy of the commons, *Science,* 162: 1243–1248 (1968).

KASTING, MARTHA. *Concepts of Math for Business: The Mathematics of Finance.* UMAP Modules in Undergraduate Mathematics and Its Applications: Modules 370–372. COMAP, Inc., Arlington, Mass., 1980.

KLEINBAUM, DAVID G., AND ANNA KLEINBAUM. *Adjusted Rates: The Direct Rate.* UMAP Modules in Undergraduate Mathematics and Its Applications: Mod-330. COMAP, Inc., Arlington, Mass., 1980. Reprinted in *The UMAP Journal,* 1(1): 49–80 (1980); and in *UMAP Modules: Tools for Teaching 1980,* Birkhäuser, Boston, 303–334. A beginning exploration into the structure of populations, which explains, for instance, the paradox of how a Third World country can have a lower overall mortality rate than the United States, yet have a higher mortality rate for every age group.

LINDSTROM, PETER A. *Nominal vs. Effective Rates of Interest.* UMAP Modules Undergraduate Mathematics and Its Applications: Module 474. COMAP, Inc., Arlington, Mass., 1988. Reprinted in *UMAP Modules: Tools for Teaching 1988,* Paul J. Campbell (ed.), COMAP, Inc., Arlington, Mass., 21–53. A learning module about the difference between nominal and effective rates of interest and how to calculate them. Gives examples of banks using particular options for calculating interest.

LUDWIG, DONALD, RAY HILBORN, AND CARL WALTERS. Uncertainty, resource exploitation, and conservation: Lessons from history, *Science,* 260: 17, 36 (April 2, 1993).

MEADOWS, DONELLA H., DENNIS L. MEADOWS, AND JØRGEN RANDERS. *Beyond the Limits: Confronting Global*

Collapse, Envisioning a Sustainable Future, Chelsea Green, Post Mills, Vt., 1992.

OLINICK, MICHAEL. Modelling depletion of nonrenewable resources, *Mathematical Computer Modelling,* 15(6): 91–95 (1991).

OPHULS, WILLIAM, AND A. STEPHEN BOYAN, JR. *Ecology and the Politics of Scarcity Revisited,* W. H. Freeman, New York, 1992.

POPULATION REFERENCE BUREAU. *Annual World Population Data Sheet,* 777 14 St. N.W., Suite 800, Washington, D.C. 20005.

SAFINA, CARL. The world's endangered fisheries, *Scientific American,* 273(5) (November 1995): 46–53.

SCHWARTZ, RICHARD H. *Mathematics and Global Survival,* 3rd ed., Ginn, Needham Heights, Mass., 1993.

VEST, FLOYD, AND REYNOLDS GRIFFITH. The mathematics of bond pricing and interest rate risk, *Consortium (COMAP),* No. 59 (Fall 1996): HiMAP Pullout Section 1–6.

SUGGESTED WEB SITES

U.N. Population Division. **http://www.popin.org/** Population statistics and estimates for all countries.

Population Reference Bureau. **http://www.prb.org/** Population statistics and rates of growth by regions.

Easter Island Home Page. **http://www.netaxs.com/~trance/rapanui.html** Dozens of links to sites about Easter Island.

SKILLS CHECK

1. If you deposit $1000 at 6.2% simple interest, what is the balance after three years?

   (a) $1186.00
   (b) $1197.77
   (c) $1224.63

2. Suppose you invest $250 in an account that pays 4.5% interest compounded quarterly. After 30 months, how much is in your account?

   (a) $279.08
   (b) $279.59
   (c) $279.71

3. Suppose you deposit $15 at the end of each month into a savings account that pays 2.5% interest compounded monthly. After a year, how much is in the account?

   (a) $184.50
   (b) $182.50
   (c) $182.08

4. What is the APY for 5.90% compounded monthly?

   (a) 5.90%
   (b) 6.06%
   (c) 6.08%

5. If a bond matures in 3 years and will pay $10,000 at that time, what is the fair value of it today, assuming the bond has an interest rate of 6% compounded annually?

   (a) $8200.00
   (b) $8396.19
   (c) $8352.70

6. If you buy a house by taking a 20-year mortgage for $40,000 at an interest rate of 8% compounded monthly, how much will the monthly payments be?

   (a) $359.82
   (b) $334.58
   (c) $296.09

7. Suppose you buy a new tractor for $60,000. It depreciates steadily at 7% per year. When will it be worth approximately $10,000?

   (a) After about 12 years
   (b) After about 24.5 years
   (c) After about 26.5 years

EXERCISES   ▲ Optional.   ■ Advanced.   ◆ Discussion.

The exercises below require a scientific calculator with buttons for powers y^x, exponential e^x, and natural logarithm $\ln x$.

The Mathematics of Geometric Growth

1. You deposit $1000 at 8% per year. What is the balance at the end of one year, and what is the annual yield, if the interest paid is

   (a) simple interest?
   (b) compounded annually?
   (c) compounded quarterly?
   (d) compounded daily?

2. Repeat Exercise 1, but for $1000 at 3% per year.

3. *Zero-coupon bonds* are securities that pay no current interest but are sold at a substantial discount from redemption value. The difference between purchase price and redemption value provides income to the bondholder at the time of redemption or resale. If the interest rate in the economy is now 7%, what should be the price of a zero-coupon bond that will pay $10,000 eight years from now? (Use daily compounding.)

4. Repeat Exercise 3, but for a current interest rate of 5% and a zero-coupon bond that will pay $10,000 five years from now.

5. *The rule of 72* is a rule of thumb for finding how long it takes money at interest to double: if $100r\%$ is the annual interest rate, then the doubling time is approximately $72/100r$ years.

   (a) Calculate the balance at the end of the predicted doubling time for each $1000, with annual compounding, for the small growth rates of 3%, 4%, and 6%.
   (b) Repeat part (a), for the intermediate interest rates of 8% and 9%.
   (c) Repeat part (a), for the larger interest rates of 12%, 24%, and 36%.
   (d) What do you conclude about the rule of 72?

6. More frequent compounding yields greater interest, but with diminishing returns as the frequency of compounding is increased. For small interest rates, there is little difference in yield for compounding annually, quarterly, monthly, daily, or continuously. Investigating doubling times with continuous compounding leads to understanding why the rule of 72 of Exercise 5 works. Recall that for continuous compounding at annual rate r, the balance A at the end of m years is Pe^{rm} for an initial principal of P. Let D be the number of years that it takes for the initial principal to double. Then we have $2P = A = Pe^{rD}$, so $e^{rD} = 2$. Taking the natural logarithm of both sides yields $rD = \ln 2$, where ln stands for the natural logarithm, represented on a calculator by a button marked either $\ln$ or LN (not $\log$ or $\log_{10}$, which stands for a different kind of logarithm). Using the button gives $\ln 2 = 0.693$. So we have $rD = 0.693$, from which we can determine D if we know r.

Calculate the doubling times for continuous compounding at 3%, 6%, and 9%, and compare them with those predicted by the rule of 72. What do you conclude? Why do you think people prefer a rule of 72 over a rule of 69.3?

7. Suppose that on the report for your money market account this month, the initial balance was $7373.98, the report was for 28 days, and the final balance was $7416.59. Calculate the annual yield.

8. Repeat Exercise 7, but for the previous month, which had an initial balance of $7331.35, a period of 31 days, and a final balance of $7373.93.

A Limit to Compounding

9. [Contributed by John Oprea of Cleveland State University.] Use your calculator to evaluate for $n = 1, 10, 100, 1000$, and $1,000,000$:

  (a) $\left(1 + \frac{1}{n}\right)^n$
  (b) $\left(1 + \frac{2}{n}\right)^n$
  (c) As n gets larger, what numbers are the expressions in parts (a) and (b) tending toward?

10. Use your calculator to evaluate for $n = 1, 10, 100, 1000$, and $1,000,000$:

  (a) $\left(1 - \frac{1}{n}\right)^n$
  (b) $\left(1 - \frac{2}{n}\right)^n$
  (c) As n gets larger, what numbers are the expressions in parts (a) and (b) tending toward?

11. You have $1000 on deposit at your bank at an annual rate of 4%. How much interest do you receive after one year, if the bank compounds

  (a) continuously?
  (b) daily, using the 360 over 360 method?
  (c) daily, using the 365 over 365 method?

12. Suppose that you have a bank account with a balance of $5432.10 at the beginning of the year and $5632.10 at the end of the year. Your bank advertises "continuous compounding," but

in fact compounds continuously over each 24-hour day and posts interest to accounts daily.

  (a) What effective rate did you receive?
  (b) What nominal rate is the calculation based on?
  (c) What difference is there between what the bank is doing and true continuous compounding?

A Model for Accumulation

13. Suppose that you want to save up $2000 for a trip abroad two years from now. How much do you have to put away each month in a savings account that earns 5% interest compounded daily?

14. Repeat Exercise 13, except that you have found a better deal, 7% interest compounded daily.

15. You want to buy a car and you need to borrow $7000 of the cost. You can get a 48-month loan from the car dealer at 8.9%. What is your monthly payment?

16. Suppose that you and two friends decide to live off campus in your senior year. One of them (who has wealthy parents) suggests that instead of renting an apartment, you could buy a house together, live in it for your senior year, then rent it or else sell it. Assuming that you could get a mortgage for $60,000 to buy a house near your college, what would be the monthly mortgage payment for a 30-year loan at 7.5%?

17. Suppose that your bill for credit card charges shows $2575.83 due (including any finance charges), with a minimum payment of $72 and monthly interest rate of $r = 1.366\%$.

  (a) Assuming monthly compounding, what is the APR for this card? What is the APY?
  (b) If you make no more charges on the card and pay $72/month as soon as you get each bill, how long will it take to pay off the total? (*Hint*: The amortization

formula can be changed algebraically into the form

$$(1 + r)^n = \frac{d}{d - rP}$$

Note that by making the first payment right away, you immediately reduce the principal P to be amortized to $2575.83 - $72.00 = 2503.83; if you delayed payment in any month, you would incur additional daily interest on the amount due. Evaluate the right-hand side. Then use the power key $\boxed{y^x}$ on your calculator to raise the value of $(1 + r)$ to various powers n until you find the smallest value for n that makes the left-hand side larger than the right-hand side.

(c) According to the regulations for this card, the minimum required payment for this card is supposed to be the greater of $20 or 2% of the balance (rounded up to the next higher dollar amount). Neglect the rounding up and assume that you pay exactly 2% of the current balance each month. Notice that with you making a payment of 2% and the bank charging interest of 1.366%, each month you in effect reduce the balance to $(1 - 0.02)(1.01366) = 99.33868\%$ of what it was the previous month. How long will it take to reduce the balance of $2575.83 to $1000? (Again, assume that you make payments right away.)

(d) Continuing part (b): Once the balance is down to $1000, the minimum payment is $20. How long does it take to pay off a balance of $1000 by making minimum payments?

(e) Making the minimum payment each month, approximately how much interest will you pay by the time you pay off the original $2575.83? (*Hint:* You won't be off by more than $10 if you estimate the last payment to be $10.)

(f) (Requires spreadsheet) As you may have noticed, contrary to what the card regulations say, the card issuer in fact appears to demand for balances over $1000 a minimum payment of $20 *plus* 2% of the balance (rounded up to the nearest dollar). (We will neglect the rounding.) Step through the payments and balances one month at a time on your spreadsheet, to determine how long it will take to reduce the balance to below $1000.

■ 18. A family struggles for the first few years after their child is born but finally is able to start saving toward the child's college education when the child goes to kindergarten at age 5. If the family saves $100 per month in an account paying 5.5% interest compounded continuously, how much will they have for college expenses 13 years hence?

In the savings formula and in the amortization formula, the interest rate r appears twice. The particular ways that r is involved in those equations make it impossible to solve them algebraically to get an explicit formula for r. However, with the help of a spreadsheet, you can find r approximately when the other quantities are given. Exercises 19 to 22 treat such situations.

19. (Requires spreadsheet) Suppose that your parents are willing to lend you $20,000 for part of the cost of your college education and living expenses. They want you to repay them the $20,000, without any interest, in a lump sum 15 years after you graduate, when they will be about to retire and move. Meanwhile, you will be busy repaying federally guaranteed loans for the first 10 years after graduation. But you realize that you can't repay the lump sum without saving up. So you decide that you will put aside money into an interest-bearing account every month for the five years before the payment is due. You feel comfortable with the idea of putting aside $275 a month (the amount of the payment on your government loans). How high an annual nominal interest rate on savings do you need to

accumulate the $20,000 in 60 months, if interest is compounded monthly? Enter into a spreadsheet the values $d = 275$, $r = 0.05$ (annual rate), $n = 60$, and the savings formula with r replaced by $r/12$ (the monthly interest rate). You will find that the amount accumulated is not enough. Change r to 0.09—it's more than enough. Try other values until you determine r to two decimal places.

20. (Requires spreadsheet)   Suppose that you decide to lease a car. At the end of the 48-month lease period, you would need to make a lump-sum $4000 payment if you want to keep the car. You decide to save up, just in case you decide to keep the car; if you don't keep this car, you will have saved a good down payment on a new car. You feel comfortable with saving $70/month (over and above your lease payments). How high an annual nominal interest rate on savings do you need for that to be enough to accumulate the $4000 in 48 months, assuming that interest is compounded monthly?

21. (Requires spreadsheet)   On May 20, 1998, a single winner won the largest (till then) Powerball lottery jackpot of $192.5 million, to be paid as an annuity in 25 equal annual installments of $7.7 million each, the first payment being right away. Instead of installment payments, however, the winner chose an instant lump sum of $104.3 million. That would make sense, particularly if the winner could earn a higher rate of interest than the annuity is based on. The present value of the payment k years from now is given by the compound interest formula $A = P(1 + r)^k$, where $P = 7.7$ million and r is the unknown rate of interest built into the annuity. The complete stream of payments has present value (in millions of dollars)

$$104.3 = 7.7\,[1 + (1 + r) + (1 + r)^2 + \cdots + (1 + r)^{24}]$$

where, by the geometric series formula, the right-hand side is also equal to

$$104.3 = 7.7\left[\frac{(1 + r)^{25} - 1}{r}\right]$$

(Notice that this is the same as the savings formula.) Enter $r = .05$ (annual rate) and the formula given earlier; the result is smaller than 104.3. For $r = .06$, the result is larger than 104.3. Make changes in the value of r until you have determined to two decimal places the rate r that gives the closest value to 104.3. Is the rate that you have found the nominal rate or the effective rate?

■ 22. (Requires spreadsheet)   A 1990 advertisement reads, "If you had put $100 per month in this fund starting in 1980, you'd have $37,747 today." Assume that deposits were made on the last day of the month, starting in January 1980, through December 1989, and that interest is paid monthly on the last day of the month (120 months).

(a) How much money was deposited during this period?

(b) What annual rate of interest, compounded monthly, would lead to the result described in the advertisement? And what is the annual yield?

Exponential Decay

23. Suppose inflation proceeds at a level rate of 4% per year from mid-1997 through mid-2001.

(a) Find the cost in mid-2001 of a basket of goods that cost $1 in mid-1997.

(b) What will be the value of a dollar in mid-2001 in constant mid-1997 dollars?

24. Suppose you bought a car in early 1996 for $10,000. If its value in current dollars depreciates steadily at 12% per year, what will be its value in current dollars in early 2001?

25. If there is also 3% annual inflation from 1996 through 2001, what will be the value of the car in Exercise 24 in early 2001 in "inflation-adjusted" (mid-1996) dollars?

26. For many years, China has been the world's most populous country. In mid-1998, the population of India was 988.7 million with a

growth rate of 1.9% per year, while the population of China (excluding Hong Kong) was 1.243 billion with a growth rate of 1.0%. If these rates of increase stay constant, when will the population of India be greater than that of China?

Growth Models for Biological Populations

27. In its estimates for doubling times for populations in the world, the Population Reference Bureau uses a rule of 70, similar to (but more accurate than) the rule of 72 used in banking. As noted in Exercise 6, a rule of 69.3 would be even more accurate; but the difference between that and the rule of 70 is only 1%. Apply the rule of 70 to estimate the doubling times for the following populations (figures are for mid-1998).

  (a)   Africa, 763 million, 2.5%
  (b)   United States, 270 million. 0.6%
  (c)   China, 1.243 billion, 1.0%
  (d)   The world as a whole, 5.926 billion, 1.4%

Nonrenewable Resources

28. In 1990 the known global oil reserves totaled 917 billion barrels. Consumption, which had been 53.4 million barrels per day in 1983, rose an average of about 1.7% per year through 1990, when the consumption was about 60 million barrels per day.

  (a)   What was the static reserve for oil in 1990?
  (b)   If the rate of increase in consumption stays constant at 1.7%, what was the exponential reserve for oil in 1990?
  (c)   What considerations may affect these reserves over time?

29. Aluminum is the most abundant structural metal in the earth's crust. The world demand for new supplies of aluminum in 1983 was 16.5 million metric tons, while the known reserves were then 21,000 million metric tons.

  (a)   What was the static reserve for aluminum in 1983?
  (b)   In 1983, the demand for new aluminum was projected to increase at 4% per year at least through the year 2000. For that rate of increase, what was the exponential reserve for aluminum in 1983?
  (c)   What considerations may affect these reserves over time?

Renewable Resources

30. A reproduction curve for a population is shown in the figure below. Estimate the equilibrium population size and the maximum sustainable yield. (The units are in thousands.)

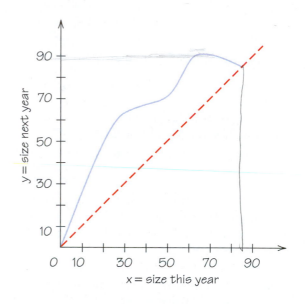

31. Suppose that a reproduction curve for a certain population is as in the accompanying figure (see facing page), where the units are in thousands.

  (a)   Estimate the sustainable yield corresponding to a population of size 10,000 remaining after the harvest.
  (b)   Estimate the maximum sustainable yield.

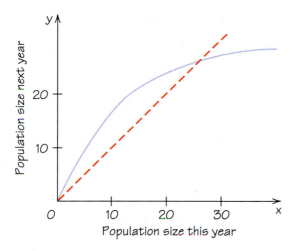

Additional Exercises

32. An oft-heard claim is that "the amount of information in the world doubles every three days." Presumably the claim refers to the amount of data, which can be quantified in terms of number of bits. (A bit is the smallest unit of storage in a computer.) Show that the claim is absolutely preposterous, by doing a little arithmetic and comparing your result with the estimated number of particles in the universe (10^{70}). In particular:

    (a) Start with one bit of data and double the number of bits every third day. How long does it take to get past 10^{70}? (*Hint:* Don't just keep multiplying by 2 over and over. Convince yourself that since the amount of data increases by a factor of 2 every three days, then it increases by a factor of $2^2 = 4$ every six days, a factor of $4^2 = 16$ every twelve days, a factor of $16^2 = 256$ every twenty-four days, and so forth.)

    (b) Part (a) involves a lot of multiplying by 2, even if you do it efficiently. Another approach is to use the fact that $2^{10} = 1024 \approx 1000$. Thus, the amount of data increases by a factor of more than 1000 every $3 \times 10 = 30$ days, or every month (except February, but the 31-day months

make up for it). By when will the total be sure to be past 10^{70}?

33. An old legend tells of a wizard who agreed to save a kingdom provided that the king would agree to a "modest" reward. The wizard asked to be given merely as much grain as would put one kernel on the first square of a chessboard, two kernels on the second, four on the third, eight on the fourth, and so forth, up through the sixty-fourth square. The king agreed, the wizard saved the kingdom, but the king was completely unable to honor the agreement. Why? [*Hints:* Notice that $1 = 2^1 - 1$, and $(1 + 2) = 2^2 - 1$, and $(1 + 2 + 4) = 2^3 - 1$; generalize to arrive at a total for the number of kernels. A kernel of rice is about a quarter of an inch long and about a sixteenth of an inch wide and a sixteenth of an inch high. So about a thousand kernels will fit in a cubic inch (you should verify this calculation). Calculate the total volume of kernels.]

34. Surprise! Just for fun, one of your friends wrote your name on an Illinois State Lottery ticket, and you are the sole winner of $40 million! You discover, however, that you don't get the $40 million all at once; in fact, it is paid in 20 annual installments. All you get right away is the first installment of $2 million (minus 20% withheld against federal income tax due, and whatever you think your friend deserves for the favor). So, what is the prize really worth to you? That depends on the rate of inflation over the years. Assume a constant rate of inflation over the 19 years until your last payment and calculate the present value of your prize winnings by using the formula for present value combined with the formula for the sum of a geometric series. Do the calculation for rates of interest of

    (a) 3%
    (b) 6%
    (c) 9%

Actually, the checks will come not from the state of Illinois but from an insurance company from which Illinois purchases an annuity (a contract to pay a certain amount each year for a specified number of years). The price of the annuity depends on current long-term interest rates.

◆ 35. By the time that there is concern about using up a nonrenewable resource, it may be too late. Suppose that a resource has a static reserve of 10,000 years but consumption is growing at 3.5% per year.

(a) How long will the resource last?
(b) How long before half the resource is gone?
(c) How much longer will the resource last if after half of it is gone, consumption is stabilized at the then-current level?
(d) What implications do you see to your answers?

◆ 36. In mid-1998, the population of the world was 5.926 billion and increasing at 1.33% per year.

(a) Project the world's population to mid-2000, to mid-2025 (by which time you will likely have finished having children, if you do), and to mid-2050 (by which time you will likely have retired).
(b) What are the assumptions involved in your projections?
(c) You can make a more refined model, which will give more realistic answers, by dividing the countries of the world into three groups that have differing rates of increase (see the table below).

Group	Population Mid-1998 (billions)	Rate of Growth (%)
More developed countries	1.178	0.1
Less developed countries (excluding China)	3.505	2.0
China	1.243	1.0

To get a projection for the world's population, project each group separately and add the totals. Redo your projections for the years 2025 and 2050. Do you find the differences from your earlier projections to be significant?

(d) Will the world be able to support the numbers of people that you project? What problems will these greater numbers of people cause? What could be done to avert those problems? Do you think that anything will be done before there is some kind of worldwide crisis?

TECHNOLOGY CORNER

Modeling Compound Interest

The spreadsheet in Figure 20.11 models an investment of annual payments. In this example, a $100 payment is made each year, and an annually compounded interest rate of 5% = .05 is assumed. The added interest at entry **D3** is computed as =**B3*E2** and the balance at entry **E3** is computed as =**E2 + C3 + D3**. The year number at entry **A3** is computed as =**A2 + 1**. These relatively defined computations can then be copied from the third row to subsequent rows. At the third annual payment, a total of $315.25 has accumulated.

TASK 1. Extend the spreadsheet to model 18 years of annual payments. Through these years, what is the total accumulated interest added to the $1800 investment?

	A	B	C	D	E
1	Year	Annual interest rate	Payment	Interest	Balance
2	0				$0.00
3	1	0.05	$100.00	$0.00	$100.00
4	2	0.05	$100.00	$5.00	$205.00
5	3	0.05	$100.00	$10.25	$315.25

FIGURE 20.11

TASK 2. Suppose the investment realizes a more aggressive annual interest rate. Examine the effects of slight changes to the annual interest rate. What must the interest rate be in order to double the $1800 investment (for a total of $3600) at the eighteenth payment? What interest rate would triple the investment at the eighteenth payment?

Modeling Debt Payments

This spreadsheet can also model payments against a debt. To model a $1000 loan, change the initial balance entry **E2** to -1000, as shown in Figure 20.12. Typically the spreadsheet will display this negative amount in red or within parentheses. At the end of the year, the $100 payment is credited and $50 in interest is charged against the account, for a balance of $950.

TASK 3. How many annual payments are required before the $1000 debt is repaid and a positive balance is shown? How much interest is charged for this loan?

TASK 4. Examine the effects of larger annual payments. How large must each payment be in order to pay off the loan in 10 years?

	A	B	C	D	E
1	Year	Annual interest rate	Payment	Interest	Balance
2	0				($1,000.00)
3	1	0.05	$100.00	-$50.00	($950.00)
4	2	0.05	$100.00	-$47.50	($897.50)
5	3	0.05	$100.00	-$44.88	($842.38)

FIGURE 20.12

Exploration

Suppose the annual interest rate is 5% and the annual payment is $100. If the initial loan is $1800, how many payments are required? How does the schedule change if the initial loan is $2000?

writing projects

1 ▶ Based on the calculations you did in Exercise 36 and the discussion you had with other members of the class, write a short essay in the form of a guest editorial for a newspaper. Describe your projections and how you arrived at them, how serious a problem you think population growth is, what problems it is likely to cause, what you think needs to be done, and what the implications are for your own life.

2 ▶ Identify a particular regional, national, or world nonrenewable primary resource (e.g., coal) or secondary resource (e.g., electric power). Research how much of it is available now and what the current rate of consumption is. Determine the static reserve. Estimate the growth rate in consumption, taking into account human population increase, and determine the exponential reserve. What social and technological factors contribute to the increasing rate of consumption? Brainstorm how those factors could be changed.

3 ▶ Identify a particular regional, national, or world renewable resource (e.g., timber, clean drinking water). Research how much of it is produced now, how much is harvested now, and what the current rate of consumption is. Estimate the growth rate in consumption, taking into account human population increase. For how long can this resource continue to meet the demand? What social and technological factors contribute to the increasing rate of consumption? Brainstorm how those factors could be changed.

4 ▶ In recent years, incentives from automobile manufacturers to potential customers have taken the form of offering either a reduced interest rate on the loan for the car or else a rebate (reduction in price) on the cost itself. In fall 1998 you could by a Dodge Neon for $11,998 with a 1.9% interest loan or else

get a $1500 rebate but have to finance at a higher rate (either through the auto dealer or elsewhere).

Suppose that you could afford a $2000 down payment and could get a loan from a credit union at 6.0%.

    (a) What is your monthly payment if you choose the rebate and take out a 48-month loan with the credit union for the reduced price minus your down payment?

    (b) What is your monthly payment if you choose the 1.9% 48-month loan for the original price minus your down payment?

    (c) Suppose that when the dealer realizes that you prefer the option in part (a), she offers you a further combined option: a rebate of $1000 with a 3.9% interest rate. How does this compare?

    (d) Locate current advertised incentives for a car that you would like to buy and compare them.

5 ▶ You want to buy a house for which you need to borrow $100,000. You have the option of a 15-year mortgage or a 30-year mortgage, both at 7.9%.

    (a) What are your monthly payments in each case?

    (b) How much interest do you pay, and what is the total amount that you pay, in each case?

    (c) Suppose that you anticipate inflation to be 3% per year for the duration of the mortgage. What is the value in today's dollars of the stream of payments that you will make under the 15-year mortgage? Under the 30-year mortgage? (*Hint:* Use the formula for the sum of a geometric series.)

    (d) Use a spreadsheet to prepare an amortization table for each loan, showing for each month how much interest is paid and how much principal is repaid.

ANSWERS SECTION CONTENTS

ANSWERS TO SKILLS CHECK EXERCISES

CHAPTER 1
1. (a)
2. (c)
3. (a)
4. (b)
5. (a)
6. (b)
7. (c)

CHAPTER 2
1. (c)
2. (b)
3. (b)
4. (b)
5. (c)
6. (b)
7. (b)

CHAPTER 3
1. (c)
2. (c)
3. (c)
4. (b)
5. (a)
6. (b)
7. (b)

CHAPTER 4
1. (b)
2. (a)
3. (b)
4. (b)
5. (b)
6. (c)
7. (c)

CHAPTER 5
1. (a)
2. (b)
3. (a)
4. (c)
5. (c)
6. (b)
7. (c)

CHAPTER 6
1. (b)
2. (b)
3. (a)
4. (b)
5. (c)
6. (b)
7. (c)

CHAPTER 7
1. (c)
2. (a)
3. (a)
4. (c)
5. (c)
6. (b)
7. (b)

CHAPTER 8
1. (a)
2. (c)
3. (b)
4. (b)
5. (b)
6. (a)
7. (c)

CHAPTER 9
1. (a)
2. (c)
3. (b)
4. (b)
5. (b)
6. (c)
7. (b)

CHAPTER 10
1. (b)
2. (b)
3. (c)
4. (b)
5. (b)
6. (a)
7. (c)

CHAPTER 11
1. (d)
2. (c)
3. (a)
4. (a)
5. (a)
6. (a)
7. (b)

CHAPTER 12
1. (b)
2. (c)
3. (c)
4. (b)
5. (b)
6. (b)
7. (a)

CHAPTER 13
1. (b)
2. (c)
3. (a)
4. (b)
5. (c)
6. (b)
7. (a)

CHAPTER 14
1. (c)
2. (a)
3. (b)
4. (a)
5. (a)
6. (b)
7. (c)

CHAPTER 15
1. (c)
2. (c)
3. (b)
4. (a)
5. (c)
6. (b)
7. (a)

CHAPTER 16
1. (c)
2. (a)
3. (b)
4. (c)
5. (b)
6. (c)
7. (c)

CHAPTER 17

1. (a)
2. (a)
3. (a)
4. (b)
5. (b)
6. (c)
7. (b)

CHAPTER 18

1. (b)
2. (b)
3. (a)
4. (c)
5. (c)
6. (b)
7. (c)

CHAPTER 19

1. (b)
2. (a)
3. (a)
4. (a)
5. (b)
6. (a)
7. (c)

CHAPTER 20

1. (a)
2. (b)
3. (c)
4. (b)
5. (b)
6. (b)
7. (b)

CHAPTER 1

1. $A:1$; $B:3$; $C:3$; $D:3$; and $E:0$. The graph shows that geographically E is isolated, perhaps on an island or a different continent than the other cities.

3. No, the loop does not join two different vertices.

5. Remove the edges dotted in the figure below and the remaining graph will be disconnected.

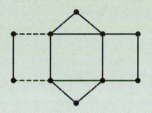

7. Discussion. Answers will vary.

9. The supervisor is not satisfied because all of the edges are not traveled upon by the postal worker. The worker is unhappy because the end of the worker's route wasn't the same point as where the worker began. The original job description is unrealistic because there is no Euler circuit in the graph.

11.

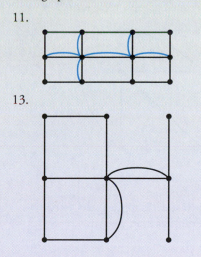

13.

15. Edge 3 or 6 could be chosen, but not edge 2.

17.

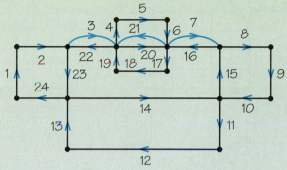

19. Remove the vertical edge in the middle.

21.

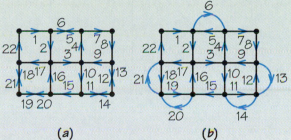

 (a)   (b)

23.

25.

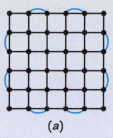

(a)

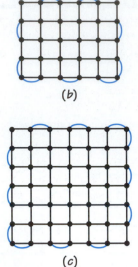

(b)

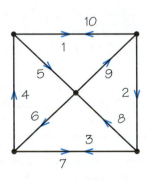

(c)

27.

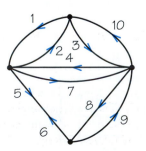

29. The graph is similar to the one in Exercise 28, except 3 of the bridges are represented by 2 edges, as shown below. This graph needs eulerization, but we don't show it. A circuit with one repeated edge is shown on this graph.

31.

33. Both graphs (b) and (c) have Euler circuits. The valences of all of the vertices in (a) are odd, which makes it impossible to have an Euler circuit there.

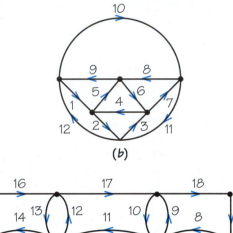

(b)

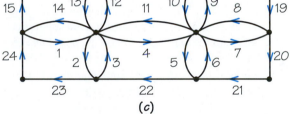

(c)

35. There are many such graphs. Here is one:

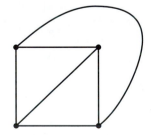

37. Graph (b).

39. Yes, because each street is represented by two edges, every vertex has even valence.

41.

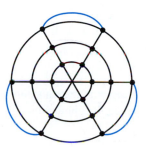

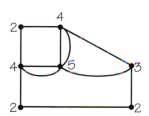

43. When you attach a new edge to an existing graph, it gets attached at two ends. At each of its ends, it makes the valence of the existing vertex go up by one. Thus the increase in the sum of the valences is two. Therefore, if the graph had an even sum of the valences before, it still does, and if its valence sum was odd before, it still is.

45.

The graph is connected.

47. Discussion. Answers will vary.

CHAPTER 2

1. (a) $X_1, X_6, X_5, X_2, X_3, X_4, X_1$.
   (b) $X_1, X_6, X_7, X_8, X_9, X_{10}, X_{11}, X_{12}, X_5, X_4,$ X_3, X_2, X_1.
   (c) $X_1, X_4, X_5, X_8, X_9, X_6, X_7, X_2, X_3, X_1$.
   (d) $X_1, X_2, X_5, X_8, X_3, X_4, X_7, X_6, X_1$.
   (e) $X_1, X_{10}, X_7, X_6, X_9, X_5, X_4, X_3, X_2, X_8, X_1$.

3. (a) For the graphs in (a)–(d) no Hamiltonian circuit would exist after X_1 is deleted along with the edges attached to it. For (e), $X_2, X_8,$ $X_{10}, X_7, X_6, X_9, X_5, X_4, X_3, X_2$ is a Hamiltonian circuit.

5. Other Hamiltonian circuits include $ABIGDCEFHA$ and $ABDCEFGIHA$.

7. (a) Any Hamiltonian circuit would have to use the edges X_4X_1 and X_4X_6 (to visit X_4), X_1X_2 and X_2X_3 (to visit X_2), and X_7X_5 and X_5X_1 (to visit X_5). This forces three edges to be used at X_1, which is not possible in a Hamiltonian circuit.
   (b) Any circuit that included X_4X_5 and X_6X_7 could not visit X_8 and X_9.

9. (a) Yes.
   (b) No Hamiltonian circuit.
   (c) No Hamiltonian circuit.

11. The n-cube has 2^n vertices, and the number of edges of the n-cube is equal to twice the number of edges of an $(n-1)$-cube plus 2^{n-1}. A formula for this number is $n2^{n-1}$.

13. (a) Hamiltonian circuit, yes; Euler circuit, no.
    (b) Hamiltonian circuit, yes; Euler circuit, no.
    (c) Hamiltonian circuit, yes; Euler circuit, no.
    (d) Hamiltonian circuit, no; Euler circuit, no.

15. Examples include inspection of traffic control devices at corners and placing new hour stickers on mailboxes located at street corners.

17. (a) $9 \cdot 8 \cdot 7 \cdot 6 \cdot 5 = 15,120$.
    (b) $(26)(26)(26) = 17,576$.

19. (a) $7 \times 6 \times 5 \times 4 \times 3 = 2520$.
    (b) $7 \times 7 \times 7 \times 7 \times 7 = 16,807$.
    (c) $(7)^5 - 7 = 16,800$.

21. (a) $26(26)(26)(10)(10)(10) - (26)(26)(26) =$ $(26)^3(10^3 - 1)$.
    (b) Answers will vary.

23. These graphs have 6, 10, and 15 edges, respectively. The n vertex complete graph has $[n(n-1)]/2$ edges. The number of TSP tours is 3, 12, and 60, respectively.

25. (a)

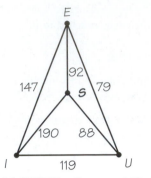

(b) (1) *UISEU;* mileage = 119 + 190 + 92 + 79 = 480.
     (2) *USIEU;* mileage = 88 + 190 + 147 + 79 = 504.
     (3) *UIESU;* mileage = 119 + 147 + 92 + 88 = 446.

(c) *UIESE* (Tour 3).

(d) No.

(e) Starting from *U*, one gets (see answer (b)) Tour 1. From *S* one gets Tour 2; from *E* one gets Tour 2; and from *I* one gets Tour 1.

(f) Tour 2. No.

27. *FMCRF* gets her home in 32 minutes.

29. *MACBM* takes 345 minutes to traverse.

31. A traveling salesman problem.

33. The complete graph shown has a different nearest-neighbor tour that starts at *A* (*AEDBCA*), a sorted-edges tour (*AEDCBA*), and a cheaper tour (*ADBECA*).

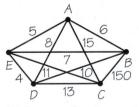

35. Optimal tour is the same, but its cost is now 3460 + 15(30) = 3910.

37. (a) a. Not a tree since there is a circuit. Also, the wiggled edges do not include all vertices of the graph.

b. The circuit does not include all the vertices of the graph.

(b) a. The tree does not include all vertices of the graph.

b. Not a circuit.

(c) a. Not a tree.

b. Not a circuit.

(d) a. Not a tree.

b. Not a circuit.

39. (a) 1, 2, 3, 4, 5, 8.
     (b) 1, 1, 1, 2, 2, 3, 3, 4, 5, 6, 6.
     (c) 1, 1, 1, 2, 2, 2, 2, 2, 3, 3, 3, 3, 4, 4, 4, 5, 5, 6, 7.
     (d) 1, 2, 2, 3, 3, 3, 4, 5, 5, 5, 6, 6.

41. Yes. At each stage of applying the algorithm for this graph, there is no choice about which edge to choose.

43. (a)

(b) Driving distances between three houses on a rural road provides one example.

45. Yes. Change all the weights to negative numbers and apply Kruskal's algorithm. The resulting tree works, and the maximum cost is the negative of the answer you get. If the numbers on the edges represent subsidies for using the edges, one might be interested in finding a maximum-cost spanning tree.

47. A negative weight on an edge is conceivable, perhaps a subsidization payment. Kruskal's algorithm would still apply.

49. (a) True.   (b) False.   (c) True.
     (d) False.   (e) Not necessarily.

51. Two different trees with the same cost are shown:

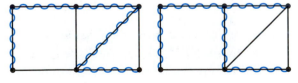

53.

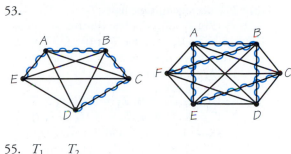

55.

$T_1 \quad T_2$

$T_3 \quad T_4$

$T_5 \quad T_6$

57. Answers will vary.

59. Reduce T_5's time by 2. T_1, T_2, T_4, T_7 now will also be a critical path.

61. (a) a. Add edge AB.
   b. Add edge $X_1 X_3$.
   (b)

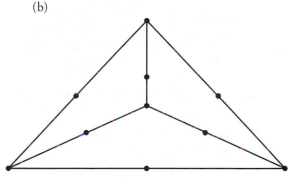

   (c) Yes: $ADGFBEC$. Figure (a).
   Yes: $X_1, X_2, X_9, X_8, X_7, X_6, X_5, X_4, X_3$. Figure (b).
   (d) Yes. A worker who must do an inspection of sites on her way to work.

63. With no other restrictions, 10^7. With no other restrictions, 9×10^2.

65. Optimal tour is the same, but its cost has now doubled to 9040.

CHAPTER 3

1. (a) Operating room schedules, doctor schedules, emergency room staffing schedules, etc.
   (b) Schedules for the trains or buses and their crews, etc.
   (c) Scheduling runway use, reservation agents, food service for planes, etc.
   (d) Schedules for each mechanic, radiator repair, etc.
   (e) Schedules for waiters, waitresses, dish cleaning, etc.
   (f) Schedules for washing clothes, cleaning rooms, dusting, etc.
   (g) Schedules for bus run, recess duty, etc.
   (h) Day, night, afternoon shift schedules, etc.
   (i) Firefighter shift schedules, schedules for checking if equipment on trucks is in repair, etc.

3. Jocelyn must pack, get to the airport, make various connections, perhaps kennel her dog, etc. Processors include plane, bus, taxi (to get to the airport), and Jocelyn herself. Unless she can get a friend to help her pack or take her dog to the kennel, none of the tasks can be done simultaneously.

5. (a) Processor 1: T_1, T_2, T_3, T_5, T_7; Processor 2: Idle 0 to 2, T_4, T_6, idle 4 to 5.
   (b) Processor 1: T_1, T_2, T_3, T_6, T_7; Processor 2: Idle 0 to 2, T_4, T_5, idle 4 to 5.
   (c) Yes.
   (d) No.

7. (a) Processor 1: T_1, T_3, T_4, T_6, T_7, T_9, T_{11}, idle 42 to 45. Processor 2: T_2, T_5, T_8, T_{10}.
   (b) Processor 1: T_1, T_6, idle 13 to 15; T_5, T_7, T_{11}, idle 34 to 38; T_{10}. Processor 2: T_2, T_9, idle 21 to 27; T_8, idle 38 to 45. Processor 3: T_3, T_4, idle 15 to 45.

9. (a) The critical path, which has length 17, is T_1 T_2 T_3.
   (b) T_1, T_4, T_5, T_2, T_6, T_7, T_3 is the list to be used. The one processor would have the tasks scheduled on it: T_1, T_4, T_5, T_2, T_6, T_7, T_3.

(c) T_6, T_1, T_7, T_2, T_4, T_3, T_5 would be the list. The resulting schedule on one processor would be: T_1, T_7, T_4, T_2, T_5, T_6, T_3.

(d) No idle time. Their completion times are the same.

(e) Earlier completion of tasks giving rise to cash payments.

(f) The required schedule is Processor 1: T_1, T_2, T_7; Processor 2: T_4, T_5, T_6, T_3, idle 19 to 21.

(g) The completion time does not halve. As the number of processors goes up, the completion time may decrease, but at some point the length of the critical path will govern the completion time rather than the number of processors.

(h) (i) Completion time goes down by 7.

   (ii) Completion time is 19 for two processors using the decreasing time list.

11. (a) $5! = 120$.

   (b) No.

   (c) No. First, while processor 1 works on T_1 processor 2 must be idle. Second, the task times are integers with sum 31. If there are two processors, one of the processors must have idle time since when 2 divides 31 there is a remainder of 1.

   (d) No.

13. Using the order-requirement digraph shown and any list with one or more processors yields the same schedule:

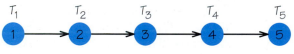

15. (a) One reasonable possibility is (time in min):

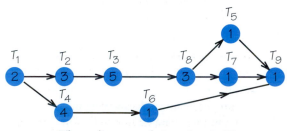

The earliest completion time is 15.

(b) The decreasing-time list is T_3, T_4, T_2, T_8, T_1, T_5, T_6, T_7, T_9. The schedule is Processor 1: T_1, T_4, T_6, idle 7 to 10, T_8, T_5, T_9; Processor 2: idle 0 to 2, T_2, T_3, idle 10 to 13, T_7, idle 14 to 15.

17. (a) Task times: $T_1 = 3$, $T_2 = 3$, $T_3 = 2$, $T_4 = 3$, $T_5 = 3$, $T_6 = 4$, $T_7 = 5$, $T_8 = 3$, $T_9 = 2$, $T_{10} = 1$, $T_{11} = 1$, and $T_{12} = 3$. This schedule would be produced from the list: T_1, T_3, T_2, T_5, T_4, T_6, T_7, T_8, T_{11}, T_{12}, T_9, T_{10}.

   (b) Task times: $T_1 = 3$, $T_2 = 3$, $T_3 = 3$, $T_4 = 2$, $T_5 = 2$, $T_6 = 4$, $T_7 = 3$, $T_8 = 5$, $T_9 = 8$, $T_{10} = 4$, $T_{11} = 7$, $T_{12} = 9$, $T_{13} = 3$. This schedule would be produced from the list: T_1, T_5, T_7, T_4, T_3, T_6, T_{11}, T_8, T_{12}, T_9, T_2, T_{10}, T_{13}.

19. (a) (i) Processor 1: T_1, T_3, T_5, T_7, T_9; Processor 2: T_2, T_4, T_6, T_8, idle 20 to 25. (ii) Processor 1: T_9, T_6, T_5, T_2, T_1; Processor 2: T_8, T_7, T_4, T_3, idle 22 to 23.

   (b) The list for (ii) is optimal.

21. Such criteria include decreasing length of the times of the tasks, order of size of financial gains when each task is finished, and increasing length of the times of the tasks.

23. The task times total to 34. Since (34/3) rounded up is 12, the earliest completion time is 12.

25. (a) The tasks are scheduled on the machines as follows: Processor 1: 12, 13, 45, 34, 63, 43, 16, idle 226 to 298; Processor 2: 23, 24, 23, 53, 25, 74, 76; Processor 3: 32, 23, 14, 21, 18, 47, 23, 43, 16, idle 237 to 298.

   (b) The tasks are scheduled on the machines as follows: Processor 1: 12, 24, 14, 34, 25, 23, 16, 16, 76, idle 183 to 240; Processor 2: 23, 23, 21, 63, 43, idle 173 to 240; Processor 3: 32, 23, 53, 74, idle 182 to 240; Processor 4: 13, 45, 18, 47, 43, idle 166 to 240.

   (c) The decreasing-time list is 76, 74, 63, 53, 47, 45, 43, 43, 34, 32, 25, 24, 23, 23, 23, 23, 21, 18, 16, 16, 14, 13, 12.

The tasks are scheduled on three machines as follows: Processor 1: 76, 45, 43, 24, 23, 18, 16, 13; Processor 2: 74, 47, 34, 32, 23, 21, 14, 12, idle 257 to 258; Processor 3: 63, 53, 43, 25, 23, 23, 16, idle 246 to 258.

The tasks are scheduled on four machines as follows: Processor 1: 76, 43, 24, 23, 16, idle 182 to 194; Processor 2: 74, 43, 25, 23, 16, 13; Processor 3: 63, 45, 32, 23, 18, 12, idle 193 to 194; Processor 4: 53, 47, 34, 23, 21, 14, idle 192 to 194.

(d) The new decreasing-time list is 84, 82, 71, 61, 55, 45, 43, 43, 34, 32, 25, 24, 23, 23, 23, 23, 21, 18, 16, 16, 14, 13, 12.

The tasks are scheduled as follows: Processor 1: 84, 45, 43, 25, 23, 23, 16, 12; Processor 2: 82, 55, 34, 32, 23, 18, 14, 13; Processor 3: 71, 61, 43, 24, 23, 21, 16, idle 259 to 271.

27. (a) One such rule, admittedly artificial, could be: if by keeping a machine voluntarily idle, there is a longer task that becomes ready one time unit later, keep the machine idle.

(b) If a longer task becomes ready at a certain time than the remaining time on a task currently scheduled, schedule the longer task and reschedule the interrupted task later. An assumption must be made whether or not an interrupted task must be resumed on the machine it was originally scheduled on or can be rescheduled on any machine that becomes free.

29. Examples include jobs in a videotape copying shop, data entry tasks in a computer system, scheduling nonemergency operations in an operating room. These situations may have tasks with different priorities, but there is no physical reason for the tasks not to be independent, as would be the case with putting on a roof before a house had walls erected.

31. (a) Each task heads a path of length equal to the time to do that task.

(b) (i) The worst finish time is
$(2 - \frac{1}{3})(450) = 750$

(ii) The worst finish time, if the decreasing-time list is used, is
$[\frac{4}{3} - 1/(3)(3)](450) = 550$

33. The times to photocopy the manuscripts, in decreasing order, are 120, 96, 96, 88, 80, 76, 64, 64, 60, 60, 56, 48, 40, 32. Packing these in bins of size 120 yields Bin 1: 120; Bin 2: 96; Bin 3: 96; Bin 4: 88, 32; Bin 5: 80, 40; Bin 6: 76; Bin 7: 64, 56; Bin 8: 64, 48; Bin 9: 60, 60. Nine photocopy machines are needed to finish within 2 minutes using FFD. The number of bins would not change, but the placement of the items in the bins would differ for worst-fit decreasing.

35. (a) Using the next-fit algorithm, the bins are filled as follows: Bin 1: 12, 15; Bin 2: 16, 12; Bin 3: 9, 11, 15; Bin 4: 17, 12; Bin 5: 14, 17; Bin 6: 18; Bin 7: 19; Bin 8: 21; Bin 9: 31; Bin 10: 7, 21; Bin 11: 9, 23; Bin 12: 24; Bin 13: 15, 16; Bin 14: 12, 9, 8; Bin 15: 27; Bin 16: 22; Bin 17: 18.

(b) The decreasing list is 31, 27, 24, 23, 22, 21, 21, 19, 18, 18, 17, 17, 16, 16, 15, 15, 15, 14, 12, 12, 12, 12, 11, 9, 9, 9, 8, 7.

The next-fit decreasing schedule is Bin 1: 31; Bin 2: 27; Bin 3: 24; Bin 4: 23; Bin 5: 22; Bin 6: 21; Bin 7: 21; Bin 8: 19; Bin 9: 18, 18; Bin 10: 17, 17; Bin 11: 16, 16; Bin 12: 15, 15; Bin 13: 15, 14; Bin 14: 12, 12, 12; Bin 15: 12, 11, 9; Bin 16: 9, 9, 8, 7.

(c) The worst-fit schedule using the original list is Bin 1: 12, 15, 9; Bin 2: 16, 12; Bin 3: 11, 15; Bin 4: 17, 12; Bin 5: 14, 17; Bin 6: 18, 7; Bin 7: 19, 9; Bin 8: 21, 15; Bin 9: 31; Bin 10: 21, 9; Bin 11: 23, 8; Bin 12: 24; Bin 13: 16, 12; Bin 14: 27; Bin 15: 22; Bin 16: 18.

(d) The worst-fit decreasing schedule would be Bin 1: 31; Bin 2: 27, 9; Bin 3: 24, 12; Bin 4: 23, 12; Bin 5: 22, 12; Bin 6: 21, 15; Bin 7: 21, 15; Bin 8: 19, 17; Bin 9: 18, 18; Bin 10: 17, 16; Bin 11: 16, 12, 8; Bin 12: 15, 14, 7; Bin 13: 11, 9, 9.

37. Discussion. Answers will vary.

39. The total performance time exceeds what will fit on 4 disks. Using FFD, one can fit the music on 5 disks.

41. The proposed heuristic may fill many bins to capacity, but the computation to find weights summing to exactly W may be very time-consuming.

43. There is an example of a bin-packing problem for which a given list takes a certain number of bins, and when an item is deleted from the list, more bins are required. In this example, the deleted item is not first in the list.

45. (a) The vertices in Figures (b), (d), (e), and (f) can be colored with 3 colors, but the vertices in Figures (a) and (c) cannot be colored with 3 colors.
    (b) The vertices in all the figures except (c) can be colored with 4 colors.
    (c) The chromatic number for (a) is 4, for (b) is 3, for (c) is 5, for (d) is 2, for (e) is 3, and for (f) is 2.

47. (a) Construct the graph shown below:

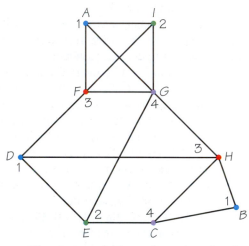

The vertices of this graph can be colored with no fewer than four colors (1, 2, 3, 4 are used to denote the colors in the figure). Hence, 4 tanks can be used to display the fish.
    (b) The coloring in (a) shows that one can display 2 types of fish in 3 of the tanks, and 3 types of fish in one tank. Since 4 does not divide 9, one cannot do better.

49. (a) The graph for this situation is shown in the next column. The vertices can be labeled with the colors 1, 2, 3 as shown.
    (b) Since the vertices can be colored with 3 colors (and no fewer), the minimum number of time slots for scheduling the committees is 3.

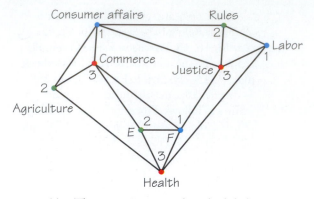

(c) The committees can be scheduled in 3 rooms during each time slot. This might be significant if there were only 3 rooms that had microphone systems.

51. (a) Three time slots. To solve this problem draw a graph by joining the vertices representing two committees if there is no × in the row and column of the table for these two committees.
    (b) It is possible to three-color this graph so that each of the 3 colors is used 3 times. This means that one needs 3 rooms to arrange the scheduling of the 9 committees.

53. Start at any vertex of the tree and label this vertex with the color 1; color any vertex attached by an edge to this vertex with color 2. Continue to color the vertices in the tree in this manner, alternating the use of colors. If some vertex were attached to both a vertex colored 1 and another vertex colored 2, at some stage this would imply the graph had a circuit (of odd length), which is not possible since trees have no circuits of any length.

55. For graph (a), 4 colors; graph (b) 4 colors; graph (c) 3 colors; graph (d) 3 colors; graph (e) 3 colors; graph (f) 5 colors; graph (g) 5 colors; graph (h) 4 colors. The minimum edge coloring number of any graph is either the maximal valence or one more than the maximal valence. This theorem is due to the Russian mathematician Vizing.

57. (a) Identical machines, typists who type the same number of words per minute, etc.
    (b) Runways at an airport in different directions, humans with different levels of skills, etc.

59. No. Machine 2 was idle at the time T_{10} was started, so T_{10} should have been assigned to machine 2. This schedule could not arise from independent tasks, since when machine 2 finished task 2, it could have started on task 8, 9, 10, or 11.

61. (a) Packing boxes of the same height into crates; packing want ads into a newspaper page.
     (b) We assume, without loss of generality, $p \geq q$. One heuristic, similar to first-fit, orders the rectangles $p \times q$ as in a dictionary (i.e., $p \times q$ listed prior to $r \times s$ if $p > r$ or $p = r$ and $q \geq s$). It then puts the rectangles in place in layers in a first-fit manner; that is, do not put a rectangle into a second layer until all positions on the first layer are filled. However, extra room in the first layer is "wasted."
     (c) The problem of packing rectangles of width 1 in an $m \times 1$ rectangle is a special case of the two-dimensional problem, equivalent to the bin-packing problem we have discussed.
     (d) Two 1×10 rectangles cannot be packed into a 5×4 rectangle, even though there would be an area of 20 in this rectangle.

63. (a) (i) The schedule with four secretaries is as follows: Processor 1: 25, 36, 15, 15, 19, 15, 27; Processor 2: 18, 32, 18, 31, 30, 18; Processor 3: 13, 30, 17, 12, 18, 16, 16, 16, 14; Processor 4: 19, 12, 25, 26, 18, 12, 24, 9.

          The schedule with five secretaries is as follows: Processor 1: 25, 25, 31, 12, 16, 14; Processor 2: 18, 12, 17, 12, 15, 30, 9; Processor 3: 13, 32, 26, 16, 15, 18; Processor 4: 19, 36, 18, 19, 24; Processor 5: 30, 18, 15, 18, 16, 27.

          (ii) The decreasing-time list is 36, 32, 31, 30, 30, 27, 26, 25, 25, 24, 19, 19, 18, 18, 18, 18, 18, 17, 16, 16, 16, 15, 15, 15, 14, 13, 12, 12, 12, 9.

          The schedule using this list on four processors would be Processor 1: 36, 25, 19, 18, 17, 16, 13, 9; Processor 2: 32, 26, 25, 18, 16, 15, 12; Processor 3: 31, 27, 24, 18, 16, 15, 12, 12; Processor 4: 30, 30, 19, 18, 18, 15, 14.

          The schedule using this list on five processors would be Processor 1: 36, 24, 18, 16, 14, 12; Processor 2: 32, 25, 18, 18, 15, 12; Processor 3: 31, 25, 19, 18, 15, 9; Processor 4: 30, 27, 18, 17, 15, 13; Processor 5: 30, 26, 19, 16, 16, 12.

          (iii) The five-processor decreasing-time schedule is optimal (time 120), but the four decreasing-time schedule is not. One can see this since when the task of length 17 scheduled on processor 1 and the task of length 18 on processor 3 are interchanged, the completion time is reduced to 154 from 155 for the four-processor decreasing-time schedule.

     (b) As a bin-packing problem, each bin will have a capacity of 60. Using the decreasing list we obtain the following packings:
          (i) (First-fit decreasing): Bin 1: 36, 24; Bin 2: 32, 27; Bin 3: 31, 26; Bin 4: 30, 30; Bin 5: 25, 25, 9; Bin 6: 19, 19, 18; Bin 7: 18, 18, 18; Bin 8: 18, 17, 16; Bin 9: 16, 16, 15, 13; Bin 10: 15, 15, 14, 12; Bin 11: 12, 12.
          (ii) (Next-fit decreasing): Bin 1: 36; Bin 2: 32; Bin 3: 31; Bin 4: 30, 30; Bin 5: 27, 26; Bin 6: 25, 25; Bin 7: 24, 19; Bin 8: 19, 18, 18; Bin 9: 18, 18, 18; Bin 10: 17, 16, 16; Bin 11: 16, 15, 15; Bin 12: 15, 14, 13, 12; Bin 13: 12, 12, 9.
               (Worst-fit decreasing): Bin 1: 36, 24; Bin 2: 32, 26; Bin 3: 31, 27; Bin 4: 30, 30; Bin 5: 25, 25; Bin 6: 19, 19, 18; Bin 7: 18, 18, 18; Bin 8: 18, 17, 16; Bin 9: 16, 16, 15, 12; Bin 10: 15, 15, 14, 13; Bin 11: 12, 12, 9.
          (iii) Since the total weight of all the objects is 596, a minimum of 10 bins is required. However, since there are no small weights, there is no way to achieve 10 bins, and in fact, 11 bins is optimal.

65. The bins have a capacity of 120. (First-fit): Bin 1: 63, 32, 11; Bin 2: 19, 24, 64; Bin 3: 87, 27;

Bin 4: 36, 42; Bin 5: 63. This schedule would take five station breaks; however, the total time for the breaks is under 8 minutes.

The decreasing list is 87, 64, 63, 63, 42, 36, 32, 27, 24, 19, 11. (First-fit decreasing): Bin 1: 87, 32; Bin 2: 64, 42, 11; Bin 3: 63, 36, 19; Bin 4: 63, 27, 24. This solution uses only four station breaks.

67. $T_1, T_2, T_3, T_4, T_8, T_9, T_{10}, T_{11}, T_5, T_6, T_7, T_{12}$.

69. (a) Graph (a) 4 colors; graph (b) 2 colors; graph (c) 4 colors; graph (d) 4 colors; graph (e) 2 colors; graph (f) 3 colors. Coloring the maps of countries in an atlas would be one application of face colorings of graphs.

CHAPTER 4

1. (a)

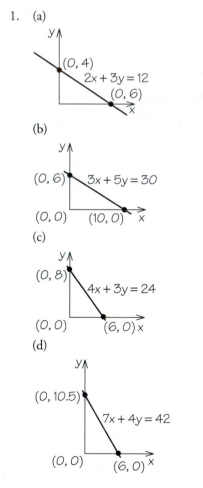

(b)

(c)

(d)

(e)

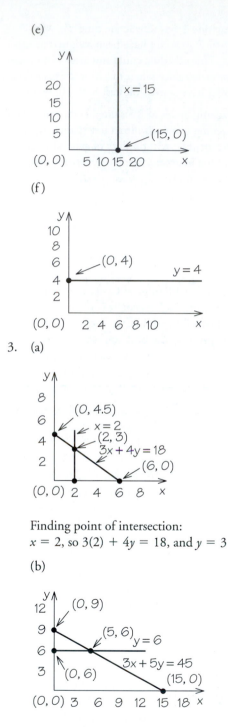

(f)

3. (a)

Finding point of intersection:
$x = 2$, so $3(2) + 4y = 18$, and $y = 3$

(b)

Finding point of intersection:
$y = 6$, so $3x + 5(6) = 45$, and $x = 5$

5. (a)

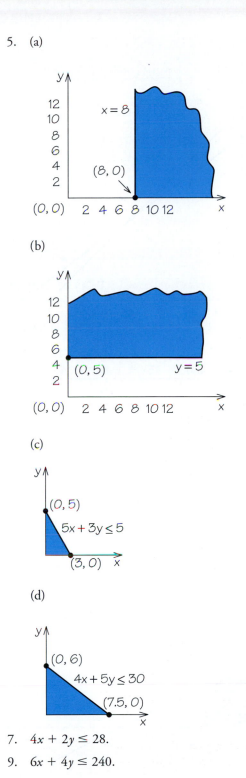

(b)

(c)

(d)

7. $4x + 2y \le 28.$

9. $6x + 4y \le 240.$

11.

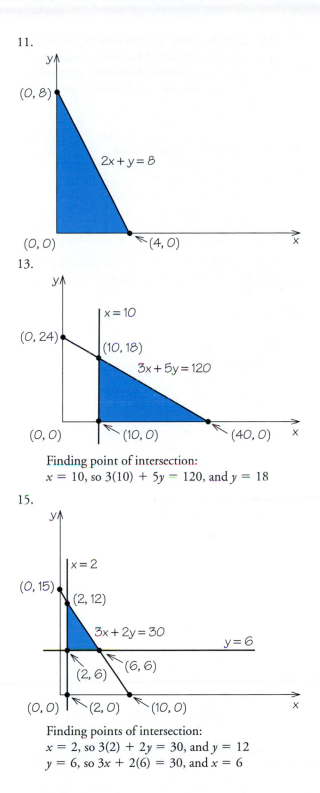

13.

Finding point of intersection:
$x = 10$, so $3(10) + 5y = 120$, and $y = 18$

15.

Finding points of intersection:
$x = 2$, so $3(2) + 2y = 30$, and $y = 12$
$y = 6$, so $3x + 2(6) = 30$, and $x = 6$

17. (a)   (2, 4) is a point of the feasible region of Ex-
          ercise 11, but not of Exercises 13 and 15.
    (b)   (10, 6) is a point of the feasible region of Ex-
          ercise 13, but not of Exercises 11 and 15.

(b)

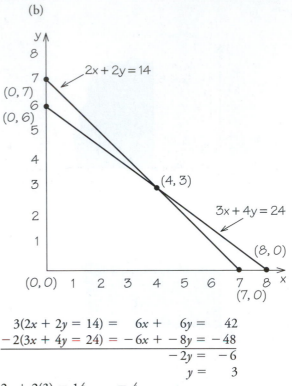

19.   (0, 0): 0 skateboards and 0 dolls.
      Profit = $2.30(0) + $3.70(0) = $0.
      (0, 30): 0 skateboards and 30 dolls.
      Profit = $2.30(0) + $3.70(30) = $111.
      (12, 0): 12 skateboards and 0 dolls.
      Profit = $2.30(12) + $3.70(0) = $27.60.

      Optimal production policy: make 0 skateboards
      and 30 dolls for a profit of $111.

21.   (a)

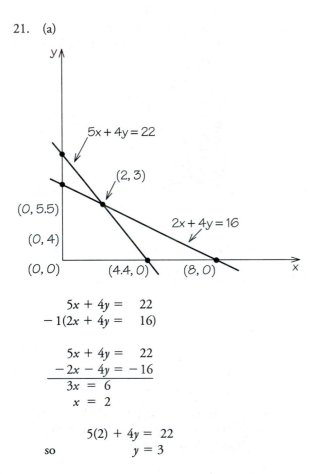

$$3(2x + 2y = 14) =\quad 6x +\quad 6y =\quad 42$$
$$-2(3x + 4y = 24) = -6x + -8y = -48$$
$$\overline{\qquad\qquad\qquad\qquad -2y = \quad -6}$$
$$y = \quad 3$$

$2x + 2(3) = 14$, so $x = 4$

23.

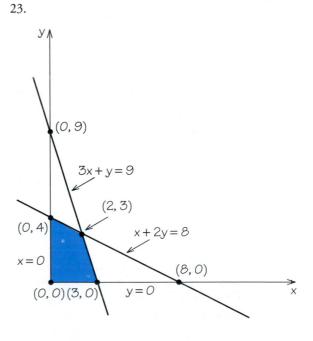

$$5x + 4y =\quad 22$$
$$-1(2x + 4y =\quad 16)$$

$$5x + 4y =\quad 22$$
$$-2x - 4y = -16$$
$$\overline{3x = 6}$$
$$x = 2$$

$$5(2) + 4y = 22$$
so $\qquad\qquad y = 3$

25.

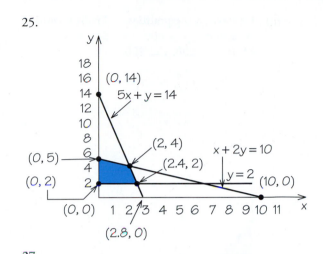

(c)

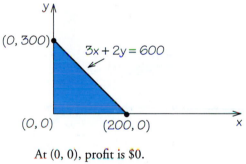

(d) **Profit**
At (100, 30), profit = $560.
At (100, 150), profit = $800.
At (180, 30), profit = $960.*
Make 180 shirts and 30 vests.

   With zero minimums, the feasible region looks like this:

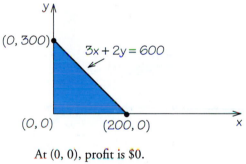

At (0, 0), profit is $0.
At (0, 300), profit is $600.
At (200, 0), profit is $1000.*
Make 200 shirts and no vests.

27.

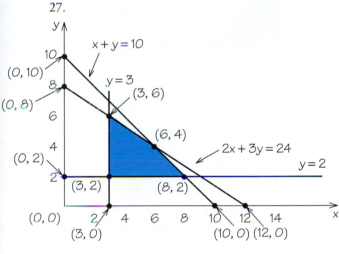

29. (a) (4, 2) is a point of the feasible region of Exercise 27, but not of Exercises 23 and 25.
    (b) (1, 3) is a point of the feasible region of Exercises 23 and 25, but not of Exercise 27.

31. (a)

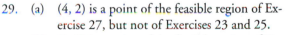

	Cloth (600 yds)	Mins	Profit
Shirts, x items	3	100	$5
Vests, y items	2	30	$2

(b) **Constraint inequalities** **Profit formula**
Cloth: $3x + 2y \leq 600$ $\$5x + \$2y$
Mins: $x \geq 100, y \geq 30$

33. (a)

	Time (90 min)	Profit
Mail order, x	10	$30
Voice-mail order, y	15	$40

(b) **Constraint inequalities** **Profit formula**
Time: $10x + 15y \leq 90$ $\$30x + \$40y$
Mins: $x \geq 0, y \geq 0$

(c)

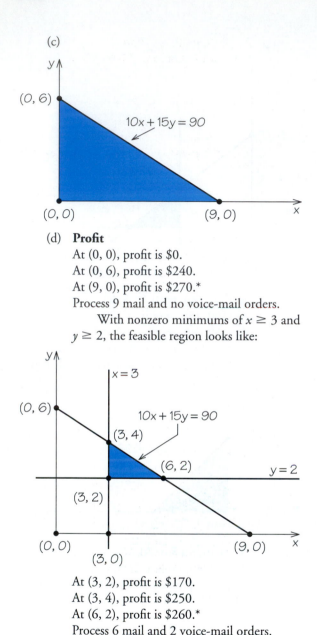

(d) **Profit**
At (0, 0), profit is $0.
At (0, 6), profit is $240.
At (9, 0), profit is $270.*
Process 9 mail and no voice-mail orders.
    With nonzero minimums of $x \geq 3$ and $y \geq 2$, the feasible region looks like:

At (3, 2), profit is $170.
At (3, 4), profit is $250.
At (6, 2), profit is $260.*
Process 6 mail and 2 voice-mail orders.

35. (a)

	Breads (600)	Mins	Profit
Multigrain			
x loaves	1	100	$8
Herb			
y loaves	1	200	$10

(b) **Constraint inequalities**   **Profit formula**
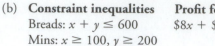
Breads: $x + y \leq 600$ $8x + $10y$
Mins: $x \geq 100, y \geq 200$

(c)

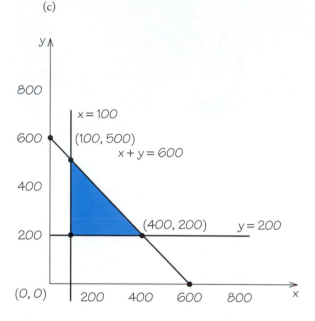

(d) **Profit**
At (100, 200), profit = $2800.
At (100, 500), profit = $5800.*
At (400, 200), profit = $5200.
Make 100 multigrain and 500 herb loaves.
    With zero minimums, $x \geq 0, y \geq 0$, feasible region is:

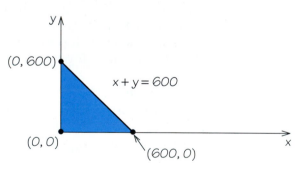

At (0, 0), profit = $0.
At (0, 600), profit = $6000.*
At (600, 0), profit = $4800.
Make no multigrain and 600 herb loaves.

37. (a)

	Layout (12 hr)	Content (16 hr)	Profit
"Hot," x	1.5	1	$50
"Cool," y	1	2	$250

(b) **Constraint inequalities**   **Profit formula**
Oven: $1.5x + 1y \le 12$ $\$50x + \$250y$
Prep: $1x + 2y \le 16$
Mins: $x \ge 0, y \ge 0$

(c)

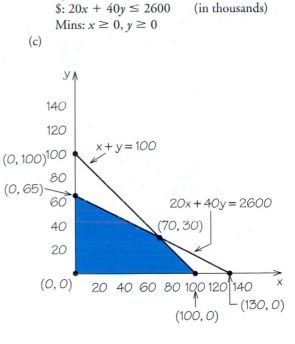

(d) **Profit**
At $(0, 0)$, the profit is $0.
At $(0, 8)$, the profit is $2000.*
At $(4, 6)$, the profit is $1700.
At $(8, 0)$, the profit is $400.
Maintain no "hot" and 8 "cool" sites.
     With nonzero minimums of $x \ge 2$ and $y \ge 3$, we get this feasible region:

At $(2, 3)$, profit is $850.
At $(2, 7)$, profit is $1850.*
At $(4, 6)$, profit is $1700.

At $(6, 3)$, profit is $1050.
Maintain 2 "hot" and 7 "cool" sites.

39. (a)

	Space (100 acres)	Money in thousands ($2600)	Profit in thousands
Modest, x houses	1	$20	$25
Deluxe, y houses	1	$40	$60

(b) **Constraint inequalities**   **Profit formula**
Space: $1x + 1y \le 100$ $\$25x + \$60y$
$: $20x + 40y \le 2600$ (in thousands)
Mins: $x \ge 0, y \ge 0$

(c)

(d) **Profit**
At $(0, 0)$, profit = $0.
At $(0, 65)$, profit = $3,900,000.*
At $(70, 30)$, profit = $3,550,000.
At $(100, 0)$, profit = $2,500,000.
Build no modest and 65 deluxe houses.
     With nonzero minimums of $x \ge 20$ and $y \ge 20$, the feasible region looks like this:

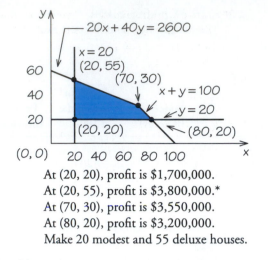

At (20, 20), profit is $1,700,000.
At (20, 55), profit is $3,800,000.*
At (70, 30), profit is $3,550,000.
At (80, 20), profit is $3,200,000.
Make 20 modest and 55 deluxe houses.

41. (a)

	Bird Count (100)	Cost $ (2400)	Profit
Pheasants, x	1	$20	$14
Partridges, y	1	$30	$16

(b) Constraint inequalities   Profit formula
Count: $1x + 1y \leq 100$ $14x + 16y$
$: 20x + 30y \leq 2400$
Mins: $x \geq 0, y \geq 0$

(c) Feasible Region

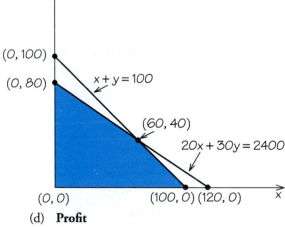

(d) Profit
At (0, 0), profit is $0.
At (0, 80), profit is $1280.
At (60, 40), profit is $1480.*

At (100, 0), profit is $1400.
Raise 60 pheasants and 40 partridges.
With nonzero minimum of $x \geq 20$ and $y \geq 10$, there is no change because the optimal production policy obeys these minimums.

43. (a)

	Shaper (50)	Smoother (40)	Painter (60)	Profit
Toy A, x	1	2	1	$4
Toy B, y	2	1	3	$5
Toy C, z	3	2	1	$9

(b) Constraint inequalities
Shaper: $1x + 2y + 3z \leq 50$
Smoother: $2x + 1y + 2z \leq 40$
Painter: $1x + 3y + 1z \leq 60$
Mins: $x \geq 0, y \geq 0, z \geq 0$
Profit formula
$4x + 5y + 9z$

(c) Optimal product policy
Make 5 toy A, no toy B, 15 toy C for a profit of $155.

45. (a)

	Chocolate (1000 lb)	Nuts (200 lb)	Fruit (100 lb)	Profit
Special, x boxes	3	1	1	$10
Regular, y boxes	4	0.5	0	$6
Purist, z boxes	5	0	0	$4

(b) Constraint inequalities   Profit formula
$3x + 4y + 5z \leq 1000$ $\$10x + \$6y +$
$1x + 0.5y + 0z \leq 200$ $\$4z$
$1x + 0y + 0z \leq 100$

(c) Make 100 boxes of Special, 175 boxes of Regular, and 0 boxes of Purist.

47. A feasible region has infinitely many points; the corner point principle tells us we only need to evaluate the profit formula at a few of those points (the corner points), not all of them.

49. (a)

	Time (240 min)	Profit
Business, x calls	4	$0.50
Charity, y calls	6	$0.40

(b)

Constraint inequalities	Profit formula
Time: $4x + 6y \leq 240$	$0.50x + $0.40y
Mins: $x \geq 0, y \geq 0$	

(c)

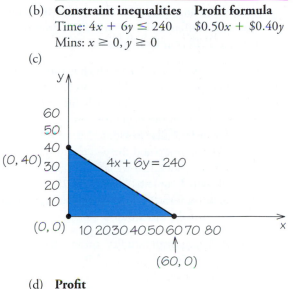

$4x + 6y = 240$

(0, 40)

(0, 0) (60, 0)

(d) **Profit**
At (0, 0), profit is $0.00.
At (0, 40), profit is $16.00.
At (60, 0), profit is $30.00.*
Make 60 business and no charity calls.

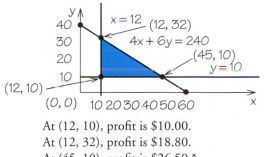

$x = 12$ (12, 32)
$4x + 6y = 240$
(45, 10)
$y = 10$
(12, 10)
(0, 0)

At (12, 10), profit is $10.00.
At (12, 32), profit is $18.80.
At (45, 10), profit is $26.50.*
Make 45 business and 10 charity calls.

51. (a)

	Machine (12 hr)	Paint (16 hr)	Profit
Bikes, x	2	4	$12
Wagons, y	3	2	$10

(b)

Constraint inequalities	Profit formula
Mach: $2x + 3y \leq 12$	$12x + $10y
Paint: $4x + 2y \leq 16$	
Mins: $x \geq 0, y \geq 0$	

(c)

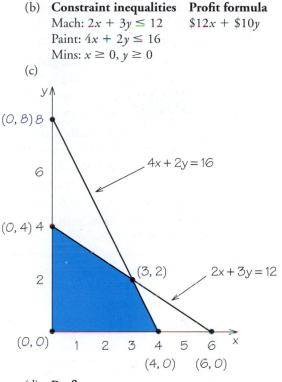

(0, 8)8

$4x + 2y = 16$

(0, 4) 4

(3, 2) $2x + 3y = 12$

(0, 0) 1 2 3 4 5 6
(4, 0)   (6, 0)

(d) **Profit**
At (0, 0), profit is $0.
At (0, 4), profit is $40.
At (3, 2), profit is $56.*
At (4, 0), profit is $48.
Make 3 bikes and 2 wagons.
 With nonzero minimums of $x \geq 2$ and $y \geq 2$ there will be no change because the optimal production policy obeys these minimums.

CHAPTER 5

1. *Population:* Employed adult women. *Sample:* The 68 women who returned the questionnaire.

3. *Population:* "Constituents," perhaps adults in her district. *Sample:* The 361 who wrote. Those who trouble to write are not representative—they feel strongly about this issue.

5. The results are not trustworthy because of voluntary response: only those who feel strongly will trouble to pay for a call.

7. People may not be truthful when speaking to a police officer. We expect less criticism of the police than if black civilian interviewers were employed.

9. If we assign labels 00 to 19 in alphabetical order, line 132 gives 08 = Foreign Languages, 17 = Sociology, 02 = Chemistry, 05 = Economics, and 16 = Psychology.

11. Label students 000 to 449 in alphabetical order (001 to 450 is also correct). Line 120 gives the first 5 members to be those labeled 281, 242, 123, 131, and 209.

13. (a) If labels 00 to 24 are assigned to the members in alphabetical order, the tickets go to 21 = Wang, 15 = Myrdal, 01 = Binet, 03 = Blum, and 17 = Spencer. Note that 21 is repeated and that it is necessary to continue to the next line of the table. (b) The answers obtained will depend on the parts of the table used. In the long run, we expect an average of 2 of the 5 tickets to go to women. (c) A rough empirical answer is based on how many of your 20 samples included cases in which no women received tickets. (In fact, the probability that no tickets go to women is about 0.056. It is somewhat unlikely that no women will receive tickets.)

15. 46% of the sample believes in life on other planets. (A recent opinion poll found this result.) We can be confident that between 43% and 49% of all adults believe in extraterrestrial life.

17. No, we can't be certain. Only 95% of all samples capture the truth about the population within their announced margin of error.

19. The effect (if any) of the tea is confounded with the effect of visits and conversation with college students. The visits alone might make the residents more cheerful.

21. Women who already feel receptive toward the baby may be more likely to take the trouble to nurse. So the mother's existing attitude is confounded with the effect of nursing.

23. A treatment (treadmill) is imposed, so this is an experiment.

25. (a) The effect of the drug would be confounded with the placebo effect and any other effects of being in a study. (b) Follow Figure 5.6, with 150 subjects in each group, placebo and hydroxyurea as the two treatments, and count and duration of pain episodes as the response variable. (c) Randomization and comparison assure that the only systematic difference between the two groups is the actual effect of hydroxyurea.

27. (a) Because students choose which version to take, there may be systematic differences between the two groups of students. Any such differences are confounded with the method of instruction. (b) The outline is similar to Figure 5.6, with 15 students in each group and the two teaching methods as the treatments. If we label the subjects 00 to 29, Group 1 contains 10, 07, 24, 25, 04, 14, 27, and so on until 15 are chosen. The remaining 15 subjects make up Group 2.

29. "Controlled scientific studies" means "randomized comparative experiments." By randomly assigning patients and comparing a group that meditates to a group treated identically except for the meditation, we can isolate the effect of meditation.

31. This problem is best done by assigning a different starting point to each of several students and combining their results. In the randomization of the previous problem (with labels in alphabetical order), two of the eight asterisks are assigned to Group 1.

33. To do this, choose a simple random sample of 5 to form Group 1. Then choose a simple random sample of 5 of the remaining 15 for Group 2, and another simple random sample of 5 of the remaining 10 for Group 3. The 5 who still remain are Group 4. It is best to relabel the 10 who remain after the second stage as 0 to 9 to speed the third sample. If the initial labels are 00 to 19, Group 1 contains 03, 04, 12, 13, and 15; Group 2 contains 17, 07, 10, 05, and 00; and the members of Group 3 depend on relabeling.

35. The average earnings of men exceeded those of women by so much that it is very unlikely that the chance selection of a sample would produce so large a difference if there were not a difference in the entire student population. But the black–white difference was small enough that it might be due to the accident of which students were chosen for the sample.

37. Question A gave 80%. The wording of Question A encourages "Yes" responses. Question B encourages "No" responses by citing the "right to contribute."

39. *Population:* All registered voters in the Second Congressional District. *Sample:* The 800 voters interviewed. The results of a larger sample are less variable, so the margin of error for our conclusion will be smaller.

41. Ann Landers's poll relies on voluntary response. It attracts readers with strong feelings, especially those with negative feelings toward their children. The random sample gives everyone the same chance, and so is much more trustworthy. The voluntary response poll gives the result 70% "No" when the truth about the population is close to 90% "Yes." Such polls give *no* useful information about anyone except the actual respondents.

43. (a) No. All states have populations very much larger than 2000. When this is true, the margin of error depends only on the size of the sample, not on the size of the population. (b) The sample sizes vary, so the margins of error will also vary.

45. The experimenter, who led the meditation group and no doubt wants to demonstrate the effectiveness of meditation, also did the final interview and rated the subjects' anxiety. He knows the meditation group well by now and cannot do an unbiased evaluation. The evaluation should be done by someone who is blind in the sense of not knowing what treatment any subject received.

47. (a) A direct comparison will eliminate the possibility that unusual nerve responses are due to something else in the diet or environment of the rats. (b) The design is similar to Figure 5.6, with 10 rats in each group and diets with and without DDT as the treatments. If the rats are labeled 00 to 19, the DDT group contains rats 07, 10, 05, 00, 15, and so on. The randomization is tedious because half the rats must be chosen. The remaining 10 form the control group.

49. (a) The effect of the drug would be confounded with the placebo effect. (b) There are 3 treatments, so follow the model of Figure 5.7 with new drug, aspirin, and placebo as the treatments and degree of pain relief as the outcome. (c) No. Knowing you are getting "only a placebo" might reduce the placebo effect. (d) Yes, because "degree of pain relief," which is subjective, might be influenced by the behavior of the medical personnel.

51. Discussion. Answers will vary.

53. (a) If the speeds are tried in order, any variable that changes over time will be confounded with conveyor speed. For example, the temperature of the solder might gradually increase over time. (b) The outline is similar to Figure 5.7, with 10 boards per group and the three conveyor speeds as the three treatments. (c) The labels are 01 to 30 (remember all must have the same number of digits). Group 1 (20 feet per second) contains 20, 03, 30, 13, 12, 07, 14, 24, 06, and 16. Continuing, Group 2 (25 feet per second) contains 27, 19, 09, 08, 17, 02, 05, 25, 18, and 22. The remaining boards form Group 3 (30 feet per minute). Because these numbers decide the order of processing, the sequence of processing speeds is 30, 25, 20, 30, 25, 20, 20, 25, 25, 30, 30, 20, 20, 20, 30, 20, 25, 25, 25, 20, 30, 25, 30, 20, 25, 30, 25, 30, 30, 20.

55. "Highly significant" means that a difference this large would almost never appear in a sample of ads just by chance. So we have strong evidence of a systematic brand effect among all ads.

CHAPTER 6

1. The individuals are 1998 motor-vehicle models. The variables are vehicle type, transmission type, number of cylinders, and city and highway miles per gallon.

3. The distribution is roughly symmetric, with center near noon (12 hours after midnight). There are no outliers or gaps.

5. (a)

48	8
49	
50	7
51	0
52	6799
53	04469
54	2467
55	03578
56	12358
57	59
58	5

   (b) The distribution is roughly symmetric, with one observation (4.88) slightly outlying.

7. The five-number summary for men is 46.9, 47.4, 51.9, 62.0, 62.9, and for women is 33.1, 38.2, 42, 49.55, 54.6. Men as a group have higher body mass than women, and their masses are somewhat more spread out.

9. (b) $M = 50.7\%$. (c) $Q_3 = 58.1\%$, so that the 1964 (Johnson defeats Goldwater), 1972 (Nixon defeats McGovern), and 1984 (Reagan defeats Mondale) elections were landslides.

11. The five-number summaries are as follows. Beef: 111, 140, 152.5, 178.5, 190. Meat: 107, 139, 153, 179, 195. Poultry: 87, 102, 129, 143, 170. Beef and meat have quite similar distributions, whereas poultry hot dogs as a group have fewer calories.

13. $M = 5.46$, $Q_1 = 5.295$, and $Q_3 = 5.615$; the five-number summary is 4.88, 5.295, 5.46, 5.615, 5.85. In a symmetric distribution, the two quartiles will fall about the same distance from the median, as will the two extremes. In this case, the quartiles are 0.165 and 0.155 from the median, and the extreme observations are 0.58 and 0.39 from the median. Note the effect of the low observation, 4.88.

15. The few very large incomes in the right tail of the skewed distribution pull up the mean. So $675,000 is the mean.

17. $s^2 = 15^2 = 225$.

19. (a) The explanatory variable x is powerboat registrations. (b) Here is the scatterplot:

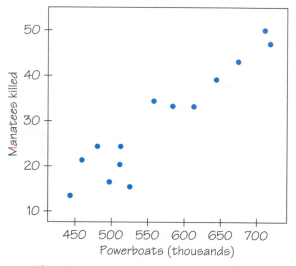

   There is an increasing and roughly straight-line overall pattern, but the points are not tightly clustered about a straight line. There are no clear outliers (1983 is closest to being an outlier).

21. (a) Choose 2 values for "weeks" on the x-axis, find the values of pH from the equation, plot the two (x, y) points, and draw the line through them. We see that pH goes down over time, by an average of 0.0053 each week. (b) For $x = 1$, pH $= 5.4247$. For $x = 150$, pH $= 4.635$. (c) The slope is -0.0053, which says that pH decreases at the rate of 0.0053 per week.

23. The result will depend on the line drawn, but should be roughly 200 to 210 manatees killed. Two million boats is a very different environment from that represented by our data. So a line based

on our data says nothing about that different environment.

25. The correlation is $r = -0.17$. Correlation measures only straight-line relationships. This relationship is very strong but curved.

27. The correlation would be $r = 1$, because there is a perfect straight-line relationship.

29. (a) There is a general increasing straight-line pattern. Spaghetti and snack cake both fall above the overall pattern; that is, the estimated calories for these two foods are unusually high relative to their true calories. (b) $r = 0.8245$. This describes the reasonably strong straight-line pattern of the plot. (c) r would not change if we added 100 to every guess. (d) For the remaining eight foods, $r = 0.9837$. Removing the two points makes the straight-line relationship stronger.

31. The regression line is $y = 11.06 - 0.0147x$.

33. Large fires cause more damage and also require more firefighters to extinguish. So the correlation is due to the size of the fires, not to a direct link between number of firefighters and damage.

35. (c) Both correlations equal 0.253; scales do not affect r.

37. (a) Round to the nearest hundred, so that Alaska's entry 4273 becomes 43. Then make a stemplot (a histogram is also fine):

```
 0 | 55666779
 1 | 022226778
 2 | 05679
 3 | 233789
 4 | 3447
 5 | 123458
 6 | 17
 7 | 34
 8 | 0
 9 | 6
10 |
11 | 28
12 | 1
13 |
14 | 4
```

Three states have populations so large that we have omitted them: New York, Texas, and California. California is certainly an outlier. It is a matter of judgment whether New York and Texas are outliers or just the upper tail of a strongly skewed distribution. The strong skewness reflects the fact that there are a few large states and many smaller ones.

The five-number summary describes this skewed distribution: 481, 1243, 3699, 6092, 31,878. In particular, the median population of a state is 3,699,000.

39. (a) For Table 6.4, Exercise 8 found the five-number summary to be 16, 25, 26, 29, 33. So $IQR = 29 - 25 = 4$, $1.5IQR = 6$, and a suspected low outlier falls below $25 - 6 = 19$. The Rolls Royce (16) is suspect. (b) For Table 6.1, the five-number summary is 5.2, 11.4, 12.7, 13.8, 18.5. So $IQR = 13.8 - 11.4 = 2.4$ and $1.5IQR = 3.6$. Suspected outliers lie below $11.4 - 3.6 = 7.8$ or above $13.8 + 3.6 = 17.4$. Thus, Alaska (5.2) and Florida (18.5) are suspect.

41. The mean is 141.8 days and the median is 102.5 days. Because the distribution is extremely right-skewed, the mean is much larger than the median.

43. Discussion. Answers will vary.

45. A single high outlier is enough. For the data 1, 1, 2, 3, 3, 4, 28, the third quartile is 4 and the mean is $42/7 = 6$.

47. (a) The regression line has slope 1.707 and intercept 6.083. (b) We predict $y = 9.07\%$. This is $\bar{y}$, as expected.

49. (a) All four sets of data have $r = 0.8162$ and regression line $y = 3 + 0.5x$ to a close approximation. (b) Here are the plots:

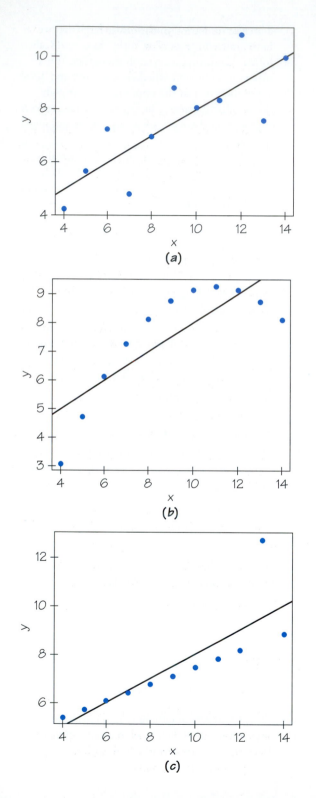

(a)

(b)

(c)

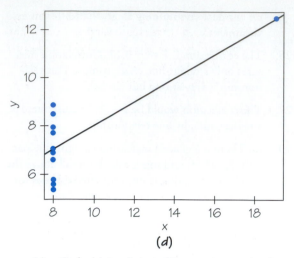

(d)

(c) Only (a) is a "normal" regression setting in which the line is useful for prediction. Plot (b) is curved, (c) has an extreme outlier in y, and (d) has all but one x identical. The lesson: plot your data before calculating.

51. (a) Here is the plot:

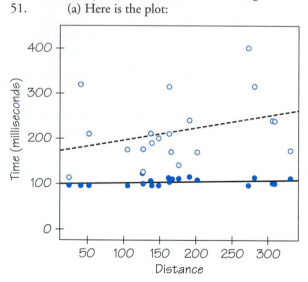

(b) We know the subject is right-handed because times with the right hand are much lower and more uniform. There is little time–distance relationship for the right hand. Time for the left hand increases a bit with distance, but with great scatter. (c) The regression lines appear on the plot given in part (a). This is an unusual example: for the right hand, $r = 0.3047$ because the plot pattern, though strong, is almost flat—this says that there is little relationship and so r is not large. For the left hand, $r = 0.3184$, because the scatter about the line means that the relationship is not strong.

CHAPTER 7

1. Results will vary.

3. Results will vary.

5. In a very large number of deals, you will be dealt three of a kind 1/50 of the time.

7. (a) $S = \{0, 1, 2, 3, 4, 5, 6, 7, 8, 9, 10\}$. (b) $S = \{0, 10, 20, 30, 40, 50, 60, 70, 80, 90, 100\}$. (c) $S = \{Yes, No\}$.

9. With obvious abbreviations, $S = \{TMS, TMN, TFS, TFN, CMS, CMN, CFS, CFN\}$.

11. (a) 0.1. (b) 0.3. (c) 0.5, 0.4.

13. 0.67, 0.33.

15. (a) BBB, BBG, BGB, GBB, BGG, GBG, GGB, BBB each have probability 1/8 = 0.0125.
(b) The model is

Girls	0	1	2	3
Probability	0.125	0.375	0.375	0.125

(c) 0.375 + 0.125 = 0.5. (d) 4/8 = 0.5.

17. $(19 \times 6 \times 19)/(20 \times 6 \times 20) = 0.9025$.

19. There are $10^4 = 10{,}000$ possible PINs. Of these, $9^4 = 6561$ have no 0s. So the probability of at least one 0 is 3439/10,000 = 0.3439.

21. $\mu = 1.5$.

23. $\mu = \$0.50$ (or $-\$0.50$ if we count the $1 cost to play).

25. (a) 12/38 = 0.316. (b) $-2/38 = -\$0.053$.

27. (b) $\mu = 141.8$. Results will vary for parts (c) and (d). (e) At 141.8.

29. (a) 2.5% (half of 5%). (b) 64 inches and 74 inches. (c) 16% (half of 32%).

31. 1.6 ± 0.17.

33. (a) 50%. (b) 2.5% (half of 5%). (c) The quartiles

are 93.25 and 126.75; the center half of all scores lies between the quartiles.

35. (a) 0.5, 0.16. (b) 0.5, 0.025.

37. About 4.9% $(7/\sqrt{2})$.

39. $\sigma = 1.394$; the column bet and "red or black" have the same mean outcome, but the variation (as measured by σ) is larger for the column bet. In the short run, a gambler is more likely to win (or to lose a lot) playing column bets.

41. $S = \{0, 1, 2, 3, \ldots\}$ (all nonnegative whole numbers) is the simplest choice, because we do not have to decide a largest possible amount.

43. In a shuffled deck, all 13 possible outcomes are equally likely, so each has probability 1/13. Any assignment that obeys Laws 1 and 2 is legitimate.

45. (a) $26 \times 26 \times 26 \times 10 \times 10 \times 10 = 17{,}576{,}000$. (b) $4 \times 26 \times 26 \times 10 \times 10 \times 10 = 2{,}704{,}000$. (c) $36^6 = 3.65616 \times 10^{15}$.

47. There are 16 possibilities: BBBB, BBBG, BBGB, BGBB, GBBB, BBGG, BGBG, GBBG, GBGB, BGGB, GGBB, GGGB, GGBG, GBGG, BGGG, GGGG. (a) 8/16 = 0.5. (b) 5/16 = 0.3125. (c) 10/16 = 0.625.

49. (a) The mean is $-\$0.25$. The standard deviation is $1.30. (b) The mean is $-\$0.28$, so Mark 2 is less favorable. The standard deviation is $2.85.

51. (a) 300. (b) No difference. (c) No. If decisions were based on maximizing the mean number of survivors, we would always choose the second program.

53. (a) The median (same as the mean) is 10%. (b) 9.6% to 10.4%. (c) 9.866% to 10.134%.

55. (a) 234 and 298 days. (b) Shorter than 234 days.

57. 245.5 days or shorter.

CHAPTER 8

1. 65 is a statistic, 63 a parameter.

3. 48% is a statistic, 52% a parameter.

5. Sketch the curve, then mark the axis: center at 75%, standard deviation 1.936% (distance to change-of-curvature points).

7. 1.18%, 1.26%, 1.29%, 1.26%, 1.18%.

9. If we repeated Gallup's sampling process, we might get a different answer, but 95% of all samples will give an answer that is within ± 3% of the percent of all adults who favor immersion. Gallup announces the margin of error to allow for this variation and indicate how accurate his result will usually be.

11. $\hat{p} = 66\%$, so the confidence interval is 66% ± 7.0%.

13. (a) $\hat{p} = 66\%$ had a TV in their room, confidence interval 66% ± 2.93%; $\hat{p} = 18\%$ favored Fox, confidence interval 18% ± 2.37%. (b) Our margins of error are a bit smaller than ± 3%. This is in part because news reports give one margin of error that covers all $\hat{p}$'s.

15. Only (c). The margin of error includes only the random sampling error described by the sampling distribution of the statistic.

17. The margin of error would be greater than ± 3 points. Smaller sample sizes result in wider intervals for the same level of confidence. (Because the poll did not use a simple random sample, we cannot calculate the margin of error.)

19. Normal with mean = 12 cm and standard deviation $\sigma_{\bar{x}} = 0.002$ cm.

21. (a) Normal with mean 0 meter and standard deviation $\sigma_{\bar{x}} = 0.0173$ meter. (b) Between ± 0.0346 meter.

23. 3.4137 ± 0.00115 grams.

25. $2\sigma/\sqrt{12} = 0.0005774$. Because of the $\sqrt{n}$, multiplying the sample size by 4 always halves the margin of error.

27. 4950 ± 167.6 bacteria per milliliter.

29. Center line = 75°, control limit = 75° ± 0.75°.

31. Center line = 5 grams, control limits = 5 ± 0.00173 grams.

33. The control charts in Exercises 33 to 35 have center line (drawn solid) at 11.5 and control limits (drawn dashed) at 11.2 and 11.8. In this case,

samples 12 and 20 fall above the upper control limit. The last 11 points lie above the center line. It appears that the mean shifted upward at about sample 11.

35. Samples 19 and 20 fall above the upper control limit. The last 11 points lie above the center line. The run of 9 rule signals at sample 18.

37. The percentages of students who smoke for each parent condition are: both parents smoke, 22.5%; one parent smokes, 18.6%; neither parent smokes, 13.9%. There is a clear association between parent smoking and student smoking, with students of smoking parents being more likely to smoke themselves.

39. (a) Alaska: 501/3775 = 13.3%, America West: 787/7225 = 10.9%. (b) For Los Angeles,

$$\text{Alaska Airlines } \frac{62}{559} = 11.1\%$$

$$\text{America West } \frac{117}{811} = 11.4\%$$

For Phoenix,

$$\text{Alaska Airlines } \frac{12}{233} = 5.2\%$$

$$\text{America West } \frac{415}{5255} = 7.9\%$$

and so on. (c) America West flies most often from sunny Phoenix, where there are few delays. Alaska Airlines flies most often from Seattle, where fog and rain cause frequent delays.

41. No. A confidence interval for the *mean* of a distribution tells us nothing about where the middle 95% of the observations making up the distribution lie.

43. (a) 47% ± 3%. (b) Another sample would probably give a different percent. We must take into account this sampling variability when announcing a conclusion about the population. (c) This particular result (47% ± 3%) was obtained by a method that in 95% of all samples gives an interval covering the true population percent.

45. (a) 20% ± 5.66%. (b) 80% ± 8%.

47. (a) The distribution is somewhat skewed to the right. (b) $\bar{x} = 7.075\%$, so a 95% confidence interval is 7.075% ± 1.058%. (c) Yes. The entire 95% confidence interval lies above 5.5%, so we are 95% confident that the true mean is greater than 5.5%.

49. 59.3% ± 4.01%. The 68% confidence interval is half as wide as the 95% confidence interval (one standard deviation rather than two) because a smaller margin of error is sufficient if we allow lower confidence in the result.

51. (a) $\hat{p} \pm 1.28\sqrt{\hat{p}(100 - \hat{p})/n}$. (b) 59.3% ± 5.13%.

53. (a) $\bar{\bar{x}} = 3.064\%$. (b) The limits are $\bar{\bar{x}} \pm 3\bar{s}/\sqrt{n}$, or 3.064% ± 11.574%. (c) Points 1, 4, and 5 lie outside the control limits. There are no runs of 9 on one side of the center line. The plot shows that Wal-Mart stock was more volatile early in the period covered by the data.

55. We would not deprive you of the joy of creation by giving this away.

CHAPTER 9

1. (a) 51593-2067; 2. (b) 50347-0055; 1. (c) 44138-9901; 1.

3. (a) 20782-9960. (b) 55435-9982. (c) 52735-2101.

5. If a double error in a block results in a new block that does not contain exactly two long bars, we know this block has been misread. If a double error in a block of five results in a new block with exactly two long bars, the new block gives a different digit than the original one. If no other digit is in error, the check digit catches the error, since the sum of the 10 digits will not end in 0. So, in every case an error has been detected. Errors of the first type can be corrected just as in the case of a single error. When a double error results in a legitimate code number, there is no way to determine which digit is incorrect.

7. 3.

9. 3.

11. 5.

13. 2.

15. X.

17. 9.

19. 2.

21. F.

23. No. The computer only needs to know which digit is the check digit.

25. (a) 7. (b) 4. (c) 7. (d) 2.

27. 0-669-09325-4.

29. The check digit would be the same.

31. S000, S200, L550, L300, E663, O451.

33. 42758.

35. March 29, female; September 17, male.

37. If you replace each a in the strings by a short bar and each b by a long bar, the resulting Postnet bar code represents the digits 1, 2, 3, 4, 5, 6, 7, 8, 9, 0, in order.

39. Substitution of b for a where $|b - a| = 5$ in positions 1, 5, 7, 9, and 11 is undetected; all errors in position 3 are undetected; substitution of b for a where $b - a$ is even in position 8 is undetected; the transposition $ab \rightarrow ba$ changes the sum used to calculate the check digit by $b - a$.

41. 5.

43. Since many people don't like to make their age public, this method is used to make it less likely that people would notice that the license number encodes year of birth.

45. The combination 72 contributes $7 \cdot 1 + 2 \cdot 3 = 13$ or $7 \cdot 3 + 2 \cdot 1 = 23$ (depending on the location of the combination) toward the total and 3 toward the check digit (since only the last digit of the total matters). The combination 27 also contributes 3 toward the check digit. So, the error is not detected. When the combination 26 con-

tributes 0 to the check digit, the combination 62 contributes 2 to the check digit. Also, when the combination 26 contributes 2 to the check digit, the combination 62 contributes 0 to the check digit. In both cases the check digit for the number resulting from the transposition error will not match the check digit for the correct number.

47. The Canadian scheme detects any transposition error involving adjacent characters. Also, there are 21,866,000 possible Canadian codes, but only 100,000 U.S. 5-digit ZIP codes. Hence the Canadian scheme can target a location more precisely.

CHAPTER 10

3. (a) 6. (b) 3.

5. 1001101.

7. 000000, 100011, 010101, 001110, 110110, 101101, 011011, 111000.

9. 0000000, 1000001, 0100111, 0010101, 0001110, 1100110, 1010100, 1001111, 0110010, 0101001, 0011011, 1110011, 1101000, 1011010, 0111100, 1111101. No, since 1000001 has weight 2.

11. 000000, 100101, 010110, 001011, 110011, 101110, 011101, 111000. 001001 is decoded as 001011; 011000 is decoded as 111000; 000110 is decoded as 010110.

13. a and b.

15. 23, 49, 16.

17. 13.

19. The integer x is encrypted as $(x + 3) \bmod 26$.

21. 111101000111001010; AABAACAEADB.

23. t, n, and r; e.

25. In the Morse code a space is needed to determine where each code word ends. In a fixed-length code of length k, a word ends after each k digit.

27. 00000000, 00010111, 00101110, 01001011, 10001101, 11000110, 10100011, 10011010, 01100101, 01011100, 00111001, 11101000, 11010001, 10110100, 01110010, 11111111.

The code will detect any three errors or correct any single error.

29. $2^5 = 32$.

31. 0000, 1012, 2021, 0111, 0222, 1120, 2210, 2102, 1201.

33. $3^4 = 81$; $3^6 = 729$.

CHAPTER 11

1. A dictatorship satisfies condition (2): If a new election is held and every voter (in particular, the dictator) reverses his or her ballot, then certainly the outcome of the election is reversed. A dictatorship also satisfies condition (3): If a single voter changes his or her ballot from being a vote for the loser of the previous election to being a vote for the winner of the previous election, then this single voter could not have been the dictator (since the dictator's ballot was not a vote for the loser of the previous election). Thus, the outcome of the new election is the same as the outcome of the previous election. A dictatorship, however, fails to satisfy condition (1): If the dictator exchanges marked ballots with any voter whose marked ballot differs from that of the dictator, then the outcome of the election is certainly reversed.

3. Minority rule satisfies condition (1): An exchange of marked ballots between two voters leaves the number of votes for each candidate unchanged, so whichever candidate won on the basis of having fewer votes before the exchange still has fewer votes after the exchange. Minority rule also satisfies condition (2): Suppose candidate X receives n votes and candidate Y receives m votes, and candidate X wins because $n < m$. Now suppose that a new election is held, and every voter reverses his or her vote. Then candidate X has m votes and candidate Y has n votes, and so candidate Y is the new winner. Minority rule, however, fails to satisfy condition (3): Suppose, for example, that there are 3 voters, and that candidate X wins with 1 out of the 3 votes. Now suppose that one of the 2 voters who voted for candidate Y reverses his or her vote. Then candidate X would have 2 votes, and candidate Y would have 1 vote, thus resulting in a win for candidate Y.

5. (a) Plurality: *A* (with 4 first-place votes).
   (b) Borda: *B* (with 15 points).
   (c) Hare: *C* (first *D* is eliminated, then *B*).
   (d) Sequential pairs with *A, B, C, D* agenda: *D*.

7. (a) Plurality: *A*.
   (b) Borda: *D*.
   (c) Hare: *E*.
   (d) Sequential pairs with *B, D, C, A, E* agenda: *E*.

9. (a) Plurality: *A*.
   (b) Borda: *D*.
   (c) Hare: *B*.
   (d) Sequential pairs with *B, D, C, A* agenda: *B*.

11. (a) Plurality satisfies Pareto: If everyone prefers *B* to *D*, then *D* has no first-place votes at all. Thus, *D* cannot be among the winners in plurality voting.
    (b) Plurality satisfies monotonicity: If an alternative wins on the basis of having the most first-place votes, then moving that alternative up one spot on some list (and making no other changes) neither decreases the number of first-place votes for the winning alternative nor increases the number of first-place votes for any other alternative. Hence, the original winner remains a winner in plurality voting.

13. (a) A Condorcet winner always wins the kind of one-on-one contest that is used to produce the winner in sequential pairwise voting.
    (b) Moving an alternative up one spot on some list only improves that alternative's chances in one-on-one contests.

15. (a) If the first election is contested using plurality voting, then *A* wins with two first-place votes. If the second election is contested the same way, then *A* and *B* tie with two first-place votes. Thus, *B* has gone from nonwinner status to winner status even though no voter reversed the order in which he or she had *B* and the winning alternative from the previous election (i.e., *A*) ranked.
    (b) If the Hare system is used instead of plurality, we still have *A* winning the first election,

and *A* and *B* tying for the win in the second election. Thus, the argument here is the same as in part (a).

17. Alternative *A* wins if the agenda is *D, C, B, A*. Alternative *B* wins if the agenda is *A, C, D, B*. Alternative *C* wins if the agenda is *D, B, A, C*. Alternative *D* wins if the agenda is *B, A, C, D*.

19. Alternative *D* is eliminated first, with *B* and *C* simultaneously eliminated at the next stage. Thus, *A* is the winner. Now suppose the voter on the far right moves *A* up. Then *D* is eliminated first, but only *B* gets eliminated in stage 2. Now *A* has 8 first-place votes to 9 for *C*, so *A* is eliminated and *C* is the winner.

21.

A	*J*	*I*	*H*	*G*	*F*	*E*	*D*	*C*	*B*
B	*A*	*J*	*I*	*H*	*G*	*F*	*E*	*D*	*C*
C	*B*	*A*	*J*	*I*	*H*	*G*	*F*	*E*	*D*
D	*C*	*B*	*A*	*J*	*I*	*H*	*G*	*F*	*E*
E	*D*	*C*	*B*	*A*	*J*	*I*	*H*	*G*	*F*
F	*E*	*D*	*C*	*B*	*A*	*J*	*I*	*H*	*G*
G	*F*	*E*	*D*	*C*	*B*	*A*	*J*	*I*	*H*
H	*G*	*F*	*E*	*D*	*C*	*B*	*A*	*J*	*I*
I	*H*	*G*	*F*	*E*	*D*	*C*	*B*	*A*	*J*
J	*I*	*H*	*G*	*F*	*E*	*D*	*C*	*B*	*A*

23. Consider the following sequence of preference lists:

Number of Voters

Rank	1	1	1
First	*A*	*B*	*A*
Second	*B*	*C*	*C*
Third	*C*	*A*	*B*

Alternative *A* is a Condorcet winner, and thus it must be the unique winner of the election contested under our hypothetical voting rule. Therefore, *A* is a winner and *B* is a nonwinner (for *this* sequence of preference lists).

Because our hypothetical voting rule satisfies independence of irrelevant alternatives, we know that alternative *B* will remain a nonwinner as long as no voter reverses his or her ordering of *B* and *A*. But to arrive at the preference lists from the voting paradox, we can move *C* (the alternative that is irrelevant to *A* and *B*) up one slot in the third voter's list. Thus, because of IIA, we know that alternative B is a nonwinner when our voting rule is confronted by the preference lists from the voting paradox of Condorcet.

The argument showing that C is a nonwinner is similar.

25. (a) $3! + 3(2!) + 3(1!) + 0! = 16.$
    (b) $3!$ (no ties) $+ 3(2)$ (two tied) $+ 1$ (three tied) $= 13.$

27. Answers will vary.

29. (a) Plurality: C.
    (b) Borda: E.
    (c) Sequential pairs with A, B, C, D, E agenda: E
    (d) Hare: D.

31. (a) A.
    (b) B.
    (c) There would be no difference in the ranking of the nominees.

CHAPTER 12

1. (a) For the 9-member committee, winning coalitions and blocking coalitions both require 5 voters. For the 8-member committee, winning coalitions also require 5 voters, but blocking coalitions must have four or more voters. (b) Winning coalitions require 6 or more votes, for both the 8- and 9-member committees. Blocking coalitions require 4 or more votes (9-member committee) or 3 or more votes (8-member committee). (c) The entire committee is the only winning coalition (8- and 9-member committees), and any coalition with one or more voters is a blocking coalition.

3. (a) (1), $\{A\}$, $\{A, B\}$; (2), $\{A\}$, $\{A, B\}$; (3) A; (4), B
    (b) (1), $\{A, B\}$, $\{A, C\}$, $\{A, B, C\}$; (2), $\{A, B\}$, $\{A, C\}$, $\{A, B, C\}$; (3), none; (4), none.
    (c) (1), $\{A, B\}$, $\{A, C\}$, $\{A, B, C\}$, (2), $\{A, B\}$, $\{A, C\}$, $\{A, B, C\}$; (3), none; (4), none.
    (d) (1), $\{A, B\}$, $\{A, C\}$, $\{A, B, C\}$; (2), $\{A\}$, $\{A, B\}$, $\{A, C\}$, $\{A, B, C\}$; (3), A; (4), none.
    (e) (1), $\{A, B\}$, $\{A, C\}$, $\{A, B, C\}$, $\{A, B, D\}$, $\{A, C, D\}$, $\{A, B, C, D\}$; (2), $\{A, B\}$, $\{A, C\}$,

$\{A, B, C\}$, $\{A, B, D\}$, $\{A, C, D\}$, $\{A, B, C, D\}$; (3), none; (4), D.
    (f) (1), $\{A, B\}$, $\{A, C\}$, $\{A, B, C\}$, $\{A, B, D\}$, $\{A, C, D\}$, $\{A, B, C, D\}$; (2), $\{A, B\}$, $\{A, C\}$, $\{A, B, C\}$, $\{A, B, D\}$, $\{A, C, D\}$, $\{A, B, C, D\}$; (3), none; (4), D.
    (g) (1), $\{A, B\}$, $\{A, C\}$, $\{A, B, C\}$, $\{A, B, D\}$, $\{A, C, D\}$, $\{A, B, C, D\}$; (2), $\{A, B\}$, $\{A, C\}$, $\{A, B, C\}$, $\{A, B, D\}$, $\{A, C, D\}$, $\{A, B, C, D\}$; (3), none; (4), D.
    (h) (1), all coalitions including A and at least two others; (2), all coalitions including A and at least two others; (3), none; (4), none.

5. As the quota increases, we have to eliminate some winning coalitions.
    (a) With a quota of 52, $\{A, D\}$ is a losing coalition.
    (b) With a quota of 55, $\{A, C\}$ is also losing.
    (c) With a quota of 58, all two-voter coalitions are losing, but coalitions of three or four voters are winning.

7. (a)

Voter	Combinations
A	Y Y Y Y Y Y Y Y N N N N N N N N
B	Y Y Y Y N N N N Y Y Y Y N N N N
C	Y Y N N Y Y N N Y Y N N Y Y N N
D	Y N Y N Y N Y N Y N Y N Y N Y N

   (b) $\{A, B, C, D\}$, $\{A, B, C\}$, $\{A, B, D\}$, $\{A, B\}$, $\{A, C, D\}$, $\{A, C\}$, $\{A, D\}$, $\{A\}$, $\{B, C, D\}$, $\{B, C\}$, $\{B, D\}$, $\{B\}$, $\{C, D\}$, $\{C\}$, $\{D\}$, $\{\ \}$.
   (c) Each subset is the coalition of those voting Y in one of the voting coalitions.
   (d) (i), 1; (ii), 4; (iii), 6.

9. $(12, 4, 4, 4)$.

11. (a) $(4, 0)$.
    (b) $(4, 4, 4)$.
    (c) $(4, 4, 4)$.
    (d) $(4, 2, 2)$.
    (e) $(8, 8, 8, 0)$.
    (f) $(8, 8, 8, 0)$.
    (g) $(8, 8, 8, 0)$.
    (h) $(12, 12, 12, 12, 12)$.

13. (a) 15.
    (b) 4950.
    (c) 4950.
    (d) 252.

15. (a) $\{A, B\}$ and $\{A, C, D\}$.
    (b) $\{A\}$, $\{B, C\}$, and $\{B, D\}$.
    (c) (8, 6, 2, 2).
    (d) (Not unique) [5 : 3, 2, 1, 1].

17. The four ordinary members can pass a motion that the chair opposes, since she does not have a veto. Thus the minimal winning coalitions are $\{C, M_1\}$, $\{C, M_2\}$, $\{C, M_3\}$, $\{C, M_4\}$, and $\{M_1, M_2, M_3, M_4\}$, all of which have a total weight of 4.

19. (a) [4 : 2, 1, 1, 1].
    (b) [6 : 2, 2, 1, 1, 1].
    (c) This system is not equivalent to a weighted system.

21. All four-voter systems can be presented as weighted voting systems.

Minimal Winning Coalitions	Weights
$\{A, B, C, D\}$	[4 : 1, 1, 1, 1]
$\{A, B\}$, $\{A, C, D\}$	[5 : 3, 2, 1, 1]
$\{A, B, C\}$, $\{A, B, D\}$	[5 : 2, 2, 1, 1]
$\{A, B\}$, $\{A, C\}$, $\{A, D\}$	[4 : 3, 1, 1, 1]
$\{A, B\}$, $\{A, C\}$, $\{B, C, D\}$	[5 : 3, 2, 2, 1]
$\{A, B\}$, $\{A, C, D\}$, $\{B, C, D\}$	[4 : 2, 2, 1, 1]
$\{A, B, C\}$, $\{A, B, D\}$, $\{A, C, D\}$	[4 : 2, 1, 1, 1]
$\{A, B\}$, $\{A, C\}$, $\{A, D\}$, $\{B, C, D\}$	[4 : 3, 2, 1, 1]
$\{A, B, C\}$, $\{A, B, D\}$, $\{A, C, D\}$, $\{B, C, D\}$	[3 : 1, 1, 1, 1]

23. $(\frac{1}{2}, \frac{1}{6}, \frac{1}{6}, \frac{1}{6})$.

25. (a) The dean has a Shapley–Shubik index of $\frac{1}{2}$, and each faculty member has an index of $\frac{1}{6}$.
    (b) The dean and provost have Shapley–Shubik indices of $\frac{7}{20}$, and each faculty member has an index of $\frac{1}{10}$.
    (c) Each of the administrators has a Shapley–Shubik index of $\frac{13}{105}$, while each faculty member has an index of $\frac{11}{70}$.

27. Among the 100 small shareholders, there will be an average of 50 yes votes, with a standard deviation of 5. The big shareholder will be a critical

voter if the number of small shareholders voting yes is between 41 and 60; that is, within two standard deviations from the mean. By the $68–95–99.7$ percent rule, the big shareholder will be a critical voter in 95% of the voting combinations. A small shareholder can be a critical voter only when joined by 60 other small shareholders (and not the big shareholder), or when joined by 40 small shareholders and the big shareholder. The probability that the small shareholder vote will break $60–40$ and the big shareholder will be on the right side is, by the same reasoning, less than 2.5%. Thus, the big shareholder is more than $95/2.5 = 38$ times as powerful as the small shareholder.

29. $\left(\frac{7}{12}, \frac{1}{4}, \frac{1}{12}, \frac{1}{12} \right)$.

31. (e).

33. (a) $C_3^5 + C_4^5 = 10 + 5 = C_4^6$.
    (b) $C_5^9 + C_6^9 = 126 + 84 = C_6^{10}$.
    (c) The coalitions that do not include the chair must contain k of the n ordinary members; thus there are C_k^n such coalitions. Coalitions that the chair belongs to have only $k - 1$ of the ordinary members, so there are C_{k-1}^n of them. Since every k-member coalition either includes the chair of doesn't include the chair, we can obtain the total number of k-member coalitions by adding C_k^n and C_{k-1}^n.

35. If there are $2m$ voters, a given voter is critical in a winning coalition if and only if the coalition has exactly $m + 1$ votes, so there will be no extra votes. That means he or she must be joined by m of the $2m - 1$ other voters. Thus, the voter is critical in C_m^{2m-1} winning coalitions and an equal number of blocking coalitions. Since there are 2^{2m} voting combinations in all, the probability of casting a critical vote is

$$\frac{2C_m^{2m-1}}{2^{2m}}$$

The following table lists the probabilities.

Number of Voters	2	4	6	8	10	12	14
Probability	$\frac{1}{2}$	$\frac{3}{8}$	$\frac{5}{16}$	$\frac{35}{128}$	$\frac{63}{256}$	$\frac{231}{1024}$	$\frac{429}{2048}$

37. [9:4, 4, 4, 1, 1, 1, 1, 1].

39. (a) 16.
    (b) 12.
    (c) 4.
    (d) If the senators vote independently, each will be a critical voter in 12 of the 32 voting combinations. If we assume the combinations are equally likely, each senator has probability $\frac{3}{8}$ of being a critical voter. The pact makes {A, B} a critical voter in $\frac{3}{4}$ of the voting combinations in which A and B vote together. C has probability $\frac{1}{4}$ of being a critical voter.

CHAPTER 13

1. Calvin gets the cannon, 43% of the unopened chest, the doubloon, the sword, the cannon ball, the wooden leg, the flag, and the crow's nest (for a total of 61.5 of his points). Hobbes gets the rest.

3. Answers will vary.

5. Mary receives the car and gives John $15,081.25.

7. Mary receives the car, and John receives the house and pays Mary $13,668.75.

9. E receives the Duesenberg and Cord and pays $8500, F receives the Bentley and Aston-Marton and pays $7500, and G receives the Ferrari plus $16,000.

11. Carol chooses the investments first. The final allocation gives Carol the investments, the boat, and the washer–dryer, while it gives Bob the car, the television, and the CD player.

13. Fred chooses the boat first. The final allocation gives Fred the boat, the car, and the motorcycle, while it gives Mark the tractor, the truck, and the tools.

15. The chooser.

17. (a)

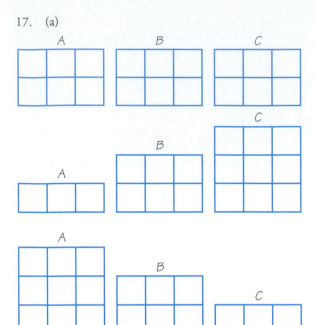

(b) Player 2 finds B acceptable (6 square units) and C acceptable (9 square units). Player 3 finds A acceptable (9 square units) and B acceptable (6 square units).

(c) Player 3 chooses A (9 square units). Player 2 chooses C (9 square units). Player 1 chooses B (6 square units). Yes. Player 2 chooses C (9 square units). Player 3 chooses A (9 square units). Player 1 chooses B (6 square units).

19. (a)

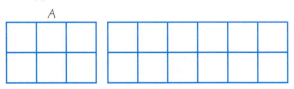

(b) Player 2 will view A as being only 3 square units, and thus he will pass.

(c) Player 3 will view A as being 9 square units, and will thus diminish it to yield A' as follows:

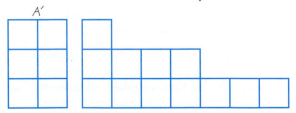

(d) Player 3 gets the piece cut off the cake (A'), because he was the last player to diminish it. He thinks it is 6 square units. (The player receiving the first piece always thinks it is $1/n$ of the cake, assuming that all n players interpret "acceptable" in this way and all follow the prescribed strategies.)

(e) If Player 1 cuts the rest, he will make each piece 7 square units. Player 2 will choose the rightmost piece, which he thinks is 10 square units.

(f) If player 2 cuts the rest, he will make each piece 8 square units. Player 2 will choose the leftmost piece, which he thinks is $8\frac{2}{3}$ square units.

(g) Player 1 will cut off 6 squares again. Player 2, thinking it is 5 square units, will pass. Player 1 receives the piece, and Player 2 gets what is left (which he thinks is 11 square units).

(h) Player 2 will cut off 6 squares. Player 1, thinking it is 7 square units, will trim it and take it. Player 2 will then receive what is left, which he thinks is 11 square units.

21. (a)

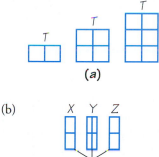

(**a**)

(b)

(**b**)

(c) Player 3 chooses any one of the three; he thinks they are all 2 square units. Player 1 chooses either of the remaining two; he thinks both are $\frac{2}{3}$ square unit. Player 2 receives the remaining piece; he thinks it is $\frac{4}{3}$ square units.

23. Player 2 trims four pieces to create a five-way tie for largest. Player 3 trims two pieces to create a

three-way tie for largest. Finally, player 4 trims one piece to create a two-way tie for largest.

25. Player 1 will think the leftover from the eleventh stage is at most $(\frac{4}{5})^{11}$ of the whole cake, which is approximately 0.086. Hence, this is less than one-tenth of the cake.

27. Bob, Carol, and Ted each divide the piece he or she has in four parts (equal in his or her own estimation). Alice then chooses one of Bob's four pieces, one of Carol's four pieces, and one of Ted's four pieces.

29. (a) The knife on the left would be at the point where the other knife started. (Thus, the portion between the knives would be the complement of the piece A.)

(b) If, for example, Carol thinks the portion between the knives at the beginning (i.e., piece A) is of size less than one-half, then she definitely will think the portion between the two knives at the end (i.e., the complement of piece A) is of size greater than one-half. Because this portion of cake between the two knives goes from being of size less than one-half in her estimation to being of size greater than one-half in her estimation, there must be a point where it is of size exactly one-half in her estimation. An analogous argument applies if Carol thinks that A is of size greater than one-half.

CHAPTER 14

1.

Party	Vote	Quota	Lower Quota	Apportionment
Social Democrats	323,839	23.0369	23	23
Democratic Socialists	880,702	62.6524	62	63
Christian Democrats	5,572,614	396.4309	396	396
Greens	1,222,498	86.9674	86	87
Communists	111,224	7.9124	7	8
Totals	8,110,867	577.0000	574	577

3. The apportionments are given in the following table:

State	Old Census	New Census
A	42	43
B	27	26
C	30	29
D	1	2
Totals	100	100

States B and C had population increases and decreased apportionments. Although the population of state D decreased slightly, its apportionment increased. This is an example of the population paradox.

5. If the fractional part of q is less than 0.5, then $q + 0.5$ is still less than $\lceil q \rceil$. Therefore $\lfloor q + 0.5 \rfloor = \lceil q \rceil = \langle q \rangle$ in this case. If the fractional part of q is greater than or equal to 0.5, then $q \times 0.5 \geq \lceil q \rceil$ so $\lfloor q + 0.5 \rfloor = \lceil q \rceil = \langle q \rangle$.

7.

Class	Enrolled	**Apportionments**		
		Hamilton	Jefferson	Webster
Geometry	76	3	3	3
Algebra	19	1	0	1
Calculus	20	1	1	1
Total	115	5	4	5
Multiplier	—		1.15	1

With the Jefferson method, geometry and algebra are tied for the fifth section. They have identical critical multipliers, $\frac{23}{19}$.

9. (b)

State	Quota	Hamilton	Jefferson	Webster
National	87.85	88	90	90
Splinter #1	1.26	2	1	1
Splinter #2	1.25	2	1	1
Splinter #3	1.24	1	1	1
Splinter #4	1.23	1	1	1
Splinter #5	1.22	1	1	1
Splinter #6	1.21	1	1	1
Splinter #7	1.20	1	1	1
Splinter #8	1.19	1	1	1
Splinter #9	1.18	1	1	1
Splinter #10	1.17	1	1	1
Total	100	100	100	100
Inf. factor		—	1.025	1.019

(c) With this example, all of the divisor methods violate the quota condition.

11. Massachusetts gets the seat.

13. Algebra, 3 sections; geometry and calculus, 1 section each. The deflation factor was 0.919.

15. (a) The triangle is a right triangle, since

$$AB + \left(\frac{A - B}{2}\right)^2 = AB + \frac{A^2 - 2AB + B^2}{4}$$
$$= \frac{A^2 + 2AB + B^2}{4}$$
$$= \left(\frac{A + B}{2}\right)^2$$

Since the hypotenuse is always the longest side, the arithmetic mean is greater than the geometric mean.

(b) Hill–Huntington rounds q upward when q is greater than the geometric mean of $\lfloor q \rfloor$ and $\lceil q \rceil$, while Webster rounds up when q is greater than the arithmetic mean. Since the geometric mean is less, Hill–Huntington rounds up all numbers that Webster does, and some that Webster doesn't. Thus, if $\langle q \rangle = \lceil q \rceil$, Webster has rounded up. Hill–Huntington does the same, and so the inequality is an equality. On the other hand, if Webster rounds down, so that $\langle q \rangle = \lfloor q \rfloor$, then Hill–Huntington may still round up, in which case $\langle q \rangle < \langle\langle q \rangle\rangle$, or it may round down, so that equality holds.

(c) The sum of the rounded quotas under the Webster method is less than or equal to the sum of the Hill–Huntington rounded quotas, because the inequality says that each individual Webster rounded quota is less than or equal to the corresponding Hill–Huntington rounded quota. Therefore, if the sum of the rounded quotas is greater than the house size under Webster, so that Webster must deflate, Hill–Huntington will certainly have to deflate, and may have to deflate more than Webster. This favors small states. If the Webster rounded quotas add up to the house size, so that Webster is neutral, Hill–Huntington rounded quotas may still add up to more than the house size, making deflation necessary and thus favoring small states. Finally, if Webster requires inflating the quotas, because the sum of the rounded quotas is less than the house size (this would favor large states), Hill–Huntington may require less or no inflation.

17. Let $p_1 = 1,000,000$, $p_2 = 6,000,000$, and $h = 10$. The tentative apportionment is $n_1 = 2$, $n_2 = 9$, for a total of 11 seats. The states are tied when it comes to relinquishing a seat.

19. 10.8%.

21. (a) Ohio, 573,017; Kansas, 621,400.
    (b) 8.44%.
    (c) 21.67%.

23. The difference in district populations is
$$\frac{p_A}{a_A} - \frac{p_B}{a_B} = \frac{a_B p_A - a_A p_B}{a_A a_B}$$
where I have simplified by combining both fractions over a common denominator. To obtain the relative difference, I divide by the smaller district population, p_B/a_B. After cancellation, this gives the required formula.

The state with the smaller representative share is A, so the relative difference is

$$\left(\frac{a_B}{p_B} - \frac{a_A}{p_A} \right) \div \left(\frac{a_A}{p_A} \right) \times 100\%$$

$$= \left(\frac{p_A a_B - a_A p_B}{p_A p_B} \right) \times \left(\frac{p_A}{a_A} \right) \times 100\%$$

$$= \frac{p_A a_B - p_B a_A}{p_B a_A} \times 100\%.$$

25. (a) The sum of the quotas is h, and, unless each quota is a whole number, the total will increase when rounding occurs. (b) We can view this method as a divisor method where the house size is whatever the sum of the upper quotas turns out to be. From this viewpoint, the actual quotas would be larger than the computed quotas, since their sum would be the sum of the actual apportionments. They would have to be deflated down to the original quotas. Deflation always favors small states. Thus California, the most populous state, would be against this method.

27. The Hamilton and Webster methods award 49 seats to the Liberals. The Jefferson method awards 48, with a tie for the 49th seat.

29. The Webster method would transfer one seat from Vermont to Pennsylvania.

31. (a) 12,606.
    (b) 8994.

33. (a) Let $n = \lfloor q \rfloor$. If q is between n and $n + 0.4$, then the Condorcet rounding of q is equal to n. Since $q + 0.6 < n + 1$ in this case, it is also true that $\lfloor q + 0.6 \rfloor = n$. On the other hand, if $n + 0.4 \leq q < n + 1$, then the Condorcet rounding of q is $n + 1$, and also $n + 1 \leq q + 0.6 < n + 1.6$, so $\lfloor q + 0.6 \rfloor = n + 1$.

    (b) The method favors small states, since numbers will be rounded up more often than down; and this makes it more likely that the quotas will be adjusted downward.

    (c) $m_i = (n_i + 0.4)/q_i$ if the total apportionment must increase; $m_i = (n_i - 0.6)/q_i$ if it must decrease.

35. Let $f_i = q_i - [q_i]$ denote the fractional part of the quota for state i. Since the Hamilton method as-

signs to each state either its lower or its upper quota, each absolute deviation is equal to either f_i (if state i received its lower quota) or $1 - f_i$ (if it received its upper quota). For convenience, let's assume that the states are ordered so that the fractions are decreasing, with f_1 the largest and f_n the smallest. If the lower quotas add up to $h - k$, where h is the house size, then states 1 through k will receive their upper quotas. The maximum absolute deviation will be the larger of $1 - f_k$ and f_{k+1}. To achieve any other apportionment that satisfies the quota condition, we would have to start by transferring a seat from a state j, where $j \leq k$ to a state l, where $l > k$. The new absolute deviations would be f_j (since now state j has its lower quota) and $1 - f_l$ (because state l has its upper quota). Because of the way the fractions have been ordered, we have $f_j \geq f_{k+1}$ and $1 - f_l \geq 1 - f_k$. Therefore, the absolute deviation for one of states j and l will be equal to or exceed the maximum absolute deviation of the Hamilton apportionment. This proves that no apportionment that meets the quota condition has a lower maximum absolute deviation. Apportionments that do not satisfy the quota condition always have maximum absolute deviation in excess of 1, while Hamilton apportionments always have maximum absolute deviation less than 1.

CHAPTER 15

1. (a) and (b) Saddlepoint at row 1 (maximin strategy), column 2 (minimax strategy), giving value 5. (c) Row 2 and column 1.

3. (a) No saddlepoint. (b) Rows 1 and 2 are both maximin strategies; column 1 is the minimax strategy. (c) None.

5. (a) and (b) Saddlepoint at row 3 (maximin strategy), column 2 (minimax strategy), giving value -20. (c) Columns 1 and 2.

7. Batter's optimal mixed strategy is (1/4, 3/4), and pitcher's is (1/4, 3/4), giving value .275.

9. Saddlepoint is "not cheat" and "audit," giving value $-\$100$.

11. (a)

	Officer Does Not Patrol	Officer Patrols
You park in street	0	-40
You park in lot	-32	-16

(b) You: $(\frac{2}{7}, \frac{5}{7})$; officer: $(\frac{1}{7}, \frac{4}{7})$; value: $-\$22.86$.
(c) It is unlikely that the officer's payoffs are the opposite of yours—that she always benefits when you do not.
(d) Use some random device, such as a die with seven sides.

13. (a) Move first to the center box; if your opponent moves next to a corner box or to a side box, move to a corner box in the same row or column. There are now six more boxes to fill, and you have up to three more moves (if you or your opponent does not win before this point), but the rest of your strategy becomes quite complicated, involving choices like "move to block the completion of a row/column/diagonal by your opponent."
(b) Showing that your strategy is optimal involves showing that it guarantees at least a tie, no matter what choices your opponent makes.

15. Player I should play H, winning 1 on average.

17. (a) Player II should avoid "call" because "fold" dominates it.
(b) Player I: $(\frac{1}{3}, \frac{2}{3}, 0)$; player II: $(\frac{2}{3}, 0, \frac{1}{3})$; value: $-\frac{1}{12}$.
(c) Player II. Since the value is negative, player II's average earnings are positive and player I's are negative.
(d) Yes. Player I bets first while holding L with probability $\frac{2}{3}$. Player II raises while holding L with probability $\frac{1}{3}$, so sometimes player II raises while holding L.

19. The Nash equilibria are (4, 3) and (3, 4). [It would be better if the players could flip a coin to decide between (4, 3) and (3, 4).]

21. These choices give x as an outcome. X certainly would not want to depart from a strategy that

yields a best outcome; furthermore, neither Y's departure to another outcome in the first column, nor Z's departure to another outcome in the second row, can improve on x for these players. It seems strange, however, that Z would choose x over z, since z is sincere and dominates x. Thus, there seem few if any circumstances in which this Nash equilibrium would be chosen.

23. X no longer has a dominant strategy, so one must consider two possibilities: (1) that X votes for x, as assumed in the 3×3 outcome matrix in Figure 15.4; and (2) that X votes for y (X would never vote for his worst choice, z), as assumed in the 3×3 outcome matrix in Figure 15.5. In the case of (1), Y's strategy y dominates x and z, and Z's strategy x is dominated by y and z, giving a reduced 1×2 matrix, in which Z would choose y, yielding y as the outcome if X chose x. In the case of (2), Y's strategy of y and Z's strategy of z are dominant, yielding y as the outcome if X chose y. In both cases, note that Y would choose y; knowing this, Z would also choose y if Z wanted to prevent the possibility that x would be chosen (x is Z's worst outcome). X's tacit deception of announcing for y, and then voting for it, would induce Z to vote for z, but y would still be the outcome. If X actually voted for x, Y's deception would be revealed, but then there would be a three-way tie, leaving unclear what would be the outcome, and therefore whether revealed deception was worthwhile.

25. B will shoot C, because it leads to $(3, 3, 1)$, which is better for B than $(2, 2, 2)$. Because $(3, 3, 1)$ is also better for A than either $(1, 1, 4)$ or $(1, 4, 1)$—the survivors of the other branches that A can choose—A will not shoot initially, and B will shoot C.

27. B will be indifferent between shooting or not shooting C, because whatever B does, he or she will be shot in the end by A.

29. (a) No saddlepoint. (b) Row 2 is the maximin strategy; column 1 is the minimax strategy. (c) None.

31. (a) Four saddlepoints at the four 5s in the payoff matrix. (b) Rows 1 and 3 are the maximin strategies; columns 2 and 4 are the minimax strategies; the saddlepoints at the four intersections of these rows and columns give the same value of 5. (c) Rows 2 and 4.

33. (a) Whatever box the first player chose, choose a box as close as possible to that box. If there are several equally close boxes (e.g., that are all adjacent to the box the first player chose), choose one of these closest boxes at random. (b) No.

35. (a) Leave umbrella at home if there is a 50% chance of rain; carry umbrella if there is a 75% chance of rain.

   (b) Carry umbrella in case it rains.

   (c) Saddlepoint at "carry umbrella" and "rain," giving value -2.

37. Player II's first strategy is dominant; $(3, 4)$ is a Nash equilibrium.

39. Consider the 7-person voting game in which 3 voters have preference xyz (one of whom is chair), 2 voters have preference zxy, and 2 voters have preference zyx. Then for the 3 xyz voters, voting for both x and y dominates voting for only x; and for the 2 zyx voters, voting for only z dominates voting for both z and y. With the dominated strategies of x and zy eliminated, in the second-reduction matrix z dominates zy for the 2 zyx voters, yielding the sophisticated outcome z, which is the chair's worst outcome.

CHAPTER 16

1. (a) 1. (b) 3; 9 times as large. (c) 4; 24 in.². (d) Almost, but not exactly. (e) The 4-by-6 prints are almost twice as expensive per square inch of paper. (f) 79 cents; $1.46.

3. (a) 1/45. (b) The volume of the real human is $45^3 = 91,125$ times as large as the volume of the figure. (c) 450 cm = 4.5 m.

5. (a) Always. (b) Sometimes. (c) Always. (d) Sometimes. (e) Always. (f) Sometimes. (g) Sometimes (when the rectangle is also a square). (h) Always. (i) Never. (j) Sometimes.

7. (a) The new altar would have a volume 8 times as large—not "8 times greater than" or "8 times larger than," and definitely not "twice as large"—as the old altar. (b) $\sqrt[3]{2} \approx 1.26$.

9. The writer of the ad meant that the volume was 2.5 times as much before packaging. Since 2.5 bags have been compressed to one bag, the new volume is $1/2.5 = 0.4$ "times as much as" before. We could also correctly say that the peat moss has been compressed "to 40% of its original volume" or "by 60%," or that the compressed volume is "60% less than" the original volume.

11. (a) $26.70. (b) $482.57. (c) $60.12. (d) 1970: $1.09; 1974: $2.40.

13. 36 mpg.

15. (a) 0.00013 ton. (b) We assume that all parts of the scale model are made of the same materials as the real locomotive. (c) 0.27 lb. (d) 0.12 kg. (e) 0.00012 metric ton.

17. $1.29.

19. 185 m, or 607 ft.

21. (a) 900 lb/ft^3. (b) Almost twice as dense. (c) Since 230 lb of compost is supposed to add about 5%, the original should be about 230 lb divided by 0.05, or 4600 lb. The revised quotation should say that the mineral soil weighs about 4500 lb.

23. (a) 400,000 lb. (b) 28 lb/in.^{2}.

25. 470,000 lbs, or almost 240 tons.

27. $\sqrt{12} \times 20$ mph $= 69$ mph.

29. A small warm-blooded animal has a large surface-area-to-volume ratio. Pound for pound, it loses heat more rapidly than a larger animal, hence must produce more heat per pound, resulting in a higher body temperature.

31. $A \propto d^2$ and $A \propto M^{3/4} \propto (d^2 h)^{3/4} = d^{3/2} h^{3/4}$, so $d^2 \propto d^{3/2} h^{3/4}$, hence $d^{1/2} \propto h^{3/4}$ and $d \propto h^{3/2}$.

33. 9 ft 3 in. to 11 ft 9 in. (in modern times there have been men over 9 ft tall); 282 cm to 358 cm.

35. It has disproportionately large wings compared to geometric scaling up of a bird, hence lower wing loading and lower minimum flying speed. Also, in part it glides rather than flies.

37. It is the outside of the tree branches that the lights are strung around, so that in effect you are covering the outside "area" of the tree (thought of as a cone) with strings of lights. Hence, the number of strings needed grows in proportion to the square of the height: a 30-ft tree will need $5^2 = 25$ times as many strings as a 6-ft tree. However, you could also argue that a 30-ft tree is meant to be viewed from farther away, so that the strings of lights would produce the same effect as on the shorter tree if they were strung farther apart, so you wouldn't need quite so many.

39. 1973: $49,500, $7,600, $38,000; 1979: $29,300, $20,900, $34,900; 1998: $35,200, $12,400, $25,900, $12,400, $5,200.

41. (a) $20 \left(\dfrac{60}{30}\right)^{1/4} = 20 \cdot 2^{1/4} = 23.8$ m.
    (b) 480 years.
    (c) 16,000 years.

WP1. A human grows from a height (length) of between 1 and 2 ft to a height usually between 5 and 6 ft, hence by a scaling factor of between 2.5 and 6. Under proportional scaling, its weight would have to go up by the cube of the scaling factor, hence by a factor of between $2.5^3 = 15.6$ and $6^3 = 216$; so it would have a weight between $15.6 \times 10 = 156$ lb and $216 \times 5 = 1,080$ lb. But the vast majority of human adults weight between 100 and 200 lbs.

WP3. (a) The picture shows the dollar bill shrinking in both length and width, even though the value shrinks only once. To use area to reflect the purchasing power of the dollar, the 1993 dollar should have about 5 times the area shown (and the other depictions also adjusted accordingly). (b) It is not indicated whether the graphic depicts the decline in percentage of doctors devoted solely to family practice or the decline in the total number of doctors. Taken as the former, a 55% decrease appears in terms of area as a shrinking by 80%, and in terms of implied volume as a decrease of 90%. c. Simply monstrous! The line for 27.5 mpg, which is about $1\frac{1}{2}$ as much as 18 mpg, is about 9 times as long as the line for 18 mpg.

WP5. Answers will vary.

CHAPTER 17

1. 5, 8, and 13.

3. Answers will vary.

5. (a), (b) The digits after the decimal point do not change. (c) $\phi^2 = \phi + 1$. (d) $1/\phi = \phi - 1$.

7. (a) 9. (b) 16.

9. (a) 4, 7, 11, 18, 29, 47, 76, 123. (b) 3, 1.333, 1.75, 1.571, 1.636, 1.611, 1.621, 1.617, 1.618. The ratios approach ϕ.

11. Answers will vary.

13. The seventh number is $5m + 8n$, and the total is $55m + 88n$.

15. All are true.

17. (a) B, C, D, E, H, I, K, O, X. (b) A, H, I, M, O, T, U, V, W, X, Y. (c) H, I, N, O, S, X, Z.

19. (a) MOM, WOW (both either horizontally or vertically); MUd and bUM reflect into each other. (b) pod rotates into itself; MOM and WOW rotate into each other. (c) Here are some possibilities: NOW NO; SWIMS; ON MON; CHECK BOOK BOX; OX HIDE.

21. (a) $c5$. (b) $c12$. (c) $c22$.

23. (a) $c6$. (b) $d2$. (c) $c16$.

25. (a) Vertical. (b) Vertical and every multiple of 45°. (c) Vertical and every multiple of 72°. (d) Vertical and horizontal. (e) None.

27. For all parts, translations. (a) Reflection in vertical lines through the centers of the **A**s or between them. (b) Reflection in the horizontal midline. (c) Reflection in the horizontal midline, reflections in vertical lines through the centers of the **O**s or between them; 180° rotation around the centers of the **O**s or the midpoints between them; glide reflections. (d) None, other than translations.

29. (a) $d3$. (b) $d1$. (c) $c1$.

31. (a) Yes. (b) Yes.

33. (a) $\langle T, H | H^2 = I, T \circ H = H \circ T \rangle = \{ \ldots , T^{-1}, I, T^1, \ldots ; \ldots , H \circ T^{-1}, H, H \circ T, \ldots \}$. (b) $\langle G, R | R^2 = I, R \circ G = G^{-1} \circ R \rangle = \{ \ldots , G^{-2} = T^{-1}, G^{-1}, I, G^1, G^2 = T, \ldots ; \ldots , R \circ G^{-1}, R, R \circ G, \ldots \}$.

35. $\langle R, H | R^4 = I, H^2 = I, R \circ H = H \circ R^{-1} \rangle = \{I, R, R^2, R^3, H, H \circ R, H \circ R^2, H \circ R^3\}$, where R is a rotation by 90° and H is a reflection across a line of symmetry.

37. $p111, p1a1, p112, pm11, p1m1, pma2, pmm2$.

39. $pmm2, p1a1, pma2, p112, pmm2$ (perhaps), $p1m1, pma2, p111$.

41. (a) Reflection in a vertical line. (b) Glide reflection. (c) See the figure below.

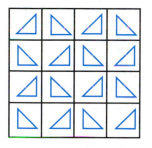

(d) cm.

43. Answers will vary.

WP1. (a) 1, 1, 3, 5, 11, 21, 43, 85, 171, 341, 683, 1365. (b) $B_n = B_{n-1} + 2B_{n-2}$. (c) 1, 3, 1.667, 2.2, 1.909, 2.048, 1.977, 2.012, 1.994, 2.003, 1.999. (d) $x = 2, -1$; we discard the -1 root. (e) $B_n = [2^n - (-1)^n]/3$.

WP3. (a) 58. (b) 12. (c) $(89000 + 5)/144 = 618$, so take soundings at 618 meters from each end, that is, at $x = 0.382$ and $x = 0.618$. These give soundings of depths 326 m and 382 m, so we discard the left region from 0 to 382 m. Since the sounding done already in the remaining region was at 382 m from the right end, the next sounding should be at 382 m from the left end, that is, at $x = 0.764$. (d) 11.

CHAPTER 18

1. Exterior: 135°. Interior: 45°.

3. $180° - \frac{360°}{n}$.

5. A regular polygon with 12 sides has interior angles of 150°, and a regular polygon with 8 sides has interior angles of 135°. No integer combination of these numbers can add up to 360°.

13. The truth table is as follows:

P	Q	¬P	¬Q	P⇔Q	¬(P⇔Q)	P∧¬Q	¬P∧Q	(P∧¬Q)∨(¬P∧Q)	¬(P⇔Q)⇔(P∧¬Q)∨(¬P∧Q)
T	T	F	F	T	F	F	F	F	T
T	F	F	T	F	T	T	F	T	T
F	T	T	F	F	T	F	T	T	T
F	F	T	T	T	F	F	F	F	T

15. The truth table is as follows:

P	Q	R	Q∧R	P∨(Q∧R)	P∨Q	P∨R	(P∨Q)∧(P∨R)	[P∨(Q∧R)]⇔[(P∨Q)∧(P∨R)]
T	T	T	T	T	T	T	T	T
T	T	F	F	T	T	T	T	T
T	F	T	F	T	T	T	T	T
T	F	F	F	T	T	T	T	T
F	T	T	T	T	T	T	T	T
F	T	F	F	F	T	F	F	T
F	F	T	F	F	F	T	F	T
F	F	F	F	F	F	F	F	T

17. The truth table is as follows:

P	Q	P ⊻ Q
T	T	F
T	F	T
F	T	T
F	F	F

19. (a) The truth table is as follows:

P	Q	P⇔Q	P∧¬Q	(P⇔Q)⇒(P∧¬Q)	¬[(P⇔Q)⇒(P∧¬Q)]
T	T	T	F	F	T
T	F	F	T	T	F
F	T	F	F	T	F
F	F	T	F	F	T

This is not a tautology.

(b) The truth table is as follows:

P	Q	¬P	¬Q	¬P∧¬Q	P∧Q	¬(P∧Q)	(¬P∧¬Q)⇔¬(P∧Q)
T	T	F	F	F	T	F	T
T	F	F	T	F	F	T	F
F	T	T	F	F	F	T	F
F	F	T	T	T	F	T	T

This is not a tautology.

(c)   The truth table is as follows:

P	Q	$\neg P$	$\neg Q$	$P \Rightarrow \neg Q$	$\neg P \Leftrightarrow (P \Rightarrow \neg Q)$
T	T	F	F	F	T
T	F	F	T	T	F
F	T	T	F	T	T
F	F	T	T	T	T

This is not a tautology.

21. Axioms: (1) M.
        (2) $B \Rightarrow \neg M$.
        (3) $\neg B \Rightarrow \neg E$.
        (4) $M \Rightarrow (\neg B \vee \neg E)$.

Statement	Justification
M	Axiom 1
$B \Rightarrow \neg M$	Axiom 2
$\neg\neg M$	Double negation
$\neg B$	Modus tollens
$\neg B \Rightarrow \neg E$	Axiom 3
$\neg E$	Modus ponens

Conclusion: M, $\neg B$, and $\neg E$.

23. Axioms: (1) $\neg I \Rightarrow (S \Rightarrow \neg A)$
        (2) $I \Rightarrow G$
        (3) $F \Rightarrow S$
        (4) $\neg S \Rightarrow H$
        (5) A
        (6) $\neg G$

Statement	Justification
$\neg G$	Axiom 6
$I \Rightarrow G$	Axiom 2
$\neg I$	Modus tollens
$\neg I \Rightarrow (S \Rightarrow \neg A)$	Axiom 1
$S \Rightarrow \neg A$	Modus ponens
A	Axiom 5
$\neg\neg A$	Double negation
$\neg S$	Modus tollens
$F \Rightarrow S$	Axiom 3
$\neg F$	Modus tollens
$\neg S \Rightarrow H$	Axiom 4
H	Modus ponens

Conclusion: $\neg G$, $\neg I$, A, $\neg S$, $\neg F$, and H.

25. The sentence is as follows:

$\forall x \, \exists y \, [(y > x) \wedge \forall u \, \forall v \, [(u > 1 \wedge v > 1) \Rightarrow$
$\neg (y = u \cdot v)]$.

CHAPTER 20

1. (a) \$1080.00; 8.000%. (b) \$1080.00; 8.000%.
     (c) \$1082.43; 8.243%. (d) \$1083.28; 8.328%.

3. \$5712.39.

5. (a) \$2032.79; \$2025.82; \$2012.20.
     (b) \$1999.00; \$1992.56. (c) \$1973.82;
     \$1906.62; \$1849.60. (d) For small and interme-
     diate interest rates, the rule of 72 gives good
     approximations to the doubling time.

7. 7.81%.

9. (a) 2, 2.59, 2.705, 2.7169, 2.718280469. (b) 3,
     6.19, 7.245, 7.3743, 7.389041321. (c) $e =$
     2.718281828 . . . ; $e^2 = 7.389056098$. . . .
     Your calculator may give slightly different an-
     swers, because of its limited precision.

11. In all cases, \$40.81, not taking into account any
      rounding to the nearest cent of the daily posted
      interest.

13. Using either "360 over 360" and 30-day months,
      or "365 over 365" and $30\frac{5}{12}$-day months: \$79.40.

15. \$173.87 (rounded up to the nearest cent, so as to
      pay the complete amount).

17. (a) 16.39%; 17.68%. (b) 48 more months. (You
      pay \$72 right away, \$72/month for 47 more
      months, then a final payment of \$35.91.) (c) 143
      months, or almost 12 years. And you still have
      \$1000 to go. (d) The first payment reduces the
      balance to \$980. Then it takes 82 more pay-
      ments, or almost 7 years. (e) While the balance is
      above \$1000, the interest totals

$\$2575.83(0.98)(0.01366) [1 + 0.9933868$
$+ 0.9933868^2 + \cdots + 0.9933868^{142}]$

$= \$2575.83(0.0133868)\dfrac{1 - (0.9933868)^{143}}{1 - 0.9933868}$

$= \$3195.25$

which a spreadsheet will confirm. For the balances
under \$1000, the geometric series formula does

not apply and we must resort to a spreadsheet, finding $645.96. The total interest is $3841.21, about one and a half times the original principal. (f) 50 payments.

19. 7.61%.

21. 5.66%. It is the effective rate.

23. (a) $(1.04)^4 = $1.17. (b) $1/1.17 = $0.85.

25. $10,000(1 - 0.12)^5(1 - 0.03)^5 \approx $4500.

27. (a) 28 yrs. (b) 117 yrs. (c) 70 yrs. (d) 50 yrs.

29. (a) 1,300 yrs. (b) 100 yrs. (c) Would tend to increase the indexes: greater efforts to recycle aluminum—spurred by the immense amount of electricity required to process aluminum ore—may reduce the need for new supplies; rate of growth of demand for new aluminum may sink from 4% to a value closer to the rate of increase of world population, 1.7%.

31. (a) About 15; 35.

33. About 70 mi³.

35. (a) 170 yrs. (b) 150 yrs. (c) 28 yrs. (d) By the time half the resource is gone, freezing the consumption level will not extend the life of the resource by very much.

WP1. Answers will vary.

WP3. Answers will vary.

WP5. (a) $726.81 (30-year); $949.89 (15-year).
(b) $261,651.60, of which $161,651.60 is interest (30-year); $170,980.20, of which $70,980.20 is interest (15-year).
(c) $90,461.19 (30-year); $93,985.33 (15-year).
(d) Answers will vary.

ANSWERS TO TECHNOLOGY CORNER EXERCISES

CHAPTER 1

Task 1.

	A	B	C	D	E	F	G
1	1		1				
2	1			1			
3			1	1			
4			1		1		
5			1			1	
6			1				1
7				1		1	
8				1			1
9					1	1	
10					1		1

Task 2.

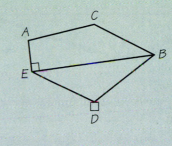

Task 3. For example:

	A	B	C	D	E	F	G	H	I	J
1	1	1								
2	1		1							
3	1			1						
4	1				1					
5	1					1				
6	1						1			
7		1	1							
8		1		1						
9		1			1					
10			1			1				
11			1				1			
12				1	1					
13				1		1				
14					1	1				
15						1		1		
16							1	1		
17							1		1	
18									1	1
19		1				1				
20		1								1
21										
22										
23	6	6	4	4	4	6	4	2	2	2

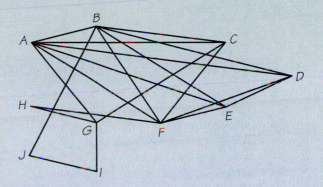

for which one possible Euler circuit is FHGIJBAGCBFDEACFADBEF.

Exploration.   If the graph is not connected, the columns of the spreadsheet can be separated into two groups which share no row elements. In the example created in the previous answer, the graph is connected.

CHAPTER 2

TASK 1.   This procedure is the same as that of Kruskal's algorithm.

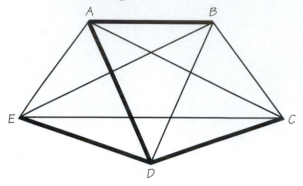

TASK 2.   The spanning tree is built from these edges: *AF, DE, EF, BF, AC.*

TASK 3.   The circuit is built from these edges: *AF, DE, EF, AC, BC, BD.*

Exploration.   The first and second sorted edges will always be used. These procedures model the "sorted edge" algorithms of the textbook.

CHAPTER 3

TASK 1.   If jobs are assigned in order of length and every person gets 10 jobs, then the loads are more equable: 33, 35, and 37 hours. However, it is possible to allocate these jobs so that each person has a 35-hour load. For example, the 33-hour and 37-hour employees can exchange a 4-hour task and a 6-hour task.

TASK 2.   Jobs can be allocated so that each person has a 35-hour load, but in doing so the people will no longer have the same number of jobs. For example, the jobs can be allocated so that one person has all five 6-hour jobs and one of the 5-hour jobs, another person has three of the 10-hour jobs and one of the 5-hour jobs, and a third person has the remaining two 10-hour jobs and the remaining three 5-hour jobs.

TASK 3.   It is possible to allocate the jobs so that each person has a 35-hour load. For example, allocate to one person three 11-hour tasks and one 2-hour task, allocate to another person three 8-hour tasks and one 11-hour task, allocate to a third person the five 2-hour tasks and the remaining 11-hour and 8-hour tasks.

TASK 4.   While other algorithms may allocate the items differently, seven bins will be required.

1	6	5	4	2	6	5
2	2	6	5	3	2	6
3	3	2	6	4	3	
4	4	3	1	5	4	
5	1			1		
1						
16	16	16	16	15	15	11

Exploration.   Seven employees are required. It is possible to assign the tasks so that each of seven employees has a 15-hour workload.

CHAPTER 4

TASK 1.   A production of 2 pints of Wholesome and 3 pints of Yummy yields a profit of $54.

TASK 2.   A production of 6 pints of Wholesome and 1 pint of Yummy yields a profit of $82.

TASK 3.   The critical points are $(0,0)$, $(0,5)$, $(20/3, 0)$, and $(6,1)$.

TASK 4.   After guaranteeing that at least 2 pints of Yummy are produced, you can produce as much as 4.5 pints of Wholesome. The resulting profit is $74.

Exploration.   Regardless of the situation, at least one maximal production mix can be found.

CHAPTER 5

TASK 1. Spreadsheet entries will vary.

TASK 2. Some of the variation may be due to human bias in naming "random numbers."

TASK 3. For example, a command **=BandBetween(1,3)** can be used to assign one of three exercise regimens to each person in the class.

TASK 4. If each decision entry uses a command such as **=BandBetween(0,1)** to determine whether or not to use a particular drug, it is possible for some people to receive no drugs. Alternately, a single command such as **=BandBetween(1,7)** can determine which of the seven drug combinations is received: *A, B, C, AB, AC, BC, ABC*.

Exploration. Histograms for the larger data sets should show less variance.

CHAPTER 6

TASK 1. Spreadsheet entries will vary, but will model the example.

TASK 2. After ordered, the average of the 25th and 26th entries is the median. The average of the 12th and the 13th entries is the first quartile. The average of the 37th and 38th entries is the third quartile.

TASK 3. Results will vary. See, for example, the following data and scatterplot in the next column.

Black	White (x)	Sum (y)	x^2	xy
1	2	3	4	6
6	5	11	25	55
1	5	6	25	30
5	4	9	16	36
4	5	9	25	45
5	6	11	36	66
5	6	11	36	66
6	5	11	25	55
2	1	3	1	3
3	3	6	9	18
2	5	7	25	35
3	4	7	16	28
5	4	9	16	36
3	3	6	9	18
2	3	5	9	15
6	3	9	9	27
4	5	9	25	45
3	2	5	4	10
3	6	9	36	54
6	6	12	36	72
sums	83	158	387	720

Least squares slope	1.511163
y intercept	1.628672

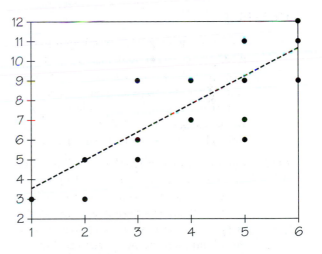

TASK 4. Results will vary, depending on the data. Estimates based on this model may be highly inaccurate.

Exploration. Any change in these values is due to sampling variability. Because the outcomes of a *single* die are equally likely, those measures of spread and average do not change due to the sample size.

CHAPTER 7

TASK 1.   For example, if the jackpot were increased from $1000 to $1125, the casino world earn 4.955 cents for each dollar game.

TASK 2.   Of the 53^3 possible outcomes, 4 will earn a Super Jackpot. Hence, the probability of pulling three identical aces is $4/53^3$. There are 48 remaining ways to earn a jackpot, for a probability of $48/53^3$. If the Super Jackpot is set at $2700, the jackpot is set at $1000, and the small prize remains at $10, then the game earns 5.168 cents for each dollar game.

prize	probability	prize*probability
$ 2,700.00	2.68678E-05	0.07254
$ 1,000.00	0.000341375	0.34137
$ 10.00	0.053440088	0.53440
	total	0.94832
	cost	$ 1.00
	average outcome	−0.05168

TASK 3.   Generally, most of these simulations will lose money.

TASK 4.   Generally, the smaller the jackpots, the more return in a typical round of play. This paradox is due to the fact that jackpots will be rarely attained.

Exploration. On average, tens of thousands of plays are required.

CHAPTER 8

TASK 1.   If in at least 19 of the 20 experiments the number of "1"s falls between 2 and 8 out of 10, then random number generator falls within the acceptable range.

TASK 2.   When 100 samples are taken, 95% of the time the observed sample $\hat{p}$ is within the interval: $.5 \pm .1$, or between .4 and .6. That is, between 40 and 60 of 100 samples should be "1"s (at least 95% of the time) if the "coin" is fair.

TASK 3.

38.82	st. dev. for sample	0.05
38.76	st. dev. for average	0.022361
38.75		
38.75	sample mean	38.778
38.81	confidence interval	38.73328
	(95% confidence)	38.82272
193.89 sum		

TASK 4.   The sample mean $\hat{\mu}$ will be approximately 25.5. The confidence interval will be $\hat{\mu} \pm 2 \cdot .1/\sqrt{5}$, or approximately $25.5 \pm .8944$.

Exploration. The scenario depends greatly on your anticipated costs.

CHAPTER 9

TASK 1.   Digits "0" and "9" can be exchanged without detection.

TASK 2.   The number is legitimate when sum/9 is a whole number. Therefore, the given number is legitimate.

	A	B	C	D
1	American Express Travelers Cheque digits			
2	3			
3	2			
4	9			
5	1			
6	0			
7	2			
8	3			
9	9			
10	1			
11	6			
12				
13	36	sum		
14	4	sum/9		

TASK 3. **Yes.** For example, the third and fourth digits can be exchanged without detection by the check digit.

TASK 4. Detection of scrambled digits varies according to the specific ISBN.

	A	B	C	D
1	ISBN Digits	Weights	Digit*Weight	
2	0	10	0	
3	7	9	63	
4	1	8	8	
5	6	7	42	
6	7	6	42	
7	2	5	10	
8	8	4	32	
9	4	3	12	
10	1	2	2	
11	9	1	9	
12				
13			220	sum

CHAPTER 10

TASK 1. For example, these code words are valid: 0001011, 1110100. No valid code word has one, two, five, or six "1" digits.

TASK 2. For example, single-digit detection will depend on the digit sums selected.

	A	B	C	D
1	1		sum of 1,2,3,4,5:	4
2	1		sum of 6,7,8,9,10:	2
3	0		sum of 1,3,5,7,9:	2
4	1		sum of 2,4,6,8,10:	4
5	1			
6	1			
7	0			
8	0			
9	0			
10	1			

TASK 3. Yes, the encoding and decoding routines should work properly.

TASK 4. For example,

	A	B	C
1		p	101
2		q	103
3		n=pq	10403
4		m=lcm(p-1,q-1)	5100
5		r	11
6		s	1391
7		rs mod m	1

Exploration. Larger p and q values create codes that are much harder to break.

CHAPTER 11

TASK 1. For example, Jan can assign Atlanta 7 points, Fresno 5 points, Cincinnati 1 point, and Evansville 2 points.

TASK 2. For example, Kim can assign Cincinnati 7 points and Boston 5 points, so that Cincinnati again has the most points.

TASK 3. For example, Kim can vote for his top five choices, in which case Gainesville will tie with Denver. It is not possible for Kim to cast his votes so that another city beats Denver.

TASK 4. For example, if Jan votes for her top four choices and Kim votes for her top five choices, Gainesville receives the most votes.

Exploration. Results will vary, depending on the diversity of responses.

CHAPTER 12

TASK 1. A motion favored by any two voters passes.

TASK 2. The outcomes of [6:5, 4, 3] and [8:7, 6, 5] are the same as those of [5:4, 3, 2].

TASK 3. 6

TASK 4.   When $q = 7$, the Banzhaf power index is (12, 4, 4, 4). When $q = 9$, the Banzhaf power index is (10, 6, 2, 2).

Exploration.   For example, when $q = 12$, all players have equal power. For example, when $q = 13$, the power is not equal.

CHAPTER 13

TASK 1.

	A	B	C	D	E	F	G
1		Adam	Beth	Chris	Danielle		Max Price
2	Car	5000	5500	5200	5600		5600
3	House	85000	90000	86000	88000		90000
4	Boat	2000	1600	2400	2200		2400
5	Jewelry	2000	2000	2000	3000		3000
6							
7	Estate sum	94000	99100	95600	98800		
8	Estate portion	23500	24775	23900	24700		
9	Items received		-90000	-2400	-8600		
10	Balance	23500	-65225	21500	16100	surplus:	-4125
11	Surplus funds	1031.25	1031.25	1031.25	1031.25		
12	Total received	24531.25	-64193.75	22531.25	17131.25		
13			and House	and Boat	and Car, Jewelry		

TASK 2.   Answers will vary, depending on the bids. Each child will recieve the items for which he or she placed the higher bid. Depending on their bids, some cash may be transferred from one child to the other.

TASK 3.   If Jill changes her bids to slightly overbid Jack for the house and slightly underbid Jack for the car and boat, then Jack's portion of the house can drop to approximately 26%.

	A	B	C	D	E
1		Jack	Jill	ratio:Jack/Jill	
2	House	70	72	0.97222222	
3	Car	20	19	1.05263158	
4	Boat	10	9	1.11111111	
5					
6	Total	100	100		
7					
8	Assets	Jack	Jill		
9	House	18.2	53.28	part to Jack:	0.26
10	Car	20			
11	Boat	15			
12	Total	53.2	53.26		

TASK 4.   If Jack assigns one point each to the car and the boat and the remaining 98 points to the house, then he will receive almost half (about 49.5%) of the house, as well as the car and the boat.

	A	B	C	D	E
1		Jack	Jill	ratio:Jack/Jill	
2	House	98	100	0.98	
3	Car	1	0	#DIV/0!	
4	Boat	1	0	#DIV/0!	
5					
6	Total	100	100		
7					
8	Assets	Jack	Jill		
9	House	48.51	50.5	part to Jack:	0.495
10	Car	1			
11	Boat	1			
12	Total	50.51	50.5		

Exploration.

	A	B	C	D	E	F	G
1		Adam	Beth	Chris	Danielle		Max Price
2	Car	5000	5500	5200	5600		5600
3	House	85000	90000	86000	88000		90000
4	Boat	2000	1600	2400	2200		2400
5							
6	Estate sum	92000	97100	93600	95800		
7	Estate portion	46000	29130	9360	9580		
8	Items received		-90000	-2400	-5600		
9	Balance	46000	-60870	6960	3980	surplus:	-3930
10	Surplus funds	1965	-1179	-393	-393		
11	Total received	47965	-62049	6587	3587		
12			and House	and Boat	and Car		

CHAPTER 14

TASK 1.   Using the Hamilton method, 5 sections for Precalculus, 10 for Calculus I, 4 for Calculus II, 7 for Calculus III, 1 for Advanced Calculus, 3 for Differential Equations, 1 for Geometry, 5 for Linear Algebra, 2 for Numerical Analysis, and 1 for Modern Algebra. Recomputing for 37 sections, Precalculus reduces to 4 sections and the 1 section of Modern Algebra is eliminated.

TASK 2.   Changing from the Hamilton method to the Jefferson method, Calculus I and Calculus III gain a section; Advanced Calculus and Modern Algebra lose their only sections.

TASK 3. Using the Webster method, 5 sections for Precalculus, 11 for Calculus I, 4 for Calculus II, 7 for Calculus III, 1 for Advanced Calculus, 3 for Differential Equations, 1 for Geometry, 5 for Linear Algebra, 2 for Numerical Analysis, and none for Modern Algebra. Recomputing for 35 sections, Precalculus reduces to 4 sections, Calculus I reduces to 9 sections, and Calculus III reduces to 6 sections.

TASK 4. Using the Hill–Huntington method, 4 sections for Precalculus, 9 for Calculus I, 4 for Calculus II, 6 for Calculus III, 1 for Advanced Calculus, 3 for Differential Equations, 1 for Geometry, 4 for Linear Algebra, 2 for Numerical Analysis, and 1 for Modern Algebra. When the number of sections increases to 41, Precalculus and Linear Algebra each get an additional section, while Calculus I and III get two additional sections apiece. The apportionments for the other subjects remain unchanged.

Exploration. The methods round to a nearby whole number. When the sizes are scaled, a quota that was previously far from a whole number might now be very close to a whole number.

CHAPTER 15

TASK 1. Pitcher's mix changes to an equal mix; batter's expectations change to 60% fastballs and 40% curveballs. The batter's overall hit average increases to 250.

TASK 2. A hit average of almost .530 is required.

TASK 3. Pitcher mixes 20% fastballs, 80% curveballs, and no knuckleballs. Batter anticipates 40% fastballs, 20% knuckleballs, and 40% curveballs.

TASK 4. Pitcher mixes approximately even proportions of fastballs, curveballs, and knuckleballs. Batter anticipates about 50% fastballs, 33% knuckleballs, and about 17% curveballs.

Exploration. For instance, the pitcher could elect to throw knuckleballs and fewer fastballs. If this

occurred, then the batter would also update her anticipated mix.

CHAPTER 16

TASK 1. $7500 in today's dollars is about $1063 in 1950 dollars, so the tractor increased about $163 in 1950 dollars. $900 in 1950 dollars is about $6350 in today's dollars, so the tractor increased about $1050 in today's dollars.

TASK 2. Assuming today's minimum wage is $5.50, the equivalent minimum wage surpassed $1 in the early 1960s. It surpassed $2 in the 1970s, and surpassed $3 and $4 in the 1980s.

TASK 3. For example, a one-story 55 ft by 55 ft house provides approximately the same floor space and less external woodwork.

TASK 4. The footing will be minimized when it is square. A house approximately 45 ft by 45 ft will provide the necessary floor space.

Exploration. The amount of roofing, in each case, can be computed by multiplying the footing by 13/12.

CHAPTER 17

TASK 1. The four decimal places are fixed after the 13th term, 233.

TASK 2. The four decimal places are fixed after the 12th term, 322.

TASK 3. The four decimal places are fixed at 1.8392 after the 16th term, 4063.

TASK 4. The sequence drifts toward the same number regardless of the values of the first three terms.

Exploration. About 5 terms are required for each additional two decimal digits.

CHAPTER 18

TASK 1. Regular polygons that have a whole number interior angle (in degrees) include those with 3, 4, 5, 6, 8, 9, 10, 12, 15, 18, and 20 sides. Other regular polygons with this feature include those with 24, 30, 36, 40, 45, 60, 72, 90, 120, 180, and 360 sides.

	A	B	C
1	Number of Sides	Exterior Angle	Interior Angle
2	3	120	60
3	4	90	90
4	5	72	108
5	6	60	120
6	7	51.4286	126.571
7	8	45	135
8	9	40	140
9	10	36	144
10	11	32.7273	147.273
11	12	30	150
12	13	27.6923	152.308
13	14	25.7143	154.286
14	15	24	156
15	16	22.5	157.5
16	17	21.1765	158.824
17	18	20	160
18	19	18.9474	161.053
19	20	18	162

TASK 2. If the polygon has more than six sides, its interior angle is more than 120° and less than 180°. The sum of two such angles is less than 360°, and the sum of three such angles is more than 360°.

TASK 3. Two hexagons and two triangles joined at each vertex form a simiregular tiling.

TASK 4. A square, hexagon, and 12-gon joined at each vertex form a semiregular tiling.

Exploration. Yes, the hexagons and triangles must alternate about each vertex.

CHAPTER 19

TASK 1.

	A	B	C	D	E	F	G	H
1	P	Q	P and Q	P or Q	not P	not Q	not P and not Q	not P or not Q
2	TRUE	TRUE	TRUE	TRUE	FALSE	FALSE	FALSE	FALSE
3	TRUE	FALSE	FALSE	TRUE	FALSE	TRUE	FALSE	TRUE
4	FALSE	TRUE	FALSE	TRUE	TRUE	FALSE	FALSE	TRUE
5	FALSE	FALSE	FALSE	FALSE	TRUE	TRUE	TRUE	TRUE

TASK 2. Every column is different. These eight logical statements are distinct.

TASK 3.

	A	B	C	D	E	F	G	H	I
1	P	Q	R	P and Q	P and R	Q and R	P or Q	P or R	Q or R
2	TRUE	TRUE	TRUE	TRUE	TRUE	TRUE	TRUE	TRUE	TRUE
3	TRUE	FALSE	TRUE	FALSE	TRUE	FALSE	TRUE	TRUE	TRUE
4	FALSE	TRUE	TRUE	FALSE	FALSE	TRUE	TRUE	TRUE	TRUE
5	FALSE	FALSE	TRUE	FALSE	FALSE	FALSE	FALSE	TRUE	TRUE
6	TRUE	TRUE	FALSE	TRUE	FALSE	FALSE	TRUE	TRUE	TRUE
7	TRUE	FALSE	FALSE	FALSE	FALSE	FALSE	TRUE	TRUE	FALSE
8	FALSE	TRUE	FALSE	FALSE	FALSE	FALSE	TRUE	FALSE	TRUE
9	FALSE	FALSE	FALSE	FALSE	FALSE	FALSE	FALSE	FALSE	FALSE

TASK 4. The statements are logically equivalent.

Exploration. For example, P or (Q and R).

CHAPTER 20

TASK 1. A total of $1013.24 in interestr is paid.

	A	B	C	D	E
1	Year	Annual Interest Rate	Payment	Interest	Balance
2	0				$0.00
3	1	0.05	$100.00	$0.00	$100.00
4	2	0.05	$100.00	$5.00	$205.00
5	3	0.05	$100.00	$10.25	$315.25
6	4	0.05	$100.00	$15.76	$431.01
7	5	0.05	$100.00	$21.55	$552.56
8	6	0.05	$100.00	$27.63	$680.19
9	7	0.05	$100.00	$34.01	$814.20
10	8	0.05	$100.00	$40.71	$954.91
11	9	0.05	$100.00	$47.75	$1102.66
12	10	0.05	$100.00	$55.13	$1257.79
13	11	0.05	$100.00	$62.89	$1420.68
14	12	0.05	$100.00	$71.03	$1591.71
15	13	0.05	$100.00	$79.59	$1771.30
16	14	0.05	$100.00	$88.56	$1959.86
17	15	0.05	$100.00	$97.99	$2157.86
18	16	0.05	$100.00	$107.89	$2365.75
19	17	0.05	$100.00	$118.29	$2584.04
20	18	0.05	$100.00	$129.20	$2813.24
21					
22	sum			$1013.24	

TASK 2.   An interest rate of 7.6% each year will double the investment after 18 years. A rate of 11.7% will triple the investment.

TASK 3.   The loan is paid after 15 years, including interest of $421.07.

TASK 4.   Payments of approximately $130 will repay the loan in 10 years.

Exploration.   A loan of $1800 requires 25 payments. A loan of $2000 requires 30 payments and a small 31st payment.

Cover: Baseball, Alan Schein/ The Stock Market; nautilus, James Handklev/ Tony Stone Images; sunflower, H. Lloyd/ The Stock Market; coin, Superstock; houses, Superstock; air traffic controller, Roger Tully/ Tony Stone Images.

PART I *(left):* Letter carrier, Lawrence Migdale/ Tony Stone Images; data entry pool, Michael Rosenfeld/ Tony Stone Images. *(right):* Video conference, Steven Peters/ Tony Stone Images; nurses, Roger Tully/ Tony Stone Images.

Chapter 1 3: *(Left)* Steven Peters/ Tony Stone Images; *(center)* Roger Tully/ Tony Stone Images; *(right)* Superstock. **6:** Spotlight 1.1, Portrait by Emanuel Handmann, Bildnis des Mathematikers, 1753, Oeffentliche Kunstsammlung Basel, Kunstmuseum. **7:** Spotlight 1.2, Thomas Magnanti. **19:** Figure 1.20a, Superstock.

Chapter 2 31: *(left)* Steven Peters/ Tony Stone Images; *(center)* Roger Tully/ Tony Stone Images; *(right)* Charles Thatcher/ Tony Stone Images. **33:** Lawrence Migdale/ Tony Stone Images. **46:** Steven Peters/ Tony Stone Images. **50:** Roger Tully/ Tony Stone Images.

Chapter 3 72: Roger Tully/ Tony Stone Images. **73:** Roger Tully/ Tony Stone Images. **75:** Roger Tully/ Tony Stone Images. **89:** Michael Rosenfeld/ Tony Stone Images.

Chapter 4 115: B/W Archive Photos/ American Stock. **116:** General Motors. **152:** Figure 4.22, Courtesy of AT&T Labs. **153:** Figure 4.23, Courtesy of AT&T Labs.

PART II *(left):* Coin, Superstock. *(right):* Survey, Andy Sacks/ Tony Stone Images; dice, Superstock; laptop, Charles Thatcher/ Tony Stone Images.

Chapter 5 167: Andy Sacks/ Tony Stone Images. **170:** Andy Sacks/ Tony Stone Images. **182:** Spotlight 5.1, University of London. **188:** Spotlight 5.2 AP/Wide World Photos.

Chapter 6 204: Charles Thatcher/ Tony Stone Images. **209:** Charles Thatcher/ Tony Stone Images. **211:** Spotlight 6.1, Kip Brundage/ Woodfin Camp & Associates. **232:** Figure 6.12, Courtesy of Daniel Scheirer, Brown University.

Chapter 7 251: Ken Whitmore/ Tony Stone Images. **252:** Superstock. **253:** Superstock. **256:** Spotlight 7.1, *(left)* The Granger Collection, New York. **256:** Spotlight 7.1, *(right)* The Granger Collection, NY. **277:** Figure 7.14, Ken Whitmore/ Tony Stone Images. **278:** Spotlight 7.2, New York Lottery Games.

Chapter 8 294: Busco/ The Image Bank.

PART III *(left):* Bee, Scott Camazine. *(right):* Bar code scanner, Stewart Cohen/ Tony Stone Images; woman with credit card, Russell Illig/ PhotoDisc.

Chapter 9 331: Stewart Cohen/ Tony Stone Images. **342:** Stewart Cohen/ Tony Stone Images. **346:** Scott Camazine/Sue Trainor.

Chapter 10 358: *(inset)* Frank Rossotto/ The Stock Market; *(background)* Stewart Cohen/ Tony Stone Images. **360:** Spotlight 10.1, Rex Ridenouse. **362:** Spotlight 10.2, Cour-

tesy of Neil Sloane/ AT&T Labs. **365:** Spotlight 10.3, Bettmann-UPI/ Corbis. **367:** Spotlight 10.4, Jessie MacWilliams. **371:** Spotlight 10.5, Matthew Mulbry. **372:** Christopher Morris/ Black Star.

PART IV *(left):* Baseball game, Alan Schein/ The Stock Market; voting, Robert E. Daemmrich/ Tony Stone Images; chess, Dan Bosler/ Tony Stone Images. *(right):* Cake, Superstock; convention, Ron Edmonds/ AP/Wide World Photos.

Chapter 11 385: *(left)* Alan Schein/ The Stock Market; *(right, inset)* Ron Edmonds/ AP/Wide World Photos; *(right, background)* Robert E. Daemmrich/ Tony Stone Images. **386:** Halstead/ Gamma-Liaison. **388:** Tom Horan/ Sygma. **402:** Spotlight 11.1, L.A. Cicero/ Stanford University News Service.

Chapter 12 416: *(right, background and inset)* Robert E. Daemmrich/ Tony Stone Images. **417:** Ron Edmonds/ AP/Wide World Photos. **420:** White-Packard/ The Image Bank. **422:** Spotlight 12.2, *(left)* Lloyd S. Shapeley; *(center)* AP/Wide World Photos; *(right)* Courtesy Yale School of Management Public Affairs Office.

Chapter 13 454: Superstock. **457:** Alan Schein/ The Stock Market. **466:** Spotlight 13.1, Superstock. **477:** Marc Deville/ Gamma-Liaison.

Chapter 14 489: *(left , background)* Alan Schein/ The Stock Market; *(right, inset)* National Portrait Gallery/ Art Resource, NY; *(right, background)* Robert E. Daemmrich/ Tony Stone Images. **490:** Brad Markel/ Gamma-

INDEX